The Oxford Handbook of Job Loss and Job Search

OXFORD LIBRARY OF PSYCHOLOGY

OXFORD LIBRARY OF PSYCHOLOGY

The Oxford Handbook of Job Loss and Job Search

Edited by

Ute-Christine Klehe

Edwin A. J. van Hooft

OXFORD
UNIVERSITY PRESS

OXFORD
UNIVERSITY PRESS

Oxford University Press is a department of the University of Oxford. It furthers
the University's objective of excellence in research, scholarship, and education
by publishing worldwide. Oxford is a registered trade mark of Oxford University
Press in the UK and certain other countries.

Published in the United States of America by Oxford University Press
198 Madison Avenue, New York, NY 10016, United States of America.

Library of Congress Cataloging-in-Publication Data
Names: Klehe, Ute-Christine, 1975–editor. | Hooft, Edwin A. J. van, editor.
Title: The Oxford handbook of job loss and job search /
edited by Ute-Christine Klehe, Edwin A. J. van Hooft.
Description: New York, NY : Oxford University Press, [2018] |
Includes bibliographical references and index.
Identifiers: LCCN 2017055016 | ISBN 9780199764921 (hardcover : alk. paper)
Subjects: LCSH: Unemployment—Social aspects. | Unemployed. |
Job hunting. | Employment (Economic theory)—Social aspects.
Classification: LCC HD5708 .O97 2018 | DDC 331.13/7—dc23
LC record available at https://lccn.loc.gov/2017055016

9 8 7 6 5 4 3 2 1

Printed by Sheridan Books, Inc., United States of America

CONTENTS

About the Editors   vii

Contributors   ix

Table of Contents   xiii

Chapters   1–590

Index   591

ABOUT THE EDITORS

Ute- Christine Klehe

Ute-Christine Klehe chairs the team of Work and Organizational Psychology at Justus-Liebig-University Giessen (Germany). Her research addresses career self-management and career transitions, particularly when faced with economic stressors, as well as personnel selection and performance. It has been published in outlets such as the *Journal of Applied Psychology, Personnel Psychology*, the *Journal of Vocational Behavior*, the *Journal of Organizational Behavior*, and others.

Edwin A. J. van Hooft

Edwin A. J. van Hooft is an Associate Professor of Work and Organizational Psychology at the University of Amsterdam, the Netherlands. His research interests include motivation and self-regulation (procrastination, goal orientation, intention-behavior consistency), job search behavior, job loss, reemployment, recruitment, and assessment. His work has appeared in journals such as *Journal of Applied Psychology, Personnel Psychology, Journal of Vocational Behavior, Journal of Occupational and Health Psychology*, and *Academy of Management Journal*.

CONTRIBUTORS

Clare Bambra
Institute of Health & Society
Newcastle University
Newcastle-upon-Tyne, England, UK

Wendi Benson
Department of Psychology
Washington State University Vancouver
Vancouver, Washington, USA

William A. Borgen
Department of Educational and
    Counseling Psychology and Special
    Education
University of British Columbia
Vancouver, British Columbia, Canada

Wendy R. Boswell
Mays Business School
Texas A&M University
College Station, Texas, USA

Gina M. Bufton
School of Psychology
Georgia Institute of Technology
Atlanta, Georgia, USA

Lee D. Butterfield
Adler School of Professional Psychology
Vancouver, British Columbia, Canada

James E. Coverdill
Department of Sociology
University of Georgia
Athens, Georgia, USA

Serge P. da Motta Veiga
Department of Management
Lehigh University
Bethlehem, Pennsylvania, USA

Nele De Cuyper
Department of Occupational and
    Organisational Psychology and
    Professional Learning
University of Leuven
Leuven, Belgium

Irene E. de Pater
NUS Business School
National University of Singapore
Singapore

Hans De Witte
Department of Occupational and
    Organisational Psychology and
    Professional Learning
University of Leuven
Leuven, Belgium

Eva Derous
Department of Personnel Management,
    Work and Organizational Psychology
Ghent University
Ghent, Belgium

Terje A. Eikemo
Department of Sociology and
    Political Science
Norwegian University of Science
    and Technology
Trondheim, Norway

Norman Feather
School of Psychology
Flinders University
South Adelaide, Australia

William Finlay
Department of Sociology
University of Georgia
Athens, Georgia, USA

Rita Fontinha
Henley Business School
University of Reading
Reading, England, UK

Monica L. Forret
Department of Managerial Studies
St. Ambrose University
Davenport, Iowa, USA

Richard G. Gardner
Mays Business School
Texas A&M University

College Station, Texas, USA

Arie Glebbeek
Department of Sociology
University of Groningen
Groningen, the Netherlands

Alice Hassel
Department of Organizational and Social
  Psychology
University of Erlangen—Nuremberg
Erlangen, Germany

Bonnie Hayden Cheng
Department of Management and
  Marketing
The Hong Kong Polytechnic University
Hung Hom, Hong Kong

Lixin Jiang
Department of Psychology
University of Wisconsin—Oshkosh
Oshkosh, Wisconsin, USA

Ruth Kanfer
School of Psychology
Georgia Institute of Technology
Atlanta, Georgia, USA

Derin Kent
Smith School of Business
Queen's University
Kingston, Ontario, Canada

Mari Kira
Department of Psychology
University of Michigan
Ann Arbor, Michigan, USA

Ute-Christine Klehe
Department of Psychology
The University of Giessen
Giessen, Germany

Jessie Koen
Faculty of Social Sciences
University of Amsterdam
Amsterdam, the Netherlands

Gary P. Latham
Rotman School of Management
University of Toronto
Toronto, Ontario, Canada

Xian Li
NUS Business School
National University of Singapore
Singapore

Colin Lindsay
Strathclyde Business School
University of Strathclyde
Glasgow, Scotland, UK

Edwin A. Locke
Robert H. Smith School of Business
The University of Maryland
College Park, Maryland, USA

Robyn Maitoza
Department of Behavioral Sciences
York College
York, Pennsylvania, USA

Mary B. Mawritz
LeBow College of Business
Drexel University
Philadelphia, Pennsylvania, USA

Julie M. McCarthy
Rotman School of Management
University of Toronto Scarborough
Scarborough, Ontario, Canada

Frances M. McKee-Ryan
The College of Business
University of Nevada, Reno
Reno, Nevada, USA

Klaus Moser
Department of Organizational and Social
  Psychology
University of Erlangen—Nuremberg
Erlangen, Germany

Karsten I. Paul
Department of Organizational and Social
  Psychology
University of Erlangen—Nuremberg
Erlangen, Germany

Richard H. Price
Institute for Social Research
University of Michigan
Ann Arbor, Michigan, USA

Tahira M. Probst
Department of Psychology
Washington State University Vancouver
Vancouver, Washington, USA

Julia Richardson
School of Human Resource
  Management
York University
Toronto, Ontario, Canada

Ann Marie Ryan
Department of Psychology
Michigan State University
East Lansing, Michigan, USA

Alan M. Saks
Centre for Industrial Relations and
Human Resources
University of Toronto
Toronto, Ontario, Canada

Adrian Sinfield
School of Social and Political Science
The University of Edinburgh
Edinburgh, Scotland, UK

Els Sol
Amsterdam Institute for Advanced Labour
Studies
University of Amsterdam
Amsterdam, the Netherlands

Zhaoli Song
NUS Business School
National University of Singapore
Singapore

Shu Hua Sun
Freeman School of Business
Tulane University
New Orleans, Louisiana, USA

Daniel B. Turban
Department of Management
University of Missouri
Columbia, Missouri, USA

Arne Uhlendorff
Center for Research in Economics and
Statistics
Paris Graduate School of Economics,
Statistics and Finance
Paris, France

Gerard J. van den Berg
Department of Economics
University of Mannheim
Mannheim, Germany

Anja Van den Broeck
Research Centre for Work and
Organisation Studies
University of Leuven
Leuven, Belgium

Edwin A. J. van Hooft
Department of Work and Organizational
Psychology
University of Amsterdam
Amsterdam, the Netherlands

Greet Van Hoye
Department of Personnel Management,
Work, and Organizational Psychology
Ghent University
Ghent, Belgium

Maarten Vansteenkiste
Department of Developmental,
Personality, and Social Psychology
Ghent University
Ghent, Belgium

Annelies E. M. van Vianen
Department of Work and Organizational
Psychology
University of Amsterdam
Amsterdam, the Netherlands

Amiram D. Vinokur
Institute for Social Research
University of Michigan
Ann Arbor, Michigan, USA

Meghna Virick
School of Management
San Jose State University
San Jose, California, USA

Jelena Zikic
School of Human Resource
Management
York University
Toronto, Ontario, Canada

TABLE OF CONTENTS

1. Introduction: What to Expect   1
   Ute-Christine Klehe and *Edwin A. J. van Hooft*

SECTION I   •   From the Start: Historic Perspective and Job Insecurity

2. Historical Background to Research on Job Loss, Unemployment, and Job Search   9
   Norman Feather
3. Job Insecurity and Anticipated Job Loss: A Primer and Exploration of Possible Interventions   31
   Tahira M. Probst, Lixin Jiang, and *Wendi Benson*

SECTION II   •   Consequences of Job Loss and Unemployment

4. Individual Consequences of Job Loss and Unemployment   57
   Karsten I. Paul, Alice Hassel, and *Klaus Moser*
5. Job Loss, Unemployment, and Families   87
   Frances M. McKee-Ryan and *Robyn Maitoza*
6. Unemployment and Its Wider Impact   99
   Adrian Sinfield
7. Insecurity, Unemployment, and Health: A Social Epidemiological Perspective   111
   Clare Bambra and *Terje A. Eikemo*

SECTION III   •   Theoretical Perspectives to Job Loss and Job Search

8. Goal Setting and Control Theory: Implications for Job Search   129
   Gary P. Latham, Mary B. Mawritz, and *Edwin A. Locke*
9. Job Loss and Job Search: A Social-Cognitive and Self-Regulation Perspective   143
   Ruth Kanfer and *Gina M. Bufton*
10. Understanding the Motivational Dynamics Among Unemployed Individuals: Refreshing Insights from the Self-Determination Theory Perspective   159
    Maarten Vansteenkiste and *Anja Van den Broeck*

11. Motivation and Self-Regulation in Job Search: A Theory of Planned Job Search Behavior   181
    Edwin A. J. van Hooft

12. Self-Regulatory Perspectives in the Theory of Planned Job Search Behavior: Deliberate and Automatic Self-Regulation Strategies to Facilitate Job Seeking   205
    Edwin A. J. van Hooft

13. New Economy Careers Demand Adaptive Mental Models and Resources   223
    Annelies E. M. van Vianen and *Ute-Christine Klehe*

14. Economic Job Search and Decision-Making Models   243
    Gerard J. van den Berg and *Arne Uhlendorff*

SECTION IV • Components and Phases of Job Search

15. Job-Search Behavior as a Multidimensional Construct: A Review of Different Job-Search Behaviors and Sources   259
    Greet Van Hoye

16. Networking as a Job-Search Behavior and Career Management Strategy   275
    Monica L. Forret

17. Contingency Headhunters: What They Do—and What Their Activities Tell Us About Jobs, Careers, and the Labor Market   293
    James E. Coverdill and *William Finlay*

18. Who is Searching for Whom? Integrating Recruitment and Job Search Research   311
    Serge P. da Motta Veiga and *Daniel B. Turban*

19. Through the Looking Glass: Employment Interviews from the Lens of Job Candidates   329
    Julie M. McCarthy and *Bonnie Hayden Cheng*

20. Reemployment Quality, Underemployment, and Career Outcomes   359
    Meghna Virick and *Frances M. McKee-Ryan*

SECTION V • Career Transitions

21. Job Search and the School-to-Work Transition   379
    Alan M. Saks

22. Employed Job Seekers and Job-to-Job Search   401
    Wendy R. Boswell and *Richard G. Gardner*

23. Job-Search Behavior of the Unemployed: A Dynamic Perspective   417
    Zhaoli Song, Shu Hua Sun, and *Xian Li*

SECTION VI · Special Populations

24. Too Old to Tango? Job Loss and Job Search Among Older Workers   433
    Ute-Christine Klehe, Irene E. de Pater, Jessie Koen, and *Mari Kira*
25. Nontraditional Employment: The Careers of Temporary Workers   465
    Nele De Cuyper, Rita Fontinha, and *Hans De Witte*
26. International Job Search   481
    Jelena Zikic, Derin Kent, and *Julia Richardson*
27. By Any Other Name: Discrimination in Resume Screening   501
    Eva Derous and *Ann Marie Ryan*

**SECTION VII · Programs to Support Job-Search and
End Spells of Unemployment**

28. The Evaluation of Reemployment Programs: Between Impact Assessment
    and Theory-Based Approaches   525
    Arie Glebbeek and *Els Sol*
29. Job Loss: Outplacement Programs   547
    William A. Borgen and *Lee D. Butterfield*
30. Work First Versus Human Capital Development in Employability
    Programs   561
    Colin Lindsay
31. The JOBS Program: Impact on Job Seeker Motivation, Reemployment,
    and Mental Health   575
    Richard H. Price and *Amiram D. Vinokur*

Index   591

Introduction: What to Expect

Ute-Christine Klehe *and* Edwin A. J. van Hooft

Abstract

We often associate job search with job loss, an adverse and often traumatic experience with dire consequences to individuals, their families, and societies overall. Yet job search happens far more often in better circumstances, such as when people start out on their careers, move between jobs, or follow less traditional career paths. In either case, this self-regulatory behavior is worth investigation from many different perspectives. The current handbook thus offers the first comprehensive overview of the literatures on job loss and job search, discussing the antecedents and consequences of job loss as well as different situations besides job loss that may call for an intense job search. Further, the handbook discusses the diverse theoretical and methodological perspectives from which job search has been studied, the situation of special populations, and the types of interventions that have been developed when job search proves unsuccessful in the face of unemployment.

Key Words: job insecurity, job loss, job search, employment, unemployment, reemployment, networking, career transition

The Rationale of *The Oxford Handbook of Job Loss and Job Search*

Whenever we talk about job loss and job search, the intuitive place to start is the Great Recession in the first decade of this century. In the course of only a few years, millions of people lost their jobs with little hope of regaining employment in economies that were faltering. Since then some countries have fully recovered, while others still suffer. Yet also irrespective of one specific crisis or another, new threats to employment emerge as jobs fall prey to increasing automatization and faltering international trade alliances. Overall, it is a cornerstone of contemporary economies to see employment statistics shift and change more rapidly than they have in earlier times. Relatedly, individuals enjoy less predictability about what their careers may look like in the coming five, ten, or fifteen years. The need to address the prospect of changing jobs, losing jobs, possibly changing careers, and starting anew has become more common.

The issues of job loss and job search are not only relevant during an economic crisis. Rather, job search is and always has been an integral part of careers under more stable economic circumstances, such as when new entrants to the labor market seek out their first employment, when mature job seekers seek fresh challenges in new organizations or even new countries, or when economies change and organizations go under while new ones emerge. Therefore, while this handbook was conceived in the context of great economic uncertainties, the topics of job loss and job search are timeless. And as the chapters of this handbook will show, the scope and relevance of this book extend beyond any crisis situation.

Given their prevalence and importance, job loss and job search have been studied from many different perspectives, such as psychology, sociology, labor studies, and economics. Yet quite surprisingly, the current handbook appears to be the first one trying to bring these different perspectives together in one comprehensive volume. We hope that it will thus turn into a major reference for both scholars and practitioners working in areas such as job loss, unemployment, career transitions, outplacement, and job search.

The Scope and Structure of This Handbook

The goal in assembling the *Oxford Handbook of Job Loss and Job Search* was to offer a comprehensive, multidisciplinary, and timely overview of the state of theory and empirical knowledge on the various perspectives from which to study job loss and job search; to identify best practices, where applicable; and to point readers toward stimulating directions for future research.

In this endeavor, we drew on the support of a great cast of international experts from diverse scientific disciplines. Overall, the 31 chapters of this handbook combine the insights from 57 authors located in eight countries on four continents of the world. Given the self-regulatory nature of the job-search activity itself, many scholars come from a psychological background, yet others work in the sciences of counseling, sociology, labor studies, management, and economics. Altogether, they offer a rich and detailed account of the literatures on job loss and job search, while also pointing out relevant questions for future research; and they pay particular attention to the usability of this knowledge for practice, often adding a list of practical recommendations at the end of their chapter.

While each chapter can stand on its own, a reading of this literature will also provide a sense of the richness and interconnectedness of the different topics discussed. The cross-links between topics are too numerous to discuss at this stage, yet we asked authors to consider them when writing their respective chapters. We also asked authors to cross-read and comment upon each other's contributions. The result is not only a series of stand-alone chapters but also a carpet of interweaving patterns and topics for discussion, which, we hope, will both deepen and enrich readers' understanding of the topic areas discussed and offer avenues and suggestions for informed practice and scientific inquiry.

In terms of structure, we divided this handbook into seven sections, covering background information, the consequences of job loss, motivational and other theories on job loss and job search, different behaviors relevant in the job-search process, different career transitions during which job search is particularly relevant, specific populations of job seekers, and interventions designed to help job seekers in the process of going back to work.

From the Start: Historic Perspective and Job Insecurity

More specifically, the first section addresses the starting points of job loss, unemployment, and job search, both from historic and sequential perspectives. Here, **Norman Feather** leads us back to the beginnings of the field, beginning in another period of great economic turmoil (i.e., the 1930s). The value of this chapter lies not only in its description of fundamental studies on the effects of unemployment and on how people try to cope (e.g., Jahoda's Marienthal studies or Bakke's research in Greenwich and New Haven, among others) but also in highlighting how acute and generalizable some of these findings have remained across the decades. He follows the development of research over time, discussing the increasing breadth of research interests (e.g., focusing on more diverse populations, forms of coping, and mediating and moderating factors), but he also provides a taste of the diversity of methodologies employed in the field of unemployment and job search.

Next, **Tahira M. Probst**, **Lixin Jiang**, and **Wendi Benson** adopt a chronological perspective, as job loss often casts a shadow long before it actually happens. For this purpose, they first discuss the dimensionality of job insecurity (subjective vs. objective, qualitative vs. quantitative, cognitive vs. affective) and then combine the literatures on job insecurity and anticipated job loss from a multilevel perspective into an integrative framework. This allows them to discuss individual, occupational, organizational, and societal antecedents of perceived job insecurity and anticipated job loss, as well as individual and organizational consequences and the organizational and societal factors that may help mitigate these negative effects.

Consequences of Job Loss and Unemployment

The second section of his handbook then addresses the consequences of job loss and unemployment from an increasingly wide angle. First, **Karsten I. Paul**, **Alice Hassel**, and **Klaus Moser** discuss the individual consequences of job loss. They report meta-analytic findings on the effects of unemployment on different aspects of mental health, and they then discuss the state of knowledge regarding the possibility of reverse causality as well as different mediators, moderator variables, and coping mechanisms.

Yet, job loss not only affects the individual alone but also casts wider circles. First, **Frances M. McKee-Ryan** and **Robyn Maitoza** discuss how job loss affects families, including partners and children, discussing ripple and crossover effects on topics such as relationship quality and children's mental health, development, and educational attainment, as well as the social resources that families provide and the effects of social roles and identities related to families.

Then, **Adrian Sinfield** offers a passionate debate on the effect of unemployment on societies overall, showing how it affects poverty and exclusion not only for the unemployed themselves but also for other groups in a diverse society. He further discusses wider implications for the distribution of resources, power, and opportunity across a society.

Finally, **Clare Bambra** and **Terje A. Eikemo** combine the perspectives on societal differences and the effects of unemployment on mental health by addressing the topic from a social epidemiology and cross-cultural perspective. They show how the understanding and handling of unemployment differs among clusters of countries representing different welfare state policies and social safety nets and how these different systems influence people's experiences during unemployment.

Theoretical Perspectives on Job Loss and Job Search

The following two sections of the handbook then address the topic of job search, approaching it from different perspectives. The third section pays credit to the fact that job search is a taxing motivational task, and thus it addresses the process of job search from differing theoretical perspectives grounded in psychology, career studies, and economics.

First, **Gary P. Latham, Mary B. Mawritz**, and **Edwin A. Locke** compare and contrast the implications of both goal-setting theory and control theory on job search behavior, using the chapter also to highlight overlaps and differences between these two sets of theories and to present research findings deriving from these two lines of literature.

Second, **Ruth Kanfer** and **Gina Bufton** review social-cognitive and self-regulatory perspectives on coping with involuntary job loss and subsequent job search. They draw from and combine a wide array of social-cognitive and self-regulatory theories into a chronological model that addresses both the

more reactive effects and coping responses with job loss and also the more proactive job-search process characterized by goal generation, goal choice, goal striving, self-monitoring, evaluation, and reaction.

Maarten Vansteenkiste and **Anja van den Broeck** add insights from self-determination theory to the literature on job search and unemployment. They convincingly argue for why and how self-determination theory may be able to account for a number of the findings known from the literature on unemployment, and how it can inform future thinking and practice on unemployment, job search, and wellbeing. Of particular relevance in these arguments is a consideration of people's intrinsic versus extrinsic work goals and their type of motivation to search for a new job, as well as their possible motivations to not search, leading to a number of promising research propositions.

In the next two chapters **Edwin A. J. van Hooft** focuses on motivational and self-regulatory predictors and mechanisms that are important in the job-search process. The first chapter addresses the job-search process from the perspective of the theory of planned behavior, arriving at a theory of planned job-search behavior (TPJSB). Theoretical underpinnings are described, and the research on global-level, contextual, and situational predictors of job-search intentions and behavior are discussed. The second chapter zooms in on the gap between job-search intentions and behavior, taking a self-regulatory perspective. The chapter provides some hands-on suggestions based on self-regulatory theories on how to reduce this distinction.

The following two chapters widen the theoretical perspective somewhat further. First, **Annelies E. M. van Vianen** and **Ute-Christine Klehe** address the issue from a careers perspective. Building on recent career theories that pay credit to the increasingly unpredictable, nonlinear, and uncertain nature of careers, they present a model based on identity and coping during career transitions, which implies that coping with identity threats, changing one's mental model of careers, and needing to adapt to frequent and unpredictable career transitions becomes more characteristic of contemporary careers.

Finally, **Gerard J. van den Berg** and **Arne Uhlendorff** address the topic of job search from an economics perspective. Following the basic premise that individuals try to maximize their expected utility based on the information available to them, this perspective assumes a greater level of rationality than most psychological approaches, while also taking into consideration job seekers' imperfect information in their decision-making process, the role of their reservation wage, and the way that utilities may change over time.

Components and Phases of Job Search

The fourth section then focuses on the specific forms and dimensionality of job search. It starts with a systematic overview by **Greet van Hoye** on the multitude of ways in which we can understand job search, organizing the respective literature along the dimensions of direction, effort, and intensity. Her discussion of diverse preparatory and active job-search behaviors, different job-search strategies, and indicators of job-search quality and dynamics, among others, give a first indication of the multifaceted perspective needed to fully grasp the nature of job search.

Next, **Monica Forret** dives into one particular form of job-search behavior that is still relatively understudied, even though it has proven to be particularly helpful in past research, namely networking job search. Using social network theory as a conceptual basis, the chapter outlines the use of networking, not only in the context of job search specifically but also for careers in general, and explains why some groups and individuals may be more successful at their networking attempts than others.

In some cases candidates may find themselves in a situation as described by **James E. Coverdill** and **William Finlay**, who address the situation of "job seekers" who may not even have known that they are seeking new employment but who are recruited to change jobs via the intervention of a headhunter. While largely understudied in the classic job-search literature, headhunters are, after all, a major matchmaker at least among professionals and managers undertaking job-to-job transitions.

Conceptually, this also touches upon the chapter by **Serge P. da Motta Veiga** and **Daniel B. Turban** on integrating the job-search and organizational-recruitment perspectives, as both processes happen simultaneously, after all, and both aim for the mutual outcome of securing a good match between the candidate and the organization.

Job search and pursuit processes commonly include a job interview stage, as **Julie M. McCarthy** and **Bonnie Hayden Cheng** discuss. They address the interview experiences from a candidate's perspective, addressing candidate characteristics like gender, age, or race; candidate behaviors, like impression management and communication style;

and candidate reactions, like interview anxiety and justice perceptions, all of which influence both the process and the resulting candidate performance as well as candidates' attraction to the organization.

Finally, **Meghna Virick** and **Frances M. McKee-Ryan** address the topic of the quality of employment obtained upon reemployment. More specifically, they focus on the issue of underemployment that many job seekers face upon reemployment, particularly job seekers of particularly vulnerable groups, such as older job-seekers, women, and ethnic minorities. While research on underemployment is as of now relatively underdeveloped, the authors provide us with a breadth of theoretical perspectives from which to study the phenomenon of underemployment and thus also with useful directions for future research.

Career Transitions

The fifth section addresses different career transitions during which job search plays a pivotal role. The first of these phases, which is relevant for just about anyone at some point in their life, is the school-to-work transition. In his chapter, **Alan M. Saks** presents an integrated model that embeds job search within the context of the school-to-work transition and shows how different phases of this transition require different kinds of behaviors. Thus, job search ideally follows a phase of career planning and development to ensure that the seeker has actually developed a vocational self-concept and work-role identity, has acquired the necessary work-related knowledge and skills, and has a plan and objectives for his or her career and thus also a direction for the actual search. Job search itself implies the use of both formal and informal job information sources as well as preparatory and active job-search behaviors. Finally, the school-to-work transition ends with a phase of work adjustment in the found job characterized by information and feedback seeking as well as networking and relationship building.

Some of these topics also reemerge when people do not start out searching for their first job but move between jobs in the context of a job-to-job search. Special about this situation, of course, is that job seekers may be searching not only for something (pull factors) but also in order to evade unwanted aspects of their current job (push factors). Thus, **Wendy R. Boswell** and **Richard G. Gardner** discuss in detail the different objectives that may drive job seekers toward their search. These cognitions, in turn, both influence and are influenced by job seekers' quit cognitions and job-search behaviors. While this process may or may not result in a subsequent job change, it will also influence job seekers' subsequent attitudes and behaviors toward their work and bear consequences for the job seeker's context (e.g., in terms of group and organizational culture and interpersonal relations).

Finally, **Zhaoli Song, Shu Hua Sun**, and **Xian Li** address the most dire phase in which to undertake job search, namely in the context of unemployment. After addressing the unique aspects of unemployment that influence job search, the chapter highlights antecedents and outcomes of this behavior during unemployment and pays special credit to the dynamic nature of job search, outlining findings and different models describing the development of job search over time. Additionally, this chapter provides an overview of the pros and cons of different research approaches to job search, specifically multiwave longitudinal methods, diary methods, and experience-sampling methods, as well as suitable ways to analyze the resulting data.

Special Populations

The sixth section of the handbook focuses on specific populations whose examination warrants special attention, both for their growing prevalence and their unique challenges in the labor market. The first of these chapters by **Ute-Christine Klehe, Irene E. de Pater, Jessie Koen**, and **Mari Kira** focuses on older job-seekers, highlighting their vulnerability to possible job loss and to stereotypes that may lower their perceived employability. This mismatch of stereotypes and perceived employability places older workers in precarious situations regarding the threat of losing their jobs, the loss of latent functions associated with work, having different and fewer coping options than younger job-seekers, and facing fewer chances of finding reemployment.

The situation of nontraditional and particularly temporary workers is often precarious, as discussed by **Nele DeCuyper, Rita Fontinha**, and **Hans De Witte**. This growing group of workers can sometimes hope for the eventual option of permanent employment, yet for many, temporary employment is part of a vicious circle between unstable employment and subsequent unemployment. On the negative side, such a vicious circle is kept in place by the dual nature of the labor market, including lower job quality, lower investments on the part of employers, and negative stereotyping of temporary workers. On the positive side, however, it raises employees' constant awareness of the importance of maintaining and broadening their employability and managing their own careers.

Such awareness is also very common in the next special population discussed, namely that of international job seekers who independently of any one organization seek employment in a country different from their home. In their chapter, **Jelena Zikic, Derin Kent**, and **Julia Richardson** discuss the diverse contextual and personal factors that drive this international job search in general and specific job-search behaviors in particular, as well as international job-seekers' post-migration investment in their human capital. Quite common among this population, however, is a lack of employment in their field of study and the experience of underemployment, although there are several contextual factors in terms of country of origin, time in the host country, and domestic labor demand that may mitigate such effects.

One issue that may remain, however, is that of discrimination. In line with this thought, the last chapter in this section by **Eva Derous** and **Ann Marie Ryan** addresses the situation of ethnic minorities, and particularly reasons why their job search is often far less successful than that of majority members. For this purpose, they focus on the resume screening phase and discuss current psychological perspectives and empirical findings on ethnic discrimination. More specifically, they discuss the human-capital versus hiring-discrimination perspectives on discriminatory hiring, followed by different social-psychological insights, each of which offers a different perspective on the puzzle. Finally, they discuss the effects of applicants and job and recruiter characteristics, and they end with a critical reflection on some common practical recommendations.

Programs to Support Job Search and End Spells of Unemployment

This leads us to the final section of this handbook. This section discusses different types of programs designed to bring unemployed job seekers closer to the labor market.

First, **Arie Glebbeek** and **Els Sol** discuss the rather divergent and at points nonconclusive findings on the macro-level effects of reemployment programs. Taking a critical stance toward the experimental and meta-analytic methods used for evaluating and comparing programs, they argue that a major issue in macro-level policy evaluations is the "black box character" of many experimental evaluations, which offer little information about the content of the programs evaluated. Rather, any evaluation should also consider the theories behind the programs and thus the mechanism via which the programs intend to reach these goals.

Next, **William A. Borgen** and **Lee D. Butterfield** discuss the case of outplacement counseling, which is usually offered to displaced workers by specialized outplacement firms at the expense of downsizing organizations. As their discussion shows, we actually know far less about outplacement than is warranted, given its frequent use. That said, the chapter does provide readers with available information on the history and typical services offered by outplacement firms, on measures of success, on factors that help or hinder this success, and on challenges related to outplacement counseling.

Then, **Colin Lindsay** takes a critical comparative view of two types of programs dominant in the services offered to unemployed job seekers, namely human capital versus work first programs. While human capital programs seek to enhance job seekers' long-term employability through investments in their human capital via education and training, work first programs build on the assumption that "any job is better than no job" and thus try to place people into any available job opportunity as quickly as possible. In his chapter, Lindsay identifies the differences in rationales, content, and outcomes of these types of programs, and he advocates for a more holistic view of the factors affecting the unemployed.

Finally, **Richard H. Price** and **Amiram D. Vinokur** present the conceptual framework, learning processes, and outcomes obtained from one prime human capital development program, namely the JOBS program. The JOBS program is likely the best-validated counseling program offered to unemployed job seekers worldwide. At the core of this elaborate training lies the acquisition of relevant job-search skills and techniques to maintain one's motivation to continue searching despite the likely setbacks. For this purpose, the program integrates active learning techniques such as modeling and role-plays, techniques known to build self-efficacy and inoculation against setbacks, and the creation of a supportive environment through unconditional positive regard, supportive feedback, and other components.

Conclusion

Overall, the handbook thus combines a rich combination of perspectives and disciplines addressing the nature, antecedents, consequences, and processes underlying job loss and job search. Each chapter is rich in theory and discussion of empirical findings, while also offering not only a list of practical implications for job seekers, practitioners, and policy makers but also the outspoken call for more and richer research. We hope that both will help to foster the science and practice of job search and of helping people in the dire situation of having lost their jobs, given that both job loss and the need to search for a job—be it the first or a job elsewhere—are here to stay.

From the Start: Historic Perspective and Job Insecurity

Historical Background to Research on Job Loss, Unemployment, and Job Search

Norman Feather

Abstract

This chapter provides a selective review of past research on job loss, unemployment, and job search up to the beginning of the 1990s. The Great Depression studies in the 1930s at Marienthal by Jahoda and colleagues and by Bakke at Greenwich and New Haven are described, along with other research at the time. These early studies sowed the seeds for subsequent research programs in England, Europe, and Australia; the theories that emerged from this early and later research are described. They include stage theory, deprivation theory, agency theory, and vitamin theory. Other more general approaches—such as stress and coping models and expectancy-value theory—are also described as relevant to the unemployment experience. The historical review provides lessons about the importance of using a variety of methodologies that include descriptive field research, survey and questionnaire studies, longitudinal research, and research across cultures. It also suggests that progress will involve the application of midrange theories about work, paid employment, and unemployment targeted to particular issues such as psychological well-being, health-related problems, social and family effects, and job-search behavior.

Key Words: great Depression studies, 1980s research, midrange theories

In this chapter I review studies of the psychological impact of unemployment that date from the 1930s and 1940s through to the beginning of the 1990s. The review is necessarily brief and focuses on some of the major contributions that emerged in the years of the Great Depression and subsequently. The review does not consider more recent contributions. This handbook provides a wide range of chapters that reflect where research stands at the present time. It will be obvious from these chapters that research on job loss, unemployment, and job search has developed rapidly in recent years and that researchers have investigated a wide range of interesting and important questions. However, it is useful to set a historical framework so that we can see how the seeds of questions posed in current research were sown many years ago. The issues raised then remain salient today, and we now have the advantage of examining them using new theoretical approaches and more sophisticated methodologies and forms of analysis.

Much of the present review is distilled from the introductory chapters of my book, *The Psychological Impact of Unemployment* (Feather, 1990), a monograph that provides a historical overview of classic studies and related theory followed by a summary of findings from my research program at Flinders University. I refer readers to this monograph for a much more detailed account of unemployment research up to that time.

Studies from the Great Depression

I note in my monograph that there is a literature that considers unemployment across history in relation to public policies, social attitudes (e.g., Garraty, 1978), and historical precursors of the sociopsychological effects of unemployment (e.g., Kelvin & Jarrett, 1985). For example, Kelvin and

Jarrett described a fourteenth-century English ordinance that distinguished between "sturdy beggars" who were fit for work and the "deserving poor" who were sick, old, and incapacitated. Charity was to be withheld from the sturdy beggars because there was a shortage of labor due to the devastation of the Black Death. Those who were able bodied were valued for rational economic reasons rather than because of a social ethic that working was somehow fulfilling a moral virtue. Fryer and Payne (1986) referred to a *Bibliography of Unemployment and the Unemployed* (Taylor, 1909), which listed 800 books, articles, and pamphlets; these were prepared for a royal commission in England that considered the poor laws and the relief of distress from unemployment. That is, issues concerning work, employment, and unemployment surfaced in past times in response to changing economic and political circumstances and philosophies, along with attempts to deal with the effects of unemployment and poverty. These are great social issues that affect the lives of all people.

Publications on unemployment tend to follow rapid increases in unemployment rates. Thus, there was a spate of publications during the 1930s and 1940s relating to the Great Depression (e.g., Bakke, 1933, 1940a, b; Eisenberg & Lazarsfeld, 1938; Jahoda, Larzarsfeld, & Zeisel, 1933; Komarosky, 1940; Pilgrim Trust, 1938). These early studies were conducted in a different era. The standard of living was lower, life expectancy was shorter and health care was much less advanced, welfare schemes were more limited in scope, less of the population stayed in school and went on to higher education, technological advances were much less sophisticated, the focus was more on unemployed males who came from semiskilled and unskilled jobs, and many other social and economic differences existed as compared with today. Furthermore, the methodologies used in these studies were often limited, based on small samples and case histories.

Yet it would be wrong to dismiss this research out of hand. Some studies have deservedly achieved the status of classic investigations because they combined different methodologies in their enquiries and provided a richness of detail that is often missing from current research. They were the source of important ideas about the functions of work and employment and about how unemployment affects the lives of those who experience it.

A major contribution in the 1930s was the sociographic study of people living in the Austrian village of Marienthal, people whose livelihoods depended on a flax factory. When the factory closed down in 1929, the inhabitants of Marienthal experienced a period of prolonged unemployment. A group of researchers led by Marie Jahoda and Paul Lazarsfeld came to the Marienthal community in order to investigate the effects of this closure over a number of months (Jahoda et al., 1933). The Marienthal study has classic status in the unemployment literature. It is a prime example of what can be achieved by obtaining both quantitative and qualitative data about unemployment in field research involving detailed observations of life in a small community.

Many different sorts of information were obtained in this study (Fryer, 1987, 1992; Jahoda et al., 1933). This was possible because, in addition to the leaders, the team included four physicians and six other researchers, including students in law, social work, economics, and psychology. Members of the community also assisted in various ways. The information that they collected included the compilation of family files and detailed life histories; how people used their time; reports and complaints sent to the industrial commission; school essays on "What I want most of all," "What I want to be," and "What I want for Christmas"; a prize essay competition on "How I see my future"; family records of meals and what children took to school for their lunches the day before and the day after relief money was paid; the Christmas presents children received; medical tests; performance at school; and how much money was spent at different locations. The research also obtained information from political clubs and other organizations; statistical data on accounts at the local cooperative store; loans from the public library; membership of clubs; election results; newspaper subscriptions; age distributions; births, deaths, and marriages; and migration figures as well as some household statistics. I offer this detail so as to indicate the richness of the information that was obtained at that time, enabling triangulation of data to bring out consistency and a deep understanding of how unemployment affected the community.

The Marienthal researchers also showed ethical responsibility in giving back to the community. They launched special projects that were of use, such as arranging for the distribution and repair of clothing, setting up gymnastics courses, organizing essay prize competitions, and arranging free medical consultations. Thus they became part of the community during their research at Marienthal, helping in various ways as well as obtaining the information they asked for.

Jahoda (1979) has summarized some of the main findings from the Marienthal study:

> the study showed that being unemployed is something very different from having leisure time. The unemployed decreased their attendance of clubs and voluntary organizations, their use of the free library, their reading habits. Their sense of time disintegrated, having nothing to do meant that they became less able to be punctual for meals or other arrangements. Budgeting, so much more necessary than before, was progressively abandoned. While family relations continued in established patterns longer than other relations and activities, there was some evidence that they, too, deteriorated and family quarrels increased. (p. 309)

Jahoda et al. (1933) distinguished four different attitudes that they observed could occur among the unemployed in Marienthal. The most common attitude was *resignation*, with "no plans, no relation to the future, no hopes, extreme restriction of all needs beyond the bare necessities, yet at the same time maintenance of the household, care of the children, and an overall feeling of relative well-being" (p. 53). This attitude was distinguished from an *unbroken* attitude, where the unemployed person showed continued attempts to find employment, maintained the household and care of the children, and displayed subjective well-being and hopes and plans for the future. Two other attitude groups were distinguished, each of which was described as *broken*. One group involved those unemployed people who were in *despair*, showing depression, hopelessness, feelings of futility, no further attempts to find work or to improve the situation in some way, and a backward comparison of the present with a better past. The final attitude group was characterized by *apathy*. It was associated with a disordered household where the children were dirty and neglected, passivity was a dominant reaction, and there was no effort to improve the situation; in these households no attempts to plan for the immediate or distant future were made.

These four attitudes were correlated with level of income. The shift from resignation and unbroken attitudes to the broken attitudes of despair and apathy was associated with "the narrowing of economic resources and the wear and tear on personal belongings. At the end of this process lies ruin and despair" (p. 87). Thus financial hardship was a key factor affecting people's lives. The consequences of unemployment were closely intertwined with the consequences of poverty.

In her later writings Jahoda (1982, 1988) referred to categories of experience such as a habitual time structure for the waking day, which she deemed to be basic and that people were assumed to lose when they became unemployed. I will return to this form of analysis later in this chapter when I summarize some of the theoretical ideas that have emerged from unemployment research.

Jahoda conducted another sociographic study in the 1930s in South Wales in the Eastern Valley of Monmouthshire (Jahoda, 1987). She became associated with a small group of Quakers who set up a cooperative enterprise to help unemployed miners. They found that the normal attitude of the miners was one of resignation. Jahoda noted that the fact that they received an unemployment allowance may have produced less serious effects of unemployment as compared with the despair and apathy found in the Marienthal study. Note, however, that resignation was the dominant attitude in both of these studies. Only 7% of families in Marienthal were classified as "in despair" or "apathetic," whereas 70% of families in Marienthal also showed resignation.

Fryer (1992) notes that the Marienthal report did not refer much to previous research on unemployment and mental health. He states that the original intention of the Marienthal study was to investigate the use of leisure time rather than unemployment, but the researchers changed their tack. Jahoda et al. (1933) did briefly mention an earlier study in York by Rowntree and Lasker (1911) as "the first sociographic study of unemployment" (p. 105); see also Dooley, Catalano, and Hough (1992). Jahoda et al. also referred to research on the "European laborer" conducted by Le Play in the mid-nineteenth century that used detailed observations of events, compilation of source material, and the engagement of the observer in the field of enquiry. So there was some historical background to the methods used in Marienthal.

Leaving Marienthal I now turn to another major set of studies that were conducted by Bakke (1933, 1940a, b) during the 1930s. Bakke obtained descriptions based on personal contact as well as other kinds of information that he used to present a detailed description of the lives of unemployed people. In his study of working-class families conducted in Greenwich, a borough of London, that he published in *The Unemployed Man* (Bakke, 1933), he immersed himself in the community and conducted interviews with workers, particularly those who were unemployed; interviews with other members of the community;

arranged for the unemployed men to keep time diaries; observed the life circumstances of the unemployed while living among them; and obtained statistical information concerning school attendance, marriage, health, unemployment, visits to the unemployment exchange, church activity, and other activities of interest. So again we see, as in the Marienthal study, attention to a wide array of descriptive information in order to get a deep understanding of the impact that unemployment had on individuals and their families in these early years of the Great Depression.

Bakke (1933) provided important information about the work environment in which his families lived and the features of this environment that shaped their attitudes toward work and getting a job. O'Brien (1985, 1986), in an analysis of the relevance of Bakke's contributions, noted Bakke's emphasis on the development of feelings of insecurity and powerlessness or external control.

The insecurity reported by male workers had a number of sources: the development of new machinery, fear among young workers that they might lose their jobs if their wages or unemployment insurance became too high, fear that they might be displaced by women in their jobs, uncertainty about how migrating labor might affect prospects for employment, and concern about the restrictions of job opportunities because older men were holding on to their jobs even if they were receiving pensions.

The feelings of powerlessness or external control involved beliefs by the unemployed workers that their destinies were controlled by others, that they were not masters of their own fate, and that luck had an important role in determining whether or not they had employment. The workers were suspicious of employers and about any plans for cooperation between the worker and the employer. As O'Brien (1986) noted, however, Bakke (1933) emphasized the shaping influence of the context of work and that there were differences between unskilled and skilled workers in the incentives that were available and the attitudes that they developed on the job. More skilled men had greater satisfaction in their jobs beyond the mere reward of money. For the unskilled worker, the major satisfaction from work was the immediate reward of a wage. But if the wages were close to the dole, there would be more temptation to remain on the dole as long as possible. So for both unskilled and skilled workers "the conditioning power of the job soon makes its influence felt" (Bakke, 1933, p. 33).

Bakke (1933) also indicates that the workers hestudied displayed personal foresight in reacting to their lot. Some joined "slate clubs" or savings associations that enabled them to put money aside for the future; some took out private insurance against misfortune; some joined trade unions; others joined clubs or lodges, thereby extending their range of contacts who might be able to assist them in some way. The development of foresight was associated with various factors in the work environment and the rewards that this environment offered. Bakke recognized that "The long arm of income, as it places people automatically within certain fields of possible achievement, is a factor constantly to be reckoned with. Income, steadiness of income, skill, education, all of these are the high fences that surround the fields" (p. 45).

The unemployed men in the Bakke (1933) study were not active in organized political protests, but they became discouraged, felt insecure, and had diminished self-confidence. Unemployment insurance benefits helped to moderate some of the effects of unemployment, enabling the unemployed to buy food and to reduce the risks of ill health. Bakke noted that most of the unemployed continued to seek employment and tried to fill their time in meaningful ways, although their low levels of income limited what they could do.

Bakke (1940a, b) conducted a subsequent study of unemployed workers in New Haven, Connecticut, that again provided a wealth of detail. Here, in a different culture, he found effects that were similar to those of the Greenwich study and evidence for the shaping effects of the work environment on general beliefs and attitudes.

It should be clear that these descriptive sociographic studies by Jahoda and her associates and by Bakke shared many important features. The researchers in both investigations obtained a wealth of information about the widespread effects of unemployment on the lives of those in each respective community. The magnitude of these effects was associated with available income; that is, the effects were intertwined with relative poverty. The effects also varied across people, depending on social context (e.g., the family situation) and demographic variables (e.g., age and sex) but also on preestablished frames of mind (e.g., beliefs about degree of personal control over events), capacities (e.g., self-reliance, coping skills) and how skilled or unskilled the person was. Some of these variables were a product of previous unemployment experience and other socializing influences in the unemployed person's life. The studies were a rich mine for theories about the impact of unemployment, some of which are reviewed later in this chapter.

The pioneering work of Jahoda et al. and Bakke was supported by other studies conducted in the 1930s. For example, research by the Pilgrim Trust (1938) set out to study the effects of long-term unemployment in six towns (Deptford; Leicester; Liverpool; Blackburn; Crook, County Durham; and Rhondda) in the United Kingdom. These were selected to enable comparison between two prosperous towns, two with a mixture of employment and unemployment, and two that were especially depressed economically. Information on a wide range of variables was collected (e.g., age, previous occupation, family size, income, health, attitudes, leisure activities, club membership, employment record). The results of this study again drew attention to the negative effects of poverty as a cause of anxiety and deteriorating physical health. Unemployment assistance helped to relieve the burden, but there was not much scope for moving beyond the "dead level" of daily life. Families who had children to support were worse off and among the unemployed there was evidence of anxiety, restlessness, and nervousness as well as depression, hopelessness, apathy, and feelings of loneliness and isolation reflecting a lack of structure and purpose in daily life. A vicious cycle resulted, with increasing negative reactions making the person more unfit for work.

The report of the Pilgrim Trust also noted how work provides meaning and structure in everyday life. Thus

> Work provides for most people the pattern within which their lives are lived and when this pattern is lost they have thrown on them a responsibility which, in the case of most unemployed men, their working lives in no way qualified them to bear—the responsibility for organising their own existence. They fall in ultimately with some new makeshift pattern. (p.149)

Similar findings were obtained by the Carnegie Trust (1943) in their study of unemployed youth. These young people tried to fill their days with various activities such as reading newspapers and magazines, listening to the radio, and going to the cinema and dances, but their attempts were limited by lack of money and sometimes poor health. It was difficult for them to establish regular routines and to maintain their self-respect.

There were many other studies of the effects of unemployment during the 1930s, some of which referred to the negative effects of failure and other emotional reactions (Israeli, 1935), to how length of unemployment was associated with changes in attitudes (e.g., Beales & Lambert, 1934; Zawadski & Lazarsfeld, 1935), and to the effects of unemployment on the unemployed man and his family (Komarovsky, 1940). An influential article by Eisenberg and Lazarsfeld (1938) reviewed over 100 studies, some of which concerned the effects of unemployment on personality traits, interests and habits, moral attitudes, attitudes toward religion, and political attitudes. The Eisenberg and Lazarsfeld review also noted research that considered different attitudes among the unemployed and how these differences were related to social and economic status, age, gender, personality, economic resources, and length of unemployment. Their review also described research on the effects of unemployment on children and youth. They concluded that young people suffered similar effects to adults, but because young people were going through a transition period between childhood and maturity, the effects of unemployment were probably more lasting.

An influential contribution of the Eisenberg and Lazarfeld (1938) review was their summary of findings about the stages of unemployment effects. On the basis of the studies reviewed, they concluded that

> First there is shock, which is followed by an active hunt for a job, during which the person is still optimistic and unresigned; he still maintains an unbroken attitude. Second, when all efforts fail, the individual becomes pessimistic, anxious, and suffers active distress; this is the most crucial state of all. And, third, the individual becomes fatalistic and adapts himself to his new state but with narrower scope. He now has a broken attitude. (p. 378)

They also proposed that this sequence of changes would be moderated by individual differences relating to status, age, gender, personality, and other variables, thus limiting the generalization that they made.

The body of research on the psychological impact of unemployment produced in the 1930s set the stage for much that was to come later. In the next section I refer selectively to some of the contributions that were made up to around the 1990s.

Research up to the 1990s

Research on unemployment declined for a time following the Great Depression. The Second World War and postwar reconstruction affected employment rates and changes in the labor market. The 1960s and 1970s saw the publication of case studies, quantitative research, and reviews, some of which dealt with job loss, others with the effects of being unemployed (e.g., Cobb & Kasl, 1977; Daniel, 1974; Harrison, 1976; Hill, 1977, 1978; Marsden & Duff, 1975; Sinfield, 1968, 1970, 1981; Tiffany, Cowan, & Tiffany, 1970; Wedderburn, 1964). Jahoda (1979, 1982) compared the impact of unemployment in the 1930s with its impact in the 1970s and 1980s and argued that psychological responses to unemployment in the 1970s and 1980s "can with greater confidence than in the past be attributed to the absence of a job not just to restricted finances" (Jahoda, 1982, p. 58).

The increase in unemployment levels from 1975 onward was followed by a rise in publications and led to an extensive literature describing research from British, American, European, and Australian research teams. There is not space to review this literature in detail. A lot of the studies in the 1980s and 1990s issued from the MRC/SSRC Social and Applied Psychology Unit at the University of Sheffield, from research groups at Flinders University and the University of Adelaide in Australia, from North American teams from the Institute for Social Research at the University of Michigan and elsewhere, and from research groups in Europe (e.g., in Amsterdam) and elsewhere. There were extensive reviews at the time (e.g., Feather, 1989a; Fryer & Payne, 1986; Warr, Jackson, & Banks, 1988); special journal issues concerned with unemployment and its effects (*Social Science and Medicine* in 1987; the *Journal of Social Issues* in 1988, and the *Journal of Occupational and Organizational Psychology* in 1992); and books, monographs, and edited volumes that dealt with the psychology of work, job loss, and unemployment (e.g., Banks & Ullah, 1988; Barling, 1990; Feather, 1990; O'Brien, 1986; Fineman, 1983, 1987; Fryer & Ullah, 1987; Warr, 1987; A. H. Winefield et al., 1993). In the mid-1990s, Winefield (1995) updated the Fryer and Payne (1986) review in a paper that cited a large number of studies, noting different theoretical approaches and suggesting directions for future research. A more recent collection of papers focuses on the health effects of unemployment and on interventions to limit these effects (Kieselbach, Winefield, Boyd, & Anderson, 2006).

These later studies incorporated improvements in methodology and statistical analysis. Many of them involved survey designs with questionnaires and interviews and targeted different populations (e.g., young people, adults). Other procedures were also used (e.g., personal document analysis, time budget analysis, depth interviewing). Psychological scales with known test characteristics were included to measure such variables as psychological well-being, life satisfaction, proneness to psychiatric disorder, positive and negative affect, self-esteem, depressive symptoms, anxiety, work values, cognitive difficulties, external locus of control, and causal attributions. Physiological measures were also obtained involving biochemical analysis of blood and urine in some of the American studies concerned with job termination (e.g., Cobb & Kasl, 1977). In addition, questionnaires were also constructed to measure health and behavioral changes following job loss. There was increasing recognition of the need to strengthen inferences by including specially selected control groups (e.g., people in employment), employing longitudinal designs that followed up unemployed people over time or that studied school leavers (e.g., Feather & O'Brien, 1986a,b; Winefield et al. 1993), obtaining measures prior to and after job loss, and applying sophisticated multivariate procedures to achieve statistical control over such variables as social class, education, and income.

Some studies focused on the analysis of aggregate data following the contributions of Brenner (1973, 1979a,b). In one of his studies Brenner found that admissions to New York State public hospitals between 1914 and 1967 increased as the state's manufacturing employment index decreased. This aggregate-level research attracted a lot of comment (e.g., Kasl, 1982; Warr, 1985, 1987), especially in regard to how one interprets the relations that were found. An economic downturn may provoke new illness for various reasons, but it may also uncover previous illness that was contained or held in check under more benign conditions of a higher employment rate (O'Brien, 1986; Warr, 1987). Moreover, various authors have pointed out that it is hazardous to generalize from aggregate studies to effects at the individual level (e.g., Warr, 1987). By doing so one commits the ecological fallacy. Relations may differ at the individual level as compared with the macrolevel.

Some studies have attempted to link information from aggregate-level and individual-level studies (e.g., Catalano & Dooley, 1983; Dooley, Catalano, & Rook, 1988). Dooley and Catalano (1984) argue that an increased unemployment rate may increase mental health problems because it has direct effects on individuals via job loss but also because of other more extended consequences that affect individuals, families, and the community in subtle and gradual ways, and not only in relation to those who lose their jobs. The spouses and children may suffer, and there may be more family conflict; workers who lose their jobs may have to bear the psychological cost of retraining and relocating; they may also end up in lower-status occupations and suffer anxiety and insecurity as they anticipate job loss or move from one job to another; they may remain in unsatisfactory working conditions; and they may suffer cuts in social services and welfare payments as the bargaining power of organized labor is undermined (see also Dooley & Catalano, 1980).

The individual-level studies conducted during the 1980s showed a range of negative effects in relation to such variables as psychological well-being, physical and mental health, and coping behavior. Some unemployed people coped better than others, but in general the effects were negative. As noted earlier, there have been many reviews summarizing findings from both cross-sectional and longitudinal studies of the effects of unemployment and prospective or "before/after" studies of job loss. My 1990 book noted some of these summaries (Feather, 1990, p. 22). There I concluded that the research recognized that

> the psychological impact of unemployment varies considerably depending on the people who are unemployed and the circumstances under which they live. In some cases negative effects on mental and physical health may be slight, in other cases much more severe. Among the important variables that influence the outcome are length of unemployment, age, gender, ethnic background, social class, employment commitment, financial strain, prior job experience, and social support. (p. 22)

In his 1987 book *Work, Unemployment, and Mental Health*, Warr concluded that "the findings . . . leave no doubt that unemployment has substantial harmful effects upon many individuals and their families. Futhermore, the consequences are likely in practice to be more serious than is revealed in survey investigations" (p. 207).

Similarly, Fryer and Payne (1986) recognized the negative effects of unemployment and job loss, noting that "among that large majority whose experience is generally worsened by job loss there is still a wide range of reactions, partly because of wide variations in economic and social circumstances but also because of wide individual differences in the ability to cope with economic, social, and psychological pressures" (p. 259).

These reviews show a fair degree of consensus about the negative effects of unemployment across a wide range of variables and about the variables that moderate these effects. Some selected studies follow. In research conducted in Michigan, Kessler, Turner, and House (1987, 1988) distinguished between modifying and mediating variables. Ways of coping (assessed in terms of financial adjustment, avoidance of intrusive thoughts, and active problem solving), social support and a positive self-concept were significant modifiers of the health-damaging effects of unemployment, attenuating the effects of unemployment on ill health. Kessler et al. found two clear variables that mediated the negative effects of unemployment, namely financial strain and the presence or absence of other stressors. Social support (among the unmarried), a positive self-concept, and coping all reduced the damage that unemployment inflicted.

The results of a study by Whelan (1992) in the Republic of Ireland also showed that poverty and lifestyle deprivation played a major role in mediating the impact of unemployment on individuals and their families. Financial stress and strain were also important variables investigated in the Sheffield and Flinders programs of research (Feather, 1990; Warr, 1987), along with many other variables in these wide-ranging and productive programs.

Some other investigations at the time focused on the effects of anticipated termination of employment and reactions to subsequent job loss (e.g., Cobb & Kasl, 1977; Iverson & Sabroe, 1988; Kasl & Cobb, 1982). The psychological effects of job insecurity were also described in relation to the work situation and the anticipation of possible job loss in a volume edited by Hartley et al. (1991). In other studies job-seeking behavior was investigated along with other variables such as social support that related to successful coping (e.g., Feather, 1990, 1992; Feather & O'Brien, 1987; Vinokur & Caplan, 1987). For example, Feather and O'Brien (1987) found that job-seeking behavior was positively related to job valence and negative affect about unemployment but unrelated to control-optimism (see also Feather 1989a). Other studies using either quantitative or more qualitative methodologies were concerned with the effects of unemployment on family members (e.g., Allat & Yeandle, 1992; Elder & Caspi, 1988; Fagin & Little, 1984; Liem & Liem, 1988; Whelan, 1992).

These studies are only a sample of the research that was under way in the 1980s and the beginning of the 1990s. Burchell (1992) criticized psychologists who studied the effects of unemployment for their failure to take account of the nature of the labor market and the ebb and flow of available jobs, some being part-time, some of higher quality than others, some restricted to particular skills. He proposed that psychologists working in this area should become more acquainted with the economic and sociological literature on how the labor market affects the behavior of the unemployed. The point is well taken.

The studies following the Great Depression and thereafter advanced our understanding about how job loss and periods of unemployment affect people in regard to their psychological well-being and other variables. They also provide ideas about how we might account for some of these effects in terms of theoretical frameworks. I turn to these theoretical ideas in the next section.

Theoretical Approaches

The Marienthal study and other studies during the Great Depression were essentially descriptive. At the end of their review Eisenberg and Lazarsfeld (1938) noted the need for theoretical ideas that could guide research on the effects of unemployment. Later, Marie Jahoda cautioned against applying overly individualistic theories from social psychology and experimental psychology and argued that a social psychological approach should put equal emphasis on understanding the social and psychological dimensions and "the fit or misfit between socially imposed experiences and human needs" (Jahoda, 1988, p. 18). Theories that focused on an individual's needs and cognitions were seen to "have a bearing on only one dimension of the inevitably two-dimensional interaction between individual psychological processes and institutional arrangements that constrain or enable the conduct of social life" (p. 19).

For Jahoda (1992), "No single theory about the psychological impact of unemployment exists; none is likely to emerge. But there is much good thought and increasing concern with the utilization of concepts developed in the experimental sciences" (p. 357).

One is reminded that Lewin (1936) emphasized not only the individual's "life space," involving the person and his or her currently perceived psychological environment, but also the "foreign hull" and alien factors that are outside the person's control and impinge on the life space in an ever-changing world.

In my 1990 monograph I discussed some of the theoretical ideas that came from unemployment research from up to the beginning of the 1990s as well as other more general theoretical approaches that appeared relevant to the analysis of the psychological impact of job loss and unemployment (Feather, 1990). The more specific theories included stage theories (Eisenberg & Lazarus, 1938; Zawadski & Lazarsfeld, 1935); Jahoda's functional or deprivation approach (Jahoda, 1979, 1981, 1982, 1988); a focus on job content and locus of control (O'Brien, 1986); agency theory (Fryer, 1986, 1988; Fryer & Payne, 1986; Hartley & Fryer, 1984); and Warr's vitamin model (1987). The more general theories cover self-concept theory, stress and coping models, expectancy-value theory, causal attribution theory, helplessness/hopelessness theory, self-efficacy theory, and lifespan developmental psychology.

We could now add other theoretical approaches to this list. For example, Winefield (1995) included frustration-aggression theory in the theories he described. Creed and Bartrum (2006) included theories relating to Karasek's (1979) job demands-control theory, cybernetic theories, and theories concerned with cognitive appraisal and the emotions. We could also add to the list theories concerned with self-determination and self-regulation. Some of these theoretical approaches are the subject of later chapters in this handbook (see Kanfer and Bufton, this volume; Latham, Mawritz, & Locke, this volume; Van Hooft, this volume; Vansteenkiste & Van den Broeck, this volume).

Here I selectively focus on four of the more specific approaches (stage theory, functional or deprivation theory, agency theory, the vitamin model) and two of the more general approaches (stress and coping models, expectancy-value theory) that relate to the research contributions discussed so far.

Stage Theories

As noted previously, Eisenberg and Lazarsfeld (1938) described stages through which unemployed people were assumed to move as their unemployment continued (see also Beales & Lambert, 1934; Jahoda et al., 1933; Zawadski & Lazarsfeld, 1935). These early statements were mainly based on biographies, memoirs, case histories, and interviews. In the 1970s both Harrison (1976) and Hill (1978) described stage models, drawing both on the 1930s statements and in the latter case on sampling unemployed people in a cross-sectional study with different periods of unemployment. Jahoda's (1979) conclusion in the late 1970s about findings from the 1930s is consistent with the Eisenberg and Lazarsfeld (1938) statement and with most of the other summaries. She concluded that the early studies

> do establish at least the temporal priority of unemployment to the decay of self-esteem and morale. The process is not a smooth curve. More often the onset of unemployment produces an immediate shock effect which is followed by a period of almost constructive adaptation in which some enjoy their free time and may engage in active job-search; but deterioration follows quickly, with boredom and declining self-respect ending in despair or fatalistic apathy. (p. 310).

Harrison's (1976) description of stages was basically similar. Like Eisenberg and Lazarsfeld, he recognized that there would be differences in the way people reacted to their unemployment. He argued that those less likely to suffer would be those with adequate financial resources, those who saw their unemployment as somehow legitimate in relation to their perceived social role, those who were close to retirement, and those whose aspirations and expectations were low to begin with. Those who were ambitious and successful in their previous jobs would find prolonged unemployment especially stressful (see also Bakke, 1933).

Hill's (1977, 1978) model was more in line with the sequence of stages commonly described in relation to bereavement, namely denial, anger, grief, and depression, with a gradual movement toward some form of acceptance and recovery. How strong the initial reactions were would depend on how strongly the unemployed person was identified with the previous job, just as stronger reactions to bereavement are related to strength of attachment to the person who has died.

In the 1980s Fineman (1983, pp. 8–12) described other stage models as they applied to white-collar unemployment. These models were similar to those already described, with a shift from initial shock to a degree of acceptance. Some of these models derived from the life crisis model proposed by Fink (1967). In other cases they came from observations of unemployed managers and professionals (e.g., Powell & O'Driscoll, 1973). Fineman (1983) commented that there may be a lot of variation between individuals in their responses over time and that this variation "may be as (or more) important to understanding the impact of unemployment than a search for similarities and invariant patterns" (p.11). He was cautious about the use of stage theory, arguing that it is "unclear whether the unemployed experience moving in and out of phases, or whether the phases represent mere labels of convenience for the observer/investigator" (p. 11).

My own conclusion about stage theories of unemployment effects also regards them as descriptive accounts and as not having the status of explanations (Feather, 1990, p. 29). Then I noted that stage theories that come from the unemployment literature add to a long history of other theories proposing sequential changes that are assumed to occur in the course of development or that describe how people deal with negative events in their lives, such as bereavement or other life traumas.

Stage theories have had their fair share of critics (e.g., Bandura, 1986, pp. 483–485; Silver & Wortman, 1980). In the case of unemployment, the literature amply shows that there are differences in the way people react when they become unemployed, and that these differences depend on a range of variables that include financial status, social support, experience with past stressors, personality, coping skills, past job status, employment commitment, the current labor market, the quality or lack of quality of the unemployment experience, and so on. As noted previously, some of these variables were acknowledged by stage theorists in the 1930s (e.g., Eisenberg & Lazarsfeld, 1938), but without much theoretical elaboration of their effects. The idea that there is a set pattern of stages that most unemployed people go through oversimplifies the reactions to unemployment that occur and fails to deal with the causal processes that determine differences in how people react to job loss and continuing unemployment. Aggregate trends conceal important individual differences.

Deprivation Theory

In her later writings, Jahoda (1979, 1981, 1982) developed ideas about the manifest and latent functions of employment, stimulated by the Marienthal research and by other research on the psychological impact of unemployment. She proposed that the most important manifest function of employment was to provide a wage and that being deprived of a regular salary would have multiple effects on psychological well-being, the family, and many other aspects of daily life. The

Marienthal study provided many examples of the negative effects of economic deprivation and the association between broken and unbroken attitudes and level of income.

Paid employment as a social institution was also assumed by Jahoda (1982) to provide a number of latent functions that encompassed certain broad categories of experience that are

> enforced on the overwhelming majority of those who participate in it: the imposition of a time structure, the enlargement of the scope of social activities into areas less emotionally charged than family life, participation in a collective purpose and effort, the assignment by virtue of employment of status and identity, and required regular activity. These categories of experience . . . follow necessarily from the structural forms of modern employment. (p. 59)

Jahoda (1982) then linked these categories of experience to psychological well-being: "To the extent that these categories of experience have become a psychological requirement in modern life, the unemployed will suffer from their absence unless through their own deliberate efforts they have found alternative ways of satisfying these requirements" (p. 59). Although there are "other institutions that enforce one or more of these categories on their participants . . . none of them combines them all with as compelling a reason as earning one's living" (p. 59). Thus the loss of a job was assumed to deprive a person of both the manifest and latent benefits of having paid employment. Jahoda proposed that these functions relate to basic human needs, and she drew on Freud's (1930) ideas that work is a person's strongest tie to reality.

Jahoda's discussion of the manifest and latent functions of employment was criticized on the basis that it seemed to conceive of the person as a passive object, at the mercy of social institutions and external forces (e.g., Fryer, 1986; Fryer & Payne, 1986; Hartley & Fryer, 1984). To my mind this criticism was overdrawn. Jahoda's discussion of employment and unemployment was carefully nuanced and was presented as a framework of ideas rather than a well-developed theory. Her analysis recognized that employment as well as unemployment can have negative effects of people, depending on its quality—a point taken up in subsequent Australian research by O'Brien and Feather (1989) and Winefield, Tiggemann, & Goldney (1988) as well as Warr (1987). Similarly, her interest in time structure and its importance in daily life stimulated research on structure and purpose in the use of

time and the development of a time-structure questionnaire (Bond & Feather, 1988; Feather, 1989b, 1990; Feather & Bond, 1983) that was used in a number of later studies. Her focus on the different functions of employment suggested links between psychological well-being and the degree to which a person's current situation satisfied the needs implied by the manifest and latent functions and how one might alleviate any deficiencies that were present. These ideas influenced a lot of subsequent research, some of which involved developing measures of the latent functions and testing their effects on psychological well-being; see Creed & Bartrum (2006) for a review.

Agency Theory

Fryer's (1986) agency theory was a reaction to Jahoda's analysis. He argued for the importance of recognizing that people display personal agency in the way they react to events in their lives. Whether they are in paid employment or are unemployed, they actively strive, make decisions, plan for the future, set goals, initiate new activities, try to influence events, are guided by values and purposes, organize and structure information, and attempt to have some control over the events and outcomes that affect their lives. The agentic features of individuals can be blocked both in paid employment and in unemployment, and this frustration of agency was assumed by Fryer to have negative consequences as far as psychological well-being was concerned.

Fryer and his colleagues published research showing purposeful and constructive behaviors in small samples of unemployed people (e.g., Fryer, 1988; Fryer & McKenna, 1987; Fryer & Payne, 1984). The emphasis on personal agency is an important feature of some of the theories concerning goal setting, self-regulation, and self-determination to be described in subsequent chapters in this handbook (see Kanfer and Bufton, this volume; Latham, Mawritz & Locke, this volume; Van Hooft, this volume; Vansteenkiste & Van den Broeck, this volume). It complements Jahoda's emphasis on the importance of paid employment as a social institution and her focus on the loss of the features of paid employment that she assumed would occur when a person no longer had a job.

Note, however, that Jahoda (1982) did recognize that the individual has a need to understand the world so as "to make sense of events, to see through the baffling diversity of appearances to the underlying meaning of it all" (p. 69) and a need "for some degree of control over one's immediate environment" (p.70). She did not see her approach as diametrically opposed to agency theory. In fact, she saw each approach as not theories in the true sense of the word but as involving differences in emphasis. In her view (Jahoda, 1992) the "agency approach has led to a greater emphasis on the study of poverty in unemployment, making economic hardship a central explicator of the psychological impairment. The deprivation "theory" leads to more sociological considerations of employment as a dominant social institution: exclusions from it leaves psychological needs unmet" (p. 356).

The Vitamin Model

Warr's vitamin model was a development from earlier statements where he distinguished between good and bad jobs (Warr, 1983); it was similar in some respects to Jahoda's analysis. He developed his earlier ideas further and extended them to the condition of unemployment. In the vitamin model, Warr (1987) listed nine features of the environment that were assumed to relate to mental health. These features were opportunity for control, opportunity for the use of skill, externally generated goals, variety, environmental clarity, availability of money, physical security, opportunity for interpersonal contact, and valued social position. These nine features were assumed to overlap so that, for example, valued social position would be associated with more availability of money, and increased personal control might carry with it greater opportunity for the use of skill and for variety in a job.

The list of environmental features proposed by Warr encompassed the manifest and latent functions of paid employment that were described by Jahoda, but they were more extensive. They were assumed to influence mental health analogously to the way vitamins affect physical health. Just as vitamins are beneficial to physical health up to a certain level and just as a deficiency in vitamins can impair physical health, so the environmental features were assumed to be beneficial up to a certain level and their absence would tend to impair mental health.

An interesting feature of Warr's vitamin model was the assertion that the positive advantage conferred by some of the environmental features on mental health levels reached a plateau after an initial rise in the presence of that feature. Warr termed these features the constant effect (CE) vitamins. For other environmental features, the initial advantage and plateau for mental health conferred by these features was assumed to be followed by a falling off or decrement in mental health if these

features were excessive. Warr termed these the additional decrement (AD) vitamins. He proposed that the CE vitamins were money, physical security, and valued social position; the AD vitamins were externally generated goals, variety, environmental clarity, control, skill use, and interpersonal contact. For the AD vitamins, a person could have too much of a good thing.

Warr applied the vitamin model to a wide range of topics in his book *Work, Unemployment, and Mental Health* (Warr, 1987)—see also Warr, Jackson, and Banks (1988). The model implied that negative effects on well-being would tend to be associated with the transition from employment to unemployment because of decrements in the nine environmental features. However, these negative effects would depend on the amount of change in the environmental vitamins. For example, a shift to unemployment from a low-skilled and routine job with low wages would not be as dramatic as a shift from a highly skilled job with high wages, variety, and opportunities for control. In both cases the negative effects would be buffered if there were welfare or redundancy payments or if some environmental features like opportunities for interpersonal contact continued to be preserved. The unemployment experience would also vary for different subgroups depending on the presence or absence of the CE and AD environmental features. Warr (1987) discussed the psychological effects of unemployment for middle-aged men, teenagers, women, and the long-term unemployed. Research by the Sheffield group also showed the importance of personal commitment to paid employment as a variable affecting psychological well-being after job loss (e.g. Warr, 1987; Warr, Jackson, & Banks, 1988).

Warr's model can be applied not only to the description and comparison of jobs and unemployed situations but also to other kinds of environment, such as the family, hospitalization, leisure activities, and retirement. The model proposes that nonlinear effects could occur between mental health and environmental features and implies that the design of research should allow for these effects. Warr (1987) conceived of mental health as involving five main components: affective well-being, competence, autonomy, aspiration, and integrated functioning. Research from the Sheffield group in the 1980s was discussed by Warr in relation to the vitamin model.

Subsequent research to test Warr's vitamin model has mainly been conducted in the context of employment rather than job loss. The research also relates to other theoretical perspectives on job characteristics such as the Job Characteristics Model (Hackman & Oldham, 1980) and the Demand-Control-Support Model (Karasek, 1979; Karasek & Theorell, 1990). Not all of Warr's vitamins are included in these studies. The focus has been more on variables such as job demands, job autonomy, and social support in the workplace.

Empirical evidence concerned with the vitamin model was reviewed by de Jonge and Schaufeli (1998). They concluded that the evidence was somewhat conflicting. In their own investigation involving a large sample of Dutch health care workers, they found partial support for the non-linear relationship between job characteristics (job demands, job autonomy, social support) and employee well-being (job satisfaction, job-related anxiety, and emotional exhaustion), consistent with the vitamin model (see also Warr, 1990). In contrast, Jeurissen and Nyklicek (2001) found limited support in a much smaller sample of predominantly female nurses in a health-care organization. Much may depend upon the types of workers who were sampled and the nature of the work they performed. In the meantime, there is a need to go beyond studies of stress in the workplace and to update research on the vitamin model and unemployment, adding to the earlier studies that came from the Sheffield group.

It should be clear that the theoretical ideas put forward by both Warr and Jahoda had a situational focus. They were not concerned with a detailed analysis of underlying human needs or with personality differences but with environmental features (in the case of Warr) and functional analyses of the social institution of employment (in the case of Jahoda). Both approaches stimulated research and both remain as important contributions. However they left some questions unanswered. For example, are some of Warr's environmental variables more important than others? Would that depend on context (e.g., length of unemployment, age to retirement)? How do the vitamins cluster together? Are they related to underlying needs? Does Jahoda's manifest function of paid employment (providing an income) override the other functions in its effects? How does the manifest function interact with the latent functions? Their approaches, however, focused on situation-centred variables for good reason. Situations may be easier to modify than people, providing more opportunity for interventions that improve the situation of people who are either in bad jobs or in unemployment that varies in its quality (Feather,

1990, p. 45). Thus they had policy implications as well as research implications.

Stress and Coping Models

The models described so far are those that emerged after the Great Depression and in the 1980s, influenced by the research available at the time. They were more specifically targeted to the analysis of work and unemployment and their effects on psychological well-being. In my book *The Psychological Impact of Unemployment* (Feather, 1990), I also described more general theoretical approaches that would also be relevant to the analyses of unemployment effects.

One framework that I discussed concerned stress and coping. Loss of a job may be viewed as a stressful event with which the unemployed person has to cope in some way both emotionally and behaviorally. There is a vast literature that considers how people cope with stress and negative events in their lives (Feather, 1990, p. 55). This literature emphasizes how a person appraises a stressful situation and the coping reactions that may follow (e.g., Lazarus & Folkman, 1984; Pearlin & Schooler, 1978).

According to Lazarus and Folkman (1984), "Psychological stress is a particular relationship between the person and the environment that is taxing or exceeding his or her resources and endangering his or her well-being" (p. 19). They distinguished between a *primary appraisal* ("Am I in trouble or being benefited, now or in the future, in what way?) and a *secondary appraisal* ("What if anything can be done about it?") Coping with the situation involved *emotion-focused coping* (regulating the emotional response to the problem) and *problem-solving coping* (managing or altering the problem that is causing the distress). Lazarus and Folkman also discuss resources that could help to buffer the effects of stress (e.g., health and energy, positive beliefs, problem-solving skills, social support, social skills, material resources) and constraints that might restrict the use of resources (e.g., personal and environmental constraints and level of threat). The distinctions made by Lazarus and Folkman have obvious relevance to the situation of unemployment. For example, types of emotion-focused and problem-solving coping among unemployed people might involve defensive strategies such as denial, positive comparisons that compare self with others who are less fortunate, justifications, reappraisals, downsizing one's goals and aspirations, seeking support from others, and other types of active problem solving; see also Taylor (1986) for a detailed treatment of the coping process, which takes account of both internal and external sources of resources or impediments. The literature on stress and coping has expanded considerably since the 1980s, but these earlier contributions are still clearly relevant.

Some of the North American studies in the 1980s described how people coped with changes in their work situation, as in the pioneer study conducted by Kasl and Cobb, who investigated the effects on male workers of plant closure and job loss in both a large metropolitan area and a rural community (Cobb & Kasl, 1977; Kasl & Cobb, 1982). For example, Kasl and Cobb (1982) included both objective and subjective measures in their study (e.g., blood and urine specimens, blood pressure, pulse rate, self-blame, reported health, perceived social support, work-role deprivation, personality variables). Other North American studies at the time considered the effects of economic change (see Dooley & Catalano, 1980, Dooley, Catalano, & Rook, 1988) and coping reactions to the stress produced by unemployment (e.g., Elder & Caspi, 1988; Kessler, Turner, & House, 1988). Studies in Australia, the United Kingdom, and Europe also referred to the stress of unemployment and the coping reactions that followed. Many of these studies assessed financial stress and strain (e.g., Feather, 1989b; Rowley & Feather, 1987; Warr, 1987; Whelan, 1992).

Most of these studies were not integrated into formal stress and coping models. They dealt more generally with the types of stress that could follow job loss (e.g., financial stress) and how the unemployed person coped with this stress in family life and elsewhere. Examples of more formal models were those proposed by Fineman and by Payne and Hartley; see Feather (1990, pp. 61–62). Fineman (1983, 1987) developed a stress model that he applied to white-collar unemployment and that took account of the threat impact of unemployment as a stressor and the forms of coping behavior that followed. This model was clearly indebted to earlier analyses by Howard and Scott (1965) and Lazarus (1966) and took account of the demands of unemployment, its impact and threat, effects on personality, ways of coping, and stress and strain. Payne and Hartley (1987) described a model proposing that "the stressfulness of the environment is a function of the relative balance between the problems facing the unemployed and the degree of support and/or constraint under which these problems are faced" (p. 33). Ways of helping individuals to deal with

the stress that follows job loss and unemployment (e.g., the JOBs intervention program) are reviewed in later chapters in this handbook (see Price & Vinokur, this volume).

This brief review concerned with stress and coping models is highly selective, dealing with only some of the ideas put forward at the time (see also Dohrenwend & Dohrenwend, 1974; Hamilton, Hoffman, Broman, & Rauma, 1993; Kinicki & Latack, 1990; Leana & Feldman, 1992; Schaufeli, 1992; Vinokur, Caplan, & Williams, 1987). Kessler, Price, and Wortman (1985) provided a convenient summary of the wider literature in an article in the *Annual Review of Psychology*, where they reviewed social factors in psychopathology and concluded that the common conception of the stress process is

the notion that stress exposure sets off a process of adaptation. It is recognized that this process unfolds over time and it acknowledges that this process is modified by structural factors as well as by personal dispositions and vulnerabilities. There is growing recognition that the analysis of this process requires longitudinal methods. Also, it is becoming increasingly clear that experimental interventions are required to unravel the parts of this process that link stress and health. (p. 565)

Clearly these discussions of stress, appraisal, and ways of coping are relevant to our understanding of how the unemployed cope with their situation.

Expectancy-Value Theory

So far in this historical review I have been concerned with research and theory that connected job loss and unemployment with psychological well-being and ways of coping. At some time after job loss, however, most unemployed people start to look for another job. In the 1980s I used the general framework of expectancy-value theory to model job-seeking behavior.

This framework came from motivational theory and it assumes that what a person does bears some relation to the expectations or beliefs that a person holds and to the subjective value of the outcomes that might occur following the action. The expectations encompass both beliefs about whether a particular action can be performed to some required standard and beliefs about the various positive and negative consequences that might occur as a result of the action. The subjective values (or valences) of these possible consequences are assumed to be determined by a person's needs and values and by the social norms that prevail in the context in which the behavior occurs. Back in 1959 I described various expectancy-value models (Feather, 1959), and I updated the picture in 1982 in my edited book *Expectations and Actions* (Feather, 1982). There have been further developments since then; see Feather, 1990, pp. 62–66) and Feather (1992).

Using this approach, one would predict that job-seeking behavior following job loss would be positively related to the strength of an unemployed person's expectation that he or she would succeed in obtaining a particular job and also on how much the person valued that job (Feather, 1990, 1992). This hypothesis was tested in studies conducted in the Flinders program in the 1970s and 1980s (Feather, 1990; Feather & Davenport, 1981; Feather & O'Brien, 1987). The results were mixed for the expectancy variable but supported the influence of job valence or work value on job search. For example, Feather and Davenport (1981) found that measures of confidence about finding a job, need for a job, and negative affect about unemployment predicted effort expended, but Feather and O'Brien (1987) found that a general measure of control-optimism did not predict how frequently an unemployed person looked for a job. A measure of job valence based on a person's expressed need for a job and negative affect about being unemployed did predict in the expected direction (see also Feather, 1990, 1989b). In the Feather and O'Brien (1985) study, control-optimism was negatively related to both duration of unemployment and number of previous job applications. Thus unsuccessful experience in the job market was associated with lower expectations of finding a job, as would be expected.

Ullah and Banks (1985) conducted a related study in the United Kingdom that was influenced by the Feather and Davenport (1981) research and also by the Fishbein and Ajzen (1975) theoretical approach to attitude-behavior relations. They found that lower expectations of finding a job, a less positive job-search attitude, and lower levels of employment commitment were significantly associated with lower levels of reported job-seeking activity for all three measures used. They also found that long spells of unemployment were associated with lower expectations of getting a job and with a less positive job-search attitude.

In other related research that used unemployed adults in southeast Michigan, Vinokur and Caplan (1987) found support for predictions based on the Fishbein and Ajzen (1975) attitude-behavior model. They found that the intention to try hard to seek reemployment was the main significant predictor of job-seeking behavior in the four-month period they identified. This intention was related to attitude toward job-seeking and to subjective norms. Vinokur and Caplan (1987) also found that the negative effects of an unsuccessful job search on mental health can be counteracted by social support.

More recent studies of job-search behavior are described in later chapters of this handbook along with the theoretical ideas that guided them (e.g., Boswell, & Gardner, this volume; Saks, this volume; Song, Sun, & Li, this volume; Van Hooft, this volume). The 1980s research showed that the expectancy-value theoretical framework was a viable way of analyzing job-seeking behavior, but the results implied that relations between expectations and job search were not always in the positive direction as predicted but were more complexly determined. Some of the possible reasons for this complexity were canvassed at the time (e.g., Feather, 1990, pp. 206–207; 1992). Here I again note some possible variables that may have underlined this complexity: Measures of expectations in some studies may not have been closely targeted to a person's goals (e.g., the control-optimism measure used by Feather and O'Brien may have been too general); expectations may have been high but job search may be inhibited by barriers and costs associated with looking for a job (e.g, the cost of transport); external forces (e.g., the need to qualify for social welfare benefits, parental or family concerns) may pressure an unemployed person to look for a job even though that person has a low expectancy of finding one; those unemployed individuals with high confidence about finding a job may take "time out" and delay their job search; job search may be inhibited by a restricted labor market for many types of jobs, resulting in a narrow range of mostly low expectations; and the value of having a job may override a person's expectations of finding one regardless of the odds. These different possibilities would undermine a simple positive relation between the expectation that a job would be found and actions directed toward finding the job.

Other Theoretical Approaches

I have also suggested some other more general theoretical approaches that might usefully be applied to the analysis of job loss and the impact of unemployment (Feather, 1990). For example, how a person reacts to losing a job may relate to the causal attributions he or she makes for the loss (e.g., lack of ability or skill, lack of effort, sickness, external conditions in the labor market, bad luck).

These reactions may also involve feelings of help-lessness and hopelessness and beliefs that nothing can be done to change the situation. They may also vary according to beliefs about self-efficacy involving the degree to which an unemployed person believes that he or she is able to perform the necessary actions to get a job. How people react to unemployment may also depend on the values they hold and on where they are in the life-cycle (young, middle-aged, or older). Research in the 1980s related reactions to job loss and unemployment to attribution theory (Feather, 1983a, 1983b, 1983c, 1985, 1990; Feather & Barber, 1983; Feather & Davenport, 1981; Furnham, 1982; Weiner, 1986, 1995); helplessness/hopelessness theory (Abramson, Seligman, & Teasdale, 1978); attitudes and values (Feather, 1985); and life-cycle differences (Feather, 1990; Warr, 1987). Bandura (1982) discussed the effects of self-efficacy judgments and outcome beliefs on how a person reacts to positive or negative outcomes. I also related self-efficacy theory to unemployment effects (Feather, 1990, pp. 73–77), and noted Bandura's (1982) statement that

> When people have a low sense of personal efficacy and no amount of effort by themselves or others produces results, they become apathetic and resigned to a dreary life. The pattern in which people see themselves as ineffectual but see similar others enjoying the benefits of successful effort is apt to give rise to self-disparagement and depression. Evident successes of others make it hard to avoid self-criticism. (p. 141)

These general approaches as well as those specifically targeted to the conditions of employment and unemployment continue to be appropriate for current research on job loss, unemployment, and job search. Other theoretical approaches have emerged since then, some of which are the focus of later chapters in this handbook (e.g., goal setting and control theory, Latham, Mawritz, & Locke, this volume; social cognitive and self-regulation theory, Kanfer & Bufton, this volume; self-determination theory, Vansteenkiste & Van den Broeck, this volume; theory of planned behavior; Van Hooft, this volume). In applying theoretical models to the analysis of reactions to unemployment, we should be careful to avoid approaches that are overly individualistic and that neglect the situational context that follows job loss. The positive and negative features of a person's prior employment situation and current unemployment situation are variables that always have to be considered. An interactionist

approach that considers both person and situation variables is necessary.

Finally, there would seem to be scope for applying ideas that come from research on justice to the analysis of reactions to unemployment. As noted previously, a distinction was made in early times between the deserving poor and the sturdy beggars. Deservingness is a justice-related concept that is relevant to how a person perceives positive or negative outcomes that relate to self or other. I have proposed a model (Feather, 1999) that conceptualizes deservingness in terms of the evaluative structure of action/outcome relations and that uses a balance principle (Heider, 1958). Research on deservingness, employment, and unemployment was conducted by Feather and Dawson (1998). In its more recent development, the structural model was extended to the analysis of discrete emotions that were proposed to follow deserved or undeserved positive or negative outcomes such as success or failure in applying for a job (Feather, 2006; Feather & McKee, 2009; Feather, McKee, & Bekker, 2011). This approach focuses on perceived justice and injustice, especially deservingness and undeservingness, and it can be applied to the analysis of feelings such as anger, guilt, and shame that may follow loss of a job and also to how people react to the unemployment of others. These variables that have to do with deservingness and entitlement have been neglected in research on job loss, unemployment, and job search. They are important variables that should be considered more in future research.

Other research reviewed by Dalbert (2006) has considered how belief in a just world (BJW) affects a person's reactions to unemployment. The studies showed that BJW can be an adaptive resource in how people cope with the challenge of job loss. Those with a strong BJW may cope better in various ways than those with a weaker BJW even though they may also perceive their own unemployment as unfair. But the longer the unemployment continued the more difficult it became for them to find meaning in their fate.

These new lines of research highlight the importance of relating how people react to job loss to justice-related variables. Beliefs about deservingness and entitlement should affect the emotions that are experienced and the way in which unemployed people cope with their negative condition. Discrete emotions such as anger, guilt, and shame that relate to beliefs about deservingness and entitlement may have different effects on how the unemployed person reacts in terms of such behaviors as an active job search, partial withdrawal from the labor market, or protest behaviors either by the unemployed or by others in attempts to redress injustice (e.g., Feather, 2006; Feather & Bond, 1984; Feather, Woodyatt, & McKee, 2011).

Concluding Comments

In this historical review I have focused on early studies from the Great Depression of the 1930s and later contributions that take us up to the beginning of the 1990s. The literature is extensive, and I have necessarily been selective in my focus. It should be apparent, however, that current research on job loss, unemployment, and job search has an important historical background that is both empirical and theoretical and contains the seeds of much of what is being done in the present. Similar issues occupy the attention of current researchers, and there is good reason to look back to see what has been done before.

As the chapters in this handbook show, there are new questions being asked that relate to social and economic change and technological development. Some of these questions relate to the effects of computer and electronic technologies; some concern the representation of women in the workforce and ways of balancing employment and child care; some involve new styles of management; some concern changes in the nature of the labor market and the availability of social welfare; some relate to the emergence of casual and contract employment and intermittent changes in a person's employment history; some relate to employment over the life cycle and the shift to retirement. Yet some central issues remain the same. How psychological well-being and health relate to changes in employment status and how people cope with short- and longer-term unemployment in their daily lives remain basic questions that need to be addressed in the context of the changes that occur in the social and economic environment and in the culture as a whole.

This historical review teaches us some lessons. The Marienthal research and other studies from the Great Depression remind us of the importance of descriptive fieldwork where detailed information of different kinds is collected, enabling the researcher to build up a picture of what it means to be unemployed in the person's social and family context. It helps us to put flesh on the bones of bare statistics. The introduction over time of longitudinal designs as well as advances in statistical procedures enables some leverage on questions of causality such as whether unemployment is a cause of reduced psychological well-being and other negative outcomes or whether personal deficiencies that are already present lead to unemployment and diminished chances of being selected for a job (the social causation versus drift hypotheses; see Dooley et al., 1988). As is often the case in these kinds of discussions, both factors seem to be involved, and the social and personal factors interact often in complex ways. Other lessons remind us that both employment and unemployment vary in their good and bad features and that the effects of job loss and unemployment can be buffered by social support, welfare payments, and other factors. Still other lessons point to the need to examine effects in different cultures where there may be different attitudes and values and different ways of supporting the unemployed (e.g., Schaufeli & van Yperen, 1992). The background historical literature is not culture-bound. Studies have been conducted across a range of cultures that have included Australia, Austria, England, Ireland, the Netherlands, the United States, and even a Scottish island (Harding & Sewell, 1992).

The message from this review is clear. Unemployment has negative effects that vary in their magnitude depending on variables that relate both to the individual and the situational context. Having some financial support that lifts people out of relative poverty buffers these negative effects, so that people may be able to maintain their households, pay their mortgages, cover the cost of transport, and obtain other necessities that money can buy. Financial stress and strain are the great enemies. The past research tells us this. It also tells us that good employment enhances psychological well-being because of the latent functions and "vitamins" that the institution of employment provides in various degrees, enabling a person to contact with the world outside the family, to satisfy basic needs, and to find structure and purpose in their use of time. The absence of these features has negative effects for most people, although there may be differences between people in which features they regard as important. The research also tells us that people are usually not passive in the face of unemployment. Most make active choices and plan for the future, although negative effects become more dramatic in recalcitrant environments where desired jobs are no longer available and valued goals are out of range.

Finally, the past literature warns us against attempts to construct an overarching theory to account for the effects of job loss and unemployment.

A key message from my 1990 book was the importance of using midrange theories, targeted to particular topics such as psychological well-being and job search, that consider both personal characteristics and environmental features and have regard to underlying processes and the dynamics of change both in individuals and in environments over time (Feather, 1990). That message has not changed. The task remains a complex one, engaging multidisciplinary efforts from social psychologists, sociologists, economists, and other social scientists. The focus should extend beyond psychological well-being and health-related issues to other possible social consequences of unemployment such as the breakup of families, the temptation to engage in social protest, and antisocial behaviors such as crime and delinquency, drug-taking, and so forth.

This review of the past history of unemployment research has provided examples of seminal studies and ideas that continue to influence the field. Their influence is evident in the following chapters of this handbook.

Appendix

I list below a short set of recommendations for practitioners and policymakers that are suggested by the research described in this historical review. The list is by no means complete, but it samples some of the major implications of the research that I reviewed.

• The importance of considering not only the financial resources available to those without jobs but also their need for assistance in terms of how they organize their budgets and how they deal with the loss of the time structure and the other "vitamins" that employment provides in part or whole.

• The importance of considering not only characteristics of the unemployed person—such as his or her age, sex, marital status, health, personality, competence and interpersonal skills—but also the social context in which the job loss occurs, such as the social and organizational context of the person's previous employment and its quality, the person's family situation, and the availability of social support within the family and the community—or, more formally, from the employment agencies.

• The importance of considering the nature of the person's previous employment and how it might shape expectations about what new job opportunities are possible and desirable in a changing labor market.

• The importance of considering variables (personal and social) that might help to buffer the negative effects of job loss, leading to resilience in the face of misfortune and positive ways of coping, and also variables that impede positive coping.

• The importance of considering what kinds of jobs are available in the labor market and whether they meet the same kinds of needs and provide the same kinds of "vitamins" and financial security when compared with the job that was lost.

• The importance of considering how job search relates to realistic or unrealistic beliefs and expectations about the likelihood of finding a suitable job and on how these job expectations are influenced by job availability and the person's past record of success or failure in job applications.

• The importance of considering the stress and strain associated with job loss, the emotions that occur, and the coping strategies that are adopted.

• The importance of conducting fine-grain fieldwork studies that go beyond surveys; that is, studies that look closely at the unemployed person in his or her social context.

• The importance of disentangling the effects of poverty from the other negative effects of unemployment that relate to losing the benefits of having a job.

• The importance of recognizing that a multidisciplinary approach is necessary in the study of job loss, unemployment, and job search involving contributions from psychologists, sociologists, economists, and other social scientists.

• The importance of recognizing the effects of different types of employment (full-time, casual, and contract), good and bad forms of employment and unemployment, and between patterns of employment and unemployment as people move in and out of the labor market.

• The importance of recognizing both social causation and drift into unemployment relating to psychological deficits as factors that may lead to job loss and unemployment, both of which affect an unemployed person's psychological well-being and subsequent job search.

• The importance of studying the role of job-search institutions set up to manage unemployment. How much do they enhance the opportunities for the unemployed to find employment? How much do they alter the attitudes and expectations of the unemployed towards seeking employment?

References

Abramson, L. Y., Seligman, M.E.P., & Teasdale, J. D. (1978). Learned helplessness in humans: Critique and reformulation. *Journal of Abnormal Psychology, 87,* 49–74.

Allat, P., & Yeandle, S. (1992). *Youth unemployment and the family: Voices of disordered times.* London: Routledge.

Bakke, E. W. (1933). *The unemployed man.* London: Nisbet.

Bakke, E. W. (1940a). *Citizens without work.* New Haven, CT: Yale University Press.

Bakke, E.W. (1940b). *The unemployed worker.* New Haven, CT: Yale University Press.

Bandura, A. (1982). Self-efficacy in human agency. *American Psychologist, 37,* 122–147.

Bandura, A. (1986). *Social foundations of thought and action: A social cognitive theory.* Englewood Cliffs, NJ: Prentice-Hall.

Banks, M. H., & Ullah, P. (1988). *Youth unemployment in the 1980s: Its psychological effects.* London: Croom Helm.

Barling, J. (1990). *Employment, stress, and family functioning.* Chichester, UK: Wiley.

Beales, H. L., & Lambert, R. S. (1934). *Memoirs of the unemployed.* London: Gollancz.

Bond, M. J., & Feather, N. T. (1988). Some correlates of structure and purpose in the use of time. *Journal of Personality and Social Psychology, 55,* 321–329.

Brenner, M. H. (1973). *Mental illness and the economy.* Cambridge, MA: Harvard University Press.

Brenner, M. H. (1979a). Influence of the social environment on psychopathology: The historical perspective. In J. E. Barrett, R. M. Rose, & G. L. Kerman (Eds.), *Stress and mental disorder.* New York: Raven Press.

Brenner, M. H. (1979b). Unemployment, economic growth and mortality. *Lancet, 1,* 672.

Burchell, B. (1992). Towards a social psychology of the labour market: Or why we need to understand the labour market before we can understand unemployment. *Journal of Occupational and Organisational Psychology, 65,* 345–354.

Carnegie Trust (1943). *Disinherited youth: A survey* 1936–1939. London: T. & A. Constable.

Catalano, R. A., & Dooley, C. D. (1983). Health effects of economic instability: A test of the economic stress hypothesis. *Journal of Health and Social Behavior, 24,* 46–60.

Cobb, S., & Kasl, S. V. (1977). *Termination: The consequences of job loss.* Cincinatti: U.S. Department of Health, Education, and Welfare.

Creed, P. A., & Bartrum, D. (2006). Explanations for deteriorating wellbeing in unemployed people: Specific unemployment theories and beyond. In T. Kieselbach, A. H. Winefield, C. Boyd, & S. Anderson (Eds.), *Unemployment and health: International and interdisciplinary perspectives* (pp.1–20). Brisbane: Australian Academic Press.

Dalbert, C. (2006). Justice concerns and mental health during unemployment. In T. Kieselback, A. H. Winefield, C. Boyd, & S. Anderson (Eds.), *Unemployment and health: International and interdisciplinary perspectives* (pp. 35–50). Brisbane: Australian Academic Press.

Daniel, W. W. (1974). *A national survey of the unemployed.* London: Political and Economic Planning Institute.

de Jonge, J., & Schaufeli, W. B. (1998). Job characteristics and employee well-being: A test of Warr's Vitamin Model in health care workers using structural equation modelling. *Journal of Organizational Behaviour, 19,* 387–407.

Dooley, C. D., & Catalano, R. A. (1980). Economic change as a cause of behavioral disorder. *Psychological Bulletin, 87,* 450–468.

Dooley, C. D., & Catalano, R. A. (1984). The epidemiology of economic stress. *American Journal of Community Psychology, 12,* 387–409.

Dooley, C. D., Catalano, R. A., & Rook, K. S. (1988). Personal and aggregate unemployment and psychological symptoms. *Journal of Social Issues, 44,* 107–123.

Dooley, C. D., Catalano, R. A., & Hough, R. (1992). Unemployment and alcohol disorder in 1910 and 1990: Drift versus social causation. *Journal of Occupational and Organizational Psychology, 65,* 277–290.

Dohrenwend, B. S., & Dohrenwend, B. P. (Eds.). (1974). *Stressful life events: Their nature and their effects.* New York: Wiley.

Eisenberg, P., & Lazarsfeld, P. F. (1938). The psychological effects of unemployment. *Psychological Bulletin, 35,* 358–390.

Elder, G. H., & Caspi, A. (1988). Economic stress in lives: Developmental perspectives. *Journal of Social Issues, 44,* 25–45.

Fagin, L., & Little, M. (1984). *The forsaken families.* Harmondsworth: Penguin.

Feather, N. T. (1959). Subjective probability and decision under uncertainty. *Psychological Review, 66,* 150–164.

Feather, N. T. (Ed.) (1982). *Expectations and actions: Expectancy-value models in psychology.* Hillsdale, NJ: Erlbaum.

Feather, N. T. (1985). Attitudes, values, and attributions: Explanations of unemployment. *Journal of Personality and Social Psychology, 48,* 876–889.

Feather, N. T. (1989a). The effects of unemployment on work values and motivation. In U. W. Kleinbeck, H. H. Quast, H. Thierry, & H. Hacker (Eds.), *Work motivation* (pp. 201–229). Hillsdale, NJ: Erlbaum.

Feather, N. T. (1989b). Reported changes in behaviour after job loss in a sample of older unemployed men. *Australian Journal of Psychology, 41,* 75–85.

Feather, N. T. (1990). *The psychological impact of unemployment.* New York: Springer-Verlag.

Feather, N. T. (1992). Expectancy-value theory and unemployment effects. *Journal of Occupational and Organizational Psychology, 65,* 315–330.

Feather, N. T. (1999). *Values, achievement, and justice: Studies in the psychology of deservingness.* New York: Kluwer Academic/Plenum.

Feather, N. T. (2006). Deservingness and emotions: Applying the structural model of deservingness to the analysis of affective reactions to outcomes. *European Review of Social Psychology, 17,* 38–73.

Feather, N. T., & Barber, J. G. (1983). Depressive reactions and unemployment. *Journal of Abnormal Psychology, 92,* 185–195.

Feather, N. T., & Bond, M. J. (1983). Time structure and purposeful activity among employed and unemployed university graduates. *Journal of Occupational Psychology, 56,* 241–254.

Feather, N. T., & Bond, M. J. (1984). Potential social action as a function of expectation-outcome discrepancies among employed and unemployed university graduates. *Australian Journal of Psychology, 36,* 205–217.

Feather, N. T., & Davenport, P. R. (1981). Unemployment and depressive affect: A motivational and attributional analysis. *Journal of Personality and Social Psychology, 41,* 121–144.

Feather, N. T., & Dawson, S. (1998). Judging deservingness and affect in relation to another's employment or unemployment: A test of a justice model. *European Journal of Social Psychology, 28,* 361–381.

Feather, N. T., & McKee, I. R. (2009). Differentiating emotions in relation to deserved or undeserved outcomes: A retrospective study of real-life events. *Cognition and Emotion*, *23*, 955–977.

Feather, N. T., McKee, I. R., & Bekker, N. (2011). Deservingness and emotions: Testing a structural model that relates emotions to the perceived deservingness of positive or negative outcomes. *Motivation and Emotion*, *35*, 1–13.

Feather, N. T., & O'Brien, G. E. (1986a). A longitudinal analysis of the effects of different patterns of employment and unemployment on school-leavers. *British Journal of Psychology*, *77*, 459–479.

Feather, N. T., & O'Brien, G. E. (1986b). A longitudinal study of the effects of employment and unemployment on school-leavers. *Journal of Occupational Psychology*, *59*, 121–144.

Feather, N. T., & O'Brien, G. E. (1987). Looking for employment: An expectancy-value analysis of job-seeking behaviour among young people. *Journal of Occupational Psychology*, *78*, 251–272.

Feather, N. T., Woodyatt, L., & McKee, I. R. (2011). Predicting support for social action: How values, justice-related variables, discrete emotions, and outcome expectations influence support for the stolen generations. *Motivation and Emotion*. DOI 10.1007/s11031–001-9262-5.

Fineman, S. (1983). *White collar unemployment: Impact and stress*. Chichester: Wiley.

Fineman, S. (Ed.) (1987). *Unemployment: Personal and social consequences*. London: Tavistock.

Fink, S. L. (1967). Crisis and motivation—A theoretical model. *Archives of Physical Medicine and Rehabilitation*, *43*, 592–597.

Fishbein, M., & Ajzen, I. (1975). *Belief, attitude, intention, and behavior: An introduction to theory and research*. Reading, MA: Addison-Wesley.

Freud, S. (1930). *Civilization and its discontents*. London: Hogarth.

Fryer, D. (1986). Employment deprivation and personal agency during unemployment: A critical discussion of Jahoda's explanation of the psychological effects of unemployment. *Social Behaviour*, *1*, 3–23.

Fryer, D. (1987). Monmouthshire and Marienthal: Sociographies of two unemployed communities. In D. Fryer & P. Ullah (Eds.), *Unemployed people: Social and psychological perspectives* (pp. 47–73). London: Tavistock.

Fryer, D. (1988). The experience of unemployment in social context. In S. Fisher & J. Reason (Eds.), *Handbook of life stress, cognition and health* (pp. 211–238). Chichester: Wiley.

Fryer, D. (1992). Editorial: Introduction to *Marienthal and Beyond*. *Journal of Occupational and Organizational Psychology*, *65*, 257–268.

Fryer, D. M., & McKenna, S. P. (1987). The laying off of hands—Unemployment and the experience of time. In S. Fineman (Ed.), *Unemployment: Personal and social consequences* (pp. 47–72). London: Tavistock.

Fryer, D. M., & Payne, R. L. (1984). Pro-active behaviour in unemployment: Findings and implications. *Leisure Studies*, *3*, 273–295.

Fryer, D. M., & Payne, R. L. (1986). Being unemployed: A review of the literature on the psychological experience of unemployment. In C. L. Cooper & I. Robertson (Eds.), *International review of industrial and organizational psychology* (pp. 235–278). Chichester: Wiley.

Fryer, D., & Ullah, P. (Eds.) (1987). *Unemployed people: Social and psychological perspectives*. Milton Keynes, UK: Open University Press.

Furnham, A. (1982). Explanations for unemployment in Britain. *European Journal of Social Psychology*, *12*, 335–352.

Garraty, J. A. (1978). *Unemployment in history: Economic thought and public policy*. New York: Harper & Row.

Hackman, J. R., & Oldman, G. R. (1980). *Work redesign*. Reading, MA: Addison Wesley.

Hamilton, V. L., Hoffman, W. S., Broman, C. L., & Rauma, D. (1993). Unemployment, distress, and coping: A panel study of autoworkers. *Journal of Personality and Social Psychology*, *65*, 234–247.

Harding, L., & Sewel, J. (1992). Psychological health and employment status in an island community. *Journal of Occupational and Organizational Psychology*, *65*, 269–275.

Harrison, R. (1976). The demoralizing experience of prolonged unemployment. *Department of Education Gazette*, *84*, 339–348.

Hartley, J., & Fryer, D. (1984). The psychology of unemployment: A critical appraisal. In G. M. Stephenson (Ed.), *Progress in applied social psychology* (Vol. 2, pp. 3–30). Chichester: Wiley.

Hartley, J., Jacobson, D., Klandermans, B., & van Vuuren, T. (1991). *Job insecurity: Coping with jobs at risk*. London: Sage.

Heider, F. (1958). *The psychology of interpersonal relations*. New York: Wiley.

Hill, J.M.M. (1977). *The social and psychological impact of unemployment*. London: Tavistock.

Hill, J.M.M. (1978). The psychological impact of unemployment. *New Society*, *43*, January, 118–120.

Howard, A., & Scott, R. A. (1965). A proposed framework for the analysis of stress in the human organism. *Behavioral Science*, *10*, 141–166.

Israeli, N. (1935). Distress in the outlook of Lancashire and Scottish unemployed. *Journal of Applied Psychology*, *19*, 67–69.

Iverson, L., & Sabroe, S. (1988). Psychological well-being among unemployed and employed people after a company closedown: A longitudinal study. *Journal of Social Issues*, *44*, 141–152.

Jahoda, M. (1979). The impact of unemployment in the 1930s and 1970s. *Bulletin of the British Psychological Society*, *32*, 309–314.

Jahoda, M. (1981). Work, employment, and unemployment: Values, theories, and approaches in social research. *American Psychologist*, *36*, 184–191.

Jahoda, M. (1982). *Employment and unemployment: A social-psychological analysis*. Cambridge, UK: Cambridge University Press.

Jahoda, M. (1987). Unemployed men at work. In D. Fryer & P. Ullah (Eds.) *Unemployed people: Social and psychological perspectives* (pp. 1–73). Milton Keynes, UK: Open University Press.

Jahoda, M. (1988). Economic recession and mental health: Some conceptual issues. *Journal of Social Issues*, *44*, 13–23.

Jahoda, M. (1992). Reflections on Marienthal and after. *Journal of Occupational and Organizational Psychology*, *65*, 355–358.

Jahoda, M., Lazarsfeld, P. F., & Zeisel, J. (1933). *Marienthal: The sociography of an unemployed community*. (English translation, 1971). Chicago: Aldine.

Jeurissen, T., & Nyklicek, I. (2001). Testing the Vitamin Model of job stress in Dutch health care workers. *Work & Stress*, *15*, 254–264.

Karasek, R. A. (1979). Job demands, job decision latitude, and mental strain: Implications for job redesign. *Administrative Science Quarterly 24*, 285–308.

Karasek, R. A., & Theorell, T. (1990). *Healthy work: Stress, productivity and the reconstruction of working life.* New York: Basic Books.

Kasl, S. (1982). Strategies of research on economic instability and health. *Psychological Medicine, 12,* 637–649.

Kasl, S., & Cobb, S. (1982). Variability of stress effects among men experiencing job loss. In L. Goldberger & S. Breznitz (Eds.), *Handbook of stress: Theoretical and clinical aspects* (pp. 445–465). New York: Free Press.

Kelvin, P., & Jarrett, J. E. (1985). *Unemployment: Its social psychological effects.* Cambridge, UK: Cambridge University Press.

Kessler, R. C., Price, R. H., & Wortman, C. B. (1985). Social factors in psychology: Stress, social support, and coping process. *Annual Review of Psychology, 36,* 531–572.

Kessler, R. C., Turner, J. B., & House, J. S. (1988). Effects of health in a community survey: Main, modifying, and mediating effects. *Journal of Social Issues, 44,* 69–85.

Kessler, R. C., Turner, J. B., & House, J. S. (1987). Intervening processes in the relationship between unemployment and health. *Psychological Medicine, 17,* 949–9961.

Kieselbach, T., Winefield, A. H., Boyd, C., & Anderson, S. (2006). *Unemployment and health: International and interdisciplinary perspectives.* Brisbane: Australian Academic Press.

Kinicki, A. J., & Latack, J. C. (1990). Explication of the construct of coping with involuntary job loss. *Journal of Vocational Behaviour, 36,* 339–360.

Komarovsky, M. (1940). *The unemployed man and his family: The effect of unemployment upon the status of the man in 59 families.* New York: Dryden.

Lazarus, R. S. (1966). *Psychological stress and the coping process.* New York: McGraw-Hill.

Lazarus, R. S., & Folkman, S. (1984). *Stress, appraisal, and coping.* New York: Springer-Verlag.

Leana, C. R., & Feldman, D. C. (1992). *Coping with job loss: How individuals, organizations, and communities respond to lay offs.* Lexington, MA: Lexington Books.

Liem, R., & Liem, J. H. (1988). Psychological effects of unemployment on workers and their families. *Journal of Social Issues, 44,* 87–105.

Lewin, K. (1936). *Principles of topological psychology.* New York: McGraw-Hill.

Marsden, D., & Duff, E. (1975). *Workless: Some unemployed men and their families.* Harmondsworth: Penguin.

O'Brien, G. E. (1985). Distortion in unemployment research: The early studies of Bakke and their implications for current research on employment and unemployment. *Human Relations, 38,* 877–894.

O'Brien, G. E. (1986). *Psychology of work and unemployment.* Chichester: Wiley.

O'Brien, G. E., & Feather, N. T. (1989). The relative effects of unemployment and quality of employment on the affect, work values and personal control of adolescents. *Journal of Occupational Psychology, 63,* 151–165.

Payne, R. L., & Hartley, J. (1987). A test of a model for explaining the affective experience of unemployed men. *Journal of Occupational Psychology, 60,* 31–47.

Pearlin, L. J., & Schooler, D. (1978). The structure of coping. *Journal of Health and Social Behavior, 19,* 2–21.

Pilgrim Trust (1938). *Men without work.* Cambridge, UK: Cambridge University Press.

Powell, D. H., & O'Driscoll, S.P.F. (1973). Middle class professionals face unemployment. *Society, 10,* 18–26.

Rowntree, B. S., & Lasker, B. (1911). *Unemployment: A social study.* London: Macmillan.

Schaufeli, W. B. (1992). Unemployment and mental health in well- and poorly- educated school-leavers. In K. Verhaar & L. Jansma (Eds.), *On the mysteries of unemployment* (pp. 253–271). Deventer, Holland: Kluwer.

Schaufeli, W. B., & Van Yperen, N. W. (1992). Unemployment and psychological distress among graduates: A longitudinal study. *Journal of Occupational and Organizational Psychology, 65,* 291–305.

Silver, R. L., & Wortman, C. B. (1980). Coping with undesirable life events. In J. Garber & M.E.P. Seligman (Eds.), *Human helplessness: Theory and applications.* (pp. 279–340). New York: Academic Press.

Sinfield, A. (1968). *The long term unemployed.* Paris: Organisation for Economic Co-operation and Development.

Sinfield, A. (1970). Poor and out-of-work in Shields. In P. Townsend (Ed.), *The concept of poverty* (pp. 220–235). London: Heinemann.

Sinfield, A. (1981). *What unemployment means.* Oxford, UK: Martin Robertson.

Taylor, F. I. (1909). *A bibliography of unemployment and the unemployed.* London: P. S. King & Son.

Taylor, S. E. (1986). *Health psychology.* New York: Random House.

Tiffany, D. W., Cowan, J. R., & Tiffany, P. M. (1970). *The unemployed: A social psychological portrait.* Englewood Cliffs, NJ: Prentice-Hall.

Ullah, P., & Banks, M. H. (1985). Youth unemployment and labour market withdrawal. *Journal of Economic Psychology, 6,* 51–64.

Vinokur, A., & Caplan, R. D. (1987). Attitudes and social support: Determinants of job-seeking behavior and well-being among the unemployed. *Journal of Applied Social Psychology, 17,* 1007–1024.

Vinokur, A., Caplan, R. D., & Williams, C. C. (1987). Effects of recent and past stress on mental health: Coping with unemployment among Vietnam veterans and nonveterans. *Journal of Applied Social Psychology, 17,* 710–730.

Warr, P. B. (1983). Work, jobs and unemployment. *Bulletin of the British Psychological Society, 36,* 305–311.

Warr, P. B. (1985). Twelve questions about unemployment and health. In B. Roberts, R. Finnegan, & D. Gallie (Eds.), *New approaches to economic life.* Manchester, UK: Manchester University Press.

Warr, P. B. (1987). *Work, unemployment, and mental health.* Oxford, UK: Clarendon Press.

Warr, P. B. (1990). Decision latitude, job demands, and employee well-being. *Work and Stress, 4,* 285–294.

Warr, P. B., Jackson, P. R., & Banks, M. H. (1988). Unemployment and mental health: Some British studies. *Journal of Social Issues, 44,* 47–68.

Wedderburn, D. (1964). *White collar redundancy.* Department of Applied Economics Occasional Papers, No. 1, University of Cambridge.

Weiner, B. (1986). *An attributional theory of motivation and emotion.* New York: Springer-Verlag.

Weiner, B. (1995). *Judgments of responsibility: A foundation for a theory of social conduct.* New York: Guilford.

Whelan, C. T. (1992). The role of income, life-style deprivation and financial strain in mediating the impact of unemployment on psychological distress: Evidence from the Republic of Ireland. *Journal of Occupational and Organizational Psychology, 65,* 331–344.

Winefield, A. H. (1995). Unemployment: Its psychological costs. In C. L. Cooper & I. T. Robertson (Eds.). *International review of industrial and organisational psychology* (Vol 10, pp. 169–212). Chichester: Wiley.

Winefield, A. H., Tiggemann, M., & Goldney, R. D. (1988). Psychological concomitants of satisfactory employment and unemployment in young people. *Social Psychiatry and Psychiatric Epidemiology, 23,* 149–157.

Winefield, A. H., Winefield, H. R., & Tiggemann, M. (1993). *Growing up with unemployment: A longitudinal study of its psychological impact.* London: Routledge.

Zawadski, B., & Lazarsfeld, P. F. (1935). The psychological consequences of unemployment. *Journal of Social Psychology, 6,* 224–251.

Job Insecurity and Anticipated Job Loss: A Primer and Exploration of Possible Interventions

Tahira M. Probst, Lixin Jiang, *and* Wendi Benson

Abstract

Given the increasing prevalence of job insecurity across the globe, the purpose of this chapter is to identify variables operating at the individual, occupational, organizational, and societal levels that have been found to influence employee perceptions of job insecurity and to discuss the outcomes (related to organizational well-being and employee well-being) that accrue as a result of such insecurity. In doing so, we bring together two disparate bodies of literature on economic stress (job insecurity and anticipated job loss) by integrating them into a comprehensive model that explicitly advocates a multilevel perspective and acknowledges that employees are embedded in multiple intersecting and influential contexts (e.g., socioeconomic conditions). Although a vast body of research suggests that the consequences of job insecurity are largely negative, this chapter also explores organizational- and societal-level interventions to attenuate these negative consequences.

Key Words: job insecurity, anticipated job loss, socioeconomic conditions, economic stress, intervention, multilevel model, organizational well-being, employee well-being

Economic crises such as the Great Recession of 2007–2009 have raised the salience of job insecurity in the popular press, and a growing body of empirical research indicates that the fear of losing one's job is a persistent and increasingly common stressor for many of today's workers. For example, as early as 1997 (a time of great economic growth in the United States), a study commissioned by the Organization for Economic Co-operation and Development (OECD) found that 52% of workers in the United States saw their jobs as being insecure and only 48% were satisfied with their security. More than a decade later and in the immediate aftermath of the Great Recession, a survey conducted by the American Psychological Association (2010) found nearly identical numbers, with 49% of respondents reporting worries about the future stability of their jobs. Such findings are certainly not confined to the United States. That same OECD

study found a 12% decline in the proportion of European employees who felt that their jobs were secure. Similar trends have also been observed in Asia (Zhao, Rust, McKinley, & Edwards, 2010), where market reforms have had a significant impact on employment security.

Given the increasing prevalence of job insecurity across the globe, the purpose of this chapter is to identify the myriad different variables operating at the individual, occupational, organizational, and societal levels that have been found to influence employee perceptions of job insecurity and to discuss the outcomes that accrue as a result of such insecurity. While there have been many recent meta-analyses and reviews of job insecurity, we believe that this chapter offers three unique perspectives. First, rather than focusing solely on the extensively studied outcomes of job insecurity, we concentrate on identifying predictors of job insecurity and anticipated job loss. In doing so, our chapter also brings together two disparate bodies of literature (job insecurity and anticipated job loss) and integrates these into a comprehensive model. Finally, we expand beyond the traditional individual-level focus to explicitly advocate a multilevel perspective that considers variables operating within each stage of the process. We argue that a complete understanding of the experience of job insecurity requires an acknowledgment that employees are embedded in multiple intersecting and influential contexts.

We begin our chapter with a brief discussion of the construct of job insecurity and its intersection with anticipated job loss, noting some of the most pressing controversies and debates within the field. Next, we present an overview of our overarching multilevel model of the antecedents and consequences of job insecurity. The remainder of the chapter considers each section of the model in greater detail (e.g., multilevel antecedents as well as individual and organizational outcomes). Finally, because it is important to understand not only the causes and consequences of job insecurity but also the ways of coping with such insecurity, we devote the final section of our chapter to research on moderator variables that may serve as a springboard to the development of practical intervention strategies.

The Nature of Job Insecurity

While the term *job insecurity* is commonly bandied about (indeed, a Lexis-Nexis search found more than 3,000 newspaper articles on the topic just within a year), consensus among job insecurity researchers regarding a commonly accepted definition and understanding of the construct has been surprisingly difficult to achieve. Job insecurity has been variously defined as "perceived powerlessness to maintain desired continuity in a threatened job situation" (Ashford, Lee, & Bobko, 1989); "perceived level of stability and continuance of one's job" (Probst, 2003); and "concern about the future permanence of the job" (Van Vuuren & Klandermans, 1990), to name a few. As Klandermans and Van Vuuren (1999) noted more than a decade ago, agreement regarding the appropriate definition and underlying dimensionality of the job insecurity construct is elusive, and it remains so to date. The areas under debate include whether job insecurity is a subjective experience or an objective state; whether job insecurity is a unidimensional or multidimensional construct; whether job insecurity is best conceptualized as a quantitative or qualitative construct; and whether it is theoretically

or practically meaningful to differentiate between cognitive and affective insecurity.

Subjective Versus Objective Insecurity

Job insecurity is most commonly conceptualized as a subjective phenomenon that is best understood and described "in the eye of the beholder" (e.g., Davy, Kinicki, & Scheck, 1997; Greenhalgh & Rosenblatt, 1984; Probst, 2002a; Sverke & Hellgren, 2002) and is often measured by asking employees to indicate their perceived likelihood of job loss. From this perspective, job insecurity can be defined as *the perception that the future of one's job is unstable or at risk*, regardless of any actual objective level of job security. Such a conceptualization explicitly relies upon potentially fallible individual perceptions regarding the future of one's job, which can be colored by economic, social, organizational, and individual characteristics (Sinclair, Sears, Probst, & Zajack, 2010). Therefore, it is possible to have a job that is objectively secure but subjectively perceived to be insecure by the employee holding that position (and vice versa).

Although subjective assessments of job insecurity are most common, there are ways to measure job insecurity objectively. For example, employees who are hired on a temporary contract have less objective security than employees who are permanent (De Cuyper & De Witte, 2006; De Witte & Naswall, 2003; Pearce, 1998). Additionally, government agencies can provide estimates of the job outlook for various occupations based on whether employment opportunities within these occupations are expected to be growing, stable, or declining over the next decade (e.g., the US Department of Labor's *Occupational Outlook Handbook*). Organizations can also objectively identify positions within their company as being more or less likely to be outsourced, eliminated, retained, or expanded in the future. Often this assessment can be made by upper-level management based on annual strategic planning and company economic forecasts. Once organizational plans for restructuring or downsizing are decided, employees may or may not receive advance notice of job loss. Thus objective job insecurity can also be conceptualized as advance notice of impending job loss.

The literature on impending job loss looks at outcomes of having received an actual layoff notice, but before the employee's actual departure date. While layoff notices can certainly be quite abrupt and immediate in nature, frequently employees are given some advance notice—either because it is required by law (e.g., the WARN Act), or because the organization needs a some transition time (e.g., in the event of a plant closure). For the purposes of the current chapter, we define anticipated job loss as *advance notice of involuntary job loss due to layoffs* rather than as job loss due to being fired for cause.[1]

Mohr (2000) incorporates many of these different aspects of objective insecurity by conceptualizing job insecurity as a process involving four different stages. The first stage is a state of public awareness that jobs in general might be insecure (e.g., during times of national recession and high unemployment). The second stage refers to objective job insecurity at the organizational level due to instability within the organization (e.g., following sharp declines in an organization's profits or pending merger/acquisition). The third stage is "acute" objective job insecurity when real threats to job loss are apparent at an individual level (e.g., following an announcement of impending downsizing). Finally, the fourth stage of objective job insecurity reflects anticipated job loss, when dismissals are already arranged.

Unlike many subjective forms of job insecurity, in the case of advance notice of layoffs there is no ambiguity regarding one's job security (i.e., it is known that the job will end on a set date). Thus, while the stressor of impending job loss remains, the employee can begin to prepare and plan for reentry into the job market (Swaim & Podgursky, 1990). On the other hand, in situations where the future of one's job is uncertain, the focus is on coping with the stress of perceived job insecurity in the face of such continued ambiguity (Probst, 2008). While impending job loss is distinct from the conceptualization of job insecurity, as noted earlier, many researchers include some proxy of anticipated or guaranteed job loss (e.g., permanent versus fixed employment contracts) as a global measure of job insecurity (e.g., Amabile & Conti, 1999; Holden, Scuffham, Hilton, Vecchio, & Whiteford, 2010; Mauno, Kinnunen, Mäkikangas, & Nätti, 2005; Probst, 2002b).

Interestingly, research generally has found that subjective perceptions of job insecurity are more closely associated with employee job- and health-related outcomes than objective job insecurity. For example, De Witte and Näswall (2003) found that subjective insecurity was a stronger predictor of job satisfaction and organizational commitment than objective insecurity (i.e., in the case of a temporary rather than permanent position). Similarly, Probst (2003) found that subjective job insecurity was a

better predictor of physical health, psychological distress, and job stress than an objective measure of organizational change.

Dimensionality of the Job Insecurity Construct

There has also been much debate regarding the dimensionality of the job insecurity construct. In their seminal article on the topic, Greenhalgh and Rosenblatt (1984) defined job insecurity as "perceived powerlessness to maintain desired continuity in a threatened job situation" (p. 438), and a subsequent multidimensional measure based on this definition (Ashford, et al., 1989) calculates job insecurity as a function of (1) the range and valence of job features that could be in jeopardy; (2) the subjective probability of losing each feature; (3) the valence of one's job and the perceived likelihood of job loss; and (4) one's perceived powerlessness to counter job threats. Other researchers prefer a global (i.e., unidimensional) definition of job insecurity that focuses primarily on the perceived probability of job loss (e.g., Klein Hesselink & Van Vuuren, 1999) by asking participants to indicate "the likelihood of losing their job in the next year," or "if they expected a change in their employment for the worse" (e.g., Büssing, 1986; Dooley, Rook, & Catalano, 1987). Some measures (e.g., Probst, 2003) ask employees to reflect on the future of their job by indicating if their job is "secure," "up in the air," "unknown," etc. Although the jury is still out regarding an empirical basis for recommending a unidimensional or multidimensional measure, it is perhaps not surprising that multi-item scales tend to be more predictive of outcomes than single-item measures of job insecurity (Sverke, Hellgren, & Näswall, 2002), which often underestimate the size of these relationships.

Qualitative Versus Quantitative Job Insecurity

Hellgren, Sverke, and Isaksson (1999) argue that another important theoretical distinction concerns the relationship between qualitative and quantitative job insecurity, where the former reflects potential loss of valued job features and the latter reflects potential loss of the job itself. Blau, Tatum, McCoy, and Ward-Cook (2004) found support for this argument by using confirmatory factor analysis to demonstrate that job insecurity has at least three distinct facets (i.e., fear of job loss itself, loss of coworkers, loss of desirable work conditions) with differing predictors and relations with organizational withdrawal. However, Reisel and Banai (2002) found that the threat of job loss (quantitative insecurity) was a better predictor of employee attitudes and behaviors than the threatened loss of job features. Further, a global (unidimensional) measure of job insecurity generally explained more variance than a multidimensional measure.

Affective Versus Cognitive Job Insecurity

Yet a fourth and growing debate among researchers concerns the affective versus cognitive nature of the job insecurity construct. Both involve subjective perceptions. However, whereas cognitive job insecurity reflects perceptions regarding the *likelihood* of negative changes to one's job, (e.g., threat of job loss or loss of valued job features), affective job insecurity refers to *emotional and attitudinal reactions* to that potential loss (e.g., concern, worry, anxiety). Increasingly, researchers argue that both need to be measured in order to adequately capture the full domain (e.g., Borg & Elizur, 1992; Probst, 2003, 2008; Reisel & Banai 2002), and empirical evidence appears to support the validity of making this distinction (Huang, Lee, Ashford, Chen & Ren, 2010). Further, by making this important distinction, researchers can better explore potential moderators that might explain why employees with the same subjective perceptions of cognitive insecurity may have very different affective responses to that perception.

Despite these lingering unresolved issues regarding the conceptualization and measurement of job insecurity, there is little debate among researchers regarding the overwhelmingly adverse effects of job insecurity (see Sverke et al., 2002; and Cheng & Chan, 2008 for meta-analyses). While significantly less is known about the conditions that prompt perceptions of job insecurity, it is clear that relevant variables are operating at multiple levels and drawn from a variety of sources. Below we introduce a comprehensive model of job insecurity that attempts to delineate the known antecedents and consequences of job insecurity, as well as identify important mediating and moderating variables.

While it is important to keep in the mind the unresolved debates reviewed above regarding the nature of the job insecurity construct itself, for the purposes of this model, we would like to make explicit the following assumptions. First, we are primarily interested in subjective job insecurity; therefore when we use the term *job insecurity*, we are referring to subjective cognitive perceptions that one's job is at risk. Second, the extent to which one

has negative affective reactions to the cognitive perception of job insecurity and/or anticipated job loss will be a function of individual, organizational, and socioeconomic moderators. Finally, we take a unidimensional approach to job insecurity and argue that the primary concern of job insecurity pertains to the potential loss of one's job, rather than the loss of specific desired job features (i.e., quantitative rather than qualitative job insecurity).

A Comprehensive Model of Job Insecurity: An Overview

Figure 3.1 presents an overview of our proposed model of job insecurity; subsequent sections in this chapter provide greater detail regarding the specific variables contained within each category. We recognize our review of the literature is by no means exhaustive. To do so would require much more space that allotted; therefore we acknowledge the somewhat selective nature of the variables examined.

We propose that socioeconomic conditions, organizational features, and employee characteristics all influence employee perceptions of job insecurity. Most contemporary models of stress acknowledge that a complete understanding of the structure and process of stress invariably requires a consideration of such individual, group and environmental/situational characteristics operating at different levels (Sulsky & Smith, 2005). For example, the cognitive-transactional model of stress (Lazarus & Launier, 1978) posits that perception of and reactions to potential stressors such as job insecurity will vary within and across individuals and may differ over occasions and time. Whether the potential stressor is perceived to be stressful depends on characteristics of the individual (e.g. needs, abilities, personality) and contextual variables related to the situation (e.g. demands, resources). Therefore, we acknowledge that individual, organizational, and socioeconomic variables may moderate not only the relationship between predictors and perceptions of job insecurity but also the relationship between perceived job insecurity and negative affective, attitudinal, and cognitive outcomes.

Further, we expect that negative cognitive, affective and attitudinal reactions will result in reduced employee well-being and more negative employee behaviors. While many theories (e.g., demands-control model [Karasek, 1979]; P-E fit model [French, Caplan, & Van Harrison, 1982, Van Harrison, 1978]; and job demands- resources model [Demerouti, Bakker, Nachreiner, &

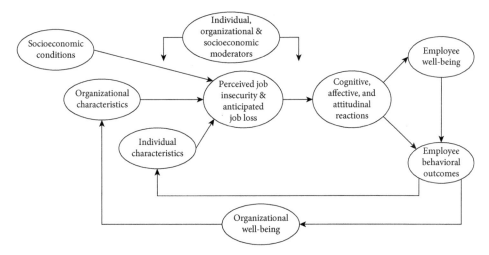

Figure 3.1 A comprehensive model of the antecedents and consequences of job insecurity and anticipated job loss.

Schaufeli, 2001]) would make similar predictions, we believe that Hobfall's (1989, 2001) conservation of resources (COR) theory provides an excellent and intuitive explanation for the causes of job insecurity and why it often (but not always) leads to an adverse outcome. COR posits that people strive to obtain, build, and protect that which they value (e.g., resources). When these resources are lost or threatened with loss, psychological stress occurs. Job insecurity, of course, inherently implies a threat of resource loss in the form of lost employment and income or loss of valued aspects of one's job.

COR also predicts that individuals with greater resources are more capable of resource gain and those with limited or fewer resources are more susceptible to resource loss. Thus a lack of resources can not only cause stress but access to resources can potentially buffer the stressor-strain relationship. Again we argue that such resources may accrue from the individual, organizational, and/or socioeconomic levels to moderate the effects of job insecurity. In turn, these outcomes are expected to influence organizational well-being in terms of productivity, innovation, customer service, safety, and other organizationally relevant factors.

Finally, we posit that the system is a nonrecursive one—one in which individual behavioral outcomes may alter individual characteristics also found at the antecedent stage. Similarly, the lack of organizational well-being may in turn affect organizational characteristics that render organizations more vulnerable to additional layoffs and future organizational decline (c.f., Morris, Cascio, & Young, 1999; Greenhalgh, 1983).

Antecedents of Perceived Job Insecurity and Anticipated Job Loss

In the following sections, we expand upon the above model in greater detail, specifically identifying where empirical research has found supporting evidence and noting where research gaps still remain. We begin with a review of antecedents of perceived job insecurity and anticipated job loss. Many of these antecedents are variables that not only increase the likelihood that one will perceive their job to be insecure (i.e., subjective job insecurity), but are also variables that objectively increase the likelihood of future job loss (i.e., objective insecurity).

Socioeconomic Antecedents

Despite their intuitive importance, the effects of broad socioeconomic indices on perceptions of job insecurity have been given insufficient attention in organizational psychology, where the vast majority of research has focused on individual-level predictors of individual-level outcomes (Cooper, 2011; Probst, 2010; Sinclair, Sears, Probst, & Zajack, 2010). Nonetheless, we propose (like Mohr, 2000) that socioeconomic factors such as mass layoff events, national and local unemployment and underemployment rates, economic conditions, and occupational forecasts may all serve to influence the extent to which employees perceive their jobs to be a risk (see also Bambra & Eikemo, this volume).

During the 2007–2009 recession, nearly 65,000 mass layoff events occurred in the United States alone (Bureau of Labor Statistics, 2010). A mass layoff event is any organizational layoff that involves fifty or more employees. Although empirical research has yet to be conducted on this, one might expect that an increase in the number of mass layoff events would prompt an increased amount of concern on the part of employees who wonder if their organization will be next. Indeed, empirical research has shown that an increase in national unemployment rates is accompanied by increased fears among employees that their job may be the next to fall (Anderson & Pontusson, 2007).

Despite this, researchers (Feldman, 1996; McKee -Ryan, & Harvey, 2011) have argued that a more telling indicator than the unemployment rate regarding the health of the economy may be the underemployment rate (i.e., the extent to which individuals are employed in jobs that are below their working capacity). As the state of an economy worsens, underemployment rates also increase owing to lower levels of job creation and a scarcity of high-wage jobs (Jefferson & Preston, 2010; Tam, 2010). Such underemployment has been found to be predictive of employee job insecurity as well (e.g., McGuiness & Wooden, 2009).

Finally, government estimates regarding the expected growth or decline in one's occupation may also be expected to predict employee job insecurity. Such estimates include the predicted employment change and job prospects for the upcoming decade (*Occupational Outlook Handbook* [OOH], 2010). While employment change describes the economic forces that will influence future employment in an occupation, the job prospects indicator signifies whether the occupation is expected to have a large or small number of job openings relative to the number of qualified applicants. Clearly individuals employed in shrinking occupations (e.g., production and manufacturing) (OOH, 2010) might experience lower job security since the former employees might face fewer employment alternatives and more competition for available openings. Conversely, individuals employed in growing occupations (e.g., health care, which is expected to increase by 21% over the next decade) might have higher levels of job security perceptions as greater market demands create more job openings.

Indeed, recent analyses appear to support this contention. Jiang, Probst, and Sinclair (2013) utilized multilevel modeling to evaluate the extent to which the anticipated 10-year employment change (OOH, 2010) accounted for individual-level differences in perceived job security. In support of their predictions, they found that occupational outlook accounted for 21.8% of the variance in between-occupation job security intercepts.

Organizational Antecedents

ORGANIZATIONAL CHANGE

A growing body of evidence suggests that formal announcements of layoffs, an upcoming merger or acquisition, organizational restructuring, and downsizing are all organizational change characteristics that may either presage anticipated job loss and/or increase employee job insecurity perceptions (Ashford et al., 1989; De Cuyper, De Witte, Vander Elst, & Handaja, 2010; Marks & Mirvis, 1985; Olson & Tetrick, 1988; Probst, 2002a, 2003b; Roskies & Louis-Guerin, 1990; Turnley & Feldman, 1999). For example, Probst (2003b) found that employees affected by organizational restructuring reported greater job insecurity than individuals not affected by the reorganization; further, their insecurity was greater after the restructuring announcement than before.

JOB TECHNOLOGY CHANGE

An additional antecedent of job insecurity may be related to changing organizational technology. A change in the technological systems of an organization can have a profound effect on job security (Greenspan, 1996), particularly if the changing technology might result in obsolescence of skills and/or positions, thus leading to greater job insecurity among those who have difficulty in learning new skills and technology and those whose positions might be made redundant by the new technology (Green, Felstead, & Burchell, 2000; Hulin & Roznowski, 1985). Increasing automation, for example, is a bigger driver of job loss than outsourcing (Khanna & Khanna, 2012), and some argue that this accounts for the increasing gap between stagnant employment trends and increasing corporate profits (Brynjolfsson & McAfee, 2011).

ORGANIZATIONAL PERFORMANCE

As early as 1984, Greenhalgh and Rosenblatt (1984) predicted that organizational performance would influence employees' perception of job security. However, little research actually tested this proposition until recently. Debus, König, and Kleinmann (2011) used multilevel modeling with 640 respondents nested in fifty companies to demonstrate that objective company performance accounted for a significant amount of the variance in employee job insecurity perceptions. In other words, employees in poorer-performing organizations reported significantly higher levels of job insecurity than employees in better-performing companies.

INDUSTRY SECTOR

In general, public sector employees appear to have greater perceived job security than their private sector counterparts. In a study of employees in fifteen European countries, Clark and Grey (1997) found greater proportions of private sector workers reported perceived job insecurity and anticipated job loss than their public sector counterparts. Similar results were found among individuals working in state-owned firms in China (Gong & Chang, 2008) and public sector employees in the United States (Jiang, Probst, & Sinclair, 2013).

Individual Antecedents

Individual-level antecedents comprise a variety of individual differences that increase an individual's susceptibility to being laid off or perceiving their job to be insecure, including employee demographics, personality, employment contract, union status, proximity to the organizational core, job performance, and prior layoff experiences.

DEMOGRAPHICS

Research on demographic predictors of job insecurity has generally not produced consistent results (e.g., Mauno & Kinnunen, 2002; Muñoz de Bustillo & De Pedraza, 2010). Moreover, such demographic variables typically explain only a small part of variance of job insecurity (Kinnunen & Natti, 1994; Muñoz de Bustillo & De Pedraza, 2010). However, significant results have been found for age, generation, race, and foreign status. Specifically, some research indicates that older employees experience higher levels of job insecurity (Probst et al., 2011), whereas other studies find that insecurity lessens with age (e.g., Näswall, Sverke, & Hellgren, 2005). Independent of age, additional research (Kowske, Rasch, & Wiley, 2010), has found that baby boomer employees (born between 1943 and 1960) reported the lowest levels of job security compared with generation X employees (born between 1961 and 1981) and millennial employees (born after 1982). Recent data from European countries (Muñoz de Bustillo & De Pedraza, 2010) suggests that affective job insecurity increases with age, but that education was related to fewer fears of job loss.[2]

Race also appears to be a predictor of perceived job insecurity in that Black Americans report higher levels of job insecurity compared with Whites (Fullerton & Wallace, 2007; Manski & Straub, 2000). For example Fullerton and Wallace (2007) examined data from the General Social Survey (from 1977 to 2002) and found that being a Black American was a significant predictor of lower levels of job security, even after controlling for age, generation, education, job status, and occupation. In addition to higher levels of perceived job insecurity, Black Americans also have more negative perceptions of positive job-search outcomes as compared with White Americans (Manski & Straub, 2000). See Derous and Ryan (this volume) for more information on disadvantaged job seekers (including ethnic minorities). Finally, foreign employees with temporary visas are often faced with considerable uncertainty about the length and conditions of their stay in the host country. Not surprisingly, Soylu (2008) found that foreign workers had higher levels of perceived insecurity compared to permanent residents and US citizens (see also Zikic, Kent, & Richardson, this volume, for more information on international workers).

PERSONALITY

Perceptions of job insecurity appear to be primarily influenced by personality traits associated with a negative outlook. For example, Tivendell and Bourbonnais (2000) found that of all of the "Big 5" personality characteristics, neuroticism was the only significant predictor of job insecurity perceptions among a sample of Canadian federal employees facing downsizing. Other studies have found a positive relationship between neuroticism and job insecurity perceptions even after controlling for the effects of job characteristics (e.g., Blackmore & Kuntz, 2011; Slack, 2004). Research also suggests that negative (not positive) affect has a significant positive relationship with perceptions of job insecurity (Mak & Mueller, 2000). Thus individuals with personality characteristics associated with a negative outlook on life may be more prone to judge their employment situation as insecure as compared with individuals having a more positive outlook on life in general.

JOB TENURE

The frequent implementation of "last hired, first fired" policy lends credence to the suggestion that job longevity or organizational seniority may provoke feelings of security (Luthans & Sommer, 1999). However, empirical research (Green, et al., 2000; Erlinghagen, 2008) suggests instead a U-shaped relationship, indicating a relatively high level of job insecurity among employees with very short and very long job tenures. This may be owing to skill obsolescence among older employees and worries about age discrimination should they lose their jobs.

EMPLOYMENT CONTRACT

Employment contract refers to the contractual relationship that an employee has with his or her organization. This includes whether the worker is employed on a temporary or contingent basis versus a permanent one; whether the worker is employed part-time versus full-time; and whether the job falls under union jurisdiction. Nonbinding, temporary, or part-time contracts are expected to result in lower job security and a higher likelihood of resulting in unemployment because these characteristics implicitly suggest a briefer tenure with the organization than a binding, permanent, full-time contract would suggest. Indeed, researchers consider temporary contracts to be a form of "objective" job insecurity (e.g., De Witte & Näswall, 2003; De Cuyper & De Witte, 2006; Pearce, 1998). Additionally, previous studies have found that temporary workers report greater subjective insecurity compared with permanent employees (e.g., Kinnunen & Nätti, 1994; Muñoz de Bustillo & De Pedraza, 2010; Sverke et al., 2000). Therefore the type of employment contract clearly appears to operate as an antecedent to subjective insecurity.

Interestingly, when permanent employees (i.e., those with greater "objective" job security) perceive job insecurity, they seem to experience more negative responses than temporary employees. This suggests that contract may also operate as a moderator, in addition to an antecedent. For example, De Cuyper and De Witte (2006) found that job insecurity was related to lower job satisfaction and organizational commitment, but only among permanent employees; no effects were seen for temporary employees. Similarly, Mauno et al. (2005) found job insecurity had greater negative effects on permanent workers than fixed-term workers. These results suggest that job insecurity may result in negative effects only if job security was an expected part of the job, whereas perceiving job insecurity in an already insecure position (i.e., temporary workers) did not result in more negative effects. Thus, while many deplore the growth of flexible work arrangements (i.e., nonpermanent employment contracts), and argue that most employees with fixed or temporary contracts would prefer permanent ones (Brewster, Mayne, & Tregaskis, 1997), it appears that the added insecurity of such positions does not necessarily lead to more negative outcomes because security was not an expected benefit of the job in the first place. Future research should explore not only the nature of the contract but also whether the individual prefers a temporary or a permanent contract. See De Cuyper, Fontinha and De Witte (this volume) for more information on job loss and job-search outcomes for temporary workers.

UNION MEMBERSHIP

Union affiliation might be expected to result in higher perceptions of job security and less unemployment than no union affiliation. Because union employees have some formal recourse when they perceive their jobs to be threatened and often are mandated by law to participate in any organizational mass layoff plans, one might expect that, all other things being equal, they would be less immediately susceptible to the economic stressors of unemployment and job insecurity. Drawing on 1997 survey data from fifteen OECD countries, Anderson and Pontusson (2007) found that union membership was associated with higher job security perception.

PROXIMITY TO CORE TECHNOLOGY

Hulin and Roznowski (1985) have argued that the proximity of one's job in relation to the organizational technology can often be more important than the job itself in determining the security or vulnerability of that position. Positions can be classified into two different categories: (1) those that are core or essential (D'Aveni, 1989) to transforming organizational input into organizational output and (2) those that are located in the buffering or peripheral systems of an organization. According to Hulin and Roznowski (1985), all components other than the core technology systems exist solely to support the core activities. Thus these buffering or peripheral positions are more likely to be seen as unnecessary or easily replaced than those found in the core organizational systems. And it is exactly these buffering functions that are increasingly being cut by organizations. Empirical support for this proposition is evidenced by the large numbers of organization that downsize by cutting layers of middle management, organizational bureaucracy, and other nonessential positions (D'Aveni, 1989). While we would predict, therefore, that employees holding peripheral positions would experience more job insecurity, empirical data on this issue are just beginning to emerge (e.g., Wagenaar et al., 2011) and remain scant.

PERFORMANCE-RELATED VARIABLES

Although not extensively studied, one would expect that the job performance of employees would influence the likelihood of layoff. Just as employers terminate employment for cause (i.e., due to poor job performance), research indicates that poorly performing employees are at greater risk of being selected for layoff during times of organizational change and downsizing (Bishop, 1990). Additionally, excessive absenteeism may also be a performance-related risk factor, given that research has found that higher rates of absenteeism among government workers were related to lower levels of job security (Probst, 2002).

Research has also shown that workers who file grievances are less likely to be promoted, receive lower performance evaluations following the grievance activity, and have higher voluntary and involuntary turnover rates (Carnevale, Olson, & O'Connor, 1992; Lewin, 1987). In addition, Probst (2002) found a significant negative relationship between government employee rates of grievance filing and their job security perceptions. Thus, although employees may be utilizing a company-endorsed grievance system, doing so may come at a price to the employee's job security, upward job mobility, and employment.

CAREER HISTORY

An employee's career history is also expected to be related to his or her vulnerability to job insecurity (see also van Vianen & Klehe, this volume). Research (Kjos, 1988; Leana, Feldman, & Tan, 1998) suggests that employees who have been laid off in the past or laid off for longer periods of time and those who have reached a plateau in their careers are more likely to face underemployment. Feldman (1996) suggests that this may be due to a marketplace stigma associated with having been laid off. In support of this, Erlinghagen (2008) found that the experience of prior unemployment was positively related to perceived job insecurity and anticipated job loss, although this relationship weakened the longer the time that had elapsed since the period of unemployment.

Consequences of Job Insecurity

Over two decades of research have demonstrated that job insecurity is directly and indirectly related to a multitude of consequences that negatively impact employees and organizations. As depicted in Figure 3.1, the nomological net of job insecurity includes a wide variety of initial reactions and subsequent consequences related to the perceived instability in the continuance of one's job. Research suggests that the perception of job insecurity generates cognitive, affective, and attitudinal reactions that result in diminished employee well-being and negative changes in behavior. The negative consequences of job insecurity on employees have the potential to extend beyond the employee to family members, fellow employees, and to the well-being of their organization. The following sections detail empirical support for this portion of the model.

Cognitive, Affective, and Attitudinal Reactions to Job Insecurity

The most immediate reactions to job insecurity involve cognitive deficits, negative emotions, and dissatisfaction often rivaling that of actual job loss (Dekker & Schaufeli, 1995; Latack & Dozier, 1986). In other words, the anticipation and ambiguity associated with the expected event can be a greater source of anxiety than the event itself (Lazarus & Folkman, 1984). Experimental research has found that perceived job insecurity impacts cognitive reasoning negatively and that the mere threat of a layoff has detrimental effects on creative problem solving (Probst, Stewart, Gruys, & Tierney, 2007). Job insecurity may reduce employee creativity because of decreased cognitive flexibility (Carnevale & Probst, 1998), behavioral rigidity (Cameron, Sutton, & Whetton, 1988), or increased risk aversion (Cascio, 1993) due to increased fear of conflict and expectations of competition over resources.

Not surprisingly, a number of researchers have proposed that the uncertainty regarding potential job loss (i.e., job insecurity) may serve as a precursor to numerous negative emotional reactions (Ito & Brotheridge, 2007; Roskies & Louis-Guerin 1990; Strazdins, D'Souza, Lim, Broom, & Rodgers 2004) including heightened anger, alarm, fear, anxiety, and resentment. Although this proposition is not as well studied in the literature, evidence appears to support it (e.g., Probst, 2002, 2008; Reisel et al., 2010).

While a nascent but growing body of research examines the affective and cognitive consequences of insecurity, the vast majority of research has focused on the negative impact of job insecurity on job-related attitudes. Indeed, two meta-analytic summaries of dozens of studies indicate that job insecurity has a consistently negative relationship with job satisfaction, organizational commitment, trust in management, and job involvement (Cheng & Chan, 2008; Sverke et al., 2002).

Consequences of Job Insecurity for Employee Well-Being

The cognitive, affective, and attitudinal reactions associated with job insecurity have widespread implications for overall employee well-being and work behavior. Research indicates that job insecurity is a consistent predictor of psychological distress (Catalano, Rook & Dooley, 1986; Dekker & Schaufeli, 1995; Mohr, 2000; Probst 2000, 2002a, 2003), negative general mental health (Cheng & Chan, 2008; Sverke et al., 2002), anxiety, depression, somatization, and hostility (Kuhnert, Sim, & Lahey, 1989). Additionally, Roskies and Louis-Guerin (1990) found that perceived job insecurity was a better predictor of metal health outcomes than objective risk of job loss, suggesting again that subjective appraisals of the potential job loss threat are key to understanding employee reactions to that threat.

Because it is also possible that one's mental state can be an antecedent rather than a consequence of perceived job insecurity, Ibrahim, Smith, and Muntaner (2009) tested this possibility with longitudinal data from the Canadian National Population Health Survey. They found that a model using job insecurity at time 1 to predict depression, distress, and health at time 2 was a significantly better fit to the data than a model predicting time 2 job insecurity with depression, distress, and health at time 1. That is, job insecurity is best conceptualized as a predictor rather than a consequence of decreased psychological well-being.

Job insecurity also has negative physical health implications for employees; these have been shown to be on par with the health effects of a serious illness (Burgard, Brand, & House, 2009). One of the earliest studies on this topic found that the stress of possible termination is associated with physiological responses such as increased norepinephrine excretion, serum creatinine levels, serum uric acid levels, and serum cholesterol levels (Cobb, 1974). More recent studies across ten European countries have shown that job insecurity is linked to decrements in general physical health (Cheng & Chan, 2008; Sverke et al., 2002), poor eating habits (Hannerz, Albertsen, Nielsen, Tüchsen, & Burr, 2004), high blood pressure, high cholesterol (Pollard, 2001), high injury rates (Quinlan, 2005), and negative perceptions of good health (László et al., 2010).

Most studies examining the relation between job insecurity and health are cross-sectional and fail to account for the impact of actual job loss, thus limiting our understanding of how fluctuations in employment conditions and perceptions of such conditions impact worker health over time. However, one study by Burgard, Brand, and House (2009) addresses this limitation by examining episodic and persistent job insecurity and job loss over extended periods of time ranging from 3 to 10 years. Results indicate that persistent job insecurity is consistently associated with significantly worse self-rated health than episodic or no job insecurity even after controlling for objective job loss over time, prior health, job characteristics, and sociodemographic characteristics (Burgard et al., 2009).

The negative effects of job insecurity on well-being are not limited to the employee alone. Limited research on the crossover effects of job insecurity on couples and families indicates that the economic worries of one partner are related to the other partner's job security (Mauno & Kinnunen, 2002) and that a parent's job insecurity negatively impacts his or her children's perceptions of work, work beliefs, and work attitudes (Barling, Dupré, & Hepburn, 1998) as well as their performance in school (Barling & Mendelson, 1997). Job insecurity also has a negative impact on spousal relations (Scherer, 2009; Westman, Etzion, & Danon, 2001), work-family conflict, and life satisfaction (Scherer, 2009). Job insecurity has even been shown to predict family planning (Scherer, 2009).

Behavioral Consequences of Job Insecurity

Considering the great deal of strain induced by perceived job insecurity, it is no surprise that job insecurity is also associated with changes in employee behavior with respect to turnover intentions, safety, productivity, and other aspects of performance. Cheng and Chan's (2008) meta-analysis indicates that job insecurity has a small but negative impact on overall work performance. However, Cheng and Chan also suggest that the impact of job insecurity on performance may have been underestimated owing to the complexity of the relationship. While some research has found monotonic negative relationships between insecurity and performance (e.g., Abramis, 1994), others (e.g., Brockner, Grover, Reed, & DeWitt, 1992) have found a nonlinear relationship between insecurity and work effort; that is, the highest levels of work effort were found under conditions of moderate job insecurity, whereas the lowest levels were seen under very low and very high levels of insecurity. One interpretation of this is that a little insecurity may be a good thing for motivating work effort. Another study conducted in an experimental laboratory setting (Probst, 2002b) found that the threat of layoffs increased sheer productivity, but the quality of the work products decreased. Thus the extent to which job insecurity is found to be related to performance may be driven in part by how performance is operationalized in a given study.

Job insecurity has also been indirectly related to work performance through its impact on related variables such as lower creativity (Probst, Stewart, Gruys, & Tierney, 2007), absenteeism, work task avoidance, tardiness (Probst, 1998), workplace bullying (DeCuyper, Baillien, & DeWitte, 2009) and decreased organizational citizenship behaviors among permanent-status employees (Feather & Rauter, 2004; Reisel et al., 2007).

In addition to on-the-job behaviors associated with job insecurity, job insecurity is also associated with the propensity for one to change careers voluntarily (Cheng & Chan, 2008; Sverke et al., 2002). A recent longitudinal field study found that job insecurity was the only organizational factor that predicted career/occupation change even after controlling for personality, demographics, education, tenure, salary, job satisfaction, and turnover intentions (Carless & Arnup, 2011). Similarly, job insecurity has also been shown to predict increases in turnover intentions. In their meta-analysis, Cheng & Chan (2008) reported a corrected correlation of .32 between the two variables, suggesting that job insecurity accounts for 10% of the variance in intentions to quit.

Unfortunately little consensus has emerged regarding actual job-search behaviors. On the one hand, Reisel and Banai (2002) found that job insecurity predicted job-search behaviors that were seen as precursors to turnover. On the other hand, Klehe et al. (2011) found that advance notice of job loss resulted in more proactive career-related behaviors as compared with employees who were still uncertain regarding the future of their jobs. In other words, employees who anticipated job loss (having actually received a layoff notice) engaged in more proactive career planning and exploration than employees who were still uncertain about the future of their jobs (i.e., job insecurity). Interestingly, Waters (2007) found that individuals who voluntarily chose redundancy engaged in more proactive job-search behaviors than individuals who became redundant involuntarily. Together, these studies suggest while job insecurity is related to greater turnover intentions and eventual career

change, proactive career and job-search behaviors may be prompted more by the immediacy of the anticipated job loss and the voluntary nature of that loss. Clearly, however, more research is needed on this topic.

An emerging body of literature also indicates that job insecurity has a negative effect on the safety-related behaviors of employees. A longitudinal study from Parker, Axtell, and Turner (2001), one of the first studies on this topic, found that job insecurity was a predictor of safety compliance among 161 glass manufacturing employees. A second study (Probst & Brubaker, 2001) found that the effects of job insecurity on safety compliance were mediated by the effects of insecurity on safety knowledge and safety motivation. In turn, lower compliance resulted in more accidents and injuries. A subsequent comprehensive review of more than ninety studies conducted in Europe, North and South America, Asia, and Africa (Quinlan, 2005) found evidence of a consistent adverse associations between precarious employment, job insecurity, and occupational safety outcomes such as injury rates, safety knowledge, and safety compliance.

A Note on Mediation

As is apparent from the above review, much of the research investigating consequences of job insecurity have not explicitly tested the extent to which these relationships are in fact mediated by cognitive, affective, and attitudinal reactions to job insecurity (as posited in Figure 3.1). However, researchers who have tested these more complex models have generally found support for the hypothesized mediated effects. For example, Probst (2002) found that the effects of cognitive perceptions of job insecurity on turnover, physical and mental health, and work withdrawal were fully mediated by satisfaction with one's job security, job satisfaction, and affective reactions. Another study conducted by Davy, Kinicki, and Scheck (1991) also found that the relationship between job insecurity and turnover was fully mediated by job satisfaction and organizational commitment, which is consistent with models of turnover (e.g., Porter, Steers, Mowday, & Boulian, 1974; Steers & Mowday, 1981). Yet other research (e.g., Staufenbiel & König, 2010) found evidence for both direct and mediated effects. Thus while much of the research reviewed above primarily tested direct relationships between job insecurity and its consequences, we expect that the effects are largely mediated by the cognitive, affective, and attitudinal reactions, although some direct effects may be possible as well.

Organizational Consequences of Job Insecurity

Although most research considers the impact of job insecurity on the affected employee, many of the individual-level consequences of job insecurity have serious implications for the well-being or health of his or her organization. A healthy work organization can be characterized both in terms of its financial success and the health of its workforce (Sainfort, Karsh, Booske, & Smith 2001), both of which are at risk when employees perceive their jobs to be insecure. Research indicates that amid organizational downsizing, the environment for organizational creativity suffers as employees report significantly less freedom, challenge, access to resources, supervisory encouragement, work-group support, and organizational encouragement (Amabile & Conti, 1999). From a financial standpoint, less creativity among its employees may make an organization less competitive and less profitable as innovation suffers.

In fact, research indicates that job insecurity is directly related to organizational-level outcomes. For example, Reisel, Chia, and Maloles (2005) found that job insecurity was a significant predictor of organizational performance (i.e., perceived overall customer service performance, customer effectiveness, organizational adaptation to changing competitive conditions, and esprit de corps among coworkers) even after controlling for demographics, customer-related rules and procedures, and financial, technological, and managerial resources. Similarly, Reisel, Chia, Maloles, and Slocum (2007) found that job insecurity was directly and indirectly (through job satisfaction) related to organizational performance (i.e., customer satisfaction, growth, market share, new products, retaining customers, attracting new customers).

Evidence for Positive Outcomes of Job Insecurity

As the preceding section illustrates, research has typically focused on the many downsides of job insecurity. However, some research has found evidence of positive outcomes. For example, Aletraris (2010) found that job insecurity was positively related to job satisfaction (especially for men) in a sample of 3,854 temporary workers in Australia. Another recent study (Staufenbiel & König, 2010) found that although job insecurity is indirectly (through job dissatisfaction and lowered affective commitment)

related to negative job-related consequences, job insecurity was directly related to better performance, decreased absenteeism, and lower turnover intentions. Staufenbiel and König (2010) noted that despite the negative impact of job insecurity on work attitudes, job insecurity can motivate employees to work harder and be more dedicated to avoid negative consequences (e.g., layoffs or firings). Laboratory research manipulating the threat of layoffs has found similar productivity gains, although these effects disappeared once the threat of layoffs was removed (Probst, 1998, 2002b; Probst et al., 2007). Together, these studies suggest that perceived job insecurity may serve as a motivating force for employees under certain circumstances. However, additional research is needed to examine what factors prompt positive versus negative reactions to job insecurity.

Moderators of the Effects of Perceived Job Insecurity
The Search for Possible Interventions

Despite the overwhelming evidence indicating that perceived job insecurity has grave negative implications for individuals, organizations, and society, there are unfortunately few realistic options to eliminate the occurrence of layoffs, downsizing, and many of the other precursors to perceived job insecurity. Thus organizational researchers and practitioners must be concerned with ways to mitigate the negative impact of job insecurity by developing intervention strategies targeted at those who are most at risk of involuntary job loss and/or perceived job insecurity. Research on such moderators can be broadly classified into either variables involving individual differences or higher-level moderators (e.g., those operating at the organizational and sociocultural levels).

While empirical evidence exists for the presence of a variety of individual-level moderators (e.g. cultural values [König, Debus, Häusler, Lendenmann, & Kleinmann, 2010; Probst & Lawler, 2006], spirituality [Probst & Strand, 2010; Schreurs et al., under review], affectivity [Chan, Kwok, & Yeung, 2004; Roskies, Louis-Guerin, & Fournier, 1993], locus of control [König et al, 2010; Näswall et al., 2005; Orpen, 1994], self-efficacy [Feng, Lu, & Siu, 2008; Probst, 2001]), many of these variables represent traitlike individual difference characteristics that are relatively stable and therefore less amenable to modification or intervention. Therefore we intentionally restrict our discussion below to those individual-level moderating variables that might

Table 3.1. A Practical Checklist for Practitioners and Employees to Alleviate the Negative Effects of Job Insecurity and Anticipated Job Loss

1. Offer employees opportunities for more job control and autonomy.

2. Foster high quality relationships between supervisors and their employees based on mutual respect, obligation, and trust.

3. Facilitate open two-way communication and flow of information between employees and management, particularly during times of organizational transition.

4. Encourage employee participation into organizational decision making processes.

5. Promote a positive organizational climate that values justice, mutual trust, and employee safety.

6. If notice of layoffs will be given, avoid abrupt announcements with no warning. Conversely, also avoid extremely lengthy rollouts that only serve to prolong the anxiety.

7. Proactively seek out job skills training opportunities to maintain competitiveness on the job market.

8. Develop strong social and professional networks that can not only serve as needed sources of social support, but also facilitate the search for a new job if needed.

---

serve as fruitful avenues to explore as springboards for the development of potential invention strategies. At the same time, we also consider related organizational and sociocultural interventions that may alleviate the negative effects of job insecurity. Table 3.1 summarizes these findings into a practical checklist to serve as a guide to practitioners and employees working in organizations where concerns regarding job insecurity and/or anticipated job loss are prevalent.

Alleviating Effects of Job Insecurity via Enhanced Employability

Whereas the traditional psychological contract involves an implicit exchange of hard work and loyalty in return for job security and continued employment, the contemporary contract suggests that employees need to be loyal to themselves, their work, and their profession (Arthur & Rousseau, 1996; Granrose & Baccili, 2006). Rather than creating a self-identity based on an affiliation with an organization, employees might be committed to an organization only to the extent that the organization can fulfill their current career needs and goals. In return, organizations are expected to provide training in skills that will increase the future employability of the worker in the event of a layoff.

Thus it has been argued that the concepts of job security and *lifetime employment* are being replaced by the notion of *lifetime employability* (Kanter, 1989; Kluytmans & Ott 1999). While high employability does not necessarily prevent the threat of job loss, it may act as a valuable resource in the event that an employee does become unemployed (Baruch, 2001). Therefore interventions that increase an employee's ability to compete for alternative employment options in the labor market may attenuate the negative consequences of job insecurity (Fugate, Kinicki, & Ashforth, 2004; Greenhalgh & Rosenblatt, 1984; Näswall, 2004, 2005; Sverke & Hellgren, 2002). Indeed, a growing body of empirical results has found that the interaction between job insecurity and employability explains a significant proportion of the variance in depression (Kuhnert & Vance, 1993), irritation/strain (Büssing, 1999), psychosomatic complaints (Büssing, 1999; Mohr, 2000), and life satisfaction (Silla, De Cuyer, Gracia, Peiró, & De Witte, 2009), although results were not supportive for anxiety (Kuhnert & Vance, 1993; Mohr, 2000), psychological distress (Silla et al., 2009), or job satisfaction (Büssing, 1999).

A more recent study examined multiple different possible employee reactions to job insecurity (e.g., exit, voice, and loyalty) (Berntson, Näswall & Sverke, 2010) as a function of employability and found that employees with higher levels of employability tended to exit more, voice less (i.e., refrained from trying to encourage the organization to move in the desired direction), and have less loyalty toward their organizations in times of job insecurity. Such findings indicate that highly employable individuals may tend to respond to insecurity via turnover (i.e., withdrawing from the situation) instead of attempting to change the current employment situation (via voice), perhaps owing to the available job alternatives that might better fulfill their career goals (Pfeffer, 1998).

Together, these studies also suggest there are advantages and disadvantages of the purported new psychological contracts. On the one hand, employers may not be able to provide guarantees of job security, but they can provide access to job skills training and other avenues for fostering continuous employee improvement. On the other hand, while such efforts may increase the employability of workers and buffer some of the adverse effects of perceived job insecurity, the studies reviewed above are somewhat mixed regarding whether this will lead to higher levels of employee turnover in response to job insecurity because of a possible increase in alternative employment opportunities. Clearly, this is an area ripe for further investigation at the individual, organizational, and societal levels. In addition, there are likely other individual-differences variables that are relevant to understanding how employees will respond to insecurity (e.g., boundaryless career orientation in terms of mobility preference, Arthur & Rousseau, 1996).

Alleviating Effects of Job Insecurity via Enhanced Support Systems

In their seminal article on job insecurity, Greenhalgh and Rosenblatt (1984) proposed that social support would increase employees' ability to cope with the stress of job insecurity. Although they originally considered support originating from nonwork sources, the empirical evidence suggests that social support obtained from a variety of different work and nonwork sources might have beneficial effects. Specifically, researchers found that support originating from others at the workplace (e.g., colleagues and/or supervisors) could alleviate the negative effects of job insecurity on work-related outcomes, ranging from job satisfaction, proactive job search, noncompliant job behaviors, to work involvement (Kinnunen & Natti, 1994; Lim, 1996). When it comes to non-work-related support (e.g., support from family and/or friends), it was found that such support could attenuate the negative consequences of job insecurity on life satisfaction (Lim, 1996), mental health complaints, and somatic complaints (Näswall, Sverke,& Hellgren, 2005). On the other hand, however, other studies failed to establish any interaction between job insecurity and work-related (Dekker & Schaufeli, 1995) or non-work-related (Mohr, 2000) support.

These mixed results might arise from the complexity of the social support construct, the forms of which can be categorized as emotional support, instrumental support, and informative support (Fenlason & Beehr, 1994; House, 1981; Scheck, Kinicki & Davy, 1997). In examining the effects of social support on employee outcomes of job insecurity, combining forms of and resources from social support might produce different results. Thus more empirical evidence is required to explore the boundary conditions of social support in terms of job insecurity.

Supervisors may also play a pivotal role in supporting employees by providing emotional, instrumental, or informative support. For example, such support may be in the form of relaying regular, systematic, and accurate information to the workforce. In a representative sample of Finnish employees, Kinnunen and Natti (1994) found a significant link between perceived job insecurity and relations with supervisors.

Building upon leader-member exchange (LMX) theory, Probst (2011) predicted that high quality LMX would buffer the relationship between job insecurity and supervisor satisfaction, safety knowledge, reported accidents, and physical health conditions. LMX consists of the levels of respect, trust, and mutual obligation perceived between employees and their supervisors (Graen & Uhl-Bien, 1995). Results from 212 employees of a copper mine in the United States supported those predictions and revealed that positive LMX attenuated the adverse effects of job insecurity on supervisor satisfaction, workplace accidents, and health conditions, whereas the positive effects of LMX on safety knowledge are only seen under conditions of high job security. Similarly, with a sample in a state-owned enterprise in China, researchers (Loi, Ngo, Zhang, & Lau, 2011) found that LMX attenuated the effects of job insecurity on employee altruism, such that job insecurity was related to lower levels of altruism only under conditions of low LMX.

In tough economic times, organizations may have little control over the job insecurity of employees. However, they do have some control over the leadership practices within their organization. Taken together, the above results suggest that fostering positive LMX between supervisors and employees may mitigate the negative effects of job insecurity in difficult times.

At the societal level, there also appears to be evidence that support structures offered by the social safety net may moderate reactions to insecurity. Debus, Probst, König, and Kleinmann (2012) examined the effects of country-level differences in the social safety net (including unemployment assistance, duration of benefits, job skills retraining programs, and the like) on employee reactions to perceived job insecurity. Using nationally representative individual-level data from 15,200 employees nested within twenty-four countries and country-level data on the social safety net from economic security indices provided by the International Labor Organization (2004), they found that employees living in countries with more robust social safety nets had fewer negative attitudinal reactions with respect to job satisfaction and organizational commitment in response to job insecurity compared to employees in countries with weaker social safety nets. These data suggest that societal-level support structures may also mitigate some of the adverse effects of job insecurity (see also Bambra & Eikemo, this volume).

Alleviating Effects of Job Insecurity via Enhanced Control

Just as individuals require vitamins for maintaining their physical health, Warr (1987) proposed there are nine "vitamins" individuals need for psychological health, including opportunity for control, opportunity for skill use, externally generated goals, variety, environmental clarity, availability of money, physical security, opportunity for interpersonal contact, and valued social position. Many of these "vitamins" (similar to the needs identified in Jahoda's [1982] latent deprivation model) are threatened under conditions of job insecurity and anticipated job loss which are often accompanied by lack of control over the future of one's position and a lack of communication by upper management about the future of one's position or indeed the future fate of the company. Furda and Meijman (1992, as cited in De Witte, 1999) specifically call out two separate aspects of uncertainty that accompany job insecurity: (1) a lack of predictability regarding the future and (2) a lack of control over that future. Therefore organizational interventions that act to reduce unpredictability by increasing information regarding the future of one's job or that address the perceived powerlessness of employees by enhancing control via increased participative decision making may serve to attenuate the negative effects of job insecurity.

Initial research on these issues is promising. Perceived powerlessness appears to influence both the primary and secondary appraisals of job insecurity. Reisel (2003) found that powerlessness significantly moderated the relationship between antecedents of job insecurity (e.g., environmental threats, role ambiguity, job alternatives) and the perception of job insecurity. Perceived powerlessness has also been shown to moderate the effects of perceived insecurity on job satisfaction, irritation/strain, psychosomatic complaints, and other health outcomes (Barling & Kelloway, 1996).

Whereas job insecurity is associated with a lack of control perceived by employees, participative decision making has been found to be effective within organizations precisely because it allows employees to have a substantial voice in job-related decisions. Therefore Probst (2005) has argued that organizations that provide their employees with participative decision-making opportunities offer their employees the chance to regain control over important aspects of their jobs that is otherwise lost under conditions of job insecurity.

A series of studies conducted within the past few years appears to support this contention. Mikkelsen and Saksvik (1999) found that during periods of organizational restructuring workgroups exposed to an organizational intervention consisting of increased employee control, decision making, and participation experienced fewer negative health and stress effects than control work groups. Likewise, Bordia et al. (2004) found that participative decision making reduces employee uncertainty during periods of organizational change and averts the damaging effects of such uncertainty by increasing employee feelings of control. Similarly, Probst (2005a) reported that employees with greater participative decision-making opportunities experienced fewer negative job-related consequences related to job satisfaction and turnover intentions as a function of job insecurity as compared with employees who had fewer participative decision-making opportunities. In addition, results from a cross-sectional study of 3,881 employees from twenty organizations in Belgium revealed that organizational participation attenuated the negative relationship between job insecurity and work engagement such that when the participation level was high, the negative relationship between job insecurity and work engagement was weaker than when participation levels were perceived to be low and average (Elst, Baillien, De Cuyper, & De Witte, 2010).

Similar research also suggests that workplace control (i.e., the ability to protect oneself from negative events at work) may be an important moderator of the stress associated with job insecurity (e.g., Büssing, 1999). Based on data from 187 black South African gold miners, Barling and Kelloway (1996) concluded that perceived workplace control moderated the relationship between job insecurity and somatic symptoms and blood pressure. Job insecurity was positively associated with somatic symptoms and blood pressure when perceived workplace control was low but unrelated to these outcomes when perceived workplace control was high. Recently, results from a heterogeneous sample of 1,368 Belgian employees revealed that workplace control mitigated the negative effects of job insecurity on a short-term health outcome (need for recovery) and a long-term health outcome (impaired general health) (Schreurs, van Emmerik, Notelaers, & De Witte, 2010).

Thus there appears to be growing evidence that organizations may mitigate the negative impact of job insecurity by increasing the extent to which employees have control over their jobs and voice in organizational decision-making processes.

Alleviating Effects of Job Insecurity via Enhanced Communication

As noted above, organizations may also potentially alleviate the negative effects of job insecurity via interventions that reduce the unpredictability regarding the future fate of one's position and/or organization. Indeed, even when the outcome itself is not positive, advance notice regarding the future of one's job appears to be beneficial. Specifically, research indicates that some of the negative consequences of job loss can be mitigated by advanced notice of the impending job loss. For example, Addison and Blackburn (1995) and Swaim and Podgursky (1990) found that it took less time for employees to become reemployed after job loss if they were given advance notice. Similarly, Klehe et al. (2011) found that advance notice of redundancy resulted in more active career behaviors compared to employees who were still uncertain regarding the future of their jobs. Further, Brewington et al. (2004) found a negative relationship between length of job loss notice and job loss grief (i.e., grief, guilt, despair, rumination, and depersonalization), such that greater advance notice was related to less grief. On the other hand, research by Probst and Collison (2006) identified a curvilinear relationship between length of job loss notice and outcomes, suggesting that the most positive outcomes may be observed when there is a moderate amount of advance notice, rather than too little (e.g., no notice) or too much (e.g., greater than 60 days) advance notice.

Other research in this area has focused on the overall quality and extent of organizational communication with employees. As early as 1990, the National Institute for Occupational Safety and Health (NIOSH) began recommending that organizations reduce ambiguity regarding the future of employee jobs by informing employees in a timely fashion of impending organizational changes that may affect their job security or their opportunities for career development and advancement (Sauter, Murphy, & Hurrell, 1990). One of the major sources of stress during times of organizational change is the uncertainty associated with such change and the overreliance on the rumor mill in the absence of factual information that can exacerbate employee anxiety (Buono & Bowditch, 1989).

To assess whether enhanced organizational communication could dampen the dysfunctional effects of an organizational merger, Schweiger and DeNisi (1991) examined the effectiveness of a "realistic merger preview" in reducing employee uncertainty. Analogous to a realistic job preview, a realistic merger preview provides detailed information regarding the timeline of the merger, how the merger will affect employees, and other pertinent information. In their longitudinal field experiment, Schweiger and DeNisi (1991) were able to provide realistic merger previews to employees in one plant, while having a control plant where the merger was managed in a more traditional format. Although both plants experienced initial negative effects as a result of the announced upcoming merger, the plant that was offered a realistic merger preview rebounded more quickly from the negative effects, whereas employees in the control plant continued to report negative job attitudes, a lack of trust in the company, and lower levels of self-reported performance 4 months following the merger announcement. Thus, as the authors noted, "a realistic merger preview seems to function at least as an inoculation that makes employees resistant to the negative effects of mergers and acquisitions, and its effects may go beyond that" (p. 129).

A more recent study (Jiang & Probst, 2011) found that organizational communication was critical in attenuating the negative effects of job insecurity on employee safety and health outcomes and job attitudes. In this multiorganizational field study, it was found that when job security was high, there were no differences in outcomes between employees who perceived low versus high levels of organizational communication. However, when employees felt their jobs were insecure, employees who had positive perceptions of their organization's communication reported half as many accidents, less than one third as many near accidents, higher job satisfaction, and fewer physical ailments than employees who were dissatisfied with the level of communication within the organization.

The preceding studies suggest that organizational communication can play a pivotal role in preventing or attenuating the negative effects of job insecurity, downsizings, and mergers on employee physical and psychological outcomes. This kind of proactive intervention should be even more attractive to organizations when one considers the relatively low cost involved with opening the lines of communication with employees.

Alleviating Effects of Job Insecurity via Organizational Justice and Trust

Although it is more difficult to design interventions to address the more nebulous constructs of organizational justice and trust in management, research indicates that these variables may also play an important role in determining the way in which employees react to job insecurity. According to Mayer, Davis, and Schoorman (1995) there are three important characteristics associated with trust—that is, belief in the ability, benevolence, and integrity of the focal entity (in this case, the organization). A lack of trust in upper management may make an already difficult situation even more ambiguous and unpredictable. Consistent with such a prediction, Probst et al. (2011) in a study of university employees facing repeated rounds of budget cuts and layoffs found that the relationships between job insecurity and burnout, psychological distress, role ambiguity, role overload, and work dissatisfaction were stronger for employees who had low levels of trust in upper management (i.e., the individuals in positions of power to make the decisions about the upcoming cuts and layoffs).

Gleenhalgh and Rosenblatt (1984) theorized that organizational norms of fairness would also influence the perceptions and outcomes of job insecurity. Organizational justice consists of the shared perceptions of individuals within an organization regarding the subjective perceptions of fairness related to organizational processes, outcomes, and treatment of organizational members (Colquitt et al., 2001). Ensuring high levels of organizational justice—while not eliminating employee job insecurity per se—may nonetheless be an effective mechanism to alleviating employee discomfort regarding the process, outcomes, and treatment of individuals affected by job insecurity or anticipated job loss (Elovainio et al., 2005; Judge & Colquitt, 2004; Thau, Aquino, & Wittek, 2007). Consistent with such a prediction, Sora et al. (2010) found that organizational justice buffered the negative effects of job insecurity on job satisfaction and turnover intentions in a sample composed of 597 employees nested in twenty-nine Spanish organizations.

Attenuating Adverse Safety Outcomes of Insecurity via a Positive Organizational Safety Climate

A final organizational-level moderator that shows promise in attenuating some of the negative effects of job insecurity involves the organizational safety climate. Organizational climate can be viewed as a set of underlying values, beliefs, and principles that employees perceive are held within their organization. These perceptions serve as a frame of reference for employees to guide normative and adaptive work behavior by providing cues regarding expected behavior-outcome contingencies (Schneider, 1975). Organizational safety climate then can be defined as a unified set of cognitions held by workers regarding the safety aspects of their organization (Zohar, 1980), including management values, safety communication, safety training, and safety systems (Neal, Griffin, & Hart, 2000).

As noted earlier, research indicates that job insecurity has a detrimental effect on employee safety attitudes, behaviors, and outcomes (Grunberg, Moore, & Greenberg, 1996; Probst, 2002; Probst & Brubaker, 2001). However, the effects of job insecurity on safety appear to be moderated by the extent to which the organization is seen as valuing and emphasizing safety. In a study of light manufacturing employees, Probst (2004) found that when employees perceived a weak organizational safety climate, job insecurity was related to lower levels of safety knowledge, less employee safety compliance, a greater number of employee accidents, more near miss incidents, a greater likelihood of workplace injury, and a greater incidence of repetitive motion injuries. However, when employees perceived that the organizational safety climate was strong, the slope of the relationships between job insecurity and these safety outcomes was consistently attenuated. Research by Parker et al. (2001) suggests that job insecurity can even result in positive safety effects, depending on the strength of the organizational safety climate. In their longitudinal study of 161 employees in a glass manufacturing setting, they found—contrary to their hypothesis—that job insecurity was related to more positive safety behaviors among these employees. They ascribed these initially counterintuitive findings to the extensive efforts on the part of the organization via organizational safety campaigns, new safety training programs, and other safety initiatives to clearly convey to employees the importance of safety. As a result, employees faced with job insecurity and the threat of unemployment focused more (not less) on safety perhaps due to their organization's strong emphasis on safety.

These results suggest that particularly during times of organizational transition and employee job insecurity, it is wise for organizations to consistently send a strong message regarding the importance of safety to their employees. Organizations that do so may be able to reap added benefits in terms of reduced accidents and injuries even in the face of threatened layoffs or job uncertainty. It is important to note, however, that during times of layoffs, it may be very difficult to convince employees and managers that safety is truly valued as being equal to or better than other job performance measures, such as productivity or quality (Probst & Brubaker, 2007).

Conclusion

Given the increasing prevalence of job insecurity across the globe, this chapter has identified some of the myriad variables operating at the individual, occupational, organizational, and societal levels that have been found to influence employee perceptions of job insecurity and anticipated job loss. In doing so, we have attempted to integrate two disparate bodies of literature (job insecurity and anticipated job loss) into a comprehensive model that explicitly advocates a multilevel perspective. Given that employees are embedded in multiple intersecting and influential contexts, such a consideration of variables operating at multiple levels within each stage of the process is critical.

In turn, we also reviewed the large extant body of literature regarding the complex and wide array of consequences of such insecurity at the individual and organizational levels. Although the vast majority of this research suggests these consequences are largely negative, there is a growing body of literature aimed at identifying interventions at the individual, organizational, and even societal levels to attenuate these negative consequences. Thus the last section of the chapter focuses on reviewing some of the more promising avenues and developing a practical checklist for practitioners and employees alike. Such interventions range from those that are relatively low in cost and easy to implement (e.g., enhanced organizational communication) to those that would require fundamental, extensive (and costly) modifications to the very fabric of the social safety net within a country. Together, the evidence suggests that these interventions may be effective at alleviating some of the negative consequences of a stressor that plagues many of today's employees around the globe.

Notes

1. It is also important to recognize that many job insecurity researchers operationalize job insecurity as anticipated job loss (i.e., the likelihood of losing one's job). Therefore, while we make a distinction between subjective job insecurity and anticipated job loss in this chapter, we have to acknowledge there is significant construct overlap in the empirical literature.

2. Research also suggests that advancing age, in addition to possibly acting as an antecedent of job insecurity, may moderate reactions to such insecurity. For example, Cheng and Chan (2008) found that older employees experience more adverse psychological and physiological health-related consequences in response to job insecurity as compared with their younger counterparts. On the other hand, older employees are less likely to quit in response to job insecurity, possibly because they have fewer perceived opportunities. See Klehe, De Pater, Koen, and Kira, this volume, for a more in-depth consideration of older workers.

References

Abramis, D. J. (1994). Relationship of job stressors to job performance: Linear or an inverted-U? *Psychological Reports, 75*, 547–558.

Addison, J. T., & Blackburn, M. (1995). Advance notice and job search: More on the value of an early start. *Industrial Relations, 34*, 242–244.

Aletraris, L. (2010). How satisfied are they and why? A study of job satisfaction, job rewards, gender, and temporary agency workers in Australia. *Human Relations, 63*, 1129–1155.

Amabile, T. M., & Conti, R. (1999). Changes in the work organization for creativity during downsizing. *Academy of Management Journal, 42*, 630–640.

American Psychological Association (2010). *Stress in America findings.* Washington, DC: APA.

Anderson, C. A., & Pontusson, J. (2007). Workers, worries and welfare states: Social protection and job insecurity in 15 OECD countries. *European Journal of Political Research, 46*, 211–235. doi: 10.1111/j.1475-6765.2007.00692.x

Arthur, M. B., & Rousseau, D. M. (Eds.). (1996). *The boundaryless career: A new employment principle for a new organizational era.* New York: Oxford University Press.

Ashford, S., Lee, C., & Bobko, P. (1989). Content, causes, and consequences of job insecurity: A theory based measure and substantive test. *Academy of Management Journal, 32*, 803–829.

Barling, J., & Kelloway, E. K. (1996). Job insecurity and health: The moderating role of workplace control. *Stress Medicine, 12*, 253–259.

Barling, J., & Mendelson, M. B. (1997). Parents' job insecurity affects children's grade performance through the indirect effects of beliefs in an unjust world and negative mood. *Journal of Occupational Health Psychology, 4*, 347–355.

Barling, J., Dupre, K. E., & Hepburn, C. G. (1998). Effects of parents' job insecurity on children's work beliefs and attitudes. *Journal of Applied Psychology, 83*, 112–118.

Baruch, Y. (2001). Employability: A substitute for loyalty? *Human Resource Development International, 4*, 543–566.

Berntson, E., Näswall, K., & Sverke, M. (2010). The moderating role of employability in the association between job insecurity and exit, voice, loyalty and neglect. *Economic and Industrial Democracy, 31*, 215–230. doi: 10.1177/0143831X09358374

Bishop, J. H. (1990). Job performance, turnover, and wage growth. *Journal of Labor Economics, 8*, 363–386.

Blackmore, C., & Kuntz, J. R. C. (2011). Antecedents of job insecurity in restructuring organizations: An empirical investigation. *New Zealand Journal of Psychology, 40*, 7–18.

Blau, G., Tatum, D. S., McCoy, L., & Ward-Cook, K. (2004). Job loss, human capitol job feature, and work condition job feature as distinct job insecurity constructs. *Journal of Allied Health, 33*, 31–41

Bordia, P., Hobman, E., Jones, E., Gallois, C., & Callan, V. J. (2004). Uncertainty during organizational change: Types, consequences, and management strategies. *Journal of Business and Psychology, 18*, 507–532.

Borg, I., & Elizur, D. (1992). Job insecurity: Correlates, moderators, and measurement. *International Journal of Manpower, 13*, 13–26.

Brewington, J., Nassar-McMillan, S., Flowers, C., & Furr, S. (2004). A preliminary investigation of factors associated with job loss and grief. *The Career Development Quarterly 53* (September): 78–83.

Brewster, C., Mayne. L., & Tregaskis, O. (1997). Flexible staffing in Europe. *Journal of World Business, 32*, 133–151.

Brockner, J., Grover, S., Reed, T. F., & DeWitt, R. L. (1992). Layoffs, job insecurity, and survivors' work effort: Evidence of an inverted-U relationship. *Academy of Management Journal, 35*, 413–425.

Brynjolfsson, E. & McAfee, A. (2011). *Race against the machine: How the digital revolution is accelerating innovation, driving productivity, and irreversibly transforming employment and the economy.* Lexington, MA: Digital Frontier Press.

Buono, A. F., & Bowditch, J. L. (1989). *The human side of mergers and acquisitions: Managing collisions between people, cultures, and organizations.* San Francisco: Jossey Bass.

Bureau of Labor Statistics (2010). Mass layoff statistics. Available at: http://www.bls.gov/mls/ (Retrieved October 13, 2012.)

Burgard, S. A., Brand, J. E., & House, J. S. (2009). Perceived job insecurity and worker health in the United States. *Social Science & Medicine, 69*, 777–785.

Büssing, A. (1986). Worker responses to job insecurity: A quasi-experimental field investigation. In G. Debus & H. W. Schroiff (Eds.), *The psychology of work and organization.* (pp. 137–144). North Holland: Elsevier Science Publishers.

Büssing, A. (1999). Can control at work and social support moderate psychological consequences of job insecurity? Results from a quasi-experimental study in the steel industry. *European Journal of Work and Organizational Psychology, 8*, 219–242.

Cameron, K. S., Sutton, R. I., & Whetton, D. A. (1988). *Readings in organizational decline: Frameworks, research and prescriptions.* Cambridge, MA: Ballinger.

Carless, S. A., & Arnup, J. L. (2011). A longitudinal study of the determinants and outcomes of career change. *Journal of Vocational Behavior, 78*, 80–91.

Carnevale, P. J., Olson, J. B., & O'Connor, K. M. (1992, June). Reciprocity and informality in a laboratory grievance system. Paper presented at the International Association of Conflict Management, Minneapolis, MN.

Carnevale, P. J., & Probst, T. M. (1998). Social values and social conflict in creative problem solving and categorization. *Journal of Personality and Social Psychology, 74*, 1300–1309.

Cascio, W. (1993). Downsizing: What do we know? What have we learned? *Academy of Management Executive, 7*, 95–104.

Catalano, R., Rook, K., & Dooley, D. (1986). Labor markets and help-seeking: A test of the employment security hypothesis. *Journal of Health and Social Behavior, 27*, 277–287.

Chan, W., Kwok, K., & Yeung, S. A. (2004). Facing challenging circumstances: Optimism and job insecurity. *Journal of Psychology in Chinese Societies, 5*, 81–95.

Cheng, G. H.-L., & Chan, D. K.-S. (2008). Who suffers more from job insecurity? A meta-analytic review. *Applied Psychology: An International Review, 57*, 272–303. doi: 10.1111/j.1464–0597.2007.00312.x

Clark, A., & Grey, A. (1997). Is job insecurity on the increase in OECD countries? DEELSA, OECD, mimeografado, Março.

Cobb, S. (1974). Physiologic changes in men whose jobs were abolished. *Journal of Psychosomatic Research, 18*, 245–258.

Colquitt, J. A., Conlon, D. E., Wesson, M. J., Porter, C. O., & Ng, K. Y. (2001). Justice at the millennium: A meta-analytic review of 25 years of organizational justice research. *Journal of Applied Psychology, 86*, 425–445.

Cooper, C. L. (2011). Stress in the post-recession world. *Stress and Health 26*, 261. doi: 10.1002/smi.1352

D'Aveni, R. A. (1989). The aftermath of organizational decline: A longitudinal study of the strategic and managerial characteristics of declining firms. *Academy of Management Journal, 32*, 577–605.

Davy, J. A., Kinicki, A. J., & Scheck, C. L. (1991). Developing and testing a model of survivors' responses to layoffs. *Journal of Vocational Behavior, 38*, 302–317.

Davy, J. A., Kinicki, A. J., & Scheck, C. L. (1997). A test of job security's direct and mediated effects on withdrawal cognitions. *Journal of Organizational Behavior, 18*, 323–349.

De Cuyper, N., & De Witte, H. (2006). The impact of job insecurity and contract type on attitudes, well-being and behavioural reports: A psychological contract perspective. *Journal of Occupational and Organizational Psychology, 79*, 395–409.

De Cuyper, N., Baillien, E., & DeWitte, H. (2009). Job insecurity, perceived employability and targets' and perpetrators' experiences of workplace bullying. *Work & Stress, 23*, 206–224.

De Cuyper, N., De Witte, H., Vander Elst, T., & Handaja, Y. (2010). Objective threat of unemployment and situational uncertainty during a restructuring: Associations with perceived job insecurity and strain. *Journal of Business and Psychology, 25*, 75–85. doi: 0.1007/s10869-009-9128-y

De Witte, H. & Näswall, K. (2003). Objective versus subjective job insecurity: Consequences of temporary work for job satisfaction and organizational commitment in four European countries. *Economic and Industrial Democracy, 24*, 149–188.

De Witte, H. (1999). Job insecurity and psychological well-being: Review of the literature and exploration of some unresolved issues. *European Journal of Work and Organizational Psychology, 8* (2), 155–177.

Debus, M. E., König, C., & Kleinmann, M. (April 2011). The building blocks of job insecurity perceptions: the impact of company performance and personality on perceived job insecurity. Poster presented to the Society for Industrial and Organizational Psychology, Chicago.

Debus, M. E., Probst, T. M., König, C. J., & Kleinmann, M. (2012). Catch me if I fall! Country-level resources in the job insecurity-job attitudes link. *Journal of Applied Psychology, 97*, 690–698.

Dekker, S. W. A., & Schaufeli, W. B. (1995). The effects of job insecurity on psychological health and withdrawal: A longitudinal study. *Australian Psychologist, 30*, 57–63. doi: 10.1080/00050069508259607

Demerouti, E., Bakker, A. B., Nachreiner, F., & Schaufeli, W. B. (2001). The job demands-resources model of burnout. *Journal of Applied Psychology, 86*, 499–512.

Dooley, D., Rook, K. S., & Catalano, R. (1987). Job and non-job stressors and their moderators. *Journal of Occupational Psychology, 60*, 115–132.

Elovainio, M., Van den Bos, K., Linna, A., Kivimäki, M., Ala-Mursula, L., Pentti, J., & Vahtera, J. (2005). Combined effects of uncertainty and organizational justice on employee health: Testing the uncertainty management model of fairness judgments among Finnish public sector employees. *Social Science and Medicine, 61*, 2501–2512. doi: 10.1016/j.socscimed.2005.04.046

Elst, T. V., Baillien, E., De Cuyper, N., & De Witte, H. (2010). The role of organizational communication and participation in reducing job insecurity and its negative association with work-related well-being. *Economic and Industrial Democracy, 31*, 249–264. doi: 10.1177/0143831X09358372

Erlinghagen, M. (2008). Self-perceived job insecurity and social context: A multi-level analysis of 17 European countries. *European Sociological Review, 24*, 183–197. doi: 10.1093/esr/jcm042

Feather, N. T., & Rauter, K. A. (2004). Organizational citizenship behaviours in relation to job status, job insecurity, organizational commitment and identification, job satisfaction and work value. *Journal of Occupational and Organizational Psychology, 77*, 81–94.

Feldman, D. C. (1996). The nature, antecedents, and consequences of underemployment. *Journal of Management, 22*, 385–407.

Fenlason, K. J., & Beehr, T. A. (1994). Social support and occupational stress: Effects of talking to others. *Journal of Organizational Behavior, 15*, 157–175. doi: 10.1002/job.4030150205

French, J. R. P., Caplan, R. D., & Van Harrison, R. (1982). *The mechanisms of job stress and strain.* New York: Wiley.

Fugate, M., Kinicki, A. J., & Ashforth, B. E. (2004). Employability: A psycho-social construct, its dimensions and applications. *Journal of Vocational Behavior, 65*, 14–38.

Fullerton, A. S., & Wallace, M. (2007). Traversing the flexible turn: US workers' perceptions of job insecurity, 1977–2002. *Social Science Research, 36*, 201–221.

Furda, J., & Meijman, T. (1992). Druk en dreiging, sturing of stress. In J. Winnubst & M. Schabracq (Eds.), *Handboek Arbeid en Gezondheid Psychologie. Hoofdthema's* (pp. 127–144). Utrecht, The Netherlands: Uitgeverij Lemma.

Goog, Y., & Chang, S. (2008). Institutional antecedents and performance consequences of employment security and career advancement practices: Evidence from the People's Republic of China. *Human Resource Management, 47*, 33–48. doi: 10.1002/hrm.20196

Graen, G. B., & Uhl-Bien, M. (1995). Relationship-based approach to leadership: Development of leader-member exchange (LMX) theory of leadership over 25 years: Applying a multi-level multi-domain perspective. *Leadership Quarterly, 6*, 219–247. doi.org/10.1016/1048-9843(95)90036-5

Granrose, C. S., & Baccili, P. A. (2006). Do psychological contracts include boundaryless or protean. careers? *Career Development International, 11*, 163–182.

Green, F, Felstead, A., & Burchell, B (2000). Job insecurity and the difficulty of regaining employment: an empirical study of unemployment expectations. *Oxford Bulletin of Economics and Statistics, 62*(Special Issue): 855–883.

Greenhalgh, L., & Rosenblatt, Z. (1984). Job insecurity: Toward conceptual clarity. *Academy of Management Review, 3*, 438–448.

Greenspan, A. (1996). Address: Job insecurity and technology. In J. C. Fuhrer and J. Sneddon Little, eds., *Technology and Growth Conference Proceedings* (pp. 173–181). Boston: Federal Reserve of Boston Press.

Grunberg, L., Moore, S., & Greenberg, E. (1996). The relationship of employee ownership and participation to workplace safety. *Economic and Industrial Democracy, 17*, 221–241.

Hannerz, H., Albertsen, K., Nielsen, M. L., Tüchsen, F., & Burr, H. (2004). Occupational factors and 5-year weight change among men in a Danish national cohort. *Health Psychology, 23*, 283–288.

Hellgren, J., Sverke, M., & Isaksson, K. (1999). A two-dimensional approach to job insecurity: Consequences for employee attitudes and well-being. *European Journal of Work and Organizational Psychology, 8*, 179–195.

Hobfoll, S. E. (1989). Conservation of resources: A new attempt at conceptualizing stress. *American Psychologist, 44*, 513–524. doi: 10.1037/0003-066X.44.3.513

Hobfoll, S. E. (2001). The influence of culture, community, and the nested-self in the stress process: Advancing conservation of resources theory. *Applied Psychology: An International Review, 80*, 337–421. doi: 10.1111/1464-0597.00062

Holden, L., Scuffham, P. A., Hilton, M. F., Vecchio, N. N., & Whiteford, H. A. (2010). Work performance decrements are associated with Australian working conditions, particularly the demand to work longer hours. *Journal of Occupational and Environmental Medicine, 52*, 281–290.

House, J. S. (1981). *Work stress and social support.* Reading, MA: Addison-Wesley.

Huang, G., Lee, C., Ashford, S., Chen, Z., & Ren, X. (2010). Affective job insecurity: a mediator of cognitive job insecurity and employee outcomes relationships. *International Studies of Management and Organization, 40*, 20–39.

Hulin, C. L., & Roznowski, M. (1985). Organizational technologies: Effects on organizations' characteristics and individuals' responses. *Research in Organizational Behavior, 7*, 39–85.

Ibrahim, S., Smith, P., & Muntaner, C. (2009). A multi-group cross-lagged analyses of work stressors and health using Canadian national sample. *Social Science & Medicine, 68*, 49–59.

International Labor Organization. (2004). *Economic security for a better world.* Geneva, Switzerland: Author.

Ito, J. K., & Brotheridge, C. M. (2007). Exploring the predictors and consequences of job insecurity's components. *Journal of Managerial Psychology, 22*, 40–64.

Jahoda, M. (1982). *Employment and unemployment: A social-psychological analysis.* Cambridge, England: Cambridge University Press.

Jefferson, T., & Preston, A. (2010), Negotiating fair pay and conditions: Low paid women's experience and perceptions of labour market deregulation and individual wage bargaining. *Industrial Relations Journal, 41*, 351–366. doi: 10.1111/j.1468-2338.2010.00573.x

Jiang, L., & Probst, T. M. (April 2011). Organizational communication: A buffer in times of job insecurity? In M. Krischer (chair), Individual and organizational strategies for coping with job insecurity. Symposium presented at the 2011 Conference of the Society for Industrial and Organizational Psychology, Chicago.

Jiang, L., Probst, T. M., & Sinclair, R. R. (2013). Perceiving and responding to job insecurity: The importance of multilevel contexts. In A. Antoniou & C. Cooper (Eds.), *The Psychology of the Recession on the Workplace* (pp. 176–195). Cheltenham, UK: Edward Elgar.

Judge, T. A., & Colquitt, J. A. (2004). Organizational justice and stress: The mediating role of work–family conflict. *Journal of Applied Psychology, 89*, 395–404. doi: 10.1037/0021-9010.89.3.395

Kanter, R. M. (1989). *When giants learn to dance: Mastering the challenges of strategy, management and careers in the 1990s.* New York: Basic Books.

Karasek, R. (1979). Job demands, job decision latitude and mental strain: Implications for job redesign. *Administrative Science Quarterly, 24*, 285–306. doi: 10.2307/2392498

Khanna, P., & Khanna, A. (2012). Is your job robot-proof? Available at: http://www.forbes.com/sites/ciocentral/2012/06/07/is-your-job-robot-proof/

Kinnunen, U., & Natti, J. (1994). Job insecurity in Finland: Antecedents and consequences. *The European Work and Organizational Psychologist, 4*, 297–321. doi: 10.1080/13594329408410490

Kjos, D. (1988). Job search activity patterns of successful and unsuccessful job seekers. *Journal of Employment Counseling, 5*, 4–6.

Klandermans, B., & van Vuuren, T. (1999), Job insecurity. *Special Issue of the European Journal of Work and Organizational Psychology, 8*, 145–314.

Klehe, U.-C., Zikic, J., van Vianaen, A. E. M., & DePater, I. E. (2011). Career adaptability, turnover, and loyalty during organizational downsizing. *Journal of Vocational Behavior, 79*, 217–229.

Klein Hesselink, D. J., & van Vuuren, T. (1999). Job Flexibility and job insecurity: The Dutch case. *European Journal of Work and Organizational Psychology, 8*, 273–93.

Kluytmans, F., & Ott, M. (1999). The management of employability in the Netherlands. *European Journal of Work and Organizational Psychology, 8*, 261–72.

König, C. J., Debus, M. E., Häusler, S., Lendenmann, N., & Kleinmann, M. (2010). Examining occupational self-efficacy, work locus of control and communication as moderators of the job insecurity relationship-job performance. *Economic and Industrial Democracy, 31*, 231–247. doi: 10.1177/0143831X09358629.

Kowske, B., Rasch, R. L., & Wiley, J. W. (2010). Millennials' (lack of) attitude problem: An empirical examination of generational effects on work attitudes. *Journal of Business and Psychology, 25*, 265–279. doi: 10.1007/s10869-010-9171-8

Kuhnert, K., Sims, R., & Lahey, M. (1989). The relationship between job security and employees health. *Group and Organization Studies, 14*, 399–410.

Kuhnert, K. W., & Vance, R. J. (1993). Job insecurity and moderators of the relation between job insecurity and employee adjustment. In J. Campbell Quick, L. R. Murphy & J. J. Hurrel (Eds.), *Stress and well- being at work* (pp. 48–63). Washington, DC: American Psychological Association.

László, K. D., Pikhart, H., Kopp, M. S., Bobak, M., Pajak, A., Malyutina, S., Salavecs, G., & Marmont, M. (2010). Job insecurity and health: A study of 16 European countries. *Social Science & Medicine, 70*, 867–874.

Latack, J. C., & Dozier, J. B. (1986). After the axe falls: Job loss on a career transition. *Academy of Management Review, 11*, 375–392.

Lazarus, R., & Folkman, S. (1984). *Stress, appraisal and coping.* New York: Springer.

Lazarus, R. S., & Launier, R. (1978). *Stress-related transactions between person and environment.* In L. A. Pervin, & M. Lewis

(Eds.), *Perspectives in Interactional Psychology* (pp. 287–327). New York: Plenum.

Leana, C. R., Feldman, D. C., & Tan, G. Y. (1998). Research predictors of coping behavior after a layoff. *Journal of Organizational Behavior, 19*, 85–97.

Lewin, D. (1987). Dispute resolution in the non-union firm: A theoretical and empirical analysis. *Journal of Conflict Resolution, 31*, 465–502.

Lim, V. K. G. (1996). Job insecurity and its outcomes: Moderating effects of work-based and nonwork-based social support. *Human Relations, 49*, 171–194. doi: 10.1177/001872679604900203

Loi, R., Ngo, H., Zhang, L., & Lau, V. P. (2011). The interaction between leader-member exchange and perceived job security in predicting employee altruism and work performance. *Journal of Occupational and Organizational Psychology, 4*, 1–17. doi: 10.1348/096317910X510468

Luthans, B., & Sommer, S. M. (1999). The impact of downsizing on workplace attitudes. *Group and Organization Management, 24*, 46–70.

Mak, A. S., & Mueller, J. (2000). Job insecurity, coping resources, and personality dispositions in occupational strain. *Work & Stress, 14*, 312–328.

Manski, C. F., & Straub, J. D. (2000). Worker perceptions of job insecurity in the mid-1990s: Evidence from the survey of economic expectations. *The Journal of Human Resources, 35*, 447–479.

Marks, M. L., & Mirvis, P. (1985). Merger syndrome: Stress and uncertainty. *Mergers and Acquisitions, 20*, 70–76.

Mauno, S., & Kinnunen, U. (2002). Perceived job insecurity among dual-earner couples: Do its antecedents vary according to gender, economic sector and the measure used? *Journal of Occupational and Organizational Psychology, 75*, 295–314.

Mauno, S., Kinnunen, U., Mäkikangas, A., & Nätti, J. (2005). Psychological consequences of fixed-term employment and perceived job insecurity among health care staff. *European Journal of Work and Organizational Psychology, 14*, 209–237.

Mayer, R. C., Davis, J. H., & Schoorman, F. D. (1995). An integrative model of organizational trust. *The Academy of Management Review, 20*, 709–734.

McKee-Ryan, F. M., & Harvey, J. (2011). "I have a job, but . . .": A review of underemployment. *Journal of Management, 37*, 962–996. doi: 10.1177/0149206311398134

Mikkelsen, A., & Saksvik, P. O. (1999). Impact of a participatory organizational intervention on job characteristics and job stress. *International Journal of Health Services, 29*, 871–93.

Mohr, G. B. (2000). The changing significance of different stressors after the announcement of bankruptcy: A longitudinal investigation with special emphasis on job insecurity. *Journal of Organizational Behavior, 21*, 337–359. doi: 10.1002/(SICI)1099–1379(200005)21:3<337::AID-JOB18>3.0.CO;2-G

Muñoz de Bustillo, R., & De Pedraza, P. (2010). Determinants of job insecurity in 5 European countries. *European Journal of Industrial Relations, 16*, 5–20. doi: 10.1177/0959680109355306

Näswall, K., Sverke, M., & Hellgren, J. (2005). The moderating role of personality characteristics on the relation between job insecurity and strain. *Work & Stress, 19*, 37–49.

Näswall, K. (2004). The buffering effect of employability on job insecurity outcomes. Poster presented at the XXVIII International Congress of Psychology, August 8–13, Beijing, China.

Näswall, K. (2005). Job insecurity and well-being: Moderating factors of a negative relationship. Paper presented at the 12th European Congress on Work and Organizational Psychology, May 12–15, Istanbul.

Neal, A., Griffin, M. A., & Hart, P. M. (2000). The impact of organizational climate on safety climate and individual behavior. *Safety Science, 34*, 99–109. doi: 10.1016/S0925-7535(00)00008-4

Olson, D. A., & Tetrick, L. E. (1988). Organizational restructuring: The impact on role perceptions, work relationships and satisfaction. *Group and Organization Studies, 13*, 374 –388.

Orpen, C. (1994). The effects of self-esteem and personal control on the relationship between job insecurity and psychological well-being. *Social Behavior and Personality 22*, 53–55. doi: 10.2224/sbp.1994.22.1.53

Parker, S. K., Axtell, C. M., & Turner, N. (2001). Designing a safer workplace: Importance of job autonomy, communication quality, and supportive supervisors. *Journal of Occupational Health Psychology, 6*, 211–228.

Pearce, J. L. (1998). Job insecurity is important, but not for the reasons you might think: The example of contingent workers. In C. Cooper and D. M. Rousseau (Eds.), *Trends in Organizational Behavior* (Vol. 5, pp. 31–46). Chichester, UK: Wiley.

Pfeffer, J. (1998). *The human equation: Building profits by putting people first*. Boston, MA: Harvard Business School.

Pollard, T. M. (2001). Changes in mental well-being, blood pressure and total cholesterol levels during workplace reorganization: The impact of uncertainty. *Work and Stress, 15*, 14–28.

Porter, L. W., Steers, R. M., Mowday, R. T., & Boulian, P. V. (1974). Organizational commitment, job satisfaction, and turnover among psychiatric technicians. *Journal of Applied Psychology, 59*, 603–609.

Probst, T. M. (1998). Antecedents and consequences of job insecurity: Development and test of an integrated model. Unpublished doctoral dissertation. University of Illinois at Urbana-Champaign.

Probst, T. M. (2002a). The impact of job insecurity on employee work attitudes, job adaptation, and organizational withdrawal behaviors, In J. M. Brett and F. Drasgow (Eds.), *The psychology of work: Theoretically based empirical research* (pp. 141–168). Mahwah, NJ: Erlbaum.

Probst, T. M. (2002b). Layoffs and tradeoffs: Production, quality, and safety demands under the threat of job loss. *Journal of Occupational Health Psychology, 7*, 211–220.

Probst, T. M. (2003b). Exploring employee outcomes of organizational restructuring: A Solomon four-group study. *Group and Organization Management. 28*, 416–439.

Probst, T. M. (2004). Safety and insecurity: Exploring the moderating effect of organizational safety climate. *Journal of Occupational Health Psychology, 9*, 3–10.

Probst, T. M. (2005). Countering the negative effects of job insecurity through participative decision making: Lessons from the demand-control model. *Journal of Occupational Health Psychology, 10*, 320–329.

Probst, T. M. (2008). Job insecurity. In C. L. Cooper & J. Barling (Eds.), *Handbook of organizational behavior* (pp. 178–195). Thousand Oaks, CA: Sage.

Probst, T. M. (2009). Job insecurity, unemployment, and organizational well-being: Oxymoron or possibility? In S. Cartwright and C. L. Cooper (Eds.), *The Oxford handbook of organizational well-being* (pp. 398–410). Oxford, UK: Oxford University Press.

Probst, T. M. (2010). Multi-level models of stress and well-being. *Stress and Health, 26*, 95–97.

Probst, T. M. (2011, April). *Leader-Member Exchange: How supervisor-employee relationships moderate outcomes of job insecurity*. In M. Krischer (chair), Individual and Organizational Strategies for Coping with Job Insecurity. Symposium presented at the 2011 Conference of the Society for Industrial and Organizational Psychology, Chicago.

Probst, T. M., & Brubaker, T. L. (2001). The effects of job insecurity on employee safety outcomes: Cross-sectional and longitudinal explorations. *Journal of Occupational Health Psychology, 6*, 139–159.

Probst, T. M., & Collison, J. (2006). "You're laying me off WHEN??" The effects of layoff notice as viewed by HR. Unpublished manuscript, Washington State University, Vancouver.

Probst, T. M., & Lawler, J. (2006). Cultural values as moderators of the outcomes of job insecurity: The role of individualism and collectivism. *Applied Psychology: An International Review, 55*, 234–254. doi: 10.1111/j.1464-0597.2006.00239.x

Probst, T. M., & Strand, P. (2010). Perceiving and responding to job insecurity: A workplace spirituality perspective. *Journal of Management, Spirituality and Religion, 7*, 135–156.

Probst, T. M., Benson, W., Graso, M., Jiang, L., & Olson, K. (2011). Effects of the budget cuts on faculty, staff, and administrative professions: A feedback report to WSU. Prepared for faculty, staff, and administrators at Washington State University.

Probst, T. M., Stewart, S., Gruys, M. L., & Tierney, B. W. (2007). Productivity, counterproductivity, and creativity: The ups and downs of job insecurity. *Journal of Occupational and Organizational Psychology, 80*, 479–497.

Probst, T. M. (2001, May). Self-efficacy for adapting to organizational transitions: It helps, but only when the prospects are bright. Paper presented to the 2001 Western Psychological Association, Maui, HI.

Probst, T. M. (2003a). Development and validation of the Job Security Index and the Job Security Satisfaction Scale: A classical test theory and IRT approach. *Journal of Occupational and Organizational Psychology, 76*, 451–467.

Quinlan, M. (2005). The hidden epidemic of injuries and illness associated with the global expansion of precarious employment. In C. L. Peterson & C. Mayhew (Eds.), *Occupational health and safety: International influences and the new epidemics* (pp. 53–74). Amityville, NY: Baywood Publishing.

Reisel, W. D. (2003). Predicting job insecurity via moderating influence of individual powerlessness. *Psychological Reports, 92*, 820–822.

Reisel, W. D., & Banai, M. (2002). Comparison of a multidimensional and a global measure of job insecurity: Predicting job attitudes and work behaviors. *Psychological Reports, 90*, 913–922.

Reisel, W. D., Chia, S. L., & Maloles, C. M. (2005). Job insecurity spillover to key account management: Negative effects of performance, effectiveness, adaptiveness, and esprit de corps. *Journal of Business and Psychology, 19*, 483–503.

Reisel, W. D., Chia, S.-L., Maloles, C. M., & Slocum, J. W. (2007). The effects of job insecurity on satisfaction and perceived organizational performance. *Journal of Leadership & Organizational Studies, 14*, 106–116.

Reisel, W. D., Probst, T. M., Chia, S-L., Maloles, C. M., & Konig, C. K. (2010). The effects of job insecurity on job satisfaction, organizational citizenship behavior, deviant behavior, and negative emotions of employees. *International Studies of Management and Organization, 40*(1), 74–91.

Reisel, W. D., Probst, T. M., Chia, S., Maloles, C. M., Brown, J. W. & Hazen, J. (2007). *An examination of the effects of job insecurity on job satisfaction, organizational citizenship behavior, deviant behavior, and negative emotions of employees*. Poster presented to the 2007 Conference of the Institute of Behavioral and Applied Management, Reno, NV.

Roskies, E., & Louis-Guerin, C. (1990). Job insecurity in managers: Antecedents and consequences. *Journal of Organizational Behavior, 11,* 345–359. doi: 10.1002/job.4030110503

Roskies, E., Louis-Guerin, C., & Fournier, C. (1993). Coping with job insecurity: How does personality make a difference? *Journal of Organizational Behavior, 14,* 617–630.

Sainfort, F., Karsh, B., Booske, B. C., & Smith, M. J. (2001). Applying quality improvement principles to achieve healthy work organizations. *Journal of Quality Improvement, 27,* 469–483.

Sauter, S., Murphy, L. R., & Hurrell, J. J. (1990). A national strategy for the prevention of work related psychological disorders. *American Psychologist, 45,* 1146–1158.

Scheck, C. L., Kinicki, A. J., & Davy, J. A. (1997). Testing the mediating processes between work stressors and subjective well-being. *Journal of Vocational Behavior, 50,* 96–123. doi: 10.1006/jvbe.1996.1540

Scherer, S. (2009). The social consequences of insecure jobs. *Social Indicators Research, 93,* 527–547.

Schneider, B. (1975). Organizational climate. *Personnel Psychology, 28,* 447–479.

Schreurs, B. H. J., van Emmerik, H., De Cuyper, N., Probst, T. M., van den Heuvel, M., & Demerouti, E. (2011, August). Praying for security: The role of religion in moderating outcomes of job insecurity. Paper presented to the Annual Conference of the Academy of Management, San Antonio, TX.

Schreurs, B., van Emmerik, H., Notelaers, G., & De Witte, H. (2010). Job insecurity and employee health: The buffering potential of job control and job self-efficacy. *Work and Stress, 24,* 56–72. doi: 10.1080/02678371003718733

Schweiger, D. M., & DeNisi, A. S. (1991). Communication with employees following a merger: a longitudinal field experiment. *Academy of Management Journal, 34,* 110–35.

Silla, I., De Cuyer, N., Gracia, F. J., Peiró, J. M., & De Witte, H. (2009). Job insecurity and well-being: Moderation by employability. *Journal of Happiness Studies, 10,* 739–751. doi 10.1007/s10902-008-9119-0

Sinclair, R., Sears, L. E., Probst, T. M., & Zajack, M. (2010). A multilevel model of economic stress and employee well-being. In J. Houdmont & S. Leka (Eds.), *Contemporary Occupational Health Psychology: Global Perspectives on Research and Practice* (Vol. *1,* pp. 1–21). Hoboken, NJ: Wiley-Blackwell.

Slack, K. J. (2004). Examining job insecurity and well-being in the context of the role of employment. *Dissertation Abstracts International: Section B: The Sciences and Engineering, 65*(9), 4884.

Sora, B., Caballer, A., Peiró, J. M., Silla, I., & Gracia, F. J. (2010). Moderating influence of organizational justice on the relationship between job insecurity and its outcomes: A multilevel analysis. *Economic and Industrial Democracy, 31,* 613–637. doi: 10.1177/0143831X10365924

Soylu, A. (2008). Causes and consequences of work stress: A comparison of foreign and American workers in the United States. Ph.D. dissertation, Temple University, Philadelphia. AAT: 3300379.

Staufenbiel, T., & König, C. J. (2010). A model for the effects of job insecurity on performance, turnover intention, and absenteeism. *The British Psychological Society, 83,* 101–117.

Steers, R. M., & Mowday, R. T. (1981). Employee turnover and post-decision justification. In L. L. Cummings & B. M. Staw (Eds.), *Research in organizational behavior* (Vol. 3, pp. 235–282). Greenwich, CT: JAI Press.

Strazdins, L., D'Souza, R. M., Lim, L. L., Broom, D. H., & Rodgers, B. (2004). Job strain, job insecurity, and health: rethinking the relationship. *Journal of Occupational Health Psychology, 9,* 296–305. doi: 10.1037/1076-8998.9.4.296

Sulsky, L., & Smith, C. S. (2005). *Work stress.* Belmont CA: Wadsworth.

Sverke, M., & Hellgren, J. (2002). The nature of job insecurity: Understanding employment uncertainty on the brink of a new millennium. *Applied Psychology: An International Review, 51,* 23–42.

Sverke, M., Hellgren, J., & Näswell, K. (2002). No security: A meta-analysis and review of job insecurity and its consequences. *Journal of Occupational Health Psychology, 7,* 242–264.

Swaim, P., & Podgursky, M. (1990). Advance notice and job search: The value of an early start. *The Journal of Human Resources, 25,* 141–178.

Tam, H. (2010). Characteristics of the underemployed and the overemployed in the UK. *Economic & Labor Market Review, 4,* 8–20.

Thau, S., Aquino, K., & Wittek, R. (2007). An extension of uncertainty management theory to the self: The relationship between justice, social comparison orientation, and antisocial work behaviors. *Journal of Applied Psychology, 92,* 250–258. doi: 10.1037/0021-9010.92.1.250

Tivendell, J. & Bourbonnais, C. (2000). Job insecurity in a sample of Canadian civil servants as a function of personality and perceived job characteristics. *Psychological Reports, 87,* 55–60.

Turnley, W. H., & Feldman, D. C. (1999). The impact of psychological contract violations on exit, voice, loyalty and neglect. *Human Relations, 52,* 895–922.

Van Harrison, R. (1978). Person-environment fit and job stress. In C. L. Cooper, & R. Payne (Eds.), *Stress at work* (pp. 175–208). Chichester, UK: Wiley.

van Vuuren, C. V., & Klandermans, P. G. (1990). Individual reactions to job insecurity: An integrated model. In P. J. D. Drenth & J. A. Sergeant (Eds.), *European perspectives in psychology* (pp. 133–146). Chichester, UK: Wiley.

Wagenaar, A. F., Kompier, M. A., Houtman, I. L., van den Bossche, S., Smulders, P., & Taris, T. W. (May 2011). Can labour contract differences in health and in work-related attitudes be explained by quality of working life and/or work insecurity? Paper presented at the Work, Stress, and Health Conference, Orlando, FL.

Warr, P. B. (1987). *Work, unemployment, and mental health.* Oxford, UK: Clarendon Press.

Westman, M., Etzion, D., & Danon, E. (2001). Job insecurity and crossover of burnout in married couples. *Journal of Organizational Behavior, 22,* 467–481.

Zhao, J., Rust, K. G., McKinley, W., & Edwards, J. C. (2010). Downsizing, ideology and contracts: A Chinese perspective. *Chinese Management Studies, 4,* 119–140.

Zohar, D. (1980). Safety climate in industrial organizations: Theoretical and applied implications. *Journal of Applied Psychology, 65,* 96–102.

Consequences of Job Loss and Unemployment

Individual Consequences of Job Loss and Unemployment

Karsten I. Paul, Alice Hassel, *and* Klaus Moser

Abstract

Scholars from several different fields have studied the individual consequences of job loss and unemployment since the beginning of the twentieth century. This chapter provides a review of some important results of this research with special emphasis on the effects of unemployment on mental health. Among the topics reviewed are the size and practical relevance of these effects and the question of causality (i.e., does job loss really cause distress or are people with distress symptoms more likely to lose their jobs and remain unemployed for a longer time?) Results of moderator variables are also reviewed, as well as those concerning coping mechanisms. Then theories concerning the question of why unemployment impairs mental health (mediating mechanisms) are described, along with empirical results. Finally, some selected research findings for other outcome dimensions, ranging from physical health to political attitudes, are reported. The chapter ends with a discussion of the practical consequences of the reviewed research findings and the identification of research gaps.

Key Words: unemployment, job loss, health, distress, attitudes, causation, moderation, mediation, review

Introduction

During times of peace, full employment (i.e., unemployment rates below 3%) has been rare in North America and western Europe during the twentieth and twenty-first centuries (Dormois, 2004; Niess, 1979; OECD, 2000, 2004, 2010; United States Department of Labor, 1990). Thus unemployment is a chronic problem of modern societies. Furthermore, unemployment is a global problem: In 2011 the worldwide number of people who were unemployed was as large as 197 million, representing 6% of the global labor force (International Labour Office, 2012). For psychologists, the following questions arise: How does unemployment affect people's lives? Are the effects of unemployment mainly of a financial nature, or are they more severe, possibly impairing physical and psychological health?

Already in the first decades of the twentieth century psychologists began to offer answers to these questions—for example, Jahoda, Lazarsfeld,

and Zeisel (1933/1975) in their famous *Marienthal* study. Since that time psychologists and researchers from other disciplines have gathered a huge amount of data concerning the psychological effects of unemployment. Today several reviews in *narrative form* are available that give an overview of the research of the past decades (e.g., Catalano, 1991; DeFrank, & Ivancevich, 1986; Dooley, Fielding, & Levi, 1996; Eisenberg & Lazarsfeld, 1938; Ezzy, 1993; Frese & Mohr, 1978; Fryer & Payne, 1986; Hammarström, 1994; Hanisch, 1999; Kasl, Rodriguez, & Lasch, 1998; Wanberg, Kammeyer-Mueller, & Shi, 2001; Warr & Parry, 1982; Winefield, 1995; Feather, this volume).

Recent meta-analyses have provided quantitative estimates of the effects of unemployment and job loss on mental health (Foster, 1991; McKee-Ryan, Song, Wanberg, & Kinicki, 2005; Murphy & Athanasou, 1999; Paul & Moser, 2009). Furthermore, these studies analyzed a large number of moderator variables, both on the individual level (for example, occupational status or duration of unemployment) as well as on the level of countries (for example, income disparity), enabling us to obtain a clearer picture of the circumstances under which the effects of unemployment are particularly strong or comparatively weak. This kind of knowledge is important, since it can help to identify groups of people in need of help and can lead to the development of improved intervention strategies. The important question of causality (i.e., whether unemployment causes distress or whether persons with mental health symptoms are more likely to lose their jobs and to stay unemployed for a prolonged time) was also scrutinized in these meta-analyses.

The current chapter gives an overview over the research results concerning the psychological consequences of unemployment and job loss, particularly its effects on mental health and well-being. It is mainly based on the findings of two recent meta-analyses concerning this topic that synthesized a large number of primary studies, but it also includes the findings of relevant primary studies.

McKee-Ryan, Song, Wanberg, and Kinicki (2005) included 104 studies in their meta-analysis, of which 32 had a longitudinal design. The outcome variables they studied were mental health, life satisfaction, marital satisfaction, and subjective and objective physical health. Paul and Moser's (2009) meta-analysis included 237 cross-sectional and 87 longitudinal studies. The outcome variables they studied were mixed symptoms of distress, depression, anxiety, psychosomatic symptoms, self-esteem, and subjective well-being. Since a meta-analysis of the intercorrelations of these six variables demonstrated that they are highly linked, a composite for overall mental health was also computed for each sample and then meta-analyzed. [1]

The chapter begins by taking a quick look into the history of unemployment and its definition in order to contextualize the findings of almost 100 years of psychological research on this issue. Then the main effects of unemployment on mental health are reviewed, followed by moderator effects on the individual level and the level of countries. After that, research results on coping strategies and the problem of causality are described. The next section reviews some important theoretical accounts explaining the effects of unemployment on mental health. Then research on the important question whether a job is *always* better than unemployment is discussed. Finally, effects of unemployment on

relevant psychological variables other than mental health are briefly reviewed. Discussions of the practical and political consequences of psychological unemployment research and of unresolved research questions conclude this chapter.

Unemployment in History

Through the ages there have been people who—from a modern perspective—could be considered "unemployed." Around 450 BCE, for example, statesman and general of Athens Pericles undertook "vast projects of buildings and designs of work" with the goal "that the undisciplined and mechanic multitude . . . should not go without their share of public salaries, and yet should not have them given for sitting still and doing nothing" (Plutarch, cited after Garraty, 1978, p. 13). In the Bible we can also find references to people who have problems finding work:

> For the kingdom of heaven is like unto a man that is a householder, which went out early in the morning to hire labourers into his vineyard. And when he had agreed with the labourers for a penny a day, he sent them into his vineyard. . . . And about the eleventh hour he went out, and found others standing idle, and saith unto them, Why stand ye here all the day idle? They say unto him, Because no man hath hired us. *(Matthew 20: 1–7)*

However, for a very long time in the history of humanity unemployed people were not perceived as a distinct group; they rather were seen as a part of the large class of paupers. The concept of "unemployment" as we know it today did not emerge before the industrial revolution (Garraty, 1978; Niess, 1979). This was the time when the relationship between employer and employee, which is common in modern societies, was established and when the new capitalist methods of production were repeatedly accompanied by waves of recession and mass unemployment. These frequent fluctuations in the business cycle forced European and northern American societies to accept the idea that there is not always enough work for everyone who is willing and able to work—an attitude that had dominated the thinking of earlier centuries. This process of understanding was a slow one; therefore the modern English word *unemployment* (and the German equivalent *Arbeitslosigkeit*) did not come into general use until 1890. That was also the time when most of the modern practices concerned with the unemployment phenomenon were created, such as the regular collection of unemployment statistics and the establishment of unemployment insurance systems (Garraty, 1978; Niess, 1979).

In the twentieth century, unemployment stood among the most challenging economic problems: Even in the world's most economically powerful nation, the United States, more than a million people were unemployed in every year since 1929 (the only exception being the war year of 1944). In the years preceding World War II and in the early 1980s, more than 10 million US citizens were involuntarily out of work (United States Department of Labor, 1990, 2009). Similar pictures emerged for other western countries in the last century.

In 2011, the world regions with the highest unemployment rates were North Africa with 10.9% and the Middle East with 10.2% (International Labour Office, 2012). Thus unemployment today is a problem not only of western economies but of the whole world.

We can conclude that unemployment is a phenomenon that has probably accompanied humankind during most periods of recorded history and is currently a global problem.

Definitions

To define unemployment is not as trivial as it might appear at first glance. The definitions of unemployment used in different countries concur only partly, and even within a country different institutions sometimes adhere to different definitions (Hollederer, 2002). However, contemporary national definitions of unemployment are usually oriented toward the definition of the International Labour Office and regularly include its main elements. This definition can be seen as an international compromise and consists of three core elements:

> "The 'unemployed' comprise all persons above a specific age who during the reference period were (a) 'without work,' i.e., were not in paid employment or self-employment . . .; (b) 'currently available for work,' i.e., were available for paid employment or self-employment during the reference period; and (c) 'seeking work,' i.e., had taken specific steps in a specified reference period to seek paid employment or self-employment." (International Labour Office, 2000a, p. 429)

This definition includes not only situational aspects (nonemployment) but also motivational aspects ("seeking work") and medical and legal aspects (being "available for work"). While the first criterion is obviously necessary in order to distinguish unemployed from employed persons, the second and the third criteria help to distinguish unemployed persons from persons who are out of the labor force, such as homemakers, students, disabled people, retirees, prisoners, etc.).

Thus, although the common definition of unemployment was developed by labor statisticians, scholars in the field of psychological unemployment research usually adhere to a conceptualization of unemployment that is very similar to the one cited above, because it is the "official" definition that is used by the state authorities and by other sciences, particularly economics. However, there are exceptions. Marie Jahoda, for example, one of the most renowned psychologists concerned with unemployment, used a broader definition: "All those can be considered as unemployed, who have no job but would like to have one, or have to rely on financial support in order to survive as long as they don't have a job" (1986, p. 32, translation into English by the authors).

Consequences: Unemployment and Mental Health
Main Effects of Unemployment

The pivotal question that was most intensively scrutinized in the realm of psychological unemployment research was that of the possible effects of unemployment on mental health. Does job loss lead to distress? And if so, is this effect large enough to be of relevance for individual lives and—on an aggregate level—for public health?

The recently published meta-analyses (McKee-Ryan, Song, Wanberg, & Kinicki, 2005; Paul & Moser, 2009) are in good agreement with each other with regard to the answers to these questions. Both meta-analyses found a clear association between unemployment and mental health: The difference between employed and unemployed persons with regard to mental health was of medium size in both studies (about half of a standard deviation).

Since effect sizes are abstract entities and are not easy to interpret, Paul and Moser (2009) also meta-analyzed the results of those studies that reported prevalence rates for cases of clinically relevant psychological disorders among employed and unemployed people. This analysis demonstrated that the effect of unemployment on mental health has considerable practical importance, because the average prevalence rate of psychological disorders among employed persons was 16%, while it was 34% among unemployed people (Paul & Moser, 2009).

In other words, being unemployed is associated with a doubled risk of clinically relevant mental health problems—a finding that shows the importance of unemployment and its consequences for public health.

Some authors (e.g., Frese & Mohr, 1978) have argued that unemployment is particularly likely to cause depression-like symptoms. However, separate meta-analyses for specific indicators of mental well-being (anxiety, depression, reduced subjective well-being/life satisfaction, and reduced self-esteem) revealed that the effect sizes were similar for all of these indicator variables of mental health. The only exception was psychosomatic complaints (i.e., a group of symptoms at the borderline between psychological and physical health), for which Paul and Moser (2009) found only a small effect size. Thus the effect of unemployment on mental health was found to be very broad, affecting all aspects of psychological health, most of these being of similar magnitude. In other words, there exists no specific cluster of symptoms that could be called the typical "unemployment syndrome."

Moderators of the Effects of Unemployment on Mental Health

Knowledge about moderators gives us a more detailed picture of the effects of unemployment and helps us to identify the most distressed groups who might be seen as most appropriate targets for intervention. Furthermore, those groups of unemployed persons who suffer less from their situation than others possibly provide us with information of how to cope with unemployment and could therefore be helpful in developing interventions. The meta-analyses have tested moderators on both the individual level, analyzing characteristics of the employed or unemployed persons, and on the level of countries, analyzing characteristics of the nations in which the research studies were conducted. The latter analyses shed some light on the effects of sociopolitical decisions that influence the lives of unemployed people.

Moderators on the Individual Level
Gender

Men were often assumed to suffer more from unemployment than women. The conventional masculine identity in western societies is to a very large degree defined by having a job and being the provider ("breadwinner") of a family; thus this role is threatened by unemployment at its core

(Komarovsky, 1940; McFayden, 1995; Nixon, 2006). That is, men are assumed to have a stronger commitment to the work role than women, resulting in greater distress when they are deprived of this role. Women, on the other hand, have alternative roles at their disposal, which can serve as substitutes for employment (Shamir, 1985). On the financial side, the traditional distribution of roles should also result in more distressing effects of unemployment on males, because men still earn more money than women, resulting in a greater reduction of the household income in case of male job loss compared with female job loss. In contrast, when they are unemployed, women can expect more financial support from their husbands than men can from their wives (Leana & Feldman, 1991; Shamir, 1985). Furthermore, men still have more attractive jobs than women with regard to other aspects as well (e.g., hierarchical position, decision latitude, social exchange, etc.). Like the financial aspect, this means a more severe loss for men than for women when a job is lost (Mohr, 1993). In addition, stigmatization may be stronger against unemployed men than against unemployed women (Kulik, 2000; Shamir, 1985). Staying with the traditional distribution of roles, employed women, on average, still spend more time on domestic work than do their spouses. This results in a dual burden, of which a woman is relieved when she loses her job. The negative effects of unemployment thus might be diminished by the lessened stress of multiple role engagement (Mohr, 1993; Muller, Hicks, & Winocur, 1993; Warr & Parry, 1982). In sum, a lot of arguments have been put forward endorsing the assumption that unemployment has more severe health effects on men than on women.

Of course, these arguments in favor of more severe negative effect among men have not remained undisputed. First, gender roles have changed in the last decades. There have been substantial alterations in women's work patterns, which may affect their reactions to unemployment and bring them closer to men in suffering from the related distress (Kulik, 2000). In addition, the status of the role of housewife and mother might be lower than it was in the past, reducing the possible beneficial effects of this alternative role. Furthermore, gender equality still being incomplete, women might still experience discrimination in many labor markets, reducing their chances of reemployment and increasing their likelihood of being reemployed in less attractive jobs (Fielden & Davidson, 2001; Perrucci, Perrucci, & Targ, 1997). Knowledge of their poor reemployment prospects might further diminish unemployed women's well-being.[2]

Empirically, the assumption of more severe health effects of unemployment among men in comparison with women has been clearly supported. In Paul and Moser's (2009) meta-analysis, gender (measured by the percentage of female participants in a sample) was found to be a significant moderator: For samples with a large proportion of female participants, the effect sizes were weaker than for samples with a small proportion of female participants. These authors also tested whether males and females had become more similar during the last decades with regard to their reactions to unemployment. However, they could not identify signs of an interaction effect between gender and the year of data collection. Thus the changes in the female gender role that occurred during the last decades were not (yet?) strong enough to substantially influence the effects of unemployment on male and female mental health. The difference between employed and unemployed persons with regard to depression, anxiety, and similar symptoms is still considerably larger among men than among women.

Then again, McKee-Ryan et al. (2005) analyzed correlates of mental health and life satisfaction separately for unemployed people (without considering employed comparison groups). They found a small yet significant correlation between gender and mental health. But, surprisingly, unemployed men reported slightly *better* mental health and slightly *more* life satisfaction than unemployed women. An explanation for this slightly puzzling pattern of findings might be that employed men receive more psychological benefits from their jobs than employed women do. The lack of benefits associated with unemployment, on the other hand, is similar for both genders. Thus, men losing a job lose many psychological benefits, causing large mental health differences between unemployed and employed men. Women, on average, receive fewer benefits from their jobs; consequently the mental health differences between employed and unemployed women are smaller, as reported by Paul and Moser (2009). In other words, the loss is apparently larger for men, but the psychological end state during unemployment is similar for members of both genders.

Socioeconomic Status

Contrasting theoretical arguments have been posed for the moderating role of socioeconomic status. Several scholars have argued that individuals of higher socioeconomic status (i.e., with higher income and better education) can be expected to suffer more from unemployment than individuals of lower status because they generally lose more attractive jobs. This concerns job aspects such as income, reputation, physical work conditions, and promotion opportunities as well as task content or intrinsic motivational potential (Eisenberg & Lazarsfeld, 1938; Kaufman, 1982; Payne, Warr, & Hartley, 1984).

Furthermore, for high-status individuals, their jobs very often are important aspects of their identity: "consequently, job loss is probably a greater blow to the ego and self-esteem of professionals than of other workers, and the former would be expected to experience more severe psychological stress" (Kaufman, 1982, p. 25). The stigmatization followed by unemployment is, in addition, possibly more pronounced for persons of higher status: White-collar or professional unemployment is rare and harder to justify than blue-collar unemployment (McFayden, 1995).

Then again, the "higher fall" that individuals with higher socioeconomic status have to suffer when facing unemployment could be balanced by various advantages and options they may have available. They usually have better financial and social resources and may possess better coping strategies than low-status persons (Kulik, 2000; Little, 1976; Payne, Warr, & Hartley, 1984; Schaufeli & van Yperen, 1992). Furthermore, even if the job among high-status persons is an important aspect of identity, educational attainment could serve as an alternative provider of status and identity and thus reduce the negative mental health effects. Unemployed engineers, for example, will still see themselves and will still be respected by other people as engineers. Unemployed assembly line workers do not have this advantage. In addition, unemployment rates are usually higher among groups of lower socioeconomic status. The prospects of a difficult yet unavoidable job hunt may be rather depressing and have additional negative mental health effects.

Empirically, a significant moderator effect was found in the Paul and Moser (2009)-meta-analysis for occupational status, with mental health differences between employed and unemployed persons being larger among people with blue-collar occupations in comparison to those with white-collar occupations (including professionals). In good agreement with these findings, McKee-Ryan et al (2005) found significantly better mental health and life satisfaction among unemployed persons with high education versus those with low education. In summary, the frequently expressed assumption that unemployment has more severe consequences for people of high socioeconomic status versus those of low status is not supported empirically. Quite to the contrary, meta-analytic findings demonstrate that those members of a society who have to content themselves with the less desirable social positions are more vulnerable to the negative psychological effects of unemployment.

Duration of Unemployment

Since the beginning of psychological unemployment research, the question of whether there is a pattern of discernable stages of the psychological reactions to unemployment has frequently been discussed. The cumulative stress model of unemployment distress argues for a linear deterioration of mental health with increasing duration of unemployment. According to this line of thinking, unemployed workers may become more discouraged over time by continuing failures in job seeking. Furthermore, financial pressures may become greater as time passes, savings are used up, and personal or household items wear out or break down and require repair or replacement (Jackson & Warr, 1984; Warr, Jackson, & Banks, 1982).

However, a range of more complex stage models was also formulated to describe the psychological deterioration process associated with unemployment. All of these models assume that job loss is followed by a specific sequence of reactions that should be identical for all unemployed persons. Eisenberg and Lazarsfeld (1938), for example, proposed a three-phasic model:

> First there is shock, which is followed by an active hunt for a job, during which the individual is still optimistic and unresigned; he still maintains an unbroken attitude. Second, when all efforts fail, the individual becomes pessimistic, anxious, and suffers active distress; this is the most crucial state of all. And third, the individual becomes fatalistic and adapts himself to his new state but with a narrower scope. He now has a broken attitude. (p. 378) *(See also Feather, this volume.)*

Other stage models have been proposed that differ from Eisenberg and Lazarsfeld's in number and descriptions of the phases (e.g., Amundson & Borgen, 1982; Dreiss, 1983; Harrison, 1976; Kaufman, 1982). Some stage models are formulated in analogy to the process of grief (Hill, 1978; Raber, 1996; see also Archer & Rhodes, 1987, 1993, for a explicitly "nonstage" grief model of job loss), and

one stage model was even formulated in analogy to the process of dying (Winegardner, Simonetti, & Nykodym, 1984).

Although the proposed stage models differ, most of them share the assumption that in the first weeks after job loss the mental health of unemployed persons is comparatively good, followed by a severe deterioration in the months that follow. After this crisis (and possibly other intermediate phases), a final stage of adaptation and stabilization at a low level of mental health is usually proposed. Warr and Jackson (1987) assume that this adaptation is the result of either the development of interests and activities outside the labor market that act as substitutes for paid employment and are associated with increased levels of aspiration, autonomy, and sense of competence (constructive adaptation) or is the result of a simple reduction in employment commitment that is not associated with aspirations, autonomy, and sense of competence (resigned adaptation).

Empirically, McKee-Ryan et al. (2005) found a significantly higher distress level for persons who were unemployed for up to 6 months versus those who were unemployed for more than 6 months. Furthermore, in a more fine-grained analysis, Paul and Moser (2009) found a significant curvilinear association, with stress symptoms sharply increasing during the first 9 months of unemployment, followed by stabilization at a medium level of distress during the second year (see Figure 4.1). This meta-analysis also found hints of a significant cubic association, meaning that people who were unemployed for a very long time (> 2.5 years) experienced a renewed increase of symptom levels. However, owing to the dearth of studies with people who have been unemployed for extremely long times, these results were not stable (the effect was reduced to marginal significance after exclusion of a probable outlier study). Thus the issue of renewed deterioration of mental health after very long durations of unemployment is in need of further research.

Age

It is often assumed that persons of middle age suffer most from unemployment, while younger and older persons are less severely affected (e.g., Broomhall & Winefield, 1990; Eisenberg & Lazarsfeld, 1938; Fryer, 1997b; Hepworth, 1980; Winefield, 1995). Reasons cited in this context are higher family responsibilities of middle-aged people (Jackson & Warr, 1984) and their allegedly stronger career commitment (Lahelma, 1989).

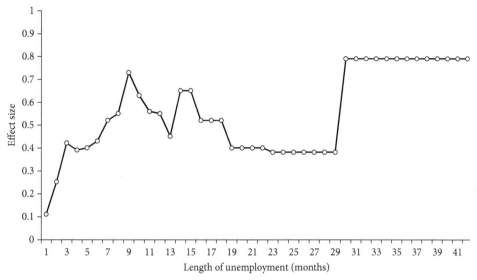

Figure 4.1 Unemployment duration and impaired mental health.
Note: For each time interval of unemployment duration a separate meta-analysis was conducted. The breadth of time intervals varied: one month for months 1 to 13, two months for months 14 and 15, three months for months 16 to 18, four months for months 19 to 22, seven months for months 23 to 29, and thirteen months for months 30 to 42. One outlier study with an unemployment duration of 74 months was not included in the diagram. Altogether, 18 separate meta-analyses were conducted for this diagram with an average number of primary studies of $k = 8.8$. A positive effect size means that unemployed persons have a worse mental health than employed persons.
Source: Paul, K. I., & Moser, K. (2009). Unemployment impairs mental health: Meta-analyses. *Journal of Vocational Behavior, 74*, 264–282. doi:10.1016/j.jvb.2009.01.001

However, there are also arguments against the hypothesis that younger and older unemployed workers suffer less than middle-aged unemployed workers. For example, the physical, social, and emotional problems that are part of the maturation process may be compounded with the stress of unemployment among youths, making the experience of unemployment more detrimental for them than for adults (Gurney, 1980). The first job has been called "the capitalist equivalent of initiation rites in primitive society" (Windschuttle, 1979, p. 65, as cited in Tiggemann & Winefield, 1984, p. 34). This modern rite helps young people to establish some independence from their parents and to consolidate a sense of personal identity as an adult. Thus unemployment may act as an obstacle to healthy personality development among youths and possibly has especially negative effects in this age group.

At the other end of the age continuum, older persons are often confronted by severely adverse stereotypes (Posthuma & Campion, 2009) that undermine their alleged employability (Klehe, de Pater, Koen, & Kira, this volume). They experience discrimination in the labor market and have very poor prospects of finding reemployment; if they do find it, they often suffer severe cuts in income (Adler & Hilber, 2009). Their knowledge of these

poor prospects can have a negative impact on their mental health. Furthermore, qualitative data indicate that workers over the age of 45 experience identity changes during job search, often in an unfavorable direction (i.e., starting to define themselves as "old") (Berger, 2006). (For information on older job seekers, see also Klehe et al., this volume).

The meta-analytic results concerning age as a moderator variable are not completely conclusive: McKee-Ryan et al. (2005) found significantly larger effect sizes for school-leaver samples than for adult samples. Paul and Moser (2009) found a nonsignificant U-shaped curvilinear association, with unemployed youths and unemployed older adults close to retirement showing the most severe distress symptoms, while unemployed middle-aged people were characterized by comparatively weak distress levels. The authors conducted several additional analyses in order to test whether the results changed when some outlying studies were removed, when possibly biasing design variables were controlled (for example the language in which the study was published), or when the influence of other relevant substantive variables, such as marital status, was controlled. In these analyses, some evidence supporting the curvilinear association was found. However, this finding was not stable across analyses, possibly owing to insufficient test power. Further meta-analytic research with more primary studies is needed here.

In summary, the traditional assumption that unemployment hits middle-aged persons more severely than youths or older persons was not in the least empirically endorsed by the existing meta-analyses. On the contrary, there is some empirical evidence that unemployed adolescents (and possibly also older workers) might have a particularly high risk of negative effects on their mental health.

Year of Data Collection

In the 1950s and 1960s, when unemployment rates were low in most western countries, many economists and politicians—as well as ordinary people—assumed that unemployment was a problem of the past. The general expectation for the future was permanent full or almost full employment (Garraty, 1978; Jahoda, 1982).

When mass unemployment came back during the recession of the early 1970s, it came as a surprise to unprepared societies and optimistic individuals who had hoped to be employed continuously throughout their lives. When these hopes were suddenly frustrated, the distressing effects of unemployment were often particularly strong (Jahoda, 1982). After this period, when unemployment rates remained high during much of the following decades in many countries, a slight cultural change has been assumed to have taken place, characterized by what has been called a "normalization" of unemployment, meaning that being unemployed became more socially acceptable and less stigmatizing (Schaufeli & van Yperen, 1992; Sheeran, Abrams, & Orbell, 1995). As a result, weaker differences between unemployed and employed persons in more recent studies as compared with older studies can be expected.

However, this hypothesis cannot be supported empirically. Paul and Moser (2009) found a zero association between effect size and the year in which a study's data were collected. This result remained stable when design characteristics were controlled that have a significant influence on the effect sizes of psychological unemployment studies, such as whether a written test was used versus an oral interview. Changes in research methods could therefore not be shown to be the cause of the unexpected lack of a significant time effect. However, the number of primary studies that were conducted before 1980

using quantitative empirical methods (which can be used in modern meta-analysis) is much smaller than the number of usable studies conducted after 1980. Thus the certainty with which we can estimate the psychological impact of unemployment in past times is limited.

In sum, the assumption that societies somehow got "used to" unemployment and that the negative effects on mental health were less severe in more recent studies was not endorsed meta-analytically. Despite some uncertainty due to the small number of older studies, unemployment nowadays appears to be as bad for health as it was in the decades after the Second World War.

Other Demographic Variables

Other demographic variables that were tested meta-analytically for moderator effects were whether unemployed people belonged to an ethnic or cultural minority group and whether they were married or not. However, no clear and stable moderator effects were found for these variables (Paul & Moser, 2009).

Moderator Effects—Summary

Meta-analytic moderator tests conducted by McKee-Ryan et al. (2005) as well as Paul and Moser (2009) have demonstrated that the negative effects of unemployment on mental health are larger in male than in female groups and in blue-collar than in white-collar groups. Furthermore, there is a curvilinear relation between length of unemployment and distress, with a sharp increase in distress during the first 9 months and a subsequent stabilization of mental health at levels that are less severe but are still considerably distressing in comparison to mental health among the employed. There are also signs of a further increase in distress among those who are unemployed for a very long time, but this is a preliminary finding. Another preliminary finding in need of further scrutiny is that youths and possibly also older people versus persons of middle age have an elevated risk of experiencing negative mental health effects as a result of unemployment.

Thus male blue-collar workers who are unemployed for more than half a year represent a group who are particularly threatened by the negative mental health effects of unemployment; they, in particular, should not be neglected when decisions are made about how to distribute financial and other resources and interventions aimed at helping the unemployed to cope with their situation.

Differences Between Countries

An advantage of meta-analytic methods is that they facilitate moderator tests on the country level. Researchers can compare groups of countries and test whether aspects of the economic system or the policies regarding unemployment are associated with high or low levels of distress among unemployed people. In the following paragraphs, we briefly review the meta-analytic moderator tests conducted by Paul and Moser (2009) for differences between countries. (For a further discussion of country differences, see Bambra & Eikemo, this volume.)

Economic Development

The renowned Marienthal study demonstrated that unemployment accompanied by absolute poverty (i.e., a level of poverty characterized by starvation and a lack of clothing as well as health care) leads to severe negative psychological reactions. It induces despair and apathy in a large proportion of the individuals experiencing it (Jahoda, Lazarsfeld, & Zeisel, 1933/1975).

It seems reasonable to assume that, in most societies, unemployed people are typically more in danger of absolute poverty than other social groups. Since the level of a country's economic development is negatively associated with the percentage of persons who are doomed to live under conditions of absolute poverty (United Nations Development Programme, 2003) and since unemployed people usually belong to the poorer strata of a society, it could be expected that unemployment in less developed countries is more harmful than unemployment in more affluent countries.

Empirically, this assumptions was clearly endorsed: The difference between more and less developed countries was highly significant in Paul and Moser's (2009) analyses regardless whether the GDP per capita or the Human Development Index[3] (HDI) was used as indicator variable of development. In both analyses differences between unemployed and employed persons concerning their mental health were significantly greater in less developed countries than in more affluent countries.

Income Inequality

Citizens of egalitarian countries typically have a better level of health and a higher average life expectancy than those of countries with an unequal distribution of income (Wilkinson, 1996). Strong social cohesion is probably an important mediator of this effect, as social cohesion is better in more egalitarian societies than in societies characterized by inequality (Wilkinson, 1996). Since a reduction of social contacts is a frequently reported effect of job loss on the individual level (Jahoda, 1982; Warr, 1987), unemployment is likely to have more severe effects in less egalitarian societies because unemployed persons may be more in danger of "dropping out" and of losing basic social and emotional bonds. Furthermore, their income loss will probably be comparatively small in more egalitarian countries and comparatively large in countries where the differences between the poor and the wealthy are large.

In line with this reasoning, Paul and Moser (2009) found moderating effects of income inequality: In countries with high levels of inequality (measured either as high Gini scores[4] or as large proportions of poor citizens), the negative mental health effects of unemployment were stronger than in more egalitarian countries. Note that among the countries represented in this meta-analysis, income inequality was also strongly and significantly negatively correlated with unemployment protection standards. In more egalitarian countries, the unemployment protection system was clearly more generous. It may be this specific aspect of an egalitarian society that has particular relevance for unemployed people and determines their comparatively good mental health (see the next paragraph).

Unemployment Protection

The extent of protection that a state offers to people who have lost their jobs probably determines the economic pressure they experience to a large degree. Furthermore, the availability of money is assumed to be an important mediator of distress in all theoretical accounts dealing with the psychological effects of unemployment (Fryer, 1986, 1997a; Jahoda, 1981, 1982, 1997; Warr, 1987). Since the protection systems differ widely between countries with regard to the ratio of wage replacement, duration of coverage, and percentage of unemployed persons who receive benefits (International Labour Office, 2000b), it can be expected that the generosity of the public unemployment protection system moderates the mental health effects of unemployment.

The empirical results concerning this assumption are unequivocal with regard to the pattern of results, although the findings are not always significant. McKee-Ryan et al. (2005) found the expected pattern of results with larger differences in mental health between employed and unemployed people in countries with a restrictive system versus those with a generous system. However, this moderator test was not significant. Paul and Moser (2009) also found the expected pattern, and in this case the moderator test was also significant. Note that owing to the larger number of primary studies included in this meta-analysis, the power of this test was larger than that of the test conducted by McKee-Ryan et al. (2005).

In summary, there is empirical evidence supporting the view that a social system offering good protection against unemployment reduces the detrimental impact of job loss on mental health.

Labor Market Opportunities

A bad economic climate, expressing itself in a high unemployment rate, might be particularly threatening to unemployed persons because they perceive lowered opportunities for their job search and a lowered likelihood of reemployment, resulting in a depressed mood (Dooley, Catalano, & Rook, 1988, McKee-Ryan et al., 2005). Furthermore, high national unemployment rates can be expected to lengthen the average duration of unemployment. As long-term unemployment is more damaging to mental health than short-term unemployment, this effect should also contribute to increased distress levels among unemployed persons in countries with high unemployment rates.

Then again, high unemployment rates may also reduce feelings of stigma resulting from unemployment, since so many other people have lost their jobs, too. Furthermore, high unemployment rates may have a negative impact on the mental health of *employed* persons, as they could trigger fears of job loss and could increase average levels of job stress due to the loss in bargaining power of employed individuals and their unions (Dooley, Catalano, & Rook, 1988). This would lead to smaller differences in distress levels between employed and unemployed people.

In line with these ambivalent arguments, McKee-Ryan et al. (2005) were not able to identify a significant moderator effect of national unemployment rates on the mental health effects of unemployment. Paul and Moser's (2009) test was more powerful because of the larger number of primary studies in their meta-analysis. They found a marginally significant moderating effect: In countries with higher unemployment rates, stronger effect sizes emerged than in countries with lower unemployment rates. This would mean that high unemployment rates go along with even more detrimental

effects of unemployment for the individuals. Yet this marginal significance vanished when outlying studies were excluded and important design features controlled. Furthermore, for an alternative measures of the quality of labor market opportunities (Labor Market Security Index[5] [LMSI]), no significant result emerged. Contrary to this, a recent study found that the negative effect of unemployment on subjective well-being is *weaker* in countries with high unemployment rates (Mikucka, in press). Therefore it is still unclear whether a moderating effect of labor market opportunities really exists. One reason for this ambiguous result pattern may be the high variability of unemployment rates within specific countries. Often, unemployment rates are high in one part of the country while there is labor shortage in other parts. Since the studies were conducted on the level of countries, they were unable to explain this variability *within* countries. (See also Probst, Jiang & Benson, this volume, for the effects of job insecurity on mental health).

Collectivism/Individualism

Individualistic societies are societies "in which the ties between individuals are loose: Everyone is expected to look after him/herself and his/her immediate family only" (Hofstede, 2001, p. 225). In contrast, collectivistic societies are societies "in which people from birth onwards are integrated into strong, cohesive in-groups, which throughout people's lifetime continue to protect them in exchange for unquestioning loyalty" (Hofstede, 2001, p. 225). People in individualistic societies are more satisfied with their lives than people in collectivistic societies (Diener, Diener, & Diener, 1995). However, it has been hypothesized that this pattern may be reversed in times of stress (Diener et al., 1995). Persons in individualistic societies usually feel greater personal responsibility for their success as well as their failures. Therefore when they lose their jobs they may be more distressed than people in collectivistic societies, who feel less personal responsibility and can rely on strong social networks to help them cope with unemployment.

A study in Italy, where the northern and southern parts of the country differ considerably with regard to individualism/collectivism, partly endorsed the assumption that this variable moderates the mental health effects of unemployment (Martella & Maass, 2000). These authors drew matched samples from a northern and a southern Italian city that were comparable with regard to population size and social composition. They found that the differences in well-being between unemployed and employed individuals were considerably larger in the individualistic north than in the collectivistic south, as expected. However, it is unclear whether other differences between northern and southern Italy might have caused the observed differences.

Meta-analytic findings concerning the proposed moderator effect of individualism/collectivism were inconclusive. Meta-analytic differences between unemployed and employed people were larger in countries with an individualistic culture than in those with a collectivistic culture, as expected, but this result was not significant (Paul & Moser, 2009). The authors conducted additional analyses in order to control the influence of a few outlier studies and the biasing effect of some design variables. In some of these additional analyses, a significant moderator effect was identified, and in others not. Nevertheless, a recent comparison of 42 European countries found the expected moderating effect of individualism/collectivism on the well-being of unemployed people (Mickuka, in press). Thus there is some empirical evidence now that culture is a moderator of unemployment distress. It would be interesting to know whether other cultural variables (e.g., masculinity/femininity) also have such a moderating effect.

Coping Strategies

The question of coping strategies is an important one because knowledge about successful methods of coping with their difficult situations could be very helpful for unemployed people. Researchers have scrutinized different aspects of the coping process in relation to unemployment. Some studies, for example, were concerned with individual characteristics and environmental objects or environmental conditions that can act as coping resources—for example, social support. Other studies pertaining to the topic of coping with unemployment were concerned with cognitive appraisal, asking questions such as: Do unemployed people attribute the loss of their job externally or internally (Prussia, Kinicki, & Bracker, 1993)? What are their expectations concerning reemployment (Wanberg, 1997)? A third group of studies tested the effects of specific coping behaviors such as distancing from job loss (an example for emotion-focused coping [Kinicki & Latack, 1990]) or seeking retraining (an example of problem-focused copping [Leana & Feldman, 1990]).

MyKee-Ryan et al. (2005) have meta-analyzed studies concerned with the influence of these variables on unemployed people's well-being. They found that personal and situational coping resources had positive effects, mitigating the negative impact of job loss. For example, core self-evaluations such as self-esteem, locus of control, self-efficacy, and emotional stability (Judge, Locke, & Durham, 1997) had strong positive relationships with mental health and subjective well-being among unemployed persons. Social support and good financial resources were also positively correlated with mental health and subjective well-being.

On the level of appraisal, regarding job loss as a negative life event was associated with poorer mental health. Furthermore, internal attributions of job loss were related to lower subjective well-being, while unemployed people with positive reemployment expectations had higher levels of mental health.

Finally, problem-focused coping behaviors such as seeking retraining or seeking to relocate and emotion-focused coping behaviors such as seeking counseling or community activism were both positively correlated to mental health. However, job-search activity, which can also be seen as a problem-focused coping behavior, did not fit into this general pattern. Instead, high job-search effort was associated with *lowered* mental health. This effect was weak yet significant, indicating that job search, while certainly necessary in order to escape the harmful situation of unemployment, might be an additional burden for individuals that further threatens their health.

In summary, unemployed people strongly benefit from good access to different kinds of coping resources. Cognitive appraisals are also important, since people who do not blame themselves for their job loss and who avoid pessimism concerning their chances of reemployment fare better psychologically. Finally, problem-focused as well as emotion-focused coping strategies have been shown to be helpful with regard to the mental health of unemployed persons.

One caveat, however, is necessary with regard to pessimism/optimism concerning one's chances for reemployment: In a study with unemployed German blue-collar workers, Frese and Mohr found—similar to the meta-analytic results reported above—a significant negative correlation between hope for reemployment and depression (Frese, 1987; Frese & Mohr, 1987). Thus, cross-sectionally, being optimistic and hopeful had a positive effect on mental health. But when the analysis was extended from cross-sectional to longitudinal data, the result pattern changed in a very meaningful way: While hope was negatively predictive for depression among those persons who found a new job between the first and the second measurement point, meaning that people who were optimistic and then found a job felt better, it was *positively* predictive for depression among those unemployed men who were still unemployed at the second measurement time. In other words: When one's optimism is crushed and the expected new job does not show up, the initially positive effect of hope is reversed and the formerly optimistic unemployed person feels even worse than the pessimist. Thus recommending an optimistic attitude to unemployed people might be not only useless but even harmful under certain circumstances. Instead, Frese's (1987) suggestion of an "existentialistic attitude towards unemployment" might be a better recommendation: "One knows that it will be extremely hard to find a job, but at the same time one does not give up trying" (p. 214). (See also Song, Sun, & Li, this volume, on job seeking among unemployed individuals).

Tackling the Problem of Causality by Means of Longitudinal Studies

Intuitively, most people will probably assume that the high levels of distress frequently observed among unemployed persons are the direct consequence of unemployment. However, this could be a premature conclusion, because other processes that can explain these elevated levels of distress are also plausible. The selection hypothesis is particularly relevant in this context. This hypothesis implies that the relationship between unemployment and reduced mental health is caused by selection processes in the labor market penalizing people with impaired mental health. Individuals with mental health problems possibly have a higher probability of losing their jobs and—when unemployed—need more time to find new employment (Frese & Mohr, 1978; Mastekaasa, 1996; Toppen, 1971; Winefield, 1995). Unemployment thus is conceptualized as a consequence of mental health problems in this hypothesis, not as its cause. Mastekaasa (1996) proposed a theoretical model of labor market mechanisms that could explain such an effect: Mental health problems may increase absenteeism, which increases the likelihood of dismissal. Such problems may also directly influence hiring decisions, when the employer is able to recognize an applicant's mental health state and assumes, for example, that an applicant who gives

an impression of being depressed will be less productive as an employee than other applicants. Furthermore, psychological problems could reduce the effort and efficiency of a person's job search to some extent. Self-esteem, for example, has been shown to be significantly correlated with the intensity of job-search behavior (Kanfer, Wanberg & Kantrowitz, 2001) and is probably low among persons with mental health problems. All these labor market processes would increase the proportion of persons with impaired mental health among the unemployed, explaining the observed mean difference between employed and unemployed people.

However, there is no reason why causation and selection should be mutually exclusive processes, and it is possible that both contribute to the accumulation of mental health symptoms among the unemployed. By meta-analyzing longitudinal studies, it is possible to shed some light on the question of causation.

Significant changes in mental health coming along with transitions into or out of unemployment were found in several meta-analyses endorsing the assumption that unemployment impairs mental health: When people lost their jobs, deteriorations in mental health occurred. When unemployed persons found new jobs, their mental health improved (McKee-Ryan et al., 2005; Murphy & Athanasou, 1999; Paul & Moser, 2009). There was also a significant reduction in distress symptoms for young persons who found jobs after school. For youths becoming unemployed after school a weak nonsignificant increase of distress symptoms was found. Such a stagnation of mental health is unusual in this age group, since the comparison group of young people who stayed in the education system also showed a significant improvement of their mental health, similar to the improvement in youths who changed from education to employment (Paul & Moser, 2009). Thus, these results with young people also support the assumption that unemployment has a causal effect on mental health, because it obviously blocks psychological processes with positive outcomes that are typical for this age group.

Unexpectedly, the effect size for the improvement of mental health that accompanied reemployment was in all three meta-analyses considerably larger than the effect size for the deterioration associated with job loss. This is a surprising result, since it means that a cycle of job loss, unemployment, and reemployment would, overall, be a *positive* experience for the individual, resulting in better mental health at the end than in the beginning. Additional analyses (Paul & Moser, 2009) showed that the most plausible explanation for this finding is the measurement effect: People who are asked repeatedly for their mental health status generally tend to report a slight improvement, even when nothing has happened that is likely to cause such an improvement. Continuously employed persons, for example, showed such improvements, although their employment situation remained stable during the course of longitudinal studies. Thus the positive effect of reemployment is probably overestimated and the negative effect of job loss underestimated in longitudinal studies because of these measurement effects.

The conclusion that unemployment causes mental health impairment is also endorsed by the result of specific studies that can be seen as "natural experiments,"—that is, as situations where the selection of persons to one of two treatment conditions is done by chance and any kind of self-selection is ruled out, enabling researchers to draw firmer conclusions about the direction of causal effects than are usually possible in field studies. These studies are concerned with factory closures: When an entire factory is shut down, one can assume that psychological symptoms among the laid-off workers result from unemployment, not selection processes. Indeed, a separate meta-analysis of such plant-closure studies conducted by Paul and Moser (2009) found that the effect sizes for the impact of unemployment on mental health were only slightly smaller in these studies compared with other studies, again endorsing the assumption that unemployment impairs mental health.

Yet the selection hypothesis was also endorsed empirically, because distress preceded subsequent layoffs among employed persons and it also preceded subsequent reemployment among unemployed persons and among school leavers. In other words, during the course of a longitudinal study, already at the first measurement point (T1) when both groups were still employed, employed persons who lost their jobs showed more signs of distress than continuously employed persons (Paul & Moser, 2009). Furthermore, continuously unemployed persons showed more symptoms of distress at T1, when both groups were still unemployed, than those unemployed persons who were successful at finding new jobs relatively quickly. A similar result was found for school graduates: Youths without a job after finishing school (T2) showed more symptoms of distress while at school (T1) than those who managed to find a job after school.

All these effects were small in size but significant. Thus the causal link from mental health to employment status was supported in these analyses, but it is small in comparison to the reverse effect of employment status to mental health.[6]

A third explanation for the association between unemployment and mental health is the influence of a third variable that causes both—unemployment as well as mental health. Physical illnesses have been mentioned in this context because they can lead to job loss and are probably able to reduce subjective well-being and mental health. If that were true, the correlation between mental health and unemployment would be a purely statistical one with no substantive meaning beyond showing the importance of physical health as a cause of job loss as well as distress (Winefield, 1995).

However, the direct effect of physical illness upon mental health could be weaker than commonsense assumptions might expect, because even in the case of such a severe illness as cancer, surprisingly good coping has been found (Beutel, 1988; de Haes & van Knippenberg, 1985). Furthermore, the common definitions of unemployment require unemployed people to be available for the labor market, excluding persons with severe physical illnesses that impair their ability to work. Thus, those kinds of illnesses that are most likely to reduce mental health are probably rare among unemployed people because they diminish a person's work ability and lead to a re-classification of an unemployed person as an acute medical patient or a disability pensioner. In good agreement with this point, a large-scale analysis of German health insurance data showed that, in comparison with employed people, unemployed people had a strongly increased prevalence of mental health diagnoses but only a slightly elevated prevalence of diagnoses of physical illnesses (Grobe, Dörning, & Schwartz, 1999).

McKee-Ryan et al. (2005) reported medium to large effect sizes for the difference between unemployed and employed people with regard to physical health. However, these results were based on small numbers of primary studies. Furthermore, in Paul and Moser's (2009) meta-analysis, the effect of unemployment on psychosomatic symptoms—a variable with an obvious physical component, as scales measuring psychosomatic symptoms consist mainly of widespread bodily symptoms such as headaches and back pain—was considerably weaker than the mean effect sizes for "pure" psychological indicators of mental health. In summary, the empirical findings for the association of unemployment and physical health are mixed, but there is no indication that this association is larger than the association between unemployment and mental health. This finding argues against the hypothesis of physical illnesses as third variable causing unemployment and distress. If physical health were the crucial factor, its association with unemployment should be larger than the association between unemployment and mental health, which according to this hypothesis is only an indirect effect.

In summary, there is evidence for social causation (i.e., unemployment impairs mental health) as well as selection effects. Thus unemployment is both a cause as well as a consequence of mental health problems. And although the effect sizes for the selection effects were small, their importance should not be underestimated. Small effects can be important practically, especially when the outcome variable is difficult to influence and depends on many other things (Prentice & Miller, 1992), as is the case with one's success and failure in the labor market. The significant selection effects show us that our labor markets function in a way that creates additional disadvantages for those people who are already disadvantaged with regard to their mental health. This problem is probably particularly severe when unemployment rates and job insecurity are high and competition for jobs is strong. In this situation, it is even more important to improve unemployed people's mental health than it would be in any case.

Explanations of the Negative Mental Health Effects of Unemployment

We have seen so far that there is clear evidence of the negative effects of unemployment on mental health. This leads to the question of *why* unemployment impairs health (i.e., the question of mediating processes that trigger this effect).

Several general psychological theories have been applied to the problem of unemployment—for example, helplessness theory (Baum, Fleming, & Reddy, 1986; Frese & Mohr, 1978; Kirchler, & Kirchler, 1989; Lynd-Stevenson, 1996; Ostell, & Divers, 1987; Rodriguez, 1997; Rothwell, & Williams, 1983; Tiggemann, Winefield, Goldney, & Winefield, 1992; Tiggemann, Winefield, Winefield, & Goldney, 1991a,b; Winefield, Tiggemann, & Smith, 1987), Weiner's (1985) attributional theory (Winefield, Tiggemann, Winefield, & Goldney, 1993), expectancy-value theory (Feather, 1990; Feather & Barber, 1983; Feather & Davenport, 1981; Winefield et al., 1993; see also

Feather, this volume), self-determination theory (Vansteenkiste, Lens, De Witte, De Witte, & Deci, 2004; see also Vansteenkiste & Van den Broeck, this volume); Erikson's (1959) developmental theory (Gurney, 1980; Meeus, Deković & Iedema, 1997; Winefield, Winefield, Tiggemann, & Goldney, 1991; Winefield et al., 1993), stress and coping models (Latack, Kinicki, & Prussia, 1995; Kinicki, Prussia, & McKee-Ryan, 2000; Leana & Feldman, 1988, Leana, Feldman, & Tan, 1998; Price, Van Ryn, & Vinokur, 1992), social comparison theory (Sheeran, Abrams, & Orbell, 1995), symbolic interactionism (Sheeran, & Abraham, 1994), self-discrepancy theory (Sheeran & McCarthy, 1992), self-consistency theory (Shamir, 1986), cognitive adaptation theory (Wanberg, 1997), stigma theory (McFayden, 1995), alienation theory (Kieselbach, 1998), object relations theory (Raber, 1996), and psychoanalysis (Rupp, 1988). However, the most influential were three specific theories that were originally developed within the field of psychological unemployment research: Jahoda's latent-deprivation model, Warr's vitamin model, and Fryer's agency-restriction approach. They are briefly reviewed below, together with a new theoretical approach that was recently formulated.

According to Jahoda's (1981, 1982, 1997) latent deprivation model, employment has not only a manifest function (earning a living) but also "latent functions" that are important for mental health. She specified five latent functions of employment: "time structure, an enlarged social network, participation in collective efforts, definition of social identity, and required regular activity" (Jahoda, 1997, p. 318). Jahoda (1983) stated that these latent functions correspond to "deep seated needs" (p. 298). Therefore the amount of access to the latent functions should have a direct impact upon a person's mental health because it determines the level of need satisfaction an individual experiences. In modern societies, employment is assumed to be the only institution that can provide the latent functions in a sufficient amount. Other institutions, such as organized religion or voluntary associations, cannot serve as substitutes for employment to a satisfying degree (Jahoda, 1988). Therefore employment is usually necessary in order to be psychologically healthy, while unemployed persons are at risk of experiencing distress symptoms and a loss of well-being.

Warr's (1987) vitamin model is similar to Jahoda's (1981, 1982, 1997) deprivation theory in assuming that certain characteristics of the environment predict the mental well-being of a person. But the environmental features specified by Warr (1987) show only a partial overlap with those specified by Jahoda (1981, 1982, 1997): opportunity for control, opportunity for skill use, externally generated goals, variety, environmental clarity, availability of money, physical security, opportunity for interpersonal contact, and valued social position. Warr hypothesized that the environment influences mental health "in a manner analogous to the effect of vitamins on physical health" (Warr, 1987, p. 9). Thus low levels of the nine environmental features are assumed to have negative effects on mental health, while increasing levels are assumed to have positive effects on mental health. However, an increase beyond a certain limit should not result in further improvements. For some of the environmental features (e.g., physical security), very high levels are hypothesized to have no additional impact at all. Other environmental features are even thought to be harmful in very high doses (e.g., variety). Unemployed persons are typically confronted with an environment that contains only limited amounts of each of Warr's (1987) "vitamins." According to the vitamin model, this group of persons should thus be characterized by mental health problems.

Fryer (1986) stressed the importance of the basic view of human nature that is implied in a theoretical model. According to him, situation-centered theories such as Jahoda's or Warr's conceptualize aspects of the situation as the main determinants of human mental health and are thus based on a view of the person as a passive, reactive, dependent, and mainly extrinsically motivated being. In contrast to this, Fryer (1986, 1997a) proposes a more person-centered theoretical approach. He assumes humans to be "agents actively striving for purposeful self-determination, attempting to make sense of, initiate, influence, and cope with events in line with personal values, goals, and expectations of the future" (1997a, p. 12). However, unemployment severely restricts and frustrates agency as well as undermines planning and purposeful action because it is usually associated with poverty, future insecurity, and low social power. In other words: "agency theory tries to focus upon what people bring with them to a situation which is unfamiliar and problematical rather then upon what is taken away from them" by the loss of employment (1986, p. 16). We can conclude that in Fryer's (1986) agency restriction theory human beings are assumed to feel a "desire for self-directedness" (p. 16), which is frustrated

by unemployment and the poverty that is often associated with unemployment, resulting in distress and low well-being.

A fourth theoretical approach that was recently proposed is concerned with the incongruence of unemployed people's work values and life goals on the one hand and their actual employment situation on the other hand (Paul & Moser, 2006). Meta-analytic results showed that work values, such as employment commitment, are stable and remain unchanged when people lose their jobs. In general, employed and unemployed persons' levels of employment commitment are very similar and both groups attribute a strong positive value to having a job (Paul & Moser, 2006). Similar findings were found for life goals: Both groups regard similar goals as important for their lives (Paul, Vastamäki, & Moser, 2014). However, unemployed persons report lower levels of current realization of their life goals compared to employed persons and are pessimistic concerning the future attainability of these goals. Thus, unemployment obviously does not change people's value and goal systems, but it hurls people in a situation of incongruence: The discrepancy between what they think is important with regard to work and their current life situation is much larger for unemployed persons than for employed persons. Since high levels of incongruence between individual goals and perceived goal attainment have been shown to be a cause of the formation and maintenance of psychopathological symptoms (Grawe, 2004), it is straightforward to assume that this process is also one of the mediators of unemployment distress. In summary, the incongruence hypothesis states that a lack of congruence between a person's work related goals and values and his or her current employment situation is a typical characteristic of unemployment. It also states that this lack of congruence is psychologically pathogenic and causes the distress symptoms that can often be found among unemployed people.

Empirically, all four aforementioned theoretical models have been supported by several independent studies. Particularly, Jahoda's latent deprivation theory has instigated a comparatively large corpus of research that usually endorsed the model (e.g., Creed & Macintyre, 2001; Paul & Batinic, 2010). However, even in this case some important questions remain unanswered. There exist, for example, only a few longitudinal studies, and the existing studies are often restricted to a subfacet of the model but do not test the whole proposed mediation process (e.g., Hoare & Machin, 2010; Selenko, Batinic, & Paul, 2011).

Warr's (1987, 2007) vitamin model is based on older empirical research concerning the effects of environmental characteristics on human well-being. Subsequent direct tests of the model, particularly its assumptions concerning curvilinearity, were partly supporting it (e.g., De Jonge & Schaufeli, 1998; Jeurissen.& Nyklíček, 2001). However, there are only a few tests of the model using samples of unemployed persons (Warr, Butcher, Robertson, & Callinan, 2004).

Specific tests of Fryer's agency restriction model are also not abundant, but the existing studies support the model (Creed & Klisch, 2005; Fryer & McKenna, 1984). Furthermore, the importance of the main proposed mediator variable in this model, (i.e., a person's financial situation) has received support in a large number of studies not specifically concerned with Fryer's theory (e.g., Whelan, 1992).

Finally, the incongruence model was clearly supported by meta-analytic results on employment commitment (Paul & Moser, 2006) and recently found further support in primary studies specifically designed to test its assumptions (Creed, Lehmann, & Hood, 2009; Paul, Vastamäki, & Moser, 2012).

In summary, with regard to the question of why unemployment causes mental health impairments, several promising theories have been proposed and successfully tested. However, which of the models has the most explanatory power is still unclear.

Is a Job Always Better Than Unemployment?

Marie Jahoda's opinion towards employment was remarkably positive. She wrote: "Employment is psychologically supportive, even when conditions are bad" (Jahoda, 1981, p. 188). Thus Jahoda assumed not only that employment *on average* was more beneficial than unemployment for mental health but also obviously assumed that *any* kind of job was better than unemployment, at least in developed countries where certain minimum standards of safety measures, work hours, and so on exist.

The question whether a job is *always* better than being unemployed in developed countries is highly relevant, since it pertains to the question of whether creating low-quality jobs ("McJobs") could be a justifiable way to combat mass unemployment. Thus Jahoda's contentious statements stimulated intense theoretical controversies (see Fryer, 1986, 1992) as well as empirical studies. O'Brien and Feather (1990), for example, operationalized "quality of employment" with a scale measuring "skill utilization" (p. 156). Persons in qualitatively poor employment did not differ from unemployed persons with regard

to mental health in their sample. Furthermore, several authors report that people who had been unemployed and then found a new job, but one they were not satisfied with, felt as bad as unemployed persons (e.g., Leana & Feldman, 1995; Wanberg, 1995). Winefield and colleagues (1991) did a similar study with school leavers. They found that youths who found satisfactory jobs after school showed a decrease of depressive symptoms, while there was no decrease of symptoms for youths who became unemployed after school or found only unsatisfactory jobs. Paul and Batinic (2010) compared workers doing unskilled manual work—a kind of work that is usually regarded as less preferable than skilled manual work or nonmanual work—with unemployed people. They found that persons in those unattractive jobs reported more latent benefits and slightly less distress than unemployed persons.

In summary, this interesting strand of research is not yet completely conclusive and can certainly be criticized. (Is, for example, a very subjective and unspecific measure of job quality such as "satisfaction" appropriate when the outcome variable is mental health?) Nevertheless, most of the available empirical evidence suggests that low-quality jobs are not better than unemployment with regard to mental health, and trying to solve the unemployment problem by the creation of such low-quality jobs might possibly result in an improvement for the government budget (because of the larger number of employed taxpayers), but it would not improve public health.

Then again, if one turns around the original perspective of this research, these results are an impressive illustration how strong the effects of unemployment are: Even if you have a really unattractive job, you will probably not feel worse than the average unemployed person.

Other Consequences of Unemployment— From Physical Health to Political Attitudes

While most psychological research on the effects of unemployment was concerned with mental health, other outcome variables have also been scrutinized. Important topics were, for example, physical health, health behavior, immune function, hostility and aggression, employment commitment, political attitudes, sexual behavior, and family formation. Findings from each of these diverse fields are briefly reviewed below.

Physical Health and Health Behavior

As has already been said in Section "Tackling the Problem of Causality by Means of Longitudinal

Studies", the meta-analytic findings for the association between unemployment and physical health agreed that there probably is an association, although they differ with respect to the size of the effect. The results of the most recent primary studies scrutinizing the effects of unemployment on physical health are also not straightforward when considered together. Some recent studies found a negative impact of unemployment on self-assessed health (e.g., Åhs & Westerling, 2006; Bambra & Eikemo, 2009), but it is not completely clear whether the dependent variables in these studies on self-rated health (e.g., "longstanding illness," "general health") confound physical health with mental health. There are also studies explicitly differentiating mental and physical health that did not find negative effects of unemployment on physical health (Galic & Sverko, 2008). A very interesting new step in this field of research is a recently published meta-analysis on the association between unemployment and mortality (Roelfs, Shor, Davidson, & Schwartz, 2011). According to this meta-analysis, after adjustment for age and other covariates, the risk of death is 63% higher among currently or formerly unemployed persons compared with employed persons. This effect was higher for men than for women. Furthermore, unemployment was primarily associated with an increased mortality risk for people in their early and midcareers, while the association was weaker (yet still significant) for people in their late careers.

A part of this effect on mortality might be due to causes that usually are not regarded as elements of "physical health," such as traffic accidents or suicides (see Platt, 1985, for a review on unemployment and suicide). Nevertheless, this finding endorses the assumption that unemployment considerably impairs physical health, since the aforementioned other causes of death probably comprise only a small percentage of the higher overall mortality that was found among unemployed people in this meta-analysis.

Also pertaining to the question of physical health, research on health behavior has demonstrated that unemployment is associated with problematic patterns of drug use. Unemployed people drink significantly more alcoholic beverages than employed people do (Rásky, Stronegger, & Freidl, 1996), and a longer duration of unemployment is longitudinally associated with a higher likelihood of becoming a heavy drinker (Mossakowski, 2008). Unemployed persons also have a higher risk of hospitalization due to alcohol-related conditions (Eliason & Storrie, 2009). In addition, they are more often smokers, and as smokers they consume more tobacco than their employed counterparts do (Fagan, Shavers, Lawrence, Gibson, & Ponder, 2007; Hammarström & Janlert, 2002; Rásky, Stronegger, Freidl, 1996). Unemployed people also use illegal drugs more frequently (Hammarström, 1994).

Furthermore, unemployed persons are significantly less motivated to reduce weight and to change dietary habits than employed people are (Rásky, Stronegger, & Freidl, 1996). They also exercise and brush their teeth less often (Rásky et al., 1996) and have an increased risk of hospitalization due to traffic accidents (Eliason & Storrie, 2009).

In sum, unemployed people's health-related habits and behavior patterns appear to be more risky and less beneficial for their heath than the habits of persons with a job are. These behavioral differences are probably an important part of an explanation for the reduced levels of physical health and elevated mortality risks of unemployed individuals (see above). The question how these differences can be explained (whether they are, for example, a consequence of the elevated distress levels that are caused by unemployment) has not yet been answered as far as we know.

Another important result pertaining to the question of the reasons for the reduced physical health levels and higher mortality of unemployed people is the finding that immune function declines after job loss and recovers when an unemployed person finds a new job (Cohen, Kemeny, Zegans, Johnson, Kearney, & Stites, 2007). In line with this, unemployed individuals were found to have more traces of cortisol in different segments of their hair, indicating chronically elevated physiological stress levels (Dettenborn, Tietze, Bruckner, & Kirschbaum, 2010).

Sexual Behavior and Family Formation

Partly related to questions of health and health behavior, differences between different employment status groups with regard to sexual behavior, fertility, and family life have also been observed. It has been shown that being unemployed or having an insecure job can delay couple formation and marriage (Ekert-Jaffe, & Solaz, 2001). In Germany, unemployment leads to the postponement of reproduction, although the process that causes this postponement appears to be different between East and West Germany: While in West Germany family formation is delayed, especially when the male partner is unemployed, the process is primarily influenced by the employment situation of the woman in East Germany and not so much by that of her partner (Gebel & Giesecke, 2009). Unemployment—not only of mothers but also of fathers—is also associated with an increased risk for stillbirth (Reime, Jacob, & Wenzlaff, 2009).

Then again, unemployed adolescents engage in high levels of sexual activity with a comparatively large number of different partners but with a low rate of condom use in comparison to adolescents who are still in school or who attend university (Buzwell & Rosenthal, 1995). Furthermore, in Australia, rates of pregnancy and live births were higher among young unemployed women than among young employed women (Kelaher, Dunt, & Dodson, 2007).

In summary, the results of some studies seemingly indicate that unemployment handicap family formation and fertility. However, the process leading to this outcome appears to differ between countries and even parts of the same country (see the German study by Gebel & Giesecke; 2009). Furthermore, other studies imply that unemployment can increase pregnancy and birth rates at very young ages, when having children is often perceived as problematic in western societies because of the immaturity of the teenage parents. Thus evidence concerning the effects of unemployment on sexual behavior, family formation, and fertility is not really conclusive at the moment, but the existing studies on the topic rarely report any outcomes of unemployment that would be desirable for a developed society.

Hostility and Aggression

With regard to the question of effects of unemployment on hostility and aggression, particularly in intimate relationships, the picture is rather bleak. In general, unemployed individuals score significantly higher on self-report measures of hostility than employed persons do (Fischer, Greitemeyer & Frey, 2008; Singh, Kumari, & Singh, 1992; Stokes & Cochrane, 1984). This general tendency to report more hostility expresses itself on a personal level in the higher frequency of intimate partner violence that has been observed among unemployed people. Unemployed women are often in danger of becoming victims of intimate partner violence (Kimerling, Alvarez, Pavao, Mack, Smith, & Baumrind, 2009). Furthermore, couples where the male partner is unemployed are at risk of both increased levels of male-to-female violence (Cunradi, Todd, Duke, & Ames, 2009) as well as

increased levels of female-to-male violence (Newby, Ursano, McCarroll, Martin, Norwood, & Fullerton, 2003). Finally, instances of abuse or neglect of children occur more often in families suffering from parental unemployment (Christoffersen, 2000). In summary, unemployment is not only likely to impact family formation negatively (see the preceding paragraph) but also has disruptive influences on existing families. Thus, in several ways, unemployment threatens what is often regarded as the core institution of a functioning society.

Attitudes

Unemployment also exerts an influence on people's attitudes. Related to the aforementioned findings concerning hostility and aggression are results regarding the political attitudes of unemployed people. Several studies have revealed not only a widespread detachment from mainstream political parties but also from the government and the political system in general (Banks & Ullah, 1987; Breakwell, 1986; Plunkett, 1995). Hostility toward foreigners is also more prevalent among unemployed persons than among those who are employed (Bacher, 2001). Furthermore, unemployment is often accompanied by the endorsement of radical political action (Breakwell, 1986; Clark, 1985; de Witte, 1992; Gaskell & Smith, 1985) and sometimes even by the endorsement of violent political action (Gaskell & Smith, 1985) and a tendency to favor extremist political parties (Banks & Ullah, 1987).

Perhaps contributing to this feeling of detachment from and sometimes hostility toward society is the effect that unemployment has on beliefs regarding control: Jobless persons have been repeatedly reported to perceive events as being beyond their personal control and to believe that chance or powerful others controls their lives (Gaskell, & Smith, 1985; Layton, 1987; O'Brien, & Kabanoff, 1979). Interestingly, however, unemployment is not accompanied by a reduction of employment commitment and work values related to the traditional Protestant work ethic (at least among the jobless people with short- or medium-term unemployment, who formed the large majority of participants in the studies meta-analyzed by Paul and Moser [2006]). This lack of a change is noteworthy, because high levels of employment commitment and Protestant work ethic are associated with more distress among unemployed persons, and a reduction of theses work values could help to ameliorate this distress.

Related to the aforementioned effects of unemployment on health and mortality is a recent study concerning the role of sense of coherence. This sense represents a person's "feeling of confidence that one's internal and external environments are predictable and that there is a high probability that things will work out as well as can reasonably be expected" (Antonovsky, 1979, p. 10). Consisting of the subdimensions comprehensibility, manageability, and meaningfulness, it represents a highly important stress resistance resource and is highly relevant for both mental and physical health. Sense of coherence has recently been shown to be weakened among unemployed people and to gain strength after reemployment, rendering it a possible mediator of the negative effects of unemployment on health (Vastamäki, Moser & Paul, 2009).

In summary, it can be said that the worrying effects of unemployment on health are aggravated by negative effects in several other areas, such as health behavior, attitudes, and family lives. The findings that indicate problems with family formation among unemployed people, elevated partner violence, and a tendency to feel alienated from the democratic political system demonstrate that the negative effects of unemployment go far beyond the health impairments that were usually the focus of research interests. Unemployment affects not only the unemployed persons themselves but also others related to them and the society as a whole. (See also McKee-Ryan & Maitoza, this volume, and Sinfield, this volume).

Conclusions
Practical Conclusions on the Individual and Collective Level

Unemployment has a negative effect on mental health; that is, the health level of unemployed persons is half a standard deviation below the health level of employed persons (Paul & Moser, 2009). This effect is of considerable practical importance, as it is equivalent to a strong increase, from 16% to 34%, in the rates of psychological problems among unemployed people.

On the individual level, we believe that therapists and other members of the health-care system should consider these findings in their therapeutic strategies for persons without jobs. As unemployment itself can cause distress, the employment situation should not be underestimated in comparison to other potentially pathogenic factors (e.g., problematic intimate relationships).[7] It could also be advisable to include elements of outplacement counseling (see

Borgen & Butterfield, this volume) and job search–oriented interventions (see Glebbeek & Sol, this volume; Latham, Mawritz, & Locke, this volume; Lindsay, this volume; Price & Vinokur, this volume; Van Hooft, this volume) into the treatment of clients who are unemployed.

Furthermore, counselors and other practitioners who are involved in planning interventions for unemployed people can be advised to create the intervention in a way that provides for as many of the latent benefits of employment (Jahoda, 1982, 1983, 1997) as possible. In other words, what the unemployed person does during the intervention should be useful for other people, should be something he or she can be proud of or at the very least need not be ashamed of, should entail positive contacts with other people, should entail sufficient activities (instead of, for example, the passive reception of lectures), and should help to give a clear structure to the participant's day and week.

Counselors might also bear in mind that loving your work does not improve your well-being if you don't have a job. Thus interventions that primarily aim at "increasing work motivation" or a similar goal could often be ill advised, since most unemployed persons already have a high level of employment commitment, which has detrimental effects on mental health in this group. For specific subgroups of unemployed persons, those who have particularly bad prospects for reemployment (for example, older persons close to retirement age with physical health impediments), it might even be advisable to intentionally *reduce* their employment commitment in order to stabilize their mental health.

Insofar as counselors offer social support, they represent a helpful coping resource themselves. Other coping resources resemble stable personality traits, such as self-esteem or emotional stability. They might be difficult to train, but some change could certainly be achieved. Cognitive appraisals such as attributions of job loss and reemployment expectations should be more open to change—for example by a Socratic dialogue—and have been shown to be influential in terms of well-being. In general, problem-focused as well as emotion-focused coping strategies can be recommended for unemployed persons.

For unemployed men, counseling should also incorporate a discussion of gender role expectations. Does the client feel unmanly because of his job loss? Does he think he is a failure? How appropriate is the expectation that men must always be strong and thus always succeed in the labor market? What makes a man a good father? Is it solely the ability to provide material support, even in modern welfare states? These and similar questions might be able to weaken those cognitive concepts that can have detrimental effects on men who are unemployed.

A very positive piece of news is the finding that it is obviously possible to recover completely from all mental health issues after reemployment. This, at least, is what the longitudinal data imply. Thus the distress that is caused by mass unemployment would disappear if unemployment could be eliminated.

On the collective level, the research results reviewed here have important implications for social policies and the health care system. Since unemployment is a prevalent problem that affects a significant part of the labor force in most countries and since it has been shown to cause mental health problems, it can be concluded that unemployment is an economic phenomenon with a considerable negative impact on public health. As a consequence, it can be expected that a country's health-care system, particularly its mental health branch, will be more strained when unemployment is high than when unemployment is low. Since the mental health status of unemployed persons is better in countries with a generous unemployment protection system, the costs of this system may not be as high as they appear to be, because the generous protection system, by stabilizing the unemployed, helps to keep the costs of the health-care system down.

With regard to the demographic moderator effects that were identified, one consequence could be to steer the allocation of public resources according to these results—for example, by giving special support to people who have been found to suffer most from unemployment, particularly unemployed youths and male blue-collar workers experiencing long-term unemployment.

In economically more developed countries, the effects of unemployment are not as pronounced as in less developed countries. The same is true for more egalitarian societies (where the level of unemployment protection usually is higher) in comparison with less egalitarian societies. Yet both goals—economic development and income equality—may compete with each other. Nevertheless, there are countries, like Canada and Sweden, that have managed to achieve both goals simultaneously—that is, both development and income equality. As a result unemployment is a weaker threat to public health there.

In sum, the devastating effects of unemployment have been demonstrated by a very large number of researchers. The results differ only in details, and the main outcome is a clear and unequivocal warning that unemployment is a severe risk to public mental health. Furthermore, this effect on health is aggravated by other negative effects, such as increased drug abuse, delayed family formation, partner violence, and political alienation.

Research Gaps

After 100 years of psychological unemployment research (if we take Rowntree and Lasker's study from 1911 as the starting point), there are a large number of studies providing a lot of knowledge about the psychological effects of joblessness. But despite this huge amount of information, it is our impression from several years of close contact with the research field that many questions remain unresolved.

For example, the mediating processes responsible for the transmission of unemployment into mental health symptoms are not yet fully understood. We cannot be sure whether Jahoda's (1982, 1997) model includes all the relevant psychological needs likely to be influenced by unemployment. One might argue that at least competence is a need that is probably reduced during unemployment and is also highly relevant for psychological well-being, but it is not included in Jahoda's model (see also Vansteenkiste & Van den Broeck, this volume). Other psychological needs that should be scrutinized for the same reasons are autonomy, security, and stimulation (Sheldon, Elliott, Kim, & Kasser, 2001). Furthermore, other theoretical approaches such as Fryer's (1986, 1997a) agency restriction model or the incongruence model (Paul & Moser, 2006) have been studied even less than Jahoda's model and are also in need of further scrutiny.

There is also a need for a more detailed analysis of the moderator effects and their theoretical explanations. These explanations often consist only of a few post hoc arguments that are frequently reproduced in different articles but infrequently tested. There are exceptions, of course. Shamir (1985), for example, directly compared different explanations for the finding that men suffer more from unemployment than women. He found that less financial difficulties but not lower employment commitment or the availability of alternative roles explained the better mental health of the women in his Israeli sample (see also Waters & Moore, 2002). Yet such studies that directly test different explanations for moderator effects against each other are rare and should be done more often in our eyes in order to get a clearer and more generalizable picture of what causes these effects.

There are also some underresearched variables that deserve more attention in our opinion, even if existing tests have not (yet) endorsed their status as moderators. For example, few studies were especially concerned with the problems of unemployed parents, although these problems may be serious, particularly for impoverished single mothers and for men who stick to their traditional role as a family provider. As a result, meta-analytic tests comparing parents and nonparents were planned but not realized owing to a lack of usable studies in recent meta-analyses (Paul & Moser, 2009).

Studies on the mental health of older unemployed workers are also not numerous as far as we know, although this is a very timely research topic. Almost all industrialized societies experience demographic changes that will lead to a higher proportion of elder persons in the labor market in the near future. This also means more unemployed persons in an advanced age. Yet we do not know much about the specific experience of job loss and job search when one's physical fitness starts to decline and when the general perception of one's personality is dominated by stereotypes such as "loyal," "less cooperative," and "resists change more often," etc. (Hassell & Perrewe, 1995, p. 465; see also Klehe et al., this volume).

Another interesting yet neglected research topic is unemployment in rural environments. While few people are still living in such an environment today, it represents something like a "different world" within urbanized industrialized societies, and it might be helpful to study unemployment there in order to get a better understanding of the experience of unemployment in urban surroundings. Are the typically closer social bonds in a village a blessing for unemployed people because they lead to more social support or are they a bane owing to stronger stigmatization as compared with the circumstances in a more anonymous city environment? Is the closeness of food plants (combined with farmers who turn a blind eye) still an important and economically very helpful asset for rural unemployment persons, as it was in Marienthal 80 years ago (Jahoda, Lazarsfeld & Zeisel, 1933)? We do not really know the answers to these questions since—to the best of our knowledge—only two studies were specifically concerned with unemployment in rural environments in the last decades (Harding & Sewel, 1992; Leeflang, Klein-Hesselink, & Spruit, 1992).

Furthermore, nonwestern countries are still strongly underrepresented in the English-language literature on the psychological effects of unemployment, thus limiting the generalizability of conclusions based on this literature to three continents: North America, Europe, and Australia/New Zealand (and even these continents are not fully represented owing to the small number of studies from eastern Europe). Thus, more studies from nonwestern countries, especially from countries with values concerning work and employment that differ from the western ones, could possibly be very helpful to improve the understanding of the negative mental health effects of unemployment. For example, one of the few studies from Africa showed that the moderator effect of gender, which was demonstrated in western studies, does not exist in South Africa, where the experience of unemployment appears to be equally negative for women and men (Griep, Rothmann, Vleugels, & De Witte, 2012). Thus looking at nonwestern cultures might teach us a lot about the variability of the psychological effects of unemployment.

Another neglected topic is the question for the positive consequences of unemployment. Asking this question might be surprising to the reader after studying a chapter full of information about the negative effects of unemployment. However, recent research on posttraumatic growth (Tedeschi & Calhoun, 2004; Zoellner & Maercker, 2006) has demonstrated that individuals who experience highly stressful live events sometimes are able to use this experience as an opportunity for further psychological development. This may also be possible in the case of unemployment; here coping strategies such as positive reappraisal and sense making might also occur, as in other instances of posttraumatic growth, and might also have positive long-term effects. However, while growth is one possible outcome of a challenging experience, such an experience can also result in what has been named "survival" (i.e., a continued existence at a lower level of psychological adjustment compared with prechallenge) (O'Leary & Ickovics, 1995).

Currently studies that specifically measured features of posttraumatic growth in jobless and formerly jobless people are still lacking. However, a few empirical studies have already demonstrated that for a subgroup of people, the experience of unemployment appears to be a positive one. Fryer and Payne (1984), for example, managed to identify a small group of persons who were described by community workers as coping exceptionally well with unemployment. Interviews showed that these people were characterized by a high level of proactivity and very strong political, religious, or other values. They also distinguished work, as purposeful activity, from employment, the social institution, and generally viewed the latter as an overly restrictive and life-inhibiting arrangement. Unemployment, on the other hand, provided them with a unique opportunity to pursue their individual goals, something they cherished as a highly meaningful experience, an experience that their former jobs had never given them.

Jones (1989) also described a group of unemployed persons—about one tenth of his sample—who were able to personally profit from unemployment. They saw job loss as a "blessing in disguise" (p. 53) because it liberated them from an unsatisfactory job impinging on their happiness and gave them the necessary motivation and opportunity to change their careers in a direction more in line with their true values and goals. Unusually, this group was characterized by an *improvement* of mental health with lengthening joblessness. Similar results were reported in a study scrutinizing older unemployed managers (Zikic & Richardson, 2007). Many of these managers appreciated that unemployment gave them an opportunity for a "time out" (p. 62), a period of time, similar to a sabbatical, that they could use for nonprofessional activities such as housing renovation or sports but also for self-reflection and a thorough reevaluation of their lives. This often resulted in a better understanding of their previous organizational roles and their relationships with colleagues and often inspired them to reconstruct their personal relationships and to explore completely new career opportunities. In line with these findings, Koen, Klehe, Van Vianen, Zikic, and Nauta (2010) were recently able to demonstrate that a high level of career decisiveness (i.e., knowledge what one wants in a future job) has a strong positive effect on subsequent reemployment quality. Deliberate career planning has also been shown to lead to high quality reemployment (Zikic & Klehe, 2006). Thus the opportunity to reflect and redirect one's former choices might indeed have positive long-term consequences for at least some unemployed people.

From a theoretical point of view it might also be promising to compare unemployed persons with other persons who are also out of employment but who do not fit the definition of unemployment, such as homemakers or retirees. There are some indications that unemployed persons feel bad not only in comparison to people who work but also in comparison to these latter groups (Paul & Moser, 2006, 2010). One may then ask what it is that allows people in these groups to sustain a better mental health despite the apparent lack of employment that they share with unemployed persons.

Furthermore, the dynamics of the relationship between the bureaucrat and his/her unemployed "client" might be a fascinating avenue for further research. Unemployed persons' dependency on financial aid forces them into a relationship with public service employees that is characterized by power asymmetry and the potential for massive conflict. In the popular media one can sometimes find reports of violence occurring between these groups (e.g., Diehl, 2012), and a recent study showed that—on average—German job agency employees deal with alcohol-intoxicated customers and verbal threats several times each week, some sort of turmoil or riot at least once a week, and direct and massive forms of violence about once or twice a year (Deutsche Gesetzliche Unfallversicherung, 2011). They also report a perceived lack of security and are characterized by a high level of emotional exhaustion. Some information on this topic can also be found in qualitative studies of unemployed persons, showing that they do not feel comfortable in their relationship with agency employees, experiencing it as oppressive and demeaning (e.g., Drewery, 1998; Fryer & Fagan, 2003). In sum, there are few but strong empirical hints that the relationship between agency employees and unemployed persons is a rather problematic one. We clearly need more knowledge about this relationship, experienced by almost every unemployed person, which could be highly relevant to their mental health as well as that of the agency workers.

Finally, new research methods developed in the last decades might be very helpful in studies involving the unemployed persons. Experience sampling is particularly promising here (Hektner, Schmidt, & Csikszentmihalyi, 2007). Traditionally, research with unemployed persons has been done via questionnaire or interview, two methods that usually imply a comparatively large time lag between the psychological event that is being scrutinized and its recording. Diary studies or experience sampling methods enable a much more fine-grained, detailed, and close-to-real-life analysis of psychological processes and might be a interesting alternative. Currently there seem to be very few studies that use such a method in order to study mental health processes among the unemployed persons (e.g., Džuka,, 2001). Another methodological advance that has recently been used more often comprises longitudinal designs with several time points, which enable scholars to conduct more convincing tests of the causal processes involved in the dynamic of unemployment and mental health (e.g., Lucas, Clark, Georgellis, & Diener, 2004; Selenko, Batinic, & Paul, 2011).

In summary, much has already been done in this highly important research field, but several important questions remain only partly answered, for example: Has unemployment comparable effects on mental health in all parts of the world? Which factors moderate the negative effects of unemployment? How can these moderating effects be explained? What are the exact causal mechanisms that mediate the negative effects of unemployment? Which ways of coping are the most helpful for unemployed persons? Why do other people who are out of employment, such as homemakers or retirees, feel better than unemployed people do? Even if the net effect of job loss on mental health is negative, do there exist specific positive outcomes, too? And so on. There is much that still needs to be done.

Notes

1. Two older meta-analyses (Foster, 1991; Murphy & Athanasou, 1999) are not included in the present review because they are based on very small numbers of studies (10 and 9, respectively), limiting the generalizability of their findings.
2. Note that the last argument is possibly outdated. Since about the year 2000, unemployment rates for men have started to be higher than for women in several countries, a development that was intensified by the recent economic crisis (International Labour Office, 2011).
3. The Human Development Index (HDI) is an index that measures a country's level of development through the use of three factors: longevity (mean life expectancy in the nation), knowledge (rate of literacy and school population), and purchasing power (GDP per person) (Sotelo & Gimeno, 2003).
4. The Gini score measures the extent to which the distribution of income among individuals or households within a country deviates from a perfectly equal distribution. High Gini scores indicate a high level of economic inequality in a country (UNDP, 2003).
5. The LMSI is a complex composite of several indicators of the "level of access to reasonable income-earning activities" in a country. It was developed and published by the International Labour Organization (International Labour Office, 2004, p. 131).
6. Note that anticipation effects might play a biasing role here: Many employed people whose jobs are endangered and many unemployed persons with low chances for finding a new job will probably suspect that things are not looking well for them, and this knowledge could possibly cause distress. If so, it's not distress that leads to unemployment in these

cases, but anticipated unemployment that leads to distress. Disentangling such anticipation effects is extremely difficult though, even with longitudinal research designs.
7. A hint that such a tendency toward underestimation of the negative effect of unemployment exists and is widespread can be found in the accounts of unemployed survivors of suicide attempts, who usually claim relationship problems as the main reason for their wish to die, although research shows that unemployment also plays a major role as a risk factor for suicide (see Platt, 1985).

References

Adler, G., & Hilber, D. (2009). Industry hiring patterns of older workers. *Research on Aging, 31*(1), 69–88.

Åhs, A., & Westerling, R. (2006). Self-rated health in relation to employment status during periods of high and of low levels of unemployment. *European Journal of Public Health, 16,* 294–304. doi:10.1093/eurpub/cki165

Amundson, N. E., & Borgen, W. A. (1982). The dynamics of unemployment: Job loss and job search. *Personnel & Guidance Journal, 60,* 562–564.

Antonovsky, A. (1979). *Health, stress and coping.* San Francisco: Jossey-Bass.

Archer, J., & Rhodes, V. (1987). Bereavement and reactions to job loss: A comparative review. *British Journal of Social Psychology, 26,* 211–224.

Archer, J., & Rhodes, V. (1993). The grief process and job loss: A cross-sectional study. *British Journal of Psychology, 84,* 395–410.

Bacher, J. (2001). In welchen Lebensbereichen lernen Jugendliche Ausländerfeindlichkeit? Ergebnisse einer Befragung bei Berufsschülerinnen und Berufsschülern [In which environments do adolescents learn hostility towards foreigners? Questionnaire results of technical school students.]. *Kölner Zeitschrift für Soziologie und Sozialpsychologie, 53,* 334–349. doi:10.1007/s11577-001-0042-1

Bambra, C., & Eikemo, T. A. (2009). Welfare state regimes, unemployment and health: A comparative study of the relationship between unemployment and self-reported health in 23 European countries. *Journal of Epidemiology and Community Health, 63,* 92–98. doi:10.1136/jech.2008.077354

Banks, M. H., & Ullah, P. (1987). Political attitudes and voting among unemployed and employed youth. *Journal of Adolescence, 10,* 201–216. doi:10.1016/S0140-1971(87)80088-X

Baum, A., Fleming, R., & Reddy, D. M. (1986). Unemployment stress: Loss of control, reactance and learned helplessness. *Social Science & Medicine, 22,* 509–516. doi:10.1016/0277-9536(86)90016-X

Berger, E. D. (2006). 'Aging' identities: Degradation and negotiation in the search of employment. *Journal of Aging Studies, 20,* 303–316.

Beutel, M. (1988). *Bewältigungsprozesse bei chronischen Erkrankungen* [Coping processes during chronic illness]. Weinheim, Germany: Edition Medizin.

Breakwell, G. M. (1986). Political and attributional responses of the young short-term unemployed. *Political Psychology, 7,* 575–586. doi:10.2307/3791257

Broomhall, H. S., & Winefield, A. H. (1990). A comparison of the affective well-being of young and middle-aged unemployed men matched for length of unemployment. *British Journal of Medical Psychology, 63,* 43–52.

Buzwell, S., & Rosenthal, D. (1995). Exploring the sexual world of the unemployed adolescent. *Journal of Community & Applied Social Psychology*, 5, 161–166. doi:10.1002/casp.2450050303

Catalano, R. (1991). The health effects of economic insecurity. *American Journal of Public Health*, 81, 1148–1152. doi:10.2105/AJPH.81.9.1148

Christoffersen, M. (2000). Growing up with unemployment: A study of parental unemployment and children's risk of abuse and neglect based on national longitudinal 1973 birth cohorts in Denmark. *Childhood: A Global Journal of Child Research*, 7, 421–438. doi:10.1177/0907568200007004003

Clark, A. W. (1985). The effects of unemployment on political attitude. *Australian & New Zealand Journal of Sociology*, 21, 100–108. doi:10.1177/144078338502100106

Cohen, F., Kemeny, M. E., Zegans, L. S., Johnson, P., Kearney, K. A., & Stites, D. P. (2007). Immune function declines with unemployment and recovers after stressor termination. *Psychosomatic Medicine*, 69, 225–234. doi:10.1097/PSY.0b013e31803139a6

Creed, P. A. & Klisch, J. (2005). Future outlook and financial strain: Testing the personal agency and latent deprivation models of unemployment and well-being. *Journal of Occupational Health Psychology*, 10, 251–260. doi: 10.1037/1076-8998.10.3.251

Creed, P. A., Lehmann, K., & Hood, M. (2009). The relationship between core self-evaluations, employment commitment and well-being in the unemployed. *Personality and Individual Differences*, 47, 310–315. doi:10.1016/j.paid.2009.03.021

Creed, P. A., & Macintyre, S. R. (2001). The relative effects of deprivation of the latent and manifest benefits of employment on the well-being of unemployed people. *Journal of Occupational Health Psychology*, 6, 324–331. doi:10.1037/1076-8998.6.4.324

Cunradi, C. B., Todd, M., Duke, M., & Ames, G. (2009). Problem drinking, unemployment, and intimate partner violence among a sample of construction industry workers and their partners. *Journal of Family Violence*, 24, 63–74. doi:10.1007/s10896-008-9209-0

de Haes, J. C., & Van Knippenberg, F. C. (1985). The quality of life of cancer patients: A review of the literature. *Social Science & Medicine*, 20, 809–817. doi:10.1016/0277-9536(85)90335-1

De Jonge, J., & Schaufeli, W. B. (1998). Job characteristics and employee well-being: A test of Warr's vitamin model in health care workers using structural equation modelling. *Journal of Organizational Behavior*, 19, 387–407. doi:10.1002/(SICI)1099-1379(199807)19:4<387::AID-JOB851>3.0.CO;2-9

DeFrank, R. S., & Ivancevich, J. M. (1986). Job loss: An individual level review and model. *Journal of Vocational Behavior*, 28, 1–20. doi:10.1016/0001-8791(86)90035-7

Dettenborn, L. L., Tietze, A. A., Bruckner, F. F., & Kirschbaum, C. C. (2010). Higher cortisol content in hair among long-term unemployed individuals compared to controls. *Psychoneuroendocrinology*, 35, 1404–1409. doi:10.1016/j.psyneuen.2010.04.006

Deutsche Gesetzliche Unfallversicherung (2011). *Arbeitsbelastungen und Bedrohungen in Arbeitsgemeinschaften nach Hartz IV—Abschlussbericht* [Pressures at work and threats in job centres after Hartz IV—final report]. Meckenheim, Germany: Deutsche Gesetzliche Unfallversicherung.

de Witte, H. (1992). Unemployment, political attitudes and voting behaviour. *Politics & the Individual*, 2, 29–41.

Diehl, J. (2012). Angriff im Jobcenter: Tödliche Stiche in der Abteilung "Visionen 50plus". [Attack in the job center: Fatal knife stabs in the department, Visions 50plus".] *Spiegel Online*. Available at: http://www.spiegel.de/panorama/justiz/jobcenter-neuss-familienvater-ersticht-seine-sachbearbeiterin-a-858111.html (Retrieved November 17, 2012.)

Diener, E., Diener, M., & Diener, C. (1995). Factors predicting the subjective well-being of nations. *Journal of Personality and Social Psychology*, 69, 851–864. doi:10.1037/0022-3514.69.5.851

Dooley, D., Catalano, R., & Rook, K. S. (1988). Personal and aggregate unemployment and psychological symptoms. *Journal of Social Issues*, 44(4), 107–123.

Dooley, D., Fielding, J., & Levi, L. (1996). Health and unemployment. *Annual Review of Public Health*, 17, 449–465. doi: 10.1146/annurev.pu.17.050196.002313

Dormois, J.-P. (2004). *The French economy in the twentieth century*. Cambridge, UK, and New York: Cambridge University Press.

Dreiss, J. E. (1983). The stages of terminating: When mental health workers face job loss. *Community Mental Health Journal*, 19, 3–16. doi: 10.1007/BF00778675

Drewery, W. (1998). Unemployment: What kind of problem is it? *Journal of Community & Applied Social Psychology*, 8, 101–118. doi: 10.1002/(SICI)1099-1298(199803/04)8:2<101::AID-CASP461>3.0.CO;2-C

Džuka, J. (2001). Time sampling of unemployment experiences by Slovak youth. In H. Brandstätter & A. Eliasz (Eds.), *Persons, situations and emotions: An ecological approach* (pp. 147–162). New York: Oxford University Press.

Eisenberg, P. P., & Lazarsfeld, P. F. (1938). The psychological effects of unemployment. *Psychological Bulletin*, 35, 358–390. doi:10.1037/h0063426

Ekert-Jaffe, O., & Solaz, A. (2001). Unemployment, marriage, and cohabitation in France. *The Journal of Socio-Economics*, 30, 75–98. doi:10.1016/S1053-5357(01)00088-9

Erikson, E. H. (1959). Identity and the life cycle. *Psychological Issues*, 1, 50–100.

Eliason, M., & Storrie, D. (2009). Job loss is bad for your health—Swedish evidence on cause-specific hospitalization following involuntary job loss. *Social Science & Medicine*, 68, 1396–1406. doi:10.1016/j.socscimed.2009.01.021

Ezzy, D. (1993). Unemployment and mental health: A critical review. *Social Science & Medicine*, 37, 41–52. doi:10.1016/0277-9536(93)90316-V

Fagan, P., Shavers, V., Lawrence, D., Gibson, J., & Ponder, P. (2007). Cigarette smoking and quitting behaviors among unemployed adults in the United States. *Nicotine & Tobacco Research*, 9, 241–248. doi:10.1080/14622200601080331

Feather, N. T. (1990). *The psychological impact of unemployment*. New York: Springer.

Feather, N. T., & Barber, J. G. (1983). Depressive reactions and unemployment. *Journal of Abnormal Psychology*, 92, 185–195. doi:10.1037/0021-843X.92.2.185

Feather, N. T., & Davenport, P. R. (1981). Unemployment and depressive affect: A motivational and attributional analysis. *Journal of Personality and Social Psychology*, 41, 422–436. doi:10.1037/0022-3514.41.3.422

Fielden, S. L., & Davidson, M. J. (2001). Stress and gender in unemployed female and male managers. *Applied Psychology: An*

International Review, *50*, 305–334. doi:10.1111/1464-0597.00060

Fischer, P., Greitemeyer, T., & Frey, D. (2008). Unemployment and aggression: The moderating role of self-awareness on the effect of unemployment on aggression. *Aggressive Behavior, 34*, 34–45. doi:10.1002/ab.20218

Foster, C. (1991). "Because no man hath hired us": A study of the impact of unemployment on mental health through the analysis of linear structural relationships. Unpublished dissertation. Waltham, MA: Brandeis University.

Frese, M. (1987). Alleviating depression in the unemployed: Adequate financial support, hope and early retirement. *Social Science & Medicine, 25*(2), 213–215.

Frese, M., & Mohr, G. (1978). Die psychopathologischen Folgen des Entzugs von Arbeit: Der Fall Arbeitslosigkeit [The psychopathological consequences of the loss of work: The case of unemployment]. In M. Frese, S. Greif, & N. B. Brenner (Eds.), *Industrielle Psychopathologie* (pp. 282–320). Bern, Switzerland: Huber.

Fryer, D. (1986). Employment deprivation and personal agency during unemployment: A critical discussion of Jahoda's explanation of the psychological effects of unemployment. *Social Behaviour, 1*, 3–23.

Fryer, D. (1992). Psychological or material deprivation: Why does unemployment have mental health consequences? In E. McLaughlin (Ed.), *Understanding unemployment* (pp. 103–125). London: Routledge.

Fryer, D. (1997a). Agency restriction. In N. Nicholson (Ed.), *The Blackwell encyclopedic dictionary of organizational psychology* (p. 12). Oxford, UK: Blackwell.

Fryer, D. (1997b). International perspectives on youth unemployment and mental health: Some central issues. *Journal of Adolescence, 20*, 333–342. doi:10.1006/jado.1997.0089

Fryer, D., & McKenna, S. P. (1984). Perceived health during lay off and early unemployment. *Occupational Health*, May 1984, 201–206.

Fryer, D., & Payne, R. (1984). Proactive behaviour during unemployment: Findings and implications. *Leisure Studies, 3*, 273–295.

Fryer, D., & Payne, R. (1986). Being unemployed: A review of the literature on the psychological experience of unemployment. In C. L. Cooper & I. T. Robertson (Eds.), *International review of industrial and organizational psychology* (pp. 235–278). Chichester, UK: Wiley.

Galić, Z., & Šverko, B. (2008). Effects of prolonged unemployment and reemployment on psychological and physical health. *Review of Psychology, 15*, 3–10.

Garraty, J. A. (1978). *Unemployment in history*. New York: Harper & Row.

Gaskell, G., & Smith, P. (1985). An investigation of youths' attributions for unemployment and their political attitudes. *Journal of Economic Psychology, 6*, 65–80. doi:10.1016/0167-4870(85)90006-6

Gebel, M., & Giesecke, J. (2009). Ökonomische Unsicherheit und Fertilität. Die Wirkung von Beschäftigungsunsicherheit und Arbeitslosigkeit auf die Familiengründung in Ost- und Westdeutschland [Economic insecurity and fertility. The effects of job insecurity and unemployment on family formation in East and West Germany]. *Zeitschrift für Soziologie, 38*, 399–417.

Griep, Y., Rothmann, S., Vleugels, W., & De Witte, H. (2012) psychological dimensions of unemployment: A gender comparison between Belgian and South African unemployed. *Journal of Psychology in Africa, 22*(3), 303–314.

Grawe, K. (2004). *Psychological therapy*. Seattle: Hogrefe & Huber.

Grobe, T. G., Dörning, H., & Schwartz, F. W. (1999). *GEK-Gesundheitsreport 1999. Schwerpunkt: Arbeitslosigkeit und Gesundheit* [GEK health report 1999. Main focus: Unemployment and health]. Sankt Augustin, Germany: Asgard.

Gurney, R. M. (1980). The effects of unemployment on the psycho-social development of school-leavers. *Journal of Occupational Psychology, 53*, 205–213.

Hammarström, A. (1994). Health consequences of youth unemployment: Review from a gender perspective. *Social Science & Medicine, 38*, 699–709. doi:10.1016/0277-9536(94)90460-X

Hammarström, A. A., & Janlert, U. U. (2002). Early unemployment can contribute to adult health problems: Results from a longitudinal study of school leavers. *Journal of Epidemiology and Community Health, 56*, 624–630. doi:10.1136/jech.56.8.624

Hanisch, K. A. (1999). Job loss and unemployment research from 1994 to 1998: A review and recommendations for research and intervention. *Journal of Vocational Behavior, 55*, 188–220. doi:10.1006/jvbe.1999.1722

Harding, L., & Sewel, J. (1992). Psychological health and employment status in an island community. *Journal of Occupational and Organizational Psychology, 65*, 269–275.

Harrison, R. (1976). The demoralising experience of prolonged unemployment. *Department of Employment Gazette, 84*, 339–348.

Hassell, B. L. & Perrewe, P. L. (1995). An examination of beliefs about older workers: Do stereotypes still exist? *Journal of Organizational Behavior, 16*, 457–468.

Hektner, J. M. Schmidt, J. A. Csikszentmihalyi, M. (2007). *Experience sampling method: Measuring the quality of everyday life*. Thousand Oaks, CA: Sage.

Hepworth, S. J. (1980). Moderating factors of the psychological impact of unemployment. *Journal of Occupational Psychology, 53*, 139–146.

Hill, J. (1978). The psychological impact of unemployment. *New Society, 19*, 118–120.

Hoare, P., & Machin, M. (2010). The impact of reemployment on access to the latent and manifest benefits of employment and mental health. *Journal of Occupational and Organizational Psychology, 83*, 759–770. doi:10.1348/096317909X472094

Hofstede, G. (2001). *Cultures consequences: Comparing values, behaviors, institutions, and organizations across nations*. 2nd ed. Thousand Oaks, CA: Sage.

Hollederer, A. (2002). Arbeitslosigkeit und Gesundheit: Ein Überblick über empirische Befunde und die Arbeitslosen- und Krankenkassenstatistik. [Unemployment and health: A review of empirical evidence and of statistics concerning unemployment and health insurance]. *Mitteilungen aus der Arbeitsmarkt- und Berufsforschung, 35*, 411–428.

International Labour Office (2000a). *Yearbook of labour statistics* (58th issue). Geneva: International Labour Office.

International Labour Office (2000b). *World labour report 2000: Income security and social protection in a changing world*. Geneva: International Labour Office.

International Labour Office (2004). *Economic security for a better world*. Geneva: International Labour Office.

International Labour Office. (2011). *Key indicators of the labor market*, 7th ed. Geneva: International Labour Office.

International Labour Office. (2012). *Global employment trends*. Geneva: International Labour Office.

Jackson, P. R., & Warr, P. B. (1984). Unemployment and psychological ill-health: The moderating role of duration and age. *Psychological Medicine: A Journal of Research in Psychiatry and the Allied Sciences, 14*, 605–614. doi:10.1017/S003329170001521X

Jahoda, M. (1981). Work, employment, and unemployment: Values, theories, and approaches in social research. *American Psychologist, 36*, 184–191. doi:10.1037/0003-066X.36.2.184

Jahoda, M. (1982). *Employment and unemployment*. Cambridge, UK: Cambridge University Press.

Jahoda, M. (1983). *Wieviel Arbeit braucht der Mensch? Arbeit und Arbeitslosigkeit im 20. Jahrhundert* [How much work do human beings need? Employment and unemployment in the twentieth century]. Weinheim, Germany: Beltz.

Jahoda, M. (1986). *Wieviel Arbeit braucht der Mensch?* 3rd rev. ed. [How much work do human beings need?] Weinheim, Germany: Beltz.

Jahoda, M. (1988). Economic recession and mental health: Some conceptual issues. *Journal of Social Issues, 44*(4), 13–23.

Jahoda, M. (1997). Manifest and latent functions. In N. Nicholson (Ed.), *The Blackwell encyclopedic dictionary of organizational psychology* (pp. 317–318). Oxford, UK: Blackwell.

Jahoda, M., Lazarsfeld, P. F., & Zeisel, H. (1933/1975). *Die Arbeitslosen von Marienthal* [Marienthal: The sociography of an unemployed community]. Konstanz, Germany: Verlag für Demoskopie.

Jeurissen, T., & Nyklíček, I. (2001). Testing the vitamin model of job stress in Dutch health care workers. *Work & Stress, 15*, 254–264. doi:10.1080/02678370110066607

Jones, L. P. (1989). A typology of adaptations to unemployment. *Journal of Employment Counseling, 26*(2), 50–59.

Judge, T. A., Locke, E. A., & Durham C. C. (1997). The dispositional causes of job satisfaction: A core evaluations approach. *Research in Organizational Behavior, 19*, 151–188.

Kanfer, R., Wanberg, C. R., & Kantrowitz, T. M. (2001). Job search and employment: A personality–motivational analysis and meta-analytic review. *Journal of Applied Psychology, 86*, 837–855. doi:10.1037/0021-9010.86.5.837

Kasl, S. V., Rodriguez, E., & Lasch, K. E. (1998). The impact of unemployment on health and well-being. In B. P. Dohrenwend (Ed.), *Adversity, stress, and psychopathology* (pp. 111–131). Oxford, UK: University Press.

Kaufman, H. G. (1982). *Coping with the stress of job loss and underemployment*. Hoboken, NJ: Wiley.

Kelaher, M., Dunt, D., & Dodson, S. (2007). Unemployment, contraceptive behaviour and reproductive outcomes among young Australian women. *Health Policy, 82*, 95–101. doi:10.1016/j.healthpol.2006.08.002

Kieselbach, T. (1998). Arbeitslosigkeit und Entfremdung [Unemployment and alienation]. *Journal für Psychologie, 6*, 38–52.

Kimerling, R., Alvarez, J., Pavao, J., Mack, K. P., Smith, M. W., & Baumrind, N. (2009). Unemployment among women: Examining the relationship of physical and psychological intimate partner violence and posttraumatic stress disorder. *Journal of Interpersonal Violence, 24*, 450–463. doi:10.1177/0886260508317191

Kinicki, A. J., & Latack, J. C. (1990). Explication of the construct of coping with involuntary job loss. *Journal of Vocational Behavior, 36*, 339–360. doi:10.1016/0001-8791(90)90036-2

Kinicki, A. J., Prussia, G. E., & McKee-Ryan, F. M. (2000). A panel study of coping with involuntary job loss. *Academy of Management Journal, 43*, 90–100. doi:10.2307/1556388

Kirchler, E., & Kirchler, E. (1989). Individuelle Erfahrungen mit Arbeitslosigkeit: Grundriss eines psychologischen Wirkungsmodells [Individual experiences of unemployment. Sketch of a psychological model of its effects]. *Zeitschrift für Arbeits- und Organisationspsychologie, 33*, 168–177.

Koen, J., Klehe, U. C., Van Vianen, A. E. M., Zikic, J., & Nauta, A. (2010). Job-search strategies and reemployment quality: The impact of career adaptability. *Journal of Vocational Behavior, 77*, 126–139. doi: 10.1016/j.jvb.2010.02.004

Komarovsky, M. (1940). *The unemployed man and his family: The effect of unemployment on the status of the man in 59 families*. New York: Dryden Press.

Kulik, L. (2000). Jobless men and women: A comparative analysis of job search intensity, attitudes toward unemployment and related responses. *Journal of Occupational and Organizational Psychology, 73*, 487–500. doi:10.1348/096317900167173

Lahelma, E. (1989). Unemployment, re-employment and mental well-being: A panel survey of industrial job seekers in Finland. *Scandinavian Journal of Social Medicine, Supplementum 43*.

Latack, J. C., Kinicki, A. J., & Prussia, G. E. (1995). An integrative process model of coping with job loss. *Academy of Management Review, 20*, 311–342. doi:10.2307/258849

Layton, C. (1987). Levels of state anxiety for males facing redundancy and subsequently reporting to be employed or unemployed. *Perceptual and Motor Skills, 65*, 53–54.

Leana, C. R., & Feldman, D. C. (1988). Individual responses to job loss: Perceptions, reactions, and coping behaviors. *Journal of Management, 14*, 375–389. doi:10.1177/014920638801400302

Leana, C. R., & Feldman, D. C. (1990). Individual responses to job loss: Empirical findings from two field studies. *Human Relations, 43*, 1155–1181. doi:10.1177/001872679004301107

Leana, C. R., & Feldman, D. C. (1991). Gender differences in responses to unemployment. *Journal of Vocational Behavior, 38*, 65–77. doi:10.1016/0001-8791(91)90018-H

Leana, C. R., & Feldman, D. C. (1995). Finding new jobs after a plant closing: Antecedents and outcomes of the occurrence and quality of reemployment. *Human Relations, 48*, 1381–1401.

Leana, C. R., Feldman, D. C., & Tan, G. Y. (1998). Predictors of coping behavior after a layoff. *Journal of Organizational Behavior, 19*, 85–97. doi:10.1002/(SICI)1099-1379(199801)19:1<85::AID-JOB838>3.0.CO;2-Y

Leeflang, R. L. I., Klein-Hesselink, D. J., & Spruit, I. P. (1992). Health effects of unemployment—I.Long-term unemployed men in a rural and an urban setting. *Social Science and Medicine, 34*, 341–350.

Lynd-Stevenson, R. (1996). A test of the hopelessness theory of depression in unemployed young adults. *British Journal of Clinical Psychology, 35*, 117–132.

Little, C. B. (1976). Technical-professional unemployment: Middle-class adaptability to personal crisis. *The Sociological Quarterly, 17*, 262–274. doi:10.1111/j.1533-8525.1976.tb00978.x

Lucas, R. E., Clark, A. E., Georgellis, Y., & Diener, E. (2004). Unemployment alters the set point for life satisfaction. *Psychological Science, 15,* 8–13. doi: 10.1111/j.0963-7214.2004.01501002.x

Martella, D., & Maass, A. (2000). Unemployment and life satisfaction: The moderating role of time structure and collectivism. *Journal of Applied Social Psychology, 30,* 1095–1108. doi:10.1111/j.1559-1816.2000.tb02512.x

Mastekaasa, A. (1996). Unemployment and health: Selection effects. *Journal of Community & Applied Social Psychology, 6,* 189–205. doi:10.1002/(SICI)1099-1298(199608)6:3<189::AID-CASP366>3.0.CO;2-O

McFayden, R. G. (1995). Coping with threatened identities: Unemployed people's self-categorizations. *Current Psychology: Development, Learning, Personality, Social, 14,* 233–257.

McKee-Ryan, F., Song, Z., Wanberg, C. R., & Kinicki, A. J. (2005). Psychological and physical well-being during unemployment: A meta-analytic study. *Journal of Applied Psychology, 90,* 53–76. doi:10.1037/0021-9010.90.1.53

Meeus, W., Deković, M., & Iedema, J. (1997). Unemployment and identity in adolescence: A social comparison perspective. *The Career Development Quarterly, 45,* 369–380.

Mikucka, M. (in press). Does individualistic culture lower the well-being of the unemployed? Evidence from Europe. *Journal of Happiness Studies.* Doi: 10.1007/s10902-013-9445-8

Mohr, G. (1993). Industriearbeiterinnen sieben Jahre später: Arbeitssuchende Frauen im Vergleich mit wieder erwerbstätigen Frauen und Hausfrauen [Female industrial workers seven years later: Job searching women in comparison to reemployed women and homemakers]. In G. Mohr (Ed.), *Ausgezählt: Theoretische und empirische Beiträge zur Psychologie der Frauenerwerbslosigkeit* (pp. 187–204). Weinheim, Germany: Deutscher Studien Verlag.

Mossakowski, K. N. (2008). Is the duration of poverty and unemployment a risk factor for heavy drinking? *Social Science & Medicine, 67,* 947–955. doi:10.1016/j.socscimed.2008.05.019

Muller, J., Hicks, R. R., & Winocur, S. S. (1993). The effects of employment and unemployment on psychological well-being in Australian clerical workers: Gender differences. *Australian Journal of Psychology, 45,* 103–108. doi:10.1080/00049539308259126

Murphy, G. C., & Athanasou, J. A. (1999). The effect of unemployment on mental health. *Journal of Occupational and Organizational Psychology, 72,* 83–99. doi:10.1348/096317999166518

Newby, J. H., Ursano, R. J., McCarroll, J. E., Martin, L. T., Norwood, A. E., & Fullerton, C. S. (2003). Spousal aggression by US Army female soldiers toward employed and unemployed civilian husbands. *American Journal of Orthopsychiatry, 73,* 288–293. doi:10.1037/0002-9432.73.3.288

Niess, F. (1979). *Geschichte der Arbeitslosigkeit.* Köln: Pahl-Rugenstein.

Nixon, D. (2006). "I just like working with my hands": Employment aspirations and the meaning of work for low-skilled unemployed men in Britain's service economy. *Journal of Education and Work, 19,* 201–217. doi:10.1080/13639080600668051

O'Brien, G. E., & Feather, N. T. (1990). The relative effects of unemployment and quality of employment on the affect, work values and personal control of adolescents. *Journal of Occupational Psychology, 63,* 151–165.

O'Brien, G. E., & Kabanoff, B. (1979). Comparison of unemployed and employed workers on work values, locus of control and health variables. *Australian Psychologist, 14,* 143–154. doi:10.1080/00050067908260434

OECD (2000). *OECD Employment Outlook 2000.* Paris: OECD Publishing.

OECD (2004). *OECD Employment Outlook 2004.* Paris: OECD Publishing.

OECD (2010). *OECD Employment Outlook 2010.* Paris: OECD Publishing.

O'Leary, V. E., & Ickovics, J. R. (1995). Resilience and thriving in response to challenge: An opportunity for a paradigm shift in women's health. *Women's Health: Research on Gender, Behavior, and Policy, 1,* 121–142.

Ostell, A., & Divers, P. (1987). Attributional style, unemployment and mental health. *Journal of Occupational Psychology, 60,* 333–337.

Paul, K. I., & Batinic, B. (2010). The need for work: Jahoda's latent functions of employment in a representative sample of the German population. *Journal of Organizational Behavior, 31,* 45–64. doi:10.1002/job.622

Paul, K., & Moser, K. (2006). Incongruence as an explanation for the negative mental health effects of unemployment: Meta-analytic evidence. *Journal of Occupational and Organizational Psychology, 79,* 595–621. doi:10.1348/096317905X70823

Paul, K. I., & Moser, K. (2009). Unemployment impairs mental health: Meta-analyses. *Journal of Vocational Behavior, 74,* 264–282. doi:10.1016/j.jvb.2009.01.001

Paul, K. I., Vastamäki, J., & Moser, K. (2014). *Unemployment and life goals.* Manuscript submitted for publication. University of Erlangen-Nuremberg, Germany.

Payne, R., Warr, P., & Hartley, J. (1984). Social class and psychological ill-health during unemployment. *Sociology of Health & Illness, 6,* 152–174. doi:10.1111/1467-9566.ep10778241

Perrucci, C. C., Perrucci, R., & Targ, D. B. (1997). Gender differences in the economic, psychological and social effects of plant closings in an expanding economy. *The Social Science Journal, 34,* 217–233. doi:10.1016/S0362-3319(97)90052-5

Platt, S. (1985). Suicidal behaviour and unemployment: A literature review. In G. Westcott, P. G. Svensson, & H. F. K. Zöllner (Eds.), *Health policy implications of unemployment* (pp. 87–132). Copenhagen, Denmark: World Health Organization.

Plunkett, M. (1995). The effects of unemployment on social and political attitudes. *Dissertation Abstracts International Section A: Humanities and Social Sciences, 56*(6-A).

Posthuma, R. A., & Campion, M. A. (2009). Age stereotypes in the workplace: Common stereotypes, moderators, and future research directions. *Journal of Management, 35*(1), 158–188.

Prentice, D. A., & Miller, D. T. (1992). When Small Effects Are Impressive. *Psychological Bulletin, 112* (1), 160–164.

Price, R. H., Van Ryn, M., & Vinokur, A. D. (1992). Impact of a preventive job search intervention on the likelihood of depression among the unemployed. *Journal of Health and Social Behavior, 33,* 158–167. doi:10.2307/2137253

Prussia, G. E., Kinicki, A. J., & Bracker, J. S. (1993). Psychological and behavioral consequences of job loss: A covariance structure analysis using Weiner's (1985) attribution model. *Journal of Applied Psychology, 78,* 382–394. doi:10.1037/0021-9010.78.3.382

Raber, M. J. (1996). Job loss and dislocated workers: A stage theory model for treatment. *Employee Assistance Quarterly, 12*(2), 19–32. doi:10.1300/J022v12n02_02

Rásky, É., Stronegger, W., & Freidl, W. (1996). Employment status and its health-related effects in rural Styria, Austria. *Preventive*

Medicine: An International Journal Devoted to Practice and Theory, 25, 757–763. doi:10.1006/pmed.1996.0116

Reime, B., Jacob, C., & Wenzlaff, P. (2009). Is parental unemployment related to an increased risk for stillbirths? *Journal of Public Health, 17*, 363–369. doi:10.1007/s10389-009-0262-9

Rodriguez, Y. (1997). Learned helplessness or expectancy-value? A psychological model for describing the experiences of different categories of unemployed people. *Journal of Adolescence, 20*, 321–332. doi:10.1006/jado.1997.0088

Roelfs, D. J., Shor, E., Davidson, K. W., & Schwartz, J. E. (2011). Losing life and livelihood: A systematic review and meta-analysis of unemployment and all-cause mortality. *Social Science & Medicine, 72*, 840–854. doi:10.1016/j.socscimed.2011.01.005

Rothwell, N., & Williams, J. (1983). Attributional style and life-events. *British Journal of Clinical Psychology, 22*, 139–140.

Rowntree, B. S., & Lasker, B. (1911). *Unemployment: A social study.* London: Macmillan.

Rupp, K. J. (1988). Arbeitslosigkeit als Sozialisation? Ein tiefenpsychologisches Konzept ihrer Analyse und institutionellen Beeinflussung [Unemployment as a problem of socialization? A depth-psychological concept for analyzing institutional countermeasures]. *Gruppendynamik, 19*, 275–283.

Schaufeli, W. B., & VanYperen, N. W. (1992). Unemployment and psychological distress among graduates: A longitudinal study. *Journal of Occupational and Organizational Psychology, 65*, 291–305.

Selenko, E., Batinic, B., & Paul, K. I. (2011). Does latent deprivation lead to psychological distress? Investigating Jahoda's model in a four-wave study. *Journal of Occupational and Organizational Psychology, 84*, 723–740. doi: 10.1348/096317910X519360

Shamir, B. (1985). Sex differences in psychological adjustment to unemployment and reemployment: A question of commitment, alternatives or finance?. *Social Problems, 33*, 67–79. doi:10.1525/sp.1985.33.1.03a00060

Shamir, B. (1986). Self-esteem and the psychological impact of unemployment. *Social Psychology Quarterly, 49*, 61–72. doi:10.2307/2786857

Sheeran, P., & Abraham, C. S. (1994). Unemployment and self-conception: A symbolic interactionist analysis. *Journal of Community & Applied Social Psychology, 4*, 115–129. doi:10.1002/casp.2450040205

Sheeran, P., Abrams, D., & Orbell, S. (1995). Unemployment, self-esteem, and depression: A social comparison theory approach. *Basic and Applied Social Psychology, 17*, 65–82. doi:10.1207/s15324834basp1701&2_4

Sheeran, P., & McCarthy, E. (1992). Social structure, self-conception and well-being: An examination of four models with unemployed people. *Journal of Applied Social Psychology, 22*, 117–133. doi:10.1111/j.1559-1816.1992.tb01525.x

Sheldon, K. M., Elliott, A. J., Kim, Y., & Kasser, T. (2001). What is satisfying about satisfying events? Testing 10 candidate psychological needs. *Journal of Personality and Social Psychology, 80*, 325–339.

Singh, L. B., Kumari, R., & Singh, I. K. (1992). Extent of hostility in educated Indian unemployed youth: A micro analysis. *International Journal of Psychology, 27*, 89–97. doi:10.1080/00207599208246868

Sotelo, M. J., & Gimeno, L. (2003). What does human development index rating mean in terms of individualism/collectivism? *European Psychologist, 8*, 97–100.

Stokes, G., & Cochrane, R. (1984). A study of the psychological effects of redundancy and unemployment. *Journal of Occupational Psychology, 57*, 309–322.

Tedeschi, R. G., & Calhoun, L. G. (2004). Posttraumatic growth: Conceptual foundations and empirical evidence. *Psychological Inquiry, 15*, 1–18.

Tiggemann, M., & Winefield, A. H. (1984). The effects of unemployment on the mood, self-esteem, locus of control, and depressive affect of school-leavers. *Journal of Occupational Psychology, 57*, 33–42.

Tiggemann, M., Winefield, A. H., Winefield, H. R., & Goldney, R. D. (1991a). The prediction of psychological distress from attributional style: A test of the hopelessness model of depression. *Australian Journal of Psychology, 43*, 125–127. doi:10.1080/00049539108260135

Tiggemann, M., Winefield, A. H., Winefield, H. R., & Goldney, R. D. (1991b). The stability of attributional style and its relation to psychological distress. *British Journal of Clinical Psychology, 30*, 247–255.

Tiggemann, M., Winefield, H. R., Goldney, R. D., & Winefield, A. H. (1992). Attributional style and parental rearing as predictors of psychological distress. *Personality and Individual Differences, 13*, 835–841. doi:10.1016/0191-8869(92)90058-W

Toppen, J. T. (1971). Underemployment: Economic or psychological? *Psychological Reports, 28*, 111–122.

United Nations Development Programme. (2003). *Human development report 2003: Millenium development goals: A compact among nations to end human poverty.* New York: Oxford University Press.

United States Department of Labor. (1990). Employment status of the civilian noninstitutional population, 1929 to date. *Employment and Earnings, 37*, 160–171.

United States Department of Labor. (2009). Employment status of the civilian noninstitutional population 16 years and over, 1970 to date. *Employment and Earnings, 56*.

Vansteenkiste, M., Lens, W., De Witte, S., De Witte, H., & Deci, E. L. (2004). The "why" and "why not" of job search behaviour: Their relation to searching, unemployment experience, and well-being. *European Journal of Social Psychology, 34*, 345–363. doi:10.1002/ejsp.202

Vastamäki, J., Moser, K., & Paul, K. (2009). How stable is sense of coherence? Changes following an intervention for unemployed individuals. *Scandinavian Journal of Psychology, 50*, 161–171. doi:10.1111/j.1467-9450.2008.00695.x

Wanberg, C. R. (1995). A longitudinal study of the effects of unemployment and quality of reemployment. *Journal of Vocational Behavior, 46*, 40–54.

Wanberg, C. R. (1997). Antecedents and outcomes of coping behaviors among unemployed and reemployed individuals. *Journal of Applied Psychology, 82*, 731–744. doi:10.1037/0021-9010.82.5.731

Wanberg, C. R., Kammeyer-Mueller, J. D., & Shi, K. (2001). Job loss and the experience of unemployment: International research and perspectives. In N. Andeson, D. S. Ones, H. K. Sinangil, & C. Viswesvaran (Eds.), *Handbook of industrial, work and organizational psychology* (pp. 253–269). London: Sage.

Warr, P. B. (1987). *Work, unemployment and mental health.* Oxford, UK: Clarendon Press.

Warr, P. B. (2007). *Work, happiness and unhappiness.* Mahwah, NJ: Erlbaum.

Warr, P., & Jackson, P. (1987). Adapting to the unemployed role: A longitudinal investigation. *Social Science & Medicine, 25*, 1219–1224. doi:10.1016/0277-9536(87)90369-8

Warr, P., & Parry, G. (1982). Paid employment and women's psychological well-being. *Psychological Bulletin, 91*, 498–516. doi:10.1037/0033-2909.91.3.498

Warr, P., Jackson, P. R., & Banks, M. H. (1982). Duration of unemployment and psychological well-being in young men and women. *Current Psychological Research, 2*, 207–214.

Warr, P., Butcher, V., Robertson, I., & Callinan, M. (2004). Older people's well-being as a function of employment, retirement, environmental characteristics and role preference. *British Journal of Psychology, 95*(3), 297–324. doi: 10.1348/0007126041528095

Waters, L. E., & Moore, K. A. (2002). Predicting self-esteem during unemployment: the effect of gender, financial deprivation, alternate roles, and social support. *Journal of Employment Counseling, 39*, 171–189.

Weiner, B. (1985). An attributional theory of achievement motivation and emotion. *Psychological Review, 92*, 548–573. doi:10.1037/0033-295X.92.4.548

Whelan, C. T. (1992). The role of income, life-style deprivation and financial strain in mediating the impact of unemployment on psychological distress: Evidence from the Republic of Ireland. *Journal of Occupational and Organizational Psychology, 65*, 331–344.

Wilkinson, R. G. (1996). *Unhealthy societies: The afflictions of inequality.* London: Routledge.

Windschuttle, K. (1979). *Unemployment.* London: Penguin.

Winefield, A. H. (1995). Unemployment: Its psychological costs. In C. L. Cooper & I. T. Robertson (Eds.), *International review of industrial and organizational psychology* (Vol. *10*, pp. 169–212). Chichester, UK: Wiley.

Winefield, A. H., Tiggemann, M., & Smith, S. (1987). Unemployment, attributional style and psychological well-being. *Personality and Individual Differences, 8*, 659–665. doi:10.1016/0191-8869(87)90063-8

Winefield, A. H., Tiggemann, M., Winefield, H. R., & Goldney, R. D. (1993). *Growing up with unemployment: A longitudinal study of its psychological impact.* New York: Taylor & Frances/Routledge.

Winefield, A. H., Winefield, H. R., Tiggemann, M., & Goldney, R. D. (1991). A longitudinal study of the psychological effects of unemployment and unsatisfactory employment on young adults. *Journal of Applied Psychology, 76*, 424–431. doi:10.1037/0021-9010.76.3.424

Winegardner, D., Simonetti, J. L., & Nykodym, N. (1984). Unemployment: The living death? *Journal of Employment Counseling, 21*(4), 149–155.

Zikic, J., & Klehe, U. C. (2006). Job loss as a blessing in disguise: The role of career exploration and career planning in predicting reemployment quality. *Journal of Vocational Behavior, 69*, 391–409. doi: 10.1016/j.jvb.2006.05.007

Zikic, J., & Richardson, J. (2007). Unlocking the careers of business professionals following job loss: Sensemaking and career exploration of older workers. *Canadian Journal of Administrative Sciences, 24*, 58–73. doi: 10.1002/CJAS.5

Zoellner, T., & Maercker, A. (2006). Posttraumatic growth in clinical psychology—A critical review and introduction of a two component model. *Clinical Psychology Review, 26*, 626–653.

Job Loss, Unemployment, and Families

Frances M. McKee-Ryan *and* Robyn Maitoza

Abstract

The detrimental effects of job loss and unemployment are not limited to the unemployed worker but ripple out to affect those closest to him or her. These ripple effects most notably impact the unemployed worker's family, including a spouse or partner and/or children. In this chapter, we summarize previous research related to the impacts on marital or partner relationships and families and the particular effects of unemployment on children. For couples and families, we explore the financial or economic stressors and strain brought about by job loss; the direct, crossover, and relationship quality effects of stress and reduced mental health among unemployed workers and their spouses; protective resources for coping with job loss, such as social support and family resilience; and the social roles and identity of the unemployed worker. For children, we focus on mental health, child development, and educational/human capital attainment. We then offer suggestions for future research on families facing unemployment.

Key Words: unemployment, job loss, families, children, marriage, relationship quality, financial strain, identity, roles

Introduction

The detrimental outcomes of job loss and unemployment on individuals are well documented (e.g., Feather, this volume; McKee-Ryan, Song, Wanberg, & Kinicki, 2005; Paul, Hassel, & Moser, this volume; Paul & Moser, 2009). The effects of the unemployment experience also extend to others close to the unemployed worker, notably his or her spouse or significant other, child or children, and families (e.g., Ström, 2003). The impact of job loss and unemployment on the family has been recognized since the 1930s, beginning with research conducted by Jahoda and by Bakke (see Feather, this volume, for a review). Coming out of the global recession that began in 2007, millions of families in the United States and around the world are affected by unemployment. In fact the percentage of families with at least one unemployed member nearly doubled in just four years (Bureau of Labor Statistics, 2011). Moreover, the jobs recovery tends

to lag other economic indicators as the broader economy recovers (Summers, 2010). During previous recessions, the unemployment rate among families declined more slowly than the unemployment rate in general (cf. Gray, Edwards, Hayes, & Baxter, 2009).

Yet the effects of job loss and unemployment on families are relatively understudied, primarily because families are complex systems and the effects of unemployment are difficult to tease out from the myriad influences on families and family members' well-being (cf. Strom, 2003). Evidence for negative effects of unemployment on spouses, children, and families is accumulating (cf. Lobo & Watkins, 1995; Strom, 2003), but the causal mechanism through which unemployment operates to affect families is not well understood. Price, Choi, and Vinokur (2002; see also Price & Vinokur, this volume, for a summary of the JOBS intervention program) note that job loss and unemployment can "trigger a cascade" of secondary stressors for the unemployed worker. These additional stressors also affect families. This cascade results in complex models of the effects of unemployment on families. Rather than studying these effects with a particular theoretical lens, researchers tend to employ one or more of the following perspectives to explain how unemployment affects families, as summarized in Figure 5.1. Research has focused on (1) the financial or economic stressors and strain brought about by job loss, (2) the direct, crossover and relationship quality effects of stress and reduced mental health among unemployed workers and their spouses, (3) the cascade of stressors brought about by job loss, (4) protective personal and family resources for coping with job loss, and (5) social family roles and the identity of the unemployed worker. As noted, research tends to examine multiple perspectives simultaneously and there is no clear research paradigm guiding this research, although most research reflects studies of unemployment as a major life stressor and invokes stress and coping models for individuals and families (cf. Lazarus & Folkman, 1984). The goal of this chapter is to provide a high-level overview of research on the spouse and family effects of unemployment. We first summarize pathways through which unemployment affects spouses and families (see Figure 5.1) and then review research on the more specific effects of unemployment on children. It should be noted that we focus more narrowly on workers who have lost their jobs and have been unemployed for less than two years. This focus is necessary because as unemployment becomes chronic and long-term, the effects of unemployment on families become more entangled with the effects of poverty more generally.

Job loss and/or reduced hours generally lead to a reduction in household income, for which families may or may not be prepared. Agency restriction theory (Fryer, 1986) highlights the role of income as a manifest (versus latent) benefit of employment, noting that the detrimental effects unemployment arise from the restricted ability of unemployed workers to control and organize their lives and lifestyles because of the lack of economic resources. Although unemployment insurance (UI) provides some relief, UI typically does not replace the unemployed worker's former salary. Reductions in household income can affect the family and its ability to make rent or mortgage payments; buy food and other necessities; or have disposable income for extracurricular activities, hobbies, and entertainment. It may also result in the loss of health insurance benefits and access to medical care. UI compensation provides a limited protective effect on the detrimental outcomes of unemployment (cf. Artazcoz, Benach, Borrell, & Cortes, 2004); single-parent families in particular are likely to face considerable distress due to unemployment (Gray et al., 2009). Two-income families may experience lesser effects, since the likelihood of both members becoming unemployed at the same time is lower; however, these families are also likely to be dependent on both incomes. While some households have "emergency

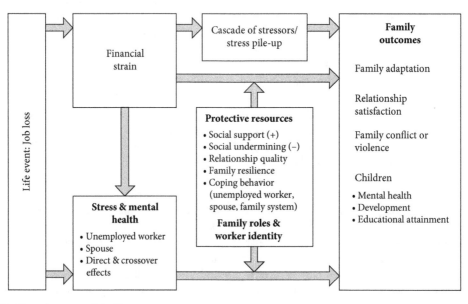

Figure 5.1 Unemployment and families.

funds" in the form of savings or investments, many face an immediate financial crisis from unemployment. For example, Anong and DeVany (2010) found that only 1 in 12 households have at least six months of living expenses available in liquid assets. They further report that larger households were less likely to have emergency funds available, and that workers employed in industries likely to be adversely affected by a recession were unlikely to have emergency funds saved up.

The inability to pay bills or meet expenses is called economic or financial distress, strain, or hardship and seems to affect outcomes more strongly than absolute levels of financial resources (McKee-Ryan et al., 2005). Economic hardship leads to increased depression and anxiety for both unemployed workers and their spouses (e.g., Creed & Klisch, 2005; Price et al., 2002; Vosler & Page-Adams, 1996; Weckström, 2012; Westman et al., 2004). Economic hardship also affects marital adjustment negatively (e.g., with less agreement on major decisions, more conflict, and reduced engagement in outside interests) for both husbands and wives, both directly and through psychological distress (Kinnunen & Feldt, 2004). This sequence of events was also linked to a higher probability of divorce (Conger et al., 1990). Among a sample of Asian couples, economic hardship affected marital roles (the way household tasks, child-care responsibilities, and earned income were shared) and psychological well-being but not social support or family relations (Ishii-Kuntz, Gomel, Tinsley, & Parke, 2010). In a sample of newlywed couples, stressful events (including job loss) and facing financial strain were related to increased negativity among both husbands and wives (Williamson, Karney, & Bradbury, 2013). Having a negative future outlook partially mediated the relationship between economic hardship and psychological well-being (Creed & Klisch, 2005). Moreover, reduced access to material resources affects children's well-being (Lempers, Clark-Lempers, & Simons, 1989). The new jobs obtained after a spell of unemployment often lead to underemployment or jobs that are of lower quality, including either working for less pay or in a short-term, part-time, or contract position (Feldman, 1996; McKee-Ryan & Harvey, 2011; Virick & McKee-Ryan, this volume). Insecure employment (for contract employees) was also associated with increased financial strain, work-family conflict, and disagreements with partners, along with decreased life satisfaction and physical health (Probst, Jiang, & Benson, this volume;

Scherer, 2009). Hence underemployment also affects couples and families adversely.

Economic strain is both a help and a hindrance to becoming reemployed: Financial hardship serves to motivate the job seeker, on one hand, but the depressive symptoms brought about by economic strain also inhibit job-search behavior (Vinokur & Schul, 2002). Kanfer, Wanberg, and Kantrowitz's (2001) meta-analysis demonstrated a significant positive effect of financial need on job search ($r_c = .21$) yet a negative link to later employment status ($r_c = -.11$). However, financial need was also associated with a shorter duration of unemployment ($r_c = -.07$), suggesting that people in financial need may settle for whatever job comes along first. UI and other forms of short-term income replacement (e.g., stop-gap jobs, part-time or contract work) often fail to alleviate the financial hardship brought about by job loss (McKee-Ryan & Harvey, 2011; Scherer, 2009), and the family continues to be adversely affected.

In sum, the economic strain or hardship brought about by job loss and unemployment is associated with detrimental effects on unemployed workers and their families. Economic hardship is often conceptualized as a mediator between unemployment and detrimental outcomes or as the first step in a causal chain for a host of additional stressors and negative effects (e.g., Price et al., 2002).

Stress and Mental Health—Direct, Crossover, and Relationship Quality Effects

A majority of the studies examining how the unemployment of one spouse affects the well-being of the other indicate that there is a negative association between one spouse's unemployment and the other spouse's well-being (e.g., Giatti et al., 2008; Strom, 2003; Whelan, 1992). However, the relationship is not clear cut because the partner's well-being, the role of financial strain, and other mediating and moderating factors may play a role. Thus the exact causal mechanism through which this occurs is not known. In particular, job loss and unemployment can affect couples in three ways: (1) by experiencing common stressors, (2) by transmitting stress to the other partner, or (3) in declining relationship quality among the partners.

Howe, Levy, and Caplan (2004) tested these three competing models of how job loss affects couples. Results indicated that all three models were supported by the data, leading the team to suggest that the stress of job loss and unemployment accumulates over time in a chain, whereby common stressors are experienced by both partners who each transmit stress to the other, ultimately affecting the quality of the relationship. Kinnunen and Feldt (2004) found that economic strain and psychological distress affected marital adjustment for husbands and wives negatively, but only the husband's length of unemployment affected wife's relationship quality. There were no other significant crossover paths. Westman et al. (2004) found both a contemporaneous and a cross-lagged effect of spouses' anxiety on each other in a sample of unemployed workers and their spouses. Their results also supported the common stressor model, whereby the economic hardship created by job loss affects both unemployed workers and their spouses.

More recently, Song, Foo, Uy, and Sun (2011) looked at the distress experienced by unemployed workers and their working spouses in China to examine the direct crossover of stressors (stress of one spouse demonstrating a correlation with strain for the other spouse), indirect or mediating crossover (through marital support), and the domain stressor (work stress for employed workers and unemployment stress for unemployed workers) model. Results supported the direct crossover model and further revealed that financial strain and job search contributed to the daily distress of unemployed workers, while work-family and family-work conflict, but not work stress, were linked to increased distress for employed spouses. Similar to Westman et al. (2004), the mediating model of marital support buffering the effects of stressors on distress was not supported. Interestingly, the unemployed worker may or may not accurately assess the effect of unemployment of spouses and children. In a sample of unemployed workers in Finland, only one third indicated that job loss had negatively affected spouses and children (Weckström, 2012).

Cascade of Stressors

As mentioned previously, losing a job often leads to a cascade of additional stressors: financial strain, lifestyle changes, a move to less expensive housing, and disruption of social relationships are all possible outcomes. Job loss can throw a family into crisis mode, and this crisis can allow additional stresses to "pile up" on the family. This process is explained by the double ABCX model, formulated by McCubbin and Patterson (1983).

McCubbin and Patterson describe the process by which families interpret a stressful event and subsequently adjust and adapt. The first step is to identify the *stressor* (A)—the life event or transition that may cause a change in the family's structure (e.g., job loss)—and the stressors' associated *hardships*—the demands on the family that result from the stressor (e.g., financial strain). Next is an assessment of the *resources* (B) that the family possesses for dealing with the stressor. Taken together, these factors result in the *subjective meaning* (C) of the event to the family, or an appraisal of the significance of the event. *Family stress* occurs when family members perceive that the demands outweigh the resources available and that change is needed, leading to identification of a *crisis* (X) that must be addressed by the family system (though not necessarily labeled as a crisis by the family).

As the family addresses the initial stressor and the resulting crisis, additional cascading stressors arise, labeled aA by McCubbin and Patterson (1983). For example, when a primary breadwinner in a family is laid off from his/her job (A), a formerly nonworking spouse may have to return to the workforce (aA). The family system now has two major stressors to address. This is called a "pile up" of stressors. The family system is now addressing the second stressor before the first stressor had been resolved and a new equilibrium reached. In addition, the family may experience additional daily hassles or microstressors resulting from unemployment. While not additional major stressors, these hassles also require resources. The family then assesses its resources (bB), as resources may have been expended or new resources may have been identified over time. The family then interprets the events for subjective meaning (cC). Reframing the situation as a challenge or opportunity is a useful approach for families. In this stage, families need to clarify the issues and hardships so they can be addressed, recognize and affirm emotional responses, and focus on the family unit as a continued source of emotional and social development for family members (McCubbin & Patterson, 1983).

This discussion highlights the fact that addressing the primary and subsequent stressors is a process that evolves over time, and that the process is dynamic and somewhat unpredictable. Families simultaneously address multiple stressors while working to resolve the family disruption. However, the goal of this coping process may not be to return to the prestressor state within the family but to adapt as a family to a new equilibrium. Successful adaptation occurs when there is a balance between individual family members' needs and the family system, when there is a sense of coherence (balancing control and trust) within the family, and when the family appropriately fits in with its community and context (McCubbin & Patterson, 1983).

Protective Resources for Coping with Job Loss—Social Support, Social Undermining, and Family Resilience

Being married or in a committed relationship seems to provide a protective effect on the mental health and well-being of unemployed workers, as unmarried unemployed workers fare worse than their married counterparts on outcomes such as somatic complaints, depression and anxiety, and life satisfaction (e.g., Hamilton, Broman, Hoffman, & Renner, 1990; Leana & Feldman, 1991; Weckström, 2012). Among unemployed workers, lacking social support is linked to facing greater problem severity and the use of avoidance coping (Walsh & Jackson, 1995) as well as increased illness (Schwarzer, Jerusalem, & Hahn, 1994), psychosomatic symptoms (Viinamäki, Koskela, & Niskanen, 1993), distress (Gowan, Riordan, & Gatewood, 1999), and depression (Vinokur et al., 1996; Vosler & Page-Adams, 1996). Preexisting family relations or problems also influence spousal well-being during unemployment (e.g., Liem & Liem, 1988; Lobo & Watkins, 1995). For example, couples whose relationships are marked by dysfunctional conflict and fighting or who are prone to negative communication patterns may find that unemployment exacerbates conflict and strife within their relationships.

Spouses and families affect the coping behaviors of the unemployed worker by providing or withholding social support as a protective resource for the stress accompanying job loss (Conger, Rueter, & Elder, 1999; Kinicki et al., 2000). Spouses can also undermine the job seeker (e.g., Vinokur, Price, & Caplan, 1996; Vinokur & van Ryn, 1993). Social support includes providing encouragement, listening and making the unemployed worker feel cared for, building the worker's self-confidence, and helping with job search. Social undermining, in contrast, entails criticism, insults, angry or disdainful communication, and getting on the nerves of the job seeker. Thus the presence of a spouse or partner does not automatically make life better for unemployed workers but depends on the degree to which the spouse behaves in a way that increases the efficacy of the job seeker by providing emotional and practical support. Those closest to the unemployed worker may also be detrimental to the job seeker, undermining his or her confidence and providing an additional source of stress.

An interview study of male job losers and their families highlighted that the emotions experienced by the job seeker as he negotiated the search process affected his spouse and children, that the emotions of the job seeker and his spouse influenced each other, and that the family worked to regain a sense of normalcy after job loss (Buzzanell & Turner, 2003). In a sample of middle-aged Chinese men, worsened mental health was reported by unemployed men with lowered household income; they quarreled with their wives and expressed anger to their families. Interestingly, unemployed men were less likely to display lowered mental health when their family members grumbled at them regarding their job loss and when they felt less sorry for the family for their unemployment (Chiu & Ho, 2006), thus highlighting the complex relationships between family variables and the effects of unemployment.

Research focusing on families and their adaptation to short-term challenges and longer-term crises also highlights the role of family resilience (e.g., Walsh, 2003) in the process of coping with job loss and unemployment. Walsh (2003) defines resilience as the ability to withstand and rebound from disruptive life challenges and notes that family resilience derives from effective family functioning within the family unit rather than from a collection of resilient individuals within the family. Hallmarks of resilient families are found within (1) the family belief system, (2) the organizational patterns within the family, and (3) the communication and problem solving used within the family. For the family belief system, families tend to fare better when they make meaning out of their adversity and cognitively reframe it as a challenge to be faced by the family, maintain a positive and optimistic outlook, and view the situation in a transcendent or spiritual way, looking for the opportunity to grow and change from the experience. For organizational patterns, resilient families tend to be flexible and adaptable, to seek interconnectedness with each other while respecting personal boundaries, and to build social and financial resources they can mobilize to deal with stressors or crises. For communication and problem solving, resilience derives from clear communication, sharing emotions and empathizing with one another, and working together to collaboratively solve problems. Walsh further notes that the life stage of the family affects resilience and coping patterns; for example, coping with unemployment is different for families with young children in the home versus those with high school or college-aged children.

Taken together, research highlights the importance of resources for the unemployed worker and his or her family in coping with job loss and unemployment. Specifically, the worker and his or her spouse can support or undermine one another; family resilience leads to more positive outcomes for the family; and support from friends, relatives, and the broader community can provide another resource for families coping with unemployment.

Unemployed Workers' Identities and Family Roles

Job loss also has the potential to affect the unemployed worker's sense of self and his or her identity (e.g., Buzzanell & Turner, 2003; Van Vianen & Klehe, this volume). Because work is such an integral and important aspect of life, unemployment can significantly alter the roles one fulfills both at work and at home. Identity theory suggests that the more central a role is to the person's sense of self or identity, the greater the potential impact of the loss of that role (e.g., Ashforth, 2001; Thoits, 1995). The damaging effect of role loss—without the potential confound of financial impact—was demonstrated by Schlenker and Gutek (1987). These researchers followed two groups of social workers as one group was demoted to a lower status position (e.g., the role loss group) while the other served as a control with no status change. Results revealed that the role-loss/demoted social workers displayed lower self-esteem, job satisfaction, and life satisfaction and increased intention to quit relative to the control group. However, these demoted workers maintained both professional involvement and identification as social workers. The researchers thus concluded that the loss of an important role and the resulting hit to the ego experienced by this group of professionals had contributed to the detrimental outcomes. It is important to note that these effects occurred independently of financial impacts, as there was only a status change and not a loss of income among the workers.

In the context of job loss and unemployment, however, multiple roles are lost, damaged, changed, or added simultaneously and, generally speaking, very quickly. Losing a job can mean losing one's career role identity as a worker, professional (e.g., CPA, construction worker, etc.), or industry member, but it can also affect family or household role identities, such as breadwinner or financial supporter, and shift them to other roles that are deemed to be of lower status or less important (as subjectively determined), such as child-care provider or homemaker. Such identity and role changes also potentially create subtle and overt shifts in the power dynamics of a household.

Hence job loss can affect family structures, but family members may not be aware of the extent of the changes (Lara & Kindsvatter, 2010). For example, the proportion of domestic duties completed by men and women may shift and be different than among working spouses (Strom, 2003). Because a newly unemployed worker is now home at different times, for example, chores and roles may shift. This type of adaptation may be unplanned and result in family members being "out of sorts" with each other without consciously knowing the root cause of their unhappiness or shifted roles. As mentioned, unemployment can also affect the power balance in a family, particularly when the "breadwinner" becomes unemployed.

Moreover, job loss can be emasculating and require men to reconconstruct their masculine identities (Buzzanell & Turner, 2003; Sherman, 2009) and roles (Chiu & Ho, 2006). Sherman's (2009) ethnographic study of rural couples affected by the loss of jobs due to the main employer leaving town identified two very different adaptations to job loss. First, couples that adhered to strict gender roles and masculine identities she labeled "rigid." Second, adaptive couples in which the male renegotiated a sense of male success and achievement away from breadwinner and toward good parent were labeled "flexible." The detrimental effects of unemployment—increased marital discord, seasonal and out of town work, controlling and violent behavior toward one's spouse, and drug use—tended to be concentrated among the rigid couples. At the opposite end of the spectrum, among a sample of unmarried fathers, identifying oneself as a father influenced both getting and keeping a job and being involved in his child's life (Cabrera, Fagan, & Farrie, 2008).

Although not causally connected, this identity reconstruction may also be at play in terms of family conflict and violence. Unemployment was linked to increased male-to-female partner violence among couples, including a male construction industry worker (Cunradi, Todd, Duke & Ames, 2009). Problem drinking was also a predictor of partner violence, but it did not exacerbate the effects of unemployment. Violent behavior (male-to-female) was increased only when current unemployment was considered, not as a result of several jobless spells, leading the researchers to posit that the acute stress of joblessness prompted the violent actions of males. Qualitative research suggests that anger and frustration from the daily experience of being unemployed plays out in men's aggressive or violent behavior toward their spouses (e.g., Sherman, 2009).

Interestingly, a different pattern of violence emerged when longer-term unemployment was considered. Among long-term unemployed male construction industry workers and their wives, female-to-male partner violence increased (Cunradi et al., 2009). These authors speculate that this partner violence stems from the accumulated stress of unemployment spells. If these men held traditional gender-role attitudes, they may have been less likely to adapt to new family roles, such as performing "women's work" and helping out with household chores, as they were habituated to long-term unemployment, leaving their spouses the double burden of being the breadwinners and performing household chores (e.g., Sherman, 2009). Longer-term unemployment on the part of the husband was also negatively related to the wife's marital satisfaction (Kinnunen & Feldt, 2004), suggesting that wives also have role expectations for their husbands that may be affected by unemployment.

Male Versus Female Unemployment: Same or Different?

The various and often gender-specific family roles typically engaged by men and women lead to the question of whether the genders experience unemployment in a similar manner. For example, although unemployment may be seen as more "acceptable" among women than among men, research on gendered response to unemployment is mixed (e.g., Strom, 2003). Artazcoz, Benach, Borrell, and Cortes (2004) explored gender and family role differences in mental health among employed and unemployed workers in Spain. Results revealed no gender differences among single workers but demonstrated less negative effects of unemployment for women, particularly those with children at home, than for their male counterparts. These authors note that gender, family roles, and employment type (manual versus nonmanual work) moderate the relationship between unemployment and mental health. Unemployed workers in Sweden reported lower levels of overall quality of life; educational level was associated with higher quality of life for employed but not unemployed workers. Gender differences demonstrated that unemployed women reported higher existential meaning and men

reported lower general life satisfaction (Hultman, Hemlin, & Hornquist, 2006).

Song et al. (2011), in their study in China, found a significant three-way interaction between gender, marital satisfaction, and distress among families with an unemployed spouse. Specifically, there were greater stress crossover effects for working women's husbands when they were satisfied with their marriages but lesser crossover for from working husbands to their wives in low-satisfaction marriages. The authors note that male workers tend to protect their families from work stressors, while female workers are more likely to integrate home and work domains. Westman et al. (2004) found no significant gender differences in the crossover effects of state anxiety among unemployed workers and their spouses. They note that gender effects are less likely among dual-earner professional couples. Thus there is no clear and consistent pattern of gender differences or similarities in response to job loss and unemployment. Future research is warranted, particularly since gender roles continue to shift as new generations enter the workforce (e.g., Strom, 2003) and as women begin to reshape their identities to simultaneously negotiate professional and parental roles rather than experiencing them as oppositional identities (Hodges & Park, 2013).

Family Outcomes of Unemployment

The previous sections summarized research on couples and families coping with unemployment. Among these outcomes are family adaptation, satisfaction with marital and family relationships, and family conflict and violence in addition to the individual effects on unemployed workers and their spouses. We now turn our attention to research that specifically focused on the effects of unemployment on children living within the home of an unemployed parent.

Effects of Unemployment on Children

Strom's (2003) review revealed a negative effect of unemployment on children, including negative effects on both health and educational attainment. In the following section, we summarize recent research on the effects of unemployment on children, including their mental health, development, and human capital/educational attainment.

Mental Health

As noted previously, mental health is diminished among household members of unemployed workers, including children in the home. Children in unemployed households may have a disrupted sense of security or may blame themselves for a parent's job loss (Schliebner & Peregoy, 1994). The negative relationship between unemployment and mental health is additionally expected to operate through the relationships between parents and children and the quality of parenting among unemployed workers (e.g., Strom, 2003). For example, unemployment is a risk factor for child maltreatment and neglect (cf. Euser et al., 2010). Among Dutch children, emotional and behavioral problems were more likely for children of unemployed workers. These problems were most pronounced among children with a parent who lost his or her job within the preceding 12 months versus those with more distant unemployment experiences (Harland et al., 2002). In a sample of 1,992 adolescents in Slovakia, parental support from the employed parent displayed a protective effect on adolescents' perceived health but parental support from the unemployed parent did not (Bacikova-Sleskova, Geckova, van Dijk, Groothoff & Reijneveld, 2011). The authors note that the unemployed parent's stress may inhibit the effectiveness of his or her support for children.

Child Development

Job loss affects child development (Kalil, 2009). Children from economically disadvantaged families, characterized by low-income jobs and unemployment, displayed poorer early learning. The effect was more pronounced for boys and was expected to accumulate over time and become more pronounced as the children grew and developed (Mensah & Kiernan, 2010). In Germany, rates of stillbirth were higher for unemployed workers and homemakers than for professionally employed workers (Reime et al., 2008). The authors note that this may be due to lack of economic resources, lack of social support from professional networks, a covariation with educational status, or poor health and risk behaviors. Access to prenatal care was available for the sample regardless of socioeconomic status. Unger, Hamilton, and Sussman (2004) found that adolescents were significantly more likely to try smoking for the first time after a family member lost a job.

Educational Attainment/Human Capital Attainment

Stevens and Schaller's (2011) analysis of US Census Bureau data showed that children were more likely to have to repeat a grade following a parental job loss. The timing of this increased likelihood suggests a causal relationship, and the authors posit that the shock of job loss contributes to school difficulties. Kalil and Wightman (2011) also showed that parental unemployment is significantly negatively related to children pursuing postsecondary education, and that this effect is three times stronger for Black than for White families. A study across 17 countries found a negative relationship between father's unemployment and children's literacy. However, contrary to expectations, UI levels in the given country did not lessen the effect of unemployment in this prospective study (Siddiqi et al., 2007). Children who grow up in jobless families may also lack role modeling for healthy work attitudes of the responsibility and self-discipline required for career success (Brown, 2009).

As with spouses, unemployment affects children negatively through complex causal mechanisms. Future research is needed to examine complex models, using large samples and longitudinal analyses. There is a strong need to disentangle the independent effects of unemployment from low income and poverty more generally in order to examine the effect of unemployment on children. In particular, among other potential explanations, the detrimental effects on children may arise from a lack of material resources, increased harsh parenting or family violence, the emotional unavailability of a parent who has been adversely affected by unemployment, poor communication between parent and child, and a lack of quality parenting, or "learned helplessness" on the part of children who do not perceive value in pursuing academic goals because labor force opportunities are not available,.

Conclusion

Our review of the literature reveals that the impact of unemployment ripples out to adversely affect spouses and families. Future research is warranted to unravel the effects of unemployment on spouses and families of unemployed workers, and the reciprocal effects on the unemployed worker. Based on this review, we offer the following suggestions for future research on unemployment and families: First, conduct studies with longitudinal designs. In particular, longer periods of time and more frequent time intervals are needed to obtain a better understanding of the coping strategies, consequences, and adjustments to unemployment that are made by individuals and families. Studies that follow individuals into and out of unemployment would also be helpful. In addition, long-term follow-up studies would elucidate the extent to which families and individuals are able to overcome the obstacle of unemployment in the near and long term. This type of research would allow an examination of the extent to which the effects of unemployment are more contemporaneous, additive, or permanent for families with an unemployed worker.

Second, studies with large heterogeneous samples in terms of gender, age, and job classification would be desirable. As the landscape of unemployed workers shifts to include more women, more highly educated workers, and older individuals, exploring the psychological and situational variables that might explain the differences and similarities between the groups (e.g., men and women) will become even more critical.

Third, future research should also investigate the life stage of the family of the unemployed worker in terms of early marriage, young children in the home, older children in the home and/or in college, and the stage of the "empty nest." The very limited research in this area suggests that coping with unemployment varies across life stages.

Fourth, the effects of unemployment during and after a major economic downturn should be investigated. For example, Gray et al. (2009) summarize the major effects of recessions on families as occurring primarily through the effects of unemployment and reduced working hours on the subsequent and corresponding reduction in income. They note that unemployment increases quickly during a recession and employment grows slowly during the recovery. They further note that families are also likely to face declining asset values, the concentration of disadvantage in particular geographic regions, and increased uncertainty and worry about the future. Beyond the direct effect of unemployment on families, families can also be indirectly affected by diminished job opportunities for young people, delayed retirements and reentry of retirees into the labor market, a decreased likelihood of engaging in a committed relationship, lowered fertility, and decreased quality of child care.

Finally, research should employ more complex, moderated, and mediated models of families' adjustment to unemployment. For example, both financial strain and parental well-being are expected to mediate the unemployment experience of families. These more complex models, coupled with longitudinal research designs such as multiwave or diary studies, will help to unravel the mechanisms through which unemployment affects individuals and families.

Research in these key areas will help focus future interventions targeted at minimizing the detrimental effects of unemployment on families. This focus will simultaneously reduce the cost of designing and implementing such interventions and increase the benefits to individuals and families. Key takeaways are as follows:

• Unemployment affects the unemployed worker, his or her partner or spouse, and other household members in addition to disrupting the family system.

• Unemployment may trigger a cascade of additional stressors to the family system that need to be addressed simultaneously. Among these stressors is the possibility of changed family roles and power dynamics.

• Family members and spouses need to recognize that the experience of unemployment is stressful for the job seeker and that their interaction with him or her can help or hinder the process of becoming reemployed. In particular, family members can bolster the self-confidence of the job seeker, provide practical advice and support for job seeking, and help the job seeker stay actively involved in the job-search process. Although families may experience financial distress, reminding the job seeker of the financial shortfall and the need for reemployment can inhibit rather than encourage reemployment.

• Unemployed workers need to remain emotionally involved with their family members. Although being unemployed typically means that the unemployed worker will be at home and physically present more often, that does not automatically translate into being emotionally present for family members.

• Children in the home may need reassurance from parents relating to (1) the fact that the child was not responsible for job loss, (2) making the child feel secure and reminding the child that the world remains a safe place, and (3) modeling work behavior and positive attitudes toward work so that the child maintains positive expectations about future employment opportunities and continues to see the importance of investing effort in educational pursuits.

References

Anong, S. T., & DeVaney, S. A. (2010). Determinants of adequate emergency funds including the effects of seeking professional advice and industry affiliation. *Family & Consumer Sciences Research Journal*, 38, 405–419.

Ashforth, B. E. (2001). *Role transitions in organizational life: An identity-based perspective*. Mahwah, NJ: Erlbaum.

Artazcoz, L., Benach, J., Borrell, C., & Cortes, I. (2004).Unemployment and mental health: Understanding the interactions among gender, family roles, and social class. *American Journal of Public Health*, 94, 82–88.

Bacikova-Sleskova, M., Geckova, A., van Dijk, J. P., Groothoff, J. W., & Reijneveld, S. A. (2011). Parental support and adolescents' health in the context of parental employment status. *Journal of Adolescence*, 34(1), 141–149.

Brown, J. (2009). Jobless families in a recession. *Policy*, 25(2), 5–8.

Bureau of Labor Statistics. (March 24, 2011). Employment characteristics of families—2010. News release, USDL-11-0396.

Buzzanell, P. M., & Turner, L. H. (2003). Emotion work revealed by job loss discourse: Foregrounding of feelings, construction of normalcy, and (re)instituting of traditional masculinities. *Journal of Applied Communication Research*, 3, 27–57.

Cabrera, N. J., Fagan, J., & Farrie, D. (2008). Explaining the Long Reach of Fathers' Prenatal Involvement on Later Paternal Engagement. *Journal of Marriage and Family*, 70,1094-1107.

Chiu, M.Y.L., & Ho, W.W.N. (2006). Family relations and mental health of unemployed middle-aged Chinese men. *Journal of Mental Health*, 15, 191–203.

Conger, R. D., Elder, G. H. Jr., Lorenz, F. O., Conger, K. J., Simons, R. L., Whitbeck, L. B., . . . Melby, J. N. (1990). Linking economic hardship to marital quality and instability. *Journal of Marriage and the Family*, 52, 643–656.

Conger, R. D., Rueter, M. A., & Elder, G. H. Jr. (1999). Couple resilience to economic pressure. *Journal of Personality & Social Psychology*, 76(1), 54–71.

Creed, P. A. & Klisch, J. (2005). Future outlook and financial strain: Testing the personal agency and latent deprivation models of unemployment and well-being. *Journal of Occupational Health Psychology*, 10, 251–260

Cunradi, C., Todd, M., Duke, M., & Ames, G. (2009). Problem drinking, unemployment, and intimate partner violence among a sample of construction industry workers and their partners. *Journal of Family Violence*, 24(2), 63–74.

Fryer, D. (1986). Employment deprivation and personal agency during unemployment: A critical discussion of Jahoda's explanation of the psychological effects of unemployment. *Social Behaviour*, 1, 3–23.

Giatti, L., Barreto, S. M., Comini Cesar, C. (2008). Household context and self-rated health: the effect of unemployment and informal work. *Journal of Epidemiology & Community Health*, 62, 1079–1085.

Gowan, M. A., Riordan, C. M., & Gatewood, R. D. (1999). Test of a model of coping with involuntary job loss following a company closing. *Journal of Applied Psychology*, 84, 75–86.

Gray, M., Edwards, B., Hayes, A., & Baxter, J. (2009). The impacts of recessions on families. *Family Matters*, 83, 7–14.

Hamilton, V. L., Broman, C.L., Hoffman, W.S., & Renner, D. S. (1990). Hard times and vulnerable people: Initial effects of plant closing on autoworkers' mental health. *Journal of Health and Social Behavior*, 31, 123–140.

Harland, P., Reijneveld, S. A., Brugman, E., Verloove-Vanhorick, S. P., & Verhulst, F. C. (2002). Family factors and life events as risk factors for behavioural and emotional problems in children. *European Child & Adolescent Psychiatry*, 11, 176–184.

Hodges, A. J., & Park, B. (2013). Oppositional identities: Dissimilarities in how women and men experience parent versus professional roles. *Journal of Personality and Social Psychology*, 105, 193-216.

Howe, G. W., Levy, M. L., & Caplan, R. D. (2004). Job loss and depressive symptoms in couples: Common stressors, stress transmission, or relationship disruption? *Journal of Family Psychology*, 18, 639–650.

Hultman, B., Hemlin, S., & Hornquist, J. O. (2006). Quality of life among unemployed and employed people in northern Sweden. Are there any differences? *Work*, 26, 47–56.

Ishii-Kuntz, M., Gomel, J.N., Tinsley, B. J., & Parke, R. D. (2010). Economic hardship and adaptation among Asian American families. *Journal of Family Issues*, 31, 407–420.

Kalil, A. (2009). Joblessness, family relations and children's development. *Family Matters*, 83, 15–22.

Kalil, A., & Wightman, P. (2011). Parental job loss and children's educational attainment in black and white middle-class families. *Social Science Quarterly*, 92, 57–78.

Kanfer, R., Wanberg, C. R., & Kantrowitz, T. M. (2001). Job search and employment: A personality–motivational analysis and meta-analytic review. *Journal of Applied Psychology*, 86, 837–855.

Kinicki, A. J., Prussia, G. E., & McKee-Ryan, F. M. (2000). A panel study of coping with involuntary job loss. *Academy of Management Journal*, 43, 90–100.

Kinnunen, U., & Feldt, T. (2004). Economic stress and marital adjustment among couples: analyses at the dyadic level. *European Journal of Social Psychology*, 34, 519–532

Lara, T., & Kindsvatter, A. (2010). A structural approach to assisting families recovering from job loss. *The Family Journal*, 18(4), 344–348.

Lazarus, R. S., & Folkman, S. (1984). *Stress, appraisal, and coping*. New York: Springer.

Leana, C. R., & Feldman, D. C. (1991). Gender differences in responses to unemployment. *Journal of Vocational Behavior*, 38, 65-77.

Lempers, J. D., Clark-Lempers, D., & Simons, R. L. (1989). Economic hardship, parenting, and distress in adolescence. *Child Development*, 60, 25–39.

Liem, R., & Liem, J. H. (1988). Psychological effects of unemployment on workers and their families. *Journal of Social Issues*, 44(4), 87–105.

Lobo, F., & Watkins, G. (1995). Late career unemployment in the 1990s: Its impact on the family. *Journal of Family Studies*, 1(2), 103–113.

McCubbin, H. I., & Patterson, J. M. (1983). The family stress process: The double ABCX model of adjustment and adaptation. *Marriage and Family Review*, 6, 7–37.

McKee-Ryan, F. M., & Harvey, J. (2011). "I have a job, but . . . ": A review of underemployment. *Journal of Management*, 37, 962-996.

McKee-Ryan, F. M., Song, Z, Wanberg, C. R., & Kinicki, A. J. (2005). Psychological and physical well-being during unemployment: A meta-analytic study. *Journal of Applied Psychology*, 90, 53–76.

Mensah, F. K., & Kiernan, K. E. (2010). Gender differences in educational attainment: Influences of the family environment. *British Educational Research Journal*, 36, 239–260.

Paul, K. I., & Moser, K. (2009). Unemployment impairs mental health: Meta-analyses. *Journal of Vocational Behavior*, 74, 264-282.

Price, R. H., Choi, J., & Vinokur, A. D. (2002). Links in the chain of adversity following job loss: How financial strain and loss of personal control lead to depression, impaired functioning, and poor health. *Journal of Occupational Health Psychology*, 7(4), 302–312.

Reime, B., Jacob, C., & Wenzlaff, P. (2009). Is parental unemployment related to an increased risk for stillbirths? *Journal of Public Health*, 17, 363–369.

Scherer, S. (2009). The social consequences of insecure jobs. *Social Indicators Research*, 93, 527–547.

Schlenker, J. A., & Gutek, B. A. (1987). Effects of role loss on work-related attitudes. *Journal of Applied Psychology*, 72, 287–293.

Schliebner, C. T., & Peregoy, J. J. (1994). Unemployment effects on the family and the child: Interventions for counselors. *Journal of Counseling & Development*, 72(4), 368–372.

Schwarzer, R., Jerusalem, M., & Hahn, A. (1994). Unemployment, social support and health complaints: A longitudinal study of stress in East German refugees. *Journal of Community and Applied Social Psychology*, 4, 31–45.

Sherman, J. (2009). Bend to avoid breaking: Job loss, gender norms, and family stability in rural America. *Social Problems*, 56, 599–620.

Song, Z., Foo, M.-D., Uy, M. A., & Sun, S. (2011). Unraveling the daily stress crossover between unemployed individuals and their employed spouses. *Journal of Applied Psychology*, 96, 151–168.

Siddiqi, A., Subramanian, S. V., Berkman, L., Hertzman, C., & Kawachi, I. (2007). The welfare state as a context for children's development: A study of the effects of unemployment and unemployment protection on reading literacy scores. *International Journal of Social Welfare*, 16, 314–325.

Stevens, A. H. & Schaller, J. (2011). Short-run effects of parental job loss on children's academic achievement, *Economics of Education Review*, 30, 289–299.

Ström, S. (2003). Unemployment and families: A review of research. *Social Service Review*, 77(3), 399.

Thoits, P. A. (1995). Identity-relevant events and psychological symptoms: A cautionary tale. *Journal of Health and Social Behavior*, 36, 72–82.

Unger, J. B., Hamilton, J. E., & Sussman, S. (2004). A family member's job loss as a risk factor for smoking among adolescents. *Health Psychology*, 23, 308–313.

Viinamäki, H., Koskela, K., & Niskanen, L. (1993). The impact of unemployment on psychosomatic symptoms and mental well-being. *International Journal of Social Psychiatry*, 39, 266–273.

Vinokur, A. D., Price, R. H., & Caplan, R. D. (1996). Hard times and hurtful partners, how financial strain affects depression and relationship satisfaction of unemployed persons and their spouses. *Journal of Personality and Social Psychology*, 71, 166–179.

Vinokur, A. D., & Schul, Y. (2002). The web of coping resources and pathways to reemployment following a job loss. *Journal of Occupational Health Psychology*, 7(1), 68–83.

Vinokur, A. D., & van Ryn, M. (1993). Social support and undermining in close relationships, their independent effects on the mental health of unemployed persons. *Journal of Personality and Social Psychology*, 65, 350–359.

Vosler, N. R., & Page-Adams, D. (1996). Predictors of depression among workers at the time of a plant closing. *Journal of Sociology and Social Welfare*, 23, 25–42.

Walsh, F. (2003). Family resilience: A clinical perspective. *Family Process*, 42, 1–18.

Walsh, S., & Jackson, P. R. (1995). Partner support and gender: Contexts for coping with job loss. *Journal of Occupational and Organizational Psychology*, 68, 253–268.

Weckström, S. (2012). Self-assessed consequences of unemployment on individual wellbeing and family relationships: A study of unemployed women and men in Finland. *International Journal of Social Welfare*, 21(4), 372–383.

Westman, M., Vinokur, A., Hamilton, L., & Roziner, I. (2004). Crossover of marital dissatisfaction during military downsizing among Russian army officers and their spouses. *Journal of Applied Psychology*, 89, 769–779.

Whelan, C. T. (1992). The role of income, life-style deprivation and financial strain in mediating the impact of unemployment on psychological distress: Evidence from the Republic of Ireland. *Journal of Occupational and Organizational Psychology*, 65, 331–344.

Williamson, H. C., Karney, B. R., & Bradbury, T. N. (2013). Financial strain and stressful events predict newlyweds' negative communication independent of relationship satisfaction. *Journal of Family Psychology*, 27(1), 65–75.

Unemployment and Its Wider Impact

Adrian Sinfield

Abstract

Higher unemployment affects many more people than those currently out of work. A society with unemployment remaining high for many years is very different from one providing adequate opportunities for all who want work. The lack of jobs can be a major obstacle to preventing and reducing poverty and exclusion not simply among the unemployed but also among single parents, older people, and those with disabilities. Equal opportunity programs and rehabilitation services also encounter particular difficulties. The level of unemployment has wider implications for the distribution of resources, power, and opportunity across society. But analysis and research into this wider impact remain limited. The reasons lie in part in a general shift away from structural analyses. Yet more and better understanding of the broader impact of unemployment on society may help us to take account of and respond to the experiences of those currently out of work and to the wider repercussions.

Key Words: wider unemployment, poverty, low-pay no-pay cycle, social security, stigma, inequality

Introduction

"Beyond the men and women actually unemployed at any moment, are the millions more in work at that moment but never knowing how long that work or any work for them may last" (Beveridge, 1944, pp. 247–248). This statement from the final chapter, "Full employment and social conscience," of William Beveridge's classic *Full employment in a free society* may appear obvious to any reader, but surprisingly little time has been given to considering its implications.

A society with unemployment remaining high for many years is very different from one that provides adequate opportunities for all who want work: any increase in unemployment affects many more people than those currently out of work. The level of unemployment has wider implications for the distribution of resources, power, and opportunity among different groups and classes in society. Yet nearly all the research and analysis conducted of the impact of unemployment have been on those out of work (see Paul et al., this volume, and

McKee-Ryan & Maitoza, this volume) with scant consideration to what it, or the threat of it, means to those in work or to the effects on the wider society. As a result, this chapter has to draw from sources over a considerable period of time.

The chapter examines how changing unemployment can affect the balance of power in the labor market and how the impact of this may vary across societies. The significance of higher unemployment for public and other services and the wider costs for the economy and society are discussed. The impact for different generations is also explored—those still in school, those of working age, and even after that. The final sections of the chapter consider the ways that the impact of unemployment can be modified by, for example, the effect of automatic economic and social stabilizers and the role of social security and protection in reducing the risk of poverty and exclusion, even when unemployment is high. One particularly pervasive belief that joblessness leads to crime is explored. The conclusions summarize the unequal burden of the social and economic costs of high unemployment across and within societies. While stressing that different policies can help to modify the impact, it emphasizes the value of high stable levels of employment for the sounder social development of any society.

The Balance of Power in the Labor Market

With changes in demand, the shift in the balance of power between the employer and the worker, between the employing and the working classes, is significant. The higher the unemployment, the more the balance tilts in favor of the employer: "hiring requirements tend to rise—the definition of an 'acceptable' worker is tightened up," as Lloyd Reynolds, a pioneer of labor market analysis, pointed out (Reynolds, 1951, p. 73). As a consequence, those with the least bargaining power in the labor market—such as those lacking skills and/or belonging to ethnic, religious, and other minorities—become even more vulnerable to exclusion and deprivation. The risk of low pay and poor working conditions is increased. By contrast, with lower unemployment employers may have to recruit more widely, invest more in training and recruitment, and make more adjustments to promote flexible working time that allows a "family-friendly" and better "work–life" balance for their employees.

How working relations can change after layoffs is illustrated by a Finnish national study that found the stress of increased insecurity among those that remain is likely to be exacerbated by extra work that rarely brings extra pay. "Downsizing may imply a one-sided renegotiation of the terms of the psychological contract between the organization and its employees, such that the latter (1) receive less from this relationship and (2) invest more in this relationship. Both processes may result in an imbalance between investments and rewards, which in turn may lead to lower well-being" (Kalimo, 2003, p. 9; Bambra, 2010, p. 215). This could be affected by the scale of the reductions and the broader labor market context. It is not clear if or how far the balance shifts the other way with an improvement in the labor market.

"Liability to unemployment or insecurity of tenure" is "the distinguishing feature of the proletarian estate" (G. A. Briefs, 1937, quoted in Lockwood, 1958, p. 55). This central element has clearly persisted in the United Kingdom at least: analysis over 8 years of the British Household Panel Survey showed that the two higher classes of the seven classes measured were "50% less likely to have any experience of unemployment and 75%

less likely to have 12 months or more accumulated unemployment [over the 8 years] compared to those in" the bottom two (ISER, 2002, p. 7). As Townsend showed in *Poverty in the UK*, those with unskilled jobs particularly "live in the shadow of unemployment" (Townsend, 1979, p. 601).

In societies in which this pattern persists, unemployment is not simply a "distinguishing feature" but a central element of *The hidden injuries of class* (Sennett & Cobb, 1973) that itself increases the insecurity of those more vulnerable to being out of work. "Anticipating that one will be dismissed during the next year has a quite substantial effect on worker well-being" (Kalimo, 2003, p. 9). Those in poorer-paid work with less skills are more prone to be out of work and have less resources to cope with it. For many of them unemployment is a characteristic of the job, expected and endured with greater frequency as a worker grows older or has poorer health. That experience of unemployment may itself damage health and accelerate the aging process (Bartley, Ferrie, & Montgomery, 2006).

Differences across Societies and over Time

High levels of unemployment bring "consequences so serious for the whole of society (and not just for the unemployed) that a strong case can be made for low rates of unemployment to be a national goal" was the conclusion of a pioneering study of well-being in Australia (Travers & Richardson, 1993, p. 223). A generation ago Goran Therborn examined *Why some peoples are more unemployed than others*. He called attention to the importance of a "historically deeply rooted . . . commitment to full employment" (Therborn, 1986, p. 32) leading some countries to respond to economic crises without allowing a surge in joblessness.

Differences in preventing and containing unemployment can significantly affect the ways in which unemployment impacts societies, their institutions, and their members. With the growing polarization in many labor markets across the world, the degree of commitment to full employment cross-nationally and in supranational groupings and international organizations has weakened, especially as spreading global economic and financial crises have led more governments to cut back on public spending and risk higher unemployment as growth has faltered.

The organization of the labor market in different societies is likely to affect the impact of any particular level of unemployment. Where internal labor markets have been developed with limited points of entry and greater reliance on promotion than external recruitment for most posts, the more established, skilled workers may be even better protected against loss of work whereas those unable to gain entry are left more vulnerable still to job insecurity. "The more secure are the 'ins', the greater the penalty for being an 'out'" (Kerr, 1954, p. 105). What Kerr called the "balkanization" of labor markets can become reinforced by increased unemployment, leading to wider inequalities and so reduced social mobility as the gaps between the rungs of the social ladder are widened.

This is not to argue that the maintenance of high employment by itself is sufficient to avoid problems such as these, but experience over time and across countries strongly suggests that it is a necessary requirement. Many basic social policies depend upon unemployment being kept low for their success. A comparative review of European programs to help the "hard-to-employ" led Beatrice Reubens to stress the value of low unemployment as a prerequisite for successful rehabilitation and reemployment (Reubens, 1970). "Maintenance of a high general level of economic activity has priority over improved labor market organisation . . . because it is a structural prerequisite to the latter" (Reynolds, 1951, p. 75).

The ways that society, its institutions, and its members, particularly the more powerful, regard unemployment and respond to changes in it can be critical. The fear of unemployment and its insecurity is likely to be felt differently in different societies depending not only on past experience but also on the stress they place on individual achievement and how far they believe in the openness of opportunity. The legacy of past recessions, for example, may linger for years, reinforcing resistance to change. In the United Kingdom the fear of insecurity persisted from the interwar depression into high employment years as a folk memory dominating trade union–employer relations (Burkitt & Bowers, 1979, p. 13). In the United States the interwar "depression imposed its scarcity regime and disciplines on a society accustomed to a 'politics of abundance'" (Elder, 1974, p. 284) and *The invisible scar* (Bird, 1966) was borne by many for a long time (see also Terkel, 1970; on Australia see Travers, 1986). Voting studies suggested the depression may have shaped the political views of the generations most affected for decades. Work insecurity was found to "foster a retreat from both work and the larger communal society" (Wilensky, 1961, pp. 523–524

and 539) and "can lead to a misanthropic view of society and a pessimistic view of life" (Hyman, 1979, pp. 290–293).

Some have argued that unemployment should be used as a policy tool to be increased, or allowed to increase, to keep inflation low by subduing workers' pay demands. Others have seen it as a way to control trade unions more generally. It has not only been "in the embattled right-wing camps of Thatcher and Regan" in the 1980s but "the bourgeoisie has often seen high unemployment as a means to roll back the power of the working class and the trade unions" (Therborn, 1986, p. 133). Those with considerable influence and power, and little risk of unemployment, often accept, even engineer, higher unemployment because of its presumed effect on the behavior of others, and not just those out of work. In fact, they are less concerned with jobseekers than those in work and the disciplining effect of the "reserve army of labour." "'Discipline in the factories' and 'political stability' are more appreciated by the business leaders than profits. Their class instinct tells them that lasting full employment is unsound from their point of view and that unemployment is an integral part of the 'normal' capitalist system" (Kalecki, 1943, p. 326, although the causes of the latest financial crises might lead him to modify the first sentence). However, too much unemployment may be seen as a major problem by governments, putting their own future at risk. How the issue of full employment can slip or be pushed off the political agenda is brought out well in Alan Deacon's analysis of the first generation of postwar politics in the United Kingdom (Deacon, 1981).

Later, in the early 1980s, the UK Conservative government under Margaret Thatcher believed that the unions were too powerful and the "short sharp shock" of unemployment would bring them to their senses, stopping what it saw as workers "pricing themselves out of jobs" and pushing up inflation. By contrast, in 2008, the causes of the sudden decline in demand with "the credit crunch" across many societies were generally recognized to be far from the ordinary worker whose job was at risk, and employers then were more willing to keep staff using short-time working to spread work and avoid laying them off than in the 1980s. Even then different countries acted to restore and maintain demand to very different degrees: in those that gave priority to reducing budget deficits the consequences of the recession were felt more widely with cuts to public services affecting very many more than the increased numbers out of work.

The Impact on Public and Other Services and the Wider Costs

Success in many health and personal social services requires restoring people to a "normal" life in the "community" after a particular crisis, whether it is due to some physical injury, an illness, a breakdown, or a period in prison. What this usually means is getting people back into a job since it provides the main source of regular income, status in society, a daily routine, and a range of social contacts. With unemployment rising and remaining at a high level, such rehabilitative measures are severely threatened. Higher unemployment need not have contributed to the initial problem, but it is likely to inhibit its solution and can worsen it. Equal opportunity programs to reduce discrimination against minorities also run into difficulties when job openings become limited.

The impact is further intensified by the fact that the increased unemployment itself, with more people affected by the stresses and pressures of being out of work, and for longer, places greater demands on many public services (Popay, 1983). Someone with a disability or mental illness may be able to cope while working, but the loss of their job, its resources, and its supporting structure can make their condition worse, or at least more visible, and increase their difficulties in many ways including getting back to work.

There is a double pressure imposed on government and the services. With extra spending on out-of-work benefits and the heavy loss of direct and other taxes that those now unemployed would have provided while working, public resources diminish at the same time as needs increase. The total budgetary loss to the government per person unemployed is not just the cost of the direct spending on benefits to those out of work, but income tax and social security contributions are also lost, and so too are indirect taxes as people's spending drops with their reduced income. In the United Kingdom the revenue loss has been greater than the additional spending (e.g., Unemployment Unit, 2000/2001, pp. 20–21). This lost revenue is rarely taken into account publicly in government reports or discussed in policy debates, but it adds considerably to any fiscal crisis—a point well recognized in a Swedish saying: "this country is not rich enough to afford unemployment" (quoted in the Kreisky Commission, 1989).

The costs of higher unemployment become added to the other factors making greater demands on welfare state provisions. In many countries the needs of the increased number of unemployed add to those of an already rising number of retired groups and other groups in need, and do so at a time when escalating health costs and rising expectations of public provision have been making heavier demands upon state services that are also restricted by budget deficits. Furthermore, the higher unemployment can increase the need for spending among these other groups, including those in work and others outside the labor force (see below).

Under these increased pressures of rising need and falling revenue, supply and standards in many public services are likely to decline. Those who can afford it turn to alternative forms of provision outside the state. They may purchase these services privately or support demands for increased provision by their employers. Resource problems become intensified when, as in many countries, this alternative provision through the market is supported and subsidized by tax breaks for employers and employees (e.g., tax relief for private health insurance, housing costs, and pensions). These less visible subsidies reduce public revenues even more and further squeeze public expenditure to the benefit of the better-off. This becomes one more factor leading to the widening of inequalities in resources, power, and security under the pressure of increased unemployment.

The Varying Impact across the Generations
The Impact on Those Still at School

The prevailing trends in unemployment nationally and at a local level can have an effect on education. Many teachers have spoken of the ways in which schoolchildren are affected by high unemployment with the consequential reining-in of career aspirations (Sinfield, 1981, see also McKee-Ryan and Maitoza, this volume). Young students from deprived areas or minority groups have recounted how some teachers and career advisers dismissed their hopes of entering particular careers when unemployment is high.

Those entering the labor market when demand is high can find training and work opportunities, but, as demand falls, employers cut training programs as well as recruitment. Some university graduates are forced to take jobs previously expected to be taken by sixth-formers, who in turn are pushed down the labor market with knock-on effects all the way down. During a prolonged downturn the result becomes "a lost generation," that finds new school-leavers preferred to them when demand picks up and realizes that their whole working lives may be affected by long-term political and social repercussions.

By contrast, "stable employment contributes to building up skills, work experience, and social networks, although some forms of work will also have a psychological cost. . . . The process of identity formation is, therefore, far more at risk, with accompanying rises of relationship breakdown, poor mental health, addiction, and accidental and self-inflicted harm" (Bartley et al., 2006, p. 90).

Qualitative longitudinal study on the United Kingdom has shown that "young people enter a period of economic recession with prior resources and particular trajectories already in play in their lives" (Edwards & Weller, 2010, p. 125). For those with some prior handicap the problems may be particularly acute. One institution for young people with learning disabilities developed a successful program that enabled them to develop sufficient skills to take some basic jobs at a nearby airport. The visible success of the scheme encouraged new entrants and the teachers. It also helped to enable some to make the move out into the community and generally helped to reduce the social distance from the rest of the world. With increased unemployment "able-bodied" competitors were preferred for the jobs that remained: the young people became locked into repeating training with no successful exit, and the walls of "the total institution" became higher again, reinforced by the fact that the teachers also became demoralized and sought other opportunities.

The Impact on Those of Working Age

It is not only the workers who cannot get jobs who lose when unemployment rises, but voluntary job-changing also falls as those remaining in work are more likely to cling to their jobs, however unsatisfactory, even though they resent being trapped and the stagnation of their careers. This creates a fertile ground for cynical and dismissive stories about the unemployed as scroungers that can serve to weaken public concern about the level of unemployment.

When employers set their requirements higher in looser labor markets, the chance of moving up are further limited. This can be compounded as larger organizations reduce external entry to many jobs, relying on internal promotions to reduce staff numbers. The effect on career development can be felt over many years, especially when younger generations with better training are likely to be recruited to better paid and more secure work.

The way that "aggregate unemployment adversely affects all principal wage earners in the community, not just those personally unemployed," is also brought out in a study based on telephone interviews in Los Angeles county from 1976 to 1982 (Dooley, Catalano, & Rook, 1988, pp. 117–118). It found that those already vulnerable were likely to be most affected (although it provided little on the actual effects). Similarly, in Denmark "the health consequences of unemployment and, more generally, of economic instability," according to one study of a shipyard closure over 3 years, "apply not just to unemployed people, but also to large groups of employed people whose conditions of employment are uncertain or whose jobs are temporary" (Iversen & Sabroe, 1988, pp. 149–150). The value of better, more open, and more accountable procedures on dismissals helping to reduce the stress among the workforce was noted.

Anxiety about job security as demand falls affects workers before redundancies are announced, and the impact on health may be across the labor force of a company, affecting those who retain their jobs as well (Bambra, 2010, p. 214; Beale & Nethercott, 1992). This may be all the more likely when further layoffs are expected. Those who already have health or other problems can be particularly affected by declining demand. "In times of low unemployment, the great majority of men with long-term illness are in fact employed, and thus deriving most of their income from paid work" (Bartley et al., 2006, p. 89) and are less subject to social exclusion through poverty. When demand falls, those with poor health or some disability are more likely to be edged or forced out: they may even be given incentives to take redundancy (MacKay & Davies, 2008). Higher unemployment can have particular significance for mental illness: "unemployment is a severe risk for public mental health that must be fought with all possible means" concluded a meta-analysis of studies from "26 predominantly western" countries (Paul & Moser, 2009, p. 271). Once out of work, these people experience more difficulty than others in obtaining new jobs and so have a greater risk of prolonged unemployment, poverty, and premature withdrawal from the labor market.

Unemployment and Life after Work

Unemployment impacts the lives of retired people in two ways. First, the quality of retirement is affected by how those retiring have been able to plan for that event. "Working life matters" is the subtitle of a study that examines the experience of older people (Bardasi & Jenkins, 2002). The security and rewards of their past employment have a major impact on the pension they have been able to build up, particularly private ones in which no allowance is made for contributions lost while out of work. A couple who can both plan their retirement from secure jobs are able to save for their retirement, building up their resources in their last years of work and replacing major household items, as well as retiring with adequate, if not better, pensions.

This is a very different experience from those whose last full-time jobs were 10 or even 20 years before the standard retirement age when a sudden redundancy removed the chance of building up savings, especially among those in less secure work with the least chance of generous payoffs. In the intervening years they will have exhausted any savings and may already be in debt to maintain even the limited level of living that a pension reduced by the lack of contributions from the time out of work may do little to ease. Where unemployment has been high or has increased during the last years in work, more older people will be closer in experience to the second couple: opportunities for part-time work to supplement inadequate pensions into retirement are also likely to decrease with increased unemployment.

Longitudinal studies have revealed that it is not just the quality of life that is affected by unemployment, but lives are also liable to be shortened by the experience (Bartley et al., 2006). However, a society's institutional arrangements for retirement can shape the experience: in countries in which state benefits are low, for example, the risks and effects of poverty and deprivation in old age are greater.

Second, the level of unemployment during people's retirement may also affect their resources. When and where unemployment is high, older people are more likely to be sharing the family's poverty resulting from unemployment by helping younger members instead of benefiting from the higher standard of living achieved by members in full-time employment.

Modifying the Broader Impact of Unemployment
Social and Economic Stabilizers

The ways that unemployment has an impact not only on individuals directly affected but also on other groups and on the wider society can be significantly modified. The effects vary across societies and over time: they are by no means uniform or inevitable. In particular, unemployment benefits and other financial support during unemployment can

act as an automatic economic built-in stabilizer that benefits the whole society. The partial replacement of earnings helps to limit unemployed households' drop in income: it thus maintains purchasing power in the wider economy so that demand for workers does not fall even further. Debrun and Kapoor's analysis of data from 49 industrial and developing economies led them to their subtitle: "automatic stabilizers work, always and everywhere," "strongly contributing to output stability regardless of the type of economy" (Debrun & Kapoor, 2010, p. 5).

The effect, of course, depends on the level and duration of benefits and the ease of access to them. "The more highly developed the social protection in a system and the more generous the social benefits provided, the greater the effects of automatic stabilizers on the economy are likely to be" (Euzéby, 2010, p. 74; Dolls, Fuest, & Peichl, 2012). The current trends across many countries to reduce insurance coverage, limit benefits, and tighten entitlement conditions are weakening this protection. This is all the more counterproductive when many economies are failing to maintain the growth necessary to maintain employment.

A good benefit system can be a social as well as an economic stabilizer. "It is the response to the aspirations for security in its widest sense. . . . Its fundamental purpose is to give individuals and families the confidence that their level of living and quality of life will not, in so far as is possible, be greatly eroded by any economic and social eventuality. It is the guarantee of security that matters most of all, rather than the particular mechanisms" (ILO, 1984, para. 39).

This "guarantee of security" affects those in work, increasing their willingness to risk changing jobs and reducing the immobility in the labor market that can inhibit the expansion of new industries. Both trade union and employer responses to changes in companies and in the labor market more generally are likely to be influenced by the degree of protection that is seen to be available to workers. The extension of unemployment insurance to "nearly 1 million domestic workers" in South Africa is likely to have reduced the fear of job loss for a group, predominantly women, that has long been highly vulnerable to great insecurity in the informal market (Lund, 2009, p. 302). "Additional social buffers" such as strengthening the employment and training services can also support the automatic ones (Euzéby, 2010, p. 76).

The value and importance of social security in reducing the impact of increased unemployment and preventing further effects both on the individual and the wider society have not been extensively discussed (Sinfield, 2012). This neglect is itself a reflection of "the individualisation of the social" (Ferge, 1997) that has become a dominant trend in many societies with the shift toward the market and cuts to public spending. As a consequence, there has been little comparative research into the differences in the extent of security and stability in the labor market that countries provide. One rare comparative study with data on over 15,000 employees in 24 countries concluded that the existence of a "social safety net" as well as broader societal support provided a greater sense of security (Debus, Probst, König, & Kleinmann, 2012). However, studies of the different benefit systems reveal that some, for example, offer better support to higher-paying occupations and little support to groups more marginal to the labor market, thus helping to reinforce core and peripheral polarization and the social exclusion of certain minorities; others provide stronger support for older redundant workers (Clasen, Gould, & Vincent, 1998).

The Wider Impact of the Political and Social Construction of Unemployment

In societies in which there is greater concern for work incentives, the extent to which benefits of any type help to replace lost wages and so bring greater economic and social stability is more limited. One detailed comparative analysis of 18 "rich democracies" led the U.S. author to conclude that in his own country there is "an unbalanced infatuation with trying to detect welfare disincentives and dependency" (Brady, 2009, p. 142). This is also true of the United Kingdom: 40 years ago contributory-based benefits were received by 75% of those drawing any benefits while unemployed, but the proportion has now fallen below 20%. Maximum benefit duration has been cut from 12 to 6 months and the value relative to wages has fallen by 50% in the past 30 years to some 10% of the average. Penalties and sanctions have been increased despite the lack of any evidence supporting the policy swing to "conditionality" (Sinfield, 2013).

A poor benefits system with low benefits and increased conditionality and sanctions can add to the unsettling and destabilizing effect of increased unemployment not only on individuals but also on their families and others, on communities, and on the wider institutions of society, leading to and reinforcing a second-class citizenship for certain groups and areas. The dominant public and political discourse in countries with poor benefits seems more likely to "blame the victim" out of work (Ryan, 1971) than in others with more generous, or at least more adequate, benefits. Curiously, it seems to be in places in which benefits are relatively low that there is more concern that people out of work are "resting" or "languishing" on benefits and so should be more vigorously policed and controlled to "regulate the poor" (Piven & Cloward, 1972). For example, in countries such as the United States and the United Kingdom the fear and shame of being out of work among those worried about losing their jobs are likely to be much greater than in, for example, the Scandinavian countries, although there appears to be no systematic research on this.

Acceptance of that political and social climate amid high unemployment effectively lets governments, employers, and others off the hook, reducing the pressures to bring about increased demand in the labor market, not only in reducing the numbers out of work but also in tackling problems of discrimination and equal opportunity. Higher unemployment becomes a double blow for less popular and powerful groups, weakening their position in the labor market and public support for more positive action to help them. Those out of work become blamed for high and prolonged unemployment, thus increasing the divisions and tensions in society.

These views that lay the blame for continuing unemployment on those out of work have persisted despite sound research to the contrary. For example, analyses over half a century in the United Kingdom demonstrate that changes in long-term unemployment are closely related to the changing overall level of unemployment and not to altered behavior by individuals out of work (Webster, 2005). Claims of "welfare dependency" and a "culture of entitlement" with two or more generations that have never worked are not borne out by detailed research (see especially Shildrick, Furlong, MacDonald, Roden, & Crow, 2012; on EU Eichhorn, 2013). Yet these myths continue to be supported and even fostered by politicians and media while studies reveal the myth-making and the harm it does in areas in which many are trapped in "low-pay no-pay" labor markets (Shildrick, Furlong, MacDonald, Roden, & Crow, 2012; Shildrick, MacDonald, Webster, & Garthwaite, 2012). This scapegoating not only increases pressure on many who are already vulnerable but affects their families and can reduce social cohesion in local communities leading to greater social exclusion and rejection. The persistence of stigmatizing "demonization" may be fostered by some in the belief that benefits can be cut more easily and with less political fallout when their recipients are presented as "undeserving" (Taylor-Gooby, 2012).

Poverty and Unemployment

Higher unemployment leads to an increase in poverty, as Brady's (2009) comparative analysis has shown. It affects many more than those recognized as unemployed, including, for example, single parents or older and/or disabled people who might have sought part-time work to supplement low benefits or pensions. Given the class and geographic concentration of unemployment, there is a greater risk that many in the same family may be affected with children leaving school unable to find work while their parents and their grandparents may have lost their jobs. Where previously those in work may have helped the others to bear the losses, the whole family, whether living together or not, becomes deprived. This can have a knock-on effect on a whole community with shops losing customers and closing, and the general quality of life declining in a downward spiral. Jobseekers find employers resistant to taking on workers from that area because of its reputation for high unemployment, and this only adds to the community's problems and the difficulties in overcoming them.

However, this downward trend into more and deeper poverty as unemployment increases is not inevitable and can be moderated by the strength of the economic and social stabilizers already established in countries. "Welfare generosity always has a larger effect on poverty than unemployment" is the conclusion of an 18-country study with 30 years of data (Brady, 2009, p. 143; see also Martínez, Ayala, & Ruiz-Huerta, 2001, p. 446). The benefits are not confined to the individual but extend to the broader society. Similarly, in her comparative study of European member countries Bea Cantillon concluded that "the higher the level of expenditure, the lower the level of poverty among those out of work, irrespective of the overall level of unemployment in a country. . . Rich, high employment countries where social spending is low end up with high poverty. This leads to the conclusion that, if it is possible to attain a low risk of poverty without substantial spending, it has not yet been demonstrated" (Cantillon, 2009, pp. 232 and 240).

Lower unemployment by itself does not ensure lower poverty, as particularly revealed in the United States. This emphasizes the importance of the automatic stabilizing effects of good social protection and of the need for decent work and wages to prevent subemployment with its low-pay no-pay cycle. In fact, good stabilizers and decent jobs can help to promote equality, thus reducing the impact of joblessness: the 26-country review cited earlier gives particular emphasis to the "important result that unemployment has comparatively weak malignant effects in economically highly developed countries and in countries with an egalitarian income structure (where the level of unemployment protection usually is high)" (Paul & Moser, 2009, p. 280).

Crime and Unemployment

One of the few broader issues linked with higher unemployment in the public mind is an increase in criminality. However, this may well be more of an assumption than the outcome of rigorous research. Increased crime in the past has been linked to increasing affluence and many other factors. The UK Home Office Research Unit reviewed the available literature a generation ago and briefed the press that the links between crime and unemployment were "very unclear . . . with no discernible pattern" and "no evidence of a significant relationship between the two factors." Rising crime was also "highly correlated with the consumption of ice-cream, the number of cars on the road and the gross national product" (*The Guardian*, October 2, 1982).

There appears to be a stronger link between increased unemployment and the greater likelihood that those convicted are sent to prison. This may be partly due to the fact that more of those arrested are without jobs and fines may be seen as less suitable for them; in addition, those passing sentence may believe that imprisonment may be more harmful to someone in work who will lose their job and/or that those out of work are in some way more deserving of a period in prison. If people are out of work, they may be more likely to be refused bail. And unless prisoners have a job to go to, they are also less likely to be given parole. However, higher unemployment was not found to be significantly related to increased imprisonment in one study across 18 OECD countries: there was a stronger negative relation to the level of welfare spending (Downes & Hansen, 2006, pp. 146–147), one more indication of the importance of countries' social policies in mediating the repercussions of economic change.

Conclusions

"In a society where unemployment is accepted, great material and social gaps develop, resulting in the mutual isolation and alienation of different groups. Any social order not based on full employment must imply a restriction of living conditions and a squandering of human resources" (Swedish Ministry of Labour, 1974).

Yet, as this chapter indicates, analysis and research into the wider impact of unemployment remain limited. The reasons lie at least in part in a general shift away from structural analyses. "Today social and employment policy is characterized by its avoidance of questions about the wider system, in favor of a focus on the 'margins', and its downplaying of the involuntary dimension of unemployment while opting for a very subjective and personalized approach to the problem" (Walters, 2000, p. 9; see also O'Connor, 2001, final chapter). Yet more and better understanding of the broader impact of unemployment on society, and not just those currently out of work, could be valuable to readers of a handbook of psychology as it could help to set the context within which they are able to take account of the evidence of other chapters on the experience of unemployment.

Higher unemployment can be a major obstacle to attempts to prevent or reduce poverty and other forms of disadvantage not only among the unemployed but also among single parents, older people, and those with disabilities. Equal opportunity programs and rehabilitation services face particular difficulties, especially when recovery from some crisis means return to employment, the main source for income, status, a daily routine, and social contacts. Unemployment may not have caused the initial problem, but can make its solution harder and even exacerbate it.

However, the impact of unemployment is by no means inevitable, as experience across many countries demonstrates. The welfare state and in particular the benefit systems working as social as well as economic stabilizers can help to reduce and modify its impact. More research is needed, examining unemployment as a characteristic of society and not just of those who happen to be out of work at any time, and taking account of change. "Research has not fully kept up with more recent labor market change," but it is becoming increasingly clear that "unemployment and work insecurity are part of a process through which health disadvantage is accumulated over the life-course" (Bartley et al., 2006, pp. 91 and 88; Bambra, 2011).

In 1984 I concluded an attempt to examine the wider impact of unemployment (Sinfield, 1984) by referring to a European Commission report that showed how unemployment was affecting political and public views in ways that weakened the drive toward reestablishing full employment as a high priority objective. It still appears particularly appropriate. "Rising unemployment and pressure on living standards have hardened resistance to change, at a time when change is essential for the restoration of economic health and a return to better employment" (CEC, April 1981). Three decades later I endorse that conclusion even more strongly, adding that a return to higher and better employment results in benefits not just for economic health but also for securer democratic and social development across societies.

Research Questions

What are the main ways in which the level of unemployment has an impact on the lives of all people across society, and to what extent does it differ among countries?

How does the political economy of unemployment vary across societies, and why?

What impact do the attitudes and practices of employers, employees, their associations, and unions have on unemployment and full employment over time, across industries, and across countries?

To what extent and in what ways do institutions such as the welfare state moderate the impact of unemployment not only on those out of work but also on other groups?

To what extent do attacks on those out of work "dependent on benefits" undermine public support for better structural measures to tackle unemployment and distract attention from the problems of the labor market with increasing evidence of the low-pay no-pay cycle? And how does this vary over time and across societies?

References

Bambra, C. (2010). Yesterday once more? Unemployment and health in the 21st century. *Journal of Epidemiology and Community Health*, 64(3), 213–215.

Bambra, C. (2011). *Work, worklessness, and the political economy of health*. Oxford: Oxford University Press.

Bardasi, E., & Jenkins, S. (2002). *Income in later life: Work history matters*. Bristol, CT: Policy Press.

Bartley, M., Ferrie, J., & Montgomery, S. M. (2006). Health and labour market disadvantage: Unemployment, non-employment, and job insecurity. In M. Marmot & R. G. Wilkinson (Eds.), *Social determinants of health* (2nd ed., pp. 78–96). Oxford: Oxford University Press.

Beale, N., & Nethercott, S. (1992). A critical review of the effect of factory closures on health. *Letter to British Journal of Industrial Medicine*, 49(1), 70.

Beveridge, W. H. (1944). *Full employment in a free society*. London, England: Allen & Unwin.

Bird, C. (1966). *The invisible scar*. New York, NY: McKay.

Brady, D. (2009). *Rich democracies poor societies: How politics explain poverty*. Oxford: Oxford University Press.

Burkitt, B., & Bowers, D. (1979). *Trade unions and the economy*. London, England: Macmillan.

Cantillon, B. (2009). The poverty effects of social protection in Europe: EU enlargement and its lessons for developing countries. In P. Townsend (Ed.), *Building decent societies: Rethinking the role of social security in development* (pp. 220–241). Basingstoke, England: ILO & Palgrave Macmillan.

CEC—Commission of the European Communities. (April 1981). *Problems of unemployment: Points for examination*. Brussels, Belgium: CEC.

Clasen, J., Gould, A., & Vincent, J. (1998). *Voices within and without*. Bristol, England: The Policy Press.

Deacon, A. (1981). Unemployment and politics in Britain since 1945. In B. Showler & A. Sinfield (Eds.), *The workless state* (pp. 59–88). Oxford: Martin Robertson.

Debrun, X., & Kapoor, R. (2010). *Fiscal policy and macroeconomic stability: Automatic stabilizers work, always and everywhere*. IMF Working Paper, WP/10/111. www.imf.org/external/pubs/cat/longres.cfm?sk=23818.0

Debus, M. E., Probst, T. M., König, C. J., & Kleinmann, M. (2012). Catch me if I fall! Enacted uncertainty, avoidance and the social safety net as country-level moderators of the job insecurity-job attitudes link. *Journal of Applied Psychology*, 97(3), 690–698.

Dolls, M., Fuest, C., & Peichl, A. (2012). Automatic stabilizers and economic crisis: US vs Europe. *Journal of Public Economics*, 96(3), 279–294.

Dooley, D., Catalano, R., & Rook, K. S. (1988). Personal and aggregate unemployment and psychological symptoms. *Journal of Social Issues*, 44(4), 107–123.

Downes, D., & Hansen, K. (2006). Welfare and punishment in comparative perspective. In S. Armstrong & L. McAra (Eds.), *Perspectives on punishment: The contours of control* (pp. 133–154). Oxford: Oxford University Press.

Edwards, R., & Weller, S. (2010). Trajectories from youth to adulthood: Choice and structure for young people before and during recession. *21st Century Society*, 5(2), 125–136.

Eichhorn, J. (2013). The (non-)effect of unemployment benefits: Variations in the effect of unemployment on life-satisfaction between EU countries. *Social Indicators Research*, 119:389-404.

Elder, G. H. (1974). *Children of the great depression*. Chicago, IL: University of Chicago Press.

Euzéby, A. (2010). Economic crisis and social protection in the European Union: Moving beyond immediate responses. *International Social Security Review*, 63(2), 71–86.

Ferge, Z. (1997). The changed welfare paradigm: The individualisation of the social. *Social Policy and Administration*, 31(1), 20–44.

Hyman, H. H. (1979). The effects of unemployment: A neglected problem in modern social research. In R. K. Merton, et al. (Eds.), *Qualitative and quantitative social research: Papers in honor of Paul F. Lazarsfeld* (pp. 282–298). New York, NY: Free Press.

ILO. (1984). *Into the 21st century: The development of social security*. Geneva: ILO.

ISER. (2002). Class matters. ISER Newsletter, October, 6–7—drawing on Elias, Peter & McKnight, Abigail. (2002). In D.

Rose & D. Pevalin (Eds.), *A researcher's guide to the National Statistics Socio-Economic Classification*. London: Sage (Institute of Social and Economic Research, University of Essex). www.iser.essex.ac.uk.

Iversen, L., & Sabroe, S. (1988). Psychological well-being among unemployed and employed people after a company shutdown. *Journal of Social Issues*, 44(4), 141–152.

Kalecki, M. (1943). Political aspects of full employment. *Political Quarterly*, 14(4), 322–331.

Kalimo, R., Taris, T. W., & Schaufeli, W. B. (2003). The effects of past and anticipated future downsizing on survivor well-being: An equity perspective. *Journal of Occupational Health Psychology*, 8(2), 91–109.

Kerr, C. (1954). The Balkanization of labor markets. In E. W. Bakke (Ed.), *Labor mobility and economic opportunity* (pp. 92-110). New York, NY: John Wiley.

Kreisky Commission on Employment Issues in Europe. (1989). *A programme for full employment in the 1990s: Report*. Oxford: Pergamon.

Lockwood, D. (1958). *The blackcoated worker*. London: Allen & Unwin.

Lund, F. (2009). Welfare, development and growth: Lessons from South Africa. In P. Townsend (Ed.), *Building decent societies: Rethinking the role of social security in development* (pp. 290–309). Basingstoke, England: ILO & Palgrave Macmillan.

MacKay, R. R., & Davies, L. (2008). Unemployment, permanent sickness, and nonwork in the United Kingdom. *Environment and Planning A*, 40(2), 464–481.

Martínez, R., Ayala, L., & Ruiz-Huerta, J. (2001). The impact of unemployment on inequality and poverty in OECD countries. *Economics of Transition*, 9(2), 417–448.

O'Connor, A. (2001). *Poverty Knowledge: Social science, social policy, and the poor in twentieth-century U.S. history*. Princeton, NJ: Princeton University Press.

Paul, K. I., and Moser, K. (2009). Unemployment impairs mental health: Meta-analyses. *Journal of Vocational Behavior*, 74(3), 264–282.

Piven, F. F., & Cloward, R. (1972). *Regulating the poor: The functions of public welfare*. London: Tavistock.

Popay, J. (1983). Closer to the edge. *Social Work Today*, 14, 12–14.

Reubens, B. (1970). *The hard-to-employ: European programs*. New York, NY: Columbia University Press.

Reynolds, L. (1951). *The structure of labor markets: Wages and labor mobility in theory and practice*. Westport, CT: Greenwood.

Ryan, W. (1971). *Blaming the victim*. London, England: Orbach and Chambers.

Sennett, R., & Cobb, J. (1973). *The hidden injuries of class*. New York, NY: Vintage.

Shildrick, T., Furlong, A., MacDonald, R., Roden, J., & Crow, R. (2012). *Are 'cultures of worklessness' passed down the generations?* York: Joseph Rowntree Foundation.

Shildrick, T., MacDonald, R., Webster, C., & Garthwaite, K. (2012). *Poverty and insecurity: Life in low-pay, no-pay Britain*. Bristol, England: The Policy Press.

Sinfield, A. (1981). *What unemployment means*. Oxford: Martin Robertson.

Sinfield, A. (1984). The wider impact of unemployment in OECD. In *High unemployment: A challenge for income support policies* (pp. 33–66). Paris, France: OECD.

Sinfield, A. (2012). Strengthening the prevention of social insecurity. *International Social Security Review*, 65(1), 89–106.

Sinfield, A. (2013). What unemployment means three decades and two recessions later. *Social Policy Review*, 25, 205–223.

Swedish Ministry of Labour. (1974). *Employment tomorrow: Terms of reference for the Royal Commission on Long-Term Employment*. Stockholm, Sweden: Ministry of Labour.

Taylor-Gooby, P. (2012). Beveridge overboard? How the UK government is using the crisis to permanently restructure the welfare state. *Intereconomics*, 47(4), 224–229.

Terkel, S. (1970). *Hard times: An oral history of the Great Depression*. New York, NY: Pantheon.

Therborn, G. (1986). *Why some peoples are more unemployed than others*. London: Verso.

Townsend, P. (1979). *Poverty in the United Kingdom: A survey of household resources and standards of living*. London, England: Allen Lane.

Travers, P. (1986). Contingent and noncontingent effects of unemployment. *Sociology*, 20(2), 192–206.

Travers, P., & Richardson, S. (1993). *Living decently: Material well-being in Australia*. Melbourne, Australia: Oxford University Press.

Unemployment Unit. (2001). *Working Brief* 120, December 2000/January, 20–21.

Walters, W. (2000). *Unemployment and the social: Genealogies of the social*. Cambridge, England: Cambridge University Press.

Webster, D. (2005). Long-term unemployment, the invention of "hysteresis" and the misdiagnosis of structural unemployment in the UK. *Cambridge Journal of Economics*, 29(6), 975–995.

Wilensky, H. L. (1961). Orderly careers and social participation: The impact of work history on social interpretation in the middle mass. *American Sociological Review*, 26(4), 521–539.

Insecurity, Unemployment, and Health: A Social Epidemiological Perspective

Clare Bambra *and* Terje A. Eikemo

Abstract

This chapter draws on research from social epidemiology to examine the relationships between insecurity, unemployment, and health. It outlines the rise of insecurity at work and provides a working definition. It then describes some of the key longitudinal studies that have described the relationship between job insecurity and health outcomes. The key explanations for this association are also explored. The chapter then summarizes the large literature on unemployment and health, examining mental health and suicide, mortality, self-reported health, and health behaviors. The chapter then examines international variations in the relationships between insecurity, unemployment, and health, with a particular focus on the role of welfare state policies and social safety nets. The chapter concludes by reflecting on the policy implications and highlighting key areas for future research.

Key Words: unemployment, health, insecurity, inequality, welfare state, Europe

Introduction

This chapter takes a more macro-level and sociological approach, which contrasts with the more micro-level psychological approach to job insecurity (e.g., Probst, Jiang, & Benson, this volume) and unemployment (Paul, Hassel, & Moser, this volume) taken elsewhere in this handbook. It draws on research from social epidemiology. Social epidemiology is about the social causes of disease distribution within and between societies, it is "about why different societies—and within societies, why different societal groups—have better or worse health than others" (Kreigar, 2011, vii). Firstly, the chapter outlines the rise of insecurity at work and provides a working definition. It then reviews some of the key longitudinal studies that have described the relationship between job insecurity and health outcomes, including obesity, cardiovascular disease, self-rated health, and psychological morbidity. Explanations for the association are also explored. The chapter then summarizes the large literature on unemployment and health, examining mental

health and suicide, mortality, self-reported health, and health behaviors. It also explores issues of work and social status as well as the mechanisms underpinning the negative health effect of unemployment. The chapter then examines in some detail international variations in the relationships between insecurity, unemployment, and health, with a particular focus on the role of welfare-state policies and social safety nets. The chapter concludes by reflecting on the policy implications and highlighting key areas for future research.

Job Insecurity and Health

This section starts by defining the concept of job insecurity. The relationship between job insecurity and health is then outlined, drawing on some of the key studies in the field of social epidemiology. The section concludes by exploring some of the key explanations that have been put forward to explain how job insecurity impacts on health. Paid work is of fundamental importance to individuals in modern societies, not only because it provides people with subsistence but also because paid work plays an important structuring role in status attribution (Bambra, 2011). Notably, occupation is an important determinant of social prestige (Ganzeboom, De Graaf, Treiman, & De Leeuw, 1992) and social class (Erikson & Goldthorpe, 1992), both of which are, in turn, strongly associated with various health outcomes (Eikemo, Kunst, Judge, & Mackenbach, 2008; Lahelma, Laaksonen, & Aittomäki, 2009). However, in the last few decades, working life has been subject to major transformations as a result of the international deregulation of labor markets, increased economic dependency between countries, rapidly changing consumer markets, and escalated demands for flexibility between and within organizations (László et al., 2010; Sverke, Hellgren, & Näswall, 2002). Consequently there has been an increase in labor market flexibility, temporary work (De Cuyper, Fontinha, & De Witte, this volume), and job insecurity, particularly in periods of economic recession (Sverke, Hellgren, & Näswall, 2006). These transformations to working life, particularly in the United States, Asia, and Europe during the 1980s and the 1990s, has brought the issue of insecure working conditions to the forefront among scholars and researchers (Sverke et al., 2006). These are discussed in more detail by Probst, Jiang, and Benson (this volume). It has been suggested that these changes, and particularly downsizing, may have adverse health effects (Martikainen, Mäki, & Jäntti, 2008).

Job Insecurity

Job insecurity implies a threat of job loss or a loss of any valued condition of employment (Greehalg & Rosenblatt, 1984). In general terms, job insecurity may be defined as the discrepancy between the level of security a person experiences and the level she or he might prefer (Bartley & Ferrie, 2001). The terms *flexible, precarious*, and *insecure employment* are also used in the literature to describe the increasing numbers of people who are working on either temporary contracts or no contracts, with limited or no employment or welfare rights. In this—secondary—labor market, skills, working hours, contracts, conditions, pay, and location are all more flexible (Beatson, 1995; Marmot et al., 1999). Temporary, insecure, work accounts for an average of around 15% of paid employment across the European Union (Massarelli, 2009). This amounts to 19.1 million full-time temporary workers: the so-called *precariat* (Massarelli, 2009). Across all European countries except Germany,

temporary work is considerably higher among women than men (Bambra, 2011). Job insecurity itself is discussed more by Probst and colleagues (this volume). Here we focus on its health impact.

General Overview of Job Insecurity and Health

The first studies on the association between job insecurity and health were published in the late 1970s and applied *physiological measures*. Compared with other health outcomes, only a few studies have been conducted, but the most recent ones have examined job insecurity in relation to high cholesterol (Ferrie, Shipley, Marmot, Stansfeld, & Smith, 1995), obesity (Ferrie, Shipley, Stansfeld, & Marmot, 2002), and adrenal hormones (Toivanen et al., 1996). Moreover, studies of physiological measures have revealed inconsistent results, but the strongest evidence comes from studies of hypertension from the United Kingdom's Whitehall II occupational cohort study, which indeed showed that job insecurity is associated with higher levels of blood pressure (Ferrie et al., 1995; Ferrie, Shipley, Marmot, Stansfeld, & Smith, 1998b).

In the late 1980s the term *psychological morbidity* (mental ill health, such as anxiety and depression) was increasingly used to describe the outcome. With the exception of the early Michigan study (Cobb & Kasl, 1977), these studies have shown a consistent pattern of adverse health effects from job insecurity (D'Souza, Strazdins, Lim, Broom, & Rodgers, 2003; Ferrie et al., 1998b; Ferrie, Shipley, Newman, Stansfeld, & Marmot, 2005; Rugulies, Aust, Burr, & Bültmann, 2008; Swaen, Bültmann, Kant, & van Amelsvoort, 2004), with strong evidence for a causal association (longitudinal studies have shown that job insecurity precedes the onset of ill health).

In the early 90s *self-reported morbidity* became more common (see De Witte, 1999) for a review). Here, symptom checklists were applied, which included both somatic and psychological elements (Ferrie et al., 1998b, 2002; Ferrie, Shipley, Marmot, Stansfeld, & Smith, 1998a; Mohren, Swaen, van Amelsvoort, Borm, & Galama, 2003). These studies have also demonstrated a consistent pattern—by gender and age, for example—of adverse health effects (e.g., in terms of depression and anxiety) (Ferrie et al., 2002) from job insecurity. The same is the case for studies of self-reported morbidity (László et al., 2010) and with regard to incident coronary heart disease (Lee, Colditz, Berkman, & Kawachi, 2004). Furthermore, a few studies have found associations of job insecurity to more distant health measures, such as *health care use* (Roskies & Louis-Guerin, 1990) and absence due to sickness (Kivimäki et al., 1997). For example, medication use was twice as high among insecure managers as secure ones (Roskies & Louis-Guerin, 1990), and sickness absence was 10% higher among women experiencing job insecurity (Kivimäki et al., 1997).

Given the range of health outcomes that have been applied in studies of job insecurity, it may come as a surprise that research on *disease incidence* and *mortality* is so rare. The available studies on mortality mainly come from Finland, which focus on the adverse consequences of downsizing on health among those remaining in the downsized workplaces (Martikainen et al., 2008). Vahtera et al. (2004) showed that organizational downsizing may increase absence due to sickness and the risk of death from cardiovascular disease in employees who keep their jobs.

Key Studies of Insecurity and Health

As noted above, low job security has been proven to be related to somatic outcomes, psychological morbidity, poor self-rated health, incident coronary heart disease, and many risk factors such as high cholesterol, hypertension, and obesity. However, given the multitude of studies with varying degrees of methodological limitations, it is important to identify a few key studies. For example, most studies of job insecurity to date have largely been cross-sectional. Analyzing the extent to which labor market experiences affects health outcomes is challenging because of the difficulty of following subjects longitudinally from secure employment throughout an anticipation phase toward unemployment (Ferrie et al., 1995). The ideal study design will have data before the exposure, a follow-up time that includes a period of secure employment and sufficient time for the outcome to develop, and a control group with adequately matched employment experiences (Ferrie et al., 1995).

All of these limitations were met for the first time by the Whitehall II study, because data were obtained during a phase of job security for the whole cohort. Ferrie et al. (1995) assessed the effect of anticipating job change or nonemployment on self-reported health status in a group of middle-aged male and female white-collar civil servants. They compared self-reported health status measures and health-related behaviors before and during anticipation of privatization. The authors found that, although the changes in health behaviors between cohort members moving into a period of job

insecurity and the remainder of the cohort were not significant, self-reported health status tended to deteriorate among employees anticipating privatization when compared with that of the rest of the cohort.

In a later Whitehall II study, Ferrie et al. (1998b) examined changes in the health status of civil servants whose employment security was threatened. They observed that, from a position of advantage or no difference at baseline, self-reported morbidity and physiological risk factors tended to increase among respondents from the threatened department compared with those from other departments. Significant increases were also observed for body mass index, sleeping disorders, and cholesterol concentration. The research group also performed another study that examined the effects of a major organizational change and consequent job insecurity on the health status of a cohort of 7,419 white-collar civil servants (Ferrie et al., 1998a). Compared with controls, they found that men both already working in and anticipating transfer to an executive agency experienced significant increases in self-rated poor health, long-standing illness, adverse sleep patterns, mean number of symptoms in the fortnight before questionnaire completion, and minor psychiatric morbidity. Furthermore, compared with controls, women in both exposure groups reported small increases in most self-reported morbidity measures and most clinical measurements, accompanied by slight beneficial changes in some health-related behaviors and small adverse changes in others. Significant relative increases were seen in mean number of symptoms including ischemia among women anticipating exposure and in body mass index among those exposed to agency status.

In terms of mortality, a large prospective population study performed by Pekka Martikainen and colleagues (Martikainen et al., 2008), which examined whether downsizing was associated with increased mortality among those remaining in downsized workplaces in Finland, found that there was no association between downsizing and increased mortality. It is not directly comparable to the Whitehall II study because of different outcome measures and the particular focus on downsizing, but the unique statistical design (natural experiment), the completeness of the data, and mortality as a health outcome makes it a key study within the area. The authors did not find any association between downsizing and increased all-cause mortality among those remaining in downsized workplaces, nor was a period of particular vulnerability immediately following the downsizing identified. Furthermore, no detrimental effects were observed for any particular cause of death studied (Martikainen et al., 2008).

Explanations of Job Insecurity and Health

Only a few studies have focused on developing explanations of the relationship between job insecurity and health. Ferrie et al. (2005) examined the potential of demographic, personal, material, and behavioral characteristics, other psychosocial features of the work environment, and job satisfaction with data from the Whitehall II study. In their analyses—which were controlled for age, employment grade (occupational level), and health during a prior phase of secure employment—they observed that pessimism, heightened vigilance, primary deprivation, financial security, social support, and job satisfaction explained 68% of the association between job insecurity and self-rated health in women and 36% of the same factors in men (2005). Furthermore, with the addition of job control, these factors explained 60% of the association between job insecurity and minor psychiatric morbidity and just over 80% of the association with depression in both sexes (2005). László et al. (2010) could not explain within-country variations by demographic, behavioral, work-related, or socioeconomic factors, but the authors pointed to tentative explanations at the micro-level, such as the family or the workplace context, the economic and the social network, self-esteem, and mental health. At the macro level, the authors hypothesized that the extent of labor market regulation, the degree of unionization and collective power, and investments in and the strictness of employment protection could explain cross-national variations of the relationship between job insecurity and health. However, the authors observed only minor between-country variations, leaving little room for macro-level interpretations (László et al., 2010).

Unemployment and Health[1]

The International Labour Organization defines someone as unemployed if he or she is without a job but has actively looked for one within the last 4 weeks. Studies have consistently shown that unemployment increases the chances of poor health (Bambra & Eikemo, 2009; Paul, Hassel, & Moser, this volume). Empirical studies from the recessions of the 1980s and 1990s have shown that unemployment is associated with an increased likelihood of morbidity and mortality (Bartley et al.,

2006). There are clear relationships between unemployment and increased risk of poor mental health and suicide (Platt, 1986; Montgomery et al., 1999a; Blakely et al., 2003), higher rates of all-cause and specific causes of mortality (Morris et al., 1994; Scott-Samuel, 1984; Mosser et al., 1984; Martikainen & Valkonen, 1996), self reported health and limiting long-term illness (Bartley & Plewis, 2002; Korpi, 2001), and, in some studies, a higher prevalence of risky health behaviors (particularly among young men), including problematic alcohol use and smoking (Montgomery et al., 1999b; Luoto et al., 1998). The negative health experiences of unemployment are not limited to the unemployed only but also extend to their families and the wider community (Mosser et al., 1984; see also McKee-Ryan & Maitoza, this volume; Sinfield, this volume). For example, figures from a 1984 study suggest that for every "2000 men seeking work 2 (1.94), and among their wives 1 (0.98), will die each year as a result of unemployment" (Moser et al., 1984). Unemployment therefore also has serious implications for health-service planning with, for example, increased pressures on mental health services (Watkins, 1986).

Links between unemployment and poorer health have conventionally been explained through two interrelated concepts (see also Feather, this volume): the psychosocial effects of unemployment (e.g., stigma, isolation, and loss of self-worth), and the material consequences of unemployment (e.g., wage loss and resulting changes in access to essential goods and services). The psychosocial explanation of the health effects of unemployment draws upon the "latent deprivation theory," which asserts that being employed imposes a structure for time use, enforces some level of activity, provides opportunities for contact with others, provides a sense of social status, and offers opportunities to work unison with others toward collective goals (Jahoda 1982, 59). The unemployed are, according to Jahoda (1982), deprived of these latent functions of employment and thus experience psychological distress, which may, in turn, lead to physical ill health. Materialist critics of the psychosocial explanations of unemployment and health, such as Fryer (1986), have argued that it is actually the loss of the income from employment and the control over life which an income gives, as well as the relative poverty experienced by the unemployed, which accounts for the deterioration in health.

Studies that have examined the loss of social status and the "shaming" aspects of unemployment, such as Eales (1989) or Rantakeisu and colleagues (1997), found that around one in four unemployed men had experienced feelings of shame related to unemployment and that these feelings of shame were strongly related to depression, anxiety, and minor affective disorders. Similarly, an Italian study of factory workers who were made redundant in the early 1990s recession found that mental health declined even though the material situation of the workers did not deteriorate when they were given 100% of their wages for the first 6 months of unemployment (Rudas et al., 1991). Longer term, though, the unemployed suffer from a greatly reduced income, and many unemployed people live in relative poverty. Commentators have also drawn attention to the contributory role of ill health itself as a factor behind unemployment. This "health selection" hypothesis (see Paul, Hassel, & Moser, this volume) suggests that people who are in work and experiencing illness are more likely to lose their jobs than those who are healthy, and that this will probably be attenuated in times of economic recession.

Unemployment, Mental Health, and Suicide

Unemployment is associated with a more than twofold increase in the likelihood of poor mental health. A longitudinal UK study of young men examined the relationship between unemployment and depression and anxiety (Montgomery et al., 1999a). It analyzed data for 3,241 men taken from the 1958 British Birth Cohort. Baseline measures were taken when the men were aged 23 and the follow-up was at age 33, with the outcome being the onset of depression between these ages. The study compared the onset of depression or anxiety between those who had experienced recent unemployment (those were unemployed at any point in the year before) and those who had not. It found that, after adjustment for potential confounding factors (preexisting tendency to depression, social class, education, region), the relative risk (RR) of developing symptoms resulting in consultation for the recently unemployed was 2.10 (95% CI 1.21–3.63). Excluding those men with a preexisting tendency to depression (as measured by the Malaise Inventory at age 23) increased this to 2.30 (95% CI 1.44–3.65). In addition, the study looked at the effects of accumulated unemployment (more than 3 years of unemployment) since age 23. It found that, in general, long-term unemployment of over 3 years did not significantly increase the risk of consulting a health professional about depression or anxiety (fully adjusted RR = 1.63, 95% CI 0.95–2.79)

compared with those who had not experienced unemployment. However, once those young men with a preexisting tendency to depression were excluded, long-term unemployment doubled the likelihood of depression and anxiety (fully adjusted RR = 2.04, 95% CI 1.17–3.54).

One of the most important recessions of the 1980s and 1990s examined the relationship between unemployment and suicide (Platt, 1986). Studies generally found a more than twofold increased risk of suicide (Lewis and Sloggett, 1998; Kposowa, 2001) and attempted suicide (parasuicide) among the unemployed (Platt, 1986). Parasuicide rates are over ten times higher among unemployed young men than those in employment (Dorling, 2009). For example, a paper by Blakely and colleagues (2003) used data from 2.04 million respondents to the 1991 New Zealand census. It linked census data with mortality records and examined deaths from suicide among those aged 16 to 64 years from 1991 to 1994. It found that death by suicide was more than two times more likely among the unemployed than those in employment (age-adjusted OR women = 2.46, 95% CI 1.10–5.49; age-adjusted OR men = 2.63, 95% CI 1.87–3.70). No patterning of suicide by socioeconomic status was detected. When controlled for rates of mental ill health (using population estimates of the prevalence of mental ill health), the RR of death by suicide among unemployed men compared with employed men decreased to 1.88 (95% CI 1.35–2.43). This suggests that 47% of the excess suicide deaths among unemployed working-age men were attributable to confounding by mental illness. There has been debate about whether the associations between suicide and unemployment are direct—that unemployment is a traumatic life event that increases vulnerability to suicide; indirect— that unemployment increases exposure to other risk factors for suicide (e.g., poor mental health, financial strain); or noncausal—that people with an increased risk of unemployment are also those with an increased risk of suicide (and vice versa) (Blakely et al., 2003). The indirect explanation has had the most support in the literature to date.

Unemployment and Mortality

Other causes of death are also more common among the unemployed. A prospective cohort study of 6,191 middle-aged British men (aged 40 to 59 in 1978) examined the impacts of loss of employment during the early 1980s recession on mortality (Morris et al., 1994). Baseline questionnaires were sent out from 1978 to 1980 and 5-year mortality data were obtained from death registers. The study found that men who experienced unemployment (n = 1,779) during the 5-year follow-up were twice as likely to die as those who remained continuously employed (all-cause mortality RR = 2.13, 95% CI 1.71–2.65). Controlling for smoking, weight, and alcohol consumption as well as socioeconomic status reduced the RR slightly to 1.95 (95% CI 1.57–2.43). These risks were consistent across different causes of death, with the unemployed more than twice as likely to die from cancers (fully adjusted RR = 2.07, 95% CI 1.45–2.97) and cardiovascular diseases (fully adjusted RR = 2.13, 95% CI 1.57–2.89) as the employed. However, once those who were unemployed on the grounds of illness were excluded, the relative risk of death among the "healthy unemployed" (n = 923) decreased substantially to 1.49 (95% CI 1.10–1.96) for all causes, to 1.59 (95% CI 1.00–2.51) for cancers, and to 1.64 (95% CI 1.10–2.43) for cardiovascular diseases. Although this is still an excess mortality of at least 49%, it brings into play questions about selection versus causation in the relationship between unemployment and ill health.

Unemployment, Self-Reported Health, and Limiting Long-Term Illness

The negative relationship between unemployment and health is also reflected in studies of self-reported health and limiting long-term illness (LLTI). For example, a 20-year longitudinal study of limiting long-term illness among UK men (Bartley & Plewis, 2002) found a substantially increased risk among the unemployed. Data were examined relating to 60,000 men aged 15 to 40 at the start of the 20-year study period (1971) and thus aged 35 to 60 at the end (1991). The study found a large degree of continuity in the unemployed population, concluding that over 25% of those unemployed in 1971, 30% of those unemployed in 1981, and 46% of those unemployed in both 1971 and 1981 were also unemployed in 1991. In terms of health, the study found that the odds of reporting a LLTI in 1991 increased in a graded manner depending on the number of times someone had experienced a period of unemployment in the previous 20 years: men who were unemployed in 1971 or 1981 were almost twice as likely (OR 1.88, 95% CI 1.70–2.10) than those who had been continuously employed to report LLTI; men who were unemployed in both 1971 and 1981 were three times more likely to report LLTI (OR = 3.04, 95% CI 2.18–4.24). Adjustment for low socioeconomic status reduced

these increased odds of LLTI to only 1.68 (95% CI 1.51–1.87) and 2.50 (95% CI 1.79 only 3.50) respectively, showing that unemployment had an independent relationship with increased odds of developing a LLTI. Similar findings were reported in relation to self-reported health by a Swedish study (Korpi, 2001).

Unemployment and Health Behaviors

There are some longitudinal data suggesting that unemployment also increases the likelihood of hazardous health behaviors such as smoking or excess alcohol consumption. This is particularly the case among young men. For example, a study of 2,887 men from the 1958 British Birth Cohort found an increased risk of smoking and problem drinking among those who were unemployed (Montgomery et al., 1999b). After adjustment for potential confounding factors (socioeconomic and behavioral factors before the onset of unemployment), the RR of smoking for those aged 33 who had been unemployed in the last year was 2.92 (95% CI 2.13 only 4.01), for heavy drinking it was 1.73 (95% CI 1.18 only 2.54), and having a drink problem was 2.90 (95% CI 1.99 only 4.21). In addition, the study looked at the effects of accumulated unemployment (more than 3 years of unemployment) since age 16. It found that long-term unemployment of over 3 years increased the risk of smoking: fully adjusted relative odds (RO) = 2.11, 95% CI 1.42 only 3.12), and problem drinking (fully adjusted RO = 2.15, 95% CI 1.39 only 3.33) compared with those who had never experienced unemployment. Similarly, a Finnish study of alcohol use found that associations between high levels of alcohol consumption and unemployment were consistent across periods of both high and low national unemployment levels only among poorly educated, single, unemployed men (OR = 1.6, 95% CI 1.1–2.4) (Luoto et al., 1998).

Comparative Research on Job Insecurity, Unemployment, and Health[2]
Welfare-State Regimes and Health

In narrow terms, the "welfare state" is a means of referring to the state's role in education, health, housing, poor relief, social insurance, and other social services in developed capitalist countries during the postwar period (Ginsburg, 1979, 3). The welfare state can also be considered more broadly as a particular form of state or a specific type of society that emerged in advanced market democracies in the postwar period (Pierson 1998, 7). Welfare provision, in the form of cash benefits and welfare services, is acknowledged as an important moderator in terms of the relationship between labor market position and health (Bartley & Blane, 1997; Dahl et al., 2006; Diderichsen, 2002). A crucial aspect of welfare provision, and one that most differentiates welfare states, is income maintenance (to prevent poverty), particularly during adverse events such as unemployment, old age, or long-term absence due to sickness (Diderichsen, 2002; Esping-Andersen, 1990).

Welfare states have been classified into regimes—"welfare-state regimes"—with those welfare states that are the most similar (in terms of political tradition, the principles underpinning delivery, the levels of welfare provision, etc.) being categorized into together, thus emphasizing *within* regime coherence and *between* regime differences (Eikemo & Bambra, 2008). There are various competing welfare-state regime typologies, each emphasizing different aspects of welfare-state provision, such as decommodification ("the extent to which individuals and families can maintain a normal and socially acceptable standard of living regardless of their market performance" (e.g., Esping-Andersen, 1987, 86), social expenditure levels (the amount that a country spends on social welfare (e.g., Bonoli, 1997), or political traditions (whether a country has a history of liberal, social democracy or conservative politics (e.g., Navarro & Shi, 2001) (for an overview see Bambra, 2007). Ferrera's (1996) fourfold typology, which focuses on different dimensions of how social benefits are granted and organized, has been highlighted as one of the most empirically accurate welfare-state regime typologies (Bambra, 2007). Ferrera makes a distinction between the Scandinavian, Anglo-Saxon, Bismarckian, and southern countries (Figure 7.1). More recently, the eastern European countries have begun to be considered as an additional regime type (Bambra, 2007).

Welfare-State Regimes and Social Protection for the Unemployed

Social protection (the amount of financial support provided by the state in terms of cash payments) during unemployment varies by country and welfare-state regime type. To a large degree this reflects the historical influence of differing political traditions, with those countries experiencing more postwar years of Social Democratic rule providing more generous systems of social support (Esping-Andersen, 1990). Table 7.1 breaks down the various characteristics of social protection during unemployment

by five different welfare-state regimes: Scandinavian, Anglo-Saxon, Bismarckian, southern and eastern. In essence, there are three interrelating principles underpinning provision, which are combined in different ways in different welfare systems: universalism (welfare services and cash payments are available for all citizens), social insurance (welfare services and cash payments are available only to those who have contributed previously) and means-testing (services and payments are given only to those below a certain income threshold—usually the very poor) (Diderichsen, 2002). Benefits based on universal provision do not make reference to previous contributions or means testing and are offered to all citizens on an entitlement basis as long as specific demographic, social, or health criteria are fulfilled. Often flat-rate benefits which are the same for everyone, are paid. Under social insurance, entitlement to benefits is dependent on previous contributions; in most cases subsequent benefit levels reflect previous earned income. Under means testing, entitlement is restricted on the basis of income and the (often minimal) financial support is targeted at those in most need usually after they have exhausted all other means (e.g., personal savings or social insurance) (Rhodes, 1997).

Welfare provision for the unemployed is governed by these three principles in varying ways. For example, to differing degrees of generosity, universalism is more prominent within the Scandinavian welfare states (high population coverage) and the Anglo-Saxon regimes (fixed low level benefit rates for all), while social insurance is the key component of provision within the Bismarckian, southern, and eastern European welfare states. Means testing is more commonly a characteristic of the Anglo-Saxon welfare states. For example, in the United Kingdom (Anglo-Saxon), unemployment benefit is only payable (for a maximum of 6 months) to those who fulfil the minimum National Insurance contribution requirement within the 2 years before claiming (Table 7.1). Most claimants do not meet these criteria and are therefore reliant on means-tested social assistance benefits. Unemployment protection in each welfare-state regime therefore represents a complex mix of these differing principles.

However, there are clear differences by welfare-state regime—owing to the influence of differing political traditions—in terms of how these principles are operationalized, particularly in terms of the generosity of benefits paid to the unemployed, the qualifying period and conditions, duration of

1. Scandinavian (example = Sweden)

   Characterised by universalism, comparatively generous social transfers, a commitment to full employment and income protection; and a strongly interventionist state. The state is used to promote social equality through a redistributive social security system. Unlike the other welfare state regimes, the Scandinavian regime type promotes a high level of equality via high value out of work payments and universal access to well-funded public welfare services.

2. Bismarckian (example = Germany)

   Distinguished by its 'status differentiating' welfare programs in which benefits are often earnings related (so that higher earners will receive higher out of work benefits than lower earners who lose their jobs), administered through the employer; and geared towards maintaining existing social patterns (as there will be income differences between the unemployed that reflect their previous employment). The role of the family is also emphasised and the redistributive impact is minimal (as the benefits system maintains occupational hierarchies). However, the role of the market is marginalised.

3. Anglo-Saxon (example = USA)

   State provision of welfare is minimal with large roles for private provision. Social protection levels are modest (low financial value of benefits) and often attract strict entitlement criteria which limit access. Benefits are usually means-tested and benefit recipients are often stigmatised for needing state support. In this model, the dominance of the market is encouraged both passively, by guaranteeing only a minimum, and actively, by subsidising private welfare schemes. The Anglo-Saxon welfare state regime thereby minimises the decommodification effects of the welfare state and a stark division exists between those, largely the poor, who rely on state aid and those who are able to afford private provision.

4. Southern (example = Spain)

   The southern welfare states have been described as 'rudimentary' because they are characterised by their fragmented and localised system of welfare provision which consists of diverse income maintenance schemes that range from the meagre to the generous and welfare services, particularly, the health care system, that provide only limited and partial population coverage. Reliance on the family and voluntary sector is also a prominent feature.

5. Eastern (example = Poland)

   The formerly Communist countries of East Europe have experienced the demise of the universalism of the Communist welfare state and a shift towards policies associated more with the Anglo-Saxon welfare state regime notably marketisation and decentralisation. In comparison with the other member states of the European Union, they have fairly limited welfare services.

Figure 7.1. Welfare state regimes.

benefit payments, and the waiting period before entitlement is activated. In each of these regards, the Scandinavian welfare states are generally more generous than the other welfare-state regimes (Table 7.1), particularly in comparison to the Anglo-Saxon and eastern European regimes.

Welfare-State Regimes, Unemployment, and Health

Differences in the social protection offered to the unemployed could therefore be an important moderating factor in the relationship between poverty, unemployment, and health (Bartley et al., 2006). In a recent paper (Bambra & Eikemo, 2009), we examined the extent to which relative health inequalities between unemployed and employed people varied across twenty-three European countries and by the different approaches to social protection taken by the five European welfare-state regimes (Scandinavian, Anglo-Saxon, Bismarckian, southern and eastern). The study used data from the 2002 and 2004 waves of the cross-sectional European Social Survey (37,499 respondents, aged 25 to 60). Employment status was measured as the main activity in the previous 7 days. Health variables were self-reported limiting long-term illness (LLTI) and fair/poor general health (PH).

We found that in all countries, unemployed people reported higher rates of PH than those in employment (Table 7.2). There were also clear differences by welfare-state regime. Relative inequalities between employed and unemployed were largest in

Table 7.1. Characteristics of Unemployment Protection in 23 European Countries, Ranked by Welfare State Regime

Welfare Regime (1–5, High-Low)	Country	Funding System	Qualifying Period[a]	Initial Net Replacement Rate (% of Net Average Wages)[b]	Unemployment Insurance Benefit Duration (Months)[c]	Waiting Period (Days)[d]
1. Scandinavian	Denmark	Subsidized voluntary insurance	12 months in last 3 years	70	48	0
	Finland	Voluntarily subsidized insurance and social assistance system	43 weeks in last 2 years	70	23	7
	Norway	Social Insurance	Annual earnings in last year equal to 75% of base amount.	68	36	5
	Sweden	Subsidized program of basic insurance and voluntary income-related insurance	6 months in last 12 months	75	28	5
2. Bismarckian	Austria	Social insurance	28 weeks in last 12 months	63	9	0
	Belgium	Social insurance	468 days in last 27 months	61	No limit	0
	France	Social insurance and social assistance	6 months in last 22 months	75	23	8
	Germany	Social insurance and social assistance	12 months in last 2 years	69	12	0
	Luxembourg	Social insurance	26 weeks in last 12 months	80	12	0
	Netherlands	Social insurance and social assistance	26 weeks in last 39 weeks	74	24	0
	Switzerland	Social insurance	12 months in last 2 years	77	24	5

(continued)

Table 7.1. Continued

Welfare Regime (1–5, High-Low)	Country	Funding System	Qualifying Period[a]	Initial Net Replacement Rate (% of Net Average Wages)[b]	Unemployment Insurance Benefit Duration (Months)[c]	Waiting Period (Days)[d]
3. Anglo-Saxon	Ireland	Social insurance and social assistance	39 weeks in last 12 months	49	15	3
	United Kingdom	Social insurance and social assistance	Contributions equivalent to 25 and 50 times the lower earnings limit must have been paid in the last 2 years	54	6	3
4. Southern Europe	Greece	Social insurance	125 days in last 14 months	55	12	6
	Italy	Social insurance	2 years of insurance contributions with 52 weeks contributions in last 2 years	54	6	7
	Portugal	Social insurance and social assistance	540 days in last 24 months	83	24	0
	Spain	Social insurance	12 months in last 6 years	67	21	0
5. Eastern Europe	Czech Republic	Social insurance	12 months in last 3 years	56	5	-
	Hungary	Social insurance	12 months in last 4 years	49	9	0
	Poland	Social insurance	Earnings in 18 months prior to claim must be at least equivalent to the minimum wage.	59	12	7
	Slovenia	Social insurance	12 months in last 18 months	56	8	-

[a] For unemployment insurance benefits.

[b] Net replacement rate = (benefit income when unemployed − tax on benefit income)/(earned income + benefit income when employed 2 tax on earnings and benefits)6100; it is assumed that the unemployed worker is 40 years old and has an uninterrupted employment record of 22 years. Benefits included in calculation: unemployment insurance, unemployment assistance, social assistance, family benefits, housing benefits.

[c] Months at equivalent to the initial rate for the Czech Republic, the Slovak Republic and Spain, where the benefit level declines overtime (eg, for Spain, where the nominal replacement rate declines from 70% to 60% after 6 months, the month's equivalent initial rate is calculated as 6 months plus six-sevenths of 18 months). In most countries after the insurance period ends the unemployed person is entitled to claim social assistance (which may be means-tested).

[d] No data available.

Table 7.2. Prevalence Rates, Rate Differences and Age-Standardized Odds Ratios (95% CI) of the Relationship Between Unemployment and Health by Welfare State Regime.

Welfare State Regime		Limiting Long- Term Illness (LLTI)				Poor/fair general health (PH)			
		Prevalence Employed %	Prevalence Unemployed %	Rate Difference (Unemployed—Employed)	OR for Rate Difference (95 % CI)	Prevalence Employed %	Prevalence Unemployed %	Rate Difference (Unemployed—Employed)	OR for Rate Difference (95 % CI)
Men	Scandinavian	17.5	30.3	13.5	1.96 (1.47–2.61)	18.4	17.6	17.0	2.27 (1.72–3.01)
	Bismarckian	13.7	25.1	12.0	2.21 (1.74–2.79)	20.1	19.0	19.8	2.72 (2.21–3.35)
	Anglo-Saxon	11.1	16.4	5.7	1.67 (0.99–2.81)	12.7	11.7	16.9	2.97 (1.92–4.60)
	Southern	6.8	12.5	6.2	2.07 (1.34–3.18)	21.9	21.2	12.6	1.82 (1.35–2.46)
	Eastern	17.6	27.4	10.8	1.89 (1.43–2.52)	33.1	31.6	17.8	2.15 (1.67–2.76)
Women	Scandinavian	19.4	35.3	17.0	2.28 (1.71–3.03)	17.8	35.3	18.7	2.99 (2.34–4.00)
	Bismarckian	14.8	23.5	9.4	1.87 (1.48–2.37)	21.9	34.7	13.8	2.06 (1.67–2.55)
	Anglo-Saxon	10.0	23.1	13.7	2.73 (1.50–4.95)	13.6	27.5	14.8	2.78 (1.63–4.73)
	Southern	7.8	11.8	4.5	1.52 (1.03–2.25)	30.5	39.3	10.1	1.66 (1.31–2.11)
	Eastern	18.1	24.4	7.0	1.65 (1.24–2.19)	38.4	49.0	12.0	1.76 (1.38–2.25)

Source: **European Social Survey 2002 and 2004.**

the Anglo-Saxon (men: OR_{PH} = 2.97, 1.92–4.60; women: OR_{LLTI} = 2.73, 1.50–4.95 and OR_{PH} = 2.78, 1.63–4.73) Bismarckian (men only: OR_{LLTII} = 2.21, 1.74–2.79 and OR_{PH} = 2.72, 2.21–3.35), and Scandinavian (women only: OR_{LLTI} = 2.28, 1.71–3.03 and OR_{PH} = 2.99, 2.34–4.00) regimes, and smallest in the southern (men: OR_{PH} = 1.82, 1.35–2.46; women: OR_{LLTI} = 1.52, 1.03–2.25 and OR_{PH} = 1.66, 1.31–2.11) and eastern (women only: OR_{LLTI} = 1.65, 1.24–2.10 and OR_{PH} = 1.76, 1.38–2.25) welfare-state regimes.

Our study shows that the relationship between unemployment and health is consistent across European countries, with the unemployed in each country self-reporting worse health than the employed. It seems, therefore, that even though the levels of social protection offered to the unemployed vary by welfare state (and welfare-state regime), in all countries a relationship exists between unemployment and poorer self-rated health. This suggests that current wage-replacement rates, even in the more generous welfare states, are not sufficient to overcome the financial effects of unemployment on health. On the other hand, it may indicate the importance for health of the nonfinancial losses associated with unemployment (e.g., social isolation) (Bartley et al., 2006, Rudas et al., 1991).

However, our study identified important differences in the magnitude of the relationship by welfare-state regime. Specifically, relative inequalities were found to be largest for men and women in the Anglo-Saxon countries. Wage replacement rates for the unemployed are the lowest in these welfare states, and benefits are means-tested and subject to strict entitlement rules. The unemployed in the Anglo-Saxon welfare states are therefore at a great financial disadvantage in comparison with those in employment; this may well explain the magnitude of inequality as financial strain has been found to be an important factor in the relationship between unemployment and ill health (Kessler et al., 1987). Furthermore, means-tested benefits are associated with stigma; therefore the nonfinancial problems of unemployment may be greater in the Anglo-Saxon welfare states (Diderichsen, 2002). A comparative study by Rodriguez (2001) found that in the United Kingdom, Germany, and the United States, the likelihood of reporting poor health was significantly higher among unemployed people in receipt of means-tested benefits than those in receipt of entitlement benefits. The higher inequalities in the Anglo-Saxon countries are in keeping with broader-based studies of welfare-state regimes, and health indicators have found that overall public health tends to be worse in the welfare states of the Anglo-Saxon regime.

International Variation in Job Insecurity and Health

Relatively little is known about the health-damaging effects of job insecurity in terms of international patterns (László et al., 2010). In Europe, we have mainly seen studies from the Nordic countries, the United Kingdom, and Belgium, but these were not comparative studies. In particular, more research is needed from central and eastern parts of Europe, which have experienced difficulties in the transition from a state-based to a market-oriented economy. Several papers have found that there are large and significant cross-national differences in self-perceived job insecurity in Europe (Erlinghagen, 2008; Green, Felstead, & Burchell, 2000; OECD, 1997). These studies show a similar pattern in which the Nordic countries score better than elsewhere. However, none of these studies examined associations with health. To date, only one study has conducted a comparative analysis of the association between job insecurity and health. Laszlo et al. investigated the association between job insecurity and self-rated health in approximately 23,000 working subjects aged 45 to 70 years from sixteen European countries. They found that a high proportion of the working population perceive their jobs as insecure, ranging from 14.2% in Spain to 41.7% in Poland. Notably, the eastern European countries showed consistently higher proportions compared with all other countries, the Nordic welfare-state countries had the lowest proportions (together with France and Spain), while the central European countries were placed in an intermediate position. In models adjusted for demographic, socioeconomic, work-related, and behavioral factors, they observed only modest variations of the association between job insecurity and health between European countries. Job insecurity was significantly associated with an increased risk of poor health in the Czech Republic, Denmark, Germany, Greece, Hungary, Israel, the Netherlands, Poland, and Russia, with odds ratios varying from 1.3 (in Czech Republic) to 2.0 (in Germany). Similar but nonsignificant associations were observed in Austria, France, Italy, Spain, and Switzerland. No effects were observed for Belgium and Sweden.

Concluding Comments

This chapter has provided a brief overview of the research literature on job insecurity, unemployment, and health. It has noted that although low job security has been proven to be causally related in some studies to a range of health outcomes, particularly with respect to psychological morbidity, self-reported morbidity, and mortality, this finding is not consistent across all studies and may vary internationally. Similarly, while there is increasingly strong evidence that unemployment is also causally linked to a decline in health status and increased mortality across all European countries, comparative research suggests that international variations in welfare-state polices might moderate this relationship and that therefore social safety nets matter to public health (Bartley & Blane, 1997).

The levels of welfare benefits paid to the unemployed, how they access these benefits, and for how long may all moderate the ill health effects of unemployment. Likewise, in countries with more supportive welfare-state safety nets, the ill health effects of stress and insecurity are lessened as the fear of unemployment is less (Dragano et al., 2010). This means that policymakers need to consider interventions to raise the living standards of those who are out of work. The "minimum income for healthy living" (MIHL) is potentially a way of ensuring that welfare benefits are of a sufficient level to maintain health and well-being, and that there is a right to a certain standard of living. Based on the link between income and health, Morris and colleagues (2000) have illustrated how, in relation to older people and young men, health can be improved and inequalities in health reduced via the public provision of a minimum income to meet basic and social needs relating to nutrition, physical activity, housing, psychosocial interactions, transport, medical care, and hygiene. The MIHL would include funding to enable "consumption of a healthy diet, for example five portions of fruit and vegetables a day, two portions of fish a week; expenses related to exercise costs, for example, the cost of trainers, bicycles and swimming in a local leisure centre; as well as costs related to social integration and support networks (e.g. telephone rental, television)" (Marmot, 2010, 121). In addition to the payment of out-of-work welfare benefits, governments need to increase employment rates via public investment; where this is not possible, they must fund active labor market policies (work, training, or other programs) to help the unemployed move back into employment (e.g., Lindsay, this volume; Price & Vinokur, this volume).

In terms of remaining research challenges, there is still a need for further research that provides more conclusive explanations of the causal nature of the relationship between job insecurity, unemployment, and health. This will require international longitudinal studies. Second, gender differences in the relationships should be further clarified and explained as most research to date has focused on the relationship between unemployment and health among men (Bambra, 2011). Third, studies need to examine how job insecurity is distributed by social class as well as how class impacts on the relationship between unemployment and health. Social inequalities in the distribution of these risk factors could be important in terms of explaining socioeconomic health inequalities (Bambra, 2011). Finally, there is a need for more research into international variations in the relationship between job insecurity and health, particularly by socioeconomic status. This will enable the effects of different public policy interventions to be examined. These questions will help address some of the gaps in the current social epidemiological evidence base on unemployment, insecurity, and health.

Notes

1. The section "Unemployment and Health" is reproduced from C Bambra 2011 *Work, Worklessness and the Political Economy of Health* pp. 100–129, with permission from Oxford University Press.
2. Sections "Welfare-State Regimes and Health", "Welfare-State Regimes and Social Protection for the Unemployed" and "Welfare-State Regimes, Unemployment, and Health" are reproduced from C. Bambra and T. A. Eikemo (2009), Welfare state regimes, unemployment and health: A comparative study of the relationship between unemployment and self-reported health in 23 European countries. *Journal of Epidemiology & Community Health*, 63: 92–98, with permission from the BMJ Publishing Group Ltd.

References

Bambra, C. (2007). Going beyond the three worlds: Regime theory and public health research. *Journal of Epidemiology and Community Health, 61*, 1098–1102.

Bambra, C., & Eikemo, T. A. (2009). Welfare state regimes, unemployment and health: A comparative study of the relationship between unemployment and self-reported health in 23 European countries. *Journal of Epidemiology and Community Health, 63*, 92–98

Bambra, C. (2011) *Work, worklessness and the political economy of health*. Oxford, UK: Oxford University Press.

Bartley, M., & Blance, D. (1997). Health and the lifecourse: Why safety nets matter. *British Medical Journal, 314*, 1194–1196.

Bartley, M., & Ferrie, J. (2001). Glossary: unemployment, job insecurity, and health. *Journal of Epidemiology and Community Health, 55*, 776–781.

Bartley, M. & Plewis, I. (2002). Accumulated labour market disadvantage and limiting long-term illness: Data from the 1971–1991 ONS longitudinal study. *International Journal of Epidemiology, 31*, 336–341.

Bartley, M., Ferrie, J. & Montgomery, S. (2006). Health and labour market disadvantage: Unemployment, non-employment, and job insecurity, in M. Marmot and R. G. Wilkinson (eds.) *Social determinants of health* (pp. 78–96). Oxford, UK: Oxford University Press.

Beatson, M. (1995). *Labour market flexibility*. London: Department of Employment.

Blakely, T. A., Collings, S.C.D. & Atkinson, J. (2003). 'Unemployment and suicide. Evidence for a causal association?' *Journal of Epidemiology and Community Health, 27,* 294–600.

Blakely, T., Tobias, M., & Atkinson, J. (2008). Inequalities in mortality during and after restructuring of the New Zealand economy: Repeated cohort studies. *British Medical Journal, 336,* 371–375

Bonoli, G. (1997). Classifying welfare states: A two-dimension approach. *Journal of Social Policy, 26,* 351–372.

Cobb, S., & Kasl, S. V. (1977). *Termination: The consequences of job loss.* Cincinnati, OH: National Institute for Occupational Safety and Health.

D'Souza, R. M., Strazdins, L., Lim, L. L., Broom, D. H., & Rodgers, B. (2003). Work and health in a contemporary society: Demands, control, and insecurity. *Journal of Epidemiology and Community Health, 57*(11), 849–854.

De Witte, H. (1999). Job insecurity and psychological well-being: Review of the literature and exploration of some unresolved issues. *European Journal of Work and Organizational Psychology, 8,* 155–157.

Dahl, E., Fritzell, J., Lahelma, E., Martikainen, P., Kunst, A. E. & Mackenbach, J. P. (2006) Welfare state regimes and health inequalities. In J. Siegrist & M. Marmot (eds.), *Social inequalities in health* (pp. 193–222). Oxford, UK: Oxford University Press.

Diderichsen, F. (2002). Impact of income maintenance policies. In J. Mackenbach & M. Bakker (eds.) *Reducing inequalities in health: A European perspective* (pp. 53–66). London: Routledge.

Dorling, D. (2009). Unemployment and health: Health benefits vary according to the method of reducing unemployment. *British Medical Journal, 338,* 1087.

Dragano, N., Siegrist, J. & Wahrendorf, M. (2010). Welfare regimes, labour policies and workers' health: A comparative study with 9917 older employees from 12 European countries. *Journal of Epidemiology and Community Health.* doi: 10.1136/jech2009.098541

Eales, M. J. (1989). Shame among unemployed men. *Social Science & Medicine, 28,* 783–789.

Eikemo, T. A. & Bambra, C. (2008). The welfare state: A glossary for public health. *Journal of Epidemiology and Community Health, 62,* 3–6.

Eikemo, T. A., Kunst, A. E., Judge, K., & Mackenbach, J. P. (2008). Class-related health inequalities are not larger in the East: A comparison of four European regions using the new European socioeconomic classification. *Journal of Epidemiology and Community Health, 62*(12), 1072–1078.

Erikson, R., & Goldthorpe, J. H. (1992). *The constant flux. A study of class mobility in industrial societies.* Oxford, UK: Clarendon Press.

Erlinghagen, M. (2008). Self-perceived job insecurity and social context: A multi-level analysis of 17 European countries. *European Sociological Review, 24*(2), 183–197.

Esping-Andersen, G. (1987). Citizenship and socialism: Decommodification and solidarity in the welfare state. In G. Esping-Andersen & L. Rainwater (eds.), Stagnation and renewal in social policy: The rise and fall of policy regimes. London: Sharpe.

Esping-Andersen, G. (1990). *The three worlds of welfare capitalism.* London: Polity.

Ferrera, M. (1996). The southern model of welfare in social Europe. *Journal of European Social Policy, 6,* 17–37.

Ferrie, J. (2001). Is job insecurity harmful to health? *Journal of the Royal Society of Medicine, 94,* 71–76.

Ferrie, J., Shipley, M. J., Marmot, M., Stansfeld, S., & Smith, G. D. (1995). Health effects of anticipation of job change non-employment: longitudinal data from the Whitehall II study. *British Medical Journal, 311,* 1264–1269.

Ferrie, J., Shipley, M. J., Marmot, M., Stansfeld, S., & Smith, G. D. (1998b). An uncertain future: The health effects of threats to employment security in white-collar men and women. *American Journal of Public Health, 88*(7), 1030–1036.

Ferrie, J., Shipley, M. J., Marmot, M. G., Stansfeld, S., & Smith, G. D. (1998a). The health effects of major organisational change and job insecurity. *Social Science & Medicine, 46*(2), 243–254. doi: 10.1016/S0277-9536(97)00158-5

Ferrie, J., Shipley, M. J., Newman, K., Stansfeld, S. A., & Marmot, M. (2005). Self-reported job insecurity and health in the Whitehall II study: Potential explanations of the relationship. *Social Science & Medicine, 60*(7), 1593–1602. doi: 10.1016/j.socscimed.2004.08.006

Ferrie, J., Shipley, M. J., Stansfeld, S., & Marmot, M. (2002). Effects of chronic job insecurity and change in job security on self reported health, minor psychiatric morbidity, physiological measures, and health related behaviours in British civil servants: The Whitehall II study. *Journal of Epidemiology and Community Health, 56*(6), 450–454.

Fryer, D. M. (1986). Employment, deprivation and personal agency during unemployment: A critical discussion of Jahoda's explanation of the psychological effects of unemployment. *Social Behavior, 3,* 23.

Ganzeboom, H.B.G., De Graaf, P. M., Treiman, D. J., & De Leeuw, J. (1992). A standard international socio-economic index of occupational status. *Social Science Research, 21,* 1–56.

Ginsburg, N. (1979). *Class, capital and social policy.* London: Macmillan.

Greehalg, L., & Rosenblatt, Z. (1984). Job insecurity: Towards conceptual clarity. *The Academy of Management Review, 9,* 438–448.

Green, F., Felstead, A., & Burchell, B. (2000). Job insecurity and the difficulty of regaining employment: An empirical study of unemployment expectations. *Oxford Bulletin of Economics and Statistics, 62*(Special Issue).

Jahoda, M. (1982). *Employment and unemployment. A social psychological analysis.* Cambridge, UK: Cambridge University Press.

Kessler, R. C., Turner, J. B., & House, J. S. (1987). Intervening processes in the relationship between unemployment and health. *Psychological Medicine, 17,* 949–61.

Kivimäki, M., Vahtera, J., Thomson, L., Griffiths, A., Cox, T., & Pentti, J. (1997). Psychosocial factors predicting employee sickness absence during economic decline. *Journal of Applied Psychology, 82*(6), 858–872.

Korpi, T. (2001). Accumulating disadvantage: longitudinal analyses of unemployment and physical health in representative samples of the Swedish population. *European Sociological Review, 17,* 255–74.

Kposowa, A. (2001). Unemployment and suicide: A cohort analysis of social factors predicting suicide in the US National Mortality Study. *Psychological Medicine, 31,* 127–38.

Kreigar, N. (2011). Epidemiology and the people's health. New York: Oxford University Press.

Lahelma, E., Laaksonen, M., & Aittomäki, A. (2009). Occupational class inequalities in health across employment sectors: The contribution of working conditions. *International Archives of Occupational and Environmental Health, 82*(2), 185–190.

László, K. D., Pikhart, H., Kopp, M. S., Bobak, M., Pajak, A., Malyutina, S., . . . Marmot, M. (2010). Job insecurity and health: A study of 16 European countries. Social Science & Medicine, 70(6–3), 867–874.

Lee, S., Colditz, G. A., Berkman, L. F., & Kawachi, I. (2004). Prospective study of job insecurity and coronary heart disease in US women. *Annals of Epidemiology, 14*(1), 24–30. doi: 10.1016/S1047-2797(03)00074-7

Lewis, G., & Sloggett, A. (1998). Suicide, deprivation and unemployment: Record linkage study. *British Medical Journal, 317*, 1283–1286.

Luoto, R., Poikolainen, K., & Uutela, A. (1998). Unemployment, sociodemographic background and consumption of alcohol before and during the economic recession of the 1990s in Finland. *International Journal of Epidemiology, 27*, 623–629.

Marmot, M., Siegrist, J., Theorell, T., & Feeney, A. (1999). Health and the psychosocial environments at work. In M. Marmot and R. Wilkinson (eds.), *Social determinants of health*. New York: Oxford University Press.

Marmot, M. (2010). Fair society, healthy lives: the Marmot review. London: University College.

Martikainen, P., & Valkonen, T. (1996). Excess mortality of unemployed men and women during a period of rapidly increasing unemployment. *Lancet, 348*, 909–912.

Martikainen, P., Mäki, N., & Jäntti, M. (2008). The effects of workplace downsizing on cause-specific mortality: A register-based follow-up study of Finnish men and women remaining in employment. *Journal of Epidemiology and Community Health, 62*(11), 1008–1013.

Massarelli, N. (2009). European Union Labour Force Survey: Annual results 2008. *Eurostat: Data in Focus, 33.*

Mohren, D. C., Swaen, G. M., van Amelsvoort, L. G., Borm, P. J., & Galama, J. M. (2003). Job insecurity as a risk factor for common infections and health complaints. *Journal of Occupational and Environmental Medicine, 45*(2), 123–129.

Montgomery, S. M., Cook, D. G., Bartley, M., & Wadsworth, M. E. (1999a). Unemployment pre-dates symptoms of depression and anxiety resulting in medical consultation in young men. *International Journal of Epidemiology, 28*, 95–100.

Montgomery, S. M., Cook, D. G., Bartley, M., & Wadsworth, M. E. (1999b). Unemployment, cigarette smoking, alcohol consumption and body weight in young British men. *European Journal of Public Health, 8*, 21–27.

Morris, J. K., Cook, D. G., & Shaper, A. G. (1994). Loss of employment and mortality. *British Medical Journal, 308*, 1135–1139.

Morris, J. N., Donkin, A. J., Wonderling, D., Wilkinson, P., & Dowler, E. A. (2000). A minimum income for healthy living. *Journal of Epidemiology and Community Health, 54*, 885–889.

Moser, K. A., Fox, A. J., & Jones, D. R. (1984). Unemployment and mortality in the OPCS Longitudinal Study. *Lancet, 324*, 1324–1329.

Pierson, C. (1998). Theory in British social policy. In C. Pierson & N. Ellison (eds.), *Developments in British social policy* (pp. 17–30). London: Macmillan.

Navarro, V., & Shi, L. (2001). The political context of social inequalities and health. *International Journal of Health Services Research, 31*, 1–21.

OECD. (1997). *Is job insecurity on the increase in OECD countries?* Paris: OECD.

Platt, S. (1986). Parasuicide and unemployment. *British Journal of Psychiatry, 149*, 401–405.

Rantakeisu, U., Starrin, B., & Hagquist, C. (1997). Unemployment, shame and ill health—An exploratory study. *Scandinavian Journal of Social Welfare, 5*, 13–23.

Roskies, E., & Louis-Guerin, C. (1990). Job insecurity in managers: Antecedents and consequences. *Journal of Organizational Behavior, 11*, 345–359.

Rudas, N., Tondo, L., Musio, A., & Masia, M. (1991). Unemployment and depression: Results of a psychometric evaluation. *Minerva Psichiatrica, 32*, 205–209.

Rhodes, M. (1997). The Welfare State: internal challenges, external constraints. In M. Rhodes, & A. Vincent (eds.), *Developments in Western European politics*. London: Macmillan.

Rodriguez, E. (2001). Keeping the unemployed healthy: the effect of means-tested and entitlement benefits in Britain, Germany and the United States. *American Journal of Public Health, 91*, 1403–11.

Rugulies, R., Aust, B., Burr, H., & Bültmann, U. (2008). Job insecurity, chances on the labour market and decline in self-rated health in a representative sample of the Danish workforce. *Journal of Epidemiology and Community Health, 62*(3), 245–250.

Scott-Samuel, A. (1984). Unemployment and health. *Lancet, 324*, 1465.

Sverke, M., Hellgren, J., & Näswall, K. (2002). No security: A meta-analysis and review of job insecurity and its consequences. *Journal of Occupational Health Psychology, 7*, 242–264.

Sverke, M., Hellgren, J., & Näswall, K. (2006). *Job insecurity. A literature review.* Stockholm: National Institute for Working Life and The Swedish Trade Unions in Co-operation.

Swaen, G. M., Bültmann, U., Kant, I., & van Amelsvoort, L. G. (2004). Effects of job insecurity from a workplace closure threat on fatigue and psychological distress. *Journal of Occupational and Environmental Medicine, 46*(5), 443–449.

Toivanen, H., Lansimies, E., Jokela, V., Helin, P., Penttila, I., & Hanninen, O. (1996). Plasma levels of adrenal hormones in working women during an economic recession and the threat of unemployment: Impact of regular relaxation training. *Journal of Psychophysiology, 10*, 36–48.

Vahtera, J., Kivimäki, M., Pentti, J., Linna, A., Virtanen, M., Virtanen, P., & Ferrie, J. E. (2004). Organisational downsizing, sickness absence, and mortality: 10-town prospective cohort study. *British Medical Journal, 328*(7439), 555.

Watkins, S. (1986). Economic adversity and health: Policy implications. In F. Eskin (ed.), *Unemployment: A challenge to public health* (pp. 1–72). Manchester, UK: Manchester Centre for Professional Development.

Theoretical Perspectives to Job Loss and Job Search

Goal Setting and Control Theory: Implications for Job Search

Gary P. Latham, Mary B. Mawritz, *and* Edwin A. Locke

Abstract

The benefit of using theories in the behavioral sciences for job search is that they facilitate predicting, explaining, and influencing behavior. This chapter compares and contrasts two such theories, namely, goal setting and control theory. Empirical research, emanating from these two theories on job search, is reviewed. The chapter closes with a checklist for job seekers and suggestions for future research.

Key Words: goal setting theory, inductive theory building, verbal self-guidance, control theory

Introduction

The primary purposes of this chapter are (1) to review two theories of motivation, namely, goal setting and control theories, and (2) to compare and contrast the two with regard to their applicability for pursuing a job.[1] The chapter is organized such that first, goal setting theory is explained. Second, empirical research based on this theoretical framework is reviewed with a focus on the benefits of setting a specific, challenging goal to obtain employment. Third, control theory is discussed with regard to its applicability for job search. Fourth, empirical research on this theory is reviewed. Finally, control theory is discussed in terms of its similarities and differences with goal setting theory, again with an emphasis on its relevance for job search. The chapter closes with a checklist for job seekers and suggestions for future research.

Prior to the 1960s, advances in knowledge of employee motivation were limited because most research consisted of atheoretical one-shot studies that were not part of a programmatic thrust. Thus, inductive theories could not be readily built. A drawback of conducting research in this manner is that it did not provide a framework for predicting, explaining, or influencing behavior in

organizations. Application was tantamount to "this intervention worked here; let's try it again there." But no theories were developed to show evidence of generality, or to identify mediators and moderators of the observed effects.

Inductive Theory Building

Locke and Latham's (1990, 2002, 2013; Latham & Locke, 2007) theory of goal setting was inductively developed over a 25-year period. The advantages of induction rather than deduction to build a theory have been explained in detail elsewhere (Locke, 2007). In brief, deduction is useful in developing a theory only if the data have been collected through induction. Consider the famous example put forth by Socrates. All men are mortal is an inductive generalization without which the rest could not follow. The conclusion is already implicit in the premise; the conclusion, that Socrates is mortal, makes it explicit. The syllogism connects an established inductive generalization to an observed fact, namely, that Socrates is a man. Unlike induction, there is nothing logically new in a deduction.

As Hambrick (2007, p. 1346) has argued, the requirement by many social science journal editors to deductively develop a theory prior to, rather than after, conducting research retards the field's ability to attain its primary goal: understanding. "Our field's theory fetish, for instance, prevents the reporting of rich detail about interesting phenomena for which no theory yet exists. And it bans reporting of facts—no matter how important or competently generated . . ., but that once reported, might stimulate the search for an explanation." Typically a deductively derived theory is simply "constructed" to demonstrate a researcher's preconceived thinking, or worse, biases. Consequently, deduction has seldom led to the development of rigorously developed, validated theories. In contrast to the social sciences, Harriman (2010) provided evidence on how modern physics progressed due to the use of the inductive method to develop theory.

Goal Setting Theory

Goal setting theory, as noted earlier, was developed inductively (Locke & Latham, 2005), and therefore makes valid predictions within the scope of the established theory. The theory states that (1) a specific high goal leads to higher performance than setting no goal or even setting a vague one such as to do your best; (2) the higher the goal, the higher your performance; (3) feedback or knowledge of results, incentives, participation in decision making, and the like affect behavior only to the extent that they lead to the setting of and commitment to a specific high goal (see Figure 8.1). The theory differentiates between proximal and distal goals (Latham & Seijts, 1999) and between performance and learning goals (Winters & Latham, 1996).

Proximal and distal goals have a hierarchical relationship in that proximal goals facilitate the attainment of distal goals. They do so by indicating progress or the lack thereof toward the attainment of the distal goal. Thus they suggest whether the plan for goal attainment is appropriate, or a change in strategy is required. Strategy/plan is a mediator that explains the beneficial effect of the goal–performance relationship (Latham & Arshoff, in press). For example, when people are searching for a job, they may set a distal goal. In the absence of

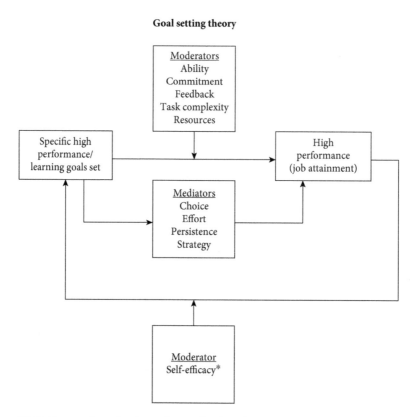

Goal setting theory

* Self efficacy mediates the effects of assigned goals and its effects are mediated by self-set goals; self-efficacy may also have a direct effect on performance.

Figure 8.1 Goal setting theory.

setting and attaining proximal goals, they may become discouraged and abandon the distal goal when a job offer is not imminent. Examples of proximal goals include updating your resume by the end of today, reading the want ads in X papers a day, making Y cold calls weekly, and networking with Z people monthly.

Although goal theory asserts that people can pursue multiple goals at the same time, it is not known how many goals people can pursue simultaneously. Presumably the answer depends on many context factors including moderator variables (Locke & Latham, 1990). Moderator variables or boundary conditions are synonymous with interactions; they specify the conditions under which a theory will or will not be applicable. Goal setting theory includes five moderators that were identified inductively through empirical research. First, an individual must have the *ability (knowledge, skill)* to attain the goal. Otherwise, goal attainment is impossible, and goal commitment is likely to be low if it exists at all. As Fugate, Kinicki, and Asforth (2004) noted, ability enables job applicants to be attractive to potential employers, and thus attain their goal of finding employment.

Second, a person must be *committed* to attaining the goal. In regard to a job search, goal commitment refers to the importance or centrality that an individual places on obtaining a job. Ability, no matter how impressive, is irrelevant if a person has no desire to attain the goal of becoming employed.

Third, *feedback* is critical for self-regulation in goal pursuit. Feedback enables people to track progress toward a goal and thereby to ascertain whether they have an appropriate strategy or plan for goal attainment and/or whether they need to increase their effort to do so. What contributes to the difficulty in mastering golf, for example, is the lack of feedback as to what an individual did correctly/incorrectly in hitting the ball. Hence, Michael Jordan, the former basketball star, had himself video-taped as he went from one hole to the next so that he could immediately see what he was doing when he swung at the ball. Similarly, it is not uncommon for unemployed people to send out hundreds of job applications. Yet, often the only information they subsequently receive is a one- to two-sentence rejection letter. Constructive feedback as to why they were rejected is missing (e.g., typing errors that suggest they are not conscientious; unexplained omissions; resume not tailored to the job opening). Hence they do not know what they need to do to attain their goal. Job applicants

need to actively seek feedback from respected others on ways they can improve their job search.

Fourth, consistent with ability moderating the strength of the positive linear relationship between the difficulty level of a specific goal to which you are committed to attaining is the *complexity* of the task. Specific high-performance goals have a highly positive effect only on the performance of tasks that are straightforward for a person.

When an individual has yet to acquire the knowledge or skill to perform a task, as is common in searching for a job (Bolles, 1989), a goal for a specified high level of performance (e.g., obtain a job in 6 months) may have a deleterious effect on performance. In such cases, a *learning* rather than a performance goal should be set (Winters & Latham, 1996). A learning goal focuses attention on the discovery of the requisite knowledge, process, or procedures to attain a goal (e.g., ways to attain a job) rather than on a specific performance outcome (e.g., obtain the job). As previously stated, obtaining a job is a complex task for most people. Setting a performance goal that "by March 1st I will have a job in profession A, at location B, with a salary of C" may decrease rather than increase their chances of obtaining a job. Instead, people should focus on discovering and mastering specific processes/steps they will take to secure a job. That is, they should set learning goals.

Van Hooft and Noordzij (2009) conducted a training program on goal setting for job seekers who were registered with a reemployment counseling agency in the Netherlands. Regardless of an individual's goal orientation (Dweck, 1986), the workshop on setting learning goals led to more time and effort spent on job search behaviors and higher reemployment probabilities than the workshop on setting performance goals or the control condition in which no specific goal for job search was set. It is noteworthy that research has shown that setting learning goals is especially helpful when ability (Seijts & Latham, 2011) and achievement motivation are low (Elliot & Harackiewitz, 1994).

Job rejections can be especially hard on highly conscientious job seekers. This is because they are typically ambitious; they want to succeed. Cianci, Klein, and Seijts (2010) found that these people react more negatively and experience greater tension when they receive negative feedback than people who are less conscientious. In addition, these researchers discovered that when a specific high-performance goal is followed by negative feedback, the resulting tension leads to poor performance for those who are conscientious. But this was not the case when a specific, high-learning goal was set.

Note that there is a linear relationship between the difficulty of a learning goal and performance on tasks that are complex for people (Latham, Seijts, & Crim, 2008). With regard to a job search, an individual may want to set learning goals for customizing a resume for different types of jobs, effective and efficient ways to network, and how to make successful "cold calls."

Finally, all of this becomes negligible if *situational* variables, the fifth moderator in goal setting theory, mitigate goal pursuit (e.g., a rapid downturn in the economy; a high unemployment rate in the person's occupation). People must have the necessary resources to attain a specific, high goal (e.g., a laptop).

Four mediators (causal mechanisms) explain the positive effects of specific high goals on an individual's performance. First, a specific goal affects *choice*; the goal focuses an individual's attention and subsequent actions on X to the relative exclusion of Y or Z. Wanberg, Hough, and Song (2002) found that goal specificity, defined as clarity as to the type of career, work, or job desired, increased the intensity of an individual's job search. It directed attention and effort toward targeted activities relevant to the job search. Cote, Saks, and Zikic (2006) too found that job search clarity is positively related to job search intensity. Specific, distal, and proximal goals for a job search keep an individual focused and decrease the chances for that person to become distracted.

Second and third, a specific high goal affects both *effort* (e.g., job search intensity) and *persistence* until the goal (e.g., obtaining a job) is attained. Prussia, Fugate, and Kinicki (2001), for example, found that the setting of goals by unemployed manufacturing workers was positively related to job search effort, and effort in turn was positively related to securing a job.

Fourth, commitment to a specific, high goal cues the recall of extant *strategies* or knowledge, or it motivates the development of a new plan for attaining the goal of job attainment. Planning is especially relevant to the issue of multiple goals (Latham & Arshoff, in press). This is because planning, as Hua and Frese (2013) noted, specifies the steps and substeps for goal attainment, such as securing a job. The different goals are prioritized, and the substeps make clear the ways to attain these multiple goals. Planning can identify whether the multiple goals are nested in one another or are reciprocally interdependent.

Consistent with research findings on learning goals, Koen, Klehe, VanVianen, Ziki, and Nauta (2010) found that a focused strategy, in which people have identified their top job choice, reduced the likelihood of haphazard job-seeking behavior and hence contributed to the number of job offers. This is because a focused plan specifies the requisite actions for goal attainment. A more general exploratory strategy reduced the quality of reemployment 8 months later.

Goal theory focuses on affect in addition to performance (Locke & Latham, 1990, 2013). A goal, such as job attainment, is both an end to aim for and a standard for assessing your achievement. Positive affect, including pride in performance, is experienced when a specific high goal is attained or exceeded, whereas negative affect is experienced when a goal is not reached (Mento, Locke, & Klein, 1992). Goal attainment typically leads to setting an even higher goal, such as a job promotion within a specific time period, when people have self-efficacy that they can master the task and that they can indeed find a job (Bandura, 1997). Furthermore, people with high self-efficacy persist in goal pursuit despite experiencing setbacks to goal attainment (Bandura, 1997; Locke & Latham, 1990). Thus, the degree of discrepancy between a person's performance and the goal is not definitive; an individual's response depends on how that discrepancy is cognitively processed and the decisions a person makes as a result (e.g., the goal could be lowered, kept the same, raised, or abandoned).

Goal Setting Research

Approximately 400 studies led to the development of goal theory (Locke & Latham, 1990). As of the new millennium, more than 1000 studies have been conducted on one or more aspects of this theory (Mitchell & Daniels, 2003; Latham & Pinder, 2005). One of the first field experimental tests of the theory involved engineers/scientists. Using a 3 (assigned goal, participatively set goal, and do your best) × 3 (praise, public recognition, and a monetary bonus) factorial design that included a comparison group, Latham, Mitchell, and Dossett (1978) found, consistent with goal theory, that employees who were urged to do their best to obtain a high performance appraisal performed no better than those in the comparison group even though the former were rewarded with praise, public recognition, or a monetary bonus. In addition, employees who had a specific high goal performed significantly higher than those in the comparison group, as well as those who were rewarded with praise, public recognition, or a monetary bonus for high performance, but had no specific high-performance goal. Goal commitment did not differ between those with a participatively set or an assigned goal. But, in the participative condition, employees set significantly higher goals than the employees who were assigned goals by their supervisor. Consistent with the theory, the higher the goal, the higher the employee's performance.

Self-set goals are the core of self-management/self-regulation. Frayne and Latham (1987) developed a 7-week training program on the self-management of job attendance for state government unionized workers in the United States. For sundry reasons, these individuals perceived obstacles to them coming to work as insurmountable. For example, some were single parents of children under 5 years of age who were consistently sick. As a result, those employees in both the experimental and control group were in danger of being subjected to progressive disciplinary action leading to job termination.

The training program included the necessity for setting distal and proximal goals for monthly and weekly attendance. Obtaining feedback by using charts and graphs to self-monitor goal progress was stressed. This step was necessary because many employees were unaware of how many days they were absent from the workplace. A behavioral contract was written by each employee to self-specify the rewards (e.g., a beer) and punishers (e.g., housework) that would be self-administered contingent on goal progress or the lack thereof. The result was job attendance significantly higher than that of the control group. Nine months later the control group received the same training in self-management. As was the case in the original group trained in self-management, employee self-efficacy for coming to work and actual job attendance increased significantly (Latham & Frayne, 1989). This training intervention can be adapted easily to self-management of the job search process.

Social cognitive theory (Bandura, 1986) is related to goal setting theory in that one of its three central variables is goal setting. In addition, social cognitive theory stresses the importance of outcome expectancy, namely enabling people to see the relationship between what they are doing and attaining their goal. The majority of studies on social cognitive theory, however, have focused on a third variable, self-efficacy (Bandura, 1997), that is, domain, specific confidence in being able to attain a given level of performance. High self-efficacy is important because people may see what is required of them to attain a specific high goal, but lack the confidence that they can do so. Thus, self-efficacy is arguably the most important variable in this theory of personal agency because it refers to people's beliefs in their capability to exercise control not only over their own functioning, but in addition, over environmental events. Van Ryn and Vinokur (1992) found that job search self-efficacy had relatively durable effects on an individual's intention to seek a job over time despite repeated failures to obtain employment.

Bandura's research (1986, 1997, 2001) shows that when people are confronted by obstacles to goal attainment, they engage in self-enabling or self-debilitating self-talk depending on whether their self-efficacy is high or low (Bandura, 2001). Self-efficacy predicts goal choice (e.g., a high goal). It often has a main effect on performance (including persistence) independently of goals. Self-efficacy, however, is affected by goal assignment because assigning a high goal is typically a signal that the person who assigned the goal believes this individual can attain it. People with high self-efficacy have greater commitment to a high goal than people with low self-efficacy that the goal is attainable. Finally, high self-efficacy is important because it has a reciprocal effect with discovering an appropriate strategy, and being open to feedback showing a change in strategy is needed (Latham & Seijts, 1999). A meta-analysis revealed that self-efficacy has a medium-sized correlation with the number of job offers an individual receives (Kanfer, Wanberg, & Kantrowitz, 2001).

FUNCTIONAL VERSUS DYSFUNCTIONAL SELF-TALK AFFECTING SELF-REGULATION

Meichenbaum (1977) developed a methodology for training people to change their dysfunctional to functional self-talk. This verbal self-guidance (VSG) involves three steps: (1) observing a trainer model the desired task, (2) performing the task while verbally instructing yourself overtly, and (3) performing the task while verbally instructing yourself covertly. Although the effectiveness of this training has been assessed primarily in clinical psychology settings, Brown (2003) found that VSG was also effective in increasing the collective efficacy for, as well as actual team-playing skills of, college students in their respective study groups. VSG training has been shown to be especially effective in enabling people to obtain a job.

Millman and Latham (2001) conducted a study with displaced managers in Toronto who had been out of work for 13 months despite the services of an outplacement agency. In the time period in which the study was conducted, there was an economic recession. Media reports were repeatedly emphasizing the futility in seeking jobs. Setting a specific goal for reemployment was accompanied by seven 2.5-hour VSG training sessions to ensure goal commitment. Because self-talk occurs on a continuous basis, it plays a central role in self-regulation. Through negative self-talk, and a job seeker's ability for symbolic visualization and forethought, a single failure in obtaining a job may be experienced repeatedly (Bandura, 1986). Training to change negative self-talk into positive self-guidance fosters goal commitment and hence persistence in the job search process. Thus this training was conducted in recognition that one or more failure experiences can undermine self-efficacy and your confidence that a job will be found.

Goal setting, followed by training in VSG, led to significantly higher self-efficacy regarding reemployment, and a significantly greater number of displaced managers finding jobs within 9 months of training relative to the displaced managers in the control group. VSG enables people to act in accordance with the beliefs they express to themselves.

In a field experiment involving Native North Americans in high school, Latham and Budworth (2006) subsequently assessed the effectiveness of training in VSG to increase self-efficacy for the goal to obtain a job. They hypothesized that (1) the job search self-efficacy of participants receiving training in VSG is significantly higher than those who do not receive training, (2) self-efficacy is positively correlated with performance in a mock selection interview conducted by white managers unaware of who received training in VSG, and (3) participants trained in VSG are significantly more likely to become employed than are those in the control group. The hypotheses were supported. VSG training resulted in higher job search self-efficacy, higher evaluations in the mock selection interview conducted by managers, and subsequently a greater number of meaningful jobs than was the case for those who were not trained in VSG.

In a third field experiment, Yanar, Budworth, and Latham (2009) examined the effectiveness of this technique for enabling Muslim women in Turkey, who were over the age of 40, to attain their goal to become reemployed. In the time interval when this field experiment was conducted, 71.3% of men were employed while the same was true for only 26.9% of women. Turkish culture has been characterized by patriarchy and low gender egalitarianism (Fikret Pasa, Kabasakal, & Bodur, 2001; Kagitcibasi, 1986). Despite the fact that Turkey has laws that prohibit sex and age discrimination in the workplace, the legal system has not resulted in changes in lifestyle (Kagitcibasi, 1986). Women who are actively involved in the Turkish labor force typically drop out when they have children (Tasci & Tansel, 2005). Yet, many female managers have reported that family duties per se did not interfere with their reemployment outside the home. Aycan (2004, p. 465) found that the barrier to women reentering the workforce was lack of self-confidence: "The greatest of all barriers against women is their low self-confidence. At the sight of the first disappointment or a problem, the ones with low self-confidence are the ones who give up and use children and husband as an excuse."

In short, both person and environmental factors often limit the employment of women over the age of 40 in Turkey. Consequently, goal setting and VSG training in self-efficacy for goal attainment were given to women who had been randomly assigned to an experimental group. The mean age of the women in this field experiment was 48 years. More than half of them had worked previously in managerial positions. Many of them had been unemployed for 3 years.

Training in VSG was provided in four 90-minute sessions over four consecutive days.[2] In the first session, trainees stated their beliefs to one another as to why they were unable to attain their goal of obtaining a job and listed the environmental barriers they perceived were preventing them from doing so (e.g., "this is a bad economy," "I am too old for the jobs I want," "After spending a long time at home, I am not confident I will perform well if I do get a job").

A trainer modeled for the trainees how to change their dysfunctional talk to functional self-talk (e.g., "Because of my past experiences, I know what I am capable of doing, and I am very determined to get what I want," "My age means I have a lot of experience in social relations, which helps me to solve problems in the workplace effectively"). The trainer modeled the functional statements overtly before asking the trainees to do likewise overtly, and then covertly.

On the second day, the training session focused on job search channels. The trainees were given job advertisements from a local recruitment paper. They were asked to discuss why they would not consider applying for the jobs advertised. The trainees were then asked to record their negative self-statements (e.g., "They already indicated that they were looking for someone who is much younger than I am. How can I send my resume to them?"). Second, the trainees watched the trainer engage in VSG by changing dysfunctional to functional self-statements ("I have far more experience than people younger than I who are likely to apply for this job"). Third, they were requested to engage in VSG overtly and to do so again covertly changing their dysfunctional to functional self-talk. In short, training in VSG taught these trainees to eliminate dysfunctional self-talk about their job application by asking them to verbalize positive statements that can be made about a particular job posting (e.g., "Look, they want someone who has experience in sales. I do have sales experience from different companies. My age means that I have a lot of experience in social relations too. I can add a cover letter to my resume and tell them they should consider my experience").

On the third day, the training focused on the selection interview and the overall selection process. In dyads, the trainees practiced VSG in "mock" interviews. Practice interview questions were taken from a Turkish human resources website. While answering interview questions (e.g., Why do you think you are suitable for the job?), they used VSG to increase their self-efficacy with respect to giving appropriate answers (e.g., "I can answer this question in a confident manner; I will talk about my competencies suitable for the job. I will not let myself focus on my age or my responsibilities at home").

On the fourth and final day of this training program, the trainees rehearsed VSG relative to all of the job search activities they had been taught. The women were also encouraged to continue using VSG at home before applying for the jobs, and again while preparing for an employment interview.

Given their goal to get a job, those given VSG attained significantly higher job search self-efficacy with regard to reemployment than their counterparts in the control group. In addition, they persisted in job search behavior significantly more so than those in the control group, who also had the goal to get a job but no VSG training. Job search self-efficacy completely mediated the effect of this intervention on job search behavior. Consequently, a significantly greater number of women who received this training attained their goal of employment in their

area of interest within 6 months to 1 year following training than did the women in the control group.

Before leaving this topic, it should be noted that VSG training includes aspects of both a performance and a learning goal. The performance goal/desired outcome was to obtain a job. The VSG training focused a person's attention on ways to obtain the job.

Control Theory

Control theory has a very different history than goal theory. Control theory was developed deductively, based on cybernetic engineering by Powers (1978), and later refined by two social psychologists, Carver and Scheier (1981), as well as many others in the field of organizational behavior (e.g., Klein, 1989). As Locke (1991) noted, the original theory was based on a mechanical model, namely, that of torpedoes and thermostats. The object (e.g., thermostat) detects a signal that is then compared to a standard (e.g., the preset temperature). If there is a discrepancy between the signal and the standard, the object is programmed to reduce the discrepancy.

Initially, control theory used inanimate terms. This is because the object in the theory was not a person, rather it was an effector. The detection of a discrepancy was not done by a mind, it was done by a comparator. The use of mechanistic language was subsequently eliminated by Carver and Scheier (1981). The effector became a person, the comparator became a cognitive judgment, and the standard became a goal.

As control theory evolved, it borrowed heavily from goal theory and other cognitive theories (Klein, 1989). For example, Campion and Lord (1982) stated that an individual's motivation is a function of the discrepancy between behavior and the goal to which a person is committed. Note that goal commitment is a moderator in goal theory. Control theory currently states that people are motivated by their desire to minimize the discrepancy between their behavior and their goal that has yet to be attained. When people receive feedback that their performance has led to goal attainment, the theory states that effort and persistence cease. However, when feedback indicates a negative discrepancy between performance and an individual's goal, this theory states that then, and only then, will an individual attempt to reduce the discrepancy by increasing effort and/or lowering the goal (Klein, 1989). Thus, the basic premise of control theory is that it is this feedback loop that motivates an individual's behavior. Discrepancy reduction is the primary motivator of the action an individual initiates. This loop is shown in Figure 8.2.

As an example, consider an experienced pharmaceutical salesperson who is searching for a new job. The salesperson produces a certain level of sales performance (i.e., output), which in turn affects this individual's perception of his or her performance. Information regarding the job market provides the salesperson with knowledge of what level of sales performance is necessary to be considered for a desired position in another organization (i.e., a goal). The salesperson compares actual performance to the standard. If the salesperson perceives that he or she is failing to meet the standard, the theory suggests that the person will likely take corrective action to increase sales performance in order to reduce the discrepancy, such as increasing effort. Note that effort is a mediator in goal theory.

Although control theory draws upon many goal theory concepts, it differs from goal theory in two points of emphasis: goal theory begins with *discrepancy creation* (Bandura & Locke, 2003). This is because goal setting and attainment are requirements for survival. Goal-directed action is required by all living organisms. If an organism does not attain goals commensurate with its needs, the organism perishes. In nonconscious organisms, goal-directed action is automatic, programmed by evolution. In the lower animals, consciousness directs goal-directed action, but the types of goals pursued are again set by evolution. For example, a hungry lion sees a zebra and chases it. If lions chased only shadows, the species would expire.

In contrast to the mechanistic roots of control theory, goal theory has biological roots in that the essence of living action is goal directedness. Unlike lower forms of life, human beings have the ability and the need to choose goals volitionally. Only their internal organs and bodily systems function automatically in accordance with the thermostat model (e. g., body temperature regulation). A human being cannot survive by automatic processes alone. An individual has to acquire knowledge, set and choose goals to attain, and take actions to pursue them. This is a life-long process. Choose goals, work to attain them, and set new goals. Failure to set and pursue new goals results in stagnation, lack of adaptation to the environment, and ultimately in death. Hence, goal theory begins with the setting of a goal, which volitionally creates a performance discrepancy. Goal theory views discrepancy reduction as a *correlate* of goal-directed behavior rather than as the prime motivator. In short, both theories emphasize discrepancy reduction, but they differ as to where the motivation sequence begins. The difference is essentially an approach versus an avoidance focus. Goal theory states that people set goals for future performance; control theory states that people strive to avoid a discrepancy between their present performance and their goal. Only goal theory emphasizes both discrepancy production and reduction.

The second crucial difference between these two theories is that control theory denies the effect of self-efficacy on motivation despite the many empirically documented links to goal theory noted earlier. Between-subject correlations of self-efficacy with

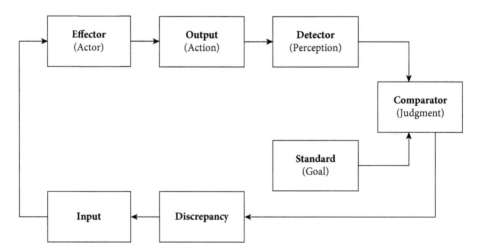

Control Theory: The Negative Feedback Loop (Locke, 1991)

Figure 8.2 Control theory: the negative feedback loop (Locke, 1991).

performance are said by control theorists to be epiphenomenal because they believe incorrectly that self-efficacy simply reflects past performance (e.g., Vancouver, 2000). Voluminous studies have refuted this claim (e.g., Bandura, 1997, 2012; Bandura & Locke, 2003).

The negative feedback loop in control theory includes affect (Carver & Scheier, 1981). Affect has been a focus of goal setting research since the 1960s (Locke & Latham, 1990). Carver and Scheier (1981) argued that the rate of discrepancy reduction is positively associated with satisfaction. Locke, Cartledge, and Knerr (1970) found that satisfaction was affected by the perceived instrumentality of performance on a given trial for attaining an end goal. Goal theory research has shown that the actual degree of deviation from the goal also affects satisfaction (Locke & Latham, 1990).

Advocates of control theory have attempted to circumvent the problem posed by the argument that discrepancy reduction alone is the prime motive of behavior. The theory currently posits goals at various levels of abstraction, namely at the higher-order goal level (the superordinate goal), at the intermediate level, and at the lower-order level (the subordinate goal) (Boekaerts, de Koning, & Vedder, 2006). Short-term, behavioral goals, it is claimed, are regulated by feedback loops at lower levels, whereas long-term, abstract goals are regulated by feedback loops at higher levels. The theory further states that the goals for lower-order feedback loops are determined by the output of higher-order feedback loops. Lower-order goals are linked to goals located higher in the goal system (Carver & Scheier, 1981). Their pursuit signals the means by which higher-level goals are attained (Lord & Levy, 1994).

In the context of a job search, control theory suggests that to obtain a job (i.e., a higher-level goal), a job applicant might set a goal to acquire the specific skills necessary to perform the job (i.e., a lower-level goal). This in turn might lead to setting a specific goal to obtain a formal education (i.e., another lower-level goal). The problem for control theory is that this does not resolve the issue of postulating discrepancy reduction as *the* primary motive. The feedback loops are merely embedded in other loops. But, there has to be a starting point. Biologically speaking, the ultimate basis for goal-directed action is the need to survive. This means there is a continual process of setting and working to attain a goal. If revisions of control theory state that the starting point at the highest level is discrepancy *creation* due to the choice of a goal, then control theory will lose its primary distinction from goal theory (aside from its failure to specify moderators and mediators and its rejection of self-efficacy as a motivator).

As with goal theory, control theory asserts that individuals often pursue multiple goals. As noted above, control theory suggests that goals are hierarchically arranged, such that higher-level goals influence the setting of lower-level goals, the means by which they are attained, and that an individual's goals may conflict and/or may be pursued simultaneously. The idea of goal hierarchy is an important aspect of control theory (although value hierarchies are an important part of many psychological theories) and has been used to explain motivation in a number of different contexts, including purchasing decisions (e.g., Gutman, 1982) and job search activities (e.g., Steel, 2002).

Empirical Research on Control Theory

Empirical research shows that the size of the discrepancy between an individual's actual output and the standard (e.g., the goal) influences the extent to which people increase their performance (Campion & Lord, 1982; Kernan & Lord, 1990). For example, Hollenbeck (1989) developed and empirically examined a control theory model to explain employee reactions (e.g., job satisfaction, organizational commitment, voluntary turnover). His model incorporates three "core elements" of control theory as predictors of employee reactions: (1) discrepancies between standards/goals and perceptions, (2) expectations regarding future discrepancies (i.e., outcome expectancies), and (3) self-focus (i.e., the ability to recognize that goals/standards exist and an awareness of the negative emotions associated with the discrepancy). Consistent with both goal theory and social–cognitive theory, Hollenbeck found that both perceptions of discrepancies and outcome expectancies influence employee reactions. These relationships are moderated by self-focus, such that high self-focus strengthens the relationships.

Additionally, two laboratory experiments conducted by Kernan and Lord (1991) found support for the crucial role of discrepancies and goal level in explaining employee reactions. Employee performance and satisfaction were positively related when performance and goal difficulty level were aligned. This finding replicates goal theory findings.

Control Theory and Job Search

Control theory has been used to explain aspects of the job search process. Steel (2002) used the negative feedback loop described by control theory to propose that when individuals make contact with concrete employment prospects, they receive feedback from the job market on their employability. Negative feedback from the job market may result in adjustments of employment expectations (e.g., decreases in estimations of perceived job alternatives). It may also trigger a reassessment of thoughts and feelings regarding the status quo [e.g., (dis)satisfaction with the present job]. Regardless of the outcome, job market feedback provides recipients with a better understanding of their employment prospects. Note that feedback is a moderator variable in goal theory.

Additionally, Wanberg, Zhu, and Van Hooft (2010) used control theory to explain job search efforts. They hypothesized that low perceived progress toward attaining a job (i.e., "I had an unproductive day in relation to my job search") highlights a discrepancy between desired and actual progress. This, they said, results in increased effort. They also hypothesized that high perceived progress leads to a decrease in effort. Consistent with control theory, the results of this study revealed that the more (or less) progress participants made on a given day, the less (or more) time they spent searching for a job the subsequent day. Note that effort and persistence are mediators in goal theory.

In addition to explaining changes in expectations and attitudes regarding current and prospective employment, control theory has been used to explain applicants' job search behaviors when multiple goals are set. As mentioned, the theory suggests that lower-level goals are linked to higher-level goals in that the pursuit of lower goals signals the means by which higher goals can be obtained. Suppose a job applicant who is trying to obtain a job (i.e., a lower-level goal) also has a higher-level goal of having a work–life balance. Control theory suggests that the job search process will be influenced by this higher-order goal of work–life balance. For example, the individual may forego certain job search activities, such as acquiring the formal education necessary to obtain the job desired, because doing so conflicts with the ability to increase time with family and friends. To date, these examples are inferences drawn from control theory and hence are subjects for future research.

CRITICAL DIFFERENCES BETWEEN GOAL SETTING AND CONTROL THEORIES FOR JOB SEARCH

Job search, as defined by Kanfer, Wanberg, and Kantrowitz (2001), is a purposeful, volitional pattern of action that begins with the setting of and commitment to an employment goal. It is the goal that activates a job search.

The crucial difference between goal setting and control theory is their respective fundamental assumptions regarding *the* source of motivation. The underlying assumption of control theory is that people are only motivated by discrepancy reduction between a goal and their behavior. For example, when their goal to attain a job is met, the motivation to act to further attain this goal ceases. However, goal setting theory, as well as social cognitive theory, states that motivation is a result of goal performance discrepancy production as well as reduction. Thus, those people who have high self-efficacy for job search, upon attaining a job, will likely set a specific high goal for job promotion, or to search for an even better job elsewhere. As long as a person strives to live, setting goals is a continuous process.

As noted earlier, the feedback loop in control theory is based on the adaptation of Powers' (1978) cybernetic engineering to organizational psychology. A heat pump moves the temperature to a predetermined set point (e.g., 70°F) and then stops. People, too, may very well stop when their goal to obtain employment is attained. Alternatively, they may immediately set a new and higher goal. For example, as VanHoye and Saks (2008) pointed out, a job search goal is not restricted to obtaining a job. A job search goal for an employed individual may be to seek bargaining leverage to improve their present job situation. A goal for both unemployed and employed individuals might be to develop a network of professional relationships. Control theory may or may not be correct in predicting that search behavior ceases when a job is secured. Goal setting theory is more likely correct in predicting that goal attainment leads to the setting of higher goals for a better job, greater leverage with your employer, and a larger social network. In short, basing a theory of motivation in the workplace on a machine metaphor is incompatible with employee consciousness and volition. It is incompatible with the nature of the life process.

As stated previously, one benefit of control theory for people engaged in a job search is that it stresses the importance of a goal hierarchy in which lower-order goals are linked to higher-level goals and represent the means by which higher-level goals are accomplished. But there is still the problem of what initiates action. Research on goal setting theory has shown that people can effectively prioritize their goals and act in accordance with those priorities (Locke & Latham, 1990, 2013).

As argued previously, the advantage of an inductively derived theory in the social sciences is that it provides a framework, based on empirical research, for predicting, explaining, and influencing behavior. The advantages of using goal setting theory as a framework for job search is the emphasis that the theory places on (1) goal specificity, (2) goal difficulty, (3) moderators and mediators of goal effectiveness, (4) self-efficacy, including ways to increase your self-efficacy through verbal self-guidance to obtain a job despite the difficulties encountered in goal pursuit, and (5) the setting of a learning versus a performance goal for job search. In sum, goal setting is a more complete theory and has a more logically justifiable starting point than control theory. Consistent with goal setting theory, Kanfer et al. (2001) argued that job search refers to a pattern of thinking, affect, and behavior that can be evaluated along choice/duration (e.g., search activities), effort (e.g., frequency of search activity), and persistence, that is, the mediators in goal setting theory.

In summary, putting theoretical issues aside, an argument can be made that the practical implications of goal setting and control theories for conducting a job search are more similar than they are different. Both theories stress the importance of setting a specific, high goal and both stress the importance of performance feedback in relation to goal attainment. However, as noted earlier, control theory fails to distinguish between a learning and a performance goal, and worse, it denies the importance of self-efficacy in the job search process.

A Job Seeker's Checklist

The research findings discussed in this chapter suggest the following action steps for job seekers:

1. Determine whether you currently have the ability to obtain a job that is meaningful for you.

2. If you have the ability and you are committed to obtaining a job, set a specific goal in terms of the time-frame (e.g., 6 months) that is difficult yet obtainable.

3. If you lack the ability to obtain the type of job you desire, set a specific learning goal for the procedures/processes you will master within a specified time-frame before you set a distal performance goal.

4. When feedback indicating poor performance on a task is likely, set learning rather than performance goals. This is especially important if you are a highly conscientious individual.

5. Set proximal/subgoals in addition to your distal goal for obtaining a job. Do so for the day, week, and month.

6. Monitor your self-talk. Focus on ways to turn your dysfunctional self-talk into functional self-talk.

7. Write a behavioral contract to yourself that specifies your performance and/or learning goals as well as ways you will reward yourself for goal progress and the ways you will punish yourself for procrastination.

8. Actively seek feedback from trusted others on what you are doing well and how you can improve your job search. Make them comfortable giving you their suggestions.

9. Once you attain a meaningful job, set a distal learning or performance goal, plus proximal goals, for a promotion. There is a saying that obstacles are the frightful things you see only when you take your mind off your goal.

10. Keep in mind the acronym SMART (Mealiea and Latham, 1996). Regardless of whether you set a learning or a performance goal, it should be Specific, Measurable, Attainable, Relevant and have a Timeframe.

Future Research

Many of the suggestions in this chapter for obtaining a job are logical inferences derived from goal and control theories. The following questions should be answered through empirical research:

1. Should job seekers be encouraged to set goals for employment in a wide range of positions for which they may not be qualified, or should they be much more specific?

2. Are people more likely to obtain a job when a learning rather than a performance goal is set?

3. Is there a point in the job search process when an individual should switch from a learning to a performance goal?

4. What are the effective ways job seekers can obtain feedback on what they should start doing, stop doing, or be doing differently to attain proximal and distal goals for employment?

5. When people obtain a job, do they rest on their laurels as suggested by control theory? Do they set higher goals, as suggested by goal theory (e.g., increasing your network, obtaining a promotion)?

6. Can self-management training programs be developed for job seekers that lead to employment?

7. Can VSG training programs for job seekers be developed to change their dysfunctional self-talk to functional self-talk so that their job search self-efficacy for job attainment is increased and a job is actually obtained? Does the time interval between the VSG training have a larger effect on efficacy beliefs when they are assessed relatively sooner rather than later following training in VSG or other self-regulation interventions?

8. Do the answers to the above questions change as a function of a job seeker's age (e.g., those in their 20s versus those in their 50s)?

9. As Kanfer et al. (2001) queried, does the type of performance goal set affect job search behavior (e.g., pay level, location, required hours, type of work)?

10. How might individuals most in need of a job search intervention be identified?

Notes

1. The comparison of goal setting and control theories was done at the request of the editors. Preparation of this chapter was funded in part by a grant from the Social Sciences and Humanities Council, Canada to Gary P. Latham. We thank Howard Klein for a critical review of this chapter.
2. This explanation is taken from Yanar, Budworth, and Latham (2009).

References

Aycan, Z. (2004). Key success factors for women in management in turkey. *Applied Psychology: An International Review, 53,* 453–477.

Bandura, A. (1986). *Social foundations of thought and action: A social-cognitive theory.* Englewood Cliffs, NJ: Prentice-Hall.

Bandura, A. (1997). *Self-efficacy, the exercise of control.* New York: Freeman.

Bandura, A. (2001). Social cognitive theory of mass communication. *Media Psychology, 3,* 265–299.

Bandura, A. (2012). On the functional properties of self-efficacy revisited. *Journal of Management, 38,* 9–44.

Bandura, A., & Locke, E. A. (2003). Negative self-efficacy and goal effects revisited. *Journal of Applied Psychology, 88,* 87–89.

Boekaerts, M., de Koning, E., & Vedder, P. (2006). Goal-directed behavior and contextual factors in the classroom: An innovative approach to the study of multiple goals. *Educational Psychologist, 41,* 33–51.

Bolles, R. N. (1989). *What color is your parachute?* Berkeley, CA: Ten Speed.

Brown, T. C. (2003). The effect of verbal self-guidance training on collective efficacy and team performance. *Personnel Psychology, 56,* 935–964.

Campion, M. A., & Lord, R. G. (1982). A control systems conceptualization of the goal-setting and changing process. *Organizational Behavior and Human Decision Processes, 30,* 265–287.

Carver, C. S., & Scheier, M. F. (1981). *Attention and self-regulation: A control theory approach to human behavior.* New York: Springer-Verlag.

Cianci A. M., Klein, H. J., & Seijts, G. (2010). The effect of negative feedback on tension and subsequent performance: The main and interactive effects of goal content and conscientiousness. *Journal of Applied Psychology, 95,* 618–630.

Cote, S., Saks, A. M., & Zikic, J. (2006). Trait affect and job search outcomes. *Journal of Vocational Behavior, 68,* 233–252.

Dweck, C. S. (1986). Motivational processes affecting learning. *American Psychologist, 41,* 1040–1048.

Elliot, A. J., & Harackiewicz, J. M. (1994). Goal setting, achievement orientation, and intrinsic motivation: A mediational analysis. *Journal of Personality and Social Psychology, 66,* 968–980.

Fikret Pasa, S., Kabasakal, H., & Bodur, M. (2001). Society, organizations, and leadership in Turkey. *Applied Psychology: An International Review, 50,* 559–589.

Frayne, C. A., & Latham, G. P. (1987). The application of social learning theory to employee self-management of attendance. *Journal of Applied Psychology, 72,* 387–392.

Fugate, M., Kinicki, A. J., & Ashforth, B. E. (2004). Employability: A psycho-social construct, its dimensions, and applications. *Journal of Vocational Behavior, 65,* 14–38.

Gutman, J. (1982). A means-end chain model based on consumer categorization. *The Journal of Marketing, 46,* 60–72.

Hambrick, D. C. (2007). The field of management's devotion to theory: Too much of a good thing? *Academy of Management Journal, 50,* 1346–1353.

Harriman, D. (2010). The logical leap: Induction in physics. *Physics Today, 63,* 48–50.

Hollenbeck, J. R. (1989). Control theory and the perception of work environments: The effects of focus of attention on affective and behavioral reactions to work. *Organizational Behavior and Human Decision Processes, 43,* 406–430.

Hua, S. S., & Frese, M. (2013). Multiple goal pursuit. In E. A Locke & G. P. Latham (Eds.), *New developments in goal and task performance* (pp. 177–194). New York: Routledge.

Kagitcibasi, C. (1986). Status of women in Turkey: Cross cultural perspectives. *International Journal of Middle East Studies, 18,* 485–499.

Kanfer, R., Wanberg, C. R., & Kantrowitz, T. M. (2001). Job search and employment: A personality-motivational analysis and meta-analytic review. *Journal of Applied Psychology, 86,* 837–855.

Kernan, M. C., & Lord, R. G. (1990). Effects of valence, expectancies, and goal-performance discrepancies in single and multiple goal environments. *Journal of Applied Psychology, 75,* 194–203.

Kernan, M. C., & Lord, R. G. (1991). An application of control theory to understanding the relationship between performance and satisfaction. *Human Performance, 4,* 173–185.

Klein, H. J. (1989). An integrated control theory model of work motivation. *Academy of Management Review, 14,* 150–172.

Koen, J., Klehe, U. C., VanVianen, A. E. M., Zikic, J., & Nauta, A. (2010). Job-search strategies and reemployment quality: The impact of career adaptability. *Journal of Vocational Behavior, 77,* 126–139.

Latham, G. P., & Arshoff, A. S. (in press). Planning: A mediator in goal setting theory. In M. Frese & M. D. Mumford (Eds.), *Organization planning: The psychology of performance.* New York: Taylor & Francis.

Latham, G. P., & Budworth, M. H. (2006). The effect of training in verbal self-guidance on the self-efficacy and performance of Native North Americans in the selection interview. *Journal of Vocational Behavior, 68,* 516–523.

Latham, G. P., & Frayne, C. A. (1989). Self management training for increasing job attendance: A follow-up and a replication. *Journal of Applied Psychology, 74,* 411–416.

Latham, G. P., & Locke, E. A. (2007). New developments in and directions for goal-setting research. *European Psychologist, 12,* 290–300.

Latham, G. P., Mitchell, T. R., & Dossett, D. L. (1978). The importance of participative goal setting and anticipated rewards on goal difficulty and job performance. *Journal of Applied Psychology, 63,* 163–171.

Latham, G. P., & Pinder, C. (2005). Work motivation theory and research at the dawn of the 21st century. *Annual Review of Psychology, 56,* 485–516.

Latham, G. P., & Seijts, G. (1999). The effects of proximal and distal goals on performance on a moderately complex task. *Journal of Organizational Behavior, 20,* 412–429.

Latham, G. P., Seijts, G., & Crim, D. (2008). The effects of learning goal difficulty level and cognitive ability on strategies and performance. *Canadian Journal of Behavioural Science, 40,* 220–229.

Locke, E. A. (1991). Goal theory vs. control theory: Contrasting approaches to understanding work motivation. *Motivation and Emotion, 15,* 9–28.

Locke, E. A. (2007). The case for inductive theory building. *Journal of Management, 33,* 867–890.

Locke, E. A., Cartledge, N., & Knerr, C. S. (1970). Studies of the relationship between satisfaction, goal-setting, and performance. *Organizational Behavior and Human Performance, 5,* 135–158.

Locke, E. A., & Latham, G. P. (1990). *A theory of goal setting & task performance.* Englewood Cliffs, NJ: Prentice Hall.

Locke, E. A., & Latham, G. P. (2002). Building a practically useful theory of goal setting and motivation: A 35-year odyssey. *American Psychologist, 57,* 705–717.

Locke, E. A., & Latham, G. P. (2005). Goal setting theory: Theory by induction. In K. Smith & M. Hitt (Eds.), *Great minds in management: The process of theory development* (pp. 128–150). New York: Oxford University Press.

Locke, E. A., & Latham, G. P. (2013). *New developments in goal setting and task performance.* New York: Routledge Academic.

Lord, R. G., & Levy, P. E. (1994). Moving from cognition to action: A control theory perspective. *Applied Psychology: An International Review, 43,* 335–398.

Meichenbaum, D. (1977). *Cognitive-behavior modification: An integrative approach.* New York: Plenum.

Mento, A. J., Locke, E. A., & Klein, H. (1992). Relationship of goal level to valence and instrumentality. *Journal of Applied Psychology, 77,* 395–405.

Mealiea L., & Latham, G. P. (1996). *Skills for managerial success.* Chicago: Irwin.

Millman, Z., & Latham, G. P. (2001). Increasing re-employment through training in verbal self-guidance. In M. Erez, U. Kleinbeck, & H. K. Thierry (Eds.), *Work motivation in the context of a globalizing economy.* Mahwah, NJ: Lawrence Erlbaum.

Mitchell, T. R., & Daniels, D. (2003). Motivation. In W. C. Borman, D. R. Ilgen, & R. J. Klimoski (Eds.), *Comprehensive handbook of psychology: Industrial organizational psychology* (Vol. 12, pp. 225–254). New York: Wiley & Sons.

Powers, W. (1978). Quantitative analysis of purposive systems: Some spadework at the foundations of scientific psychology. *Psychological Review, 85,* 417–435.

Seijts, G. H., & Latham, G. P. (2011). The effect of commitment to a learning goal, self-efficacy, and the interaction between learning goal difficulty and commitment on performance in a business simulation. *Human Performance, 24,* 189–204.

Steel, R. P. (2002). Turnover theory at the empirical interface: Problems of fit and function. *Academy of Management Review, 27,* 346–360.

Tasci, H. M., & Tansel, A. (2005). Unemployment and transition in the Turkish labor market: Evidence from individual level data, IZA Discussion Papers, 1663.

Van Hooft, E.A.J., & Noordzij, G. (2009). The effects of goal orientation on job search and reemployment: A field experiment among unemployed job seekers. *Journal of Applied Psychology, 94,* 1581-1590.

Van Hoye, G., & Saks, A. M. (2008). Job search as goal-directed behavior: Objectives and methods. *Journal of Vocational Behavior, 73,* 358–367.

Van Ryn, M., & Vinokur, A. D. (1992). How did it work? An examination of the mechanisms through which an intervention for the unemployed promoted job search behavior. *American Journal of Community Psychology, 20,* 577–597.

Vancouver, J. B. (2000). Self-regulation in industrial/organizational psychology: A tale of two paradigms. In M. Boekaerts, P. R. Pintrich, & M. Zeidner (Eds.), *Handbook of self-regulation* (pp. 303–341). San Diego, CA: Academic Press.

Wanberg, C. R., Hough, L., & Song, Z. (2002). Predictive validity of a multidisciplinary model of reemployment success. *Journal of Applied Psychology, 87,* 1100–1120.

Wanberg, C. R., Zhu, J., & Van Hooft, E. A. J. (2010). The job search grind: Perceived progress self-reactions, and self-regulation of search effort. *Academy of Management Journal, 53,* 788–807.

Winters, D., & Latham, G. P. (1996). The effect of learning versus outcome goals on a simple versus a complex task. *Group and Organization Management, 21,* 236–250.

Yanar, B., Budworth, M. H., & Latham, G. P. (2009). The effect of verbal self-guidance training for overcoming employment barriers: A study of Turkish women. *Applied Psychology: An International Review, 58,* 586–601.

Job Loss and Job Search: A Social-Cognitive and Self-Regulation Perspective

Ruth Kanfer *and* Gina M. Bufton

Abstract

This chapter reviews social-cognitive and self-regulatory perspectives on involuntary job loss and subsequent job search. We begin by organizing different social-cognitive and self-regulatory perspectives along the temporal continuum of job loss and job search, and discuss the experience of job loss and its impact on the individual during subsequent job search. Using a motivational/self-regulatory frame, we then review findings related to goal generation and goal striving and outline important considerations for research design, including temporal, social, and measurement issues. Finally, we highlight the successes that have been made in the field thus far, and provide suggestions for promising future research avenues.

Key Words: job loss, job search, unemployment, reemployment, self-regulation, coping

Over the past decade, an unemployment storm has traversed the developed world. Although a complete account of the reasons for the sudden rise in unemployment over the past decade is beyond the scope of this chapter, it is important to note the multiplicity of factors that have contributed to the large-scale job losses and rising unemployment rates: the economic turbulence of the early twenty-first century, globalization, the rapid, large-scale introduction of new workplace technologies, and the mounting impact of demographic realities on national labor supplies. In the United States, the overall jobless rate at the end of 2014 was 5.6% (8.7 million persons), with 2.8 million persons unemployed for longer than 27 weeks (U.S. Department of Labor, 2015). Older workers faced substantially longer job searches than mid-career workers, and younger workers were more likely to stop looking for work than other age groups (Ilg, 2010). The negative consequences of economic events on the most vulnerable segments of the workforce have galvanized public and scientific interest in identifying key determinants and consequences of job loss and job search.

Research on job loss and job search has waxed and waned over the past century, largely in concert with economic conditions. During most of the twentieth century, research often focused on the reemployment of individuals who lost their jobs due to mass plant layoffs and the quality of their reemployment (e.g., Clague & Couper, 1931). Two implicit assumptions in this research were that a layoff was a unique event in work life, and that workers who obtained reemployment would remain in the new job through retirement. Today, however, it is clear that job loss and job search are no longer one-time events for most workers, and that job loss and job search have become an integral part of the modern employment experience. For example, findings from the National Longitudinal Survey of Youth database indicate that members of the latter portion of the baby boomer cohort (born 1957–1964) experienced an average of 4.8 unemployment spells from the beginning of their careers during the period 1978–2002 (U.S. Department of Labor, 2010). The frequency of job loss and the duration of job search across the work lifespan are complexly determined by economic conditions, industry sector, and worker characteristics (e.g., education, skills). However, the frequency of unemployment spells observed in the U.S. workforce is consistent with the notion that successful work adjustment over the lifespan requires competencies in coping with job loss and in making effective job, organizational, and even career transitions.

In accord with changes taking place in the world of work, research on job loss and job search has also evolved. As the number and length of unemployment spells have increased, researchers have begun to examine the impact that unemployment has on workers' mental and physical health (McKee-Ryan, Song, Wanberg, & Kinicki, 2005; Paul & Moser, 2009; also see Wanberg, 2012; Paul, Hassel, & Moser, this volume). Research has also expanded from simply measuring reemployment success to examining a range of outcomes related to reemployment quality (e.g., type of reemployment, comparable pay and benefits to old job, new job satisfaction; see Wanberg, Kanfer, Paulson, & Zhang, 2014; also see Virick & McKee-Ryan, this volume).

Greater diversity in age, gender, and ethnicity in the labor market, along with uneven rates of unemployment across industry sectors, have also increased research attention to the context in which job loss and job search takes place. Job loss may occur early or late in an individual's career, in a sector of the economy that is growing (e.g., programming) or declining (e.g., plant assembly), in times when financial concerns are more or less important to the individual, and in varying points of the individual's employability, in terms of health, motives, portfolio of job skills, and learning competencies. To date, most psychological studies that attempt to examine the impact of context on job search activities use demographic information (e.g., age, job industry, job tenure, gender) to evaluate contextual influences, but such studies rarely have sufficient sample size or information to consider the joint impact of different contextual variables on job search strategies and reemployment outcomes. For example, psychological studies of job search following reemployment often use "convenience" samples comprised of individuals laid off from a specific organization or those who have registered for unemployment insurance in a particular location or region. Although these studies enable detailed examination of the psychological processes associated with job search behavior, they often do not permit an examination of the influence of environmental or individual circumstances. Alternatively, research by labor economists on reemployment outcomes often uses large and diverse samples that allow for an evaluation of an individual's age, gender, health, and job history on reemployment probability and reemployment characteristics. However, data from these larger studies are often insufficient for examining the microanalytic processes by which individuals form and change reemployment goals and job search strategies over time (Wanberg, Kanfer, Hamann, & Zhang, 2015). Identifying the key person characteristics and environmental variables that affect individual job search and reemployment outcomes represents a daunting but critical challenge for advancing research in this field.

Increased recognition of the interplay between person characteristics and the external environment in which job loss and job search occur has slowly begun to encourage cross-disciplinary exchange between psychologists, organizational scientists, and economists. In the spirit of this trend, the purpose of this chapter is twofold. First, we summarize the contributions that psychological theories, in particular social-cognitive and self-regulation perspectives, have made to the understanding of worker affect, cognition, and behavior in the context of job search following involuntary job loss. Second, we present a broad research agenda for future work that may inform and contribute to an interdisciplinary approach for understanding and mitigating the impact of job loss on job search and reemployment outcomes. Accordingly, the focus of this chapter is limited to adult members of the workforce (typically aged 18–65 years) who experience involuntary loss of their primary job and then seek new employment. We do not address issues related to job search among new workforce entrants (see Saks, this volume), job search among employed individuals (see Boswell & Gardner, this volume), or job loss and job search among postretirement workers. More comprehensive reviews of the theoretical and research literature on unemployment, job search, and reemployment that fall beyond the scope of this chapter can be found in Fryer and Payne (1986), Hanisch (1999), Kanfer, Wanberg, and Kantrowitz (2001), McFadyen and Thomas (1997), Saks, Brown, and Lent (2005), Wanberg (2012), Gowan (2014), and in other chapters in this volume.

This chapter is organized into three sections. In the first section, we review the theoretical underpinnings of social-cognitive and self-regulation approaches to job loss and job search and discuss these and alternative perspectives in terms of understanding the impact of job loss. In the second section, we summarize the psychological research on job search following job loss. In the third and final section, we summarize progress in the field and propose a research agenda to address abiding issues and practical problems that unemployed job seekers confront during prolonged periods of job search.

Social-Cognitive/Self-Regulation Perspectives

Social-cognitive and self-regulatory theories of human behavior posit that human behavior can be understood as the result of continuous, reciprocal interactions between three input classes: environmental variables, intrapersonal processes, and genetic/biological factors (F. Kanfer & Schefft, 1988). Theorizing by Bandura (1977, 1986), Fishbein and Ajzen (1975), F. Kanfer (1977), Lazarus and Folkman (1984), Locke and Latham (1990), and Weiss and Cropanzano (1996) provides the broad foundations for a common social-cognitive perspective on job loss and job search. These motivational theories emphasize the psychological mechanisms and processes by which an individual responds to his or her environment and manages his or her cognitions, affect, and behaviors for the purpose of coping with job loss and gaining reemployment.

Different theories that may be considered to fall within the broad social-cognitive perspective all emphasize person–environment transactions, but each focuses on different aspects of the process. Figure 9.1 provides a heuristic model of the job loss–job search process and associated theories that have been used to investigate different aspects of the process. As shown in Figure 9.1, affective reactions to the layoff event and coping strategies for dealing with job loss are distinguished from job search activities directed toward reemployment. Although the two systems are related, broad worker affect models and job loss-specific theories differ in terms of the portion of the process emphasized. For example, Affective Events Theory (Weiss & Cropanzano, 1996) focuses on the individual's affective, cognitive, and behavioral reactions to a specific event that has taken place, such as being laid off by your supervisor. In contrast, Fishbein and Ajzen (1975) and Locke and Latham (1990) focus on the person, social, and contextual factors that influence behavioral intentions and goal choice, respectively. Similarly, Bandura (1977, 1986) and F. Kanfer (1977) focus on the self-regulatory processes (e.g., self-monitoring, self-evaluation/progress; self-reactions/efficacy) that follow from purposive goal adoption. These broad social-cognitive formulations have also been used to develop situation-specific models of job loss and job search described later in this chapter.

As indicated in Figure 9.1, self-regulatory processes instigated to cope with the affect and stress following a negative life event and processes directed toward reemployment are distinguishable but closely related. An individual's reaction to job

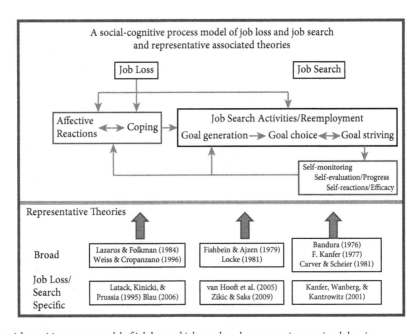

Figure 9.1 A social-cognitive process model of job loss and job search and representative associated theories.

loss and subsequent coping strategies are posited to influence the development of initial reemployment and job search goals that consequently affect job search activities. Over time, however, perceptions of poor progress in obtaining reemployment and declines in self-efficacy during unemployment can lead to stress and the need to activate emotion-focused coping strategies, as well as reconsideration of job opportunities and revision of the job search goal.

Figure 9.1 provides an overview of the processes and mechanisms involved in job loss and job search. Person and situation factors, although not shown in the figure, are further posited to exert influence throughout the job loss–job search process. Meta-analytic findings by Kanfer et al. (2001), for example, indicate a significant relationship between personality traits and other noncognitive variables on job search behavior and reemployment. Similar findings for the role of personality and affective variables on the use of job coping strategies have also been found (e.g., Leana & Feldman, 1998).

Reactions to job loss. For most persons, involuntary job loss represents a major, negative life event. The Lazarus and Folkman (1984) Transactional Model of Stress and Coping and Weiss and Cropanzano's (1996) Affective Events Theory provide two complementary frameworks for understanding the process by which individuals cope with stressful events. According to the Lazarus and Folkman model (1984), the impact of external events is mediated by the individual's appraisal. Primary appraisals of an event define the event's controllability, relevance, and stressfulness for the individual. Primary appraisals also determine the need for secondary appraisals that activate the individual's self-regulatory coping processes. In the context of involuntary job loss, the associated feelings of uncontrollability and stress typically activate secondary appraisals that guide the adoption of subsequent coping strategies. The Lazarus and Folkman (1984) model focuses on coping and the development of coping strategies for dealing with the change in internal or external demands placed on the individual by the event. For individuals who experience involuntary job loss, coping strategies may involve management of cognitive or behavioral activities to address the negative emotions and/or problems that occur as a result of the stressful event.

The Lazarus and Folkman (1984) model builds upon a self-regulation conceptualization of the coping process by distinguishing different types of coping in terms of the focus and the cognitive/behavioral strategies used. According to Lazarus and Folkman (1984), coping strategies may be broadly organized into one of two major coping categories: problem-focused strategies and emotion-focused strategies (See Hanisch, 1999 for a review). Problem-focused coping strategies are aimed at managing the event that is causing the problem (e.g., increasing job search efforts). In contrast, emotion-focused strategies are directed toward managing the emotional distress that follows from the event (e.g., reducing negative affect through exercising). Research investigating the different coping strategies employed by persons experiencing job loss suggests that individuals often employ both types of strategies during unemployment. Several studies show that the use of job search-related, problem-focused coping strategies is positively related to reemployment (e.g., Caplan, Vinokur, Price, & van Ryn, 1989). However, emotion-focused coping strategies that reduce negative affect can also be helpful for job search and reemployment (e.g., Leana & Feldman, 1998; Wanberg, Basbug, Van Hooft, & Samtani, 2012; also see Gowan & Gatewood, 1997 for a review).

The Weiss and Cropanzano (1996) Affective Events Theory (AET) is similar to the Lazarus and Folkman (1984) model in its focus on affective reactions to past events, but AET is more focused on the process by which affective reactions may yield nonconscious, affect-driven behaviors that are independent of work attitudes. For example, individuals who unexpectedly receive a pink slip may demonstrate greater irritability in the home context, although their attitude toward the organization remains positive and they engage in problem-focused coping strategies.

Generating reemployment intentions and goals. In contrast to reactive processes associated with job loss, several motivational theories address the determinants and mechanisms by which individuals develop proactive reemployment and job search goals. Fishbein and Ajzen's Theory of Reasoned Action (TRA; 1975) specifies the social, cognitive, and affective determinants of a behavioral intention. Although behavioral intentions and goals are not conceptually identical, they are closely related. Behavioral intentions refer to actions, such a filling out a job application. In contrast, goals may involve behavior, but are typically anchored around a higher-order desired outcome, such as obtaining reemployment.

According to the TRA, individuals develop a behavioral intention based on an integration of beliefs about the value of the behavior, expectancies about their ability to successfully perform the behavior, and the individual's beliefs about whether other persons who are important to them think they should engage in the behavior. A unique aspect of the TRA model compared with other formulations is its emphasis on the interpersonal context. All else being equal, individuals are more likely to fill out a job application if they believe that their spouse wants them to, as opposed to those individuals who do not have such interpersonal influences. In the job search context, these socially derived beliefs may promote job search activity even when the individual thinks the behavior is unlikely to yield benefit.

Lent, Brown, and Hackett (1994) provide another social-cognitive formulation, the Social-Cognitive Career Theory (SCCT), which emphasizes the determinants of career development and choice. According to this theory, an individual's career goals and behaviors are determined by self-efficacy, outcome expectations, and perceived barriers (e.g., discrimination, financial constraints) and supports (e.g., family, social network). Two aspects distinguish the SCCT model from other social-cognitive models. First, the SCCT model focuses on goal generation variables related to career, that is, to career exploration, career planning, and career and job goals. These variables provide the context for the generation of career goals that influence self-regulatory processes during the job search. Second, the SCCT model emphasizes the contextual factors (perceived barriers and supports) that play a role in goal generation. These variables, such as social support and financial resources, also play an important role in goal decision and goal commitment during a prolonged job search. Although many of the studies that provide support for SCCT involve young adults entering the workforce, SCCT provides a conceptual basis for identifying relevant goal generation variables and understanding the direction and persistence of job search activities for individuals in all stages of work life.

Yet another popular theory in industrial/organizational psychology is Locke's goal setting theory (Locke, Shaw, Saari, & Latham, 1981; Locke & Latham, 1990; see also Latham, Mawritz, & Locke, this volume). Although the initial formulations of this theory emphasized the impact of goal generation and goal attributes, later research has focused on the mechanisms by which goal attributes affect goal striving and self-regulatory processes. According to Locke and his colleagues, goals represent the most proximal influences on action by directing attention, mobilizing on-task effort, encouraging task persistence, and facilitating the development of strategies for goal accomplishment. Organizational research on goal setting and performance provides evidence that different goal attributes have varying effects on self-regulation processes, which in turn contribute to performance. Results of numerous studies show that individuals who adopt specific and difficult goals outperform individuals with less specific and/or easy goals (see Locke et al., 1981). However, research findings in this area also indicate that goals are less effective in promoting performance when self-efficacy for goal attainment is low (see Locke & Latham, 1990), when goals activate disruptive, off-task emotional processing (e.g., Kanfer & Ackerman, 1989; Wanberg, Zhu, Kanfer, & Zhang, 2012), when individuals are not committed to goal attainment (e.g., Locke, Latham, & Erez, 1988), and when goals focus on distal rather than proximal outcomes (e.g., Latham & Seijts, 1999). In the context of job search, goal setting theory suggests a beneficial effect for establishing specific, difficult job search goals (versus vague, distal reemployment goals), provided the individual is committed to the goal and the goal does not instigate disruptive emotional processing.

Goal striving and self-regulated job search. Theories and research on goal striving have dominated both the general motivational science and job search literatures over the past few decades. The focus of these theories is largely based on the mechanisms by which individuals accomplish purposive goals and the impact that goal attributes have on self-regulation processes for goal attainment.

Theories of self-efficacy by Bandura (1977) and self-regulation by F. Kanfer (1977) focus directly on the determinants, mechanisms, and consequences of purposive goals that activate and maintain self-regulatory processes for goal accomplishment. F. Kanfer's self-regulation model (1977) describes the intervening self processes by which individuals strive for goal attainment. According to this model, self-regulation involves three interrelated sets of activities: self-monitoring, self-evaluation, and self-reactions. Self-monitoring refers to the attention that an individual gives to behaviors and events related to the goal. Failure to self-monitor, or failure to self-monitor information related to goal accomplishment, precludes the opportunity to evaluate goal progress. In the context of job search, self-monitoring typically refers to keeping track of your own job search activities. Self-evaluation refers to the comparative evaluation of the goal state to the current state. Individuals who set vague job search goals or fail to monitor their job search activity can be expected to experience difficulty in judging their goal progress. Self-reactions are the natural consequence of self-evaluations and typically refer to the affective/motivational responses that an individual has toward the discrepancy between the desired goal and current progress. In contrast to self-efficacy expectations that refer to judgments about future capabilities to accomplish a goal (Bandura, 1977), self-reactions refer to satisfaction/dissatisfaction with past accomplishments. Of course, dissatisfaction with goal progress may exert an initial positive effect on effort allocations as individuals seek to reduce the discrepancy between current and desired states. Over time, however, sustained dissatisfaction with goal progress is likely to exert a negative effect on self-efficacy for future goal accomplishment. Negative goal progress over a protracted period of time may also weaken self-efficacy to a point at which the individual abandons job search and/or reemployment goals. Self-reactions to goal progress serve an informational and motivational function in the self-regulation cycle. Depending on the context and level of self-efficacy, individuals who are dissatisfied with goal progress might alter their job search goals, job search strategy, and/or the amount of effort devoted to accomplishing the goal.

Bandura's theory of self-efficacy (1977) builds upon and expands the self-regulation formulation by delineating the role of self-efficacy in self-regulation processing. According to Bandura (1977), individuals make self-efficacy judgments about their future capability for organizing and executing a behavior or course of action requisite for goal accomplishment on the basis of four inputs: past performance, vicarious experiences (such as observing models), verbal persuasion, and feedback from emotional arousal. Self-efficacy judgments are particularly important for the initiation of behavior, such that low levels of self-efficacy may moderate the impact of behavioral intentions on action. Accordingly, self-efficacy has been shown to be positively related to job search activities and reemployment outcomes in a number of job search studies (see Kanfer et al., 2001).

A third influential formulation of self-regulation dynamics is Carver and Scheier's Cybernetic Control Theory (Carver & Scheier, 1981). This theory has its roots in both social-cognitive and cybernetic systems. In contrast to other social-cognitive formulations, control theories highlight the self-evaluative process by which individuals modify their goals and/or effort over time and in response to feedback. Although control theories have not frequently been used as a foundation for studies of job search, findings from this perspective may help to explain the conditions that affect job search goal revision and/or withdrawal.

Social-cognitive formulations of goal striving focus on the psychological mechanisms by which individuals cope with adversity and accomplish desired goals in environments that provide little or no direct support. These conceptualizations differ from more purely behavioral theories that tend to focus on observable behaviors, response consequences, and reward contingencies. Social-cognitive theories accord central roles to goals, self-efficacy, and self-regulation in modulating thoughts, feelings, and behavior during the goal striving process. Social-cognitive approaches are also often regarded as theories of motivation and overlap in different ways with other general motivation theories, such as Deci and Ryan's Self-Determination Theory (SDT; 1985) and resource allocation models by Kanfer and Ackerman (1989) and Naylor, Pritchard, and Ilgen (1980).

Summary. As shown in Figure 9.1, the proposed social-cognitive process of job loss and job search encompasses both reactions to the loss event and proactive processes directed toward finding reemployment. Although self-regulation is involved in reactions to both job loss and job search, the targets and strategies used for successful modulation of affect and behavior differ between the two processes. Likewise, the pattern and effectiveness of different coping strategies for modulating negative affect about job loss are likely to differ from coping strategies used to modulate negative affect related to job search frustration and disappointment. General theories within the broader social-cognitive perspective tend to focus on different aspects of the job loss–job search process, although there is greater overlap between theories that address goal constructs (e.g., SCCT, Goal Setting Theory, Self-Efficacy, Self-Regulation). In the next section, we highlight theory and research findings on job loss and job search grounded in different social-cognitive approaches, and identify some current gaps in our knowledge.

Job Loss

Involuntary job loss is a negative and stressful event for employees and their managers. Informing an employee that he or she is being laid off the job is one of the most dreaded tasks in management, and how employees react and cope with this event over time often affects not only the manager and the employee, but co-workers and the employee's family and friends (see, for example, McKee-Ryan & Maitoza, this volume). Disbelief, anger, disappointment, fear, and anxiety are common immediate emotional reactions to the news of job loss. Job loss also frequently cues thoughts and affect associated with the anticipated negative economic and psychological consequences of unemployment.

Latack, Kinicki, and Prussia (1995) and Gowan and Gatewood (1997) both proposed models of coping with involuntary job loss that build upon the Lazarus and Folkman (1984) stress and coping theory, although the Latack et al. (1995) model is also influenced by self-efficacy and cybernetic control theories. Organizational studies of coping following job loss have tended to organize coping strategies into two broad categories, problem-focused coping and emotion-focused coping. Findings from several studies (e.g., Kinicki, Prussia, & McKee-Ryan, 2000; Leana & Feldman, 1998) show a positive relationship between job-seeking social support and the use of problem-focused coping strategies, although Leana and Feldman (1998) found that both types of coping strategies were positively related to reemployment. Gowan, Riordan, and Gatewood (1999) examined the determinants and consequences of three coping strategies (problem-focused, emotion-focused, and symptom-focused strategies) in a sample of workers who had been laid off several months prior to the study. They found that human capital variables and cognitive appraisal of the job loss event were related to the developed coping strategies, and that the coping strategies used were differentially related to reemployment and distress. Specifically, individuals who used distancing and social support strategies reported less emotional distress, but only distancing strategies were related to reemployment. (Distancing is an emotion-focused coping strategy in which an individual reexamines his or her personal experiences as an observer, which may promote a more objective self-understanding.) Gowan et al. (1999) suggest that the use of distancing coping strategies following job loss may help persons reconcile the negative emotions associated with loss and reduce the likelihood that these emotions impair job-seeking activities.

Studies to date on strategies for coping with job loss have focused broadly on coping strategies during unemployment, including job search activities. As such, it is unclear how coping with the job loss event itself may differ from coping strategies adopted during the job search. Emotional responses and economic problems experienced as direct consequences of job loss may change over time, and may affect the ability to establish effective reemployment goals and to self-manage job search activities. Although there is obviously no clear line between the reaction to job loss and the initiation of job search, it would be helpful to better understand the factors that affect this transition, as well as the consequences of different transition patterns on job search activities and reemployment outcomes.

In a related vein, relatively few studies have examined how individuals cope with the change in daily routines and patterns of social exchange caused by involuntary job loss. Whether job exit occurs within hours, days, weeks, or even months, job loss removes individuals from the "normal," orderly, information-rich environment of the workplace and places them in an ill-defined environment in which there are often few explicit consequences for daily behavior, few opportunities for teamwork, and fewer available sources for obtaining feedback about behavior. Nonetheless, individuals in this new environment are often expected to develop new goal hierarchies, behavioral routines, and social, informational networks. Not surprisingly, research findings on older American time use by employment status show that unemployed males aged 55–69 years reported 1.4 hours more television watching and 0.3 hours more sleeping per week than employed males in the same age group (Krantz-Kent & Stewart, 2007). It may be useful for future studies to examine whether individual differences in strategies used to cope with the change in daily environment also aid in the prediction of job search intensity and mental health.

Although the immediate negative effects of job loss are widely acknowledged, some researchers suggest that job loss may have a longer-term positive effect on employment among some individuals who are able to explore career options and to direct their search toward jobs that provide a better person–job fit (Eby & Buch, 1995; Latack & Dozier, 1986; Zikic & Klehe, 2006). Latack and Dozier (1986) proposed that job loss may promote effective job search and job growth among some people in certain circumstances. Findings by Eby and Buch (1995) also provide support for this model and indicate that gender, context, and financial factors play key roles in the extent to which individuals experience involuntary job loss in a positive light. As Latack and Dozier (1986) note, however, perceptions of career growth following involuntary job loss are likely to occur over time and among individuals who have emotionally accepted the loss. For those who have difficulty accepting the job loss, the increase in autonomy brought about by involuntary job loss is likely to be accompanied by decreased feelings of control and increased uncertainty about the future and finances—consequences that counteract the potential positive effect associated with greater autonomy. Building on the Lazarus and Folkman (1984) model, these theories about the impact of job loss can be reconciled by distinguishing between primary and secondary appraisals. Specifically, even if the primary appraisal of the job loss event is negative, the secondary appraisal of the event as an opportunity for growth (i.e., cognitive reappraisal) may be a useful coping strategy for promoting job search.

A common assumption in most job loss–job search research is that individuals who lose their jobs want to find reemployment. In the modern work environment and among an age-diverse workforce, this assumption may not always hold true. In an aging workforce, for example, not all older workers who lose their jobs want to remain in the labor force. Older workers with sufficient financial resources may, for example, choose to retire rather than seek reemployment. Workers with young children and those with other sources of financial support may choose to stay at home rather than seek reemployment. At a broader level, the experience of job layoff may also modify the individual's expectations about employment goals and work itself. Among individuals who have experienced prior job layoffs, reemployment goals may be less attractive than self-employment goals. For individuals who perceive the job loss event as a violation of the psychological employer–employee contract, subsequent reemployment goals may emphasize transactional features, such as pay, rather than relational features, such as co-worker relationships. Because reemployment goals set the stage for self-regulatory processes during the job search, understanding the impact of the job loss event on work-related goal generation activities in a more diverse labor force and marketplace appears to be an important direction for future research.

Blau (2008) proposed another approach for understanding the impact of job loss on job search and reemployment outcomes based on the application of a stage-based grief model. Building on the Kubler-Ross (1970) model, Blau (2008) proposed that job loss activates a developmental grieving process, characterized by early feelings of denial, followed by anger, bargaining, depression, willingness to explore, and, finally, acceptance. Similar to the explanation offered by Gowan et al. (1999), Blau (2008) suggested that an effective job search (exploration) would be less likely during the early stages of grief and would be more likely during the later stages when the individual has achieved resolution about his or her job loss. Findings by Blau (2008) and Archer and Rhodes (1987, 1993, 1995) provide partial support of this model in results that show a temporal decline in some grieving characteristics during unemployment.

Job Search and Reemployment Outcomes

Since the early 1980s, many organizations and countries have established programs aimed at assisting workers who have been downsized or laid-off from their jobs. One of the first demonstrations of how social-cognitive interventions might assist job losers appeared in a series of studies conducted by Caplan, Vinokur, Price, van Ryn, and their colleagues at the University of Michigan in the 1980s through the early 2000s (Caplan, Vinokur, Price, & van Ryn, 1989; van Ryn & Vinokur, 1992; Vinokur & Caplan, 1987; Vinokur & Schul, 2002; see also Price & Vinokur, this volume). Working from the Lazarus and Folkman (1984) framework, these researchers conducted a series of field experiments among unemployed adults that showed that coping and job search strategy training had a positive effect on unemployed workers' reemployment success and mental health.

With the introduction of the self-efficacy construct by Bandura (1977), job search researchers shifted their attention to investigating the role of job search self-efficacy on job search behavior and employment outcomes (Blau, 1994; Eden & Aviram, 1993; Kanfer & Hulin, 1985; Schmit, Amel, & Ryan, 1993; Schwab, Rynes, & Aldag, 1987; Wanberg et al., 1996, 1999). These studies provide support for the positive relationship between job search self-efficacy and job search behaviors (Kanfer & Hulin, 1985), mental health (Caplan et al., 1989), and employment outcomes (see Kanfer et al., 2001).

Social-cognitive and self-regulatory models posit that goals set the stage for self-management. Although attention has been directed toward the goal development portion of the job loss–job search process, research streams tend to be disparate and to conceptualize reemployment and job search goals in different ways. Three broad streams of research in this area may be identified. One stream of research, appearing primarily in the economics literature, focuses on the determinants and consequences of reservation wages on job search activities and reemployment outcomes (see Van den Berg & Uhlendorff, this volume). In these studies, reservation wage is typically defined as the lowest pay that an unemployed individual will accept for employment. In contrast to psychological studies that tend to conceptualize employment goals in terms of a maximally satisfying future state, the reservation wage represents the anticipated minimum standard that the individual will accept. Studies on the determinants of reservation wages show that person characteristics (e.g., gender, education level), contextual factors (e.g., duration of unemployment), and environmental factors (e.g., availability and level of unemployment insurance) influence reservation wage.

One particularly interesting study by Brown and Taylor (2011) found that individuals who reported reservation wages above the wage that would be predicted also engaged in higher levels of job search and were more likely to find employment than individuals with lower reservation wages. These findings led Brown and Taylor (2011) to interpret reservation wages as an index of reemployment motivation. In light of the growing research interest in the role of career exploration influences on goal development, it would also be useful to examine the impact of career exploration activities on reservation wage setting and flexibility during the job search. Psychological studies to investigate reservation wage represent a natural next step in the integration of economic advances and social-cognitive formulations.

A second stream of research on job search and reemployment goal setting stems from studies that extend SCCT to evaluate the impact of career exploration variables on goal choice and ensuing job search behaviors. Studies by Cote, Saks, and Zikic (2006) and Wanberg et al. (2002) examined job search clarity, assessing the extent to which the individual had a "clear idea" of search objectives. Findings from these studies indicated a positive relationship between search clarity and job search intensity. Koen, Klehe, Van Vianen, Zikic, and Nauta (2010) examined the influence of four career-related activities on three job search strategies

that varied in terms of their focus and subsequent reemployment quality. Their results suggested that career exploration that resulted in career decision making and a focused job search strategy was associated with high reemployment quality as well as more job offers.

Zikic and Saks (2009) proposed a model based on theorizing in the career literature that takes into account career and training determinants of reemployment and job search goal clarity. Consistent with their model, Zikic and Saks (2009) found that higher levels of career-related activities were related to higher levels of job search goal clarity and job search self-efficacy. Similarly, Fort, Jacquet, and Leroy (2011) applied Lent, Brown, and Hackett's (1994) SCCT to investigate the impact of self-efficacy among unemployed job seekers on employment goal precision, and the impact of employment goal precision on job search behaviors, search effort, and search planning. In contrast to Zikic and Saks (2009), however, Fort et al. (2011) found no significant impact of goal precision on job search behaviors. Fort et al. (2011) speculated that the divergence in their results may have stemmed from a difference in goal precision measurement, indicating a need for future research in this domain.

The studies on career adaptability and their effects on job search behavior and outcomes represent an exciting new direction toward understanding the forces that shape an unemployed worker's job search and employment goals. In particular, findings by Koen et al. (2010) suggest that an optimal sequence of career activities prior to a job search may promote career decision making. Consistent with Gollwitzer and Bayer's (1999) distinction between deliberation and implementation phases of action, a job-searching individual first explores different jobs, then makes a career path decision, and finally launches into a focused action sequence.

A third, newer stream of research highlights the collective impact of individual differences in affective motive tendencies and goal orientation on reemployment goals and job search (Creed, King, Hood, & McKenzie, 2009; Saitere, 2010; van Hooft & Noordzij, 2009; Van Dam & Menting, 2012; Wanberg, Zhu, Kanfer, & Zhang, 2012). These studies emphasize the role of broad individual differences in appetitive and avoidance motives and cognitive tendencies on self-regulatory processes during job search and reemployment outcomes. Individuals high in appetitive or approach motives are oriented toward opportunities for personal growth and achievement, whereas those high in avoidant or aversive motives are oriented toward avoiding failure and criticism (see Kanfer, 2012). Findings to date provide stronger support for the facilitative role of high levels of approach or appetitive motivation tendencies on job search and reemployment outcomes, as opposed to avoidance or aversive motivation tendencies. Findings by Wanberg et al. (2012) further distinguish the impact of these tendencies on individuals' mean level of job search activities over time and on their self-regulatory processes within weekly episodes of self-regulated job search. Examination of traits at these two levels suggests that goal interventions may be more useful for persons low in approach motivation early in the job search.

Although there is growing interest and evidence regarding how person characteristics and activities related to career exploration may contribute to the development of job search, reemployment, and career goals, further research is needed to evaluate the impact of person and career exploration variables on the individual's goal structure and goal attributes related to reemployment. In addition, it is important to understand whether broad traits (e.g., conscientiousness, openness, and extraversion) exert widespread or discrete effects on different aspects of the employment goal structure (e.g., reemployment commitment, reservation wage) and the job search process (e.g., job search strategies). In addition, research appears warranted in other areas of self-regulatory processing, such as self-monitoring and feedback seeking. Inaccurate self-monitoring of job search progress, for example, may hinder reemployment self-efficacy and preclude the individual from effective self-regulation during the job search.

Temporal Considerations

Job search occurs over time and fluctuates as a function of person and situation factors. The intensity of an individual's job search activity may change on a weekly basis, for example, as a result of illness, home responsibilities, job openings, or the individual's motivation. Over time and on average, however, job search intensity and mental health tend to decline during unemployment (McKee-Ryan et al., 2005; Krueger & Mueller, 2010). What is not yet well understood is the potential moderating role of person factors and self-regulatory processes in mitigating these declines. Accordingly, organizational researchers have begun to use longitudinal research designs that permit analysis of these

questions among persons who experience involuntary job loss (e.g., Barber, Daly, Giannantonio, & Phillips, 1994; Galic, 2011, Wanberg et al., 2005, 2010, 2012). Findings by Wanberg et al. (2012) suggest that although job search intensity tends to decline over time, mental health during unemployment appears to stabilize. These preliminary findings suggest that adoption of a slower-paced job search schedule at the onset of job seeking may support mental health and sustain job search activities longer.

A second temporal perspective that has recently gained more attention pertains to the individual's life stage, and the effects of age cohort and career status at which job loss and job search occur (Adams & Rau, 2004). Findings from studies of nationally representative samples indicate a developmental pattern in which (all other things being equal) younger workers change jobs more frequently than older workers. As such, the individual's age and cohort at the time at which job loss occurs may have different meanings and implications for reemployment goals. Involuntary job loss among younger workers may be appraised as a less stressful event than among mid-life or older workers with heavier financial burdens and lower expectancies of reemployment success. Nonwork circumstances, such as caregiving, also tend to increase with age, and may also interfere with job search activities and limit the individual's range of reemployment options. For older workers, involuntary job loss after a long job tenure may be associated with difficulties in job search due to age discrimination, skill obsolescence, or poor social networks for learning about new job possibilities. Furthermore, research in the cognitive aging and adult development literatures indicates a variety of age-related changes in cognition, affect, and motives that may affect work motivation and work-related competencies (see Kanfer & Ackerman, 2004). In the context of job search, these age-related differences may also affect the use of different job search strategies during the search. For example, as employers increasingly rely on the Internet for professional job postings, older workers less familiar with Internet job seeking may miss job opportunities.

Social Influences

Another area of growing research activity pertains to the role that interpersonal factors play in job search and reemployment outcomes. Drawing from Fishbein and Ajzen's TRA, van Hooft and his colleagues (Van Hooft, Born, Taris, & Van der

Flier, 2006a, 2006b; Van Hooft, Born, Taris, Van der Flier, & Blonk, 2005; Van Hooft & De Jong, 2009; also see Song, Wanberg, Niu, & Xie, 2006; Van Hooft, this volume) have shown that interpersonal factors have a significant effect on job search behavior. Future research to extend these assessments to normative beliefs about the influence of co-workers on individual action may be used to more fully capture the influence of interpersonal forces on behavior. Along similar lines, another important aspect of social influence relates to the individual's social capital, such as the density, form, and use of his or her social network (van Hoye, van Hooft, & Lievens, 2009; Wanberg, Kanfer, & Banas, 2000). Results of these studies suggest that further examination of social network characteristic effects (e.g., network size, density, composition, use, and type) may yield important insight into the dynamics of reemployment goal revision change and the patterning of job search behavior.

Measurement Issues

Most studies employ self-report measures of job loss coping strategies, reemployment and job search goals, job search behaviors, and reemployment outcomes, but researchers vary widely in the aspect of the job loss–job search process they evaluate. Kanfer et al. (2001) found that the most frequently assessed index of job search was job search intensity, or the frequency with which job seekers engaged in a specific set of search behaviors (such as preparing a resume) during a specific period of time. Following Blau (1994), several researchers have further distinguished between preparatory job search behaviors (e.g., reviewing employment ads) and active job search behaviors (e.g., contacting an employer).

The use of job search intensity measures that simply sum job search activities undertaken during a specific time period is problematic for two reasons. First, inventories of job search behaviors tend to be generic and thus may overlook search activities unique to a specific locale or industry. For example, individuals looking for work as a member of a boat crew may benefit from attending boating events and making regular visits to area marinas—social activities that may be of little benefit for individuals seeking work in telephone sales. Second, most intensity measures typically accord all job search behaviors an equal value with respect to effort and meaning, regardless of whether the behavior entails preparing a resume or attending a job fair. In reality, job search activities differ in terms

of degree of effort, skill, and functionality in different occupational sectors. For example, filling out a job application in person may be considered more appropriate behavior in retail sales than in professional fields, such as for a position as a program analyst. Unweighted, aggregate measures of job search intensity do not readily permit analysis of whether changes in job search intensity reflect an overall reduction in search activity and/or a change in job search strategy.

Another frequent method for assessing job search activity has been the measurement of subjective job search effort. In contrast to intensity measures, job search effort measures typically ask the individual to indicate the extent of time or mental effort directed toward job seeking using a graded scale. In their meta-analysis of the determinants and consequences of job search activities, Kanfer et al. (2001) found that both search intensity and subjective job search effort measures were significantly related to job search self-efficacy, though in opposite directions. Although a positive relationship between search efficacy and search intensity makes sense, it is less clear why subjective effort should be negatively related to search efficacy. One possibility is that subjective measures may partially capture the cognitive, attentional resource costs associated with self-regulatory activities. That is, individuals who perceive that they have expended a lot of cognitive energy on managing their job search activities may also perceive themselves as less capable than individuals with more effective management skills.

A final concern related to the measurement of job search activities relates to the frequent lack of information about an individual's search behavior goals or intentions. From a social-cognitive perspective, changes in job search intensity may arise from a change in the individual's search goal and/or a problem implementing the goal or intention. As such, differences in job search intensity measures between individuals are often interpreted in terms of personality traits, when in fact they may be due to more malleable factors, such as illness, poor self-management skill, or discouragement.

Similar to assessments of job search behaviors, measures to assess job search success and reemployment outcomes have rarely been linked to the individual's employment goals. Brasher and Chen (1999) noted the lack of consistency in measures of employment outcomes following job search, and argued that different patterns of job search behavior might be more or less effective for different employment goals. For example, the most commonly assessed employment outcome measure, employment status, does not permit an evaluation of the extent to which the obtained job represents a goal accomplishment or a satisfying outcome following downward employment goal revision. Consistent with econometric studies, psychological research investigating the impact of self-regulatory processes on reemployment success requires a more precise evaluation of reemployment goals within factors such as content, pay, and work conditions. In a recent meta-analysis of the relationship between age and reemployment outcomes following job loss, Wanberg, Kanfer, Hamann, and Zhang (2015) proposed a four-part framework of the reemployment outcome criterion space, distinguishing between reemployment status and speed, reemployment basis (e.g., job type), person–demand job fit, and intrinsic job rewards.

In summary, the field is likely to benefit from the development of a wider variety of measures to assess goals and activities related to job search and reemployment. In addition to self-report measures, researchers should consider the use of other ratings (e.g., spouse), the use of online daily record sheets to monitor the type and duration of search activities, and measures that assess social network characteristics. With respect to reemployment goals, research is needed to develop and validate measures that assess relevant attributes of the reemployment goal. Qualitative research to identify job search strategies in terms of coordinated patterns of thought, affect, and behavior, rather than just intensity or activity type, may also be useful for revealing different multidimensional strategies (e.g., social support groups coupled with online training for job search skills) for accomplishing longer-term search, reemployment goals, and goals related to personal well-being.

At the same time, further research attention is needed to understand the choice of reemployment outcomes that go beyond the simple employed/unemployed dichotomy. As suggested by Wanberg et al. (2014), employment outcomes may vary in terms of their "satisfactoriness" along a number of dimensions, including amount of work (part-time versus full-time), job conditions, and job demands. Understanding the profile of reemployment outcomes associated with different employment goals is likely to yield new knowledge about the relationship between goals and job search strategies.

Summary and Research Agenda

Few life events and environments make as many demands on self-processes as adult job loss and job search. Individuals must cope with the emotional sting of being involuntarily let go from their jobs and the angst that often accompanies coping with the effects of job loss on finances, professional identity, the elimination of routines organized around work, the resource demands associated with identifying a viable reemployment goal, the development of a job search strategy, and the allocation of resources to sustain job search motivation in the face of obstacles and poor information feedback. During economic downturns, sustained job search motivation over periods of a year or longer is exhausting and untenable for most people. The depletion of personal resources ultimately requires that individuals revise their employment goals and/or reduce their job search effort. Although such changes may have a protective effect for the individual in the long run, revising or abandoning employment goals often comes at a high cost to self-concept.

Over the past few decades, research on job search and employment outcomes in the psychological literature has steadily coalesced around a common paradigm that emphasizes social-cognitive/self-regulatory processes. Early applications of these formulations during the last part of the twentieth century have yielded new knowledge about the crucial role that person characteristics play in sustaining a job search. Recent investigations have extended these formulations into two promising directions. One stream of research has focused on the social and career-related determinants of employment goals and job search. The second stream of research has focused on the role of individual differences in personality and motivational traits on the self-regulation of behavior and affect during job search. Examination of intraindividual changes in these microanalytic processes over time provides support for the conceptualization of job search following job loss as a self-managed activity.

Nonetheless, a host of theoretical and practical questions remain. To conclude, we suggest three topic areas and related questions that appear to have strong potential for informing social policy makers, improving organizational practices, and assisting unemployed workers seeking reemployment.

1. *Individual differences and the context of job loss and job search.* Layoffs and unemployment rates differ by market sector, as do the person

and situation characteristics of workers in various sectors. Although involuntary job loss may be unavoidable, individual differences in person characteristics and the individual's life context appear to play an important role in the success that individuals experience in coping with job loss, making the transition to reemployment, and regaining sense of well-being. More interdisciplinary research to investigate the multilevel, multidimensional influences on reemployment goal development and goal choice is needed. Following the lines of work by Wanberg, Hough, and Song (2002), McArdle, Waters, Briscoe, and Hall (2007), and Meyers and Houssemand (2010), such studies should incorporate economic, sociocultural, and socioprofessional variables.

Another area in which more research is needed pertains to age-related differences on the job loss–job search process. Among younger workers, prolonged periods of involuntary joblessness may preclude the development of general work competencies, with potentially long-term negative effects on career adjustment and success. In this group, research and interventions are needed to promote the development of effective self-management skills. In contrast, among older workers, prolonged periods of unemployment may strain financial resources and impair mental and physical health. For this group, research and interventions are needed to assist workers in sustaining employability.

2. *Reemployment goals.* Research on reemployment goals is developing in exciting new ways. For the past few decades, researchers have focused largely on job search behaviors as the proximal determinants of reemployment success. However, new approaches highlight the importance of *how* employment and job search goals are formulated. These goals set the direction and demand for self-regulated job search behaviors and may exert an even stronger impact on reemployment outcomes than search activities per se. More information is needed about the determinants of reemployment goal structures and their malleability as a function of individual differences in traits, work competencies, and intervention effectiveness (e.g., career exploration). Recent work on career exploration activities suggests that such activities may have a beneficial effect on job search and reemployment outcomes *if* the consequences of these activities lead to career decision making and a sense of confidence.

Research on reemployment goals suggests a new direction for the field aimed at an abiding problem: namely, understanding the processes by which an individual makes the psychological transition from the experience of involuntary job loss to looking (forward) to reemployment. Intervention programs have long recognized the importance of shifting the job loser's mindset, but we still know relatively little about the person and situation factors that can hinder the transition or undermine reemployment commitment. Understanding the personal meaning of the job loss experience to the individual, how career exploration may facilitate the transition to reemployment, and for whom job search interventions are most important are crucial steps in this direction.

3. *Mitigating the use of inaccurate stereotypes in employment decision making.* In poor economic times, industry sector and human capital may account for most of the variance in the probability and speed of reemployment following job loss (see, e.g., Sverko, Galic, Sersic, & Galesic, 2008). Thus, reemployment success may be particularly difficult for older workers and workers with lower levels of formal education in declining industry sectors. This does not make the job search less important for these individuals, but it does increase the likelihood that it will last longer. Nonetheless, it is important for both researchers and employers to recognize that human capital measures (such as education level, job history, and length of unemployment) are not univocally determined by the individual, but represent historical characteristics of the individual that only partially capture individual differences in knowledge, abilities, emotion regulation, and motivation at the time of application. Such measures may also correspond poorly with the human capital needed to perform the job, such as when the decision to hire an electrician is unduly influenced by the length of his or her latest unemployment spell. Research on age discrimination further indicates that employers sometimes make employment decisions based on inaccurate stereotypes about the learning and performance competencies of older workers. Research is needed to identify the use of potentially inaccurate or inappropriate stereotypes in employment decisions, and to develop reliable and valid indices for the assessment of the individual's personal and social capital at the time of application.

Acknowledgments

We wish to thank Phillip Ackerman and Margaret Beier for their insightful comments on earlier drafts of this chapter.

References

Adams, G., & Rau, B. (2004). Job seeking among retirees seeking bridge employment. *Personnel Psychology*, 57, 719–744.

Archer, J., & Rhodes, V. (1987). Bereavement and reactions to job loss: A comparative review. *Journal of Social Psychology*, 26, 211–224.

Archer, J., & Rhodes, V. (1993). The grief process and job loss: A cross-sectional study. *British Journal of Psychology*, 84, 395–411.

Archer, J., & Rhodes, V. (1995). A longitudinal study of job loss in relation to the grief process. *Journal of Community and Applied Social Psychology*, 5, 183–188.

Bandura, A. (1977). Self-efficacy: Toward a unifying theory of behavioral change. *Psychological Review*, 84, 191–215.

Bandura A. (1986). *Social foundations of thought and action: A social cognitive theory*. Englewood Cliffs, NJ: Prentice Hall.

Barber, A. E., Daly, C. L., Giannantonio, C. M., & Phillips, J. M. (1994). Job search activities: An examination of changes over time. *Personnel Psychology*, 47, 739–766.

Blau, G. (1994). Testing a two-dimensional measure of job search behavior. *Organizational Behavior and Human Decision Processes*, 59, 288–312.

Blau, G. (2006). A process model for understanding victim responses to worksite/function closure. *Human Resource Management Review*, 16, 12–28.

Blau, G. (2008). Exploring antecedents of individual grieving stages during an anticipated worksite closure. *Journal of Occupational and Organizational Psychology*, 81, 529–550.

Brasher, E. E., & Chen, P. Y. (1999). Evaluation of success criteria in job search: A process perspective. *Journal of Occupational and Organizational Psychology*, 72, 57–70.

Brown, S., & Taylor, K. (2011). Reservation wages, market wages and unemployment: Analysis of individual level panel data. *Economic Modeling*, 28, 1317–1327.

Caplan, R. D., Vinokur, A. D., Price, R. H., & van Ryn, M. (1989). Job seeking, reemployment, and mental health: A randomized field experiment in coping with job loss. *Journal of Applied Psychology*, 74, 759–769.

Carver, C. S., & Scheier, M. F. (1981). *Attention and self-regulation: A control theory approach to human behavior*. New York, NY: Springer-Verlag.

Clague, E., & Couper, W. J. (1931). The readjustment of workers displaced by plant shutdowns. *Quarterly Journal of Economics*, 45, 309–346.

Cote, S., Saks, A. M., & Zikic, J. (2006). Trait affect and job search outcomes. *Journal of Vocational Behavior*, 68, 233–252.

Creed, P. A., King, V., Hood, M., & McKenzie, R. (2009). Goal orientation, self-regulation strategies, and job-seeking intensity in unemployed adults. *Journal of Applied Psychology*, 94, 806–813.

Deci, E. L., & Ryan, R. M. (1985). *Intrinsic motivation and self-determination in human behavior*. New York, NY: Plenum.

Eby, L. T., & Buch, K. (1995). Job loss as career growth: Responses to involuntary career transitions. *Career Development Quarterly*, 44, 26–43.

Eden, D., & Aviram, A. (1993). Self-efficacy training to speed reemployment: Helping people to help themselves. *Journal of Applied Psychology*, 78, 352–360.

Fishbein, M., & Ajzen, I. (1975). *Belief, attitude, intention, and behavior*. Reading, MA: Addison-Wesley.

Fort, I., Jacquet, F., & Leroy, N. (2011). Self-efficacy, goals, and job search behaviors. *Career Development International*, 16, 469–481.

Fryer, D., & Payne, R. (1986). Being unemployed: A review of the literature on the psychological experience of unemployment. In C. L. Cooper & I. T. Robertson (Eds.), *International review of industrial and organizational psychology* (Vol. 1, pp. 235–278). Chichester, UK: Wiley.

Galic, Z. (2011). Job search and (re)employment: Taking the time-varying nature of job-search intensity into consideration. *Revija Socijainu Politiku*, 1, 1–23.

Gollwitzer, P. M., & Bayer, U. (1999). Deliberative versus implemental mindsets in the control of action. In S. Chaiken & Y. Trope (Eds.), *Dual-process theories in social psychology* (pp. 403–422.). New York, NY: Guilford Press.

Gowan, M. A. (2014). Moving from job loss to career management: The past, present, and future of involuntary job loss research. *Human Resource Management Review*, 24, 258–270.

Gowan, M. A., & Gatewood, R. D. (1997). A model of response to the stress of involuntary job loss. *Human Resource Management Review*, 7, 277–298.

Gowan, M. A., Riordan, C. M., & Gatewood, R. D. (1999). Test of a model of coping with involuntary job loss following a company closing. *Journal of Applied Psychology*, 84, 75–86.

Hanisch, K. A. (1999). Job loss and unemployment research from 1994 to 1998: A review and recommendations for research and intervention. *Journal of Vocational Behavior*, 55, 188–220.

Ilg, R. (2010). Long-term unemployment experience of the jobless. *Issues in Labor Statistics, Summary 10-05*. http://www.bls.gov/opub/ils/summary_10_05/long_term_unemployment.htm.

Kanfer, F. H. (1977). The many faces of self-control or behavior modification changes its focus. In R. Stuart (Ed.), *Behavioral self-management*. New York, NY: Bruner/Mazel.

Kanfer, F. H., & Schefft, B. K. (1988). *Guiding the process of therapeutic change*. Champaign, IL: Research Press.

Kanfer, R. (2012). Work motivation: Theory, practice, and future directions. In S. W. J. Kozlowski (Ed.), *The Oxford handbook of industrial and organizational psychology* (pp. 455–495). Oxford, UK: Blackwell.

Kanfer, R., & Ackerman, P. L. (1989). Motivation and cognitive abilities: An integrative/aptitude-treatment interaction approach to skill acquisition. *Journal of Applied Psychology—Monograph*, 74, 657–690.

Kanfer, R., & Ackerman, P. L. (2004). Aging, adult development and work motivation. *Academy of Management Review*, 29, 1–19.

Kanfer, R., & Hulin, C. L. (1985). Individual differences in successful job searches following lay-off. *Personnel Psychology*, 38, 835–847.

Kanfer, R., Wanberg, C. R., & Kantrowitz, T. M. (2001). Job search and employment: A personality-motivational analysis and meta-analytic review. *Journal of Applied Psychology*, 86, 837–855.

Kinicki, A. J., Prussia, G. E., & McKee-Ryan, F. M. (2000). A panel study of coping with involuntary job loss. *Academy of Management Journal*, 43, 90–100.

Koen, J., Klehe, U.-C., Van Vianen, A. E. M., Zikic, J., & Nauta, A. (2010). Job-search strategies and reemployment quality: The impact of career adaptability. *Journal of Vocational Behavior*, 77, 126–139.

Krantz-Kent, R., & Stewart, J. (2007). How do older Americans spend their time? *Monthly Labor Review*, 130, 8–26.

Krueger, A. B., & Mueller, A. (2010). Job search and unemployment insurance: New evidence from time use data. *Journal of Public Economics*, 94, 298-307.

Kubler-Ross, E. (1970). *On death and dying*. New York, NY: Collier Books/Macmillan.

Latack, J. C., & Dozier, J. B. (1986). After the ax falls: Job loss as a career transition. *Academy of Management Review*, 11, 375–392.

Latack, J. C., Kinicki, A. J., & Prussia, G. E. (1995). An integrative process model of coping with job loss. *Academy of Management Review*, 20, 311–342.

Latham, G. P., & Seijts, G. H. (1999). The effects of proximal and distal goals on performance on a moderately complex task. *Journal of Organizational Behavior*, 20, 421–429.

Lazarus, R. S., & Folkman, S. (1984). *Stress, appraisal, and coping*. New York, NY: Springer.

Leana, C. R., Feldman, D. C., & Tan, G. Y. (1998). Predictors of coping behavior after a layoff. *Journal of Organizational Behavior*, 19, 85–97.

Lent, R. W., Brown, S. D., & Hackett, G. (1994). Toward a unifying social cognitive theory of career and academic interest, choice, and performance. *Journal of Vocational Behavior*, 45, 79–122.

Locke, E. A., & Latham, G. P. (1990). *A theory of goal setting and task performance*. Englewood Cliffs, NJ: Prentice-Hall.

Locke, E. A., Latham, G. P., & Erez, M. (1988). Resolving scientific disputes by the joint design of crucial experiments by the antagonists: Application to the Erez-Latham dispute regarding participation in goal setting. *Journal of Applied Psychology*, 73, 753–772.

Locke, E. A., Shaw, K. N., Saari, L. M., & Latham, G. P. (1981). Goal setting and task performance: 1969–1980. *Psychological Bulletin*, 90, 125–152.

McArdle, S., Waters, L., Briscoe, J. P., & Hall, D. T. (2007). Employability during unemployment: Adaptability, career identity and human and social capital. *Journal of Vocational Behavior*, 71, 247–264.

McFadyen, R. G., & Thomas, J. P. (1997). Economic and psychological models of job search behavior of the unemployed. *Human Relations*, 50, 1461–1484.

McKee-Ryan, F. M., Song, Z., Wanberg, C. R., & Kinicki, A. (2005). Psychological and physical well-being during unemployment: A meta-analytic study. *Journal of Applied Psychology*, 90, 53–76.

Meyers, R., & Houssemand, C. (2010). Socioprofessional and psychological variables that predict job finding. *Revue Europeenne de Psychologie Appliqué*, 60, 201–209.

Naylor, J. C., Pritchard, R. D., & Ilgen, D. R. (1980). *A theory of behavior in organizations*. New York, NY: Academic Press.

Paul, K. I., & Moser, K. (2009). Unemployment impairs mental health: Meta-analyses. *Journal of Vocational Behavior*, 74, 264–282.

Saitere, S. (2010). Job search intentions of the unemployed in Latvia: The role of emotions, motives, and prospects. *Baltic Journal of Psychology*, 11, 18–36.

Saks, A. M., Brown, S. D., & Lent, R. W. (2005). Job search success: A review and integration of the predictors, behaviors, and outcomes. In S. D. Brown & R. W. Lent (Eds.), *Career development and counseling: Putting theory and research to work* (pp. 155–179). Hoboken, NJ: John Wiley & Sons.

Schmit, M. J., Amel, E. L., & Ryan, A. M. (1993). Self-reported assertive job-seeking behaviors of minimally educated job hunters. *Personnel Psychology*, 46, 105–124.

Schwab, D. P., Rynes, S. L., & Aldag, R. J. (1987). Theories and research in job search and choice. In K. Rowland & G. Ferris (Eds.), *Research in personnel and human resources management* (Vol. 5, 129–166). Greenwich, CT: JAI Press.

Song, Z., Wanberg, C., Niu, X., & Xie, Y. (2006). Action-state orientation and the theory of planned behavior: A study of job search in China. *Journal of Vocational Behavior*, 68, 490–503.

Sverko, B., Galic, Z., Sersic, D. M., & Galesic, M. (2008). Unemployed people in search of a job: Reconsidering the role of search behavior. *Journal of Vocational Behavior*, 72, 415–428.

U.S. Department of Labor, Bureau of Labor Statistics. (2010, September 10). *Number of jobs held, labor market activity, and earnings growth among the youngest baby boomers: Results from a longitudinal survey*. Retrieved from http://www.bls.gov/news.release/archives/nlsoy_09102010.pdf

U.S. Department of Labor, Bureau of Labor Statistics. (2015, January 9). *The Employment Situation Summary*. Retrieved from http://www.bls.gov/news.release/pdf/empsit.pdf

Van Dam, K., & Menting, L. (2012). The role of approach and avoidance motives for unemployed job search behavior. *Journal of Vocational Behavior*, 80, 108–117.

Van Hooft, E. A. J., Born, M. P., Taris, T. W., & Van der Flier, H. (2006a). The cross-cultural generalizability of the theory of planned behavior: A study on job seeking in the Netherlands. *Journal of Cross-Cultural Psychology*, 37, 127–135.

Van Hooft, E. A. J., Born, M. P., Taris, T. W., & Van der Flier, H. (2006b). Ethnic and gender differences in applicants' decision-making processes: An application of the theory of reasoned action. *International Journal of Selection and Assessment*, 14, 156–166.

Van Hooft, E. A. J., Born, M. P., Taris, T. W., Van der Flier, H., & Blonk, R. W. B. (2005). Bridging the gap between intentions and behavior: Implementation intentions, action control, and procrastination. *Journal of Vocational Behavior*, 66, 238–256.

Van Hooft, E. A. J., & De Jong, M. (2009). Predicting job seeking for temporary employment using the theory of planned behavior: The moderating role of individualism and collectivism. *Journal of Occupational and Organizational Psychology*, 82, 295–316.

Van Hooft, E. A. J., & Noordzij, G. (2009). The effects of goal orientation on job search and reemployment: A field experiment among unemployed job seekers. *Journal of Applied Psychology*, 94, 1581–1590.

Van Hoye, G., Van Hooft, E. A. J., & Lievens, F. (2009). Networking as job search behavior: A social network perspective. *Journal of Occupational and Organizational Psychology*, 82, 661–682.

Van Ryn, M., & Vinokur, A. D. (1992). How did it work? An examination of the mechanisms through which an intervention for the unemployed promoted job-search behavior. *American Journal of Community Psychology*, 20, 577–597.

Vinokur, A., & Caplan, R. D. (1987). Attitudes and social support: Determinants of job-seeking behavior and well-being among the unemployed. *Journal of Applied Social Psychology*, 17, 1007–1024.

Vinokur, A. D., & Schul, Y. (2002). The web of coping resources and pathways to reemployment following a job loss. *Journal of Occupational Health Psychology*, 7, 68–83.

Wanberg, C. R. (2012). The individual experience of unemployment. *Annual Review of Psychology*, 63, 369–396.

Wanberg, C., Basbug, G., Van Hooft, E. A., & Samtani, A. (2012). Navigating the black hole: Explicating layers of job search context and adaptational responses. *Personnel Psychology*, *65*, 887-926.

Wanberg, C. R., Glomb, T. M., Song, Z., & Sorenson, S. (2005). Job-search persistence during unemployment: A 10-wave longitudinal study. *Journal of Applied Psychology*, *90*, 411–430.

Wanberg, C. R., Hough, L. M., & Song, Z. (2002). Predictive validity of a multidisciplinary model of reemployment success. *Journal of Applied Psychology*, *87*, 1100–1120.

Wanberg, C. R., Kanfer, R., & Banas, J. T. (2000). Predictors and outcomes of networking intensity among unemployed job seekers. *Journal of Applied Psychology*, *85*, 491–503.

Wanberg, C. R., Kanfer, R., Hamann, D. J., & Zhang, Z. (2015). *Age and reemployment success after job loss: An integrative model and meta-analysis*. Unpublished manuscript.

Wanberg, C. R., Kanfer, R., & Rotundo, M. (1999). Unemployed individuals: Motives, job-search competencies, and job-search constraints as predictors of job seeking and reemployment. *Journal of Applied Psychology*, *84*, 897–910.

Wanberg, C. R., Watt, J. D., & Rumsey, D. J. (1996). Individuals without jobs: An empirical study of job-seeking behavior and reemployment. *Journal of Applied Psychology*, *81*, 76–87.

Wanberg, C. R., Zhu, J., Kanfer, R., & Zhang, Z. (2012). After the pink slip: Applying dynamic motivation frameworks to the job search experience. *Academy of Management Journal*, *55*, 261–284.

Wanberg, C. R., Zhu, J., & Van Hooft, E. A. J. (2010). The job search grind: Perceived progress, self-reactions, and self-regulation of search effort. *Academy of Management Journal*, *53*, 788–807.

Weiss, H. M., & Cropanzano, R. (1996). Affective Events Theory: A theoretical discussion of the structure, causes, and consequences of affective experiences at work. *Research in Organizational Behavior*, *18*, 1–74.

Zikic, J., & Klehe, U. (2006). Job loss as a blessing in disguise: The role of career exploration and career planning in predicting reemployment quality. *Journal of Vocational Behavior*, *57*, 379–394.

Zikic, J., & Saks, A. M. (2009). Job search and social cognitive theory: The role of career-relevant activities. *Journal of Vocational Behavior*, *74*, 117–127.

Understanding the Motivational Dynamics Among Unemployed Individuals: Refreshing Insights from the Self-Determination Theory Perspective

Maarten Vansteenkiste *and* Anja Van den Broeck

Abstract

Although the role of motivation has been emphasized in the field of unemployment and job search, the motivational dynamics underlying unemployed individuals' behavior have not yet received the attention they deserve. In this chapter, we present a motivational perspective grounded in self-determination theory (SDT), a macrotheory focusing on human motivation in the social context. We discuss basic principles of SDT and formulate seven propositions that have direct relevance for the fields of unemployment and job search. In discussing these propositions, we elucidate similarities and differences between SDT and various frameworks in the unemployment and job search literature and cover the available empirical evidence in the realm of SDT in these fields. Given that the literatures on job search and unemployment have been developed fairly independently, we conclude that SDT represents a promising theory to bridge these two fields and may equally provide useful guidelines for practitioners in the field.

Key Words: job search, unemployment, self-determination theory, motivation

In the context of unemployment, political leaders often have their mouths full of the fact that unemployed people need to be "activated." The term *activation* basically implies that we need to find ways to motivate unemployed individuals in general and at-risk groups (e.g., long-term unemployed, elderly unemployed) in particular. Specifically, we need to stimulate those unemployed who would not be sufficiently active and motivated by themselves to search for employment. Although it is clear that (at least some) unemployed individuals need to be activated or motivated, the way to do so varies widely across political parties and ideologies. Depending on one's political affiliation, an activation policy can take the form of being highly prescriptive and controlling or rather supportive, taking the unemployed

person's rhythm, situation, and personal choices into consideration.

For instance, at least in Belgium, a *do ut des* credo seems to be increasingly adopted by different political parties, suggesting that in return for their unemployment benefits unemployed people *must* search for a job and *have* to accept any job that is offered to them, particularly after multiple refused job offers or a certain amount of time. Consistent with this idea and in light of the recent worldwide financial crisis, consensus in Europe is growing that the unemployment benefits of the passive unemployed should be gradually withdrawn. Such a measure would subject inactive unemployed individuals to financial pressures and eventually help to speed their reemployment process, thereby reducing the percentage of long-term unemployed individuals. Yet research does not provide evidence for such reasoning, as financial hardship fails to predict job-search behavior, reemployment, let alone quality of reemployment.

In addition to the plea for a gradual withdrawal of unemployment benefits, some political parties also suggest investing in the creation of additional jobs, such that unemployed individuals would be offered a broader array of positions. This would increase the chances that they would accept jobs that fit their interests and preferences. Although governmental policies represent a mix of prescriptive, sanctioning, supportive, and facilitative measures, this cocktail can vary widely from one country to another, with resulting implications for the unemployed.

Indeed, the efficacy of these various policy measures at the macrolevel can be understood from a psychological and, more specifically, *motivational* perspective. Unemployed individuals find themselves embedded within a broader societal context that impacts their individual motivation because unemployed individuals interact with unemployment counselors and employers who are equally affected by the policy installed by their local and national governments (Deci & Ryan, 2012). To fully understand how unemployed individuals are affected, we argue that it is critical to consider the amount and type of job-search motivation fostered by different societal policies, employers, and individual unemployment counselors.

The importance of studying motivational dynamics was already highlighted by Marie Jahoda (1981) more than three decades ago. She noted that "motivation . . . is obviously relevant for understanding people at work or without it" (p. 184). Although motivational dynamics have received quite some attention by scholars in the unemployment literature (Creed, King, Hood, & McKenzie, 2009; Kanfer, Wanberg, & Kantrowitz, 2001), the attempts to study motivational processes were not systematically informed by more general social-motivation theories (Feather, 1990; Jahoda, 1981). In line with Feather's call to directly ground unemployment research in such midrange or grand psychological theories, we present the self-determination theory (SDT) view (Deci & Ryan, 2000; Ryan & Deci, 2000a) on the motivational dynamics involved in unemployment. SDT is a macrotheory of human motivation, emotion, and personality that has been under development for more than forty years, following the seminal work of Edward Deci and Richard Ryan. In its current status, SDT comprises six different minitheories

(Deci & Ryan, 2014; Vansteenkiste, Niemiec, & Soenens, 2010), all of which yield relevance for the domain of unemployment. Rather than presenting these six minitheories in an exhaustive and theory-driven fashion, we chose to organize the chapter around four larger sections, that is, (1) the energetic basis of motivation: psychological need satisfaction; (2) the "why" of behavior; (3) the "what" of behavior; and (4) facilitating motivation: the role of contextual need support. Each of these sections begins with a discussion of the basic features of the SDT framework. The provided theoretical basis then allows us to formulate seven propositions that have direct relevance to the fields of unemployment and job search. In discussing these propositions, we indicate similarities and differences between SDT and various other frameworks within the literature on unemployment and job search, including Jahoda's model (Jahoda, 1981, 1982), Fyer's agency model (Fryer, 1986), expectancy-valence models (Feather, 1990), and current self-regulation models (Wanberg, Zhu, Kanfer, & Zhang, 2012). We cover the limited available research on SDT in the domains of unemployment and job search and provide a number of future research directions.

The Energetic Basis of Motivation: Psychological Need Satisfaction

One of the central assumptions of SDT is that people are inherently proactive—that is, they have the potential to act on and master both the internal (i.e., drives and emotions) and the external (i.e., environmental) forces they encounter rather than being passively controlled by those forces. Further, SDT assumes that through their activity, humans steadily move toward increasing levels of psychological growth and integration. Yet, this proactivity and growth does not take place automatically but needs to be facilitated by the social environment in the form of the support of the basic psychological needs for autonomy, competence, and relatedness (Deci & Ryan, 2000; Deci & Vansteenkiste, 2004; Ryan & Deci, 2000a).

Psychological needs have been defined as "innate psychological nutriments that are essential for ongoing psychological growth, integrity, and well-being" (p. 229). Because of their inborn character, the psychological needs are considered part of human nature (Deci, 1992); their satisfaction is said to be fundamental for individuals' wellness and psychological health. Specifically, just as plants need sunshine and water to flower, human beings need to experience the satisfaction of these needs, according to SDT, to be optimally motivated and to feel well, both psychologically and physically. Yet SDT also recognizes that people have vulnerabilities—such as those for being aggressive, defensive, or passive—and maintains that the active frustration and blocking of these very same psychological needs awakens these vulnerabilities (Ryan & Deci, 2000b; Vansteenkiste & Ryan, 2013).

Within SDT, three inborn needs are identified: that is, the needs for autonomy, competence, and relatedness. Autonomy concerns the desire to experience personal ownership over one's actions, thoughts, and emotions and to engage in an activity with a sense of volition and psychological freedom. When this need is satisfied, unemployed persons likely feel that they are searching for a job out of volition and that they can be themselves without feeling the obligation to hide or suppress feelings like resentment, fear, or sadness. Competence concerns the desire to feel effective in what one does and in mastering new skills in the process. When this need is satisfied, unemployed persons will feel that they are making progress toward their desired goals (e.g., writing an application letter). Finally, relatedness refers to the desire to develop satisfying and deeply anchored relationships. Unemployed people who feel understood by their partners or an unemployment counselor in coping with the frustration that goes along with being unemployed experience a sense of relatedness and connection.

In line with SDT, several studies have demonstrated that need satisfaction relates positively to indices of well-being (e.g., life satisfaction, vitality) and negatively to indices of ill-being (e.g., depressive symptoms). Need satisfaction plays a role at different levels of generality, with differences in need satisfaction between persons, groups, and nations accounting for differences in well-being among individuals (e.g., Wilson, Rogers, Rogers, & Wild, 2006), groups (e.g., Meyer, Enström, Harstveit, Bowles, & Beevers, 2007; Vansteenkiste, Lens, Soenens, & Luyckx, 2006), and nations (e.g., Sheldon, Cheng, & Hilpert, 2011), respectively. Need satisfaction has been found to play a critical role at the within-person level as well, with daily fluctuations in autonomy, competence, and relatedness being uniquely associated with daily differences in well-being (e.g., Ryan, Bernstein, & Brown, 2010) and bulimic symptoms (Verstuyf, Vansteenkiste, Soenens, Mouratidis, & Boone, 2013). Finally, need satisfaction has been found to predict optimal functioning in domains as diverse

as schooling, exercise, work, and psychotherapy (see Deci & Ryan, 2000, and Vansteenkiste et al., 2010, for general overviews) and in both individualistic and collectivistic cultures (e.g., Chen, Vansteenkiste, Beyers, Soenens, & Van Petegem, 2013). Herein, we suggest that psychological need frustration can help to account for the observed decrements in well-being among unemployed individuals, which leads to the formulation of our first proposition.

Proposition One: The Frustration of the Basic Psychological Needs Can Account for the Negative Impact of Unemployment on Well-Being

Dozens of studies have examined whether unemployed individuals experience less psychological and physical health and more ill-being relative to employed individuals. Recent meta-analytical reviews (McKee-Ryan, Song, Wanberg, & Kinicki, 2005; Paul & Moser, 2009; Wanberg, 2012) provide a summary of these studies, showing that unemployed individuals report lower psychological health (e.g., lower self-worth and more worries, fear, and depressive symptoms) and physical health (e.g., more heart trouble and hypertension) than their employed counterparts. These differences were more pronounced among men, blue-collar workers, the long-term unemployed, and school leavers. Moreover, the association between employment status and psychological health is not only a concurrent one but a change from employment to unemployment has been found to cause increased in distress. Although less psychologically adjusted employees might have a greater likelihood of becoming unemployed, research mostly supports the notion that that becoming unemployed causes a change in well-being (Creed & Bartrum, 2006).

Several models in the organizational/industrial literature—such as Jahoda's latent deprivation model (Jahoda, 1982) and Warr's vitamin model (Warr, 1987)—help to account for these findings. Jahoda (1982) argues that, besides the manifest function of providing financial benefits, employment serves several important latent functions: that is, time structure, social contact, collective purpose, social identity or status, and regular activity. Because unemployed individuals are denied these experiential categories, they display deficits in well-being. In a similar vein, Warr (1987) suggests that the unemployed are relatively deprived of environmental aspects, such as opportunities to develop their skills and social support. According to Warr, these aspects serve as "vitamins" that improve—to a certain degree—individuals' well-being. Although Fryer and Payne (1986) recognize the importance of these benefits, they emphasize, in their agency restriction model, the manifest function of employment more strongly. The decrease or loss of income places a financial burden on unemployed individuals, which is highly distressing. In line with these arguments, the deprivation of these latent and manifest functions has been found to account for the observed decrements in well-being among unemployed individuals, with financial strain being an especially strong predictor of unemployed individuals' experiences of distress (e.g., Creed & Klisch, 2005; Paul & Batinic, 2010).

Although appealing, these accounts are rather *descriptive* in nature, as the provided explanation is not tied to or guided by a formal theory. Such more global, social-psychological theories have received increasing attention in the field of unemployment and job search. One such promising framework is self-determination theory (SDT). From an SDT-perspective, as already noted, humans' innate basic psychological needs must be satisfied if they are to flourish. We maintain that, on *average*, unemployed individuals might be more prone to experience frustration of their psychological needs. For instance, they must often handle financial and social pressures during their job search, and their job search increasingly becomes a daunting duty, such that their need for autonomy is frustrated. Their daily activities may feel like a "chain of obligations" and "musts." Moreover, unemployed individuals might also start to doubt their capacities. Especially in the case of prolonged unemployment, which often goes together with an increasing number of rejections, their need for competence might be actively frustrated (Vansteenkiste, De Witte, & Lens, 2006). Finally, their social networks might gradually erode, to a point where they feel socially isolated or excluded from society, which frustrates their need for relatedness (Underlid, 1996).

Notably, meaningful links can be drawn between the three psychological needs identified within SDT and the manifest and latent functions identified by Jahoda, Warr, and Fryer and Payne. For instance, the deprivation of social contact reduces opportunities for relatedness satisfaction and may even elicit feelings of loneliness. The lack of time structure and regular activity in one's life might preclude one's opportunities for the experience of competence, because ill-structured days might leave one with the feeling that one is unable to achieve any outcome. Further, because occupying a job is central to one's identity, the unemployed may feel that their lack of work alienates them from their preferences and ideals, thereby having a negative impact on their need for autonomy. Finally, financial strain might result in unwanted pressures, worries, and stress, thus further frustrating the need for autonomy. Future research may jointly assess these latent and manifest functions (e.g., Muller, Creed, Waters, & Machin, 2005; Paul & Batinic, 2010) and the satisfaction of the basic psychological needs among unemployed individuals so as to examine these associations and their explanatory role in the link between unemployment status and well-being.

The "Why" of Behavior

According to SDT, satisfaction of the basic psychological needs for autonomy, competence, and relatedness provides the energetic basis for optimal forms of motivation. The more that these psychological needs are satisfied during the job search, the more unemployed persons develop an autonomous, relative to controlled, job-search motivation. Autonomous and controlled motivations reflect different categories or reasons for engaging in a particular behavior (e.g., job searching). In the context of unemployment, the type of job-search motivation is said to contribute to various outcomes, such as unemployment experience, job-search intensity, job-search quality, and employability as well as speed and quality of reemployment.

As can be noticed in Figure 10.1, autonomous and controlled motivation include different motivational subtypes. The prototype of autonomous motivation is intrinsic motivation (Ryan & Deci, 2000a). In the case of *intrinsic motivation*, people engage in an activity for the inherent pleasure and satisfaction it provides (Deci, 1975). For instance, unemployed persons may derive a sense of enjoyment from exploring the job market and trying to find a job that meets their interests. Curiosity forms the impetus for intrinsically motivated behavior and at least some people, perhaps especially school leavers, are simply very curious to find out which jobs are available on the job market. Because individuals are spontaneously following their interests during such explorative behavior, intrinsic motivation is said to represent the hallmark of autonomous or volitional behavior.

Although some unemployed might experience searching for a job as enjoyable, for many such individuals searching for a job is a rather unpleasant duty that requires considerable effort (Van Hooft,

Wanberg, & Van Hoye, 2013). Also, some unemployed individuals lose interest in searching over time owing to repeated rejections (Vansteenkiste et al., 2006). In spite of the lack of enjoyment (i.e., intrinsic motivation) of searching as such, unemployed individuals can still be autonomous in their search given that they have accepted the reason for doing so as their own. This process has been labeled the process of "internalization" and has been intensively studied within SDT. Conceptually, internalization refers to incorporating the value or reason for engaging in a particular behavior (e.g., job searching) into one's own value system, so that the searchers experience a sense of personal ownership over their behavior (Deci & Ryan, 2000). Because this process can be variably successful, different regulatory subtypes have been distinguished, with some being rather controlled and others being more autonomous in nature.

Controlled regulation entails engaging in an activity out of a sense of pressure, and two subtypes have been discerned (see Figure 1). The first form of controlled regulation involves the execution of behaviors to comply with external demands (i.e., *external regulation*). Such external pressures can be tangible or rather social in nature: One can engage in the activity to obtain a contingent material reward or to avoid a tangible threatening punishment, or one can engage in the activity to gain social appreciation or to avoid criticism. For instance, school leavers who search to avoid further nagging of their parents display external regulation, just like the long-term unemployed looking for jobs because they have difficulties making ends meet. This external form of motivation has received quite some attention in past unemployment research, as the role of financial pressures in the job-search process and well-being of unemployed individuals has been extensively studied (e.g., McKee-Ryan et al., 2005).

Notably, the pressure to search does not necessarily reside in external forces, as people can also pressure themselves into the activity—for instance, by linking their behavioral regulation to threats of self-imposed guilt, shame, or a loss of self-worth. This second type of controlled regulation is labelled *introjected* regulation. Although the behavioral regulation has been taken in this case and introjected regulation thus constitutes internal regulation, the reason for performing the activity has not yet been fully accepted as one's own (i.e., partial internalization). As result, the behavioral engagement is experienced as internally conflicted, tense, and pressured. Unemployed persons who search because they feel ashamed of being jobless or because they

Lack of Intention	Intentional Behavior				
Amotivation	Extrinsic Motivation				Intrinsic Motivation
Nonregulation	External Regulation	Introjected Regulation	Identified Regulation	Integrated Regulation	Intrinsic Regulation
Lack of expectations Lack of valuation	External expectations Threatening sanctions Controlling rewards	Guilt, Shame, Anxiety Contingent self-worth	Conscious valuation Personal meaning	Fit with other values Harmony, coherence	Interest, enjoyment, pleasure Curiosity
Lack of Motivation	Controlled Motivation "Mustivation"		Autonomous motivation "Wantivation"		
Least Self-Determined					*Most Self-Determined*

Figure 10.1 Schematic representation of the types of motivation and regulation within self-determination theory. *Source*: Adapted from Ryan & Deci, 2000a.

believe they are taking advantage of society display introjected regulation, just like the school leavers who are searching because they are afraid of coming across as lazy. Likely, individuals with a strong Protestant work ethic (Furnham, 1987) might display a mix of this internally pressuring type of job-search regulation in combination with more fully internalized types of job search regulation.

Parallel to the bifurcation of controlled motivation, different subtypes of autonomous motivation have been proposed. When unemployed people have internalized the reason for engaging in job search, they are said to display *identified* regulation—that is, they concur with the personal importance of job searching. In the case of identification, unemployed people search for a job because they perceive searching and finding work as personally meaningful for a self-selected goal, like developing their talents or personality. The highest level of internalization is achieved when one not only concurs with the value of searching as such but also perceives fit between the value attached to searching for a job and other personally held values and ideals. This has been labeled *integrated* regulation. When integrated, the values and ideals of unemployed individuals form a coherent and harmonious whole, such that their job searching emanates from themselves. For instance, the unemployed searching for a job because they believe that work allows them to offer their children a better education would display integrated regulation. Similarly, employed job seekers often search for a different employment to better coordinate their different roles, like being a caring mother and an engaged employee.

Autonomous and controlled motivated behavior is intentional in nature; that is, the behavior is oriented toward achieving a particular outcome. Amotivation, in contrast, is characterized by a lack of intention. When amotivated, people do not or rather passively engage in the required behavior; they are said to go "through the motions." Amotivaton may result from the feeling that one is incapable of engaging in a particular behavior (efficacy expectation), that the required activity does not bring the desired outcome (outcome expectation), or because one devalues the activity altogether (Ryan, Lynch, Vansteenkiste, & Deci, 2011). For instance, an unemployed person who does not know how to start a job search displays amotivation, just like those who believe that they will not be hired even when they would perform well in a job interview.

The distinction between autonomous and controlled motivation and amotivation has been proven useful in predicting one's performance, persistence, and well-being in a wide variety of life domains, including sport, education, work, and psychotherapy (Deci & Ryan, 2000; Vansteenkiste, Niemiec et al., 2010). Yet it is only recently that these motivational dynamics were studied in the job-search and unemployment domain, which leads to the formulation of our second proposition.

Proposition Two: The Type of Job-Search Motivation Matters for Unemployed People's Job Search Intensity and Unemployment Experience

In one of the first studies on job-search motivation, Vansteenkiste, Lens, Dewitte, De Witte, and Deci (2004) developed the self-regulation/job search questionnaire, which taps into unemployed individuals' autonomous and controlled reasons for job searching. In two large samples of long-term unemployed individuals, the various SDT-based job-search motives could be factor-analytically distinguished and the retained factors correlated in meaningful ways with other constructs. For instance, both autonomous and controlled motivation correlated positively with job commitment (Warr et al., 1981), which is in line with the idea that they both reflect a certain degree of motivation (convergent validity). Further, controlled motivation correlated positively with financial concerns, while autonomous motivation related positively to job-search optimism and the expectancy to find a job, and amotivation correlated negatively with job-search optimism and the expectancy to find a job. These findings highlight that the different types of behavior regulation associate with different constructs (divergent validity).

Next, the pattern of external outcomes associated with both types of motivation was markedly different: While autonomous motivation was positively related to job search behavior over the past three months, controlled motivation and amotivation were unrelated to job-search behavior. In addition to this behavioral outcome, a number of general well-being outcomes (i.e., general health, life satisfaction, self-actualization) and unemployed individuals' positive and negative experiences of their unemployment situation were assessed. Negative experiences concern unemployed individuals' feeling of social isolation, worthlessness, and meaningfulness (De Witte & Wets, 1996). Positive experiences tap the extent to which unemployed individuals feel more relaxed since they became jobless and were able to enjoy their spare time. Across the two studies, autonomous motivation related positively to self-actualization, was unrelated to life satisfaction and general health, and associated negatively with the positive experience of one's unemployment. It seems plausible that autonomously motivated unemployed, who likely have a sincere interest in getting a job, have difficulty in enjoying their free time; yet, through their searching, they feel that they are actualizing their potential and don't feel devalued as persons. In contrast, controlled motivation and amotivation related positively to negative experiences of unemployment and negatively to general well-being. Thus the more individuals report controlled motives or amotivation, the more they experience their unemployment status as negative and the more they pay a price for it in well-being.

In a recent study, Koen, Klehe, and Van Vianen (in press) studied the role of motivation in a sample of long-term unemployed individuals who were following a mandatory reemployment course. Results showed that unemployed, who displayed relatively more autonomous than controlled reasons for searching, reported an increase in job searching and employability after the termination of the reemployment course. Apparently, the relatively more autonomously motivated unemployed were capable of extracting greater benefits from the mandatory course.

These motivational dynamics were also found to be relevant among school leavers undertaking their first steps on the job market. Specifically, in a study among twelfth- and thirteenth-grade school leavers (Soenens & Vansteenkiste, 2005), a relatively autonomous motivation for searching was found to relate positively to the intention to search for a job in the future as well as to school leavers' exploration and commitment of their vocational identity. Exploration and commitment represent two critical identity dimensions in Marcia's classic identity status paradigm (Kroger & Marcia, 2011; Marcia, 1966). Exploration of one's vocational identity refers to exploring different options on the job market, while commitment refers to making a particular job choice which one fully endorses and feels certain about. School leavers' type of job search motivation was found to be implicated in their identity formation (LaGuardia, 2009; Ryan & Deci, 2003; Soenens & Vansteenkiste, 2011): Autonomously motivated school leavers have more energy available to explore different job openings and are more capable of committing themselves to a particular option. They might commit themselves more

easily because they are in better contact with their preferences, interests, and values, such that they have a clearer view of what sort of job they really value and want. We would predict that such sincere interest and personal valuation of a particular job would also be sensed by interviewers during a job application, such that autonomously motivated candidates may be more quickly hired. This hypothesis deserves to be tested in future research.

A short-term longitudinal study by Grant, Nurmohamed, Ashford, and Dekas (2011) provides some preliminary evidence for this hypothesis. Specifically, in a sample of job applicants, they found that taking initiative during the job search process related to a greater number of job offers in case the job applicants scored high on autonomous and low on controlled job-search motivation. The fact that only the combined presence of high autonomous and low controlled motivation yielded a long-term benefit suggests that applicants' job search motivation should be of very high quality to get translated in positive outcomes over the longer term.

Apart from studies among job seekers, the relevance of the distinction between autonomous and controlled motivation has recently been studied among part-time workers (Halvari, Vansteenkiste, Brorby, & Karlsen, 2013). Specifically, Norwegian part-time working nurses, who are generally encouraged to search for full-time jobs, indicated their reasons for searching for a full-time employment. Replicating the findings among job seekers, autonomous job-search motivation related positively to the self-reported search for a full-time position. Further, controlled motivation was unrelated to job search but also negatively related to the positive experience of one's spare time as a part-time worker.

To summarize, the aforementioned studies indicate that autonomous and controlled motivation represent qualitative different types of motivation, with autonomous motivation yielding more desirable correlates than controlled motivation. From an applied perspective, this implies that it is not only critical that unemployed individuals get activated and motivated but also that they display the "right" type of motivation. These findings are perhaps counterintuitive, because unemployment counselors, unemployed people, and scholars frequently assume that unemployed individuals' level of motivation is of critical importance, regardless of the type of motivation. Specifically, more strongly motivated jobless people are assumed to more quickly find a (new) job, presumably because they put greater effort into their searching. Yet based on SDT, we maintain that it is important to move beyond merely considering unemployed individuals' intensity of motivation and to additionally consider the sort or type of motivation they display. In line with these claims, Vansteenkiste, Lens, De Witte, and Feather (2005) found that, autonomous and controlled motivation accounted for an incremental variance in unemployed individuals' job search, unemployment experience, and well-being after controlling for unemployed people's amount of job search motivation, operationalized in terms of the expectancy to find a job and employment commitment, as detailed in expectancy-valence theory (Feather, 1990, 1992; Feather & Davenport, 1981).

In our view, the research available to date indicates that studying unemployed individuals' quality of motivation represents a fruitful avenue for future research. Specifically, longitudinal studies would need to examine whether the type of job-search motivation (i.e., autonomous or controlled) relates to (1) quality of job search (Van Hooft, Wanberg, & Van Hoye, 2013), (2) attributions for being rejected during an application interview (Weiner, 1985), (3) speed, and (4) quality of (re)employment. We elaborate on these issues below.

Although many scholars (e.g., Kanfer et al., 2001; Van Hoye, this volume; Vinokur & Schul, 2002; Wanberg, Hough, & Song, 2002) emphasize the importance of unemployed people's job-search quality, in the majority of studies the assessment of job-search behavior has been limited to its intensity. High-quality job search has been defined "performing one's job search activities in such a way that those meet/exceed the expectations of the demanding parties of the labour market (e.g., selection organization, recruiters, assessors, hiring managers, counsellors)" (Van Hooft, et al., 2013, p. 7). We would expect that although controlled motivation might engender some behavioral engagement, autonomous motivation especially would relate to high-quality behavior. For instance, autonomously motivated individuals might submit more carefully crafted job applications, might perceive an application interview as a challenge rather than a threat, and might come across as more enthusiastic and authentically interested during such an interview. Consistent with such predictions, previous research in the academic domain indicates that whereas controlled motivation engenders superficial learning, autonomous motivation relates to deep-level learning (e.g., Benware & Deci, 1984; Vansteenkiste, Simons, Lens, Soenens, & Matos,

2005), predicts a lowered threat response to a stressful event (Hodgins, et al., 2010), and relates to higher engagement as rated by external observers (e.g., Aelterman et al., 2012; Reeve, Jang, Carrell, Jeon, & Barch, 2004). In this context, it would also be interesting to examine relations between different motivations and the active (i.e., focused and exploratory) and passive (i.e., haphazard) job-search strategies outlined by Crossley and Highouse (2005). Autonomous job seekers are most likely to be focused in their job search, perhaps after a period of broader exploration of different options (see Soenens & Vansteenkiste, 2005). Because of the lack of a clear view of their vocational identity, amotivated individuals might engage in the trial-and-error approach characteristic of the haphazard strategy.

Quality of job-search motivation might also predict one's reaction to failure during the job-search process. Because controlled motivated individuals' ego and self-worth are more contingent upon the outcome of job search, they might engage in more self-handicapping prior to the application interview to protect their ego (e.g., Hodgins, Yacko, & Gottlieb, 2006). They might also experience a rejection as a stronger blow to their self-worth as compared with autonomously oriented individuals. In an attempt to protect their self-worth, they may react more defensively, thereby providing external attributions for their failure (e.g., the attitude of the interviewer). Autonomously oriented unemployed individuals might be more open to feedback (Hodgins & Knee, 2002), thereby trying to understand why they are not accepted for a job and perceiving the feedback as a source of information for taking new steps in their job search and personal development.

Regarding the speed of reemployment, the available research suggests autonomous motivation will relate to a quicker reemployment. Yet unemployed individuals who are subjected to financial pressures might also find employment, albeit the type of accepted job might be different. One potential explanatory mechanism in this process forms job flexibility (Reilly, 1998)—that is, the strictness of the demands of jobless people regarding their future jobs (De Witte, 1993). Because controlled motivated individuals may be more ready to sacrifice the content of their job to gain quick employment, they may apply for a diversity of jobs in order to become engaged quickly. In contrast, because autonomous motivated unemployed people are committed to a particular vocational identity, they might be more picky and selective in their job search and only apply for jobs that really fit their interests. This more focused job search likely results in reemployment of a better quality (Crossley & Highhouse, 2005), as indexed by higher job satisfaction, engagement, and less absenteeism (Koen, Klehe, & Van Viaenen, 2010). The focused search of autonomously oriented individuals would allow them to occupy high-quality jobs with greater opportunities for basic psychological need satisfaction (Van den Broeck, Vansteenkiste, De Witte, Soenens, & Lens, 2010).

Future longitudinal work may also examine how people's motivational regulations change as a function of their unemployment duration. Because unemployment duration may affect unemployed people's experiences of need satisfaction, their motivational regulation may change. For instance, because continued unemployment often goes hand in hand with repetitious rejections and hence competence-thwarting experiences, unemployed individuals may lose their eagerness to spontaneously explore the job market and instead become apathic (i.e., amotivated; see Vansteenkiste, et al., 2006). Also, the searching might be experienced as increasingly autonomy-thwarting because the searching is experienced as a daunting duty. Said differently, owing to increasing experiences of need frustration associated with longer unemployment duration, unemployed people's reasons for searching will become increasingly alien to their sense of self. This leads us to elaborate in the next section on the meaning of the notion of self as defined in SDT and modern self-regulation models.

Proposition Three: The Notion of "Self" Carries a Different Meaning in Modern Self-Regulation Models Compared with SDT

Since the millennium, self-regulation models have received increasing attention within the field of unemployment research (Kanfer, Wanberg, & Kantrowitz, 2001; Wanberg, Zhu et al., 2012). Because the term self-regulation surfaces in the SDT vocabulary, it is critical to discuss whether the SDT's view on self-regulation resembles the notion of self-regulation as used in the job-search literature. We argue that these notions of self-regulation are not equivalent, because the notion of "self" carries a different meaning in the SDT and job-search literature, which yields important theoretical and practical implications.

Within the self-regulation models in the job-search literature, job seeking is conceived as a goal-setting process—that is, as "a purposive, volitional pattern of action that begins with the identification and commitment to pursuing an employment goal" (Kanfer et al., 2001, p. 838). Self-regulated job seekers are said to be capable to effectively cycle through different phases of the job-search process (Van Hooft et al., 2013). Self-regulatory job seekers are, for example, able to establish a desired job-seeking goal to which they are committed (e.g., writing two application letters a week). They carefully plan their job-search activities—for instance, by forming implementation intentions (Gollwitzer, 1990) specifying when, where, and how they will realize their plans. During their actual job search, they engage in a variety of processes to monitor their progress. On encountering obstacles (e.g., rejection during a job interview), they are capable of handling the resulting disruptive emotions. Self-regulatory job seekers are also persistent and able to modify their strategies so as to increase the probability of achieving their goals. Apart from specifying these different stages, scholars in the job-search literature focus on three key self-regulatory strategies: (1) work commitment, which refers to the desire to close the gap between one's current unemployment and being employed; (2) emotion control, which involves the use of self-regulatory strategies to cope with negative emotions such as shame, guilt, and anger; and (3) motivation control, which involves the engagement in a variety of strategies (e.g., self-talk and visualizing positive outcomes) to facilitate persistence during the job search process (e.g., Creed et al., 2009).

Although this brief discussion does not justify the richness of these self-regulation models (see Latham et al., this volume, for a more extensive presentation), we want to address three key points in discussing this self-regulation view in relation to SDT. First, by describing the self-regulatory stages and by identifying the self-regulatory strategies of the job search process, these self-regulation models primarily indicate how job searchers can embark and successfully engage in the job-search process. Put briefly, these phases and strategies denote the *how* of job search. Yet, cycling through these phases and engaging in these strategies requires energy and hence a motivational basis. Current self-regulation models in the job-search literature, perhaps owing to their rather descriptive focus, are more silent about the factors that supplement this energy (Ryan & Deci, 1999). By considering the job-search process as a goal-related endeavor, it remains unclear where these goals come from in the first place. SDT can fill this theoretical gap, as its organismic approach provides the basis for gaining insight into the process of goal-selection and hence, the *why* of job-search behavior. Further, the interface between the social environment and the living organism endowed with psychological needs fuels individuals' goals with psychological meaning and provides the necessary energy for continued goal pursuit (Ryan & Deci, 1999).

Of course, the *why* of behavior will relate to the *how* of job search. Yet not all types of job-search motivation are equally predictive of the engagement in self-regulatory strategies. As noted above, autonomous but not controlled motivation was found to be associated positively with job commitment (Soenens & Vansteenkiste, 2005). Further, both types of motivation are differentially related to a variety of emotional coping strategies, with autonomous motivation being positively related to the positive reinterpretation of one's unemployment situation and controlled motivation being related to mental disengagement, denial, and drug use. Finally, as for engagement in motivational control strategies, autonomously motivated job searchers were found to engage in a variety of proactive job-search strategies, such as planning and the suppression of competing activities (Vansteenkiste, 2010).

Second, the engagement in goal-related activities (e.g., planning) can by itself be motivated by very different reasons. For instance, an unemployed person could choose to make up a plan for the upcoming week (e.g., writing an application letter) because she really believes that making a plan is helpful in achieving her desired goals. Alternatively, she might also feel pressured to make up a plan only because an employment counselor insisted upon her doing so. From a SDT-perspective, however, the reasons underlying these self-regulatory strategies will determine their effectiveness. If the planning is controlled rather than autonomously motivated, it is less likely that job seekers will stick to their planning, instead putting off their job search (Senécal & Guay, 2000; Van Hooft et al., 2005). In line with these claims, experimental work by Koestner, Lekes, Powers, and Chicone (2002) demonstrates that the formulation of implementation intentions—that is, a self-regulatory strategy recommended in the job search literature (Van Hooft et al., 2013)—resulted in more goal progress when participants had autonomous rather than controlled reasons for pursuing these goals.

A third issue concerns the meaning attributed to the term *self*. As noted by Ryan and Deci (1999),

in many contemporary self-regulation models, "self is synonymous with person, such that all of one's psychic make-up is self" (p. 195). The notion of self then refers to the fact that an unemployed person is internally, rather than externally, regulating his or her job search behavior. SDT converges with contemporary self-regulation models on the idea that an unemployed person can better search out of internal than external reasons. Yet different types of internal regulation are distinguished, some being more coercive, internally conflicted, and hence alien to the growth-oriented self (i.e., introjected regulation as part of controlled regulation) whereas others are more volitional, authentic, and hence congruent with the growth-oriented self (i.e., autonomous regulation). As such, not all job-search strategies considered to be self-regulated from a self-regulation perspective represent true or volitional self-regulation from the SDT viewpoint! In this respect, we argue that we need to be careful in the use of the term *volitional*, which was used by Kanfer et al. (2001, p. 838) to characterize job seeking as a self-regulatory process. This is because not all unemployed individuals engage in self-regulatory job-search strategies, as advocated in self-regulation models, volitionally or willingly. This is not just an issue of terminology, as different types of internal regulation have been found to yield different correlates, with internally conflicted relative to internally harmonious types of regulation leading to an emotional cost (e.g., Assor, Vansteenkiste, & Kaplan, 2009; Koestner & Losier, 2002).

At the practical level, this analysis suggests that unemployment counselors may not want to foster *any* type of internal regulation but rather promote autonomous types of internal regulation. A concrete example might help to illustrate this point. Many politicians and unemployment counselors alike emphasize that unemployed individuals need to learn to take *responsibility* for their situation and that the activation of unemployed individuals involves highlighting this responsibility. Considered from the process of internalization, the notion of responsibility has an ambiguous meaning, as it can be indicative of one's autonomous commitment to search for a job or may suggest an internal demand pushing one to take up one's responsibility (see Miller, Das, & Chakravarthy, 2011). In daily practice, at least some unemployment counselors point to the responsibility of unemployed individuals in a guilt-inducing way—for instance, by conveying the message that inactive job searchers are lazy or are taking advantage of society. In facing such guilt-inducing language, unemployed people might feel devalued and, for this reason, take up their responsibility for internally pressuring reasons. They might have the impression that unemployment counselors are projecting their own work ethic on them, thereby bypassing their reasons for not searching. From the SDT perspective, it is critical to be open to unemployed people's reasons for not searching, as the lack of engagement in job-search behavior can represent a self-endorsed choice or a sign of oppositional defiance, as highlighted in proposition four.

Proposition Four: Not Searching Can Represent a Self-Endorsed Choice or an Indication of Oppositional Defiance

Most motivation theories restrict themselves to asking why individuals engage or fail to engage in a *target* activity. Yet, given the constant flux of people's activities (Atkinson & Birch, 1970), their motivation for a target activity likely also depends on their reasons for engaging in *alternative* activities. This implies that people's nonengagement in the target activity is not necessarily function of their amotivation but could also represent a fully endorsed choice because they give priority to an alternative activity. For instance, an unemployed person might decide not to search for a job because he gives priority to taking care of his sick mother or to pursue vocational training. Alternatively, individuals may have the impression they are not allowed to engage in the target activity because they feel pressured or seduced to take part in such alternative activities. For instance, an unemployed person might not search because his wife wants him to take care of the children or because he would feel like a bad father if he did not take sufficiently care of his children.

Consistent with this idea, Vansteenkiste et al. (2004) examined whether the autonomously controlled motivation distinction can be applied to both the engagement and nonengagement in job-search behavior. In addition to being asked why they were searching for a job, long-term unemployed individuals were asked why they were not searching, thereby tapping into their autonomous and controlled motives not to search. Interestingly, the motives not to search predicted additional variance in participants' unemployment experiences and general well-being above and beyond the "classic" SDT motives to search (i.e., autonomous motivation, controlled motivation, and amotivation). Specifically, controlled motivation not to search

yielded a unique positive relation with a negative experience of one's unemployment. Autonomous motivation not to search related positively to enjoying the benefits of being unemployed (i.e., positive unemployment experience) and overall well-being while being negatively related to feeling devalued or socially isolated owing to one's unemployment (i.e., negative unemployment experience). Thus, whereas autonomous motivation to search was—as noted above—unrelated to general well-being, the often observed positive correlates for autonomous motivation were found for the construct of autonomous nonengagement. Presumably unemployment allows autonomous nonengaged individuals to achieve their ideals and values, while autonomously job-seeking individuals have not yet achieved their personally valued goal of being employed. Consistent with these findings, Halvari et al. (2013) found autonomous motivation not to search for full-time employment to relate positively to positive experiences of one's part-time position, while being negatively related to job-search intensity.

The idea that the autonomous-controlled distinction can be symmetrically applied to individuals' engagement and nonengagement is fairly novel. Thus a lot of work still can be done in this area. One intriguing possibility is that controlled nonengagement can take the form of *oppositional defiance*, in which an unemployed person aims to differentiate himself from external forces by seeking independence (Deci & Ryan, 1985; Vansteenkiste, Soenens, Van Petegem, & Duriez, 2013). For instance, an unemployed person who would react against social norms and legislations by rejecting the authority figure instantiating the norms would display oppositional defiance. Oppositional-defiant behavior is controlled in nature, because one is rebelling against pushing external (authority) figures.

Although trait differences in oppositional-defiant behavior would arise as a function of being exposed to need-thwarting experiences during childhood (Vansteenkiste & Ryan, 2013), such defiance can also be easily activated by a partner or unemployment counselor in a single conversation (i.e., at the state level). Indeed, because some unemployed people perceive searching versus not searching for a job as their personal business, they are very sensitive to any signals pushing them into a particular direction. As a result, straightforwardly activating those unemployed individuals to seek employment, especially in a controlling and forceful way, will likely elicit oppositional defiance because such people have the feeling that these activation attempts represent a threat to their autonomy, a point also central to psychological reactance theory (Brehm, 1966). Not only threats to one's autonomy but also to one's relatedness and competence may activate oppositional defiance. When unemployment counselors or family members are highly critical or cynical about a person's capacity to find a job,. that person will feel rejected (relatedness frustration) and worthless (competence frustration). Such intense experiences of need frustration may initially cause anger and opposition and, when experienced repeatedly, as is the case for long-term unemployed individuals, result in apathy and amotivation. In future work, it would be interesting to examine the interactions between unemployment counselors and unemployed individuals in terms of how need-supportive versus need-thwarting a counselor acts and whether the unemployed person displays signs of oppositional defiance. Previous research grounded in motivational interviewing (Miller & Rollnick, 2002) among alcohol addicts indicates that patients' resistance to change and long-term abstinence varies as a function of the confronting versus empathic approach of the counselor (e.g., Miller & Baca, 1983; Miller, Taylor, & West, 1980).

Another possibility for future research is to conduct diary studies (e.g., Wanberg, Zu, & Van Hooft, 2010) in which participants report on their motives for searching or not searching, need satisfaction, well-being, and job-search behavior. The researcher could examine how day-specific autonomous and controlled reasons for searching and not searching relate to each other over time. Although not framed from an SDT perspective, a diary study by Wanberg, et al. (2010) indicated that there is considerable variation in unemployed people's job-search efforts. Unemployed people also differed in terms of reasons for not searching, which nicely map onto the categories distinguished within SDT. For instance, some of commonly used reasons for not searching on a given day were "had family obligations," "wanted to do other things," and "discouragement," which nicely correspond to the categories of controlled nonengagement, autonomous nonengagement, and amotivation, respectively. Future work could also examine how these motives for searching and not searching relate to unemployed people's daily or weekly functioning, both in terms of searching efforts, progress made, and relational and personal well-being. Such an intraindividual approach seems a particularly well-suited method to study unemployed people's

motivation (and lack thereof) from a more dynamic perspective (Brown & Ryan, 2006).

Finally, it could be examined which processes explain the positive association between an autonomous motivation not to search and well-being. Because autonomous nonseekers choose to not search and give priority to other meaningful activities, they might not experience as much deprivation in the latent benefits of employment. Instead, they might experience their unemployment time as well structured and purposeful (Bond & Feather, 1988), build up a satisfying network of contacts, and be engaged in a variety of activities, which, in turn, may contribute to the satisfaction of their basic psychological needs. Given the observed well-being correlates of autonomous motivation not to search, we suggest in proposition five that motivational dynamics might play a moderating role in the unemployment/ill-being association.

Proposition Five: Quality of Motivation May Play a Moderating Role in the Unemployment/Ill-Being Association

Although meta-analytical reviews indicate that becoming unemployed yields *on average* a deterioration in well-being (McKee-Ryan, et al., 2005; Paul & Moser, 2009), considerable variation around this average effect exists, such that being unemployed might not be health-impairing for all unemployed individuals. This raises the question which variables may play a moderating role.

Various moderators have been studied in the unemployment literature, including age, gender, length of unemployment, family unemployment, local levels of unemployment, attributions of causes of job loss, personality variables and values (Creed & Bartrum, 2006). From the SDT perspective, one potential moderator involves unemployed individuals' autonomous and controlled motives for searching and not searching for a job. To further the understanding of the impact of unemployment, person-centered analyses might be useful. Such analyses allow one to identify different groups of unemployed individuals characterized by a particular *motivational profile*, that is, a combination of reasons for engaging and not engaging in job search. Such motivational profiles have been studied in the educational (e.g., Hayenga & Corpus, 2010; Vansteenkiste, Sierens et al., 2009), physical education (Haerens, Kirk, Cardon, De Bourdeauduij, & Vansteenkiste, 2010), sport (Gillet, Vallerand, & Rosnet, 2009), and work domains (Van den Broeck, Lens, De Witte, & Van Coillie, 2013). Whereas some of these retained groups were found to score relatively high on both autonomous and controlled motivation, others scored relatively low on both dimensions, and still other groups displayed a combination of high autonomous and low controlled motivation or vice versa. Interestingly, these groups differed substantially in their degree of self-regulation (e.g., time management, effort regulation) and well-being (e.g., engagement, stress), with more autonomously motivated groups displaying the most optimal outcomes.

Similar person-centered analyses could be performed among unemployed individuals to discover subgroups of the unemployed and examine mean-level differences in well-being and the use of self-regulatory search strategies. These retained motivational profiles could then be compared with the motivational profiles extracted from a matched employment group. It is possible that employed individuals who belong to a poor-quality motivation group (i.e., a group high on controlled and low on autonomous work motivation) display an equal or even lower level of well-being compared with unemployed individuals in the good-quality motivation group (i.e., high on autonomous and low on controlled job-search motivation). These analyses could further be refined by including the subdimensions of autonomous regulation (i.e., identified, integrated, and intrinsic) and controlled regulation (i.e., external and introjected) or byadding unemployed individuals' autonomous and controlled motivation not to search as additional dimensions in the person-centered analyses. Given that the dimension of autonomous motivation not to search positively relates to unemployed people's well-being (Vansteenkiste et al., 2004), a group of unemployed individuals characterized by high autonomous motivation not to search may not suffer from being unemployed. Finally, it could be examined whether differences in well-being across the motivational subgroups could be accounted for by differences in need satisfaction during unemployment.

The "What" of Behavior

Besides the reasons or behavioral regulation of unemployed individuals to search for a job or not search (i.e., the *why*), SDT also considers the type of goals or values unemployed individuals strive for (i.e., the *what*) (Deci & Ryan, 2000; Kasser & Ryan, 1996; Vansteenkiste, Soenens, & Duriez, 2008). For most unemployed individuals, finding a job is their most important goal. However, the specific goals unemployed individuals want to achieve via their work may vary considerably. Some unemployed individuals value employment in general and a specific job in particular because it allows them to meaningfully contribute to society or to develop their skills. Others value jobs that are well respected or that allow them to become materially successful. From the perspective of more quantitatively oriented theories, such as expectancy values theory and goal-setting theory, the specific goals unemployed individuals aim to achieve via their new job is of little importance as long as unemployed people highly value employment per se or are highly focused on achieving the goal of reemployment (Ryan, Sheldon, Kasser, & Deci, 1996). SDT, in contrast, maintains that the type of work goals unemployed individuals pursue during job search may yield important repercussions, as different types of goals relate differently to unemployed individuals' job flexibility, job choice, and hence also the experienced need satisfaction and well-being at their future job.

Specifically, SDT differentiates global intrinsic aspirations, such as contributing to the community, building social bonds, and developing and refining skills, from global extrinsic aspirations, such as accumulating wealth and material possessions, acquiring fame and social recognition, and having power and influence over others (Kasser & Ryan, 1996). When applied to the field of unemployment and work, an intrinsically oriented individual would value opportunities for skill development and formation at the job, while an extrinsically oriented individual would value a high-status job where he is, for example, seen as leader or a high potential. Intrinsic and extrinsic goal contents have been found to yield different well-being correlates (e.g., Kasser & Ryan, 1996) because they allow for a differential degree of need satisfaction. While intrinsic goal pursuit would be conducive to basic need satisfaction (e.g., Sebire, Standage, & Vansteenkiste, 2009), extrinsic goal pursuit would be unrelated or would even interfere with the satisfaction of one's basic psychological needs (e.g., Verstuyf, Vansteenkiste, & Soenens, 2012). In pursuing such outwardly oriented goals, one's ego and self-worth are more at stake and one is less likely to become fully immersed in the activity at hand (Schmuck, Kasser, & Ryan, 2000; Vansteenkiste, Simons, Lens, Soenens, Matos, & Lacante, 2004). Moreover, extrinsic goal-oriented individuals are more likely to adopt a competitive worldview that justifies the discrimination of threatening out-groups (Duriez, Soenens, et al., 2007) and to make use of others to get ahead in life (Sheldon, Sheldon, & Osbaldiston, 2000), behaviors that reduce one's opportunities for basic need satisfaction. Consistent with such a reasoning, the valuation of material possessions as a happiness medicine has been found to increase loneliness over time, which is indicative of relatedness frustration (Pieters, 2013). The research on individuals' work-related goals is still scarce but suggests that these different goal contents may yield a number of different correlates, both among unemployed and employed individuals, as outlined in proposition six.

Proposition Six: Intrinsic and Extrinsic Work Goals Yield Different Correlates Among Unemployed Individuals

To shed light on the different dynamics involved in the pursuit of intrinsic and extrinsic goals, Van den Broeck, Vansteenkiste, Lens, and De Witte (2010) relate these different goal contents to unemployed individuals' flexibility in accepting a job that deviates from their ideal (De Witte, 1993; Vandoorne, De Witte, & Hooge, 2000). After controlling for various background characteristics, perceived financial hardship, and general employment value, they found that intrinsic goals related positively to both training flexibility (i.e., the willingness to attend extra courses to find employment) and pay flexibility (i.e., the willingness to accept job that pays less well than what could be expected based on one's level of education or work experience). In contrast, the pursuit of extrinsic goals related negatively to these types of flexibility. This pattern of relations suggests that extrinsic goal oriented individuals adopt a less flexible attitude toward the labor market. Most importantly, they seem to reject these types of flexibility that may yield beneficial effects in the long term as they choose jobs that may offer reduced opportunities for basic psychological need satisfaction. By being strict about their pay level, extrinsically oriented individuals might end up choosing jobs that are well paid but yet are of a rather poor quality, for example, in terms of the job resources they offer (Bakker & Demerouti, 2007; Warr, 1987). By being unwilling to participate in job training, they are less likely to develop their skills and competencies. Such job training, which intrinsically oriented individuals are more likely to engage in, might, however, open up new job possibilities, which likely lead to high-quality and more enduring employment, characterized by higher levels of experienced psychological need satisfaction.

Consistent with this reasoning, Van den Broeck (2010) found in a sample of graduating university students that intrinsic and extrinsic work goals related differently to individuals' engagement and burnout assessed two years later. Intrinsic work goals related positively to engagement and negatively to burnout, while extrinsic work goals related negatively to engagement. These prospective associations could be accounted for by the fact that intrinsic work goals related positively to job resources, while extrinsic work goals yielded a negative relation. These findings provide preliminary evidence that unemployed people's goal contents relates to their future job well-being, although it remains to be studied which mechanisms can account for this association. These different goal-contents may—via the above mentioned accompanying types of flexibility—relate to the choice of jobs that differ in terms of their afforded job characteristics (self-selection mechanism). During the search for a new job, unemployed individuals with different goal contents likely pay attention to different aspects of job vacancies, with intrinsic goal oriented unemployed individuals being more attracted to vacancies highlighting job content, societal relevance, and social relations while extrinsic oriented unemployed individuals being attracted to vacancies highlighting high wages and prestigious functions. Apart from this self-selection mechanism, it is also possible that individuals with different goal-profiles evoke different job characteristics through a process of job crafting (evocative mechanism) or interpret and react to the available job characteristics differently (reactive mechanism) (see Van den Broeck, Van Ruysseveldt, Smulders, & De Witte, 2011).

Regardless of the mechanisms at work, previous work demonstrates that the pursuit of intrinsic, relative to extrinsic, work goals is associated positively with job satisfaction and work engagement and negatively with burnout and intention to turn over one's job for another (Vansteenkiste, Neyrinck et al., 2007). This relation could be accounted for by basic psychological need satisfaction at work (see also Unanue, Vignoles, Dittmar, & Vansteenkiste, in press). Along similar lines, Promislo, Deckop, Giacalone, and Jurkiewicz (2010) showed that the negative effects of a materialistic orientation are not limited to the workplace but may radiate to family life, as a materialistic orientation related to more work-family conflict. Indeed, extrinsically oriented individuals might work long hours to achieve their extrinsic ambitions, taking time away from family or leisure activities. Overall, then, the current findings suggest that to the extent that organizations attract unemployed individuals with an extrinsic, rather than an intrinsic, goal profile, their employees are more likely to display reduced job well-being and might also more easily quit their jobs.

At this point, some might argue that to the extent that extrinsic goals are central to the culture of the organization, organizations might actually benefit from hiring extrinsically oriented unemployed individuals. This position is maintained within the match perspective (e.g., Sagiv & Schwartz, 2000) and the person-environment fit paradigm (Kristof-Brown, Zimmerman, & Johnson, 2005). Indeed, it would be to the advantage of both the organization and the employees themselves if the goal profile of employees matched the goal profile encouraged within the organization's culture. Said differently, if social prestige, competition, and money are central aspects of an organization's culture, it is likely that a highly competitive and materialistically oriented unemployed individual would thrive there. From the SDT perspective, the critical question is whether such an extrinsic-extrinsic match actually creates opportunities for basic psychological need satisfaction. This might be rather unlikely, as previous work shows that extrinsically oriented business students don't display elevated well-being, although extrinsic goals are more likely present in their study environment (Kasser & Ahuvia, 2002; Vansteenkiste, Duriez, Simons, & Soenens, 2006).

Facilitating Motivation: The Role of Contextual Need Support

It is assumed that autonomous motivation and intrinsic goal pursuit can be either promoted or undermined depending on whether the environment nourishes or blocks satisfaction of basic psychological needs for autonomy, competence, and relatedness (Deci & Ryan, 2000; Ryan, 1995). Parallel to the three needs, SDT distinguishes autonomy-supportive relative to more controlling, well-structured relative to more chaotic, and involved relative to more distant social environments. To date, most of work within SDT has focused on the support of autonomy, but research witnesses an increasing interest in the topics of structure (e.g., Jang, Reeve, & Deci, 2010) and involvement (e.g., Grolnick & Ryan, 1989). The concept of need support allows one to evaluate the demotivating impact of (1) individual persons (e.g., partner, family, unemployment counselors) who interact on a frequent

basis with unemployed people and (2) the measures taken at the societal level.

Autonomy-supportive individuals dealing with unemployed people use inviting language and allow for participation and dialogue. They provide choices and give a meaningful rationale for a request. Perhaps, the core feature of autonomy support involves working from the unemployed person's frame of reference. This can be achieved by being curious about the unemployed person's view such that he feels fully understood and validated. Rather than displaying an authentic interest in the other's viewpoint, a controlling style involves approaching unemployed individuals from one's own or stereotyped (e.g., "unemployment is the result of one's own fault"; "unemployed individuals take advantage of society") standards, which are then used to judge the unemployed and to push them into action. Such coercion can be achieved by using overt (e.g., "I *count* on the fact that you write two application letters this week") or more subtle (e.g., "You get a monthly unemployment benefit, thus society expects something in return from your side") controlling language, or by threatening the unemployed person with external consequences (e.g., "If you keep on just hanging around here and stay unemployed, our marriage will fall apart"). A controlling approach then often takes the form of contingent regard (Roth, Assor, Niemiec, Ryan, & Deci, 2009), which involves buttressing one's appreciation and disappointment depending on people's effort expenditure and accomplishments.

Structure involves the setting of clear expectations and the provision of desired help, guidance, and information and, if needed, a detailed step-by-step plan, such that obstacles to reemployment are eliminated. Structuring socializing agents are stimulating and encouraging and provide competence-supportive feedback. As such, they guide the goal-setting and goal-achievement process of the unemployed individual. It is critical that structure be introduced in an autonomy-supportive way (Jang, et al., 2010; Sierens, Vansteenkiste, Goossens, Soenens, & Dochy, 2009). All too often, though, socializing agents (e.g., counselors, partners, parents) provide information that is not desired and, as a result, comes across as redundant or even irritating. Although the provision of such information is intended to be helpful, it is not perceived as such by the person being socialized because the information does not build a sense of competence. Instead, it only highlights what the person already knows. Finally, involvement is expressed through the display of a concern with the unemployed person's situation, such that the unemployed person feels fully understood.

Although the benefits of socializing agents' need support has been demonstrated in dozens of studies in domains outside the unemployment literature—including the sport, work, education, and health care domain (Deci & Ryan, 2000)—there is a paucity of work on need support in the domain of job search and unemployment, leading to proposition seven.

Proposition 7: Autonomous Motives to Search and Not to Search Can Be Facilitated by the Provision of Need Support

In one study among school leavers, Soenens and Vansteenkiste (2005) examined the role of parental and teacher autonomy support in the prediction of school leavers' relative autonomous motives for searching for a job. It was found that whereas maternal autonomy support was unrelated, both teacher and paternal autonomy support yielded a unique positive association with school leavers' relative autonomous motives for searching. Importantly, the mandatory nature of reemployment courses does not by definition elicit a controlled job-search motivation in the unemployed, since the necessity and personal usefulness of the mandatory course is well explained to the unemployed. In line with this, Koen, Klehe, and Van Viaenen (in press) show that unemployed people who perceived a mandatory course as personally meaningful had better endorsed the value of searching for a job, with increasing levels of internalization in part accounting for a positive change in employability. Yet if such courses were not perceived as personally meaningful, the unemployed likely felt that the course was yet another daunting duty from which they could extract little if any benefits.

Clearly more research is needed in this area. For instance, it needs to be demonstrated that the counselor's autonomy support, structure, and involvement relate to the unemployed person's experience of need satisfaction, which, in turn, predicts his or her motivational and emotional regulation strategies. One interesting avenue involves studying the interactions between counselors and unemployed individuals in terms of the provided need support at the *micro level* (for instance, through observations). This would help us to get a better insight in what exactly need-supportive counselors are doing and saying during these conversations (see Reeve, 2006, for an example in education) and

to shed light on the interview techniques they use (see Markland, Ryan, Tobin, & Rollnick, 2005; Vansteenkiste, Williams, & Resnicow, 2012). For instance, the language used by counselors might be quite different, with controlling counselors using more "should" language and autonomy-supportive counselors being more inviting (e.g., Vansteenkiste, Simons, Lens, Sheldon, & Deci, 2004).

Although scholars and practitioners might agree that it is critical to support unemployed people's autonomous motives for search, the question of how to deal with unemployed individuals who choose not to search might be more controversial. This issue contains at least two different layers: that is, the question (1) *whether* you need to motivate and activate unemployed individuals who are autonomously not searching for a job and, if so, (2) *how* you can motivate them. The answer to the first question will be informed by one's world view, political affiliation, and empirical and ethical considerations. As noted, empirically, the autonomous motivation not to search has been found to yield a positive relation to well-being (Vansteenkiste, Simons, Lens, Sheldon, et al., 2004), presumably because those unemployed individuals find themselves in their personal desired situation, which allows them to get their basic needs met. Also, within SDT (Ryan, Lynch, Vansteenkiste, & Deci, 2011), it has been argued that the support of autonomy is an end in itself, a goal that can be justified on ethical grounds. At times, this also implies supporting the individual's decision not to engage in a particular activity (e.g., searching). Indeed, autonomy support does not represent a motivational technique to trick unemployed individuals into searching for a job. If unemployment counselors start a dialogue with the unemployed with the explicit aim of activating them, they might come across as manipulative. Thus they would not be exercising autonomy support but some form of "pseudoautonomy support."

This does not imply that unemployment counselors need to adopt a permissive, laissez-faire attitude, as if they could not clarify their expectations or point out the consequences of nonsearching. Yet what is critical is the *timing* of and the *way* how these issues get discussed. Need-thwarting unemployment counselors directly confront unemployed persons with the consequences of their nonsearching behavior—for instance, by suggesting that finding employment is their societal duty and that not searching will be sanctioned (e.g., removal of unemployment benefits). At least some unemployed people are very much aware of the consequences of their nonsearching; hence the information provided by counselors will not be experienced as very helpful. Instead, because of its redundant character, the information might cause irritation and prompt a defensive reaction. To avoid such oppositional defiant reactions, need-supportive counselors would express interest and be curious about why the unemployed person did not search for a job over the past weeks. Through such interest taking, nonsearching unemployed persons would be validated rather than being judged for not living up to the counselor's and society's expectations.

Having addressed the reasons for not searching, autonomy-supportive counselors would choose the right moment to ask in a friendly way whether the unemployed person has reasons to search for a job. If it turns out that the reasons for not searching outweigh the reasons for searching, need-supportive unemployment counselors would respect the unemployed person's viewpoint yet point out that there might be *consequences* associated with not searching (e.g., removal of unemployment benefits). Rather than highlighting the evaluative value of these consequences by presenting them as threatening *sanctions* ("We will need to sanction you if you do not do X or Y"), the counselor would adopt a need-supportive style, thereby emphasizing the informational value of these consequences. Need-supportive counselors would, for instance, be curious to hear whether an unemployed person's viewed the consequences associated with not searching as unfair and illegitimate; they would then offer a meaningful rationale and relevant information for why such a system is installed by the government. If the unemployed person was already aware of these reasons, he or she would be asked to self-generate those reasons in order to avoid the repetition of that information.

Thus, in the end, the pros of not searching but also searching would be discussed by need-supportive counselors, yet these counselors would pay careful attention to the order and the way in which this would be done. In general, a need-supportive unemployment counselors would voice unemployed persons' reasons for not searching rather than rejecting them and pushing the them to start searching for a job. The latter approach would create tension and conflict and would be experienced as need-thwarting by both the unemployed person and the counselor, such that the unemployed person would fail to endorse the decision to start searching for a job.

At a broader level, then, need-supportive counseling does not imply that one stays silent about societal measures to foster reemployment, including the gradual removal of unemployment benefits or the necessity to participate in mandatory training programs. This would be typical for a laissez-faire approach. There are likely good reasons why governments decide to gradually remove unemployment benefits or to organize mandatory training programs. Need-supportive counsellors would discuss these reasons and would highlight the informational value of these societal measures while at the same time minimizing their controlling aspect (Deci & Ryan, 1985).

Conclusion

Rather surprisingly, the literatures on the well-being effects of unemployment and unemployed people's job search behavior have been developed fairly independently. One reason for this is perhaps that an overarching theory that allows one to study both phenomena simultaneously is currently missing. SDT might help to bridge the gap between both literatures, as SDT specifies the explanatory mechanisms (basic need satisfaction and frustration) and moderators (quality of motivation in terms of behavioral regulations and goals) of the link between unemployment and well-being. Further, the type of motives underlying search behavior relate to unemployed people's intensity of searching, employability, and their reemployment success. A lot of work still needs to be done in this area, but the few SDT-based studies on unemployment and job search and the wealth of empirical evidence in other life domains indicate that truly motivating unemployed people involves more than putting them under pressure, such that they become activated. For activation policies to be effective in the long term—that is, to promote high quality reemployment—policy makers, counselors, and family need to nurture unemployed people's basic psychological needs for autonomy, competence, and relatedness.

Practical Guidelines

• Counselors do well to move beyond considering unemployed people's level of motivation to search by also taking into account the type of reasons (autonomous or controlled) underlying unemployed people's search behavior.

- A lack of motivation to search stems not only from discouragement after repetitive rejections but could also represent a more deliberate and well-reflected choice or an attempt to defy pressuring authority figures.

- Putting pressure on people to search a job may be effective in the short term but yield considerable *collateral damage* in the long term, as indexed by lowered well-being and poor-quality reemployment.

- To foster autonomous search motivation, counselors do well to adopt a counseling style supportive of employed people's psychological needs for autonomy, competence, and relatedness.

- Autonomy support manifests through the provision of desired choice, the offering of a meaningful rationale, the unconditional acceptance of unemployed people's functioning, the use of inviting rather than controlling language, and the display of a sincere curiosity in unemployed people's reasons for both searching and not searching.

References

Aelterman, N., Vansteenkiste, M., Haerens, L., Vandenberghe, L., Demeyer, J., & Van Keer, H. (2012). Pupils' objectively measured physical activity levels and engagement as a function of between-class and between-pupil differences in motivation towards physical education: A self-determination theory approach. *Journal of Sport & Exercise Psychology, 34*, 457–480.

Assor, A., Vansteenkiste, M., & Kaplan, A. (2009). Identified versus introjected-approach and introjected-avoidance motivations in school and in sports: The limited benefits of self-worth strivings. *Journal of Educational Psychology, 101*, 482–497.

Atkinson, J. W., & Birch, D. (1970). *The dynamics of action*. New York: Wiley.

Bakker, A. B., & Demerouti, E. (2007). The job demands–resources model: State of the art. *Journal of Managerial Psychology, 22*, 309–328.

Benware, C., & Deci, E. L. (1984). Quality of learning with an active versus passive motivational set. *American Educational Research Journal, 21*, 755–765.

Bond, M. J., & Feather, N. T. (1988). Some correlates of structure and purpose in the use of time. *Journal of Personality and Social Psychology, 55*, 321–329.

Brehm, J. W. (1966). *Theory of psychological reactance*. San Diego, CA: Academic Press.

Brown, K. W., & Ryan, R. M. (2006). Multilevel modeling of motivation: A Self-determination theory analysis of basic psychological needs. In A. D. Ong & M. van Dulmen (Eds.), *Oxford handbook of methods in positive psychology* (pp. 1158–1183). New York: Oxford University Press.

Chen, B., Vansteenkiste, M., Beyers, W., Soenens, B., & Van Petegem, S. (2013). Autonomy in family decision-making among Chinese adolescents: Disentangling the dual meaning

of autonomy. *Journal of Cross-Cultural Psychology, 44*, 1184–1209.

Creed, P. A., & Bartrum, D. (2006). Explanations for deteriorating wellbeing in unemployed people: Specific unemployment theories and beyond. In T. Kieselbach (Ed.), *Unemployment and health: International and interdisciplinary perspectives* (pp. 1–20). Bowen Hills: Australian Academic Press.

Creed, P. A., King, V., Hood, M., & McKenzie, R. (2009). Goal orientation, self-regulation strategies, and job-seeking intensity in unemployed adults. *Journal of Applied Psychology, 94*, 806–813.

Creed, P., & Klisch, J. (2005). Future outlook and financial strain: Testing the personal agency and latent deprivation models of unemployment and well-being. *Journal of Occupational Health Psychology, 3*, 251–260.

Crossley, C. D., & Highhouse, S. (2005). Relation of job search and choice process with subsequent satisfaction. *Journal of Economic Psychology, 26*, 255–268.

Deci, E. L. (1975). *Intrinsic motivation*. New York: Plenum.

Deci, E. L. (1992). On the nature and functions of motivation theories. *Psychological Science, 3*, 167–171.

Deci, E. L., & Ryan, R. M. (1985). *Intrinsic motivation and self-determination in human behavior*. New York: Plenum.

Deci, E. L., & Ryan, R. M. (2000). The "what" and "why" of goal pursuits: Human needs and the self-determination of behavior. *Psychological Inquiry, 11*, 227–268.

Deci, E. L., & Ryan, R. M. (2012). Motivation, personality, and development within embedded social contexts: An overview of self-determination theory. In R. M. Ryan (Ed.), *Oxford handbook of human motivation* (pp. 85–107). Oxford, UK: Oxford University Press.

Deci, E. L., & Vansteenkiste, M. (2004). Self-determination theory and basic need satisfaction: Understanding human development in positive psychology. *Ricerche di Psicologia, 27*, 17–34.

De Witte, H. (1993). Psychological consequences of long-term unemployment: Review of the literature. *Psychologica Belgica, 33*, 1–35.

De Witte, H., & Wets, J. (1996). On the heterogeneity of the experience of long-term unemployment among young women. In P. De Goede, P. De Klaver, J. Van Ophem, C. Verhaar, & A. De Vries (Eds.), *Youth: Unemployment, identity and policy* (pp. 65–85). Avebury, UK: Aldershot.

Duriez, B., Soenens, B., & Vansteenkiste, M. (2007). In search of the antecedents of adolescent authoritarianism: The relative contribution of parental goal promotion and parenting style dimensions. *European Journal of Personality, 21*, 507–527.

Feather, N. T. (1990). *The psychological impact of unemployment*. New York: Springer-Verlag.

Feather, N. T. (1992). Values, valences, expectations, and actions. *Journal of Social Issues, 48*, 109–124.

Feather, N. T., & Davenport, P. R. (1981). Unemployment and depressive affect: A motivational and attributional analysis. *Journal of Personality and Social Psychology, 41*, 422–436.

Fryer, D. (1986). Employment deprivation and personal agency during unemployment: A critical discussion of Jahoda's explanation of the psychological effects of unemployment. *Social Behavior, 1*, 3–23.

Fryer, D., & Payne, R. L. (1986). Being unemployed: A review of the literature on the psychological experience of unemployment. In C. L. Cooper & I. Robertson (Eds.), *International* review of industrial and organizational psychology (pp. 235–278). Chichester, UK: Wiley.

Furnham, A. (1987). Work-related beliefs and human values. *Personality and Individual Differences, 8,* 627–637.

Gillet, N., Vallerand, R. J., & Rosnet, E. (2009). Motivational clusters and performance in a real-life setting. *Motivation and Emotion, 33,* 49–62.

Grolnick, W. S., & Ryan, R. M. (1989). Parent styles associated with children's self-regulation and competence in school. *Journal of Educational Psychology, 81,* 143–154.

Gollwitzer, P. M., & Brandstatter, V. (1990). Implementation intentions and effective goal pursuit. *Journal of Personality and Social Psychology, 73,* 186–199.

Haerens, L., Kirk, D., Cardon, G., De Bourdeaudhuij, I., & Vansteenkiste, M. (2010). Motivational profiles for secondary school physical education and its relationship to the adoption of a physically active lifestyle among university students. *European Physical Education Review, 16,* 117–139.

Halvari, H., Vansteenkiste, M., Brorby, S., & Karlsen, H-P. (2013). Examining antecedents and outcomes of part-time working nurses' motives to search and not-to-search for a full-time position. *Journal of Applied Social Psychology, 43,* 1608–1623.

Hayenga, A. O., & Corpus, J. H. (2010). Profiles of intrinsic and extrinsic motivation: A person-centered approach to motivation and achievement in middle school. *Motivation and Emotion, 34,* 371–383.

Hodgins, H. S., & Knee, C. R. (2002). The integrating self and conscious experience. In E. L. Deci & R. M. Ryan (Eds.). *The handbook of self-determination research,* (pp. 87–100). Rochester, NY: University of Rochester Press.

Hodgins, H. S., Yacko, H. A., & Gottlieb, E. (2006). Autonomy and non-defensiveness. *Motivation and Emotion, 30,* 283–293.

Hodgins, H. S., Weibust, K. S., Weinstein, N., Shiffman, S., Miller, A., Coombs, G., & Adair, K. C. (2010). The cost of self-protection: Threat response and performance as a function of autonomous and controlled motivations. *Personality and Social Psychology Bulletin, 36,* 184–191.

Jahoda, M. (1981). Work, employment, and unemployment: Values, theories, and approaches in social research. *American Psychologist, 36,* 184–191.

Jahoda, M. (1982). *Employment and unemployment: A sociopsychological analysis.* Cambridge, UK: Cambridge University Press.

Jang, H., Reeve, J., & Deci, E. L. (2010). Engaging students in learning activities: It's not autonomy support or structure, but autonomy support and structure. *Journal of Educational Psychology, 102,* 588–600.

Kanfer, R., Wanberg, C. R., & Kantrowitz, T. M. (2001). Job search and employment: A personality-motivational analysis and meta-analytic review. *Journal of Applied Psychology, 86,* 837–855.

Kasser, T., & Ahuvia, A. C. (2002). Materialistic values and well-being in business students. *European Journal of Social Psychology, 32,* 137–146.

Kasser, T., & Ryan, R. M. (1996). Further examining the American dream: Differential correlates of intrinsic and extrinsic goals. *Personality and Social Psychology Bulletin, 22,* 280–287.

Koen, J., Klehe, U. C., Van Vianen, A. E. M. (2010). Job search strategies and reemployment quality—The impact of career adaptability. *Journal of Vocational Behavior, 77,* 126–139.

Koen, J., Klehe, U. C., Van Vianen, A. E. M. (in press). Job search and employability after compulsory reemployment courses: The role of choice, usefulness, and motivation. *Journal of Occupational and Organisational Psychology.*

Koestner, R., & Losier, G. F. (2002). Distinguishing three ways of being highly motivated: A closer look at introjection, identification, and intrinsic motivation. In E. L. Deci & R. M. Ryan (Eds.), *Handbook of self-determination research* (pp. 101–121). Rochester, NY: University of Rochester Press.

Koestner, R., Lekes, N., Powers, T. A., & Chicoine, E. (2002). Attaining personal goals: Self-concordance plus implementation intentions equals success. *Journal of Personality and Social Psychology, 83,* 231–244.

Kristof-Brown, A., Zimmerman, R., & Johnson, E. (2005). Consequences of individuals' fit at work: A meta-analysis of person-job, person-organization, person-group, and person-supervisor fit. *Personnel Psychology, 58,* 285–342.

Kroger, J. & Marcia, J. E. (2011). The identity statuses: Origins, meanings, and interpretations. In S. J. Schwartz, K. Luyckx, & V. L. Vignoles (Eds.), *Handbook of Identity Theory and Research,* (pp. 31–54). New York: Springer.

La Guardia, J. G. (2009). Developing who I am: A self-determination theory approach to the establishment of healthy identities. *Educational Psychologist, 44,* 90–104.

Marcia, J. E. (1966). Development and validation of ego identity status. *Journal of Personality and Social Psychology, 3,* 551–558.

Markland, D., Ryan, R. M., Tobin, V. J., & Rollnick, S. (2005). Motivational interviewing and self-determination theory. *Journal of Social and Clinical Psychology, 24,* 811–831.

McKee-Ryan, F. M., Song, Z. L., Wanberg, C. R., & Kinicki, A. J. (2005). Psychological and physical well-being during unemployment: A meta-analytic study. *Journal of Applied Psychology, 90,* 53–76.

Meyer, B., Enström, M. K., Harstveit, M., Bowles, D. P., & Beevers, C. G. (2007). Happiness and despair on the catwalk: Need satisfaction, well-being, and personality adjustment among fashion models. *Journal of Positive Psychology, 2,* 2–17.

Miller, J. G., Das, R., & Chakravarthy, S. (2011). Culture and the role of choice in agency. *Journal of Personality and Social Psychology, 101,* 46–61.

Miller, W. R., & Baca, L. M. (1983). Two-year follow-up of bibliotherapy and therapist-directed controlled drinking training for problem drinkers. *Behavior Therapy, 14,* 441–448.

Miller, W. R., Taylor, C. A., & West, J. C. (1980). Focused versus broad spectrum behavior therapy for problem drinkers. *Journal of Consulting and Clinical Psychology, 48,* 590–601.

Miller, W. R., & Rollnick, S. (2002). *Motivational interviewing.* New York: Guilford Press.

Muller, J. J., Creed, P. A., Waters, L. E., & Machin, M. A. (2005). The development and preliminary testing of a scale to measure the latent and manifest benefits of employment. *European Journal of Psychological Assessment, 21,* 191–198.

Paul, K. L., & Batinic, B. (2010). The need for work: Jahoda's latent functions of employment in a representative sample of the German population. *Journal of Organizational Behavior, 31,* 45–64.

Paul, I., & Moser, K. (2009). Unemployment impairs mental health: Meta-analyses. *Journal of Vocational Behavior, 74,* 264–282.

Pieters, R. (2013). Bidirectional dynamics of materialism and loneliness: Not just a vicious cycle. *Journal of Consumer Research, 40,* 615–631.

Promislo, M. D., Deckop, J. R., Giacalone, R. A., & Jurkiewicz, C. L. (2010). Valuing money more than people: The effects of materialism on work-family conflict. *Journal of Occupational and Organizational Psychology*, *83*, 935–953.

Roth, G., Assor, A., Niemiec, C. P., Ryan, R. M., & Deci, E. L. (2009). The emotional and academic consequences of parental conditional regard: Comparing conditional positive regard, conditional negative regard, and autonomy support as parenting practices. *Developmental Psychology*, *45*, 1119–1142.

Reeve, J. (2006). Teachers as facilitators: What autonomy-supportive teachers do and why their students benefit. *Elementary School Journal*, *106*, 225–236.

Reeve, J., Jang, H., Carrell, D., Jeon, S., & Barch, J. (2004). Enhancing students' engagement by increasing teachers' autonomy support. *Motivation and Emotion*, *28*, 147–169.

Reilly, P. A. (1998). Balancing flexibility: Meeting the interests of employers and employee. *European Journal of Work and Organizational Psychology*, *7*, 7–22.

Ryan, R. M. (1995). Psychological needs and the facilitation of integrative processes. *Journal of Personality*, *63*, 397–427.

Ryan, R. M., Bernstein, J. H., & Brown, K. W. (2010). Weekends, work, and well-being: Psychological need satisfactions and day of the week effects on mood, vitality, and physical symptoms. *Journal of Social and Clinical Psychology*, *29*, 95–122.

Ryan, R. M., & Deci, E. L. (1999). Approaching and avoiding self-determination: Comparing cybernetic and organismic paradigms of motivation. In C. Carver & M. Scheier (Eds.), *Perspectives on behavioral self-regulation: Advances in social cognition* (pp. 193–215). Mahwah, NJ: Erlbaum.

Ryan, R. M., & Deci, E. L. (2000a). Self-determination theory and the facilitation of intrinsic motivation, social development, and well-being. *American Psychologist*, *55*, 68–78.

Ryan, R. M., & Deci, E. L. (2000b). The darker and brighter sides of human existence: Basic psychological needs as a unifying concept. *Psychological Inquiry*, *11*, 319–338.

Ryan, R. M., & Deci, E. L. (2003). On assimilating identities to the self: A self-determination theory perspective on internalization and integrity within cultures. In M. R. Leary & J. P. Tangney (Eds.), *Handbook of self and identity* (pp. 253–274). New York: Guilford Press.

Ryan, R. M., Lynch, M. F., Vansteenkiste, M., & Deci, E. L. (2011). Motivation and autonomy in counseling, psychotherapy, and behavior change: A look at theory and practice. *The Counseling Psychologist*, *39*, 193–260.

Ryan, R. M., Sheldon, K. M., Kasser, T., & Deci, E. L. (1996). All goals are not created equal: An organismic perspective on the nature of goals and their regulation. In P. M. Gollwitzer & J. A. Bargh (Eds.), *The psychology of action: Linking cognition and motivation to behavior* (pp. 7–26). New York: Guilford Press.

Sagiv, L., & Schwartz, S. H. (2000). Value priorities and subjective well-being: Direct relations and congruity effects. *European Journal of Social Psychology*, *30*, 177–198.

Schmuck, P., Kasser, T., & Ryan, R. M. (2000). Intrinsic and extrinsic goals: Their structure and relationship to well-being in German and U.S. college students. *Social Indicators Research*, *50*, 225–241.

Sebire, S., Standage, M., & Vansteenkiste, M. (2009). Examining intrinsic versus extrinsic exercise goals: Cognitive, affective, and behavioral Outcomes. *Journal of Sport & Exercise Psychology*, *31*, 189–210.

Senécal, C., & Guay, F. (2000). Procrastination in job seeking: An analysis of motivational processes and feelings of hopelessness. In J. R. Ferrari, & T. A. Pychyl (Eds.), Procrastination: Current Issues and New Directions (Special Issue). *Journal of Social Behavior and Personality*, *15*(5), 267–282.

Sheldon, K. M., Cheng, C., & Hilpert, J. (2011). Understanding well-being and optimal functioning: Applying the multilevel personality in context (MPIC) model. *Psychological Inquiry*, *22*, 1–16.

Sheldon, K. M., Sheldon, M. S., & Osbaldiston, R. (2000). Prosocial values and group assortation within an N-person prisoner's dilemma game. *Human Nature*, *11*, 387–404.

Sierens, E., Vansteenkiste, M., Goossens, L., Soenens, B., & Dochy, F. (2009). The synergistic effect of perceived teacher autonomy-support and structure in the prediction of self-regulated learning. *British Journal of Educational Psychology*, *79*, 57–68.

Soenens, B., & Vansteenkiste, M. (2005). Antecedents and outcomes of self-determination in 3 life domains: The role of parents' and teachers' autonomy support. *Journal of Youth and Adolescence*, *34*, 589–604.

Soenens, B., & Vansteenkiste, M. (2011). When is identity congruent with the self? A self-determination theory perspective. In S. J. Schwartz, K. Luyckx, & V. L. Vignoles (Eds.) *Handbook of identity theory and research* (pp. 381–402).

Unanue, W., Vignoles, V., Dittmar, H., & Vansteenkiste, M. (in press). Materialism and well-being in the UK and Chile: Basic need satisfaction and basic need frustration as underlying psychological processes. *European Journal of Personality*.

Underlid, K. (1996). Activity during unemployment and mental health. *Scandinavian Journal of Psychology*, *37*, 269–281.

Van den Broeck, A., Lens, W., De Witte, H., & Van Coillie, H. (2013). Unraveling the importance of the quantity and the quality of workers' motivation for well-being: A person-centered perspective. *Journal of Vocational Behavior*, *82*, 69–78.

Van den Broeck A., Van Ruysseveldt J., Smulders P. & De Witte H. (2011) Does an intrinsic work value orientation strengthen the impact of job resources? A perspective from the job demands-resources model. *European Journal of Work and Organizational Psychology*, *20*, 581–609.

Van den Broeck, A., Vansteenkiste, M., De Witte, H., Soenens, B., & Lens, W. (2010). Capturing autonomy, competence, and relatedness at work: Construction and initial validation of the work-related basic need satisfaction scale. *Journal of Occupation and Organizational Psychology*, *83*, 981–1002.

Van den Broeck, A., Vansteenkiste, M., Lens, W., & De Witte, H. (2010). Unemployed individuals' work values and flexibility: A comparison of expectancy-value theory and self-determination theory. *Applied Psychology: An International Review*, *59*, 296–317.

Vandoorne, J., De Witte, H., & Hooge, J. (2000), Werk in zicht: houding ten aanzien van arbeid en toekomstperspectief op de arbeidsmarkt [Work in sight: attitude toward work and future perspective on the labour market], in H. De Witte, J. Hooge & L. Walgrave (red.), *Jongeren in Vlaanderen: gemeten en geteld. 12—tot 18—jarigen over hun leefwereld en toekomst* (pp. 185–208). Leuven: Universitaire Pers Leuven.

Van Hooft, E. A. J., Born, M, Taris, T. W., van der Flier, H., & Blonk, R. W. B. (2005). Bridging the gap between intentions and behavior: Implementation intentions, action control, and procrastination. *Journal of Vocational Behavior, 66,* 238–256.

Van Hooft, E. A. J., Wanberg, C. R., & Van Hoye, G. (2013). Moving beyond job search quantity: Towards a conceptualization and self-regulatory framework of job search quality. *Organizational Psychology Review, 3,* 3–40.

Vansteenkiste, M. (2010, May). Motivational profiles from a self-determination theory perspective. Paper presented at the 4th Conference on Self-Determination Theory (SDT), Ghent, Belgium.

Vansteenkiste, M., De Witte, H., & Lens, W. (2006). Explaining the negative relationship between length of unemployment and the willingness to undertake job training: A self-determination perspective. In T. Kieselback & T. Winefield (Eds.), *Unemployment and health, international and interdisciplinary perspectives* (pp. 199–217). Bowen Hills: Australian Academic Press.

Vansteenkiste, M., Duriez, B., Simons, J., & Soenens, B. (2006). Materialistic values and well-being among business students: Further evidence for their detrimental effect. *Journal of Applied Social Psychology, 36,* 2892–2908.

Vansteenkiste, M., Lens, W., De Witte, H., & Feather, N. T. (2005). Understanding unemployed people's job search behavior, unemployment experience and wellbeing: A comparison of expectancy-value theory and self-determination theory. *British Journal of Social Psychology, 44,* 269–287.

Vansteenkiste, M., Lens, W., De Witte, S., De Witte, H., & Deci, E. L. (2004). The "why" and "why not" of job search behaviour: Their relation to searching, unemployment experience, and well-being. *European Journal of Social Psychology, 34*(3), 345–363.

Vansteenkiste, M., Lens, W., Soenens, B., & Luyckx, K. (2006). Autonomy and relatedness among Chinese sojourners and applicants: Conflictual or independent predictors of well-being and adjustment? *Motivation and Emotion, 30,* 273–282.

Vansteenkiste, M., Neyrinck, B., Niemiec, C. P., Soenens, B., De Witte, H., & Van Den Broeck, A. (2007). On the relations among work value orientations, psychological need satisfaction, and job outcomes: A self-determination theory approach. *Journal of Occupational and Organizational Psychology, 80,* 251–277.

Vansteenkiste, M., Niemiec, C., & Soenens, B. (2010). The development of the five mini-theories of self-determination theory: An historical overview, emerging trends, and future directions. In T. Urdan & S. Karabenick (Eds.), *Advances in motivation and achievement* (Vol. 16). Bingley, UK: Emerald Publishing.

Vansteenkiste, M., & Ryan, R. M. (2013). On psychological growth and vulnerability: Basic psychological need satisfaction and need frustration as an unifying principle. *Journal of Psychotherapy Integration, 3,* 263–280.

Vansteenkiste, M., Sierens, E., Soenens, B., Luyckx, K., & Lens, W. (2009). Motivational profiles from a self-determination theory perspective: The quality of motivation matters. *Journal of Educational Psychology, 101,* 671–688.

Vansteenkiste, M., Simons, J., Lens, W., Sheldon, K. M., & Deci, E. L. (2004). Motivating learning, performance, and persistence: The synergistic effects of intrinsic goal contents and autonomy-supportive contexts. *Journal of Personality and Social Psychology, 87,* 246–260.

Vansteenkiste, M., Simons, J., Lens, W., Soenens, B., & Matos, L. (2005). Examining the motivational impact of intrinsic versus extrinsic goal framing and autonomy-supportive versus internally controlling communication style on early adolescents' academic achievement. *Child Development, 76,* 483–501.

Vansteenkiste, M., Soenens, B., & Duriez, B. (2008). Presenting a positive alternative to materialistic strivings and the thin-ideal: Understanding the effects of extrinsic relative to intrinsic goal pursuits. In Lopez, S. J. (Ed.) *Positive psychology: Exploring the best in people* (Vol. 4, pp. 57–86). Westport, CT: Greenwood.

Vansteenkiste, M., Soenens, B., Van Petegem, S., & Duriez, B. (2014). The relation between degree and style of prohibition and adolescent internalisation and oppositional defiance. *Developmental Psychology, 50,* 229–236.

Vansteenkiste, M., Williams, G. C., & Resnicow, K. (2012). Toward systematic integration between self-determination theory and motivational interviewing as examples of top-down and bottom-up intervention development: Autonomy or volition as a fundamental theoretical principle. *International Journal of Behavioral Nutrition and Physical Activity, 9,* 23.

Verstuyf, J., Vansteenkiste, M., & Soenens, B. (2012). Eating regulation and bulimic symptoms: The differential correlates of health-focused and appearance-focused eating regulation. *Body Image: An International Journal of Research, 9,* 108–117.

Verstuyf, J., Vansteenkiste, M., Soenens, B., Boone, L., & Mouratidis, T. (2013). Daily ups and downs in Womens' binge eating symptoms: The role of basic psychological needs, general self-control and emotional eating. *Journal of Social and Clinical Psychology, 32,* 335–361.

Vinokur, A. D., & Schul, Y. (2002). The web of coping resources and pathways to reemployment following a job loss. *Journal of Occupational Health Psychology, 5,* 32–47.

Wanberg, C. (2012). The individual experience of unemployment. *Annual Review of Psychology, 63,* 369–396.

Wanberg, C., Hough, L. M., & Song, z. (2002). Predictive validity of a multidisciplinary model of reemployment success. *Journal of Applied Psychology, 87,* 1100–1120.

Wanberg, C. R., Zhu, J., Kanfer, R., & Zhang, Z. (2012). After the pink slip: Applying dynamic motivation frameworks to the job search experience. *Academy of Management Journal, 55,* 261–284.

Wanberg, C. Zu, J., & Van Hooft, A. J. (2010). The job search grind: perceived progress, self-reactions, and self-regulation of search effort. *Academy of Management Journal, 53,* 788–807.

Warr, P. (1987). *Work, Unemployment, and Mental Health,* Clarendon Press, Oxford.

Weiner, B. (1985). An attributional theory of achievement motivation and emotion. *Psychological Review, 92,* 548–573.

Wilson, P. M., Rogers, W. T., Rodgers, W. M., & Wild, T. C. (2006). The psychological need satisfaction in exercise scale. *Journal of Sport and Exercise Psychology, 28,* 231–251.

Motivation and Self-Regulation in Job Search: A Theory of Planned Job Search Behavior

Edwin A. J. van Hooft

Abstract

Job search is a difficult and complex process that demands prolonged motivation and self-regulation. Integrating insights from generic motivation theories and the job search literature, a Theory of Planned Job Search Behavior (TPJSB) is introduced as a framework for organizing the motivational and self-regulatory predictors and mechanisms that are important in the job search process. The chapter specifically focuses on the motivation-related concepts in the TPJSB, distinguishing between global-level, contextual, and situational predictors of job search intentions and job search behavior. After describing the theoretical underpinnings, empirical support for the associations in the model is presented and reviewed, and recommendations for future research are provided. Last, the moderating role of broader context factors on the TPJSB relations is discussed.

Key Words: job search, job attainment, motivation, intentions, theory of planned behavior

At any point in time, many individuals engage in job search, including school-leavers or graduating students seeking their first job, employed people looking for a job change, temporary workers in search of their next job, to-be-laid-off employees or employees in outplacement programs seeking a replacing job, unemployed people searching for reemployment, or nonworking people (re)entering the labor force (for reviews of job search in various samples of job seekers, see Boswell & Gardner, this volume; De Cuyper, Fontinha, & De Witte, this volume; Klehe, De Pater, Koen, & Kira, this volume; Saks, this volume; Song, Sun, & Li, this volume; Zikic, Kent, & Richardson, this volume). *Job search* is typically defined as specific behaviors to identify labor market alternatives, acquire information about these alternatives, and actively pursue job opportunities (Barber, Daly, Giannantonio, & Phillips, 1994; Bretz, Boudreau, & Judge, 1994), including activities such as checking online job boards, networking for job options, preparing a

résumé, making inquiries to prospective employers, and sending application letters. Extant theory and conceptual models have identified job search as an important factor in career decision-making during school-to-work transitions (Mihal, Sorce, & Comte, 1984; Saks, this volume; Soelberg, 1967); in the employee turnover process (Boswell & Gardner, this volume; Mobley, 1977; Steers & Mowday, 1981); and in the process of coping with job loss (Latack, Kinicki, & Prussia, 1995; Leana & Feldman, 1988), increasing the chances to obtain a (new) job.

Job search is a difficult, complex process. Several aspects inherent to the job search process and its context contribute to that complexity. First, for most people job search is a rather *novel, nonroutine activity* for which they have relatively little skilled experience. The job search process places people in uncertain situations that require adaptability and changes in their routines and strategies (Leana & Feldman, 1988; Noordzij, Van Hooft, Van Mierlo, Van Dam, & Born, 2013; Wanberg, 2012;

Wanberg, Basbug, Van Hooft, & Samtani, 2012). Second, job search involves a *wide array of methods and channels* to use and activities and behaviors to engage in. Moreover, these activities demand a broad range of different skills (e.g., whereas locating job vacancies requests Internet and information-seeking skills, effective networking requests social skills, and drafting a good application letter requests writing skills). Third, job search occurs in a rather *ambiguous and competitive context*. Because the labor market is complex, characterized by low transparency and high heterogeneity, it is often unclear what one needs to do exactly to locate job leads, obtain job interviews, meet the expectations of recruiting organizations, and obtain a job. Furthermore, one often has to compete against other job seekers and applicants during the job search, job pursuit, and application process. Fourth, job search is a rather *lengthy process toward a distal goal* (i.e., obtaining a job) with an abundance of obstacles, setbacks, and rejections along the way, which can easily distract job seekers' attention and undermine their motivation. Especially in times of economic turmoil, people likely experience the job search process as a black hole swallowing all their energy and efforts (Wanberg et al., 2012). Fifth, job search is a largely *self-organized and self-managed process*, often (although not always) occurring in a context with relatively little external help and steering.

Because of all these difficulties and complexities, having and maintaining motivation is of utmost importance to secure continuous job search activity. To predict and explain job search activity, previous theorizing and research has adapted various theoretical frameworks on human motivation to the context of job search. Other chapters in this volume reviewed several of these theories, including expectancy-value frameworks (Feather, this volume); goal-setting theory (Latham, Mawritz, & Locke, this volume); and Self-Determination Theory (SDT; Vansteenkiste & Van den Broeck, this volume). All of these theories specify factors that may enhance or undermine peoples' motivation to engage in job search. While motivation is essential for engaging and persisting in job search, it likely is not enough. As a consequence of the complexities, difficulties, and rejections associated with job seeking, job search activities are rarely considered to be fun, enjoyable, and entertaining. Rather, job search is often considered aversive and associated with negative emotions (Borgen & Amundson, 1987; Song, Uy, Zhang, & Shi, 2009; Wanberg, Zhu, & Van Hooft, 2010). For tasks that

are difficult, unpleasant, boring, or otherwise aversive, but are important to attain some valued goal (i.e., finding a job), people need self-regulation (e.g., regulation of effort, reminding oneself of the valued outcome, maintenance actions directed at increasing interest) to ensure task persistence and performance. Recent conceptualizations have therefore emphasized not only the motivational but also the self-regulatory nature of job search.

In this chapter and the next, I present a theoretical framework integrating both motivational and self-regulatory perspectives on job search (see Figure 11.1). This framework is grounded in Ajzen's (1991) Theory of Planned Behavior (TPB). In the present chapter, I focus on the motivational components and outline the theoretical rationales for the basic concepts and relations of the model, review empirical research, and address gaps in the literature, highlighting areas for future research. In the next chapter, I focus on the self-regulatory components and address the limitations of these highly cognitive models of motivation and self-regulation, calling for research on more automatic and nonconscious self-regulatory processes that may help people's job search.

The Job Search Process

Based on generic motivation theories (e.g., Ajzen, 1991; Gollwitzer, 1990), extant theorizing has conceptualized job search as a conscious and planned process, existing of an intentional or goal-establishment phase and a behavioral or goal-striving phase, ultimately leading to finding (new) employment (Kanfer & Bufton, this volume; Soelberg, 1967; Van Hooft & Noordzij, 2009). The *goal-establishment* or *intentional phase* in job search is a deliberative phase during which job seekers process available information, evaluate competing goals, and decide which goal(s) to pursue. This phase results in the selection of an employment goal and subsequently the formation of job search intentions.

Goals are internal representations of desired states (Austin & Vancouver, 1996), and an employment goal thus reflects the type of employment that one wants to obtain. Employment goals can vary in terms of specificity or clarity (Wanberg, Hough, & Song, 2002), for example, regarding the type of job or organization that one desires or the time frame within which one desires to obtain the goal. The identification of and commitment to an employment goal is a crucial aspect in the job search process (Kanfer, Wanberg, & Kantrowitz, 2001),

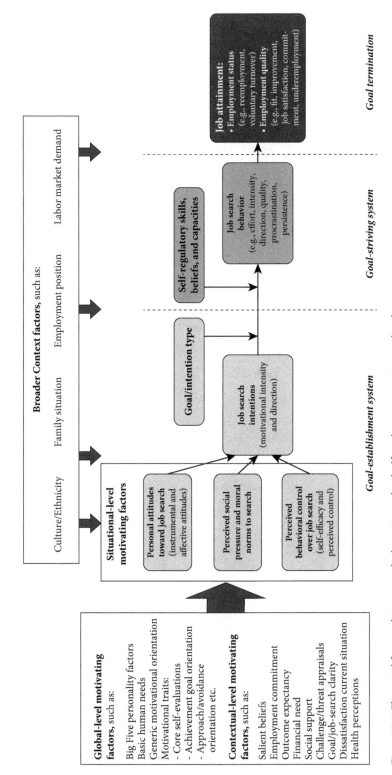

Figure 11.1 Theoretical framework integrating both motivational and self-regulatory perspectives on job seeking.

steering the subsequent formation of job search intentions.

Job search intentions capture the motivational factors that instigate job search behavior and thus reflect the strength of an individual's motivation to engage in job search. Job search intentions can be described along a *motivational direction* component, reflecting the type of job search behaviors or activities that people are planning to perform, and a *motivational intensity* component, reflecting the time, effort, and energy that people plan to allocate toward performing those activities. As with goals, intentions can vary in terms of specificity. For example, measures of general job search intentions typically encompass only the motivational intensity component, referring to how hard people are going to try to find a job or the time and effort they intend to invest in job seeking in general during a given period (e.g., Van Hooft, Born, Taris, Van der Flier, & Blonk, 2005; Wanberg, Glomb, Song, & Sorenson, 2005). Measures of specific job search intentions typically encompass both components by referring to the selection of search generators or job information sources (i.e., the formal and informal channels that job seekers use to acquire information about job opportunities) and the intended allocation of time and effort toward each of these search generators. Specific job search intention measures reflect how much time job seekers intend to spend on a number of specific job search activities, such as preparing or revising their resume, looking for job vacancies in newspapers, looking for jobs online, talking with friends or relatives about possible job leads, speaking with professional contacts about possible job leads, visiting job fairs, and contacting employment agencies (e.g., Van Hooft, Born, Taris, Van der Flier, & Blonk, 2004; Zikic & Saks, 2009).

The intentional phase is followed by a *goal-striving* or *behavioral phase*, which involves the initiation and sustained performance of the planned job search activities toward the established employment goal. It thus involves acting according to one's job search intentions and trying to achieve the employment goal. In the job search literature, this phase is typically conceptualized in terms of the motivational components *intensity* and *direction* of people's job search behaviors (Kanfer et al., 2001). For example, general job search effort measures typically refer to the actual time and effort that individuals have invested in job search in general, thus including only the motivational intensity component. More specific job search intensity measures typically refer to the actual time and effort that individuals have

invested in performing specific job search activities, such as networking, looking for job ads, and sending résumés (i.e., combining the motivational intensity and motivational direction components). In addition to motivational intensity and direction, a third component of job search behavior refers to *persistence* and other temporal factors (Kanfer et al., 2001; see also Van Hoye, this volume). Important processes in the goal-striving phase therefore also include goal shielding and maintenance, self-control, and self-monitoring (Van Hooft, Wanberg, & Van Hoye, 2013) to avoid procrastination and persist in one's job search efforts, ensuring the sustained allocation of resources toward job seeking over time until the employment goal is achieved.

The behavioral or goal-striving phase ends when people attain or abandon their employment goal (*goal termination*). A typical indicator of goal attainment in the job search literature is employment status. Depending on the sample type, employment status refers to whether graduating students have a job lined up after graduation, employed job seekers voluntarily turn over to a new job, or unemployed job seekers find reemployment. In addition to employment status as an indicator of goal attainment, it is important to distinguish employment quality indicators (Saks, 2005; Schwab, Rynes, & Aldag, 1987) as outcomes of the job search process because job quality positively affects people's well-being and reduces the likelihood of having to go through a job search again shortly after having started in the new job. Job quality outcomes include factors related to whether people found the job they were looking for (e.g., in terms of contract time, amount of hours, and wage; job improvement or career growth; underemployment); whether they (experience) fit in their new job (e.g., person–job fit; person–organization fit); and whether they have positive attitudes in their new job (e.g., job satisfaction; organizational commitment; organizational identification; intentions to stay).

A Theory of Planned Job Search Behavior

Conceptualizing job seeking as a conscious and planned behavior, existing of an intentional/goal establishment phase and a behavioral/goal-striving phase that continue until the goal is attained (or abandoned), the TPB (Ajzen, 1991) can be used to specify predictions about which factors drive people to engage in job seeking and what motivational factors affect goal attainment. Synthesizing the TPB with extant job search theorizing (Feather, 1992; Kanfer et al., 2001; Latack et al., 1995;

Leana & Feldman, 1988; Saks, 2005; Schwab et al., 1987) and motivation and self-regulation theories (e.g., Bandura, 1991; Baumeister, Vohs, & Tice, 2007; Locke & Latham, 2002; Ryan & Deci, 2000; Vallerand, 1997; Van Hooft et al., 2013) has led to the formulation of a *Theory of Planned Job Search Behavior* (TPJSB) as presented in Figure 11.1. In the following, I first describe the theoretical underpinnings of the core relationships in the TPJSB and then review the existing empirical evidence.

Theoretical Underpinnings of the Core TPJSB Relationships

Job search behavior–job attainment. The TPJSB proposes job search behavior as an important determinant of job attainment (cf. Kanfer et al., 2001; Saks, 2005; Schwab et al., 1987). First, the *intensity* of the job search behavior relates positively to job attainment. As Kanfer et al. (2001) theorized, higher exertion of effort toward a goal should result in greater probability to attain the goal. Specifically, the more time and effort individuals allocate toward a larger number of job search activities, the more likely they will generate (a greater number of) suitable job leads, and the more likely they will obtain interviews and job offers. In turn, job offers usually do not come out of the blue, occurring without any preceding engagement in job search activities.

Although intensity is an important dimension of job search behavior, the goal-striving system includes a broader array of behavioral dimensions that are often overlooked in empirical research on job seeking (see also Van Hoye, this volume). For example, as Van Hooft et al. (2013) argued, also the *quality* of the performed job search activities is an important dimension of job search behavior. Van Hooft et al. (2013) further theorized that job search quality can be conceptualized as consisting of process quality and behavior or product quality. *Process quality* refers to conducting one's job search based on cycles of planning and analysis of the performed activities and on adjustment and improvement of one's job search behavior based on such analysis and feedback from the environment. A high-quality job search process evokes a learning process, leading job seekers to learn what employers want, resulting in high-quality job search behaviors or products, that is behaviors (e.g., networking, interview behavior) and products (e.g., application letters, résumés) that meet or exceed the expectations of the demanding parties of the labor market (e.g., recruiting organizations). Given the complexity of job search behaviors as well as the ambiguity and heterogeneity of the labor market in which job seeking occurs, not only the intensity but also the quality of job search behavior likely is important in obtaining a (suitable) job.

Job search intention–job search behavior. In its core, similar to the TPB, the TPJSB conceptualizes job search intention as the most proximal predictor of job search behavior. Job search intentions reflect the strength of an individual's motivation to engage in job seeking. They specify the employment goal and indicate a readiness to perform job search activities. Therefore, the stronger people's job search intentions are, that is, the more time, effort, and energy they plan to allocate toward performing job search activities and conducting those in a high-quality manner, the stronger their motivation and the higher their readiness, and thus the more likely that their job search intentions will be acted on. Vice versa, most (high-quality) job search activities are unlikely to occur spontaneously without any preformed job search intention because job search activities usually reflect nonhabitual and often-difficult types of behavior.

Predictors of job search intention. To specify the factors that motivate people to form job search intentions and engage in job search behavior, the TPJSB integrates the TPB with insights from Vallerand's (1997) hierarchical model of motivation and SDT (Ryan & Deci, 2000). As such, motivating factors can be classified along three hierarchical levels that vary in level of generality, stability, and proximity to behavior (cf. Vallerand, 1997): (a) global-level motivating factors, referring to generalized, trait-like constructs that are stable over time and situations; (b) contextual-level motivating factors, referring to constructs concerning specific life domains (e.g., work), which are less stable and more contextual than global-level factors; and (c) situational-level motivating factors, referring to specific behaviors (e.g., job search) within specific time frames, which reflect the least stable and most contextual motivating forces.

At the lowest, most proximal level are the situational-level motivating factors personal attitude toward job search, social pressure to engage in job search, and perceived behavioral control over job search. These factors not only reflect the three predictors outlined in the TPB (Ajzen, 1991) but also are conceptually related to motivation quality (i.e., extrinsic vs. intrinsic motivation) and the three underlying basic human needs of autonomy, relatedness, and competence as proposed by SDT (Ryan & Deci, 2000; see also Vansteenkiste & Van den Broeck, this volume). According to SDT, people are motivated for behaviors that satisfy their basic needs of autonomy, relatedness, and competence, whereas factors that do not affect these needs should have minimal or no effects on motivation (Vallerand, 1997). The stronger these needs are satisfied by the behavior in question, the higher the quality of the motivation for the behavior, with motivation quality ranging from amotivation, to controlled motivation (i.e., external regulation, introjected regulation), to autonomous motivation (i.e., identified, integrated, and intrinsic regulation) (Ryan & Deci, 2000; Vansteenkiste & Van den Broeck, this volume).

More specifically, *personal attitude toward job search* can be defined as the extent to which individuals have a positive or negative evaluation of engaging in job search within a given time frame (e.g., the next month), which is conceptually related to autonomous motivation. Such an evaluation has an affective and an instrumental component. Affective job search attitudes refer to whether people evaluate job seeking as enjoyable, pleasant, and interesting (Van Hooft, Born, Taris, Van der Flier, & Blonk, 2004) and thus concern the extent to which people evaluate job seeking as inherently pleasant and rewarding. Affective attitudes are conceptually related to SDT's regulatory style of intrinsic regulation, referring to the intrinsic gratification of an activity regardless of its outcome. Instrumental job search attitudes refer to whether people evaluate job seeking as wise, beneficial, and useful (Van Hooft, Born, Taris, Van der Flier, & Blonk, 2004) and thus concern the extent to which people evaluate job seeking as instrumental in obtaining some beneficial goal (e.g., finding a job). Instrumental attitudes are conceptually related to SDT's regulatory style of identified regulation, referring to personal importance and value.

Job search attitudes are based on people's beliefs about outcomes of their job search (e.g., having a job, feeling good) and the likelihood that these outcomes will occur. People with more positive attitudes toward job search likely intend to invest more time in their job search than those with less positive evaluations of job search because they expect more valued outcomes of their job seeking. Furthermore, when people personally value the engagement in job seeking, it likely satisfies their need for autonomy, resulting in increased motivation for performing job search activities.

Perceived social pressure to search (or subjective job search norms) refers to the amount of social pressure that people perceive to engage in job search within a given time frame. Subjective job search norms are based on beliefs about expectations that others (e.g., partner, family, friends, employment counselors) have regarding the engagement in job seeking and the importance that individuals attach to complying with these normative expectations. As such, perceived social pressure resembles SDT's regulatory style of external regulation, referring to external expectations and compliance to other people's norms. Individuals likely intend to spend more time on their job search the more social pressure from important others to do so they perceive. Further, although SDT suggests that social pressure may undermine people's need for autonomy, it may still be a motivating factor as it may align with people's need for relatedness. For example, individuals are likely to engage in job seeking when this positively affects their relationship with significant others. In addition to subjective norms, Ajzen (1991) suggests that intentions may originate from feelings of moral obligation or responsibility to perform a certain behavior. Conner and Armitage (1998) suggest that moral norms should especially have an influence on the performance of behaviors with a moral or ethical dimension. With regard to job search, unemployed people or graduating students may perceive it unethical to live off social benefits and therefore perceive a moral responsibility to secure employment and engage in job search behavior. Such *moral norms to search* are more internalized than subjective norms, referring to societal values and feelings of shame and guilt, thus resembling what is labeled introjected regulation in SDT. Perceived social pressure to search and moral norms to search both represent forms of controlled motivation.

Perceived behavioral control over job search encompasses the perceived ease or difficulty of performing job search activities within a specified time frame and is based on beliefs about the presence of factors that further or hinder performing job search activities. Perceived behavior control over job search includes both control perceptions over internal factors (e.g., availability/absence of information, skills and abilities, and presence/absence of emotions and compulsions) and external factors (e.g., availability/absence of opportunities and resources, and dependence of cooperation of others). The perceptions of control over internal resources component are usually labeled job search self-efficacy, whereas the external component is referred to as perceived control. As humans want to feel competent and effective in dealing with their environment (cf. SDT), activities that satisfy the need for competence generate stronger interest and motivation. People will therefore be more motivated to perform job search activities when they are more confident in their competence to perform these activities and when they think that the performance of these activities is under their personal control. In contrast, people with little confidence and control more likely perceive job search as difficult, complex, and aversive and therefore likely are less motivated to perform job search activities.

Empirical Support for the Core TPJSB Relationships

Previous research has provided empirical support for the outlined relationships of the TPJSB in diverse samples and contexts.

Job search behavior–job attainment. Regarding the job search behavior–job attainment relationship, meta-analytic findings corroborate the proposition that people who spend more time on job seeking are more likely to obtain a job than others, with corrected correlations varying between .18 and .30, depending on sample and operationalization of job search behavior (Kanfer et al., 2001). Despite this general support, primary studies often found relatively modest relations between job search and job attainment, with null relations no exception. These meager findings may be explained by the validity of the measurement of job search intensity, as job search studies typically rely on self-reports to measure job search behavior. Van Hooft (2014) found some support for this explanation by showing that employment counselor ratings of unemployed people's job search intensity are more strongly related to reemployment status than unemployed job seekers' self-ratings.

Furthermore, almost all studies operationalized job search behavior as referring only to effort-intensity or direction of job search, ignoring temporal and quality-related components (Kanfer et al., 2001; Van Hooft et al., 2013; Van Hoye, this volume; Wanberg, 2012). Broadening the operationalization of job search behavior to include job search quality will likely increase its predictive validity (Van Hooft et al., 2013). Some initial evidence pointing in this direction is reported by Turban, Stevens, and Lee (2009), who found that job-seeking students who engaged more in metacognitive activities during their job search (e.g., high-quality indicators such

as planning, monitoring progress, and evaluation of interview performance) were more likely to obtain job interviews and job offers. In addition, regarding more specific job search quality dimensions, empirical research has illustrated the importance of planning during job search (Saks & Ashforth, 2002; Zikic & Klehe, 2006); searching with a focused or exploratory rather than a haphazard strategy (Crossley & Highhouse, 2005; Koen, Klehe, van Vianen, Zikic, & Nauta, 2010; Koen, Van Vianen, Van Hooft, & Klehe, 2016); and timeliness of performing job search activities (Turban, Lee, da Motta Veiga, Haggard, & Wu, 2013; Van Hooft, 2014) in predicting outcomes such as job interviews, job offers, or employment status.

Job search intention–job search behavior. Regarding the predictors of job search behavior and job search intention, general support has been found for the relationships as outlined by the TPJSB. Table 11.1 presents an overview of studies that tested the TPB relationships in the context of job search. A PsychInfo search using the keywords "job search OR job seeking" in combination with "planned behavior OR reasoned action OR intention" resulted in 50 hits. Of these, 19 were published studies in English that presented zero-order correlations of one or more TPB variables with job search intention using a cross-sectional design or of one or more TPB variables with job search behavior using a predictive design. Cross-sectional correlations between TPB variables and job search behavior measures were excluded from the overview because these cannot be interpreted properly as they reflect the prediction of behavior that occurred in the past.

As displayed in Table 11.1, moderate-to-strong empirical support is usually found for the relationship between job search intention and job search behavior, with correlations varying between .23 and .66. This is relatively consistent with findings on the intention–behavior relationship in general, with a meta-analysis of meta-analyses reporting an overall average correlation of .53 between intentions and behavior (Sheeran, 2002). The correlations between job search intention and behavior seem to be rather independent of time lag between the measurement of intention and behavior, although there are too few studies per category to draw firm conclusions on this. Future research is needed to examine more closely the effects of time lag and temporal stability of job search intentions on the relationship between job search intention and behavior because previous

Table 11.1 Overview of findings from empirical studies testing the relationships as predicted by the theory of planned behavior (TPB) in the context of job seeking.

Study	Sample type	Zero-order correlation with job search intention			Zero-order correlation with job search behavior			Job search intention–behavior relationship			
		Job search attitude	Perceived social pressure	Perceived behavioral control	Job search attitude	Perceived social pressure	Perceived behavioral control	Zero-order correlation	Time lag	Correspondence	Measure-type job search behavior
Caska (1998)	Students	.48[a]	.45	.27[c]							
Corbière et al. (2011)	Unemployed			.44[c]			.17 to .23[c]	.32 to .33	9 months	No	Index
Creed, Doherty, and O'Callaghan (2008)	Students	.44[a]	.47	.30[c] .31[d]	.35[a]	.40	.34[c] .21[d]	.37	4 months	Yes	Index
Lay and Brokenshire (1997)	Unemployed	.56[a] .56[b]		.59[c]	.36[a] .21[b]		.27[c]	.58	2 weeks	Yes	Index
Lin (2010)	Students	.79[a,b]	.52	.69[c] .63[d]							Internet job search
Noordzij, Van Hooft, Van Mierlo, Van Dam, and Born (2013)	Unemployed			.26 to .29[c]							
Song, Wanberg, Niu, and Xie (2006)	Unemployed	.54[a]	.68	.03[c]	.13[a]	.19	.30[c]	.23	1 month	No	Index
Van Hooft (2014)	Unemployed				.19[a]	.06	.34[c]		4 months		Index

Study	Sample										
Van Hooft, Born, Taris, and Van der Flier (2004)	Temporary workers	.52ᵃ .18ᵇ	.46	-.03ᶜ	.34ᵃ .10ᵇ	.31	-.03ᶜ	.47	4 months	Yes	Index
Van Hooft, Born, Taris, and Van der Flier (2005)	General population: Males	.58ᵃ	.43	-.03ᶜ	.41ᵃ	.31	-.02ᶜ	.54	4 months	Yes	Index
Van Hooft, Born, Taris, and Van der Flier (2005)	General population: Females	.62ᵃ	.46	.05ᶜ	.42ᵃ	.29	.04ᶜ	.51	4 months	Yes	Index
Van Hooft, Born, Taris, Van der Flier, and Blonk (2004)	Unemployed	.65ᵃ .32ᵇ	.44	.19ᶜ	.50ᵃ .23ᵇ	.23	.16ᶜ	.66	4 months	Yes	Index
Van Hooft, Born, Taris, Van der Flier, and Blonk (2004)	Employed	.58ᵃ .18ᵇ	.46	-.06ᶜ	.40ᵃ .17ᵇ	.34	.03ᶜ	.52	4 months	Yes	Index
Van Hooft, Born, Taris, Van der Flier, and Blonk (2005)	Unemployed			.11ᶜ .16ᵈ			.12ᶜ .04ᵈ	.31	4 months	Yes	Job search time/ effort
Van Hooft and De Jong (2009)	Temporary workers	.72ᵃ	.52	.48ᶜ·ᵈ	.21ᵃ	.34	.11ᶜ·ᵈ	.42	2 months	Yes	Job search time/ effort
Van Hooft and Noordzij (2009)	Unemployed							.59	2 weeks	Yes	Index

(continued)

Table 11.1 Continued

Study	Sample type	Zero-order correlation with job search intention			Zero-order correlation with job search behavior			Job search intention–behavior relationship			
		Job search attitude	Perceived social pressure	Perceived behavioral control	Job search attitude	Perceived social pressure	Perceived behavioral control	Zero-order correlation	Time lag	Correspondence	Measure-type job search behavior
Wanberg, Glomb, Song, and Sorenson (2005)	Unemployed	.09 to .25[a,b]	.65 to .77	.18 to .28[c]	.05 to .18[a,b]	.30 to .44	.12 to .23[c]	.39 to .45	2 weeks	No	Index
Wanberg, Watt, and Rumsey (1996)	Unemployed		.73	.04[c]							
Zikic and Saks (2009)	Mixed	.28[a]	.41	.43[c]	.26[a]	.22	.25[c]	.47	8 months	Yes	Index

Note. Included are only published studies in English that presented zero-order correlations among TPB variables using a cross-sectional design for the prediction of intention and a predictive design for the prediction of behavior (i.e., cross-sectional correlations between TPB variables and job search behavior measures are excluded).

[a] Instrumental job search attitude measure.

[b] Affective job search attitude measure.

[c] Job search self-efficacy measure.

[d] Perceived control over external sources measure.

research on the TPB has indicated that such factors may be important moderators (Cooke & Sheeran, 2004; McEachan, Conner, Taylor, & Lawton, 2011). Effect sizes for the job search intention–behavior relation seem to be larger for index measures (i.e., a measure consisting of an index of job search activities whereby participants have to indicate their intentions or behavior for each of the listed activities). Also, consistent with Ajzen's (1991) notion that measures of intention and behavior should correspond in specificity, target, situation, and time, effect sizes seem to be larger when using corresponding intention and behavior measures (i.e., when the job search intention and job search behavior measures use the same items with the intention items referring to the intended time or effort and the behavior items referring to the actual time or effort spent).

Predictors of job search intention. As demonstrated by the correlations in Table 11.1, *job search attitudes* are generally moderately to strongly related to job search intention. Correlations between instrumental job search attitudes and job search intentions vary between .28 and .72, whereas correlations between affective job search attitudes and job search intention vary between .18 and .56.

On average, instrumental job search attitude seems to relate stronger to job search intentions than affective job search attitude, although future meta-analytic integration is needed to test this. A stronger motivational role of instrumental attitude makes sense theoretically and can be underpinned by considering the motivational characteristics of the behavior of job seeking. Job search is a goal-directed behavior (Kanfer et al., 2001) and as such is more likely driven by goals-defined or outcome-related (i.e., extrinsic) motivation rather than experience-defined or activity-related (i.e., intrinsic) motivation. In other words, people usually engage in job search to obtain some valued goal (e.g., finding a job) rather than for the inherent value of the activity of job seeking. As such, the goals-defined motivational system (i.e., motivation originating from the willingness to reach some valued outcome by engaging in a task or activity; Ryan & Deci, 2000; Sansone & Thoman, 2005, 2006) should be more salient than the experience-defined motivational system (i.e., motivation originating from the experience of the task or activity itself as interesting or pleasant; Ryan & Deci, 2000; Sansone & Thoman, 2005, 2006) in explaining the occurrence of job seeking,

which is reflected by instrumental job search attitudes being more predictive than affective job search attitudes. In contrast, for leisure activities (e.g., going to the beach, mountain climbing, biking), affective attitudes are usually found to be more predictive than instrumental attitudes (e.g., Ajzen & Driver, 1992).

Nevertheless, motivational theories such as the SDT (Ryan & Deci, 2000) pose that intrinsic motivation rather than the more controlled forms of extrinsic motivation typically results in more persistence, deeper engagement in the activity, and more learning. Therefore, future research should examine whether affective job search attitudes are more predictive of job search behavior when a broader operationalization is used, including temporal and quality components of job search.

Table 11.1 shows relatively strong correlations between *perceived social pressure to search* and job search intention, ranging from .41 to .77. In a meta-analysis of TPB studies, Armitage and Conner (2001) report an average subjective norm–intention correlation of .34. Perceived social pressure therefore seems to be a stronger predictor of intentions in the context of job seeking than for intentions in general. A possible explanation for this finding may be that job seeking often has consequences for one's immediate social surroundings. For example, for unemployed job seekers, finding reemployment is important not only for the job seekers themselves but also for their partners or children. Van Hooft, Born, Taris, and Van der Flier (2005) found some support for this reasoning, as perceived social pressure more strongly related to job search intentions among people with a larger household.

Although perceptions of social pressure seem to be strong predictors of job search, future research is needed to determine to what extent the motivational power of social pressure holds when using broader job search conceptualizations (i.e., including not only behavioral intensity but also temporal and quality-related components). In terms of SDT, perceived social pressure maps on external regulation, which refers to relatively low-quality motivation. That is, the motivation does not originate from the activity itself or from one's own goals, but from norms and pressure of others. Although perceived social pressure may lead to forming job search intentions and performing job search behavior, it is expected to be less predictive of job search persistence, learning, and job search quality.

Moral norms have been found to predict behaviors such as refraining from dishonest actions, ethical decision-making, and telling the truth to customers, with an average moral norm–intention correlation of .50 (Conner & Armitage, 1998). In the job search literature, the concept of *moral norms to search* has received only limited research attention. In a study among high school students, Creed, Doherty, and O'Callaghan (2008) reported moderate-to-strong correlations of moral norms with job search intentions and behavior and found that it explained unique variance in job search intentions controlling for the other TPB variables. Moral norms to search therefore seem to be a promising addition to the original TPB variables, both theoretically and empirically.

Of the relationships outlined by the TPB, support for the role of *perceived behavioral control over job search* is most mixed. As presented in Table 11.1, correlations with job search intention vary between –.06 and .69 and with job search behavior between –.03 and .34. The correlations are typically lower than what is generally found in TPB studies. For example, in their meta-analysis Armitage and Conner (2001) report correlations of .43 and .37 of perceived behavioral control with intention and behavior, respectively. Armitage and Conner (2001) further found that correlations were typically stronger for the self-efficacy component as compared to perceived control over external resources component. In job search studies that used both operationalizations of perceived behavioral control (i.e., Creed et al., 2008; Lin, 2010; Van Hooft, Born, Taris, Van der Flier, & Blonk, 2005), the two components seem to be as predictive of job search intention, but in line with general TPB research, job search self-efficacy seems to be a slightly stronger predictor of job search behavior than perceived control.

Furthermore, with some exceptions (e.g., Song, Wanberg, Niu, & Xie, 2006; Van Hooft & De Jong, 2009; Wanberg, Watt, & Rumsey, 1996), perceived behavioral control seems to be a more important predictor of job search intentions and behavior in student and unemployed samples than in employed samples. For example, in a study that directly compared job search among unemployed and employed individuals, Van Hooft, Born, Taris, Van der Flier, and Blonk (2004) reported correlations of job search self-efficacy with job search intention and behavior of .19 and .16 in the unemployed sample and of –.06 and .03 in the employed sample. These findings may be explained by the fact that perceived behavioral control is often operationalized at the contextual level rather than at the situational level and has more stable, trait-like qualities.

Whereas this may not be problematic in samples of graduating students or unemployed individuals, where most participants have the goal of finding a job, it may suppress its predictive validity in employed samples. For example, an employed individual may have strong confidence in the ability to write a good application letter. However, this does not necessarily drive that individual into a job search. In other words, in employed samples there may be many individuals with high job search self-efficacy who are perfectly happy in their current jobs and therefore not likely engage in job seeking.

Contextual-Level and Global-Level Motivating Factors

In addition to the core relationships between situational-level motivating factors, job search intentions, job search behavior, and job attainment, the TPJSB can be extended toward antecedents of the situational-level motivating factors. Based on the TPB (Ajzen, 1991) and expectancy-value principles as outlined in its predecessor the theory of reasoned action (Fishbein & Ajzen, 1975; see also Feather, this volume), job search attitudes, perceptions of social pressure to search, and perceived behavioral control over job search are thought to depend on people's underlying *salient beliefs* about job seeking and having employment (Van Hooft & De Jong, 2009). Those beliefs are formed by associations of job search or having a job with other outcomes, events, or characteristics. More specifically, job search attitude depends on behavioral beliefs about having a (particular) job (e.g., "Having a job provides me with purpose in life"), weighted in a multiplicative fashion by its subjective value (e.g., "A sense of purpose is important for me"). In other words, the more positive features people attach to having a job, and the stronger they value these features, the more likely they will regard searching for a job as useful.

Second, perceived social pressure to search depends on the product of normative beliefs about job seeking (e.g., "My family thinks that I should look for a job") and the individual's motivation to comply with the different referents (e.g., "In general, I want to meet my family's expectations"). The stronger people in one's surroundings think that one should look for a job and the more one attaches value to these people's opinions, the more likely that one perceives pressure to search for a job.

Third, perceived behavioral control over job search depends on the product of control beliefs about the perceived presence of facilitating or impeding factors (e.g., "I have health problems") and the perceived power of each control belief to actually facilitate or impede performing job search behaviors (e.g., "Having health problems would likely impede my search for employment"). The more facilitating factors people experience and the higher the power of these factors to help one's job search, the easier people will perceive it to be to engage in job seeking. In contrast, the more impeding factors people experience and the higher the power of these factors to impede one's job search, the more difficult people will perceive searching for a job.

Identification of the salient underlying beliefs is important from a practical point of view, as these beliefs provide insight in the origins of attitudes and perceptions, offering more specific leads for initiating behavioral change. However, limited research on job seeking tested the belief-based underpinnings of the TPB, and only meager support has been found (Van Hooft & De Jong, 2009). In addition to methodological issues (e.g., testing for multiple interactions using a relatively modest sample size), a possible explanation for the limited support may be that belief salience is highly idiosyncratic. The potential lack of universally salient beliefs in a given sample may cause traditional research methods to find little support for the belief-based model of the TPB. Nevertheless, from a practitioner's point of view, it may be recommendable to identify a client's deeper beliefs regarding work and job search as these may provide valuable insights and starting points for changing people's job search attitudes, perceptions, intentions, and ultimate behaviors.

In addition to these specific beliefs, theory and research (e.g., Boswell, Zimmerman, & Swider, 2012; Feather, 1992; Kanfer et al., 2001; Latack et al., 1995; Leana & Feldman, 1988; Saks, 2005; Schwab et al., 1987) have identified several more general factors that may motivate or hinder people's job search (e.g., personality, core self-evaluations, motivational traits, employment commitment, outcome expectancies, financial need, social support, cognitive appraisals, goal clarity, satisfaction, and health perceptions). Based on Vallerand's (1997) hierarchical model of motivation, these factors can be classified as global-level motivating factors (e.g., personality) or contextual-level motivating factors (e.g., employment commitment).

Vallerand's (1997) hierarchical model further suggests that situational-level factors such as the TPB variables are the most proximal predictors of behavior that mediate the effects of contextual-level and global-level motivating factors. This proposition aligns with the TPB, which was originally thought to be a complete theory of the proximal determinants of behavior (Conner & Armitage, 1998; see also Ajzen, 2011; Fishbein & Ajzen, 1975), implying that the effects of other variables on behavior are completely mediated by attitude, subjective norm, perceived behavioral control, and intention. For example, as Fishbein (1980) noted, "a person does not perform a given behavior because she is a woman or educated or altruistic. . . . Instead, she ultimately performs the behavior because she believes that its performance will lead to more 'good' than 'bad' consequences and/or because she believes that most of her important others . . . think she should perform that behavior" (p. 103).

The posed completeness of the TPB has been subject of much debate in the general motivation literature (e.g., Ajzen, 1991, 2011; Conner & Armitage, 1998). In the job search literature, empirical research demonstrates the added value of including contextual-level and global-level motivators in predicting job search intention and behavior (e.g., Creed et al., 2008; Derous, Van Hooft, & Elling, 2009; Lay & Brokenshire, 1997; Van Hooft, 2014; Van Hooft, Born, Taris, Van der Flier, & Blonk, 2004; Wanberg et al., 2005; Zikic & Saks, 2009). Rather than discussing all potentially relevant factors, next I specifically review those contextual and global motivating factors that have been studied in the context of the TPB and job search (see also Figure 11.1).

Contextual-level motivation. As applied to job search, contextual-level motivating factors refer to constructs concerning the domain of employment and seeking for employment more generally (rather than during a specific time frame). These factors concern both personal and situational factors that may affect the TPB variables both separately and in interaction.

One motivational theory of contextual-level motivation factors that has been examined in the job search literature is expectancy-value theory (EVT; see, for example, Feather, 1992; Feather, this volume). The basic premise of EVT is that the intensity of people's job search behavior is a function of how much people value having a (particular) job (work valence), the strength of people's expectation that they will succeed in obtaining a (or that particular) job if they try (outcome expectancy), and their interaction. The EVT constructs of work valence and outcome expectancy are different from the TPB constructs job search attitude and perceived behavioral control over job search as the EVT constructs refer to the outcomes of one's job search behavior, whereas the TPB constructs refer to the job search behavior itself (Van Hooft, Born, Taris, Van der Flier, & Blonk, 2004). For example, perceived behavioral control over job search includes perceptions of control over job search activities, such as beliefs whether one will be able to write a good application letter. Outcome expectancies, in contrast, include perceptions regarding the outcome of finding a job, such as beliefs whether one will be able to obtain a job if one tries hard.

Work valence is conceptually similar to the concept of *employment commitment*, which is often included in research on job seeking among unemployed and graduating student samples. Employment commitment is an attitude describing the importance or centrality that individuals place on employed work and is generally found to positively predict job search intensity (Kanfer et al., 2001). This positive relationship aligns with EVT, suggesting that the more positively people value having a job, the more motivated they will be to mobilize energy and invest time and effort in their job search to obtain a job. In various TPB studies, work valence has been shown not only to positively predict job search attitudes (Caska, 1998; Van Hooft, Born, Taris, Van der Flier, & Blonk, 2004) but also to explain unique variance in job search intention and job search behavior beyond the original TPB variables (Creed et al., 2008; Van Hooft, Born, Taris, Van der Flier, & Blonk, 2004; Vinokur & Caplan, 1987). In employed samples, employment commitment has not received any research attention, most likely because it theoretically should not be a motivator for employed individuals to engage in a job search. Instead, the valence attached to finding a new or better job may be a potentially important factor that can instigate a job search among employed people.

Outcome expectancy refers to people's expectations about the likelihood of finding a (particular) job given attempts to do so. Constructs that have been studied in the job search literature that are conceptually similar include situational control (Wanberg, 1997), perceived control over job search outcomes (Saks & Ashforth, 1999), perceived instrumentality (Vinokur & Caplan, 1987), perceived reversibility of job loss (Gowan, Riordan, &

Gatewood, 1999; Leana & Feldman, 1988), job search locus of control (Van Hooft & Crossley, 2008), and reemployment efficacy (Wanberg et al., 2010). All these constructs relate to the amount of influence that job seekers believe they have over job search outcomes in terms of the chances that they perceive obtaining a job if they invest effort in finding one. In addition to EVT, behavioral coping theory (e.g., Leana & Feldman, 1988) proposes that people are more motivated to mobilize energy and invest time and effort in their job search when they perceive their efforts will more likely to result in obtaining a job. Nevertheless, empirical support for the proposed positive relationship between outcome expectancy and job search is rather mixed, with some studies reporting (modest) positive relations with job search measures (e.g., Kinicki, 1989; Taris, Heesink, & Feij, 1995; Ullah & Banks, 1985; Wanberg, 1997); some failing to find significant relationships (e.g., Feather & O'Brien, 1987; Gowan et al., 1999); and some reporting negative relationships (e.g., Liu, Wang, Liao, & Shi, 2014; Saks & Ashforth, 1999; Van Hooft, Born, Taris, Van der Flier, & Blonk, 2004).

Several explanations have been provided for the absence of a positive effect of outcome expectancy, and theoretical rationales have been offered for the negative effects (Feather, this volume; Liu et al., 2014; Saks & Ashforth, 1999; Van Hooft, Born, Taris, Van der Flier, & Blonk, 2004). For example, rather than motivating them, high outcome expectations may lead job seekers to take it easy during their job search, and switch their attention to other goals, because they perceive that also with low effort a job offer is likely. Vice versa, low outcome expectations may lead job seekers to invest extra effort in their job search to compensate the low likelihood of finding a job.

Van Hooft and Crossley (2008) interpreted these explanations from the perspective of economic rational choice theory (see McFadyen & Thomas, 1997) and control theory (Klein, 1989). Both theories suggest that people base the level of effort invested in job search on the expected marginal returns. That is, people invest the minimal amount of effort and time in job seeking that is necessary to successfully attain a suitable job, suggesting that those with high outcome expectancies will invest less time in job seeking compared to those with low outcome expectancies. Thus, summarizing previous theorizing and speculation on the outcome expectancy–job search relationship, Van Hooft and Crossley (2008) noted that two approaches can be distinguished: (a) the behavioral coping approach, which predicts a positive motivating effect of outcome expectancy, and (b) the compensatory approach, which predicts a negative motivating effect of outcome expectancy. They further theorized that, depending on the context, people will respond according to either the behavioral coping or compensatory response. More specifically, in weak situations where few external incentives or normative expectations are present, people will be more likely to respond to their personal dispositions and therefore more likely display the behavioral coping response (e.g., higher outcome expectancies induce higher job search intensity). In strong situations, however, people will be likely to act according to the situational demands, thus more likely display a compensatory response (e.g., lower outcome expectancies induce higher job search intensity to compensate). Van Hooft and Crossley (2008) used financial need as an indicator of situational strength and, consistent with this rationale, found support for the compensatory approach (i.e., outcome expectancy relates negatively to job search intensity) under conditions of high financial need only. Under conditions of low financial need, outcome expectancy was slightly positively but not significantly related to job search intensity.

Financial need or *economic hardship* has also been examined as a motivating factor of job search in itself. Economic theory (e.g., Mortensen, 1977; Van den Berg & Uhlendorff, this volume) suggests that unemployment benefits influence job search effort, such that more generous unemployment benefits lower the intensity with which unemployed people search for employment. In support of this idea, empirical support indicates that unemployed individuals invest less effort in their job search the higher their unemployment benefits (e.g., Klepinger, Johnson, & Joesch, 2002; Krueger & Mueller, 2010).

Most psychological studies focus on the more subjective notion of perceived financial need, or people's subjective sense of how adequately their current income and monetary assets meet their personal and family needs. As found by Ullah (1990), it is not so much the actual financial situation, but this subjective perceived financial need, that predicts job search intensity. More generally, Kanfer et al. (2001) reported a moderate positive correlation between financial need and job search behavior. Explaining mechanisms in the relation between financial need and job search would be the TPB variables (e.g., job search attitude and perceived social pressure to

search; Van Hooft, Born, Taris, Van der Flier, & Blonk, 2004).

However, studies that examined the effects of financial need in the context of the TPB mostly found positive direct effects of financial need on job search behavior (Vinokur & Caplan, 1987; Wanberg et al., 2005). Although evidence clearly supports the idea that financial pressure stimulates people's job search efforts, an important question remains regarding how financial need relates to the quality of people's job search behavior. As Van Hooft et al. (2013) theorized, financial need may urge people into job search without much forethought and reflection, resulting in lower goal clarity, less planning, and more haphazard job search strategies, thereby reducing people's job search quality and subsequent employment success.

In addition to perceptions of social pressure to search, other social factors may help and motivate people in the job search process. Coping theory (e.g., Latack et al., 1995; Leana & Feldman, 1988) suggests *social support* is an important resource that can help people cope constructively with job loss by reducing or diffusing negative tension and increasing positive energy. Social support in terms of showing concern and providing encouragement during the job search process can be labeled emotional social support, as it specifically aims to aid job seekers' emotional control. Emotional social support is moderately positively related to job search behavior, especially among unemployed job seekers (Kanfer et al., 2001), and predicts unique variance in job search behavior beyond the TPB variables (Vinokur & Caplan, 1987). Furthermore, social contacts can provide instrumental social support, such as giving advice, information, assistance, and feedback on job search activities, which may help job seekers form clear goals, develop suitable plans, and obtain diagnostic information about their goal striving. Although instrumental social support has been less widely studied, it seems to relate more strongly to job search behavior than emotional support (e.g., Briscoe, Henagan, Burton, & Murphy, 2012; Corbière et al., 2011; Zikic & Klehe, 2006). An explanation for these findings may be that emotional social support could also undermine job search behavior by diverting people's attention to non–problem-focused coping strategies such as distancing and engagement in nonwork activities (Gowan et al., 1999). Future research is needed to more specifically detail for which samples and in which situations specific types of social support are most useful for stimulating engagement in job search behavior.

Another core construct in coping theory that importantly affects job search behavior is people's *cognitive appraisals* of their job loss and subsequent job search. The extent to which people appraise these as a threat may negatively impact the extent to which unemployed people engage in active job search behavior (Latack et al., 1995; Leana & Feldman, 1988). Alternatively, cognitively (re) appraising job search more positively (e.g., framing job search as a challenge or nonthreatening learning situation) may help job seekers deal better with stress, difficulties, and obstacles during their job search, freeing more resources to invest in job search behavior. Although job loss and job search are commonly associated with threat appraisals, occasionally individuals may view job loss as liberating, allowing them to change their direction in life (Latack et al., 1995; Zikic & Klehe, 2006). Based on challenge-hindrance theory (LePine, Podsakoff, & LePine, 2005) and their qualitative data, Wanberg et al. (2012) suggested that especially challenge appraisals regarding job search demands induce adaptive coping responses (e.g., managing mood and motivation, help and feedback seeking, self-reflection, and learning) that are needed to successfully navigate through the job search process. The few studies that empirically examined the role of cognitive appraisals in the context of job search seem to support the beneficial impact of positive or challenge appraisals. For example, Leana, Feldman, and Tan (1998) found positive reappraisal to be a relatively strong predictor of job search behavior, and Caska (1998) reported that challenge appraisals positively related to job search intentions, explaining unique variance beyond the traditional TPB variables.

An important motivational theory with implications for job search motivation is goal-setting theory (Latham et al., this volume; Locke & Latham, 2002). At its core, goal-setting theory states that specific, difficult goals direct attention and effort toward goal-relevant activities, energize goal pursuit, make people identify and use effective task strategies, and increase persistence, thereby resulting in higher performance than vague or easy goals. In the job search literature, the goal dimension of specificity received some attention, mostly under the label of purposefulness, goal-directedness, or job search clarity (Stevens & Beach, 1996; Stumpf, Colarelli, & Hartman, 1983; Wanberg et al., 2002). For example, Wanberg et al. (2002) suggested that a lack of clarity

in terms of type of career, work, or job desired leads to uncertainty and indecision during the job search, resulting in more exploration and contemplation rather than targeted applications. Empirical findings have shown that *job search clarity* positively relates to job search intention and behavior (e.g., Côté, Saks, & Zikic, 2006; Koen et al., 2010; Wanberg et al., 2002; Zikic & Saks, 2009) and explains unique variance in job search behavior beyond the traditional TPB variables (Zikic & Saks, 2009).

An important factor that may push people into a job search is *dissatisfaction with one's current situation*. Employee turnover models (e.g., Mobley, 1977; Steers & Mowday, 1981; see also Boswell & Gardner, this volume) typically describe job dissatisfaction as causing thoughts of quitting and instigating a job search for better alternatives, which may ultimately lead to voluntary employee turnover. Although more recent theorizing has noted that employee job search and turnover are not always instigated by job dissatisfaction (Boswell, Boudreau, & Dunford, 2004; Lee & Mitchell, 1994), empirical findings suggest that the route to turnover via job dissatisfaction and job search explain the majority of turnover cases (Lee, Mitchell, Holtom, McDaniel, & Hill, 1999). In addition, in their meta-analysis, Hom, Caranikas-Walker, Prussia, and Griffeth (1992) reported a corrected correlation of –.47 between job satisfaction and search intentions. Furthermore, Van Hooft, Born, Taris, Van der Flier, and Blonk (2004) found that job satisfaction among employed people negatively predicted their job search behavior, which was only partially mediated by instrumental job search attitudes and job search intention. Dissatisfaction with one's job therefore can be considered an important motivator of employed people's job search.

In unemployed samples, dissatisfaction with one's current situation has been examined by measuring to what extent people experience their unemployment as negative or positive or more generally by measuring life dissatisfaction. Studies of unemployment negativity usually find small-to-medium positive correlations with job search measures (e.g., Prussia, Kinicki, & Bracker, 1993; Vansteenkiste, Lens, De Witte, De Witte, & Deci, 2004; Wanberg et al., 1996), indicating that being negative or dissatisfied with one's unemployment situation stimulates unemployed individuals to invest time and effort into their job search. Similarly, when people do not mind unemployment or experience their unemployment positively, they likely perceive less need to alter their employment situation by engaging in job search activities (e.g., Taris, 2002; Van Dam & Menting, 2012; Vansteenkiste et al., 2004). Regarding the more general construct of life dissatisfaction, however, empirical findings have been rather mixed, with studies reporting mostly nonsignificant correlations with job search measures (e.g., Prussia et al., 1993; Taris et al., 1995; Vansteenkiste et al., 2004). These findings can be explained by opposing theoretical rationales on the effects that life dissatisfaction may have on unemployed people's job search. On the one hand, similar to the motivating effect of job dissatisfaction for employed people, life dissatisfaction may motivate unemployed people to change their situation by looking for a job. On the other hand, life dissatisfaction may cause (or relate to) reduced well-being and lower energy levels, resulting in a lack of motivation and mental resources to invest in job seeking.

Similar reasoning has been offered for people's *perceptions of their health* situation. Taris (2002), Van Hooft (2014), and Vinokur and Schul (2002), for example, hypothesized that individuals who perceive more health problems will be less inclined to spend time on their job search than those who perceive no health problems because mental ill health induces feelings of powerlessness, which lead to lowered capacity to actively shape and influence one's environment, deplete mental and physical energy, and likely result in shifting one's priority to short-term mood regulation over long-term goal-striving. Whereas mental and physical health have often been studied in the unemployment literature, these concepts are usually included as outcomes (Bambra & Eikemo, this volume; Paul, Hassel, & Moser, this volume). The role of health (perceptions) as predictor of job search has received less attention in the job search literature. Whereas Vinokur and Schul (2002) reported nonsignificant relationships, Taris (2002) and Van Hooft (2014) found that health perceptions significantly predicted job search intention or behavior, such that those with better mental health and fewer health problems were more motivated to search for a job. Van Hooft (2014) further found that health perceptions predicted unique variance in job search behavior beyond the situational-level TPB variables.

Global-level motivation. Global-level motivating factors refer to generalized, trait-like constructs that are stable over time and situations. Examples of such global-level factors include personality traits (e.g., Big Five); basic needs and generic motivational orientations (e.g., SDT's need for autonomy,

competence, and relatedness; general levels of intrinsic/extrinsic motivation); and motivational traits (e.g., core self-evaluations, approach/avoidance orientation, achievement goal orientation). Such global-level factors affect behavior in a top-down fashion through their effects on contextual-level and situational-level motivation (cf. Vallerand, 1997). In the context of job seeking, most attention has been given to global-level factors such as Big Five personality factors (e.g., emotional stability, conscientiousness, extraversion) and motivational traits (e.g., core self-evaluations, approach/avoidance, goal orientation). Meta-analytic findings show that especially extraversion, conscientiousness, openness to experience, and self-esteem relate positively to job search intensity (Kanfer et al., 2001). However, although their effects on job search behavior have been theorized to be indirect, mediated by more proximal processes (e.g., Kanfer et al., 2001), most empirical work has resorted to examining direct effects. Among the few exceptions that investigated the effects of global-level factors in conjunction with the TPB variables are studies by Lay and Brokenshire (1997) and Wanberg et al. (2005).

For example, Lay and Brokenshire (1997) hypothesized that individuals low on conscientiousness will be more likely to perceive job search activities as less important and less pleasant (i.e., low instrumental and affective job search attitudes) and will feel less competent in performing these activities (i.e., low job search self-efficacy), which makes them less motivated to engage in such activities. In support of this line of reasoning, in a sample of unemployed job seekers, they found conscientiousness to be positively related to job search intentions, fully mediated by perceived importance, pleasantness, and competence toward job search activities.

Wanberg et al. (2005) examined the relationship of core self-evaluations (a conglomerate of self-esteem, generalized self-efficacy, locus of control, and emotional stability) with job search behavior in a multiwave study among unemployed job seekers. Their findings demonstrate that individuals with more positive core self-evaluations were more likely to display higher levels of job search intensity over time, indicating more persistence in their job search. The relationship of core self-evaluations with job search intensity remained significant when the TPB variables were included, suggesting direct effects of core self-evaluations on job search intensity.

Thus, future research is needed to investigate in more detail the top-down mechanisms by which global-level factors affect the job search process, for example, by specifying how personality traits relate to contextual-level and situational-level motivating factors that are important in predicting job search intentions and behavior. Also, future research should investigate the role of a wider variety of global-level factors, such as basic needs, generic motivational orientations, and motivational traits, in affecting job search behavior, as mediated by motivational factors at the contextual and situational level.

Summary. Various contextual-level motivating factors (i.e., work valence, financial need, social support, cognitive appraisals of job loss and subsequent job search, job search clarity, dissatisfaction, and perceived health) and global-level motivating factors (i.e., core self-evaluations) have been found to predict job search intentions or behavior beyond the situational-level TPJSB predictors. These findings contradict the original theoretical predictions of the TPB and Vallerand's (1997) hierarchical model of motivation, based on which situational-level predictors (i.e., job search attitudes, subjective job search norms, perceived behavioral control over job search) are assumed to be the most proximal predictors of job search intentions, completely mediating the effects of more distal contextual- and global-level motivators.

If we consider this theoretical prediction correct, a *methodological explanation* for finding direct effects may relate to the fact that many studies did not operationalize the situational-level TPJSB predictors in their full breadth. For example, attitude measures may not have captured all important attitudes toward job seeking, and perceptions of behavioral control over job search have often been operationalized as job search self-efficacy, leaving out the perceived control over external factors. As a consequence, variance in job search intentions is left unexplained by the situational-level TPJSB predictors, leaving room for finding direct effect relations of higher-level factors. Regarding job search behavior, variance may be left unexplained by job search intention when noncorresponding measures have been used for intention and behavior, again leaving room for finding direct effect relations between higher-level factors and job search behavior.

Alternatively, one can speculate about more *theoretical explanations* for the direct effect relations of the contextual- and global-level factors. One potential pathway to explain these findings relates to the self-regulatory nature of the job search process. Regardless of positive proximal attitudes and perceptions, and strong intentions to search, people may procrastinate or fail to enact on their job search intentions due to a lack of self-regulation skills and capacities. To the extent that global-level and contextual-level factors influence people's self-regulation, these may add to the prediction of job search behavior over and beyond the TPB variables. For example, core self-evaluations are associated with lower procrastination and improved self-regulation (e.g., Steel, 2007) and as such may directly affect job search behavior because people with more positive core self-evaluations will be more likely to self-regulate and act on their job search intentions. Another potential pathway may relate to habitual responses or nonconscious self-regulatory processes that result in the performance of job search activities without having formed specific job search intentions. In the next chapter, these self-regulatory perspectives are addressed in more detail (see Van Hooft, this volume).

The Moderating Role of the Broader Context

Importantly, the process of job seeking and obtaining a (new) job does not occur in a social vacuum. Although underexamined in psychological research, the broader context in which the job search takes place and the experience thereof by the individual job seeker may importantly affect the process and its outcomes (Wanberg et al., 2012; see also Kanfer & Bufton, this volume). Context factors refer to exogenous features of the action setting, that is, factors that are external to the individual (Kanfer, 2012), and may refer to an individual's history (e.g., employment experience); the immediate task setting (e.g., type of job search activity); the direct environment in which the job search occurs (e.g., policies of recruiting organizations, branch characteristics); the nonwork situation (e.g., family situation, caregiving demands); and the wider sociocultural or economic environment (e.g., cultural norms, labor market demand).

From the perspective of the TPB, the effects of context are posed to be indirect and should be mediated by the more proximal situation-level motivating factors. In addition to such indirect effects, Fishbein (1980) and Ajzen (1991) theorize that context variables may exert their influence in a second way, that is, by affecting the relative weights of the attitudinal, normative, and control components as determinants of job search intentions. Similarly, in the TPJSB the relative importance of job search attitudes, perceptions of social pressure to search, and perceptions of behavioral control over job search in affecting job search intentions, the relative importance of job search intentions in affecting job search behavior and the relative importance of job search behavior in predicting employment success outcomes are posed to vary depending on the broader context. While one can think of many potentially relevant context factors, next I focus on a limited selection of factors that are highly salient for job seeking (i.e., labor market, employment position) or have been studied using the TPB (i.e., culture, family situation).

Labor market demand. Job search occurs at the labor market; therefore, the economic conditions and labor market demand are important context factors likely affecting the job search process and its outcomes. Wanberg et al. (2012) conducted a qualitative study among employed and unemployed job seekers in the United States in spring 2010, when the economic conditions were relatively poor and the unemployment rate of 9.9% was relatively high. They found that over 65% of the interviewed job seekers mentioned factors related to the economic conditions when asked what situations they found difficult (i.e., challenging, demanding, frustrating, discouraging, and irritating) in their job search. The economic situation not only seemed to affect the number of available positions and the selection criteria of hiring organizations (e.g., insisting on a perfect match between applicant and job), but also altered the job search process. For example, whereas in good economic times highly qualified job seekers are likely to be headhunted by recruiters, in poor economic times the initiative in the job search process lies more with the individual job seeker. Based on these observations, labor market demand is proposed to moderate the effects of job search intensity on employment success, such that when demand is low, job search intensity is more strongly related to employment success than when demand is high (as in the latter situation it is easier to find a job without looking very hard).

Not only job search intensity but also job search quality is posed to differentially affect employment success depending on labor market demand. As Van Hooft et al. (2013) propose, when labor market demand is high, job search quality makes less of a difference because it is relatively easy to find a (new) job. In times of low demand, however, organizations can select from a larger pool of applicants. Holding applicant characteristics constant, applicants conducting a high-quality job search process are posed to be more likely to meet/exceed hiring organizations' expectations because of clearer goals, better job search strategies, improved preparation, and better self-monitoring and reflection, leading to increased learning concerning what hiring organizations are looking for.

Only limited empirical research has sought to examine the effects of the labor market on the job search process. An important reason for this are practical difficulties in operationalization and measurement of labor market demand. That is, when operationalizing it at the macro or regional level in terms of unemployment rate, it has little variance between study participants; moreover, it may not accurately reflect the demand for the individual's specific skills (e.g., labor market demand may vary substantially by occupation, job type, experience level, etc.). Alternatively, when operationalizing labor market demand at the individual level, there are few options besides using self-report measures for labor market demand (e.g., see Wanberg et al., 2002), which people likely can only assess properly after having conducted a representative job search. As Wanberg et al. (2012) found, even though people were generally aware of the poor labor market conditions in 2010, they only realized how bad things were (for them) after they engaged in a job search for a while. Nevertheless, future (meta-analytic) research should make an effort to capture labor market factors and test whether the TPJSB relations depend on the labor market demand.

Employment position. A second context factor is the current employment position of the job seeker (i.e., employed vs. unemployed) or more generally the transition type (e.g., job-to-job seeker, unemployed job seeker, new entrant to the labor market, reentering the labor market). For example, Wanberg et al. (2012) reported that unemployed job seekers experienced their employment status as a severe handicap in their job search, feeling stigmatized by potential employers for being jobless. In terms of the TPJSB relations as depicted in Figure 11.1, this would imply that job search behavior is less likely to result in employment success for unemployed than for employed job seekers. Consistent with this proposition, Kanfer et al. (2001) found that the correlation between job search intensity and employment status was higher among employed than unemployed job seekers (r_c = .38 vs. .20), although based on a relatively low number of samples (k = 2 vs. 14).

Future research is needed to examine whether this difference also applies to other dimensions of job search behavior, such as its quality, and for other employment outcomes, such as job quality. Furthermore, future research may examine the potential moderating role of unemployment duration. Assuming that the stigma of unemployment increases the longer people are unemployed, unemployment duration would act as a moderator in the job search behavior–employment success relationship, such that it becomes weaker as unemployment is prolonged.

Wanberg et al.'s (2012) findings indicate that also employed job seekers experience difficulties in the job search process because of their employment position. Specifically, engaging in a quality job search process while having to meet one's obligations in one's present job was perceived as a difficult challenge by employed job seekers. In terms of the TPJSB relations, this implies that employment position acts as a moderator, such that employed job seekers, due to their time constraints, will be less likely to translate positive job search attitudes into job search intentions, and job search intentions into actual job search behavior, as compared to unemployed job seekers.

Van Hooft, Born, Taris, Van der Flier, and Blonk (2004) conducted a study of job seeking among employed and unemployed people and indeed found that the job search attitude–job search intention–job search behavior path was weaker among employed than unemployed individuals. Future research is needed to more systematically study differences in the TPJSB relationships depending on transition type, as well as the underlying mechanisms that explain such differences.

Family situation. An important context factor that may influence the TPJSB relations is the social milieu of a job seeker. Wanberg et al.'s (2012) findings illustrate the importance of the family, as many job seekers reported difficulties regarding family relationships, personal finances, and effects on the family of their job pursuit decisions. Also Van Hooft, Born, Taris, and Van der Flier (2005) reported evidence for the importance of family situation, as household size was found to moderate the relationships of job search attitude and perceived social pressure to search with job search intentions. More specifically, perceived social pressure was a stronger predictor of job search intentions for individuals with a larger household, whereas the reverse was found for job search attitude.

Culture and ethnicity. Another moderator of the TPJSB-relations is the job seekers' ethnicity and cultural background. Even though cross-cultural research has identified many dimensions of cultural value orientations (e.g., individualism–collectivism, power distance, masculinity, future

orientation, uncertainty avoidance; Hofstede, 1980; Javidan & House, 2001), previous research on the TPB has mainly focused on the role of individualism–collectivism in affecting the TPB relationships.

Specifically, in individualistic cultures people perceive themselves as autonomous individuals who are independent of the group, which leads them to prioritize personal goals above collective goals. Therefore, their behavior is guided more by personal attitudes than social norms. Conversely, in collectivistic cultures, people are characterized more by an interdependent self-construal, leading them to prioritize goals of the in-group above their personal goals and behaving more by anticipated expectations of others or social norms of the in-group than by personal attitudes (e.g., Markus & Kitayama, 1991). Some corroborating evidence has been reported for this reasoning, such that in samples of job seekers from more collectivistic cultures, perceived social pressure to search more strongly and job search attitude more weakly predicted job search intentions than in samples of job seekers from more individualistic cultures (e.g., Song et al., 2006; Van Hooft, Born, Taris, & Van der Flier, 2004, 2006).

Rather than directly measuring people's cultural value orientations, these studies assumed cultural differences based on their ethnicity. As such an approach is based on an untested assumption of cultural homogeneity, which ignores within-group cultural differences (Fiske, 2002), it is better to directly measure cultural value orientations at the individual level. Using direct individual difference measurements of collectivism, Van Hooft and De Jong (2009) found that people low on collectivism were more strongly motivated by their personal attitudes about job seeking and less by perceptions of social pressure than people high on collectivism, supporting the impact of collectivism on the relative importance of job search attitudes and social pressure to search.

In addition to affecting the relative importance of situational-level predictors, future research should investigate whether individualism–collectivism may moderate other TPJSB relations. For example, in collectivistic cultures specific types of job search behaviors may be more or less effective as compared to individualistic cultures. Furthermore, apart from individualism–collectivism, other cultural value orientations may affect the relative importance of the TPJSB relations. As an example, cultures differ on future orientation, that is, the degree to which future-oriented behaviors such as planning, investing in the future, and delaying gratification are expected and valued (Javidan & House, 2001). Because the TPJSB is based on the assumption of rationality and planfulness, future orientation may moderate the TPJSB relations such that TPJSB relations are weaker in countries or individuals lower on future orientation. For example, intentions may be less predictive for behavior among job seekers low on future orientation because more value is placed on instant gratification and spontaneous actions than on planned behavior. Future research is needed to build and test theoretical explanations for the moderating role of these and other cultural dimensions in the TPJSB relations.

Conclusion

The present chapter introduced TPJSB, based on an integration of insights from the job search literature and generic motivation theories and models such as Ajzen's (1991) TPB, Vallerand's (1997) hierarchical model of motivation, and SDT (Ryan & Deci, 2000), applied to the job search context. A review of empirical research not only demonstrated support for most of the relationships outlined in the TPJSB, but also indicated several areas that are in need of further inspection. For example, future research should extend the job search behavior concept by including quality-related aspects in addition to intensity (see also Van Hooft et al., 2013) and test the validity of the TPJSB relations for job search quality. Also, future research should empirically test the proposed hierarchical order of motivational factors from global level via contextual level to situational level for a broader array of relevant global-level factors and by using full-breadth operationalizations of the situational-level predictors. Last, future research is needed to increase our understanding of the validity of the TPJSB relations under different labor market situations, in different cultures, and for different transition types or job seeker groups, as well as the underlying mechanisms that explain such situational differences in the TPSJB relations.

Overall, the TPSJB as discussed so far assumes that job search intentions are the main determinant of job search behavior. However, as with all resolutions, also job search intentions do not always translate into actual job search behavior. Indeed, an often-coined limitation of the general TPB is that it leaves the processes by which intentions lead to behavior unexplored. In the next chapter, I therefore extend the current description of the TPSJB by taking a self-regulatory perspective on job seeking,

discussing potentially influential moderators of the relationship between job search intentions and job search behavior.

Practical Tips

Some general tips for job seekers and employment counselors that follow from the core relations of the TPJSB are as follows:

• Even though engaging in job search activities may sometimes feel ineffective for obtaining a job, job search behavior is still the best controllable predictor of finding a job. Therefore, spending much time on a diverse set of job search activities (i.e., networking, searching for vacancies online and in traditional media, visiting various employment agencies, etc.) is beneficial to obtain employment.

• Formulate specific intentions for a wide array of different job search activities, as job search intentions are a strong predictor of actual job search behavior.

• Even though social pressure and moral norms are predictive of job search behavior, these represent rather controlled forms of motivation. In contrast, more autonomous forms of motivation, such as positive instrumental and affective attitudes toward job seeking, represent a higher quality and more sustainable form of motivation. Employment counselors should therefore focus on increasing these more autonomous forms of motivation for job seeking.

• A possible way to make job search attitudes more positive is to elicit people's underlying salient beliefs about job seeking and finding employment and intervene on these idiosyncratic beliefs.

• Other ways to improve job search attitudes are, for example, enhancing the importance that people attach to having a job, making people see job seeking as a challenge and learning experience rather than as a threat, and increasing people's clarity regarding their employment goals and job search activities that are needed to obtain those goals.

• Enhance people's self-efficacy for performing job search activities (e.g., by training job search skills), but be careful with enhancing people's confidence to find employment because this may result in reduced job search effort.

Acknowledgment

This work was supported by the FMG-UvA Research Priority Grant on Affect Regulation.

References

Ajzen, I. (1991). The theory of planned behavior. *Organizational Behavior and Human Decision Processes, 50,* 179–211.

Ajzen, I. (2011). The theory of planned behavior: Reactions and reflections. *Psychology and Health, 26,* 1113–1127.

Ajzen, I., & Driver, B. L. (1992). Application of the theory of planned behavior to leisure choice. *Journal of Leisure Research, 24,* 207–224.

Armitage, C. J., & Conner, M. (2001). Efficacy of the theory of planned behavior: A meta-analytic review. *British Journal of Social Psychology, 40,* 471–499.

Austin, J. T., & Vancouver, J. B. (1996). Goal constructs in psychology: Structure, process, and content. *Psychological Bulletin, 120,* 338–375.

Bandura, A. (1991). Social cognitive theory of self-regulation. *Organizational Behavior and Human Decision Processes, 50,* 248–287.

Barber, A. E., Daly, C. L., Giannantonio, C. M., & Phillips, J. M. (1994). Job search activities: An examination of changes over time. *Personnel Psychology, 47,* 739–766.

Baumeister, R. F., Vohs, K. D., & Tice, D. M. (2007). The strength model of self-control. *Current Directions in Psychological Science, 16,* 351–355.

Borgen, W. A., & Amundson, N. E. (1987). The dynamics of unemployment. *Journal of Counseling and Development, 66,* 180–184.

Boswell, W. R., Boudreau, J. W., & Dunford, B. B. (2004). The outcomes and correlates of job search objectives: Searching to leave or searching for leverage? *Journal of Applied Psychology, 89,* 1083–1091.

Boswell, W. R., Zimmerman, R. D., & Swider, B. W. (2012). Employee job search: Toward an understanding of search context and search objectives. *Journal of Management, 38,* 129–163.

Bretz, R. D., Boudreau, J. W., & Judge, T. A. (1994). Job search behavior of employed managers. *Personnel Psychology, 47,* 275–301.

Briscoe, J. P., Henagan, S. C., Burton, J. P., & Murphy, W. M. (2012). Coping with an insecure employment environment: The differing roles of protean and boundaryless career orientations. *Journal of Vocational Behavior, 80,* 308–316.

Caska, B. A. (1998). The search for employment: Motivation to engage in a coping behavior. *Journal of Applied Social Psychology, 28,* 206–224.

Conner, M., & Armitage, C. J. (1998). Extending the theory of planned behavior: A review and avenues for further research. *Journal of Applied Social Psychology, 28,* 1429–1464.

Cooke, R., & Sheeran, P. (2004). Moderation of cognition–intention and cognition–behaviour relations: A meta-analysis of properties of variables from the theory of planned behavior. *British Journal of Social Psychology, 43,* 159–186.

Corbière, M., Zaniboni, S., Lecomte, T., Bond, G., Gilles, P.-Y., Lesage, A., & Goldner, E. (2011). Job acquisition for people with severe mental illness enrolled in supported employment programs: A theoretically grounded empirical study. *Journal of Occupational Rehabilitation, 21,* 342–354.

Côté, S., Saks, A. M., & Zikic, J. (2006). Trait affect and job search outcomes. *Journal of Vocational Behavior, 68,* 233–252.

Creed, P. A., Doherty, F., & O'Callaghan, F. (2008). Job-seeking and job-acquisition in high school students. *Journal of Vocational Behavior, 73,* 195–202.

Crossley, C. D., & Highhouse, S. (2005). Relation of job search and choice process with subsequent satisfaction. *Journal of Economic Psychology, 26,* 810–819.

Derous, E., Van Hooft, E. A. J., & Elling, M. J. (2009, April). *An integrated motivational framework on young professionals' job search behavior.* Top poster session presented at the 24th annual meeting of the Society of Industrial and Organizational Psychology, New Orleans, LA.

Feather, N. T. (1992). Expectancy-value theory and unemployment effects. *Journal of Occupational and Organizational Psychology, 65,* 315–330.

Feather, N. T., & O'Brien, G. E. (1987). Looking for employment: An expectancy-valence analysis of job-seeking behaviour among young people. *British Journal of Psychology, 78,* 251–272.

Fishbein, M. (1980). A theory of reasoned action: Some applications and implications. In H. E. Howe & M. M. Page (Eds.), *Nebraska Symposium on Motivation* (Vol. 27, pp. 65–116). Lincoln, NE: University of Nebraska Press.

Fishbein, M., & Ajzen, I. (1975). *Belief, attitude, intention and behavior: An introduction to theory and research.* Reading, MA: Addison-Wesley.

Fiske, A. P. (2002). Using individualism and collectivism to compare cultures—A critique of the validity and measurement of the constructs: Comment on Oyserman et al. (2002). *Psychological Bulletin, 128,* 78–88.

Gollwitzer, P. M. (1990). Action phases and mind-sets. In E. T. Higgins & R. M. Sorrentino (Eds.), *Handbook of motivation and cognition: Foundations of social behavior* (Vol. 2, pp. 53–92). New York: Guilford.

Gowan, M. A., Riordan, C. M., & Gatewood, R. D. (1999). Test of a model of coping with involuntary job loss following a company closing. *Journal of Applied Psychology, 84,* 75–86.

Hofstede, G. (1980). *Culture's consequences: International differences in work-related values.* Beverly Hills, CA: Sage.

Hom, P. W., Caranikas-Walker, F., Prussia, G. E., & Griffeth, R. W. (1992). A meta-analytical structural equations analysis of a model of employee turnover. *Journal of Applied Psychology, 77,* 890–909.

Javidan, M., & House, R. J. (2001). Cultural acumen for the global manager: Lessons from project GLOBE. *Organizational Dynamics, 29,* 289–305.

Kanfer, R. (2012). Work motivation: Theory, practice, and future directions. In S. W. J. Kozlowski (Ed.), *The Oxford handbook of organizational psychology* (Vol. 1, pp. 455–495). New York: Oxford University Press.

Kanfer, R., Wanberg, C. R., & Kantrowitz, T. M. (2001). Job search and employment: A personality-motivational analysis and meta-analytic review. *Journal of Applied Psychology, 86,* 837–855.

Kinicki, A. J. (1989). Predicting occupational role choices after involuntary job loss. *Journal of Vocational Behavior 35,* 204–218.

Klein, H. J. (1989). An integrated control theory model of work motivation. *Academy of Management Review, 14,* 150–172.

Klepinger, D. H., Johnson, T. R., & Joesch, J. M. (2002). Effects of unemployment insurance work-search requirements: The Maryland experiment. *Industrial & Labor Relations Review, 56,* 3–22.

Koen, J., Klehe, U.-C., Van Vianen, A. E. M., Zikic, J., & Nauta, A. (2010). Job-search strategies and reemployment quality: The impact of career adaptability. *Journal of Vocational Behavior, 77*, 126–139.

Koen, J., Van Vianen, A. E. M., Van Hooft, E. A. J., & Klehe, U.-C. (2016). How experienced autonomy can improve job seekers' motivation, job search, and chance of finding reemployment. *Journal of Vocational Behavior, 95–96*, 31–44.

Krueger, A. B., & Mueller, A. I. (2010). Job search and unemployment insurance: New evidence from time use data. *Journal of Public Economics, 94*, 298–307.

Latack, J. C., Kinicki, A. J., & Prussia, G. E. (1995). An integrative process model of coping with job loss. *Academy of Management Review, 20*, 311–342.

Lay, C. H., & Brokenshire, R. (1997). Conscientiousness, procrastination, and person-task characteristics in job searching by unemployed adults. *Current Psychology, 16*, 83–96.

Leana, C. R., & Feldman, D. C. (1988). Individual responses to job loss: Perceptions, reaction, and coping behaviors. *Journal of Management, 14*, 375–389.

Leana, C. R., Feldman, D. C., & Tan, G. Y. (1998). Predictors of coping behavior after a layoff. *Journal of Organizational Behavior, 19*, 85–97.

Lee, T. W., & Mitchell, T. R. (1994). An alternative approach: The unfolding model of voluntary employee turnover. *Academy of Management Review, 19*, 51–89.

Lee, T. W., Mitchell, T. R., Holtom, B. C., McDaniel, L. S., & Hill, J. W. (1999). The unfolding model of voluntary turnover: A replication and extension. *Academy of Management Journal, 42*, 450–462.

LePine, J. A., Podsakoff, N. P., & LePine, M. A. (2005). A meta-analytic test of the challenge stressor-hindrance stressor framework: An explanation for inconsistent relationships among stressors and performance. *Academy of Management Journal, 48*, 764–775.

Lin, H.-F. (2010). Applicability of the extended theory of planned behavior in predicting job seeker intentions to use job-search websites. *International Journal of Selection and Assessment, 18*, 64–74.

Liu, S., Wang, M., Liao, H., & Shi, J. (2014). Self-regulation during job search: The opposing effects of employment self-efficacy and job search behavior self-efficacy. *Journal of Applied Psychology, 99*, 1159–1172.

Locke, E. A., & Latham, G. P. (2002). Building a practically useful theory of goal setting and task motivation. *American Psychologist, 57*, 705–717.

Markus, H. R., & Kitayama, S. (1991). Culture and the self: Implications for cognition, emotion, and motivation. *Psychological Review, 98*, 224–253.

McEachan, R. R. C., Conner, M., Taylor, N. J., & Lawton, R. J. (2011). Prospective prediction of health-related behaviours with the theory of planned behaviour: A meta-analysis. *Health Psychology Review, 5*, 97–144.

McFadyen, R. G., & Thomas, J. P. (1997). Economic and psychological models of job search behavior of the unemployed. *Human Relations, 50*, 1461–1484.

Mihal, W. L., Sorce, P. A., & Comte, T. E. (1984). A process model of individual career decision making. *Academy of Management Review, 9*, 95–103.

Mobley, W. H. (1977). Intermediate linkages in the relationship between job satisfaction and employee turnover. *Journal of Applied Psychology, 62*, 237–240.

Mortensen, D. T. (1977). Unemployment insurance and job search decisions. *Industrial & Labor Relations Review, 30*, 505–517.

Noordzij, G., Van Hooft, E. A. J., Van Mierlo, H., Van Dam, A., & Born, M. P. (2013). The effects of a learning-goal orientation training on self-regulation: A field experiment among unemployed job seekers. *Personnel Psychology, 66*, 723–755.

Prussia, G. E., Kinicki, A. J., & Bracker, J. S. (1993). Psychological and behavioral consequences of job loss: A covariance structure analysis using Weiner's (1985) attribution model. *Journal of Applied Psychology, 78*, 382–394.

Ryan, R. M., & Deci, E. L. (2000). Self-determination theory and the facilitation of intrinsic motivation, social development, and well-being. *American Psychologist, 55*, 68–78.

Saks, A. M. (2005). Job search success: A review and integration of the predictors, behaviors, and outcomes. In S. D. Brown & R. W. Lent (Eds.), *Career development and counseling: Putting theory and research to work* (pp. 155–179). Hoboken, NJ: Wiley.

Saks, A. M., & Ashforth, B. E. (1999). Effects of individual differences and job search behaviors on the employment status of recent university graduates. *Journal of Vocational Behavior, 54*, 335–349.

Saks, A. M., & Ashforth, B. E. (2002). Is job search related to employment quality? It all depends on fit. *Journal of Applied Psychology, 87*, 646–654.

Sansone, C., & Thoman, D. B. (2005). Interest as the missing motivator in self-regulation. *European Psychologist, 10*, 175–186.

Sansone, C., & Thoman, D. B. (2006). Maintaining activity engagement: Individual differences in the process of self-regulating motivation. *Journal of Personality, 74*, 1697–1720.

Schwab, D. P., Rynes, S. L., & Aldag, R. J. (1987). Theories and research on job search and choice. In K. M. Rowland & G. R. Ferris (Eds.), *Research in personnel and human resources management* (Vol. 5, pp. 129–166). Greenwich, CT: JAI Press.

Sheeran, P. (2002). Intention-behavior relations: A conceptual and empirical review. In W. Stroebe & M. Hewstone (Eds.), *European review of social psychology* (Vol. 12, pp. 1–36). Chichester, UK: Wiley.

Soelberg, P. O. (1967). Unprogrammed decision making. *Industrial Management Review, 8*, 19–29.

Song, Z., Uy, M. A., Zhang, S., & Shi, K. (2009). Daily job search and psychological distress: Evidence from China. *Human Relations, 62*, 1171–1197.

Song, Z., Wanberg, C., Niu, X., & Xie, Y. (2006). Action–state orientation and the theory of planned behavior: A study of job search in China. *Journal of Vocational Behavior, 68*, 490–503.

Steel, P. (2007). The nature of procrastination: A meta-analytic and theoretical review of quintessential self-regulatory failure. *Psychological Bulletin, 133*, 65–94.

Steers, R. M., & Mowday, R. T. (1981). Employee turnover and post-decision accommodation processes. *Research in Organizational Behavior, 3*, 235–281.

Stevens, C. K., & Beach, L. R. (1996). Job search and job selection. In L. R. Beach (Ed.), *Decision making in the workplace: A unified perspective* (pp. 33–49). Mahwah, NJ: Erlbaum.

Stumpf, S. A., Colarelli, S. M., & Hartman, K. (1983). Development of the Career Exploration Survey (CES). *Journal of Vocational Behavior, 22*, 191–226.

Taris, T. W. (2002). Unemployment and mental health: A longitudinal perspective. *International Journal of Stress Management, 9*, 43–57.

Taris, T. W., Heesink, J. A. M., & Feij, J. A. (1995). The evaluation of unemployment and job-searching behavior: A longitudinal study. *Journal of Psychology, 129*, 301–314.

Turban, D. B., Lee, F. K., da Motta Veiga, S. P., Haggard, D. L., & Wu, S. Y. (2013). Be happy, don't wait: The role of trait affect in job search. *Personnel Psychology, 66*, 483–514.

Turban, D. B., Stevens, C. K., & Lee, F. K. (2009). Effects of conscientiousness and extraversion on new labor market entrants' job search: The mediating role of metacognitive activities and positive emotions. *Personnel Psychology, 62*, 553–573.

Ullah, P. (1990). The association between income, financial strain and psychological well-being among unemployed youth. *Journal of Occupational Psychology, 63*, 317–330.

Ullah, P., & Banks, M. (1985). Youth unemployment and labour market withdrawal. *Journal of Economic Psychology, 6*, 51–64.

Vallerand, R. J. (1997). Toward a hierarchical model of intrinsic and extrinsic motivation. In M. P. Zanna (Ed.), *Advances in experimental social psychology* (Vol. 29, pp. 271–360). San Diego, CA: Academic Press.

Van Dam, K., & Menting, L. (2012). The role of approach and avoidance motives for unemployed job search behavior. *Journal of Vocational Behavior, 80*, 108–117.

Van Hooft, E. A. J. (2014). Motivating and hindering factors during the reemployment process: The added value of employment counselors' assessment. *Journal of Occupational Health Psychology, 19*, 1–17.

Van Hooft, E. A. J., Born, M. P., Taris, T. W., & Van der Flier, H. (2004). Job search and the theory of planned behavior: Minority–majority group differences in the Netherlands. *Journal of Vocational Behavior, 65*, 366–390.

Van Hooft, E. A. J., Born, M. P., Taris, T. W., Van der Flier, H., & Blonk, R. W. B. (2004). Predictors of job search behavior among employed and unemployed people. *Personnel Psychology, 57*, 25–59.

Van Hooft, E. A. J., Born, M. P., Taris, T. W., & Van der Flier, H. (2005). Predictors and outcomes of job search behavior: The moderating effects of gender and family situation. *Journal of Vocational Behavior, 67*, 133–152.

Van Hooft, E. A. J., Born, M. P., Taris, T. W., Van der Flier, H., & Blonk, R. W. B. (2005). Bridging the gap between intentions and behavior: Implementation intentions, action control, and procrastination. *Journal of Vocational Behavior, 66*, 238–256.

Van Hooft, E. A. J., Born, M. P., Taris, T. W., & Van der Flier, H. (2006). The cross-cultural generalizability of the theory of planned behavior: A study on job seeking in the Netherlands. *Journal of Cross-Cultural Psychology, 37*, 127–135.

Van Hooft, E. A. J., & Crossley, C. D. (2008). The joint role of locus of control and perceived financial need in job search. *International Journal of Selection and Assessment, 16*, 258–271.

Van Hooft, E. A. J., & De Jong, M. (2009). Predicting job seeking for temporary employment using the theory of planned behaviour: The moderating role of individualism and collectivism. *Journal of Occupational and Organizational Psychology, 82*, 295–316.

Van Hooft, E. A. J., & Noordzij, G. (2009). The effects of goal orientation on job search and reemployment: A field experiment among unemployed job seekers. *Journal of Applied Psychology, 94*, 1581–1590.

Van Hooft, E. A. J., Wanberg, C. R., & Van Hoye, G. (2013). Moving beyond job search quantity: Towards a conceptualization and self-regulatory framework of job search quality. *Organizational Psychology Review, 3*, 3–40.

Vansteenkiste, M., Lens, W., De Witte, S., De Witte, H., & Deci, E. L. (2004). The "why" and "why not" of job search behaviour: Their relation to searching, unemployment experience, and well-being. *European Journal of Social Psychology, 34*, 345–363.

Vinokur, A. D., & Caplan, R. D. (1987). Attitudes and social support: Determinants of job-seeking behavior and well-being among the unemployed. *Journal of Applied Social Psychology, 17*, 1007–1024.

Vinokur, A. D., & Schul, Y. (2002). The web of coping resources and pathways to reemployment following a job loss. *Journal of Occupational Health Psychology, 7*, 68–83.

Wanberg, C. R. (1997). Antecedents and outcomes of coping behaviors among unemployed and reemployed individuals. *Journal of Applied Psychology, 82*, 731–744.

Wanberg, C. R. (2012). The individual experience of unemployment. *Annual Review of Psychology, 63*, 369–396.

Wanberg, C. R., Basbug, G., Van Hooft, E. A. J., & Samtani, A. (2012). Navigating the black hole: Explicating layers of job search context and adaptational responses. *Personnel Psychology, 65*, 887–926.

Wanberg, C. R., Glomb, T. M., Song, Z., & Sorenson, S. (2005). Job-search persistence during unemployment: A 10-wave longitudinal study. *Journal of Applied Psychology, 90*, 411–430.

Wanberg, C. R., Hough, L. M., & Song, Z. (2002). Predictive validity of a multidisciplinary model of reemployment success. *Journal of Applied Psychology, 87*, 1100–1120.

Wanberg, C. R., Watt, J. D., & Rumsey, D. J. (1996). Individuals without jobs: An empirical study of job-seeking behavior and reemployment. *Journal of Applied Psychology, 81*, 76–87.

Wanberg, C. R., Zhu, J., & Van Hooft, E. A. J. (2010). The job-search grind: Perceived progress, self-reactions, and self-regulation of search effort. *Academy of Management Journal, 53*, 788–807.

Zikic, J., & Klehe, U.-C. (2006). Job loss as a blessing in disguise: The role of career exploration and career planning in predicting reemployment quality. *Journal of Vocational Behavior, 69*, 391–401.

Zikic, J., & Saks, A. M. (2009). Job search and social cognitive theory: The role of career-relevant activities. *Journal of Vocational Behavior, 74*, 117–127.

Self-Regulatory Perspectives in the Theory of Planned Job Search Behavior: Deliberate and Automatic Self-Regulation Strategies to Facilitate Job Seeking

Edwin A.J. van Hooft

Abstract

Because job search often is a lengthy process accompanied by complexities, disruptions, rejections, and other adversities, job seekers need self-regulation to initiate and maintain job search behaviors for obtaining employment goals. This chapter reviews goal/intention properties (e.g., specificity, proximity, conflicts, motivation type) and skills, beliefs, strategies, and capacities (e.g., self-monitoring skills and type, trait and momentary self-control capacity, nonlimited willpower beliefs, implementation intentions, goal-shielding and goal maintenance strategies) that facilitate self-regulation and as such may moderate the relationship between job search intentions and job search behavior. For each moderator, a theoretical rationale is developed based on self-regulation theory linked to the theory of planned job search behavior, available empirical support is reviewed, and future research recommendations are provided. The importance of irrationality and nonconscious processes is discussed; examples are given of hypoegoic self-regulation strategies that reduce the need for deliberate self-regulation and conscious control by automatizing job search behaviors.

Key Words: job search, self-regulation, motivation, intention–behavior gap, procrastination, goal orientation, theory of planned behavior

In the previous chapter (see Van Hooft, this volume), I introduced a Theory of Planned Job Search Behavior (TPJSB) to outline the motivational antecedents of job search behavior and job attainment, based on a synthesis of insights from the job search literature (e.g., Kanfer, Wanberg, & Kantrowitz, 2001) and generic motivational theories and models such as Ajzen's (1991) Theory of Planned Behavior (TPB), Vallerand's (1997) hierarchical model of motivation, and Self-Determination Theory (Ryan & Deci, 2000). The TPJSB conceptualizes job search as a conscious and planned behavior, consisting of an intentional or goal establishment phase, a behavioral or goal-striving phase, and a goal termination phase (i.e.,

when the goal is obtained or abandoned). In addition, the TPJSB provides a hierarchical framework of motivational antecedents of job search intentions and behavior, distinguishing between proximal situational-level motivating factors (i.e., affective and instrumental job search attitudes indicating autonomous motivation, perceived social pressure and moral norms to search indicating controlled motivation, and job search self-efficacy and perceived control over job search indicating availability of resources) and more distal contextual-level (e.g., beliefs about job search and employment, employment commitment, social support, financial need, health perceptions) and global-level factors (e.g., personality, basic needs, motivational traits).

Based on Ajzen's (1991) TPB, in its core the TPJSB conceptualizes job search intentions as the most immediate determinant of job search behavior, with job search intentions reflecting the intensity and direction of people's motivation to engage in job search (Van Hooft, this volume). While motivation is essential for engaging and persisting in job search (as also indicted by the moderate-to-strong correlations between job search intentions and job search behavior; see Van Hooft, this volume), it likely is not enough. Because of the complexities, difficulties, and rejections that people inevitably encounter during their job search, job seeking is often considered aversive. For tasks that are difficult, unpleasant, boring, or otherwise aversive, but that are important to attain some valued goal (i.e., finding a job), people need self-regulation to initiate and maintain behavior, regulate their emotions and effort, and recoup after failures to ensure task persistence and sustained performance until the goal is achieved.

In the present chapter, I take a self-regulation perspective on job search. I extend the theoretical framework presented in the previous chapter with self-regulatory concepts as moderators in the job search intention–job search behavior relationship, leading to the full TPJSB as displayed in Figure 12.1. I integrate recent theory and empirical findings of the general self-regulation literature and the job search literature to identify self-regulation concepts that are important or seem promising in the context of job search, outline the theoretical rationales for their moderating role in the TPJSB, review available empirical research, present some new data, and highlight areas where future research is needed. Last, I address the limitations of highly cognitive models of motivation and self-regulation, calling for research on more automatic and nonconscious self-regulatory processes that may help people's job search.

The Intention–Behavior Gap

The theoretical model as displayed in Figure 12.1 is grounded in Ajzen's (1991) TPB, which describes human behavior as rational and planned, with intentions as the main driver of behavior. This basic relation between intentions and behavior notwithstanding, intentions often do not translate into actual behavior. Sheeran (2002), for example, meta-analyzed meta-analyses of the intention–behavior relationship across domains and found an overall sample-weighted average correlation of .53, indicating that intentions on average

account for 28.1% of the variance in behavior. Similarly, as displayed in Table 11.1 of the previous chapter (see Van Hooft, this volume), correlations between job search intentions and job search behavior vary between .23 and .66, averaging around .46. This means that job search intentions explain about 20% of the variance in job search behavior, leaving 80% of the variance unexplained. To a certain degree, these correlations may be underestimations of the true job search intention–job search behavior relationship because of methodological issues (cf. Ajzen, 1991; Sutton, 1998). Examples of such issues include the following: (a) Job search intentions may have changed shortly after their measurement; (b) there may have been a lack of correspondence or compatibility between the job search intention and behavior measures in terms of specificity, target, situation, and time (e.g., when the intention measure is more general whereas the behavior measure represents an index of job search activities or when the intention measure refers to another time period than the behavior measure); (c) different response scales may have been used for the job search intention and behavior measures; (d) random measurement error; and (e) restriction of range.

However, even when taking such methodological problems into account, job search intentions likely still are no perfect predictors of actual job search behavior. A substantive discrepancy between intentions and behavior can take two forms: (a) job search intentions that are not acted on and (b) job search behaviors occurring without job search intentions. Combining a selected set of studies on health-related behaviors, Sheeran (2002) concluded that the lack of consistency between intentions and behavior is mainly due to failing to act on intentions rather than acting without intentions. With regard to job seeking, a reanalysis of previous data (i.e., Van Hooft, Born, Taris, & Van der Flier, 2004; Van Hooft, Born, Taris, Van der Flier, & Blonk, 2004, 2005; Van Hooft & De Jong, 2009) shows that 21.3% to 69.1% (mean = 46.4%) of the people with job search intentions at Time 1 had not acted upon these at Time 2, whereas 3.2% to 36.4% (mean = 17.8%) of the people with no job search intentions at Time 1 actually had spent time on job seeking at Time 2 (see Table 12.1). Thus, although there were differences between samples, in general it seems that not acting on job search intentions explains a greater share of the intention–behavior gap than acting without job search intentions.

Whereas the TPB falls short of explaining the intention–behavior gap, theory and research on

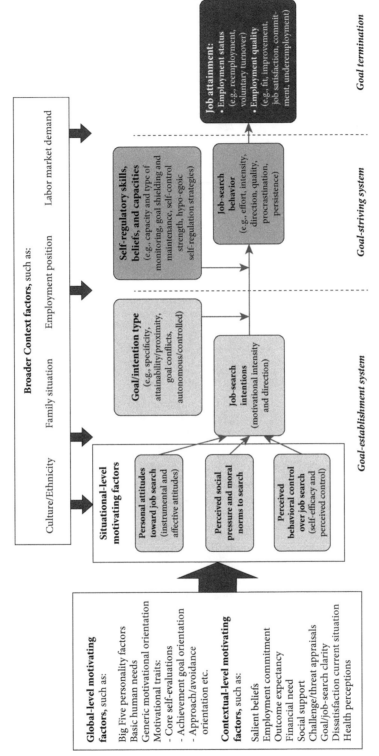

Figure 12.1 Overview of the Theory of Planned Job Search Behavior (TPJSB) integrating motivational and self-regulatory perspectives on job seeking.

Table 12.1 Percentages of people who acted versus did not act on their job search intentions

Sample type	Dataset	T1–T2 time lag (months)	T1 Intend to search			T1 Not intend to search		
			n	T2 did search (%)	T2 did not search (%)	n	T2 did search (%)	T2 did not search (%)
Employed individuals ($N = 999$)	Van Hooft, Born, Taris, Van der Flier, and Blonk (2004)	4	340	30.9	69.1	659	3.2	96.8
Unemployed individuals ($N = 395$)	Van Hooft, Born, Taris, Van der Flier, and Blonk (2004, 2005)	4	227	43.6	56.4	168	7.7	92.3
Temporary workers ($N = 412$)	Van Hooft, Born, Taris, and Van der Flier (2004)	4	228	61.8	38.2	184	23.9	76.1
Temporary workers ($N = 86$)	Van Hooft and De Jong (2009)	2	75	78.7	21.3	11	36.4	63.6

Note. Job search intentions were measured at Time 1 (T1) and job search behavior at Time 2 (T2) with a question asking how much time or how many hours per week the participant intended to invest in job seeking in the next *X* months versus had invested in job seeking in the last *X* months (with *X* the number of months between the T1 and T2 measurement). For the present analysis, the responses were dichotomized to create a categorical variable indicating whether people reported at T1 whether they did versus did not intend to spend time on a job search and a categorical variable indicating whether they reported at T1 whether they actually did or did not spend time on their job search.

self-regulation (e.g., Baumeister & Heatherton, 1996; Baumeister, Vohs, & Tice, 2007; Inzlicht, Legault, & Teper, 2014; Metcalfe & Mischel, 1999; Ryan & Deci, 2000; Sansone & Thoman, 2005, 2006; Van Hooft, Wanberg, & Van Hoye, 2013; Zimmerman, 2000) offer a variety of perspectives that are useful for building a more comprehensive theory of explaining job search behavior. In the present chapter, I focus on a set of moderators that can explain when job search intentions are more or less likely to result in initiation and maintenance of the intended job search behaviors. To organize the set of moderators, I first define and describe self-regulation based on the most prominent self-regulation theories and models.

The Functioning of Self-Regulation

Definitions of self-regulation (e.g., Karoly, 1993; Zimmerman, 2000) characterize self-regulation as intraindividual processes (deliberate or automated) that enable people to initiate and maintain their goal-directed activities and guide their goal attainment over time and across changing situations. It includes the control by the human self to modulate thoughts, affect, attention, behaviors, or task performance to reach the goal. Self-regulation is needed when there is a discrepancy between one's

current and desired state or, alternatively, when one's immediate urges are in conflict with one's long-term valued goals. Based on dual-process models such as Metcalfe and Mischel's (1999) hot-/cool-system framework or Strack and Deutsch's (2004) reflective–impulsive system model, it can be argued that people have to engage in self-regulation when a stimulus is perceived that activates the hot system/impulsive system (i.e., a hot stimulus), thereby thwarting one's goal-directed volition or reasoned intentions stored in the reflective system. Such hot stimuli can include not only pleasurable activities, habits, impulses, temptations, or cravings that are not beneficial for obtaining one's goals but also urges like refraining from engaging in a difficult or tiring task, not resuming task behavior after distractions or failure, or remaining lazy while you actually have to do something.

In other words, self-regulation is needed in two types of dilemmas or situations. First, when an activity has short-term benefits (e.g., it feels good, it gratifies an immediate need) but long-term costs, people have to self-regulate to refrain from such activities. This inhibitory type of self-control needed in a delayed-cost dilemma situation is what De Boer, Van Hooft, and Bakker (2011, 2015) labeled stop-control, defined as self-regulation aimed at short-term attractive but long-term undesirable behavior in order not to perform this behavior. Second, when an activity has short-term costs (e.g., it is aversive) but long-term benefits, people have to self-regulate to engage in such activities. This initiatory type of self-control needed in a delayed-benefit dilemma situation is what De Boer et al. (2011, 2015) labeled start-control, defined as self-regulation aimed at short-term unattractive but long-term desirable behavior in order to perform this behavior.

Many process models of self-regulation (e.g., Austin & Vancouver, 1996; Carver & Scheier, 1982; Gollwitzer, 1990; Kanfer, 1990; Karoly, 1993; Van Hooft et al., 2013; Zimmerman, 2000; see also Kanfer & Bufton, this volume) distinguish between several phases of self-regulation, linked in a cyclical fashion. In their core, all such process models of self-regulation are based on cybernetic control theory (e.g., Carver & Scheier, 1982). Control theory describes the functioning of self-regulation along a negative-feedback loop, which starts with the *setting of a goal* representing the desired state. In the *monitoring function*, information is then collected to determine the present state, which is compared to this desired state. When the monitoring function detects a discrepancy between the desired and present state, this information is fed forward to the *operating function*, which needs to initiate or inhibit behavior to reduce the discrepancy. Importantly, social cognitive theory (e.g., Bandura, 1991; Zimmerman, 2000) adds to this reactive discrepancy reduction system the notion that people can, and also deliberately and proactively do, create discrepancies by setting goals that challenge their current status (Phillips, Hollenbeck, & Ilgen, 1996; see also Latham, Mawritz, & Locke, this volume).

Conceptualizing Self-Regulation in the TPJSB

As applied to job search, self-regulation thus becomes salient when the goal of searching for a (new) job is activated (a long-term valued goal) and the goal-directed behavior of job seeking is thwarted (e.g., by distractions, other life goals, failures, fatigue, negative emotions, distress, discouragement, cognitions about the difficulty of job search activities, etc.). In terms of the TPJSB, self-regulation is needed when people have to initiate job search behaviors as planned in their job search intentions (i.e., start-control) and when people have to maintain their planned job search behaviors,

shielding these behaviors from short-term urges (i.e., stop-control).

The present formulation of a TPJSB extends previous applications of the TPB to job search by incorporating mechanisms that facilitate or hinder the translation of job search intentions into actual job search behavior. The self-regulation functioning as described in the preceding section, distinguishing between a goal establishment system and a goal-striving system (consisting of a monitoring and an operating function), suggests that self-regulation can also fail because of dysfunctions in each of these systems (cf. Baumeister & Heatherton, 1996; Inzlicht et al., 2014). Self-regulatory failures, or in other words failures in transforming job search intentions into actual job search behaviors, can thus be described along these two systems. Therefore, in the TPJSB two specific clusters of moderators in the intention–behavior relationship are proposed: (a) aspects related to the type of goals and intentions formulated in the goal establishment system (see "Goal/intention type" box in Figure 12.1) and (b) aspects related to the monitoring and operating function of the goal-striving system (see "Self-regulatory skills, beliefs, and capacities" box in Figure 12.1).

Intention–Behavior Moderators Related to Qualities of the Goal Establishment System

The goal establishment phase in job search refers to a cognitive phase during which job seekers process available information and evaluate competing goals, resulting in a selection of one or more employment goals and the formation of job search intentions. These goals and intentions can vary along dimensions such as specificity, proximity, conflictual properties, and content (e.g., with respect to the underlying motivation type). Such properties of goals and intentions have implications in terms of the self-regulation processes needed to initiate and maintain the striving for the employment goal(s) and enact on the intended job search behaviors, and as such may act as moderators of the job search intention–behavior relation.

Goal specificity. Goal specificity is a first important moderator in the job search intention–behavior relationship. Goal-setting theory (Locke & Latham, 2002; see also Latham et al., this volume) suggests that when goals are *vague* rather than *specific*, self-regulation more likely fails because monitoring discrepancies and progress toward vague and ill-defined goals is difficult, if not impossible. In other words, job search intentions that are formulated in general, nonmeasurable terms (e.g., "I intend to engage in job seeking") are less likely to translate into actual job search behavior than specific, measurable job search intentions (e.g., "I intend to spend 2 hours each day next week looking for vacancies online"). Although previous research indicates initial indirect support for this prediction as job search intention–behavior correlations seem higher for index measures than for general measures as discussed in the previous chapter (see Table 11.1 in Van Hooft, this volume), future research is needed to test this more rigorously.

Goal proximity. Second, when goals are *unrealistic* or *very distal* rather than *attainable and more proximal*, self-regulation more likely fails because the discrepancy may be too large, which subsequently overtaxes the operating function. As Van Hooft and colleagues (2013) argued, the specification of one's distal goals in a hierarchical fashion of more proximal subgoals helps to make the cognitive transition from goal establishment into planning and execution of the goal pursuit. Such proximal goals further facilitate the self-regulation process because attaining subgoals leads to self-satisfaction and feelings of progressive mastery of the job search process (cf. Bandura, 1991). For example, when people only set the goal of obtaining a job (which is a rather distal goal in most situations) without furnishing it with more proximal subgoals (i.e., breaking it down in steps that will ultimately lead to the goal of obtaining a job), self-regulation more likely fails because the discrepancy between one's current state and the ultimate goal may feel too large to overcome and progress toward the distal goal of obtaining a job may feel too limited. Future research should examine the validity of this prediction in the context of job search, for example, by testing whether job search intentions are more strongly related to actual job search behavior when these serve proximal rather than distal job search goals.

Goal conflicts. Third, when job search goals are *incompatible* or *in conflict* with other goals that people have, effective self-regulation of the job search process is threatened. Job search typically occurs in a context where people have other goals. For example, employed job seekers need to balance their job search time with their regular job obligations, which may be challenging (e.g., Wanberg, Basbug, Van Hooft, & Samtani, 2012). Student job seekers often conduct their job search in the final stages of their studies, which raises issues of switching between their study requirements and job search goals. Also, unemployed job seekers have been found to combine their job search with pursuing other goals. For example, in their daily diary study, Wanberg, Zhu, and Van Hooft (2010) observed a vacillating pattern of the time that unemployed job seekers spent on job search activities, whereby more search time on one day is followed by less search time the following day. Frequently reported reasons for not working on one's job search on a given day included "had family obligations" (35.4%) and "wanted to do other things" (15%), illustrating the multiple-goal context in which job seeking occurs.

Other goals can undermine people's self-regulation in their job search in several ways. For example, other goals may distract people from enacting their job search intentions. This is especially likely when the behaviors for such other goals are more attractive in the short term (e.g., they feel good or they gratify an immediate need). Furthermore, other goals may tax people's self-regulation for job search because when multiple goals conflict, people need to make choices between those goals and switch among different goal-relevant behaviors, which may deplete people's self-control strength (Baumeister et al., 2007), resulting in reduced self-regulatory performance, which hampers the enactment of intended job search behaviors.

Alternatively, other goals may also serve as a functional distraction to people's job search. For example, in Wanberg et al.'s (2010) study, 13.6% of the unemployed job seekers responded that they needed a break from their job search when asked for the reasons for not spending time on job seeking. Similarly, Gowan, Riordan, and Gatewood (1999) found that engagement in nonwork activities (e.g., community and leisure activities) reduces distress among laid-off job seekers. As such, devoting time to other life goals may also support people's self-regulation in their job search because it helps them recoup from their stressful job search experiences and replenish their emotional energy. Similarly, research on ego depletion has found that positive emotions help replenish the self after depletion, improving self-regulation on subsequent tasks (Tice, Baumeister, Shmueli, & Muraven, 2007). Further research in the context of job search is therefore needed to more closely examine when the pursuit of other goals that compete for resources with job search activities may hamper versus help people's self-regulation toward their job search goals.

Job search goals and activities may compete for limited resources not only with other life goals, but also with each other. Job search involves a wide array of methods and includes many different activities (e.g., networking, searching online job boards, drafting application letters, etc.) that can all serve to obtain the same goal. Furthermore, job seekers may simultaneously pursue various different jobs, for which they need to engage in different activities toward different organizations. Dividing one's ultimate, distal goal of obtaining a (new) job into lower-order goals (e.g., obtaining job interviews with companies X and Y), and setting proximal goals for job search activities needed to obtain such lower-order goals, creates a complex hierarchical multiple-goal system. Theory and research on multiple-goal regulation are still in infancy but seem to indicate that resource allocation toward goals in a multiple-goal context is driven by the perceived discrepancy of the goal, the urgency or remaining time of the goal, the perceived control over the attainability of the goal, the value of the goal, and individual differences in motivational orientation (e.g., Mitchell, Harman, Lee, & Lee, 2008; Schmidt & DeShon, 2007; Schmidt, Dolis, & Tolli, 2009). In addition, in a situation of multiple lower-order goals (i.e., many job opportunities) and multiple job search methods that can be used to pursue each of these job opportunities, job seekers have to prioritize their goals and activities and make numerous choices along the way. Whereas having choices may be motivating, research has indicated that when the number of options to be considered becomes extensive people may feel confused and overwhelmed (e.g., see Chua & Iyengar, 2006), resulting in avoidance of making choices and hampering self-regulation.

Future studies are needed that conceptualize and examine job search as a multiple-goal system to shed light on the mechanisms that help or hinder the enacting of job search intentions toward multiple job options and for multiple job search activities in concert. The TPJSB may provide a valuable framework for modeling and investigating job seeking in a multiple-goal context. For example, concepts such as job search attitude, intention, and behavior can be operationalized for specific jobs or job search activities, using a multilevel between-individuals design (cf. Jaidi, Van Hooft, & Arends, 2011).

Motivation quality of the goals. Fourth, self-determination theory (Ryan & Deci, 2000; see also Vansteenkiste & Van den Broeck, this volume) suggests that self-regulation becomes easier when goals reflect more *self-determined* or *autonomous* rather than *controlled* types of motivation. Intrinsic motivation is the type of motivation that is the most self-determined. When goal-directed activities are intrinsically motivating, self-regulation is not needed to perform such tasks as those are inherently pleasurable, interesting, and fun. The reflective and impulsive systems are aligned, and no delayed-benefit or delayed-cost dilemma is present. Extrinsically motivated activities, however, represent tasks that are not necessarily fun or interesting by themselves. Instead, these serve a goal or identity that is personally valued or valued by important others and as such pose a delayed-benefit dilemma.

Extrinsic motivation comes in various types, ranging from autonomous or highly self-determined to controlled or non-self-determined. When goals are more autonomously motivated, they are more internally driven and personally meaningful (i.e., the delayed benefit is more direct and closer to the self) and therefore result in more self-alignment and less conflict with other goals, which makes self-regulation easier. In contrast, when goals are more controlled by others, they are more externally driven and less personally meaningful (i.e., the delayed benefit is more indirect) and therefore result in more conflict with other goals, making self-regulation more difficult.

Indeed, Moller, Deci, and Ryan (2006) reported three studies that indicate that making autonomous choices is motivating whereas making controlled choices is depleting. Similarly, Muraven (2008) found that when people did not eat cookies for more autonomous rather than controlled reasons, they performed better on a handgrip task, indicating that their self-regulatory strength was less depleted. In the context of the TPB, Sheeran, Norman, and Orbell (1999) found that intentions that are based on personal attitudes (i.e., autonomous motivation) are enacted on more so than intentions that are based on subjective norms (i.e., controlled motivation).

Altogether, these studies suggest that self-regulation is easier and less depleting when people's goals and intentions are more autonomously motivated (i.e., initiated and sustained by one's self) rather than controlled by others (i.e., initiated by feeling pressured, coerced, or seduced). Future research should therefore include the type of motivation for people's goals and intentions in the context of job search, as this may importantly moderate the relationship between job search intentions and behavior.

Intention–Behavior Moderators Related to Qualities of the Goal-Striving System

The goal-striving phase in job search refers to processes involving actual initiation of the planned job search behaviors and sustained performance of job search activities toward the established employment goal(s). Moderators related to the goal-striving system can be divided between those that affect the monitoring function (i.e., keeping track of the behaviors and progress and comparing the present state to the desired state to detect discrepancies) and those that affect the operating function (i.e., initiating or inhibiting behavior to reduce perceived discrepancies between the present and desired state).

Monitoring function. Regarding the monitoring of behavior and progress, self-regulation is jeopardized when people fail to pay attention to their valued longer-term goals or to their current state/behavior, such that effective monitoring of discrepancies between those goals and current state or behavior is hampered. For example, some people have better *self-monitoring skills* than others, which should improve subsequent self-regulation. Furthermore, when people (temporarily) lack the *capacity to transcend* an immediate tempting or emotional situation, they more likely engage in immediate gratification, forgetting their long-term goals (Baumeister & Heatherton, 1996). In the context of job seeking, some evidence supports the existence of individual differences in monitoring one's job search activities and progress and its relevance for obtaining employment goals (Turban, Stevens, & Lee, 2009). Future research should examine whether concepts related to self-monitoring skills and capacities may help improve our understanding of self-regulation failures during job seeking.

In addition to the capacity for monitoring, the type of monitoring may help or hinder self-regulation. When people monitor discrepancies in an *ego-threatening* way (e.g., interpreting failures as indicators of poor ability, leading to reduced self-worth), self-regulation is more difficult than when discrepancies are monitored in a nonjudgmental and accepting way (e.g., interpreting failures as indicators of lack of effort or use of poor strategies and viewing those as learning opportunities) because attention is shifted away from the goal striving toward ego protection (cf. Kanfer & Ackerman, 1989; Kluger & DeNisi, 1996). Some illustrative support for this mechanism is provided by research on error orientation, which shows that people who interpret errors in a learning-oriented fashion have

more on-task thoughts and better emotion control and are engaged in more meta-cognition, resulting in better performance (Dimitrova, Van Dyck, Van Hooft, & Groenewegen, 2015; Keith & Frese, 2005), whereas people who are error avoidant draw their attention more to the self during error-prone activities (Van Dyck, Van Hooft, De Gilder, & Liesveld, 2010).

In the context of job search, similar illustrative evidence has been found for the harming role of ego-threatening monitoring. More specifically, job seekers with a stronger performance goal orientation (PGO; i.e., a focus on demonstrating one's competence and thereby gaining positive judgments and avoiding negative judgments; Dweck, 1986) were found to be less likely to translate their job search intentions into actual job search behavior as compared to job seekers scoring low on PGO (Van Hooft, 2006). Data were collected in a two-wave longitudinal design in the Netherlands, using a mixed sample of job seekers ($N = 59$; 50.8% male; $M_{age} = 29.0$, $SD = 7.9$; 39.0% graduating students, 20.3% unemployed, and 40.7% employed). PGO (eight items; $\alpha = .73$; Button, Mathieu, & Zajac, 1996) and job search intention (two items; $\alpha = .65$; Van Hooft et al., 2005) were assessed at Time 1 and job search behavior (2 items; $\alpha = .83$; Van Hooft et al., 2005) was assessed 1 month later at Time 2. Results indicate that job search intention was strongly positively related to job search behavior ($r = .70$, $p < .001$). However, regression analysis showed that PGO moderated this relationship ($\beta = -.25$, $p < .05$), such that the intention–behavior relationship was significantly weaker at high levels of PGO ($B = 0.48$) than at low levels of PGO ($B = 1.08$), $t(55) = -2.54$, $p < .05$, although both simple slopes were significantly different from zero, $t(55) = 2.47$, $p < .05$, and $t(55) = 7.37$, $p < .001$, respectively (see Figure 12.2). Thus, goal orientation was found to moderate the intention–behavior relation, such that job seekers high on PGO had lower intention–behavior consistency than job seekers low on PGO. These findings suggest that job seekers who are more inclined to interpret failures in an ego-threatening way (i.e., high PGO) have more difficulty with self-regulation as demonstrated by a lower likelihood of acting on their job search intentions.

More direct evidence for the link between PGO and self-regulatory failure can be found in additional nonpublished data collected in the Van Hooft and Noordzij (2009) study. Specifically, in this field experiment among 109 unemployed job seekers, those

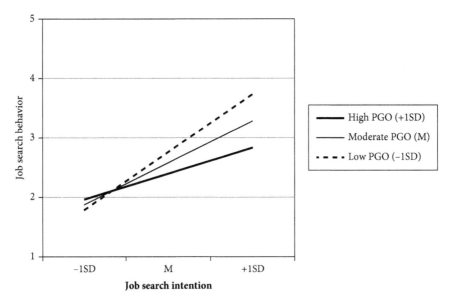

Figure 12.2 Simple regression slopes of job search intention on job search behavior for low (*M* − 1 *SD*), moderate (*M*), and high (*M* + 1 *SD*) levels of performance goal orientation (PGO).

who were trained in adopting a PGO toward their job search reported more procrastination of job search activities (measured with one face-valid item, i.e., "How often have you procrastinated intended job search activities in the last 2 weeks?" with response options ranging from 1 = never to 5 = often) in the follow-up measurement 2 weeks later as compared to the other groups ($\beta_{\text{PGO-training}}$ = .25, $p < .05$). Thus, inducing job seekers with a PGO resulted in more self-regulatory failures as indicated by increased levels of job search procrastination.

Together, these findings suggest that monitoring discrepancies during goal striving in an ego-threatening way increases the likelihood of self-regulatory breakdowns (such as procrastination and failures to act on intentions). In practice, it is therefore advisable to reduce job seekers' PGO toward job search and strengthen their learning goal orientation toward job search. Van Hooft and Noordzij (2009; see also Noordzij, Van Hooft, Van Mierlo, Van Dam, & Born, 2013) developed a training on learning goal orientation in job search, during which job seekers learned to frame their job search as a learning situation. Specifically, trainees were instructed to set specific, attainable, and moderately difficult learning goals for their job search and were encouraged to identify possible obstacles, focus on different strategies, view error and failure as learning opportunities, and look for ways to improve their job search skills. During the training, a climate of development and improvement was

created by giving both positive and negative feedback. Noordzij et al. (2013) found that the training indeed increased people's learning goal orientation toward job search. Importantly, using field experimental designs among samples of unemployed job seekers, both Van Hooft and Noordzij (2009) and Noordzij et al. (2013) found that the learning goal orientation training increased reemployment probabilities.

Apart from goal orientation, future research should examine the role of other psychological constructs that relate to monitoring discrepancies in a nonjudgmental and accepting way (e.g., self-compassion, mindfulness) in improving self-regulation during job seeking. Also, future research should investigate the role of monitoring during the job search process more directly, outlining the effects of different types of monitoring on task-related versus ego-related attention and self-regulation of job search activities.

Operating function. Regarding the operating function, self-regulation can fail because the stimulus that activates the hot system is too strong to override (*stimulus strength*) or because the detected discrepancy between the current and desired state is too large (*discrepancy size*). In such cases, the self-control demands that are put on the operating system are too large to overcome. Independent of the stimulus strength or discrepancy size, self-regulation can fail because people lack the ability, temporary strength, or motivation to implement the behaviors needed to reduce the discrepancy between their current and desired state. That is, people vary in their levels of self-control ability, with some having overall higher levels of *trait self-control* than others (e.g., De Boer et al., 2011; Tangney, Baumeister, & Boone, 2004), allowing for better initiating or inhibiting behavior to reduce the detecting discrepancies. Also in the context of job search, individual differences in self-regulatory traits and states have been shown to be important (Baay, De Ridder, Eccles, Van der Lippe, & Van Aken, 2014; Song, Wanberg, Niu, & Xie, 2006; Van Hooft et al., 2005; Wanberg, Zhu, Kanfer, & Zhang, 2012). For example, in a study among unemployed job seekers in China, Song et al. (2006) found that job seekers with higher levels of action control had a higher job search intention–behavior consistency than job seekers with lower levels of action control.

Furthermore, according to the limited resource model of self-regulation, the exertion of self-control relies on some limited resource, which becomes depleted after use, leading to a temporary *state of ego depletion* that impairs subsequent self-control (Baumeister et al., 2007; Muraven & Baumeister, 2000). Alternatively, according to the mechanistic process model of ego depletion (Inzlicht & Schmeichel, 2012), engaging in self-control efforts is posed to temporarily shift motivation and attention toward immediate gratification, leading to *reduced motivation* for subsequent self-regulation. Several strategies have been documented in the self-regulation literature that people may use to support the operating system's functioning. These strategies aim at (a) making self-regulation less needed, (b) making self-regulation easier, or (c) increasing self-regulation strength.

First, self-regulation is less needed when the operating system is less taxed because the initiation of intended goal-directed actions is preprogrammed by *implementation intentions* (Gollwitzer, 1999). Implementation intentions are if–then plans that link a goal-directed action to the occurrence of a certain situation (e.g., "If it's Monday morning 10 a.m., then I will sit down at my computer and write the application letter for job X"). Implementation intentions have been found to facilitate action initiation for a wide variety of behaviors (see Gollwitzer, 1999). In the context of job seeking, Van Hooft et al. (2005) also found support for the value of implementation intentions, showing that people who specifically planned when, where, and how to perform their job search activities reported higher job

search intensity 4 months later. Thus, implementation intentions reduce the demands posed on the operating function because the initiation of planned job search activities is more automated, requiring less conscious control (i.e., less self-regulatory resources).

Self-regulation is also less needed when hot stimuli such as pleasurable activities, habits, impulses, temptations, or cravings that are not beneficial for obtaining one's goals are *physically or mentally avoided*. In their hot-/cool-system framework, Metcalfe and Mischel (1999) further specified this by describing three categories of strategies to control hot stimuli that distract people from their goal striving: (a) avoidance of hot stimuli or avoiding paying attention to hot stimuli, (b) shifting the attention away from the hot stimulus by seeking actual or cognitive distraction, or (c) reconstrual of the meaning of the hot stimulus such that it is less tempting. A practically helpful technique to facilitate the activation of control strategies to shield goal-directed behavior from unwanted influences is the formation of *goal-shielding implementation intentions* (Achtziger, Gollwitzer, & Sheeran, 2008). These refer to if–then statements that specify a mental link between potential factors that inhibit the goal-striving process (e.g., distractions, temptations, unanticipated obstacles, inner disruptive states such as discouragement) in the if component and link it to an instrumental coping response in the then component. Such goal-shielding implementation intentions make self-regulation less needed when disruptions or distractions occur because the needed coping responses are already specified and therefore easily available.

Second, self-regulation can be made easier by *goal maintenance strategies* that serve to keep the goal that one is striving for accessible, active, and valuable. Specific examples of such goal maintenance strategies are to bolster the goal's value and its associated activities by reminding oneself and elaborating on what makes the attainment of the goal (e.g., finding a job) important by reconsidering the personal benefits and providing meaningful rationales (e.g., Inzlicht et al., 2014; Trope & Fishbach, 2000; Van Hooft et al., 2013). Furthermore, self-regulation may be facilitated by imposing additional self-rewards on completion of aversive tasks that are needed in the goal-striving process (i.e., difficult job search activities, job search tasks that one feels uncomfortable about such as networking). Alternatively, rather than making the completion of the job search activities more rewarding, self-regulation becomes easier when the activities themselves are made less aversive and more intrinsically rewarding and interesting. This can be done by applying interest-enhancing strategies, aimed at cognitively or behaviorally transforming an uninteresting but important activity to create a more interesting experience (Sansone & Thoman, 2005). In the context of job search, interest-enhancing strategies have not received much attention yet but may, for example, involve performing job search activities with others, framing the job search activities as learning opportunities, or choosing pleasant surroundings. Importantly, what makes an activity more interesting differs between individuals, depending on personalities, preferences, and values (Sansone & Thoman, 2006).

Alternatively, self-regulation can be made easier by bolstering people's *beliefs in nonlimited willpower*. Job, Dweck, and Walton (2010) proposed that people differ in their implicit beliefs whether self-control or willpower is a limited resource that is easily depleted after using it or whether self-control relies on nonlimited resources and that engaging in a strenuous task can even activate and increase self-control resources. In a series of lab studies, Job et al. (2010) found that when people believe that willpower is nonlimited rather than easily depleted, they are less vulnerable to the ego depletion effect and better able to self-regulate on a second task that poses a demand on people's self-control. Similarly, based on their studies using repeated self-regulation tasks, Converse and DeShon (2009) suggest that instilling a high-exertion climate, which communicates a strong norm regarding the level of effort and persistence expected and rewarded, is likely to induce a process of psychological adaptation toward self-regulation, resulting in improved self-regulation. Subsequent research by Vohs, Baumeister, and Schmeichel (2013) indicates that the beneficial effects of such beliefs in nonlimited willpower may be restricted to situations of mild depletion and are nullified or even reversed in cases of severe depletion. Field research among students in an academic setting, however, seems to indicate that a mindset of nonlimited willpower relates to improved self-regulation over time (e.g., less procrastination, higher grades), especially under conditions of high self-regulatory demands (Job, Walton, Bernecker, & Dweck, 2015). Because job search can be characterized as a situation posing repeatedly high demands on people's self-regulation, instilling a mindset of nonlimited willpower may be beneficial in initiating and maintaining job search

activities over time. Future research, however, is needed to verify this prediction.

Third, although the capacity for self-control has trait-like qualities, with some people having higher self-control skills and capacities than others (De Boer et al., 2011; Tangney et al., 2004), previous research seems to suggests that people may be able to *increase self-control strength* with training (see Baumeister, Gailliot, DeWall, & Oaten, 2006; Muraven, 2010). Specifically, the strength model of self-regulation (Baumeister et al., 2007; Muraven & Baumeister, 2000) suggests that the regular practice of small self-regulatory exercises (e.g., small acts that involve the inhibition of attractive emotions, urges, and thoughts or initiation of unattractive behaviors) can increase self-regulatory strength that generalizes to other tasks that require self-control.

In support of this idea, several experimental studies showed that practicing with self-control acts such as cutting back on sweets, squeezing a handgrip, maintaining one's posture, physical exercise, regular study activities, controlling one's mood, or keeping track of finances for a given time results in increased self-regulation performance in other domains (Baumeister et al., 2006; Muraven, 2010; Muraven, Baumeister, & Tice, 1999; Oaten & Cheng, 2006). Future research is needed to examine whether such self-control training programs are also beneficial for increasing the intensity, quality, and persistence of people's job search behavior.

Summary

The present formulation of the TPJSB emphasizes the importance of incorporating self-regulatory mechanisms in the study of job search. Extending previous self-regulation conceptualizations and models of job search (e.g., Kanfer & Bufton, this volume; Kanfer et al., 2001; Van Hooft et al., 2013; Wanberg et al., 2010), the present chapter describes a variety of constructs that may support self-regulation in the job search process by facilitating the initiation and maintenance of job search behaviors and inhibition of internal or external distractions. Several qualities of goals or intentions formed in the goal establishment system (e.g., specificity, proximity, absence of goal conflicts, autonomous goal types) and self-regulatory skills, beliefs, and capacities related to the goal-striving system (e.g., self-monitoring skills and capacity, non-ego-threatening self-monitoring, trait self-control, implementation intentions, goal-shielding strategies, goal maintenance strategies, nonlimited willpower mindsets, self-control strength) are proposed to positively influence the translation of job search intentions into actual job search behaviors. However, most of the proposed mechanisms are based on the general self-regulation literature, with only limited empirical evidence available regarding job search. Thus, for almost all identified constructs, future research is needed to examine their value in the context of job search.

Nonconscious Self-Regulation

The TPJSB as well as the job search literature in general are grounded in the assumption that job search is a deliberate and rational process toward a conscious employment goal. Previous social psychological research has criticized the assumption of consciousness and intentionality as causal drivers of human behavior, suggesting that most (if not all) behavior is governed largely by automatic and unconscious processes (e.g., Bargh & Chartrand, 1999). Human behavior may be automatically initiated, for example, by mere perceptions of other people's behavior, situational cues or primes, implicit goals or needs, norms, or habits (e.g., Bargh & Chartrand, 1999; Fitzsimons & Bargh, 2004; Shantz & Latham, 2009). More specifically, effective self-regulation can occur, and is even posed to typically occur, without conscious guidance because conscious self-regulation is effortful and depleting (Fitzsimons & Bargh, 2004).

Also in the TPB literature, the notion of automaticity has received extensive attention. Specifically, the TPB has been criticized as an adequate model of human behavior because of its focus on conscious and rational processes (Ajzen, 2011; Ajzen & Fishbein, 2000). Opposing the assumption of the TPB that behavior is solely caused by intentions, in reality behavior is posed to often occur unintentionally and automatically, that is, without a conscious act of will and outside people's conscious awareness.

Ouellette and Wood (1998) theorized that whether behavior is caused by intentions depends on the behavioral context. Specifically, in contexts that encourage habit formation (e.g., routine and frequent behaviors), behavior is triggered by environmental cues, requiring little or no conscious and deliberate control. In these cases, habits rather than intentions determine behavior. In contexts that are complex or changing (e.g., difficult and novel behaviors), behavior is posed to be guided more by conscious processes and deliberate control. In these cases, intentions are driving behavior. Supporting their assumptions, Ouellette and Wood (1998) found in a meta-analysis that

intention was a stronger predictor of behaviors that are performed irregularly in unstable contexts, whereas past behavior (as a proxy for habit strength) is a stronger predictor of behaviors that are performed regularly in stable contexts. Because job search typically is a novel and complex behavior, occurring in an ambiguous and changing environment (Van Hooft, this volume; Van Hooft et al., 2013), this reasoning and findings suggest that conscious processes such as the formation of job search intentions are a more important mechanism in explaining job search behavior than automatic and unconscious processes.

Nevertheless, job search can also be characterized as a highly emotional and often-irrational process, which may undermine the translation of job search intentions into actual job search behavior. Also, routinization of job search activities and habit formation may occur when the job search process prolongs, resulting in the performance of job search behaviors without conscious intention formation. Therefore, theorizing and research in the field of job search should consider the inclusion of irrationality, automaticity, and unconscious processes more explicitly in conceptual models and study designs. This call mimics Krieshok, Black, and McKay's (2009) analysis of the broader career decision-making literature, suggesting that even though both rational and intuitive processes are intertwined in effective judgment and decision-making, the latter has been largely ignored in vocational research.

The importance of incorporating automatic and nonconscious processes also pertains to self-regulation during the job search process. Deliberate or conscious self-regulation is effortful and consumes substantial cognitive and physical resources (Baumeister et al., 2007; Kanfer & Ackerman, 1989), which may lead to temporary ego depletion, hindering subsequent self-regulation (Muraven & Baumeister, 2000), or to reduced motivation for subsequent self-regulation (Inzlicht & Schmeichel, 2012). To maintain the performance of job search behavior over time and persisting until the attainment of the employment goals, people may want to resort to less effortful control strategies.

In this context, Leary, Adams, and Tate (2006) introduced the term *hypoegoic self-regulation*, which refers to intentionally and consciously taking steps that later reduce the need for deliberate executive control over the behaviors that are needed to obtain the goal. Hypoegoic self-regulation strategies may function to either reduce the need for deliberate self-control to initiate goal-directed activities (i.e., start-control; De Boer et al., 2011) or inhibit goal-disruptive thoughts and activities (i.e., stop-control; De Boer et al., 2011).

An example of a hypoegoic self-regulation strategy to support action initiation is a strategy discussed previously, namely, the formation of *implementation intentions* (Gollwitzer, 1999), as these reduce the need for deliberate start-control by automatizing the initiation of intended job search behaviors. Another similar strategy is the creation of *job search habits and routines*, as these reduce the need for conscious intention formation and deliberate start-control by routinization of job search activities. Recent research on health-related, exercise, and study behaviors has indeed demonstrated that people with higher self-control abilities actually use less self-control but make better progress toward their goals because they rely on beneficial habits (Galla & Duckworth, 2015). Furthermore, the use of *subconscious goal primes* (i.e., the subconscious activation of an individual's goals by external cues) may facilitate action initiation without conscious self-regulation because these direct attention toward goal-relevant items, supporting the automated initiation of goal-directed behavior. Similar to research by Shantz and Latham (2009) demonstrating the effects of goal primes on achievement motivation and work performance, job search studies should seek to examine whether the use of subconscious goal primes (e.g., pictures) could improve the performance of job search activities.

An example of a hypoegoic self-regulation strategy to support inhibition of goal-disruptive thoughts and activities is a strategy discussed previously, namely, the formation of *goal-shielding implementation intentions* (Achtziger et al., 2008), as these reduce the need for deliberate stop-control by automatizing the activation of goal-shielding responses when temptations and distractions occur. Another example is the practice of *mindfulness*. Mindfulness refers to a mode of awareness, alertness, and nonjudgmental acceptance that is evoked by the self-regulation of attention toward the present moment and current experience (Bishop et al., 2004). Attention has a limited capacity, and mindfulness is a method to focus attention on the present moment and behavior, facilitating inhibition of goal disruptions. That is, by acknowledging thoughts and feelings as they arise, just observing and accepting them rather than seeing them as distractions, and subsequently directing attention back to the present behavior elaborative processing is prevented. This reduces abstract, critical, and evaluative self-thoughts and heightens the acceptance of the present reality, freeing attentional resources for task engagement. Such present-focused awareness is supposed to result in increased behavioral control by nonconscious and automatic processes, reducing the cognitive load of conscious self-control (Leary et al., 2006).

Consistent with this rationale, Chatzisarantis and Hagger (2007) argue that mindfulness should facilitate a successful translation of intentions into behavior because it strengthens the ability to control habits, thoughts, and emotions that run counter to the ongoing behavioral intention. In two studies, Chatzisarantis and Hagger (2007) indeed found that mindfulness moderated the intention–behavior relationship in the context of engaging in physical activities and reduced the negative effects of counterintentional habits (i.e., binge drinking) on engagement in physical activities. Because job search is a behavior that people often have to perform in a reality that they do not like (e.g., being unemployed, having received a rejection), with plenty of counterintentional thoughts, emotions, and habits (e.g., self-doubts, discouragement, procrastination), mindfulness training seems a promising avenue to support people in their job search. However, future research is needed to empirically test these assumptions.

Conclusion

The present chapter extended the TPJSB described in the previous chapter (Van Hooft, this volume) by including a selection of (potential) moderators of the job search intention–job search behavior relationship. Scientific research has corroborated common observations in practice that intentions are not always acted on. Regarding job search, even though job search intentions and job search behavior are strongly correlated, a reanalysis of previous data revealed that many people with job search intentions do not act on these as planned. To successfully translate job search intentions into actual job search behavior, people have to use self-regulation to initiate goal-directed behaviors (i.e., start-control) and inhibit non-goal-directed distractions (i.e., stop-control). Conscious self-regulation, however, is difficult.

To ease self-regulation and facilitate the translation of job search intentions into job search behavior, job search goals and job search intentions should be specific rather than vague, proximal and attainable rather than distal, aligned rather than in conflict with other goals, and based on autonomous rather than controlled motives. Furthermore, several self-regulatory skills, beliefs, and strategies may moderate the relationship between job search intentions and job search behavior by reducing the need for self-regulation, by facilitating conscious self-regulation, or by supporting nonconscious self-regulation. Examples of these are self-monitoring skills and type (e.g., learning goal orientation), trait and momentary self-control capacity, nonlimited willpower beliefs, implementation intentions, goal-shielding and goal maintenance strategies, and hypoegoic self-regulation strategies (e.g., routinization, mindfulness). While the present chapter has offered theoretical rationales for these moderators, empirical support in the context of job search appears to be largely lacking. Self-regulation processes related to the translation of job search intentions into job search behavior therefore seem a fruitful avenue for future research.

Practical tips

The following are some general tips for job seekers and employment counselors that may facilitate the initiation and continued performance of job search behaviors over time:

• Translate the general goal of obtaining a (new) job into clear and specific (sub)goals to guide the job search.

• When the ultimate goal is relatively difficult to reach (i.e., a dream goal), it is important to think of a pathway to reach that dream goal. For employment counselors, it is important to realize that rather than dismissing the dream goal as unreachable, it is better and more motivating to help job seekers set smaller goals that are easier to obtain (but still are in the direction of the dream goal). This way, job seekers can self-regulate more easily, experience progress, and build self-efficacy.

• Support people's need for autonomy in setting goals and formulating job search intentions. Rather than coercing, controlling, or pressuring people, it is better to support people with identifying and formulating self-aligned goals and intentions and sustain their self-determination. This enhances people's motivation quality and facilitates their self-regulation.

• Frame and monitor job search in a non-ego-threatening way. Rather than evoking competition and emphasizing outcomes, it is better to approach job search as a learning situation. Employment counselors should support job

seekers to set specific, attainable, and moderately difficult learning goals for their job search and encourage them to identify possible obstacles, focus on different strategies, view error and failure as learning opportunities, and look for ways to improve their job search skills.

• Formulate specific if–then plans for important job search activities that you find difficult to start with (e.g., "If it's Monday morning 10 a.m., then I will sit down at my computer and write the application letter for job X").

• Such if–then plans can also be formulated for known obstacles or disruptions. That is, make specific plans for coping strategies that are effective to deal with the disruptions (e.g., "If I feel that I want to stop job seeking and do something more fun, I will think of why the search for a job is important and beneficial for me," or "If I feel discouraged when searching for vacancies, I will tell myself that discouragement is OK and then refocus on the search for vacancies").

• Realize that willpower is a plentiful resource and that engaging in strenuous job search activities strengthens willpower and may increase self-control resources.

• Practice with small self-control acts, such as cutting back on sweets, maintaining a straight posture, engaging in physical exercise, controlling mood and emotions, or keeping track of finances. Such practice may result in increased willpower, facilitating the performance and maintenance of job search activities.

• Form job search habits to make your job search tasks more routine. Routinization of job search activities reduces the need for conscious control and therefore facilitates the performance of job search activities over time.

• Take a mindfulness training class to facilitate the nonjudgmental acceptance of the present reality and improve the handling of disruptive thoughts and emotions during job search.

Acknowledgment

This work was supported by the FMG-UvA Research Priority Grant on Affect Regulation.

References

Achtziger, A., Gollwitzer, P. M., & Sheeran, P. (2008). Implementation intentions and shielding goal striving from unwanted thoughts and feelings. *Personality and Social Psychology Bulletin, 34*, 381–393.

Ajzen, I. (1991). The theory of planned behavior. *Organizational Behavior and Human Decision Processes, 50*, 179–211.

Ajzen, I. (2011). The theory of planned behavior: Reactions and reflections. *Psychology and Health, 26*, 1113–1127.

Ajzen, I., & Fishbein, M. (2000). Attitudes and the attitude-behavior relation: Reasoned and automatic processes. *European Review of Social Psychology, 11*, 1–33.

Austin, J. T., & Vancouver, J. B. (1996). Goal constructs in psychology: Structure, process, and content. *Psychological Bulletin, 120*, 338–375.

Baay, P. E., De Ridder, D. T. D., Eccles, J. S., Van der Lippe, T., & Van Aken, M. A. G. (2014). Self-control trumps work motivation in predicting job search behavior. *Journal of Vocational Behavior, 85*, 443–451.

Bandura, A. (1991). Social cognitive theory of self-regulation. *Organizational Behavior and Human Decision Processes, 50*, 248–287.

Bargh, J. A., & Chartrand, T. L. (1999). The unbearable automaticity of being. *American Psychologist, 54*, 462–479.

Baumeister, R. F., Gailliot, M., DeWall, C. N., & Oaten, M. (2006). Self-regulation and personality: How interventions increase regulatory success, and how depletion moderates the effects of traits on behavior. *Journal of Personality, 74*, 1773–1801.

Baumeister, R. F., & Heatherton, T. F. (1996). Self-regulation failure: An overview. *Psychological Inquiry, 7*, 1–15.

Baumeister, R. F., Vohs, K. D., & Tice, D. M. (2007). The strength model of self-control. *Current Directions in Psychological Science, 16*, 351–355.

Bishop, S. R., Lau, M., Shapiro, S., Carlson, L., Anderson, N. D., Carmody, J., . . . Devins, G. (2004). Mindfulness: A proposed operational definition. *Clinical Psychology: Science and Practice, 11*, 230–241.

Button, S. B., Mathieu, J. E., & Zajac, D. M. (1996). Goal orientation in organizational research: A conceptual and empirical foundation. *Organizational Behavior and Human Decision Processes, 67*, 26–48.

Carver, C. S., & Scheier, M. F. (1982). Control theory: A useful conceptual framework for personality-social, clinical, and health psychology. *Psychological Bulletin, 92*, 111–135.

Chatzisarantis, N. L. D., & Hagger, M. S. (2007). Mindfulness and the intention-behavior relationship within the theory of planned behavior. *Personality and Social Psychology Bulletin, 33*, 663–676.

Chua, R. Y.-J., & Iyengar, S. S. (2006). Empowerment through choice? A critical analysis of the effects of choice in organizations. *Research in Organizational Behavior, 27*, 41–79.

Converse, P. D., & DeShon, R. P. (2009). A tale of two tasks: Reversing the self-regulatory resource depletion effect. *Journal of Applied Psychology, 94*, 1318–1324.

De Boer, B. J., Van Hooft, E. A. J., & Bakker, A. B. (2011). Stop and start control: A distinction within self-control. *European Journal of Personality, 25*, 349–369.

De Boer, B. J., Van Hooft, E. A. J., & Bakker, A. B. (2015). Self-control at work: Its relationship with contextual performance. *Journal of Managerial Psychology, 30*, 406–421.

Dimitrova, N., Van Dyck, C., Van Hooft, E. A. J., & Groenewegen, P. (2015). Don't fuss, focus: The mediating effect of on-task thoughts on the relationship between error approach instructions and task performance. *Applied Psychology: An International Review, 64*, 599–624.

Dweck, C. S. (1986). Motivational processes affecting learning. *American Psychologist, 41*, 1040–1048.

Fitzsimons, G. M., & Bargh, J. A. (2004). Automatic self-regulation. In R. F. Baumeister & K. D. Vohs (Eds.),

Handbook of self-regulation: Research, theory, and applications (pp. 151–170). New York: Guilford Press.

Galla, B. M., & Duckworth, A. L. (2015). More than resisting temptation: Beneficial habits mediate the relationship between self-control and positive life outcomes. *Journal of Personality and Social Psychology, 109*, 508–525.

Gollwitzer, P. M. (1990). Action phases and mind-sets. In E. T. Higgins & R. M. Sorrentino (Eds.), *Handbook of motivation and cognition: Foundations of social behavior* (Vol. 2, pp. 53–92). New York: Guilford.

Gollwitzer, P. M. (1999). Implementation intentions: Strong effects of simple plans. *American Psychologist, 54*, 493–503.

Gowan, M. A., Riordan, C. M., & Gatewood, R. D. (1999). Test of a model of coping with involuntary job loss following a company closing. *Journal of Applied Psychology, 84*, 75–86.

Inzlicht, M., Legault, L., & Teper, R. (2014). Exploring the mechanisms of self-control improvement. *Current Directions in Psychological Science, 23*, 302–307.

Inzlicht, M., & Schmeichel, B. J. (2012). What is ego depletion? Toward a mechanistic revision of the resource model of self-control. *Perspectives on Psychological Science, 7*, 450–463.

Jaidi, Y., Van Hooft, E. A. J., & Arends, L. R. (2011). Recruiting highly educated graduates: A study on the relationship between recruitment information sources, the theory of planned behavior, and actual job pursuit. *Human Performance, 24*, 135–157.

Job, V., Dweck, C. S., & Walton, G. M. (2010). Ego depletion—Is it all in your head? Implicit theories about willpower affect self-regulation. *Psychological Science, 21*, 1686–1693.

Job, V., Walton, G. M., Bernecker, K., & Dweck, C. S. (2015). Implicit theories about willpower predict self-regulation and grades in everyday life. *Journal of Personality and Social Psychology, 108*, 637–647.

Kanfer, R. (1990). Motivation theory and industrial/organizational psychology. In M. D. Dunnette & L. M. Hough (Eds.), *Handbook of industrial and organizational psychology* (pp. 75–170). Palo Alto, CA: Consulting Psychologists Press.

Kanfer, R., & Ackerman, P. L. (1989). Motivation and cognitive abilities: An integrative/aptitude-treatment interaction approach to skill acquisition. *Journal of Applied Psychology, 74*, 657–690.

Kanfer, R., Wanberg, C. R., & Kantrowitz, T. M. (2001). Job search and employment: A personality-motivational analysis and meta-analytic review. *Journal of Applied Psychology, 86*, 837–855.

Karoly, P. (1993). Mechanisms of self-regulation: A systems view. *Annual Review of Psychology, 44*, 23–52.

Keith, N., & Frese, M. (2005). Self-regulation in error management training: Emotion control and metacognition as mediators of performance effects. *Journal of Applied Psychology, 90*, 677–691.

Kluger, A. N., & DeNisi, A. (1996). The effects of feedback interventions on performance: A historical review, a meta-analysis, and a preliminary feedback intervention theory. *Psychological Bulletin, 119*, 254–284.

Krieshok, T. S., Black, M. D., & McKay, R. A. (2009). Career decision making: The limits of rationality and the abundance of non-conscious processes. *Journal of Vocational Behavior, 75*, 275–290.

Leary, M. R., Adams, C. E., & Tate, E. B. (2006). Hypo-egoic self-regulation: Exercising self-control by diminishing the influence of the self. *Journal of Personality, 74*, 1803–1831.

Locke, E. A., & Latham, G. P. (2002). Building a practically useful theory of goal setting and task motivation. *American Psychologist, 57*, 705–717.

Metcalfe, J., & Mischel, W. (1999). A hot/cool-system analysis of delay of gratification: Dynamics of willpower. *Psychological Review, 106*, 3–19.

Mitchell, T. R., Harman, W. S., Lee, T. W., & Lee, D.-Y. (2008). Self-regulation and multiple deadline goals. In R. Kanfer, G. Chen, & R. D. Pritchard (Eds.), *Work motivation: Past, present, and future* (pp. 197–231). New York: Routledge.

Moller, A. C., Deci, E. L., & Ryan, R. M. (2006). Choice and ego-depletion: The moderating role of autonomy. *Personality and Social Psychology Bulletin, 32*, 1024–1036.

Muraven, M. (2008). Autonomous self-control is less depleting. *Journal of Research in Personality, 42*, 763–770.

Muraven, M. (2010). Building self-control strength: Practicing self-control leads to improved self-control performance. *Journal of Experimental Social Psychology, 46*, 465–468.

Muraven, M., & Baumeister, R. F. (2000). Self-regulation and depletion of limited resources: Does self-control resemble a muscle? *Psychological Bulletin, 126*, 247–259.

Muraven, M., Baumeister, R. F., & Tice, D. M. (1999). Longitudinal improvement of self-regulation through practice: Building self-control strength through repeated exercise. *The Journal of Social Psychology, 139*, 446–457.

Noordzij, G., Van Hooft, E. A. J., Van Mierlo, H., Van Dam, A., & Born, M.Ph. (2013). The effects of a learning-goal orientation training on self-regulation: A field experiment among unemployed job seekers. *Personnel Psychology, 66*, 723–755.

Oaten, M., & Cheng, K. (2006). Improved self-control: The benefits of a regular program of academic study. *Basic and Applied Social Psychology, 28*, 1–16.

Ouellette, J. A., & Wood, W. (1998). Habit and intention in everyday life: The multiple processes by which past behavior predicts future behavior. *Psychological Bulletin, 124*, 54–74.

Phillips, J. M., Hollenbeck, J. R., & Ilgen, D. R. (1996). Prevalence and prediction of positive discrepancy creation: Examining a discrepancy between two self-regulation theories. *Journal of Applied Psychology, 81*, 498–511.

Ryan, R. M., & Deci, E. L. (2000). Self-determination theory and the facilitation of intrinsic motivation, social development, and well-being. *American Psychologist, 55*, 68–78.

Sansone, C., & Thoman, D. B. (2005). Interest as the missing motivator in self-regulation. *European Psychologist, 10*, 175–186.

Sansone, C., & Thoman, D. B. (2006). Maintaining activity engagement: Individual differences in the process of self-regulating motivation. *Journal of Personality, 74*, 1697–1720.

Schmidt, A. M., & DeShon, R. P. (2007). What to do? The effects of discrepancies, incentives, and time on dynamic goal prioritization. *Journal of Applied Psychology, 92*, 928–941.

Schmidt, A. M., Dolis, C. M., & Tolli, A. P. (2009). A matter of time: Individual differences, contextual dynamics, and goal progress effects on multiple-goal self-regulation. *Journal of Applied Psychology, 94*, 692–709.

Shantz, A., & Latham, G. P. (2009). An exploratory field experiment of the effect of subconscious and conscious goals on employee performance. *Organizational Behavior and Human Decision Processes, 109*, 9–17.

Sheeran, P. (2002). Intention-behavior relations: A conceptual and empirical review. In W. Stroebe & M. Hewstone (Eds.), *European review of social psychology* (Vol. 12, pp. 1–36). Chichester, UK: Wiley.

Sheeran, P., Norman, P., & Orbell, S. (1999). Evidence that intentions based on attitudes better predict behaviour than intentions based on subjective norms. *European Journal of Social Psychology, 29*, 403–406.

Song, Z., Wanberg, C., Niu, X., & Xie, Y. (2006). Action–state orientation and the theory of planned behavior: A study of job search in China. *Journal of Vocational Behavior, 68*, 490–503.

Strack, F., & Deutsch, R. (2004). Reflective and impulsive determinants of social behavior. *Personality and Social Psychology Review, 8*, 220–247.

Sutton, S. (1998). Predicting and explaining intentions and behavior: How well are we doing? *Journal of Applied Social Psychology, 28*, 1317–1338.

Tangney, J. P., Baumeister, R. F., & Boone, A. L. (2004). High self-control predicts good adjustment, less pathology, better grades, and interpersonal success. *Journal of Personality, 72*, 271–324.

Tice, D. M., Baumeister, R. F., Shmueli, D., & Muraven, M. (2007). Restoring the self: Positive affect helps improve self-regulation following ego depletion. *Journal of Experimental Social Psychology, 43*, 379–384.

Trope, Y., & Fishbach, A. (2000). Counteractive self-control in overcoming temptation. *Journal of Personality and Social Psychology, 79*, 493–506.

Turban, D. B., Stevens, C. K., & Lee, F. K. (2009). Effects of conscientiousness and extraversion on new labor market entrants' job search: The mediating role of metacognitive activities and positive emotions. *Personnel Psychology, 62*, 553–573.

Vallerand, R. J. (1997). Toward a hierarchical model of intrinsic and extrinsic motivation. In M. P. Zanna (Ed.), *Advances in experimental social psychology* (Vol. 29, pp. 271–360). San Diego, CA: Academic Press.

Van Dyck, C., van Hooft, E. A. J., De Gilder, D., & Liesveld, L. C. (2010). Proximal antecedents and correlates of adopted error approach: A self-regulatory perspective. *The Journal of Social Psychology, 150*, 428–451.

Van Hooft, E. A. J. (2006, May). Intentions that do not result in behavior: The role of goal commitment and goal orientation. In S. Y. Wu & D. B. Turban (Chairs), *Intentions, goal orientations, and social networks in the job search*. Symposium conducted at the 21st annual meeting of the Society of Industrial and Organizational Psychology, Dallas, TX.

Van Hooft, E. A. J., Born, M. P., Taris, T. W., & Van der Flier, H. (2004). Job search and the theory of planned behavior: Minority–majority group differences in the Netherlands. *Journal of Vocational Behavior, 65*, 366–390.

Van Hooft, E. A. J., Born, M. P., Taris, T. W., Van der Flier, H., & Blonk, R. W. B. (2004). Predictors of job search behavior among employed and unemployed people. *Personnel Psychology, 57*, 25–59.

Van Hooft, E. A. J., Born, M. P., Taris, T. W., Van der Flier, H., & Blonk, R. W. B. (2005). Bridging the gap between intentions and behavior: Implementation intentions, action control, and procrastination. *Journal of Vocational Behavior, 66*, 238–256.

Van Hooft, E. A. J., & De Jong, M. (2009). Predicting job seeking for temporary employment using the theory of planned behaviour: The moderating role of individualism and collectivism. *Journal of Occupational and Organizational Psychology, 82*, 295–316.

Van Hooft, E. A. J., & Noordzij, G. (2009). The effects of goal orientation on job search and reemployment: A field experiment among unemployed job seekers. *Journal of Applied Psychology, 94,* 1581–1590.

Van Hooft, E. A. J., Wanberg, C. R., & Van Hoye, G. (2013). Moving beyond job search quantity: Towards a conceptualization and self-regulatory framework of job search quality. *Organizational Psychology Review, 3,* 3–40.

Vohs, K. D., Baumeister, R. F., & Schmeichel, B. J. (2013). Erratum to "Motivation, Personal Beliefs, and Limited Resources All Contribute to Self-Control" [*Journal of Experimental Social Psychology, 48* (2012) 943–947]. *Journal of Experimental Social Psychology, 49,* 184–188.

Wanberg, C. R., Basbug, G., Van Hooft, E. A. J., & Samtani, A. (2012). Navigating the black hole: Explicating layers of job search context and adaptational responses. *Personnel Psychology, 65,* 887–926.

Wanberg, C. R., Zhu, J., Kanfer, R., & Zhang, Z. (2012). After the pink slip: Applying dynamic motivation frameworks to the job search experience. *Academy of Management Journal, 55,* 261–284.

Wanberg, C. R., Zhu, J., & Van Hooft, E. A. J. (2010). The job-search grind: Perceived progress, self-reactions, and self-regulation of search effort. *Academy of Management Journal, 53,* 788–807.

Zimmerman, B. J. (2000). Attaining self-regulation: A social cognitive perspective. In M. Boekaerts, P. R. Pintrich, & M. Zeidner (Eds.), *Handbook of self-regulation* (pp. 13–39). San Diego, CA: Academic Press.

13 New Economy Careers Demand Adaptive Mental Models and Resources

Annelies E. M. van Vianen *and* Ute-Christine Klehe

Abstract

Volatile economic and labor market circumstances have significant effects on the development of people's work careers; thus recent literature on careers has started to take into account the reality of increasingly unpredictable, nonlinear, and inherently uncertain careers. In this chapter we argue that careers in the new economy require, first, that people learn to cope with identity threats; second, that they need to change their mental models of careers; and third, that they must develop the resources to adapt to more frequent and unpredictable career transitions. Specifically we address three themes that we consider at the core of adaptation to nonlinear careers: people's work-related identities, their conceptualization of career success, and their adaptability resources. We build a model called "identity and coping during career transitions" (ICCT), which integrates theories on identity, careers, and adaptability and could serve as an agenda for future research. Finally, we provide some guidelines for practitioners and organizations.

Key Words: career, career interruption, work-related identities, adaptability resources

Introduction

Technological progress, competitive forces, and an ever-changing economic climate are reducing the prevalence of lifelong employment and enhancing the call for workers' adaptability and lifelong learning in order to remain attractive within the labor market (Fugate, Kinicki, & Ashforth, 2004). Volatile economic and labor market circumstances have significant effects on the development of people's work careers.

The concept of career is generally defined as "the evolving sequence of a person's work experiences over time" (Arthur, Hall, & Lawrence, 1989, p. 8). Super (1980) conceived this sequence of experiences as being more or less linear, with fixed career stages through which career paths develop. Each career stage represents a major goal (growth, exploration, establishment, maintenance, and disengagement) and is largely bound to someone's age. For example, the stage of exploration is expected between ages 14 to 24 and the stage of

establishment concerns the period between 25 and 44. Around the age of 45, people are thought to arrive at the goal of career consolidation, the typical midlife maintenance stage, involving the preservation of an occupational role.

Social cognitive career theory (Lent, Brown, & Hackett, 1994, 2000) also approaches careers as a sequence of experiences, but these experiences are not necessarily captured in stages. Both experience and environment shape people's occupational interests and choices. Through learning experiences, people learn to know the outcomes of their choices and get insight into their competencies. These outcome and self-efficacy expectations affect the career goals that people select. Hence social cognitive career theory describes careers as a sequence of expectancy-driven choices through which people develop their self-concepts. Although not explicitly argued, this theory also assumes that one's self-concept in terms of career grows toward stabilization and thus tends to become more predictable over time.

In contrast, protean career theory (Hall, 2002) and the "life design" career approach (Savickas, Nota, Rossier, Dauwalder, Duarte, Guichard, et al., 2009) no longer hold to the idea of career predictability. Instead, these theories see careers as interacting with changing economic and social conditions, which are by definition unpredictable. Here, careers no longer follow a specific path but are characterized by volatile movements as people adapt to shifting environments and to dynamic personal needs and values. Because collective career stages are no longer functional in a changing labor market, a life design perspective views careers as individual and flexible scripts in which work and nonwork activities are interwoven (Savickas et al., 2009). People's lives will unfold as sequences of career minicycles, each involving explorative and developmental activities that may or may not build on earlier work and nonwork experiences.

This short overview of mainstream career theories (see also Van Vianen, De Pater, & Preenen, 2009) exemplifies a major shift in career models in the literature: from linear prescriptions to dynamic processes (Savickas et al., 2009). This shift in thinking about careers primarily emanated from changing economic and labor market conditions and has not resulted from advancements in scientific knowledge about the psychological processes that are associated with careers. Rather, current career literatures seem to argue that people need to adapt their own career conceptualizations and behaviors to the new prevailing career realities.

Yet many people still reflect on their careers in a more traditional way, that is, with a focus on linearity, success, and security. It is of no surprise that they do so, since these standard mental models have been stressed in discourses about employment and are based on the idea that work should fulfill innate human needs such as security and predictability. Indeed, seminal self-regulation theories (e.g., Vohs & Baumeister, 2004) elucidate that people have an innate drive to protect and recover their equilibrium, preferably with a minimum of effort and costs. On the other hand, it has also been argued that despite their security needs, humans are remarkably capable of adapting to changing environments (e.g., Wang, Novemsky, & Dhar, 2009) and are even inclined to create change by seeking challenges in their work and lives (Bandura, 1991; Preenen, De Pater, Van Vianen, & Keijzer, 2011).

Since employment has traditionally been associated with security rather than challenge, people may need guidance to view their careers in terms of unpredictability, nonlinear progress, and uncertainty (see also Bloch, 2005; Pryor & Bright, 2007), so that they may develop a different perspective toward both job insecurity and job loss. Whereas job insecurity and job loss are traditionally treated as major life events that threaten to disrupt one's progress and signals of career failure (e.g., Feldman, Leana, & Bolino, 2002; Leana, Feldman, & Tan, 1998), people today may come to view job insecurity and job loss as normal events in the course of their careers— and as not necessarily welcome but possibly enriching opportunities to reorient themselves (e.g., Feldman & Leana, 2000; Zikic & Klehe, 2006; Zikic & Richardson, 2006).

In this chapter we propose a theoretical model in which career transitions are conceptualized in terms of the possible loss of work-related identity. Consequently coping responses to career transitions are seen as responses to identity threats. First we argue that nonlinear careers in the new economy require the ability to make identity shifts. Second, we contend that responses to possible identity threats depend on the type and strength of work-related identities and on the career models that people bear in mind, such as their definition of career success. Finally, we reason that more frequent and unpredictable career transitions essentially require the development of adaptability resources.

Work-Related Identities

Individuals have multiple identities that differ in importance but together constitute their core sense of self. That is, they have a personal identity, which is the unique set of characteristics that differentiate them from others, and multiple social identities, which are categorizations of the self into different social groups based on gender, race, occupational roles, work team, and so forth (e.g., Kreiner, Hollensbe, & Sheep, 2006).

In addition, employees can have different orientations toward work. They may, for example, view work as a means to earn money to meet their needs, as a way to advance and receive prestige, or as an enjoyable activity through which they can contribute to society (e.g., Berg, Grant, & Johnson, 2010). These work orientations influence how an employee's personal identity is formed, how employees identify with what they are doing, and how they identify themselves with specific work-related social groups.

The career literature distinguishes several work-related identity concepts, such as organizational and professional (or occupational) identities.

Employees' work-related identities are important because they affect all sorts of work behaviors (e.g., Walsh & Gordon, 2008) and they may also affect employees' responses to work-related events such as job insecurity and job loss. Organizational identity regards an individual's identification with the organization, which is based on feelings of similarity between his or her self-concept and his or her perceptions of the organization's identity. The more similarity individuals perceive, the more strongly they will identify with the organization. Furthermore, since individuals preferably associate themselves with high-status groups (e.g., Walsh & Gordon, 2008), organizational identification is also strengthened if individuals perceive that the organization provides them with self-enhancing status. Employees with a strong organizational identity are embedded in their organization: they perceive a fit with the organization, they have strong ties with other people and activities in the organization, and they want to stay (Ng & Feldman, 2009). On the whole, these employees define themselves by "where they work" (Pratt, Rockmann, & Kaufmann, 2006, p. 236).

Professional identity concerns the extent to which employees define themselves in terms of their profession and professional roles (Ibarra, 1999). Employees with a strong professional identity view their profession as critical to their goals and core sense of self (e.g., Randel & Jaussi, 2003). The organization in which they perform the profession is generally less important. For example, a researcher may see herself more as a scientist than as an employee at the university where she works. The development of a strong professional identity may originate in several factors (Brooks, Riemenschneider, Hardgrave, & O'Leary-Kelly, 2011). First, individuals may have a specific desire to define themselves by their membership in a profession (Brooks et al., 2011). Second and relatedly, individuals may experience positive public perceptions of their profession; identification is thus self-enhancing. Third, individuals may perceive similarity with and have ties to others in the profession and professional associations. Hence employees with a strong professional identity not only define themselves by "what they do" (Pratt et al., 2006, p. 236), but also by "what they are" professionally.

A third work-related identity that is not necessarily bound to specific professions but is associated with professional roles and activities is "calling," defined as "a consuming, meaningful passion people experience toward a domain" (Dobrow & Tosti-Kharas, 2011, p. 1005). Calling reflects identification with a role or mission (e.g., helping people), which can be fulfilled within or without an organization or profession. Therefore calling domains can encompass more than just work; for example, they may include volunteer and family activities. Individuals with a calling orientation toward work "expect work to be both purposeful and inherently meaningful" (Carcador, Dane, & Pratt, 2011, p. 367), and they view their activities as inseparable from their lives (Wrzesniewski, McCauley, Rozin, & Schwartz, 1997). They define themselves by their passion.

As stated above, individuals differ in the importance they attribute to different identities. That is, an individual may have a strong organizational identity but a weak professional identity and no specific calling. To date, little is known about how work-related identities may interfere with individuals' responses to job insecurity and job loss. It seems plausible to assume that strong work-related identities will make individuals more vulnerable to work-related stressors such as job insecurity and job loss. Job loss, for example, is a direct threat to these identities because it implies the loss of important parts of an individual's core self (e.g., Berger, 2006). It is conceivable that such an identity threat will evoke negative cognitive and emotional responses and that the strength of these responses may differ for different identity threats. We address identity threats and their possible effects in the following section.

Work-Related Identity Threats

Job insecurity and job loss imply the possible—at least temporary loss of one's organizational and/or professional identities and perhaps a threat to the fulfillment of one's work-related calling. The more self-defining a person's organization, profession, or work activity is, the greater the psychological distress that may be experienced during job loss. Employees with a strong organizational identity are no longer members of company X or Y. Similarly, employees with a strong professional identity may not only lose their work but also their self-definition as, for example, a doctor, a researcher, or a construction worker, and employees with a calling orientation toward work activities lose their main purpose in life if this calling cannot be passed on to other domains. As a consequence, employees with strong work-related identities may suffer severely when faced with possible unemployment.

In addition, the type of work-related identity may affect people's responses differently. Job insecurity and job loss may be more difficult for individuals with strong organizational identities than for those with strong professional identities because losing one's job does not necessarily mean the loss of one's professional identity, whereas it definitely means the loss of one's organizational identity. Some empirical evidence for such reasoning may be research findings showing that job loss had less effect on mental health among more highly educated than less educated people (see Paul, Hassel, & Moser, this volume).

Generally, unemployment has often proved to be among the most stressful, depressing, and literally sickening experiences that people can encounter (McKee-Ryan, Song, Wanberg, & Kinicki, 2005; Paul et al., this volume; Paul & Moser, 2009; Price, Choi, & Vinokur, 2002), leading—just like other economic stressors, like job insecurity and underemployment—to impaired mental health, depressive symptoms, learned helplessness, anxiety, and decreased positive affect and self-esteem (Dooley, Prause, & Ham-Rowbottom, 2000; Sverke, Hellgren, & Näswall, 2002). Especially severe negative responses during unemployment tend to go together with inactivity, limited job-search activities, and thus lower chances of finding reemployment (e.g., Kanfer, Wanberg, & Kantrowitz, 2001; Song, Sun, & Li, this volume). Individuals with strong work-related identities may be particularly vulnerable to these harmful consequences of unemployment.

Alternatively, it could be argued that strong work-related identities—professional identity and calling in particular—may facilitate rather than hinder recovery from job loss and thus may encourage rather than discourage job-search activities. In order to preserve their identity, these unemployed people may be strongly motivated to find reemployment in a comparable job domain. Moreover, job seekers with a strong professional identity may concentrate their search efforts on a small number of relevant jobs that fit with their identity. Indeed, prior research has shown that familiarity with a specific field of work is an important condition for a successful job change (e.g., Ibarra, 2003) and that a clear vision of what type of job to aspire to upon reemployment is positively related to finding a job (Koen, Klehe, Van Vianen, Zikic, & Nauta, 2010).

To date, there is only one study that we know of that directly addressed employees' responses to job insecurity and job loss from an identity perspective. Tosti-Kharas (2012) reasoned that remaining identified with a former organization or profession may help job seekers to preserve a sense of self-enhancement, belongingness, and prestige. The resulting self-esteem and self-efficacy, in turn, both contribute to psychological well-being (general positive affect and emotional control and low depression and anxiety) during unemployment (McKee-Ryan et al., 2005) and that these may support the job search (Kanfer et al., 2001).

Thosti-Kharas's study involved two small samples of highly educated individuals. The first sample concerned individuals who were already unemployed and they, thus, reported their identification with their former organization. The group in the second sample became unemployed over time and reported their identification with the organization while still being employed (time 1) and during unemployment (time 2). Positive relationships were found between organizational identification and well-being, but only when both these variables were measured simultaneously during unemployment. Organizational identification before job loss (only measured in the second sample of employed individuals at time 1) was unrelated to later well-being (during unemployment at time 2). Apparently, for some of these individuals, organizational identification had changed in response to their unemployment.

Given these preliminary and weak findings and the lack of other studies that examined job loss from an identity perspective, we may have to look at adjacent lines of research to learn more about how people with different work-related identities may respond to these threatening events—namely, at research on work-role centrality, voluntary turnover, and job dissatisfaction. Work-role centrality is a concept that directly refers to work-related identity and is therefore relevant to discuss. Research on voluntary turnover and job dissatisfaction is relevant as well, because this research may inform us about the relationship between work-related identities and people's willingness to change jobs. We address these literatures first before discussing identity literatures that reflect on people's general responses toward identity threats.

Work-role centrality is defined as "the importance and significance of working in an individual's overall life or the degree of cognitive investment into the work role" (McKee-Ryan et al., 2005, p. 62). It encompasses measures such as employment importance, employment commitment, work involvement, valence of work, and the Protestant work ethic, all referring to the belief that work is crucial for one's well-being and purpose in life. McKee-Ryan et al. conducted a meta-analysis examining the human capital, demographic, and psychological correlates of worker well-being during unemployment. Unemployed individuals' work-role centrality, more so than human capital and demographic variables, could explain their well-being: The more central the work-role was, the lower mental health and life satisfaction were. Based on these findings, the researchers advocated specific job-loss interventions that help people to deal with personal identity threats. Their findings are consistent with identity theory, which claims that identity loss is a serious threat to general well-being (Ashforth, 2001).

Social identity theory suggests that individuals will not easily leave groups they strongly identify with. Khapova and colleagues (Khapova, Arthur, Wilderom, & Svensson, 2007) examined how professional identity related to employees' turnover intentions. They found that professionals in the information technology sector who had a strong professional identity aimed to change their jobs more often than professionals who reported a weaker professional identity. This finding seems to indicate that, under propitious economic conditions, professionals with a strong professional identity seek to advance their professional position. The benefits of a job move (e.g., development of one's professional role and further strengthening of one's professional identity) are then larger than the costs (leaving the organization and loss of organizational identity).

Recent research on calling, a construct that incorporates professional identity, revealed findings that speak against the idea that a strong professional identity would lead to voluntary job changes. Cardador et al. (2011) found that a calling orientation related negatively to turnover intention because employees with a calling more strongly identified with their organization. These results are consistent with those found in identity research that indicated that attachment to one's work and role may generalize to other foci of identification, such as the organization (Rothbard & Edwards, 2003; Sluss & Ashforth, 2008). The underlying mechanisms of this generalization are thought to be twofold. First, people strive toward self-consistency and therefore align different identification targets with each other (Swann, Griffin, Predmore, & Gaines, 1987). Second, people may perceive the organization to be instrumental to the fulfillment of their calling,

such as by providing the means for pursuing their calling (e.g., training, working with specific types of products or clients). Cardador et al. (2011) indeed found that organizational instrumentality could explain the higher organizational identification and lower turnover intentions of people with a calling orientation. In addition, employees who have a low calling orientation typically value salary and status rather than meaningfulness in their job (e.g., Duffy & Sedlacek, 2007). These employees in particular are motivated to leave their organization if a job change involves financial or status gain.

Yet, what happens when employees with a calling orientation are dissatisfied with their jobs because they are unable to be involved in work that answer their calling? The organization is less instrumental, then, for the fulfillment of a calling. In line with Khapova et al.'s (2007) research, these individuals may want to leave their jobs to pursue their calling elsewhere (Duffy, Dik & Steger, 2011). Berg et al. (2010) conducted interviews with employees who dealt with unanswered callings owing to specific job duties in their current jobs. They found that these employees used active coping, in the form of crafting their job or leisure activities, as a strategy to deal with their unanswered callings. They focused on specific tasks by dedicating more time and effort to those work aspects that related to their (unanswered) calling, added specific tasks to their jobs, or pursued leisure activities that fulfilled their calling. Furthermore, they also became involved in role reframing by cognitively adjusting their job responsibilities toward their (unanswered) calling. Through these coping techniques they experienced more meaning and enjoyment at work.

On the whole, turnover research has shown that employees who combine their calling orientation with a strong organizational identity are reluctant to change jobs. Employees with a strong professional identity are more in favor of changing jobs, especially if they see opportunities to advance their professional identity by finding employment elsewhere. In addition, research on unanswered callings suggests that employees with a calling orientation preferably put effort into (cognitively) changing the content of their current job rather than in finding another job. They may particularly do so in an unfavorable labor market when there are no options for advancement or when finding employment in a similar job but in a different organization is difficult. Hence literatures in other domains than mainstream identity research suggest that strong work-related identities are related to intentions to remain in the present job, particularly when a strong professional identity or calling orientation is supported by the organization and organizational identity is thus high as well. Therefore strong work-related identities seem not very compatible with the new economy career model involving regular voluntary and involuntary job moves.

We, however, believe that the psychological consequences of job insecurity and job loss will be different for employees having different career orientations. Those who see work as a means to earn income or status will suffer from unemployment primarily because of the loss of income and status. On the other hand, those who view their career in light of a calling or a professional or organizational identity have to deal with similar consequences, but in addition to this also with the loss of a core element of identity and meaning in life. The question then is how employees with strong work-related identities may cope with the (possible) loss of their core identity. Are identities, for example, easy to abandon or change under times of economic or labor market pressures? And, could some identities be more beneficial for searching for and gaining of (satisfying) reemployment than others? To answer this question, we need to turn to the identity literature.

Coping with Identity Threat

In a situation of job insecurity or job loss, individuals' work-related identities likely affect their ability to cope adequately with this unfortunate state of affairs. Individuals whose professional or organizational identity has become more differentiated from their personal identity—that is, those who have separated their self-identities from their profession and/or organization (Kreiner et al., 2006)—may have less to lose when their work-related identities are threatened, making it easier for them to cope with the threat of unemployment, whereas those with strong work-related identities may be particularly vulnerable and may, therefore, struggle most with such life events.

The further people are in their work careers the more deeply they tend to integrate their professional roles into their personal identities. Therefore identity may play a particular role for older workers who tend to identify strongly with their lifetime professions (Berger, 2006) and who are more likely than younger workers to show additional role behaviors (Ng & Feldman, 2008) associated with the notion of a corporate identity (Van der Heijde & Van der Heijden, 2006). Letting

go of their work-related identities by changing jobs, changing organizations, or stepping into early retirement may thus be a particular challenge for them (Hanisch, 1999).

Employees may use different strategies to respond to severe identity threats, and these strategies may vary for different identities (i.e., organizational versus professional identities). First, because job loss is inherently associated with releasing work-related identities, employees may try to abandon some of their work-related identities, especially as the duration of unemployment progresses. This may particularly be the case for organizational identity, because if one is no longer a member of a social group one is less likely to remain emotionally connected to that group. Rather, probably after a transitional stage in which existing social identities gradually diminish, people may start to identify themselves with new and more salient social contexts.

However, this so-called identity-exit response seems less likely with regard to one's professional identity. Generally people do not abandon their professional identity that easily (Petriglieri, 2011); moreover, this identity seems unrelated to the stability or insecurity of the job. Brooks et al. (2011) found that employees' professional identity was unrelated to uncertainty in the profession (stability of the profession, security of jobs). Instead, the strength of professional identity was primarily determined by individual factors, such as a person's need for professional identification, perceptions of similarity with other professionals, and perceptions of a profession's image. Also, Walsh and Gordon (2008) have argued that professional identity will be as prominent for more traditional employees (who expect linearity and relative stability in their careers) as it is for more boundaryless employees (who view careers as volatile and without bounds). Hence, identity-exit responses are highly unlikely for people's professional identity unless an identity threat is so strong that preserving that identity has become a mission impossible.

Petriglieri (2011) describes two other coping responses that people pursue in order to counteract an identity threat, namely denying the threat or convincing others of the identity's value for the group (i.e., the organization). This seems indeed to happen when employees face job insecurity, as when they are informed that they are on the list of those who may be laid off.

Klehe and colleagues (Klehe, Zikic, Van Vianen, & De Pater, 2011), for example, found that employees who experienced job insecurity were neither activated to search for another job outside the organization nor involved in career planning. Although not examined, these employees may instead have tried to preserve their social and professional identities—for example, by putting effort into convincing the company of the added value of their professional roles. These *identity-protection* responses are focused on the source of the threat (i.e., the organization) and not on individual adjustment (Petriglieri, 2011).

The second category of coping strategies is focused on the threatened identities with the aim of making them less vulnerable to impairment; this involves *identity-restructuring* responses (Petriglieri, 2011). The identity-exit response, as discussed above, is the most radical identity-restructuring strategy. Two other types of responses are less drastic—namely, diminishing the threatened identity's importance or changing its meaning. For example, in times of job insecurity, employees may come to view their organizational identity as less important than alternative social identities, a notion in line with findings that job insecurity diminishes not only workers' satisfaction, trust, and physical and mental well-being but also their organizational commitment and job involvement while at the same time fostering turnover intentions (Sverke et al., 2002). Imagine a person who has devoted most of his or her effort and time to his or her organization at the cost of other (former) valuable social groups. When job loss is at hand, this person may decide to shift his or her focus to these other groups. Another identity-restructuring response in times of job insecurity may be that people do not give up their professional identity but instead give a different meaning to their profession—for example, by defining their profession in broader terms. Rather than seeing oneself exclusively as a software developer, one may reframe his or her profession in terms of a broad spectrum of information and communications technology activities. This shift in focus will likely facilitate a movement to adjacent professional domains.

Identity-restructuring responses seem most adequate in times of job insecurity and unemployment. Furthermore, according to McConnell's (2011) multiple self-aspect framework, these responses are also most likely pursued. The multiple self-aspect framework (MSF) views the self as a "collection of multiple, context-dependent self-aspects" (p. 5). Self aspects and associated attributes (such as characteristics, behaviors, or affect) are activated by an individual's context. Hence, work-related self-aspects are highly accessible when one has a secure job, whereas non-work-related aspects of self (and related attributes) become more accessible in times of unemployment. The unemployment context activates a broadening of or gradual shift toward other self aspects.

Furthermore, MSF argues that different self aspects are associated with different affective states as derived from a person's appraisal of a particular self aspect. This implies that during times of unemployment, when non-work-related self aspects have become more accessible, individuals' general affect may depend relatively more on the appraisal of their nonwork selves and associated attributes. However, if work remains highly central to an individual's self-concept (i.e., no identity-restructuring takes place), work-related self aspects (i.e., the loss of these aspects) may remain to have a strong impact on an individual's general affect even during unemployment. According to MSF, this will particularly be the case if work-related attributes are not associated with non-work-related aspects of self.

Imagine Susan, who is a university professor (a work-related self aspect), a job that is associated with attributes such as intelligence, conscientiousness, and creativity. Susan is also the mother of two boys (nonwork self aspect) and she plays the violin in an amateur orchestra (nonwork self aspect). Her motherhood is associated with attributes such as femininity and caring, and her musical activity is associated with attributes such as team membership, conscientiousness, and musicality. Owing to personnel cutbacks at her university, Susan loses her job. How will she react? If her professorship becomes less central to her self-concept, her affective responses will primarily depend on affects that are associated with the activities in her private life—that is, the extent to which she feels satisfied with and is recognized for her motherhood and leisure activities. If, however, her professorship remains highly central to her self-concept, she will feel desperate and/or depressed. Yet her music activity may give her some relief, since this activity includes an attribute that is associated with her work-related self (i.e., conscientiousness). In other words, the MSF suggests that unemployment may be less detrimental for the affective responses of individuals with strong work-related identities when work and nonwork self aspects are positively connected, or when individuals' self aspects share attributes that are positively appraised.[1]

Identity research has shown that identities are subject to change and dependent on changes in context, comparisons (similarities) with others, and status attributions of the group to which one belongs (Walsh & Gordon, 2008). Hence employees' work-related identities may change as well when changes in work conditions, professional groups, and status occur (Pratt et al., 2006). When faced with job loss, individuals with a strong professional identity or calling orientation may initially stick to their identity and try to find employment in a job that fits with their professional identity and calling. This is particularly true of older workers who lose their jobs, since older workers often continue to identify with work and the work ethic to the same degree as when they were first employed, even after long periods of unemployment (Berger, 2006; Rife & First, 1989). However, when no such job is available and the period of unemployment lengthens, identity changes are necessary for finding reemployment and progressing in one's career. Note that identity changes can also take the wrong direction: Long-term unemployed individuals may customize their identity toward the social group of the unemployed. For example, in view of the low status associated with unemployment, they may frame their position in light of being a member of a group that objects to society or that is not given fair opportunities by society.

To summarize, identity theory and research suggest that strong work-related identities may hinder adaptation to changing environmental conditions, whether this includes changes in functions and jobs or job insecurity and job loss. Viewed from an identity perspective, flexible and unpredictable careers will less likely occur spontaneously because many employees tend to identify strongly with their organization, profession, and work activities. They prefer to hold on to or strengthen rather than abandon their work-related identities. However, when forced by economic conditions, they can be able to restructure work-related identities by diminishing their organizational ties or by broadening their professional scope and shifting their focus to other meaningful activities. Although a strong professional identity seems beneficial in times of economic turbulence, since it motivates people to search for alternative employment in the areas of their expertise, it could become a hindrance in times when work contents and roles shift as well. In that case, a restructuring of one's professional identity is warranted, which can be more easily realized to the extent that work and nonwork activities and affects are tied to each other.

Future research is needed that investigates how people's inherent predisposition toward identity formation can get along with a new economy mindset: Identity formation may promote or hinder the development of flexible mental career models. On the one hand, a strong professional identity may inspire people to search for a job and explore their options during times of unemployment. A strong professional identity may thus initially help people to view their job loss as a challenge for finding alternative and even better job options. However, as the time of unemployment lengthens and the optimal job that matches with an individual's identity is not available, a strong professional identity may gradually become a burden and negatively affect one's mental health. Consequently the original challenge turns into a threat when an identity shift has not been made. In essence, the ease with which people are able to make identity shifts determines their adaptation in times of change and thus their career flexibility.

Future research could further investigate the possible divergent effects of different work-related identities on people's responses to job insecurity and unemployment over time. Our model of identity and coping during career transitions (ICCT) may function as a guide for a future research agenda. This research should be particularly focused on the factors that impact upon and promote identity shifts because we expect that these shifts will be beneficial for people's mental health and self-regulation (i.e., job search) during unemployment. In our ICCT model we have included five factors that we believe are directly and/or indirectly important for people's coping responses (among which their identity shifts): (1) work-orientation (identity-based versus instrumental-based), (2) cognitive appraisal of the transition (challenge or threat), (3) mental models of career (traditional or nontraditional) and career success, (4) non-work-related identities and aspects of self, and (5) career adaptability.

In the next paragraph, we address people's mental models of careers as fed by their definition of career success and we discuss how societal and individual notions of career success may influence individual responses toward job insecurity and job loss. Thereafter, we reflect on the basic resources (career adaptability) that people need to deal with careers in the new economy.

Mental Models of Careers: Career Success

Career success is generally defined as "the positive psychological or work-related outcomes or achievements one accumulates as a result of work experiences" (Seibert, Crant, & Kraimer, 1999, p. 417). This definition includes two forms of career success: objective and subjective. Objective career success refers to tangible and quantifiable manifestations of careers such as salary, salary growth, and job level throughout one's career (e.g., Heslin, 2005). Subjective career success frames people's careers in terms of their experiences— that is, how they feel about their work over the course of their working lives. It has been mostly operationalized as job satisfaction, stay intentions, involvement, health, and need fulfillment. In addition, a career is perceived as successful if an individual experiences that he or she achieves goals that are personally meaningful (Mirvis & Hall, 1994).

Objective and subjective career success are distinct constructs yet also related to each other. First, they seem to share some of their determinants. A meta-analysis conducted by Ng, Eby, Sorensen, and Feldman (2005) showed that several factors outside the individual, such as career sponsorship (from senior managers and mentors) and training and skill development opportunities (as provided by the organization), were related to both objective and subjective career success. Second, experiences of career success are influenced by the social context in which individuals live (Gunz & Heslin, 2005). For example, in a context in which objective vertical career progress is viewed as the main indicator of career success, people may adopt this norm and also perceive their careers in terms of upward mobility rather than fulfillment of intrinsic needs. Dries (2011) argued that this societal norm explains why so many people feel unsuccessful about their careers: Only a few people are actually able to advance upwardly in their careers.

Whether subjective career perceptions are influenced by societal norms may depend on the extent to which individuals rely on their own personal standards and goals (self-referent subjective success) or compare themselves to a reference group or external standard (other-referent subjective success) (Abele & Spurk, 2009; Heslin, 2005). Employees with a calling orientation will take the self as the main referent for establishing their career success. They may experience their career as successful if their inner goals are fulfilled and they view work as meaningful. However, employees with a job or career orientation may primarily use others as referents to establish their career success. More specifically, employees with a job orientation work for financial rewards (Wrzesniewski et al., 1997) and will likely assess their career success by comparing their own income to the incomes of relevant others. Employees with a career orientation adhere to social

status, power, and prestige; they may tend to compare their own prestige and achievements with those of others.

The distinction between self- and other-referent foci for career success was confirmed by Dries, Pepermans, and Carlier (2008), who investigated the spontaneous conceptualizations that managers use in thinking about their careers. The managers conceptualized career success along two dimensions, intrapersonal and interpersonal, each consisting of two components: achievement and affect. Intrapersonal achievement concerns success criteria such as self-development and creativity, whereas interpersonal achievement refers to advancement and the factual contribution that one makes to the organization. Individuals' affect that is associated with career success may concern feelings of security and satisfaction (intrapersonal affect) or feelings such as recognition and perceived contribution to the organization (interpersonal affect).

The division between intrapersonal or self-referent and interpersonal or other-referent experiences of career success nicely reflects the performance/mastery divide in goal orientation theory (e.g., Elliot, 1999; Elliot & Covington, 2001), which argues that people are differently oriented toward comparing and competing with others (other-referent) or toward their own accomplishments and development (self-referent).

Abele and Spurk (2009) conducted a longitudinal study in which they examined relationships between subjective self-referent, subjective other-referent, and objective career success among a sample of graduated professionals. Objective career success was measured with income and hierarchical status, self-referent career success was measured as overall job satisfaction, and other-referent career success was seen as perceived career development in comparison with fellow graduates. The researchers reasoned that relationships among these measures would be different for different career phases, with objective success having a stronger influence on individuals' other-referent career experiences at career entry than in later career phases (establishment and advancement phases). In addition, objective as well as subjective career success will change over time; thus changes in one success criterion could affect changes in other criteria.

It has been shown that initial objective career success was positively related to initial other-referent career success, which, in turn, had a positive impact on growth in objective career success over time. Furthermore, changes in objective career success went together with changes in other-referent career success over time. People who reach higher job levels and progress in their salary are typically regarded as successful and are thus more likely to perceive themselves as successful (e.g., Ng et al., 2005). Abele and Spurk (2009) furthermore found that initial job satisfaction (self-referent career success) had a positive effect on later objective career success. This finding is consistent with prior research (e.g., Ng et al.) showing that some individuals are more disposed to experiencing a satisfying career than others because of their greater emotional stability, proactivity, and internal locus of control. These personality characteristics are also beneficial for work performance and promotions.

On the whole, Abele and Spurk's (2009) study indicated that objective, initial self-referent and other-referent career success in early careers are all important for objective career success over time. Early objective career success goes together with early other-referent success experiences, because individuals feel that they measure up to the societal norm (of objective success). This early other-referent success experience plus early job satisfaction promote future objective career success. Consequently, if employees experience job insecurity (often resulting in lower job satisfaction) or job loss (low career success) early in their careers, it could have a negative effect on their future objective career success. In the next paragraph we further address the possible consequences of career interruptions for careers.

Career Interruptions: Are They Good or Bad?

Career interruptions due to unemployment tend to harm people's well-being (McKee-Ryan et al. 2005) and may also impair their careers. Most literatures on job loss and unemployment emphasize the negative effects of temporary unemployment for people's careers (e.g., De Cuyper, Fontinha, & De Witte, this volume; Leana et al., 1998; McKee-Ryan et al., 2005). For example, a career interruption may lead to underemployment, including work at lower levels and with a lower salary than in a prior job (Feldman & Leana, 2000; Virick & McKee-Ryan, this volume). Above we have described research that showed that early career experiences have an effect on later career success. This research suggests that career interruptions in early careers can have negative consequences for later career development. At the same time, in many societies career interruptions in early careers seem

to become the norm rather than the exception. For example, European governments promote temporary employment contracts so as to enhance labor market flexibility (Gebel, 2012). These temporary jobs are mostly available for career starters; therefore many young adults will be confronted with job uncertainty and periods of unemployment early in their careers.

Gebel (2012) investigated the consequences of these temporary jobs and unemployment for careers. Specifically, he compared the wages and employment opportunities of temporarily employed entrants in Germany and the United Kingdom with those of comparable entrants (i.e., who are similar with respect to other relevant characteristics) but employed in permanent contracts. A first observation was that temporarily employment generally lasted for not more than five years. Further, the initial wage gap between temporarily and permanent employees rapidly decreased when temporary employees found permanent jobs. Actually, temporarily employed entrants were better off than permanently employed entrants who nevertheless lost their job and reentered in temporary jobs. Finally, the unemployment risks of temporary and permanent employees were similar in Germany, but they were higher for temporary as compared with permanent employees in the United Kingdom.

All in all, temporary employment and job uncertainty in early careers seem not necessarily detrimental for people's later career success. Moreover, the effects of early career interruptions seem to depend on societal economic conditions and norms. If the societal context dictates that careers should start with uncertain temporary jobs (thereby setting lower early objective success norms), negative career effects may be less likely to occur. On the contrary, if temporary employment interruptions are used for learning and personal development, they may ultimately result in better-fitting jobs and thus better options for career advancement. Furthermore, while unemployment is undoubtedly often an aversive state, the need to decide on the characteristics of suitable work and then search for it during temporary unemployment may particularly help career starters to gain a better understanding of the environment and their personal strengths and values, which, in turn, may lead to finding a better-fitting job and career (DiRenzo & Greenhaus, 2011). Indeed, some individuals may appreciate the period of unemployment as an opportunity to reflect on the direction of their lives and careers (Jones, 1989; Zikic & Richardson, 2007).

However, job uncertainty and periods of unemployment are likely harmful for employees in later career stages. Regarding indicators of objective career success, results from large-scale survey work in the United States convincingly show that the average displaced worker in his or her fifties experienced a loss in earnings of nearly 40% (Couch, 1998) and that the earning losses were still at 40% four years after job displacement. Six or more years after displacement they still ranged from 23% to 29% (Chan & Stevens, 2001), beside serious losses in fringe benefits, which may be just as large as the losses in direct earnings (Haider & Stephens, 2001).

Regarding indicators of subjective career success, Finnish researchers (Mauno, Feldt, Tolvanen, Hyvönen, & Kinnunen, 2011) investigated the consequences of career disruptions (dismissals, layoffs, unemployment) among mainly male managers. As in prior studies (e.g., Paul & Moser 2009), they found that career disruptions were associated with lower subjective well-being and more stress-related health symptoms. Additionally, they found that employees who had experienced a career disruption at an earlier career stage were more likely to have more career disruptions in later years. Thus negative career disruptions seemed to accumulate over an individual's career. This finding suggests that these people were not able to find fitting jobs early in their careers, which may have resulted in lower well-being and a higher vulnerability to subsequent job loss. Low subjective well-being at one point in time indeed increased the likelihood of job loss in the following time period. The researchers reasoned, however, that subjective well-being has a dispositional component, whereas stress-related health symptoms are state-like personal outcomes. Hence, people's dispositional well-being influences later career outcomes (such as job loss) and these negative outcomes, in turn, cause stress-related health symptoms. All in all, people's basic level of well-being more than their career disruptions may influence career success in the end. Initial self-referent perceptions of success (satisfaction and general well-being) and the way in which individuals attribute meaning to temporary career interruptions (cognitive appraisal) are more significant for career development than career interruptions as such.

Individual differences in (subjective) meaning making during unemployment are also related to gender. Although gender roles have changed over the years, women are still expected to identify more with their caregiving roles, such as taking care of the home and children, than men. For this reason,

women may suffer less from unemployment than men, especially when they have children. Forret, Sulliven, and Mainiero (2010) indeed found that men more often viewed their unemployment as a personal defeat (they felt ashamed, isolated, and angry), whereas women more often reported to view their unemployment as an opportunity to make a new start (new challenges, rediscovery of the self). However, these gender differences only concerned men and women with children. Male and female participants without children did not differ in their responses to unemployment. All in all, these findings again point to the role of personal identities that affect well-being in times of unemployment. The consequences of unemployment for people's well-being are more severe if individuals have strong work-related personal identities and weak non-work-related identities.

As argued above, older employees in particular will have a stronger work-related personal identity owing to their longer work history. They should show more negative responses to job insecurity and unemployment than younger employees. Research among a group of older unemployed managers and professionals indeed revealed that many of these employees experienced negative emotions such as disappointment, anxiety, sadness, and loss, and they viewed their environment as harsh (Gabriel, Gray, & Goregaokar, 2010). At the same time, these older employees varied in the way they experienced their unemployment: some lingered in mourning about the end of their career, whereas others considered it as a temporary disruption or detached themselves from their professional career and sought to make the best out of their situation.

To summarize, people's responses to career interruptions depend on societal norms, the use of self- and other-referent foci for establishing career success, and cognitive framing of career interruptions. The more career interruptions are accepted as "normal," the more self-referent focused people are and the more they perceive the interruption as an opportunity to find a better future work fit. They will also be likely to experience less sorrow from temporary unemployment and be more likely to live up to the new economy career model. That is, self-focused perceptions of career success will facilitate adequate coping with identity threats (see Figure 13.1).

So far we have discussed adaptations of individuals' mental models with regard to their identities and definitions of career success that are necessary to meet the characteristics of new

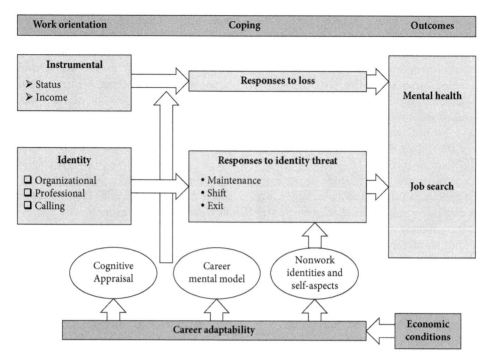

| Work orientation | Coping | Outcomes |

Figure 13.1 Identity and coping during career transitions.

economy (i.e., unpredictable) careers including insecurity and disruptions. In the next paragraph we discuss the basic resources that individuals need in order to effectively deal with possible loss and identity threats.

Career Adaptability

Unpredictable careers request that individuals have the ability to foresee and cope with career transitions. Career construction theory refers to this ability as *career adaptability*, which concerns "the resources for coping with current and anticipated tasks, transitions, and traumas in occupational roles" (Savickas & Porfeli, 2012, p. 662). These resources encompass: concern, control, curiosity, and confidence.

Concern (about the future) regards the extent to which individuals look ahead and prepare for what might come next. *Control* concerns individuals' responsibility for shaping the self and the environment through self-discipline, effort, and persistence. *Curiosity* refers to the exploration of possible selves and alternative scenarios, and reflection on various situations and roles by means of information-seeking activities. *Confidence* concerns individuals' perception that they can actualize their choices, such as finding a suitable job. Individuals who display high levels of concern, control, curiosity, and

confidence are thought to be well prepared to a volatile labor market in which they will be frequently confronted with uncertain job situations.

Particularly during times of unemployment, the four sources of adaptability together will likely facilitate positive cognitive appraisal, flexible mental models of careers, and a better integration of work and nonwork aspects of self (see Figure 13.1). Specifically, people who feel confident will be less likely to appraise job insecurity and job loss as a threat, and people who rate high on concern, control, and curiosity will be more likely to adopt a self-referent focus and a flexible mental model toward their careers. Further, people who are concerned with their careers and who explore their possible and alternative selves will be better able to integrate work and nonwork self aspects and make necessary identity shifts. Hence career adaptability will promote coping with unemployment, self-regulation, and ultimately the finding of good reemployment.

Koen and colleagues (Koen, Klehe, Van Vianen, Zikic, & Nauta, 2010) investigated whether and how career adaptability influenced the way in which people searched for jobs and the quality of their reemployment. They used an earlier measure of the four adaptability dimensions and described these as planning (looking ahead to one's future career), decision making (knowing what career to pursue), exploration (looking around at various career options), and confidence (having a feeling of self-efficacy to successfully execute the activities needed to achieve one's career goals). They were particularly interested in how these adaptability dimensions would relate to individuals' job search strategies and whether these strategies, in turn, were conducive to finding a suitable job.

Job seekers' adaptability was indeed found to be related to the use of specific job-search strategies. First, individuals who were high on the adaptability measures of exploration and confidence used an exploratory job-search strategy. That is, they were dedicated to their job search and were motivated to fully explore their options by gathering job-related information from various sources, such as friends, family, and former employers. In contrast, individuals who were high on career planning but reported lower exploration abilities more often used a focused job-search strategy. They concentrated their search efforts on a small number of carefully screened employers and applied only for jobs that fitted their needs, qualifications, and interests. Finally, individuals who showed lower adaptability with regard to planning and decision making tended to use a haphazard strategy. That is, their job-search activities were best to characterize as trial and error or the passive gathering of relevant and irrelevant information. These individuals were undecided about what kind of career to pursue.

The adaptability factors of decision making and confidence were—irrespective of one's job search strategy—directly and positively related to the chance of finding a fitting job. The adaptability factors were also indirectly related to finding a job (but not necessarily a fitting one) through the use of exploratory and focused job-search strategies. Hence career adaptability both directly and indirectly (through the use of specific job-search strategies) affected people's reemployment. Although the four adaptability dimensions are necessary for making career transitions in that they initiate and direct job-search activities, they do not guarantee that individuals will find the best-fitting job (Koen et al., 2010; Zicik & Klehe, 2006). For example, curiosity (self and environmental exploration) may not automatically result in better job choices (see also Zikic & Hall, 2009). We see three reasons why curiosity, although necessary, may not result in the best job choice. First, more (self and environmental) information makes the decision process more complex and people are generally not capable to adequately

deal with lots of information. Although more information may trigger rational decision making it may also suppress intuitive thoughts, whereas both rational thinking and intuition seem more optimal for making better decisions (see Van Vianen et al., 2009). Second, more is not always better, because it is the *quality* rather than the amount of information that will contribute to making better decisions. Third, the job search context, that is, whether one seeks a job while being unemployed or employed, may affect the job choice decision process and subsequently the quality of the final job choice.

The research on career adaptability generally argues that career adaptability is particularly triggered during periods of transition such as unemployment (Savickas, 1997). Moreover, although adaptability is conceptualized as ability (Savickas & Porfeli, 2012), this ability can fluctuate as influenced by the situational context. This was nicely illustrated in research that showed different adaptability responses for employees who experienced job insecurity on the one hand and employees who faced actual job loss on the other hand (Klehe et al., 2011). Career planning and exploration were higher among the latter group of employees as compared with the first one. Hence security of (future) job loss rather than feelings of job insecurity—when keeping one's job is yet uncertain—seem to induce adaptive behaviors. It is however, the question whether individuals also remain adaptable *after* job loss and as the duration of their employment lengthens.

Adaptability During Long-Term Unemployment

Unemployment causes stress and is a serious threat to people's work-related identities and careers. Stress during unemployment not only includes worries about the loss of income, professional and organizational identities, and possible career options but also involves worries about making the right decisions while searching for a new job. People have a natural tendency to avoid negative emotions, such as stress. They therefore sometimes procrastinate with regard to decision-related activities rather than engaging in these activities in order to quickly solve the decision problem. Unemployed people face a dilemma: They can reduce their unemployment stress by finding reemployment through job search, but at the same time they can avoid job-search stress by doing nothing.

Job search is stressful for two reasons. First, job seekers are often faced with a lack of sufficient information about suitable job alternatives (De Goede, Van Vianen, & Klehe, 2011). This ambiguity is less of a problem if the search process is appraised as a challenge because experienced challenge tends to facilitate cognitive adjustment (Kassam, Koslov, & Berry Mendes, 2009), which may positively influence career decision making. However, if job seekers perceive the job-seeking process as difficult and threatening, they may rather tend to opt for suboptimal choices. They may, for example, choose a job because of its nearby location rather than its suitable content.

Second, job seekers are dependent on the types of jobs that are available at the labor market, and these jobs may not be their favorite ones. If there are few job positions available, as during economic crises, job seekers may have to choose from less optimal job alternatives. Generally people experience more decision stress if they have to choose among relatively unattractive as opposed to highly attractive alternatives (Botti & Iyengar, 2004). This means that job seekers experience more decision stress under negative economic circumstances; they may have to reconcile themselves to a job choice that seems less optimal for their career.

All in all, people's initial concern, control, curiosity, and confidence before job loss come under pressure after they have actually lost their jobs and are unemployed. Unemployment and related job-search stress can reduce job seekers' career concern when it seems useless to plan ahead. It can also reduce their control when persistence seems not necessarily to result in better outcomes, and it can reduce their confidence when finding an optimal job seems no longer an option. Moreover, as the time of unemployment lengthens, not only individuals' adaptability resources become depleted but also their job skills and job-related networks decrease, which further diminishes their chances of finding reemployment (Aaronson, Mazumder, & Schechter, 2010).

For these reasons, many governments seek ways to bring long-term unemployed people back into the labor market by offering them educational programs and skill training. These training efforts aim to support or raise individuals' adaptability, to increase their social capital (social skills and network), human capital (work experience, training, skills and knowledge), and to strengthen their career identity (work values and motivation to work) (Koen et al., 2010; Price & Vinokur, this volume). Yet, it is conceivable that the reemployment motivation of long-term employed people reaches a point that they are no longer willing to participate in reemployment interventions. In that case, reemployment services may consider to enforce such interventions (e.g., Petrongolo, 2009), although such strategy seems opposed to prevailing psychological theories on human motivation that stress voluntary participation as a prerequisite for successful intervention (e.g., Deci & Ryan, 2000; see also Vansteenkiste & Van den Broeck, this volume).

Recently Koen and colleagues (in press) examined the effect of mandatory interventions for people's skill development, motivation, job-search behaviors, and chances of finding reemployment. They showed that the mandatory nature of reemployment interventions is not necessarily detrimental for people's development, provided that they find a course useful for finding reemployment. In addition, when people had some choice in participating in the intervention but experienced the intervention as useless, their motivation for finding reemployment decreased and thereby negatively influenced skill development and job-search intensity. Hence having a choice whether to participate in an intervention is less important for people's development and reemployment than the experienced usefulness of an intervention. The findings of this study further stress the point that reemployment interventions should be person-adaptive.

Overall, extant research indicates that career adaptability is a prerequisite for finding reemployment because it supports self-regulation during job search. We have argued that career adaptability promote self-regulation because its four components (resources) facilitate positive cognitive appraisal, self-referent and flexible career mental models, and the integration of work and nonwork related self aspects. At the same time, individuals' career adaptability fluctuates as influenced by contextual conditions and particularly in stressful times of unemployment, it does not guarantee the finding of a suitable job. Reemployment interventions, eventually mandatory ones, are then needed to sustain or improve unemployed people's level of adaptability and to update their knowledge and skills. Hence, new economy nonlinear careers require high levels of career adaptability as well as the continuous support and development of expertise, knowledge and experience (Rothwell & Arnold, 2007). Society as a whole and organizations in particular should provide the means for preserving high levels of adaptability and employability in the form of customized methods and programs.

Discussion

In this chapter we have argued that careers no longer involve a prescribed route to a final career destination. Careers have become discontinuous and less predictable, requiring employees to prepare themselves to changing work conditions, job uncertainty, and frequent reflections on their own preferences and abilities and the career opportunities available at the labor market. Current and future careers cannot be predicted from a one-time vocational choice early in individuals' careers, but will often involve frequent and temporary career choices that may not always logically follow upon each other. Furthermore, work and nonwork activities may more often alternate and may become more aligned with each other.

We proposed that many employees may still adhere to the traditional conception of careers and therefore experience difficulties with job uncertainty and job loss. Specifically, they may frame temporary unemployment as a threat for work-related identities and/or as a loss of instrumental revenues. Furthermore, they may hold a traditional view on career success as involving a sequence of ascending job levels and salaries which is launched by early-career success. Finally, they may lack adaptability resources to prepare themselves for and to cope with career transitions.

Unpredictable careers require adjustments of work-related identities, and we have argued that these adjustments are possible yet difficult. Identity formation develops naturally and therefore cannot easily be regulated consciously. For example, it is not useful to coach employees that they should form weakly work-related identities in order to be better prepared for future job changes. However, it is conceivable that employees who frequently have to move from one job to another or who frequently experience job insecurity in their careers will develop weaker work-related identities in the end. If so, this may mean that a "boundaryless mindset" will harm employees' work involvement, which will have negative effects on organizational commitment and performance (e.g., Duffy et al., 2011; Wrzesniewski et al., 1997). Preliminary research findings show, however, no support for this contention: only mobility preference (individuals' low desire to stay with a single employer) was negatively related to organizational commitment, whereas a boundaryless mindset was unrelated to organizational commitment (Briscoe & Finkelstein, 2009).

A boundaryless mindset is an opportunity-driven orientation to the career and involves the willingness to cross organizational and employment boundaries when one sees opportunities to do so (e.g., Arthur, 1994). Hence, employees with boundaryless mindsets may wish to be flexible on the labor market because they see options for further advancement of their professional identity or calling. Labor market reality may, however, not accord with such opportunistic expectations. In case of job loss, boundaryless employees with strong professional identities may initially focus on finding a job in a similar profession. Yet if no such job is available, they have to adjust their professional identity.

Under tough economic conditions or in a changing labor market, strong work-related identities may help people to maintain a sense of belonging and self-esteem (Tosti-Kharas, in press), yet may hinder them in adjusting successfully or finding suitable reemployment. They need to psychologically disengage from their professional identity or restructure it by, for example, ascribing a broader meaning to their profession, adjusting perceptions of the self, and constructing other self-narratives (Ibarra & Barbulescu, 2010). Furthermore, based on the MSF, it is conceivable that consistency among work- and non-work-related attributes could help these individuals to restructure their identities and to cope more successfully with times of unemployment.

Unpredictable or new economy careers also require that people rebuild their assumptions about careers and career success and develop a new economy career orientation that includes self-referent perceptions of career success, mobility values, portable competencies, self-directedness, and autonomy (e.g., Creed, Macpherson, & Hood, 2011). A new economy orientation may be helpful in times of unemployment in that it may facilitate shifts in work-related identities.

Individuals' career mental model develops at a younger age when they have early work experiences and need to make a career choice (Loughlin & Barling, 2001; Van Vianen, Dalhoeven, & De Pater, 2011). Therefore it is particularly important to make young adults aware that career choices "should not be associated with planning a far future "(Van Vianen et al., 2009, p. 305), that career paths are unpredictable, and that career success is a relative concept in that it is a matter of individual standards and goals. Viewed from this perspective, we have argued that temporary employment in early careers may help to construct rather than demolish people's careers. Through temporary employment, career starters enrich their work-role experiences and they learn to deal with job insecurity and identity shifts.

Little is yet known about how people's definitions of career and career success may shift over time as affected by their own unique career trajectory as well as changing societal conditions. We have argued that careers are for the large part socially constructed and therefore that current economic and labor market mechanisms may cause a shift in people's thoughts about their careers. For example, a career may no longer be seen as successful when a person has reached higher levels of professional expertise or higher hierarchical levels but instead has regularly moved among jobs and/or has been self-employed during his or her career. Similarly, job insecurity and job loss may no longer be associated with unsuccessful careers but instead as common periods of career reflection.

Finally, careers in the new economy require adaptability—that is, having the resources for coping with (anticipated) transitions, as indicated by high levels of career concern, control, curiosity, and confidence. These resources will promote positive cognitive appraisal, self-referent and flexible career mental models, and the integration of work- and non-work-related aspects of self. However, adaptability resources are particularly provoked by adverse economic conditions and setbacks. Therefore careers in the new economy require that individuals receive support for maintaining or improving their adaptability resources.

Recommendations for Practice

• Employees, managers, and employment counselors need to prepare employees for the reality of volatile, unpredictable, and nonlinear career paths characterized by numerous voluntary and involuntary career transitions.

• People's reactions (well-being and job-search approach) to job insecurity and job loss depend on their work-related identities. Generally the more self-defining a person's organization, profession, or work activity is, the greater the psychological distress experienced during (possible) job loss.

• Because a specific identity tends to deepen with time, older workers in particular may suffer from the identity loss incurred through job loss.

• It is important to differentiate between the various forms of identity (organizational,

professional, and calling) that may characterize workers, as each of these may have distinct effects in times of job insecurity and job loss.

• A strong organizational identity may prevent employees from taking the necessary career steps in times of organizational downturns and may cause severe suffering in times of job loss.

• A high work-role centrality and strong professional identity may be a motivating asset during the search for a new job, but it may also become a stressor when no suitable employment option emerges. Because distress during unemployment often incurs inactivity and resignation, work-role centrality and professional identity may end up being a double-edged sword in terms of helping people find reemployment.

• While individuals do not easily leave groups with which they strongly identify, identities can often be restructured by exiting a threatened identity, diminishing its subjective importance, or changing its meaning. As a consequence, an organizational identity during employment may not generalize to peoples' sense of identity once they are unemployed.

• Identities are more easily restructured when the content of the threatened identity links to other identities relevant to one's self-concept. Thus when one can find overlaps in content between work and nonwork self-aspects, unemployment may be less detrimental to affected individuals' well-being.

• In discussing a successful career, it is important to consider not only the objective success or a subjective comparison to relevant others but also the fulfillment of one's own goals and standards. The latter may be easier for workers with a calling orientation than for those with a career orientation to their work.

• While job loss often leads to a lower reemployment status and wages, particularly among older workers, such career disruptions can prove to be a "blessing in disguise," depending largely on people's career adaptability.

• Generally, unstable career prospects need not always be automatically bad. Particularly among job starters, they may present a temporary phenomenon during entry into the labor market, yet they should then also include a strong focus on learning and personal development.

• Career adaptability (i.e., career concern, control, curiosity, and confidence) can be a great asset during unemployment in terms of fostering both job-search strategies that lead to finding a job in the first place and in ensuring that the new job will be one of high-quality.

• Of particular benefit, both for careers in general and also during times of unemployment, is career planning (the behavioral component of career concern).

• Far less certain are the benefits of career exploration (the behavioral component of career curiosity). While usually embraced in theory and practice, current findings on the effects of career exploration (particularly self-exploration) on reemployment quality are far less convincing.

• It would be wrong to assume that a looming career transition automatically triggers career-adaptive behavior. While this seems to be true in case of job loss, job uncertainty seems to have a rather contrary and inhibiting effect.

• While career adaptability generally seems to suffer during prolonged unemployment, employment interventions can help to rebuild it as long as these interventions are seen as useful for finding reemployment. Far less relevant, however, is whether job seekers participate in these interventions out of free choice or whether these interventions are mandatory in nature.

Acknowledgment

This publication was supported by the FMG-UvA Research Priority Grant on Affect Regulation.

Note

1. Note that if individuals' self-aspects are more strongly connected (through their associated attributes), individuals' general affect is also more vulnerable to any negative feedback that they may receive on these attributes. For example, if an attribute (e.g., intelligence) is associated with several self-aspects and an individual receives negative feedback on this attribute (e.g., low intelligence) in one domain, the negative consequences of this feedback for a person's mood will spread to other domains as well, resulting in a general negative affect.

References

Aaronson, D., Mazumder, B., & Schechter, S. (2010). What is behind the rise in long-term unemployment? *Economic Perspectives, 34*(2), 28–51.

Abele, A. E., & Spurk, D. (2009). The longitudinal impact of self-efficacy and career goals on objective and subjective career success. *Journal of Vocational Behavior, 74*(1), 53–62.

Arthur, M. B. (1994). The boundaryless career: A new perspective for organizational inquiry. *Journal of Organizational Behavior, 15*(4), 295–306.

Arthur, M. B., Hall, D. T., & Lawrence, B. S. (1989). Generating new directions in career theory: The case for a transdisciplinary approach. In M. B. Arthur, D. T. Hall, &

B. S. Lawrence (Eds.), *Handbook of career theory* (pp. 7–25). Cambridge, UK: Cambridge University Press.

Ashforth, B. E. (2001). *Role transitions in organizational life: An identity-based perspective.* Mahwah, NJ: Erlbaum.

Bandura, A. (1991). Social cognitive theory of self-regulation. *Organizational Behavioral and Human Decision Processes, 50*, 248–287.

Berg, J. M., Grant, A. M., & Johnson, V. (2010). When callings are calling: Crafting work and leisure in pursuit of unanswered occupational callings. *Organization Science, 21*(5), 973–994.

Berger, E. D. (2006). "Aging" identities: Degradation and negotiation in the search for employment. *Journal of Aging Studies, 20*(4), 303–316.

Bloch, D. P. (2005). Complexity, chaos, and nonlinear dynamics: A new perspective on career development theory. *Career Development Quarterly, 53*(3), 194–207.

Botti, S., & Iyengar, S. (2004). The psychological pleasure and pain of choosing: When people prefer choosing at the cost of subsequent satisfaction. *Journal of Personality and Social Psychology, 87*(3), 312–326.

Briscoe, J. P., & Finkelstein, L. M. (2009). The "new career" and organizational commitment. Do boundaryless and protean attitudes make a difference? *Career Development International, 14*(3), 242–260.

Brooks, N. G., Riemenschneider, C. K., Hardgrave, B. C., & O'Leary-Kelly, A. M. (2011). IT professional identity: Needs, perceptions, and belonging. *European Journal of Information Systems, 20*(1), 87–102.

Cardador, M. T., Dane, E., & Pratt, M. G. (2011). Linking calling orientations to organizational attachment via organizational instrumentality. *Journal of Vocational Behavior, 79*(2), 367–378.

Chan, S. W., & Stevens, A. H. (2001). Job loss and employment patterns of older workers. *Journal of Labor Economics, 19*(2), 484–521.

Couch, K. A. (1998). Late life job displacement. *Gerontologist, 38*(1), 7–17.

Creed, P., Macpherson, J., & Hood, M. (2011). Predictors of "new economy" career orientation in an Australian sample of late adolescents. *Journal of Career Development, 38*(5), 369–389.

De Goede, M. E. E., Van Vianen, A. E. M., & Klehe, U.-C. (2011). Attracting applicants on the web: PO fit, industry culture stereotypes, and website design. *International Journal of Selection and Assessment, 19*(1), 51–61.

Deci, E. L., & Ryan, R. M. (2000). The "what" and "why" of goal pursuits: Human needs and the self-determination of behavior. *Psychological Inquiry, 11*(4), 227–268.

DiRenzo, M. S., & Greenhaus, J. H. (2011). Job search and voluntary turnover in a boundaryless world: A control theory perspective. *Academy of Management Review, 36*(3), 567–589.

Dobrow, S. R., & Tosti-Kharas, J. (2011). Calling: The development of a scale measure. *Personnel Psychology, 64*(4), 1001–1049.

Dooley, D., Prause, J., & Ham-Rowbottom, K. A. (2000). Underemployment and depression: Longitudinal relationships. *Journal of Health and Social Behavior, 41*(4), 421–436.

Dries, N. (2011). The meaning of career success. Avoiding reification through a closer inspection of historical, cultural, and ideological contexts. *Career Development International, 16*(4), 364–384.

Dries, N., Pepermans, R., & Carlier, O. (2008). Career success: Constructing a multidimensional model. *Journal of Vocational Behavior, 73*(2), 254–267.

Duffy, R. D., Dik, B. J., & Steger, M. F. (2011). Calling and work-related outcomes: Career commitment as a mediator. *Journal of Vocational Behavior, 78*(2), 210–218.

Duffy, R. D., & Sedlacek, W. E. (2007). The presence of and search for a calling: Connections to career development. *Journal of Vocational Behavior, 70*(3), 590–601.

Elliot, A. J. (1999). Approach and avoidance motivation and achievement goal. *Educational Psychologist, 34*(3), 169–189.

Elliot, A. J., & Covington, M. V. (2001). Approach and avoidance motivation. *Educational Psychology Review, 13*(2), 73–92.

Feldman, D. C., & Leana, C. R. (2000). A study of reemployed challenges after downsizing. *Organizational Dynamics, 29*(1), 64–75.

Feldman, D. C., Leana, C. R., & Bolino, M. C. (2002). Underemployment and relative deprivation among re-employed executives. *Journal of Occupational and Organizational Psychology, 75*(4), 453–471.

Forret, M. L., Sullivan, S. E., & Mainiero, L. A. (2010). Gender role differences in reactions to unemployment: Exploring psychological mobility and boundaryless careers. *Journal of Organizational Behavior, 31*(5), 647–666.

Gabriel, Y., Gray, D. E., & Goregaokar, H. (2010). Temporary derailment or the end of the line? Managers coping with unemployment at 50. *Organization Studies, 31*(12), 1687–1712.

Gebel, M. (2012). Early career consequences of temporary employment in Germany and the UK. *Work, Employment and Society, 24*(4), 641–660.

Gunz, H. P., & Heslin, P. A. (2005). Reconceptualizing career success. *Journal of Organizational Behavior, 26*(2), 105–111.

Haider, S. J., & Stephens, M. J. (2001). "The impact of displacement on older workers" (DRU-2631-NIA—Labor and population program working paper series 01–13, prepared for the National Institute on Aging). Santa Monica, CA: Rand.

Hanisch, K. H. (1999). Job loss and unemployment research from 1994 to 1998: A review and recommendations for research and interventions. *Journal of Vocational Behavior, 55*(2), 188–220.

Heslin, P. A. (2005). Conceptualizing and evaluating career success. *Journal of Organizational Behavior, 26*(2), 113–136.

Ibarra, H. (1999). Provisional selves: Experimenting with image and identity in professional adaptation. *Administrative Science Quarterly, 44*(4), 764–791.

Ibarra, H. (2003). *Working identity: unconventional strategies for reinventing your career.* Boston: Harvard Business School Press.

Ibarra, H., & Barbulescu, R. (2010). Identity as narrative: Prevalence, effectiveness, and consequences of narrative identity work in macro work role transitions. *Academy of Management Review, 35*(1), 135–154.

Jones, L. P. (1989). A typology of adaptations to unemployment. *Journal of Employment Counseling, 26*(2), 50–59.

Kanfer, R., Wanberg, C. R., & Kantrowitz, T. M. (2001). Job search and employment: A personality-motivational analysis and meta-analytic review. *Journal of Applied Psychology, 86*(5), 837–855.

Kassam, K. S., Koslov, K., & Berry Mendes, W. (2009). Decisions under distress: Stress profiles influence anchoring and adjustment. *Psychological Science, 20*(11), 1394–1399.

Khapova, S. N., Arthur, M. B., Wilderom, C. P. M., & Svensson, J. S. (2007). Professional identity as the key to career change intention. *Career Development International, 12*(7), 584–595.

Klehe, U.-C., Zikic, J., Van Vianen, A. E. M., De Pater, I. (2011). Career adaptability, turnover and loyalty during organizational downsizing. *Journal of Vocational Behavior, 79*(1), 217–229.

Koen, J., Klehe, U.-C., & Van Vianen, A. E. M. (2010). "Development of job-search and employability over time: A matter of motivation?" Paper presented at the Academy of Management, Montreal Canada, August 2010.

Koen, J., Klehe, U.-C., Van Vianen, A. E. M., Zikic, J., & Nauta, A. (2010). Job-search strategies and reemployment quality: The impact of career adaptability. *Journal of Vocational Behavior, 77*(1), 126–139.

Koen, J., Klehe, U. C., & Van Vianen, A. E. M. (in press). Job-search and employability after compulsory reemployment courses: The role of choice, usefulness and quality of motivation. *Applied Psychology: an International Review.*

Kreiner, G. E., Hollensbe, E. C., & Sheep, M. L. (2006) Where is the "me" among the "we"? Identity work and the search for optimal balance. *Academy of Management Journal, 49*(5), 1031–1057.

Leana, C. R., Feldman, D. C., & Tan, G. Y. (1998). Predictors of coping behavior after a layoff. *Journal of Organizational Behavior, 19*(1), 85–97.

Lent, R. W., Brown, S. D., & Hackett, G. (2000). Contextual supports and barriers to career choice: A social cognitive analysis. *Journal of Counseling Psychology, 47*(1), 36–49.

Loughlin, C., & Barling, J. (2001). Young workers' work values, attitudes, and behaviours. *Journal of Occupational and Organizational Psychology, 74*(4), 543–558.

Mauno, S., Feldt, T., Tolvanen, A., Hyvönen, K., & Kinnunen, U. (2011). Prospective relationships between career disruptions and subjective well-being: Evidence from a three-wave follow-up study among Finnish managers. *International Archives of Occupational and Environmental Health, 84*(5), 501–512.

McConnell, A. R. (2011). The multiple self-aspects framework: Self-concept representation and its implications. *Personality and Social Psychology Review, 15*(1), 3–27.

McKee-Ryan, F., Song, Z., Wanberg, C. R., & Kinicki, A. J. (2005). Psychological and physical well-being during unemployment: A meta-analytic study. *Journal of Applied Psychology, 90*(1), 53–76.

Mirvis, P. H., & Hall, D. T. (1994). Psychological success and the boundaryless career. *Journal of Organizational Behavior, 15*(4), 365–380.

Ng, T. W. H., Eby, L. T., Sorensen, K. L., & Feldman, D. C. (2005). Predictors of objective and subjective career success: A meta-analysis. *Personnel Psychology, 58*(2), 367–408.

Ng, T. W. H., & Feldman, D. C. (2008). The relationship of age to ten dimensions of job performance. *Journal of Applied Psychology, 93*(2), 392–423.

Ng, T. W. H., & Feldman, D. C. (2009). Occupational embeddedness and job performance. *Journal of Organizational Behavior, 30*(7), 836–891.

Paul, K. I., & Moser, K. (2009). Unemployment impairs mental health: meta-analyses. *Journal of Vocational Behavior, 74*(3), 264–282.

Petriglieri, J. L. (2011). Under threat: Responses to and the consequences of threats to individuals' identities. *Academy of Management Review, 36*(4), 641–662.

Petrongolo, B. (2009). The long-term effects of job search requirements: Evidence from the UK JSA reform. *Journal of Public Economics, 93*(11–12), 1234–1253.

Pratt, M. G., Rockmann, K. W., & Kaufmann, J. B. (2006). Constructing professional identity: The role of work and identity learning cycles in the customization of identity among medical residents, *Academy of Management Journal, 49*(2), 235–262.

Preenen, P. T. Y., De Pater, I. E., Van Vianen, A. E. M, & Keijzer, L. (2011). Managing voluntary turnover through challenging assignments. *Group and Organization Management, 36*, 308–344.

Price, R. H., Choi, J. N., & Vinokur, A. D. (2002). Links in the chain of adversity following job loss: How financial strain and loss of personal control lead to depression, impaired functioning, and poor health. *Journal of Occupational Health Psychology, 7*(4), 302–312.

Pryor, R. G. L., & Bright, J. E. H. (2007). Applying chaos theory to careers: Attraction and attractors. *Journal of Vocational Behavior, 71*(3), 375–400.

Paul, K. I., Hassel, A., & Moser, K. (in press). Individual consequences of job loss and unemployment. In Klehe, U.-C. & van Hooft, E. A. (Eds.) *Oxford handbook of job loss and job search*. New York: Oxford University Press.

Randel, A. E. & Jaussi, K. S. (2003). Functional background identity, diversity, and individual performance in cross-functional teams. *Academy of Management Journal, 46*(6), 763–774.

Rife, J. C., & First, R. J. (1989). Discouraged older workers—An exploratory study. *International Journal of Aging & Human Development, 29*(3), 195–203.

Rothbard, N. P., & Edwards, J. R. (2003). Investment in work and family roles: A test of identity and utilitarian motives. *Personnel Psychology, 56*(3), 699–729.

Rothwell, A., & Arnold, J. (2007). Self-perceived employability: Development and validation of a scale. *Personnel Review, 36*(1), 23–41.

Savickas, M. L. (1997). Career adaptability: An integrative construct for life-span, life-space theory. *The Career Development Quarterly, 45*(3), 247–259.

Savickas, M., Nota, L., Rossier, J., Dauwalder, J. P., Duarte, M. E. C, Guichard, J., . . .; Van Vianen, A. E. M. (2009). Life design: A paradigm for career construction in the 21st century. *Journal of Vocational Behavior, 75*(3), 239–250.

Savickas, M. L., & Porfeli, E. J. (2012). The career adapt-abilities scale: Construction, reliability, and measurement equivalence across 13 countries. *Journal of Vocational Behavior, 80*, 661–673.

Seibert, S. E., Crant, J. M., & Kraimer, M. L. (1999). Proactive personality and career success. *Journal of Applied Psychology, 84*(3), 416–427.

Sluss, D. M., & Ashforth, B. E. (2008). How relational and organizational identification converge: Processes and conditions. *Organization Science, 19*(6), 807–823.

Super, D. E. (1980). A life-span, life-space approach to career development. *Journal of Vocational Behavior, 16*(3), 282–298.

Sverke, M., Hellgren, J., & Näswall, K. (2002). No security: a meta-analysis and review of job insecurity and its consequences. *Journal of Occupational Health Psychology, 7*(3), 242–264.

Swann, W. B., Griffin, J. J., Predmore, S. C., & Gaines, B. (1987). The cognitive-affective crossfire: When self-consistency confronts self-enhancement. *Journal of Personality and Social Psychology, 52*(5), 881–889.

Tosti-Kharas, J. (2012). Continued organizational identification following involuntary job loss. *Journal of Managerial Psychology*, 829–847.

Van der Heijde, C. M., & Van der Heijden, B. I. J. M. (2006). A competence-based and multidimensional operationalization and measurement of employability. *Human Resource Management, 45*(3), 449–476.

Van Vianen, A. E. M., Dalhoeven, B. A. G. W., & De Pater, I. E. (2011). Aging and training and development willingness: Employee and supervisor mindsets. *Journal of Organizational Behavior, 32*(2), 226–247.

Van Vianen, A. E. M., De Pater, I. E., & Preenen, P. T. Y. (2009). Adaptable careers: Deciding less and exploring more. *Career Development Quarterly, 57*(4), 298–310.

Vohs, K. D., & Baumeister, R. F. (2004). Understanding self-regulation. In R. F. Baumeister & K. D. Vohs (Eds.), *Handbook of self-regulations: Research, theory, and applications* (pp. 1–9). New York: Guilford Press.

Walsh, K., & Gordon, J. R. (2008). Creating an individual work identity. *Human Resource Management Review, 18*(1), 46–61.

Wang, J., Novemsky, N., & Dhar, R. (2009). Anticipating adaptation to products. *Journal of Consumer Research, 36*, 149–159.

Wrzesniewski, A., McCauley, C., Rozin, P., & Schwartz, B. (1997). Jobs, careers, and callings: People's relations to their work. *Journal of Research in Personality, 31*(1), 21–33.

Zikic, J., & Hall, D. T. (2009). Toward a more complex view of career exploration. *The Career Development Quarterly, 58*(2), 181–192.

Zicik, J., & Klehe, U.-C. (2006). Job loss as a blessing in disguise: The role of career exploration and career planning in predicting reemployment quality. *Journal of Vocational Behavior, 69*(3), 391–409.

Zikic, J., & Richardson, J. (2007). Unlocking the careers of business professionals following job loss: Sensemaking and career exploration of older workers. *Canadian Journal of Administrative Sciences-Revue Canadienne Des Sciences De L Administration, 24*(1), 58–73.

Economic Job Search and Decision-Making Models

Gerard J. van den Berg *and* Arne Uhlendorff

Abstract

The economic job search theory is based on the assumption that individuals have imperfect information about jobs and wages. It takes time to find an acceptable job and individuals have to make decisions about their job search behavior. The optimal job search behavior is characterized by the reservation wage, that is, the wage above which job offers are accepted, and by the search effort. Both components depend on factors such as the income during job search and the probability of receiving a job offer. Search effort can be described by the amount of resources used for finding a job, which includes time but can also include the type of search channels. We present the basic models of economic job search theory and selected empirical findings, in which we focus on the job search behavior of unemployed individuals.

Key Words: job search theory, unemployment duration, reservation wage, search effort

Introduction

Psychologists and economists have studied the determinants and outcomes of the job search process for several decades. However, the theoretical and empirical approaches are quite different. The aim of this chapter is to provide an overview of the basic models of economic job search theory including selected empirical findings. Traditional neoclassical labor market models are unable to explain long spells of possibly involuntary unemployment. In these models individuals have perfect information about the labor market, which implies that time and cost of looking for a job do not play a role in the individual labor supply decision. In contrast to this, one main assumption of job search theory is that individuals have only imperfect information about jobs and wages. It is assumed that the unemployed know the probability of receiving a job offer with a specific wage, but they do not know for sure when they will receive which job offer. In other words wage offers occur randomly from the point of view of the individual and it usually takes some time and

can involve some effort for a worker to get a good job offer with an acceptable wage. This generates probability distributions for observed labor market outcomes such as unemployment and job durations and wages. The imperfect information is usually denoted by the phrase "search frictions"; employers are also faced with these search frictions since they do not know when they will find a worker for a job vacancy.[1] These models have proven to be fruitful tools for the understanding of unemployment duration and the effectiveness of labor market policies aimed at bringing the unemployed back to work.

We focus on the decision problem of unemployed individuals with imperfect information. According to the standard assumption in economic models unemployed individuals choose their job search behavior to maximize their (expected) utility. Given their information about the labor market they choose an optimal reservation wage, that is, the wage at which the benefits or the expected utility of continued search are just equal to the additional search costs. Search costs include monetary and nonmonetary costs. Any wage above the reservation wage is accepted, whereas any offer below the reservation is rejected. Starting with a basic stationary model in which it is assumed that components such as the job offer arrival rate do not vary over time, we discuss important extensions including the introduction of nonstationarity—models in which, for example, the amount of unemployment benefits could change over time—and the introduction of endogenous search effort—models in which the unemployed individuals choose how much of their resources to invest in a job search. Search effort can be modeled and measured as the time spent for a job search, but there also exist studies that model the choice between different search channels that might have different productivities. In these models concepts such as social networks can be incorporated, which might have an impact on the quantity and the quality of job offers. Recently psychological concepts such as the locus of control have also been taken into account in economic job search models. We do not discuss the search process and the production functions of firms nor equilibrium search models. For surveys that include these models see, for example, Mortensen and Pissarides (1999), Rogerson, Shimer, and Wright (2005), and Eckstein and van den Berg (2007).

The theoretical models on the job search behavior of unemployed individuals have been structurally estimated using data on individual labor market outcomes including unemployment duration, job duration, and wages. "Structural" here means that the theoretical framework is assumed to describe the empirical distribution of durations and wages and that the structural parameters are estimated directly based on the observed data. The main advantage of structural models is that they allow for an evaluation of counterfactual policies, that is, policies that have not been implemented in reality. Moreover, these models have been used to interpret estimates of reduced-form duration models, that is, models in which functions of the structural parameters are estimated rather than a direct estimation of structural parameters. The common feature of both approaches is that they are based on search models that describe the duration in unemployment until the unemployed received a job offer with a wage above the reservation wage. The main empirical framework for analyzing job search behavior and job search outcomes therefore involves duration models, which are, for example, described in Lancaster (1990) and van den Berg (2001).

In contrast to other social sciences, in economics the individual decision problem is usually presented in a rather formal way. In economic models it is assumed that the individual maximizes his or her expected utility based on the available information. Moreover, in the standard model it is assumed that the individual is aware of the consequences of his or her behavior on the probability of future outcomes and takes this into account. These models might often sound unrealistic from a psychological point of view. However, in economics we are usually not interested in explaining the behavior of a specific individual. Instead, economists are interested in average outcomes of individual behavior—for example, the average impact of an extension of unemployment benefit payments on job search behavior—and the aggregated (equilibrium) outcome—such as the number of employees in a specific sector. Although economic models often appear (especially to noneconomists) to be based on very simple assumptions, these simplifying assumptions have the advantage of keeping the models mathematically tractable and permitting concrete predictions about economic decisions and outcomes to be made. Moreover, the formal presentation ensures a rigorous analysis of the decision problems and the aggregation of individual behavior.

This chapter is organized as follows: the next section presents the basic job search model, followed by sections that introduce nonstationarity to the decision problem and that then discuss the extension to on-the-job search. We then introduce an endogenous job search effort followed by a section that presents the idea of different search channels, which is related to the role of social networks in the job search process. Two studies are then discussed that analyze the impact of policy measures on the job search behavior of unemployed individuals in the context of job search models; this is followed by a discussion of recent approaches to take personality traits into account when modeling job search decisions. The conclusions end the chapter.

Basic Search Model with a Stationarity Assumption

We start by considering the basic job search model for the behavior of unemployed workers. This model has been discussed extensively; see for example Mortensen (1986) (accordingly, the exposition follows that of Mortensen, 1986, and also van den Berg, 2001). It aims to describe the behavior of unemployed individuals in a dynamic and uncertain environment. Job offers arrive at random intervals following a Poisson process with arrival rate λ. A job offer is a random drawing (without recall) from a wage offer distribution with distribution function $F(w)$ In this stylized model it is assumed that all jobs are fulltime jobs and for simplicity we start with the assumption that search effort is exogenously given and is the same for everybody, that is, the search behavior does not include the choice about the individual search effort. Every time an offer arrives, the decision has to be made as to whether to accept the offer or reject it and search further. Once a job is accepted it will be held forever at the same wage, so job-to-job transitions are excluded. It is assumed that individuals know the arrival rate λ and the wage offer distribution F but that they do not know in advance when job offers arrive and what wages are associated with them. During the period of unemployment a benefit b is received. Unemployed individuals aim at maximizing their own expected present value of income over an infinite horizon. The subjective rate of discount is denoted by ρ. A high ρ implies that individuals value current income flows more than future income flows compared to individuals with a low discount rate. In general, a job offer will be accepted if the expected present value of utility resulting from accepting this job—which in this model corresponds for simplicity to the present value of income—is higher than the expected present value of continuing to look for a job.

The variables λ, w, b, and ρ are measured per unit time period. It is assumed that the model is stationary. This means that λ, F, b, and ρ are assumed to be constant, and, in particular, are independent of unemployment duration and calendar time and independent of all events during unemployment. To ensure that attention is restricted to economically meaningful cases, and to guarantee the existence of the optimal strategy, we assume that $0 < \lambda, E_F(w), b, \rho < \infty$. For ease of exposition we take F to be continuous. Let R denote the expected present value of search when following the optimal strategy. Because of the stationarity assumption and the infinite-horizon assumption, the unemployed individual's perception of the future is independent of time or unemployment duration, so the optimal strategy is constant during the period of unemployment and R does not depend on the elapsed unemployment duration t. It is well known (see, e.g., Mortensen, 1986) that there is a unique solution to the Bellman equation for R, satisfying

$$\rho R = b + \lambda \, E_w \max\left\{0, \frac{w}{\rho} - R\right\} \tag{1}$$

A Bellman equation describes the value of a decision problem at a certain point in time. In this decision problem, the individual maximizes the value of the current utility and the discounted value of the future payoffs. In equation (1), the expectation is taken over the wage offer distribution F. Equation (1) has a familiar structure (see, e.g., Pissarides, 1990). The return of the asset R in a small interval around t equals the sum of the instantaneous utility flow in this interval and the expected excess value of finding a job in this interval. When an offer of w arrives at t then there are two options: (1) to reject it (excess value zero), and (2) to accept it (excess value $w/\rho - R$). It is clear that the optimal policy is to choose option (2) iff $w > \rho R$. Therefore, the optimal strategy of the worker can be characterized by a reservation wage ϕ: a job offer is acceptable iff its wage exceeds ϕ, with $\phi = \rho R$. Using equation (1), ϕ can be expressed in terms of the model determinants,

$$\phi = b + \frac{\lambda}{\rho} \int_\phi^\infty \bar{F}(w)\,dw \tag{2}$$

This equation implies that when receiving a job offer the individuals compare the utility of accepting a job offer with the utility of continuing to search for another job. If the wage is below ϕ, the job offer is rejected. It is possible to easily generalize ϕ to not only consist of a wage but also depend on other nonmonetary characteristics. Note that the equation has a unique solution for ϕ. The model implies that reservation wages are increasing in unemployment benefits and in the job offer arrival rate. This is quite intuitive as both components increase the expected present value of being unemployed. The unemployment benefits b have a direct impact because they increase the income during the job search, whereas the increased job offer arrival rate λ has an impact on the expected present value of unemployment because it increases the probability of receiving a suitable job offer in the future.

The hazard (or exit rate out of unemployment, or transition rate from unemployment into employment) ϑ equals the product of the job offer arrival rate and the conditional probability of accepting a job offer,

$$\theta = \lambda \bar{F}(\phi) \tag{3}$$

Obviously, the exit rate out of unemployment is higher the higher the job offer arrival rate and the lower the reservation wage. As a result of the stationarity assumption, θ does not depend on the elapsed duration of unemployment. Consequently, the duration of unemployment t has an exponential distribution with parameter θ. The average unemployment duration is given by

$$T_u = \frac{1}{\lambda \bar{F}(\phi)} \tag{4}$$

This implies that an increase in the unemployment benefits should lead to an increase of the average unemployment duration. Moreover, the individuals should end up on average with better jobs in the sense that they have on average a higher wage. In contrast to this, the impact of an increase in the job arrival rate on the unemployment duration is theoretically ambiguous as on the one hand it leads to an increase in the reservation wage but on the other hand it leads to an increase in the probability of receiving an acceptable job offer for a given reservation wage.

An individual who is unemployed and actively searching for a job may drop out of the labor force at some point of time during unemployment. The standard job search model can be extended by allowing for transitions from unemployment to nonparticipation; see, for example, van den Berg (1990b). In this model the optimal strategy of an unemployed individual depends on the expected utility of becoming a nonparticipant. If the latter is high with respect to the expected utility of becoming employed then it is optimal to accept a job offer only if the wage corresponding to it is very high. Transitions into nonparticipation might occur, for example, when an unemployed individual becomes disabled, retires, or returns to school.

Versions of the stationary job search model have been structurally estimated with individual data on unemployment durations and wages. "Structural" here means that the theoretical framework is assumed to describe the empirical distribution of durations and wages. This enables estimation of the determinants λ, F,. . . of individual behavior. See Flinn and Heckman (1982), Narendranathan and Nickell (1985), and van den Berg (1990b) for examples of this and see Wolpin (1995) for a survey.

Search Models that are Nonstationary

The stationarity assumption made in the previous section is often unrealistic. The model parameters may change over time because of duration dependence of the amount of unemployment benefits, a stigma effect of being long-term unemployed, policy changes, or business cycle effects. Sooner or later these features of the labor market and personal characteristics of job searchers are recognized and used in determining the optimal strategy. So, generally, the optimal strategy is not constant in case of nonstationarity. Two types of nonstationarity can be distinguished: (1) nonstationarity without anticipation, that is, the individuals do not know that the environment is changing, and (2) nonstationarity with anticipation, that is, the individuals know that the environment is changing over time and take these future changes into account.

No Anticipation

We start with assuming that the individual's search environment is subject to unanticipated changes in the values of the structural determinants. Thus, the values of these determinants may change over the duration, but the individual always thinks that they will remain constant at their current values. This might be a reasonable assumption in case of a change in λ that is due to a random macroeconomic shock, or in case of a change in b that is due to a sudden change in the benefits system.

By exploiting the analogy to the stationary model, we obtain the following equations for the reservation wage function $\phi(t)$, giving the reservation wage at time t and the hazard function $\theta(t)$,

$$\phi(t) = b(t) + \frac{\lambda(t)}{\rho(t)} \int_{\phi(t)}^{\infty} \bar{F}(w|t)\, dw \tag{5}$$

$$\theta(t) = \lambda(t) \bar{F}(\phi(t)|t) \tag{6}$$

where $F(w|t)$ denotes the wage offer distribution at time t (so it should not be interpreted as a distribution conditional on the realization of a random duration variable). The reservation wage might change over time depending on realizations of $b(t), \lambda(t), \rho(t)$, and $F(w|t)$ at t, but future values of these parameters do not have any impact on the behavior in t. In general, $\theta(t)$ varies with t. See Narendranathan (1993) for a structural empirical analysis of a nonstationary model without anticipation.

With Anticipation

In many cases it is not realistic to assume that individuals do not anticipate changes in the values of λ, F, and b. In this section we consider nonstationarity with anticipation along the lines of van den Berg (1990a).[2] The structural determinants λ, F, and b are allowed to vary over the duration t in a deterministic way (so dependence on past offer arrival times or wage levels associated with rejected offers is ruled out). This entails that the process with which job offers arrive is a nonhomogeneous Poisson process. We assume that job searchers have perfect foresight in the sense that they correctly anticipate changes in the values of λ, F, and b. In other words, we expect people to know how these are related to t. As usual, individuals do not know in advance when job offers arrive, or which w is associated with them. Finally, we assume that λ, F, and b are constant for all sufficiently high t. The latter implies that the optimal strategy is also constant for sufficiently high t.

Let $R(t)$ denote the expected present value of search if the unemployment duration equals t, when following the optimal strategy. There is a unique continuous solution to the Bellman equation for $R(t)$, satisfying

$$\rho R(t) = \frac{dR(t)}{dt} + b(t)$$
$$+ \lambda(t) \, \mathrm{E}_{w|t} \max \left\{ 0, \frac{w}{\rho} - R(t) \right\} \qquad (7)$$

at points at which $R(t)$ is differentiable in t, where the expectation is taken over the wage offer distribution $F(w|t)$ at t. Note the similarity to equation (1) above. The return of the asset $R(t)$ in a small interval around t equals the sum of the appreciation of the asset in this interval, the instantaneous utility flow in this interval, and the expected excess value of finding a job in this interval. The optimization problem is similar to the search model without anticipating changes over time, see equation (5), but now the individual takes the changes of the present value of search over time $(dR(t)/dt)$ into account. The optimal strategy can be characterized by a reservation wage function $\phi(t)$ that gives the reservation wage at time t. Using the fact that $\phi(t) = \rho R(t)$, it follows that

$$\phi(t) = \frac{dR(t)}{dt} + b(t)$$
$$+ \frac{\lambda(t)}{\rho} \int_{\phi(t)}^{\infty} (w - \phi(t)) dF(w|t) \qquad (8)$$

$$\frac{d\phi(t)}{dt} = \rho\phi(t) - \rho b(t)$$
$$- \lambda(t) \int_{\phi(t)}^{\infty} (w - \phi(t)) dF(w|t) \qquad (9)$$

This differential equation has a unique solution for $\phi(t)$, given the boundary condition that follows from the assumption that the model is stationary for all sufficiently high t.

The hazard function $\theta(t)$ now equals

$$\theta(t) = \lambda(t) \overline{F}(\phi(t)|t) \qquad (10)$$

In general, $\vartheta(t)$ varies with t. This model implies that any future shift in the time path of exogenous variables that benefits the expected discounted lifetime income induces job searchers to be more selective in their search process. An example of this could be the introduction of an intensive job search assistance program for unemployed individuals that starts after a specific time spent in unemployment. This program might increase the probability of receiving job offers, and therefore it would induce the unemployed to increase their reservation wage even before they entered the program.

For examples of structural empirical analyses of nonstationary models with anticipation, see Wolpin (1987), van den Berg (1990a), Engberg (1991), and Garcia-Perez (1998). Frijters and van der Klaauw (2006) extend the nonstationary framework of van den Berg (1990a) by allowing for endogenous nonparticipation, that is, individuals might choose to leave the labor force at some point of time during unemployment. van den Berg (1990a) provides an empirical application for the nonstationary model that focuses on the consequences of a downward shift in the level of benefits after some time of unemployment. In economics, the elasticity describes the degree to which one economic variable induces a change in another economic variable, that is, the elasticity corresponds to the ratio of the relative change in one variable and the relative change in another variable. It appears that the elasticity of duration with respect to the level of benefits after the shift is much larger than the elasticity with respect to the level before the shift.

There also exist numerous reduced form studies on the impact of changes in the benefit duration— a nonstationarity in $b(t)$—on the probability of leaving unemployment for a job. In reduced form studies the underlying structural parameters of the decision problem is not estimated directly. Instead, functions of the structural parameters are estimated. Meyer (1990), Katz and Meyer (1990), Card and Levine (2000), and Addison and Portugal (2008) find in the United States a sharp increase in the exit rate from unemployment before benefits are exhausted. For Europe, Hunt (1995) for Germany, Lalive (2008) for Austria, Røed and Zhang (2003) for Norway, and van Ours and Vodopivec (2008) for Slovenia find that benefit extensions reduce job finding rates and create a spike around benefit exhaustion.

The empirical evidence for the effect of unemployment insurance on postunemployment outcomes is rather mixed. Whereas, for example, Belzil (2001) analyzes unemployment experience and employment duration in the context of the Canadian unemployment insurance reform and finds a weak positive relationship between reemployment duration and unemployment benefit generosity, Card et al. (2007) find for Austria that an increase in benefit entitlement length reduces job-finding rates but does not have any effect on subsequent job match quality, measured in wage growth and job duration. Similarly, van Ours and Vodopivec (2008) find no effect on the quality of postunemployment jobs for Slovenia, whereas Caliendo, Tatsiramos, and Uhlendorff (2013) provide evidence that finding a job close to and shortly after benefit exhaustion is associated with less stable employment patterns and lower reemployment wages.

Search in Employment

The assumption made in the previous sections that unemployed individuals will keep a job forever once they receive a suitable job offer does not seem to be very realistic. This assumption can easily be relaxed. First, models can be extended by including a separation probability ϑ, that is, a probability that the job match ends involuntarily from the perspective of the worker. Second, the model can be extended to allow the worker to search further for better matches after accepting a job offer and a job match has been formed. These so-called on-the-job search models aim to describe the behavior of employed individuals who search for a better job (see Mortensen, 1986, for an overview).

In the basic on-the-job search model, a job is characterized by its wage w, which is taken to be constant within a job. For a working individual, the search environment is specified in exactly the same way as previously done for an unemployed individual. In particular, we assume the model to be

stationary. The optimal strategy is constant during a job spell, and the expected present value of search $R(w)$ when following the optimal strategy in a job with wage w satisfies

$$\rho R(w) = w + \lambda_e \, \mathrm{E}_{w^*} \cdot \max\left\{0, R\left(w^*\right) - R(w)\right\} \quad (11)$$

where the expectation is taken with respect to the distribution F of wage offers w^*. Clearly, the optimal strategy is such that a job is accepted if and only if the offered wage w^* exceeds the current wage w, so it suffices to compare instantaneous income flows (i.e., the optimal strategy is "myopic"), and the reservation wage simply equals the current wage. The job offer arrival rate during employment is given by λ_e, which differs from the job offer probability during λ_u. For a given current wage w, the hazard of the job duration distribution (or exit rate out of the present job) equals

$$\theta = \lambda_e \bar{F}(w) \quad (12)$$

As a result, the duration of a job with a wage w has an exponential distribution with this parameter ϑ. Note that models of repeated search are informative on the joint distribution of consecutive job durations.

The possibility of on-the-job search has implications for the optimal strategy of unemployed job seekers. If the difference in the job offer arrival rates between job search during unemployment and job search during employment $\lambda_u - \lambda_e$ is large, the value of searching for a job during unemployment is relatively high—which implies a relatively high reservation wage during unemployment—compared to a situation in which the difference $\lambda_u - \lambda_e$ is rather small. If there would be no difference between the job offer arrival rates (and if the search costs are the same for unemployed and employed workers) this would imply that every job offer with a wage above b would be accepted. If $\lambda_e > \lambda_u$ this would imply that the reservation would be even below b, because in this situation an employed worker has a higher probability of receiving a suitable job offer than an unemployed job seeker. However, this does not seem to be a realistic assumption. The unemployed job seeker is able to devote much more time to job search activities, which should result in more job offers. Moreover, unemployed job seekers usually receive referrals to job vacancies by their case workers, which is not the case for employed workers.

If, during employment, exogenous separations occur at a rate δ, then this does not affect the optimal strategy. The exit rate out of the present job then equals $\lambda_e \bar{F}(w) + \delta$. See Flinn (1996) for an example of the structural estimation of this model with job duration data.[3]

Burgess (1989) introduces a rather manageable type of nonstationarity in this model. The individual's search environment (i.e., λ and F) is subject to shocks that are not job specific but rather act similarly on all employed workers. The shocks may be anticipated or unanticipated. It is intuitively obvious that this nonstationarity does not change the optimal strategy: it remains optimal to accept another job if and only if its wage exceeds the current wage.

Endogenous Search Effort

The job search model can be extended by assuming that individuals not only make a decision about the optimal stopping rule—the reservation wage above which every job offer is accepted—but that they also decide about the intensity of their search. Similar to what was assumed previously, we assume in this section that each unemployed individual searches sequentially for a job in a stationary environment. However, now job offers arrive for a given search effort s with arrival rate $\lambda(s)$. This arrival rate depends positively on an individual's search effort when the marginal return to search effort is decreasing (i.e., $\lambda' > 0$ and $\lambda'' < 0$). Similar to the sections above, job offers are independent draws from a wage distribution $F(w)$, which is known by the unemployed. Each unemployed individual faces search costs $c(s)$, which are increasing in search effort (i.e., $c' > 0$ and $c'' > 0$).

In this model the reservation wage depends on the search effort, which has an impact on the job offer arrival, but also goes along with some costs. The utility flow during unemployment is given by $(b - c(s))$. The reservation wage is given by

$$\phi = b - c(s) + \lambda(s) \mathrm{E}_w \max\left\{0, \frac{w}{\rho} - R\right\} \quad (13)$$

Unemployed individuals choose both their search effort s and reservation wage ϕ so as to maximize their discounted expected utility R. We can solve for the optimal search effort s^* by differentiating the relation (13) with respect to s and solving for s^* such that $\partial\phi/\partial s = 0$. Specifically,

$$c'\left(s^*\right) = \frac{\lambda'\left(s^*\right)}{\rho} \int_\phi^\infty \left(w - \phi\right) dF\left(w\right). \quad (14)$$

Equation (14) implies that individuals choose their optimal search effort by equating the marginal cost of job search with the marginal benefits associated with additional search, that is, an increased probability of receiving a job offer paying more than their reservation wage.

This model implies that an increase in the income during unemployment b next leads to an increase in the reservation wage additionally to a lower amount of search effort. The reason for this is that an increase in the utility flow during unemployment leads to an increase in the reservation wage, which for a given search effort decreases the probability of receiving a job offer above ϕ. To equalize the marginal benefits and costs of the search effort the optimal strategy implies that the unemployed lowers the search effort.

This model can be extended to allow for changes in the job arrival rate depending on the state of the economy. It can be shown that given the multiplicative impact of the state of the employment on $\lambda(s)$, the unemployed lower their reservation wage and decrease their search effort. The implications are quite intuitive. Conditional on search intensity, in a better state of the economy with a higher demand for labor individuals receive more job offers. For them remaining unemployed and waiting for new job offers have a higher expected utility, which leads to a higher reservation wage. For a given amount of search and a specific reservation wage, the marginal returns of search are also higher in periods with a higher demand for labor. So, to equalize the marginal returns and marginal costs of search, individuals search more if the state of the economy is better.

For an example of a structural estimation of a model with endogenous job search effort see Bloemen (2005). In contrast to the basic model with search effort he allows for the choice of different channels of search, because search is measured by several indicators in his data set, and his model incorporates on-the-job search. His findings suggest, for example, that the number of applications affects the arrival rate significantly for unemployed individuals.

Social Networks and Informal Search Channels

Social networks are an important source of information in the labor market and many workers find jobs through friends and relatives. Seminal studies by Rees (1966) and Granovetter (1995) show that a considerable part of the working population relies on personal contacts to obtain information about job offers. The widespread use of informal search channels has given rise to an extensive body of literature investigating the effect of networks and informal search on labor market outcomes.

One reasonable assumption is that informal job contacts reduce informational asymmetry by lowering uncertainty about the job match quality for both employees and the employers (see, e.g., Montgomery, 1991). In terms of labor market outcomes this mechanism should lead to higher wages and longer job tenure. However, the empirical evidence is rather mixed. In particular, it has been found that informal search success can be associated with a premium as well as penalty in terms of wages and employment stability (compare, e.g., Ioannides & Datcher Loury, 2004, and Mouw, 2003, for overviews). More recent studies focus on the quality of the information transmitted via the network. It is argued that the productivity of the network is determined by the characteristics of individuals composing the network, and it is expected that the employment status of individuals within a network is correlated with each other (compare Calvo-Armengol & Jackson, 2007).

In the analysis of job search with multiple search channels it is usually assumed that the choice of a particular search channel and the channel specific search effort is determined by the relative efficiency of that channel in generating acceptable job offers. In the optimum, an individual equalizes the marginal returns of the different search channels. For a general job search model with two search channels, informal and formal search, see van den Berg and van der Klaauw (2006). Formal search usually includes formalized search methods such as personnel advertisements and the public employment office whereas informal search occurs when, for example, unemployed workers receive job offers through a referral by an employed worker, a friend, or a relative.

An early example of a study on the determinants of the choice of search methods and its effectiveness is Holzer (1988). Using a sample of unemployed youth—who are interviewed at different points in time during their unemployment spell—his findings suggest that the main determinants of search channel use are the relative costs in terms of time spent on a particular channel for generating job offers and acceptances. More recently Weber

and Mahringer (2008) conducted a similar analysis, looking at the job search choices of newly employed workers in Austria. In line with the previous studies they find that contacting friends is one of the most often used search methods. Moreover, they find evidence that job search via the public employment office usually does not pay off for the job seekers.

An example of a study analyzing the impact of social networks on job search channels and search outcomes is Whaba and Zenou (2005). They use population density as a proxy for the size of social networks and find—based on cross-sectional data for Egypt—that the probability of finding a job through friends and relatives increases and is concave with population density. Mouw (2003) explicitly considers the relationship between specific network characteristics and the use of informal search channels. However, he does not find any evidence for a positive relationship between the "quality" of a network, for example, the proportion of friends in similar jobs, and the use of informal search channels. Caliendo, Schmidl, and Uhlendorff (2011) analyze the relationship between social networks and the job search behavior of unemployed individuals in Germany. Their findings suggest that individuals with larger networks use informal search channels more often and that they have higher reservation wages.

A structural analysis of the differences between formal and informal search is conducted by Koning, van den Berg, and Ridder (1997). In their analysis they find no evidence for differences in the wage offer distributions between formal and informal search channels, but there is an increased exit rate from unemployment for the use of informal channels compared to formal channels. However, they do not find any significant effect for a social network indicator—reflecting the number of friends—on the exit rate from unemployment to employment via informal channels.

Active Labor Market Policy and Job Search Behavior

Job search theory can be used to understand the impact of policy measures on the job search behavior and the employment outcomes of unemployed individuals. This is especially true for measures that aim to influence the search behavior of unemployed workers directly, such as monitoring and counseling schemes. In a monitoring scheme caseworkers might, for example, ask the job seekers to prove their job search effort, whereas in counseling schemes unemployed individuals are supported in their search, for example, by informing them about job vacancies. The job search theory helps to understand how and why measures might work and which could be ways to improve existing policy programs. In this section we present two examples for policy evaluations in the context of job search theory.

van den Berg and van der Klaauw (2006) theoretically and empirically analyze the effect of counseling and monitoring in a job search model with two search channels and endogenous search effort, allowing for formal and informal job search. Job offers arrive from the formal search channel with the arrival rate λ_1 and from the informal search channel with the arrival rate λ_2, with both arrival rates depending on the search specific search efforts s_1 and s_2. They assume that counseling is increasing the job arrival rate of formal job search λ_1. They show that this should lead to an increase in the optimal reservation wage. A higher value of λ_1 improves the present value of the unemployed worker and therefore he or she becomes more selective concerning the wages offered. If formal job search becomes more efficient, individuals also substitute an informal job search effort into a formal job search effort. Counseling might also increase the arrival rate of informal jobs λ_2. However, the results hold as long as the increase in λ_1 is larger than the increase in λ_2. Additionally, van den Berg and van der Klaauw (2006) assume that monitoring concerns the formal job search effort s_1 but not the informal search effort. This is plausible since the caseworkers of an unemployment insurance agency can, for example, check the number of times the unemployed responds to a job advertisement, but it would be much more difficult for a caseworker to measure how often an individual asks friends or relatives about job openings. In the case that monitoring implies a binding minimum search effort s_1, which is above the optimal individual search level, the marginal returns to formal job search effort are lower than the marginal costs. Even if job seekers would engage only in additional fake job applications, the marginal costs of search would be higher than the marginal returns. It can be shown that the optimal reservation wage is decreasing in the binding minimum level required for search effort. Unemployed workers are forced to behave suboptimally, which implies that being unemployed becomes less attractive, and therefore they are willing to accept jobs with lower wages.

Based on data from a social experiment with relatively well-qualified job seekers in the Netherlands van den Berg and van der Klaauw (2006) find no evidence that counseling has a significant impact on the exit rate to work. However, because the counseling component of the policy experiment was rather a low-intensity job search assistance, high-intensity job search assistance programs might have a more positive effect on job finding rates. In addition to that their results show that monitoring of relatively well-qualified individuals leads to inefficient substitution of search methods or channels, whereas the exit rate out of unemployment is not affected.

Fougère, Pradel, and Muriel (2009) develop a partial two-channel model in which one channel has a fixed and the other one has an endogenous search intensity. They use this model to analyze the impact of an increase in the job offer arrival rate of the formal search channel λ_1—contacts to employers through the public employment agency—on the job search behavior and the exit probability from unemployment to work. In their theoretical model they assume that the private search method is costly and unemployed individuals choose the optimal level of search effort for this channel, whereas the formal search channel is costless and exogenously given. They show that an increase in the exogenous job offer arrival rate through the public employment agency has a theoretically ambiguous effect. For a given amount of search effort, the reservation is increasing in λ_1, since the probability of receiving a suitable job offer in the future is increasing, which implies an increase of the present value of continuing search. In addition to that this also leads to a lower optimal search intensity for the informal search channel. They estimate a structural model based on French data to analyze whether these effects outweigh the direct positive impact of an increased job offer arrival rate λ_1 on the exit rate. Their results suggest that the exit rate from unemployment increases with λ_1 and that this is true especially for low-skilled workers. The search effort seems to be especially costly for low-skilled workers, which implies that increasing the job offers through the public employment agency for this group seems to be beneficial.

Job Search Behavior and Personality Traits

In economics there exists an increasing number of studies analyzing the impact of personality traits on economic outcomes. The empirical evidence indicates a positive correlation between noncognitive skills and economic outcomes such as wages or educational choices; see, for example, Almlund et al. (2011) for an overview. Some of these differences in economic outcomes between individuals might be driven by different search behavior. In this section we present two articles that incorporate personality traits into a job search model that are usually not taken into account in "standard" economic analysis. In psychology there exist several studies on the relationship between various personality characteristics and job search behavior. For a corresponding meta-analysis see Kanfer, Wanberg, and Kantrowitz (2001).

Standard job search theory assumes that unemployed individuals have perfect information about the effect of their search effort on the job offer arrival rate. This assumption can be relaxed by incorporating psychological concepts in the job search model. Caliendo, Cobb-Clark, and Uhlendorff (2014) present a job search model that assumes that each individual has a subjective belief about the impact of his or her search effort on the rate at which job offers arrive. This subjective belief depends in part on individuals' "locus of control," which is defined as a generalized expectation about the internal versus external control of reinforcement (Rotter, 1966). A person whose external locus of control dominates tends to believe that much of what happens is beyond his or her control. Life's outcomes are instead attributed to other forces, such as fate or luck, rather than to your own actions. In contrast, a person with an internal locus of control sees future outcomes as being contingent on his or her own decisions and behavior.

They assume that each individual has a subjective belief—given by $(\lambda^*(s, loc))$—about the effect of s on λ, which depends on the extent to which an individual has an internal locus of control (loc). Individuals with an internal locus of control believe that increased search effort results in a relatively large increase in the job offer arrival rate. In contrast, individuals who believe that their own behavior does not influence future outcomes believe that additional search effort has little effect on the rate at which job offers arrive. In other words $\dfrac{\partial \lambda^*(s, loc)}{\partial s}$ is assumed to be higher for those with a more internal locus of control than for those with a more

external locus of control, that is, $\dfrac{\partial^2 \lambda^*(s, loc)}{\partial s \partial loc} > 0$.

They model individuals' locus of control to have a multiplicative impact on the subjective beliefs about arrival rates: $\lambda^*(s, loc) = \lambda(s)f(loc)$, with $f'(loc) > 0$. Consistent with this model and based on German data, they find empirical evidence that individuals with an internal locus of control search more and that individuals who believe that their future outcomes are determined by external factors have lower reservation wages.

Della Vigna and Paserman (2005) analyze the effects of impatience on job search outcomes. Impatience implies that individuals assign lower values to future outcomes. Impatience has two effects on the job search behavior. On the one hand, individuals who are more impatient exert less effort because they assign a lower value to the future benefits of search. This should lead to a lower arrival rate and a lower exit probability from unemployment. On the other hand, more impatient individuals have a lower reservation wage because they should prefer to accept a wage offer today rather than to continue to search and to wait for a better offer. In addition to impatience they introduce an alternative type of time preference to the job search model. The standard model is based on the assumption of exponential time discounting. This implies a constant discount rate over time. Additionally, they consider the case of hyperbolic time preferences. Hyperbolic time preferences go along with a high discounting in the short run and low discounting in the long run. The two types of time preferences imply different theoretical predictions for the outcomes of the job search behavior.

Della Vigna and Paserman (2005) estimate their job search models based on longitudinal data sets from the United States. They find a negative correlation between impatience measures and the exit rate from unemployment, even if they control for a wide range of observable characteristics. Impatience is negatively correlated with search effort, while they do not find evidence for a correlation with the reservation wage. These results are in line with the model based on hyperbolic discounting.

These examples demonstrate that the incorporation of—from an economic point of view—"nonstandard" personal characteristics such as the locus of control and impatience in economic models of job search behavior can improve our understanding of heterogeneous patterns of job search behavior and employment outcomes in the data.

Conclusions

In this chapter we have presented the basic models of economic job search theory. In contrast to traditional neoclassical labor market models—which are based on the assumption that workers and firms have imperfect information about the labor market—these models are able to explain long spells of involuntary unemployment. The models have proven to be fruitful tools for enhancing our understanding of unemployment durations and the effectiveness of labor market policies aimed at bringing the unemployed back to work.

The empirical findings clearly indicate that unemployed job seekers are changing their job search behavior in response to changes in financial incentives such as the generosity of unemployment benefits and to changes in the design of active labor market policy programs such as counseling and monitoring programs. In the context of unemployment insurance systems the empirical evidence suggests that longer unemployment benefit entitlement as well as higher benefit payments lead to on average longer unemployment durations. However, this does not imply that a low level of benefit generosity is always the optimal policy. First, unemployment benefits insure workers against income loss in case of (involuntary) job loss. The value of this insurance obviously depends on the generosity of the benefits. Second, although the evidence is mixed, there exist some studies showing that jobs that are found around the exhaustion point of the unemployment benefits are less stable and go along with lower wages than jobs found before. These trade-offs have to be taken into account when evaluating the design of an unemployment insurance system. For a recent overview of the labor market effects of unemployment insurance design see Tatsiramos and van Ours (2014).

The models have been extended in several directions. We have discussed some of these extensions including the incorporation of concepts such as social networks and informal search and of psychological characteristics such as personality traits. We expect that the increasing availability of data on job search behavior and their determinants will lead to further extensions and improvements of job search theory and will enhance our understanding of job search outcomes. An example for a promising direction that we have not discussed in this chapter is the incorporation of subjective expectations about search outcomes in job search models. The study of van den Berg, Bergemann, and Caliendo (2009) is an example for such an approach in the context of job search behavior of unemployed workers. They show that expected participation in active labor market programs generate negative ex ante effects on the reservation wage and positive effects on search effort. Another promising direction for future research is the increasing use of exogenous variation in policy parameters to estimate structural job search models. The better availability of administrative data over long periods will allow researchers to make more use of changes over time or of discontinuities in labor market institutions to estimate the causal effects of specific programs and to identify the structural parameters of the job search models without relying mainly on parametric assumptions about the model specification.

Notes

1. In 2010 Peter Diamond, Dale T. Mortensen, and Christopher A. Pissarides received the Nobel Prize for their analysis of markets with search frictions. The labor market is one prominent example of a market with search frictions.
2. Some special cases of this model have been examined earlier; see, for example, Mortensen (1986).
3. The empirical analysis of so-called equilibrium search models, which endogenize the wage offer distribution F, often involves the joint estimation of the distributions of unemployment durations and job durations. See, for example, Van den Berg and Ridder (1998) and Bontemps, Robin, and Van den Berg (2000).

References

Addison, J. T., & Portugal, P. (2008). How do different entitlements to unemployment benefits affect the transitions from unemployment into employment? *Economics Letters*, 101, 206–209.

Almlund, M., Duckworth, A. L., Heckman, J. J., & Kautz, T. (2011). Personality psychology and economics. In E. A. Hanushek, S. Machin, & L. Woessmann (Eds.), *Handbook of the economics of education* (pp. 1–181). Amsterdam: Elsevier.

Belzil, C. (2001). Unemployment insurance and subsequent job duration: Job matching vs. unobserved heterogeneity. *Journal of Applied Econometrics*, 16, 619–633.

Bloemen, H. G. (2005). Job search, search intensity and labor market transitions: An empirical exercise. *Journal of Human Resources*, 40, 231–269.

Bontemps, C., Robin, J.M., & van den Berg, G.J. (2000): Equilibrium search with continuous productivity dispersion: theory and non-parametric estimation. *International Economic Review*, 41, 305–358.

Burgess, S. (1989). The estimation of structural models of unemployment duration with on-the-job search. Working paper, University of Bristol, Bristol.

Caliendo, M., Cobb-Clark, D., & Uhlendorff, A. (2014). Locus of control and job search strategies. *Review of Economics and Statistics*. Forthcoming.

Caliendo, M., Schmidl, R., & Uhlendorff, A. (2011). Social networks, job search methods and reservation wages: Evidence for Germany. *International Journal of Manpower*, 32(7), 796–824.

Caliendo, M., Tatsiramos, K., & Uhlendorff, A. (2013). Benefit duration, unemployment duration and match quality: A regression-discontinuity approach. *Journal of Applied Econometrics*, 28(4), 604–627.

Calvo-Armengol, A., & Jackson, M. O. (2007). Networks in labor markets: Wag and employment dynamics and inequality. *Journal of Economic Theory*, 132, 27–46.

Card, D., Chetty, R. & A. Weber (2007). Cash-on-hand and competing models of Intertemporal behavior: new evidence from the labor market, *Quarterly Journal of Economics*, 122, 1511–1560.

Card, D., & Levine, P. B. (2000). Extended benefits and the duration of UI spells: Evidence from the New Jersey Extended Benefit Program. *Journal of Public Economics*, 78, 107–138.

Della Vigna, S., & Paserman, M. D. (2005). Job search and impatience. *Journal of Labor Economics*, 23, 527–588.

Eckstein, Z. & G.J. van den Berg (2007). Empirical labor search: a survey, *Journal of Econometrics*, 136, 531–564.

Engberg, J. (1991). The impact of unemployment benefits on job search: Structural unobserved heterogeneity and spurious spikes. Working paper, Carnegie-Mellon University, Pittsburgh.

Flinn, C. J. (1996). Labor market structure and welfare: A comparison of Italy and the U.S. Working paper, New York University, New York.

Flinn, C. J., & Heckman, J. J. (1982). New methods for analyzing structural models of labor force dynamics. *Journal of Econometrics*, 18, 115–168.

Fougère, D., Pradel, J., & Roger, M. (2009). Public employment offices and the transition rate from unemployment to employment. *European Economic Review*, 53, 846–869.

Frijters, P., & van der Klaauw, B. (2006). Job search with nonparticipation. *Economic Journal*, 116, 45–83.

Garcia-Perez, J. I. (1998). Non-stationary job search with firing: A structural estimation. Working paper, CEMFI, Madrid.

Granovetter, M. S. (1995). *Getting a job: A study of contacts and careers*. Chicago: University of Chicago Press.

Holzer, H. (1988). Search method use by unemployed youth. *Journal of Labor Economics*, 1, 1–20.

Hunt, J. (1995). The effect of the unemployment compensation on unemployment duration in Germany. *Journal of Labor Economics*, 13, 88–120.

Ioannides, Y. M., & Loury, L. D. (2004). Job information networks, neighborhood effects, and inequality. *Journal of Economic Literature*, 4, 1056–1093.

Kanfer, R., Wanberg, C. R., & Kantrowitz, T. M. (2001). Job search and employment: A personality-motivational analysis and meta-analytic review. *Journal of Applied Psychology*, 86, 837–855.

Katz, L. F., & Meyer, B. D. (1990). The impact of the potential duration of unemployment benefits on the duration of unemployment. *Journal of Public Economics*, 41, 45–72.

Koning, P., van den Berg, G. J., & Ridder, G. (1997). A structural analysis of job search methods and subsequent wages. Tinbergen Institute Discussion Papers, 97-082/3.

Lalive, R. (2008). How do extended benefits affect unemployment duration? A regression discontinuity approach. *Journal of Econometrics*, 142, 785–806.

Lancaster, T. (1990). *The econometric analysis of transition data*. Cambridge: Cambridge University Press.

Meyer, B. D. (1990). Unemployment insurance and unemployment spells. *Econometrica*, 58, 757–782.

Montgomery, J. D. (1991). Social networks and labor market outcomes: Toward an economic analysis. *American Economic Review*, 81, 1408–1418.

Mortensen, D. T. (1986). Job search and labor market analysis. In O. Ashenfelter & R. Layard (Eds.), *Handbook of labor economics*. Amsterdam: North-Holland.

Mortensen, D. T., & Pissarides, C. A. (1999). New developments in models of search in the labor market. In O. Ashenfelter & D. Card (Eds.), *Handbook of labor economics* (Vol. III). Amsterdam: North-Holland.

Mouw, T. (2003). Social capital and finding a job: Do contacts matter. *American Sociological Review*, 68, 868–898.

Narendranathan, W. (1993). Job search in a dynamic environment—an empirical analysis. *Oxford Economic Papers*, 45, 1–22.

Narendranathan, W., & Nickell, S. J. (1985). Modelling the process of job search. *Journal of Econometrics*, 28, 28–49.

Pissarides, C. A. (1990). *Equilibrium unemployment theory*. Oxford: Basil Blackwell.

Rees, A. (1966). Information networks in labor markets. *American Economic Review*, 56, 559–566.

Røed, K., & Zhang, T. (2003). Does unemployment compensation affect unemployment duration? *Economic Journal*, 113, 190–206.

Rogerson, R., Shimer, R., & Wright, R. (2005). Search-theoretic models of the labor market: A survey. *Journal of Economic Literature*, 53, 846–869.

Rotter, J. B. (1966). Generalized expectancies for internal versus external control of reinforcement. *Psychological Monographs: General & Applied*, 80, 1–28.

Tatsiramos, K., & van Ours, J. (2014). Labor market effects of unemployment insurance design. *Journal of Economic Surveys*, 28, 284–311.

van den Berg, G. J. (1990a). Nonstationarity in job search theory. *Review of Economic Studies*, 57, 255–277.

van den Berg, G. J. (1990b). Search behaviour, transitions to nonparticipation and the duration of unemployment. *Economic Journal*, 100, 842–865.

van den Berg, G. J. (2001). Duration models: Specification, identification, and multiple durations. In J. J. Heckman & E. Leamer (Eds.), *Handbook of econometrics* (Vol. V). Amsterdam: North Holland.

van den Berg, G. J., Bergemann, A., & Caliendo, M. (2009). The effect of active labor market programs on not-yet treated unemployed individuals. *Journal of the European Economic Association*, 7, 606–616.

van den Berg, G.J. & G. Ridder (1998). An empirical equilibrium search model of the labor market. *Econometrica*, 66, 1183–1221.

van den Berg, G.J. & B. van der Klaauw (2006). Counseling and monitoring of unemployed workers: Theory and evidence from a controlled social experiment, *International Economic Review*, 47, 895–936.

van Ours, J. C., & Vodopivec, M. (2008). Does reducing unemployment insurance generosity reduce job match quality? *Journal of Public Economics*, 92, 684–695.

Weber, A., & Mahringer, H. (2008). Choice and success of job search methods. *Empirical Economics*, 35, 153–178.

Whaba, J., & Zenou, Y. (2005). Density, social networks and job search methods: Theory and applications to Egypt. *Journal of Development Economics*, 78, 443–473.

Wolpin, K. I. (1987). Estimating a structural search model: the transition from school to work, *Econometrica*, 55, 801–817.

Wolpin, K. I. (1995). *Empirical methods for the study of labor force dynamics*. Luxembourg: Harwood Academic Publishers.

Components and Phases of Job Search

Job-Search Behavior as a Multidimensional Construct: A Review of Different Job-Search Behaviors and Sources

Greet Van Hoye

Abstract

Both theoretical models of job search and empirical research findings suggest that job-search behavior is not a unidimensional construct. This chapter addresses the multidimensionality of job-search behavior and provides a systematic review of the different job-search behaviors and sources studied in the job-search literature and their relationships with antecedent variables and employment outcomes. Organized within three major dimensions (effort/intensity, content/direction, and temporal/persistence), job-search effort and intensity, job-search strategies, preparatory and active job-search behaviors, formal and informal job sources, specific job-search behaviors, job-search quality, job-search dynamics, and job-search persistence are discussed. This review strongly suggests that it is essential to consider all the dimensions of job-search behavior for understanding job-search success in both practice and research. This study points to a number of key implications for job seekers and employment counselors as well as crucial directions for future research.

Key Words: job-search behavior, job-search effort, job-search intensity, job-search strategy, job source, networking, job-search quality, job-search dynamics

Introduction

As individuals search for work following graduation or job loss or to pursue career opportunities, job search has become so pervasive and frequent that it is now considered to be an integral part of working life. At the same time there has been a dramatic increase in research on job search and unemployment, including a meta-analysis that has identified job-search behavior as a major determinant of finding employment (Kanfer, Wanberg, & Kantrowitz, 2001). However, various definitions of what constitutes job-search behavior exist, and most of them suggest that it is not a unidimensional construct. Accordingly, different operationalizations of job-search behavior have been used in previous research (Wanberg, 2012). Whereas some studies have focused on the time and effort that job seekers invest in their search, others have looked

at the nature of the sources used to identify job opportunities or the specific search activities that people engage in. Given that most research has only included one or a few aspects of job-search behavior, it is difficult to integrate previous findings and there is a lack of a clear understanding of the different dimensions of job-search behavior and how they relate to each other as well as to antecedent variables and outcomes. Such understanding is important, given that some research suggests that the predictors and consequences of job search depend on the specific job-search behaviors or sources applied (Saks, 2006; Van Hoye, Van Hooft, & Lievens, 2009). As such differences are ignored by a unidimensional approach, a multidimensional perspective on job-search behavior is likely to enhance our knowledge of the job-search process and to improve our prediction of crucial employment outcomes.

Therefore the purpose of this chapter is to put forth job-search behavior as a multidimensional construct and to review the different job-search behaviors and sources identified in the job-search literature and their relationships with other variables. By doing so, previous research on job-search behavior is systematically integrated and key gaps in our current knowledge are revealed. Ultimately this chapter aims to create awareness among researchers as well as job seekers and employment counselors that effective job-search behavior goes a long way beyond merely putting a lot of effort into job search and that considering all the dimensions of job-search behavior is essential for understanding job-search success in both research and practice.

Definition and Dimensions of Job-Search Behavior

Even though various definitions of job-search behavior exist, most of them have recognized its multidimensional nature. For instance, Schwab, Rynes, and Aldag (1987) proposed that job-search behavior consists of the sources used to acquire information about job vacancies as well as the intensity with which such information is pursued. Soelberg (1967) developed a sequential model of job-search behavior and distinguished a phase of planning job search (i.e., allocating resources to job search and identifying search generators or sources to produce initial job alternatives) from a job search and choice phase (i.e., activating search generators, collecting information on job alternatives, and evaluating job alternatives [Power & Aldag, 1985]). Similarly, Barber, Daly, Giannantonio, and Phillips (1994) have suggested that the term *job-search behavior* refers to identifying the existence of job opportunities and gathering more detailed information on selected job alternatives.

More recently, Kanfer et al. (2001) defined job-search behavior as the product of a dynamic self-regulatory process that begins with the identification of and commitment to an employment goal. This goal subsequently activates search behavior designed to bring about the desired goal. Accomplishing or abandoning the employment goal is posited to terminate the job-search process and associated job-search efforts and activities. Given that job-search behavior is largely self-regulated, Kanfer et al. (2001) further conceptualized that it is likely to vary across individuals along three major dimensions: effort/intensity (effort and frequency of job-search activity), content/direction (activities engaged in and quality of these activities), and temporal/persistence (dynamic processes and persistence in job search).

This chapter builds on the multidimensionality of job-search behavior implied by these definitions and relies on the three dimensions proposed by Kanfer et al. (2001) to organize, review, and discuss the different kinds of job-search behaviors and sources that have been studied in the literature (see Table 15.1 for a nonexhaustive overview). Whereas previous research has mainly focused on the effort/intensity dimension, research on the other two dimensions (i.e., the content and dynamics of job-search behavior) is relatively scarce but equally or even more important.

Job-Search Effort and Intensity

The vast majority of job-search studies have operationalized job-search behavior in terms of effort or intensity, which essentially refers to how hard one tries to find a job. Measures of *job-search effort* assess the general amount of energy and time devoted to job search, with no reference to specific job-search behaviors (e.g., "Within the last six months, I focused my time and effort on job-search activities," rated on a 5-point Likert-scale ranging from 1 = strongly disagree, to 5 = strongly agree (Blau, 1993). Measures of job-search intensity require individuals to indicate the frequency with which they have engaged in a number of specific job-search activities during a given time period (e.g., "Within the last six months, I talked with friends or relatives about possible job leads," rated on a 5-point scale, with 1 = never (0 times), 2 = rarely (1 or 2 times), 3 = occasionally (3 to 5 times), 4 = frequently (6 to 9 times), and 5 = very frequently (at least 10 times [Blau, 1994]). Typically, these items are averaged to produce a composite score of overall job-search intensity (Kopelman, Rovenpor, & Millsap, 1992).

On a theoretical level, both job-search effort and intensity assess the extent to which individuals engage in job search. However, job-search effort refers more to the subjectively felt investments made in job search, which can be cognitive, emotional, and/or behavioral, whereas job-search intensity focuses more on the level of performing concrete search behaviors (Saks, 2005). In addition to this theoretical distinction, there are some methodological differences. Compared to general measures of job-search effort, asking more concretely how many times individuals have carried out specific behaviors is likely to aid correct recall and reduce exaggeration (Kanfer et al., 2001). In addition, the detailed response scale provides a more objective

Table 15.1 Multidimensional Overview of Job-Search Behaviors and Sources

Dimension		Job-Search Behaviors and Sources		
Effort/intensity	Job-search effort	Job-search intensity		
Content/direction		Preparatory job-search behavior	Job-search strategies	Job-search quality
		Formal job sources		
		Job ads	Focused	Goal
		Job sites	Exploratory	establishment
		Employment agencies	Haphazard	Planning
		Public employment service	Maximizing	Goal striving
		Campus recruitment	Satisficing	Reflection
		Recruitment events		
		Informal job sources		
		Rehires		
		Networking		Quality social
		Active job search behavior		network
		Contacting employers		Assertive job-
		Submitting applications		search behavior
		Walk-ins		
		(Job interviews)		
Temporal/ persistence	Changes over time	Changes over time	Changes over time	Changes over time

frame of reference that allows for a better comparison across individuals (e.g., checking job sites for vacancies four times a month might be experienced as a large effort by one job seeker but as a small effort by someone else). There is also an important caveat, however, as measures of job-search intensity require a better knowledge of the studied sample of job seekers than effort measures. Specifically, the list of job-search activities included needs to be exhaustive and representative for the ways in which individuals look for jobs (Kanfer et al., 2001). In addition, the exact response scale and time period must be chosen deliberately to allow for sufficient interindividual variation. In line with these similarities and distinctions, research generally finds that job-search effort and intensity represent related but distinct constructs (Blau, 1993; Saks, 2006).

The effort/intensity dimension of job-search behavior is the only one that had been sufficiently investigated to be included in the job-search meta-analysis of Kanfer et al. (2001). Results indicate that both job-search effort and intensity were significantly and positively related to finding employment. Moreover, the best predictors of job-search effort and intensity combined were extraversion, conscientiousness, openness to experience, employment commitment, and self-efficacy. However, notable differences emerged in the pattern of relationships with antecedents and outcomes. Overall, job-search intensity tended to show stronger relationships with individual difference and situational antecedent variables than job-search effort. Moreover, for a few antecedents, relations were in the opposite direction. For instance, individuals higher in neuroticism reported more job-search effort but less job-search intensity. More neurotic job seekers are more likely to experience negative feelings during job search, thus needing to invest more time in managing their emotions, leaving less time for carrying out concrete search behaviors (Zimmerman, Boswell, Shipp, Dunford, & Boudreau, 2012). This might explain why their subjectively felt effort is higher, whereas their intensity of performing search behaviors is lower.

With respect to outcomes, Kanfer et al.'s (2001) meta-analysis showed that job-search effort was more strongly related to employment status and to shorter job-search duration, whereas job-search intensity was a better predictor of job offers. Job offers represent a proximal job-search outcome, whereas employment status and job-search duration are more distal employment outcomes (Brasher & Chen, 1999). Investing more time in concrete search behaviors (captured best by job-search intensity) is likely to produce more job interviews and offers, but actually obtaining employment is dependent on many other factors, some of which might be included only in measures of job-search effort (e.g., proper planning, thorough preparation).

In sum, these meta-analytical findings provide further support for job-search effort and intensity being related yet distinct constructs, which capture only partially overlapping aspects of job-search behavior and explain both shared and unique variance in job-search success (Kanfer et al., 2001).

Content and Direction of Job-Search Behavior

To find information on job opportunities and follow up on them, job seekers can apply a myriad of different sources and behaviors. For instance, to identify potential jobs, individuals can consult job ads in newspapers, listings on job sites, or people they know that are working for the company. To gather in-depth information on vacancies and apply for them, job seekers can contact prospective employers by phone or pay them a visit (i.e., walk-in) or submit an online application. Even though it is likely that people prefer certain search methods over others and that the outcomes of job search differ according to the methods applied (Saks, 2006), the often used global measures of job-search effort and intensity are not able to grasp these differences. Therefore we also need to consider the specific content and direction of the search activities that job seekers engage in (Kanfer et al., 2001). To this end, different job-search strategies, preparatory and active job-search behaviors, formal and informal job sources, and specific job-search behaviors are discussed in this section. In addition, the quality with which these various search activities are carried out is also addressed.

Job-Search Strategies

On the basis of image theory, Stevens and Beach (1996) suggested that the job-search process starts with the adoption of a goal. Whereas some job seekers might have a clear idea of the type of job they desire (which is also referred to as job-search clarity, Wanberg, Hough, & Song, 2002), others might have only a very fuzzy idea. These variations in goal clarity are assumed to be related to differences in strategies for goal achievement (Stevens & Beach, 1996). When the goal is clearly defined, job search will be more focused on specific sources that are likely to offer desired job features. When the goal is more diffuse, job seekers are likely to use a broader range of sources to learn about multiple types of job options. Along these lines, previous research has identified three distinct strategies for searching information about possible jobs (Crossley & Highhouse, 2005). Job seekers

applying a *focused search strategy* concentrate their efforts on a small number of carefully screened potential employers, identified early in the search process. They have clear employment goals and only apply for jobs that they are qualified for and are interested in. Job seekers following an *exploratory search strategy* have some idea of the type of job they want, but still are open to opportunities that may present themselves. Therefore they examine several potential employment options and actively gather job-related information from various sources. Job seekers using a *haphazard search strategy* do not have a clear idea of what they are looking for and apply a trial-and-error approach to their search. They passively gather information both inside and outside their area of educational and vocational experience.

Research on these job-search strategies is scarce, but there is some evidence that they represent a useful dimension of job-search behavior related to employment outcomes. A haphazard strategy seems to be the least preferable one as it relates negatively to the number of job offers, satisfaction with the job-search process, and satisfaction with the new job (Crossley & Highhouse, 2005). On the contrary, a focused search strategy appears to produce the most positive outcomes, given its positive relationship with job offers, job-search satisfaction, and job satisfaction (Crossley & Highhouse, 2005; Koen, Klehe, Van Vianen, Zikic, & Nauta, 2010). An exploratory strategy relates positively to number of job offers and job-search satisfaction but negatively to reemployment quality (Crossley & Highhouse, 2005; Koen et al., 2010).

Koen et al. (2010) also investigated how the four dimensions of career adaptability relate to individuals' use of the different job-search strategies. Career decision making (i.e., certainty about what career to pursue) and planning (i.e., future career orientation and planfulness) were negatively associated with the use of a haphazard search strategy. Career exploration (i.e., exploring career options) and confidence (i.e., self-efficacy beliefs about achieving career goals) were positive predictors of applying an exploratory strategy. A focused search strategy was positively predicted by career planning and negatively by career exploration.

Another approach to job-search strategies is based on decision-making theory (Van den Berg & Uhlendorff, this volume) and distinguishes a *maximizing* strategy from a *satisficing* strategy. Whereas maximizers look for the single best option, requiring an exhaustive search of all possibilities, satisficers seek until they encounter a "good enough" option that crosses the threshold of acceptability (Iyengar, Wells, & Schwartz, 2006). Research indicates that graduating students who apply a maximizing strategy to their job search obtain objectively better employment outcomes (i.e., 20% higher starting salaries) than students following a satisficing strategy (Iyengar et al., 2006). However, maximizers are less satisfied with these outcomes and experience more negative affect throughout the job-search process. Given that maximizers investigate more options, engage in more social comparisons, and are fixated on securing the best option, they are more likely to have unrealistically high expectations and to feel regret for missed options. Therefore, job seekers following a maximizing decision-making strategy seem to be "doing better" objectively, but are "feeling worse" subjectively, at least in the short term (Iyengar et al., 2006).

Clearly more research is needed in this area, given that job-search strategies seem to be important predictors of job-search success. For instance, despite the conceptual link between job-search goals and strategies, this relationship has not yet been empirically investigated (Van Hoye & Saks, 2008). Moreover, strategies seem to be related to the quality of job-search behavior (see further on), given that they affect the search behaviors that job seekers will perform in order to realize their goals as well as the likelihood of success (Van Hooft, Wanberg, & Van Hoye, 2013).

Preparatory and Active Job-Search Behaviors

On the basis of sequential models of the job-search process (Barber et al., 1994; Soelberg, 1967), Blau (1994) distinguished between preparatory and active job-search behaviors. In the *preparatory search* phase, individuals gather information about potential job leads through various sources such as job ads, job sites, and friends. Subsequently, job seekers follow up on these job leads by performing *active job-search behavior* such as contacting and applying to prospective employers. Measures of preparatory and active job-search behavior are typically based on intensity measures (Saks, 2006). Instead of calculating an overall score of job-search intensity, separate scores are computed to reflect the frequency of performing either preparatory (e.g., read the help wanted/classified ads in a newspaper) or active (e.g., fill out a job application) job-search activities (Blau, 1993). As such, measures of preparatory and active job-search behavior reflect both the effort/intensity and content/direction dimensions of Kanfer et al.'s

(2001) framework. In this chapter, they are placed under the content/direction dimension, given that the content of job-search behavior (i.e., preparatory versus active) is explicitly considered.

Findings indicate that both preparatory and active job-search behavior are positively related to employment outcomes (Saks & Ashforth, 1999). However, active job-search behavior is a stronger predictor (Blau, 1993; Saks, 2006; Saks & Ashforth, 2000) and in line with a sequential view on job search, it mediates the effects of preparatory search behavior (Blau, 1994). Moreover, individuals do not always actively pursue their job search after the preparatory phase—for instance, when no attractive job options have been identified. Along these lines, Blau (1994) found that the relationship between preparatory and active job-search behavior was stronger for job seekers with higher job-search self-efficacy beliefs.

In terms of antecedents, higher financial need and job-search self-efficacy are related to a higher intensity of both preparatory and active job-search behaviors (Blau, 1994; Crossley & Stanton, 2005; Saks & Ashforth, 1999, 2000). In addition, among employed job seekers, active job-search behavior is predicted by lower job satisfaction and organizational commitment (Blau, 1994).

Conceptually related to active job-search behavior is the construct of job-seeking assertiveness, which refers to the ability to identify one's rights and choices during job search and to act upon them while respecting the rights and choices of others (Schmit, Amel, & Ryan, 1993). *Assertive job-search behaviors* include directly contacting employers for information on job openings and making follow-up calls regarding the status of an application (Becker, 1980). Contrary to the intensity-based measurement of active job-search behavior, the Assertive Job-Hunting Survey (Becker, 1980) requires job seekers to indicate how likely they are to perform the listed assertive search behaviors. Despite this methodological difference, active and assertive job-search behaviors are conceptually related (but not the same), as they both involve behaviors associated with contacting and applying to potential employers. However, assertive job-search behavior also reflects elements of job-search quality (see further on), as it assesses not only whether these search behaviors (e.g., contacting employers) are likely to be performed (e.g., "I avoid contacting potential employers by phone or in person because I feel they are too busy to talk with me", reverse coded) but also how well they are likely to be carried out (e.g., "I would ask an employer who did not have an opening if he knew of other employers who might have job openings"). Even though assertive search behaviors are often recommended in the popular job-search literature, almost no empirical research has examined their effects. As a notable exception, Schmit et al. (1993) reported a positive relationship between job seeking assertiveness and finding a job.

Formal and Informal Job Sources

As outlined in the previous section, preparatory job search consists of collecting job-related information from various sources (Blau, 1994). Both the recruitment and job-search literature have generally divided these different means through which job seekers learn about job opportunities into formal and informal sources (Saks, 2005; Zottoli & Wanous, 2000). *Formal job sources* are public intermediaries that exist primarily for recruitment purposes, including employment agencies, job ads, and campus placement offices (Barber et al., 1994). *Informal job sources* involve either no intermediaries (e.g., rehires and walk-ins) or private intermediaries such as current or former employees, friends, relatives, or acquaintances (Saks & Ashforth, 1997). Measures of job sources typically present individuals with a list of various formal and informal sources and ask them to indicate whether or not they have used each particular source (Saks, 2006). These items are then summed to reflect overall usage of formal versus informal job sources. Alternatively, intensity-based measures might be used, as these allow to capture variations into the extent to which each source has been used (e.g., once versus multiple times [Van Hoye & Lievens, 2009]).

Considerable empirical evidence suggests that job seekers are more likely to find employment as well as to obtain higher-quality jobs (i.e., higher job satisfaction, better fit perceptions, lower turnover) through the use of informal job sources than through formal sources (Granovetter, 1995; Zottoli & Wanous, 2000). Two major theoretical explanations for these source differences have been investigated, both of which have received some empirical support (Breaugh, 2008; Griffeth, Hom, Fink, & Cohen, 1997; Saks, 1994; Williams, Labig, & Stone, 1993; Zottoli & Wanous, 2000). The realistic information hypothesis states that informal sources provide more accurate and specific information about what the job entails than formal sources (Breaugh, 2008). This allows job seekers to apply for jobs that better fit their interests and skills as well as to submit better-prepared applications, thus

increasing the likelihood of positive employment outcomes. In addition, a substantial proportion of job opportunities is never communicated through formal sources, so if job seekers do not include informal sources in their search, they are not even aware of these vacancies and hence cannot apply (Granovetter, 1995).

The individual differences hypothesis proposes that informal sources are used by other types of job seekers than formal sources (Williams et al., 1993). These preexisting differences would then explain the later differences in employment outcomes between formal and informal job sources instead of source usage as such. For instance, Ellis and Taylor (1983) found that individuals with lower self-esteem were more likely to rely on formal sources for identifying job opportunities. Similarly, Saks and Ashforth (2000) observed that job seekers with higher job-search self-efficacy beliefs made more use of informal job sources. Given that self-esteem and job-search self-efficacy are positively associated with receiving job offers, finding employment, and shorter search duration (Kanfer et al., 2001), these underlying individual differences might (partly) explain the effects of formal and informal source usage on employment outcomes. In further support of this assumption, Kirnan, Farley, and Geisinger (1989) observed that job seekers applying through informal sources had higher scores than applicants from formal sources on a biographical inventory used in the selection procedure to assess applicants' educational and work-related background. Again, these results suggest that higher-quality applicants, with higher chances of job-search success, are more likely to rely on informal sources in their job search, implying that individual differences offer an alternative explanation for the effects of job-source usage on employment outcomes.

Even though informal sources of job information typically yield better search results than formal sources, evidence suggests that sometimes formal sources perform better (e.g., Saks & Ashforth, 1997) and informal sources can even have negative effects (Saks, 2006). Along these lines, Van Hoye et al. (2009) found that the effects of networking on employment outcomes were more beneficial when the contacts in job seekers' social networks were of higher quality (see the next section). This implies that informal job sources are more likely to produce better outcomes when higher-quality sources are used (e.g., contacts with high-level jobs rather than low-level jobs). This may explain why minority group members (whose network might contain fewer majority group and high-level contacts [Elliott, 2001]) and students (with less developed professional networks [Saks, 2006]) might benefit less from using informal sources in their job search.

Specific Job-Search Behaviors and Sources

Given that overall job-search intensity can be split up into preparatory and active job-search behavior and that preparatory job search is further divided into using formal and informal job sources, the next logical step would be to investigate specific job-search activities. However, contrary to recruitment research that has more extensively studied distinct recruitment sources such as job ads (e.g., Walker, Feild, Giles, & Bernerth, 2008), job sites (e.g., Dineen & Noe, 2009) and word-of-mouth (e.g., Van Hoye & Lievens, 2009), surprisingly little job-search research has examined job seekers' use of particular search behaviors and sources (see also da Motta Veiga & Turban, this volume).

One of the few specific job-search behaviors that has been examined to some extent is *networking* (Forret, this volume), which involves contacting relatives, friends, and other people for information and leads about job opportunities (Wanberg, Kanfer, & Banas, 2000). Job seekers' intensity of networking has been found to relate positively to number of job offers (Van Hoye et al., 2009) as well as finding employment (Wanberg et al., 2000; Zikic & Klehe, 2006) and to explain incremental variance in job offers beyond other preparatory job-search behaviors (Van Hoye et al., 2009). Moreover, the effectiveness of networking behaviors seems to depend on the quality of the contacts in job seekers' social networks. Along these lines, Van Hoye et al. (2009) observed that job seekers who engaged in networking more frequently were more likely to find employment when the educational and occupational status of the other people in their network was higher. In addition, networking intensity was more positively related to job-organization fit when the ties making up job seekers' social networks were weaker (e.g., vague acquaintances) rather than stronger (e.g., close friends). This is consistent with Granovetter's (1995) strength-of-weak-ties hypothesis, which states that weak ties are more likely to move in different social circles and thus have access to unique and therefore more useful job information than strong ties.

In terms of antecedents, both individual differences and situational variables predict job seekers' use of networking. Job seekers with higher levels of extraversion and networking comfort (i.e., positive attitude toward using networking as a job-search method) more frequently engage in networking behaviors (Van Hoye et al., 2009; Wanberg et al., 2000). In addition, individuals with larger social networks and stronger ties in their networks spend more time on networking during job search (Van Hoye et al., 2009).

Future research on networking might benefit from applying recent developments in the recruitment literature that have resulted in an integrative conceptual model of word-of-mouth as a recruitment source (see Van Hoye, 2014). *Word-of-mouth* is defined as an interpersonal communication, independent of the organization's recruitment activities, about an organization as an employer or about specific jobs (Van Hoye & Lievens, 2009). While word-of-mouth in general can be initiated by the source (e.g., current employee) as well as by the recipient (i.e., job seeker) and can be driven by various motives (e.g., satisfaction of the source or coincidence), networking consists of word-of-mouth initiated by job seekers with the explicit motive to gather job-related information (Van Hoye et al., 2009). The theoretical model developed by Van Hoye (2014) integrates research findings from both literatures and highlights that word-of-mouth as a source of employment information affects both individual job-search outcomes (e.g., job offers) and organizational prehire (e.g., application decisions) as well as posthire recruitment outcomes (e.g., job satisfaction). Moreover, various process variables are proposed that might help to explain the impact of word-of-mouth, such as accessibility, diagnosticity, credibility, media richness, and realism (cf. the realistic information hypothesis). The integrative model further suggests that the use of word-of-mouth is determined by the characteristics of its recipient (cf. the individual differences hypothesis), its source, and the organization involved, as well as by the interactions between these characteristics. Relevant recipient characteristics include personality, self-evaluations, motives, and social network; whereas personality, expertise, motives, and tie strength are key source attributes. With respect to the recruiting organization, the employer brand, organizational justice, referral bonuses, and other recruitment practices need to be considered. In addition to their role as determinants, these characteristics might also moderate the effects of word-of-mouth on job-search and recruitment outcomes. Finally, the characteristics of word-of-mouth—such as its valence, content, and medium—are also likely to affect its impact.

Unfortunately almost no research has investigated job seekers' use of other specific search behaviors besides networking. On the basis of measures of job-search intensity, which are composed of various search activities, Van Hoye and Saks (2008) distinguished six specific job-search behaviors: *looking at job ads in newspapers or journals, visiting job sites,* networking, *contacting employment agencies* (Coverdill & Finlay, this volume), *contacting employers,* and *submitting applications.* In a sample of employed job seekers, they found that job-search objectives were differentially related to the use of these specific search activities. Whereas job seekers with the objective of finding a new job engaged more frequently in all these activities, passive job seekers who aimed to stay aware of alternative job opportunities made more use of passive search methods, such as looking at job ads and visiting job sites. Job seekers with the objective of developing a network of professional relationships applied more search behaviors involving human contact, such as networking and contacting employers, and job seekers wanting to obtain bargaining leverage against their employer contacted other employers more frequently. These findings suggest that different objectives for engaging in job search are likely to elicit the use of different search methods that are most suited to accomplish those objectives. However, more research is needed to determine whether the various search behaviors actually lead to the desired outcome. Such research is essential if we want to provide guidance to job seekers as to what specific search methods they should apply, given their particular objectives. Along these lines, Van Hoye et al. (2009) observed that looking at job ads in newspapers or journals was negatively related to (re)employment quality, whereas relying on the *public employment service* was a positive predictor of job offers but a negative predictor of finding employment.

As already pointed out with respect to networking, it would be worthwhile for future research on specific job-search behaviors and sources to apply insights from the recruitment literature (Uggerslev, Fassina, & Kraichy, 2012; see also da Motta Veiga & Turban, this volume). First, job seekers are likely to vary in the extent to which they receive employment information from a particular source (Saks & Ashforth, 1997). This implies that a Likert-type scale measuring the intensity of using a specific source seems more appropriate than a simple yes/no response scale measuring whether or not any information was received from that source (Van Hoye & Lievens, 2009). Second, on the basis of their

review of the recruitment source literature, Zottoli and Wanous (2000) have suggested that differences between job sources need to be investigated at three levels of specificity: between theoretically relevant categories (e.g., formal versus informal sources), but also between individual sources across (e.g., employment agencies versus networking) and within (e.g., re-hires versus networking) categories, and even within sources. For instance, future research on job advertisements might differentiate between print and Internet advertising. In turn, print advertising could be subdivided into job advertisements in national magazines, regional papers, and local free sheets, whereas Internet advertising might be split up into corporate websites, job boards, and sponsored banners (Van Hoye, 2012).

Furthermore, with respect to categorizations of job sources, Cable and Turban (2001) borrowed from the marketing literature to suggest two additional theoretically relevant dimensions, beyond the distinctions between preparatory and active search behaviors and between formal and informal job sources. Their model posits that job seekers are influenced by employment information from a wide variety of sources, not restricted to those that organizations intentionally incorporate in their recruitment activities. The first dimension therefore refers to the degree of control the organization has over the source. Company-dependent sources such as advertising are part of the organization's recruitment activities and can be directly managed to communicate the intended message to job seekers. On the contrary, company-independent sources such as word-of-mouth cannot be directly controlled by the organization but can only be influenced indirectly through other recruitment activities. The second dimension of experiential versus informational sources represents the degree to which a source allows job seekers to acquire information through personal, vivid media (e.g., recruitment event) versus impersonal, pallid media (e.g., recruitment brochure). Both company-independent and experiential sources are proposed to have a larger impact owing to their higher credibility (Van Hoye, 2012).

Finally, *going on job interviews* (McCarthy & Cheng, this volume) is sometimes considered to be a specific job-search behavior. In fact, it is often included as an item in measures of overall job-search intensity (Kopelman et al., 1992) and active job-search behavior (Blau, 1994). However, it might be more appropriate to consider the number of job interviews attended as one of the criteria for evaluating job-search success (Brasher & Chen,

1999). Theoretical models of job search (Brasher & Chen, 1999; Saks, 2005) have distinguished various types of outcomes of job-search behaviors, including job-search outcomes (e.g., job interviews, job offers), quantitative employment outcomes (e.g., employment status, exhaustion of unemployment benefits), qualitative employment outcomes (e.g., job-organization fit, job satisfaction; Virick & McKee-Ryan, this volume), and psychological well-being (e.g., stress, anxiety; Paul, Hassel, & Moser, this volume). As already noted, job-search outcomes such as job interviews are the most proximal outcomes of job-search behavior, whereas quantitative and qualitative employment outcomes represent more distal outcomes. While job-search behavior is most directly related to receiving invitations for job interviews, many other factors besides job-search behavior are likely to determine whether or not an individual actually obtains employment (Saks, 2005). In fact, there is some support for an unfolding model of job-search success in which job-search behavior leads to job interviews, interviews result in job offers, and more job offers lead to employment (Saks, 2006). This attests to the importance of using job interviews as a criterion for evaluating the effectiveness of job-search behaviors. In any case, researchers should avoid including job interviews in both measures of the predictor (job-search behavior) and the criterion (job-search success), as this is likely to lead to inflated and biased results.

Quality of Job-Search Behaviors

According to Kanfer et al. (2001), the content/direction dimension of job-search behavior not only refers to the specific activities that job seekers engage in, but also to the *quality* with which these activities are being performed. Spending much time on job-search activities does not necessarily imply that job search is done effectively, which might explain the relatively small meta-analytic effects of job-search effort and intensity on employment outcomes (Kanfer et al., 2001). In other words, the effectiveness of job-search behavior is likely to not only depend on the specific search activities selected and the intensity of performing them, but also on how well job seekers carry out the chosen search activities (Wanberg et al., 2002).

Despite the intuitive appeal of these assumptions and their far-reaching implications, very little research has been conducted in this area. As discussed earlier, research on networking as a job-search behavior suggests that its effects depend on the quality of the contacts in job seekers' social networks (Van

Hoye et al., 2009). Similar reasoning might apply to other preparatory and active job-search behaviors. For instance, web-based job search is likely to be more effective when multiple job sites as well as employer recruitment sites are consulted or when more relevant keywords are used. The effects of reading job ads might depend on the quality and the diversity of the screened newspapers and journals. The quality of contacting employment agencies and employers seems highly dependent on job seekers' self-presentation skills whereas submitting carefully crafted job applications tailored to the specific vacancy is likely to be more successful than sending out numerous one-size-fits-all applications or resumes with a poor layout and spelling errors. Research on job-search quality is crucial if we are to advise and train job seekers on how they should best carry out the specific job-search behaviors that are most likely to help them accomplish their particular job-search and employment objectives.

Taking a broader (i.e., not limited to job-search behaviors) perspective toward conceptualizing job-search quality, Van Hooft et al. (2013) propose a *four-phased cyclical self-regulatory model.* This model posits that a high-quality job search consists of a highly self-regulated process, starting with goal establishment and followed by planning, goal striving, and reflection. In each of these phases, key components of job-search quality are delineated that contribute to a successful job search. In the goal establishment phase, job seekers should select a clear goal for their search (e.g., find a better-paying job), commit to it, and translate it into lower-level goals (e.g., be invited for an interview at company X offering above market salaries). In the next phase of planning, job seekers need to select a behavioral strategy that should be followed to realize their goals and decide on which sources of job information they will rely. As already noted, an exploratory or focused job-search strategy is preferred over a haphazard strategy and multiple job sources should be used, with an emphasis on (but not limited to) informal sources. In addition, job seekers should form concrete intentions, set priorities and deadlines, and thoroughly prepare for the planned activities. The third phase of goal striving involves the sustained performance of the planned search behaviors as job seekers move toward their goals. As there are likely to be many obstacles and setbacks during job search, job seekers must apply self-regulatory techniques that help to initiate and maintain the planned search activities, such as self-control, self-monitoring, goal shielding, and task-related feedback-seeking. In the final phase of reflection, job seekers have to evaluate whether their search has been effective and whether revisions to their goals, planning, or behavior are necessary. At this stage, evaluating errors and failures in a learning-oriented way and attributing them to internal but changeable causes should be beneficial. In addition, the model poses that job seekers should administer self-rewards contingent on their performance, which is likely to motivate their continued effort and persistence. To realize a high-quality job search, job seekers should cycle through these four phases in the proposed sequence (often multiple times) and follow the recommendations made in each phase. Further research is needed to validate this self-regulatory model of job-search quality and test all its propositions so that it might serve as a framework for future job-search research as well as practice.

Job-Search Dynamics and Persistence

So far, we have discussed various job-search activities as well as the intensity and quality with which they are performed as key components of job-search behavior. However, hardly anyone finds a job in just one day, and more often than not the entire job-search process takes several months or even longer. This implies that temporal aspects of job search should also be considered (Song, Sun, & Li, this volume). Over time, job-search behavior may *change* in intensity or direction as self-reactions or feedback from the environment influence self-regulatory mechanisms which, in turn, affect behavior (Kanfer et al., 2001). For instance, after several unsuccessful applications, job seekers might decide to lower their goals, to change their search strategy, or to rely on other sources for collecting information on job opportunities. Moreover, job seekers are also likely to vary in the *persistence* with which they sustain their job-search behavior, especially when confronted with difficulties, discouragements, and uncertainty (Wanberg, Glomb, Song, & Sorenson, 2005). To grasp these dynamic aspects of the job-search process, it is obviously not sufficient to assess job-search behavior at merely one point in time (either in research or in practice), longitudinal measurement with multiple time waves is required.

Only a few studies have examined the dynamics of job-search behavior. Barber et al. (1994) propose three alternative models that might explain changes in job-search behavior that occur over time. First, the sequential model is based on various conceptualizations of job search as a phased process, in which job-search activities follow a logical and systematic sequence (Blau, 1994; Soelberg, 1967). This model suggests that job seekers first search broadly to identify as many job opportunities as possible (cf. preparatory job-search behavior) and then acquire more in-depth information about selected opportunities and actually apply for them (cf. active job-search behavior). When this does not result in desired job offers, job seekers might need to return to earlier stages. Second, the learning model posits that job-search behavior changes over time because job seekers learn more effective and more efficient search techniques as their search progresses (Barber et al., 1994). This learning can be the result of personal experience, observing the success of others, feedback from recruiters, advice from job-search counselors, job-search training, or reading popular job-search books. Third, whereas both the sequential and the learning model emphasize cognitive processes, the emotional response model focuses on emotional reactions to job search (Barber et al., 1994). Job search can be very stressful, and the longer the search lasts, the more job seekers are confronted with rejections and uncertainty, resulting in accumulated levels of stress and frustration. This might cause them to withdraw from job search in general or from specific job-search behaviors that are experienced as more stressful.

To test the implications of these three models, Barber et al. (1994) examined the job-search behaviors of graduating students early in their search, at graduation, and 3 months after graduation for those who remained unemployed. First of all, their findings confirm that job seekers do change their search behavior over the course of time. Furthermore, the observed changes were most in line with the sequential model. As students moved from initial search to late search, their job-search effort and use of formal sources decreased and they were less likely to look for information related to obtaining jobs. Moreover, students who remained unemployed and needed to extend their search seemed to return to earlier stages as their job-search effort and reliance on formal sources increased again. Saks and Ashforth (2000) provide further support for the latter findings, as they observed that students who were still unemployed at graduation increased their job-search effort, use of formal sources, and active job-search behavior in the months following graduation. In addition, increases in job-search effort and active job-search behavior seemed to be effective, as they resulted in a higher number of job interviews. It should be noted that the job-search process of graduating students is likely to be more sequential than for other groups of job seekers, such as job losers and employed job seekers (Boswell, Zimmerman, & Swider, 2012). Unique to the job-search process of new entrants is that it coincides with the natural cycle of students' progression through their educational programs, with the end date of graduation known months or even years in advance. In addition, employers' campus recruitment activities (e.g., placing job postings, scheduling interviews) are also in tune with this educational cycle, creating even more sequential effects on students' job search.

If we really want to understand the fluctuations in job search as well as the reasons for them on a day-to-day or week-to-week basis, it is imperative to measure job-search behavior at considerably more points in time. To this end, Wanberg et al. (2005) investigated changes in unemployed individuals' job-search intensity in a ten-wave longitudinal study. Consistent with previous research findings in student samples (Barber et al., 1994; Saks & Ashforth, 2000), job seekers somewhat decreased their search intensity over time but then increased their search intensity again when they remained unemployed, providing some support for a sequential model of the dynamics of unemployed job seekers' search behavior. This slight convex trend was observed for most of the specific job-search behaviors as well, including looking for job opportunities in newspapers or on the internet, networking, contacting employers, and submitting applications. An opposite, concave trend was observed for contacting private or public employment agencies. Moreover, in line with the theory of planned behavior (Ajzen, 1991), subjective norms and job-search self-efficacy beliefs at any given time predicted job-search intensity in the following 2 weeks and these effects were mediated by job-search intentions. In addition, job seekers with higher core self-evaluations showed higher job-search persistence, as evidenced by higher average levels of search intensity over time. Finally, a dynamic assessment of job-search behavior did not improve the prediction of reemployment beyond a static assessment, as time 1 and cumulative job-search intensity were equally positively related to reemployment.

In another multiple time wave study, Wanberg, Zhu, and Van Hooft (2010) applied self-regulation theory to examine daily changes in unemployed persons' job-search effort over a three-week period. On average, people spent 3.56 hours a day on job-search activities (ranging from 0.4 to 8.6 hours), but job-search effort showed strong vacillations over time. Reasons provided for putting in less effort on a given day included family obligations, not feeling well, wanting to do other things, needing a break, and discouragements. Furthermore, job seekers who exerted less search effort and perceived lower job-search progress on one day reported higher levels of search effort the following day, and vice versa. In addition, lower positive affect on a given day was related to lower search effort the next day for more state-oriented job seekers (i.e., with a lower ability to detach from negative thoughts), but to higher effort for more action-oriented individuals (i.e., with a higher disengagement ability). These findings provide some support for an emotional response model of job-search changes and suggest that job seekers need self-regulation to manage negative emotions over time and sustain their job-search efforts. This might be especially true for unemployed job seekers, as compared to students or employed job seekers (Boswell et al., 2012).

In further support of a self-regulatory perspective on the dynamics of job search, Wanberg, Zhu, Kanfer, and Zhang (2012) found that unemployed job seekers with higher approach-oriented trait motivation (i.e., tendency to engage in goal striving for the purpose of personal growth and developing competencies) showed higher levels of job-search intensity and mental health, both at the start of and over the course of their unemployment. These effects were mediated by weekly changes in the self-regulatory state variable of motivation control (i.e., intentional cognitive redirection of attention, use of goal setting, and/or use of environmental management strategies to stay on course and sustain effort). In addition, some support was found for the sequential model, as job seekers reported a decline in the weekly hours spent on job search ($M = 14.5$ hours, range = 11.2–17.8) over time, with a slight increase in later months. Finally, the findings demonstrate the importance of job-search persistence, as unemployed individuals who maintained high levels of job-search intensity over the duration of their job search had more interviews and found jobs more quickly.

Relationships Within and Between Dimensions of Job-Search Behavior

This chapter relies on the three dimensions of job-search behavior proposed by Kanfer et al. (2001)—effort/intensity, content/direction, and temporal/persistence—to organize and review the different kinds of job-search behaviors and sources studied in prior research. In fact, the main strength of this multidimensional approach is that it enables to encompass and highlight all the relevant aspects of job-search behavior that should be taken into account when designing job-search studies and interventions. However, from the preceding review, it is clear that these three dimensions of job-search behavior are not independent from each other, as significant relationships exist both within and between dimensions of job-search behavior. Some of these connections become apparent in looking at the overview of job-search behaviors shown in Table 15.1. For instance, if a study were to measure specific job-search behaviors with an intensity-based scale at multiple points in time, all three dimensions would be taken into account, and the same measures would also allow to examine overall job-search intensity, preparatory and active job-search behavior, formal and informal job sources, and changes in job-search behavior. Depending on the research questions and context, researchers can then decide whether they need to include additional aspects of job-search behavior that require another measure, such as job-search strategies or job-search quality. In conclusion, this multidimensional review of job-search behavior does not necessarily imply that all dimensions and behaviors should be measured in any given situation or that separate measures should be used for each individual construct. Instead, it offers a framework that both researchers and practitioners can rely on to identify all possibly relevant aspects of job-search behavior, allowing them to make an informed decision on which behaviors to focus on in their particular context and how these might be measured.

Implications for Job Seekers and Employment Counselors

The above discussion of job-search behavior as a multidimensional construct and the review of the different job-search behaviors and sources studied to date strongly imply that we need to take all the dimensions of job-search behavior into account if we want to understand and improve job-search success. Therefore this chapter has a number of key implications for job seekers and employment counselors.

Implications for Job Seekers

• Consider job search to be your full-time job. Make and follow a planning and devote a minimum amount of hours to job search every day. The more time and effort you invest in job search and the more intensely you engage in a

greater number of search activities, the higher your chances of receiving job interviews and offers, and of finding employment.

• Think about what you are trying to achieve through job search and what kind of job you are looking for. Formulate clear job search and employment goals and select the job-search behaviors that are most likely to help you realize your goals. Adopting such a focused search strategy increases the likelihood of finding high-quality employment.

• Realize that job search is a sequential process in which both preparatory and active job-search behaviors are necessary. However, active search behaviors such as contacting employers and submitting applications are key for job-search success. Even though active search might seem more stressful, it is essential to act upon the information gathered on job opportunities and to progress from preparatory to active search.

• Do not rely on just a single job-search behavior or source but engage in multiple and diverse search activities. It seems especially important to include informal job sources in your search and to spend sufficient time on networking and developing your social network. Focus on contacting people with a higher educational and occupational status and people that you are less acquainted with to ask for information and advice on jobs, as this increases the effectiveness of networking behaviors.

• Engaging in appropriate job-search behaviors with a high intensity is not sufficient; you should also carry out these behaviors in a high-quality manner. If you are less confident about your job-search skills, seek advice and feedback from others, refer to job-search handbooks, or follow job-search training.

• Be aware that job search can be a long and stressful process and that you will be confronted with difficulties, rejections, and uncertainty. Seek support from your social environment and persist in your job-search activities. Regularly reflect on your job search and revise your goals, strategy, or job-search behavior if necessary.

Implications for Employment Counselors

• Realize that even though job-search effort and intensity are important determinants of job-search success, they represent merely one dimension of job-search behavior. To provide the best possible guidance to job seekers, first try to obtain a complete picture of their current job search and also consider the specific job-search behaviors and sources that they rely on as well as the quality of their search activities.

• Make job seekers aware of the importance of clear and specific goals for their job search. Help them to clarify, formulate, and periodically revise their job-search and employment objectives and to translate these objectives into job-search strategies and behaviors that are most suited to accomplish them. Pay particular attention to job seekers using a haphazard search strategy.

• Encourage job seekers to include informal sources in their search for information on job opportunities and to follow up with active and assertive search behaviors. Strengthening job seekers' self-efficacy beliefs (e.g., through training) is likely to increase their use of these specific sources and behaviors. Assist job seekers in developing their social network and in achieving higher levels of networking comfort.

• Try to enhance the quality with which job seekers perform various job-search activities through advice and training. Point out the value of high-quality contacts (i.e., high-status and weak ties) for networking and offer opportunities for developing and practicing self-presentation and job-search skills.

• To capture the dynamics of job search, meet with job seekers and assess their job-search behaviors at multiple moments in time. Help them to deal with discouragements and uncertainty and to persist in their job search. Highlight the importance of resuming their search activities and disengaging from negative thoughts and emotions after an "off-day."

Future Research Directions

A review of the literature on job-search behaviors and sources from a multidimensional perspective reveals numerous gaps in our current knowledge and highlights the urgent need for future research in this area. With respect to the three main dimensions that were used to categorize the different aspects of job-search behavior, we can conclude that the effort/intensity dimension has been the main focus of previous research, including a meta-analysis (Kanfer et al., 2001). Therefore the most pressing and valuable directions for future research involve the other two dimensions and include the study of specific job-search behaviors, the quality of job-search behaviors, the dynamics of job-search behavior, and

the (inter)relationships between different job-search behaviors, goals, and outcomes.

First, most job-search research has used general measures of job-search behavior that combine a variety of job-search activities to derive an overall intensity measure with little attention to the specific behaviors performed (Kanfer et al., 2001). As a result, we know virtually nothing about the use and effectiveness of specific job-search behaviors, with the exception of networking (Wanberg et al., 2000). Research that focuses on and measures specific search behaviors is important because there is some evidence that job seekers differ in their use of specific methods (Wanberg et al., 2005) and that the predictors and consequences of job search depend on the applied search behaviors (Van Hoye et al., 2009). This is a key topic for future research if we are to provide guidance to job seekers as to what search behaviors they should be engaging in to a greater or lesser extent. We need to know what job-search activities should be applied by particular job seekers, when they should apply them, what activities are most effective for specific job-search and employment goals, and what activities are most effective for certain types of jobs and occupations. For instance, with respect to networking, some evidence suggests that it is particularly suited for job seekers with the objectives of finding a (new) job and of developing a professional network (Van Hoye & Saks, 2008; Van Hoye et al., 2009). However, networking seems less effective in terms of employment outcomes for job seekers whose social network mostly contains strong low-status ties (Van Hoye et al., 2009). In addition, there might be cultural differences with respect to the prevalence, appropriateness, and effectiveness of networking that need to be further explored (Van Hoye et al., 2009; Wanberg et al., 2000). Moreover, not much is known about the type of jobs for which networking as a job-search behavior is most effective, it seems plausible though that networking might be especially suited for finding higher-level jobs and jobs involving more interpersonal contacts, particularly with people outside the organization.

Second, the effectiveness of job-search behavior is not only determined by the specific search activities selected and their intensity, but also by the quality with which these activities are performed (Wanberg et al., 2002). Job-search quality represents a crucial area for future research that previous studies have hardly touched upon. We need to know what constitutes high-quality job-search behavior, how it can be stimulated or trained, and how it contributes to various indicators of job-search success including employment quality. Prior research on networking quality might be extended by investigating how other particular aspects of networking such as the manner in which social ties are contacted (e.g., too timid versus too pushy) or the level of rapport building impact its effectiveness. Similar issues should be examined for all other specific search behaviors as well. For instance, what constitutes a high-quality web-based job search? Should job seekers use national or regional sites, general or job-specific sites, job sites or employer recruitment sites? How many different sites should be consulted and what keywords generate a higher probability of success? Answers to these and many other questions would be highly useful, as they would allow us to advise and train job seekers on how they should best carry out the specific job-search activities that are most suited for accomplishing their job-search and employment goals.

Third, when investigating specific job-search behaviors and their quality, the dynamics of job search should also be taken into account. There is already some evidence suggesting that job seekers' use of specific search activities fluctuates over time (Wanberg et al., 2005). It would be interesting to examine whether the same is true for job-search quality and how these changes can be explained. Whereas the sequential model has been most often applied for describing changes in the use of job-search behaviors (Barber et al., 1994), the learning and emotional response models may hold more promise for explaining fluctuations in the quality of those behaviors. On the basis of the learning model, one would predict that the quality of job-search behaviors increases over time as job seekers learn from their own experiences and advice from others. The emotional response model might lead to an opposite prediction of decreasing job-search quality over time, as job seekers are faced with rejections and uncertainty evoking negative emotions and stress that may impair their job-search performance. Future research should examine the validity of these predictions for different job-search behaviors and determine whether the learning and emotional effects on the quality of job-search behavior are affected by other individual and situational variables, such as job-search self-efficacy and action-state orientation (Wanberg et al., 2010).

Fourth, research on different job-search behaviors is fragmented and scarce and has typically focused on only one or a few behaviors at a time. As a result, we know very little of how the different (sub)dimensions of job-search behavior relate to each other as well as to antecedent variables and outcomes. Therefore a particularly promising avenue for future research would be to include multiple operationalizations of job-search behavior in a single study. This would allow determining their mutual relationships as well as their relative effects on job-search success. A worthwhile effort in this direction was conducted by Saks (2006) who examined the combined and differential effects of five job-search behaviors (job-search effort, preparatory search behavior, active search behavior, informal sources, formal sources) on various employment outcomes, with active job-search behavior emerging as the key predictor of search success. Further research should also include antecedent variables, specific job-search behaviors, and job-search quality. Ideally, such research should also produce a validated questionnaire encompassing all dimensions and relevant aspects of job-search behavior, which would be a highly valuable instrument for job seekers and employment counselors (self-)assessing the totality of one's search activities.

Finally, several theoretical models of job search (Kanfer et al., 2001; Stevens & Beach, 1996) imply that different job-search and employment goals are likely to elicit the use of different job-search behaviors that are (thought to be) most suited to accomplish those objectives. Even though hardly any research has been conducted in this area, some evidence suggests that distinct objectives for engaging in job search are differentially related to the use of specific job-search behaviors (Van Hoye & Saks, 2008) and to job-search outcomes (Boswell, Boudreau, & Dunford, 2004). Future research should extend these findings to various employment goals and should investigate the relationships between goals, job-search strategies, job-search behaviors, and outcomes. This type of research would greatly improve our knowledge of what job-search strategies and behaviors are most effective for obtaining the outcomes associated with particular objectives. For instance, although employees engaging in job search with the objective of obtaining bargaining leverage against their current employer seem more likely to engage in active search behaviors such as contacting other employers (Van Hoye & Saks, 2008) and to actually use leverage later on (Boswell et al., 2004), we do not yet know whether search behaviors mediate the effect of this objective on search outcomes. In addition, much less is known about the outcomes of other objectives such as staying aware of alternative job opportunities and developing a network of professional relationships or about the (other) objectives of unemployed job seekers (e.g., searching to comply with unemployment benefits regulations) and how they relate to job-search behavior as well as outcomes.

Conclusion

This chapter strongly argues for conceptualizing and measuring job-search behavior as a multidimensional construct. As such, the effectiveness of job-search behavior is determined by the specific search activities engaged in, the intensity and quality with which these activities are performed, as well as changes in these activities over time. All these dimensions of job-search behavior need to be taken into account for understanding and improving job-search success. Whereas previous research has mainly focused on the intensity dimension, future research on the content and dynamic dimensions would greatly enhance our knowledge of the multidimensionality of job-search behavior.

Acknowledgment

This work was supported by a postdoctoral fellow grant from the Research Foundation Flanders (FWO).

References

Ajzen, I. (1991). The theory of planned behavior. *Organizational Behavior and Human Decision Processes, 50*, 179–211.

Barber, A. E., Daly, C. L., Giannantonio, C. M., & Phillips, J. M. (1994). Job search activities: An examination of changes over time. *Personnel Psychology, 47*, 739–766.

Becker, H. A. (1980). The Assertive Job-Hunting Survey. *Measurement and Evaluation in Guidance, 13*, 43–48.

Blau, G. (1993). Further exploring the relationship between job search and voluntary individual turnover. *Personnel Psychology, 46*, 313–330.

Blau, G. (1994). Testing a two-dimensional measure of job search behavior. *Organizational Behavior and Human Decision Processes, 59*, 288–312.

Boswell, W. R., Boudreau, J. W., & Dunford, B. B. (2004). The outcomes and correlates of job search objectives: Searching to leave or searching for leverage? *Journal of Applied Psychology, 89*, 1083–1091.

Boswell, W. R., Zimmerman, R. D., & Swider, B. W. (2012). Employee job search: Toward an understanding of search context and search objectives. *Journal of Management, 38*, 129–163.

Brasher, E. E., & Chen, P. Y. (1999). Evaluation of success criteria in job search: A process perspective. *Journal of Occupational and Organizational Psychology, 72*, 57–70.

Breaugh, J. A. (2008). Employee recruitment: Current knowledge and important areas for future research. *Human Resource Management Review, 18*, 103–118.

Cable, D. M., & Turban, D. B. (2001). Establishing the dimensions, sources and value of job seekers' employer

knowledge during recruitment. In G. R. Ferris (Ed.), *Research in Personnel and Human Resources Management, Volume 20* (pp. 115–163). New York: Elsevier Science.

Crossley, C. D., & Highhouse, S. (2005). Relation of job search and choice process with subsequent satisfaction. *Journal of Economic Psychology, 26*, 255–268.

Crossley, C. D., & Stanton, J. M. (2005). Negative affect and job search: Further examination of the reverse causation hypothesis. *Journal of Vocational Behavior, 66*, 549–560.

Dineen, B. R., & Noe, R. A. (2009). Effects of customization on application decisions and applicant pool characteristics in a web-based recruitment context. *Journal of Applied Psychology, 94*, 224–234.

Elliott, J. R. (2001). Referral hiring and ethnically homogeneous jobs: How prevalent is the connection and for whom? *Social Science Research, 30*, 401–425.

Ellis, R. A., & Taylor, M. S. (1983). Role of self-esteem within the job search process. *Journal of Applied Psychology, 68*, 632–640.

Granovetter, M. S. (1995). *Getting a job: A study of contacts and careers* (2nd ed.). Chicago: University of Chicago Press.

Griffeth, R. W., Hom, P. W., Fink, L. S., & Cohen, D. J. (1997). Comparative tests of multivariate models of recruiting sources effects. *Journal of Management, 23*, 19–36.

Iyengar, S. S., Wells, R. E., & Schwartz, B. (2006). Doing better but feeling worse: Looking for the "best" job undermines satisfaction. *Psychological Science, 17*, 143–150.

Kanfer, R., Wanberg, C. R., & Kantrowitz, T. M. (2001). Job search and employment: A personality-motivational analysis and meta-analytic review. *Journal of Applied Psychology, 86*, 837–855.

Kirnan, J. P., Farley, J. A., & Geisinger, K. F. (1989). The relationship between recruiting source, applicant quality, and hire performance: An analysis by sex, ethnicity, and age. *Personnel Psychology, 42*, 293–308.

Koen, J., Klehe, U. C., Van Vianen, A. E. M., Zikic, J., & Nauta, A. (2010). Job-search strategies and reemployment quality: The impact of career adaptability. *Journal of Vocational Behavior, 77*, 126–139.

Kopelman, R. E., Rovenpor, J. L., & Millsap, R. E. (1992). Rationale and construct validity evidence for the job search behavior index: Because intentions (and New Year's resolutions) often come to naught. *Journal of Vocational Behavior, 40*, 269–287.

Power, D. J., & Aldag, R. J. (1985). Soelberg's job search and choice model: A clarification, review, and critique. *Academy of Management Review, 10*, 48–58.

Saks, A. M. (1994). A psychological process investigation for the effects of recruitment source and organization information on job survival. *Journal of Organizational Behavior, 15*, 225–244.

Saks, A. M. (2005). Job search success: A review and integration of the predictors, behaviors, and outcomes. In S. Brown & R. Lent (Eds.), *Career development and counseling: Putting theory and research to work* (pp. 155–179). Hoboken, NJ: Wiley.

Saks, A. M. (2006). Multiple predictors and criteria of job search success. *Journal of Vocational Behavior, 68*, 400–415.

Saks, A. M., & Ashforth, B. E. (1997). A longitudinal investigation of the relationships between job information sources, applicant perceptions of fit, and work outcomes. *Personnel Psychology, 50*, 395–426.

Saks, A. M., & Ashforth, B. E. (1999). Effects of individual differences and job search behaviors on the employment status of recent university graduates. *Journal of Vocational Behavior, 54,* 335–349.

Saks, A. M., & Ashforth, B. E. (2000). Change in job search behaviors and employment outcomes. *Journal of Vocational Behavior, 56,* 277–287.

Schmit, M. J., Amel, E. L., & Ryan, A. M. (1993). Self-reported assertive job-seeking behaviors of minimally educated job hunters. *Personnel Psychology, 46,* 105–124.

Schwab, D. P., Rynes, S. L., & Aldag, R. J. (1987). Theories and research on job search and choice. In K. M. Rowland & G. R. Ferris (Eds.), *Research in personnel and human resources management* (Vol. 5, pp. 129–166). Greenwich, CT: JAI Press.

Soelberg, P. O. (1967). Unprogrammed decision making. *Industrial Management Review, 8,* 19–29.

Stevens, C. K., & Beach, L. R. (1996). Job search and job selection. In L. R. Beach (Ed.), *Decision making in the workplace: A unified perspective* (pp. 33–47). Hillsdale, NJ: Lawrence Erlbaum.

Uggerslev, K. L., Fassina, N. E., & Kraichy, D. (2012). Recruiting through the stages: A meta-analytic test of predictors of applicant attraction at different stages of the recruiting process. *Personnel Psychology, 65,* 597–660.

Van Hooft, E. A. J., Wanberg, C. R., & Van Hoye, G. (2013). Moving beyond job search quantity: Towards a conceptualization and self-regulatory framework of job search quality. *Organizational Psychology Review, 3,* 3–40.

Van Hoye, G. (2012). Recruitment sources and organizational attraction: A field study of Belgian nurses. *European Journal of Work and Organizational Psychology, 21,* 376–391.

Van Hoye, G. (2014). Word of mouth as a recruitment source: An integrative model. In K. Y. T. Yu & D. M. Cable (Eds.), *The Oxford Handbook of Recruitment* (pp. 251–268). New York: Oxford University Press.

Van Hoye, G., & Lievens, F. (2009). Tapping the grapevine: A closer look at word-of-mouth as a recruitment source. *Journal of Applied Psychology, 94,* 341–352.

Van Hoye, G., & Saks, A. M. (2008). Job search as goal-directed behavior: Objectives and methods. *Journal of Vocational Behavior, 73,* 358–367.

Van Hoye, G., Van Hooft, E. A. J., & Lievens, F. (2009). Networking as a job search behaviour: A social network perspective. *Journal of Occupational and Organizational Psychology, 82,* 661–682.

Walker, H. J., Feild, H. S., Giles, W. F., & Bernerth, J. B. (2008). The interactive effects of job advertisement characteristics and applicant experience on reactions to recruitment messages. *Journal of Occupational and Organizational Psychology, 81,* 619–638.

Wanberg, C. R. (2012). The individual experience of unemployment. *Annual Review of Psychology, 63,* 369–396.

Wanberg, C. R., Glomb, T. M., Song, Z., & Sorenson, S. (2005). Job-search persistence during unemployment: A 10-wave longitudinal study. *Journal of Applied Psychology, 90,* 411–430.

Wanberg, C. R., Hough, L. M., & Song, Z. (2002). Predictive validity of a multidisciplinary model of reemployment success. *Journal of Applied Psychology, 87,* 1100–1120.

Wanberg, C. R., Kanfer, R., & Banas, J. T. (2000). Predictors and outcomes of networking intensity among unemployed job seekers. *Journal of Applied Psychology, 85,* 491–503.

Wanberg, C. R., Zhu, J., Kanfer, R., & Zhang, Z. (2012). After the pink slip: Applying dynamic motivation frameworks to the job search experience. *Academy of Management Journal, 55,* 261–284.

Wanberg, C. R., Zhu, J., & Van Hooft, E. A. J. (2010). The job search grind: Perceived progress, self-reactions, and self-regulation of search effort. *Academy of Management Journal, 53,* 788–807.

Williams, C. R., Labig, C. E., Jr., & Stone, T. H. (1993). Recruitment sources and posthire outcomes for job applicants and new hires: A test of two hypotheses. *Journal of Applied Psychology, 78,* 163–172.

Zikic, J., & Klehe, U. C. (2006). Job loss as a blessing in disguise: The role of career exploration and career planning in predicting reemployment quality. *Journal of Vocational Behavior, 69,* 391–409.

Zimmerman, R. D., Boswell, W. R., Shipp, A. J., Dunford, B. B., & Boudreau, J. W. (2012). Explaining the pathways between approach-avoidance personality traits and employees' job search behavior. *Journal of Management, 38,* 1450–1475.

Zottoli, M. A., & Wanous, J. P. (2000). Recruitment source research: Current status and future directions. *Human Resource Management Review, 10,* 353–382.

Networking as a Job-Search Behavior and Career Management Strategy

Monica L. Forret

Abstract

Networking is often cited as a key to job-search success; however, relatively little scholarly research on networking as a job-search behavior exists. The purpose of this chapter is to review the literature on networking and its relevance for job-search success and career management more broadly. The use of networking for both obtaining new jobs at different employers as well as advancing upward in one's current organization is considered. This chapter describes the importance of networking for developing career competencies, how networking can enhance a job seeker's social network, and barriers faced by women and minorities in building their social networks. The multiple ways in which networking has been measured are described, along with the antecedents and outcomes of networking behavior pertinent to job seekers. This chapter discusses the implications of networking as a job-search behavior for job seekers, career counselors, and organizations and concludes with future research suggestions for scholars.

Key Words: networking, jobs, networking behavior, job search, careers, advancement

In 2012, according to the CareerXroads annual source of hire study, which includes data from 37 large US-based organizations from a variety of industries (Crispin & Mehler, 2013), 25% of external hires were made through referrals, and current employees filled 42% of all job openings (e.g., through internal moves or promotions). A 2007 Hudson survey based on a poll of 2,024 US workers showed that networking was cited as the most common method workers and managers used to obtain their current jobs. The use of social relations to find jobs is a global phenomenon. In their study of respondents from twenty-eight countries who reported how they had located their present jobs, Franzen and Hangartner (2006) showed a widespread use of personal contacts, ranging from 26% in Finland to 83% in the Philippines. Furthermore, research by Booz Allen Hamilton (2006) for the Direct Employers Association showed that referrals from networks and social networking websites had the best value for companies, surpassing

other sources such as employment websites and campus recruiting. A Society for Human Resource Management (2002) search tactics poll indicated that 95% of job seekers used personal contacts/networking to look for a job, and the majority (78%) stated that personal contacts/networking was the most effective job-search tactic.

In view of these statistics, it is no surprise that networking is considered a key to job-search success. Newspaper and magazine articles abound encouraging individuals to tap their contacts in search of new job prospects. Many popular books on networking have been written—such as Fisher and Vilas's *Power Networking*, RoAne's *The Secrets of Savvy Networking*, and Zack's *Networking for People Who Hate Networking*—to provide job seekers with advice on developing their networking abilities. Participation in social networking sites such as LinkedIn and Facebook is a widely accepted means of searching for new jobs. However, in light of the seemingly ubiquitous advice on networking for job seekers, academic research on networking as a job-search behavior lags far behind (Van Hoye, Van Hooft, & Lievens, 2009).

The purpose of this chapter is to provide the first review of the literature on networking and its relevance for job-search success and career management. To accomplish this objective, first, I more fully explicate the construct of networking behavior and discuss why networking is so critical for careers in today's fast-changing economy. Second, I utilize social network theory as a basis for describing how and why networking can benefit individuals in their job search; I also discuss barriers faced by women and minorities that may inhibit the effectiveness of their networking behavior. Third, I describe the multiple ways in which networking has been operationalized in the academic literature, along with measures more specific to job-search behavior. Fourth, research on antecedents of networking pertinent to job seekers is examined to illustrate why some individuals are more adept at networking behavior than others. Fifth, I describe research on networking pertaining to job-search processes along with other key outcomes associated with networking behavior. Sixth, I provide implications of networking research to help job seekers, career counselors, and organizations seeking to fill positions. Seventh, I propose an agenda for future research by scholars interested in studying networking behavior as it pertains to job-search and career management.

Definition of Networking Behavior

Networking behavior refers to proactive attempts by individuals to develop and maintain relationships with others for the purpose of work or career benefits (Forret & Dougherty, 2001). According to Wayne Baker (2000), "the goal of building networks is to contribute to others" (p. 70). The notion of effective networkers as self-centered individuals who exploit others is a popular myth (Anand & Conger, 2007). Instead, effective networking behavior involves developing trusting relationships with others. In helping individuals, by, for instance, providing information, advice, support, friendship, or resources (Tichy, Tushman, & Fombrun, 1979), a foundation is built for further interaction. Providing assistance to others invokes the norm of reciprocity (Gouldner, 1960) such that when an individual needs help, support will be forthcoming. Networking effectively is also about sharing. Cross, Parker, Prusak, and Borgatti (2001) describe four

qualities of relationships that help promote knowledge sharing in organizations; these qualities portray characteristics of high-quality relationships that can be developed through networking behavior when individuals focus on developing and maintaining contacts with others.

According to Cross et al. (2001), individuals must first be aware of the knowledge and expertise of the other person with whom they seek to build a relationship. To gain a solid understanding of another person's background requires effective listening and a desire to ask questions and gain knowledge of the other person's competencies. Second, maintaining a relationship once developed is vital for gaining access, when needed, to the other person. If active give and take has been missing from the relationship, tapping one's network only when a favor is desired can be perceived as "usury" by network members. Third, contacts who are willing to engage in active problem solving are beneficial from the standpoint of sharing information. And fourth, the sharing of knowledge is most likely to occur in relationships where individuals feel comfortable admitting their questions, insecurities, or anxieties with another person without fear of rejection. These four characteristics of high-quality relationships can be developed through appropriate networking behavior. Taken as a whole, networking behaviors are primarily concerned with the development and maintenance of relationships that may result in mutual job and career benefits.

Networking behavior may help individuals in their job search and career management in multiple ways—for instance, by providing them with information, emotional social support, feedback, and instrumental support. For example, individuals seeking a job change often begin by contacting their colleagues, acquaintances, family, and friends to let them know that they are interested in finding a new job and to inquire about job leads or opportunities (Wanberg, Kanfer, & Banas, 2000). Individuals struggling in their job search may turn to close friends for emotional support as well as advice on how they might refine their strategies (Brown & Konrad, 2001). Instrumental support is gained when well-placed colleagues within an organization provide significant influence when decisions about hiring, promotions, and transfers are being made (Tichy et al., 1979). Furthermore, by virtue of the trusting relationships they have developed and maintained through their networking behavior, individuals who are not even seeking new positions may be actively recruited by their contacts for new job opportunities leading to subsequent unexpected job changes.

Networking is one of various job-search methods (see Derous & Ryan, this volume). Although individuals commonly engage in networking behavior for the purpose of finding a new job, multiple goals for the job search may exist, depending on the job seeker. Boswell, Zimmerman, and Swider (2012) have distinguished between new entrants to the labor market, those who have lost their jobs, and employed job seekers and compared the various kinds of search objectives held by members of these groups. For instance, employed job seekers may be looking for a new job, trying to stay aware of alternatives, developing a network of professional relationships, or seeking a job offer to use as leverage against an employer (Boswell, Boudreau, & Dunford, 2004; Boswell et al., 2012; Van Hoye & Saks, 2008). Those who are not employed may be searching to help them weigh alternatives, such as furthering their education, accepting a new position, or remaining unemployed (Boswell et al., 2012). Depending on the goals held by job seekers, the number and types of networking behavior may vary greatly.

Networking Behavior Develops Career Competencies

In their 2009 review of the careers literature, Sullivan and Baruch emphasized the importance of developing relationships for the successful enactment of careers. Changes in the workforce—including massive restructurings, unprecedented technological advances, and increased competition due to globalization—highlight the perils of isolation for job seekers. Careers are no longer considered "bounded," unfolding in one or two organizations across the working life of an individual (Arthur & Rousseau, 1996). Rather, careers are now considered to be "boundaryless," since individuals may change jobs rapidly within their current organizations (moving up, down, or laterally) or across organizational, occupational, industry, or national borders to pursue new opportunities (Sullivan, 1999). Recent research has focused on both the psychological and physical mobility of individuals (Sullivan & Arthur, 2006) as they contemplate their desires and readiness to make career changes (i.e., psychological mobility) as well as their ability to relocate themselves and their families (i.e., physical mobility), given existing ties to their current jobs and communities (Feldman & Ng, 2007; Holtom, Mitchell, & Lee, 2006). Similarly, writings on the protean career (Briscoe & Hall, 2006; Hall, 2002) emphasize the importance of maintaining employability in the increasingly uncertain job market. Adaptation to changes in the workplace calls for conducting self-assessments to ascertain areas in need of development, obtaining or upgrading one's skills so as to remain marketable, and networking in order to learn about new job opportunities or get help in navigating the changing work terrain (Hall, 2002; Mirvis & Hall, 1996).

Inkson and Arthur (2001) discuss three career competencies that are vital to remaining competitive in one's career: knowing why, knowing how, and knowing whom. All three competencies are important for the job-search process. First, the knowing-why competency refers to an individual's career identity. Those who have developed this competency understand what gives them purpose in their working lives and how they would like to expend their energies. Such knowledge provides individuals with a greater sense of what types of jobs would be more appealing to them and satisfy their needs and values. Second, the knowing-how competency refers to an individual's human capital—that is, the past investments that he or she may have made. Human capital includes a person's past work experiences, education, training, skills, and abilities (Becker, 1975). Essentially, human capital represents what an individual knows that can be applied to a job. In looking for a new job, the job seeker will compare the requirements of each position with his or her background and skill set to determine whether there is an appropriate fit. Third, the knowing-whom competency refers to one's social capital. This represents the resources available to a person within his or her network of contacts (Baker, 2000; Nahapiet & Goshal, 1998) and is critical for career success (Seibert, Kraimer, & Liden, 2001; Wanberg, 2012). Most important for the job-search process, social capital can provide one with job leads as well as with ideas, information, social support, opportunities, and other resources that may be beneficial for finding jobs. Whom an individual knows can provide numerous benefits, as social capital extends to the contacts of the other person. That is, a person may gain not only from information provided by a contact but also by those people who are part of the contact's network.

Networking behavior can be utilized to develop all three career competencies. Although commonly associated with the knowing-whom competency, since networking behavior can enlarge an individual's network of contacts, reciprocal linkages exist between the knowing-whom, knowing-how, and knowing-why competencies (Inkson & Arthur, 2001). For example, a person who has a strong knowing-whom competency can benefit from the reputation that he or she has developed. Such people may be sought out for interesting jobs or challenging assignments that can enhance their knowing-how competency. Hence, as a result of their contacts and reputation, they may be approached by others about applying for jobs. Meanwhile, in the process of working toward their new pursuits, they can enlarge the number of people in their personal contact networks. Moreover, those who have cultivated a professional network strengthen their knowing-why competency (i.e., career identity), and those with a strong knowing-why competency tend to be more comfortable contacting individuals in their field in order to develop professional relationships, thus further enhancing their knowing-whom competency.

Networking as a Method of Building Contacts That May Be Useful in the Job-Search Process

Social network theory can help to explain how networking behaviors can benefit job seekers (Wanberg, 2012). Brass (2004) defines a social network as a series of nodes (i.e., individuals) and a set of ties indicating the presence (or absence) of a relationship between the nodes. As described by Forret (2006) and Van Hoye et al. (2009), networking behaviors can influence the structure and composition of social networks, which in turn can affect an individual's subsequent networking behavior. Key characteristics of a social network include its size, the strength of the relationships within it, the pattern of those relationships, and the resources to which members of the network have access.

First, *network size* refers to the number of members in a social network (Brass, 2004). Accordingly, those who have larger social networks have more people to consult in seeking information about job opportunities. For example, in results from their longitudinal study of 1,177 unemployed Flemish job seekers, Van Hoye et al. (2009) showed that network size was positively associated with the amount of time spent networking. Research has also examined the effects that size has on specific types of social networks. For instance, in her study of the socialization of auditors, Morrison (2002) showed that having a larger friendship network helped integrate the auditors into the organization, and having a larger information network increased the auditors' organizational knowledge and ability to perform

the work. Moreover, Podolny and Baron (1997), in their study of managers and professionals of a high-tech firm, found that the size of an individual's strategic information network was positively related to number of promotions. By participating in networking behaviors, individuals can develop larger social networks that can help them to search for jobs, become integrated into organizations, and be nominated for promotions.

Second, *strength of ties* refers to the degree of closeness that distinguishes a relationship. Strong ties are depicted by frequent communication, greater intimacy, and more emotional investment in the relationship (Granovetter, 1973). According to Granovetter's strength-of-ties hypothesis, those with whom we have strong ties (i.e., close friends) are more likely to know one another and hence to be a source of identical information benefits, in contrast to those with whom we have weak ties (i.e., acquaintances). Because our acquaintances tend to move in different social circles, they do not share information with one another. Therefore those in the latter group should be a richer source of unique information about job openings. Granovetter (1974) found that job seekers with weak ties were more successful in finding jobs than those with strong ties. Additional evidence for the importance of weak ties was shown by Brown and Konrad (2001) in their longitudinal study of displaced job seekers. Job seekers from declining industries who utilized their weak ties had greater gains in terms of salary and occupational status upon being reemployed. Furthermore, Van Hoye et al. (2009) found that time spent networking resulted in a better job-organization fit for reemployed job seekers with weaker ties in their social network, providing added support for Granovetter's hypothesis.

However, strong ties can still be beneficial for the job-search process. In the Brown and Konrad (2001) study, both displaced job seekers from declining as well as growing industries tended to contact their strong ties first to help them obtain a job. Similarly, Van Hoye et al. (2009) found that unemployed job seekers who had stronger ties tended to spend more time networking in their job search. Individuals may feel more comfortable discussing their fears and concerns about finding a job and asking for assistance with their stronger ties, who are more likely to engage in higher levels of problem solving and exploration of potential opportunities with job seekers (Brown & Konrad, 2001). Furthermore, owing to the higher level of risk and effort involved, strong ties may be more critical for the transfer of sensitive information in job-search processes, such as the level of salary offered for a position (Seidel, Polzer, & Stewart, 2000). Overall, whereas weak ties may be more helpful for acquiring job leads, stronger ties appear to be more beneficial for obtaining emotional social support as well as assistance in career exploration and decision making.

Third, Burt's (1992) structural hole theory addresses the *pattern of relationships* in a social network. That is, a social network can be depicted as a web, with ties (i.e., links) connecting the members of a social network who know one another. In the absence of a tie between any two members of a social network, a structural hole exists. According to Burt (1992), structural holes provide two types of benefits. First, individuals can obtain more diverse information (e.g., such as information about job openings) from members of a social network who do not know one another. Second, structural holes permit an individual to control the flow of information between network members, thus serving a bridging function that can be utilized to advantage. Findings by Burt (1992) as well as Podolny and Baron (1997) showed that structural holes were positively related to upward mobility within organizations. Furthermore, Rodan and Galunic (2004) found that structural holes were related to higher managerial performance and innovation due to the greater access to heterogeneous knowledge.

Fourth, the *resources held* by members of a social network include a range of benefits that may be helpful to the job seeker. Tichy et al. (1979) classified these benefits into four categories: information, friendship, materials/services, and influence. For example, individuals may participate in networking behaviors in order to obtain information about job opportunities, get needed social support while they are searching for a job, receive coaching to help them perform better in job interviews, and leverage influence to help them obtain an interview and/or job offer. Having powerful members in one's social network can provide valuable benefits for those searching for jobs. In their research on job seekers, Lin, Ensel, and Vaughn (1981) found that the status of the network member had a strong effect on the prestige of the attained job. Although tie status was not positively related to time spent networking in their longitudinal study, Van Hoye et al. (2009) found that tie status moderated the relationship between time spent networking and whether job seekers became reemployed. Job seekers who had higher-status ties in their social network were more likely to have jobs at time 2 in the study.

These results indicate that networking behaviors focused on cultivating relationships with high-status contacts can provide substantial job-search assistance.

Taken as a whole, networking behavior can be utilized to help shape the structure and composition of an individual's social network and may provide valuable assistance during a job search. Networking behavior can increase the size of an individual's network, can result in the development of both strong and weak ties, can be used to influence the pattern of connections among network members, and can impact the level of resources available in a social network. However, this should not be taken to suggest that all job seekers can derive equal benefits from their social networks.

Barriers Faced by Women and Minorities in Building and Utilizing Their Social Networks

Research from sociodemographic perspectives shows that women and minorities tend to have less influential and fewer well-developed social networks; clearly this can inhibit their opportunities in the external labor market as well as within their current organizations (Brass, 1985; Chapple, 2002; Dreher & Cox, 1996, 2000; Ibarra 1992, 1995; Wanberg, 2012; see Derous & Ryan, this volume, on disadvantaged groups, and Zikic, Kent, & Richardson, this volume, on international job seekers). Forret (2006) discusses the similarity-attraction paradigm, tokenism theory, and existing organizational structures as three explanations for the barriers women and minorities face in developing or utilizing their social networks.

First, according to the similarity-attraction paradigm (Byrne, 1971), individuals are attracted to those like themselves on such characteristics as gender, race, and ethnicity. This similarity makes communication with others easier and more frequent, facilitating the development of trusting relationships (Roberts & O'Reilly, 1979) and social networks. However, utilization of social networks can be particularly problematic for women and minorities. According to Chapple (2002), chronically unemployed women may have few weak ties in the labor market to provide them with information about better job opportunities, so they rely on strong ties, which tend to connect them with low-paying jobs. Huffman and Torres (2001) and Straits (1998) found that women tend to use fewer personal contacts than men in searching for jobs. However, when women do use informal sources, they are more likely to end up in female-dominated jobs (which tend to be less well paid) than women using formal sources (Drentea, 1998; Straits, 1998). Looking at the careers of male and female managers, Brett and Stroh (1997) found that pursuing an external labor market strategy (i.e., changing employers frequently to advance one's career) benefited men but not women in terms of salary progression. Furthermore, in examining race in addition to gender, Dreher and Cox (2000) found that pursuing an external labor market strategy increased the compensation of White males only. These results suggest that in searching for a new employer, similarity with majority group members, who tend to hold more power and influence in hiring decisions, is important. The similarity effect also appears to make it difficult for even highly educated women and minorities to establish strong ties with members of the majority group. For example, Dreher and Cox (1996) found that although individuals with White male mentors received higher compensation, African American, Hispanic, and female MBAs were less likely to establish mentoring relationships with White male mentors. Considering the benefits of having a strong advocate on one's behalf when promotional opportunities arise, the lack of strong ties with those in higher-level positions can be particularly detrimental for women and minorities.

Second, according to tokenism theory (Kanter, 1977), it can be risky for members of the majority group to strongly support a woman or minority for a new job or promotion in light of the higher visibility, added pressures to perform, and increased awareness throughout the organization should the individual fail in the position. Lack of strong sponsorship eliminates any perceived need to deflect attention from oneself should the woman or minority candidate not succeed in the new job. Furthermore, when an easily identifiable minority group exists in an organization, boundary heightening can occur, such that women and minorities are excluded from venues where opportunities for informal socialization take place during the regular work day or after hours (Kanter, 1977). Such informal gatherings can be vital for learning about new organizational initiatives, job opportunities, important background information on job assignments and people, and can result in the development of stronger ties with colleagues. Exclusion from such informal networks and lack of culture fit were far more likely to be cited as barriers to their career advancement by women executives than by male executives (Lyness & Thompson, 1997).

Third, where women and minorities are located within their organizational structures also influences their interaction patterns with organizational members (Brass, 2004; Brass, Galaskiewicz, Greve, & Tsai, 2004; Podolny & Baron, 1997). This has implications for upward advancement. According to Pfeffer (1989), it is critical to examine the structure of individual jobs to make sure women and minorities are located in positions that have career ladders. Lack of experience in line positions has been commonly cited as a barrier to the advancement of women and minorities (Wellington, Kropf, & Gerkovich, 2003). Individuals holding line positions with profit-and-loss responsibilities have more access to powerful decision makers and better opportunities to demonstrate their worth to the organization. Although holding staff positions may offer women and minorities chances to develop relationships throughout the organization, the lack of line experience limits their opportunities to reach the highest levels.

Overall, whereas networking behavior can facilitate the development of more effective social networks in searching for new jobs or for advancing in one's current organization, women and minorities face additional challenges that can inhibit their efforts. The following paragraphs examine the variety of ways in which scholars measured an individual's networking behavior.

Measurement of Networking Behavior

Networking behavior has long been of interest to practitioners; relatively speaking, however, it has only recently gained momentum in the scholarly literature. There is no single scale of networking behavior that has received wide acceptance and usage in research studies. Rather, networking behavior has been operationalized in several ways, including both general measures of networking behavior and measures more directly related to job-search processes. Below the more general networking measures are described first. These tend to focus either on the networking behaviors utilized, the targets of the networking behavior, or the resources obtained through networking, as all of these measures have implications for the job-search process. Second, networking behavior scales are described that focus more specifically on networking for jobs.

In an observation study of fifty-two managers, Luthans, Rosenkrantz, and Hennessey (1985) found that successful managers were more likely to engage in networking behavior, which they described as the extent to which managers interacted with outsiders and participated in socializing/politicking behaviors. In a later attempt to develop a comprehensive measure of networking behaviors, Forret and Dougherty (2001) conducted a factor analysis on data collected from managers and professionals. The factor analysis results of their twenty-eight-item scale resulted in five different types of networking behavior: maintaining contacts, socializing, engaging in professional activities, participating in church and community, and increasing internal visibility in one's organization. Behaviors such as socializing/politicking and increasing internal visibility may be especially helpful for upward movement in organizations, whereas behaviors such as interacting with outsiders or engaging in professional activities may help individuals make external job changes.

Several measures of networking behavior have been developed that focus on the target of the behavior. Primarily, research has examined whether individuals participate in networking behaviors either internally in one's organization or externally with individuals outside one's organization. In their study of managers from several companies, Michael and Yukl (1993) developed an eleven-item internal networking scale (e.g., attend meetings, ceremonies, or social events in the organization) and an eight-item external networking scale (e.g., go to lunch or dinner with externals). In their study of career self-management, Sturges, Guest, Conway, and Davey (2002) developed a seven-item scale of networking behaviors which focus primarily on networking internally (e.g., I have talked to senior management at company social gatherings). Eby, Butts, and Lockwood (2003) measured the career competency of knowing-whom in their research on career success by developing a three-item scale capturing the extent to which individuals are well-connected within their organizations (e.g., I have a lot of contacts within the organization) and a three-item scale assessing the breadth of their external networks (e.g., I regularly network with individuals outside my organization). A forty-four-item networking behavior scale developed by Wolff and Moser (2006) includes twenty-two items measuring internal and twenty-two items measuring external networking behavior (see also Wolff, Schneider-Rahm, & Forret, 2011). A unique aspect of this scale is that the internal and external dimensions are each composed of three subdimensions: building, maintaining, and using. Hence the scale examines the degree to which individuals engage in building internal contacts, maintaining internal contacts, and using

internal contacts, as well as building, maintaining, and using their external contacts. Taken as a whole, the implications of the internal and external scales for job seekers is that those who are interesting in obtaining promotions in their organization may choose to focus their networking efforts internally, whereas those who are interested in obtaining a position with another organization may instead focus their networking efforts externally. Individuals may also network externally in the hope of obtaining a job offer that they can use as leverage with their current employer to gain additional compensation or promotion opportunities (Boswell et al., 2004, 2012; Van Hoye & Saks, 2008).

Three studies have focused primarily on the resources available through networking behaviors. In their early study of employees of a municipal bureaucracy, Gould and Penley (1984) employed a two-item scale to assess the degree to which employees (1) built a network of contacts in the organization for obtaining information and (2) built a network of friendships in the organization to help further their careers. The six-item scale developed by Bozionelos (2003) assessed the expressive resources (e.g., social support available) and instrumental resources (e.g., influence available) from contacts within an organization. In addition, Ferris et al. (2005) developed a six-item networking ability scale (one of the subscales of their political skill inventory). The networking ability scale measures the extent to which individuals spend time and effort networking with others and their ability to utilize their contacts for support when needed. These three measures tend to emphasize the influence available from an individual's contacts that may be particularly helpful finding new job opportunities as well as helpful social support.

Few measures have been developed with a more specific emphasis on networking for jobs. It should be noted that networking is usually incorporated in job-search behavior or intensity scales, particularly those that are based on Blau's (1994) preparatory and active job-search behavior measures. Specifically with regard to job-search behaviors, Wanberg et al. (2000) developed an eight-item networking comfort scale (e.g., I am comfortable asking my friends for advice regarding my job search) to determine the ease with which individuals were able to contact their friends or acquaintances about job opportunities. Also specific to the job-search process, Wanberg et al. (2000) developed a nine-item networking intensity scale. Six items ask respondents about the frequency in which they have utilized behaviors (e.g., contacting people to ask for job-search advice or leads) within the previous 2 weeks, and three items evaluating the thoroughness of the networking efforts (e.g., letting people know you are searching for a job). More recently, Van Hoye et al. (2009) devised a two-item measure to assess the time spent networking. Job seekers were asked to indicate, for the previous 3 months or until they became reemployed, how much time they spent on (1) contacting people they know to help them find a job and (2) asking people they knew about job leads. In a slightly different vein, Van Hoye and Saks (2008) developed a three-item measure (e.g., developing new professional relationships) to ascertain the extent to which developing a network of professional relationships is a job-search objective. Based on Forret and Sullivan's (2002) discussion of the importance of developing diverse social networks, Forret, Sullivan, and Samtani (2011) developed a twenty-item scale to find out about assistance received in the job search from (1) family and friends, (2) contacts in the profession, (3) contacts on networking sites, (4) contacts in the local community, and (5) current and former work colleagues. Respondents indicated with regard to each group of individuals whether their contacts provided them with information about job opportunities, recommended them for a job, helped them obtain a job interview, and helped them obtain a job offer.

As seen above, the multiple ways in which networking behavior has been measured unfortunately may cause the field to grow more slowly than what might otherwise have been the case. On the other hand, the diversity of measures has added new dimensions to ways of considering networking behavior. Most of the networking measures described have been utilized in only one or a very few number of studies. For scholars interested in studying networking behavior related to the job-search process, it is key to evaluate precisely what aspect of networking behavior is of interest and to select measures appropriate to the goals of the research project in order to develop a more solid base of research findings.

Antecedents of Networking Behavior

Although job seekers are constantly encouraged to engage in networking behavior, many individuals find networking difficult. Antecedents of networking behavior that have implications for job seekers fall primarily into the categories of (1) personality and attitudinal variables and (2) job characteristics.

First, of the Big Five personality dimensions, extraversion has the strongest support as a predictor of networking behavior (Forret & Dougherty, 2001; Simmons, 2010; Van Hoye et al., 2009; Wanberg et al., 2000; Wolff & Moser, 2006). Conscientiousness has received mixed results as an antecedent (Bozionelos, 2003; Van Hoye et al., 2009; Wanberg et al., 2000), and few studies have linked agreeableness, openness to experience, and neuroticism with networking behavior (Bozionelos, 2003; Wanberg et al., 2000). Extraversion refers to individuals who are more sociable, active, assertive, and who gain their energy from interacting with other people (Digman, 1990; Goldberg, 1993; McCrae & Costa, 1987). As such, it is easier for extraverted individuals to approach people whom they do not know to initiate conversations as well as to interact more frequently with people they do know. For example, Forret and Dougherty (2001) found that extraversion was significantly related with four of the five types of networking behaviors studied (i.e., maintaining contacts, socializing, engaging in professional activities, and increasing internal visibility), and Simmons (2010) found extraversion to be strongly related to both internal and external networking behavior.

In their study of unemployed job seekers, Wanberg et al. (2000) found that both extraversion and conscientiousness predicted networking intensity; however, when networking comfort was added to the regression equation the results for conscientiousness disappeared. More recently, Van Hoye et al. (2009) found that extraversion, but not conscientiousness, was positively related to the amount of time job seekers spent networking. In his examination of instrumental and expressive network resources, Bozionelos (2003) found conscientiousness to be negatively related to instrumental network resources. Bozionelos (2003) hypothesized that individuals who are more conscientious (i.e., dependable and industrious) would be more likely to concentrate on their prescribed job duties, expect to be promoted based on merit, and less likely to participant in informal influence mechanisms such as networking.

As alluded to by Bozionelos (2003), individuals who perceive networking as an informal mechanism to utilize for advancement purposes (in contrast to formal merit-based processes), may be uncomfortable participating in networking behavior. Forret and Dougherty (2001) found that those holding a more favorable attitude toward workplace politics were more likely to increase their internal visibility in the organization. Moreover, Wanberg et al. (2000) showed that unemployed job seekers who were more comfortable with networking conducted their job search with higher networking intensity. Furthermore, in their qualitative study of employed and unemployed job seekers with professional and managerial backgrounds, Wanberg, Basbug, Van Hooft, and Samtani (2012) found that many job seekers expressed great concern over the quality of their network, difficulties obtaining assistance from their contacts, and discomfort with networking. Networking ability is considered a key dimension of the political skill inventory developed by Ferris et al. (2005). Overall, those who are more comfortable networking (Wanberg, 2012; Wanberg et al., 2000, 2012), who hold more favorable attitudes toward workplace politics (Forret & Dougherty, 2001) and who evaluate themselves more favorably in networking ability (Ferris et al., 2005) should be more likely to participate in networking behavior.

Self-esteem and proactive personality have also been shown to be related to networking behavior. Self-esteem refers to an individual's general sense of worth, opinion, and regard for oneself (Brockner, 1988). Individuals who are higher in self-esteem are more confident in themselves and what they have to offer to others (Brockner, 1988; Campbell, 1990). This should translate into beliefs they would be good exchange partners in that they have valuable resources (e.g., information, services, support) to benefit others in an exchange relationship. Forret and Dougherty (2001) found that self-esteem was positively related to the networking behaviors of maintaining contacts, engaging in professional activities, and increasing internal visibility. Proactive personality also significantly predicted networking ability in Thompson's (2005) study of 126 supervisor-subordinate relationships, further emphasizing the importance of assertiveness and confidence in developing relationships with others. Other variables such as affective organizational commitment (Sturges et al., 2002), self-monitoring behavior, interpersonal trust, work-related achievement motivation, and career orientation (Wolff & Moser, 2006) have been found to be positively related to networking behavior reflecting the significance of developing trust in relationships, sensitivity to impressions conveyed to others, and the value of networking to the successful attainment of work and career goals.

Second, with regard to job characteristics, the amount of networking behavior tends to be positively associated with how dependent individuals are on others for their job performance (Michael & Yukl, 1993). Michael and Yukl (1993, p. 330) define *dependency* as "the extent to which cooperation and support from a person are needed to carry out a manager's job responsibilities effectively." Individuals may be dependent upon both internal as well as external constituents. Specifically, those in jobs that require frequent interactions with others, such as sales jobs, engage in higher levels of networking behavior. For instance, Michael and Yukl (1993) found that marketing managers networked more frequently with individuals outside the organization than production or accounting managers. Similarly, Forret and Dougherty's (2001) results showed that those holding sales or marketing jobs were more likely to engage in maintaining contacts. Likewise, in their survey of nurses in a large hospital, Brown and Konrad (1996) found that greater task instability and decision-making autonomy were positively related to intraunit and interunit networking behavior.

In addition, the organizational level of the job an individual holds has been shown to be related to networking behavior (Carroll & Teo, 1996; Forret & Dougherty, 2001; Michael & Yukl, 1993; Wolff & Moser, 2006). As individuals advance through the ranks of an organization, there tends to be greater need to serve as boundary spanners, interacting both with others inside the organization and across departmental lines along with more frequent interactions with those outside the organization (e.g., customers, suppliers, stakeholders in the community). For example, in their comparison of the social networks of managers and nonmanagers, Carroll and Teo (1996) found that managers were more likely to belong to outside organizations such as professional associations, service clubs, and societies (e.g., charitable organizations, chambers of commerce). Connections made with influential members of other organizations can assist in future collaborations and serve as useful sources of information. To satisfactorily meet the requirements of certain positions in organizations, it is essential to develop and maintain beneficial relationships with a wide variety of contacts.

The personality and attitudinal variables discussed above as well as the job-related characteristics hold several implications for job seekers. First, although personality is relatively stable over time, job seekers who are more introverted or less assertive can still utilize coaching, seminars, or books to help them strategize ways to be more comfortable approaching people they do not know. According to

Anand and Conger (2007), the best networkers are not 'born" but rather work very hard at developing their skills, investing both time and effort. Second, by understanding that networking is about helping others (Baker, 2000), job seekers may develop more favorable attitudes toward networking behavior, which can help them increase their participation in networking. Third, by focusing on contributions made in their current organizations, job seekers may become more confident in their networking ability and their abilities to help others. Fourth, job seekers who are applying for jobs that entail frequent interactions with individuals and boundary-spanning responsibilities should highlight their past cross-functional experiences as well as their involvement with members of external organizations (e.g., professional associations, service clubs) to emphasize their previous efforts in developing effective social networks.

Outcomes of Networking for Job-search Processes

Strangely, in light of the popularity of networking as a job-search technique, relatively little research has studied the effectiveness of networking for job-search success. Job-search success can be operationalized in many different ways (Brasher & Chen, 1999; Saks, 2006; Van Hoye et al., 2009; Wanberg et al., 2000) including job-search outcomes (e.g., number of job interviews and offers), employment outcomes (e.g., employment status, speed of reemployment, exhaustion of unemployment benefits), and quality of employment (e.g., job satisfaction, person-organization fit, and intentions to quit) (Van Hoye et al., 2009). As noted by Brasher and Chen (1999), these various outcomes often have weak correlations among them making it important to examine a wide variety of success measures.

In one of the first studies of networking behavior for job-search success, Wanberg et al. (2000) showed in their examination of unemployed job seekers that networking intensity was related to a lower likelihood of running out of unemployment benefits and a higher likelihood of becoming reemployed at time 2. However, neither of those findings remained statistically significant once general job-search intensity was entered into the regression equations. Networking intensity was not related to speed of reemployment, and those who did report finding jobs through networking did not report subsequently higher job satisfaction or lower intentions to quit than those who found their jobs through alternative means. However, Wanberg et al. (2000) did report that 36% of the respondents in their study indicated finding jobs through networking. In their longitudinal study of unemployed Flemish job seekers, Van Hoye et al. (2009) found that time spent networking was positively related to number of job offers but not to employment status or job-organization fit. It should also be noted that time spent networking explained additional variance in number of job offers beyond time spent looking at print advertising, searching for jobs on the Internet, or using a public employment service. In another longitudinal study by Wolff and Moser (2010) using survey data collected in three waves from 166 employed individuals in Germany, results showed that both internal and external networking behavior were positively associated with changing employers.

In his study of five job-search behaviors among 255 business school undergraduates who were approaching graduation, Saks (2006) found that contrary to expectations, the use of informal job sources (e.g., friends, relatives, employees of organization) was negatively related to number of job offers and employment status. Saks (2006) suggested that informal sources may no longer be as effective for finding jobs owing to the more rigorous selection processes (e.g., testing, structured interviews) utilized by organizations. Alternatively, given the additional resources (e.g., campus placement services, employers actively recruiting on campus) available to college graduates, it may be that formal sources are more important at this early stage in their careers. In contrast to findings by Saks (2006), Fernandez and Weinberg (1997), in their study of 5,568 individuals who inquired about four types of entry-level employment opportunities at a large retail bank, found strong support that individuals who were referred by current bank employees were significantly more likely to obtain job interviews and subsequent job offers. Overall, further research is needed on the effectiveness of networking behaviors for the job-search process, utilizing a wide variety of success outcomes and considering the current employment status of the job seeker as well as the job seeker's experience and career stage.

Besides searching for jobs at new employers, research has found networking to be particularly helpful for advancing in one's organization. Luthans et al. (1985) found networking to be related to promotions in their study of managers from public and private organizations.

Similarly, Michael and Yukl (1993) found that both internal as well as external networking was related to rate of advancement, although the results were stronger for internal networking. Bozionelos (2003) concluded that instrumental network resources, but not expressive, predicted organizational level. Forret and Dougherty (2004) found that the networking behavior of increasing internal visibility was significantly related to number of promotions; however, subsequent analysis showed that this relationship held for men but not for women. Furthermore, in their longitudinal study, Wolff and Moser's (2010) results showed that internal (but not external) networking behavior significantly predicted promotions. Taken as a whole, the strongest support exists for networking within the organization as a predictor of advancement.

While evidence exists for the vital role that networking plays in both finding a new employer and advancing in one's organization, research has also demonstrated other important outcomes of networking behavior, particularly with regard to compensation, perceptions of career success, job performance, and other important attitudes. Several studies have shown that networking behavior is related to compensation (Blickle et al., 2012; Bozionelos, 2008; Forret & Dougherty, 2004; Forret & McCallum, 2010; Gould & Penley, 1984; Wolff & Moser, 2009) and career satisfaction measures (Bozionelos, 2003, 2008; Eby et al., 2003; Forret & Dougherty, 2004; Forret & McCallum, 2010; Wolff & Moser, 2009). Networking ability is related to supervisor ratings of employee job performance (Thompson, 2005), and significantly predicted sales volume in a sample of insurance salespersons (Blickle et al., 2012). In their qualitative study of faculty members, Gersick, Bartunek, and Dutton (2000) describe a number of reasons (e.g., collegiality, advice, support, other's power and control) for the importance of professional relationships. With regard to attitudinal outcomes, Bozionelos (2008) found that expressive network resources were positively related to affective commitment and instrumental (career-oriented) network resources were negatively related to continuance commitment. McCallum and Forret's (2009) results showed that internal networking behavior was positively related to job satisfaction, affective commitment, and normative commitment, whereas external networking was negatively related with normative commitment. Furthermore, Eby et al. (2003) found that breadth of both internal and external networks predicted

perceptions of internal and external marketability in their study of alumni. In sum, the above results demonstrate that networking behavior contributes substantially to a wide range of career outcomes beyond jobs and advancement.

Implications for Individuals, Counselors, and Organizations

In light of the above research findings on networking behavior and the importance of building social networks to support job-search efforts, a number of implications exist for individual job seekers as well as for career counselors helping individuals progress in their careers. Furthermore, networking is also important for managers of organizations as they seek to develop individuals internally for promotions and look externally to fill open positions. Factors to consider include the following.

For Individuals

• Identify career goals and type of job sought. This will enable individuals to reflect on how to expand their networking behaviors to reach people they would like to meet and how they might be of assistance to them. Individuals should consider their social network critically to determine whether they have built relationships within their organization, profession, and community.

• Develop a diverse social network, including both individuals from majority and minority groups. While it is more comfortable to network with those who share one's own characteristics and this can provide emotional and career support, particularly for minorities, developing friendships with members of the majority group in an organization can provided added instrumental benefits.

• Take advantage of the norm of reciprocity by organizing contact information for social network members in order to efficiently assist others by making referrals or providing needed information. Being organized also helps job seekers in contacting others about job opportunities and being able to promptly thank others for their support.

• Review and update online profiles to project a professional image. Consider whether information displayed on social networking sites such as Facebook or LinkedIn would be appealing to potential employers and conveys the desired impression.

• Fit opportunities for networking into each week. It is critical not to let relationships vital to one's career lapse or to be perceived as interested in someone only when a favor is needed. Schedule lunches or send notes to contacts to help maintain relationships.

• Although social capital is instrumental for career success, it is also important to focus on human capital. Individuals will not recommend or refer others for jobs if they believe there are gaps in skills or expertise. Seek to gain the knowledge, skills, abilities, and experiences to remain marketable so contacts are comfortable in making a recommendation or referral.

For Counselors

• Help job seekers analyze their social networks to see how they might be made more effective. Consider the size of their social network, the number of strong and weak ties, whether the social network contains a lot of redundancy (i.e., contacts who all know one another), and the diversity of the individuals in the social network. Examine what vital contacts are missing from the social network that individuals should be developing.

• Identify barriers to networking that prevent job seekers from reaching out to others. Examine fears (e.g., rejection), personality traits (e.g., introversion), and other barriers (e.g., lack of time) that may discourage job seekers from proactively contacting individuals who would be willing to help them.

• Discuss and role play strategies that will make it easier for job seekers to initiate contact with others and to maintain those relationships. Assist job seekers in becoming more comfortable introducing themselves to strangers or initiating conversations with acquaintances. Devise strategies to help individuals schedule time for networking on a weekly basis.

• Enable job seekers to effectively solicit assistance from others. Job seekers need to ask about job or career opportunities from their contacts in a manner that is not perceived as demanding, but in such a way that contacts are willing to share information or ideas they have with the job seeker.

• Help individuals examine their career identities and what types of jobs they would find energizing. Determine the necessary knowledge, skills, abilities, and experiences individuals must

have to put themselves in a strong position for their desired jobs.

For Organizations

• Strong commitment from senior management for development of employees is needed to help ensure a pipeline of solid performers for leadership roles. This includes making sure individuals have the requisite skills and contacts to perform effectively at higher-level positions. Evaluate managers on their ability to develop their employees for such roles.

• Utilize cross-functional teams, project groups, job rotation, and challenging job assignments in order for employees to get the experience they need to progress and develop a network of contacts throughout the organization.

• Hold events to promote interaction among employees, and consider forming network groups (e.g., a new employee group) to provide opportunities for individuals to meet others with similar interests or concerns who can provide professional as well as social support.

• Provide both time and financial support for employees to actively participate in professional organizations, community groups (e.g., United Way), service organizations (e.g., Rotary, chambers of commerce), and other volunteer organizations. The relationships developed help employees become engaged in their local communities, provide employees with knowledge that may benefit their organizations, and may assist employees in identifying prospective hires for their organizations.

• Examine the layout of the organization. Determine whether departments or functions where a high level of cooperation is needed are located close to one another to facilitate informal interactions among employees that can help improve the efficiency and effectiveness of the organization.

Agenda for Future Research

Although networking is a highly popular method of searching for jobs, research has lagged behind on suggestions for how to effectively utilize networking for job-search behavior. With this in mind, four areas for future research seem most apparent and are discussed below: the efficacy of social networking for obtaining jobs, how employers use information gained from social networking sites in their selection decisions, potential negative consequences of an individual's networking behavior, and the effectiveness of training and coaching strategies to enhance networking abilities.

First, with the explosive growth of social networking sites such as Facebook and LinkedIn, little is known about the effectiveness of social networking for finding a job as well as the profile of job seekers using social networking. While anecdotal accounts about the effectiveness of sites such as LinkedIn abound (Brandel, 2009; Eccles, 2009; Kim, 2010), little academic research has examined the effectiveness of social media for job-search success. In a recent survey of 1,202 employed and unemployed job seekers who subscribed to an online job-search service, Sullivan, Forret, and Agrawal (2013) found that assistance received from social media contacts on sites such as Facebook and LinkedIn were related to obtaining job interviews but not job offers. Moreover, their results indicated that employed job seekers received less assistance from their social media contacts than those who were unemployed, suggesting that employed job seekers may be reluctant to publicize their interest in finding new jobs for fear of retribution from their current employers. More research is needed to examine whether social networking sites are more likely to be used for job searches by younger individuals, the highly educated, the unemployed, by males or females, or by members of certain racial or ethnic groups. Furthermore, studies are needed to test whether social networking sites are more effective for obtaining certain types of jobs (e.g., technical, professional), and whether the jobs found through social networking sites are of higher or lower quality (e.g., in terms of salary or person-organization fit) than might have been found through other means. Also, it would be beneficial to learn how best to phrase a request when searching for a new job to enhance the likelihood of assistance being received. Clearly opportunities abound for studies in this area.

Second, organizations are utilizing social networking for recruiting and selection purposes. The 2010 Jobvite Social Recruiting Survey of over 600 human resources professionals indicated that 73% use social networks or social media to support their recruitment efforts and 58% have successfully hired using social media. In examining which social media are used in recruiting, survey results indicated that LinkedIn (78%) is used most often, followed by Facebook (55%), Twitter (45%), blogs (19%), YouTube (14%), and MySpace (5%). However,

concerns exist as to how organizations may be utilizing the information available about applicants on sites such as Facebook or LinkedIn. Social networking website pages often contain photos and content that may affect selection decisions (e.g., the applicant's marital status, race, religion, or number of children) that can present legal issues if a potential employer asked for this information (Kluemper & Rosen, 2009; Slovensky & Ross, 2012). In addition, online profiles often contain content (e.g., alcohol and drug use, sexual activities) that potential employers find unprofessional and that has been used to eliminate job candidates (Finder, 2006). In a laboratory study where 148 undergraduate students evaluated hypothetical job candidates, Bohnert and Ross (20010) showed that candidates with a social networking website emphasizing a professional or family orientation were evaluated more favorably than those with a site emphasizing alcohol-related activities. Other recent research by Karl, Peluchette, and Schlaegel (2010) has examined characteristics of those more likely to post questionable material on their Facebook profiles. These researchers showed that persons high in conscientiousness, agreeableness, and emotional stability were less likely to post content of a problematic nature; those high in compulsive Internet use and US (in contrast to German) students were more likely to place such material on their profiles. More research on how companies are using the information they obtain from social networking sites along with how job applicants can present an attractive profile to potential employers is needed.

Third, more research needs to be performed on what Wolff, Moser, and Grau (2008) refer to as the dark side of networking. Networking is viewed as an informal means of influence that can benefit an individual's career. Such influence can take widely differing forms, including providing job-search assistance, information, advice, support, or advocacy. Networking has been viewed as a "political" behavior (e.g., Ferris et al., 2005), and individuals who have less favorable perceptions of workplace politics are less likely to engage in networking behavior (Forret & Dougherty, 2001). If individuals are perceived as having obtained jobs or promotions through the influence of their contacts, do they suffer negative reactions from their peers? How might such negative reactions impact the future job performance of persons whose contacts helped them obtain jobs or promotions? Research on nepotism shows that individuals hired with the help of relatives or friends can expect perceptions of unfairness by their coworkers (Van Hooft & Stout, 2012). Common and rather cynical phrases such as "It's who you know, not what you know" may pervade the culture of an organization if members believe that individuals are not being promoted based on merit but only because they have close friends and/or relatives in positions of influence. An organizational culture where jobs and promotions are viewed as political or due to favoritism is likely to result in low morale and less engagement by employees (Van Hooft & Stout, 2012). Moreover, those who obtain jobs with the assistance of their contacts and who do not have the necessary human capital to succeed may find help from their peers less forthcoming. Furthermore, it would be interesting to explore other potential drawbacks to a heavy reliance on contacts with others. For instance, do members of the organization such as peers or managers perceive them as "operators" or "players"—as being too ambitious and self-centered on their own careers? Perceptions might arise as to how much time is spent networking as opposed to performing their jobs. Likewise, although today individuals change jobs and organizations far more frequently than in the past, it may be that those who develop reputations as "players" may find job offers drying up if hiring managers believe they will not stay very long, as they appear to be constantly in search of greener pastures.

Fourth, research is needed on training and coaching interventions for job seekers who are uncomfortable or ineffective in their networking behavior. As previously discussed, individuals who are more introverted and have lower self-esteem are less likely to engage in networking behavior (Forret & Dougherty, 2001), which may inhibit their job search. Research studies are needed to examine the most effective techniques to help individuals overcome barriers to networking. De Janasz and Forret (2008) provide four exercises utilized with undergraduate and graduate business students to increase their awareness of the importance of networking and to build their comfort and skills when networking. Similarly, job counselors may assist job seekers through by having job seekers practice introductions and developing rapport. With all of the opportunities available for job seekers to participate in to develop their social network (e.g., professional organizations, service clubs, social activities, network groups), research is needed to ascertain what types of activities and groups tend to be more helpful for finding jobs. This would help job seekers to utilize their time and energy wisely and

to be more strategic in their networking behavior. However, because benefits from networking are reaped as a result of contributing to others (Baker, 2000), job seekers should not expect early returns from their participation in such groups.

Conclusion

This is an exciting time for networking, job-search, and career management scholars. Networking as a job-search behavior represents a rich field of study that has wide-ranging practical implications for job seekers, career counselors, and organizations. With the increasing awareness of the importance of interpersonal skills and relationships for organizational advancement, along with the rapid rise of social networking sites that can dramatically enlarge a job seeker's social network, much more research is needed to enable job seekers to successfully navigate the shifting career terrain to enhance both their internal and external mobility. Becoming proficient in networking helps to develop a job seeker's career competencies; this can open both anticipated as well as unexpected job opportunities in the marketplace.

Acknowledgments

I would like to thank Drs. Sherry Sullivan, Hans-Georg Wolff, Greet Van Hoye, Ute-Christine Klehe, and Edwin Van Hooft for their helpful comments on this chapter.

References

Anand, N., & Conger, J. A. (2007). Capabilities of the consummate networker. *Organizational Dynamics, 36*(1), 13–27. DOI: 10.1016/j.orgdyn.2006.12.001

Arthur, M. B., & Rousseau, D. (1996). *The boundaryless career.* New York: Oxford University Press.

Baker, W. E. (2000). *Achieving success through social capital: Tapping the hidden resources in your personal and business networks.* San Francisco: Jossey-Bass.

Becker, G. S. (1975). *Human capital.* Chicago: University of Chicago Press.

Blau, G. (1994). Testing a two-dimensional measure of job search behavior. *Organizational Behavior and Human Decision Processes, 59,* 288–312. DOI: 10.1006/obhd.1994.1061

Blickle, G., John, J., Ferris, G. R., Momm, T., Liu, Y., Haag, R., Meyer, G., Weber, K., & Oerder, K. (2012). Fit of political skill to the work context: A two-study investigation. *Applied Psychology: An International Review, 61,* 295–322. DOI: 10.1111/j.1464-0597.2011.00469.x

Bohnert, D., & Ross, W. H. (2010). The influence of social networking web sites on the evaluation of job candidates. *Cyberpsychology, Behavior, and Social Networking, 13,* 341–347. DOI: 10.1089/cyber.2009.0193

Booz Allen Hamilton. (2006). Direct Employers Association recruiting trends survey. Available at: http://www.jobcentral.com/pdfs/DEsurvey.pdf

Boswell, W. R., Boudreau, J. W., & Dunford, B. B. (2004). The outcomes and correlates of job search objectives: Search to leave or searching for leverage? *Journal of Applied Psychology, 89*, 1083–1091. DOI: 10.1037/0021-9010.89.6.1083

Boswell, W. R., Zimmerman, R. D., & Swider, B. W. (2012). Employee job search: Toward an understanding of search context and search objectives. *Journal of Management, 38*, 129–163. DOI: 10.1177/0149206311421829

Bozionelos, N. (2003). Intra-organizational network resources: Relation to career success and personality. *The International Journal of Organizational Analysis, 11*, 41–66.

Bozionelos, N. (2008). Intra-organizational network resources: How they relate to career success and organizational commitment. *Personnel Review, 37*(3), 249–263. DOI: 10.1108/00483480810862251

Brandel, M. (2009). Laid off? Here's your net. *Computerworld, 43*(26), 16–19.

Brasher, E. E., & Chen, P. Y. (1999). Evaluation of success criteria in job search: A process perspective. *Journal of Occupational and Organizational Psychology, 72*, 57–70.

Brass, D. J. (1985). Men's and women's networks: A study of interaction patterns and influence in an organization. *Academy of Management Journal, 28*, 327–343.

Brass, D. J. (2004). A social network perspective on human resources management. In G. R. Ferris (Ed.), *Research in personnel and human resources management* (Vol. *13*, pp. 39–79). Greenwich, CT: JAI Press.

Brass, D. J., Galaskiewicz, J., Greve, H. R., & Tsai, W. (2004). Taking stock of networks and organizations: A multilevel perspective. *Academy of Management Journal, 47*, 795–817.

Brett, J. M., & Stroh, L. K. (1997). Jumping ship: Who benefits from an external labor market career strategy? *Journal of Applied Psychology, 82*, 331–41.

Briscoe, J. P., & Hall, D. T. (2006). The interplay of boundaryless and protean careers: Combinations and implications. *Journal of Vocational Behavior, 69*, 4–18.

Brockner, J. (1988). *Self-esteem at work.* Lexington, MA: Lexington Books.

Brown, D. W., & Konrad, A. M. (1996). Task complexity and information exchange: The impact of nurses' networking activities on organizational influence. *Sociological Focus, 29*, 107–124.

Brown, D. W., & Konrad, A. M. (2001). Granovetter was right: The importance of weak ties to a contemporary job search. *Group & Organization Management, 26*, 434–462.

Burt, R. (1992). *Structural holes.* Cambridge, MA: Harvard University Press.

Byrne, D. E. (1971). *The attraction paradigm.* New York: Academic Press.

Campbell, J. D. (1990). Self-esteem and clarity of the self-concept. *Journal of Personality and Social Psychology, 59*, 538–549.

Carroll, G. R., & Teo, A. C. (1996). On the social networks of managers. *Academy of Management Journal, 39*, 421–440.

Chapple, K. (2002). "I name it and I claim it—in the name of Jesus, this job is mine": Job search, networks, and careers for low-income women. *Economic Development Quarterly, 16*, 294–313. DOI: 10.1177/089124202237195

Crispin, G., & Mehler, M. (2013). *Sources of hire 2013: Perception is reality.* Available at: http://www.careerxroads.com/news/sourcesofhire2013.pdf

Cross, R., Parker, A., Prusak, L., & Borgatti, S. P. (2001). Knowing what we know: Supporting knowledge creation and sharing in social networks. *Organizational Dynamics, 20*, 100–120.

De Janasz, S., & Forret, M. (2008). Learning the art of networking: A critical skill for enhancing social capital and career success. *Journal of Management Education, 32*, 629–650. DOI: 10.1177/1052562907307637

Digman, J. M. (1990). Personality structure: Emergence of the five-factor model. *Annual Review of Psychology, 41*, 417–440.

Dreher, G. F., & Cox, T. H. Jr. (1996). Race, gender, and opportunity: A study of compensation attainment and the establishment of mentoring relationships. *Journal of Applied Psychology, 81*, 297–308.

Dreher, G. F., & Cox, T. H. Jr. (2000). Labor market mobility and cash compensation: The moderating effects of race and gender. *Academy of Management Journal, 43*, 890–900.

Drentea, P. (1998). Consequences of women's formal and informal job search methods for employment in female-dominated jobs. *Gender & Society, 12*, 321–338. DOI: 10.1177/0891243298012003005

Eby, L. T., Butts, M., & Lockwood, A. (2003). Predictors of success in the era of the boundaryless career. *Journal of Organizational Behavior, 24*, 689–708. DOI: 10.1002/job.214

Eccles, R. (2009). Link in, get hired. *Corporate Meetings & Incentives, 28*(11), 12–16.

Feldman, D. C., & Ng, T. W. H. (2007). Careers: Mobility, embeddedness, and success. *Journal of Management, 33*, 350–377. DOI: 10.1177/0149206307300815

Fernandez, R. M., & Weinberg, N. (1997). Sifting and sorting: Personal contacts and hiring in a retail bank. *American Sociological Review, 62*, 883–902.

Ferris, G. R., Treadway, D. C., Kolodinsky, R. W., Hochwarter, W. A., Kacmar, C. J., Douglas, C., & Frink, D. D. (2005). Development and validation of the political skill inventory. *Journal of Management, 31*, 126–152. DOI: 10.1177/0149206304271386

Finder, A. (June 11, 2006). When a risqué online persona undermines a chance for a job. *New York Times.* Available at: http://www.nytimes.com

Forret, M. L. (2006). The impact of social networks on the advancement of women and racial/ethnic minority groups. In Margaret F. Karsten (Ed.), *Gender, ethnicity, and race in the workplace* (Vol. *3*, pp. 149–166). Westport, CT: Praeger.

Forret, M. L., & Dougherty, T. W. (2001). Correlates of networking behavior for managerial and professional employees. *Group & Organization Management, 26*, 283–311.

Forret, M. L., & Dougherty, T. W. (2004). Networking behaviors and career outcomes: Differences for men and women? *Journal of Organizational Behavior, 25*, 419–437. DOI: 10.1002/job.253

Forret, M. L., & McCallum, S. (August 2010). Career success: An examination of the relationships of networking and mentoring. Paper presented at the meeting of the Academy of Management, Montreal, Canada.

Forret, M. L., & Sullivan, S. E. (2002). A balanced scorecard approach to networking: A guide to successfully navigating career challenges. *Organizational Dynamics, 31*(3), 245–258.

Forret, M. L., Sullivan, S. E., & Samtani, A. (2011). The effectiveness of traditional and social networking for job search success. Manuscript in preparation.

Franzen, A., & Hangartner, D. (2006). Social networks and labour market outcomes: The non-monetary benefits of social capital. *European Sociological Review, 22,* 353–368. DOI: 10.1093/esr/jcl001

Gersick, C. J., Bartunek, J. M., & Dutton, J. E. (2000). Learning from academia: The importance of relationships in professional life. *Academy of Management Journal, 43,* 1026–1044.

Goldberg, L. R. (1993). The structure of phenotypic personality traits. *American Psychologist, 48,* 26–34.

Gould, S., & Penley, L. E. (1984). Career strategies and salary progression: A study of their relationships in a municipal bureaucracy. *Organizational Behavior & Human Performance, 34,* 244–265.

Gouldner, A. W. (1960). The norm of reciprocity: A preliminary statement. *American Sociological Review, 25,* 161–178.

Granovetter, M. (1973). The strength of weak ties. *American Journal of Sociology, 78,* 1360–1380.

Granovetter, M. S. (1974). *Getting a job: A study of contacts and careers.* Cambridge, MA: Harvard University Press.

Hall, D. T. (2002). *Careers in and out of organizations.* Thousand Oaks, CA: Sage.

Holtom, B. C., Mitchell, T. R., & Lee, T. W. (2006). Increasing human and social capital by applying job embeddedness theory. *Organizational Dynamics, 35,* 316–331. DOI: 10.1016/j.orgdyn.2006.08.007

Hudson North America. (February 21, 2007). It still comes down to who you know: Hudson survey finds networking, personal contacts best way to land a job. Available at: http://us.hudson.com/node.asp?kwd=02-21-07-networking-survey

Huffman, M. L., & Torres, L. (2001). Job search methods: Consequences for gender-based earnings inequality. *Journal of Vocational Behavior, 58,* 127–141. DOI: 10.1006/jvbe.2000.1770

Ibarra, H. (1992). Homophily and differential returns: Sex differences in network structure and access in an advertising firm. *Administrative Science Quarterly, 37,* 422–447.

Ibarra, H. (1995). Race, opportunity, and diversity of social circles in managerial networks. *Academy of Management Journal, 38,* 673–703.

Inkson, K., & Arthur, M. B. (2001). How to be a successful career capitalist. *Organizational Dynamics, 30,* 48–61.

Jobvite. (2010). 2010 social recruiting survey. Available at: http://recruiting.jobvite.com/resources/social-recruiting-survey.php

Kanter, R. M. (1977). Some effects of proportions on group life: Skewed sex ratios and responses to token women. *American Journal of Sociology, 82,* 965–990.

Karl, K., Peluchette, J., & Schlaegel, C. (2010). Who's posting Facebook faux pas? A cross-cultural examination of personality differences. *International Journal of Selection and Assessment, 18,* 174–186. DOI: 10.1111/j.1468-2389.2010.00499.x

Kim, M. J. (2010). Network via social media: Twitter and LinkedIn can help your job hunt. *U.S. News & World Report, 147*(11), 53.

Kluemper, D. H., & Rosen, P. A. (2009). Future employment selection methods: Evaluating social networking web sites. *Journal of Managerial Psychology, 24,* 567–580. DOI: 10.1108/02683940910974134

Lin, N., Ensel, W. M., & Vaughn, J. C. (1981). Social resources and strength of ties: Structural factors in occupational status attainment. *American Sociological Review, 46,* 393–405.

Luthans, F., Rosenkrantz, S. A., & Hennessey, H. W. (1985). What do successful managers really do? An observation study of managerial activities. *Journal of Applied Behavioral Science, 21,* 255–270.

Lyness, K. S., & Thompson, D. E. (1997). Above the glass ceiling? A comparison of matched samples of female and male executives. *Journal of Applied Psychology, 82,* 359–375.

McCallum, S., & Forret, M. L. (August 2009). The relationship of networking behaviors to job satisfaction and organizational commitment. Paper presented at the meeting of the Academy of Management, Chicago, IL.

McCrae, R. R., & Costa, P. T. Jr. (1987). Validation of the five-factor model of personality across instruments and observers. *Journal of Personality and Social Psychology, 52,* 81–90.

Michael, J., & Yukl, G. (1993). Managerial level and subunit function as determinants of networking behavior in organizations. *Group & Organization Management, 18,* 328–351.

Mirvis, P. H., & Hall, D. T. (1996). New organizational forms and the new career. In D. T. Hall (Ed.), *The career is dead—long live the career: A relational approach to careers* (pp. 72–101). San Francisco: Jossey-Bass.

Morrison, E. (2002). Newcomers' relationships: The role of social network ties during socialization. *Academy of Management Journal, 45,* 1149–1160.

Nahapiet, J., & Goshal, S. (1998). Social capital, intellectual capital, and the organizational advantage. *Academy of Management Review, 23,* 242–266.

Pfeffer, J. (1989). A political perspective on careers: Interests, networks, and environments. In M. B. Arthur, D. T. Hall, & B. S. Lawrence (Eds.), *Handbook of career theory* (pp. 380–396). Cambridge, UK: Cambridge University Press.

Podolny, J. M., & Baron, J. N. (1997). Resources and relationships: Social networks and mobility in the workplace. *American Sociological Review, 62,* 673–693.

Roberts, K. H., & O'Reilly, C. A. III (1979). Some correlations of communication roles in organizations. *Academy of Management Journal, 22,* 42–57.

Rodan, S., & Galunic, C. (2004). More than network structure: How knowledge heterogeneity influences managerial performance and innovativeness. *Strategic Management Journal, 25,* 541–562. DOI: 10.1002/smj.398

Saks, A. M. (2006). Multiple predictors and criteria of job search success. *Journal of Vocational Behavior, 68,* 400–415. DOI: 10.1016/j.jvb.2005.10.001

Seibert, S. E., Kraimer, M. L., & Liden, R. C. (2001). A social capital theory of career success. *Academy of Management Journal, 44,* 219–237.

Seidel, M. D. L., Polzer, J. T., & Stewart, K. J. (2000). Friends in high places: The effects of social networks on discrimination in salary negotiations. *Administrative Science Quarterly, 45,* 1–24.

Simmons, H. S. (2010). Demographics, personality and networking behavior (Unpublished master's thesis). Ludwig Maximilians University, Munich.

Slovensky, R., & Ross, W. H. (2012). Should human resource managers use social media to screen job applicants? Managerial and legal issues in the USA. *Info, 14*(1), 55–69. DOI: 10.1108/14636691211196941

Society for Human Resource Management (2002). Society for Human Resource Management research: Search tactics poll. Available at: http://www.shrm.org/research/surveyfindings/documents/search%20tactics%20poll.pdf

Straits, B. C. (1998). Occupational sex segregation: The role of personal ties. *Journal of Vocational Behavior, 52,* 191–207. DOI: 10.1006/jvbe.1997.1598

Sturges, J., Guest, D., Conway, N., & Davey, K. M. (2002). A longitudinal study of the relationship between career management and organizational commitment among graduates in the first ten years at work. *Journal of Organizational Behavior, 23,* 731–748. DOI: 10.1002/job.164

Sullivan, S. E. (1999). The changing nature of careers: A review and research agenda. *Journal of Management, 25,* 457–484.

Sullivan, S. E., & Arthur, M. (2006). The evolution of the boundaryless career concept: Examining physical and psychological mobility. *Journal of Vocational Behavior, 69,* 19–29. DOI: 10.1016/j.jvb.2005.09.001

Sullivan, S. E., & Baruch, Y. (2009). Advances in career theory and research: A critical review and agenda for future exploration. *Journal of Management, 35,* 1542–1571.

Sullivan, S. E., Forret, M. L. & Agrawal, A. (2013). Social media: An examination of effectiveness for employed and unemployed job seekers. Manuscript in preparation.

Thompson, J. A. (2005). Proactive personality and job performance: A social capital perspective. *Journal of Applied Psychology, 90,* 1011–1017. DOI: 10.1037/0021-9010.90.5.1011

Tichy, N. M., Tushman, M. L., & Fombrun, C. (1979). Social network analysis for organizations. *Academy of Management Review, 4,* 507–519.

Van Hooft, E. A. J., & Stout, T. (2012). Nepotism and career choice, job search, and job choice. In Robert G. Jones (Ed.), *Nepotism in organizations,* pp. 67–91. New York: Routledge.

Van Hoye, G., & Saks, A. M. (2008). Job search as goal-directed behavior: Objectives and methods. *Journal of Vocational Behavior, 73,* 358–367. DOI: 10.1016/j.jvb.2008.07.003

Van Hoye, G., Van Hooft, E. A. J., & Lievens, F. (2009). Networking as a job search behaviour: A social network perspective. *Journal of Occupational and Organizational Psychology, 82,* 661–682. DOI: 10.1348/096317908X360675

Wanberg, C. R. (2012). The individual experience of unemployment. *Annual Review of Psychology, 63,* 369–396. DOI: 10.1146/annurev-psych-120710-100500

Wanberg, C., Basbug, G., Van Hooft, E. A. J., & Samtani, A. (2012). Navigating the black hole: Explicating layers of job search context and adaptational responses. *Personnel Psychology, 65,* 887–926. DOI: 10.1111/peps.12005

Wanberg, C. R., Kanfer, R., & Banas, J. T. (2000). Predictors and outcomes of networking intensity among unemployed job seekers. *Journal of Applied Psychology, 85,* 491–503. DOI: 10.1037/0021-9010.85.4.401

Wellington, S., Kropf, M. B., & Gerkovich, P. R. (2003). What's holding women back? *Harvard Business Review, 81*(6), 18–19.

Wolff, H. G., & Moser, K. (2006). Entwicklung und validierung einer networking skala [Development and validation of a networking scale]. *Diagnostica, 52*(4), 161–180.

Wolff, H. G., & Moser, K. (2009). Effects of networking on career success: A longitudinal study. *Journal of Applied Psychology, 94,* 196–206. DOI: 10.1037/a0013356

Wolff, H. G., & Moser, K. (2010). Do specific types of networking predict specific mobility outcomes? A two-year prospective study. *Journal of Vocational Behavior, 77,* 238–245. DOI: 10.1016/j.jvb.2010.03.001

Wolff, H. G., Moser, K., & Grau, A. (2008). Networking: Theoretical foundations and construct validity. In J. Deller (Ed.), *Readings in applied organizational behavior from the Lüneburg Symposium* (pp. 101–118). Mehring, Germany: Rainer Hampp.

Wolff, H. G., Schneider-Rahm, C. I., & Forret, M. L. (2011). Adaptation of a German multidimensional networking scale into English. *European Journal of Psychological Assessment, 27*(4), 244–250. DOI: 10.1027/1015-5759/a000070

Contingency Headhunters: What They Do—and What Their Activities Tell Us About Jobs, Careers, and the Labor Market

James E. Coverdill *and* William Finlay

Abstract

This chapter overviews the work of contingency headhunters, who earn a fee from a client company when a candidate they have identified and presented is hired. It begins by describing the financial footing of the industry and the three central activities of headhunting: establishing business relationships with client companies, identifying and presenting candidates for positions, and facilitating encounters between clients and candidates. A second section explores how headhunters provide insights into who is on the market for a new job, who fits a job well, and who appears to fit a job well. In a third section, it draws out several issues that demand more scholarly attention, such as a lack of information about the industry, international practices, client companies, and consequences for clients and candidates of headhunter-facilitated job changes. A final section offers guidelines for individuals who might encounter or use a headhunter.

Key Words: contingency headhunters

Introduction

Headhunters interpose themselves between firms and workers to facilitate matches in the external labor market. After agreeing to a business relationship with a headhunter, client firms pay a fee when a candidate identified and presented by the headhunter is hired. Headhunters thus represent profit-seeking labor market intermediaries whose mere existence highlights profound limitations in the neoclassical notions that labor-market information is complete and that markets are competitive. Sociologists who study matching processes in the labor market, along with many economists, have long recognized the limitations of the neoclassical model (e.g., Autor, 2009; Granovetter, 1995). As Autor (2009) affirmed, labor-market information is rarely complete, symmetric, or costless, and workers rarely resemble homogeneous commodities. Labor-market intermediaries—such as network contacts (friends, relatives, and acquaintances), online

recruiting, and of course headhunters—thrive on the challenges of incomplete information, costly search, and variation across workers.

Scholarly attention to headhunters is warranted on both empirical and theoretical grounds. In the United States, data from the National Organizations Survey indicate that about 20% of all organizations "frequently" use employment agencies to recruit managerial and administrative workers (Kalleberg et al., 1996, p. 138). A 1995 survey of firms in the United States with between 100 to 1,000 employees found that 30% of such firms "regularly" use headhunters (*The Fordyce Letter*, December 1995). Terpstra's (1996) survey of 201 human-resource executives indicated that headhunters were among the three top-ranked sources of high-quality, high-performing employees. More recently, a 2007 international survey of workers, reported in Nakamura et al., (2009, p. 44), showed that 55% of those aged 25 to 44 found "recruitment consultants / headhunters" to be "useful."

Others have spoken more generally about the "explosive growth" of private search firms and how labor-market changes may be increasing the relative efficacy of those intermediaries (Rynes et al., 1997). While these estimates and assessments remain rough approximations, they support the conclusion that headhunters play a prominent role in many labor markets and therefore merit attention on empirical grounds alone.

Recent theorizing also highlights the importance of labor-market intermediaries such as headhunters. The traditional framing of research on turnover intentions and behavior gives dissatisfaction a central role (e.g., Mobley, 1977; Hom et al., 1992; Boswell & Gardner, this volume), suggesting that employees tend to be *pushed* into the external labor market by negative job-related perceptions and attitudes. Many instances of turnover, however, do not follow that logic, a pattern that sparked the development of Lee and Mitchell's (1994) "unfolding model" of voluntary employee turnover and Lee et al.'s (2008) theorizing about unsolicited job offers as "shocks" that prompt turnover.[1] Holtrom et al. (2005) argue that shocks cause voluntary turnover more often than accumulated job dissatisfaction. Unsolicited job offers, which prompted about 25% of turnover in Holtom et al. (2005) and Lee et al. (2008), represent an especially intriguing shock that may *pull* employees into the external labor market. This sort of market pull goes well beyond a consideration of favorable market conditions—such as broad indicators of unemployment rates or job growth in a particular labor-market segment—because it points to activities on the part of intermediaries, both formal and informal, not conditions alone. Lee and his colleagues note that little is known about why some individuals are targeted for recruitment by intermediaries, producing what they call a critical gap in the literature (2008).

Headhunters represent one source of what can be interpreted as "unsolicited" job offers, and a careful study of how they work offers insights into a key *pull* dimension of employee turnover and the operation of labor markets.

A related but distinct rational for exploring headhunters lies in the changing character of careers (see also van Vianen & Klehe, this volume). In recent years, organizations have increasingly turned to the external labor market to acquire new capabilities (Greenhaus, Callanan, & DiRenzo, 2008), a pattern that implies a loss of opportunities for vertical career advancement within a single employment setting (Direnzo & Greenhaus, 2011). The notions of "boundaryless" careers and organizations (Ashkenas et al., 2002; Arthur & Rousseau, 1996) coincide with diminished feelings of job security among workers and trust in employers (Fullerton & Wallace, 2007; Smithson & Lewis, 2000). This "new deal" means that labor markets, and the institutions that operate within them to match individuals and jobs, play increasingly important roles in shaping inter-organizational careers (Cappelli & Hamori, 2007; King, Burke, & Pemberton, 2005).

The portrait of headhunting that we present in this chapter is based primarily on our occupational case study of headhunters who worked with companies and job candidates in the United States (Finlay & Coverdill, 2007). Interview and fieldwork data were collected from contingency headhunters located in a major metropolitan area in the southeastern United States. We conducted thirty-four one- to three-hour semi-structured interviews with headhunters randomly selected by area of specialization from the directory of the state association of contingency recruiting firms. Most firms in our sample (75%) work with clients and candidates all over the country (a national market) and fill a wide range of positions, such as accounting, administrative and office support, banking, data processing engineering, finance, insurance, legal and medical support, and sales. All names of headhunters and their firms are pseudonyms; areas of specialization are noted in parentheses when quotations are used.

We also carried out 150 hours of fieldwork at five different headhunting firms and another 150 hours at luncheons, training sessions, and conferences sponsored by the state and national associations of contingency headhunters. Fieldwork in the headhunting firms allowed us to observe how headhunters handled clients and candidates. We covered the range of headhunting firms by doing fieldwork in one large firm with over 100 headhunters, in three firms with three to five headhunters, and with a solo practitioner.[2] Our presence at luncheons, training sessions, and conferences gave us further insight into the practice and business of headhunting. We were able to speak with headhunters we had not yet encountered and follow up with those we had interviewed or observed on the job. In both fieldwork settings, we took extensive notes while in the setting or shortly after departing.

We augment our primary data with information from industry sources, insider accounts of headhunting, and a small body of recent scholarship.

Like most industries, headhunters have a key publication (*The Fordyce Letter*) oriented to practicing headhunters, and there are several insightful books and popular-press articles on headhunting by industry insiders. The evidence focuses largely on headhunters—not job candidates or client companies—and thus supports an *occupational case study* of headhunting based primarily on its practice in the United States. As we describe later in the chapter, research has largely overlooked international aspects of headhunting along with the perspectives and experiences of clients and candidates vis-à-vis headhunters and the business of headhunting.

The balance of the chapter unfolds in four additional sections. In the next (second) section, we provide an overview of the main activities and challenges of contingency headhunters. We first describe the financial footing of the business and then turn to the three key activities of headhunters: establishing business relationships with client companies; identifying and presenting candidates for positions; and then working to facilitate encounters and negotiations between clients and candidates. In the third section, we focus on three insights into external labor markets provided by the practice of headhunting. In short, headhunters shed light on who is on the job market, who fits a job well, and who appears to fit a job well. In a fourth section, we point to several issues that merit attention, such as a lack of information about the industry as a whole, international practices, client companies, and consequences for the many individuals who change jobs through headhunters. A fifth and final section offers suggestions for individuals who might encounter or use a headhunter.

The Work of Contingency Headhunters: An Overview

The activities, motivations, and challenges of contingency headhunting are the foci of this section. We begin with the financial footing of headhunting, noting by whom headhunters are paid, for what, when, and how placement fees are structured. Unlike personal contacts, the ubiquitous informal intermediaries in the labor market, headhunting is a profit-driven business with a simple financial structure that shapes incentives and behavior. We then turn to the three critical activities of headhunters.

The Financial Footing

Headhunters deviate radically from the private employment agencies of the past (Martinez, 1976). Until the 1970s, job candidates usually paid a fee to an agency to help them secure work, often paying the fee even if they were not placed. That meant that job seekers, not employers, typically shouldered the cost of agency-brokered placements. In that era, it was reasonable to argue that employment agencies were best understood as a "last resort" for those who lacked the right personal contacts or social resources (e.g., Granovetter, 1995). During the 1970s, payment of fees shifted from individuals seeking work to employers seeking workers. Today, our best estimate is that over 95% of private employment agencies, which we call headhunting firms to distinguish them from their organizational predecessors, charge employers the placement fee. In a fiduciary and practical sense, the clients of headhunters are candidate-seeking firms, not job-seeking individuals.

The placement fee and the work it entails take two main forms. Headhunters who work on retainer are given an exclusive contract by a client to identify and present candidates for a position. They charge expenses and a fee that customarily equals one-third of the candidate's expected compensation during the first year. These recruiters typically work on top-level corporate searches and include large, multi-national firms such as Heidrick & Struggles, Korn/Ferry International, and Egon Zehnder. In contrast, contingency headhunters are usually in competition to make a particular placement, with the winner-take-all fee going to the one who supplies the candidate who is actually hired. Contingency fees range from 10% to more than 30% of the employee's first-year salary; survey evidence suggests that fees of 25 to 29% are most common (Sendouts, 2010). They fill office-support positions at the low end to professional, technical, and mid-level managerial positions at the high end, with salaries ranging from about $25,000 to $200,000. We estimate that contingency headhunters—the focus of our chapter—make up about 75% of all headhunters (see also Fisher 2001), handle more than 90% of all placements, and account for about half of all industry revenue (Burton, 2003).[3]

Fees are a constant challenge for headhunters and a perennial theme of conference sessions with titles like "Fees: How to Negotiate, How to Structure." When they acquire regular clients, few headhunters maintain standard rates because clients expect discounts. For example, Doug (who places with food producers) noted that his standard fee was 35%. He had recently conducted a series of searches for a client and had, eventually, agreed to reduce his fee to 25%. Likewise, Gail (office support) said she was willing to accept a 15% fee "because I'm going to get repeat business during the course of the year. That's more important to me than having to keep that pipeline going with new business." One typical response to fee-cutting pressures is to request an exclusive, a practice nicely illustrated by George (accounting and finance): "You want a reduced rate, everybody wants a deal, right, so I'll say, okay, I'm going to do it for less, but I want an exclusive for a 60-day period."[4]

Establishing Business Relationships with Client Companies

The first of the three core activities of headhunters involves establishing business relationships with hiring companies. The first step is to obtain a job order, also called a search assignment, which is an agreement whereby a headhunter will identify and present candidates and receive a fee if one of those candidates is hired. Before extending a job order, firms need to decide whether the task of recruiting candidates will be performed internally by a human resources (HR) department, externally by a headhunter, or by a combination of the two. As might be expected, headhunters experience sharp and often abrupt temporal shifts in their ability to secure job orders, with the 1990s boom turning to bust over the past few years. For example, one headhunter, commenting on the Asian market for financial placements, said it was "very quiet for the first eight months" of 2009 before "everything came back in a very big fashion" (Morrow, 2010, p. 99). In the United States, the biggest problem facing headhunters in 2010 was securing job orders (Sendouts 2010).

The externalization of a recruitment effort to a headhunter is driven by a mix of economic and political rationales. The economic benefits of using a headhunter can include their ability to locate and assess candidates from a narrow labor-market niche both quickly and competently because they place such candidates routinely, rather than episodically like HR, and thus maintain extensive databases and networks. Headhunters also tout their ability to enlarge the talent pool by enticing those who are contentedly employed, perhaps at a competing firm, into the market. In these ways, headhunters sell the externalization of recruitment on economic grounds: speed, exhaustiveness, and the quality of the candidates they identify and present (see also Cappelli & Hamori, 2007, p. 332–34). Headhunters also offer two political rationales for the externalization of recruitment. In one, they claim to increase the control that hiring managers have over

the hiring process because headhunters represent a dedicated and dependent external agent who must, unlike HR, please the hiring manager. Headhunters permit hiring managers to circumvent to some extent an overburdened and perhaps unresponsive human resources department. A second political rationale comes in using a headhunter as a form of cover. In some cases, competitors, clients, and customers might be ideal sources for job candidates, but overt and direct poaching of employees can inflame passions and endanger relationships. Headhunters allow hiring managers to cloak if not conceal such poaching.[5]

Job orders are generated through *cold calls*, in which a headhunter calls employers and inquires as to whether they have any positions that need to be filled, *client calls*, in which a headhunter either contacts, or is contacted by, an employer, who asks if the headhunter would be willing to undertake a search assignment, and *marketing calls*, in which a headhunter contacts employers to gauge interest in a specific candidate promoted by the headhunter. Headhunters use all three methods but especially value client calls. Many headhunters argued that economic success stems from making repeated placements with the same employers. Gail (office support) observed that "those who don't know how to build those relationships [with clients] are not going to be long-term in this business." Larry (retail and restaurant management) opined that "the cost of getting new business as opposed to repeat business is very high. Very high!"

All three methods have advantages and disadvantages. Nearly all headhunters dislike making cold calls because success is unlikely. For example, Gail (office support) claimed that "you can make seventy-five calls and not get one [job order]," and conference seminars often have titles such as "Taking the Cold Out of Cold-Call Marketing." Onerous cold calls can nonetheless unearth new clients and generate business. Headhunters prefer marketing calls to cold calls because they are less likely to be rebuffed. In a marketing call, the headhunter approaches an established or prospective client to describe a candidate whose qualifications and accomplishments may entice. Headhunters call these candidates "MPCs"—most placeable candidates—and use them as bait to fish for job orders. Especially in a poor economy, marketing calls can produce placements: "70% of my firm's placements since November 2008 have been with companies which had no openings when we called, but met the candidate [an MPC] and were so impressed they created a position and paid a fee" (McNulty 2010).

Headhunters relish making or taking client calls for three reasons. First, job orders derived from client calls are generally thought to involve less competition, which then boosts the chances the headhunter will successfully fill the position. With job orders generated by cold calls, the typical assumption is that competition may be fierce, prompting less investment and less hope of a placement. Second, every conversation with a client is seen as representing a business opportunity if handled properly. For example, the industry newsletter *The Fordyce Letter* offers advice on turning a typical client comment—"we're not hiring"—into discussions that net job orders. As Fisher (2009) put it, "you have to identify the customer's pain points or critical business issues and then convert that into a job order." Through relationships and conversations with clients, headhunters uncover "pain points" that prompt job orders. And third, client calls are valued because they allow further payoffs to a headhunter's investment in learning a company's culture and needs. One Canadian headhunter put it this way: "We know the kind of culture that is there and the kind of person that will do best in that culture" (Gagné, 2006).

Repeat business from only a few clients, however, can be problematic because of client dependence and opportunism. Many noted that revenue can drop dramatically if a key client stops hiring or shifts to another headhunter. Repeat clients also demand discounts, a practice that lowers the luster of repeat business. Building relationships with repeat clients, touted as key to economic success, thus makes headhunters vulnerable and dependent. In addition, headhunters never discount the risk that a client will hire a candidate provided by another headhunter or an internal search, even if they are assured that it is an exclusive job order and there are no internal candidates. Client opportunism looms as a substantial concern among headhunters.

Identifying Potential Job Candidates

Before the 1970s, employment agencies were passive. Given that individuals seeking jobs approached them, the pool of candidates served by an agency largely amounted to whoever came through the door. The function of the employment agent was to persuade companies to hire candidates the agency had in stock. What that entailed, as Martinez (1976) showed, was a game of manipulated expectations: a candidate entered the agency with one kind of job in mind and the agent worked to shift his expectations so that he would consider a broad range of jobs and hence be easier to place. In contrast, contemporary headhunters devote considerable time and resources to identifying, assessing, and stockpiling candidates, activities which justify the moniker "headhunters." They seek and generate candidates, rather than waiting for candidates to present themselves. They concentrate primarily, albeit not exclusively, on the employed. One headhunter spoke for many in saying that "[a]n employment agency is in the business of finding jobs for people; we're a recruiting firm so we're in the business of finding people for jobs." Another, with extensive experience in the consumer-goods sector, emphasized the hunt in headhunting: "In my 27 years as a recruiter, I can count on one hand the number of unsolicited résumés that have ended up as candidates. It's like winning the lottery" (Demos, 2010).[6]

Identifying candidates requires effort because many strong prospects are not actively searching and may have little interest in changing jobs. Headhunters find these people and turn them into candidates through persistence, persuasion, and in some cases deception. They often have to trick their way into learning the names of prospects, who they then persuade to become candidates. Assembling a roster of candidates is a two-stage process. First, headhunters must identify prospects who are likely to qualify as candidates. Second, they must contact prospects to assess fit and to pitch the opportunity if they qualify. In some cases, this process can involve an extraordinary amount of contact in any given sector of the labor market. For example, one industry publication estimated that "more than two-thirds of employed IT pros have been approached by headhunters at least once since the beginning of the year [2010]" (Davis, 2010).

Headhunters identify candidates using a multitude of methods, often in combination. Some are found in the candidate databases headhunters generate and update regularly. These databases are built by a mixture of relentless networking and candidate-provided materials (résumés and so forth) that can be either solicited or unsolicited. Our observations and interviews suggest that a candidate who dovetails well with an outstanding job order will not be dismissed, regardless of how he or she came to the attention of a headhunter. A first step is thus to ask, "Do I already know someone who might fit a particular job order?" In most cases, it is in a headhunter's interest to match job orders and candidates quickly because doing so impresses clients (provided that the candidates are good and fit the position) and increases the likelihood of filling the position if there is competition from other headhunters.

If a hunt is necessary, then headhunters normally begin by calling people they know who might be able to suggest a name or two. Typically these will be former candidates who the headhunter placed in jobs similar to that for which he is recruiting. Those who are a level above the targeted position are also contacted, as they may know emerging stars. In addition, many make cold calls and explore company websites. Cold calls can involve trickery if not outright deception in order to obtain names and extension numbers, whereas website and other online sources are largely unobtrusive.[7] Online sources, however, can be limited, especially in some sectors, such as law. One industry newsletter noted that "firms that once put up rich offerings about their associates have cut back to a minimum, with no direct phone numbers, nothing about specialty areas and often nothing to indicate who might be in that very poachable three-to-six-year term on the job" (Carter, 2005). Information gleaned from networking calls and online sources augments candidate databases, even if it does not advance a front-burner job order.

The hunt for candidates is largely unconstrained. One notable exception is that a firm may, for a period of time, be deemed "off limits" as a source of candidates for a particular headhunter because she placed a candidate there recently and thereby made it a client. Without exception, all headhunters with whom we spoke had off-limits policies. All condemned so-called "front door / back door recruiting," which entails placing a candidate with a client at the same time they are recruiting someone out of the firm for another client. Nearly all, however, had rather flexible interpretations of off-limits policies. For example, few refused to work with a candidate they had placed if the candidate made the first move by soliciting their help. Specific functions, units, or divisions—rather than a client's entire firm—were sometimes seen as the proper universe for an off-limits policy. In addition, how long a client is protected by an off-limits policy following a placement varies widely; in general, more business, and especially more recent business, buy a client greater protection from being targeted as a source of candidates by a particular headhunter. In no case is a firm seen as off limits to *all* headhunters simply because it worked recently with one or more headhunters or headhunting firms.[8]

Once a potential candidate is identified, the next step is to pitch the position and assess qualifications and interest. A typical pitch includes a description of the job and questions designed to assess the prospect's interest in the position. Rich (who places engineers) put it this way: "when I'm recruiting, I don't call up and say, "Hey, are you interested in a job?" I paint a picture, a mental picture or a quick picture of the position that I have available to try and whet this person's appetite." When a headhunter "qualifies a candidate," she assesses whether he can do the job, whether he would leave his current job, and whether he fits the client's culture. A headhunter's primary concern during the initial stages of a search is to ensure that any candidate who might be qualified is not overlooked; the narrowing of the list occurs later. Unqualified or mismatched prospects who nonetheless impress can bolster a headhunter's database and network.

Two recent studies provide additional insights into these issues. A first, by Hamori (2010), explored outcomes for financial-services executives by analyzing a database of prospective candidates created and used by a large, multinational retained headhunting firm. Results show that the database overrepresented individuals employed in admired, top-performing firms. Getting onto the firm's "radar screen" thus appears to be at least partly triggered by firm, not individual, characteristics. Interestingly, however, prospects who became candidates disproportionately worked at firms experiencing performance or reputational difficulties. In addition, the 3.5% of prospects who became candidates and were placed by the headhunting firm were more likely than those who changed jobs by other means to have moved to a larger firm (54 vs. 24%), changed industry segment (72 vs. 55%), or subsequently received a promotion (36 vs. 26%). Information about salaries, race, ethnicity, and gender, however, was not mentioned or explored.

A second study (Dreher, Lee, & Clerkin, 2011) addressed some of those limitations. They collected survey evidence from a roster of high earners maintained by a global association for retained headhunting in order to explore who headhunters contact, compensation advantages of external labor-market shifts, and race/gender effects. Results suggest three key patterns: white males are more likely than other race/sex groups to be contacted by headhunters; white males benefit most from external labor-market moves; and contacts with headhunters (but not necessarily placement by a headhunter) moderate the relationship between compensation and mobility in the external labor market. It is thus possible that long-standing forms of race and gender discrimination may be piqued and perpetuated by the practices of headhunters.

In this and other areas of headhunting, our strong sense is that international practices are similar to those in the United States, although they have received little scholarly attention. For example, a UK-based headhunter recently described her search for candidates in a way that squares well with what we learned from US-based headhunters (quoted in Woolnough, 2008, p. 25):

> We call our contacts, search our databases, look at conference lists, ring college course directors and other similar organisations. We call in favors, call people we have already placed, call people who we thought were great but the last client didn't agree. We ask: "Are you interested or do you know anyone else we should speak to?" It takes hours of concentrated research that would bring most HR departments to a grinding halt—at least three weeks doing nothing else.

Likewise, trade publications such as the UK-based *Accountancy Magazine* regularly feature the views of headhunters (e.g., Freebairn, 2008), views that overlap greatly with those offered by the headhunters we interviewed and observed in the United States.

Matchmaking with Clients and Candidates

Headhunters insist that the two essential ingredients of headhunting—a company that extends a job order and the identification of worthy candidates—come together as a placement only if they engage in matchmaking activities (see also da Motta Veiga & Turban, this volume). Once a headhunter has obtained a job order and one or more candidates, she must present them to the client in a way that makes them appear attractive, yet without deal-breaking exaggeration on the headhunter's part. Simultaneously, she must prep the client to sell themselves to the candidate when they meet during the interview. Finally, if her client makes an offer, she must ensure that the content and tone of the offer will meet the candidate's expectations and stroke his ego. These matchmaking activities are the ultimate determinant of any headhunter's success, for regardless of how good she is at getting job orders from clients and identifying worthy candidates, until her clients offer jobs to her candidates and until the candidates accept these offers, she will not earn any fees.

The matchmaking efforts of headhunters stem from complexities inherent in labor markets. The labor market is distinct from other markets in that what is sold—labor—involves people who have idiosyncratic interests, preferences, and desires. A consequence is that the primary parties to the exchange—employers and job candidates—require what we call a "double sale" for a placement to occur. Employers, who are customarily viewed as buyers, must also typically sell job candidates on the position and company, and this is definitely the case when a candidate is employed and largely content. One Canadian headhunter put it this way: "You've got to sell the job, sell the future, the company and the industry" (Holloway, 2002). Job seekers, in contrast, are typically seen as those who need to sell their merits to an employer, but they are buyers as well because they must be sufficiently enticed before they will make a move. The headhunter's task is to complete this double sale—to make sure that her client selects her candidate and that her candidate accepts her client—in order to earn a fee. She must prepare both client and candidate to both buy and sell. While each slips into the buyer's role with ease, headhunters argue that they must often be taught and coached to sell so that the other buys.

Matchmaking activities constitute third-party impression management. Headhunters are engaged in impression management from the outset, for this is how they persuade clients and candidates to enact the dual roles of buyer and seller. Their efforts to create a favorable image of the candidate in the mind of the client and an equally favorable image of the client in the mind of the candidate are what we term *direct* impression management. In these exchanges, a headhunter deals with a client or candidate directly in an effort to shape their impression of the other. Their efforts to get clients and candidates to present themselves during interviews and other encounters in a light that headhunters know will be pleasing to the other party are what we call *indirect* impression management. Headhunters not only pick candidates who they believe possess the characteristics and qualities desired by their clients, but they also try to make sure that the candidates themselves highlight these characteristics and qualities when they encounter clients.

Matchmaking involves both bridging and buffering. In a bridging role, headhunters try to facilitate the coming together of clients and candidates and the perception of common interests and rapport. The third-party impression management described thus far is a bridging activity because headhunters bring together two parties who would otherwise be unconnected. They are filling "structural holes," to use Burt's (1992) terminology. The buffering role, an opposite of the bridging role, requires headhunters to come between the various parties who are involved in the hiring in order to buffer them from each other. They could be said to be creating structural holes, which they subsequently fill. As one headhunter put it, "I wear the asbestos suit," by which he meant that he was positioned to take heat from one or more parties to an extent that others could not. Another said that "[y]ou have to trust the headhunter can communicate with the client and reinforce why you are the best candidate for the job" (McCool 2007). During the hiring process, any one of three potentially difficult relationships—client and candidate, hiring manager and their human resources department, and client and source organization—may be strained. In the buffering role, the headhunter's job is to absorb conflicts and prevent them from scuttling the placement.

Selected Insights into External Labor Markets from a Study of Headhunters

Given that headhunters interact with many clients and candidates, they are in an unusual position to gain and offer insights into hiring processes in an external labor market. In this section, we describe how headhunters provide insights into who is on the market for a new job, who fits a job well, and who appears to fit a job well.

Who Is on the Job Market?

Little scholarly attention has been given to the question of who is on the job market. Headhunters routinely lure employees into the job market because they believe that exceptional candidates are successful in, and content with, their job—and are therefore not "looking" for another job. In their view, however, no job is perfect, which means that even those who are content might still improve their lot. A headhunter's skill lies in identifying, highlighting, and then manipulating impediments to an employee's more complete satisfaction or, as Scott (engineering and insurance) put it, "finding and pounding the wound."

Wounds vary across labor-market segments. For example, a lack of exposure to new or emerging technologies is a common wound only in technical fields like engineering and information technology. Six general wounds include companies, bosses, responsibilities and duties, opportunities for career advancement, geographic location, and salary. Salary is the least preferred wound because it is easily rectified by a counter-offer. Headhunters seek and value non-financial wounds because they are best healed by a new job in new organization, as noted by Doug (food production): "Just giving somebody more money does not address those concerns [non-financial wounds]. If the problems are with your boss, your boss's boss, or anything like that, that hasn't changed [if salary alone changes]."

Finding and pounding wounds serve two main purposes for headhunters. First, wounds tell them how to present a job to the prospect: once a headhunter knows what a prospect wants, he can sell a job in terms of how it addresses those needs. Second, wounds help a headhunter "close" a candidate on an actual or prospective offer. Headhunters embrace what Prus (1989) calls "closing by inquiry," in which, having located the prospect's wounds, they will ask a version of the following question: "If I find you a job which addresses this need [referring back to the wounds], and if the money is right, will you consider it seriously?" If the prospect hesitates, it lets the headhunter know that she does not yet have a candidate. A similar process emerges when an offer is extended. At that point, headhunters shift verb tense, saying that "I found you a job which addresses your wounds" as they work to close the candidate on the offer. Headhunters gain psychological leverage with candidates by identifying and needling wounds.

Wounds are the mechanism by which headhunters turn otherwise content, non-searching employees, into job candidates. But why do they bother to woo anyone into the market when there are already many actively seeking jobs? Headhunters focus on the contentedly employed who are not on the market for two reasons: beliefs about adverse selection and the need to sell their services. Although headhunters did not use the expression "adverse selection," they worked from an implicit theory that tags those who are unemployed or eager to change jobs as the most risky and hence least desirable candidates. Headhunters reason that job loss often hinges at least partly on comparative performance, and that there may be hard-to-detect reasons for a person's unemployment. Likewise, the eager-to-move employed may be spurred by an employer who appropriately devalues their modest contributions and thereby generates dissatisfaction, a main rational for voluntary turnover among the employed (e.g., Griffeth, Hom, & Gaertner, 2000; van Hooft et al., 2004, p. 27; Boswell, Roehling, & Boudreau,

2006, p. 786). In short, headhunters fear that the eager and the unemployed may be job-market lemons, although our evidence suggests that many work with both groups. In contrast, headhunters believe that those who are not eager to change jobs—the contentedly employed—probably lack the baggage of the unemployed or eager.[9] Commenting on the recent economic downturn, one headhunter put this more as a company preference: "Companies are not using me for people out on the street. They're looking at us for corporate raid of competitors, to look for the stars that weathered the storm, so to speak" (Zmuda, 2009). Most abstractly, headhunters believe that random draws from pools of the contentedly employed, the unemployed, and the eager-to-move would show that the former yields the best candidates.

A second reason why headhunters especially value the contentedly employed stems from their need to persuade companies that they offer a distinctive service that merits a large fee. It is difficult to sustain that argument if all they do is run advertisements or solicit materials from unemployed or eager job searchers. If they identify and woo the contentedly employed, then they tap into a pool of candidates largely hidden from employers who recruit on their own. Scott (engineering and insurance) argued that "there are always those hidden people and a lot of times they [clients] want to find those hidden people. They want to find the people that are happy." Searching for "hidden people" and persuading them to become candidates helps sell headhunting services, a point noted by Gail (office support): "And that's one of the things that I sell my clients. I tell them . . . the top professionals, they are not looking in the newspaper, because they are happy where they are. And you want somebody who's happy where she is." A sales strategy is thus built upon a theory that touts the value of non-searching candidates.

That sales strategy dovetails with recent attention in the management literature to human and social capital. For example, some claim that the most powerful source of long-term competitive advantage is human and social capital (e.g., Becker, Huselid, & Ulrich, 2001; Pfeffer, 1995). Similarly, and in words that would prompt shouts of approval from the headhunters we observed, McDonnell (2011, p. 169) claimed that "[w]orkforce demographics and skills shortages are likely to make the "war for talent" fiercer than ever before." No doubt, beliefs about a fierce "war for talent" and a competitive imperative to land "top talent" (see also Faulconbridge et al., 2009) help sustain, if not fuel, the business of headhunting and a preference for non-searching candidates.

Who Is Right for the Job?

Headhunters rely primarily on what they call specs, hot buttons, and chemistry in evaluating prospects and thereby assessing "who is right for the job." Shorthand for "position specifications," specs have much in common with job advertisements and include a description of the position, a salary or salary range, and required experience and education. Specs tend to be a knock-out factor because some prospects will not "meet the specs" and will therefore not become viable candidates. Headhunters believe that top candidates will not only meet the specs but will also have the right hot buttons and chemistry. Hot buttons are highly specific and often idiosyncratic skills and experiences that a client may be unable or unwilling to articulate but will recognize—and prize—when interviewing candidates. Baseline skills noted in the specs are augmented by hot buttons, which make a particular employer sufficiently enthusiastic about a particular candidate to extend an offer. In the words of one headhunter, hot buttons are "the solution to the problem that motivated the employer to seek to fill the position."

Hot buttons are context specific, varying widely across positions, hiring managers, departments, companies, and over time for even the most narrowly-defined occupations. For example, the hot buttons for one engineering position were successful experience in designing jigs and fixtures and performing vendor quality audits. A hot button can be a higher level of education than is stated in the specs or experience with a particular previous employer. One headhunter knew, for example, that managers at Coca-Cola Foods were always enthusiastic about candidates who had worked at General Foods or Proctor & Gamble, although that background was never in the specs. In some cases, hiring managers seek particular qualities in candidates regardless of the exact position they would fill, thus pegging hot buttons to the manager, not the position. Hot buttons indicate a candidate's ability to do *the* job, not *a* job, in the *client's* company, not just *a* company.

In contrast, chemistry involves an interpersonal compatibility between the candidate and the hiring manager that stems from similarities in their backgrounds, interests, and personalities. It is also based on a compatibility between the candidate and the client company's culture, norms, and strategies.[10] In short, chemistry is a synonym for candidate fit at two levels, interpersonal and company (e.g., Chatman, 1991; Kristof-Brown, 2000; Rynes & Gerhart, 1990). For example, one headhunter, who placed information technology specialists, described fitting the candidate to the hiring manager: "We're trying to find a personality match. If I have a very nebbish character [a hiring manager], he's very introverted and I'm dealing with a guy [a potential candidate] who's very extroverted on the other side, well that's not going to work. Why waste my time even if he's qualified. Likes hire likes—so much for diversity." Another described how he interrogates candidates for evidence of non-work activities that might generate good chemistry: "I'm looking at what you do on the weekends, family, do you play golf, do you play tennis, do you like to read? Try to find out as much as I can because people hire people just like themselves."

Virtually every headhunter we spoke with or observed emphasized both the critical importance of chemistry and its highly contextual character. Gail's (office support) description of the role of chemistry is typical: "If they're all qualified, they all have the degrees, the background, the skill level that they're looking for, they're going to go with the one that they feel the best about, and that's chemistry. And that's the thing that's the crucial element." Many headhunters claim that especially good chemistry can overcome skill deficits, whereas exceptional skill can never overcome poor chemistry. As Jeff (information technology) put it, "If they don't like them, they don't hire them. If they like them, they will make allowances in other areas." Importantly, what enlivens chemistry in one context can kill it in another.

Hot buttons and chemistry-enhancing qualities are either discovered or constructed. Some employers understand and share relevant information, which then allows a headhunter to simply discover those qualities. Doug (food production), for example, described how he would directly question the hiring authority: "Look, what are the three or four most important things to you in evaluating whether this person's going to be right?" In many cases, hiring managers do not know and thus cannot share relevant hot buttons, which are then constructed through dialogue. Headhunters construct hot buttons in two ways. A first is to ask about important upcoming projects that the new hire will be involved in or will spearhead, what the new hire will do during a typical day, or what specific outcomes will be expected. Headhunters aim to generate a statement of this sort: "My understanding is that the new hire will need to accomplish X and Y, and that if I find a candidate with X and Y capability, then you will be interested in them." A second approach to constructing hot buttons and assessing chemistry involves paying attention to how clients respond to early candidates. A first candidate "tests the job order" by determining the degree of divergence between abstract selection criteria and the concrete evaluation of a flesh-and-blood candidate. Headhunters claim that clients often see positive or negative aspects of a candidate that then play a central role in defining what is sought in the new hire.

Hot buttons and chemistry are best understood as discovered and constructed through an evolving sequence of interactions. Headhunters clearly become involved in shaping—not just understanding—job definitions and selection criteria, thus making the matter of "who is right for the job?" less straightforward than the specs might otherwise imply.

Who Appears Right for the Job?

Headhunters work to grasp hot buttons and chemistry because those two issues are critical to finding good candidates and making placements. In particular, when a client fails to share hot buttons or collaborate in their construction, headhunters believe that a placement will be a long shot. As George (accounting and finance) commented, "I'm just basically throwing résumés out there, and we tend not to do that." More generally, a headhunter's ability to "control the process" through third-party impression management requires a firm grasp on hot buttons and chemistry. Social scientists have shown how job candidates strive to manage the impressions that interviewers form of them (e.g., Bolino et al., 2008; Giacalone & Rosenfeld, 1989; Gilmore & Ferris 1989; Macan, 2009; Rosenfeld, Giacalone, & Riordan, 1995). Except for a few brief comments by Rosenfeld et al. (1995, p. 40–41, 61, 96–97), that literature has been silent on the role of third parties in impression management, what Rosenfeld et al. (1995, p. 40) call "self-presentation by proxy." Kacmar, Delery, and Ferris (1992, p. 1254) hinted at the importance of third parties by saying that "the particular characteristics of the situation or context, and the behavior that is situationally defined as appropriate, will contribute to the success or failure of different impression management tactics." The situational appropriateness of a candidate's presentation, what Baumeister (1982) dubbed "audience-specific self presentation," surely influences the effectiveness of impression management strategies. The problem of situational appropriateness is profound because interviewers differ in their responses to candidates (e.g., Bretz, Rynes, & Gerhart, 1993; Mayfield & Carlson, 1966) and because candidates rarely know how best to present themselves in different contexts (e.g., Liden & Parsons, 1989; Fletcher, 1989). A lack of context-specific information puts candidates at risk of engaging in situationally inappropriate behavior (Fletcher, 1989).

Beginning with the résumé (Kaplan & Fisher, 2009) and running through the interview, job candidates are challenged to provide what we call "autobiographical accounts" of their strengths, background, skills, and approaches to various situations. In an unstructured interview, candidates might be asked to respond to a very general tell-me-about-yourself question; even in a structured, behavior- or situation-based interview, candidates confront general questions regarding how they acted (or might act) in specific situations (Bolino et al., 2008). Questions of this sort are difficult to answer, as an unabridged account would be absurdly long, thus requiring rather savage editing to pare the account to a suitable length for a résumé or interview. The risk, of course, is that the abridged autobiography will not highlight qualities the client seeks in a new hire even if the candidate perfectly meets the client's needs. A form of narrative sampling variability means that even the most honest job candidate can construct and deliver many different autobiographical accounts, some of which will pack more punch than others for a particular position or hiring manager. The problem is that most candidates can offer only one abridged account, and they may not select the one with the most punch. A similar problem plagues candidate efforts to reveal chemistry-enhancing attributes. Many experiences, values, and interests relevant to chemistry might not surface spontaneously, and would thus have no bearing on perceived chemistry.

Another challenge for prospective employees is being able to determine what a hiring manager or interviewer is looking for during an interview or assessment. Research on the concept of ATIC (Ability to Identify Criteria) has found that some people are better able than others to identify which performance criteria are most relevant in settings in which they are being assessed, especially when the selection procedures are nontransparent (e.g., Kleinmann, Ingold, Livens, Jansen, Melchers, & Konig, 2011; Melchers et al., 2009). Candidates

who lack this skill will be systematically disadvantaged during job interviews.

We argue that third parties, especially those well-positioned and motivated to gather and share information about a hiring manager's attributes and hiring preferences, represent a *social solution* to the problems of situational appropriateness, the autobiographical question, and an ATIC deficit. By gathering information about hot buttons and chemistry and then arming candidates with that information, headhunters increase the likelihood that candidates will craft situationally-appropriate self presentations and will understand what is being probed by particular interview questions. Michelle (accounting and human resources) summarized why she engages in impression management ("candidate prep" in her terms): "I mean we're grooming people so they put their best foot forward. Not so much so that we're trying to change who they are and they're going to turn into this monster two days later. *It's just that everything in life is presentation* [her oral emphasis]. And if something is presented more favorably, people feel better about buying it. And it's just marketing and packaging." Further, by sharing information with clients about candidates, headhunters make it more likely that clients will view candidates positively.

The emphasis headhunters place on impression management sheds light on the role of luck and a weakness of structured interviews. First, headhunters argue that minor—if not trivial—differences between candidates often determine who gets an offer. Most typically, getting the nod can be seen as a matter of luck, especially if what distinguishes the top candidate from the others is not a generally advantageous attribute (e.g., nebbishness).[11] For headhunters, luck can be engineered to at least some extent by preparing candidates to be situationally appropriate. Second, the widespread use of candidate reconnaissance by headhunters casts doubt on an argument in the impression-management literature. After a candidate meets a client, a headhunter will typically have an extensive debriefing conversation with her, thereby learning who she met and what questions were posed. Headhunters thus use candidates to learn more about hiring managers and interview protocols. A number of scholars (e.g., Bolino et al., 2008; Lievens & Peeters, 2008; Macan, 2009) argue that opportunities for (and consequences of) impression management on the part of candidates may be dampened by the use of structured interviews, especially the use of more standardized questioning. Candidate reconnaissance, however, provides headhunters with a "cheat sheet," packed with insider information, that empowers and encourages them to coach subsequent candidates especially well when interviews have a structured, predictable format. For headhunters, structured interviews thus greatly enhance opportunities for—and the likely success of—impression management.[12]

Future Directions

We position our research and much of what is offered in this chapter as an occupational case study of headhunters. In short, we describe what headhunters do and what insights they offer for students of labor markets and matching processes. That focus is driven by large gaps in our understanding of the business and practice of headhunting. We outline five issues here

Headhunting Firms and the Practice of Headhunting

There is little solid information on headhunting firms in the United States or other countries. We therefore know little about the number of firms, their characteristics, and how they change over time either domestically or internationally. Recently, however, the analysis of the internationalization of producer services has captured the attention of economic geographers, netting valuable insights into the global spread of retained headhunting (Faulconbridge, Hall, & Beaverstock, 2008), although none to our knowledge have yet explored contingency headhunting, the mainstay of the industry. We know little about the earnings of headhunters themselves, their staying power in the occupation, or what other occupations may serve as feeders into headhunting or as next steps if its appeal wanes.

The practice of headhunting itself also remains fallow ground in part because of the largely qualitative character of research conducted thus far. The character of qualitative evidence, for example, does not support fine subdivisions, wherein differences between occupational niches worked by headhunters can be compared confidently. There is a need for representative, quantitatively-focused evidence on the practice and business of headhunting. In addition, new developments in the field, such as the increasing use of the Internet, and social-networking sites in particular, deserve attention. As online recruitment comes to play a more prominent role in the labor market, headhunters continue to tout their access to the contentedly employed,

who, they argue (perhaps correctly, perhaps not), ignore both online and offline information about job opportunities.

Client Companies and the Use of Headhunters

We have described how headhunters snare client companies and candidates. That, however, is only one side of the story, and we know little about the process whereby companies that enter the external labor market come to use the services of a headhunter. Recent work by Beaverstock, Faulconbridge, and Hall (2010) on elite, retained headhunters in Europe has begun to add to our understanding of this process by noting the important role of labor regulation. For example, labor regulation effectively prohibited headhunting in Germany until the late 1990s, and it continues to limit the work of headhunters (Beaverstock et al., 2010, p. 837). Similar work in other parts of the world is necessary to better understand the possibilities and limits of efforts by headhunters to move search outside of firms and their internal labor markets.

In the United States, our research shows that headhunters hedge bets by evaluating job orders and clients, investing more in some searches than others. We strongly suspect that client companies engage in parallel hedges, perhaps using headhunters in a strategic way to evaluate their internal capacity to recruit and evaluate candidates. Given that contingency headhunters are paid only if one of the candidates they identify and present is hired, there is nothing to stop a company from giving a job order to one or more headhunters while also conducting a full-scale, traditional recruitment effort. Whether that strategy is common or rare is currently unknown. We are also uncertain about the veracity of one of the central claims of headhunters, namely that they alone can raid a client's competitors and customers with impunity. We know of a few instances of headhunter-within-HR arrangements (e.g., Carter, 2006; Griffin, 2008), but little is known as to the effectiveness, advantages, or sustainability of that practice.

A critical issue centers on the consequences of using headhunters for hiring organizations. A simple question has yet to be explored systematically: Are headhunter-produced candidates better in one or more ways? There is thus a complete lack of evidence as to whether the use of headhunters confers advantage or disadvantage, in either the short- or long-term, with respect to the cost of recruitment and selection, the productivity or contributions of the new hire, the likelihood of separation, and so forth. Headhunters, of course, trumpet the value of their candidates, especially the contentedly employed, but those claims may be more rhetoric than reality. Terpstra (1996) claimed that human-resource executives put headhunters among the three top-ranked sources of high-quality, high-performing employees, but he provided no sense of how, or on what grounds, that assessment was made. One business-press piece recently questioned the wisdom of a "war for talent" and the need to get the "top talent" headhunters purport to purvey by arguing that "good enough hires" may be better for firms (Pooley, 2007). A similar theme was explored through interviews with retained headhunters in Europe (Faulconbridge et al., 2009). A key conclusion of that analysis was that headhunters promulgate the "war for talent" theme in part to move recruitment outside of firms and their internal labor markets into global, external labor markets that headhunters create—and from which they profit.

Candidates, Source Companies, and Headhunters

Cost is a long-standing theme in the literature on employed job search (e.g, Bretz, Boudreau, and Judge, 1994, p. 277). Search behavior, whether or not it leads to turnover, can be costly in two ways. First, it consumes time and energy that could be put to other uses (March & Simon, 1958), such as time spent preparing resumes, planning, and then communicating with potential employers, perhaps face to face, in a way that takes time away from work. Second, it may foster psychological processes associated with withdrawal behavior and reduce commitment to one's current job and employing organization (Locke, 1976). In short, search may leave us with one foot out the door, a posture that may reduce contributions, team orientations, and the like. Although these general processes have not received much empirical attention, they have received absolutely no attention with regard to the business of headhunting. For example, headhunters routinely contact many employed individuals in the process of identifying, screening, and then wooing candidates. What costs, if any, are incurred by those activities? What happens to the contentedly employed after being wooed for a position that ultimately falls through? Does the experience prompt withdrawal behavior, reduce commitment, or spur an active job search? Are those who are regularly contacted by headhunters for information transformed in some way by the experience? Importantly, these potential

consequences can occur for both individuals and companies, especially if one or more headhunters prospect intensively for candidates in a particular company, thus targeting it as a source company. At present, we know nothing whatsoever about these issues, which amount to an externality of the business of headhunting.

Impression Management, Realistic Job Previews, and the Ability to Identify Criteria

Our research shows that headhunters do far more than simply identify prospects and hope for the best when they come into contact with client companies. Rather, they strive to manage contacts, the flow of information, and the formation of impressions by clients of candidates and candidates of clients. They are thus very much in the business of impression management. They must, however, be mindful of over-selling either side on the other, as client disappointment or a quick departure of the new hire can unravel the client-headhunter relationship. They must, then, attend to two key issues, each of which present interesting twists in the context of headhunting. First, they must provide something akin to a realistic job preview, which in general is understood to involve the presentation of both favorable and unfavorable job-related information to job candidates (e.g., Phillips, 1998). And second, they must be able to identify the most salient, targeted interview dimensions, in order to choose suitable candidates and prepare them to excel during the interview. That "ability to identify criteria" (ATIC) among job candidates has been the subject of important new research (e.g., Kleinmann et al., 2011; Melchers et al., 2009).

Both issues represent untilled research terrain when it comes to headhunters. Although reviews of the large literature on realistic job previews have suggested that they have at most modest effects (Phillips, 1998; Rynes & Cable, 2003), in the case of headhunted candidates some tempering of expectations is surely critical. As Westphal (2010, p. 324) put it, "to the extent that the job characteristics portrayed by impression managers are decoupled from the actual characteristics experienced by occupants, impression management directed at potential job candidates can reduce person-job fit, thus reducing the ultimate satisfaction and performance of the job holder, and increasing turnover." How realistic tempering of expectations is accomplished is unclear, especially in light of the imperative that headhunters generate sufficient interest to lure the contentedly employed into the labor market.

Headhunting might well be a critical research site to explore the content and delivery of realistic job previews. Likewise, research on ATIC has focused on job candidates, but the ability is surely key to the effectiveness of headhunters as they identify and prepare candidates for interviews. Attention could be profitably shifted to them, focusing on how they work to identify criteria, variations across headhunters in that ability, and how their effectiveness and candidate outcomes might well be related to that ability. In both cases, research on realistic job previews and ATIC might well profit by focusing on the work and activities of headhunters.

Candidates and Headhunters

Although headhunters are emphatic in stressing that they work for client companies, and are in the business of finding people for jobs (not jobs for people), their success hinges on their ability to convince people to take new jobs. Headhunters make much of the idea that they help candidates to "leverage" and "advance" their careers. Prospects, of course, have to believe that in order to become candidates and placements. But there is little evidence at this point to support the claims of headhunters that their candidates do exceptionally well in the labor market with respect to pay, promotions, prestige, future opportunities, or any such outcome. Dreher, Lee, and Clerkin (2011) suggest that white males are more likely than other race/sex groups to be contacted by headhunters and may benefit most from external labor-market moves. In addition, there is little information as to who gets on a headhunter's radar screen and is contacted by them as a source or prospect, who becomes a candidate, or who actually makes a job change through a headhunter. As noted earlier, Hamori (2010) found that for financial-services executives, those employed in admired, top-performing firms were overrepresented on the search firm's "radar screen" (i.e., be identified as a prospect), whereas those who worked at firms experiencing performance or reputational difficulties were overrepresented among candidates.

Other qualities of headhunter-produced candidates remain unclear as well. For example, there have been no empirical efforts to measure headhunter-produced candidates on the "Job Search Behavioral Index" (Kopelman, Rovenpor, & Millsap, 1992) to confirm that they are less engaged in search than those who are "on" the job market. Nor have headhunter-produced candidates been compared to others to determine if factors such as job satisfaction, perceived organizational success, level, tenure, gender, cognitive ability, and age remain significant predictors of job search activity and turnover (e.g., Boudreau, et al., 2001; Boswell, Roehling, & Boudreau 2006). Without solid information of that sort, it is impossible to determine if those working with headhunters represent a distinctive group of job candidates. Moreover, we do not know if the identification and screening practices of headhunters disadvantage members of any race, sex, or ethnic group and thus have an "adverse impact" (Zedeck, 2010), a possibility suggested by our research and that of Dreher, Lee, and Clerkin (2011).

In closing, headhunters represent a theoretically and empirically meaningful labor-market intermediary that merits more research attention in the United States and elsewhere.

Practical Advice: Brief Answers to Six Common Questions About Headhunters

1. *Why would a headhunter call?* Headhunters call to *get acquainted*, wherein she introduces herself and then wants to find out more about what you do; *recruit candidates*, wherein she aims to gauge your interest and suitability for a position she is trying to fill; or *seek information*, wherein she asks you to suggest names of people who might fit a particular position or to comment on someone you know who is being considered for a position. Calls can be mixtures of the three types. Always strive to assess her knowledge of your labor-market niche, whether she listens carefully, and whether she is the kind of person you might want to work with in the future.

2. *Why take a call from a headhunter?* Even if you are contentedly employed, developing a relationship with a headhunter can provide you with useful information about your industry and occupation and put (or keep) you on a headhunter's radar screen. Headhunters appreciate courtesy and candor, and rely on both to succeed. It is an advantage to be known and liked by a headhunter.

3. *What can headhunters do that I cannot?* Headhunters talk to employers and employees every day and thus know their segment of the labor market well. They also have access to a portion of the proverbial "hidden" job market (jobs that are not advertised). If you fit a position, they will strive to get your résumé in front of the right person and will help you to look your best if you get an

interview. They also assist in negotiating the terms of an offer.

4. *Can I contact a headhunter directly?* Although headhunters target and woo the contentedly employed, it would be a mistake to conclude that they neither solicit nor welcome being contacted by an active job seeker. If you opt to contact a headhunter, then keep expectations in check, as headhunters can be swamped with unsolicited material, and approach one or more headhunters who work your specific occupation or industry.

5. *Can I tell if a headhunter is any good?* A reasonable approach is to listen carefully, ask questions, and reflect on how the relationship progresses. Listen for signs that the headhunter knows his industries, companies, and positions well, even if he could not do the jobs himself (few can and even fewer believe it essential). Ask about positions filled and candidates placed. Note whether he contacts you as promised, whether he shares the company's take on you after an interview, and whether his pre-interview descriptions of companies and jobs and interviewers are for the most part consistent with what you learn on the interview. Good information and communication are markers of a relationship worth maintaining.

6. *Can I assess a headhunter's ethics?* Given that headhunters routinely provide another search at no cost if a new hire does not work out or leaves quickly, it is risky for them to oversell or misrepresent candidates or companies because that might require another search, tarnish their reputation, and diminish if not halt job orders from a client. It is possible that a headhunter will share your résumé widely or otherwise broadcast your availability. If you want to be highly discrete, then you should be emphatic about that, insist that nothing be shared without your permission, and state that you will terminate the relationship if your wishes are not honored. However, there is no way to guarantee discretion, so there is always some risk that others will learn that you are on the market, or at least testing the waters.

Notes

1. Lee and Mitchell (1994) conceptualize a "shock" as a distinguishable event that "jars" employees into thinking about their job situation and perhaps quitting voluntarily. It generates information or has meaning that cannot readily be ignored.
2. More information about the types of headhunters interviewed and observed, the firms in which they work, and the range of what is found in the industry can be found in Finlay and Coverdill (2007, pp. 6–12 and 19–23).
3. Estimates of these values are based on anecdotal evidence. Given that no governmental or authoritative source tracks headhunting firms or placements, industry-provided figures are the best available (but of course remain suspect). Reynolds (2001, p. 34) has stated that headhunting firms are evenly split between retainer and contingency formats; McCool (2008b, p. 72) suggests that about 66 percent of the roughly 6,000 "executive search firms" in the United States operated on contingency. We believe that both authors underestimate the contingent-firm segment. McCool focuses attention on the upper end of headhunting, which is not the mainstay of contingency headhunting, and Reynolds runs a retained-search firm and expresses clearly a strong preference for retained over contingent forms of headhunting. As for numbers of placements, contingency headhunters work more job orders simultaneously and earn lower fees, both of which lead to more placements per time period. Both sources (Reynolds, 2001, pp. 27–38; McCool, 2008b, pp. 72–74) offer partisan but informative discussions of differences between retainer and contingent headhunting. Both worked in retained search and, in our view, oversell its virtues and distinctiveness. Cappelli and Hamori (2007, pp. 334–336) also offer a brief but more balanced overview.
4. A typical defense of the fees headhunters charge was penned by Paul Hawkinson (2005), a prominent figure in the history of contingency recruiting and founder of *The Fordyce Letter*.
5. See Gardner, Stansbury, and Hart (2010) for an informative discussion of employee "poaching" or "lateral hiring" and its associated ethical issues for both employers and employees.
6. How much attention unsolicited material received was difficult to assess because headhunters emphasized the "hunt" for candidates. Evidence suggests that even elite retainer firms make use of candidate-provided materials. For example, Jenn (2005, p. 52) reports that Egon Zehnder International (a global retainer firm) receives "250 unsolicited CVs each week" and that they "claim to read all the CVs." Likewise, the giant retainer firm Heidrick & Struggles maintains a website option for "resume/CV submission," available at: (http://www.heidrick.com/SubmitResume/Pages/ResumeCVSubmission.aspx (Accessed 3/5/12.)
7. Miller (2000) and Kitanaka (2008) offer brief and interesting descriptions of misrepresentation and trickery used by headhunters to identify candidates. Both are consistent with our data.
8. The business press occasionally covers strategies firms use to protect themselves from raids by headhunters. One former corporate HR staffer described how "Our company became known as a gold mine for talented employees, which we began losing at an alarming rate" (Ryan, 2005). Instead of bolstering gatekeeping defenses by further training receptionists to detect and deflect headhunters' calls, they began a policy whereby employees could "Earn cash for every headhunter conversation you report to HR." This gave the company what they saw as competitive intelligence about competitors and allowed them to forge closer bonds with their employees.
9. The contentedly employed present other challenges, such as a strong incentive to remain window shoppers in the face of new opportunities. In addition, recent evidence suggests that the economic downturn in the United States,

if not elsewhere, has made it more difficult to convince these candidates to consider new opportunities (Sendouts, 2009). Some suggest that this is due to the housing-market difficulties in the United States, the reluctance of many employers to offer assistance in buying or selling homes, and concerns about how a loss of tenure after a job change may pose a last-in-first-out risk (Zmuda, 2009).

10. A helpful discussion of culture and fit by a former head-hunter is found in McCool (2008a).

11. See Coverdill and Finlay (1998, pp. 121–123) for a more elaborate discussion of luck and labor market success.

12. Candidate-provided information about structured interviews nonetheless sheds little light on how responses to questions were assessed. Headhunters, however, routinely speak with the client, not just the candidate, after an interview, and in those conversations they focus on what was deemed strong and weak about the candidate's capabilities and performance and whether, in general, the candidate would meet the client's needs. Information from candidates is thus supplemented and informed by postinterview conversations with clients.

References

Arthur, M. B., & Rousseau, D. M. (1996). *The boundaryless career: A new employment principle for a new organizational era.* New York: Oxford University Press.

Ashkenas, R., Ulrich, D., Jick, T., & Kerr, S. (2002). *The boundaryless organization: Breaking the chains of organizational structure.* 2nd ed. San Francisco: Jossey-Bass.

Autor, D. H. (2009). Studies of labor market intermediation: Introduction. In D. H. Autor (Ed.), *Studies of labor market intermediation* (pp. 1–22). Chicago: University of Chicago Press.

Baumeister, R. F. (1982). A self-presentational view of social phenomena. *Psychological Bulletin*, 91, 3–26.

Beaverstock, J. V., Faulconbridge, J. R., & Hall, S. J. E. (2010). Professionalization, legitimization and the creation of executive search markets in Europe. *Journal of Economic Geography*, 10, 825–843.

Becker, B. E., Huselid, M. A., & Ulrich, D. (2001). *The HR scorecard: Linking people, strategy, and performance.* Boston: Harvard Business School Press.

Bolino, M. C., Kacmar, K. M., Turnley, W. H., & Gilstrap, J. B. (2008). A multi-level review of impression management motives and behaviors. *Journal of Management*, 34, 1080–1109.

Boswell, W. R., Roehling, M. V., & Boudreau, J. W. (2006). The role of personality, situational, and demographic variables in predicting job search among European managers. *Personality and Individual Differences*, 40, 783–794.

Boswell, W. R., & Gardner, R. G. (2012). Employed job-seekers and job-to-job search. In U.-C. Klehe & E. A. van Hooft (Eds.) *Oxford handbook of job loss and job search.* New York: Oxford University Press.

Boudreau, J. W., Boswell, W. R., Judge, T. A., & Bretz, R. D. Jr. (2001). Personality and cognitive ability as predictors of job search among employed managers. *Personnel Psychology*, 54, 25–50.

Bretz, R. D., Rynes, S. L. & Gerhart, B. (1993). Recruiter perceptions of applicant fit: Implications for individual career preparation and job search behavior. *Journal of Vocational Behavior*, 43, 310–327.

Bretz, R. D. Jr., Boudreau, J. W., & Judge, T. A. (1994). Job search behavior of employed managers. *Personnel Psychology*, 47, 275–301.

Burt, R. S. (1992). *Structural holes: The social structure of competition.* Cambridge, MA: Harvard University Press.

Burton, M. D. (2003). *Headhunters* by Finlay & Coverdill (review). *Industrial & Labor Relations Review*, 56(3), 555–556.

Cappelli, P., & Hamori, M. (2007). The institutions of outside hiring. In H. Gunz & M. Peiperl (Eds.), *Handbook of career studies* (pp. 327–349). Los Angeles: Sage.

Carter, T. (2005). Hidden assets. *ABA Journal*, 91(7), 27.

Carter, T. (2006). On the hunt for laterals. *ABA Journal*, 92(10), 27–28.

Chatman, J. A. (1991). Matching people and organizations: Selection and socialization in public accounting firms. *Administrative Science Quarterly*, 36, 459–484.

Coverdill, J. E., & Finlay, W. (1998). Fit and skill in employee selection: Insights from a study of headhunters. *Qualitative Sociology* 21(2):105–127.

Davis, J. Dice: Full-time IT job listings jump as headhunters circle. *Channel Insider*, (May 18), 1.

Demos, T. (2010). How can I get a headhunter interested in me? *Fortune*, 161(5), 40.

DiRenzo, M. S., & Greenhaus, J. H. (2011). Job search and voluntary turnover in a boundaryless world: A control theory perspective. *Academy of Management Review*, 36(3), 567–589.

Dreher, G. F., Lee, J. -Y., & Clerkin, T. A. (2011). Mobility and cash compensation: The moderating effects of gender, race, and executive search firms. *Journal of Management*, 37(3), 651–681.

Faulconbridge, J. R., Hall, S. J. E., & Beaverstock, J. V. (2008). New insights into the internationalization of producer services: Organizational strategies and spatial economies for global headhunting firms. *Environment & Planning*, 40(1), 210–234.

Faulconbridge, J. R., Beaverstock, J. V., Hall, S., & Hewitson, A. (2009). The 'war for talent': The gatekeeper role of executive search firms in elite labour markets. *Geoforum*, 40, 800–808.

Finlay, W., & Coverdill, J. E. (2007). *Headhunters: Matchmaking in the labor market* (paperback edition with a new afterword). Ithaca, NY: Cornell University Press.

Fisher, A. (2001). Survivor guilt and oily headhunters. *Fortune*, 144(7), 268.

Fisher, D. (2009). The toughest objection of them all. *The Fordyce Letter* (June 3). Available at: www.fordyceletter.com (Accessed 3/5/12.)

Fletcher, C. (1989). Impression management in the selection interview. In R. A. Giacalone & P. Rosenfeld (Eds.), *Impression management in the organization* (pp. 269–281). Hillsdale, NJ: Erlbaum.

Freebairn, M. (2008). The headhunter will see you now. *Accountancy Magazine*, (November), 54.

Fullerton, A. S., & Wallace, M. (2007). Traversing the flexible turn: US workers' perceptions of job security, 1977–2002. *Social Science Research*, 36, 201–221.

Gagné, C. (2006). Search & employ. *Canadian Business*, 79(2), 62–63.

Gardner, T. M., Stansbury, J., & Hart, D. (2010). The ethics of lateral hiring. *Business Ethics Quarterly*, 20(3), 341–346.

Giacalone, R. A., & Rosenfeld, P. (Eds.). (1989). *Impression management in the organization*. Hillsdale, NJ: Erlbaum.

Gilmore, D. C., & Ferris, G. R. (1989). The politics of employment interview. In Robert W. Eder & Gerald R. Ferris (Eds.), *The employment interview: Theory, research, and practice* (pp. 195–203). Newbury Park, CA: Sage.

Granovetter, M. (1995). *Getting a job: A study of contacts and careers*, 2nd ed. Chicago: University of Chicago Press.

Greenhaus, J. H., Callanan, G. A., & DiRenzo, M. S. (2008). A boundaryless perspective on careers. In J. Barling & C. L. Cooper (Eds.) *The SAGE handbook of organizational behavior* (pp. 277–299). Los Angeles: Sage.

Griffeth, R. W., Hom, P. W., & Gaertner, S. (2000). A meta-analysis of antecedents and correlates of employee turnover: Update, moderator tests, and research implications for the next millennium. *Journal of Management*, 26(3), 463–488.

Griffin, G. (2008). Inside knowledge. *The Lawyer*, (March 3).

Hamori, M. (2010). Who gets headhunted—And who gets ahead? The impact of search firms on executive careers. *Academy of Management Perspectives*, 24(4), 46–59.

Hawkinson, P. (2005). Why recruiters are worth what they charge. *The Fordyce Letter* (November 1). Available at: www.fordyceletter.com (Accessed 3/5/12.)

Holloway, A. (2002). Finding the right fit. *Canadian Business*, 75(22), 119.

Holtom, B. C., Mitchell, T. R., Lee, T. W., & Inderrieden, E. J. (2005). Shocks as causes of turnover: What they are and how organizations can manage them. *Human Resource Management*, 44(3), 337–352.

Hom, P. W., Caranikas-Walker, F., Prussia, G. E., & Griffeth, R. W. (1992). A meta-analytical structural equations analysis of a model of employee turnover. *Journal of Applied Psychology*, 77(6):890–909.

Jenn, N. G. (2005). *Headhunters and how to use them: A guide for organisations and individuals*. London: The Economist.

Kacmar, K. M., Delery, J. E., & Ferris, G. R. (1992). Differential effectiveness of applicant impression management tactics on employment interview decisions. *Journal of Applied Social Psychology*, 22, 1250–1272.

Kalleberg, A. L., David K., Marsden, P. V., & Spaeth, J. L. (1996). *Organizations in America: Analyzing their structures and human resource practices*. Thousand Oaks, CA: Sage.

Kaplan, D. M., & Fisher, J. E. (2009). A rose by any other name: Identity and impression management in résumés. *Employment Responsibilities and Rights Journal*, 21, 319–332.

King, Z., Burke, S., & Pemberton, J. (2005). The "bounded" career: An empirical study of human capital, career mobility and employment outcomes in a mediated labour market. *Human Relations*, 58(8):981–1007.

Kitanaka, A. (2008). Sneaky things that bad headhunters do: The top five. *J@pan Inc*, 76(March/April), 41.

Kleinmann, M., Ingold, P. A., Lievens, F., Jansen, A., Melchers, K. G. & König, C. J. (2011). A different look at why selection procedures work: the role of candidates' ability to identify criteria. *Organizational Psychology Review*, 1(2), 128–146.

Kopelman, R. E., Rovenpor, J. L., and Millsap, R. E. (1992). Rationale and construct validity evidence for the Job Search Behavior Index: because intentions (and New Year's resolutions) often come to naught. *Journal of Vocational Behavior* 40:269-287.

Kristof-Brown, A. L. (2000). Perceived applicant fit: distinguishing between recruiters' perceptions of person-job and person-organization fit. *Personnel Psychology*, 53, 643–671.

Lee, T. H., Gerhart, B., Weller, I., & Trevor, C. O. (2008). Understanding voluntary turnover: Path-specific job satisfaction effects and the importance of unsolicited job offers. *Academy of Management Journal*, 51(4), 651–671.

Lee, T. W., & Mitchell, T. R. (1994). An alternative approach: The unfolding model of voluntary employee turnover. *Academy of Management Review*, 19(1), 51–89.

Liden, R. C., & Parsons, C. K. (1989). understanding interpersonal behavior in the employment interview: A reciprocal interactional analysis. In Robert W. Eder & Gerald R. Ferris (Eds.), *The employment interview: Theory, research, and practice* (pp. 219–232). Newbury Park, CA: Sage.

Lievens, F., & Peeters, H. (2008). Interviewers' sensitivity to impression management tactics in structured interviews. *European Journal of Psychological Assessment*, 24(3), 174–180.

Locke, E. A. (1976). The nature and causes of job satisfaction. In Marvin D. Dunnette (Ed.) *Handbook of industrial and organizational psychology* (pp. 1297–1349). Chicago: Rand McNally.

Macan, T. (2009). The employment interview: A review of current studies and directions for future research. *Human Resource Management Review*, 19, 203–218.

March, J. G., & Simon, H. A. (1958). *Organizations*. Hoboken, NJ: Wiley.

Martinez, T. (1976). *The human marketplace: An examination of private employment agencies*. New Brunswick, NJ: Transaction Books.

Mayfield, E. C., & Carlson, R. E. (1966). Selection interview decisions: First results from a long-term research project. *Personnel Psychology*, 19, 41–53.

Miller, C. (2000). Have you been called by this headhunter? *Money*, 29(9), 26.

McCool, J. D. (2007). How to let the headhunter do the job. *BusinessWeek Online*, November 27, p. 27.

McCool, J. D. (2008a). Culture club. *BusinessWeek Online*, March 4, p. 28.

McCool, J. D. (2008b). *Deciding who leads: How executive recruiters drive, direct & disrupt the global search for leadership talent*. Mountain View, CO: Davies-Black Publishing.

McDonnell, A. (2011). Still fighting the "war for talent"? Bridging the science versus practice gap. *Journal of Business and Psychology*, 26(2), 169–173.

McNulty, N. (2010). "Comment" on American heroism in the 21st century. *The Fordyce Letter* (July 19). Available at: www.fordyceletter.com (Accessed 3/5/12.)

Melchers, K. G., Klehe, U. C., Richter, G. M., Kleinmann, M., König, C. J., & Lievens, F. (2009). 'I know what you want to know': The impact of interviewees ability to identify criteria on interview performance and construct-related validity. *Human Performance*, 22, 355–374.

Mobley, W. H. (1977). Intermediate linkages in the relationship between job satisfaction and employee turnover. *Journal of Applied Psychology*, 62(2), 237–240.

Morrow, R. (2010). Headhunters poll 2010: Full results revealed. *Asiamoney*, 21(2), 99.

Nakamura, A. O., Shaw, K. L., Freeman, R. B., Nakamura, E., & Pyman, A. (2009). Jobs online. In D. H. Autor (Ed.), *Studies* of labor market intermediation (pp. 27–64). Chicago and London: University of Chicago Press.

Pfeffer, J. (1995). Producing sustainable competitive advantage through the effective management of people. *Academy of Management Executive*, 9(1), 55–69.

Phillips, J. M. (1998). Effects of realistic job previews on multiple organizational outcomes: A meta-analysis. *Academy of Management Journal*, 41(6), 673–690.

Pooley, E. (2007). Don't believe the hype. *Canadian Business*, 80(3), 60–61.

Prus, R. C. (1989). *Making sales: Influence as interpersonal accomplishment*. Newbury Park, CA: Sage.

Reynolds, S. S. (2001). *Be hunted! 12 secrets to getting on the headhunter's radar screen*. Hoboken, NJ: Wiley.

RRosenfeld, P., Giacalone, R. A., & Riordan, C.A. (1995). *Impression management in organizations: Theory, measurement, practice*. London: Routledge.

Ryan, L. (2005). A ju-jitsu attack on headhunters. *Business Week Online*, June 9.

Rynes, S. L., & Cable, D. M. (2003). Recruitment research in the twenty-first century. In W. C. Borman, D. R. Ilgen, & R. J. Klimoski (Eds.) *Handbook of psychology: Industrial and organizational psychology* (Vol.12, pp. 55–76). Hoboken, NJ: Wiley.

Rynes, S., & Gerhart B. (1990). Interviewer assessments of applicant 'fit': An exploratory investigation. *Personnel Psychology*, 43, 13–35.

Rynes, S. L, Orlitzky, M. O., & Bretz, R. D. Jr. (1997). Experienced hiring versus college recruiting: Practices and emerging trends. *Personnel Psychology*, 50, 309–339.

Sendouts. (2009). 2009 Recruiter economic survey. Available at: www.sendouts.com (Accessed 3/5/12.)

Sendouts. (2010). 2010 Summer recruiting survey: Forecast is sunny. Available at: www.sendouts.com (Accessed 3/5/12.)

Smithson, Janet, & Lewis S. (2000). Is job insecurity changing the psychological contract? *Personnel Review*, 29(6), 680–702.

Terpstra, D. E. (1996). The search for effective methods. *HR Focus*, 73(5), 16–17.

Van Hooft, E. A. J., Born, M. Ph., Taris, T. W., Van Der Flier, H., & Blonk, R. W. B. (2004). Predictors of job search behavior among employed and unemployed people. *Personnel Psychology*, 57:25–59.

Westphal, J. D. (2010). An impression management perspective on job design: The case of corporate directors. *Journal of Organizational Behavior*, 31, 319–327.

Woolnough, R. (2008). Netting the very best movers and shakers. *Resourcing*, (January/February), 23–25.

Zedeck, S. (2010). Adverse Impact: History and Evolution. In J. L. Outtz (Ed.), *Adverse impact: Implications for organizational staffing and high stakes selection* (pp. 3–27). New York: Routledge.

Zmuda, N. (2009). Recruiters say hiring is coming back to life, slowly. *Advertising Age*, 80(39), 9.

Who Is Searching for Whom? Integrating Recruitment and Job Search Research

Serge P. da Motta Veiga *and* Daniel B. Turban

Abstract

We note that organizational recruitment processes and applicant job search processes occur simultaneously; as organizations are attempting to attract qualified applicants, job seekers are searching for potential employers. Whereas the job search literature examines various outcomes within-subjects across organizations, the recruitment literature examines similar outcomes between-subjects within an organization. Thus, although the recruitment and job search literatures have developed relatively independently, we believe that it would be useful to integrate theories and concepts from these literatures. Therefore our goal in this chapter, as we review both literatures, is to integrate relevant concepts that can stimulate future research examining recruitment and job search simultaneously rather than independently. To achieve this goal, we first provide a brief overview of the recruitment and job search literatures. As part of this overview, we review predictors of applicant attraction and job choice and of job search behaviors and outcomes. We also suggest how both literatures have been and could be further integrated. Second, we suggest how three theories (i.e., signaling, expectancy, and the theory of planned behavior) have been (and could be further) used to integrate job search and recruitment research. Finally, we propose directions for future research investigating and theorizing how and when both literatures could be further integrated.

Key Words: recruitment, job search, applicant attraction, job choice

Introduction

Attracting qualified applicants is an extremely important human resources practice (Barber, 1998; Chapman, Uggerslev, Carroll, Piasentin, & Jones, 2005). Specifically, the utility of selection practices depends in part on the quality of the applicant pool and whether the top applicants accept job offers (e.g., Boudreau & Rynes, 1985; Carlson, Connerley, & Mecham, 2002; Murphy, 1986). Thus, not surprisingly, many studies have investigated predictors of applicant attraction and job choice, frequently focusing on firms' recruitment practices and job and organizational attributes (e.g., Collins, 2007; Turban & Cable, 2003). From an organization's perspective, both recruitment and selection practices occur simultaneously, resulting in numerous studies that examine how selection practices influence

applicants' reactions (e.g., Chan & Schmitt, 2004; Collins, 2007). From an individual applicant's perspective, intentions and behaviors toward a specific potential employer are components of the applicant's job search process, which typically involves multiple possible employers. Specifically, as individuals conduct their job search, they are exposed to various recruitment practices and obtain information about job and organizational attributes, which may influence their subsequent job search activities.

Thus we argue that recruitment and job search are "two sides of the same coin." On one side, recruiting applicants is an essential human resource practice for organizations looking to attract and select the best potential applicants. On the other side, job seekers are searching for the best possible job and can be attracted to apply for jobs at specific organizations. We argue that a firm's recruitment processes not only influence an applicant's attraction to that firm but also may influence the applicant's job search processes. Similarly, we expect that how an applicant searches for a job will influence how a potential employer is perceived during the job search process. Interestingly, the job search literature examines various job search outcomes for an applicant across time and organizations, whereas the recruitment literature examines similar outcomes for applicants (and potential applicants) within a specific organization and period of time. Therefore, although the recruitment and job search literatures have developed somewhat independently, we believe that it may be useful to integrate such literatures in an attempt to stimulate further research.

Although an extensive amount of research examining recruitment outcomes has taken an organizational perspective (e.g., Barber, 1998; Chapman et al., 2005), it is critical to note that applicants' intentions and behaviors are also important aspects of the job search process (e.g., Jaidi, Van Hooft, & Arends, 2011; Schreurs, Derous, Van Hooft, Proost, & De Witte, 2009). Specifically, we argue that an organization's recruitment practices not only influence applicants' attraction to the firm (e.g., Barber, 1998; Collins, 2007) but also impact applicants' job search processes and behaviors. For example, a delay in responding to an applicant following an interview may not only influence the applicant's attraction to the firm but also influence the intensity of subsequent job search behaviors. The applicant may indeed decide to put more intensity in job seeking to find alternative opportunities.

This chapter thus aims at making two general contributions. First, we provide a brief overview of the recruitment and job search literatures, including predictors of applicant attraction and job choice and of job search behaviors and outcomes. Second, as we review these literatures, we integrate relevant concepts that can stimulate future research examining recruitment and job search together rather than independently. We then review three theories (i.e., signaling, expectancy, and the theory of planned behavior), which have been utilized and could be further used to integrate recruitment and job search concepts. Finally, we propose how future research could integrate both literatures theoretically, methodologically, and empirically. We should note that although most chapters in this handbook adopt a perspective that focuses solely on the individual job seeker, we also include the organizational

perspective, as we argue that potential employers' recruitment practices and activities can influence individuals' job search behaviors and outcomes.

Brief Overview of the Recruitment and Job Search Literatures
Recruitment Literature Overview

Most scholars define employee recruitment as the organizational practices that influence the number and quality of individuals who apply for vacant positions (e.g., Barber, 1998; Chapman et al., 2005; Rynes, 1991). For example, Breaugh (2008) noted that important recruitment objectives include attracting qualified applicants and processing applicants quickly in order to fill positions with qualified workers, although he also included the job performance and retention of new hires as important objectives. Barber (1998) noted that the recruitment process includes these three phases: generating applicants, maintaining applicant status, and influencing job choice. In the *generating applicants* phase, organizations attempt to attract quality applicants to apply for positions with them. During the *maintaining applicant status* phase, organizations attempt to keep applicants interested in the firm as they are exposed to the organization's selection practices (i.e., interviews, site visits). When a job offer is made, the organization attempts to *influence job choice*, such that applicants will accept the jobs offered. In general, the recruitment literature has attempted to predict individual-level recruitment outcomes, such as job pursuit and job choice (Barber, 1998; Breaugh, 2008; Chapman, et al., 2005; Rynes, 1991). Specifically, Chapman et al. (2005) meta-analyzed 71 studies and found that the recruitment outcomes of job pursuit intentions, job-organization attraction, acceptance intentions, and job choice were predicted by job and organizational characteristics, applicant perceptions of the recruiting process, recruiter behaviors, perceived fit, and hiring expectancies.

Thus recruitment is predominantly perceived and studied as an organizationally driven process. Specifically, organizations try to influence quality candidates to apply, to keep those quality applicants interested in the firm as an employer, and ultimately to influence the best applicants to accept a job offer. Although there is a wide range, the predictors of applicant attraction and job choice can be divided into five relatively broad categories: organizational characteristics (e.g., reputation), job characteristics, recruitment processes (e.g., recruitment lags), recruiter behaviors, and other predictors (e.g., fit perceptions) (Breaugh, 2008; Chapman et al., 2005; Dineen & Soltis, 2010; Rynes & Cable, 2003). We briefly review representative findings from each of these five categories, including some of the most commonly investigated predictors, in order to provide some background about the recruitment literature. Note, however, that we do not provide an exhaustive review of all predictors of applicant attraction and job choice. Our intent is to provide a broad yet selective overview of some of the predictors of applicant attraction and job choice that may usefully inform job search research and thus drive future research bridging the gap between the recruitment and job search literatures.

Predictors of Applicant Attraction and Job Choice

ORGANIZATIONAL CHARACTERISTICS

Recruitment scholars have examined whether and how organizational characteristics influence applicants to pursue employment with some organizations rather than others (Barber, 1998; Breaugh, 2008; Dineen & Soltis, 2010; Rynes & Cable, 2003). Considerable evidence indicates that organizational characteristics, such as reputation and culture, can influence perceptions of organizational attractiveness. For example, firms with greater corporate social responsibility are seen as more attractive employers (Turban & Greening, 1997; Greening & Turban, 2000). Other organizational characteristics that have been examined include reputation and organizational image (Chapman et al., 2005; Collins & Stevens, 2002; Turban & Cable, 2003), organizational culture (Judge & Cable, 1997), firm personality (Slaughter, Zickar, Highhouse, & Mohr, 2004), firm knowledge (Cable & Turban, 2001), and corporate websites (Dineen & Noe, 2009; Williamson, Lepak, & King, 2003). For example, the size and quality of the applicant pool was related to both the firm's brand equity and reputation (Collins & Stevens, 2002; Turban & Cable, 2003). Applicant perceptions of the firm and attraction to the firm also appear to be influenced by the potential employer's websites (Allen, Mahto, & Otondo, 2007; Dineen & Noe, 2009; Williamson et al., 2003). For example, applicants reported more attraction to the firm when the website had a recruitment versus selection orientation (Williamson et al., 2003). More recently, Dineen and Noe (2009) presented evidence that customization of the web site influences the characteristics of the applicant pool. To summarize, considerable evidence indicates that organizational characteristics influence applicant attraction to the firm.

JOB CHARACTERISTICS

In addition to these organizational predictors, scholars have also examined job characteristics as predictors of applicant attraction and job choice (Dineen & Soltis, 2010). Indeed, applicants are influenced not only by characteristics of the organization but also by characteristics of the job, such as location, supportive work environment, salary, or advancement opportunities (Cable & Judge, 1994; Chapman et al., 2005; Turban, Forret, & Hendrickson, 1998). For example Turban et al. (1998) found that job characteristics—such as perceptions of potential coworkers and whether the work was challenging and interesting—were positively related to applicant attraction. Similarly, Chapman et al. (2005) found that salary and the combination of compensation and advancement were positively related to applicant attraction, although to a lesser extent than job-organizational characteristics (e.g., supportive work environment). Interestingly, research also indicates that work-life benefits of the job—such as flexible work schedules and dependent care assistance—were positively related to job pursuit intentions (Casper & Buffardi, 2004).

RECRUITMENT PROCESSES

Although job and organizational characteristics are probably the most investigated predictors, scholars have also examined the influence that recruitment processes have on applicants' intentions to pursue employment with the organization. Indeed, applicants might have initial positive perceptions of both the job and the organization but have different perceptions after experiencing the organization's recruitment processes. For example, when organizations take too long (i.e., recruitment delays) to respond to applicants following an interview or site visit, applicants are less likely to be interested in the employer (Becker, Connolly, & Slaughter, 2010; Rynes, Bretz, & Gerhart, 1991). Similarly, interview and site visit characteristics (Macan & Dipboye, 1990; Stevens, 1998; Turban, Campion, & Eyring, 1995) influence perceptions of the job and applicant attraction to the firm. Recruiters make a decision about whether to focus the interview more on evaluating applicants (a selection focus) or selling the firm to the employer (a recruitment focus) or both (Barber, Hollenbeck, Tower & Phillips, 1994; Turban & Dougherty,

1992). Evidence suggests that the interview focus influences perceptions of the organization, and although results are mixed, some evidence indicates that when interviews were high on both recruitment and selection, more applicants remained in the pool (Barber et al., 1994). Research has also examined the influence of realistic job previews on post-hire outcomes such as turnover (Breaugh, 2010; Earnest, Allen, & Landis, 2011). Specifically, realistic job previews increase the degree to which applicants perceive the job and the recruiting organization as trustworthy and honest and reduce future turnover. Thus recruitment processes influence applicants' perceptions of the employer and attraction to the employer. We also expect that an employer's recruitment processes may impact applicants' subsequent job search intensity, as described below.

RECRUITER BEHAVIORS

Another category of predictors, recruiter behaviors, is more individually oriented than the three previous ones. Evidence indicates that recruiter behaviors are related to job and organizational characteristics and to applicant attraction to the firm as an employer (Chapman et al., 2005; Harris & Fink, 1987). When recruiters are seen as more personable, competent, and informative, applicants tend to be more attracted to the firm (Chapman et al., 2005). Specifically, recruiter behaviors are thought to provide applicants with insight into what it would be like to be an employee in the firm (Rynes et al, 1991); thus these behaviors influence both perceptions of and attraction to the firm. For example, a warm and personable recruiter is more likely to indicate a warm working environment than a recruiter who is low in warmth and congeniality. In their meta-analysis, Chapman et al. (2005) found that recruiter behaviors influenced applicant attraction by influencing perceptions of job and organizational characteristics.

OTHER PREDICTORS OF APPLICANT ATTRACTION AND JOB CHOICE

A final category encompasses predictors that span across different dimensions of the recruitment literature: fit perceptions, hiring expectancies, and perceived alternatives. Considerable evidence indicates that perceptions of person-job and person-organization fit positively influence applicant attraction to a firm as well as job choice decisions (Cable & Judge, 1996; Chapman et al., 2005; Judge & Cable, 1997). Additionally, hiring expectancies tend to be positively related to application attraction (Barber,

1998; Chapman et al., 2005; Rynes, 1991; Rynes & Lawler, 1983). Specifically, when job applicants expect to be made an offer by an organization, they are more likely to be attracted to the organization as an employer and to accept an offer if they are to receive one. Interestingly, studies examining the relationship between perceived alternatives and various applicant attraction outcomes provided mixed findings (Barber, 1998; Chapman et al., 2005). For example, meta-analytic results suggested that perceived alternatives had a positive relationship with job-organization attraction and a negative relationship with acceptance intentions, although in both cases there was significant heterogeneity of the effect sizes, indicating moderation and the need for future research (Chapman, et al., 2005).

To summarize, a wide range of predictors of applicant attraction and job choice have been examined in the literature, ranging from organization and job characteristics to recruiter behaviors. We classified these predictors into three organization-level categories, one individual-level category, and one category of other predictors. We now discuss predictors of job search behaviors and outcomes, which—in contrast with the recruitment literature—are for the most part individual-level variables.

Job Search Literature Overview

The job search process involves various activities engaged in by job seekers to learn about and pursue job openings with the ultimate goal of generating job offers (Boswell, Zimmerman, & Swider, 2012). The job search process is considered a dynamic, self-regulated process in which job seekers attempt to regulate their motivations and emotions as they search for suitable employment (Boswell et al., 2012; Kanfer, Wanberg, & Kantrowitz, 2001; Wanberg, Zhu, & Van Hooft, 2010). The key outcomes examined by job search researchers are job search behaviors and the employment outcomes of whether the seeker received an offer, how many job offers were received, and the duration of the job search, although some research has also measured employment quality indicators, such as employee attitudes (Boswell & Gardner, this volume; Saks, this volume; Saks & Ashforth, 2002; Virick & McKee-Ryan, this volume). Job search behavior[1] is typically operationalized by assessing the *intensity* (frequency) with which job seekers engage in job search activities, such as revising the résumé, completing applications, or looking at the overall *effort* exhibited by the job seeker (Blau, 1994; Boswell et al., 2012; Saks & Ashforth, 2002; Van Hoye, this volume).

The job search literature has consistently been examined from an individual, self-regulated, motivational perspective (Kanfer et al., 2001). Taking such an approach has led job search scholars to predominantly examine two relatively broad categories of predictors of job search behaviors and outcomes: individual differences (e.g., personality) and self-regulatory and motivational variables (e.g., metacognitive strategies, procrastination, emotion, and motivation control). We should note, however, that these categories are not mutually exclusive or exhaustive. For example, self-efficacy, which is discussed below, can be conceptualized as a relatively stable individual difference or as a self-regulatory/motivational variable. Furthermore, other variables—such as employment commitment, financial need, and social support—although they are also important predictors of job search behaviors and outcomes, do not fit into either of these broad categories (Kanfer et al., 2001).

Predictors of Job Search Behaviors and Outcomes

INDIVIDUAL DIFFERENCES

Because job seekers approach the job search process differently, scholars have examined the role of personality characteristics in influencing job search behaviors and outcomes (Boudreau, Boswell, Judge, & Bretz, 2001; Brown, Cober, Kane, Levy, & Shalhoop, 2006; Caldwell & Burger, 1998; Saks, 2006; Tay, Ang, & Van Dyne, 2006; Turban, Stevens, & Lee, 2009). In general, considerable evidence indicates that personality characteristics impact the way job seekers behave throughout the process as well as the job search outcomes they receive. For example, conscientiousness is positively related to job search effort (Brown et al., 2006), the number of interviews, interview success, academic achievement, leadership experience (Tay et al., 2006) and job offers (Turban et al., 2009). Furthermore, extraversion is positively related to interview success (Tay et al., 2006), whereas neuroticism is positively related to job search activity among employed managers (Boudreau et al., 2001). Brown et al. (2006) also found that having a proactive personality positively influences job search success, such that more proactive job seekers are more successful in their search for employment.

In addition to personality traits, scholars have also examined the role of affect in job search (Côté, Saks, & Zikic, 2006; Crossley & Stanton, 2005;

Turban et al., 2009). Evidence indicates that positive emotions are positively related to second interviews and job offers (Turban et al., 2009) and that trait positive affectivity is positively related to job search intensity and motivation control (Côté et al., 2006; Turban, Lee, da Motta Veiga, Haggard, & Wu, 2013) and negatively to procrastination (Turban et al., 2013). Although negative affect has been included in some of these job search studies, few studies have actually found negative affect to be related to job search behaviors and outcomes (Côté et al., 2006; Crossley & Stanton, 2005). Nonetheless, Crossley and Stanton (2005) found that trait negative affectivity was negatively related to interview quality and job offers.

Finally, another individual difference, self-efficacy, also plays an important role in the job search process. Indeed, considerable evidence indicates that job seekers with a greater belief in their ability (e.g., self-efficacy) to find a job reported higher job search intensity (Côté et al., 2006; Crossley & Stanton, 2005; Ellis & Taylor, 1983; Van Hooft, Born, Taris, Van der Flier, & Blonk, 2004). Similarly, individuals with higher interviewing self-efficacy, defined as beliefs about one's interviewing capabilities, had greater interview success than individuals with lower interviewing self-efficacy (Tay et al., 2006).

SELF-REGULATORY AND MOTIVATIONAL VARIABLES

The job search process is widely accepted to be a self-regulated process, such that job seekers need to regulate their behaviors and emotions to stay motivated as they strive toward their goal of finding a job (Kanfer et al., 2001; Wanberg et al., 2010). Scholars have examined whether and how self-regulatory variables influence job search behaviors and outcomes (Creed, King, Hood, & McKenzie et al., 2009; Turban et al., 2009, 2013; Wanberg et al., 1999, 2012). For example, Turban et al. (2009) found that metacognitive activities (i.e., self-regulation activities that involve setting goals, developing plans, etc.) mediated the relationships between personality traits (i.e., extraversion and conscientiousness) and job search outcomes. Similarly, Creed et al. (2009) found that self-regulatory variables (i.e., emotion control and work commitment) mediated the relationship between job seekers' goal orientation and their job search intensity. Finally, Turban et al. (2013) found that the self-regulatory variable of procrastination mediated the relationship between positive affectivity and job search outcome.

Because job seekers need to self-motivate throughout the search process (Kanfer et al., 2001: Wanberg et al., 2010), scholars have also examined the influence that motivational variables have on job search behaviors and outcomes (Creed et al., 2009; Van Hooft & Noordzij, 2009; Van Hoye & Saks, 2009; Wanberg et al., 2012). For example, research has examined the role of motivation control in the job search (Creed et al. 2009; Turban et al., 2013; Wanberg et al., 1999, 2012). Furthermore, research has examined goal orientations and goal-directed behaviors in job search. Specifically, Creed et al. (2009) showed that learning goal orientation was positively related to job search intensity. Van Hoye and Saks (2008) found that different job search goals (e.g., finding a new job, staying aware of job alternatives) were related to different job search behaviors (e.g., looking at job ads, visiting job sites).

To summarize, we categorized job search predictors into individual differences and self-regulatory and motivational variables. Evidence indicates that variables from each of these categories influence job search behaviors and outcomes. Further, some evidence also indicates that individual differences influence job search behaviors and outcomes through self-regulatory and motivational strategies (Creed et al., 2009; Kanfer et al., 2001; Turban et al., 2009, 2013).

Integrating Recruitment and Job Search

As described above and summarized in Table 18.1, there are similarities and differences in the recruitment and job search literatures. A major difference between recruitment and job search scholars is the focus, or level of analysis. Recruitment scholars typically examine intentions and behaviors toward a specific organization, whereas job search researchers typically examine

Table 18.1 Similarities and Differences Between Recruitment and Job Search

	Recruitment	Job Search
Level of Analysis	Organizational	Individual
Main Objective	Job choice	Job offers
Proximal outcomes, predictor categories	Applicant attraction, job pursuit, job pursuit intentions, acceptance intentions Organizational characteristics; job characteristics; recruitment processes; recruiter behaviors; other predictors	Job search behaviors (and intensity) interviews, site visits: Individual differences; self-regulatory and motivational variables
Predictors	Organization reputation, brand equity, and organization website; job characteristics (e.g., location), supportive work environment, salary, and work-life benefits; interview characteristics (i.e., focus, length, structure) and recruitment delays; recruiter behaviors; fit perceptions, hiring expectancies, perceived alternatives	Job seekers' individual differences (e.g., personality, affect, self-efficacy) motivation and procrastination, and metacognitive activities commitment, financial need social support
Integrating recruitment and job search	Job seekers are involved in multiple recruitment processes for different jobs and different organizations at the same time, While recruitment research has mostly examined factors related to organizations, job search research has mostly been driven by individual factors related to job seekers	
Future research	Taking a multilevel approach (e.g., level 1, job seekers; level 2, organizations), future research could examine the influence of recruiter behaviors, recruitment processes, job characteristics, and organization characteristics on job search behaviors and outcomes	Future research could examine the role that job search behaviors and intensity, such as how the amount of time researching an organization before a visit might influence recruiter behaviors and/or the recruitment process

job search behaviors across various organizations. The outcomes are similar yet different. Recruitment scholars are most interested in job choice, typically defined as whether the applicant accepts a job offer from an employer, whereas job search scholars frequently focus on the number of job offers (choices) obtained. Thus the practical question driving much recruitment research is how to attract more qualified individuals into the applicant pool, whereas the practical question driving much job search research is how job seekers obtain employment, preferably high-quality employment. Nonetheless, both organizations and individuals have similar goals: They both want a qualified applicant filling an open position. Another area of overlap yet distinctiveness is that whereas recruitment scholars examine sources of applicants, job search scholars examine methods of finding jobs. We discuss some of the similarities and differences in these literatures before describing theoretical frameworks that we believe can be useful in integrating these research streams.

Focusing on outcomes, perhaps the "ultimate" outcome of the recruitment literature is actual *job choice*, which is whether a highly qualified applicant accepts the job offer from the organization (Barber, 1998; Chapman et al., 2005).[2] Notably, however, although recruitment scholars are interested in job choice, only a few studies have actually measured job choice (Chapman et al., 2005). Instead, researchers typically measure proximal indicators of job choice. Perhaps the most popular outcome variable is applicant attraction to the firm as an employer, which is a global evaluation of potential employers (Chapman et al., 2005). Other outcome variables include *job pursuit* and *job pursuit intentions*, which are conceptualized as an applicant's activities or intentions to pursue a job and continue in the applicant pool by attending an interview or site visit. Recruitment scholars have also examined *acceptance intentions*, or the likelihood that an applicant would accept a job offer, when actual job choice information cannot be collected (Barber, 1998; Chapman et al., 2005). In general, as might be expected, these indicators of applicant attraction tend to be relatively strongly correlated (Chapman et al., 2005). Furthermore, although there is limited evidence, acceptance intentions tend to be correlated with job choice (e.g., Chapman et al., 2005; Turban et al., 1995). To summarize, scholars interested in recruitment attempt to predict, understand, and explain the job choice of applicants, although proximal indicators of job choice are often examined.

Job search scholars are interested in understanding what leads job seekers to quickly find excellent job offers. Thus the focus is on understanding attributes and processes that lead to securing one or more job offers from good employers in a timely manner. Job search scholars have examined job search behaviors (job search intensity) and differentiated between preparatory and active job search behaviors (Blau, 1994). *Preparatory job search behaviors* include activities utilized to prepare for and learn about potential job opportunities, such as preparing or revising one's résumé, whereas *active job search behaviors* occur after job seekers have started their search—for example, by sending out résumés to potential employers or contacting them. Although researchers have combined preparatory and active job search behaviors and added or dropped items to make the scale more relevant (Saks; 2006; Saks & Ashforth, 2002), job search behavior (intensity) is perhaps the most important proximal predictor of job search outcomes (Kanfer et al., 2001).

Another example of how recruitment and job search scholars have examined similar concepts, although with a different focus and different labels, is the concept of job pursuit behavior. Recruitment scholars have conceptualized job pursuit behavior as an applicant's decision to apply for a job and to attend an interview or a site visit (Jaidi et al., 2011; Schreurs et al., 2009). Job search scholars, however, have conceptualized résumés submitted, interviews, and site visits attended as job search outcomes (Turban et al., 2009).

Similarly, whereas recruitment researchers have examined the recruitment sources through which organizations attract and find applicants (e.g., Breaugh & Starke, 2000), the job search literature has examined methods through which job seekers find and apply for jobs (e.g., Barber et al., 1994; Van Hoye, this volume; Van Hoye & Saks, 2008). For example, recruitment sources are defined as sources used by employers to find qualified applicants and are frequently categorized as internal (i.e., employee referral) and external sources (i.e., direct applications). In contrast, job search methods are defined as sources used by applicants to find jobs and are frequently categorized as formal (e.g., public employment agencies) and informal sources (e.g., friends or relatives) (Barber et al., 1994). Thus both literatures have examined sources through which both organizations and applicants look for each other, although they have a different focus and use somewhat different conceptualizations.

To summarize, although the recruitment and job search literatures have developed relatively independently, we propose that they may be fruitfully integrated; this is a major goal of our chapter. The job search literature typically focuses on behaviors that an applicant engages in, across various organizations, to obtain a job offer. Such behaviors, within a specific organization, are relevant to recruitment researchers who typically examine behaviors and attitudes of multiple applicants within an organization. Stated differently, job search research typically examines behaviors within-subjects and across organizations, whereas recruitment research typically examines behaviors across various subjects within an organization. Thus, applicants and organizations are nested within each other as an applicant has engaged in job search behaviors with multiple organizations, and organizations have multiple applicants. Note, however, that applicants may interact differently with different organizations and an organization may interact differently with different applicants. Furthermore, both applicants and organizations can have multiple interactions over time, and, importantly, actions of one party are thought to influence actions of the other party. For example, recruitment practices may influence job search behaviors toward that organization, such that recruitment delays lead job seekers to increase the intensity of their search as they look for alternative opportunities. In a recent qualitative study, Wanberg et al. (2012) found that job seekers who experienced negative experiences with recruiting organizations (e.g., lack of professionalism) developed negative attitudes toward those organizations. Similarly, job search behaviors may influence organizational practices toward the applicant, such that an applicant who has researched the organization and is thus more prepared may receive more follow-up attention from that organization. Clearly such reciprocal interactions, which unfold over time, are complex, and research is only now beginning to investigate that complexity.

Along such lines, we speculate that advances in multilevel modeling (i.e., hierarchical-level modeling) might help to advance both job search and recruitment literatures and might even help to integrate both literatures. Multilevel modeling techniques allow researchers to examine variance within subjects (applicant or organizations) over time as well as variance at different levels of analysis (at the level of the individual, the organization, or the economy). As such, multilevel modeling could be useful to examining how applicants vary over time (level 1), are different from each other (level 2), and how they vary depending on the organization (i.e., variance between organizations – level 3). We should note that job search and recruitment researchers have started using multilevel modeling to examine how recruitment activities attract applicants and how job seekers search for jobs (Collins & Stevens, 2002; Jaidi et al., 2011; Song, Uy, Zhang, & Shi, 2009; Wanberg et al., 2010, 2012). For example, using a daily diary study, Song et al. (2009) found that job seekers who experienced increased distress utilized more job search effort the following day. Interestingly, Collins and Stevens (2002) and Jaidi et al. (2011) also took a multilevel approach to examine the role of recruitment-related sources and activities on recruitment outcomes. Specifically the authors collected information from the applications about the various organizations they were interested in, allowing the examination of recruitment activities across applicants and organizations.

We suggest that multilevel modeling might be useful for understanding applicant attraction, as the recruitment literature has yet to examine how recruitment processes and the pool of applicants change over time. Further, it could be interesting to examine, from both sides (the applicant and the recruiting organization), how job search and recruitment processes unfold over time, across organizations (for job seekers), and between job seekers (for organizations). We now describe what we think are useful theoretical perspectives for integrating the recruitment and job search literatures.

Theoretical Approaches to Recruitment and Job Search

We now describe three theories that provide a framework which can help to integrate recruitment and job search in examining predictors of job search and recruitment processes. Although scholars have used various theories to examine recruitment and job search, we review only the following three theories, which we believe can help (further) integrate recruitment and job search research: signaling theory (Spence, 1973), expectancy theory (Vroom, 1964), and the theory of planned behavior (Ajzen, 1991). Throughout this section, we review these theories, how they have been used in each area, and how they could be used to integrate recruitment and job search approaches.

Signaling Theory

Signaling theory has been widely used in recruitment research but has not been used much if at all, to understand job search behaviors. As originally articulated by Spence (1973), signaling theory proposes that in situations of information asymmetry in which individuals want to make decisions, they will interpret available information as providing signals about what is unknown (for a review of signaling theory, see Connelly et al., 2011). Signaling theory has been utilized by recruitment scholars, who note that because applicants do not have complete information about what it would be like to be an employee of an organization, they interpret available information as signal(s) about the job and working conditions in the organization (Rynes, 1991). For example, job seekers are theorized to use firm reputation as a signal about job attributes and working conditions in the organization (Turban & Cable, 2003). More broadly, applicants are likely to interpret recruitment activities as providing signals about what it would be like to be an employee of the firm (Breaugh, 1992; Rynes, 1991; Turban, 2001). For example, recruitment behaviors may be interpreted such that an unfriendly recruiter may signal an unfriendly work environment (Rynes, Heneman, & Schwab, 1980; Taylor & Bergmann, 1987; Wanberg et al., 2012). Additionally, evidence indicates that applicants interpret recruitment delays as a signal of the organization's interest in them as potential employees (Becker et al., 2010; Rynes et al., 1991). What is important to highlight is that the organization may not be aware of how the applicant is interpreting information; thus organizations might be sending the wrong signal to potential applicants. In any case, signaling theory has been used to examine how various predictors—such as organizational reputation, recruiter behaviors, and recruitment delays—influence applicant perceptions of the firm as an employer (Cable & Turban, 2001; Collins, 2007; Turban, 2001; Turban & Cable, 2003).

In their review of the literature utilizing signaling theory, Connelly et al. (2011) proposed a "signaling time line" in which a signaler sends a signal to a receiver who then observes and interprets the signal and subsequently provides the signaler with feedback. We theorize, focusing on the dyad of an applicant and a potential employer, that both parties are sending signals and interpreting information from the other party as a signal. As noted above, researchers theorize that applicants interpret recruitment activities as providing signals about the working conditions in the organization. Thus, for example, firm reputation and recruiter behaviors during the interview have been conceptualized as

providing signals that influence potential applicants' perceptions of working conditions in the organization and their attraction to the organization as an employer. However, we found no research that has specifically examined whether and how applicants' job search behaviors vary depending on an organization's signals. For example, does a firm's reputation, which might be interpreted as a signal of selectivity, influence how applicants contact the firm? One might expect that if applicants perceive firms with positive reputations as more selective, they might invest more time and energy to obtain employment with such firms. Alternatively, applicants might also use specific job search methods, such as networking or internships, to increase their chances of obtaining a job at such high reputation organizations. We expect that applicant self-efficacy might moderate relationships between firm reputation and job search behaviors, such that applicants with low self-efficacy might not bother to apply to firms with excellent reputations because they do not think that they have a chance of getting a job with such firms. Note that we are attempting to extend signaling theory by examining how signals from a potential employer influence job search behaviors of applicants.

Another interesting extension of signaling theory would be to examine signals sent by job seekers to recruiting organizations, keeping in mind that applicants could be sending signals in an intentional and unintentional manner. Evidence indicates that applicants are attempting to manage the impressions that they leave with organizational representatives in an attempt to obtain a job offer (Barrick, Shaffer, & DeGrassi, 2009). For example, nonverbal behaviors during the interview may be interpreted by the interviewer as providing information about the applicant's credibility. Thus, one may consider self-presentation skills during the job search process as an attempt by the applicant to intentionally manage the signals that are communicated to potential employers. Importantly, meta-analytic results indicate that such self-presentation tactics do influence interviewer ratings, albeit more strongly in unstructured versus structured interviews (Barrick et al., 2009). Thus, applicants can influence the signals that are sent to interviewers; some evidence suggests that the applicant's handshake influences interviewer ratings of the applicant (Stewart, Dustin, Barrick, & Darnold, 2008). Apparently a quality handshake—which is measured by grip, strength, duration, vigor, and eye contact—provides a signal about the applicant's interpersonal skills.

Applicants may also be sending signals to employers that are less intentional than the self-presentation skills discussed above. For example, organizations may interpret information that applicants "publish" on social networking sites (e.g., LinkedIn, Facebook, and Twitter) as signals regarding the applicant's personality, ability, and possible fit with the organization. Of course, applicants might also intentionally attempt to signal attributes through social networking sites. For example, we know students who have joined LinkedIn with the specific purpose of attempting to signal professionalism to potential employers; we are not sure, however, whether those same students have thought about what is being signaled by their Facebook profile.

As noted above, the recruitment literature has focused predominantly on signals sent by the organization (or its recruiters), whereas the job search literature has paid little attention to examining whether and how signals sent either by the organization or by the job seekers influence job search behaviors and outcomes. Future research could examine the role of signals not only sent by the organization but also sent by job seekers (intentionally or not). For example, as suggested earlier, perhaps signals sent by job seekers through social networking sites (e.g., Facebook or LinkedIn) influence follow-up attention from employers. Additionally, research could investigate whether job seekers spend more time on social networking sites if they believe that recruiters pay attention to what they communicate through those sites, and, importantly, if they believe that such impression management activities lead to more success in the job search.

Expectancy Theory

As noted by Latham and Pinder (2005) there are various subtheories under the umbrella term *expectancy theory*, although the various expectancy theories draw from Vroom (1964; see also Feather, this volume). In general, expectancy theory is a cognitive theory proposing that individuals will choose actions that they believe will maximize their positive outcomes (pleasure) and minimize their negative ones (pain). Broadly speaking, individuals will choose actions they expect are most likely to lead to valued outcomes. As noted by Rynes (1991) in her review of the literature, firms engage in various recruitment activities in an attempt to enhance the perceived valence of a job with the firm. For example, firms create recruitment advertisements and websites and train recruiters in an attempt to

influence potential applicants' perceptions of the job and the organization.

In the recruitment literature, expectancy theory has been used to examine the concept of *hiring expectancies*, or job seekers' perceptions of the likelihood of receiving a job offer. More specifically, scholars have theorized, based on expectancy theory (Vroom, 1964), that applicants are more likely to pursue positions when they believe they have a higher likelihood of obtaining the position (i.e., higher hiring expectancies). The theory has received some support as meta-analytic results indicated that hiring expectancies were related positively to job pursuit intentions, acceptance intentions, and job choice (Chapman et al., 2005). Thus, results indicate that applicants are more attracted to and more likely to pursue employment with firms that they expect are more likely to hire them; stated differently, applicants are less likely to pursue employment with firms when they expect the firm is not likely to hire them. Importantly, evidence suggests that recruitment activities and recruiter behaviors can influence hiring expectancies and thereby have an influence on recruitment outcomes (Rynes, 1991; Chapman et al., 2005). As noted earlier, applicants tend to interpret longer recruitment delays as a signal that the firm is not interested in them; thus recruitment delays lead to lower hiring expectancies.

Several studies have also examined the role of expectancy theory in the job search process (e.g., Feather, 1990, 1992; Feather & Davenport, 1981; Feather & O'Brien, 1987; Van Hooft & Crossley, 2008; see also Feather, this volume). Consistent with expectancy theory predictions, job seekers tend to exert greater effort toward jobs that have higher valence (Feather, 1990, 1992). The effects of expectancy on job search effort are somewhat mixed. Feather and Davenport (1981) found that unemployed job seekers' expectancy to get a job was positively related to their job search effort. In contrast, however, Feather and O'Brien (1987) found that job seekers with stronger hiring expectancies submitted fewer job applications, which is interesting, as it suggests that greater expectancies lead to lower job search effort, in contrast to expectancy theory predictions. Thus the evidence suggests that job seekers exert greater effort to pursue jobs that are highly valued. The role of expectancy is less clear, however. It should be noted, however, that expectancy theory is a within-subjects theory (i.e., focusing on processes within subjects) whereas much of the research has adopted a between-subjects approach.

Future research might thus examine the role of hiring expectancies within subjects over time. For example, Feather and O'Brien (1987) found that subjects with greater hiring expectancies submitted fewer job applications. Such results are consistent with control theory (Carver & Scheier, 1981, 1982), which proposes that individuals will reduce effort if they perceive they are making good progress toward goal achievement. More broadly, future research could test the tenets of expectancy theory (i.e., expectancy, valence, and instrumentality) and examine relations of expectancy with effort throughout the job search process to determine whether and when expectancy is positively or negatively related with job search effort. We expect that the amount of time and energy spent on the job search for a particular position will be influenced by the applicant's expectancy beliefs and also by the extent to which the applicant's expectancy beliefs change during the process.

Theory of Planned Behavior

An extension of the theory of reasoned action (Fishbein & Ajzen, 1975), the theory of planned behavior (Ajzen, 1991) suggests that most conscious human behavior can be predicted by intentions, although individuals need to perceive that they control their behaviors. Ajzen (1991) further suggested that the theory of planned behavior explains how attitudes and perceptions predict human behavior. Stated differently, the theory of planned behavior assumes that human behavior (e.g., job search behavior) is explained, in large part, by attitudes and perceptions that individuals hold about some event or process. In the context of job search, the theory of planned behavior would predict that job seekers' intentions to apply or look for a job will influence their actual job search behaviors. Whether they perceive that they control their behaviors or not is theorized to be related to their belief in their job-seeking ability (i.e., job search self-efficacy). The theory of planned behavior also suggests that perceived behavioral control is likely to influence job search behaviors both indirectly (through job search intentions) and directly (Ajzen, 1991, Van Hooft et al., 2004).

The theory of planned behavior has been applied to various contexts and types of behaviors, such as choosing a career (Sutton, 1998), job search behaviors (Song, Wanberg, Niu, & Xie, 2006; Van Hooft et al., 2004; see also Van Hooft, this volume), and employee turnover (Van Breukelen, Van der Vlist, & Steensma, 2004). Van Hooft et al. (2004) used the theory of planned behavior to investigate predictors of job search intentions and behaviors among employed and unemployed people. They found that job search attitudes influenced job search intentions, which in turn influenced job search behaviors, as suggested by the theory of planned behavior.

Although Van Hooft et al. (2004) examined the role of the theory of planned behavior from a job search perspective, the theory has also received some attention in the recruitment literature (Arnold et al., 2006; Jaidi et al., 2011; Schreurs et al., 2009; Van Hooft, Born, Taris, & Van der Flier, 2006). For example, Schreurs et al. (2009) proposed and found support for a model in which perceived behavioral control and job pursuit attitudes predicted job pursuit intentions, which in turn predicted job pursuit behaviors. Jaidi et al. (2011) extended that model by also examining actual job choice; they also found support for their model and thus for the theory of planned behavior. Interestingly, these studies, although framed as recruitment studies, examined processes that are very similar to the job search process.

Although evidence seems to indicate that the theory of planned behavior is helpful in explaining job pursuit attitudes, intentions, and actual behaviors, we believe that future research could use the theory of planned behavior to incorporate organizational predictors, such as organizational attractiveness. Indeed, it would be interesting to use individual and organizational mechanisms to understand whether job seekers' attitudes and intentions change throughout the process and also whether they vary depending on the organization that is recruiting them. For example, future research could examine whether job pursuit attitudes and intentions, which lead to job pursuit and search behaviors, change once applicants have contact with an organization. Indeed, it could be interesting to examine to what extent a positive or negative experience with an interviewer influences one's general job pursuit attitudes and intentions. To achieve such research goals, collecting multiple measures over time and using multilevel modeling is necessary. Such an approach would allow scholars to understand how job search and recruitment processes unfold over time, across organizations (for job seekers), and between job seekers (for organizations).

Finally, recruitment has been viewed as a multiple-hurdle process in which organizations (attempt to) attract a large pool of qualified applicants and narrow down the pool to a smaller set of "finalists" (Carlson et al., 2002; Dineen & Soltis, 2010). Similarly, scholars have proposed that job seekers change their approach during the search (Barber et al., 1994; Song, Sun, & Li, this volume). For example, job seekers may change their job search behaviors over time either because they move to a different stage of the search process, because they learn how to master the process, or because of emotional responses during the search process. Barber et al. (1994) found support for the sequential model of change, indicating that job seekers change their behaviors because they move to a different stage of their process (e.g., from identifying a pool of potential jobs to narrowing down to a few jobs). Using a multilevel perspective, researchers could examine whether changes in job search processes are related to changes in a firm's recruitment processes. Specifically, researchers could collect data from both organizations and job seekers at different stages to examine how both job search and recruitment processes simultaneously unfold over time.

Directions for Future Research

The recruitment process and the job search process occur simultaneously; firms are attempting to attract qualified applicants and applicants are searching for potential employment opportunities. Although these processes occur simultaneously, the research areas have developed relatively independently. A major goal of our chapter is to highlight areas of overlap and to suggest where insights from one literature can inform the other. In this section, based in part on our review of the literatures and our attempts at integrating them, we describe some specific areas that we think would benefit from future research.

Considerable evidence indicates that in interpersonal interactions people have a tendency to behave in a manner that leads to confirmation of their prior beliefs (Snyder & Swann, 1978; Swann, 2011). Similarly, evidence indicates that interviewers' preinterview impressions influence how they conduct the interview in terms of questioning strategies and how they interact with the applicant (Dipboye, 1982, 1992; Dougherty, Turban, & Callender, 1994; Macan & Dipboye, 1990). More specifically, interviewers engage in confirmatory questioning in order to confirm their preinterview impressions (Binning, Goldstein, Garcia, Harding, & Scattaregia, 1988). For example, interviewers with more positive first impressions were more likely to sell the company and job to applicants (Dougherty et al., 1994).

In his model of self-fulfilling prophecy in employment interviews, Dipboye (1982, 1992) suggested that applicants may respond in a manner consistent with interviewers' expectations and may thereby fulfill the prophecy. Note, however, that a confirmatory questioning strategy is different from a self-fulfilling prophecy; a confirmatory questioning strategy can become a self-fulfilling prophecy when the applicant behaves in a manner to confirm the interviewer's initial impressions although such applicant behavior would not have occurred without the confirmatory questioning strategy. Although evidence is more supportive of the confirmatory questioning strategy effect than the self-fulfilling prophecy effect, evidence does suggest that interviewers' first impressions were related to applicants' communication style and the applicants' rapport with the interviewer (Dougherty et al., 1994). Specifically, Dougherty et al. (1994) found that interviewers' preinterview ratings of the applicant were related positively to ratings—from coders who listened to the actual audiotaped selection interviews—of how well applicants communicated their strengths to the interviewer and their rapport with the interviewer. Additional analyses indicated that the applicant's interviewer behaviors (i.e., communication style and rapport) were related to the interviewer's behaviors of positive regard during the interview. Thus, to summarize, evidence indicates that interviewer's preinterview impressions influence how applicants behave and perform during the interview, which could influence applicants' subsequent employment outcomes, such as receiving a job offer.

Although research has focused on how *interviewers'* preinterview impressions influence how they behave in the interview, we believe that *applicants'* preinterview impressions may influence interview outcomes also. For example, applicants' preinterview impressions may influence their preinterview behavior and thereby influence interview behaviors and outcomes. Evidence suggests that applicants are more attracted to firms when they have greater hiring expectancies for such firms (Chapman et al., 2005). If applicants engage in more company research for firms with greater hiring expectancies, then the applicants may be able to perform better during the interview, resulting in more positive employment outcomes. More broadly, we are suggesting that what have been considered "recruitment" variables may influence applicants' preinterview behaviors, which can then have an impact on the applicants' job search success. As another example, evidence indicates that company reputation influences applicant attitudes and behaviors toward the firm (Cable & Turban, 2001; Collins & Stevens, 2002; Collins, 2007; Turban & Cable, 2003). In particular, evidence indicates that companies with more positive reputations attracted more and higher-quality applicants (Turban & Cable, 2003). If those higher-quality applicants engaged in more preparation for the initial interviews we expect that the applicants would perform better during the interview. Future research might examine whether and how firm reputation influences applicants' job search behavior, and in particular the moderating effect of job search self-efficacy. In particular, one might expect that applicants with greater job search self-efficacy engage in higher quality job search preparations for firms with excellent reputations than applicants with less self-efficacy, who probably perceive they have a lower likelihood of receiving a job offer from a firm with an excellent reputation.

Reciprocal Processes in Interviews

We expect that applicants and organizational recruiters influence each other throughout the job search/recruitment process, although it seems likely that the reciprocal effects will be strongest in interviews. First, considerable evidence indicates recruiter behaviors influence recruitment outcomes, such as applicant attraction and job search intentions (Chapman et al., 2005). In particular, when recruiters were seen as personable and showed interest in the applicant, applicants reported greater attraction to the firm (e.g., Harris & Fink, 1987; Turban & Dougherty, 1992). Furthermore, as discussed above, some evidence indicates that recruiter behaviors can influence applicant behaviors (Dougherty et al., 1994). Thus evidence supports the conclusion that recruiters can influence applicant behaviors and attraction outcomes.

We theorize that applicants also can (and do) influence the reactions and behaviors of organizational representatives. In particular, emotional contagion theory suggests that individuals have a tendency to experience emotions that are similar to and influenced by those of others (Barsade, 2002; Kelly & Barsade, 2001). For example, controlling for initial interviews, evidence indicates that applicants' positive emotions have a positive influence on the success of obtaining second interviews (Burger & Caldwell, 2000; Turban et al., 2009). Such results led Turban et al. (2009) to suggest that applicants' positive emotions during the interview led to more favorable evaluations in the interviews because of contagion effects. Note, however, that these studies did not measure applicant or recruiter behaviors. Rather, emotions were measured and the authors proposed emotional contagion theoretical processes may have occurred.

More broadly, research might examine whether and how applicant personality characteristics influence recruiter behaviors and outcomes. In an interesting study examining customer and service provider interactions in a fast food restaurant, customer personality traits influenced displays of positive emotions by the service provider in a very brief interaction (Tan, Foo, & Kwek, 2004). Notably, service providers displayed more positive emotions to customers who were high on agreeableness and low on negative affectivity; furthermore the display of positive emotions by the service provider resulted in increased customer satisfaction. Although Tan et al. (2004) did not measure customer behaviors, presumably customers with different personality characteristics behaved differently to the service provider, which impacted the positive emotions displayed by the service provider. Note that the customer-service provider interaction is typically "scripted" and relatively short; thus the evidence provides additional support indicating that "thin slices of behavior" can predict important outcomes (Ambady & Rosenthal, 1992, 1993). By extension, research might examine how applicant personality characteristics influence recruiter behaviors, which then, presumably, influence recruitment outcomes. We believe that an employment interview is typically much longer and much less scripted than a customer-service provider interaction.

In our review of the job search and recruitment literatures we were struck by the finding that numerous studies have examined the role of job seeker personality in predicting and explaining job search success (Brown et al., 2006; Caldwell & Burger, 1998; Tay et al., 2006; Turban et al., 2009) but that few if any studies examined whether and how applicant personality influence recruitment outcomes. We expect that this disparity resulted because many recruitment scholars are interested in how an organization's recruitment activities influence applicant reactions and behaviors. In contrast, many job search scholars are interested in what leads applicants to have a more successful job search and have thus focused on applicant attributes and behaviors. With the exception of the person–organization fit literature (Cable & Judge, 1996; Kristof-Brown, Zimmerman, & Johnson, 2005; Saks & Ashforth,

2002), which measures the fit between individual and organizational attributes, there is a noticeable dearth of research examining how applicant attributes influence recruitment outcomes. Thus, a promising area for future research is the examination of how applicant characteristics and emotions influence organizational representatives and subsequent applicant reactions. More broadly, future research that examines applicant and interviewer behaviors during the initial interview is warranted, perhaps using dyadic data analysis techniques (Kenny, Kashy, & Cook, 2006).

Scholars interested in integrating the recruitment and job search literatures may elect to utilize additional research methodologies. In particular, qualitative studies of applicants may provide additional insight into how applicants search for jobs and how potential employers' recruitment activities influence job search behaviors (e.g., Wanberg et al., 2012). Specific questions that can be addressed include whether applicants prepare differently for employers based on the firm's reputation, and whether and how applicants respond differently to potential employers depending upon the initial employment interview. Evidence indicates that interviewers may focus more heavily on attracting or selecting applicants and that the interview focus influences applicant attraction and retention in the applicant pool (Turban & Dougherty, 1992; Barber et al., 1994). To the extent that applicant attraction is related to job search activities, such as sending thank-you letters or preparing for a site visit, interview focus may influence applicants' job search behaviors. We acknowledge, however, that we are speculating about this relationship, since we know of no evidence linking applicant attraction and job search behaviors, although it seems like an important area for future research. Specifically, do applicants search differently for jobs with firms for which they have more attraction toward as a potential employer? We encourage research that simultaneously examines applicants' perceptions of and reactions to potential employers and how such perceptions influence job search activities.

A promising methodological (and theoretical) development in both the job search and recruitment literatures is the tracking of applicants multiple times during their job search/recruitment process. For example, several recent studies that have examined applicant attitudes, emotions, and behaviors daily or weekly over time have provided valuable insight into job search behaviors (e.g., Song et al., 2009; Wanberg et al., 2010, 2012). As such, it could be interesting to examine not only job search behaviors, processes, and outcomes but also recruitment processes over time. For example, by collecting multiple measures throughout the recruitment process, organizations could understand why and how applicants change their intentions and perceptions about organizations over time.

Practical Implications

In addition to theoretical and empirical implications, the integration of the job search and recruitment literatures provides practical implications that highlight the importance of understanding the interactions between both job search and recruitment processes. For example, organizations need to better understand what job seekers expect from the process, whether and how job search behaviors change dependent upon organizational recruitment activities, and what organizations can do to help compensate for negative recruitment experiences. For example, an organization with a poor reputation might be able to compensate for this by highlighting interesting and challenging jobs (i.e., job characteristics). Thus, although applicants initially are less interested in such an organization, their behaviors and pursuit intentions may change at different stages of the recruitment and job search processes if the organization can compensate for negative global reputation perceptions. More broadly, it is important for organizations to understand that applicants are involved in various recruitment processes simultaneously and that they can and will change their behaviors and pursuit intentions during their job search.

From an individual perspective, job seekers need to understand what organizations are looking for, what they expect, and how they recruit their applicants. For example, career counselors could train job seekers to understand the importance of the signals they send to recruiting organizations. Similarly, career counselors could emphasize the timeliness of their job search activities, as delayed responses to organizations may influence applicants negatively. Indeed, recruiting organizations have a pool of applicants that they contact for interviews or follow-up visits. If employers do not hear back quickly from an applicant, they assume that the applicant is not interested in them as an employer (i.e., delay signals lack of interest) and move to the next applicant. More broadly, it is important for career counselors to help job seekers understand that organizations have a pool of qualified applicants and that they can and will change their recruitment intentions and preferences during the process.

Conclusion

In this chapter, we have argued that recruitment processes of organizations and job search processes of applicants occur simultaneously. Specifically, this chapter provides ideas and suggestions to integrate recruitment and job search approaches. We reviewed categories of predictors of applicant attraction and job choice, and of job search behaviors and outcomes. We discussed how three theories (i.e., signaling, expectancy, and the theory of planned behavior) could be used to integrate job search and recruitment research. Finally, we further integrated relevant concepts that can stimulate future research examining recruitment and job search processes simultaneously rather than independently.

In conclusion, both recruitment, from an organizational perspective, and job search, from an individual applicant's perspective, occur simultaneously. We suggest that recruitment and job search are "two sides of the same coin." On one side, recruiting (or attracting) applicants is an essential human resource practice for organizations looking to recruit and select the best potential applicants. On the other side, job seekers are attracted to apply for jobs at specific organizations. Thus, as job seekers engage in aspects of the job search process, they are exposed to various recruitment processes, which may influence their subsequent job search behaviors. We suggest that, although the recruitment and job search literatures have developed somewhat independently, it may be useful to integrate such literatures in an attempt to stimulate further research. As such, we hope that this chapter will stimulates future work integrating recruitment and job search research, as these are essential areas for both applicants and organizations.

Practical Recommendations
For Organizations/Recruiters

• Understand applicant expectations in terms of recruitment activities and processes and how recruiters can compensate for some negative experience.

• Understand the importance of signals sent to applicants, such as recruitment delays, as they can influence applicant attraction, job pursuit, and job choice.

For Job Seekers/Career Counselors

• Manage the signals sent to recruiters—for example, through social networking sites (Facebook, Twitter, or LinkedIn).

• Emphasize the timeliness of job search activities, as organizations may switch to another applicant if they do not hear back from their top candidate.

• Job search and recruitment are two sides of the same coin: not only may job seekers change their preference order but recruiters may also do so.

Notes

1. presumably because job seekers report the frequency (intensity) with which they engage in certain behaviors.
2. We should acknowledge, however, that scholars could argue that post-hireoutcomes, such as job performance and turnover, may also be considered important outcomes of recruitment processes.

References

Ajzen, I. (1991). The theory of planned behavior. *Organizational Behavior and Human Decision Processes*, 50, 179–211.

Allen, D. G., Mahto, R. V., & Otondo, R. F. (2007). Web-based recruitment: effects of information, organizational brand, and attitudes toward a web site on applicant attraction. *Journal of Applied Psychology*, 92, 1696–708.

Ambady, N., & Rosenthal, R. (1992). Thin slices of expressive behavior as predictors of interpersonal consequences: A meta-analysis. *Psychological Bulletin*, 111, 256–274.

Ambady, N., & Rosenthal, R. (1993). Half a minute: Predicting teacher evaluations from thin slices of behavior and physical attractiveness. *Journal of Personality and Social Psychology*, 64, 431–441.

Arnold, J., Loan-Clarke, J., Coombs, C., Wilkinson, A., Park, J., & Preston, D. (2006). How well can the theory of planned behavior account for occupational intentions? *Journal of Vocational Behavior*, 69, 374–390.

Barber, A. E. (1998). *Recruiting employees: Individual and organizational perspectives*. Thousand Oaks, CA: Sage.

Barber, A. E. Hollenbeck, J. R., Tower, S. L., & Phillips, J. M. (1994). The effects of interview focus on recruitment effectiveness: A field experiment. *Journal of Applied Psychology*, 79, 886–896.

Barrick, M. R., Shaffer, J. A., & DeGrassi, S. W. (2009). What you see may not be what you get: Relationships among self-presentation tactics and ratings of interview and job performance. *Journal of Applied Psychology*, 94, 1394–1411.

Barsade, S. G. (2002). The ripple effect: Emotional contagion and its influence on group behavior. *Administrative Science Quarterly*, 47, 644–675.

Becker, W. J., Connolly, T., & Slaughter, J. E. (2010). The effect of job offer timing on offer acceptance, performance, and turnover. *Personnel Psychology*, 63, 223–241.

Binning, J. F., Goldstein, M. A., Garcia, M. F., & Scattaregia, J. H. (1988). Effects of pre-interview impressions on questioning strategies in same- and opposite-sex employment interviews. *Journal of Applied Psychology*, 73, 30–37.

Blau G. (1994). Testing a two-dimensional measure of job search behavior. *Organizational Behavior and Human Decision Processes*, 59, 288–312.

Boswell, W. R., Zimmerman, R. D., & Swider, B. W. (2012). Employee job search toward an understanding of search context and search objectives. *Journal of Management*, 38, 129–163.

Boudreau, J. W., Boswell, W. R., Judge, T. A., & Bretz R. D. Jr. (2001). Personality and cognitive ability as predictors of job search among employed managers. *Personnel Psychology*, 54, 25–50.

Boudreau, J. W., & Rynes, S. L. (1985). Role of recruitment in staffing utility analysis. *Journal of Applied Psychology*, 70, 354–366.

Breaugh, J. A. (1992). *Recruitment: Science and practice*. Boston, MA: PWS-Kent.

Breaugh, J. A. (2008). Employee recruitment: Current knowledge and important areas for future research. *Human Resource Management Review*, 18, 103–118.

Breaugh, J. (2010). Realistic Job Previews. In R. Watkins, & D. Leigh (Eds.), *Handbook of improving performance in the workplace*, Vol. 2: *Selecting and implementing performance interventions* (pp. 203–250). New York: Wiley.

Breaugh, J. A., & Starke, M. (2000) Research on employee recruitment: So many studies, so many remaining questions. *Journal of Management*, 26, 405–434.

Brown, D. J., Cober, R. T., Kane, K., Levy, P. E., & Shalhoop, J. (2006). Proactive personality and the successful job search: A field investigation with college graduates. *Journal of Applied Psychology*, 91, 717–726.

Burger, J. M., & Caldwell, D. F. (2000). Personality, social activities, job-search behavior and interview success: Distinguishing between PANAS trait positive affect and NEO extraversion. *Motivation and Emotion*, 24, 51–62.

Cable, D. M., & Judge, T. A. (1994). Pay preferences and job search decisions: A person–organization fit perspective. *Personnel Psychology*, 47, 317–348.

Cable, D. M., & Judge, T. A. (1996). Person–organization fit, job choice decisions, and organizational entry. *Organizational Behavior and Human Decision Processes*, 67, 294–311.

Cable, D., & Turban, D. (2001). Establishing the dimensions, sources and value of job seekers' employer knowledge during recruitment. In G. Ferris (Ed.), *Research in Personnel and Human Resource Management* (Vol. 20, pp. 115–163). Greenwich, CT: JAI Press.

Caldwell, D. F., & Burger, J. M. (1998). Personality characteristics of job applicants and success in screening interview. *Personnel Psychology*, 51, 119–136.

Carlson, K. D., Connerley, M. L., & Mecham, R. L. (2002). Recruitment evaluation: The case for assessing the quality of applicants attracted. *Personnel Psychology*, 55, 461–490.

Carver, C. S., & Scheier, M. F. (1981). *Attention and self-regulation: A control theory approach to human behavior*. New York: Springer-Verlag.

Carver, C. S., & Scheier, M. F. (1982). Control theory: A useful conceptual framework for personality-social, clinical, and health psychology. *Psychological Bulletin*, 92, 111–135.

Casper, W. J., & Buffardi, L. C. (2004). Work-life benefits and job pursuit intentions: The role of anticipated organizational support. *Journal of Vocational Behavior*, 65, 391–410.

Chan, D., & Schmitt, N. (2004). An agenda for future research on applicant reactions to selection procedures: A construct-oriented approach. *International Journal of Selection and Assessment*, 12, 9–23.

Chapman, D. S., Uggerslev, K. L., Carroll, S. A., Piasentin, K. A., & Jones, D. A. (2005). Applicant attraction to organizations and job choice: A meta-analytic review of the correlates of recruiting outcomes. *Journal of Applied Psychology*, 90, 928–944.

Collins, C. J. (2007). The interactive effects of recruitment practices and product awareness on job seekers' employer knowledge and application behaviors. *Journal of Applied Psychology*, 92, 180–190.

Collins, C. J., & Han, J. (2004). Exploring applicant pool quantity and quality: The effects of early recruitment practices, corporate advertising, and firm reputation. *Personnel Psychology*, 57, 685–717.

Connelly, B. L., Certo, S. T., Ireland, R. D., & Reutzel, C. R. (2011). Signaling theory: A review and assessment. *Journal of Management*, 37, 39–67.

Collins, C. J., & Stevens, C. K. (2002). The relationship between early recruitment-related activities and the application decisions of new labor-market entrants: A brand equity approach to recruitment. *Journal of Applied Psychology*, 87, 1121–1133.

Côté, S., Saks, A. M., & Zikic, J. (2006). Trait affect and job search outcomes. *Journal of Vocational Behavior*, 68, 233–252.

Creed, P. A., King, V., Hood, M., & McKenzie, R. (2009). Goal orientation, self-regulation strategies, and job seeking intensity in unemployed adults. *Journal of Applied Psychology*, 94, 806–813.

Crossley, C. D., & Stanton, J. M. (2005). Negative affect and job search: Further examination of the reverse causation hypothesis. *Journal of Vocational Behavior*, 66, 549–560.

Dineen, B. R., & Noe, R. A. (2009). Effects of customization on application decisions and applicant pool characteristics in a web-based recruitment context. *Journal of Applied Psychology*, 94, 224–234.

Dineen, B. R., & Soltis, S. M. (2010). Recruitment: A review of research and emerging directions. In S. Zedeck (Ed.), *APA handbook of I/O psychology*: Vol. 2. *Selecting and developing members for the organization* (pp. 43–66). Washington, DC: American Psychological Association.

Dipboye, R. L. (1982). Self-fulfilling prophecies in the selection-recruitment interview. *Academy of Management Review*, 7, 579–586.

Dipboye, R. L. (1992). Social interaction in the interview. In R. L. Dipboye (Ed.), *Selection interview: Process perspective* (pp. 75–100). Cincinnati, OH: South-Western.

Dougherty, T. W., Turban, D. B., & Callender, J. C. (1994). Confirming first impressions in the employment interview: A field study of interviewer behavior. *Journal of Applied Psychology*, 79, 659–665.

Earnest, D. R., Allen, D. G., & Landis, R. S. (2011). Mechanisms linking realistic job previews with turnover: A meta-analytic path analysis. *Personnel Psychology*, 64, 865–897.

Ellis, R. A., & Taylor, M. S. (1983). Role of self-esteem within the job search process. *Journal of Applied Psychology*, 68, 632–640.

Feather, N. T. (1990). *The psychological impact of unemployment*. New York: Springer-Verlag.

Feather, N. T. (1992). Expectancy-value theory and unemployment effects. *Journal of Occupational and Organizational Psychology*, 65, 315–330.

Feather, N. T., & Davenport, P. R. (1981). Unemployment and depressive affect: A motivational and attributional analysis. *Journal of Personality and Social Psychology*, 41, 121–144.

Feather, N. T, & O'Brien, G. E. (1987). Looking for employment: An expectancy-valence analysis of job-seeking behavior among young people. *British Journal of Psychology*, 78, 251–272.

Fishbein M., & Ajzen I. (1975). *Belief, attitude, intention, and behavior: An introduction to theory and research*. Reading, MA: Addison-Wesley.

Greening, D. W., & Turban, D. B. (2000). Corporate social performance as a competitive advantage in attracting a quality workforce. *Business and Society*, 39, 254–280.

Harris, M. M., & Fink, L. S. (1987). A field study of employment opportunities: Does the recruiter make a difference? *Personnel Psychology*, 40, 765–784.

Jaidi, Y., Van Hooft, E. A. J., & Arends, L. R. (2011). Recruiting highly educated graduates: A study on the relationship between recruitment information sources, the theory of planned behavior, and actual job pursuit. *Human Performance*, 24, 135–157.

Judge, T. A., & Cable, D. M. (1997). Applicant personality, organizational culture, and organization attraction. *Personnel Psychology*, 50, 359–395.

Kanfer, R., & Hulin, C. L. (1985). Individual differences in successful job searches following lay-off. *Personnel Psychology*, 38, 835–847.

Kanfer, R., Wanberg, C., & Kantrowitz, T. (2001). Job search and employment: A personality-motivational analysis and meta-analytic review. *Journal of Applied Psychology*, 86, 837–855.

Kelly, J., & Barsade, S. (2001). Mood and emotions in small groups and work teams. *Organizational Behavior and Human Decision Processes*, 86, 99–130.

Kenny, D. A., Kashy, D. A., & Cook, W. L. (2006). *Dyadic data analysis*. New York: Guilford Press.

Kristof-Brown, A. L., Zimmerman, R. D., & Johnson, E. C. (2005). Consequences of individuals' fit at work: A meta-analysis of person-job, person-organization, person-group, and person-supervisor fit. *Personnel Psychology*, 58, 281–342.

Latham, G. P., & Pinder, C. C. (2005). Work motivation theory and research at the dawn of the twenty-first century. *Annual Review of Psychology*, 56, 495–516.

Macan, T. H., & Dipboye, R. L. (1990). The relationship of interviewers' preinterview impressions to selection and recruitment outcomes. *Personnel Psychology*, 43, 745–768.

Murphy, K. R. (1986). When your top choice turns you down: Effect of rejected job offers on the utility of selection tests. *Psychological Bulletin*, 99, 133–138.

Pinder, C. C. (1998). *Work motivation in organizational behavior*. Upper Saddle River, NJ: Prentice Hall.

Rynes, S. L. (1991). Recruitment, job choice, and post-hire consequences: A call for new research directions. In M. D. Dunnette & L. M. Hough (Eds.), *Handbook of industrial and organizational psychology* Vol. 2 (2nd ed., pp. 399–444). Palo Alto, CA: Consulting Psychologists Press.

Rynes, S. L., Bretz, R. D. Jr., & Gerhart, B. (1991). The importance of recruitment in job choice: A different way of looking. *Personnel Psychology*, 44, 487–521.

Rynes, S. L., & Cable, D. M. (2003). Recruitment research in the twenty-first century. In W. C. Borman, D. R. Ilgen, & R. J. Klimoski (Eds.), *Handbook of psychology*: Vol. 12. *Industrial and organizational psychology* (pp. 55–76). Hoboken, NJ: Wiley.

Rynes, S. L., Heneman, H. G. III, & Schwab, D. P. (1980). Individual reactions to organizational recruiting: A review. *Personnel Psychology*, 34, 823–834.

Rynes, S. L., & Lawler, J. (1983). A policy-capturing investigation of the role of expectancies in decisions to pursue job alternatives. *Journal of Applied Psychology*, 68, 620–632.

Saks, A. M. (2006). Multiple predictors and criteria of job search success. *Journal of Vocational Behavior*, 68, 400–415.

Saks, A. M., & Ashforth, B. E. (2002). Is job search related to employment quality? It all depends on the fit. *Journal of Applied Psychology*, 87, 646–654.

Schreurs, B., Derous, E., Van Hooft, E. A. J., Proost, K., & De Witte, K. (2009). Predicting applicants' job pursuit behavior from their selection expectations: The mediating role of the theory of planned behavior. *Journal of Organizational Behavior*, 30, 761–783.

Slaughter, J. E., Zickar, M. J., Highhouse, S., & Mohr, D. C. (2004). Personality trait inferences about organizations: Development of a measure and assessment of construct validity. *Journal of Applied Psychology*, 89, 85–103.

Snyder, M., & Swann, W. B. Jr. (1978). Hypothesis testing processes in social interaction. *Journal of Personality and Social Psychology*, 36, 1202–1212.

Song, Z., Uy, M. A., Zhang, S., & Shi, K. (2009). Daily job search and psychological distress: Evidence from China. *Human Relations*, 62, 1171–1197.

Song, Z., Wanberg, C. R., Niu, X., & Xie, Y. (2006). Action–state orientation and the theory of planned behavior: A study of job search in China. *Journal of Vocational Behavior*, 68, 490–503.

Spence, M. (1973). Job market signaling. *Quarterly Journal of Economics* 87, 355–374.

Stevens, C. K. (1998). Antecedents of interview interactions, interviewers' ratings, and applicants' reactions. *Personnel Psychology*, 51, 55–86.

Stewart, G. L., Dustin, S. L., Barrick, M. R., & Darnold, T. C. (2008). Exploring the handshake in employment interviews. *Journal of Applied Psychology*, 95, 1139–1146.

Sutton, S. (1998). Predicting and explaining intentions and behavior: How well are we doing? *Journal of Applied Social Psychology*, 28, 1317–1338.

Swann, W. B. Jr. (2011). Self-verification theory. In P. Van Lang, A. Kruglanski, & E. T. Higgins (Eds.), *Handbook of theories of social psychology*: Vol. 2 (pp. 23–42). London: Sage.

Tan, H. H., Foo, M. D., & Kwek, M. H. (2004). The effects of customer personality traits on display of positive emotions. *Academy of Management Journal*, 47, 287–296.

Tay, C., Ang, S., & Van Dyne, L. (2006). Personality, biographical characteristics, and job interview success: A longitudinal study of the mediating effects of interviewing, self-efficacy and the moderating effects of internal locus of causality. *Journal of Applied Psychology*, 91, 446–454.

Taylor, M. S., & Bergmann, T. J. (1987). Organizational recruitment activities and applicants' reactions at different stages of the recruitment process. *Personnel Psychology*, 40, 261–285.

Turban, D. B. (2001). Organizational attractiveness as an employer on college campuses: An examination of the applicant population. *Journal of Vocational Behavior*, 58, 293–312.

Turban, D. B., & Cable, D. M. (2003). Firm reputation and applicant pool characteristics. *Journal of Organizational Behavior*, 24, 733–751.

Turban, D. B., Campion, J. E., & Eyring, A. R. (1995). Factors related to job acceptance decisions of college graduates. *Journal of Vocational Behavior*, 47, 193–213.

Turban, D. B., & Dougherty, T. W. (1992). Influences of campus recruiting on applicant attraction to firms. *Academy of Management Journal*, 35, 739–765.

Turban, D. B., Forret, M. L., & Hendrickson, C. L. (1998). Applicant attraction to firms: Influences of organizational reputation, job and organizational attributes and recruiter behaviors. *Journal of Vocational Behavior*, 52, 24–44.

Turban, D. B., & Greening, D. W. (1997). Corporate social performance and organizational attractiveness to prospective employees. *Academy of Management Journal*, 40, 658–672.

Turban, D. B., Lee, F. K., da Motta Veiga, S. P., Haggard, D. L., & Wu, S. Y. (2013). Be happy, don't wait: The role of trait affect in job search. *Personnel Psychology*, 66, 483–514.

Turban, D. B., Stevens, C. K., & Lee, F. K. (2009). Effects of conscientiousness and extraversion on new labor market entrants' job search: The mediating role of metacognitive activities and positive emotions. *Personnel Psychology*, 62, 553–573.

Van Breukelen, W., Van der Vlist, R., & Steensma, H. (2004). Voluntary employee turnover: Combining variables from the "traditional" turnover literature with the theory of planned behavior. *Journal of Organizational Behavior*, 25, 893–914.

Van Hooft, E. A. J., Born, M. P., Taris, T. W., & Van der Flier, H. (2006). Ethnic and gender differences in applicants' decision-making processes: An application of the theory of reasoned action. *International Journal of Selection and Assessment*, 14, 156–166.

Van Hooft, E. A. J., Born, M. P., Taris, T. W., Van der Flier, H., & Blonk, R. W. B. (2004). Predictors of job search behavior among employed and unemployed people. *Personnel Psychology*, 57, 25–59.

Van Hooft, E. A. J., & Crossley, C. D. (2008). The joint role of locus of control and perceived financial need in job search. *International Journal of Selection and Assessment*, 16, 258–271.

Van Hooft, E. A. J., & Noordzij, G. (2009). The effects of goal orientation on job search and reemployment: A field experiment among unemployed job seekers. *Journal of Applied Psychology*, 94, 1581–1590.

Van Hoye, G., & Saks, A. M. (2008). Job search as goal-directed behavior: Objectives and methods. *Journal of Vocational Behavior*, 73: 358–367.

Vroom, V. H. (1964). *Work and motivation*. Hoboken, NJ: Wiley.

Wanberg, C. R., Basbug, G., Van Hooft, E. A. J., & Samtani, A. (2012). Navigating the black hole: Explicating layers of job search context and adaptational responses. *Personnel Psychology*, 65, 887–926.

Wanberg, C. R., Kanfer, R., & Rotundo, M. (1999). Unemployed individuals: Motives, job-search competencies, and job-search constraints as predictors of job seeking and reemployment. *Journal of Applied Psychology*, 6, 897–910.

Wanberg, C. R., Zhu, J., Kanfer, R., & Zhang, Z. (2012). After the pink slip: Applying dynamic motivation frameworks to the job search experience. *Academy of Management Journal*, 55, 261–284.

Wanberg, C. R., Zhu, J., & Van Hooft, E. A. J. (2010). The job search grind: Perceived progress, self-reactions, and self-regulation of search effort. *Academy of Management Journal*, 53, 788–807.

Williamson, I. O., Lepak, D. P., & King, J. (2003). The effect of company recruitment web site orientation on individuals' perceptions of organizational attractiveness. *Journal of Vocational Behavior*, 63, 242–263.

Through the Looking Glass: Employment Interviews from the Lens of Job Candidates

Julie M. McCarthy *and* Bonnie Hayden Cheng

Abstract

Job interviews are of crucial importance to the job search process. As a result, recent years have witnessed a considerable amount of research on job interviews from the perspective of candidates. While this research has provided valuable insight into candidate reactions, it has yet to have a strong impact on the actual behaviors of job candidates and organizations. Thus the goal of the current chapter is to bridge the gap between empirical knowledge and applied practice in job interviews. To accomplish this objective we first present a framework for understanding the interview process that is grounded in theoretical and empirical research. The focus of this framework is whether candidate characteristics (e.g., gender, age), behaviors (e.g., impression management, communication style), and reactions (e.g., anxiety, justice) have an effect on important interview-related outcomes, such as interview performance. This is followed by a comprehensive discussion of research relevant to each section of the framework, including impression management, the first handshake, interview anxiety, and other predictors of interview success. Implications for research and practice are discussed and a checklist for practice is provided. We conclude by highlighting how properly conducted interviews can simultaneously serve the best interest of both job applicants *and* organizations.

Key Words: job interview, job applicants, candidate reactions, impression management, anxiety, justice, interview performance.

Introduction

Research on job interviews has predominantly been conducted through the lens of organizations — focusing almost exclusively on how to improve predictive validity (Barrick, Shaffer, & DeGrassi, 2009). Findings across hundreds of studies are unequivocal and indicate that impressive levels of predictive validity can be obtained when structured job interview techniques are employed (Huffcutt & Arthur, 1994; McDaniel, Whetzel, Schmidt, & Maurer, 1994; Wiesner & Cronshaw, 1988). In recent years, however, scholars have recognized the importance of considering the interview though the lens of the job candidate. As a result, a large body of research that examines candidate perceptions of and reactions to job interviews has emerged. Several comprehensive reviews of this literature have been conducted (see Chan & Schmitt, 2004; Harris, 1989; Macan, 2009; Posthuma, Morgeson, & Campion, 2002; Ryan & Ployhart, 2000; Steiner & Gilliland, 2001), including a meta-analysis (Hausknecht, Day, & Thomas, 2004). Findings suggest that candidate characteristics, behaviors and reactions to job interviews are related to several key outcome variables, including (a) performance on selection tools; (b) perceptions of organizational attractiveness; (c) intentions to recommend the organization to other candidates; (d) intentions to litigate; and (e) intentions to accept a job offer (see Barrick et al., 2009; Bauer et al., 2001; Chapman, Uggerslev, Caroll, Piasentin, & Jones, 2005; Hausknecht et al., 2004).

This information has provided us with valuable insight into job interviews from the perspective of the candidate; however, it has been less successful in impacting what candidates and organizations can actually do to improve the interview process (Ryan & Huth, 2008). This may be in part because of the lack of a comprehensive overview that delineates the steps that candidates and organizations can take. To this end, the goal of this chapter is to provide a bridge between empirical knowledge about job interviews with applied recommendations for job candidates.

Figure 19.1 presents the conceptual framework that forms the basis for this chapter. Our framework is grounded in theoretical and empirical research and holds that candidate characteristics, candidate behaviors, and candidate reactions have important implications for job interview outcomes. The key mechanisms underlying these relations are explicated—notably stereotypes, social influence, cognitive interference, and value perceptions. It also identifies the key boundary conditions that have an impact on these relations, notably the type of job, the amount of interview structure, and candidate sincerity. As illustrated in Figure 19.1, this framework is specifically focused on the interview process from the lens of job candidates. It is important to note that other researchers have adopted a broader framework by providing more general reviews of the vast

array of studies on job interviews (see Anderson, 1992; Arvey & Campion, 1982; Harris, 1989; Huffcutt, 2011; Judge, Higgins, & Cable, 2000; Macan, 2009; McDaniel et al., 1994; Moscoso, 2000; Posthuma et al., 2002). Still others have provided general reviews of research on candidate reactions to a wide range of selection tools (see Chan & Schmitt, 2004; Hausknecht et al., 2004; Hülsheger & Anderson, 2009; Ryan & Ployhart, 2000; Steiner & Gilliland, 2001; Truxillo & Bauer, 2010; Truxillo, Bodner, Bertolino, Bauer, & Yonce, 2009). Our goal, based on the focus on candidates' perspective on job interviews, is to provide insight on how scientific findings can lead to practical recommendations.

This chapter is organized into five main parts. In the first three sections, we conduct a comprehensive review of candidate characteristics, behaviors, and reactions that may be related to interview outcomes. In doing so, we identify relevant theoretical frameworks, key research findings, and ideas for future work. Section four outlines implications for job candidates and presents recommendations on how to succeed in the job interview. The concluding section examines best practices in job interview techniques from the perspective of both job candidates and organizations. In doing so, it highlights the overlap in best practices and demonstrates that properly

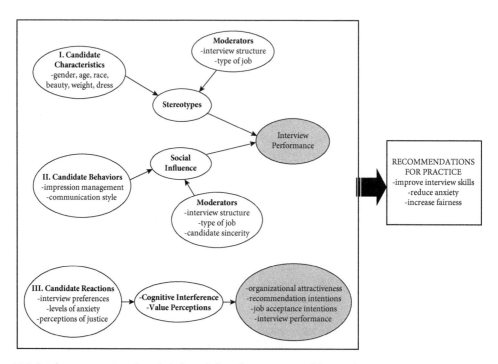

Figure 19.1 Employment interviews through the lens of job applicants: conceptual framework

conducted interviews can serve the best interest of candidates *and* organizations.

Candidate Characteristics

A number of studies have considered the extent to which candidate characteristics may have an impact on the job interview process. These studies can be broadly organized into those that examine demographic characteristics (e.g., gender, age), and those that examine the physical appearance (e.g., attractiveness, style of dress) of job candidates.

As illustrated in Figure 19.1, the focus of these studies is on the extent to which candidate characteristics influence job interview performance. Huffcutt, Van Iddekinge, and Roth (2011) have advanced a comprehensive model of interview performance and state that it "reflects how applicants behave during the interview, including what they say and what they do" (p. 354). Further, they note that interview performance includes the content of the message that the interviewee is sending, how the interviewee delivers that content, and the interviewee's nonverbal behaviors. The construct of interview performance is operationalized via interview ratings, which are typically in the form of an overall "interview" score (Barrick et al., 2009). However, it has also been assessed by obtaining ratings of candidate suitability, interview rank, intentions to hire, or intentions to recommend the candidate for a second interview (Barrick et al., 2009). Further, there is considerable variability in the actual constructs that are used to assess interview performance, as a wide variety of interview questions and scoring techniques are used (Harris, 1989). Examples of such constructs include social skills, personality traits, cognitive ability, and past experiences (Huffcutt, 2011; Posthuma et al., 2002). Of these, personality traits and social skills have been found to be the most common constructs assessed, accounting for over 60% of all rated interview characteristics (Huffcutt, Conway, Roth, & Stone, 2001). It is important to keep this variability in the operationalization of interview performance in mind in evaluating research findings and comparing results across studies.

Demographic Characteristics

Research on demographic characteristics has primarily focused on the extent to which candidate gender, race, and age influence interviewer perceptions and outcomes. This research includes studies that examine main effects, such that the performance of job candidates is directly influenced by the candidate's demographics. This research also includes studies that examine interaction effects, such that the performance of job candidates is influenced by the match (or mismatch) between the candidate's and the interviewer(s)'s demographics.

Studies examining the main effects of candidate demographic characteristics are, for the most part, founded on stereotype theory. Gender-related stereotypes reflect prejudiced attitudes toward women (Eagly & Steffen, 1984), race-related stereotypes reflect prejudiced attitudes toward minority-group members (Steele, 1997), and age-related stereotypes typically reflect prejudiced attitudes toward older workers (Rosen & Jerdee, 1976 a,b). Research findings support a main effect of gender-related stereotypes on interview performance (e.g., Adkins, Russell, & Werbel, 1994; Cable & Judge, 1997; Levashina & Campion, 2007); however, the magnitude is modest and actually suggest a slight tendency for *females* to receive higher overall ratings (average $d = .13$) (Huffcutt, 2011). Findings with respect to race and age are more robust and suggest discrimination against minorities (average $d = .36$) (Huffcutt, 2011; see also Derous & Ryan, this volume) and older applicants (Morgeson, Reider, Campion, & Bull, 2008; see also Klehe, De Pater, Koen, & Kira, this volume).

Given that job interviews are a dynamic process that involves communication between the candidate and the interviewer(s), more recent research has considered the match (or mismatch) between the demographic characteristics of the interviewer and the interviewee (e.g., Buckley, Jackson, Bolino, Veres, & Feild, 2007; Goldberg, 2005; Sacco, Scheu, Ryan, & Schmitt, 2003). These studies draw from the similarity attraction paradigm (Byrne, 1971; Newcomb, 1956). Consistent with the adage, "birds of a feather flock together," this paradigm holds that individuals with similar characteristics will be attracted to one another. Relatedly, demographic similarity theory is concerned with the extent to which people use demographic variables, such as gender and race, to determine how similar they are to others (Tsui, Egan, & O'Reilly, 1992; Tsui & O'Reilly, 1989). The key aspect of this theory is that demographic variables do not influence work outcomes on their own. Instead, an individual's demographic characteristics relative to others is what is important. Applied to job interviews, these theories suggest that candidates will be judged more favorably to the extent that they have similar characteristics and belong to similar groups as the interviewer. Findings of these studies are mixed. Specifically, some report no effects (e.g., Graves & Powell, 1995, 1996; Sacco et al., 2003), while others report small to moderate effects (e.g., Buckley et al., 2007; Lin, Dobbins, & Farh, 1992; McFarland, Ryan, Sacco, & Kriska, 2004). As discussed below, these mixed findings are likely due to differences across studies with respect to the amount of interview structure and the types of jobs examined.

In the context of job interviews, these theories predict that candidate characteristics will trigger interviewer stereotypes, which will influence interviewer ratings of candidate performance. In other words, stereotypes serve as a mechanism underlying the relation between candidate characteristics and interview performance (see Figure 19.1).

Physical Appearance

Physical appearance reflects the physical characteristics of an individual, and includes variables such as attractiveness, weight, and style of dress. A number of studies have examined the effects of physical appearance on interview outcomes by considering the extent to which, for example, more attractive candidates are deemed more suitable for a job, more likely to be hired, more likely to receive higher interview scores, and more likely to perform better on the job subsequent to being hired. Implicit personality theory (Ashmore, 1981) serves as a foundation for these studies and holds that when we are presented with information about individuals' central traits; we draw inferences and make assumptions that are not necessarily correct. In particular, we suffer from a widely shared stereotype that "what is beautiful is good" (Eagly, Ashmore, Makhijani, & Longo, 1991).

A considerable amount of research has examined this general stereotype, and meta-analytic findings indicate that individuals with a more positive physical appearance are indeed *perceived* as more socially skilled, intellectually competent, and mentally stable (Eagly et al., 1991; Feingold, 1992; Hosoda, Stone-Romero, & Coats, 2003). There is also evidence that we make these attributions instantaneously—as fast as 100 milliseconds after exposure to an individual (Willis & Todorov, 2006)! However, while we may believe that "what is beautiful is good," research indicates that attractiveness, in actuality, is trivially related to actual measures of cognitive ability and personality, suggesting that "good-looking people are not necessarily good" (Feingold, 1992). Below, we provide a more detailed perspective on the key

components of physical appearance: physical attractiveness, weight, and style of dress.

PHYSICAL ATTRACTIVENESS

Consistent with the "what is beautiful is good" stereotype, more attractive candidates are likely to receive more favorable hiring recommendations (Arvey & Campion, 1982; Gilmore, Beehr, & Love, 1986; Tews, Stafford, & Zhu, 2009), while less attractive candidates are deemed less suitable for hiring (Marlowe, Schneider, & Nelson, 1996). Barrick and colleagues (2009) conducted a meta-analytic review of research on candidate attractiveness and job interviews and found that physical appearance exhibited a strong relation with interviewer ratings of performance. In fact, physical attractiveness was found to have a stronger effect on interviewer ratings of performance than impression management behaviors, verbal communication and nonverbal communication exhibited by the candidate. The strength of this stereotype is further evidenced in a study by Rynes and Gerhart (1990), who found that physical attractiveness predicted interviewer ratings of employability over and above objective qualifications, such as past experience.

Experimental research has also been conducted to examine the specifics of the effect of physical attractiveness on hiring considerations. The bulk of this research uses the "paper people paradigm," whereby verbal descriptions and/or pictures of job candidates are rated by subjects. Overall, these studies are consistent with meta-analytic evidence and indicate that attractiveness has a significant impact on interviewer perceptions (e.g., Dipboye, Fromkin, & Wiback, 1975; Marlowe et al., 1996; Shannon & Stark, 2003). For example, Dipboye and colleagues (1975) presented students and professional interviewers with the resumes and pictures of fictitious candidates that varied on level of attractiveness. They found that both groups preferred attractive to unattractive candidates.

WEIGHT

Researchers have also started to examine the effects of candidate weight on interviewer perceptions. Drawing from implicit personality theory (Ashmore, 1981), negative stereotypes are applied to individuals who are perceived as overweight. That is, overweight individuals are typically viewed as sloppy, unattractive, dishonest, and less productive (Judge & Cable, 2011). The aversion to overweight individuals is so pervasive that even overweight people hold negative attitudes towards other overweight people (Finkelstein, DeMuth, & Sweeney, 2007).

Not surprisingly, these stereotypes exist in the workplace, such that overweight candidates and employees are rated as less desirable, less agreeable, and less stable than their non-overweight counterparts (Kutcher & Bragger, 2004; Roehling, 1999). Even experienced human resource personnel and recruitment consultants have been found to be biased against overweight candidates (Ding & Stillman, 2005). Indeed, a recent meta-analysis found that, compared with nonoverweight employees in the workplace, overweight employees were disadvantaged in terms of hiring and performance outcomes (Rudolph, Wells, Weller, & Baltes, 2009). There is even evidence that weight has profound negative effects on income levels (Judge & Cable, 2011). Perhaps unsurprisingly, these effects are more pronounced for women (Judge & Cable, 2011).

Given that these stereotypes are inaccurate (Roehling, Roehling, & Odland, 2008), it is shocking that weight can explain as much as 35% of the variance in hiring decisions (Pingitore, Dugoni, Tindale, & Spring, 1994). In fact, the stigma of obesity is so prevalent that negative perceptions are even ascribed to candidates who are *seen* with obese individuals. Hebl and Mannix (2003) demonstrated this proximity effect and found that male candidates were rated more negatively when seen with an overweight compared to a non-overweight female.

Negative biases also affect candidates who are extremely underweight. For example, Swami and colleagues have conducted research demonstrating that candidates who are emaciated (Body Mass Index less than 15), as well as candidates who are obese (Body Mass Index greater than 30), are more likely to be discriminated against in terms of hiring ratings (Swami, Chan, Wong, Furnham, & Tovée, 2008; Swami, Pietschnig, Stieger, Tovée, & Voracek, 2010). This holds true for pregnant candidates, who are viewed as less competent than their nonpregnant counterparts (e.g., Bragger, Kutcher, Morgan, & Firth, 2002; Cunningham & Macan, 2007; Masser, Grass, & Nesic, 2007). Although pregnancy is a different issue than weight, this research suggests that pregnant candidates may be viewed in the same biased manner as candidates with weight issues.

STYLE OF DRESS

The general workplace literature suggests that when employees select clothing appropriate for their work role, they feel more competent and are better able to interact with others (Rafaeli, Dutton, Harquail, & Mackie-Lewis, 1997). Not surprisingly, style of dress may also have an effect in job interview contexts (Posthuma et al., 2002). Specifically, meta-analytic research suggests that the extent to which a candidate's clothing conveys a professional appearance has a significant impact on interview scores (Barrick et al., 2009). Further, experimental research manipulating grooming and attractiveness by altering clothing, hair, makeup, and jewelry of a female candidate has found that undergraduate students are more likely to hire a well-groomed candidate than a poorly groomed candidate with identical qualifications (Mack & Rainey, 1990). In terms of specific clothing styles, Forsythe (1990; Forsythe, Drake, & Cox, 1985) examined the impact of type of clothing on managerial evaluations of female candidates. Findings indicated that females wearing more masculine clothing (e.g., dark suit) were judged to be more forceful, self-reliant, dynamic, aggressive, and decisive than those wearing feminine clothing (e.g., skirt). They were also more likely to be recommended for hire. Ultimately, conservative dress is considered to be most appropriate for both genders but is particularly preferred for female candidates (Jenkins & Atkins, 1990).

Boundary Conditions

As described above, findings are mixed with respect to whether the demographic characteristics of job candidates influence interview scores. However, findings with respect to physical appearance are more conclusive, with studies consistently indicating that physical attractiveness, weight, and style of dress are significantly related to interview outcomes. It is important to note that two boundary conditions have been found to influence the magnitude of observed relations between candidate characteristics and interview outcomes: the amount of interview structure and type of job. These conditions serve as moderators of the relation between candidate characteristics and interview performance (see Figure 19.1).

INTERVIEW STRUCTURE

The inconsistent findings with respect to demographic characteristics are partially due to inconsistencies in interview structure across past studies. Specifically, when interviews are highly structured, there is evidence that demographic similarity effects can be reduced and potentially eliminated (McCarthy, Van Iddekinge, & Campion, 2010; Sacco et al., 2003). This makes intuitive sense, as structured interviews, by their very nature, are aimed at obtaining relevant information about job candidates. At its core, structured interviews are based on a job analysis, ask the same job-relevant questions of all candidates, and are scored using anchored rating scales (Campion, Palmer, & Campion, 1997). As such, structured interviews increase the amount of individuating information about the candidate (e.g., job-relevant knowledge and skills) that is available to and used by interviewers (McCarthy et al., 2010). Further, they greatly reduce and/or eliminate irrelevant questions that may trigger biases. Thus, the effects of demographic characteristics will be stronger to the extent that unstructured interview formats are used. Unfortunately, the majority of organizations continue to use unstructured interviews, rendering the potential prevalence of demographic biases high (Parsons, Liden, & Bauer, 2001).

Relations between physical appearance and interview outcomes are also significantly reduced when structured, as opposed to unstructured, interview formats are used (Barrick et al., 2009). This holds true for overweight and pregnant candidates (Hebl, King, Glick, Singletary, & Kazama, 2007; Kutcher & Bragger, 2004). Again, this can be attributed to the fact that highly structured interviews focus attention on the relevant characteristics of candidates, reducing the effect of characteristics like attractiveness and weight.

TYPE OF JOB

The mixed findings of past research on demographic effects are also partially due to differences across job type. Specifically, certain jobs are sextyped, in that they are deemed more appropriate for females or males (Arvey, 1979; Heilman, 1983). Interviewers tend to see female candidates as more suitable for feminine-linked jobs, whereas male candidates are seen as more appropriate for masculine-linked jobs (e.g., Buttner & McEnally, 1996; Kalin & Hodgins, 1984). Similarly, older candidates are rated more favorably for jobs that are considered more suitable for older employees (Cleveland, Festa, & Montgomery, 1988; Shore & Goldberg, 2005). Thus interview scores are likely to be stronger to the extent that the job is perceived to match the demographic characteristics of the candidate.

Type of job is also a moderator of the relation between physical attractiveness and interview performance. Indeed, evidence indicates that physical attractiveness plays a pivotal role when positions entail a high level of customer contact (Tews et al., 2009; Tsai, Huang, & Yu, 2011). In fact, there is evidence that attractiveness is actually detrimental for female candidates when applying to masculine sextyped jobs where physical appearance is considered unimportant (Johnson, Podratz, Dipboye, & Gibbons, 2010).

Directions for Future Research

Existing research on candidate characteristics has been conducted relatively independently, resulting in separate research streams that focus on distinct characteristics such as race, attractiveness, and weight. Although this work has contributed greatly to our general understanding of how various characteristics impact interview outcomes, it would be particularly advantageous for research to consider the relative weight of various characteristics on interview outcomes. Tews and colleagues (2009) have provided a first glimpse of this issue by examining the relative weight that manager's place on physical attractiveness, cognitive ability, and personality during hiring decisions. They found that although physical attractiveness played a significant role, it explained only 1% of the variance in managerial ratings and was valued less than cognitive ability and conscientiousness, which explained 8% and 12% in managerial ratings respectively. To this end, additional research is needed to consider how candidate characteristics stack up to one another, as well as to assess their combined impact on various interview outcomes. Moreover, additional research is needed to determine to what extent the relative weights are influenced by job type and characteristics of the interviewer.

Candidate Behaviors

A number of studies have considered the extent to which the behaviors that candidates engage in (or fail to engage in) may impact the job interview process. These self-presentation tactics can be organized into those that examine impression management behaviors and those that examine verbal and nonverbal communication processes.

Impression Management Behaviors

Job interviews inherently reflect a process that is centered on a social exchange between individuals. As a result, candidates are motivated to use impression management behaviors in order to be perceived in a positive light (Rosenfeld, Giacalone, & Riordan, 1995; Wayne & Liden, 1995). By definition, impression management reflects "a conscious or unconscious attempt to influence images that are projected in real or imagined social interactions" (Schlenker, 1980, p. 6). A wide range of impression management behaviors have been examined, including the use of smiling, handshakes, ingratiation behaviors, self-endorsement, favors, pressure and coalition. Research indicates that these types of impression management behaviors are common, even during highly structured interviews (Levashina & Campion, 2007). Research also suggests that impression formation occurs in two steps: first impressions and general impressions (Dipboye, 2004; Kahneman, 2003). Below we discuss the theoretical frameworks underlying impression management tactics, and then discuss each in turn.

Two theoretical frameworks provide a foundation for understanding impression management tactics—interdependence theory and social influence theory. Interdependence theory (Rusbult & Van Lange, 2003) asserts that social contexts can have powerful effects on behaviors. In particular, this theory proposes that when individuals are interacting with someone whose interests differ from their own or with someone on whom they are dependent, they will be more likely to engage in self-presentation tactics in order to maximize their outcomes. Job candidates fit this description, as their interest in obtaining the job is distinct from the interviewers' interest in obtaining accurate information and hiring the strongest candidate (Barrick et al., 2009). Further, candidates are dependent on the interviewer for job success (Barrick et al., 2009). Thus, the interdependence among key players in job interview contexts promotes the use of self-presentation tactics. Social influence theory is founded on the notion that all interpersonal relationships involve social influence; as a result, individuals are motivated to use tactics to influence one another in order to get others to perceive oneself in a positive light (Cialdini & Trost, 1998; Levy, Collins, & Nail, 1998). In the context of job interviews, these theories predict that candidate impression management behaviors will yield a social influence effect, and be related to interviewer ratings of candidate performance. In other words, social influence serves as a mechanism underlying the relation between impression management behaviors and interview performance (see Figure 19.1).

FIRST IMPRESSIONS

The first stage of impression formation represents our initial judgments of others and is referred to as "first impressions" (Dipboye, 2004; Kahneman,

2003). These impressions are based on a thin slice of observational data and occur almost instantaneously, that is, within the first 39 milliseconds (Ambady & Rosenthal, 1992; Bar, Neta, & Linz, 2006; Willis & Todorov, 2006). Moreover, these first impressions are typically formed through nonverbal exchanges. That is, we form impressions of others as soon as we see them, prior to meeting or exchanging words with them (Hiemstra, 1999). In the context of job interviews, findings indicate that information communicated through the initial interaction between the candidate and interviewer, both nonverbal and verbal, can have a significant effect on interviewer impressions. For example, a study by Stewart, Dustin, Barrick, and Darnold (2008) found that a high-quality handshake (consisting of high vigor, direct eye contact, and a grip that is full, strong, and long) can result in a more favorable impression of the candidate and is more likely to be related to a positive hiring decision. Extending that research, Barrick, Swider, and Stewart (2010) found that interviewers generate impressions of candidate competence during the initial rapport-building stage of the interview, in which innocuous "small-talk" unrelated to the job is exchanged between the candidate and the interviewer. Further, they found evidence that these initial impressions predict interview outcomes beyond the potentially biasing effects of candidate-interviewer similarity and liking. This suggests that interviewers' initial evaluations are based on more than just job-relevant characteristics and incorporate liking and similarity effects.

GENERAL IMPRESSIONS

The second stage of impression formation is characterized by more rational processing of information throughout the interview (Dipboye, 2004; Kahneman, 2003). The bulk of research has focused on this second stage, measuring impression management behaviors either during or after the interview. As illustrated by Levashina and Campion (2007), impression management behaviors can have strong effects on interview outcomes, increasing the probability of a successful job interview outcome by as much as 46%.

Two main types of impression management behaviors have been studied: self-focused and other-focused tactics. Self-focused tactics occur when candidates describe themselves, their experiences and accomplishments in a positive light. This strategy focuses attention on the candidate, and includes behaviors such as self-endorsement (describing one's positive qualities) and entitlements (taking responsibility for positive events). Other-focused tactics reflect strategies that focus attention on the interviewer, and include ingratiation (flattery toward the interviewer) and favors (going out of one's way to do something for the interviewer). In 2009, Barrick and colleagues conducted a meta-analytic review of studies examining the impact of impression management on the job interview process. When the two types of impression management behaviors were considered independently, self-focused tactics demonstrated stronger effects on interviewer ratings than other-focused tactics.

Similar findings were reported in a recent empirical review of this literature conducted by Huffcutt (2011). Proost, Schreurs, De Witte, and Derous (2010) extended this research by considering the combined effect of these tactics. Results indicated that the combined use of self- and other-promotion tactics resulted in higher ratings than either tactic alone.

Another way in which researchers have distinguished impression management tactics is by differentiating between "soft" and "hard" tactics (Lamude, 1994). Soft tactics reflect the use of personal power and power sharing (e.g., ingratiation, rational persuasion). In contrast, hard tactics involve manipulation and reflect the use of position and authority (e.g., pressure, coalition tactics). McFarland, Ryan, and Kriska (2002) conducted a field study examining firefighters' use of influence tactics in job interview contexts. While soft tactics were positively associated with job interview ratings, hard tactics yielded nonsignificant relationships. Similarly, a study by Tsai, Huang, Wu, and Lo (2010) examined three soft tactics—apologies, justifications, and excuses. These particular strategies were also defensive in nature, as they involved responding to negative information. Findings indicated that when negative concerns surfaced during the interview, candidates using these soft tactics received higher ratings.

Although impression management can highlight the positive qualities of candidates and lead to higher interview ratings, candidates need to be cautious of the extent to which these tactics are used. Indeed, research demonstrates that *overuse* of impression management tactics can actually have a negative impact on interview outcomes (Baron, 1989; Bolino & Turnley, 2003). Further, there is evidence that self-promotion tactics become detrimental when the interviewer can tell that candidates are using them. Specifically, candidates who are perceived by interviewers to be using self-promotion tactics are rated lower on interview performance than candidates who are not perceived to be using self-promotion tactics (Howard & Ferris, 1996). Thus candidates are advised to use these tactics in a very cautious manner, ensuring that they are viewed as sincere. Finally, in spite of the potential power of impression management tactics, their influence is relative, as interviewers have been found to rely more heavily on job-related competencies in evaluating candidates (Lievens & Peeters, 2008).

Nonverbal and Verbal Communication

A great deal of research has also examined the effects of both verbal (e.g., speech rate and pitch) and nonverbal (e.g., eye contact) communication styles on interview outcomes. A number of theoretical paradigms have been used as the foundation for this stream of research, ranging from Brunswick's lens model (1956) to person perception and social cognition frameworks (Parsons et al., 2001), to various attribution theories (e.g., Heider, 1958). At the core, these theoretical frameworks have in common the notion that, since individuals are constantly attempting to explain others' behavior in order to make sense of what is going on around them, messages conveyed implicitly or explicitly can be misperceived. Social influence theory provides further insight into the influence of verbal and nonverbal communication styles on interview performance. Social influence theory holds that individuals are motivated to use tactics that will get others to perceive them positively (Cialdini & Trost, 1998; Levy et al., 1998). Consistent with impression management behaviors, verbal and nonverbal communication styles are expected to yield a social influence effect and, in turn, be related to interview performance. Thus, social influence also serves as a mechanism underlying the relation between candidate communication styles and interview performance (see Figure 19.1).

With regard to nonverbal communication, several studies have found that behaviors such as smiling, eye contact, and gestures are positively related to the ratings that candidates receive in the job interview (e.g., DeGroote & Motowidlo, 1999; Gifford, Ng, & Wilkinson, 1985; Imada & Hakel, 1977; Levine & Feldman, 2002; McGovern, Jones, & Morris, 1979; McGovern & Tinsley, 1978; Rasmussen, 1984; Riggio & Throckmorton, 1988). For example, a firm handshake has been demonstrated to have a positive effect on interview outcomes (Chaplin, Phillips, Brown, Clanton, & Stein, 2000;

Stewart et al., 2008). Further, eye contact has been found to determine perceptions of competence and strength of character (Anderson, 1991). There is also evidence that interviewers infer social skills from nonverbal behaviors, such as the speed of candidate gestures and the amount of time candidates spend talking (Gifford et al., 1985).

With regard to verbal communication, evidence suggests that factors such as speech rate, pitch, fluency, the use of hedges ("um" and "ah"), and use of sophisticated language, are all related to interview outcomes (DeGroot & Motowidlo, 1999). The content of responses that candidates provide to interviewers can also have an effect on interview outcomes. For example, unfavorable information provided by the candidate has been found to have a greater impact on interview ratings than favorable information (Bolster & Springbett, 1961; Constantin, 1976). This is consistent with evidence that negative life events carry more weight than positive life events (Baumeister, Bratslavsky, Finkenauer, & Vohs, 2001). Finally, many of the impression management tactics described in the previous section involve the use of verbal communication (e.g., self-endorsements, entitlements, ingratiation) and have been found to have significant effects on interviewer perceptions of candidates (e.g., Barrick et al., 2009).

Research has also provided substantial support for the joint effects of nonverbal and verbal communication on job interview performance. A combination of nonverbal and verbal communication may signal trustworthiness, likability, and credibility of candidates (DeGroot & Motowidlo, 1999; Nighswonger & Martin, 1981). Burnett and Motowidlo (1998) found that individuals asked to play the role of a recruiter who received both verbal and nonverbal information about the target candidate had improved predictions of performance compared with those who received nonverbal information only and those who received verbal information only. Similarly, DeGroot and Motowidlo (1999) found that candidate vocal cues (e.g., pitch variability, pauses) and visual cues (e.g., smiling, gaze) had a significant effect on evaluations of candidate performance during the interview and on the job. Rasmussen (1984) also found a significant interaction between nonverbal and verbal communication in simulated lab interviews. When interviews that contained high quantities of verbal content (i.e., where the candidate presented much job-relevant information), high amounts of nonverbal behavior produced higher overall interview ratings

than low amounts of nonverbal behavior. In contrast, when interviews contained low quantities of verbal content (i.e., where the candidate presented little job-relevant information), high amounts of nonverbal behavior produced lower overall ratings.

In terms of the relative effectiveness of nonverbal and verbal communication, findings are mixed. Some research suggests that nonverbal communication is more strongly associated with interview outcomes. This is consistent with the old adage "actions speak louder than words." Indeed, it is often easier to make judgments of others by relying on peripheral factors, such as nonverbal cues, than by carefully and deliberately processing the verbal content conveyed by others (Petty & Cacioppo, 1986). Empirically, this is supported by the meta-analytic review conducted by Barrick and colleagues (2009), who found that nonverbal communication demonstrated stronger relations with interview ratings than verbal information. On the other hand, there is some evidence to suggest that information conveyed verbally is more important than nonverbal cues. For example, Peeters and Lievens (2006) examined verbal communication (i.e., self-promoting utterances, entitlements, and enhancements) and nonverbal communication (i.e., smiling, hand gestures, nodding, and eye contact). Findings indicated that both tactics demonstrated significant correlations with interview ratings, but verbal self-promotion tactics were most strongly related to positive interview scores. Overall, research evidence suggests that both verbal and nonverbal communications ultimately impact interviewer perceptions and ratings and that neither should be underestimated.

Boundary Conditions

As described above, research indicates that impression management behaviors can have significant effects on job interview outcomes. In particular, the use of self-focused and soft impression management tactics is related to higher interview scores. Both nonverbal and verbal communication has also been found to influence interview scores, with their combined influence proving to have the strongest effects. However, the relation between these candidate behaviors and interview performance is dependent on three key boundary conditions: the amount of interview structure, the type of job, and candidate sincerity. These conditions serve as moderators of the relation between candidate behaviors and interview performance (see Figure 19.1).

INTERVIEW STRUCTURE

Consistent with the effects of demographic characteristics on interview outcomes, the influence of impression management tactics on interview performance is reduced when structured as opposed to unstructured interview formats are used (Barrick et al., 2009). Structured interviews focus attention on the relevant knowledge, skills, abilities, and other attributes (KSAOs) of the candidate, rendering additional behaviors, such as impression management tactics, less powerful. Thus, although impression management tactics are related to job interview performance, they are less likely to bias evaluations during structured interview sessions.

Research has also demonstrated that the effect of nonverbal communication is attenuated when structured interview formats are used. Specifically, Tsai, Chen, and Chiu (2005) examined the extent to which job candidates used friendly nonverbal cues such as smiling and nodding. They found that the influence of these nonverbal cues on interview performance was reduced when structured interviews were employed. Again, this can be attributed to the fact that structured interviews focus on a wide range of KSAOs that extend beyond communication skills. Additional research that explores this question with verbal communication would be valuable.

TYPE OF JOB

Type of job may also moderate relations between candidate behaviors and interview performance (Stevens & Kristof, 1995). Tsai and colleagues (2005) found evidence that impression management tactics were significantly related to interview scores for jobs that required high levels of customer contact. In contrast, impression management tactics were not related to interview scores for jobs that did not require high levels of customer contact. Surely industries requiring a high level of customer contact would benefit from hiring employees who were able to manage their impressions in a positive manner. Although not yet examined empirically, similar findings are expected when verbal and nonverbal communication are considered. Specifically, candidates who are verbally expressive may be rated more favorably when applying for jobs that require high levels of interaction (i.e., in service industries), whereas candidates who are verbally reserved may be rated more favorably for jobs that require minimal interpersonal contact (i.e., in high tech industries).

CANDIDATE SINCERITY

As previously indicated, a caveat in using impression management tactics concerns the authenticity with which these strategies are displayed. Specifically, interviewers have negative impressions of candidates whom they perceive to be engaged in high levels of insincere impression management (Howard & Ferris, 1996). For example, there is evidence that "false smiling" during job interviews results in less favorable impressions than does "genuine smiling" (Ekman, Friesen, & Ancoli, 1980; Woodzicka, 2008; Woodzicka & LaFrance, 2005). Thus, candidates should use impression management tactics carefully, ensuring that they are not perceived as insincere (Dipboye, 1992). One way that this can be accomplished is to make sure that what candidates portray outwardly to interviewers, whether it be the impression management strategies they engage in, what they say verbally, or how they act nonverbally, matches how candidates really feel inside, so as not to come across as insincere. Indeed, a disconnect between the two signals insincerity, whereas alignment signals sincerity and results in higher evaluations (Weisbuch, Ambady, Clarke, Achor, & Weele, 2010). Combined, these findings suggest that the relation between impression management tactics and interview scores will be moderated by perceived candidate sincerity, such that higher scores will be obtained when candidates are viewed as genuine.

Directions for Future Research

There are a number of valuable avenues for future research in this area. The majority of past work has focused on examining isolated candidate behaviors and failed to consider whether combinations of behavioral tactics are related to interview outcomes. This is surprising, given that, from a practical point of view these tactics are unlikely to be used in isolation. Falbe and Yukl (1992) were the first to examine the effectiveness of combined influence tactics. They found that using a combination of tactics was typically better than using a single tactic, as long as the combination did not involve hard tactics. More recently, Peeters and Lievens (2006) examined self-focused impression management tactics (i.e., self-promotion, entitlements) along with nonverbal communication behaviors (i.e., smiling, eye contact). While both tactics demonstrated significant relations with interview ratings, impression management tactics were more strongly related to positive interview scores. Additional research that examines the combined effects of various tactics is likely to prove invaluable.

It would also be useful to consider whether interviewers can be trained to recognize what types of impression management tactics candidates are using. Levashina and Campion (2006, 2007) have suggested that there may be important differences between "honest impression management behaviors," whereby candidates portray a positive image without being deceptive, and "dishonest impression management behaviors" wherein deceit is used. These concepts are closely aligned with "surface acting" and "deep acting" strategies from the emotion regulation literature (Grandey, 2003). Applied to job interviews, surface acting represents an attempt to be portrayed in a positive light by modifying one's facial features and/or behaviors without changing one's inner feelings in line with what is displayed (e.g., dishonest impression management), while deep acting represents an attempt to seem genuine or authentic by modifying one's feelings to match what is displayed (e.g., honest impression management). The literature on emotion regulation may serve as a valuable theoretical framework for future research in this area.

Finally, as noted by Huffcutt (2011), additional research examining social skills in job interview contexts would be valuable. In particular, the core components of emotional intelligence (perceiving emotions, using emotions, understanding emotions, and regulating emotions) (Salovey & Mayer, 1990) may have notable implications for job interview performance. Candidates who are able to use their emotions effectively—for example, by accurately perceiving an interviewer's mood, having a good grasp of the dynamics of the interaction, and using their emotions to guide thinking and facilitate performance—are likely to be better positioned to convey a positive impression. Unfortunately, few studies have examined these possibilities. An exception is Fox and Spector (2000), who conducted an empirical study and found that emotional intelligence, general intelligence, and practical intelligence are all related to interview outcomes. Additional work on emotional intelligence and job interviews is needed.

Candidate Reactions

There has also been a considerable amount of research examining candidate reactions to job interviews. This research can be divided into that which considers candidate preferences for different types of selection tools and that which focuses on candidate responses (i.e., anxiety, justice) to job interviews.

Candidate Preference for Types of Job Interviews

Job interviews are not only the most widely used selection tool in the corporate world but also the most preferred by job candidates. Hausknecht and colleagues (2004) conducted a meta-analytic review of the literature and found that interviews were rated as the most preferred selection tool, ranked higher than work samples, resumes, and psychometric tests. This finding holds across cultures, with interviews receiving high levels of favorability not only in the United States, but also in France, Germany, Belgium, Greece, Spain, Portugal, the Netherlands, and Vietnam (Anderson, Salgado, & Hülsheger, 2010; Anderson & Witvliet, 2008; Hausknecht et al., 2004; Hoang, Erdogan, Truxillo, & Bauer, 2010; Moscoso & Salgado, 2004; Nikolaou & Judge, 2007; Steiner & Gilliland, 1996).

There is also evidence indicating that job candidates prefer face-to-face interviews over videoconferencing or telephone-based interviews (Chapman & Rowe, 2002; Chapman, Uggerslev, & Webster, 2003; Silvester, Anderson, Haddleton, Cunningham-Snell, & Gibb, 2000). For example, Chapman and colleagues (2003) studied university students who were applying for jobs in 346 different organizations and found that face-to-face interviews were perceived as higher on procedural justice and led to higher job acceptance intentions. Bauer, Truxillo, Paronto, Weekley, and Campion (2004) also examined candidate reactions to interview formats and found that face-to-face interviewers were rated higher on several interpersonal justice dimensions, such as interpersonal treatment and two-way communication. Candidates also reported significantly higher organizational attractiveness and lower intentions to litigate in the face-to-face condition. These findings are not surprising, as interviews that are conducted in person promote a more natural flow of conversation and are a better medium for conveying and understanding feelings and emotions (Chapman & Rowe, 2001).

Research also indicates that candidates prefer unstructured interviews over structured interviews (Chapman & Rowe, 2002; Chapman & Zweig, 2005; Kohn & Dipboye, 1998; Latham & Finnegan, 1993). This may be because of a number of factors, including the fact that the formal nature of structured interviews makes it more difficult for candidates to manage impressions (Chapman &

Rowe, 2002; Posthuma et al., 2002). Further, candidate perceptions of control and opportunity to voice their opinions are restricted in structured interviews (Madigan & Macan, 2005). Relatedly, structured interviews have been found to be significantly related to candidate feelings of anxiety (McCarthy & Goffin, 2004).

Candidate Responses to Job Interviews

Candidate reactions to the job interview process can be quite variable, ranging from highly positive to highly negative. Negative reactions (i.e., low justice, high anxiety, low motivation) have been found to have detrimental effects on the selection process, including reduced job acceptance intentions, lower perceptions of organizational attractiveness, and fewer intentions to recommend the organization to other candidates (Hausknecht et al., 2004). This is highly problematic, as top candidates are likely to be interviewing at multiple organizations and often receive multiple job offers (Blau, 1992). Thus even small changes in the attractiveness of the organization may have a substantial effect on their intentions and behaviors (Chapman et al., 2003). Moreover, there are substantial financial costs associated with having candidates drop out of the employment pool (Boudreau & Rynes, 1985). To date, two key reactions have dominated job interview research: anxiety and justice.

JOB INTERVIEW ANXIETY

The interview process is a daunting experience for many candidates (McCarthy & Goffin, 2004). Most candidates consider the employment interview as their only chance of making a solid first impression. To compound matters, the outcome of an interview can be a life-changing event, such as a major career shift or a move to a new city. Thus, many have experienced feelings of nervous tension and trepidation when walking into a job interview, with shaking hands, fast heartbeats, and cold, sweaty palms. Moreover, these behavioral and physiological effects have been found to persist for the duration of the interview (Young, Behnke, & Mann, 2004).

However, interview anxiety has been found to extend beyond physiological manifestations to include dimensions such as interpersonal anxiety and performance anxiety (McCarthy & Goffin, 2004). This makes intuitive sense, as interviews represent a strong situation with highly evaluative interpersonal processes that are typically conducted by a stranger and are not under the candidates' control. Specifically, McCarthy and Goffin (2004)

developed a model of job interview anxiety which contains five dimensions: appearance anxiety, communication anxiety, social anxiety, behavioral anxiety, and performance anxiety (see Table 19.1 for descriptions). This model was supported by data from 276 job candidates undergoing selection interviews for a wide range of managerial and professional positions. Findings indicated that candidates experience varying levels of the five interview anxiety types.

Cognitive interference theories provide the foundation for understanding the relation between interview anxiety and performance in the interview. A number of theories are subsumed under the rubric of *cognitive interference*, including processing efficiency theory (Eysenck & Calvo, 1992); attentional control theory (Eysenck, Derakshan, Santos, & Calvo, 2007); interference theory (Wine, 1980), the elaboration likelihood model (Petty & Cacioppo, 1986), and integrative resource theory (Kanfer & Ackerman, 1989). Common to each of these theories is the proposition that anxiety interferes with people's ability to focus on and process events, resulting in lower levels of interview performance. For example, the cognitive load model states that people have finite amounts of processing power, and that anxiety impairs this processing power by interfering with their ability to attend to and process performance-relevant information (Barlow, 2002; Kanfer & Ackerman, 1989). Indeed, anxiety has been shown to impair task performance by interfering with reasoning abilities, semantic memory retrieval processes (Zeidner, 1998), information acquisition (Barber, Hollenbeck, Tower, & Phillips, 1994) and working memory performance (Shackman et al., 2006).

Consistent with cognitive interference models, empirical evidence indicates that anxiety is negatively linked to job interview performance (Arvey, Strickland, Drauden, & Martin, 1990; Ayres & Crosby, 1995; Cook, Vance, & Spector, 2000; McCarthy & Goffin, 2004). For example, McCarthy and Goffin (2004) found that the five interview anxiety dimensions, as a set, were negatively related to job interview performance. Further, when specific dimensions of interview anxiety were considered, the communication and appearance anxiety dimensions revealed the strongest relations with interviewer ratings of performance. This is consistent with a series of studies conducted by Ayres and colleagues (Ayres, Ayres, & Sharp, 1993; Ayres & Crosby, 1995; Ayres, Keereetaweep, Chen, & Edwards, 1998), who found that candidates high on communication anxiety were rated as less suitable, less effective communicators, and were less likely to be offered a job. This is also consistent with the fact that candidates with high levels of interpersonal anxiety are perceived as less attractive (Hawkins & Stewart, 1990) and less intelligent (Richmond, Beatty, & Dyba, 1985).

There is also evidence that interviewers may have difficulty perceiving candidate levels of anxiety (Barrick, Patton, & Haughland, 2000; Feiler & Powell, 2013; McCarthy & Goffin, 2004), suggesting that anxiety is not a readily observable feeling. This finding is important for at least two reasons. First, this finding suggests that candidates may be hiding or suppressing their true levels of anxiety. In 2009, Sieverding examined emotional suppression and interview anxiety in a simulated job interview paradigm. Findings indicated that candidates, particularly males, feel compelled to suppress their feelings of anxiety. Results also revealed that suppressors were viewed as more confident by interviewers than nonsuppressors. In other words, "playing it cool" may help to increase job interview performance. Given that interviewers may have difficulty recognizing feelings of anxiety in candidates, job interview preparation programs would benefit from training candidates to develop more confidence or self-efficacy (e.g., chapter by da Motta Veiga and Turban, this volume). Second, this finding provides further support for cognitive interference as the mechanism underling the anxiety-performance link. Specifically, the observed low levels of interview performance for anxious candidates are not simply due to interviewers perceiving candidates to be anxious and hence rating them low. Instead, they are more likely due to the fact that anxiety directly impacts candidates' cognitive processing capabilities, which interferes with their interview performance. Hence, cognitive interference serves as a mechanism underlying the relation between candidate anxiety and interview performance (see Figure 19.1).

JOB INTERVIEW JUSTICE

In spite of the fact that the interview is an anxiety-evoking process, it is consistently perceived to be one of the most "fair" selection procedures. This perception is generalizable to other countries (Anderson & Witvliet, 2008; Hausknecht et al., 2004). Perceptions of fairness, or justice, with respect to job interviews can be classified into concerns regarding whether the procedure is fair (procedural justice) (Greenberg, 1993) and concerns regarding whether

the outcome of the interview was fair (distributive justice) (Greenberg, 1993). A meta-analytic review of justice reactions across seventeen countries was recently conducted by Anderson and colleagues (2010). Findings indicated that interviews were consistently perceived to be high on procedural justice across all countries. Indeed, when compared with other selection techniques, job interviews are ranked at or near the top with respect to procedural justice across a host of countries, including the United States, France, Singapore, Greece, Italy, Turkey, Romania, and the Netherlands (Anderson & Witvliet, 2008; Bertolino & Steiner, 2007; Bilgic & Acarlar, 2010; Ispas, Ilie, Iliescu, Johnson, & Harris, 2010; Nikolaou & Judge, 2007; Phillips & Gully, 2002; Steiner & Gilliland, 1996).

Research has also considered candidate perceptions of justice with respect to interview structure. Chapman and Zweig (2005) obtained detailed information about how candidates perceive the various components of interview structure as outlined by Campion and colleagues (1997). Findings indicated that low levels of procedural justice were obtained when interviews were conducted by a panel, and candidates were discouraged from asking questions. Given that the use of a panel is an important component of interview structure (Campion et al., 1997); techniques to increase the perceived justice of panels are needed. Extending this research to other cultures would also be advantageous. Dipboye, Macan, and Shahani-Denning (2012) propose that highly structured interview formats may be more accepted in cultures that are high on power distance (i.e., that accept and expect unequal distributions of power) and uncertainty avoidance. Panel interviews may be better received in collectivistic cultures.

There is also evidence that interviews will be perceived as unfair if they include discriminatory questions, such as age, gender, marital status, handicaps and ethnicity. Although such questions are illegal, they are not uncommon (Bennington, 2001; Keyton & Springston, 1992; McShulskis, 1997; Saunders, 1992). Woodzicka and LaFrance (2005) examined the effects of sexually discriminatory questions (e.g., "Do you have a boyfriend?") in simulated job interviews. Female participants who were presented with these discriminatory questions spoke less fluently, gave lower-quality answers, and asked fewer job relevant questions. Saks and McCarthy (2006) examined a wider range of discriminatory questions (age, marital and child status, handicaps, and arrest record). These questions had a significant negative effect on participant's reactions to the interview and interviewer, as well as intentions to pursue employment, accept a job offer, and recommend the organization to others. Thus organizations that request discriminatory information are creating negative candidate perceptions and placing themselves at a recruiting disadvantage.

Justice perceptions may also have an impact on interview outcomes. Gilliland's (1993) seminal model of candidate reactions predicts that justice perceptions can influence candidate attitudes (e.g., organizational attractiveness), intentions (e.g., to recommend the selection process to others), and behaviors (e.g., interview performance). Fairness heuristic theory (Lind, 2001) provides a foundation for understanding these effects, as it asserts that people seek out fairness information in order to determine the extent to which they are valued by the organization (Lind & Tyler, 1988). In an interview context, the theory predicts that employees will feel valued when they perceive the job interview process to be fair. It further predicts that the manner in which interviewers treat candidates will influence perceptions of justice. Whereas fair treatment communicates respect and value toward candidates, unfair treatment communicates disrespect (Tyler & Lind, 1992). Therefore fairness heuristics, in the form of value perceptions, serve as a mechanism underlying the relation between candidate perceptions of justice and interview outcomes (see Figure 19.1).

Several studies have examined perceived justice in selection contexts and meta-analytic findings indicate that perceptions of procedural justice are related to organizational attractiveness, intentions to recommend the selection process to others, and job acceptance intentions (Chapman et al., 2005; Hausknecht et al., 2004). In terms of applying Gilliland's (1993) predictions in interview situations, Bauer and colleagues (2001) found that candidates who reported higher levels of social justice (i.e., treatment of candidates) and structural justice (i.e., procedural justice) with respect to job interviews were more likely to view the organization as attractive and recommend the organization to others.

Directions for Future Research

Although existing research has provided important insights into candidate reactions to the interview process, we suggest three areas for future research. First, future research should expand the focus of candidate reactions by considering additional reactions, such as motivation and anger.

Considerable research on motivation with respect to selection tests has been conducted (Hausknecht et al., 2004; McCarthy, Hrabluik, & Jelley, 2009); however, studies have yet to explore candidate motivation in job interview contexts. Candidate levels of motivation are deemed important by recruiters (Atkins & Kent, 1988) and are likely to have important implications for key interview outcomes, such as interview performance and recommendation intentions. It would also be valuable to examine motivation in the context of racial and gender differences with an emphasis on stereotype threat (Ployhart, Ziegert, & McFarland, 2003). Further, this research could examine how different motivational theories applied to candidate reactions would impact the interview process. For example, McClelland (1985) suggests that individuals are primarily motivated by the needs for power, affiliation, or achievement. Future research can examine whether candidates who are driven by varying levels of each of these motivation types perform better on interviews. Sanchez, Truxillo, and Bauer (2000) have developed an expectancy-based model of test-taking motivation (VIEMS) that would be useful to apply to interview contexts. Also, motivational theories such as goal-setting theory (Latham, Mawritz, & Locke, this volume; Locke & Latham, 2002) could be applied to train candidates to perform better in interviews, for example, by encouraging candidates to set specific goals for the interview. This could also potentially contribute toward lowering interview anxiety.

Candidate anger is another valuable avenue for future studies, particularly as it relates to feelings of anxiety, perceptions of justice, and the use of discriminatory questions. Some initial work with respect to candidate anger has been conducted by Segers-Noij, Proost, van Dijke, and von Grumbkow (2010), who examined candidates for a penitentiary job in Belgium. Results indicated that candidate anger was strongly and negatively related to perceptions of procedural and distributive justice. Further, the negative relation between anger and procedural justice was particularly strong among candidates who reported high levels of self-referenced anxiety (i.e., the desire to meet personal performance standards) as opposed to candidates who reported high levels of other-referenced anxiety (i.e., desire to meet others performance standards). Thus, fair procedures are particularly important for individuals who are high on self-referenced anxiety.

There is also a need for research that examines how candidate emotions more generally affect the interview process and more specifically the extent to which they are related to job interview performance. Initial research suggests that positive affect is related to whether candidates receive follow-up interviews (Burger & Caldwell, 2000). Further, evidence suggests that individuals who suppress emotions during a simulated interview are considered more competent than those who do not suppress emotions (Sieverding, 2009). However, more research needs to be conducted on candidate affectivity and mood during actual job interviews as well as research examining how candidate emotions may interact with interviewer emotions in the prediction of interview outcomes.

An additional consideration for future work is the examination of candidate reactions to interviews over time. Most individuals experience several employment interviews over the span of their careers. As a result, they are likely to become more adept at interviewing, and levels of interview anxiety, motivation, and perceptions of justice may fluctuate over time. Thus, candidate reactions may actually serve as precursors to the interview, such that candidates arrive at the interview with predetermined levels of anxiety, motivation, and perceptions of justice. However, research to date has either failed to consider changes over time or has positioned factors such as interview experience as a control variable (i.e., McCarthy et al., 2009). As highlighted by Ryan and Ployhart (2000), there is reason to believe that examining the stability of candidate reactions over time will yield valuable findings. In fact, recent work by Schleicher, Van Iddekinge, Morgeson, and Campion (2010) supports this proposition in a test-taking context. Their study examined test-taking reactions and test score improvements over time and found that test-taking motivation was partially responsible for higher test score improvements among White as opposed to Black and Hispanic candidates. Conducting similar research in job interview contexts would be worthwhile. For example, longitudinal research can consider conditions under which candidate reactions play a role with respect to changes to interview scores over time.

Finally, in line with the recommendations of Macan (2009), additional research examining the specific dimensions of interview anxiety would be extremely useful. Relatedly, training programs tailored to reduce each type of anxiety may prove valuable. Programs that focus on emotional intelligence are likely to be particularly useful with respect to the management of candidate anxiety.

Candidate Recommendations

As illustrated, we have made great strides in our understanding of the variables that can influence interviewer ratings of performance. More specifically, we now know that a wide range of candidate characteristics, candidate behaviors, and candidate reactions can have significant effects on interview scores. From the lens of job candidates, these findings underscore the importance of making a strong and lasting impression during the interview. This requires a number of steps, such as conducting research on the organization, planning one's appearance, and practicing job interview behaviors. In line with our goal to bridge research and practice, we present a practical checklist that details specific steps that candidates can take to achieve their objectives. This checklist is based on theoretical and empirical research findings described in this chapter, and is presented in the Appendix.

Existing research also indicates that the level of interview structure, type of job, and candidate sincerity can reduce the potential biasing effects of candidate characteristics and behaviors. Thus when a candidate is attending an unstructured interview or applying for jobs that are not closely aligned with his or her personal characteristics (e.g., a female candidate applying for a masculine-linked job such as a police officer), they must be cognizant of the potentially biasing effects of demographics and behaviors on interview performance and work to counteract these effects. The best way this can be accomplished is by ensuring that the interview remains focused on the job candidates' individuating information (e.g., Glick, Zion, & Nelson, 1988; McCarthy et al., 2010) or the KSAOs that are required of the job. In doing so, the interviewer is less likely to focus on or be distracted by personal characteristics and/or behaviors. Certainly the use of structured interviews is the best way to ensure that the interview will be centered on the relevant KSAOs for the job. However, candidates can also facilitate this process by conducting a comprehensive self-assessment in order to become familiar with their qualifications and personal interviewing style. The checklist provided in the Appendix details steps that can help keep the interview focused on individuating information.

Finally, our review of past work emphasized the importance of increasing candidate interviewing skills, reducing candidate anxiety, and increasing candidate perceptions of justice. Below, we outline specific techniques that can be used to accomplish each of these objectives.

IMPROVING INTERVIEW SKILLS

The first strategy is to focus on improving candidates' interview skills. In line with the research on impression management, the focus of skills training is to make candidates aware of their self-presentation tactics. This is typically accomplished through practice, tutoring, and coaching (Maurer & Solamon, 2006). Research on the effectiveness of these techniques is promising, with several studies demonstrating positive relations between interview skill training and interview performance (Latham & Budworth, 2006; Maurer, Solamon, Andrews, & Troxtel, 2001; Maurer, Solamon, & Troxtel, 1998; Tross & Maurer, 1999; see also Latham, Mawritz & Locke, and Price & Vinokur, both from this volume).

In an interesting series of studies, Maurer and colleagues examined the effectiveness of an interview training program that was designed for police and firefighter candidates. The program contained several components, including the provision of information about types of job interviews, participation in role plays, and tips on how to prepare for job interviews. Findings across two separate studies indicated that individuals who voluntarily joined this coaching program demonstrated higher levels of interview performance than those who did not participate in the program (Maurer et al., 1998, 2001). Results also demonstrated that the organizationally based interview preparation strategies (e.g., participating in role plays) were more strongly related to subsequent interview performance than internally based interview preparation strategies (e.g., reading an interview training book) (Maurer et al., 2001). Finally, candidates who were well organized and thoughtful (e.g., who had organized their answers in a chronological and logical manner) were more likely to exhibit high levels of interview performance. More recently, this program has been found to enhance the validity of the selection process (Maurer, Solamon, & Lippstreu, 2008).

The studies by Maurer and colleagues (Maurer et al., 1998, 2001, 2008) suggest that having practice vocalizing responses and practicing communication styles in simulated, or mock, interviews is more beneficial than simply reading about interviewing. This is in line with research by Caldwell and Burger (1998), who found that interviewees who used social sources to prepare for the interview (i.e., talking to people at the target company, talking to people in related jobs) were more likely to receive follow-up interviews and job offers. This probably happens because interviewees who experience interpersonal coaching are more likely to stay on target and offer relevant information to interviewers. Directing attention to relevant job knowledge and skills, in turn, provides a more accurate picture of candidate abilities and may increase the validity of the interview process.

There is also evidence that interview skills can be improved through training programs that teach candidates how to successfully manage impressions. Kristof-Brown, Barrick, and Franke (2002) found evidence that trained candidates were better at self-promotion during the interview and displayed stronger levels of nonverbal communication (e.g., eye contact, smiling). These behaviors, in turn, were positively related to interview outcomes. A note of caution is in order, however, in that it is important to be perceived as sincere as in managing impressions (Howard & Ferris, 1996). This can be accomplished by ensuring a match between action and words. Making a list of qualifications and abilities ahead of time is also advantageous, as it reduces the need to exaggerate qualifications.

REDUCING ANXIETY

The second strategy is to reduce the candidate's level of anxiety. Self-efficacy training is likely to be particularly effective in this regard, as research supports the role of self-efficacy in the relationship between interview anxiety and subsequent interview performance (Leary & Atherton, 1986; Moynihan, Roehling, LePine, & Boswell, 2003; Stumpf, Brief, & Hartman, 1987). Moreover, research has found that individuals with high levels of self-efficacy are better able to cope with stressful situations at work, while individuals with low levels of self-efficacy are more likely to experience stress, leading to lower productivity (Maciejewski, Prigerson, & Mazure, 2000; Stajkovic & Luthans, 1998).

Drawing from clinical psychology, there are at least two interventions that may be particularly useful for reducing anxiety and increasing self-efficacy: verbal self-guidance (Meichenbaum, 1977), which emphasizes the use of functional self-talk as a means of increasing self-efficacy for subsequent tasks; and attributional retraining (Perry & Penner, 1990), which emphasizes the replacement of maladaptive attributions with adaptive ones in order to improve performance.

Verbal self-guidance (VSG) involves verbalizing one's thought processes during the identification, problem-solving, and solution stages in dealing with a particular problem (Brown, 2003). Part of this is functional self-talk, or talking oneself through any challenge to effective performance (Meichenbaum, 1971, 1975, 1977). That is, negative or dysfunctional self-statements (e.g., "I am so anxious during an interview that I can't think of what to say") are modified to positive or functional self-statements (e.g., "I already know what I want to convey during the interview. I can focus on communicating this to the interviewer rather than focusing on my anxiety"). The training program contains three steps. First, trainees observe a trainer modeling effective self-statements that guide an individual towards completing the task causing the anxiety. Second, trainees are taught to overtly self-instruct. Third, trainees self-instruct covertly. Although the effectiveness of VSG training on interview anxiety has not been examined, VSG has been effectively used as a training tool in other areas (Brown, 2003; Latham, Mawritz, & Locke, this volume; Latham & Budworth, 2006; Manning, White, & Daugherty, 1994; Martini & Polatajko, 1998).

Attributional retraining (AR) may also prove to be an effective strategy for helping candidates cope with interview anxiety. The foundation for AR is attribution theory (Weiner, 1985), which holds that the attributions people make for their successes or failures vary along three dimensions: internal/external, stable/unstable, controllable/uncontrollable. Attributing past failures to internal, stable and uncontrollable causes is maladaptive because these factors are viewed as unchangeable. AR teaches candidates how to adopt adaptive attributions for past failures. The focus is on helping candidates feel a sense of control over their environment and generating a sense that future success is possible (Försterling, 1985). Given that anxious individuals often feel a lack of control over their environment (Chorpita & Barlow, 1998; Watson, 1967), this treatment may prove particularly advantageous. The beneficial effects of AR on a host of organizational outcomes have been demonstrated (Jackson, Hall, Rowe, & Daniels, 2009; Struthers, Colwill, & Perry, 2006).

There is also some evidence that AR is useful in job interview contexts. Jackson et al. (2009) examined the effectiveness of AR on a sample of cooperative education students completing job interviews. Participants in the AR training condition watched a videotape depicting two students discussing the importance of adopting positive and controllable attributions, and how this strategy actually helped them improve their interview performance. In the next section of the video, a female professor described attribution theory and how

job interview success is related to the types of attributions people hold. Finally, participants in the training condition completed a writing assignment that required them to summarize and apply what they had learned to their upcoming interview. Participants in the control condition watched a videotape outlining the importance of verbal and nonverbal communication in interviews. Findings indicated that participants in the AR condition received higher levels of interview performance than participants in the control condition, particularly those who exhibited maladaptive baseline attributions. Future research should examine the mechanisms by which this treatment operates, such as lowering feelings of interview anxiety.

INCREASING JUSTICE PERCEPTIONS

Unlike interview skills training and anxiety reduction techniques, methods to increase justice perceptions lie solely in the hands of the organization. Gilliland's (1993) procedural justice framework provide clear recommendations for how organizations can ensure the interview process is viewed as fair by candidates. Paramount among Gilliland's recommendations are the following: (1) ensure the system is job-related; (2) give candidates the opportunity to perform; (3) give candidates the opportunity to challenge or modify the selection process; (4) ensure the content and procedure of the process is consistent across all candidates; (5) provide candidates with informative and timely feedback; (6) provide explanations and justification for the use of a procedure or a decision; (7) ensure that administrators are honest when communicating with candidates; (8) ensure that administrators treat candidates with warmth and respect; (9) support a two-way communication process; and (10) ensure that questions are legal and not discriminatory in nature. Bauer and colleagues (2001) have developed a comprehensive measure to assess Gilliland's rules. Their instrument is extremely useful as a foundation for future research, and as an applied organizational instrument for assessing the relative fairness of selection practices.

A number of studies have examined whether the procedural rules outlined by Gilliland (1993) are related to perceptions of justice. In 2004, Hausknecht and colleagues conducted a meta-analysis and found strong evidence in support of Gilliland's propositions. In particular, two recommendations that have consistently been found to be advantageous are the use of job-related, or face-valid, techniques, and the provision of explanations to candidates. The use of structured interviews is particularly useful in accomplishing these objectives, as items are derived from job-relevant KSAOs. This ensures that questions are specific to the job in question and reduces the potential for interviewers to touch on discriminatory issues. In turn, candidates are more motivated to take the interview seriously (Latham, Saari, Pursell, & Campion, 1980). Meta-analytic evidence also reveals that providing explanations about the job-relatedness of the selection process is positively related to candidates' justice perceptions, perceived attractiveness of the hiring organization, test-taking motivation, and test performance (Truxillo et al., 2009). More recently, evidence has been found to suggest that tailoring explanations to candidates increase perceptions of justice (Krauss, Truxillo, Bauer, & Mack, 2010). Additional research examining justice interventions (Truxillo, Bauer, & Campion, 2009), and applying Gilliland's framework to interview contexts is greatly needed.

Conclusion

This chapter provided a comprehensive review of interview research from the perspective of job candidates. We examined how candidate characteristics, behaviors and reactions in particular have significant implications for a number of interview outcomes, most notably job interview performance. We used this research as a basis for putting forth a number of recommendations for practice, as described in the previous section, and detailed in the Appendix.

Notably, our "best practice" recommendations for candidates share considerable overlap with "best practice" recommendations for organizations. Specifically, Campion and Campion (1987) outlined a number of key recommendations for conducting properly structured interviews. As highlighted in Table 19.2, several of these recommendations parallel our best practices for candidates. This consistency is encouraging for candidates and organizations alike, as it suggests that properly conducted interviews can serve the best interest of both parties. Indeed, the ultimate goal of the job candidate is aligned with the ultimate goal of interviewers: to identify and discuss job-relevant knowledge and skills. To accomplish this, both candidate and interviewer must be well prepared. When the candidate is prepared, they will focus more on individuating information and provide more job-relevant information, making the interview more valid. By engaging in

the "recommendations for practice" identified in the Appendix, the candidate will be able to show their "true self." The interviewer must also be prepared. When the interviewer is more prepared, they will use structured techniques, making the interview more valid. Interviewers must ensure that the KSAOs for the job are clearly identified through the process of a job analysis. They should use properly structured questions with anchored rating scales. They must also be trained in job interview skills. Ultimately, this dual process of preparation from both the candidate and interviewer will result in job interviews that are beneficial for all parties involved.

In conclusion, job interviews serve both a recruiting and selection function (Rynes, 1989). From a recruiting perspective, they are designed to increase the candidate's interest in the organization as a place to work. From a selection perspective, they are designed to predict which employee(s) will demonstrate successful performance on the job. As a

Table 19.1 Model of Job Interview Anxiety

Anxiety Type	Definition
Appearance anxiety	Feelings of nervousness or apprehension about one's physical appearance in job interview situations. This includes both the unchangeable (e.g., height) and changeable (e.g., hairstyle) aspects of one's appearance.
Communication anxiety	Feelings of nervousness or apprehension about one's verbal communication skills, nonverbal communication skills, and listening skills in job interview contexts.
Social anxiety	Feelings of nervousness or apprehension about one's social behavior in job interview situations (e.g., correct handshake) resulting from a desire to be liked.
Behavioral anxiety	Activation of the autonomic nervous system (e.g., fast heartbeat, shaky hands, perspiration) due to nervousness in job interview situations.
Performance anxiety	Feelings of nervousness or apprehension about one's level of performance in job interview situations.

Source: McCarthy and Goffin (2004).

Table 19.2 Structured Interview Recommendations for Interviewers and Job Candidates

Recommendations for Interviewers	Recommendations for Candidates
Develop interview based on job analysis to identify the knowledge, skills, abilities, and other attributes (KSAOs) that are relevant for the job. Use this to develop interview questions.	Conduct a personal assessment to identify the KSAOs that are relevant for the job. Use this to think about responses to interview questions.
Use structured questions (situational, past behavioral).	Become familiar with structured interview questions and think of relevant examples that illustrate your KSAOs.
Anchor rating scales for scoring answers with examples and illustrations.	Practice answering interview questions using mock interviews. Make sure to include specific examples and provide vivid details.
Take detailed notes that can be examined after the interviews.	Take detailed mental notes about the job—the interview is a two-way process, you are also interviewing them!
Use a panel interview to record and rate answers.	Focus attention on the entire panel.
Give special attention to job-relatedness and fairness.	Help make sure the interview stays on track and is job-relevant by ensuring that your answers don't include irrelevant personal stories and information.
Provide extensive interviewer training.	Take a training program that focuses on interviewing skills.

result, considering interviews from the lens of both candidates and organizations is critical. This chapter adopted the candidates' perspective and provided comprehensive coverage of the theory, research, and practical applications of job interviews. It is our hope that it stimulates future work in this important area and serves as a practical benchmark for both candidates and organizations.

Appendix

Job Candidate Checklist for Practice

Interviewing well is a skill and is not something that occurs automatically. To do well in an interview it is essential to be well prepared. Your goal is to separate yourself from others who have applied for the job by highlighting your individuating information—your skills, knowledge, and abilities. In turn, your individuating information should be targeted to the job for which you are applying.

Based on extant research, we have put together some guidelines to help with interview preparation. This process includes four key steps. It is essential to make sure that the interviewer has access to your individuating information. That is, ensure that you communicate the knowledge, skills, and abilities that you possess that are related to the job and differentiate you from other candidates. This can be accomplished by first conducting a self-assessment in order to familiarize yourself with

your qualifications and your personal style. Second, target your individuating information to the specific job for which you are applying. A resource that is particularly useful in this regard is an online tool called the O*Net (http://www.onetonline.org/). O*Net is a free online database containing thousands of job descriptions. This step will enable you to think about times when you have used specific competencies related to the position in past experiences, and to prepare relevant stories that can be shared in the interview. Third, it is important to convey a positive impression. This involves planning your appearance, practicing your response strategy and preparing a list of questions to ask the job interviewer. Fourth, it is essential to practice job interview behaviors by engaging in mock interviews. The details of these steps are discussed below.

1. Conduct a Self-Assessment

Research indicates that biases will be reduced to the extent that interviewers have access to job-relevant information. It is essential that you convey this information to interviewers. In order to promote your attributes, you must first have a solid understanding of your strengths. The process of self-evaluation is very important, as you must make yourself stand out from other candidates. To take on the competition, you need to know how you measure up against other candidates. We recommend that you prepare lists of the following.

Your Skills: Write down the knowledge, skills, and abilities that will set you apart from other candidates. Try to look for those areas where you have obtained specialized knowledge that will meet the requirements of the position. Your knowledge, skills, abilities, and other attributes (KSAOs) may be evident within specific projects you may have completed from various jobs. Thus, it is important to identify these skills prior to the interview. Your preparation will come across, and you can be more confident in responding, minimizing the need for fumbling, mumbling, and hedging responses.

Your Strengths and Weaknesses: Make a list of your strengths and weaknesses. Be specific and list past experiences that demonstrate each point. For example, instead of identifying yourself as a team player, list specific examples where you demonstrated team skills (e.g., "When I was working for Alpha Corporation, my team was faced with the following challenge . . . I was instrumental in solving this problem, as I . . . "). With respect to your weaknesses, ask yourself how you have learned from these setbacks along the way. This is critical, as your weaknesses may be uncovered during the course of the interview and the interviewer will want to see how you have learned from them.

2. *Conduct a Job Assessment*

Research indicates that one of the best ways to reduce biases among job interviewers and recruiters is to ensure that the interview remains focused on KSAOs that are required of the job. This can be accomplished by making sure that your unique characteristics, or your individuating information, is targeted to the job for which you are applying. By understanding the specific job requirements, you can match your KSAOs directly to the position in question. This will allow you to prepare stories that describe how you have used these competencies in the past.

Again, you may well find the O*Net useful here. It not only details the knowledge, skills, and abilities required of a wide variety of jobs but also provides comprehensive information about the specific tasks associated with the job, the tools and technology required for the job, and the work context for the job. It even provides the interests, work styles, and work values of the "typical" worker. By conducting a thorough job assessment, you can ensure that the information you provide in the job interview will be targeted to the requirements of the job.

3. *Manage Impressions*

Research indicates that impression management behaviors can have an influence on the outcome of job interviews. Keep the following considerations in mind:

Be Punctual: Arrive 10 to 15 minutes early for your interview—tardiness creates an impression that is difficult to erase. Giving yourself at least an extra 15 minutes will also allow you to compose yourself in the waiting room and go into the interview relaxed.

Dress Conservatively: Job interviews still follow a conservative standard. Regardless of whether you are male or female, a suit is the recommended choice of attire. In terms of color, conservative shades (e.g., navy blue, gray, or tan) are best, as they convey a professional appearance. Make sure your clothes are clean and unwrinkled or risk inferences of sloppiness. Also, remove irrelevant accessories such as hats, coats, boots, sunglasses, etc. before you go into the interview. Finally, keep jewelry and scents to a minimum.

Be Polite to Everyone: This includes the administrative assistant and receptionist out front—you would be surprised how much influence they may have in terms of the selection process!

Use Formal Titles: Address the interviewer by his or her formal title and make sure that you pronounce it correctly.

Respect the Interviewers' Space: Recognize the boundaries of your personal space and that of others. North Americans usually prefer a comfort zone of approximately 3 feet in interpersonal relationships. Be prepared not to move closer to someone who has a personal space limit smaller than your own.

Use a Proper Handshake: Use a firm handshake and make eye contact while shaking hands.

Don't Forget to Smile! Smiling is an easy way to break the ice, convey a favorable impression, and have others empathize and warm up to you. Research has shown that interviewers give higher ratings to candidates who smiled and who were positive during the course of the interview.

Maintain Eye Contact: Lack of eye contact is often perceived negatively by job interviewers. Lack of eye contact is often associated with insincerity, a trait you do not want ascribed to you during the interview. Therefore practice maintaining eye contact while speaking and listening to others. Ask your friends to practice with you and give you feedback on how well you hold eye contact with them.

Ensure Good Posture: Height is not what is important; posture is. When you are standing, stand up straight. When you are seated, make sure you sit at the front edge of the chair. Don't slouch—the interviewer may interpret this as disinterest rather than an attempt to appear relaxed.

Watch your Gestures: When you use gestures, make sure that they are natural and meaningful rather than stiff and planned. Your gestures should match the verbal content of your message so that you are perceived as sincere.

Be Organized: Be organized and thoughtful. Before answering questions, try to organize your responses in a chronological, logical, and easy to follow manner. This is likely to enhance the comprehensiveness of your responses and make it more likely that the interviewer accurately understands the message that you are trying to convey. It is acceptable to take a minute to gather your thoughts before you respond. A coherent response will go a long way.

Remember to Listen: Although it is important to convey your suitability for the job, it is also important to hear what the interviewers have to say. Remember, you are also collecting information about the position and are interviewing the organization, in a sense. Knowing when to speak and when to listen is also a skill and demonstrates your consideration for other people and shows respect.

4. Identify and Practice Behaviors

Identify your Bad Habits: As described, interviewers are strongly influenced by a candidate's behaviors. It is therefore important to understand your verbal and nonverbal behavior patterns (or habits). Get to know your body language (e.g., eye contact, facial expressions, posture, gestures) by asking people who know you well to advise you on your nonverbal communication. For example, some individuals have a tendency to sit with their arms crossed over the chest. This behavior conveys disinterest, nervousness, and/or dislike and should be avoided in job interview situations. Other "bad habits" include playing with your hair, fidgeting with eyeglasses, and staring at the ceiling or floor.

Conduct Mock Interviews: Ask a friend or relative to give you a "mock" interview and give you feedback on your personal style. A practice, or mock, interview is an opportunity to try out your interviewing techniques and answers out loud. The benefits of using a mock interview as practice should not be overlooked. This will increase your awareness of any bad habits that you may have so that you can

control them during the job interview. It also enables you to receive constructive feedback from someone who can help improve your interviewing style and presentation. Practice questions can be obtained from lists of frequently asked questions in self-help books. In preparing answers to these questions, include specific examples from your work experience and try to tailor answers for the specific position you are applying for. Try to paint a vivid picture for the interviewer so that she or he gets a strong sense of what you are trying to convey. During your mock interview, visualize yourself as confident and self-assured. Go over common questions until you can respond effortlessly. Relax, be clear, and be yourself. The practice will be well worth it—it will not only improve your interviewing skills but also help to increase your self-confidence.

References

Adkins, C. L., Russell, C. J., & Werbel, J. D. (1994). Judgments of fit in the selection process: The role of work value congruence. *Personnel Psychology, 47*(3), 605–623. doi: http://dx.doi.org/10.1111/j.1744-6570.1994.tb01740.x

Ambady, N., & Rosenthal, R. (1992). Thin slices of expressive behavior as predictors of interpersonal consequences: A meta-analysis. *Psychological Bulletin, 111*(2), 256–274. doi:10.1037/0033-2909.111.2.256

Anderson, N. (1992). Eight decades of employment interview research: A retrospective meta-review and prospective commentary. *European Work and Organizational Psychologists, 2*(1), 1–32. doi: 10.1080/09602009208408532

Anderson, N. R. (1991). Decision making in the graduate selection interview: An experimental investigation. *Human Relations, 44*(4), 403–417. doi:10.1177/001872679104400407

Anderson, N., Salgado, J. F., & Hülsheger, U. R. (2010). Candidate reactions in selection: Comprehensive meta-analysis into reaction generalization versus situational specificity. *International Journal of Selection and Assessment, 18*(3), 291–304. doi:10.1111/j.1468-2389.2010.00512.x

Anderson, N., & Witvliet, C. (2008). Fairness reactions to personnel selection methods: An international comparison between the Netherlands, the United States, France, Spain, Portugal, and Singapore. *International Journal of Selection and Assessment, 16*(1), 1–13. doi:10.1111/j.1468-2389.2008.00404.x

Arvey, R. D., & Campion, J. E. (1982). The employment interview: A summary and review of recent research. *Personnel Psychology, 35*, 281–322. doi:10.1111/j.1744–6570.1982.tb02197.x

Arvey, R. D., Strickland, W., Drauden, G., & Martin, C. (1990). Motivational components of test taking. *Personnel Psychology, 43*(4), 695–716. doi:10.1111/j.1744–6570.1990.tb00679.x

Arvey, R. D. (1979). Unfair discrimination in the employment interview: Legal and psychological aspects. *Psychological Bulletin, 86*(4), 736–765. doi:10.1037/0033-2909.86.4.736

Ashmore, R. D. (1981). Sex stereotypes and implicit personality theory. In D. L. Hamilton (Ed.), *Cognitive processes in stereotyping and intergroup behavior* (pp. 37–81). Hillsdale, NJ: Erlbaum.

Atkins, C. P., & Kent, R. L. (1988). What do recruiters consider important during the employment interview? *Journal of Employment Counseling*, 25(3), 98–103.

Ayres, J., Ayres, D. M., & Sharp, D. (1993). A progress report on the development of an instrument to measure communication apprehension in employment interviews. *Communication Research Reports*, 10(1), 87–94. doi:10.1080/08824099309359920

Ayres, J., & Crosby, S. (1995). Two studies concerning the predictive validity of the personal report of communication apprehension in employment interviews. *Communication Research Reports*, 12(2), 145–151. doi:10.1080/08824099509362050

Ayres, J., Keereetaweep, T., Chen, P., & Edwards, P. A. (1998). Communication apprehension and employment interviews. *Communication Education*, 47(1), 1–17. doi:10.1080/03634529809379106

Bar, M., Neta, M., & Linz, H. (2006). Very first impressions. *Emotion*, 6(2), 269–278. doi:10.1037/1528-3542.6.2.269

Barber, A. E., Hollenbeck, J. R., Tower, S. L., & Phillips, J. M. (1994). The effects of interview focus on recruitment effectiveness: A field experiment. *Journal of Applied Psychology*, 79(6), 886–896. doi:10.1037/0021-9010.79.6.886

Barlow, D. H. (2002). *Anxiety and its disorders: The nature and treatment of anxiety and panic* (2nd Ed.). New York: Guilford.

Baron, R. A. (1989). Impression management by candidates during employment interviews: The "too much of a good thing" effect. In R. W. Eder & G. R. Ferris (Eds.), *The employment interview: Theory, research, and practice* (pp. 204–215). Newbury Park, CA: Sage.

Barrick, M. R., Patton, G. K., & Haughland, S. N. (2000). Accuracy of interviewer judgments of job candidate personality traits. *Personnel Psychology*, 53(4), 925–951. doi:10.1111/j.1744–6570.2000.tb02424.x

Barrick, M. R., Shaffer, J. A., & DeGrassi, S. W. (2009). What you see may not be what you get: Relationships among self-presentation tactics and ratings of interview and job performance. *Journal of Applied Psychology*, 94(6), 1394–1411. doi:10.1037/a0016532

Barrick, M. R., Swider, B. W., & Stewart, G. L. (2010). Initial evaluations in the interview: Relationships with subsequent interviewer evaluations and employment offers. *Journal of Applied Psychology*, 95(6), 1163–1172. doi:10.1037/a0019918

Bauer, T. N., Truxillo, D. M., Paronto, M. E., Weekley, J. A., & Campion, M. A. (2004). Candidate reactions to different selection technology: Face-to-face, interactive voice response, and computer-assisted telephone screening interviews. *International Journal of Selection and Assessment*, 12(1–2), 135–148. doi:10.1111/j.0965-075X.2004.00269.x

Bauer, T. N., Truxillo, D. M., Sanchez, R. J., Craig, J. M., Ferrara, P., & Campion, M. A. (2001). Candidate reactions to selection: Development of the selection procedural justice scale (SPJS). *Personnel Psychology*, 54(2), 388–420. doi:10.1111/j.1744–6570.2001.tb00097.x

Baumeister, R. F., Bratslavsky, E., Finkenauer, C., & Vohs, K. D. (2001). Bad is stronger than good. *Review of General Psychology*, 5(4), 323–370. doi:10.1037/1089-2680.5.4.323

Bennington, L. (2001). Age discrimination: Converging evidence from four Australian studies. *Employee Responsibilities and Rights Journal*, 13(3), 125–134. doi:10.1023/A:1014911816746

Bertolino, M., & Steiner, D. D. (2007). Fairness reactions to selection methods: An Italian study. *International Journal of Selection and Assessment*, 15(2), 197–205. doi:10.1111/j.1468-2389.2007.00381.x

Bilgic, R., & Acarlar, G. (2010). Fairness perceptions of selection instruments used in turkey. *International Journal of Selection and Assessment*, 18(2), 208–214. doi:10.1111/j.1468-2389.2010.00502.x

Blau, D. M. (1992). An empirical analysis of employed and unemployed job search behavior. *Industrial and Labor Relations Review*, 54(4), 738–752.

Bolino, M. C., & Turnley, W. H. (2003). More than one way to make an impression: Exploring profiles of impression management. *Journal of Management*, 29(2), 141–160. doi:10.1177/014920630302900202

Bolster, B. I., & Springbett, B. M. (1961). The reaction of interviewers to favorable and unfavorable information. *Journal of Applied Psychology*, 45(2), 97–103. doi:10.1037/h0048316

Boudreau, J. W., & Rynes, S. L. (1985). Role of recruitment in staffing utility analysis. *Journal of Applied Psychology*, 70(2), 354–366. doi:10.1037/0021-9010.70.2.354

Bragger, J. D., Kutcher, E., Morgan, J., & Firth, P. (2002). The effects of the structured interview on reducing biases against pregnant job candidates. *Sex Roles*, 46(7–8), 215–226. doi:10.1023/A:1019967231059

Brown, T. C. (2003). The effect of verbal self-guidance training on collective efficacy and team performance. *Personnel Psychology*, 56(4), 935–964. doi:10.1111/j.1744–6570.2003.tb00245.x

Brunswick, E. (1956). *Perception and the representative design of psychological experiments*. Berkeley: University of California Press.

Buckley, M. R., Jackson, K. A., Bolino, M. C., Veres, J. G., & Feild, H. S. (2007). The influence of relational demography on panel interview ratings: A field experiment. *Personnel Psychology*, 60(3), 627–646. doi:10.1111/j.1744-6570.2007.00086.x

Burger, J. M., & Caldwell, D. F. (2000). Personality, social activities, job-search behavior and interview success: Distinguishing between PANAS trait positive affect and NEO extraversion. *Motivation and Emotion*, 24(1), 51–62. doi: 10.1023/A:1005539609679

Burnett, J. R., & Motowidlo, S. J. (1998). Relations between different sources of information in the structured selection interview. *Personnel Psychology*, 51(4), 963–983. doi:10.1111/j.1744–6570.1998.tb00747.x

Buttner, E. H., & McEnally, M. (1996). The interactive effect of influence tactic, candidate gender, and type of job on hiring recommendations. *Sex Roles*, 34(7–8), 581–591. doi:10.1007/BF01545034

Byrne, D. (1971). The ubiquitous relationship: Attitude similarity and attraction: A cross-cultural study. *Human Relations*, 24(3), 201–207. doi:10.1177/001872677102400302

Cable, D. M., & Judge, T. A. (1997). Interviewers' perceptions of person–organization fit and organizational selection decisions. *Journal of Applied Psychology*, 82(4), 546–561. doi: http://dx.doi.org/10.1037/0021-9010.82.4.546

Caldwell, D. F., & Burger, J. M. (1998). Personality characteristics of job applicants and success in screening interviews. *Personnel Psychology*, 51(1), 119–136. doi: 10.1111/j.1744–6570.1998.tb00718.x

Campion, M. A., & Campion, J. E. (1987). Evaluation of an interviewee skills training program in a natural field experiment.

Personnel Psychology, 40(4), 675–691. doi:10.1111/j.1744-6570.1987.tb00619.x

Campion, M. A., Palmer, D. K., & Campion, J. E. (1997). A review of structure in the selection interview. *Personnel Psychology, 50*(3), 655–702. doi:10.1111/j.1744-6570.1997.tb00709.x

Chan, D., & Schmitt, N. (2004). An agenda for future research on candidate reactions to selection procedures: A construct-oriented approach. *International Journal of Selection and Assessment, 12*(1–2), 9–23. doi:10.1111/j.0965-075X.2004.00260.x

Chaplin, W. F., Phillips, J. B., Brown, J. D., Clanton, N. R., & Stein, J. L. (2000). Handshaking, gender, personality, and first impressions. *Journal of Personality and Social Psychology, 79*(1), 110–117. doi:10.1037/0022-3514.79.1.110

Chapman, D. S., & Rowe, P. M. (2001). The impact of videoconference technology, interview structure, and interviewer gender on interviewer evaluations in the employment interview: A field experiment. *Journal of Occupational and Organizational Psychology, 74*(3), 279–298. doi: 10.1348/096317901167361

Chapman, D. S., & Rowe, P. M. (2002). The influence of videoconference technology and interview structure on the recruiting function of the employment interview: A field experiment. *International Journal of Selection and Assessment, 10*(3), 185–197. doi:10.1111/1468–2389.00208

Chapman, D. S., Uggerslev, K. L., Caroll, S. A., Piasentin, K. A., & Jones, D. A. (2005). Candidate attraction to organizations and job choice: A meta-analytic review of the correlates of recruiting outcomes. *Journal of Applied Psychology, 90*(5), 928–944. doi:10.1037/0021-9010.90.5.928

Chapman, D. S., Uggerslev, K. L., & Webster, J. (2003). Candidate reactions to face-to-face and technology-mediated interviews: A field investigation. *Journal of Applied Psychology, 88*(5), 944–953. doi:10.1037/0021-9010.88.5.944

Chapman, D. S., & Zweig, D. I. (2005). Developing a nomological network for interview structure: Antecedents and consequences of the structured selection interview. *Personnel Psychology, 58*(3), 673–702. doi:10.1111/j.1744-6570.2005.00516.x

Chorpita, B. F., & Barlow, D. H. (1998). The development of anxiety: The role of control in the early environment. *Psychological Bulletin, 124*(1), 3–21. doi:10.1037/0033-2909.124.1.3

Cialdini, R. B., & Trost, M. R. (1998). *Social influence: Social norms, conformity and compliance.* New York, NY: McGraw-Hill.

Cleveland, J. N., Festa, R. M., & Montgomery, L. (1988). Candidate pool composition and job perceptions: Impact on decisions regarding an older candidate. *Journal of Vocational Behavior, 32*(1), 112–125. doi:10.1016/0001-8791(88)90009-7

Constantin, S. W. (1976). An investigation of information favorability in the employment interview. *Journal of Applied Psychology, 61*(6), 743–749. doi:10.1037/0021-9010.61.6.743

Cook, K. W., Vance, C. A., & Spector, P. E. 2000 (2000). The relation of candidate personality with selection-interview outcomes. *Journal of Applied Social Psychology, 30*(4), 867–885. DOI: 10.1111/j.1559–1816.2000.tb02828.x

Cunningham, J., & Macan, T. (2007). Effects of candidate pregnancy on hiring decisions and interview ratings. *Sex Roles, 57*(7–8), 497–508. doi:10.1007/s11199-007-9279-0

DeGroot, T., & Motowidlo, S. J. (1999). Why visual and vocal interview cues can affect interviewers' judgments and predict job performance. *Journal of Applied Psychology, 84*(6), 986–993. doi:10.1037/0021-9010.84.6.986

Ding, V. J., & Stillman, J. A. (2005). An empirical investigation of discrimination against overweight female job candidates in New Zealand. *New Zealand Journal of Psychology, 34*(3), 139–148.

Dipboye, R. L. (1992). Social interaction in the interview. In R. L. Dipboye (Ed.), *Selection interview: Process perspectives* (pp. 75–100). Cincinnati, OH: South-Western.

Dipboye, R. L. (2004). The selection/recruitment interview: Core processes and contexts. In A. Evers, N. Anderson, & O. Voskuijl (Eds.), *The Blackwell handbook of personnel selection.* Oxford, UK: Blackwell.

Dipboye, R. L., Fromkin, H. L., & Wiback, K. (1975). Relative importance of candidate sex, attractiveness, and scholastic standing in evaluation of job candidate resumes. *Journal of Applied Psychology, 60*(1), 39–43. doi:10.1037/h0076352

Dipboye, R. L., Macan, T., & Shahani-Denning, C. (2012). The selection interview from the interviewer and applicant perspectives: Can't have one without the other. In N. Schmitt (Ed.), *The Oxford handbook of personnel assessment and selection.* New York, NY: Oxford University Press.

Eagly, A. H., Ashmore, R. D., Makhijani, M. G., & Longo, L. C. (1991). What is beautiful is good, but . . .: A meta-analytic review of research on the physical attractiveness stereotype. *Psychological Bulletin, 110*(1), 109–128. doi:10.1037/0033-2909.110.1.109

Eagly, A. H., & Steffen, V. J. (1984). Gender stereotypes stem from the distribution of women and men into social roles. *Journal of Personality and Social Psychology, 46*(4), 735–754. doi:10.1037/0022-3514.46.4.735

Ekman, P., Friesen, W. V., & Ancoli, S. (1980). Facial signs of emotional experience. *Journal of Personality and Social Psychology, 39*(6), 1125–1134. doi:10.1037/h0077722

Eysenck, M. W., & Calvo, M. G. (1992). Anxiety and performance: The processing efficiency theory. *Cognition and Emotion, 6*(6), 409–434. doi:10.1080/02699939208409696

Eysenck, M. W., Derakshan, N., Santos, R., & Calvo, M. G. (2007). Anxiety and cognitive performance: Attentional control theory. *Emotion, 7*(2), 336–353. doi:10.1037/1528-3542.7.2.336

Falbe, C. M., & Yukl, G. (1992). Consequences for managers of using single influence tactics and combinations of tactics. *Academy of Management Journal, 35*(3), 638–652. doi:10.2307/256490

Feiler, A. R., & Powell, D. M. (2013). Interview anxiety across the sexes: Support for the sex-linked anxiety coping theory. *Personality and Individual Differences, 54*(1), 12–17. doi: http://dx.doi.org/10.1016/j.paid.2012.07.030

Feingold, A. (1992). Good-looking people are not what we think. *Psychological Bulletin, 111*(2), 304–341. doi:10.1037/0033-2909.111.2.304

Finkelstein, L. M., DeMuth, R. L. F., & Sweeney, D. L. (2007). Bias against overweight job candidates: Further explorations of when and why. *Human Resource Management, 46*(2), 203–222. doi:10.1002/hrm.20157

Försterling, F. (1985). Attributional retraining: A review. *Psychological Bulletin, 98*(3), 495–512. doi:10.1037/0033-2909.98.3.495

Forsythe, S., Drake, M. F., & Cox, C. E. (1985). Influence of candidate's dress on interviewer's selection decisions.

Journal of Applied Psychology, 70(2), 374–378. doi:10.1037/0021-9010.70.2.374

Forsythe, S. M. (1990). Effect of candidate's clothing on interviewer's decision to hire. *Journal of Applied Social Psychology, 20*(19Pt1), 1579–1595. doi:10.1111/j.1559-1816.1990.tb01494.x

Fox, S., & Spector, P. E. (2000). Relations of emotional intelligence, practical intelligence, general intelligence, and trait affectivity with interview outcomes: It's not all just "G." *Journal of Organizational Behavior. Special Issue: Emotions in Organizations, 21*, 203–220. doi:10.1002/(SICI)1099-1379(200003)21:2<203::AID-JOB38>3.0.CO;2-Z

Gifford, R., Ng, C. F., & Wilkinson, M. (1985). Nonverbal cues in the employment interview: Links between candidate qualities and interviewer judgments. *Journal of Applied Psychology, 70*(4), 729–736. doi:10.1037/0021-9010.70.4.729

Gilliland, S. W. (1993). The perceived fairness of selection systems: An organizational justice perspective. *The Academy of Management Review, 18*(4), 694–734. doi:10.2307/258595

Gilmore, D. C., Beehr, T. A., & Love, K. G. (1986). Effects of candidate sex, candidate physical attractiveness, type rater and type of job on interview decisions. *Journal of Occupational Psychology, 59*(2), 103–109.

Glick, P., Zion, C., & Nelson, C. (1988). What mediates sex discrimination in hiring decisions? *Journal of Personality and Social Psychology, 55*, 178–186. doi: 10.1037/0022-3514.55.2.178

Goldberg, C. B. (2005). Relational demography and similarity-attraction in interview assessments and subsequent offer decisions: Are we missing something? *Group & Organization Management, 30*(6), 597–624. doi:10.1177/1059601104267661

Grandey, A. A. (2003). When "the show must go on": Surface acting and deep acting as determinants of emotional exhaustion and peer-rated service delivery. *Academy of Management Journal, 46*(1), 86–96.

Graves, L. M., & Powell, G. N. (1995). The effect of sex similarity on recruiters' evaluations of actual candidates: A test of the similarity-attraction paradigm. *Personnel Psychology, 48*(1), 85–98. doi:10.1111/j.1744-6570.1995.tb01747.x

Graves, L. M., & Powell, G. N. (1996). Sex similarity, quality of the employment interview and recruiters' evaluation of actual candidates. *Journal of Occupational and Organizational Psychology, 69*(3), 243–261.

Greenberg, J. (1993). The social side of fairness: Interpersonal and informational classes of organizational justice. In R. Cropanzano (Ed.), *Justice in the workplace: Approaching fairness in human resource management* (pp. 79–103). Hillsdale, NJ: Erlbaum.

Harris, M. M. (1989). Reconsidering the employment interview: A review of recent literature and suggestions for future research. *Personnel Psychology, 42*(4), 691–726. doi:10.1111/j.1744-6570.1989.tb00673.x

Hausknecht. J. P., Day, D. V., & Thomas, S. C. (2004). Candidate reactions to selection procedures: An updated model and meta-analysis. *Personnel Psychology, 57*(3), 639–683. doi:10.1111/j.1744-6570.2004.00003.x

Hawkins, K. W., & Stewart, R. A. (1990). Temporal effects of leadership style on state communication anxiety in small task-oriented groups. *Communication Research Reports, 7*(1), 3–8. doi:10.1080/08824099009359846

Hebl, M. R., King, E. B., Glick, P., Singletary, S. L., & Kazama, S. (2007). Hostile and benevolent reactions toward pregnant women: Complementary interpersonal punishments and rewards that maintain traditional roles. *Journal of Applied Psychology, 92*(6), 1499–1511. doi:10.1037/0021-9010.92.6.1499

Hebl, M. R., & Mannix, L. M. (2003). The weight of obesity in evaluating others: A mere proximity effect. *Personality and Social Psychology Bulletin, 29*(1), 28–38. doi:10.1177/0146167202238369

Heider, F. (1958). *The psychology of interpersonal relations.* New York: Wiley.

Heilman, M. E. (1983). Sex bias in work settings: The lack of fit model. *Research in Organizational Behavior, 5*, 269–298.

Hiemstra, K. (1999). Shake my hand: Making the right first impression in business with nonverbal communications. *Business Communication Quarterly, 62*(4). 71–74. doi:10.1177/108056999906200407

Hoang, T., Erdogan, B., Truxillo, D. M., & Bauer, T. N. (2010). Cross-cultural examination of candidate reactions to selection methods: U.S. and Vietnam. In T. Bauer & A. Costa (Chairs), Candidate reactions around the globe: Belgium, Greece, United States, Vietnam. Symposium conducted at the meeting of the Society for Industrial and Organizational Psychology, Chicago, IL.

Hosoda, M., Stone-Romero, E. F., & Coats, G. (2003). The effects of physical attractiveness on job-related outcomes: A meta-analysis of experimental studies. *Personnel Psychology, 56*, 431–462. doi:10.1111/j.1744-6570.2003.tb00157.x

Howard, J. L., & Ferris, G. R. (1996). The employment interview context: Social and situational influences on interviewer decisions. *Journal of Applied Social Psychology, 26*(2), 112–136. doi:10.1111/j.1559-1816.1996.tb01841.x

Huffcutt, A. I. (2011). An empirical review of the employment interview construct literature. *International Journal of Selection and Assessment, 19*(1), 62–81. doi:10.1111/j.1468-2389.2010.00535.x

Huffcutt, A. I., & Arthur, W. (1994). Hunter and hunter (1984) revisited: Interview validity for entry-level jobs. *Journal of Applied Psychology, 79*(2), 184–190. doi:10.1037/0021-9010.79.2.184

Huffcutt, A. I., Conway, J. M., Roth, P. L., & Stone, N. J. (2001). Identification and meta-analytic assessment of psychological constructs measured in employment interviews. *Journal of Applied Psychology, 86*(5), 897–913. doi: http://dx.doi.org/10.1037/0021-9010.86.5.897

Huffcutt, A. I., Van Iddekinge, C. H., & Roth, P. L. (2011). Understanding applicant behavior in employment interviews: A theoretical model of interviewee performance. *Human Resource Management Review, 21*(4), 353–367.

Hülsheger, U. R., & Anderson, N. (2009). Candidate perspectives in selection: Going beyond preference reactions. *International Journal of Selection and Assessment, 17*(4), 335–345. doi:10.1111/j.1468-2389.2009.00477.x

Imada, A. S., & Hakel, M. D. (1977). Influence of nonverbal communication and rater proximity on impressions and decisions in simulated employment interviews. *Journal of Applied Psychology, 62*(3), 295–300. doi:10.1037/0021-9010.62.3.295

Ispas, D., Ilie, A., Iliescu, D., Johnson, R. E., & Harris, M. M. (2010). Fairness reactions to selection methods: A Romanian study. *International Journal of Selection and Assessment*, *18*(1), 102–110. doi:10.1111/j.1468-2389.2010.00492.x

Jackson, S. E., Hall, N. C., Rowe, P. M., & Daniels, L. M. (2009). Getting the job: Attributional retraining and the employment interview. *Journal of Applied Social Psychology*, *39*(4), 973–998. doi: 10.1111/j.1559-1816.2009.00468.x

Jenkins, M. C., & Atkins, T. V. (1990). Perceptions of acceptable dress by corporate and non-corporate recruiters. *Journal of Human Behavior & Learning*, *7*(1), 38–46.

Johnson, S. K., Podratz, K. E., Dipboye, R. L., & Gibbons, E. (2010). Physical attractiveness biases in ratings of employment suitability: Tracking down the 'beauty is beastly' effect. *The Journal of Social Psychology*, *150*(3), 301–318. doi:10.1080/00224540903365414

Judge, T. A., & Cable, D. M. (2011). When it comes to pay, do the thin win? The effect of weight on pay for men and women. *Journal of Applied Psychology*, *96*(1), 95–112. doi:10.1037/a0020860

Judge, T. A., Higgins, C. A., & Cable, D. M. (2000). The employment interview: A review of recent research and recommendations for future research. *Human Resource Management Review*, *10*(4), 383–406. doi:10.1016/S1053-4822(00)00033-4

Kahneman, D. (2003). A perspective on judgment and choice: Mapping bounded rationality. *American Psychologist*, *58*(9), 697–720. doi:10.1037/0003-066X.58.9.697

Kalin, R., & Hodgins, D. C. (1984). Sex bias in judgments of occupational suitability. *Canadian Journal of Behavioural Science/Revue Canadienne Des Sciences Du Comportement. Special Issue: Social Psychology Applied to Social Issues in Canada*, *16*(4), 311–325. doi:10.1037/h0080862

Kanfer, R., & Ackerman, P. L. (1989). Motivation and cognitive abilities: An integrative/aptitude-treatment interaction approach to skill acquisition. *Journal of Applied Psychology*, *74*(4), 657–690. doi:10.1037/0021-9010.74.4.657

Keyton, J., & Springston, J. K. (1992). Response alternatives to discriminatory inquiries. In D. M. Saunders (Eds.), *New approaches to employee management: Fairness in employee selection* (pp. 159–184). Greenwich, CT: JAI Press.

Kohn, L. S., & Dipboye, R. L. (1998). The effects of interview structure on recruiting outcomes. *Journal of Applied Social Psychology*, *28*(9), 821–843. doi:10.1111/j.1559-1816.1998.tb01733.x

Krauss, A., Truxillo, D. M., Bauer, T. N., & Mack, K. (2010). Tailoring explanations to candidates in real time. In K. Mack & D. Truxillo (Chairs), Candidate reactions over time. Paper presented at the SIOP Annual Meeting, Chicago, IL.

Kristof-Brown, A., Barrick, M. R., & Franke, M. (2002). Candidate impression management: Dispositional influences and consequences for recruiter perceptions of fit and similarity. *Journal of Management*, *28*(1), 27–46. doi:10.1016/S0149-2063(01)00131-3

Kutcher, E. J., & Bragger, J. D. (2004). Selection interviews of overweight job candidates: Can structure reduce the bias? *Journal of Applied Social Psychology*, *34*(10), 1993–2022. doi:10.1111/j.1559-1816.2004.tb02688.x

Lamude, K. G. (1994). Supervisors' influence tactics for handling managers' resistance. *Psychological Reports*, *75*(1), 371–374.

Latham, G. P., & Budworth, M. (2006). The effect of training in verbal self-guidance on the self-efficacy and performance of native North Americans in the selection interview. *Journal of Vocational Behavior*, *68*(3), 516–523. doi:10.1016/j.jvb.2005.11.005

Latham, G. P., & Finnegan, B. J. (1993). Perceived practicality of unstructured, patterned, and situational interviews. In J. Schuler, J. L. Farr, & M. Smith (Eds.), *Personnel selection and assessment: Individual and organizational perspectives* (pp. 41–55). Hillsdale, NJ: Erlbaum.

Latham, G. P., Saari, L. M., Pursell, E. D., & Campion, M. A. (1980). The situational interview. *Journal of Applied Psychology*, *65*(4), 422–427. doi:10.1037/0021-9010.65.4.422

Leary, M. R., & Atherton, S. C. (1986). Self-efficacy, social anxiety, and inhibition in interpersonal encounters. *Journal of Social and Clinical Psychology*, *4*(3), 256–267.

Levashina, J., & Campion, M. A (2006). A model of faking likelihood in the employment interview. *International Journal of Selection and Assessment*, *14*(4), 299–316. doi: 10.1111/j.1468-2389.2006.00353.x

Levashina, J., & Campion, M. A. (2007). Measuring faking in the employment interview: Development and validation of an interview faking behavior scale. *Journal of Applied Psychology*, *92*(6), 1638–1656. doi:10.1037/0021-9010.92.6.1638

Levine, S. P., & Feldman, R. S. (2002). Women and men's nonverbal behavior and self-monitoring in a job interview setting. *Applied H.R.M. Research*, *7*(1–2), 1–14.

Levy, D. A., Collins, B. E., & Nail, P. R. (1998). A new model of interpersonal influence characteristics. *Journal of Social Behavior & Personality*, *13*(4), 715–733.

Lievens, F., & Peeters, H. (2008). Interviewers' sensitivity to impression management tactics in structured interviews. *European Journal of Psychological Assessment*, *24*(3), 174–180. doi:10.1027/1015-5759.24.3.174

Lin, T., Dobbins, G. H., & Farh, J. (1992). A field study of race and age similarity effects on interview ratings in conventional and situational interviews. *Journal of Applied Psychology*, *77*(3), 363–371. doi:10.1037/0021-9010.77.3.363

Lind, E. A. (2001). Thinking critically about justice judgments. *Journal of Vocational Behavior*, *58*(2), 220–226. doi: http://dx.doi.org/10.1006/jvbe.2001.1793

Lind, E. A., & Tyler, T. R. (1988). *The social psychology of procedural justice*. New York: Plenum Press. Available at: http://search.proquest.com/docview/617494786?accountid=14771

Locke, E. A., & Latham, G. P. (2002). Building a practically useful theory of goal setting and task motivation: A 35-year odyssey. *American Psychologist*, *57*(9), 705–717. doi:10.1037/0003-066X.57.9.705

Macan, T. (2009). The employment interview: A review of current studies and directions for future research. *Human Resource Management Review*, *19*(3), 203–218. doi:10.1016/j.hrmr.2009.03.006

Maciejewski, P. K., Prigerson, H. G., & Mazure, C. M. (2000). Self-efficacy as a mediator between stressful life events and depressive symptoms: Differences based on history of prior depression. *British Journal of Psychiatry*, *176*, 373–378. doi:10.1192/bjp.176.4.373

Mack, D., & Rainey, D. (1990). Female candidates' grooming and personnel selection. *Journal of Social Behavior & Personality*, *5*, 399–407.

Madigan, J., & Macan, T. H. (2005). Improving candidate reactions by altering test administration. *Applied H.R.M. Research*, *10*(1), 73–88.

Manning, B. H., White, C. S., & Daugherty, M. (1994). Young children's private speech as a precursor to metacognitive strategy use during task engagement. *Discourse Processes, 17*(2), 191–211. doi:10.1080/01638539409544866

Marlowe, C. M., Schneider, S. L., & Nelson, C. E. (1996). Gender and attractiveness biases in hiring decisions: Are more experienced managers less biased? *Journal of Applied Psychology, 81*(1), 11–21. doi:10.1037/0021-9010.81.1.11

Martini, R., & Polatajko, H. J. (1998). Verbal self-guidance as a treatment approach for children with developmental coordination disorder: A systematic replication study. *Occupational Therapy Journal of Research, 18*(4), 157–181.

Masser, B., Grass, K., & Nesic, M. (2007). 'We like you, but we don't want you'—The impact of pregnancy in the workplace. *Sex Roles, 57*(9–10), 703–712. doi:10.1007/s11199-007-9305-2

Maurer, T. J., & Solamon, J. M. (2006). The science and practice of a structured employment interview coaching program. *Personnel Psychology, 59*, 433–456. doi:10.1111/j.1744-6570.2006.00797.x

Maurer, T. J., Solamon, J. M., Andrews, K. D., & Troxtel, D. D. (2001). Interviewee coaching, preparation strategies, and response strategies in relation to performance in situational employment interviews: An extension of Maurer, Solamon, and Troxtel (1998). *Journal of Applied Psychology, 86*(4), 709–717. doi:10.1037/0021-9010.86.4.709

Maurer, T. J., Solamon, J. M., & Lippstreu, M. (2008). How does coaching interviewees affect the validity of a structured interview? *Journal of Organizational Behavior, 29*(3), 355–371. doi:10.1002/job.512

Maurer, T. J., Solamon, J. M., & Troxtel, D. D. (1998). Relationship of coaching with performance in situational employment interviews. *Journal of Applied Psychology, 83*(1), 128–136. doi:10.1037/0021-9010.83.1.128

McCarthy, J., & Goffin, R. (2004). Measuring job interview anxiety: Beyond weak knees and sweaty palms. *Personnel Psychology, 57*(3), 607–637. doi:10.1111/j.1744-6570.2004.00002.x

McCarthy, J., Hrabluik, C., & Jelley, R. B. (2009). Progression through the ranks: Assessing employee reactions to high-stakes employment testing. *Personnel Psychology, 62*(4), 793–832. doi:10.1111/j.1744-6570.2009.01158.x

McCarthy, J. M., Van Iddekinge, C. H., & Campion, M. A. (2010). Are highly structured job interviews resistant to demographic similarity effects? *Personnel Psychology, 63*(2), 325–359. doi:10.1111/j.1744-6570.2010.01172.x

McClelland, D. C. (1985). *Human motivation.* Glenview, IL: Scott, Foresman.

McDaniel, M. A., Whetzel, D. L., Schmidt, F. L., & Maurer, S. D. (1994). The validity of employment interviews: A comprehensive review and meta-analysis. *Journal of Applied Psychology, 79*(4), 599–616. doi:10.1037/0021-9010.79.4.599

McFarland, L. A., Ryan, A. M., & Kriska, S. D. (2002). Field study investigation of candidate use of influence tactics in a selection interview. *Journal of Psychology: Interdisciplinary and Applied, 136*(4), 383–398. doi:10.1080/00223980209604165

McFarland, L. A., Ryan, A. M., Sacco, J. M., & Kriska, S. D. (2004). Examination of structured interview ratings across time: The effects of candidate race, rater race, and panel composition. *Journal of Management, 30*(4), 435–452. doi: 10.1016/j.jm.2003.09.004

McGovern, T. V., Jones, B. W., & Morris, S. E. (1979). Comparison of professional versus student ratings of job interviewee behavior. *Journal of Counseling Psychology, 26*(2), 176–179. doi:10.1037/0022-0167.26.2.176

McGovern, T. V., & Tinsley, H. E. (1978). Interviewer evaluations of interviewee nonverbal behavior. *Journal of Vocational Behavior, 13*(2), 163–171. doi:10.1016/0001-8791(78)90041-6

McShulskis, E. (1997). Small businesses: Be aware of illegal interview questions. *HR Magazine, 42*, 22–23.

Meichenbaum, D. H. (1971). Examination of model characteristics in reducing avoidance behavior. *Journal of Personality and Social Psychology, 17*(3), 298–307.

Meichenbaum, D. H. (1975). Enhancing creativity by modifying what subjects say to themselves. *American Educational Research Journal, 12*(2), 129–145. doi:10.2307/1162416

Meichenbaum, D. H. (1977). Dr. Ellis, please stand up. *The Counseling Psychologist, 7*(1), 43–44. doi:10.1177/001100007700700103

Morgeson, F. P., Reider, M. H., Campion, M. A., & Bull, R. A. (2008). Review of research on age discrimination in the employment interview. *Journal of Business and Psychology, 22*(3), 223–232. doi:10.1007/s10869-008-9066-0

Moscoso, S. (2000). A review of validity evidence, adverse impact and candidate reactions. *International Journal of Selection and Assessment, 8*(4), 237–247. doi:10.1111/1468-2389.00153

Moscoso, S. & Salgado, J. F. (2004). Fairness reactions to personnel selection techniques in Spain and Portugal. *International Journal of Selection and Assessment, 12*(1–2), 187–196. doi:10.1111/j.0965-075X.2004.00273.x

Moynihan, L. M., Roehling, M. V., LePine, M. A., & Boswell, W. R. (2003). A longitudinal study of the relationships among job search self-efficacy, job interviews, and employment outcomes. *Journal of Business and Psychology, 18*(2), 207–233. doi: http://dx.doi.org/10.1023/A:1027349115277

Newcomb, T. M. (1956). The prediction of interpersonal attraction. *American Psychologist, 11*(11), 575–586. doi:10.1037/h0046141

Nighswonger, N. J., & Martin, C. R. (1981). On using voice analysis in marketing research. *Journal of Marketing Research, 18*(3), 350–355. doi:10.2307/3150975

Nikolaou, I., & Judge, T. A. (2007). Fairness reactions to personnel selection techniques in Greece: The role of core self-evaluations. *International Journal of Selection and Assessment, 15*(2), 206–219. doi:10.1111/j.1468-2389.2007.00382.x

Parsons, C. K., Liden, R. C., & Bauer, T. N. (2001). Person perception in employment interviews. In M. London (Ed.), *How people evaluate others in organizations* (pp. 67–90). Mahwah, NJ: Erlbaum.

Peeters, H., & Lievens, F. (2006). Verbal and nonverbal impression management tactics in behavior description and situational interviews. *International Journal of Selection and Assessment, 14*(3), 206–222. doi:10.1111/j.1468-2389.2006.00348.x

Perry, R. P., & Penner, K. S. (1990). Enhancing academic achievement in college students through attributional retraining and instruction. *Journal of Educational Psychology, 82*(2), 262–271. doi:10.1037/0022-0663.82.2.262

Petty, R. E., & Cacioppo, J. T. (1986). *Communication and persuasion: Central and peripheral routes to attitude change.* New York: Springer-Verlag.

Phillips, J. M., & Gully, S. M. (2002). Fairness reactions to personnel selection techniques in Singapore and the United States. *The International Journal of Human Resource Management*, 13(8), 1186–1205. doi:10.1080/09585190210149475

Pingitore, R., Dugoni, B. L., Tindale, R. S., & Spring, B. (1994). Bias against overweight job candidates in a simulated employment interview. *Journal of Applied Psychology*, 79(6), 909–917. doi:10.1037/0021-9010.79.6.90

Ployhart, R. E., Ziegert, J. C., & McFarland, L. A. (2003). Understanding racial differences on cognitive ability tests in selection contexts: An integration of stereotype threat and candidate reactions research. *Human Performance*, 16(3), 231-231-259. doi:10.1207/S15327043HUP1603_4

Posthuma, R. A., Morgeson, F. P., & Campion, M. A. (2002). Beyond employment interview validity: A comprehensive narrative review of recent research and trends over time. *Personnel Psychology*, 55(1), 1–81. doi: 2002–12469—00110.1111/j.1744—6570.2002.tb00103.x

Proost, K., Schreurs, B., De Witte, K., & Derous, E. (2010). Ingratiation and self-promotion in the selection interview: The effects of using single tactics or a combination of tactics on interviewer judgments. *Journal of Applied Social Psychology*, 40(9), 2155–2169. doi:10.1111/j.1559-1816.2010.00654.x

Rafaeli, A., Dutton, J., Harquail, C. V., & Mackie-Lewis, S. (1997). Navigating by attire: The use of dress by female administrative employees. *Academy of Management Journal*, 40(1), 9–45. doi:10.2307/257019

Rasmussen, K. G. (1984). Nonverbal behavior, verbal behavior, resumé credentials, and selection interview outcomes. *Journal of Applied Psychology*, 69(4), 551–556. doi:10.1037/0021-9010.69.4.551

Richmond, V. P., Beatty, M. J., & Dyba, P. (1985). Shyness and popularity: Children's views. *Western Journal of Speech Communication*, 49(2), 116–125. doi:10.1080/10570318509374187

Riggio, R. E., & Throckmorton, B. (1988). The relative effects of verbal and nonverbal behavior, appearance, and social skills on evaluations made in hiring interviews. *Journal of Applied Social Psychology*, 18(4), 331–348. doi:10.1111/j.1559-1816.1988.tb00020.x

Roehling, M. V., Roehling, P. V., & Odland, L. M. (2008). Investigating the validity of stereotypes about overweight employees: The relationship between body weight and normal personality traits. *Group & Organization Management*, 33(4), 392–424. doi:10.1177/1059601108321518

Roehling, M. V. (1999). Weight-based discrimination in employment: Psychological and legal aspects. *Personnel Psychology*, 52(4), 969–1016. doi:10.1111/j.1744–6570.1999.tb00186.x

Rosen, B., & Jerdee, T. H. (1976a). The influence of age stereotypes on managerial decisions. *Journal of Applied Psychology*, 61(4), 428–432. doi:10.1037/0021-9010.61.4.428

Rosen, B., & Jerdee, T. H. (1976b). The nature of job-related age stereotypes. *Journal of Applied Psychology*, 61(2), 180–183. doi:10.1037/0021-9010.61.2.180

Rosenfeld, P., Giacalone, R. A., & Riordan, C. A. (1995). *Impression management in organizations: Theory, measurement, practice*. London: Routledge.

Rudolph, C. W., Wells, C. L., Weller, M. D., & Baltes, B. B. (2009). A meta-analysis of empirical studies of weight-based bias in the workplace. *Journal of Vocational Behavior*, 74(1), 1–10. doi:10.1016/j.jvb.2008.09.008

Rusbult, C. E., & Van Lange, P. A. M. (2003). Interdependence, interaction and relationships. *Annual Review of Psychology*, 54, 351–375. doi:10.1146/annurev.psych.54.101601.145059

Ryan, A. M., & Huth, M. (2008). Not much more than platitudes? A critical look at the utility of candidate reactions research. *Human Resource Management Review*, 18(3), 119–132. doi:10.1016/j.hrmr.2008.07.004

Ryan, A. M., & Ployhart, R. E. (2000). Candidates' perceptions of selection procedures and decisions: A critical review and agenda for the future. *Journal of Management*, 26(3), 565–606. doi:10.1177/014920630002600308

Rynes, S. L. (1989). The employment interview as a recruitment device. (pp. 127–141). Thousand Oaks, CA: Sage. Available at: http://search.proquest.com/docview/617685168?accountid=14771

Rynes, S. L., & Gerhart, B. (1990). Interviewer assessments of candidate "fit": An exploratory investigation. *Personnel Psychology*, 43(1), 13–35. doi:10.1111/j.1744–6570.1990.tb02004.x

Sacco, J. M., Scheu, C. R., Ryan, A. M., & Schmitt, N. (2003). An investigation of race and sex similarity effects in interviews: A multilevel approach to relational demography. *Journal of Applied Psychology*, 88(5), 852–865. doi:10.1037/0021-9010.88.5.852

Saks, A. M., & McCarthy, J. M. (2006). Effects of discriminatory interview questions and gender on candidate reactions. *Journal of Business and Psychology*, 21(2), 175–191. doi:10.1007/s10869-006-9024-7

Salovey, P., & Mayer, J. D. (1990). Emotional intelligence. *Imagination, Cognition, and Personality*, 9(3), 185–211.

Sanchez, R. J., Truxillo, D. M., & Bauer, T. N. (2000). Development and examination of an expectancy-based measure of test-taking motivation. *Journal of Applied Psychology*, 85(5), 739-739-750. doi:10.1037/0021-9010.85.5.739

Saunders, D. M. (1992). *New approaches to employee management: Fairness in employee selection*, (Vol. 1). Greenwhich, CT: JAI Press.

Schleicher, D. J., Van Iddekinge, C. H., Morgeson, F. P., & Campion, M. A. (2010). If at first you don't succeed, try, try again: Understanding race, age, and gender differences in retesting score improvement. *Journal of Applied Psychology*, 95(4), 603–617. doi:10.1037/a0018920

Schlenker, B. R. (1980). *Impression management: The self-concept, social identity, and interpersonal relations*. Monterey, CA: Brooks/Cole.

Segers-Noij, M., Proost, K., van Dijke, M. H., & von Grumbkow, J. (2010). Angry candidates: The influence of procedural and distributive justice perceptions and the moderating role of test anxiety. Paper presented at the WAOP—conference, Brussels, Belgium.

Shackman, A. J., Sarinopoulos, I., Maxwell, J. S., Pizzagalli, D. A., Lavric, A., & Davidson, R. J. (2006). Anxiety selectively disrupts visuospatial working memory. *Emotion*, 6(1), 40–61. doi:10.1037/1528-3542.6.1.40

Shannon, M. L., & Stark, C. P. (2003). The influence of physical appearance on personnel selection. *Social Behavior and Personality*, 31(6), 613–624. doi:10.2224/sbp.2003.31.6.613

Shore, L. M., & Goldberg, C. B. (2005). Age discrimination in the work place. In R. L. Dipboye & A. Colella (Eds.), *The psychological and organizational bases of discrimination at work*.

Frontier Series, Society for Industrial and Organizational Psychology.

Sieverding, M. (2009). "Be cool!": Emotional costs of hiding feelings in a job interview. *International Journal of Selection and Assessment, 17*(4), 391–401. doi:10.1111/j.1468-2389.2009.00481.x

Silvester, J., Anderson, N., Haddleton, E., Cunningham-Snell, N., & Gibb, A. (2000). A cross-modal comparison of telephone and face-to-face selection interviews in graduate recruitment. *International Journal of Selection and Assessment, 8*(1), 16–21. doi:10.1111/1468–2389.00127

Stajkovic, A. D., & Luthans, F. (1998). Self-efficacy and work-related performance: A meta-analysis. *Psychological Bulletin, 124*(2), 240–261. doi:10.1037/0033-2909.124.2.240

Steele, C. M. (1997). A threat in the air: How stereotypes shape intellectual identity and performance. *American Psychologist, 52*(6), 613–629. doi:10.1037/0003-066X.52.6.613

Steiner, D. D., & Gilliland, S. W. (1996). Fairness reactions to personnel selection techniques in France and the United States. *Journal of Applied Psychology, 81*(2), 134–141. doi:10.1037/0021-9010.81.2.134

Steiner, D. D., & Gilliland, S. W. (2001). Procedural justice in personnel selection: International and cross-cultural perspectives. *International Journal of Selection and Assessment, 9*(1–2), 124–137. doi:10.1111/1468–2389.00169.

Stevens, C. K., & Kristof, A. L. (1995). Making the right impression: A field study of candidate impression management during job interviews. *Journal of Applied Psychology, 80*(5), 587–606. doi:10.1037/0021-9010.80.5.587

Stewart, G. L., Dustin, S. L., Barrick, M. R., & Darnold, T. C. (2008). Exploring the handshake in employment interviews. *Journal of Applied Psychology, 93*(5), 1139–1146. doi:10.1037/0021-9010.93.5.1139

Struthers, C. W., Colwill, N. L., Perry, R. P. (2006). An attributional analysis of decision making in a personnel selection interview. *Journal of Applied Social Psychology, 22*(10), 801–818. doi:10.1111/j.1559–1816.1992.tb00925.x

Stumpf, S. A., Brief, A. P., & Hartman, K. (1987). Self-efficacy expectations and coping with career-related events. *Journal of Vocational Behavior, 31*(1), 91–108. doi:10.1016/0001-8791(87)90037-6

Swami, V., Chan, F., Wong, V., Furnham, A., & Tovée, M. J. (2008). Weight-based discrimination in occupational hiring and helping behavior. *Journal of Applied Social Psychology, 38*(4), 968–981. doi:10.1111/j.1559-1816.2008.00334.x

Swami, V., Pietschnig, J., Stieger, S., Tovée, M. J., & Voracek, M. (2010). An investigation of weight bias against women and its associations with individual difference factors. *Body Image, 7*(3), 194–199. doi:10.1016/j.bodyim.2010.03.003

Tews, M. J., Stafford, K., & Zhu, J. (2009). Beauty revisited: The impact of attractiveness, ability, and personality in the assessment of employment suitability. *International Journal of Selection and Assessment, 17*(1), 92–100. doi:10.1111/j.1468-2389.2009.00454.x

Tross, S. A., & Maurer, T. J. (1999). Effect of interviewee coaching on structured experience—based interview processes and outcomes. Presented at the Annual Conference of the Society for Industrial and Organizational Psychology, Atlanta, GA.

Truxillo, D. M., & Bauer, T. N. (2010). Candidate reactions to selection procedures. In S. Zedeck, H. Aguinis, W. Cascio, M. Gelfand, K. Leung, S. Parker, & J. Zhou (Eds.), *APA handbook of I/O psychology. Vol. 2: Selecting members,* pp. 379–397, Washington, DC: APA Press.

Truxillo, D. M., Bauer, T. N., & Campion, M. A. (2009). Organizational justice interventions: Practicalities, concerns, and potential. *Industrial and Organizational Psychology: Perspectives on Science and Practice, 2*(2), 211–214. doi:10.1111/j.1754-9434.2009.01141.x

Truxillo, D. M., Bodner, T. E., Bertolino, M., Bauer, T. N., & Yonce, C. A. (2009). Effects of explanations on candidate reactions: A meta-analytic review. *International Journal of Selection and Assessment, 17*(4), 346–361. doi:10.1111/j.1468-2389.2009.00478.x

Tsai, W., Chen, C., & Chiu, S. (2005). Exploring boundaries of the effects of candidate impression management tactics in job interviews. *Journal of Management, 31*(1), 108–125. doi:10.1177/0149206304271384

Tsai, W. C., Huang, T.-C. & Yu, H.-H. (2011). Investigating the unique predictability and boundary conditions of candidate physical attractiveness and non-verbal behaviours on interviewer evaluations in job interviews. *Journal of Occupational and Organizational Psychology, 84*, 1–20. doi: 10.1348/2044–8325.002003

Tsai, W., Huang, T., Wu, C., & Lo, I. (2010). Disentangling the effects of candidate defensive impression management tactics in job interviews. *International Journal of Selection and Assessment, 18*(2), 131–140. doi:10.1111/j.1468-2389.2010.00495.x

Tsui, A. S., Egan, T. D., & O'Reilly, C. A. (1992). Being different: Relational demography and organizational attachment. *Administrative Science Quarterly, 37*(4), 549–579. doi:10.2307/239347

Tsui, A. S., & O'Reilly, C. A. (1989). Beyond simple demographic effects: The importance of relational demography in superior-subordinate dyads. *Academy of Management Journal, 32*(2), 402–423. doi:10.2307/256368

Tyler, T. R., & Lind, E. A. (1992). A relational model of authority in groups. (pp. 115–191). San Diego, CA: Academic Press. doi: http://dx.doi.org/10.1016/S0065-2601(08)60283-X

Watson, D. (1967). Relationship between locus of control and anxiety. *Journal of Personality and Social Psychology, 6*(1), 91–92. doi:10.1037/h0024490

Wayne, S. J., & Liden, R. C. (1995). Effects of impression management on performance ratings: A longitudinal study. *Academy of Management Journal, 38*(1), 232–260. doi:10.2307/256734

Weiner, B. (1985). An Attributional theory of achievement motivation and emotion. *Psychological Review, 92*(4), 548–573. doi:10.1037/0033-295X.92.4.548

Weisbuch, M., Ambady, N., Clarke, A. L., Achor, S., & Weele, J. V. (2010). On being consistent: The role of verbal-nonverbal consistency in first impressions. *Basic and Applied Social Psychology, 32*(3), 261–268. doi:10.1080/01973533.2010.495659

Wiesner, W. H., & Cronshaw, S. F. (1988). A meta-analytic investigation of the impact of interview format and degree of structure on the validity of the employment interview. *Journal of Occupational Psychology, 61*(4), 275–290.

Willis, J., & Todorov, A. (2006). First impressions: Making up your mind after a 100-ms exposure to a face. *Psychological Science*, *17*(7), 592–598. doi:10.1111/j.1467-9280.2006.01750.x

Wine, J. (1980). Cognitive-attentional theory of test anxiety. In I. G. Sarason (Ed.), *Test anxiety: Theory, research and applications* (pp. 349–385). Hillsdale, NJ: Erlbaum.

Woodzicka, J. A. (2008). Sex differences in self-awareness of smiling during a mock job interview. *Journal of Nonverbal Behavior*, *32*(2), 109–121. doi:10.1007/s10919-007-0046-2

Woodzicka J. A., & LaFrance, M. (2005). The effects of subtle sexual harassment on women's performance in a job interview. *Sex Roles*, *53*(1–2), 67–77. doi:10.1007/s11199-005-4279-4

Young, M. J., Behnke, R. R., & Mann, Y. M. (2004). Anxiety patterns in employment interviews. *Communication Reports*, *17*(1), 49–57.

Zeidner, M. (1998). *Test anxiety: The state of the art.* New York: Plenum Press.

Reemployment Quality, Underemployment, and Career Outcomes

Meghna Virick *and* Frances M. McKee-Ryan

Abstract

This chapter provides an overview of research on underemployment among laid-off workers, with a particular focus on workers who are more vulnerable to underemployment based on age, gender, and minority status. This review identifies issues, problems, and gaps in the current research and outlines directions for future research, specifically highlighting the importance of examining career outcomes of underemployed workers.

Key Words: underemployment, job loss, unemployment

Introduction

The pervasive effects of job loss and job search on unemployed workers and their social networks have been chronicled in the previous chapters of this volume. We now turn our attention to these employees' post-unemployment job outcomes, with a particular focus on the quality of reemployment and underemployment among previously unemployed workers. Early job loss research focused on reemployment as a dichotomous variable—did the unemployed worker find a job or not? In the mid-1990s, however, job loss researchers took note of the fact that the reemployment jobs of displaced workers varied in quality and began to focus on the quality of reemployment. This research demonstrated that laid-off workers have a tendency to accept jobs of lower quality than their former position (e.g., Gowan, Riordan, & Gatewood, 1999; Hijzen, Upward, & Wright, 2010; Kinicki, Prussia, & McKee-Ryan, 2000; Leana & Feldman, 1995; Waters, 2007). Accepting less than optimal reemployment puts unemployed individuals at an increased risk of becoming underemployed (Feldman, 1996).

Underemployment is a complex construct that has been studied from a variety of research perspectives. Though dimensionality and exact definitions vary, most agree that underemployment occurs when an employee is in some way employed in a subpar job. For this chapter, we use the conceptualization of underemployment as explicated by Feldman (1996) and colleagues (Feldman, Leana, & Bolino, 2002). They originally described underemployment as consisting of five dimensions, but subsequently narrowed the focus to the following three dimensions: being employed at a lower hierarchical level in the organization, having lower pay, and being employed in a job in which your full complement of skills is not utilized (Feldman, 1996; Feldman et al., 2002). This has been called objective underemployment. We also explore the subjective interpretation of an individual's employment situation, alternatively called subjective underemployment, relative deprivation, or perceived overqualification (McKee-Ryan & Harvey, 2011).

The goal of this chapter is to provide an overview of underemployment following involuntary job loss, to identify gaps in the literature, and to provide future research directions. To accomplish this aim, we adopt the following structure: First, we provide evidence of the prevalence of underemployment and its likelihood to increase in the near term. Second, we identify groups most at risk for underemployment. Third, we summarize research perspectives to explain underemployment. Fourth, the outcomes of underemployment are presented and discussed, including the career effects of underemployment. Finally, we provide directions for future research on underemployment following involuntary job loss.

Prevalence of Job Loss and Underemployment

Accurately capturing the extent of underemployment is difficult because of multiple conceptualizations and corresponding measurement standards. For example, the International Labor Organization (2011) classifies two types of underemployment: time-based underemployment and inadequate employment situations. The Labor Utilization framework often used in the United States is a more objective economic measure of underemployment and includes unemployed workers, discouraged workers, and low-hours and low-wage employment. This measure is popular among labor sociologists and psychologists (Friedland & Price, 2003; Jensen & Slack, 2003; Prause & Dooley, 2001). Industrial psychologists and management scholars have focused more on subjective aspects of underemployment such as perceived overqualification and underutilization of skills (Feldman et al., 2002; Maynard, Joseph, & Maynard, 2006). Despite differing conceptualizations, there is agreement that underemployment is a pervasive and widespread problem (International Labor Organization, 2011; Maynard, 2011). Additionally, although definitions of underemployment vary, policy makers and governmental organizations have been capturing some statistics to monitor levels of underemployment. For example, in Europe the Organization for Economic Cooperation and Development (OECD) computes time-related underemployment. Similarly, other organizations that collect underemployment-related statistics include the Bureau of Labor Statistics in the United States, the Office of National Statistics in the United Kingdom, and the Australian Bureau of Statistics.

Global job markets have not rebounded as quickly as other economic indicators following recent economic downturns. Thus, job loss and the corresponding underemployment (sometimes labeled as perceived overqualification or skill mismatch) levels have become a cause of concern for policy makers across the world. The issue for policy makers revolves around whether increased underemployment levels are a transitory phenomenon for employees that will resolve in a few years or whether it will become a more permanent economic fixture. Recent estimates suggest that underemployment affects as many as one in five (McGuinness, 2006) to one in three workers in the United States (Green & Zhu, 2010). Moreover, underemployment is an issue of worldwide concern, with underemployment documented in Europe (e.g., Allen & van der Velden, 2001; Tam, 2010), Asia (Sugiyarto, 2008), and Australia (Alba-Ramirez & Blázquez, 2003; Australian Bureau of Statistics, 2013; Charlesworth, 2013; Martin, 2009; Winefield, Winefield, Tiggemann, & Gouldney, 1991). Thus, across the world employees who have encountered a job loss as a result of recessions or economic downturns are faced with the dual challenge of not only finding a job, but finding a job that is at least of the same quality as the job they lost. Research indicates that previously laid-off workers are likely to find jobs that are of a lesser quality than those they held prior to becoming unemployed. Underemployment is likely to continue and increase (e.g., Australian Bureau of Statistics, 2013; Vaisey, 2006), even as countries move out of periodic global recessions that have caused widespread unemployment.

Underemployment among High-Risk Groups

Although job loss affects all workers, research indicates that certain groups of people are more vulnerable to job loss, and reemployment probabilities of workers may vary. For example, researchers have studied underemployment among youths and college graduates (Feldman & Turnley, 1995; Prause & Dooley, 2001), executives and professional employees (Leana & Feldman, 2000; McKee-Ryan, Virick, Prussia, Harvey, & Lilly, 2009), and even some specialized groups such as expatriates (Bolino & Feldman, 2000; Kraimer, Shaffer, & Bolino, 2009) and faculty members in academia (Feldman & Turnley, 2004). In addition, there is also a stream of research that focuses on the psychological, behavioral, and job search predictors of underemployment. For example, Van Hooft, Wanberg, and Van Hoye (2013) suggest that theoretical models in the job search literature should include job search quality and examine additional reemployment outcomes rather than focusing exclusively on obtaining reemployment as the outcome.

Research shows that certain groups of individuals, based on their human capital or demographic characteristics, may be at higher risk of underemployment. We first discuss age, gender, and minority status as predominant risk factors for underemployment, and subsequently draw on the job search literature to summarize the job search-related predictors of underemployment.

Age and underemployment. Underemployment appears to affect workers differently during various career stages, with particularly detrimental effects for younger and older workers. For example, Jensen and Slack (2003) found a curvilinear relationship between age and underemployment, noting that underemployment was the highest among young workers, low during middle age, and higher again as people approached retirement.

Underemployment is a significant and growing problem among young workers, as documented in several studies done on school leavers (Crown & Leavitt, 1996; Greenberger & Steinberg, 1986; Li, Gervais, & Duval, 2006; Prause & Dooley, 2001; Winefield et al., 1991). Using Current Population Survey data from the United States, Sum and Khatiwada (2010) revealed that younger workers are faced with the highest rate of underemployment across all age groups, as did Tam (2010) across workers in the United Kingdom. Similar results were discovered by Crown and Leavitt (1996), who found that underemployment was highest among workers between the ages of 18 and 24 years in the United States. Underemployment has not been an exclusive problem for recent U.S. graduates alone (Khan & Morrow, 1991), but also affects graduates in Asia, Australia, and the United Kingdom (Feather & O'Brien, 1986; Sugiyarto, 2008; Winefield, 2002). Researchers suggest that the main barriers for younger workers to obtain adequate employment include the lack of skills, qualifications, and experience (Vaughan-Jones & Barham, 2009). The long-term consequences of early career underemployment are important to study, given the potentially major ramifications on career outcomes for new entrants and school leavers based on job decisions they made in their early careers.

Older workers, on the other hand, have to deal with issues of age bias and stereotypes based on the belief that they do not have the most current skills and knowledge (Boerlijst, Munnichs, & van der Heijden, 1998; Feldman, 1996). Older workers are seen as expensive and as having a shorter organizational time span (Greller & Simpson, 1999; McGoldrick & Arrowsmith, 2001; Simpson, Greller, & Stroh, 2002). These perceptions make them more vulnerable to problems associated with reemployment upon job loss (Chan & Stevens, 2004; Koeber & Wright, 2001; Lippmann, 2008;

Virick, 2011). When older workers lose a job, they have greater difficulty finding reemployment than younger workers (Farber, Hall, & Pencavel, 1993; Koeber & Wright, 2001), and it takes older laid-off workers longer to get a job (Fallick, 1996; Farber, 2005; Kletzer, 1998; Lippmann, 2008). Turner and Whitaker (1973) found that although older laid-off workers were generally better educated and trained, they took nearly twice as long as younger colleagues to find a job. Older workers also experience greater earning loss upon reemployment (Chan & Stevens, 2004; Couch, 1998; Ong & Mar, 1992), with the loss of earnings being higher for those above the age of 50 years (Koeber & Wright, 2001).

Gender and underemployment. The research on gender and underemployment is mixed. Some studies show that underemployment is higher among women (e.g., De Jong & Madamba, 2001; Jefferson & Preston, 2010; Jensen & Slack, 2003; Mau & Kopischke, 2001; Rodriguez & Zavodny, 2003; Spalter-Roth & Deitch, 1999). For example, Slack and Jensen (2008), in a cohort analysis of underemployment in the United States from 1974 to 2004, used gender and race as control variables in their study, but found women to be disadvantaged with respect to underemployment. Spalter-Roth and Deitch (1999) found that women experienced more bouts of unemployment and comparatively inferior reemployment opportunities than their male counterparts. Along the same lines, Rodriguez and Zavodny (2003) indicate that after an involuntary job loss, women experienced longer unemployment and worked fewer hours once regaining employment. In contrast, Tam (2010), who conceptualized underemployment as a mismatch between an individual's preferred and actual number of work hours, found that underemployment is higher among men in the United Kingdom, while other studies show no effect at all (e.g., Feldman et al., 2002).

When objective indicators such as pay or hours are considered, women tend to face a disadvantage. There is a fair amount of consensus that there is a gender gap in terms of pay between men and women, and that women are underrepresented in senior ranks in companies. Our concern is whether job loss worsens this situation. In a review of the literature on underemployment, McKee-Ryan and Harvey (2011) note that certain factors exacerbate the likelihood of women experiencing higher levels of underemployment. Underemployment among women arises not only from a higher likelihood of being laid-off, but also from career breaks and career adjustments made to accommodate child rearing and family demands. In a study examining psychological distress among men and women after job loss, Leana and Feldman (1992) found no gender differences. Van Hooft, Born, Taris, and Van Der Flier (2005) also found no gender differences in the antecedents of job seeking among Dutch jobseekers. However, Leana and Feldman (1992) did find that that coping patterns differed in response to job loss. Men tended to use an active "problem-focused" approach such as networking with others, whereas women tended to use a more passive "symptom-focused" coping method such as self-assessment activities or finding social support (Leana & Feldman, 1992). These divergent coping patterns may affect the probability of being underemployed. Research also suggests that women may face more challenges concerning their networking ability and connections (Lin, 2001) and face greater barriers to advancement (Lyness & Thompson, 2000), both of which may intensify underemployment. However, as previously mentioned, the research is equivocal, and studies have shown both positive, negative, and no effect of gender on underemployment.

Race and underemployment. Research on race and underemployment shows that some groups may be affected disproportionately. For example, underemployment is higher among black and Hispanic workers than among their white counterparts (Slack & Jensen, 2002; Tigges & Tootle, 1993). More recently, Sum and Khatiwada (2010) note that in the fourth quarter of 2009, Asian workers in the United States had the lowest underemployment rate at 4.7%, followed closely by white, non-Hispanics at 5.2%. Black and Hispanic workers had higher levels of underemployment at 7.5% and 12.0%, respectively. Along the same line, De Jong and Madamba (2001) found underemployment to be higher among racial minorities in the United States compared to non-Hispanic white males. Immigrant groups also face higher underemployment than do those born in the United States (e.g., Aycan & Berry, 1996; De Jong & Madamba, 2001; Slack & Jensen, 2007). In a study of ethnic minorities in the Netherlands Van Hooft, Born, Taris, and Van Der Flier (2004) found that their perceptions of social pressure predicted their intentions to look for a new job more than nonminorities. Recent research also revealed that workers with disabilities also face increased underemployment (Konrad, Moore, Ng, Doherty, & Breward, 2013; Markel & Barclay, 2009). Contingent workers, who are not employed full-time by organizations but are mostly on a contract basis, may also be prone to underemployment if they have taken these jobs while continuing to seek a full-time position (Connelly, Wilkin, & Gallagher, 2011).

In sum, underemployment tends to affect various groups differentially. Younger, older, female, minority, and immigrant workers tend to face higher degrees of unemployment and underemployment, particularly with respect to wages and hours. However, assessing underemployment with these groups is quite complex because of unique issues particular to each of the groups. Furthermore, particularly for women and older workers, choice may play an important role in determining whether objective indicators of underemployment translate into equivalent subjective assessments of underemployment.

Education, Occupational Status, and Underemployment

There is relatively little research in the management field on the relationship between education and underemployment. Sociologists who study underemployment have noted that there is a growing discrepancy between the formal educational requirement of job applicants and the qualifications required by their employers. This has been described as the "credential gap" (Livingstone, 1998)—or as credential inflation, which occurs when people take jobs for which they have higher levels of education than are needed for the job. Evidence indicates that this credential gap is increasing across the world. Additionally, this credential inflation affects different groups differentially. For example, Batenburg and de Witte (2001) in a study of Dutch employees found that men were more likely to experience credential inflation at lower levels of education, whereas women were more likely to experience it at higher levels of education. They also found evidence of the "waiting room" phenomenon among younger workers who often take jobs that would have gone to workers with less education, thereby concluding that younger workers experience greater credential inflation than older workers.

Although there is minimal research specifically focused on underemployment by occupational level, research on age may serve as a proxy for occupational level. That is, as workers age and progress in their careers, they are likely to hold positions at higher levels in their companies. When workers are laid off, they often have difficulty replacing their job with one at the same status, hierarchical level, and pay. Van Der Werfhorst and Andersen (2005) further note that when there is overqualification in labor markets, the propensity to hire overqualified workers at one level leads to spillover effects causing downward mobility at all levels.

Job Search Behaviors and Underemployment

Although it is clear that certain groups may experience a disadvantage due to demography, another set of predictors based on the job search literature has sought to determine the factors that may affect the *quality* of reemployment. Researchers have long emphasized that the quality of employment has important outcomes (Saks & Ashforth, 2002; Schwab, Rynes, & Aldag, 1987). Job search researchers study the job search behaviors demonstrated by individuals who are seeking employment. It includes measuring the effort made and actions taken by such job seekers, such as creating a resume, reaching out to potential employers, going for job interviews, and other such behaviors aimed at seeking employment. The research is fairly conclusive that job search intensity is positively related to job attainment (Wanberg et al., 2002; Wanberg, Kanfer, & Banas, 2000). In fact, Wanberg, Basbug, Van Hooft, and Samtani (2012) observed that there has been a new focus on time- and effort-based measures of job search in the research, such as the effectiveness of networking intensity (a job search behavior) on reemployment (Van Hoye, Van Hooft, & Lievens, 2009; Wanberg et al., 2000).

It is noteworthy that although job search intensity has been shown to predict reemployment, research is sparse and inconclusive on its relationship to reemployment quality. In trying to unravel reemployment quality, there appears to be an agreement among researchers that it is multidimensional. Thus most studies capture multiple aspects of reemployment quality (with minor variations) such as job satisfaction, organizational commitment, job improvement, organizational identification, career growth, and turnover intentions. Along those lines, Wanberg, Hough, and Song (2002) found that job search clarity (the extent to which job seekers have clear job objectives) is related to reemployment quality (job-organizational fit and lower turnover intentions, but not job improvement). In an attempt to investigate the explanatory mechanisms underlying this relationship, Zikic and Klehe (2006) use the career adaptability framework to explore this issue. They found that career planning (whether individuals set goals for their careers) and career exploration (defined as an individual's investigation of various career options) were positively related to reemployment quality (job improvement, organizational identification, career growth, and turnover intentions). Koen, Klehe, Van Vianen, Zijic, and Nauta (2010) found that career decision making (the certainty with which a person knows what career to pursue) and career confidence (the degree of career-related self-efficacy) are positively related to reemployment quality (job satisfaction, turnover intentions, and need-supplies fit). Although Wanberg, Kanfer, and Rotundo (1999) found that job search self-efficacy was related to job search intensity, job search self-efficacy failed to predict job search behavior, and, in turn, reemployment quality in more recent research by Van Hooft et al. (2005). There have also been attempts to examine mediating mechanisms. For instance, Koen et al. (2010) examined three job search strategies: haphazard, focused, and exploratory strategies (Stevens & Beach, 1996). They found that exploratory and focused approaches were related to increased job offers, but not to reemployment quality. However, they did find that the focused strategy led to a decline in reemployment quality. Although this literature is fairly recent and emerging, it has clear implications for understanding underemployment among those who have experienced a job loss.

Research Perspectives to Study Job Loss and Underemployment

In this section we review the most prominent theories that have been used to explain underemployment. Although this is not necessarily the most comprehensive list, we include the theories that occupy the greatest prominence and have the greatest relevance to unemployment and underemployment. In particular, we discuss the following: theories of relative deprivation, person–job fit, human capital theory, theory of career mobility, equilibrium theory of coping model of underemployment, job search theory, and the theory of hysteresis. We review the research with a particular focus on underemployment among those who have experienced a job loss.

Relative deprivation theory. One of the most popular models for understanding underemployment has been relative deprivation theory. The term was coined by Stouffer, Suchman, DeVinney, Star, and Williams (1949) in their study of American soldiers to explain why military police, in comparison to Air Corps men, were more satisfied, even though they had lower promotion prospects. They argued that this was because military police compared their promotions with other military police, rather than Air Corps men, in essence proposing the idea of a referent comparison. Subsequently, Merton and Rossi (1957) extended that basic idea, and formally introduced the concept of the "referent other," noting that people make comparisons with others when determining what they should possess. At a personal level, relative deprivation is defined as a feeling of dissatisfaction following negative comparisons of your situation with others who make up a reference group. It has been described as "the extent of the difference between the desired situation and that of the person desiring it" (Runciman, 1966, p. 10), noting that the reference group could be an individual or an abstract idea. It was further noted that deprivation may be either personal or egoistical when comparisons are made with other people, or group or fraternal when comparisons are made as a member of a collective. Crosby (1976, 1984) noted two preconditions to having subjective feelings of deprivation: wanting X and feeling entitled to or deserving of X.

Relative deprivation theory was first applied to underemployment by Feldman, Leana, and Turnley (1997). They suggested propositions relating to (1) how people choose referent others (e.g., laid-off workers may use survivors who were not laid off as their referent other), (2) how people are affected by attribution of blame (e.g., those who blame themselves for getting laid-off will experience less relative deprivation), and (3) how people are affected by mitigating circumstances (e.g., those who are unemployed for longer durations will experience greater relative deprivation). In a subsequent empirical study, they suggest that relative deprivation incorporates the subjective experience of underemployment because it allows us to capture not only aspects of equity, but also the discrepancy arising from individual experiences. They note that "relative deprivation may be a particularly appropriate approach to examining the underemployment phenomenon because much of the dissatisfaction underemployed workers experience may be the result of their experiences with previous employers or frustrated hopes of obtaining better employment in the future rather than from injustices at the hands of their present employers" (Feldman et al., 2002, p. 457). Therefore, the subjective experience of underemployment captures the individual experiences of the past and present as well as hopes for the future. Although McKee-Ryan and Harvey (2011) note that this may introduce ambiguity due to lack of a standard referent, these experiences

are important to individuals in their assessment of underemployment.

Research shows that relative deprivation affects job satisfaction and turnover intentions (Erdogan & Bauer, 2009). In a sample of reemployed executives, relative deprivation mediated the link between objective underemployment and job satisfaction (e.g., Feldman et al., 2002). A subsequent study also showed that laid-off individuals who experience such relative deprivation (also called subjective underemployment) experience lower job satisfaction, have less commitment, and have higher intentions to quit (McKee-Ryan et al., 2009).

Person–job fit. In building a framework that advocates greater attention to subjective underemployment, Maynard et al. (2006) adopted a person–environment fit approach. The theoretical foundation of person–environment fit is based on the assumption that the greater the fit or congruence between the person and his or her environment, the more positive the outcomes (Kristof-Brown, Zimmerman, & Johnson, 2005). In the context of underemployment, the relevant degree of fit is person–job fit. Person–job fit (P-J fit) assumes that the degree of fit between the person and the job will be positively related to employee attitudes such as job satisfaction and organizational commitment.

Although no studies have directly used the P-J fit framework to study underemployment among reemployed workers, this framework has been widely used to study underemployment among other employment groups who have not experienced job loss. For example, Saks and Ashforth (2002) examined the role of P-J and person–organization (P-O) fit as mediating the relationship between job search behaviors and career planning and employment quality among graduating students in a university in the United States. They found that postentry perceptions of P-J fit mediated the relationship between career planning and employment quality (conceptualized as organizational commitment, organizational identification, job satisfaction, and turnover intentions). Their study lent support to the idea that perceptions of fit play a significant role. Saks and Ashforth (2002) further note that the lack of support between job search and employment quality may be because researchers have investigated relatively few job search variables, suggesting the need to examine additional mediating mechanisms.

Additionally, within the fit literature, two types of fit have been differentiated: demands–abilities fit and needs–supplies fit. Demands–abilities fit reflects a more objective measure and refers to whether the employee has the required skills for the job. Needs–supplies fit is more subjectively assessed and refers to whether the job offers what the employee desires or seeks in a job. The relative importance of the types of fit suggests that subjectively determined fit may be linked to more detrimental outcomes (McKee-Ryan & Harvey, 2011). Recent findings by Luksyte, Spitzmuller, and Maynard (2011) suggest that needs–supplies fit may be more relevant in the context of underemployment. They found that needs–supplies fit mediated the relationship between overqualification and counterproductive work behaviors, but demands–abilities fit did not. Their rationale for the finding is that worker needs are more relevant than job demands since underemployed incumbents are more concerned with the discrepancy between what they desire from their jobs and what they get.

Concerning subjective aspects of underemployment, Maynard and colleagues (2006) highlight that when it comes to evaluating fit, it is important to consider choice or employee desire. They suggest that a work situation should not be considered underemployment unless the worker prefers a different arrangement, pointing out that underemployment occurs only when there is a mismatch between the needs of the employee and the job, indicating that a distinction between objective and subjective underemployment is important.

Human capital theory. Human capital theory asserts that individuals seek to build their human capital by accumulating knowledge, skills, and abilities (Becker, 1964). This set of qualifications is objective and measurable. Thus, job seekers may be expected to have a certain minimum education and/or years of work experience for a particular job (Büchel, 2009). When individuals build their stock of human capital, their expectation is that organizations will reciprocate with commensurate rewards and appropriate career growth. When such career growth or rewards are not forthcoming, as is the case with underemployed individuals, it creates an imbalance. Although the disparity is favorable to the organization, it is unfavorable to the individual. This imbalance is similar to the mismatch argument underlying P-J fit theory.

Theory of career mobility. Sicherman and Galor (1990) built on work by Rosen (1972) to propose that being overqualified (which they defined as overeducated) is rewarded not only in terms of higher starting wages, but also with greater promotion potential. These expectations for future promotion opportunities may help explain why some individuals may settle for positions for which they are underemployed, and why both individuals and organizations may settle for a situation in which there is a mismatch (Büchel, 2009). Of course, Büchel (2009) also notes that the higher the expectation of promotion, the higher the likelihood that the individual may voluntarily leave the organization if the promotion does not materialize. In support of this theory, Sicherman (1991) found that overqualified employees had higher rates of promotion, although other more recent research failed to support this proposition. In particular, Büchel and Mertens (2004) found that wage growth and occupational mobility rates were lower among over-educated German workers than among adequately educated workers. Similarly, Dolton and Vignoles (2000) found that 38% of graduates in the United Kingdom were overqualified in their first job, and this percentage dropped to only 30% after 6 years. This lends support to the fact that underemployment may persist. Thus, support for this theory is mixed.

Equilibrium theory of coping. Obtaining a job was considered the goal of the unemployed person in prior research on unemployment. This focus subsequently changed into one in which the goal of the unemployed person was not simply to get a job, but to get a job that was comparable in quality to the previous job (e.g., Latack, Kinicki, & Prussia, 1995; Leana & Feldman, 1995; Wanberg, 1995) and thus return to a state of equilibrium. McKee-Ryan and colleagues (2009) argued that displaced workers do not return to a state of equilibrium until they are able to obtain reemployment in a job that is similar to the one they lost. This equilibrium also reflects whether there is a fit, using the previous job as the referent standard.

Research in this area notes that underemployment affects workers in a manner similar to unemployment, since workers in dissatisfactory new jobs continued to cope with their job loss as though they were still unemployed (Kinicki et al., 2000; Leana & Feldman, 1995). Some researchers have used job satisfaction in the new job as an indicator of underemployment, which may not be the most accurate representation of equilibrium. In a refinement of the theory of coping goals, McKee-Ryan and Kinicki (2002) suggest that those who lose their jobs make choices about their coping goals, but that overall, well-being depends on whether there is a match between the goal and the outcome. Whether there is a match may depend on something else that occurs to people when they have been unemployed for long periods, namely an adjustment of their goals. Unemployed individuals who struggle with trying to get reemployed understand that they may not be able to attain their work-related goals. For example, Niessen, Heinrichs, and Dorr (2009) found that career growth goals decreased with age among the older unemployed workers and may result in an adjustment of work-related goals. This is consistent with cognitive dissonance theory, which suggests that laid-off workers upon reemployment may rationalize their behavior. After making the choice of accepting the job, they marshal and alter thoughts, beliefs, and attitudes to make their thoughts congruent with their behavior (e.g., Festinger, 1957). In the context of underemployment, Feldman and Turnley (2004) found that those who accepted contingent employment with the goal of a better work–life balance experienced lower levels of relative deprivation. Therefore, motivations for jobs and the choices people make in their employment can also be important considerations to subjective underemployment.

Job search theory. Prior theories of job search have tended to focus on the intensity of the job search, and some process models with self-regulation frameworks have been proposed (Kanfer, Wanberg, & Kantrowitz, 2001; Saks, 2005) and have begun to incorporate reemployment quality into their frameworks (e.g., Saks, 2005). Some have used broader theories such as the theory of planned behavior to understand job search (e.g., Van Hooft et al., 2005). Wanberg et al. (1999) examined a host of individual difference variables to predict job search intensity. These were classified under three categories: job search motives (employment commitment and financial hardship), job search competencies (job search self-efficacy, motivation control, and emotion control), and job search constraints. Building on these job search frameworks, Van Hooft et al. (2013) more recently proposed a framework suggesting that reemployment quality would be better understood if we examined the quality of the job search process. They outline a four-stage self-regulatory process in which individuals should engage in goal establishment, planning the goal pursuit, goal striving, and reflection and describe the components within each of those steps. Underemployment following job loss will be more fully explained as empirical support accumulates for this framework.

Theory of hysteresis. In an attempt to enhance the study of unemployment, economists have drawn from theories in psychology to understand the behavior of the unemployed. Thus, Darity and Goldsmith (1993) propose a theory of hysteresis, in which they argue that when workers go through long spells of unemployment, the psychological effects on overall well-being may be severe enough to create learned helplessness (Seligman & Maier, 1967). This aligns with the conservation of resources (COR) theory that has been suggested as a possible theoretical framework for studying underemployment (Feldman, 2011). COR theory posits that individuals are motivated to acquire and protect resources, and when these resources are threatened individuals experience stress (Hobfoll, 1989). With long spells of unemployment and accompanying stress, unemployed workers are less likely to have the energy and resources left to find satisfactory reemployment. This deficiency in resources and accompanied helplessness may affect their job search by weakening their resolve to wait for the right job. To escape from unemployment, they may take any job—even one for which they may be underemployed. Some support for this exists among unemployed job seekers. In a study of unemployed workers, those who experienced the highest levels of distress were more likely to be reemployed at the end of 1 year (Kessler, Turner, & House, 1988). This is symptomatic of "trauma escape" behavior (Goldsmith & Darity, 1992) or weakening resistance (Robinson, 1937). Furthermore, this sense of helplessness triggered by unemployment may persist over time among reemployed workers who are underemployed (Kinicki et al., 2000). This can create a negative spiral of poor performance and subsequent unemployment, making it relevant from a careers perspective. We now turn our attention to the outcomes of underemployment following involuntary job displacement.

Outcomes of Underemployment

Jahoda's (1981) contention that bad jobs are preferable to unemployment has been refuted by others who claim that underemployment has substantially negative effects that may be comparable to that experienced when unemployed (Kinicki et al., 2000; O'Brien & Feather, 1990; Prause & Dooley, 2001; Winefield et al., 1991). For example, Winefield (2002, p. 139) notes that "inadequate employment can be just as psychologically damaging as unemployment." More recent research indicates that in addition to psychological damage, the negative effects of underemployment on careers could range from tangible and objective indicators, such as future wages or salary and earning potential, to more intangible or subjective indicators, such as job satisfaction, career satisfaction, job withdrawal attitudes and behaviors, and job performance. In this section we discuss these outcomes, starting with the more objective indicators, followed by effects on job attitudes (e.g., job satisfaction, organizational commitment), withdrawal-related attitudes and behaviors (e.g., turnover intentions, voluntary turnover, job search intentions), and job performance.

Future wages/salary and earning potential. The most significant outcome of losing a job is the loss of income, which compounds as the duration of unemployment extends (e.g., Jackson, 1999; Kinicki et al., 2000; Vinokur, Price, & Caplan, 1996). The financial effects of job loss are felt in the day-to-day functioning of the individual and the family, not only in terms of money available for expenses, but also in terms of emotional distress and psychological well-being (Brief, Konovsky, Goodwin, & Link, 1995; Nordenmark & Strandh, 1999). Furthermore, when individuals become reemployed, their earnings tend to be lower (Hijzen et al., 2010; Mallinckrodt, 1990). This is more so for long-term unemployed worker (Addison & Portugal, 1989; Couch, 1998; Perrucci, Perrucci, & Targ, 1997). These workers are in a weaker position because employers are reluctant to hire them and are more likely to look upon a person who has been unemployed for a shorter period more favorably (Budd, Levine, & Smith, 1988). As such, the long-term unemployed have lower bargaining power when their pay is being determined or negotiated. Furthermore, these effects tend to persist over time. This occurs for both older and younger workers, although the results are more pronounced for older workers (Jacobson, LaLonde, & Sullivan (1993).

Results of a longitudinal study of male and female MBAs by Reitman and Schneer (2005) indicate that the negative effects associated with a job loss in terms of wage penalties are apparent for up to 20–25 years after the gap in employment occurred. Another study showed that with younger workers, the effect of unemployment tends to be large initially, but does show some tapering (Mroz & Savage, 2006)

Job attitudes. Across a wide range of studies (Brasher & Chen, 1999; Johnson & Johnson, 2000; Johnson, Morrow, & Johnson, 2002; Khan & Morrow, 1991; Maynard, Thorsteinson, & Parfyonova, 2006) underemployment is associated with a reduction in overall job satisfaction and job facet (e.g., co-worker, job, pay, promotion, supervisor, and work) satisfaction. Research demonstrates this trend across various settings and samples such as expatriates (Bolino & Feldman, 2000; Lee, 2005), adjunct faculty (Feldman & Turnley, 2004), nonacademic university employees (Khan & Morrow, 1991), Turkish retail workers (Erdogan & Bauer, 2009), Australian retail employees forced to work part-time (Deery & Mahony, 1994), and recent university graduates (Burke, 1997). A few studies have examined underemployment and postlayoff job satisfaction among laid-off workers (e.g., Burke, 1986; Leana & Feldman, 1995; Mallinckrodt, 1990; Wanberg, 1995). In a study of 61 laid-off individuals tracked over time, Burke (1986) found that 43% of respondents reported that their new job was comparatively less desirable than their previous job. However, in a smaller study Mallinckrodt (1990) obtained retrospective ratings from 16 employees over the age of 40 years and found only partial evidence of what he called "job satisfaction skidding," or reduced satisfaction in new jobs as compared to old jobs. Although satisfaction was lower with respect to pay and benefits, it was higher with respect to the work itself, supervision, and prospects for promotion. In a subsequent study, Wanberg (1995) did not find evidence of lower new job satisfaction among reemployed workers in her sample of unemployed participants from a job service office. In both studies Wanberg (1995) and Mallinckrodt (1990) did not specifically capture aspects of underemployment, but instead compared job satisfaction in the prelayoff job with job satisfaction in the postlayoff job. In a more recent study of reemployed high tech laid-off workers, McKee-Ryan et al. (2009) found that objective underemployment was negatively related to job satisfaction both directly and through its effect on subjective underemployment. The overall research on underemployment (which includes all workers, whether they are laid-off or not), however, points to a negative relationship of –.22 between underemployment and job satisfaction across 21 studies (McKee-Ryan & Harvey, 2011).

There has also been some research that aims at a deeper understanding of this negative relationship between underemployment and job satisfaction. For example, some researchers propose that lower levels of psychological well-being, depression, and poor health that accompany underemployment may be reflected in the workplace as lower job satisfaction and commitment (Feldman & Turnley,

1995; Maynard et al., 2006). For those who experience underemployment resulting from job loss, these effects can be exacerbated because job loss is also associated with financial strain, loss of social status, loss of self-esteem, and mental health problems (Artazcoz, Benach, Borrell, & Cortes, 2004; Bartley, 1994). Other researchers have tested factors that may attenuate the negative relationship between underemployment and job satisfaction. Employee empowerment, for example, has been shown to weaken the relationship effect of perceived overqualification on job satisfaction, indicating that there may be ways that organizations can alleviate the negative effects of underemployment (Erdogan & Bauer, 2009). In that study, overqualification was found to be negatively related to job satisfaction only when employee empowerment was low.

Underemployment is also negatively related to job involvement (e.g., Burke, 1997; Feldman & Turnley, 1995) and affective commitment (Bolino & Feldman, 2000; Feldman & Turnley, 1995; Feldman et al., 2002; Maynard et al., 2006; McKee-Ryan et al., 2009) and positively related to work alienation (Lee, 2005). Evaluating the results of a study by Abrahamsen (2010) in which hours-underemployed individuals (i.e., those who worked less hours than they sought to work) did not differ in their level of commitment as compared to others, and studies by Holtom, Lee, and Tidd (2002) and Maynard et al. (2006) in which underpaid individuals were not less committed, McKee-Ryan and Harvey (2011) note that the negative relationship between underemployment and commitment may be weaker for objective indicators of underemployment than for subjective indicators. Researchers have also found that subjective underemployment was negatively related to organizational commitment among college graduates and expatriates (Bolino & Feldman, 2000; Feldman & Turnley, 1995), laid-off high-tech employees who were subsequently reemployed (McKee-Ryan et al., 2009), and reemployed laid-off executives (Feldman et al., 2002).

Withdrawal-related attitudes and turnover behaviors. Withdrawal is a reflection of the desire of the individual to leave the organization, and those who are underemployed are more likely to think of leaving their jobs and to actually search for other jobs (Burris, 1983; Wald, 2005). Both relative deprivation theory and P-J fit have been used as explanatory mechanisms for why the underemployed may have higher turnover intentions. Studies have found that reemployed laid-off workers who were underemployed tend to be dissatisfied and have higher turnover intentions (Feldman et al., 2002; McKee-Ryan et al., 2009). Maynard et al. (2006) note that employees seek to reduce discrepancies when underemployed, and choose to do so by changing jobs. Other studies have found similar results among repatriated employees (Kraimer et al., 2009) and recent college graduates (Burke, 1997). Emphasizing the importance of choice, Maynard et al. (2006) note that involuntary part-time workers report significantly greater turnover intentions than those who prefer to work part-time. Although most research has focused on turnover intentions, Erdogan and Bauer (2009) examined the relationship between perceived overqualification and actual turnover. They found that perceived overqualification was related to turnover only when employees did not feel empowered. Their results suggest a deeper look at mitigating factors that affect the relationship between underemployment and its outcomes.

Job performance. There are competing hypotheses regarding the relationship between underemployment and job performance. Feldman (1996) suggested that underemployed workers will be less motivated and constantly seek to maintain equity that may in turn lower performance. Along those lines Bolino and Feldman (2000) reported a negative relationship between underemployment and self-reported performance. They noted, however, that the underemployed employees could have deliberately rated themselves lower, knowing that their performance did not reflect their potential.

On the other hand, there is an expectation that underemployed workers possess the requisite knowledge and skills to do the job. Hence P-J fit suggests that workers should perform at high levels even if they are underemployed. To that end, some studies have found the relationship between overqualification and performance, as measured by self or supervisor reports, to be positive (e.g., Erdogan & Bauer, 2009; Fine, 2007; Fine & Nevo, 2008). Erdogan, Bauer, Peiro, and Truxillo (2011) suggest that lower work–family conflict and voluntary acceptance of the job make this outcome more likely. All told, the research on underemployment and job performance is therefore inconclusive (McKee-Ryan & Harvey, 2011), and there is tremendous opportunity in this area for future research. To date, research is lacking to evaluate the performance levels of previously downsized employees in their postlayoff jobs.

Future Directions

From previous reviews (Feldman, 1996; McKee-Ryan & Harvey, 2011) and recent research, some fairly consistent themes have emerged in the underemployment literature. There is agreement that underemployment is multifaceted and is studied by researchers across various disciplines. Evidence is also strong that those who lose their jobs are particularly vulnerable to underemployment. We identified three potential avenues for future research on underemployment following involuntary job loss. These relate to suggested theoretical frameworks, career issues (including the role of choice and adjustment of goals), and measurement problems with underemployment.

Theoretical frameworks. Job loss is clearly viewed as a career interruption, and research suggests that the scarring effects of unemployment are likely to negatively affect reemployment. Relative deprivation and P-J fit theories lend themselves to studying underemployment among laid-off workers. We offer some suggestions to extend research aligned with relative deprivation theory. In addition, we propose additional theoretical frameworks that may be suitable for studying underemployment among laid-off workers. These include conservation of resources, attribution theory, and personality theory (Feldman, 2011).

In regard to relative deprivation theory, future research would benefit from drawing on the literature on social comparisons. An implicit assumption in the job loss–underemployment literature is that laid-off individuals make intraperson temporal comparisons, namely that they compare their current situation with their situation prior to job loss. This seems plausible, but we cannot rule out the possibility that laid-off workers may start making comparisons with other groups or entities. Depending on whom they select as their referent comparison, they may respond differently to objective underemployment (Virick, 2011). Feldman and colleagues (2002) suggest that people can use multiple referents and may experience greater or less relative deprivation as a result. Research investigating questions such as at what point laid-off workers may decide to change their referent other, and start comparing themselves to different entities, would be very relevant. For example, older individuals may initially compare themselves to other laid-off workers in their company, but may subsequently start comparing themselves to other older individuals with whom they have greater demographic proximity. This may alter their response to underemployment.

Certain factors predispose laid-off individuals to underemployment. For example, financial distress may cause an individual to take a job for which he or she is underemployed. Likewise, lack of support, whether from the company in terms of outplacement assistance, or from the family, in terms of financial or social support, is an important factor. McKee-Ryan et al. (2009) showed that how workers appraise their layoff affects whether they are objectively underemployed. Yet, how individuals appraise their job loss has a lot to do with the resources at their disposal. Feldman (2011) suggests the use of COR theory for understanding underemployment. When workers lose their jobs, they lose resources (wages, self-esteem, support). However, to the extent they have greater reserves of these resources (e.g., financial savings, outplacement help, family support, or even personal attributes such as resilience), they are less likely to take a job for which they are a poor fit. Hobfoll and Lilly (1993) note that having resources may buffer stress, but suggest that minority employees, women, and elderly workers are often underemployed because they are limited in their ability to utilize their resources—even if they possess such resources—because of racism and sexism in the workplace. We therefore suggest greater exploration of COR theory to further our understanding of underemployment.

It has also been suggested that attribution theory and personality theory can enhance our understanding of underemployment. For example, Feldman (2011) recommends that future research could test attribution theory as a basis for explaining why women, minorities, and older workers may attribute their lower status to discrimination and as a result may react less negatively to underemployment. Moreover, personality characteristics (e.g., resilience, self-esteem, not giving up) may be important in identifying workers who succeed in overcoming underemployment and those who do not. Some of these may align with learned helplessness and draw from the theory of hysteresis. Other suggested personality characteristics that may be relevant include exploring the role of core self-evaluations among underemployed workers (Maynard, 2011).

Career issues. The literature on job loss has transitioned from focusing on reemployment to focusing on quality of reemployment. Because there are no guarantees that laid-off individuals will obtain jobs for which they are the right fit, research is needed that will extend to examining the longer-term effects of job loss over a person's career. Luksyte and

Spitzmuller (2011) note the need to evaluate within-person fluctuations in underemployment over time. This is consistent with researchers in the careers field who recommend greater ipsative–normative research designs that capture the career trajectory of individuals by making repeated observations of the same individual over time (Waters, 2008). We therefore call for additional longitudinal studies that track the unemployed from unemployment into reemployment and even longer over their careers to determine whether the long-term effects of unemployment linger for several years. Research on the relationship between underemployment (mostly operationalized as overeducation) and occupational mobility is equivocal in its findings. Also, it has not been studied among laid-off employees.

Testing the theory of career mobility among laid-off workers would provide insight on whether laid-off employees willingly take on jobs for which they are underemployed, and whether these are accompanied by the expectation that organizations would recognize and reward them. When individuals lose their job, they engage coping goals, defined as "an individual's desired end result that he or she seeks to accomplish in response to a perceived harm/loss or threat" (Latack et al., 1995, p. 323). Although the most desirable situation occurs when there is a match between the coping goals and the outcome, it may not occur, and the long-term unemployed realize that they may not be able to attain their work-related goals. When that happens, it is not unusual for people to adjust their goals. Therefore, to understand situations in which laid-off individuals willingly take on jobs for which they are overqualified, we need to acknowledge that people may make conscious career choices involving a shift or adjustment of their career goals (e.g., Maynard et al., 2006; McKee-Ryan & Harvey, 2011; Virick, 2011). For example, older unemployed workers may adjust their goals to reflect lower career growth (Niessen et al., 2009). They may also attempt to make their behavior and thoughts congruent by rationalizing that they really do not wish to seek high career growth (Ng & Feldman, 2009; Virick, 2011). Erdogan et al. (2011) use this rationale to explain why some underemployed workers are higher performers. In such instances, it has been suggested that such workers may not experience the negative effects of underemployment. Research on underemployment would benefit from a further exploration of these processes as they unfold among unemployed workers.

The disruption of job loss may provide unemployed workers with the space and time to think about alternatives. They may try to seek validation in other areas of their lives (such as when workers choose to focus greater attention on their families) or pursue another career (such as becoming an entrepreneur). Among older individuals, for example, certain age-related factors need to be taken into consideration when evaluating job search after unemployment. Research shows that older individuals may have different motivations to work, such as the need for social interaction, to feel productive, and to have some structure in their lives (Adams & Rau, 2004; Dendinger, Adams, & Jacobson, 2005; Kanfer et al., 2001; Mor-Barak, 1995). Feldman and Turnley (2004) found that those who accepted contingent employment with the goal of attaining a better work–life balance experienced lower levels of relative deprivation. If they experience less deprivation, then it could be argued that the resulting negative outcomes will be attenuated.

Measurement issues. Multiple operationalizations of underemployment have created challenges in studying underemployment. Nonetheless, our review of underemployment among laid-off workers suggests that objective underemployment has a more distal connection to attitudes and behavioral outcomes than subjective underemployment, so it is important to focus on the subjective perceptions. McKee-Ryan and Harvey (2011) outlined eight possible dimensions of underemployment ranging from ones that are the most objective to ones that are the most subjective: (1) Pay/Hierarchical Underemployment, (2) Hours-Underemployment, (3) Work-Status Congruence, (4) Over-Education, (5) Job Field-Underemployment, (6) Skill Underutilization, (7) Perceived Overqualification, and (8) Relative Deprivation. We concur with McKee-Ryan and Harvey (2011) that there is a need to develop standardized scales for measuring underemployment that demonstrate convergent and discriminant validity, so that there is greater consistency and comparability in underemployment research. Furthermore, it has been observed that assessments of subjective underemployment are based on self-report data, and there is a need to gather data from other sources (e.g., supervisors and peers) to assess whether there is any bias (Maynard, 2011). There have also been calls for increased qualitative and empirical research in the field of underemployment.

Summary, Conclusions, and Practical Implications

Underemployment is a troubling problem, as it is a significant by-product of the relatively high unemployment rate experienced during the recession that began in 2007. Particular attention needs to be paid to laid-off individuals who are unique in their underemployment situation. Clearly much more research is needed to understand the nuances of underemployment, both from the perspective of the individual and the organization. For individuals recovering from job loss, awareness of the trade-offs of taking a job for which they are underemployed helps them make more informed career choices. For organizations seeking to hire laid-off workers, research may be able to provide clearer guidance on how best to manage and retain overqualified workers who tend to have higher turnover intentions. We therefore encourage research designs that follow involuntarily displaced workers through their reemployment experiences to examine the long-term and career effects of their underemployment. These are likely to provide much needed guidance to both employees and organizations on how best to minimize or, alternatively, manage underemployment.

References

Abrahamsen, B. (2010). Employment status and commitment to work in professions. *Economic and Industrial Democracy, 31*(1), 93–115.

Adams, G., & Rau, B. (2004). Job seeking among retires seeking bridge employment. *Personnel Psychology, 57*(3), 719–744.

Addison, J. T., & Portugal, P. (1989). Job displacement, relative wage changes, and duration of unemployment. *Journal of Labor Economics, 7*(3), 281–302.

Alba-Ramirez, A., & Blázquez, M. (2003). Types of job match, overeducation and labour mobility in Spain. In F. Büchel, A. de Grip, & A. Mertens (Eds.), *Overeducation in Europe* (pp. 65–92). Cheltenham, UK: Edward Elgar.

Allen, J., & van der Velden, R. (2001). Educational mismatches versus skill mismatches: Effects on wages, job satisfaction, and on-the-job search. *Oxford Economic Papers, 53*(3), 434–452.

Artazcoz, L., Benach, J., Borrell, C., & Cortes, I. (2004). Unemployment and mental health: Understanding the interactions among gender, family roles, and social class. *American Journal of Public Health, 94*(1), 82–88.

Australian Bureau of Statistics. (2013). *Underemployed workers. Publication # 6265.0.* Retrieved electronically from http://www.abs.gov.au/ausstats/abs@.nsf/mf/6265.0

Aycan, Z., & Berry, J. W. (1996). Impact of employment-related experiences on immigrants' psychological well-being and adaptation to Canada. *Canadian Journal of Behavioral Science, 28*(3), 240–251.

Bartley, M. (1994). Unemployment and ill health: Understanding the relationship. *Journal of Epidemiology and Community Health, 48*(4), 333–337.

Batenburg, R., & de Witte, M. (2001). Underemployment in the Netherlands: How the Dutch 'Poldermodel' failed to close the education-jobs gap. *Work, Employment and Society, 15*(1), 73–94.

Becker, G. (1964). *Human capital: A theoretical and empirical analysis with special reference to education.* New York: Columbia University Press.

Boerlijst, J. G., Munnichs, J. M. A., & van der Heijden, B. I. J. M. (1998). The 'older worker' in the organization. In P. J. D. Drenth, H. Thierry, & C. J. deWolf (Eds.), *Handbook of work and organizational psychology* (pp. 183–214). Hove: Psychology Press.

Bolino, M. C., & Feldman, D. C. (2000). The antecedents and consequences of underemployment among expatriates. *Journal of Organizational Behavior, 21*(8), 889–911.

Brasher, E. E., & Chen, P. Y. (1999). Evaluation of success criteria in job search: A process perspective. *Journal of Occupational and Organizational Psychology, 72*(1), 57–70.

Brief, P., Konovsky, M. A., Goodwin, R., & Link, K. (1995). Inferring the meaning of work from the effects of unemployment. *Journal of Applied Social Psychology, 25*(8), 693–711.

Büchel, F. (2009). Overqualification: Reasons, measurement issues and typological affinity to unemployment. In P. Descy & M. Tessaring (Eds.), *Training in Europe: Second report on vocational training research in Europe 2000* (Vol. 2, pp. 453–560). Cedefop Reference Series. Luxembourg: Office for Official Publications of the European Communities.

Büchel, F., & Mertens, A. (2004). Overeducation, undereducation, and the theory of career mobility. *Applied Economics, 36*(8), 803–816.

Budd, A., Levine, P., & Smith, P. (1988). Unemployment, vacancies and the long-term unemployed. *The Economic Journal, 98*(393), 1071–1091.

Burke, R. J. (1986). Reemployment on a poorer job after a plant closing. *Psychological Reports, 58*(2), 559–570.

Burke, R. J. (1997). Correlates of under-employment among recent business school graduates. *International Journal of Manpower, 18*(7), 627–635.

Burris, B. H. (1983). The human effects of underemployment. *Social Problems, 31*(1), 96–110.

Chan, S., & Stevens, A. H. (2004). How does job loss affect the timing of retirement. *Contributions to Economic Analysis and Policy, 3*(1), Article 5.

Charlesworth, S. (2013). Women, work and industrial relations in Australia in 2012. *Journal of Industrial Relations, 55*(3), 371–385.

Connelly, C. E., Wilkin, C. L., & Gallagher, D. G. (2011). Understanding underemployment among contingent workers. In D. C. Maynard & D. C. Feldman (Eds.), *Underemployment: Psychological, economic and social challenges* (pp. 145–162). New York: Springer.

Couch, K. A. (1998). Late life job displacement. *The Gerontologist, 3*(1), 7–17.

Crosby, F. (1976). A model of egotistical relative deprivation. *Psychological Review, 83*(2), 85–113.

Crosby, F. (1984). Relative deprivation organizational settings. In B. M. Staw & L. L. Cummings (Eds.), *Research in organizational behavior* (Vol. 6, pp. 51–93). Greenwich, CT: JAI Press.

Crown, W. H., & Leavitt, T. D. (1996). *Underemployment and the older worker: How big a problem?* Washington, DC: AARP, Public Policy Institute.

Darity, W. Jr., & Goldsmith, A. H. (1993). Unemployment, social psychology, and unemployment hysteresis. *Journal of Post Keynesian Economics*, *16*(1), 55–71.

De Jong, G. F., & Madamba, A. B. (2001). A double disadvantage? Minority group, immigrant status, and underemployment in the United States. *Social Science Quarterly*, *82*(1), 117–130.

Deery, S. J., & Mahony, A. (1994). Temporal flexibility: Management strategies and employee preferences in the retail industry. *Journal of Industrial Relations*, *36*(3), 332–352.

Dendinger, V. M., Adams, G. A., & Jacobson, J. D. (2005). Reasons for working and their relationship to retirement attitudes, job satisfaction and occupational self-efficacy of bridge employment. *International Journal of Aging and Human Development*, *61*(1), 31–35.

Dolton, P., & Vignoles. A. (2000). The incidence and effects of overeducation in the U.K. graduate labour market. *Economics of Education Review*, *19*(2), 179–198.

Erdogan, B., & Bauer, T. N. (2009). Perceived overqualification and its outcomes: The moderating role of empowerment. *Journal of Applied Psychology*, *94*(2), 557–565.

Erdogan, B., Bauer, T. N., Peiró, J. M., & Truxillo, D. M. (2011). Overqualified employees: Making the best of a potentially bad situation for individuals and organizations. *Industrial and Organizational Psychology*, *4*(2), 215–232

Fallick, B. C. (1996). A review of the recent empirical literature on displaced workers. *Industrial and Labor Relations Review*, *50*(1), 5–16.

Farber, H. S. (2005). What do we know about job loss in the United States, 1984–2004. Working Paper 498, Industrial Relations Section, Princeton University (January).

Farber, H. S., Hall, R., & Pencavel, J. (1993). The incidence and costs of job loss: 1982–91. *Brookings Papers on Economic Activity: Microeconomics*, 73–132.

Feather, N. T., & O'Brien, G. (1986). A longitudinal analysis of the effects of different patterns of employment and unemployment on school leavers. *British Journal of Psychology*, *77*(4), 459–479.

Feldman, D. C. (1996). The nature, antecedents and consequences of underemployment. *Journal of Management*, *22*(3), 385–407.

Feldman, D. C. (2011). Theoretical frontiers for underemployment research. In D. C. Maynard & D. C. Feldman (Eds.), *Underemployment: Psychological, economic and social challenges* (pp. 277–305). New York: Springer.

Feldman, D. C., Leana, C. R., & Bolino, M. C. (2002). Underemployment and relative deprivation among re-employed executives. *Journal of Occupational and Organizational Psychology*, *75*(4), 453–471.

Feldman, D. C., Leana, C. R., & Turnley, W. H. (1997). A relative deprivation approach to understanding underemployment. In C. L. Cooper & D. M. Rousseau (Eds.), *Trends in organizational behavior* (Vol. 4, pp. 43–60). New York: John Wiley.

Feldman, D. C., & Turnley, W. H. (1995). Underemployment among recent business college graduates. *Journal of Organizational Behavior*, *16*(6), 691–706.

Feldman, D. C., & Turnley, W. H. (2004). Contingent employment in academic careers: Relative deprivation among adjunct faculty. *Journal of Vocational Behavior*, *64*(2), 284–307.

Festinger, L. (1957). *A theory of cognitive dissonance*. Stanford, CA: Stanford University.

Fine, S. (2007). Overqualification and selection in leadership training. *Journal of Leadership and Organizational Studies*, *14*(1), 61–68.

Fine, S., & Nevo, B. (2008). Too smart for their own good? A study of perceived cognitive overqualification in the workforce. *International Journal of Human Resource Management*, *19*(2), 346–355.

Friedland, D. S., & Price, R. H. (2003). Underemployment: Consequences for the health and well-being of workers. *American Journal of Community Psychology*, *32*(1–2), 33–45.

Goldsmith, A. H., & Darity, W. Jr. (1992). Social psychology, unemployment exposure and equilibrium unemployment. *Journal of Economic Psychology*, *13*(3), 449–471.

Gowan, M. A., Riordan, C. M., & Gatewood, R. D. (1999). Test of a model of coping with involuntary job loss following a company closing. *Journal of Applied Psychology*, *84*(1), 75–86.

Green, F., & Zhu, Y. (2010). Overqualification, job dissatisfaction, and increasing dispersion in the returns to graduate education. *Oxford Economic Papers*, *62*(4), 740–763.

Greenberger, E., & Steinberg, L. (1986). *When teenagers work*. New York: Basic Books.

Greller, M. M., & Simpson, P. (1999). In search of late career: A review of contemporary social science research applicable to the understanding of later career. *Human Resource Management Review*, *9*(3), 309–347.

Hijzen, A., Upward, R., & Wright, P. W. (2010). The income losses of displaced workers. *Journal of Human Resources*, *45*(1), 243–269.

Hobfoll, S. E. (1989). Conservation of resources: A new attempt at conceptualizing stress. *American Psychologist*, *44*(3), 513–524.

Hobfoll, S. E., & Lilly, R. S. (1993). Resource conservation as a strategy for community psychology. *Journal of Community Psychology*, *21*(2), 128–148.

Holtom, B. C., Lee, T. W., & Tidd, S. T. (2002). The relationship between work status congruence and work related attitudes and behaviors. *Journal of Applied Psychology*, *87*(5), 903–915.

International Labor Organization. (2011). Underemployment: Current guidelines. Retrieved from http://www.ilo.org/global/statistics-and-databases/statistics-overview-and-topics/underemployment/current-guidelines/lang-en/index.htm.

Jackson, T. (1999). Differences in psychosocial experiences of employed, unemployed, and student samples of young adults. *Journal of Psychology*, *133*(1), 49–60.

Jacobson, L., LaLonde, R., & Sullivan, D. (1993). Earnings losses of displaced workers. *American Economic Review*, *83*(4), 685–709.

Jahoda, M. (1981). Work, employment and unemployment: Values, theories and approaches in social research. *American Psychologist*, *36*(2), 184–191.

Jefferson, T., & Preston, A. (2010). Labour markets and wages in Australia in 2009. *Journal of Industrial Relations*, *52*(3), 335–354.

Jensen, L., & Slack, T. (2003). Underemployment in America: Measurement and evidence. *American Journal of Community Psychology*, *32*(1/2), 21–31.

Johnson, G. J., & Johnson, W. R. (2000). Perceived overqualification and dimensions and job satisfaction: A longitudinal analysis. *Journal of Psychology*, *134*(5), 537–555.

Johnson, W. R., Morrow, P. C., & Johnson, G. (2002). An evaluation of a perceived overqualification scale across work settings. *Journal of Psychology, 136*(4), 425–441.

Kanfer, R., Wanberg, C. R., & Kantrowitz, T. M. (2001). Job search and employment: A personality–motivational analysis and meta-analytic review. *Journal of Applied Psychology, 86*(5), 837–855.

Kessler, R. C., Turner, J. B., & House, J. S. (1988). Effects of unemployment on health in a community survey: Main, modifying, and mediating effects. *Journal of Social Issues, 44*(4), 69–85.

Khan, L. J., & Morrow, P. C. (1991). Objective and subjective underemployment relationships to job satisfaction. *Journal of Business Research, 22*(3), 211–218.

Kinicki, A. J., Prussia, G. E., & McKee-Ryan, F. (2000). A panel study of coping with involuntary job loss. *Academy of Management Journal, 43*(1), 90–100.

Kletzer, L. G. (1998). Job displacement. *The Journal of Economic Perspectives, 12*(1), 115–136.

Koeber, C., & Wright, D. W. (2001). Wage bias in worker displacement: How industrial structure shapes the job loss and earnings decline of older American workers. *Journal of Socioeconomics, 30*(4), 343–352.

Koen, J., Klehe, U. C., Van Vianen, A. E., Zikic, J., & Nauta, A. (2010). Job-search strategies and reemployment quality: The impact of career adaptability. *Journal of Vocational Behavior, 77*(1), 126–139.

Konrad, A. M., Moore, M. E., Ng, E. S., Doherty, A. J., & Breward, K. (2013). Temporary work, underemployment and workplace accommodations: Relationship to well-being for workers with disabilities. *British Journal of Management, 24*(3), 367–382.

Kraimer, M. L., Shaffer, M. A., & Bolino, M. C. (2009). The influence of expatriate and repatriate experiences on career advancement and repatriate retention. *Human Resource Management, 48*(1), 27–47.

Kristof-Brown, A. L., Zimmerman, R. D., & Johnson, E. C. (2005). Consequences of individuals' fit at work: A meta-analysis of person-job, person-organization, person-group, and person-supervisor fit. *Personnel Psychology, 58*(2), 281–342.

Latack, J. C., Kinicki, A. J., & Prussia, G. E. (1995). An integrative process model of coping with job loss. *Academy of Management Review, 20*(2), 311–342.

Leana, C. R., & Feldman, D. C. (1992). *Coping with job loss: How individuals, organizations and communities respond to layoffs.* New York: Lexington Books.

Leana, C. R., & Feldman, D. C. (1995). Finding new jobs after a plant closing: Antecedents and outcomes of the occurrence and quality of reemployment. *Human Relations, 48*(12), 1381–1401.

Leana, C. R., & Feldman, D. C. (2000). What ever happened to laid-off executives? A study of reemployment challenges after downsizing. *Organizational Dynamics, 29*(1), 64–75.

Lee, C. H. (2005). A study of underemployment among self-initiated expatriates. *Journal of World Business, 40*(2), 172–187.

Li, C., Gervais, G., & Duval, A. (2006). *The dynamics of overqualification: Canada's underemployed university graduates.* Analysis in Brief Series. Ottawa, ON: Statistics Canada. http://www.statcan.gc.ca/pub/11-621-m/11-621-m2006039-eng.htm.

Lin, N. (2001). Building a network theory of social capital. In N. Lin, K. Cook, & R. Burt (Eds.), *Social capital: Theory and research* (pp. 3–30). New York: Walter de Gruyter Inc.

Lippmann, S. (2008). Rethinking risk in the new economy: Age and cohort effects on unemployment and re-employment. *Human Relations, 61*(9), 1259–1292.

Livingstone, D. W. (1998). *The education-jobs gap. Underemployment or economic democracy.* Boulder, CO: Westview Press.

Luksyte, A., & Spitzmuller, C. (2011). Behavioral science approaches to studying underemployment. In D. C. Maynard & D. C. Feldman (Eds.), *Underemployment: Psychological, economic and social challenges* (pp. 35–56). New York: Springer.

Luksyte, A., Spitzmuller, C., & Maynard, D. C. (2011). Why do overqualified incumbents deviate? Examining multiple mediators. *Journal of Occupational Health Psychology, 16*(3), 279–296.

Lyness, K. S., & Thompson, D. E. (2000). Climbing the corporate ladder: Do female and male executives follow the same route? *Journal of Applied Psychology, 85*(1), 86–101.

Mallinckrodt, B. (1990). Satisfaction with a new job after unemployment: Consequences of job loss for older professionals. *Journal of Counseling Psychology, 37*(2), 149–152.

Markel, K. S., & Barclay, L. A. (2009). Addressing the underemployment of persons with disabilities: Recommendations for expanding organizational social responsibility. *Employee Rights and Responsibilities Journal, 21*(4), 305–318.

Martin, G. (2009). A portrait of the youth labor market in 13 countries, 1980–2007. *Monthly Labor Review, 132*(7), 3–21.

Mau, W. C., & Kopischke, A. (2001). Job search methods, job search outcomes, and job satisfaction of college graduates: A comparison of race and sex. *Journal of Employment Counseling, 38*(3), 141–149.

Maynard, D. C. (2011). Directions for future underemployment research: Measurement and practice. In D. C. Maynard & D. C. Feldman (Eds.), *Underemployment: Psychological, economic and social challenges* (pp. 253–276). New York: Springer.

Maynard, D. C., Joseph, T. A., & Maynard, A. M. (2006). Underemployment, job attitudes, and turnover intentions. *Journal of Organizational Behavior, 27*(4), 509–536.

Maynard, D. C., Thorsteinson, T. J., & Parfyonova, N. M. (2006). Reasons for working part-time: Subgroup differences in job attitudes and turnover intentions. *Career Development International, 11*(2), 145–162.

McGoldrick, A. E., & Arrowsmith, J. (2001). Discrimination by age: The organizational response. In I. Golver & M. Branine (Eds.), *Ageism in work and employment* (pp. 75–96). Burlington, VT: Ashgate.

McGuinness, S. (2006). Overeducation in the labour market. *Journal of Economic Surveys, 20*(3), 387–418.

McKee-Ryan, F., and Harvey, J. (2011). I have a job, but . . .: A review of underemployment. *Journal of Management, 37*(4), 962–996.

McKee-Ryan, F., & Kinicki, A. J. (2002). Coping with job loss: A life-facet perspective. In C. L. Cooper & I. T. Robertson (Eds.), *International review of industrial and organizational psychology* (Vol. 17, pp. 1–30). Chichester, NY: Wiley.

McKee-Ryan, F., Virick, M., Prussia, G. E., Harvey, J., & Lilly, J. D. (2009). Life after the layoff: Getting a job worth keeping. *Journal of Organizational Behavior, 30*(4), 561–580.

Merton, R., & Rossi, A. (1957). Contributions to the theory of reference group behavior. In R. Merton (Ed.), *Social theory and social structure* (pp. 225–275). New York: Free Press.

Mor-Barak, M. (1995). The meaning of work for older adults seeking employment: The generativity factor. *International Journal of Aging*, 41(4), 325–344.

Mroz, T. A., & Savage, T. H. (2006). The long-term effects of youth unemployment. *Journal of Human Resources*, 41(2), 259–293.

Ng, T. W. H., & Feldman, D. C. (2009). Age, work experience, and the psychological contract. *Journal of Organizational Behavior*, 30(8), 1053–1075.

Niessen, C., Heinrichs, N., & Dorr, S. (2009). Pursuit and adjustment of goals during unemployment: The role of age. *International Journal of Stress Management*, 16(2), 102–123.

Nordenmark, M., & Strandh, M. (1999). Towards a sociological understanding of mental well-being among the unemployed: The role of economic and psychosocial factors. *Sociology*, 33(3), 577–597.

O'Brien, G. E., & Feather, N. T. (1990). The relative effects of unemployment and quality of employment on the affect, work values and personal control of adolescents. *Journal of Occupational Psychology*, 63(2), 151–165.

Ong, P. M., & Mar, D. (1992). Post-layoff earnings among semiconductor workers. *Industrial and Labor Relations Review*, 45(2), 366–379.

Perrucci, C. C., Perrucci, R. P., & Targ, D. B. (1997). Gender differences in the economic, psychological and social effects of plant closings in an expanding economy. *Social Science Journal*, 32(2), 217–233.

Prause, J., & Dooley, D. (2001). Favorable employment status change and psychological depression: A two-year follow-up analysis of the national longitudinal survey of youth. *Applied Psychology: An International Review*, 50(2), 282–304.

Reitman, F., & Schneer, J. A. (2005). The long-term negative impacts of managerial career interruptions: A longitudinal study of men and women MBAs. *Group & Organization Management*, 30(3), 243–262.

Robinson, J. (1937). *Essays in the theory of employment*. London: Macmillan.

Rodriguez, D., & Zavodny, M. (2003). Changes in the age and education profile of displaced workers. *Industrial and Labor Relations Review*, 56(3), 498–510.

Rosen, S. (1972). Learning experience in the labor market. *Journal of Human Resources*, 7(3), 326–342.

Runciman, W. G. (1966). *Relative deprivation and social justice*. London: Routledge & Kegan Paul.

Saks, A. M. (2005). Job search success: A review and integration of the predictors, behaviors, and outcomes. In S. D. Brown & R. W. Lent (Eds.), *Career development and counseling: Putting theory and research to work* (pp. 155–179). Hoboken, NJ: Wiley.

Saks, A. M., & Ashforth, B. E. (2002). Is job search related to employment quality? It all depends on fit. *Journal of Applied Psychology*, 87(4), 646–654.

Schwab, D. P., Rynes, S. L., & Aldag, R. J. (1987). Theories and research on job search and choice. In K. M. Rowland & G. R. Ferris (Eds.), *Research in personnel and human resources management* (Vol. 5, pp. 129–166). Greenwich, CT: JAI Press.

Seligman, M. E. P., & Maier, S. F. (1967). Failure to escape traumatic shock. *Journal of Experimental Psychology*, 74(1), 1–9.

Sicherman N. (1991). "Overeducation" in the labour market. *Journal of Labour Economics*, 9(2), 101–122.

Sicherman, N., & Galor, O. (1990). A theory of career mobility. *Journal of Political Economy*, 98(1), 169–192.

Simpson, P. A., Greller, M. M., & Stroh, L. K. (2002). Variations in human capital investment activity by age. *Journal of Vocational Behavior*, 61(1), 109–138.

Slack, T., & Jensen, L. (2002). Race, ethnicity and underemployment in nonmetropolitan America: A thirty-year profile. *Rural Sociology*, 67(2), 208–233.

Slack, T., & Jensen, L. (2007). Underemployment across immigrant generations. *Social Science Research*, 36(4), 1415–1430.

Slack, T., & Jensen, L. (2008). Employment hardship among older workers: Does residential and gender inequality extend into older age? *Journals of Gerontology: Social Sciences*, 63(1), S15–S24.

Spalter-Roth, R., & Deitch, C. (1999). I don't feel right sized; I feel out-of-work sized: Gender, race, ethnicity and the unequal costs of displacement. *Work and Occupations*, 26(4), 446–482.

Stevens, C. K., & Beach, L. R. (1996). Job search and job selection. In R. Beach & P. Lee Roy (Eds.), *Decision making in the workplace: A unified perspective* (pp. 33–47). Hillsdale, NJ: Lawrence Erlbaum Associates.

Stouffer, S. A., Suchman, E. A., DeVinney, L. C., Star, S. A., & Williams, R. M. (1949). *The American soldier: Adjustment during army life*. Princeton, NJ: Princeton University Press.

Sugiyarto, G. (2008). Measuring underemployment: Does the cut-off point really matter? *Journal of the Asia Pacific Economy*, 13(4), 481–517.

Sum, A., & Khatiwada, I. (2010). Underemployment problems in U.S. labor markets in 2009: Predicting the probabilities of underemployment for key age, gender, race-ethnic, nativity, educational attainment, and occupational subgroups of U.S. workers. *Center for Labor Market Studies Publications*. Paper 27. http://hdl.handle.net/2047/d20000592.

Tam, H. (2010). Characteristics of the underemployed and the overemployed in the U.K. *Economic & Labour Market Review*, 4(7), 8–20.

Tigges, L. M., & Tootle, D. M. (1993). Underemployment and racial competition in local labor markets. *Sociological Quarterly*, 34(2), 279–298.

Turner, R. G., & Whitaker, W. M. (1973). The impact of mass layoffs on older workers. *Industrial Gerontology*, 16, 14–21.

Vaisey, S. (2006). Education and its discontents: Overqualification in America, 1972–2002. *Social Forces*, 85(2), 835–864.

Van de Werfhorst, H. G., & Andersen, R. (2005). Social background, credential inflation and educational strategies. *Acta Sociologica*, 48(4), 321–340.

Van Hooft, E. A. J., Born, M. P., Taris, T. W., & Van der Flier, H. (2004). Job search and the theory of planned behavior: Minority–majority group differences in The Netherlands. *Journal of Vocational Behavior*, 65(3), 366–390.

Van Hooft, E. A. J., Born, M. P., Taris, T. W., & Van der Flier, H. (2005). Predictors and outcomes of job search behavior: The moderating effects of gender and family situation. *Journal of Vocational Behavior*, 67(2), 133–152.

Van Hooft, E. A., Wanberg, C. R., & Van Hoye, G. (2013). Moving beyond job search quantity towards a conceptualization and self-regulatory framework of job search quality. *Organizational Psychology Review*, 3(1), 3–40.

Van Hoye, G., Van Hooft, E. A. J., & Lievens, F. (2009). Networking as a job search behaviour: A social network perspective. *Journal of Occupational and Organizational Psychology, 82*(3), 661–682.

Vaughan-Jones, H., & Barham, L. (2009). *Healthy work: Challenges and opportunities to 2030.* London: Bupa.

Vinokur, A. D., Price, R. H., & Caplan, R. D. (1996). Hard times and hurtful partners: How financial strain affects depression and relationship satisfaction of unemployed persons and their spouses. *Journal of Personality and Social Psychology, 71*(1), 166–179.

Virick, M. (2011). Underemployment and older workers. In D. C. Maynard & D. C. Feldman (Eds.), *Underemployment: Psychological, economic and social challenges* (pp. 81–103). New York: Springer.

Wald, S. (2005). The impact of overqualification on job search. *International Journal of Manpower, 26*(2), 140–156.

Wanberg, C. R. (1995). A longitudinal study of the effects of unemployment and quality of reemployment. *Journal of Vocational Behavior, 46*(1), 40–54.

Wanberg, C., Basbug, G., Van Hooft, E. A., & Samtani, A. (2012). Navigating the black hole: Explicating layers of job search context and adaptational responses. *Personnel Psychology, 65*(4), 887–926.

Wanberg, C. R., Hough, L. M., & Song, Z. (2002). Predictive validity of a multidisciplinary model of reemployment success. *Journal of Applied Psychology, 87*(6), 1100–1120.

Wanberg, C. R., Kanfer, R., & Banas, J. T. (2000). Predictors and outcomes of networking intensity among unemployed job seekers. *Journal of Applied Psychology, 85*(4), 491–503.

Wanberg, C. R., Kanfer, R., & Rotundo, M. (1999). Unemployed individuals: Motives, job-search competencies, and job-search constraints as predictors of job-seeking and reemployment. *Journal of Applied Psychology, 84*(6), 897–910.

Waters, L. (2007). Experiential differences between voluntary and involuntary job redundancy on depression, job-search activity, affective employee outcomes and re-employment quality. *Journal of Occupational and Organizational Psychology, 80*(2), 279–299.

Waters, L. (2008). The role of protean career attitude during unemployment and reemployment: A literature review and conceptual model. In K. Näswall, J. Hellgren, & M. Sverke (Eds.), *The individual in the changing work life* (pp. 328–350). Cambridge: Cambridge University Press.

Winefield, A. H. (2002). Unemployment, underemployment, occupational stress, and psychological well-being. *Australian Journal of Management, 27*(Special Issue), 137–148.

Winefield, A., Winefield, H., Tiggemann, M., & Gouldney, R. (1991). A longitudinal study of the psychological effects of unemployment and unsatisfactory employment on young adults. *Journal of Applied Psychology, 76*(3), 424–431.

Zikic, J., & Klehe, U. C. (2006). Job loss as a blessing in disguise: The role of career exploration and career planning in predicting reemployment quality. *Journal of Vocational Behavior, 69*(3), 391–401.

Career Transitions

Job Search and the School-to-Work Transition

Alan M. Saks

Abstract

The school-to-work transition (STWT) is a major life event for those who must leave behind their lives as full-time students and begin new lives as a full-time employees. Although much has been written about the STWT, the role and importance of job search has often been neglected. At the same time, research on job search has tended to treat the job-search process as an independent and isolated activity. In this chapter, I describe an integrated model of job search within the context of the STWT. It shows that job search is preceded by a career-planning and development stage and followed by a work-adjustment stage. A successful STWT requires students to engage in a number of behaviors at each stage which should result in numerous outcomes that are necessary for a successful transition to the next stage. The model shows that job search is a critical part of the STWT that connects the career-planning and development stage to the work-adjustment stage. The chapter concludes with a discussion of the implications of the model for job search and STWT research and practice.

Key Words: school-to-work transition, job search, career planning, career development, work adjustment

Students searching for employment make up a large contingent of job seekers and, not surprisingly, have been the focus of many studies on job search. In fact, college students have been used most often in studies on job search, followed by unemployed job seekers (Saks, 2005). Student job seekers differ from unemployed job seekers and job-to-job seekers in many ways. Perhaps most significant is that student job seekers are involved in much more than a job search: They are undergoing a major life transition or what is known as the *school-to-work transition* (STWT) as they leave behind their lives as scholars and begin new lives as full-time employees.

The job-search process and search success is particularly important during the STWT, as the implications and consequences extend beyond simply finding employment. For example, there is evidence that one's first job following postsecondary education is a critical factor in determining future career success and earnings (Steffy, Shaw, & Noe, 1989). Richards (1984a,b) studied the employment situation of liberal arts undergraduates one and three years after graduation and found that graduates' occupational position one year after graduation predicted outcomes two years later as well as future occupational directions. She also found a high degree of continuity in job fit (the degree of fit between educational preparation and occupational achievement) from the first year to the third year following graduation. Richards (1984a) concluded that a "graduate's occupational position the year after graduation had a great deal to do with the probable outcome 2 years later" and that "jobs in the first year after graduation are important in determining future occupational directions" (p. 317). She recommended that students receive assistance in finding their first job, which is likely to have long-term effects on vocational outcomes.

The importance of the first job and early work experiences on one's future career success was the focus of a study by Rosenbaum (1979), who analyzed the career mobility of a cohort of employees in a large corporation over a 13-year period. The results provided support for a tournament model of career mobility. Rosenbaum (1979) found that

> very early job moves are related to subsequent mobility even a decade later, after employees have moved on to second and third jobs. Indeed, *mobility in the earliest stage of one's career bears an unequivocal relationship with one's later career*, predicting many of the most important parameters of later moves: career "ceiling," career "floor," as well as the probabilities of promotion and demotion in each successive period. (p. 220)

These findings highlight the importance of the job-search process for student job seekers who are seeking employment following graduation. However, to fully understand the importance of job search for student job seekers, one must view job search as part of the larger process of the STWT rather than as an isolated and independent event.

The main objective of this chapter is to consider job search within the larger context of the STWT. Research on the STWT has tended to focus on factors that precede job search (career planning and development) and work experiences that follow job search (e.g., work adjustment) and have ignored the job-search process. Thus a complete and integrated model of the STWT should include job search as well as career planning and development and work adjustment.

The chapter begins with a description of the meaning, experience, and success of the STWT and the role of job search within the context of the STWT. I then describe an integrative model of job search and the STWT that revolves around job search, which plays a central role in the STWT. Each stage of the model consists of a number of behaviors and outcomes that have implications for the subsequent stage. Job search is treated as the most critical stage in the STWT process because it is influenced by the first stage (career planning and development), it influences the third stage (work adjustment), and it connects the first and last stage of the STWT. Let us now take a closer look at the meaning of the STWT.

The School-to-Work Transition

The STWT refers to the period and process in which young adults move from school and life as scholars and begin full-time employment (Morrison, 2002; Ng & Feldman, 2007). It actually involves a number of transitions, including the transition to an occupation, trade, or profession; the transition to a particular organization; and more generally the transition to the world of work (Morrison, 2002). For most young adults, the STWT marks the beginning of full-time employment and is the first major work adjustment of their careers (Ng & Feldman, 2007; Savickas, 1999).

Students entering the workforce for the first time as full-time workers are very different from more experienced job seekers (see, for example, Boswell & Gardner, this volume; Song, Sun, & Li, this volume; and Klehe, de Pater, Koen, & Kira, this volume for studies of different groups of more experienced job seekers). For starters, they might not have a clear idea of what type of career they are most interested in or would be most suitable for them. They might not have sufficient knowledge about careers to even know how to make a choice. Even if students do have a clear idea of the type of career they plan to pursue, they might not know how to search for a job or choose an organization where they would want to work and begin their careers. And even if a student knows how to search for work and is successful in obtaining employment, he or she might not know how to navigate within an uncertain, unfamiliar organization once employment began.

Besides the newness associated with the transition to full-time work, a key part of the transition involves a process of identity change, which occurs during the STWT (Morrison, 2002). Students must relinquish their roles as scholars and begin to identify with their work roles (Ng & Feldman, 2007). According to Ng and Feldman (2007), "the major task facing young adults during the STWT is to develop a high level of work role identification," and "young adults' ability to identify with the work role is a decisive factor in determining STWT success" (pp. 116–117).

Ng and Feldman (2007) define work role identification as "the extent to which a person spends a large amount of time in the work role, feels positively towards the work role, and is able to express his/her personal values within the work role" (p. 116). They further note that it "refers to the salience of an individual's participation and commitment to working relative to other life roles and the extent to which an individual can express his/her values through work" (p. 117). The ability to change from the student role to a work role identity as one's core life role is an important predictor of the success of the STWT (Ng & Feldman, 2007; see van Vianen & Klehe, and Klehe, de Pater, Koen, & Kira, this volume, for a discussion of work role identity in later life).

The STWT has been described as a difficult, stressful experience filled with uncertainty and anxiety (Morrison, 2002; Taylor, 1985). The experience has been eloquently described by West and Newton (1983) thus:

> It would not be surprising if many school-leavers experience a state of confusion during their transition from school to work, since within a relatively short period of time adolescents are expected to discard the role of dependent school child and assume the role of independent working adult. The consequent complex and profound changes which occur in their lives undoubtedly cause many to oscillate between feelings of anxiety and pleasure. During this period, the individual is required to choose an occupation, to find and apply for jobs, to learn the norms and values of the new world of work, to learn the intricacies of a new job and to become successfully integrated in a new organization. (p. 1)

The extent to which individuals manage and cope with the uncertainty and anxiety of the STWT has implications for how smooth the experience will be and its ultimate success. The success of the STWT has been described in terms of both objective criteria (employment versus unemployment) as well as subjective criteria (e.g., fit perceptions) (Ng & Feldman, 2007). Ng and Feldman (2007) define STWT success as "a state in which individuals are employed after leaving school, perform at levels acceptable to their employers, and have positive attitudes towards their work environments and job requirements" (p. 116).

Thus a successful STWT involves several criteria for success, including finding employment, performance proficiency once employed, and positive attitudes toward one's job and place of employment. One can further break down the criteria for success into even more specific factors, as described later in this chapter. However, for now it should be clear that a successful STWT involves outcomes and success at several stages of the process.

The success of the STWT has implications not only for individuals making the transition but also for organizations, educational institutions, and society (Morrison, 2002). For individuals, the success of the STWT can set a pattern for their future jobs and careers. As described by Ng and Feldman (2007), it can influence whether an individual will change jobs, organizations, and occupations as well as how he or she copes with future career changes. For organizations, the success of the STWT has implications for new hire productivity, the amount of training that will be needed, and the level of turnover of new hires. And for society, the STWT has implications for individuals' employment prospects and long-term employment, which can contribute to antisocial behaviors associated with unemployment (e.g., alcohol and drug abuse) and the need for government-subsidized vocational programs (Ng & Feldman, 2007). As noted by Morrison (2002), "the failure of new graduates to move effectively from school to work can be detrimental not only for those graduates but also for the organizations and professions in which they work, for the educational institutions that they have just left, and for society overall" (p. 151).

Although the STWT inevitably requires obtaining employment, the emphasis in the literature has been on success factors that occur during employment rather than on actually finding employment. As described in the next section, little attention has been given to job search in the STWT literature, even though it is critical for initial success (i.e., employment) and a successful STWT.

Job Search in the Context of the School-to-Work Transition

While the job-search literature focuses on the search behaviors and outcomes of student job seekers, the literature on the STWT has for the most part ignored the job-search process and focused on what precedes or follows job search. For example, a series of articles on career development theories and the STWT published in *Career Development Quarterly* focused primarily on facilitating individual preference and choice (Herr, 1999). As noted by Taylor (1985), vocational models "devote relatively little attention to the process through which students initially implement their vocational choices during the transition from school to work" (p. 548).

Other approaches to the STWT focus on behaviors and work outcomes on-the-job following job search. For example, Feij, Whitely, Peiro, and Taris (1995) studied the development of career-enhancing strategies (e.g., seeking advice and information from others, networking) in a sample of youth employed as machine operators and office technology workers following their transition from vocational school to full-time work. In her chapter on the STWT, Morrison (2002) focused on what happens following the transition as students begin full-time employment. According to Morrison (2002), the primary objective of the STWT is adaptation in the new organizational context. She further notes that as individuals begin their first full-time job, they face numerous challenges as they strive to achieve mastery and comfort in their new jobs and organizations. To accomplish this objective, Morrison (2002) described three key challenges and processes in the transition from school to work that individual's must master.

First, individuals need to acquire information and learn about their jobs and their responsibilities, their work groups, and the organizations. Second, they need to build relationships with coworkers and other members of their organizations, which can help them manage the transition and improve their chances of success. And third, the STWT involves a process of identity change in which each person must redefine his or her sense of self and adopt a new social identity. As described later, a number of studies have examined the relationship between various forms of proactive behavior (e.g., information seeking, relationship building) and work adjustment.

These three challenges all occur following job search and organizational entry. Clearly individuals must first search for and find employment before they confront these challenges. Furthermore, the success of their job search and the employment they obtain has important implications for the types of challenges they encounter following entry and the extent to which the STWT is successful. Therefore a fundamental and necessary component of the STWT is job search. A successful STWT also depends on earlier career-relevant tasks (e.g., career exploration, career planning) that take place prior to job search (Lent, Hackett, & Brown, 1999).

Thus, research on the STWT can be found in three related literatures: (1) career and vocational development, which focuses on career-related activities that occur prior to job search; (2) job-search research, which investigates job-search behavior and outcomes; and (3) socialization and work-adjustment research, which investigates the relationship between newcomer proactive behaviors and work adjustment. However, the bridge or connection between the first stage (career-related activities) and the third (work adjustment) is job search, which is central to a successful STWT.

The role of job search as a link between the career-development and work-adjustment stages was noted by Stevens (1973) 40 years ago, when she stated: "Job-seeking behavior is the bridge linking job choice to the desired job. Without effective job-seeking behavior, a job is not successfully obtained, and the task of adjusting to work cannot be experienced by the individual" (p. 219).

A similar point was made by Allen and Keaveny (1980) when they stated that "the job-search process is the nexus between the job choice and subsequent work adjustment and later career development" (p. 19). Thus, job search is a critical component of a successful STWT, which connects the career-planning and development stage and the work-adjustment stage.

In summary, the STWT begins before job search and continues after job search when the student begins full-time employment. And while the STWT literature has seldom focused on the job-search process, research on job search has seldom included variables that precede and follow job search. This is a serious shortcoming because, as described in the next section, career-planning and development behaviors and outcomes can influence job-search behaviors and outcomes, which in turn can influence students' adjustment to work and STWT success. In the next section, I describe an integrative model of job search and the STWT that integrates behaviors and outcomes from the three literatures that focus on the STWT.

An Integrative Model of Job Search and the School-to-Work Transition

Figure 21.1 depicts an integrative model of job search and the STWT. It shows that the STWT involves three stages that correspond to pre–job search (career planning and development), job search, and post–job search (work adjustment). The model depicts the STWT as a sequential process in which success at each stage leads to the next. Each stage involves a set of behaviors that influence a number of outcomes. The solid lines in the model represent direct relationships, while the dotted lines represent indirect or mediated relationships. With the exception of work-role identification, the outcomes at each stage are distinct. However, given the importance of the development of a work-role identity for a successful STWT (Ng & Feldman, 2007) and the fact that the adoption of a work-role identity occurs over time (Blustein, Phillips, Jobin-Davis, Finkelberg, & Roarke, 1997), work-role identification is treated as an outcome at each stage of the STWT.

In the remainder of this section, I describe the behaviors and outcomes of each stage and review the empirical research on the relationships between the behaviors and outcomes. A series of propositions on the relationships between the behaviors and outcomes within and across the stages is also provided.

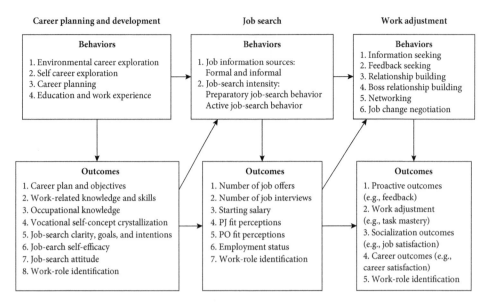

Career planning and development

Behaviors

1. Environmental career exploration
2. Self career exploration
3. Career planning
4. Education and work experience

Job search

Behaviors

1. Job information sources:
   Formal and informal
2. Job-search intensity:
   Preparatory job-search behavior
   Active job-search behavior

Work adjustment

Behaviors

1. Information seeking
2. Feedback seeking
3. Relationship building
4. Boss relationship building
5. Networking
6. Job change negotiation

Outcomes

1. Career plan and objectives
2. Work-related knowledge and skills
3. Occupational knowledge
4. Vocational self-concept crystallization
5. Job-search clarity, goals, and intentions
6. Job-earch self-efficacy
7. Job-search attitude
8. Work-role identification

Outcomes

1. Number of job offers
2. Number of job interviews
3. Starting salary
4. PJ fit perceptions
5. PO fit perceptions
6. Employment status
7. Work-role identification

Outcomes

1. Proactive outcomes
   (e.g., feedback)
2. Work adjustment
   (e.g., task mastery)
3. Socialization outcomes
   (e.g., job satisfaction)
4. Career outcomes (e.g.,
   career satisfaction)
5. Work-role identification

Figure 21.1 Integrative model of job search and the school-to-work transition.

Pre–Job Search Stage: Career Planning and Development

Prior to conducting a job search, students must engage in a variety of career-related activities that will prepare them to enter the workforce and to engage in a successful job search. As described by Savickas (1999), their ability to cope with the STWT transition is greater if students "have developed awareness of the choices to be made and of the information and planning that bear on these choices" (p. 327). In other words, students who "look ahead" and "look around" will be better prepared for job search and more likely to adjust to work. This involves developing competence and skill in five areas: self-knowledge, occupational information, decision making, planning, and problem solving (Savickas, 1999).

Morrison (2002) described a number of "pretransition" factors that can provide students with realistic information prior to the transition and can lower the uncertainty, anxiety, and stress associated with the transition and new job. It is worth noting that Morrison (2002) is referring to the influence of these factors on individuals once they have entered an organization, during the work-adjustment stage.

One reason for the difficulty that students often experience during the STWT stems from the type of information they have when they initiate their search for employment (Taylor, 1985). According to Taylor (1985), two types of information that are particularly important are occupational knowledge and crystallization of the vocational self-concept

(i.e., insight into one's relevant vocational abilities and interests).

Thus the first stage of the STWT involves career planning and other career-development behaviors that should be conducted prior to job search. In this section, I describe four career-development behaviors: environmental career exploration, self career exploration, career planning, and education and work experience. These behaviors are expected to result in the following outcomes: career plan and objectives, work-related knowledge and skills, occupational knowledge, vocational self-concept crystallization, job-search clarity (the extent to which job seekers have clear job-search objectives and a clear idea of the type of career, work, or job desired) (Wanberg, Hough, & Song, 2002), job-search goals and intentions, job-search self-efficacy (confidence in one's ability to successfully perform a variety of job-search activities) (Saks, 2006), job-search attitude, and work-role identification.

Career Exploration

According to Stumpf, Austin, and Hartman (1984), career exploration involves "purposive behavior and cognitions that afford access to information about occupations, jobs, or organizations that was not previously in the stimulus field" (p. 222). Thus career exploration involves gathering information about oneself (e.g., interests and abilities) and the environment (e.g., occupations, jobs, and organizations) (Stumpf, Colarelli, & Hartman, 1983; Werbel, 2000). It is considered to be a lifelong process that is triggered during transitions (Blustein, 1997; Savickas, 1997). According to Werbel (2000), career exploration, and the information gathering that it involves, is an important initial step that prepares job seekers to conduct an efficient and effective job search and should result in greater job-search intensity. Thus career exploration is an important component of models and theories of job search.

There are two dimensions of career exploration. *Self-exploration* involves exploring one's interests, values, skills, needs, personal goals, and experiences and reflecting on one's career to gain a deeper understanding of oneself (Stumpf et al., 1983; Werbel, 2000). Engaging in self-exploration can facilitate a clearer understanding of one's career ambitions and interest in working in different types of work environments as well as specific work activities (Zikic & Klehe, 2006). Self-exploration can also influence the job-search process because it provides greater focus and goal direction (Werbel, 2000).

Environmental exploration involves exploring various career options by collecting information about jobs, organizations, occupations or industries. This can also include learning about organizations and the demands and requirements of different jobs (Werbel, 2000). As a result, environmental exploration enables individuals to learn about different employment opportunities and to identify those that they want to pursue. This is important for job-search readiness and can result in more informed career decisions (Phillips & Blustein, 1994). That is, environmental exploration prepares and guides individuals in their job search by reducing the number of opportunities considered, providing greater focus, and making the job-search process less overwhelming and stressful (Werbel, 2000).

According to Wanberg et al. (2002), individuals who do not have clear job-search objectives might need to spend more time in career exploration owing to a lack of self-understanding and of information about the work world and job opportunities. Thus career exploration should help individuals to obtain greater clarity regarding the desired type of work, job, or career. In addition, by exploring various work options and understanding their own capabilities better, job seekers may also develop increased confidence in their ability to search for and find the right job (i.e., job-search self-efficacy).

Zikic and Saks (2009) found that environmental and self career exploration was positively related to job-search self-efficacy and that environmental career exploration was also positively related to

job-search clarity. They also found that self career exploration was positively related to job-search intention. Taylor (1985) found that college students who spent more time in vocational exploration activities had greater occupational knowledge and self-concept crystallization. According to Taylor (1985), occupational knowledge and self-concept crystallization can lessen the difficulty that students experience during the STWT.

Career Planning

Career planning involves setting career goals and formulating strategies for realizing those goals (Saks & Ashforth, 2002). According to Gould (1979), career planning facilitates the achievement of career goals and is a means of facilitating career effectiveness. Gould (1979) equates career planning with goal setting, which leads to efforts (e.g., job search) to implement goals and career plans and to a more successful career. Thus career planning enables individuals to be more focused in their job search and to find a job that is in line with their goals (Zikic & Klehe, 2006). As described by Saks and Ashforth (2002), career goals and strategies prepare individuals to search for and find jobs and organizations that will be a good fit for them (person-job fit and person-organization fit).

Education and Work Experience

Students who acquire education and work experience in general and more specifically in their chosen occupations will have a more successful STWT. For example, Morrison (2002) has described how individuals who have had relevant experience prior to the transition—such as job and professional training, prior work experience (e.g., internships, summer jobs, or part-time work), and contact with role models in their chosen professions—experience less uncertainty, anxiety, and stress during the STWT. Students who receive vocational training in school are also more likely to develop a work-role identity (Ng & Feldman, 2007). Ng and Feldman (2007) describe how work-related knowledge and skills obtained in the classroom and from vocational educational programs help to promote a high level of work-role identification, which will, in turn, positively influence STWT success.

Internships have been found to be especially effective for facilitating the STWT. Internships involve "structured and career-relevant work experiences obtained by students prior to graduation from an academic program" (Taylor, 1988, p. 393). Internships provide students not only with valuable work experience that will help them develop work-relevant knowledge and skills but also a realistic portrayal of work in general and, more specifically, a particular type of work and job as well as what it is like to work in a particular organization (Ng & Feldman, 2007). Internships increase students' access to career opportunities and the amount and quality of information that they have when they are making career decisions (Feldman & Weitz, 1990). Internships can result in better career decisions and contribute to the development of a work-role identity (Ng & Feldman, 2007).

According to Taylor (1988), internships can improve the STWT for at least three reasons. First, they result in greater crystallization of vocational self-concept and work values. Internships help students "in the crystallization of their vocational self-concept by facilitating the identification of vocationally relevant abilities, interests, and values" (Taylor, 1988, p. 393). Taylor (1988) found that compared with students who did not have an internship, interns had greater crystallization of their vocational abilities and interests during the internship period.

Second, internships lessen the reality shock of the first job. And third, they can lead to better employment opportunities. Thus work experience and internships offer a number of benefits that increase the success of the STWT. They result not only in greater crystallization of one's vocational self-concept but also prepare the student for a more successful job search and work adjustment. As noted by Richards (1984b), "recent occupational experience, and participation in prevocational programs, could serve an important function as bridges to the occupational world" (p. 302).

Propositions Regarding the Stage of Career-Planning and Development

At the end of the career-planning and development stage, students should have acquired some work-related knowledge and skills and have an understanding and awareness of their career interests and what they are looking for in terms of a job, organization, and career. They should have a career plan and job-search goals and intentions for how, when, and where they will search for a job, and a positive job-search attitude and job-search self-efficacy. They should also begin to form a work-role identity. Therefore the first proposition of this stage refers to the relationship between career-planning and development behaviors and outcomes:

Proposition 1: The behaviors at the career-planning and development stage (self career exploration, environmental career exploration, career planning, education and work experience) will be positively related to the outcomes at this stage (career plan and objectives, work-related knowledge and skills, occupational knowledge, vocational self-concept crystallization, job-search clarity, job-search goals and intentions, job-search self-efficacy, job-search attitude, and work-role identification).

In addition, there is also reason to expect the career-planning and development behaviors to be related to the behaviors and outcomes at the job-search stage. For example, in a sample of graduating college students, Werbel (2002) found that environmental career exploration was positively related to job-search intensity and initial compensation. Self-exploration was also positively correlated with job-search intensity. Steffy et al. (1989), in a sample of undergraduate business students, found that environmental career exploration prior to graduation was positively related to the number of campus screening interviews one year later.

In a study on the career exploration and interview performance and outcomes of graduate business students, Stumpf et al. (1984) found that self-exploration and environmental exploration were positively related to receiving a job offer, total call-back interviews, and total number of job offers. They also found that environmental and self/career exploration were positively related to interview readiness and recruiter ratings of interview performance. These findings suggest that career exploration results in greater interview readiness, which, in turn, relates positively to interview performance and outcome (i.e., call-back interviews and job offers).

Stumpf and Hartman (1984) found that environmental exploration prior to organizational entry results in obtaining a greater amount of career-relevant information, which leads to realistic expectations, person-job congruence, and more positive work attitudes and intentions. Zikic and Klehe (2006) found a positive relationship between environmental career exploration and reemployment quality in a sample of unemployed workers and concluded that "career-planning and environmental exploration play a key role in building successful careers" (p. 405). Thus, as noted by Werbel (2002), "career exploration is an important initial step that prepares the job seeker for a successful job search" (p. 389).

Career planning has also been linked to job search, work adjustment, and career effectiveness. For example, Gould (1979) found that more extensive career planning was related to a higher salary, greater career involvement, adaptability, and identity resolution. Saks and Ashforth (2002) found that recent graduates who did more career planning found jobs that they perceived to have higher preentry person-job (PJ) and person-organization (PO) fit as well as postentry PJ fit and job attitudes. In addition, preentry PJ fit perceptions mediated the relationship between career planning and job attitudes. Zikic and Klehe (2006) found a positive relationship between career-planning and reemployment quality in a sample of unemployed job seekers.

Internships have also been found to be related to outcomes at all stages of the STWT. This is partly due to the finding that students who participate in internships often receive job offers from the host organization (Zhao & Liden, 2011). In a study of liberal arts graduates, Richards (1984b) found that, one year after graduation, job fit (the degree of fit between educational preparation and occupational achievement) and job stability were higher for students who participated in prevocational programs (internships and work-study programs). However, the relationship between prevocational programs and job fit and stability was no longer significant three years after graduation. Further, students who participated in prevocational programs were more likely to obtain jobs related to their training and to remain in them or in similar jobs three years after graduation. Students who did not participate in prevocational programs showed more upward change over time. Thus prevocational programs "help to bridge the gap between school and employment" (Richards, 1984b, p. 290).

Student interns also have an easier STWT because they experience less reality shock when they begin a full-time job. Internships can also result in more and better employment opportunities because of greater access to informal job sources and because employers are more likely to evaluate interns more positively and hire them (Taylor, 1988). Taylor (1988) found that student interns used informal sources more frequently, received more positive evaluations from recruiters, obtained higher starting salaries, and were more satisfied with the extrinsic rewards of their new jobs. In addition, interns had stronger intentions to remain on their first jobs, and students who had higher autonomy on their internship had superior job performance.

In a study of business alumni, Gault, Redington, and Schlager (2000) found that those who participated in undergraduate internships obtained their first full-time position in less time after graduation, earned higher salaries, and reported higher levels of overall job satisfaction compared with those who did not participate in internships.

Work experience and employment prior to graduation has also been shown to be important for the STWT. While such employment might involve temporary or part-time work in low-status jobs, it provides students with work experience, a job history, and credentials, which can enhance their employability (Richards, 1984b). Richards (1984b) found that one year after graduation, students who were employed prior to graduation had higher incomes and jobs that were more stable than students who were unemployed prior to graduation. In addition, employment prior to graduation was the strongest predictor of employment status one year after graduation. Richard (1984b) suggested that the lack of recent work experience might have created a handicap in finding employment among those students who remained unemployed one year after graduation. Three years after graduation, however, pregraduation employment no longer predicted job stability or employment. It did, however, continue to predict income, and the difference had in fact widened. That is, students who were employed prior to graduation had higher incomes three years after graduation.

The outcomes of the career-planning and development stage have also been found to be related to some of the behaviors and outcomes at the job-search and work-adjustment stages. According to Taylor (1985), knowledge about the types of occupations that one is qualified can result in a more efficient and effective job search. In addition, students who have specific information about the job requirements in a particular field of study should be better at promoting themselves, thereby making themselves look more attractive to employers and increasing their chances of obtaining job offers. Students with greater self-concept crystallization should also be better at communicating their qualifications and emphasizing the match between themselves and employment opportunities (Taylor, 1985). In support, Taylor (1985) found that college students with greater occupational knowledge were more likely to receive at least one job offer by graduation and to receive more job offers than students with less occupational knowledge. Students with greater self-concept crystallization received better overall interview qualification evaluations, were more likely to receive at least one job offer at graduation, reported accepting positions with more desirable job attributes, were more confident about their job choice decisions, and were more satisfied with the type of work they would be performing.

Job-search goals have also been found to influence job-search behavior and outcomes. For example, in a study of unemployed manufacturing workers, Prussia, Fugate, and Kinicki (2001) found that reemployment coping goals (an individual's desired end result that he or she seeks to accomplish in response to a perceived harm/loss or threat such as reemployment in response to job loss) were positively related to job-search effort, and job-search effort predicted reemployment. Stevens (1973) found that students with crystallized and specific job goals were more likely to obtain employment than those who were vague and confused about their job goals. A study of vocational school students found that how they appraised their work-related goals was related to their success in finding employment. Students who appraised their work-related goals as important and had progressed in the achievement of their goals were more likely to be employed after graduation and 1½ years after graduation and to have found a job that was in their area of education (Nurmi, Salmela-Aro, & Koivisto, 2002).

Job-search clarity has also been found to predict job-search behavior and outcomes. Job seekers who lack job-search clarity may spend more time exploring different options and contemplating the future, thus reducing the intensity of their job search (Wanberg et al., 2002). Students with greater job-search clarity are more able to focus their attention and effort toward more targeted activities pertaining to job search, resulting in greater job-search intensity (Côté, Saks, & Zikic, 2006). Côté et al. (2006) found that job-search clarity of university students in their final year was positively related to their job-search intensity and mediated the relationship between several antecedent variables (e.g., positive affectivity) and job-search intensity. Wanberg et al. (2002) found that job-search clarity was positively related to fit perceptions and lower intention to quit.

Job-search self-efficacy has been found to be one of the best predictors of job-search behavior and success (Saks, 2006). It has been found to predict the use of job information sources, preparatory and active job-search behaviors, as well as the number of job interviews and job offers received, employment status, and PJ fit perceptions (Kanfer, Wanberg, & Kantrowitz, 2001; Saks & Ashforth, 1999; Saks, 2006; Wanberg, Kanfer, & Rotundo, 1999). In their meta-analysis, Kanfer et al. (2001) obtained an effect size of .27 between self-efficacy and job-search behavior.

Taken together, the above findings suggest that the behaviors and outcomes of the career-planning and development stage are related to behaviors and outcomes at the job-search stage. Theoretically speaking, many of the outcomes of the career-planning and development stage are strong predictors of job-search behavior (e.g., job-search clarity, job-search self-efficacy, job-search intentions) and have their basis in the theory of planned behavior and social cognitive theory (Zikic & Saks, 2009).

Therefore the outcomes of the career-planning and development stage are likely to be the strongest predictors of job-search behaviors. In other words, students who have been successful in achieving the outcomes of the career-planning and development stage will be more likely to engage in a vigorous and intense job search. Furthermore, the relationships between the career-planning and development behaviors and job-search behaviors are likely to be mediated through the career-planning and development outcomes given that the behaviors precede the outcomes and the outcomes are more proximal to job-search behaviors. In addition, the relationships between the career-planning and development outcomes and the job-search outcomes are expected to be mediated by the job-search behaviors that are more directly related and more proximal to job-search outcomes. This leads to the following propositions:

Proposition 2: Career-planning and development outcomes will be positively related to job-search behaviors.

Proposition 3: The relationship between career-planning and development behaviors and job-search behaviors will be mediated by career-planning and development outcomes.

Proposition 4: The relationship between career-planning and development outcomes (e.g., job-search self-efficacy) and job-search outcomes (e.g., PJ and PO fit perceptions) will be mediated by job-search behaviors.

Job-Search Stage

Job search is a process that consists of gathering information about potential job opportunities, generating and evaluating job alternatives, and choosing a job from the alternatives (Barber, Daly, Giannantonio, & Phillips, 1994). Job search is in many ways the most important stage of the STWT given that it has a direct effect on the amount and type of information that job seekers obtain about job openings, the number of job opportunities from which a job seeker may choose, and ultimately the type of job and organization in which the student job seeker will obtain employment.

Kanfer et al. (2001) have described job search as a motivational self-regulatory process that involves "a purposive, volitional pattern of action that begins with the identification and commitment to pursuing an employment goal" (p. 838). Thus, job search can be thought of as a form of goal-directed behavior (Saks, 2005). Employment goals activate job-search behaviors that are intended to lead to the employment goal. The job-search process ends when the employment goal has been achieved or is abandoned (Kanfer et al., 2001).

The job-search process has been described as a logical sequence of activities that consists of two phases—planning job search and then job search and choice (Soelberg, 1967). Job search begins with an extensive search to gather information and identify job opportunities followed by a more intensive search that involves the acquisition of specific information about jobs and organizations.

As indicated earlier, students have often been the focus of job-search research. Clearly, student job seekers are different from unemployed job seekers in many ways (see Song et al., this volume, for a more in-depth discussion of unemployed job seekers). They are younger, more educated, have fewer or no financial or family obligations, and have not suffered from the experience and consequences of job loss and unemployment. Furthermore, they usually search for employment in their final year or term prior to graduation and have access to university and college placement services as well as campus job fairs. As a result, their job search as well as some of the predictors of job-search behavior and outcomes might differ compared to unemployed or more experienced job seekers (see van Hoye, this volume, for a discussion of different job-search behaviors). For example, as described below, student job seekers might be more likely to use formal job information sources, which might be more effective for them than other job-search behaviors, such as networking (see Forret, this volume).

In this section, I describe the job-search behaviors and outcomes that have received the most

attention in research on student job seekers. Job-search behaviors have typically been described and measured in terms of job information sources used to find out about employment opportunities as well as the extent to which a job seeker engages in various job-search behaviors or what is known as *job-search intensity*.

Saks (2005) organized job-search outcomes in terms of when they occur during the job-search process noting that some outcomes occur during the job-search process itself, such as interviews and job offers, while other outcomes occur at the end of the job-search process and are the result of one's job search, such as employment status. Employment status (i.e., whether or not a job seeker has obtained employment) is the primary and most important outcome of job search, and it has been the most common outcome measured in job-search research (Kanfer et al., 2001). In addition, some studies have investigated the relationship between job search and *employment quality* (e.g., job satisfaction), which refers to outcomes that occur once the job seeker assumes a position and begins employment and represent the outcomes of the work-adjustment stage.

As shown in Figure 21.1, the behaviors at the job-search stage include job information sources (formal and informal) and job-search intensity (preparatory job-search behavior and active job-search behavior). The job-search outcomes include the number of interviews and job offers obtained, employment status, staring salary, PJ and PO fit perceptions, and work role identification.

Job Information Sources

Job information sources constitute the means by which job seekers learn about job opportunities and the jobs themselves. Job information sources have usually been categorized as either formal or informal. Formal sources involve the use of public intermediaries such as advertisements, employment agencies, and campus placement offices. Informal sources are private intermediaries such as friends, relatives, or persons who are already employed in an organization (Saks & Ashforth, 1997).

Research on job information sources has found that job seekers are more likely to obtain employment as well as higher quality employment (e.g., salary, type of position) through the use of informal sources of information (Granovetter, 1995; Schwab, Rynes, & Aldag, 1987; Taylor, 1988). In particular, friends and personal acquaintances tend to be the main source through which job seekers obtain employment.

However, there is some evidence that formal sources are more likely to result in better jobs for student job seekers. For example, Saks (2006) found that recent graduates who used more informal job information sources received fewer job offers and were less likely to have accepted a job offer in their final term prior to graduation. Allen and Keaveny (1980) found that graduates who used formal sources to find their first full-time job after graduation found jobs in higher-level occupations (white collar versus blue collar) and that were more closely related to their college training than those who used personal contacts. These differences were found to persist for business majors but not engineering technology majors. Saks and Ashforth (1997) found that recent graduates who used more formal job information sources had higher preentry perceptions of PJ and PO fit. Finally, a study by Huffman and Torres (2001) found that formal job information sources (newspaper ads, school placement offices, and private employment agencies) were related to higher earnings.

Thus when it comes to the use of job information sources, the effects on job-search outcomes depends on the source. On the one hand, informal job information sources such as friends and relatives have long been shown to be effective for obtaining employment. On the other hand, formal job information sources might be more likely to lead to a job and organization that is a better match or fit. However, the benefits of formal sources might be specific to student job seekers perhaps because of their limited network of informal job information sources and/or the many formal sources that are available to them on university and colleges campuses (e.g., career centers, job postings, campus career days, etc.).

Job-Search Intensity

Job-search intensity refers to the frequency with which job seekers, during a set period of time, engage in specific job-search behaviors or activities such as preparing a resume or contacting an employment agency (Kanfer et al., 2001). Measures of job-search intensity consist of a list of job-search activities such as "prepared/revised your résumé," "telephoned a prospective employer," or "filled out a job application." Respondents indicate how frequently they performed each activity (e.g., never to at least 10 times) over a set period of time, such as the previous three months.

Blau (1993, 1994) made a distinction between two dimensions of job-search intensity: preparatory job-search behavior and active job-search behavior. Preparatory job-search behavior involves gathering job-search information and identifying potential leads during the planning phase of job search. Active job-search behavior involves the actual job search and choice process, such as sending out résumés and interviewing with prospective employers.

Research on job search has found that students who engage in a more intense job search obtain more positive job-search outcomes. Several studies have found a positive relationship between job-search intensity and the number of job interviews and job offers received. For example, Saks and Ashforth (2000) found that job-search behavior explained a significant amount of the variance in the number of job interviews and job offers that recent graduates received four months after graduation. Werbel (2000) found that job-search intensity was positively related to initial compensation of recently graduated college students. Further, job-search intensity mediated the relationship between environmental exploration and initial compensation. Saks (2006) found that active job-search behavior was positively related to the number of job interviews and job offers that recent graduates received.

Job-search intensity has also been found to predict employment status. Saks and Ashforth (1999) found that among recent university graduates, active job-search behavior predicted employment status at the time of graduation, and preparatory job-search behavior predicted employment status four months after graduation.

Although not all studies have found support for a relationship between job-search intensity and employment status, the Kanfer et al. (2001) meta-analysis found that job-search intensity was positively related to employment status. They also found the relationship between job-search behavior and employment success was strongest for employed job seekers, followed by new entrants and unemployed job seekers. This might be because other factors, such as grade-point average, are more important predictors of job-search success for recent graduates.

There is also some evidence that a more intense job search will result in a job and organization that is perceived to be a better fit. For example, Saks and Ashforth (2002) found that job-search behavior was positively related to preentry perceptions of PJ and PO fit, which were in turn positively related to postentry perceptions of PJ and PO fit. However, Saks (2006) did not find a significant relationship between several measures of job-search behavior and fit perceptions. He speculated that this might be because students are more focused on just finding employment regardless of the fit and/or that they are more concerned about job attributes such as opportunities for advancement.

It is also worth noting that some of the job-search outcomes have been found to be related. For example, job seekers who obtain more interviews and more offers will have more opportunities to choose a job with the best staring salary and the greatest perceived fit. Saks (2006) has described how these outcomes are related in what he refers to as an unfolding model of job-search success. According to this model, job seekers who engage in a more intense job search will obtain more job interviews, more job interviews will lead to more job offers, and more job offers will result in employment and greater perceptions of PJ and PO fit.

In support of the unfolding model of job-search success, Saks and Ashforth (2000) found that an increase in job-search behaviors was related to more job interviews, more job interviews were related to more job offers, and more job offers predicted employment status. The relationship between change in job-search behavior and employment status was mediated by the number of job offers received. Saks (2006) found that the number of job interviews a student had prior to graduation was positively related to the number of job offers received and employment status as well as PO fit perceptions for those who accepted a job offer. In addition, the number of job offers a student received prior to graduation was the strongest predictor of employment status. Saks (2006) concluded that "job-search behavior has an indirect effect on employment status through job interviews and offers, and the best predictor of employment status is the number of job offers that a job seeker receives" (p. 410).

Côté et al. (2006) also found that job-search intensity was related to the number of interviews, job interviews were related to the number of job offers, and the number of job offers was related to employment status of university students in their final term prior to graduation. In a study of recent graduates at a large university, Crossley and Stanton (2005) found that job-search intensity was positively related to interview success (number of interviews and rating of interview success), and interview success was positively related to job-search success (number of job offers and a job lined up).

Research on nonstudent job seekers, however, has yet to provide support for the unfolding model of job-search outcomes, which might apply more to student job seekers. This is because recent graduates might have more opportunities than unemployed job seekers and more time to search for employment. Thus, the job-search intensity of student job seekers might be more likely to generate multiple job interviews and job offers that lead to employment as well as a job and organization that is perceived to be a good fit. Unemployed job seekers might be more inclined to accept the first job offer they receive, especially if they have been unemployed for a long period of time (see Song et al., this volume).

There is also some evidence that the relationship between job interviews and job offers and job offers and employment status is moderated by job-search self-efficacy. For example, Moynihan, Roehling, LePine, and Boswell (2003) suggested that a job seeker's effectiveness in converting job interviews into offers will depend on his or her job-search self-efficacy, because job seekers with higher job-search self-efficacy will be better at converting interviews into offers because of their greater confidence and hence performance in job interviews. As predicted, these investigators found support for the interaction effect. The relationship between the number of interviews and the number of job offers was stronger for job seekers in a sample of college graduates with higher self-efficacy.

Similarly, Saks (2006) suggested that job-search self-efficacy might moderate the relationship between job offers and employment status. He argued for a stronger relationship between job offers and employment for low self-efficacy job seekers because low self-efficacy job seekers have lower confidence in conducting a job search and obtaining employment, and will be more likely to settle on and accept early job offers, while job seekers rating high in self-efficacy are more likely to turn down job offers and continue to search for the best employment opportunity. The results did in fact indicate that student job seekers with low self-efficacy were more likely to accept a job offer as compared with high self-efficacy job seekers. Saks (2006) also found that grade-point average moderated the relationship between the number of job interviews and job offers, such that having more job interviews was more likely to result in a greater number of job offers for job seekers with higher grades (see da Motta Veiga & Turban, this volume, for more information on job choice).

Propositions Regarding the Job-Search Stage

Research on job search has found that student job seekers who use more job information sources and engage in a more intense job search are more likely to receive interviews and job offers and to obtain employment. There is also some evidence that formal job information sources and job-search intensity are associated with obtaining a higher starting salary and for obtaining a job that is perceived to be a better fit.

However, given the limited and mixed findings regarding the relative effects of informal and formal job information sources, some caution is required in making predictions and drawing conclusions about the use of each type of job information source. Thus at this time it is best to simply focus on the use of job information sources in general rather than whether they are formal or informal, since both types have been found to be effective for some outcomes. The relationships between formal job information sources and job-search outcomes for student job seekers might simply reflect the greater availability of formal job information sources on university and college campuses. As for work-role identification, previous research has not considered it as an outcome of job-search behavior. However, students who use more job information sources and engage in a more intense job search are likely to have developed a stronger work-role identity. Therefore the proposition regarding the relationship between job-search behaviors and outcomes is as follows:

Proposition 5: The behaviors at the job-search stage (formal and informal job information sources, preparatory job-search behavior, and active job-search behavior) will be positively related to the outcomes at this stage (number of job interviews and offers received, staring salary, PJ and PO fit perceptions, employment status, and work-role identification).

Although the focus of job-search research has been on the relationship between job-search behaviors and outcomes at the job-search stage, it has been suggested that job-search behaviors can also influence employment quality or outcomes at the work-adjustment stage. For example, in their model of the determinants and consequences of job-search intensity, Schwab et al. (1987) included the quality of employment as an outcome. Although this can refer to various aspects of the obtained job (e.g., pay, satisfaction with choice), the term *employment quality* has typically been used to refer to outcomes once the job seeker assumes a position and begins employment (e.g., job satisfaction). However, the results of several studies have not been supportive of a direct relationship between job-search behaviors and employment quality.

For example, Wanberg et al. (1999) did not find a significant relationship between job-search intensity and job satisfaction, job improvement, or turnover intentions. Wanberg, Kanfer, and Banas (2000) found that neither job-search intensity nor networking intensity was related to job satisfaction or turnover intentions. Werbel (2000) also did not find a significant relationship between job-search intensity and job satisfaction of college graduates.

Research on involuntary job loss has also failed to find significant relationships between job-search intensity and the quality of reemployment (Kinicki, Prussia, & McKee-Ryan, 2000). A study on unemployed persons in Croatia did not find a significant relationship between job-search intensity and job satisfaction (Sverko, Galic, Sersic, & Galesic, 2008). And although Zikic and Klehe (2006) found that career planning and environmental career exploration were positively related to reemployment quality, job-search behavior was negatively related.

Thus at this point it is not possible to conclude that job-search behavior has direct implications for employment quality or outcomes at the work adjustment stage. This, however, should not be surprising given that many other factors intervene between job-search behaviors and employment quality. As shown in Figure 21.1, job-search outcomes and behaviors at the work adjustment stage are more proximal to the work adjustment (employment quality) outcomes. Thus, one might expect job-search outcomes and behaviors at the work adjustment stage to be more strongly related to employment quality than job-search behaviors.

In fact, there is some evidence that job-search behavior is indirectly related to employment quality through job-search outcomes. For example, Steffy et al. (1989) found that the number of interviews predicted the number of job offers received by undergraduate business students, which was positively related to job satisfaction. Saks and Ashforth (1997) found that job information sources and self-esteem of recent university graduates explained a significant amount of the variance in job satisfaction, intentions to quit, stress symptoms, and turnover and these relationships were mediated by preentry fit perceptions. Thus job information sources were related to work outcomes through fit perceptions. In another study of recent university graduates, Saks and Ashforth (2002) found that job-search behavior was positively related to preentry PJ and PO fit perceptions, which were in turn positively related to postentry PJ and PO fit perceptions. Although job-search behavior was not related to job attitudes (job satisfaction and intentions to quit) or organizational attitudes (organizational commitment and organizational identification), postentry PJ and PO fit perceptions were positively related to both job and organizational attitudes.

Thus, when it comes to job search and employment quality, it seems that job-search outcomes rather than job-search behavior predicts employment quality. In other words, job-search behavior is indirectly related to employment quality through job-search outcomes. The role of fit perceptions seems to be especially important for linking job-search behavior to employment quality. According to Saks and Ashforth (2002), fit perceptions prior to entry can have long-term consequences for career success, especially for recent graduates. It might be the case that recent graduates are more inclined to obtain multiple job offers and to search for employment that is a good fit in terms of their education and career goals.

Furthermore, fit perceptions are likely to operate through the behaviors at the work adjustment stage given their greater proximity to the work adjustment outcomes. In other words, students who have greater perceptions of PJ and PO fit are more likely to engage in proactive behaviors at the work-adjustment stage. They will be more inclined to ask for feedback and information and to develop relationships and network with coworkers and members of the organization. In addition, students who have developed a stronger work role identity are also more likely to be involved in their new job and hence more likely to engage in proactive behaviors. This leads to the following propositions:

Proposition 6: PJ and PO fit perceptions and work-role identification at the job search stage will be positively related to the behaviors in the work-adjustment stage.

Proposition 7: The relationship between job-search behaviors and behaviors in the work-adjustment stage will be mediated by PJ and PO fit perceptions and work-role identification at the job search stage.

Proposition 8: The relationship between PJ and PO fit perceptions and work-role identification at the job search stage with the outcomes in the work-adjustment stage will be mediated by the work-adjustment behaviors.

Post–Job Search Stage: Work Adjustment

The final stage of the STWT occurs when the student enters the organization and begins life as a full-time employee. This marks the most dramatic part of the STWT and has in fact been the stage that has received the most attention. It is during this stage that the student must actually make the transition from full-time student to full-time employee. The outcomes of this stage have generally been referred to as employment quality, work adjustment, socialization outcomes, and career success.

Although organizations often facilitate the transition through formal orientation programs and the socialization process, new hires can play an active role during this stage by engaging in proactive behaviors. As indicated earlier, Morrison (2002) focused on this stage of the STWT by describing how newly hired students must acquire knowledge by actively seeking information, building relationships, networking, and in the process adopt a new identity and set of values (note that work role identification is also an outcome at the work-adjustment stage). Similarly, Feij et al. (1995) focused on the development and use of career-enhancing strategies of newly employed youth making the transition from vocational school to full-time employment.

Proactive behavior is the means by which newcomers actively engage with their work environment through proactive socialization strategies such as seeking information about their role and work environment to reduce uncertainty. Proactive behaviors enable newcomers to learn about their abilities, better understand the work environment and specific tasks, and adjust their behavior to improve their socialization and career success (Saks, Gruman, & Cooper-Thomas, 2011).

The most studied proactive behaviors in the socialization literature are *information seeking* (seeking information about one's job, role, work group, and the organization) Morrison, 1993a,b), *feedback seeking* (soliciting feedback about one's work and performance) (Ashford, 1986), *general socializing* (participating in social events) (Wanberg & Kammeyer-Mueller, 2000), *networking* (getting to know people outside of one's department or area) (Ashford & Black, 1996), *relationship building* (developing friendships and relationships with others) (Ashford & Black, 1996), *boss relationship building* (developing a friendship and relationship with one's boss) (Ashford & Black, 1996), and *job-change negotiation* (attempts to change or modify one's tasks) (Ashford & Black, 1996).

Research has found that proactive behaviors are related to various indicators of work adjustment such as social integration, role clarity, task mastery, job content innovation, and learning

(Ashforth, Sluss, & Saks, 2007; Chan & Schmitt, 2000; Gruman, Saks, & Zweig, 2006; Morrison, 1993a; Feij et al., 1995; Saks et al., 2011; Wanberg & Kammeyer-Mueller, 2000) as well as traditional socialization outcomes such as job satisfaction, intention to quit, turnover, and job performance (Ashford & Black, 1996; Wanberg & Kammeyer-Mueller, 2000). A meta-analysis on information seeking found that information seeking related positively to work adjustment (i.e., role clarity and social acceptance), which mediated the relationship between information seeking and socialization outcomes (e.g., job satisfaction) (Bauer, Bodner, Erdogan, Truxillo, & Tucker, 2007).

However, Saks et al. (2011) suggested that what matters most to newcomers is that they obtain what it is that they are seeking by being proactive. In other words, what students require for a successful STWT is information, feedback, and relationships. This is consistent with Morrison (2002), who indicated that a successful STWT involves acquiring knowledge and building relationships.

Saks et al. (2011) investigated the extent to which proactive behaviors are related to proactive outcomes and if proactive outcomes mediate and moderate the relationship between proactive behaviors and socialization outcomes in a sample of undergraduate students on cooperative work placements. They found that students who engaged in each of the proactive behaviors more frequently were more likely to obtain the corresponding proactive outcomes. In other words, students who engaged in more feedback and information seeking obtained more feedback and information; those who engaged in more socializing and networking developed more relationships with co-workers and organizational members from different parts of the organization; those who engaged in more boss relationship building were more likely to have developed a relationship with their boss; and those who engaged in more job change negotiation were more likely to have changed or modified their job. In addition, the proactive outcomes mediated and moderated the relationship between the proactive behaviors and socialization outcomes (e.g., job satisfaction). In other words, the proactive behaviors were more strongly related to socialization outcomes when the student received more of the corresponding proactive outcome.

Thus, in order for proactive behaviors to lead to work adjustment and socialization outcomes, newcomers must receive proactive outcomes. In other words, a new hire is not likely to be satisfied with their job if they have tried to obtain information and feedback or to make friends and develop relationships but have been unsuccessful in obtaining information and feedback and developing relationships.

As was the case with the job-search outcomes, the outcomes at this stage are also related. For example, as indicated above, the proactive outcomes have been found to be related to indicators of work adjustment (e.g., task mastery) and socialization outcomes (e.g., job satisfaction). In addition, indicators of work adjustment such as learning and role clarity have been shown to be related to socialization outcomes such as job satisfaction and organizational commitment (Ashforth et al., 2007; Bauer et al., 2007; Kammeyer-Mueller & Wanberg, 2003). Furthermore, a successful work adjustment and socialization has implications for career success and can set in motion a cycle of success (e.g., career satisfaction, promotions, salary growth) (Fang, Duffy, & Shaw, 2011). As described by Ashforth (2001), success breeds success resulting in a success spiral. Thus, initial career success has implications for future positive career consequences (Werbel, 2000). One might also speculate that work role identification will also be related to the other outcomes such that those students who have developed a stronger work-role identity will obtain more proactive outcomes and have a more positive work adjustment and socialization, and greater career success. Furthermore, as students become more adjusted and socialized, they are likely to develop a greater sense of identity with their work roles.

Propositions Regarding the Work-Adjustment Stage

In the final stage of the STWT students must successfully adjust to their new job and organization. They need to obtain information about their job, role, and the organization, receive feedback about their performance, and develop relationships with coworkers, their boss, and other members of the organization. To do so, they need to engage in a number of proactive behaviors. The research on proactive socialization has shown that newcomers who are more proactive are more likely to obtain proactive outcomes (i.e., acquire feedback and information) and to report more positive work adjustment (e.g., task mastery) and socialization outcomes (e.g., job satisfaction). Further, they are also more likely to experience success in their careers, as early success tends to lead to continued career satisfaction and success, and they are more likely to have developed a stronger work-role identity. These findings suggest the following proposition:

Proposition 9: Proactive behaviors at the work adjustment stage (information seeking, feedback seeking, relationship building, boss relationship building, networking, job-change negotiation) will be positively related to proactive outcomes (e.g., obtaining information), work-adjustment outcomes (e.g., social integration), socialization outcomes (e.g., job satisfaction), career outcomes (e.g., career satisfaction), and work-role identification.

One final proposition of the model pertains to the relationship between the behaviors and outcomes at the career-planning and development stage and the behaviors and outcomes at the work-adjustment stage. As indicated earlier, some of the career-planning and development behaviors (e.g., environmental career exploration, career planning) have been found to be related to outcomes in the work-adjustment stage. In keeping with the model in Figure 21.1 and the central role of job search, these relationships are likely to be mediated through the job-search behaviors and outcomes. Therefore the final proposition is as follows:

Proposition 10: The relationship between behaviors and outcomes at the career-planning and development stage and the outcomes at the work adjustment stage will be mediated by the behaviors and outcomes at the job-search stage.

Job Search and the School-to-Work Transition: Summary

As shown in Figure 21.1 and indicated in the propositions, the basic premise of the integrative model of job search and the STWT is that the achievement of the outcomes at each stage will lead to the behaviors at the next stage. Thus students must be successful at each stage in order to make a successful transition to the next stage. Furthermore, the strongest and most proximal predictors of the behaviors at each stage are the outcomes at the previous stages. The behaviors at each stage will be directly and most strongly related to the outcomes at the same stage and only indirectly related to behaviors and outcomes at the subsequent stage. Furthermore, the outcomes at each stage will be indirectly related to the outcomes at the next stage through the corresponding behaviors at that stage.

It should be noted that the behaviors and outcomes in the model represent those that have received the most attention in the respective literatures. Other behaviors and outcomes that are found to be important at a particular stage can be added to the model. Furthermore, interventions and training programs can also have a positive effect on the outcomes at each stage. For example, job-search workshops such as JOBS have been found to have a positive effect on job-search self-efficacy and (re) employment (Caplan, Vinokur, Price, & van Ryn, 1989; Vinokur & Schul, 1997). Zikic and Saks (2009) found that job seekers who attended more training programs and used more career resources (e.g., job-search clubs) had higher job-search clarity and job-search self-efficacy.

Although the focus of this chapter has been on college and university students, much of the literature on the STWT, particularly with respect to career development, has involved work-bound high school students. While there are differences between university/college students and high school students, especially in terms of their occupational choices and education, the model and its propositions are just as likely to apply to work-bound students. For example, Blustein et al. (1997) found that self- and environmental exploration was associated with a more successful STWT among a sample of work-bound high school students, and Creed, Doherty, and O'Callaghan (2008) found that the predictors and outcomes of job-search behavior for a sample of job seeking high school students were similar to research on adult job seekers.

An important difference, however, is that high school students who are work-bound have less education, and this can be an obstacle to finding employment. The lack of education might mean that the other behaviors during the career-planning and development stage (e.g., environmental and self career exploration) are especially important for high-school students who do not have the benefit of a college or university degree or the career- and job-search counseling services available to college and university students.

In addition, owing to their lack of postsecondary education, work-based learning (e.g., specific training opportunities) might be especially important for work-bound high school students during the career-planning and development stage (Phillips, Blustein, Jobin-Davis, & White, 2002). The availability of opportunities for growth and advancement as well as training programs to enhance career-relevant skills might be especially important for them during the work-adjustment stage (Blustein et al., 1997).

It is also important to recognize that individual differences and personality variables have been found to be important factors during each stage of the STWT. For example, Morrison (2002) described how individual differences can affect the extent to which individuals experience the STWT as uncertain and stressful. As already indicated, job-search self-efficacy has been found to be a strong predictor of job-search behavior and outcomes. In addition, individuals with high self-efficacy are more likely to experience the transition as an opportunity while those with low self-efficacy are more likely to experience more uncertainty, anxiety, and stress. In fact, Saks (1994) found that self-efficacy was negatively related to anxiety in a sample of newly hired entry-level accountants. Self-efficacy has also been found to be positively related to student's proactive behavior, job performance, job attitudes, and psychological and physical health during the work-adjustment stage (Gruman et al., 2006; Lubbers, Loughlin, & Zweig, 2005; Saks, 1995).

Morrison (2002) also suggested that individuals with high negative affectivity will experience the STWT as more stressful and anxiety-provoking than individuals who are low on negative affectivity. Positive and negative affectivity have also been linked to job search. For example, Côté et al. (2006) found that students with higher positive affectivity had higher job-search clarity and job-search intensity. Lubbers et al. (2005) found that job-related affect was positively related to the job performance and health of student interns.

Personality variables from the"Five Factor Model" have been found to be related to job search and proactive behaviors. Kanfer et al. (2001) found that extraversion (the extent to which a person is outgoing versus shy) and conscientiousness (the degree to which a person is responsible and achievement-oriented) were the strongest positive predictors of job-search intensity, followed by openness to experience (the extent to which a person thinks flexibly and is receptive to new ideas) and agreeableness (the extent to which a person is friendly and approachable), which were also significant predictors. Neuroticism (the extent to which a person is prone to experience anxiety, self-doubt, and depression and to lack emotional stability and control) was negatively related to job-search intensity. Higher levels of extraversion, conscientiousness, openness to experience, and agreeableness were related to a shorter period of unemployment. Conscientiousness was positively related to employment status, and neuroticism was negatively related

to the number of job offers and employment status. With respect to proactive behaviors, Wanberg and Kammeyer-Mueller (2000) found that extraversion was related to feedback seeking and relationship building, and openness to experience was related to feedback seeking and positive framing.

There is also some evidence that perceived control and self-esteem are related to job-search behaviors and employment status. For example, Wanberg (1997) found that unemployed job seekers who had higher levels of perceived situational control (perceived control over their unemployment situation) conducted a more intense job search. Saks and Ashforth (1999) found that perceived control (the influence and control one believes one has over the outcome of the job search) predicted the employment status of recent university graduates at the time of graduation and four months later. Self-esteem has been found to relate negatively to the use of formal job sources and positively to job-search intensity. Higher self-esteem is also associated with a shorter period of unemployment, more job offers received, and a greater likelihood of obtaining employment (Ellis & Taylor, 1983; Schmit, Amel, & Ryan, 1993).

Grade=point average has been found to be positively related to preparatory and active job-search behavior as well as employment status among a sample of recent graduates at the time of graduation and four months postgraduation (Saks & Ashforth, 1999). Steffy et al. (1989) found that grade-point average predicted the number of interviews that undergraduate business students obtained. In addition, as indicated earlier, Saks (2006) found that grade average moderated the relationship between the number of job interviews and job offers. Students with higher grades were more likely to have their job interviews result in job offers.

Some individual difference and personality variables have been found to be more strongly related to job-search behavior and outcomes for recent graduates. For example, in their meta-analysis on the predictors and outcomes of job search, Kanfer et al. (2001) found that several of the personality dimensions of the five-factor model (i.e., extraversion, neuroticism, conscientiousness) and education were more strongly related to job-search behavior for new entrants (mostly college students) than job losers, whereas several situational predictors (i.e., employment commitment and social support) were more strongly related to job-search behaviors among job losers. This might be because students have relatively little experience searching for employment, so that individual differences and personality are more important than they might be for more experienced job seekers. Along these lines, it has been suggested that job-search self-efficacy might be a more important predictor for student job seekers (van Hooft, Born, Taris, & van der Flier, 2004). Furthermore, given that employers often look at grades when hiring students, it is not surprising that grades predict job-search success for recent graduates (Saks, 2006; Saks & Ashforth, 1999).

Finally, although the emphasis of this chapter and the model has been on the role of students and the behaviors that they must engage in during each stage of the STWT, a successful STWT requires the involvement of many other stakeholders, such as educators, families, employers, and significant others. As noted by Blustein et al. (1997), "all of the players need to be active participants in the process of helping young people move from school to work" (p. 399). For example, there is considerable evidence that organization-initiated socialization practices have a strong effect on newcomers' work adjustment and socialization outcomes (Saks, Uggerslev, & Fassina, 2007). Blustein et al. (1997) have noted that employers and the job context play an important role in the STWT and the availability of supportive supervisors and coworkers is a critical factor in facilitating an individual's adjustment to work.

In summary, the integrative model of job search and the STWT focuses on the behaviors that students must engage in at each stage of the STWT. The extent to which a student engages in these behaviors will be reflected in important outcomes that signify success at each stage and predict student engagement in the required behaviors at the next stage. Thus, a successful STWT requires student engagement in key behaviors and the achievement of numerous outcomes at all three stages of the model.

Implications for Research and Practice

The model of job search and the STWT offers many avenues for future research. For starters, one might study the relationships between the behaviors and outcomes at each of the three stages. In this regard, it is important to note that while some of the behaviors have been shown to be related to particular outcomes (e.g., internships are related to greater crystallization of vocational self-concept), there are many other behavior/outcome relationships that have not be studied (e.g., internships and job-search self-efficacy). In addition, it would also be worthwhile to study the strength of the relationships between the behaviors and outcomes at each stage, as some of the behaviors might be more strongly related to and therefore more important for achieving certain outcomes. From a counseling perspective, it would be important to know what behavior to emphasize when a student needs to focus on a particular outcome. Thus research is needed to identify what behaviors at each stage are most likely to improve each of the outcomes.

Second, future research might also investigate the relationships between the behaviors and outcomes at one stage and behaviors and outcomes at subsequent stages. Here too some relationships have been studied (e.g., career exploration is related to job-search intensity and career planning is related to fit perceptions), while others have not. For example, previous research has not considered whether job-search behavior is related to proactive behaviors. Future research might try to determine the outcomes at one stage that best predict the behaviors and outcomes at the next stage.

A third area for research is to study all three stages over time in order to test the sequential nature of the STWT as a student prepares for a career, engages in job search, and then begins employment and adjusts to work. This would involve testing the proposed mediating relationships between the outcomes at one stage and the behaviors and outcomes at the subsequent stage.

A final area for research would be to focus on work-role identification, given its importance for a successful STWT at each stage. It would be interesting to study changes in work role identification across the three stages and to identify the best predictors of work-role identification at each stage and across all three stages.

The model also offers a number of implications for practice. First, it indicates the need for students to engage in a series of activities and behaviors while they are still in school before they begin to search for employment and continue on the job as they begin employment. Second, it indicates the outcomes that students should achieve at each stage before they proceed to the next stage. And third, the model can be used not only by students as a guide to monitor their progress and achievement at each stage but also by career counselors to ensure that students have performed the behaviors needed at each stage and achieved the outcomes required to succeed and make a successful transition to the next stage.

It is important to realize the practical implications of the integrative model of job search and the STWT compared with more traditional approaches to job search. The traditional approach focuses on job-search outcomes and behaviors as shown in Saks's (2005) job-search intervention framework. A career counselor would focus on the job-search behaviors that a job seeker should engage in given his or her job-search goals and recommend job-search interventions (e.g., JOBS intervention). However, in the context of the STWT, before providing job-search counseling, the counselor must first consider career-planning and development behaviors and outcomes.

Table 21.1 presents an STWT intervention framework. As shown in the table, before discussing job search, the career counselor should first evaluate the student in terms of career-planning and development outcomes and the need to engage in career-planning and development behaviors. Job search should begin only once the behaviors and

Table 21.1 School-to-Work Transition Intervention Framework

A. *Career-Planning and Development Stage*

When job search is considered within the context of the school-to-work transition, one must first consider the extent to which the student has reached a sufficient level of the outcomes of the career planning and development stage. Therefore, before discussing job search, the counselor should consider the following:

1. Does the student have a plan and objectives for his or her career?
2. What work-related knowledge and skills has the student acquired?
3. How knowledgeable is the student about occupations?
4. Has the student achieved a sufficient level of vocational self-concept crystallization?
5. Does the student have job search clarity, goals, and intentions?
6. Does the student have a high level of job search self-efficacy?
7. Does the student have a positive job-search attitude?
8. Has the student developed a work-role identity?

To the extent that a student is low on these outcomes, he or she should be instructed to engage in the career-planning and development behaviors before a job search is begun. This might involve one or more of the following:

1. Environmental career exploration
2. Self-career exploration
3. Career planning
4. Education and work experience

B. *Job-Search Stage*

Students who have engaged in the career-planning and development behaviors and have achieved a high level of the outcomes are ready to begin searching for employment. At this stage, they should be given instruction on how to search for employment and the different sources of information and job-search behaviors that can be used. The career counselor should first review the outcomes of the career-planning and development stage with particular attention to career plans and objectives, job-search clarity, goals and intentions, job-search self-efficacy and job-search attitudes. Students should then be informed of the following job-search behaviors:

1. Informal and formal job information sources
2. Preparatory job-search behaviors
3. Active job-search behaviors

C. *Work Adjustment Stage*

Students who have obtained employment should be provided with instruction and guidance on the organizational-entry/socialization/work adjustment process. They should be made aware of the importance of being proactive and the need to obtain information and feedback and to develop relationships. They should be informed of the following proactive behaviors and provided with some training that includes the opportunity to practice these behaviors:

1. Information seeking
2. Feedback seeking
3. Relationship building
4. Boss relationship building
5. Networking
6. Job-change negotiation

outcomes of the career-planning and development stage have been completed. Further, the job-search stage should be followed with some education and instruction on the proactive behaviors that an individual must engage in during the work-adjustment stage. Thus, within the context of the STWT, job-search counseling must be preceded by a review and discussion of career-planning and development behaviors and outcomes, and it must be followed by education and instruction on the organizational entry/work-adjustment stage and the need to engage in proactive behaviors to obtain important proactive outcomes, which are necessary for a successful work adjustment and socialization.

Conclusion

The STWT is a major life-changing event for students, who must relinquish and leave behind their roles as scholars and begin their careers and lives as full-time employees. During the STWT, students must make important decisions that can have immediate and long-term consequences for their adjustment to work and career success. Job search plays a significant role in the STWT and requires students to use multiple job information sources and to engage in an intense search for employment. However, as important as job search is for a successful STWT, it is only one part of a sequential process that begins with career planning and development and continues when students begin working and learn to adjust and adapt to their new jobs, roles, and organizations.

In conclusion, job search is often studied as an independent and isolated event that is primarily about finding employment. However, when it is considered within the context of the STWT, it is part of a sequential process that is influenced by behaviors and outcomes that precede it and that influence students' behaviors and outcomes once they begin their employment and careers. Job search plays a central role in the STWT and is the bridge that connects career planning and development to organizational entry and work adjustment. Given that a students' first job following graduation is a critical factor in determining their future career success, a successful STWT at all three stages of the process should be a top priority for students, educational institutions, organizations, and society.

References

Allen, R. E., & Keaveny, T. J. (1980). The relative effectiveness of alternative job sources. *Journal of Vocational Behavior*, 16, 18–32.

Ashford, S. J. (1986). Feedback seeking in individual adaptation: A resource perspective. *Academy of Management Journal*, 29(3), 465–487.

Ashford, S. J., & Black, J. S. (1996). Proactivity during organizational entry: The role of desire for control. *Journal of Applied Psychology*, 81(2), 199–214.

Ashforth, B. E. (2001). *Work transitions in organizational life: An identity-based perspective*. Mahwah, NJ: Erlbaum.

Ashforth, B. E., Sluss, D. M., & Saks, A. M. (2007). Socialization tactics, proactive behavior, and newcomer learning: Integrating socialization models. *Journal of Vocational Behavior*, 70, 447–462.

Barber, A. E., Daly, C. L., Giannantonio, C. M., & Philips, J. M. (1994). Job search activities: An examination of changes over time. *Personnel Psychology*, 47, 739–765.

Bauer, T. N., Bodner, T., Erdogan, B., Truxillo, D. M., & Tucker, J. S. (2007). Newcomer adjustment during organizational socialization: A meta-analytic review of antecedents, outcomes, and methods. *Journal of Applied Psychology*, 92, 707–721.

Blau, G. (1993). Further exploring the relationship between job search and voluntary individual turnover. *Personnel Psychology*, 46, 213–330.

Blau, G. J. (1994). Testing a two-dimensional measure of job search behavior. *Organizational Behavior and Human Decision Processes*, 59, 288–312.

Blustein, D. L. (1997). A context-rich perspective of career exploration across the life roles. *Career Development Quarterly*, 45, 260–274.

Blustein, D. L., Phillips, S. D., Jobin-Davis, K., Finkelberg, S. L., & Roarke, A. E. (1997). A theory-building investigation of the school-to-work transition. *The Counseling Psychologist*, 25, 364–402.

Caplan, R. D., Vinokur, A. D., Price, R. H., & van Ryn, M. (1989). Job seeking, reemployment, and mental health: A randomized field experiment in coping with job loss. *Journal of Applied Psychology*, 74, 759–769.

Chan, D., & Schmitt, N. (2000). Interindividual differences in intraindividual changes in proactivity during organizational entry: A latent growth modeling approach to understanding newcomer adaptation. *Journal of Applied Psychology*, 85, 190–210.

Côté, S., Saks, A. M., & Zikic, J. (2006). Trait affect and job search outcomes. *Journal of Vocational Behavior*, 68, 233–252.

Creed, P. A., Doherty, F., & O'Callaghan, F. (2008). Job-seeking and job-acquisition in high school students. *Journal of Vocational Behavior*, 73, 195–202.

Crossley, C. D., & Stanton, J. M. (2005). Negative affect and job search: Further examination of the reverse causation hypothesis. *Journal of Vocational Behavior*, 66, 549–560.

Ellis, R. A., & Taylor, M. S. (1983). Role of self-esteem within the job search process. *Journal of Applied Psychology*, 68, 632–640.

Fang, R., Duffy, M. K., & Shaw, J. D. (2011). The organizational socialization process: Review and development of a social capital model. *Journal of Management*, 37, 127–152.

Feij, J. A., Whitely, W. T., Peiro, J. M., & Taris, T. W. (1995). The development of career-enhancing strategies and content innovation: A longitudinal study of new workers. *Journal of Vocational Behavior*, 46, 231–256.

Feldman, D. C., & Weitz, B. (1990). Summer interns: Factors contributing to positive developmental experiences. *Journal of Vocational Behavior*, 37, 267–284.

Gault, J., Redington, J., & Schlager, T. (2000). Undergraduate business internships and career success: Are they related? *Journal of Marketing Education*, 22, 45–53.

Gould, S. (1979). Characteristics of career planners in upwardly mobile occupations. *Academy of Management Journal*, 22, 539–550.

Granovetter, M. S. (1995). *Getting a job*, 2nd ed. Chicago: University of Chicago Press.

Gruman, J. A., Saks, A. M. & Zweig, D. I. (2006). Organizational socialization tactics and newcomer proactive behaviors: An integrative study. *Journal of Vocational Behavior*, 69, 90–104.

Herr, E. L. (1999). Theoretical perspectives of the school-to-work transition: Reactions and recommendations. *The Career Development Quarterly*, 47, 359–364.

Huffman, M. L., & Torres, L. (2001). Job search methods: Consequences for gender-based earnings inequality. *Journal of Vocational Behavior*, 58, 127–141.

Kanfer, R., Wanberg, C. R., & Kantrowitz, T. M. (2001). Job search and employment: A personality—motivational analysis and meta-analytic review. *Journal of Applied Psychology*, 86, 837–855.

Kinicki, A. J., Prussia, G. E., & McKee-Ryan, F. M. (2000). A panel study of coping with involuntary job loss. *Academy of Management Journal*, 43, 90–100.

Lent, R. W., Hackett, G., & Brown, S. D. (1999). A social cognitive view of school-to-work transition. *The Career Development Quarterly*, 47, 297–311.

Lubbers, R., Loughlin, C., & Zweig, D. (2005). Young workers' job self-efficacy and affect: Pathways to health and performance. *Journal of Vocational Behavior*, 67, 199–214.

Morrison, E. W. (1993a). Newcomer information seeking: Exploring types, modes, sources, and outcomes. *Academy of Management Journal*, 36, 557–589.

Morrison, E. W. (1993b). Longitudinal study of the effects of information seeking on newcomer socialization. *Journal of Applied Psychology*, 78(2), 173–183.

Morrison, E. W. (2002). The school-to-work transition. In D. C. Feldman (Ed.), *Work careers: A developmental perspective*, (pp. 126–158). San Francisco: Jossey-Bass.

Moynihan, L. M., Roehling, M. V., LePine, M. A., & Boswell, W. R. (2003). A longitudinal study of the relationships among job search self-efficacy, job interviews, and employment outcomes. *Journal of Business and Psychology*, 18, 207–233.

Ng, T. W. H., & Feldman, D. C. (2007). The school-to-work transition: A role identity perspective. *Journal of Vocational Behavior*, 71, 114–134.

Nurmi, J. E., Salmela-Aro, K., & Koivisto, P. (2002). Goal importance and related achievement beliefs and emotions during the transition from vocational school to work: Antecedents and consequences. *Journal of Vocational Behavior*, 60, 241–261.

Phillips, S. D., & Blustein, D. L. (1994). Readiness for career choices: Planning, exploring, and deciding. *Career Development Quarterly*, 43, 63–73.

Phillips, S. D., Blustein, D. L., Jobin-Davis, K., White, S. F. (2002). Preparation for the school-to-work transition: The views of high school students. *Journal of Vocational Behavior*, 61, 202–216.

Prussia, G. E., Fugate, M., & Kinicki, A. J. (2001). Explication of the coping goal construct: Implications for coping and reemployment. *Journal of Applied Psychology*, 86, 1179–1190.

Richards, E. W. (1984a). Early employment situations and work role satisfaction among recent college graduates. *Journal of Vocational Behavior*, 24, 305–318.

Richards, E. W. (1984b). Undergraduate preparation and early career outcomes: A study of recent college graduates. *Journal of Vocational Behavior*, 24, 279–304.

Rosenbaum, J. E. (1979). Tournament mobility: Career patterns in a corporation. *Administrative Science Quarterly*, 24, 220–241.

Saks, A. M. (1994). Moderating effects of self-efficacy for the relationship between training method and anxiety and stress reactions of newcomers. *Journal of Organizational Behavior*, 15, 639–654.

Saks, A. M. (1995). Longitudinal field investigation of the moderating and mediating effects of self-efficacy on the relationship between training and newcomer adjustment. *Journal of Applied Psychology*, 80, 211–225.

Saks, A. M. (2005). Job search success: A review and integration of the predictors, behaviors, and outcomes. In S. Brown & R. Lent (Eds), *Career development and counseling: Putting theory and research to work* (pp. 155–179). Hoboken, NJ: Wiley.

Saks, A. M. (2006). Multiple predictors and criteria of job search success. *Journal of Vocational Behavior*, 68, 400–415.

Saks, A. M., & Ashforth, B. E. (1997). A longitudinal investigation of the relationships between job information sources, applicant perceptions of fit, and work outcomes. *Personnel Psychology*, 50, 395–426.

Saks, A. M., & Ashforth, B. E. (1999). Effects of individual differences and job search behaviors on the employment status of recent university graduates. *Journal of Vocational Behavior*, 54, 335–349.

Saks, A. M., & Ashforth, B. E. (2000). Change in job search behaviors and employment outcomes. *Journal of Vocational Behavior*, 56, 277–287.

Saks, A. M., & Ashforth, B. E. (2002). Is job search related to employment quality? It all depends on the fit. *Journal of Applied Psychology*, 87, 646–654.

Saks, A. M., Gruman, J. A., & Cooper-Thomas, H. (2011). The neglected role of proactive behavior and outcomes in newcomer socialization. *Journal of Vocational Behavior*, 79, 36–46.

Saks, A. M., Uggerslev, K. L., & Fassina, N. E. (2007). Socialization tactics and newcomer adjustment: A meta-analytic review and test of a model. *Journal of Vocational Behavior*, 70, 413–446.

Savickas, M. L. (1997). Career adaptability: An integrative construct for life-span, life-space theory. *The Career Development Quarterly*, 45, 247–259.

Savickas, M. L. (1999). The transition from school to work: A developmental perspective. *The Career Development Quarterly*, 47, 326–336.

Schmit, M. J., Amel, E. L., & Ryan, A. M. (1993). Self-reported assertive job-seeking behaviors of minimally educated job hunters. *Personnel Psychology*, 46, 105–124.

Schwab, D. P., Rynes, S. L., & Aldag, R. J. (1987). Theories and research on job search and choice. In K. M. Rowland & G. R. Ferris (Eds.), *Research in personnel and human resources management* (Vol. 5, pp. 129–166). Greenwich, CT: JAI Press.

Soelberg, P. O. (1967). Unprogrammed decision making. *Industrial Management Review*, 8, 19–29.

Steffy, B. D., Shaw, K. N., & Noe, A. W. (1989). Antecedents and consequences of job search behaviors. *Journal of Vocational Behavior*, 35, 254–269.

Stevens, N. D. (1973). Job-seeking behavior: A segment of vocational development. *Journal of Vocational Behavior*, 3, 209–219.

Stumpf, S. A., Austin, E. J., & Hartman, K. (1984). The impact of career exploration and interview readiness on interview performance and outcomes. *Journal of Vocational Behavior*, 24, 221–235.

Stumpf, S. A., Colarelli, S. M., & Hartman, K. (1983). Development of the Career Exploration Survey (CES). *Journal of Vocational Behavior*, 22, 191–226.

Stumpf, S. A., & Hartman, K. (1984). Individual exploration to organizational commitment or withdrawal. *Academy of Management Journal*, 27, 308–329.

Sverko, B., Galic, Z., Sersic, D. M., & Galesic, M. (2008). Unemployed people in search of a job: Reconsidering the role of search behavior. *Journal of Vocational Behavior*, 72, 415–428.

Taylor, M. S. (1985). The roles of occupational knowledge and vocational self-conept crystallization in students' school-to-work transition. *Journal of Counseling Psychology*, 32, 539–550.

Taylor, M. S. (1988). Effects of college internships on individual participants. *Journal of Applied Psychology*, 73, 393–401.

Van Hooft, E. A. J., Born, M. P., Taris, T. W., & Van Der Flier, H. (2004). Job search and the theory of planned behavior: Minority-majority group differences in The Netherlands. *Journal of Vocational Behavior*, 65, 366–390.

Vinokur, A. D, & Schul, Y. (1997). Mastery and inoculation against setbacks as active ingredients in the JOBS intervention for the unemployed. *Journal of Consulting and Clinical Psychology*, 65, 867–877.

Wanberg, C. R. (1997). Antecedents and outcomes of coping behaviors among unemployed and reemployed individuals. *Journal of Applied Psychology*, 82, 731–744.

Wanberg, C. R., Hough, L. M., & Song, Z. (2002). Predictive validity of a multidisciplinary model of reemployment success. *Journal of Applied Psychology*, 87, 1100–1120.

Wanberg, C. R., & Kammeyer-Mueller, J. D. (2000). Predictors and outcomes of proactivity in the socialization process. *Journal of Applied Psychology*, 85(3), 373–385.

Wanberg, C. R., Kanfer, R., & Banas, J. T. (2000). Predictors and outcomes of networking intensity among unemployed job seekers. *Journal of Applied Psychology*, 85, 491–503.

Wanberg, C. R., Kanfer, R., & Rotundo, M. (1999). Unemployed individuals: Motives, job-search competencies, and job search constraints as predictors of job seeking and reemployment. *Journal of Applied Psychology*, 84, 897–910.

Wanberg, C. R., & Kammeyer-Mueller, J. D. (2000). Predictors and outcomes of proactivity in the socialization process. *Journal of Applied Psychology*, 85(3), 373–385.

Werbel, J. D. (2000). Relationships among career exploration, job search intensity, and job search effectiveness in graduating college students. *Journal of Vocational Behavior*, 57, 379–394.

West, M., & Newton, P. (1983). *The transition from school to work*. New York: Nichols Publishing.

Zhao, H., & Liden, R. C. (2011). Internship: A recruitment and selection perspective. *Journal of Applied Psychology*, 96, 221–229.

Zikic, J., & Klehe, U. C. (2006). Job loss as a blessing in disguise: The role of career exploration and career planning in predicting reemployment quality. *Journal of Vocational Behavior*, 69, 391–409.

Zikic, J., & Saks, A. M. (2009). Job search and social cognitive theory: The role of career-relevant activities. *Journal of Vocational Behavior*, 74, 117–127.

Employed Job Seekers and Job-to-Job Search

Wendy R. Boswell *and* Richard G. Gardner

Abstract

The purpose of this chapter is to review and integrate the existing research on job-to-job search behavior. The authors provide an overview of the various job-search and employee withdrawal/turnover models followed by a review of the prior empirical findings on the processes, antecedents, and outcomes of job-search behavior within the context of employed individuals. An important focus of this paper is the authors' explicit focus on the varying objectives an employee may have for engaging in job-search activity. The chapter concludes by discussing developing issues in this research area and offering directions for future research to enhance our understanding of job-to-job search behavior.

Key Words: employee job search, turnover, employee withdrawal, job-to-job search

Employed Job Seekers and Job-to-Job Search

Employed individuals make up the largest population of potential job seekers. Understanding the job-search behavior of such individuals holds significant practical relevance for organizations owing to the tangible and intangible costs associated with employee turnover (Cascio, 2000; Hom & Griffeth, 1995). Yet there are other practical considerations involved beyond the potential for turnover when an employee searches the external market for alternative employment. An individual engaging in job search typically does so at the expense of time and energy that could be directed toward other task-related uses (March & Simon, 1958), an issue intensified by the Internet and the opportunity to peruse the market while on the job. Engaging in a search for alternative employment may also create detachment from the organization, reducing commitment and fostering psychological and behavioral withdrawal.

The purpose of this chapter is to review and integrate the extant research on the job-search behavior of employed individuals. This phenomenon is referred to as job-to-job search, although this phrase is not meant to imply that an employed individual will necessarily *leave* his or her job for a new job following a search for alternatives or even that that is the intent of the search behavior. Indeed, employed individuals may search and remain with the current employer (for a variety of reasons to be discussed) and/or may search with other motives than to quit the job for a new job (Boswell, Boudreau, & Dunford, 2002). *Job-to-job search* simply refers to the notion that an individual is currently employed and is expending effort to acquire information about labor market alternatives and generate employment opportunities (Boswell, 2006). As noted, job-to-job search has practical importance for organizations yet, interestingly, is arguably the least researched context within the job-search literature.

Figure 22.1 offers an overview of the job-to-job search process. We offer this model not as an exhaustive depiction of the various factors or precise mechanisms involved in the job-to-job search process. Rather, this figure highlights key elements (and corresponding exemplars) within the context of employee job-to-job search behavior to be discussed

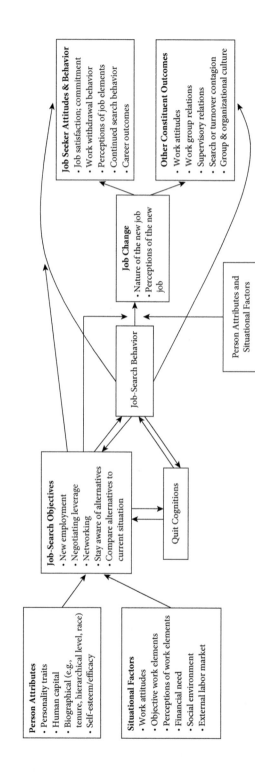

Figure 22.1 Overview of the job-to-job search process.

in this chapter. Although the links are generally consistent with existing job-search research within an employee turnover/withdrawal framework, our intent is to go beyond this perspective and also recognize the varying objectives that may underlie an employee's job-search behavior and the divergent outcomes of search other than the quit/stay decision.

We begin by presenting an overview of the existing job-search and related (e.g., turnover) process models and the empirical findings for these models. We then review the research on the specific predictors and outcomes of job-to-job search and potential moderators of the effects. We conclude the chapter by discussing developing issues in this research area and offering directions for future research to enhance our understanding of job search within the context of employed individuals.

The Process of Job-to-Job Search
Operationalizing Job Search

Job-search behavior (also referred to as job-search *activity*) has been assessed in several different ways in the job-to-job search literature, although the operationalization of the construct is generally consistent with other search contexts discussed in this volume (see Van Hoye, this volume). The two most common methods to measure job search is the effort and the intensity of the search behavior (Kanfer et al., 2001). Effort reflects the general energy and persistence that the job searcher exhibits in seeking new employment, while intensity is measured by assessing the frequency with which the searcher engages in specific job-search preparations (e.g., revising a resume, using the Internet to find job openings) and/or activities (e.g., filling out applications, interviewing with prospective employers) (Blau 1993, 1994). Research on employed job seekers in particular has commonly assessed intensity as an index of how many different search activities an individual engages in (e.g., initiated contact with a search firm, gone on an interview (e.g., Boswell, Roehling, & Boudreau, 2006; Boudreau, Boswell, Judge, & Bretz, 2001; Bretz et al., 1994; Kopelman, Rovenpor, & Millsap, 1992).

Search and Turnover Process Models in the Job-to-Job Search Context

There are various job-search theories but relatively few that explicitly focus on the process specific in the job-to-job search context (van Hooft, Born, Taris, Flier, & Blonk, 2004).

Job-search behavior in general is commonly placed within a self-regulatory perspective. As discussed in other chapters in this volume (e.g., Kanfer & Bufton, this volume; Latham, Mawritz, & Locke, this volume) search can be explained as goal-directed behavior, motivated by specific search objectives (Kanfer, Wanberg, & Kantrowitz, 2001). This self-regulatory process "begins with the identification and commitment to pursuing an employment goal. The employment goal, in turn, activates search behavior designed to bring about the goal" (Kanfer et al., 2001, p. 838). Implicit if not explicit in the literature is the assumption that the goal in the job-to-job search context is to separate from the current employer for new (presumably better) employment. However, as emphasized throughout this chapter, the goals or objectives underlying an employee's search behavior may not necessarily be for the purpose of seeking separation from a current employer, as individuals may search with other objectives in mind (Boswell, Boudreau, & Dunford, 2004). And, as suggested by Van Hoye and Saks (2008), different search objectives may result in different job-search behaviors and methods. Although these job-search behaviors may in many cases be the same regardless of the search objective (i.e., since individuals with the objective of leaving as well as those who just want to stay aware of job alternatives will both look at job ads), it is the job-search objective that drives the job-search method and ultimate outcome of the job search (Van Hoye & Saks, 2008). Certainly this is a critical component of the model shown in Figure 22.1 as search objectives are likely to influence behaviors, cognitions, and ultimately the consequences of the job-search activity.

Yet despite the potential for varying search objectives, search behavior in the job-to-job search context is commonly placed within models of employee turnover (e.g., Griffeth, Hom, & Gaertner, 2000; Hom & Griffeth, 1991; Mobley, Griffeth, Hand, & Meglino, 1979; Steers & Mowday, 1981), whereby search is the mediating process linking dissatisfaction with characteristics of the job and turnover. The basic argument is that individuals typically, though not always, search for alternative employment prior to making the quit decision. As one example, Mobley (1977) described the turnover process as a sequenced process initiated by job dissatisfaction, subsequently followed by thoughts of quitting, a cognitive evaluation of expected utility of the search, search intentions and search behavior, an evaluation of alternatives, and ultimately the decisions to leave.

Empirical tests of turnover "process models" tend to find support for the framework that voluntary turnover stems from job dissatisfaction, which leads to withdrawal cognitions, with job-search behaviors and evaluation of alternatives generated through the search as intermediary processes (Griffeth et al., 2000). If alternatives generated through search are deemed favorable for the employee, a voluntary departure from the organization for a more attractive job alternative is likely to occur (Hom & Griffeth, 1991; Hom, Griffeth & Sellaro, 1984). This basic process has generally been supported across studies, although there have been inconsistencies in regard to the temporal placement of certain variables in the process (e.g., search intent versus quit intent) as well as the effect of dissatisfaction with the job (direct versus indirect) on job-search variables (Bannister & Griffeth, 1986; Dalessio, Silverman, & Schuck, 1986). Spencer, Mowday, and Steers (1983) added the extent of search and results of search (i.e., "the results of my search are encouraging") to the framework, finding that intent to search was the strongest predictor of extent of search, which then predicted the results of search. Interestingly, this study failed to find significant effects for the search variables in predicting intent to quit, yet it found support for a feedback loop whereby what was learned during search influenced the perceived probability of finding acceptable employment, which may then presumably influence quit cognitions. A meta-analytic path model of the process by Hom et al. (1992) found that withdrawal cognitions preceded the pursuit (i.e., job search) and comparison of job alternatives. Empirical tests have also revealed an important moderating role for unemployment rate, indicating that employees assess the job market and the viability of searching for employment prior to quit decisions (Carsten & Spector, 1987; Gerhart, 1990).

It is important to note that turnover process models often vary in conceptualizing search and/or search intentions as an antecedent or consequence of quit cognitions, and the empirical findings have been somewhat equivocal (cf. Hom et al., 1984; Mobley, Horner, & Hillingsworth, 1978). On the one hand, thoughts of quitting would presumably precede actual behavior aimed at quitting. Yet searching may facilitate the intent to quit as individuals enhance their awareness of viable alternatives. Arguably the two constructs are perhaps best viewed as reciprocally related as cognitions are likely to precede goal-directed behavior, which may then help to shape subsequent intentions and decisions.

Although many turnover models have followed the sequential process model linking search to turnover (Hom, Caranikas-Walker, Prussia, & Griffeth, 1992), other research has argued for a more complex process. In this regard, a key contribution to the search and turnover literature is Lee and Mitchell's (1994) "unfolding model of voluntary turnover." This model presents alternative initiators of the turnover process beyond job dissatisfaction (a "shock"), while also recognizing that turnover is not necessarily preceded by a search for alternative employment. The unfolding model relies on image theory (Beach, 1990) to explain how turnover may be initiated by events causing an individual to evaluate his or her current employment. These events can be related to the job (e.g., a negative exchange with a supervisor, being passed over for a promotion) or may stem from external influences (e.g., an unsolicited job offer, a spouse's job transfer) that trigger separation from the employer. More specifically, the model proposes four distinct paths to turnover, two of which involve job search as a process of turnover (Lee & Mitchell, 1994).

Lee and Mitchell's model has introduced a few interesting empirical tests of the withdrawal/turnover process. In an initial test of the unfolding model, Lee, Mitchell, Wise, and Fireman (1996) used a multiple-case study design involving interviews from a sample of nurses who had recently quit their jobs. Results from this study revealed that the fourth path, which focused on the traditional accumulation of job dissatisfaction, could be separated into two different paths (4a and 4b), one involving job search and the other resulting in a more immediate path to turnover. Although this model recognizes that turnover and search processes may deviate from the traditional sequential model whereby turnover follows a search for alternatives, empirical work indicates that the majority of quit decisions are preceded by the search for alternative employment (Lee et al., 1996). Indeed, there is strong empirical evidence that greater search activity makes turnover more likely (Blau, 1993; Bretz et al., 1994; Lee, Gerhart, Weller, & Trevor, 2008).

Donnelly and Quirin (2006) extended the unfolding model by testing employees who assessed job alternatives but ultimately remained with their current jobs ("stayers") and employees who ultimately did leave their jobs ("leavers"). Among the "stayers," Donnelly and Quirin (2006) found that 73 percent engaged in decision paths involving job dissatisfaction (path 4a or 4b in Lee & Mitchell's model); however, among the "leavers" only 45 percent followed this path to actual turnover. A test of the paths that explicitly include job search as part of the process (paths 3 and 4b in Lee & Mitchell's model) revealed that economic consequences were deemed to be a deciding factor of whether the employee ultimately left the job or stayed (Donnelly & Quirin, 2006). This finding suggests that the job-search process will most likely lead to turnover when leaving the current situation is deemed most economically feasible.

Although this chapter is primarily focused on the job-search process from the perspective of the employed job seeker, it is also important to recognize the hiring organization's role in defining search and ultimately facilitating employee turnover. While the employee's motivation and opportunities represent the "supply side" of the search process, the employer's search for a qualified applicant (the "demand-side") is also relevant.[1] In particular, actions on the part of the hiring organization can help to further explain the search/turnover process, as certainly some prospective applicants are not actually searching for new employment but rather are targeted via an organization's recruitment efforts. One such action on the part of a hiring organization is engaging a headhunter to seek out qualified position candidates, a topic discussed in detail in Coverdill and Finlay's chapter in this volume. An applicant pool may thus consist of individuals actively searching to leave their present situation as well as those targeted and proactively recruited by a hiring organization. The latter situation likely reflects a hiring organization's interest in reaching passive job seekers and/or poaching from labor market competitors (Gardner, 2005), given that high quality individuals (e.g., "star" talent) (Darling, 2000) are often highly valued and rewarded by their present organizations and not necessarily seeking to change jobs. A hiring firm's proactive search for applicants, perhaps leading to an unsolicited job offer to an employed individual, further reinforces that not all employee turnover is preceded by search behavior.

Other theoretical models commonly examined in the broader job-search literature have been applied to the job-to-job search process. The theory of planned behavior (TPB) (Ajzen, 1991), for example, posits that job-search confidence in their ability to perform various job-search activities (Van Hooft, this volume; Van Hooft et al., 2004; Van

Hooft, Born, Taris, & Van der Flier, 2005). TPB describes the importance of perceived behavioral control (related to self-efficacy), arguing that it is not only an individual's skills and abilities but also available resources outside the individual's personal control that drive search behavior and search success. For example, individuals who feel that they have adequate amount of behavioral control are more likely to search for job alternatives.

Van Hooft and colleagues applied TBP (Ajzen, 1991) to examine the role of perceived behavioral control (i.e., job-search self-efficacy) as well as job-search attitude and subjective norms (i.e., pressure to look for a job) in influencing an employee's search behavior directly and indirectly through intention. Although much of the research drawing on TPB has focused on unemployed job seekers, research has generally supported the attitude-intention-behavior link across both employed and unemployed job seeker groups. In particular, van Hooft et al. (2004) conducted a study with both employed and unemployed job seekers and found that the TPB was applicable to both groups, although the attitude-intention-behavior relationship was stronger in the unemployed group than in the employed group. They attributed these differences to the possibility that unemployed individuals have a stronger desire to seek employment and that employed individuals are more likely to have other alternatives available besides searching for alternative employment, such as reconsidering their current job. This also ties to the notion that employed individuals may have varying objectives for engaging in search behavior other than to find and accept new employment. An additional explanation for the differences between unemployed and employed job seekers is that unemployed individuals have more control over the job-search process. TPB proposes that the amount of control relates to the strength of the relationship between intentions and behaviors (Ajzen, 1991). Employed individuals have less control because they have less time and fewer opportunities to engage in job searches.

Taken together, models of the search/turnover relationship suggest a complex array of factors involved in whether employee search behavior may ultimately lead to departure from an organization. Thus, although job search plays a prominent role in existing turnover theories, given the inherent connection between job search and employee

---

[1] We thank a reviewer for the suggestion to incorporate this perspective.

withdrawal from an organization, it is important to recognize job search as a construct distinct from turnover. As noted, search does not always result in turnover; additionally, not all leavers are job searchers. Accordingly we see significant value in developing models of search antecedents, behaviors, processes, and outcomes beyond the context of employee turnover.

Antecedents and Outcomes of Job-to-Job Search
Antecedents of Job-to-Job Search

What drives an employee to seek alternative employment? Bretz, Boudreau, and Judge (1994) were among the first to propose (and test) a model of job search specific to the context of employed job seekers. Bretz et al. (1994) expanded the antecedents of employee job search beyond the somewhat simplistic focus on job dissatisfaction to encompass the broader notion of employee motivation and opportunity to search. Specifically, they proposed "push" and "pull" factors that influence employed managers in particular to begin searching for alternative employment. The push process reflects a person's current work or life situation, linked to dissatisfaction with the current state of affairs, and subsequently leads to a search for alternatives (Lee & Mitchell, 1994). Push factors could be work-related (e.g., perceived organizational success, compensation level, job satisfaction), individual factors (e.g., amount of leisure time desired, work-family balance), or environmental factors (e.g., industry, publicly traded employer). Conversely, pull factors capture the challenges of searching in relation to the likelihood of finding alternative employment. In effect, an individual makes an assessment of his or her market value (or "opportunities") and contrasts this with the perceived costs of the search. Such pull factors may also include hiring firm efforts to target and attract and even "poach" (Gardner, 2005) employed talent. Testing this model, Bretz et al. found that push factors were more strongly related to job search than the pull factors, suggesting that dissatisfaction with certain elements of the job is a salient mechanism leading to job search.

The array of job-to-job search antecedents can also be generally categorized along two broad lines, as depicted in Figure 22.1: person attributes (e.g., personality, human capital) and situational factors (e.g., work elements, labor market conditions). As the research generally places job search among employed individuals within an employee withdrawal framework, the typical predictors examined often include factors in the organizational environment that may motivate a person to seek a change of employers.

Person attributes (or individual difference variables) reflect relatively enduring characteristics about an individual that may increase the propensity to seek new employment. This would include personality traits and biographical variables (Boswell et al., 2006; Boudreau et al., 2001; Zimmerman, 2008; Zimmerman, Boswell, Shipp, Dunford, & Boudreau, 2012). In regard to personality traits, Boudreau and colleagues (2001) found statistically significant effects for the "Big Five" personality traits of agreeableness, conscientiousness, extraversion, neuroticism, and openness to experience in predicting job search among employed managers. Boswell et al. (2006) found similar results for extraversion and neuroticism in a study of western European managers. We emphasize that the effect sizes for these traits, albeit statistically significant, were fairly small (ranging from .05 to .07). Most recently Zimmerman and colleagues (2012) examined the pathways (i.e., mediating mechanisms) by which extraversion and neuroticism predict job-search behavior. This study drew on an approach-avoidance framework to argue that employees search out of their desire and perceived ability to advance in their careers and/or to avoid negative aspects of their job or organization. The results of this study revealed simultaneous positive and negative effects of both extraversion and neuroticism on subsequent job-search behavior depending on the mediating mechanism involved (i.e., ambition values, job-search self-efficacy, perceived job challenge, work burnout, perceived financial inadequacy, and job satisfaction). For example, Zimmerman et al. found that extraverted individuals' higher ambition and job-search self-efficacy was associated with *greater* job search, yet such individuals' perceptions of greater job challenges and perceived alternatives were associated with greater job satisfaction and ultimately *less* job search. This research sheds light on the fairly moderate effect sizes for personality traits found in Boudreau and colleagues' studies; it suggests that individuals high in these traits are likely to experience several motivational forces related to advancing their careers and/or avoiding negative aspects of the job and that these can have "countervailing effects." The effects may in a sense be suppressed when only the direct, unmediated effects are examined. Yet by considering the multiple pathways through which extraversion and neuroticism may influence job search, we can obtain a better understanding of the key role of these traits, dependent as they are on the specific mediating mechanisms considered in facilitating or attenuating the search for alternative employment.

Several studies have examined other individual difference variables linked to an employee's tendency to engage in job-search behavior. Variables such as self-esteem or self-efficacy reflect an individual's positive self-evaluation and thus presumably may motivate him or her to enter the job market. In support of this, prior research has shown a positive link between self-esteem or self-efficacy and job-to-job-search behavior (Blau, 1994; Zimmerman et al., 2012). An individual's self-efficacy is also reflective of an individual's perception of control over the job search, which is a key element in the TPB.

Other individual difference variables examined in prior research reflect demographic and/or human capital characteristics of the job seeker. Boudreau et al. (2001), for example, found that managers higher in cognitive ability engaged in greater job-search activity. It may be that such individuals are pulled to the job market given their enhanced abilities and marketability and/or, as noted by the authors, this trait may enhance the "perceived benefit of search" (p. 44). Such ability factors may also be actively targeted by hiring firms, thus translating passive searching into a more active search process. Demographic variables are often argued to reflect an individual's human capital, thus perhaps serving to motivate an individual's search activity through enhanced perceptions of opportunities. Research has generally found a negative relationship between job search and employee level, tenure, and age (e.g., Boswell et al., 2006; Boudreau et al., 2001; Bretz et al. 1994), though again, the effect sizes are fairly small for these variables. Van Hooft et al. (2005) also found differences between minority and majority groups with regards to job search. Ethnic minorities' perceptions of social pressure predicted intentions to search for a new job more strongly that personal attitudes while majority groups were shown to have an opposite effect.

The second broad category of job-to-job search predictors includes situational variables. Given the placement of job-to-job search within the process of the employee withdrawal/turnover process, negative elements of the work environment are argued as particularly critical in "pushing" an individual to seek a new job (e.g., Blau, 1994; Bretz et al., 1994; Cavanaugh, Boswell, Roehling, & Boudreau, 2000; Dunford, Boudreau, & Boswell, 2005). Most broadly, work attitudes such as job

satisfaction and organizational commitment are significant predictors of job-search behavior (Rusbult & Farrell, 1983). Consistent with turnover research more generally, job satisfaction plays a prominent role in negatively predicting search (Boswell et al., 2006; Boudreau et al. 2001; Bretz et al. 1994), negatively relating to both preparatory and active job-search behavior (Blau, 1994). Objective factors including pay/benefits, job demands, the work environment, and perceptions of and reactions to these factors (e.g., pay equity, feelings toward the supervisor, person-organization fit) also predict job search, though are arguably more remote from the process, perhaps working through more general work attitudes (job dissatisfaction) to predict the search for alternative employment. Of particular note is the role of employee compensation in predicting job-search behavior. Interestingly, studies by Boudreau and colleagues (Boudreau et al., 2001; Bretz et al., 1994) on high-level managers have actually shown a fairly weak (negative) or even null (Boswell et al., 2006) relationship. It is likely that factors such as fairness of pay as well as financial need (cf. Blau, 1994) are more critical determinants of an individual's motivation to seek new employment than absolute pay level.

Recent work has expanded the traditional focus on situational variables reflecting job elements and perceptions of the job to also recognize the social dimension influencing job-search behavior. In particular, Felps et al. (2009) examined how coworker job attitudes and search activity can play a role in a job seeker's search behavior and ultimately his or her decision to leave an organization. The authors modeled and found support for a contagion process whereby the behaviors of coworkers spill over to influence (over and above a focal employee's own search behavior and work attitudes) employee turnover. Findings from this study reveal the important role of the social environment in the employee search and withdrawal process. Hughes, Avey, and Nixon (2010) also found that the quality of leader-member exchanges affected individuals' intentions to quit and job-search behaviors.

Another critical situational factor relevant to the search for new employment is the external labor market. Empirical findings for variables such as perceived alternative employment or opportunities as predictive of job-to-job search are fairly mixed. On the one hand, perceptions of alternatives may motivate an individual to enter to labor market due to enhanced confidence in one's ability to find a job. This contention is supported by some research showing a positive link between perceptions of alternative opportunities and job search (Blau, 1993). On the other hand, other research has shown a null effect for perceived alternatives (Boswell et al., 2006; Bretz et al., 1994), suggesting that individuals might also be less motivated to actively/intensely search due to heightened perceptions that alternatives are readily available (Boswell et al., 2006). In a sense, perceiving alternatives may act to simultaneously pull individuals into the labor market yet also attenuate the sense of urgency that may facilitate an intense search. We see alternatives as perhaps best viewed as moderating the effect of search on turnover (discussed previously and more below) rather than as a clear determinant of job-to-job-search behavior. This idea is also consistent with van Hooft and Crossley's (2008) finding that perceived financial need moderates the effect of job-search locus of control on job-search behavior. Specifically, job seeker's with an external locus of control and high financial need appear to compensate for their anticipated difficulties in finding employment through a more intense job search.

Job-to-Job Search Outcomes

Of course a key outcome to searching for employment among employed job seekers is organizational turnover (job change in Figure 22.1), as reflected in the above discussion of the job-search turnover process. As the implicit if not explicit assumption of research in this area is that individuals are searching to leave an employer, job search is often used as a proxy to organizational departure (e.g., Boudreau et al., 2001). Interestingly, prior empirical work shows a fairly modest search/turnover relationship (average weighted r = .26) (Griffeth et al., 2000). What might explain this moderate empirical relationship? Certainly, some individuals may search and not find alternative employment. In such cases, an interesting question surrounds the potential consequences for the individual and the organization of an "unsuccessful" job search. Might individuals begin to feel the present situation is acceptable perhaps through a process of cognitive dissonance (Festinger, 1957), or would individuals withdraw in other ways such as decreased performance or dysfunctional workplace behaviors? We currently have little understanding of such consequences to searching and not leaving, an issue elaborated on below in our discussion of future research.

Conversely, not all turnover is preceded by search activity. This latter argument is a key focus of Lee and colleagues' (1994, 1996) work on the "Unfolding model" (discussed above) which argues and finds that turnover can be triggered by a "shock" that motivates an individual to quit an organization without engaging in a search for alternative employment. In effect, it appears a script may be enacted which facilitates the individual's departure from an organization, perhaps leaving the labor market (e.g., to stay home with a child, to return to school) or seeking employment only after a period of unemployment, such as might be the case when a spouse relocates or an individual feels the need to leave the current situation immediately.

Some research has begun to explain the modest search/turnover link by specifically focusing on factors that may attenuate (or accentuate) the effects (person attributes and situational factors as moderators in Figure 22.1). Most common is the argument that search will lead to turnover when an individual has viable alternatives to staying with the present employer (cf. Mobley et al., 1979; Steer & Mowday, 1981). In effect, whether the search was successful in generating an attractive alternative enhances the probability of actual turnover. Yet research in this area tends to focus on characteristics of the individual or situation as proxies for "ease of movement" (March & Simon, 1958) rather than actual external offers or other search success outcomes (e.g., number of interviews). In this vein, Bretz et al. (1994) modeled opportunity to leave as an individual's human capital (e.g., age, race, education, gender). The researchers found minimal support for their hypothesis that one's opportunity to leave would interact with search behavior in predicting turnover from the firm. The weak findings may be explained by Bretz et al.'s approach of operationalizing job seeker "opportunity" as demographic variables rather than using a more direct measure. More recently, Swider, Boswell, and Zimmerman (2011) modeled several contextual factors, including labor market conditions, that may attenuate (accentuate) the relationship. More specifically, Swider and colleagues (2011) examined job satisfaction, alternative opportunities, and job embeddedness as potential moderators of the search/turnover relationship. Results showed that job search was most likely to lead to individuals actually leaving an organization when they were less satisfied with the job, had greater labor market alternatives, and were less embedded in the organization. The general conclusion is that such job seekers are more motivated, have more opportunities, and/or are less constrained thus allowing job-search activity to be more likely to lead to a viable and attractive new job. This research reinforces the concept that not all searchers are leavers and reveals important contingency factors that help to explain when turnover is most likely to result from search activity (Swider et al., 2011).

Although the general assumption is that employed individuals search with the goal to obtain new employment, this may not necessarily be the case. Arguably, individuals with alternative search objectives are less likely to convert search activity into an actual turnover decision. Such alternative objectives may include searching to network, to stay aware of the market and potential opportunities, to negotiate improved conditions with the present employer, and to investigate whether the "grass may be greener" elsewhere (cf. Boswell et al., 2002). Taking the perspective of a broadened conceptualization of search objectives, research by Boswell, Boudreau, and Dunford (2004) showed that individuals may engage in leverage-seeking searches whereby the motive driving the search activity is to obtain an external offer to enhance one's bargaining power and ultimately enhance employment conditions (e.g., pay, job promotion) with the current employer. This leverage-seeking search was not significantly related to turnover a year later, though searching "to leave" did significantly predict subsequent turnover. Thus the search/turnover link may also be dependent on one's search objectives such that there is a stronger link when individuals are searching with the objective to in fact leave the present job. This underscores the value of understanding the goal motivating an individual's search behavior (Kanfer et al., 2001), as one's objective is likely to offer insight on when search leads to turnover as well as other potential outcomes of job-search behavior.

As noted, there are other important job-to-job search outcomes to consider beyond simply the turnover decision (see Figure 22.1). Along these lines, researchers have begun to investigate the role of job search in predicting the nature of the new job (see also Virick & McKee-Ryan, this volume). For example, van Hooft et al. (2005) examined the quality of the obtained employment (Schwab, Rynes, & Aldag, 1987) by investigating individuals' satisfaction with the new job and the agreement between the job wanted and the job obtained (i.e., number of hours and type of contract) following search. Interestingly, while this study found the expected positive link between job-search activity and obtaining a new job, the extent of job search did not significantly predict satisfaction with the new job or

level of agreement between the desired and obtained job. Certainly more research is needed to clarify when and how job search can lead to more successful changes in employment, including whether an individual obtains a more satisfying, better-fitting, and more rewarding employment situation.

Looking beyond the notion of new employment and/or the nature of the job obtained, job-to-job search has additional potential outcomes for the individual during and following the search process. Recent qualitative work by Wanberg, Basbug, Van Hooft, and Samtani (2012) examined job seeker (unemployed as well as employed) responses and outcomes as individuals progressed through the search process, revealing an emergent process model whereby job search–related demands (e.g., social, task, personal) were associated with affective reactions (e.g., helplessness, frustration, loss of control, reduced self-worth) and ultimately adaptational responses (e.g., mood, feedback seeking, self-reflection, learning). The researchers also found that demands of searching were associated with specific changes in the job seeker's search behavior and intensity, attitudes toward employing firms, and feelings of stress and mental health.

Searching may also link to positive career outcomes (e.g., compensation, mobility) due to networking and enhanced recognition and generation of opportunities garnered through the labor market (cf. DiRenzo, M., & Greenhaus, 2011; Zimmerman et al., 2012). Yet searching may come at a cost as it can initiate workplace withdrawal behaviors and/or detract from task performance (Boswell et al., 2006). In addition, as discussed in detail below, it is important to consider the subsequent consequences of searching and not leaving the present situation (perhaps due to other objective for the job search or to not finding viable alternative employment). We might expect subsequent attitudes toward the job, the organization, or the supervisor to be negatively affected once an individual initiates the withdrawal process by engaging in job search. Yet if one sought new employment only to find out the alternatives were not necessarily better and/or was simply testing the market, affective reactions might actually improve following the search activity. In addition, beyond the individual job seeker, how might others in the work environment (e.g., supervisor, team members) react to and/or be impacted by a job seeker's stay decision? Boswell et al. (2004) found that the leverage-seeking search led to subsequent (one year later) pay enhancement and/or promotions (as reported by the individuals) as individuals "leverage" the alternatives generated through search. Yet the researchers noted though did not specifically examine the fact that searching to obtain leverage may have deleterious repercussions for subsequent feelings of trust, loyalty, and supervisory and work group relations despite (or perhaps because of) an individual's decision to stay with the present employer.

Conclusions and Future Research Directions

Much has been learned about antecedents of job-to-job search behavior and the link between job search and turnover. Certainly this research offers important theoretical insight into the employee withdrawal process as well as practical insight for employers looking to manage employee retention and workplace engagement. Yet there is still much to be learned about the job-search process of employed individuals. The elements highlighted in Figure 22.1 should be built upon in future research within the context of employee job-to-job search behavior. In the following section, we focus on several areas of research depicted in the model that we see as particularly critical to offering important new understanding of employee job-search behavior.

One important conclusion from recent research in this area, which stems from the modest job search-turnover empirical link, is that *not all leavers are searchers and not all searchers are leavers.* The former point is highlighted in the work by Lee and colleagues on the unfolding model of turnover showing that employees may leave (following a "shock") without engaging in a search for alternative employment. Yet perhaps most pertinent to our focus on job-search behavior is the notion that searching does not necessarily lead to turnover. A question that arises is: What are the consequences of searching and not leaving? There are likely to be consequences for multiple constituents including the job seeker, the manager, and the team/work group, particularly to the extent the other individuals are aware of the search activity. Research is needed to understand how searching and not leaving might link to subsequent job attitudes, work motivation, and related behaviors (including job performance) as well as supervisory and work group relations. This is reflected in Figure 22.1 through the arrows linking job-search behavior to both job seeker attitudes/behaviors and to other constituent outcomes as well as the indirect effects of search behavior through job change. Thus although the figure recognizes that job change has implications for

subsequent employee reactions toward the *new* job (discussed further below) and for other constituents remaining with the employer (e.g., supervisor, team members), engaging in search behavior can affect the job seeker and others within the work environment regardless of whether the search results in actual departure from the job.

Such consequences of job search are likely to depend on the individual's objectives for engaging in search behavior. This is reflected in the moderating role of job-search objectives in the search behavior-job seeker attitudes/behaviors link in the figure. For example, as discussed by Swider and colleagues (2011), a job seeker is likely to engage in other withdrawal behaviors following a search with no turnover to the extent that the individual was dissatisfied with the current situation and was thus looking to find new employment. Yet if an individual was searching with other motives in mind (e.g., networking or to "test the water"), a subsequent decision to stay may actually help to reconnect the individual to the present employer, perhaps facilitating improved job attitudes (e.g., job satisfaction, organizational commitment, engagement). Thus, although future research is needed to examine the outcomes of searching and not leaving in general, we believe such research would benefit from also incorporating the potential role of an individual's objectives for engaging in the search behavior in the first place.

There are many avenues for contributing to the research on job-to-job search, both theoretically and methodologically. Below we offer suggestions for continued research on the antecedents, outcomes, and processes of job-to-job search as well as acknowledging important methodological issues that can help to answer some of the complex questions regarding job-search behavior in this context.

Job-to-Job Search Antecedents

Above we discussed the antecedents of job search as falling under two general categories—person attributes and situational factors. Such factors are generally seen as driving an employee's desire to leave the current employer. Continued research is needed to more fully understand what drives job-to-job search behavior and specifically the factors that determine different search objectives. For example, what drives an individual to search with the intent to leave an employer versus search with other objectives in mind? There are likely characteristics of the individual (e.g., dispositional) and situational factors that come into play. Boswell and colleagues' (2004) research, discussed above, for example, found that searching to "seek leverage" against the current employer was associated with a job seeker's personal values (importance placed on reward elements), demographic characteristics (hierarchical level), work-related attitudes (career satisfaction), and perceptions of the external market (perceived alternative opportunity). Interestingly, this study, which focused on high-level managers, found no role for compensation level, suggesting that seeking leverage is motivated less by absolute pay (at least among the executives studied) and driven more by other career elements (e.g., level) as well as individual differences in valuing extrinsic rewards. We believe that research is needed to elucidate the potential differing antecedents of search dependent on an individual's specific search objective. Such research would be useful in terms of building theory regarding the role of search goals in the job-search process as well as offering practical insight for employers looking to better manage the factors that might drive different types of search and search outcomes (e.g., use of a job offer for bargaining leverage versus quitting the employer).

Researchers can look to other search contexts (discussed in this volume; e.g., Klehe, De Pater, Koen, & Kira, this volume; Saks, this volume; Song, Sun, & Li, this volume) for potential antecedents of employee job search not yet examined in the job-to-job search context. Drawing on models of expectancy, self-evaluation, and the social environment would be particularly informative. Again, this would encourage researchers to consider job-to-job search beyond the typical turnover/withdrawal framework and investigate how factors such as a job seeker's financial need, self-esteem, and personal relationships—which are commonly examined in the context of unemployment (following job loss or entering the workforce following education)—may similarly (or divergently) facilitate job-search behavior for employed individuals. We believe research linking such antecedents to specific search objectives would be particularly fruitful (as depicted at the far left of Figure 22.1).

As one example, Saks and Ashforth (2002) investigated the influence of person-job and person-organization fit perceptions on the job-search process and individuals' career development. This line of research may help to clarify additional job-search objectives and behaviors. For instance, are employed individuals searching because they are not satisfied with their jobs/careers and are experiencing a lack of person-job fit or are they experiencing a lack of person-organization fit and looking to remain within their current industry but willing to work for a competitor? These different objectives may yield different search methods, such that an individual experiencing a lack of P-O fit will search for alternative employment through network means within the current industry of employment; however, an individual experiencing a lack of P-J fit may broaden the scope of his or her search. As Saks and Ashforth (2002) note, the person-environment fit may precede job-search behaviors, and person-environment fit can also be an outcome of job-search behaviors.

Job-to-Job Search Outcomes

The notion that searching does not necessarily lead to employee turnover evokes the question as to what are other outcomes of job-search activity beyond employee turnover and related withdrawal behaviors. Certainly the literature examining alternative search objectives (e.g., "leverage-seeking search") (Boswell et al., 2006) is informative in suggesting outcomes linked to the intent of the searcher. For example, searching for leverage is conceptually linked to negotiating improved employment conditions such as higher pay, a promotion, and/or improved working conditions (Boswell et al., 2006). This suggests not only important potential outcomes of search behavior but again also highlights the value of incorporating search objectives within the model. In addition, search behavior is likely to increase an individual's knowledge of the labor market, industry, and/or potential career trajectories. Such knowledge may enhance skill sets and ultimately employability (DiRenzo, & Greenhaus, 2011). Thus how might search behavior link to longer-term career outcomes for an individual or perhaps even enhanced knowledge, skills, and abilities that can be applied to the present employer? Research has only begun to consider the role of search activity within the larger career life-cycle and/or as part of a "boundaryless career" (Arthur & Rousseau, 1996; Sullivan & Baruch, 2009). We see the merging of the job-to-job search process with the careers literature as a particularly fruitful avenue for future research (see, for example, Van Vianen & Klehe, this volume).

Following in this longer-term perspective on job-search outcomes, continued research is needed to clarify what happens to a job searcher after he or she does leave a particular employer (i.e., job change-job seeker attitudes/behaviors link in Figure

22.1). Some research has incorporated turnover destinations (e.g., promotions versus lateral moves, career changes) and/or subsequent reactions/attitudes toward the new employer (cf. van Hooft et al., 2005). Yet we have little understanding of how elements of the search process and the utilization of specific search behaviors while a person is employed at one organization might link to outcomes at another organization. Research tracking job attitudes over time and across employers suggests that one's experiences and perceptions of prior employers may have implications for subsequent job attitudes (cf. Boswell, Boudreau, & Tichy, 2005; Boswell, Shipp, Payne, & Culbertson, 2009). Similarly, how might the *experiences of searching* for a new job affect reactions toward subsequent jobs? The duration, success, and intensity (i.e., specific behaviors engaged) of a job search may also play a role in one's future employment expectations and behaviors. This again reinforces the need for a longer-term career perspective to clarify the employee job-search process and subsequent outcomes.

Process Considerations

A general issue in the job-to-job search literature is the limited focus on the dynamic process involved in searching for new employment. That is, unlike other contexts in which job search has been examined (e.g., unemployed job seekers, labor market entrants), the existing research on employed job seekers has not explicitly examined the process by which employees search for alternative employment, evaluate search alternatives, change search goals and strategies, form quit cognitions, and ultimately make a quit/stay decision. This is perhaps due to the somewhat simplistic focus on search behavior as a proximal indicator of turnover rather than as a critical construct in and of itself. Yet drawing on a self-regulatory view (Elliott & Thrash, 2002; Kanfer et al., 2001), more research is needed to uncover the dynamic processes. This would not only help to develop models specific to the job-to-job search process but also contribute practical insight on employee turnover decisions (and related withdrawal outcomes) and the potential influence of managers and organizational initiatives at various stages in the process. This dynamic job-search process is emphasized in Figure 22.1 through reciprocal relationships between various elements of the employee job-search process whereby, through job-search activity, job seekers gain new insight on their mobility and present employment situation, adjust search objectives, and behaviors accordingly, which

then helps to further shape quit cognitions and/or workplace attitudes and behaviors.

Related to the general issue of understanding the dynamic job-to-job search process is examining *how* employed individuals search. That is, what are the specific behaviors involved and what are the implications of specific behaviors for subsequent outcomes for the individual as well as others in the work environment (manager, team members)? Are certain search behaviors more/less used by employed job seekers or more/less effective at obtaining new employment (regardless of whether the intent is to leave the present employer for that "new" job)? Do search behaviors differ from that utilized in other search contexts (e.g., among unemployed individuals)? A particularly critical issue is the role of the Internet. Although the Internet has fundamentally changed the nature of job-search activity in general, its role for job-to-job search is particularly noteworthy given the potential for facilitating job search while "at work." That is, employed job seekers can actively peruse new employment opportunities while "on the clock" of their current employer. From a research standpoint, common measures of search behavior do not always assess use of the Internet as most were developed prior to its advent. And prior research findings are, in general, based on pre-Internet search. Research is needed to assess the specific role of this critical change to the search process, including the development of measures reflective of the electronic job-search environment.

Methodological Considerations

Consistent with much of the organizational behavior research, there are important methodological considerations to advance our understanding of this research area. First, as discussed above, job-to-job search research would benefit from richer measures that specifically incorporate the complexities of the Internet to an employee's search activity. In addition, we see a particularly critical role for longitudinal research involving the job-to-job search process. Existing research within a turnover framework commonly takes a single time-lag approach (time 1 minus time 2) whereby employee turnover is measured subsequent to the assessment of search behavior (e.g., Bretz et al. 1994). Research focused specifically on search behavior as the ultimate criterion has taken a similar approach, with search behavior measured subsequent to the antecedents (e.g., Zimmerman et al., 2012). Yet longitudinal research beyond a single time lag is needed to more fully uncover the dynamic process by which search unfolds over time. This would require collecting repeated measures of variables in order to assess the potential reciprocal relationships among the study variables. Further, an expanded view of search outcomes (discussed above) necessitates a longitudinal approach to capture the long-term reactions toward the new employer in the context of job change or reactions to the current employer in the context of no change.

An interesting question surrounds the "appropriate" time lag between measures of search antecedents, search-process variables, and search outcomes. Prior work has commonly relied on a six-month or one-year lag between measurement periods (e.g., Bretz et al., 1994; Zimmerman et al., 2012). This seems due as much to convenience as to theoretical arguments guiding the measurement lag. An interesting avenue of research would be to have repeated measures of satisfaction and job-search behaviors throughout defined time durations of employment to examine the interplay between the two variables. For instance, as mentioned previously, job dissatisfaction is one antecedent to job-search behaviors. When employees are dissatisfied with their current positions searches for alternative employment, does their dissatisfaction increase owing to the realization that there are better employment options? Again, the potential reciprocal relations would be important to examine. Capturing repeated measures of job-search activity can also help researchers understand the escalation of job-search behavior and changes in search behaviors in light of the job seeker's search objective.

An additional methodological consideration is to incorporate multilevel models within the job-to-job search context. Examining work group effects on job-search behavior may be fruitful in understanding the contagion of job-search behaviors (Felps et al., 2009). There may be other group-level variables that could help researchers understand the antecedents, objectives, process, and outcomes of job search. Some individuals may find themselves in highly competitive work groups where job searching to leverage their employment rewards is not an uncommon practice among members of the group. The examination of group-level variables in climate would help researchers to understand the influence of the context and social environment that are inherent in most workplaces.

A final method-related consideration is the choice of samples to investigate job-to-job search. A series of studies have focused on job-search behavior among high-level managers (e.g., Boswell, et al., 2006; Boudreau et al., 2001; Bretz et al., 1994; Zimmerman et al., 2012). These studies were made in partnership with an executive search firm, allowing the researchers to survey employed managers over time as they potentially changed employers. Research partnerships with search firms, employment agencies, or professional trade organizations in the future may similarly provide researchers with opportunities to track employed individuals, over time and even across employers, as they progress through the search process. Indeed, a challenge of assessing distant outcomes of search behaviors, such as attitudes toward a new job/ organization or search activity over multiple job changes, is the need to survey individuals across multiple employers. On the other hand, reliance on respondents through search firm/employment agency databases is likely to restrict the sample of focus to those who are actively seeking alternative employment or are in some way unique from the general population of employed individuals. We would encourage future researchers to seek out diverse samples including those individuals who are more passively seeking alternative opportunities as well as individuals with search objectives other than to leave the current employer. In addition, research focused specifically on key groups of individuals (e.g., knowledge workers) would provide valuable practical insight for organizations looking to retain their high-demand/high-value workers. Finally, studies comparing search behaviors, processes, and outcomes across industries, career stages, and generations would contribute important insight on the role of professional norms and career issues in employee job-search activity.

Practical Guidelines

• Job-search behavior is an important predictor of turnover and thus can be actively managed and, if feasible, monitored as part of an organization's retention efforts.

• Because not all searchers are leavers and not all leavers are searchers, organizations should understand the objectives (or motives) underlying an employee's search behavior as well as recognize that searching does not mean that an employee will necessarily quit. Search objectives are likely to hold implications for the outcomes following search behavior (e.g., stay versus leave, withdrawal behavior, subsequent job attitudes).

- Situational factors such as job dissatisfaction or poor job fit may "push" an individual to search for alternative employment, thus reinforcing the value of a positive work environment, effective employee relations, and fair and valuable work outcomes in curtailing job-search behavior.

- In addition, personal/individual difference factors such as external opportunities and human capital may "pull" an individual to search for alternative employment, thus suggesting the value of targeted retention efforts focusing on key and/or vulnerable employees.

- Tracking employee attitudes, perceptions, and behaviors is valuable in providing a signal of subsequent job-search activity.

- Given that individual differences (e.g., personality traits, self-esteem) have been linked to employee search behavior as well as turnover decisions, an organization can proactively "select for" subsequent employee retention during their recruitment and selection processes.

- When an employee has searched but not left it is not necessarily a "win" for an organization, as the individual's search objectives have implications for subsequent and longer-term employee attitudes and behaviors (e.g., subsequent commitment, continued search activity, withdrawal behavior).

- It is important not to be shortsighted or reactionary in regard to employee job-search behavior; job-to-job search is part of a complex process involving varying search objectives and outcomes, including potential effects on other employees and the organization's culture.

References

Ajzen, I. (1991). The theory of planned behavior. *Organizational Behavior and Human Decision Processes (Special Issue: Theories of cognitive self-regulation)*, 50, 179–211.

Arthur, M. B., & Rousseau, D. M. (1996). *The boundaryless career: A new employment principle for a new organizational era.* New York: Oxford University Press.

Bannister, B. D., & Griffeth, R. W. (1986). Applying a causal analytic framework to the Mobley, Horner, and Hollingsworth (1978) turnover model: A useful reexamination. *Journal of Management*, 12, 433–443.

Beach, L. R., (1990). *Image theory: Decision making in personal and organizational contexts.* Chichester, UK: Wiley.

Blau, G. (1993). Further exploring the relationship between job search and voluntary individual turnover. *Personnel Psychology*, 46, 313–330.

Blau, G. (1994). Testing a two-dimensional measure of job search behavior. *Organizational Behavior and Human Decision Processes*, 59, 288–312.

Boswell, W. R. (2006). Job search. In S. G. Rogelberg (Ed.), *Encyclopedia of industrial/organizational psychology* (pp. 414–416). Thousand Oaks, CA: Sage.

Boswell, W. R., Boudreau, J. W., & Dunford, B. B. (2002). The relationship between job search objectives and job search activity. Paper presented at the Society for Industrial and Organizational Psychology, Toronto, Canada.

Boswell, W. R., Boudreau, J. W., & Dunford, B. B. (2004). The outcomes and correlates of job search objectives: Searching to leave or searching for leverage? *Journal of Applied Psychology*, 89, 1083–1091.

Boswell, W. R., Boudreau, J. W., & Tichy, J. (2005). The relationship between employee job change and job satisfaction: The honeymoon-hangover effect. *Journal of Applied Psychology*, 90, 882–892.

Boswell, W. R., Roehling, M. V., & Boudreau, J. W. (2006). The role of personality, situational, and demographic variables in predicting job search among European managers. *Personality and Individual Differences*, 40, 783–794.

Boswell, W. R., Shipp, A. J., Payne, S. C., & Culbertson, S. S. (2009). Changes in job satisfaction over time: The surprising role of honeymoons and hangovers. *Journal of Applied Psychology*, 94, 844–858.

Boudreau, J. W., Boswell, W. R., Judge, T. A., & Bretz, R. D. Jr. (2001). Personality and cognitive ability as predictors of job search among employed managers. *Personnel Psychology*, 54, 25–50.

Bretz, R. D., Boudreau, J. W., & Judge, T. A. (1994). Job search behavior of employed managers. *Personnel Psychology*, 47, 275–301.

Carsten, J. M., & Spector, P. E. (1987). Unemployment, job satisfaction, and employee turnover: A meta-analytic test of the Muchinsky model. *Journal of Applied Psychology*, 72, 374–381.

Cascio, W. F. (2000). *Costing human resources: The financial impact of behavior in organizations* (4th ed). Cincinnati, OH: Southwestern.

Cavanaugh, M. A., Boswell, W. R., Roehling, M. V., & Boudreau, J. W. (2000). An empirical examination of self-reported work stress among U.S. managers. *Journal of Applied Psychology*, 85, 65–74.

Dalessio, A., Silverman, W. H., & Schuck, J. R. (1986). Paths to turnover: A re-analysis and review of existing data on the Mobley, Horner, and Hollingsworth turnover model. *Human Relations*, 39, 245–264.

Darling, A. (2000). Reaching for the stars. *Catalog Age*, 17, 113–114.

DiRenzo, M., & Greenhaus, J. (2011). Job search and voluntary turnover in a boundaryless world: A control theory perspective. *Academy of Management Review*, 36: 576–589.

Donnelly, D. P., & Quirin, J. J. (2006). An extension of Lee and Mitchell's unfolding model of voluntary turnover. *Journal of Organizational Behavior*, 27, 59–77.

Dunford, B. B., Boudreau, J. W., & Boswell, W. R. (2005). Out of the money: The impact of underwater stock options on executive job search. *Personnel Psychology*, 58, 67–101.

Elliot, A. J., & Thrash, T. M. (2002). Approach-avoidance motivation in personality: Approach and avoidance temperament and goals. *Journal of Personality and Social Psychology*, 82, 804–818.

Felps, W., Mitchell, T. R., Herman, D. R., Lee, T. W., Holtom, B. C., & Harman, W. S. (2009). Turnover contagion: How coworkers' job embeddedness and job search behaviors influence quitting. *Academy of Management Journal*, 52, 545–561.

Festinger, L. (1957). *A theory of cognitive dissonance.* Redwood City, CA: Stanford University Press.

Gardner, T. (2005). Interfirm competition for human resources: Evidence from the software industry. *Academy of Management Journal, 48*, 237–256.

Gerhart, B. (1990). Voluntary turnover and alternative job opportunities. *Journal of Applied Psychology, 75*, 467–476.

Griffeth, R. W., Hom, P. W., & Gaertner, S. A. (2000). A meta-analysis of antecedents and correlates of employee turnover: Update, moderator tests, and research implications for the next millennium. *Journal of Management, 26*, 463–488.

Hom, P. W., Caranikas-Walker, F., Prussia, G. E., & Griffeth, R. W. (1992). A meta-analytical structural equations analysis of employee turnover. *Journal of Applied Psychology, 77*, 890–909.

Hom, P. W., & Griffeth, R. W. (1991). Structural equations modeling test of a turnover theory: Cross-sectional and longitudinal analyses. *Journal of Applied Psychology, 76*, 350–366.

Hom, P. W., & Griffeth, R. W. (1995). *Employee Turnover.* Cincinnati, OH: South-Western.

Hom, P. W, Griffeth, R. W, & Sellaro, C. L. (1984). The validity of Mobley's (1977) model of employee turnover. *Organizational Behavior and Human Performance, 34*, 141–174.

Hughes, L. W., Avey, J. B., & Nixon, D. R. (2010). Relationships between leadership and followers' quitting intentions and job search behaviors. *Journal of Leadership & Organizational Studies, 17*, 351–362.

Kanfer, R., Wanberg, C. R., & Kantrowitz, T. M. (2001). Job search and employment: A personality-motivational analysis and meta-analytic review. *Journal of Applied Psychology, 86*, 837–855.

Kopelman, R. E., Rovenpar, J. L., Millsap, R. E. (1992). Rationale and construct validity evidence for the job search behavior index: Because intentions (and New Year's resolutions) often come to naught. *Journal of Vocational Behavior, 40*, 269–287.

Lee, T. H., Gerhart, B., Weller, I., & Trevor, C. O. (2008). Understanding voluntary turnover: Path-specific job satisfaction effects and the importance of unsolicited job offers. *Academy of Management Journal, 51*, 65–671.

Lee, T. W., & Mitchell, T. R. (1994). An alternative approach: The unfolding model of voluntary employee turnover. *Academy of Management Review, 19*, 51–89.

Lee, T. W., Mitchell, T. R., Wise, L., & Fireman, S. (1996). An unfolding model of voluntary employee turnover. *Academy of Management Journal, 39*, 5–36.

March, J. G., & Simon, H. A. (1958). *Organizations.* New York: Wiley.

Mobley, W. H. (1977). Intermediate linkages in the relationship between job satisfaction and employee turnover. *Journal of Applied Psychology, 62*, 237.

Mobley, W. H., Griffeth, R. W., Hand, H. H., & Meglino, B. M. (1979). Review and conceptual analysis of the employee turnover process. *Psychological Bulletin, 86*, 493–522.

Mobley, W H., Horner, S. Q, & Hollingsworth, A. T. (1978). An evaluation of precursors of hospital employee turnover. *Journal of Applied Psychology, 63*, 408–414.

Rusbult, C. E., & Farrell, D. (1983). A longitudinal test of the investment model: The impact on job satisfaction, job commitment, and turnover of variations in rewards, costs, alternatives, and investments. *Journal of Applied Psychology, 68*, 429–438.

Saks, A. M., & Ashforth, B. E. (2002). Is job search related to employment quality? It all depends on the fit. *Journal of Applied Psychology, 87*, 646–654.

Schwab, D. P., Rynes, S. L., & Aldag, R. J. (1987). Theories and research on job search and choice. *Research in Personnel and Human Resources Management, 5*, 129–166.

Spencer, D. G., Steers, R. M., & Mowday, R. T. (1983). An empirical test of the inclusion of job search linkages into Mobley's model of the turnover decision process. *Journal of Occupational Psychology, 56*, 137–144.

Steers, R. M., & Mowday, R. T. (1981). Employee turnover and postdecision accommodation processes. In L. Cummings and B. Staw (Eds.), *Research in organizational behavior* (pp. 235–281). Greenwich, CT: JAI Press.

Sullivan, S. E., & Baruch, Y. (2009). Advances in career theory and research: A critical review and agenda for future exploration. *Journal of Management, 35*, 1542–1571.

Swider, B. W., Boswell, W. R., & Zimmerman, R. D. (2011). Examining the job search-turnover relationship: The role of embeddedness, job satisfaction, and available alternatives. *Journal of Applied Psychology, 96*, 432–441.

van Hooft, E. A. J., Born, M. P., Taris, T. W., & van der Flier, H. (2005). Predictors and outcomes of job search behavior: The moderating effects of gender and family situation. *Journal of Vocational Behavior, 67*, 133–152.

van Hooft, E. A. J., Born, M. P., Taris, T. W., van der Flier, H., & Blonk, R. W. B. (2004). Predictors of job search behavior among employed and unemployed people. *Personnel Psychology, 57*, 25–59.

van Hooft, E. A. J., & Crossley, C. D. (2008). The joint role of locus of control and perceived financial need in job search. *International Journal of Selection and Assessment, 16*, 258–271.

Van Hoye, G., & Saks, A. M. (2008). Job search as goal-directed behavior: Objectives and methods. *Journal of Vocational Behavior, 73*, 358–367.

Wanberg, C. R., Basbug, G., Van Hooft, E. A. J., & Samtani, A. (2012). Navigating the black hole: Explicating layers of job search context and adaptational responses. *Personnel Psychology, 65*, 887–926.

Zimmerman, R. D. (2008). Understanding the impact of personality traits on individuals' turnover decisions: A meta-analytic path model. *Personnel Psychology, 61*, 309–348.

Zimmerman, R. D., Boswell, W. R., Shipp, A. J., Dunford, B. B., & Boudreau, J. W. 2012. Should I stay or should I go? Explaining the motivational "black box" between personality and employees' job search behavior. *Journal of Management, 38*, 1450–1475.

Job-Search Behavior of the Unemployed: A Dynamic Perspective

Zhaoli Song, Shu Hua Sun, *and* Xian Li

Abstract

Unemployment is a major social issue in modern societies. Unemployed workers obtain reemployment mainly through their job-search activities. This chapter documents the literature on the uniqueness, antecedents, and outcomes of job-search behaviors of the unemployed. Because job-search behavior has recently been examined as a dynamic process, we summarize theoretical models, research designs, and analytical approaches in studying job-search dynamics, particularly with regard to unemployed job seekers. We further suggest conceptualizing and empirically examining job-search as behavioral episodes to enhance our understanding of job-search dynamics.

Key Words: job-search behavior, unemployment, dynamics, behavioral episode

Every year, mass layoffs, firings, and turnovers cause millions of workers to lose their jobs. The unemployment problem is particularly serious during economic downturns. For example, in 2010, following the financial crisis that started in 2008, thirty-four OECD countries had a peak unemployment rate of 8.3%, representing a whopping forty-nine million unemployed workers (OECD, July 2012). To cope with unemployment, societies must generate more jobs. Simultaneously, unemployed individuals must actively search for reemployment. Given the importance of job search to unemployed individuals, this chapter is dedicated to documenting the uniqueness, antecedents, and outcomes of job-search behaviors of the unemployed. Furthermore, because job-search behavior has been conceptualized and empirically examined more recently as a dynamic process (e.g., Wanberg, Zhu, & van Hooft, 2010), we summarize theoretical models, research designs, and analytical approaches in studying job-search dynamics, particularly of unemployed job seekers. We conclude by offering directions for future research.

Job-Search Behavior of the Unemployed
Unique Aspects of Job-Search Behavior of the Unemployed

Unemployed individuals manifest job-search behavior that differs from the behavior seen in other types of job seekers (e.g., graduating students [Saks, this volume] or employed individuals [Boswell & Gardner, this volume]). For example, unemployed individuals search more intensively, through more diverse methods, and collect more offers than employed job seekers. Relationships among attitudes, intentions, and behaviors in the job-search process are stronger for unemployed individuals than for employed job seekers (Van Hooft, Born, Taris, Flier, & Blonk, 2004).

Several things account for the uniqueness of unemployed individuals' job search. First, they become unemployed because of job loss, meaning that they have often suffered from stressful life events that evoking pessimism, isolation, despair, and anger (Jahoda, 1982; Leana & Feldman, 1988). The job search is then closely linked to the grieving process (Amundson & Borgen, 1982). According to the dynamic model of unemployment, individuals can begin to search for jobs only toward the end of the grieving process, after reaching the acceptance stage (Amundson & Borgen, 1982). Many factors may influence the grieving process and engagement in job search, especially the circumstances behind losing the job, whether it was voluntary or involuntary, whether a factory was closed or the worker was fired, whether it involved a contract violation, and whether the worker had received advance notification (Addison & Portugal, 1992; Blau, 2006; Burgess & Low, 1998) Second, people who lose their jobs usually receive financial compensation, such as a retrenchment fee offered by their previous employers, unemployment insurance (UI), or welfare assistance from government agencies. Those financial aids will influence job-search patterns and unemployment duration (Devine & Kiefer, 1993). For example, job seekers who are eligible for UI tend to intensify their search when their benefits approach exhaustion (Krueger & Mueller, 2010). Third, governments and societies often provide job-search assistance for the unemployed, including job-search training, skill training, vocational counseling, and job information (Vuori & Vesalainen, 1999; Wanberg, 2012; see also Glebbeek & Sol, this volume; Price & Vinokur, this volume). Labor economists have mainly studied financial compensation and job-search assistance for their effects on job-loss impacts (Devine & Kiefer, 1991, 1993; see also Van den Berg & Uhlendorff, this volume).

Categorizations of Job-Search Behavior of the Unemployed

Unemployed job seekers may engage in various types of job-search behaviors, including using public employment offices or job-search centers, directly approaching potential employers, and seeking help from relatives, friends, or former coworkers (see also Van Hoye, this volume). Based on the types of search channels or search strategies, the literature has categorized job-search behavior of the unemployed as formal or informal (Drentea, 1998; Montgomery, 1992), preparatory or active (Blau, 1993, 1994), and focused/exploratory/haphazard (Stevens & Beach, 1996; Stevens & Turban, 2001).

Public employment offices exemplify typical formal channels. They provide employer listings to help job seekers. Informal job searches usually involve mining job seekers' social networks (Korpi, 2001; Franzen & Hangartner, 2006; Wanberg et al. 2000; see also Forret, this volume). As early as the 1960s, Rees (1966) found that most jobs were obtained through informal referrals from friends and relatives, establishing the popularity of the saying "it's not what you know, but whom you know" (Burnett, 1994). From job seekers' perspectives, their social networks may offer information about available job openings alert organizations that the job seeker is available, or even exert actual influence over hiring decisions (Lin, 2001). On the employer's side, workforce referrals provide cheap and reliable screening (Fernandez et al., 2000). Burnett (1994) compared formal and informal job-search behaviors with a sample of the unemployed and found that only a few seekers found jobs through job centers. In comparison, informal contacts with friends or acquaintances were the most often used and effective methods.

Job-search behaviors may be both preparatory and active (Blau, 1993, 1994). Preparatory search involves gathering information, revising resumes, and reading job-search publications. Active search means publicizing availability for work and actually applying for open positions. The distinction between preparatory and active search behaviors can be murky for unemployed job seekers compared with other populations, such as recent college graduates (Wanberg, 2012). For example, contacting an employment agency is typically deemed an active search behavior. However, it is preparatory behavior when the unemployed job seeker attends a job-search workshop at an agency. Likewise, some behaviors typically considered preparatory may also involve actual employment requests. Furthermore, preparatory behaviors, most suitable for employed or graduate job seekers (Saks, 2006), generally come before active behaviors (Blau, 1993, 1994). However, unemployed individuals may engage in continuous preparatory behaviors while simultaneously actively searching—for example, by revising their resumes while applying for job openings.

Successful reemployment depends on both the methods and the strategies used (Crossley & Highhouse, 2005; Kanfer et al., 2001; McArdle et al., 2007). Job seekers using *focused strategies* concentrate on one specific type of job and keep searching until they find precisely what they want; those using *exploratory strategies* fully explore all options by examining various types of jobs; those using *haphazard trial-and-error approaches* switch tactics without rationale and gather information passively (Stevens & Beach, 1996; Stevens & Turban, 2001). Among the three types of job-search strategies, one study showed that focused and exploratory strategies contribute best to the number of job offers received (Koen, Klehe, Van

Vianen, Zikic, & Nauta, 2010). However, this study also showed that 8 months later, exploratory strategies resulted in reduced reemployment quality. Haphazard strategies had no such effects. Another study identified two job-search strategies: *point strategy*, in which individuals undertake significant search costs, plan meticulously, and consider only a few options worth pursuing; and *interval strategy* in which individuals are typically averse to search costs, plan in a perfunctory manner, and accept many options as "good enough" (Wieczorkowska & Burnstein, 2004). Interval strategists, rather than point strategists, were found to have the most rapid success. For a more detailed discussion on types of job-search behavior, see Van Hoye (this volume).

Antecedents and Outcomes of Job-Search Behaviors of the Unemployed

A major theme in the unemployment job-search literature is to identify antecedents of job-search behavior or job-search effort. With so many antecedents, researchers have tried to divide them into different groups, such as personality, expectancies, self-evaluations, motivation, social contexts, and human capital variables (Kanfer, Wanberg, & Kantrowitz, 2001). In another systematic study, a multidisciplinary framework of reemployment antecedents was grouped under labor market demand, job-seeker human capital, social capital, reemployment constraints, economic need to work, job-search intensity, clarity and quality, and employer discrimination; also, a web of direct, mediated, and moderated relationships was hypothesized with reemployment outcomes (Wanberg, Hough, & Song, 2002). Similarly, a heuristic model included three variables—biological factor, motivational factor, and job-search constraints—comprising thirteen predictors that theoretically or empirically related to job-seeking behavior and employment success (Sverko, Galic, Sersic, & Galesic, 2008).

The job-search literature also consistently finds that the unemployment insurance (UI) strongly impacts job-search behavior (e.g., Burgess & Kingston, 1976; Classen, 1977; Ehrenberg & Oaxaca, 1976; Krueger & Mueller, 2010). UI is designed to provide temporary financial support to involuntarily terminated individuals while they search for work. Although UI provides only temporary support, it encourages workers to seek higher-productivity jobs (Acemoglu & Shimer, 2000). However, UI has been criticized as reducing motivation to seek employment by reducing the cost of being unemployed (Krueger & Meyer, 2002). For example, a negative relationship was found between increased UI benefits and search time per week among more than a thousand unemployed job seekers (Barron & Gilley, 1979). For UI beneficiaries, a rise in unemployment benefits has disincentive effects on the time invested in job search (Atkinson & Micklewright, 1991).

Intervention programs are another important predictor of job-search behaviors and success. Intervention programs can aim at intensifying job-search efforts (Azrin & Beasalel, 1982), enhancing job-search skills, and facilitating transition into high-quality reemployment (e.g., Caplan, Vinokur, Price, & van Ryn, 1989; Price & Vinokur, this volume), enhancing general self-efficacy (Eden & Aviram, 1993) or reemployment self-efficacy (Yanar, Budworth, & Latham, 2009; see also Latham, Mawritz, & Locke, this volume), and strengthening goal orientation (Van Hooft & Noordzij, 2009; see also Van Hooft, this volume). These studies in general found participation in intervention programs to be associated with intensified job-search effort and better employment outcomes. However, a comparative study found that participation in guidance courses, vocational training and subsidized employment had no effect on job-search effort. Only participation in guidance courses was found to predict reemployment (Vuori & Vesalainen, 1999).

The unemployment literature has examined other antecedents of job-search behavior: employability (McArdle, Waters, Briscoe, & Hall, 2007), job-search clarity (Zikic & Saks, 2009), affectivity (Côté et al., 2006), labor market interventions (Vuori & Vesalainen, 1999), cultural background (Nesdale & Pinter, 2000), and vocational maturity (Ellis et al., 1991). Although the conceptualization and typology of unemployed job-search antecedents have evolved, the fundamental tenets have remained the same: Predictor variables influence job-search behavior, which in turn influence reemployment (Schwab et al., 1987).

In contrast to studies on job-search antecedents, studies on job-search consequences are more focused and generally categorized as reemployment and well-being. Job-search intensity and reemployment are found to be positively related (e.g., Kanfer et al., 2001). In addition, reemployment reduces financial and psychological distress and restores psychosocial functioning (e.g., Bambra & Eikemo, this volume; Kessler, Turner, & House, 1989; Paul, Hassel, & Moser, this volume; Vinokur, Caplan, & Williams, 1987). However, a recent study of unemployed job seekers in China (Song, Wanberg, Niu, & Xie, 2006) found a negative relationship between job-search intensity and reemployment duration, a counterintuitive finding attributed to China's unique government reemployment interventions. This finding calls for more research in different socioeconomic contexts.

Some have criticized the current reemployment research for overemphasizing quantitative reemployment outcomes, such as the number of job offers or the speed of reemployment, and for failing to predict meaningful variance from qualitative aspects, such as satisfaction and personal fit, with the new jobs (Kanfer et al., 2001; Vinokur & Schul, 2002; Virick & McKee-Ryan, this volume; Wanberg et al., 2002). Job-search success is indeed a multidimensional construct that includes an array of employment quality measures, including salary, the degree of match between job and education, job satisfaction, intention to turn over, and tenure (Brasher & Chen, 1999). Reemployment quality outcomes also include job improvement—that is, how well the new job compares with the old job on dimensions such as salary, distance from home, job–organization fit, and intention to turn over (Wanberg et al., 2002). A positive relationship between job-search intensity and turnover intentions was found (Wanberg et al., 2002). Another study found job-search behaviors to be negatively related to job improvement, organizational identification, turnover intentions, and career growth (Zikic & Klehe, 2006). Therefore we must pay more attention to both reemployment quality and quantity as consequences of job-search behavior.

Dynamic Job-Search Behavior of the Unemployed

Job search is a dynamic process (Barber, Daly, Giannantonio, & Phillips, 1994; Kanfer, Wanberg, & Kantrowitz, 2001; McFadyen, 1995; Saks & Ashforth, 2000; Wanberg et al., 2010) Job-search changes are associated with changes in other factors, such as affect, social support, and financial conditions. The unemployed tend to follow certain trends in their search over time. A ten-wave biweekly survey of unemployed job seekers in the United States found a decreasing but convex trend of job-search intensity. Specific job-search behaviors—such as networking, sending resumes, and searching through newspapers and the Internet—showed convex trends, while searching through employment agencies showed concave trends (Wanberg et al., 2005). The overall decreasing and convex

trend of job-search intensity was replicated in a recently published weekly survey study (Wanberg, Zhu, Kanfer, & Zhen, 2012). In contrast, an economics study found that those who were eligible for UI followed a concave-shaped job search that peaked when UI approached exhaustion, while those ineligible for UI showed a constant search over time (Krueger & Mueller, 2010),

Although *trend* is an effective way to describe dynamics, not all within-person behavior changes are systematic. Another way to describe job-search dynamics is to document the within-person variability in job-search behaviors over time. Studies using weekly, biweekly, and daily surveys have found substantial within-person variances, which suggesting that job-search behaviors fluctuate over time (Wanberg et al., 2005, 2010, 2012). For example, 47% of the variance in daily job-search time was within-person (Wanberg et al., 2010). Dynamic relationships or "within-person processes" of job search have also been examined (Bolger, Davis, & Rafaeli, 2003). For example, daily distress changes were positively associated with job-search changes the next day, although average daily distress and average job-search intensity showed no significant correlation (Song et al., 2009). Obviously, job-search processes are dynamic. Modeling and examining job-search as changing processes can bring new insights.

In the next two sections, we summarize theoretical models, research designs, and analytical approaches in examining job-search dynamics.

Theoretical Models of Dynamics in Job-Search Behaviors

Researchers have proposed various theoretical models to describe and explain changes in job-search activity. In this section, we summarize five models. The first three were originally proposed by Barber et al. (1994) in a study on college job seekers; the fourth model, on identity changes of the unemployed, was proposed by McFadyen (1995); and the last model, on self-regulation, was proposed by Kanfer et al. (2001) and Wanberg et al. (2010).

Sequential Model

The sequential model (Barber et al., 1994) conceptualizes job search as an information-seeking process occurring in sequential and systematic phases (Blau, 1993; 1994; Rees, 1966). For example, extensive searches lead to intensive searches (Rees, 1966). The generalized decision-processing model describes four phases in the job-search process: identifying an ideal occupation, planning the search, searching for and selecting the job, and confirming and committing to the decision (Power & Aldag, 1985). Active searches follow preparatory searches (Blau, 1993, 1994). Those theories share a common feature—that is, search activities evolve systematically. From an information-search perspective, job seekers start by collecting information to identify as many job opportunities as possible and then narrow their focus to acquire more specific information and apply for opportunities matching their ideal jobs (Barber et al., 1994). That is, information search shifts from extensive to intensive (Rees, 1966; Barber et al., 1994). One study proposed a series of hypotheses related to changing job-search behavior; their study of university graduates partially supported the sequential model (Barber et al., 1994): As search intensity decreased over time, job seekers relied more on informal than formal sources and sought more information about the job itself rather than information about how to obtain a job.

Saks and Ashforth (2000) extended the study of Barber et al. (1994) with a two-wave design examining the changes in preparatory and active search behavior among a group of university graduates who had not found a job in their final term. The investigators found that job seekers increased their active job-search behavior, job-search intensity, and the use of formal job sources over time.

Learning Model

The learning model (Barber et al., 1994) suggests that job seekers' increased learning over time may change job-search behaviors and strategies. It explains that initially, early job seekers may lack experience or be uncertain about how to search effectively, but over time they will learn better methods (Barber et al., 1994). The learning model predicts that job seekers will increase their search intensity over time and will rely more on informal sources as their search progresses. However, empirical evidence has failed to support those predictions. Moreover, like the sequential model, the learning model is purely descriptive. Future research must examine more specifically how learning affects job-search behavior. The conceptualization of skill-acquisition processes provides a possible avenue (Kanfer & Ackerman, 1989). Specifically, resource demands—such as attention, effort, and cognitive abilities—change as people learn how to perform tasks. For example, in an experimental study in another context, self-efficacy (which is treated as an indicator of ability) was better than goals (i.e., motivation) for predicting performance initially, but in later stages, where learning happens, goals were better than self-efficacy for predicting performance (Mitchell, Hopper, Daniels, George-Falvy, & James, 1994). In the context of job search, this finding can have significant implications for practitioners who help unemployed job seekers. For example, it would suggest that in the early job-search stage, practitioners should primarily focus on helping job seekers to increase job-search skills and confidence, while as the job search goes on, practitioners should primarily focus on helping strengthen job seekers' job-search goals. However, whether these recommendations are practical for job search is open for future empirical study.

Emotional Model

The emotional model (Barber et al., 1994) explains changes in job-search activities based on emotional reactions. This differs from cognitively focused models in its special attention to emotions and stresses. Job search is often associated with anxiety, frustration, setback, rejection, and future uncertainty (Barber et al., 1994; Caplan et al., 1989; Rynes, Bretz, & Gerhart, 1991; Stumpf, Colarelli, & Hartman, 1983). Meta-analysis also shows that job search and distress correlate positively (McKee-Ryan et al., 2005; Paul, Hassel, & Moser, this volume). Although job seekers can have both positive and negative job-search experiences (Borgen & Amundson, 1984), the negative experiences, including setbacks and obstacles, have greater impacts on daily distress levels than do positive experiences (Song & Sun, 2008). Because uncertainty and rejection are almost inevitable, the search process can be stressful. Job seekers may become frustrated and even feel hopeless if the search lasts too long. They may lower their expectations and decrease search intensity over time (Barber et al., 1994). Also, since informal resources require more social skills and self-esteem than do formal resources, the emotional model predicts that job seekers will be more likely to use formal channels if their search lasts too long. Researchers have found mixed support for the hypothesized changes in job-search intensity and no support for the predicted changes in the information sources used (Barber et al., 1994). Another finding is that job seekers experience significantly lower job-search anxiety over time, probably because they are approaching the end of their job search (Saks & Ashforth, 2000).

Research on job-search dynamics are not confined to overall change patterns. Scholars have also examined how job-search and stresses are related over time (e.g., Song et al., 2009; Wanberg et al., 2012). For example, Song et al. (2009) examined the relationship between job-search and distress using a daily diary method that involved 100 unemployed job seekers in China. They tested three models: a direct relationship model examining the effect of job search on distress, a reversed relationship model examining the impact of distress on job search, and a third variable model testing how much daily financial strain accounts for the relationship between job search and distress. Results support the direct and reversed model: job search and distress have reciprocal influences over each other in the job-search processes. Drawing on a self-regulatory framework, Wanberg et al. (2012) examined the dynamics of job-search intensity and mental health over the first 20 weeks for newly unemployed individuals. They found that changes in motivation control in any given week were significantly associated with within-person changes in search intensity and mental health, and changes in self-defeating cognition from week to week were significantly associated with mental health changes.

Phase Model of Self-Categorization and Coping

The phase model of self-categorization and coping explains how unemployed individuals self-categorize and recategorize their social identity during unemployment phases and how categorizations affect coping strategies (McFadyen, 1995). This model is based on social identity theory (Tajfel & Turner, 1979) and cognitive theory of stress and coping (Folkman & Lazarus, 1980). The model suggests that the identity of the unemployed can change over time, and self-categorization of social identity may follow different stages as unemployment becomes lengthy. At the initial stage of job loss, people tend to deny their unemployment status and categorize themselves still in terms of their former occupational identity; for example, one might still identify as "a banker." Later they tend to acknowledge that their previous occupational identity is past, yet they still define themselves in terms of their former identity; for example, one might still identify as a "former banker." As time passes, it becomes increasingly difficult for them to categorize themselves in terms of their previous occupational identity. Although they acknowledge that they are unemployed, they remain reluctant to surrender their previous identity; for example, one might identify as an "unemployed banker." The final stage, which they may fail to reach, entails a complete recategorization as "unemployed." Many fail to reach the final stage of accepting the loss of occupational identity, which then leads to long-term unemployment. In addition to time or length of unemployment, several other factors affect self-categorization and recategorization processes, including whether an individual has a previous occupational identity, a commitment to that identity, a negative perception of unemployment status, an other-group categorization, a social norm or legitimacy of categorization, and control over the situation (McFadyen, 1995). Moreover, those self-categorizations affect their primary and secondary appraisals of job loss and interact with other individual and situational factors in affecting an individual's choice and types of coping strategies and job search behaviors (McFadyen, & Thomas, 1997).

Self-Regulatory Models of Job Search

Recent job-search literature tend to conceptualize job search as a dynamic, goal-directed, self-regulatory process (Kanfer, Wanberg, & Kantrowtiz, 2001; Song, Wanberg, Niu, & Xie, 2008; Van Hoye & Saks, 2008; Wanberg, Zhu, & Van Hooft, 2010). *Job search* has been defined as "a purposive, volitional pattern of action that begins with the identification and commitment to pursuing an employment goal" (Kanfer, Wanberg, & Kantrowtiz, 2001, p. 838). Studies adopting a self-regulatory perspective have illuminated personality and motivational predictors of job-search intensity, strategies, and outcomes (Kanfer, Wanberg, & Kantrowtiz, 2001; Saks & Ashforth, 1999, 2000; Van Hooft, Born, Taris, Flier, & Blonk, 2004; van Hooft & Noordzij, 2009; Wanberg, Kanfer, & Rotundo, 1999). For example, a motivational, self-regulatory framework was proposed to account for individual difference antecedents (e.g., personality, self-esteem, locus of control, and self-efficacy) of job-search behavior and employment outcomes; the meta-analytic results showed that those who reported higher levels of job-search behavior had higher reemployment probability than those who engaged in less intensive job-search behavior (Kanfer et al., 2001). Psychological variables of conscientiousness, self-esteem, and financial need significantly predicted either job search or reemployment. A two-wave study found that self-esteem and job-search self-efficacy were related to job-search intensity and outcomes (Saks & Ashforth, 2000). A field experiment comprising 109 unemployed job seekers found that a situational focus on learning goals enhances the job-search process in terms of increasing job-search behavior and ultimately the probability of reemployment (van Hooft & Noordzij, 2009).

Since self-regulation is a dynamic process that changes over time (Lord, Diefendorff, Schmidt, & Hall, 2010), scholars have gone beyond studying individual differences variables to examine changes in within-person job-search intensity and the cognitive and affective mechanisms governing such changes (e.g., Wanberg et al., 2010; Wanberg, Glomb, Song, & Sorenson, 2005). For example, guided by the theory of planned behavior (Ajzen, 1991), a ten-wave study examined the role of cognitive factors in affecting the dynamics of job-search behavior and outcomes. It found that job-search intentions mediated the relationship between subjective norms (i.e., the attitude towards the job search of significant others) and job-search self-efficacy (i.e., self-confidence in conducting the job-search behaviors well) in predicting job-search intensity, which predicted probabilities of reemployment (Wanberg et al., 2005). Furthermore, core self-evaluation (Judge, Erez, & Bono, 1998) was also found to be related to average job-search intensity over time. Recently Wanberg et al. (2010) conducted a daily diary study to examine a dynamic model of job-search effort based on social cognitive theory (Bandura, 1997) and control theory (Carver & Scheier, 1998). Their model explained how perceptions of daily job-search progress affect emotional experience and reemployment self-efficacy, which in turn impact the next-day job-search effort. They also modeled the moderating role of financial hardship, employment commitment, and action-state orientation in affecting the relationship of job-search progress, affect, and self-efficacy to job-search effort.

Moreover, several prominent self-regulation theorists have suggested that self-regulation occurs in phases (Diefendorff, & Lord, 2008; Klein, Austin, & Cooper, 2008). Bandura (1997), for example, distinguished preparatory stages and performance stages and suggests that self-efficacy, an important behavioral predictor in job search, leads to different behavioral effort or intensity in each stage. Austin and Vancouver (1996) identified four key processes of goal striving: goal establishment, planning, goal striving, and goal revision. Vancouver, More, and Yoder (2008) suggest that individuals use their efficacy beliefs differently in different stages. For example, self-efficacy was positively related to effort expenditure in the goal-establishment stage but negatively related to effort expenditure in the goal-planning stage. However, we are unaware of any job-search studies testing this proposition. Gollwitzer's (1990) Rubicon model suggests that goal pursuit could be viewed as a temporal path starting with choosing action goals through a sequential phase of planning, executing, and evaluating actions. Different mindsets are associated with different phases and lead to different cognitive and behavioral patterns (see Gollwitzer, 1990, for more information). In particular, Gollwitzer's model concerns the lack of correspondence between intention and action, and emphasizes the role of implementation intention. In a longitudinal study of unemployed individuals in Netherlands, Van Hooft et al. (2005) specifically examined and found support for the mediation role of implementation intention in the link between job-search intention and job-search behavior.

Self-regulation processes reflect the dynamic transaction between person and environment (Bandura, 1997). Indeed, contextual factors have been conceptualized as important predictors of job search from a self-regulatory perspective of job search in addition to the personal factors reviewed earlier (Kanfer et al., 2001; Saks, 2005). However, the number of contextual factors examined is rather limited, including financial difficulty and social support (Kanfer et al., 2001). Recently Wanberg, Basbug, Van Hooft, & Samtani (2012) conducted a qualitative study on the job-search context among a group of professional-level job seekers and provided in-depth understanding of five layers of job-search context. It will be useful for future quantitative studies to include some of these contextual factors in examining the job-search process.

Overall, these studies attest to the complexity of the psychological mechanisms governing the job-search process. To examine job-search dynamics, we need both the conceptual models that we have reviewed and advanced methodologies to accommodate analyses of dynamic data required for testing those models. In addition, prior job-search studies primarily focused on job-search behavior and intensity and paid less attention to the quality of job-search behavior (Wanberg, 2012; Van Hooft, Wanberg, & Van Hoye, 2013). Thus, in applying self-regulation models, it will be especially useful for researchers to pay attention to both the quantity and quality of job-search behavior. Below we discuss the methodologies that can be used to study the dynamic job-search processes.

Methodologies of Job-Search Dynamics

This section summarizes the methodologies, including research designs and analytic strategies, currently used in studying job-search dynamics.

Research Designs

Survey methods for studying job-search dynamics usually involve repeated surveys over a period of time. These designs include multiwave longitudinal methods, diary methods, and experience sampling methods.

MULTIWAVE LONGITUDINAL STUDY

Job-search dynamics are most widely studied using multiwave longitudinal methods (e.g., Creed, King, Hood, & McKenzie, 2009; Prussia, Fugate, & Kinicki, 2001; Wanberg, Kanfer, & Banas, 2000). This type of study requires researchers to collect data at least twice, with time gaps between consecutive measures spanning weeks to years. For example, van Hooft, Born, Taris, Flier, and Blonk (2004) surveyed participants twice to investigate job-search behavior and its antecedents among employed and unemployed people. Sverko, Galic, Sersic, and Galesic (2008) used three waves to investigate the relationship between job-search behavior and reemployment in Croatia. Although studies with two waves of surveys are more suited than cross-sectional designs to examine change, method scholars have suggested a minimum of three waves to uncover the complexities of change (Chan, 1998; Ployhart & Vandenberg, 2010). Recognizing that studies with fewer waves are insufficient in capturing the entire dynamic job-search process, Wanberg et al. (2005, 2012) repeated surveys biweekly for more than ten waves.

DIARY METHOD

Although multiwave longitudinal studies are well suited for understanding the dynamic aspect of job-search behavior, they cannot capture daily life events that may substantially impact job-search behavior and its outcomes. To overcome such limitation, some studies use diary methodologies to survey participants daily and continuously, perhaps for weeks (Bolger, Davis, & Rafaeli, 2003). For example, Song et al. (2009) used the diary method to examine the relationship between job search and distress of 100 unemployed job seekers in China. Participants completed paper-and-pencil surveys daily for 14 consecutive days. The study provided an in-depth examination of the nature and directionality of the relationship between job search and distress of unemployed job seekers on a day-to-day basis and illuminated the dynamic nature of the relationship. In another study, Wanberg et al. (2010) sent participants daily emails with a link to an online survey for reporting their job-search behavior at the end of each day for 3 consecutive weeks. The diary method is particularly suitable to examine within- or cross-day associations between motivational or situational factors (e.g., daily self-efficacy and daily social support) and job-search effort.

EXPERIENCE SAMPLING METHOD

The experience sampling method (ESM) studies survey participants multiple times a day for several days. Such studies are suitable for studying individuals' subjective experiences of interacting in natural environments in a way that ensures ecological validity (Csikszentmihalyi, Larson, & Prescott, 1977). Compared with diary methods, experience sampling allows researchers to collect data enabling them to study within-day dynamics and examine reported events and experiences in natural and spontaneous contexts. Thus ESM can reduce retrospective reporting biases (Bolger et al., 2003) and provides information complementary to that obtained by traditional designs (Reis, 1994). However, intensive surveys are usually costly and time-consuming, so few studies in the unemployment research field have adopted this strategy. The earliest ESM related to unemployment experience that we have identified concerns job loss and mood (Kirchler, 1984). The study asked thirty unemployed participants to report their current mood, predominant needs, and several other psychological variables at randomly selected time points during the first 6 months of unemployment. Haworth and Millar (1986) did another early study investigating intrinsic job-search motivation by asking young unemployed adults to respond to the survey six times daily for 8 days. These ESM studies provide empirical evidence at the within-person daily level, which is equally important but less documented in the literature.

The above three survey strategies vary in terms of time span and intensity. In general, multiwave surveys tend to cover a longer period of time and to be less intensive in terms of number of repeated surveys than diary studies, while ESM surveys tend to cover a shorter span and be more intensive than the other two. One critical consideration in selecting the survey strategy is how dynamic the focal phenomenon under study is. For example, mood is a fleeting construct, so a study on the relationship between mood and job search is better studied using ESM or the diary method. Reemployment success is much less changeable than mood. It tends to be realized months or even years after starting of the job search. So a study on the relationship between job-search behavior and reemployment is better studied using multiwave surveys with a time gap of several months between consecutive surveys.

Analytic Strategies

To study job-search dynamics, we must analyze data with repeated measures. Analytic strategies of job-search dynamics include repeated measure general linear modeling (GLM), multilevel modeling, latent growth modeling (LGM), and survival analysis (SA). A repeated measure GLM is useful when the primary interest is modeling the mean change of unemployed individuals over time. For example, Sverko, Galica, Sersic, and Galesic (2008) repeatedly measured individuals' employment status in two consecutive years and tested how it was influenced by a set of demographic, motivational, and job-constraint variables.

The multilevel model (also called hierarchical linear modeling, or HLM) is a more flexible and powerful approach for modeling change. It handles the violations of OLS error assumptions by tearing apart the within- and between-individual variance and examining their effects separately (Bliese & Ployhart, 2002; Hofmann, Griffin, & Gavin, 2000; Littell, Milliken, Stroup, & Wolfinger, 1996; Raudenbush, Brennan, & Barnett, 1995). In a recent study, for example, Wanberg et al. (2010) used HLM to test the within-individual relationships among perceived search progress, affect, reemployment efficacy, next-day time spent in search, and the cross-level moderating effects of financial hardship, employment commitment, and action-state orientation on the within-individual relationships.

Structure equation modeling (SEM) (Jöreskog, 1977) has a unique advantage in managing measurement error in the estimation process by using item-level information. Latent intercept and change variables may be used in any role—independent, dependent, mediating, and/or moderating. For example, to test a complicated model that comprises three patterns of crossover effect of distress caused by unemployment (i.e., direct crossover, mediating crossover, and common stressor mechanisms), Song et al. (2011) used multilevel structural equation modeling for analysis (MSEM) (Muthen & Satorra,

1989). Such a strategy accommodates the hierarchical data structure with multiple observations nested within each individual and tests the three mechanisms explaining distress crossover between partners simultaneously.

The statistic model of survival analysis, also called the hazard model, examining event change and duration, has been used to study reemployment (Singer & Willett, 2003). Wanberg et al. (2005), for example, used a proportional-hazard model (Cox, 1972) to examine reemployment probability and speed. Similarly, Pollmann-Schult and Büchel (2005) used survival analysis to monitor the transition from unemployment to employment.

One Future Direction: To Study Job Search as Behavioral Episodes

One potentially fruitful direction to enhance the study of job-search dynamics is to conceptualize and empirically examine job search as behavioral episodes. Psychology has long promoted using episodes as the natural unit of conceptualization and for the analysis of behaviors (Barker, 1963). However, organizational scholars have only recently seriously embraced this approach. In a seminal conceptual paper, Beal, Weiss, Barros, and MacDermid (2005) conceptualized job performance as behavioral episodes that are thematically organized around work-relevant immediate goals. In the work and family literature, Maertz and Boyar (2011) defined work–family conflict episodes as incidents or occurrences of work–family conflict. The episodic approach provides a refined assessment of within-person variability of behavior.

Job-search scholars generally agree that job search is an unfolding process of sequential events: For each vacancy lead, individuals will look for job information, contact the employer, submit the application, go through the job interview, and decide whether to accept or reject the offer. These search activities are behavioral episodes that have clear, immediate goals and time boundaries (Kanfer et al., 2001). Job search has been conceptualized as the unfolding process of a series of behavioral episodes: however, in terms of measurement, it usually concerns the intensity or effort of job-search activity over a specific time period. This type of lump-sum record of intensity and effort tends to neglect unique properties of each job-search activity and to mask the sequence of behaviors in pursuing each job lead. To address this research gap, we need reports of daily job-search events and the affect associated with those events across several consecutive days. We should use intensive data-collection methods such as the diary method (Bolger, et al., 2003) and the day-reconstruction method (DRM) (Kahneman, Krueger, Schkade, Schwarz, & Stone, 2004). Here we briefly illustrate two studies we conducted that tracked job-search episodes over time.

In the first study, we studied college job seekers using the DRM in a diary format to examine job-search behavioral episodes across 5 days. Participants' daily job-search events and associated psychological experiences (e.g., emotions) were reported at the end of each day (Song & Sun, 2008). Using this method, we were able to examine the refined relationship between particular job-search activity and related affect.

The second study targeted a particular job-search behavior: the job interview (Li, Lim, Song, & Chen, 2013). Immediately before and after each scheduled job interview across several months, college job seekers reported their emotions and fairness assessments of their interviews. The study showed that their fairness perceptions of the last interview were positively associated with their fairness expectations of the next interview and, in turn, influenced their fairness perception of that job interview. Although both studies examined college job seekers, similar designs can be applied to samples of unemployed individuals. We believe such effort can help us better understand the pattern of job-search behavior change and its covariates.

Researchers have long examined experiences that unemployed individuals endure during the job-search process. We now have a much better understanding on how unemployed individuals conduct their job search—the antecedents as well as outcomes of their job-search behaviors. Such knowledge can help employment counselors, job-search agencies, and policymakers better design and implement intervention programs to promote effective job search. The emerging dynamic perspective brings new insights to the current understanding. Scholars should consider these new findings and embrace more innovative perspectives and methods for revealing the nature of job-search behavior. We also believe that an understanding of the dynamic aspect of the job search can help employment practitioners design and implement more effective reemployment-intervention programs to help job seekers to remain resilient and motivated over their potentially lengthy and rough journey toward reemployment.

References

Addison, J. T., & Portugal, P. (2002). Job search methods and outcomes. *Oxford Economics*, 54, 505–533.

Ajzen, I. (1985). From intentions to actions: A theory of planned behavior. In J. Kuhl & J. Beckmann (Eds.), *Action control: From cognition to behavior* (pp. 11–39). Berlin: Springer.

Ajzen, I. (1991). The theory of planned behavior. *Organizational behavior and human decision processes*, 50(2), 179–211.

Austin, J. T., & Vancouver, J. B. (1996). Goal constructs in psychology: Structure, process, and content. *Psychological Bulletin*, 120(3), 338–375.

Azrin, N. H., & Beasalel, V. B. (1982). *Finding a job*. Berkeley, CA: Ten Speed Press.

Atkinson, A. B., & Micklewright, J. (1991). Unemployment compensation and labor market transitions: A critical review. *Journal of Economic Literature*, 29(4), 1679–1727.

Bandura, A. (1997). *Self-efficacy: The exercise of control*. New York: Freeman.

Barber, A., Daly, C., Giannantonio, C., & Phillips, J. (1994). Job search activities: An examination of changes over time. *Personnel Psychology*, 47(4), 739–766.

Barron, J. M., & Gilley, O. W. (1979). The effect of unemployment insurance on the search process. *Industrial and Labor Relations Review*, 32, 363–366.

Beal, D. J., Trougakos, J. P., Weiss, H. M. & Green, S. G. (2006). Episodic processes in emotional labor: Perceptions of affective delivery and regulation strategies. *Journal of Applied Psychology*, 91(5), 1053–1065.

Beal, D. J., Weiss, H. M., Barros, E., & MacDermid, S. M. (2005). An episodic process model of affective influences on performance. *Journal of Applied Psychology*, 90(6), 1054–1068.

Blau, G. (1993). Further exploring the relationship between job search and voluntary individual turnover. *Personnel Psychology*, 46(2), 313–330.

Blau, G. (1994). Testing a two-dimensional measure of job-search behavior. *Organizational Behavior & Human Decision Processes*, 59, 288–312.

Blau, D. M., & Robins, P. K. (1990). Job search outcomes for the employed and unemployed. *Journal of Political Economy*, 98, 637–655.

Bolger, N., Davis, A., & Rafaeli, E. (2003). Diary methods: Capturing life as it is lived. *Annual Review of Psychology*, 54, 579–616.

Borgen, W. A., & Amundson, N. E. (1984). *The experience of unemployment*. Toronto: Nelson Canada.

Brasher, E. E., & Chen, P. Y. (1999). Evaluation of success criteria in job search: A process evaluation. *Journal of Occupational and Organizational Psychology*, 72, 57–70.

Burgess, P., & Kingston, J. (1976). The impact of unemployment benefits on reemployment success. *Industrial and Labor Relations Review*, 29, 25–31.

Burnett, J. (1994). *Idle hands: The experience of unemployed: 1790–1990*. London and New York: Routledge.

Caplan, R. D., Vinokur, A. D., Price, R. H., & Van Ryn, M. (1989). Job seeking, reemployment, and mental health: A randomized field experiment in coping with job-loss. *Journal of Applied Psychology*, 74, 759–769.

Carver, C. S., & Scheier, M. F. (1998). *On the self-regulation of behavior*. New York: Cambridge University Press.

Chan, D. (1998). The conceptualization and analysis of change over time: An integrative approach incorporating longitudinal mean and covariance structures analysis (LMACS) and multiple indicator latent growth modeling (MLGM). *Organizational Research Methods, 1*, 421–483.

Classen, J. (1977). The effect of unemployment insurance on the duration of unemployment and subsequent earnings. *Industrial and Labor Relations Review*, 30, 438–444.

Cox, D. R. (1972). Regression models and life-tables (with discussion). *Journal of the Royal Statistical Society*, 34, 187–202.

Creed, P. A., King, V., Hood, M., & McKenzie, R. (2009). Goal orientation, self-regulation strategies, and job-seeking intensity in unemployed adults. *Journal of Applied Psychology*, 94, 806–813.

Crossley, C. D., & Highhouse, S. (2005). Relation of job search and choice process with subsequent satisfaction. *Journal of Economic Psychology*, 26, 255–268.

Csikszentmihalyi, M., & Larson, R. (1992. Validity and reliability of the experience sampling method. In deVries, M. (Ed.), *The experience of psychopathology: investigating mental disorders in their natural settings* (pp. 43–57). New York: Cambridge University Press.

Csikszentmihalyi, M., Larson, R., & Prescott, S. (1977). The ecology of adolescent activity and experience. *Journal of Youth and Adolescence*, 6, 281–294.

Devine, T. J., & Kiefer, N. M. (1991). *Empirical labor economics: The search approach*. New York and Oxford, UK: Oxford University Press.

Devine, T. J., & Kiefer, N. M. (1993). The empirical status of job search theory. *Labour Economics*, 1(1), 3–24.

Eden, D., & Aviram, A. (1993). Self efficacy training to speed reemployment: Helping people to help themselves, *Journal of Applied Psychology*, 78, 352–360.

Ehrenberg, R., & Oaxaca, R. (1976). Unemployment insurance, duration of unemployment and subsequent wage gain. *American Economic Review*, 66, 754–766.

Ellis, R. A., Heneman, H. G., & Lascola, C. S. (1991). Antecedents and consequences of job search intensity. Paper presented at the meeting of the academy of management, Miami, Florida.

Fernandez, R., Castilla, E. J., & Moore, P. (2000). Social capital at work: Networks and employment at a phone center. *American Journal of Sociology*, 105, 1288–1356.

Franzen, A., & Hangartner, D. (2006). Social networks and labour market outcomes: The non-monetary benefits of social capital. *European Sociological Review*, 22, 353–368.

Folkman, S., & Lazarus, R. S. (1980). An analysis of coping in a middle-aged community sample. *Journal of health and social behavior*, 21(3), 219–239.

Gollwitzer, P. M. (1990). Action phases and mind-sets. In E. T. Higgins & R. M. Sorrentino (Eds.), *The handbook of motivation and cognition: Foundations of social behavior* (Vol. 2, pp. 53–92). New York: Guilford.

Gowan, M. A., Riordan, C. M., & Gatewood, R. D. (1999). Test of a model of coping with involuntary job-loss following a company closing. *Journal of Applied Psychology*, 84, 75–86.

Hoye, G. V., & Saks, A. M. (2008). Job search as goal-directed behavior: Objectives and methods. *Journal of Vocational Behavior*, 73(3), 358–367.

Jahoda, M. (1982). *Employment and unemployment: A social psychological analysis*. New York: Academic.

Judge, T. A., Erez, A., Bono, J. E., & Thoresen, C. J. (2002). Are measures of self-esteem, neuroticism, locus of control, and generalized self-efficacy indicators of a common core construct? *Journal of Personality and Social Psychology*, 83(3), 693–710.

Kahneman, D., Krueger, D., Schkade, A., Schwarz, N., & Stone, A. (2004). A survey method for characterizing daily life experience: The day reconstruction method. *Science*, 306, 1776–1780.

Kanfer, R., & Ackerman, P. (1989). Motivation and cognitive abilities: An integrative/aptitude-treatment interaction approach to skill acquisition. *Journal of Applied Psychology*, 74(4), 657–690.

Kanfer, R., Wanberg, C., & Kantrowitz, T. (2001). Job search and employment: A personality-motivational analysis and meta-analytic review. *Journal of Applied Psychology*, 86(5), 837–855.

Kessler, R. C., Turner, J. B., & House, R. H. (1989). Unemployment, reemployment and emotional functioning in a community sample. *American Sociological Review*, 54, 648–657.

Kinicki, A. J., & Latack, J. C. (1990). Explication of the construct of coping with involuntary job loss. *Journal of Vocational Behavior*, 36, 336–360.

Kirchler, E. (1985). Job loss and mood. *Journal of Economic Psychology*, 6, 9–25.

Koen, J., Klehe U. C., Van Vianen, A. E. M., Zikic, J., & Nauta, A. (2010). Job search strategies and reemployment quality: The impact of career adaptability. *Journal of Vocational Behavior*, 77, 126–139.

Korpi, T. (2001). Good friends in bad times? Social networks and job search among the unemployed in Sweden. *Acta Sociologica*, 44, 157–170.

Krueger, A. B., & Mueller, A. (2010). Job search and unemployment insurance: New evidence from time use data. *Journal of Public Economics*, 94, 298–307.

Lazarus, R., & Folkman, S. (1984). *Stress, appraisal, and coping*. New York: Springer.

Leana, C. R., & Feldman, D. C. (1988). Individual responses to job loss: Perceptions, reaction, and coping behaviors. *Journal of Management*, 14, 375–389.

Leana, C. R., & Feldman, D. C. (1995). Finding new jobs after a plant closing: Antecedents and outcomes of the occurrence and quality of reemployment. *Human Relations*, 48, 1381–1401.

Lin, N. 2001. *Building a network theory of social capital*. In N. Lin, K. Cook, R. S. Burt (Eds.), *Social capital: Theory and research* (pp. 3–29). Hawthorne, NY: Aldine de Gruyter.

Lord, R. G., Diefendorff, J. M., Schmidt, A. M., & Hall, R. J. (2010). Self-regulation at work. *Annual review of psychology*, 61, 543–568.

Maertz, C. P., & Boyar, S. L. (2011). Work-family conflict, enrichment, and balance under "levels" and "episodes" approaches. *Journal of Management*, 37(1): 68–98.

McArdle, S., Waters, L., Briscoe, J. P., & Hall, D. T. (2007). Explicability during unemployment: Adaptability, career identity and human and social capital. *Journal of Vocational Behavior*, 71, 247–264.

McFadyen, R. G. (1995). Coping with threatened identities: Unemployed people's self-categorizations. *Current Psychology*, 14(3), 233–256.

McFadyen, R. G., & Thomas, J. P. (1997). Economic and psychological models of job search behavior of the unemployed. *Human Relations*, 50(12), 1461–1484.

McKee-Ryan, F., Song, Z., Wanberg, C. R., & Kinicki, A. J. (2005). Psychological and physical well-being during unemployment: a meta-analytic study. *Journal of Applied Psychology*, 90(1), 53–76.

Mitchell, T. R., Hopper, H., Daniels, D., George-Falvy, J., & James, L. R. (1994). Predicting self-efficacy and performance during skill acquisition. *Journal of Applied Psychology*, 79(4): 506–517.

Mitchell, T. R., & James, L. R. (2001). Building better theory: Time and the specification of when things happen. *The Academy of Management Review*, 26(4), 530–547.

Nesdale, D., & Pinter, K. (2000). Self efficacy and job seeking activities in unemployed ethnic youth. *The Journal of Social Psychology*, 140, 608–614.

OECD, OECD Harmonized unemployment rate, news release. October 2012. Available at: http://www.oecd.org/std/labourstats/HUR_NR10e12.pdf (Retrieved at March 6, 2013.)

Paul, K. I., & Moser, K. (2009). Unemployment impairs metal health: Meta analyses. *Journal of Vocational Behavior*, 74, 264–282.

Ployhart, R. E., & Vandenberg, R. J. (2010). Longitudinal research, the theory, design, and analysis of change, *Journal of Management*, 36, 94–120.

Pollmann-Schult, M., & Büchel, F. (2005). Unemployment benefits, unemployment duration and subsequent job quality: Evidence from West Germany. *Acta Sociologica*, 48, 21–39.

Price, R. H., Choi J. N., Lim, S. (2007). Beyond the iron rice bowl: Life stage and family dynamics in unemployed Chinese workers. In G. Lee and M. Warner (Eds.), *Unemployment in China: Economy, human resources and labor Markets*. New York: Routledge.

Prussia, G. E., Fugate, M., Kinicki, A. (2001). Explication of the coping goal construct: Implications for coping and reemployment. *Journal of Applied Psychology*, 86, 1179–1190.

Rees, A. (1966). Information networks in labor markets. *American Economic Review*, 56, 559–566.

Reis, H. T. (1994). Domains of experience: Investigating relationship processes from three perspectives. In R. Erber & R. Gilmore (Eds.), *Theoretical frameworks in personal relationships* (pp. 87–110). Mahwah, NJ: Erlbaum.

Rynes, S. L., Bretz, R. D. Jr., & Gerhart, B. (1991). The importance of recruitment in job choice: A different way of looking. *Personnel Psychology*, 44(3), 487–521.

Saks, A. M. (2006). Multiple predictors and criteria of job search success. *Journal of Vocational Behavior*, 68, 400–415.

Saks, A., & Ashforth, B. (2000). Change in job search behaviors and employment outcomes. *Journal of Vocational Behavior*, 56(2), 277–287.

Schwab, D. P., Rynes, S. L., & Aldag, R. J. (1987). Theories and research on job search and choice. *Research in Personnel and Human Resources Management*, 5, 129–166.

Singer, J. D., & Willett, J. B. (2003). *Applied longitudinal data analysis: Modeling change and event occurrence*. Oxford, UK: Oxford University Press.

Song, Z. L., Foo, M. D., Uy, M. A., & Sun, S. H. (2011). Unraveling the daily stress crossover between unemployed individuals and their employed spouses. *Journal of Applied Psychology*, 96(1), 151–168.

Song, Z., & Li, X. (2010). *Expectations and perceptions of organizational justice across job interviews*. Singapore: National University of Singapore.

Song, Z., & Sun, S. (2008, April). Job search and affective reactions: A diary study on college graduate job seekers. Paper presented at the 23th Annual Society for Industrial and Organizational Psychology, San Francisco.

Song, Z., Uy, M. A., Zhang, S., & Shi, K. (2009). Daily job search and psychological distress: Evidence from China. *Human Relations*, 62(8), 1171–1197.

Song, Z., Wanberg, C. R., Niu, X., & Xie, Y. (2006). Action–state orientation and the theory of planned behavior: A study of job search in China. *Journal of Vocational Behavior*, 68, 490–503.

Stevens, C. K., & Beach, L. R. (1996). Job search and job selection. In R. Beach & P. Lee Roy (Eds.), Decision making in the workplace: A unified perspective (pp. 33–47). Hillsdale, NJ: Erlbaum.

Stevens, C. K., & Turban, D. B. (2001). Impact of job seekers' search strategies and tactics on search success. Paper presented at the annual conference of the Society for Industrial and Organizational Psychology.

Stone, A. A., Schwartz, J. E., Schwarz, N., Schkade, D., Krueger, A., & Kahneman, D. (2006). A population approach to the study of emotion: Diurnal rhythms of a working day examined with the day reconstruction method. *Emotion*, 4, 39–149.

Stumpf, S. A., Colarelli, S. M., & Hartman, K. (1983). Development of the Career Exploration Survey (CES). *Journal of Vocational Behavior*, 22(2), 191–226.

Sverko, B., Galic, Z., Sersic, D. M., & Galesic, M. (2008). Unemployed people in search of a job: Reconsidering the role of search behavior. *Journal of Vocational Behavior*, 72, 415–428.

Tajfel, H., & Turner, J. C. (1979). An integrative theory of intergroup conflict. In W. G. Austin & S. Worchel (Eds.), *The social psychology of intergroup relations* (pp. 33–47). Monterey, CA: Brooks/Cole.

Van Hooft, E. A. J., Born, M. P., Taris, T. W., Van der Flier, H., & Blonk, R. W. B. (2004). Predictors of job search behavior among employed and unemployed people. *Personnel Psychology*, 57, 25–59.

Van Hooft, E. A. J., & Noordzij, G. (2009). The effect of goal orientation on job search and reemployment: A field experiment among unemployed job seekers. *Journal of Applied Psychology*, 94, 1581–1590.

Vinokur, A., Caplan, R. D., & Williams, C. C. (1987). Effects of recent and past stresses on mental health: Coping with unemployment among Vietnam veterans and nonveterans. *Journal of Applied Social Psychology*, 17, 710–730.

Vinokur, A. D., & Caplan, R. D. (1987). Attitudes and social support: Determinants of job-seeking behavior and well-being among the unemployed. *Journal of Applied Social Psychology*, 17, 1007–1024.

Vinokur, A., Price, R. H., & Caplan, R. D. (1996). Hard times and hurtful partners: How financial strain affects depression and relationship satisfaction of unemployed persons and their spouses. *Journal of Personality and Social Psychology*, 71, 166–179.

Vinokur, A., & Schul, Y. (2002). The web of coping resources and pathways to reemployment following a job loss. *Journal of Occupational Health Psychology*, 7, 68–83.

Vuori, J., & Vesalainen, J. (1999). Labor market interventions as predictors of reemployment: Job seeking activity, and psychological distress among the unemployed. *Journal of Occupational and Organizational Psychology*, 72, 523–538.

Wanberg, C. R. (1997). Antecedents and outcomes of coping behaviors among unemployed and reemployed individuals. *Journal of Applied Psychology*, 82, 731–744.

Wanberg, C. R. (2012). The individual experience of unemployment. *Annual Review of Psychology*, 63, 369–396.

Wanberg, C. R., Glomb, T., Song, Z., & Sorenson, S. (2005). Job search persistence during unemployment: A ten wave longitudinal study. *Journal of Applied Psychology*, 90, 411–430.

Wanberg, C. R., Hough, L., & Song, Z. (2002). Predictive validity of a multidisciplinary model of reemployment success. *Journal of Applied Psychology*, 87, 1100–1133.

Wanberg, C. R., Kanfer, R., & Banas, J. T. (2000). Predictors and outcomes of networking intensity among unemployed job seekers. *Journal of Applied Psychology*, 85, 491–503.

Wanberg, C. R., Kanfer, R., & Rotundo, M. (1999). Unemployed individuals: Motives, job search competencies, and job search constraints as predictors of job seeking and reemployment. *Journal of Applied Psychology*, 84, 897–910.

Wanberg, C. R., Watt, J. D., & Rumsey, D. J. (1996). Individuals without jobs: An empirical study of job-seeking behavior and reemployment. *Journal of Applied Psychology*, 81, 76–87.

Wanberg, C. R., Zhang, Z., & Diehn, E. W. (2010). Development of the "getting ready for your next job" inventory for unemployed individuals. *Personnel psychology*, 63, 439–478.

Wanberg, C. R., Zhu, J., & Van Hooft, A. J. E. (2010). The job search grind: Perceived progress, self-reactions, and self-regulation of search effort. *Academy of Management Journal*, 53, 788–807.

Wieczorkowska, G., & Burnstein, E. (2004). Hunting for a job: How individual differences in foraging strategies influence the length of unemployment group. *Processes & Intergroup Relations*, 7, 305–315.

Zikic, J., & Saks, A. M. (2009). Job search and social cognitive theory: The role of career-relevant activities. *Journal of Vocational Behavior*, 74, 117–127.

Special Populations

Too Old to Tango? Job Loss and Job Search Among Older Workers

Ute-Christine Klehe, Irene E. De Pater, Jessie Koen, *and* Mari Kira

Abstract

Older workers are often shielded from job loss by high tenure, yet are struck particularly harshly when seeking reemployment after job loss. This article combines earlier research on coping with job loss and job search with insights on employability for older workers. We outline the situation of older workers, highlighting their vulnerability to possible job-loss and to stereotypes that may lower their perceived employability. Then we outline how this may place older workers in precarious situations regarding (a) the threat of losing their jobs, (b) suffering from loss of nonmonetary benefits (or latent functions) associated with work, (c) having different and fewer coping options than younger job-seekers, and (d) facing fewer chances of finding reemployment. Older workers face an uphill battle when searching for reemployment, which is partially explained by retirement as an alternative coping reaction to age-related stereotypes, discrimination that undermines older workers' employability, and other factors.

Key Words: older workers, job loss, job search, employability, age-related stereotypes, discrimination

Across many occupations and industries, employment is not what it used to be (Hall 1996; Lippmann, 2008; Rubin & Brody, 2005). Lifetime employment has become the exception rather than the norm in a world of technological advances, global competition, state deregulation, and constantly changing market conditions—thus affecting staffing needs in organizations (Donkin, 2010). Flexible short-term contracts have become quite common (e.g., Rubin & Brody, 2005; Sparrow, 2000; Tetrick & Barling, 1995). Layoffs and downsizing—intentional and deliberate organizational decisions to reduce the workforce (Cameron, Freeman, & Mishra, 1991) —are making the nature and existence of employees' jobs less certain (Probst, 2003).

Job loss and unemployment are among the worst stressors that any employee can encounter during their working life (e.g., Probst, 2005), and the search for employment (or reemployment) is often a process troubled with setbacks and disappointments. Yet, not all groups of workers face the same likelihood and consequences of job loss. In this chapter, we focus on the job loss and job search process among older workers who may have organized their whole careers around stable career models (Lippmann, 2008; Rubin & Brody, 2005) and who, due to stereotypes pertaining to their employability (McFadyen, 1995, 1995; Posthuma & Campion, 2009), may face even greater barriers toward suitable reemployment. For this purpose, we first outline the situation of older workers in the workforce, highlighting their vulnerability to a possible job-loss. Then, we will draw on earlier conceptual work on job loss and coping with job loss (Jahoda, 1982; Latack, Kinicki, & Prussia, 1995) in order to depict a chronological process model of anticipatory job insecurity, job loss, and subsequent unemployment (see Figure 24.1). At each stage of the process, we outline the general situation, challenges, and tasks that affect workers in general and older workers in particular. We especially outline the losses that

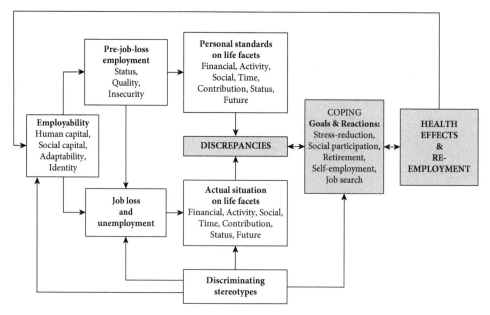

Figure 24.1 A process model of older job-seekers starting position in terms of stereotypes, employment situation, and employability, their job loss, coping responses, and outcomes.

older workers experience due to job loss and unemployment and review the consequences of these losses for unemployed people's psychological and physical health. We also recognize the different coping options available to older workers in order to reestablish their wellbeing.

The Precarious Situation of Older Workers: Employability and Stereotypes

In a not so distant past, many workers could rely on the same organization to offer income and employment throughout their entire careers. Today, such job security is the exception rather than the norm, and workers need to increasingly manage and rely on their own employability, that is, their ability *"to deal effectively with the career-related changes occurring in today's economy"* (Fugate, Kinicki, & Ashforth, 2004, p. 14). While various models on employability differ somewhat, most of them understand this ability as a multidimensional concept consisting of workers' social and human capital, their personal adaptability, and their identity narratives. Unfortunately, stereotypes about older workers often suggest that they are less employable than their younger colleagues. In the following discussion, we describe these stereotypes in connection with the various dimensions of employability. Subsequently, we outline how the alleged lower employability of older workers may place them in a precarious situation in regard to (a) the

threat of losing their jobs; (b) suffering particularly harshly from the loss of nonmonetary benefits (or latent functions) associated with work, such as time structure, social contacts, collective purpose, identity, and activity (Jahoda, 1982); (c) having different and possibly fewer coping options available to them; and (d) facing fewer chances of finding reemployment (see Figure 24.1).

Social capital. Social capital, the goodwill inherent in social networks (Fugate et al., 2004, p. 23), depicts components such as recognition by important key figures, but also more plainly the sheer size, strength, and quality of one's social network. As we will discuss in more detail in the section on job-search strategies, social network features will also play a major role in older unemployed workers' job-search efforts, given that social networks tend to decrease with age and with unemployment (Creed & Macintyre, 2001; Paul & Batinic, 2010) and that relying on good networks is often one of the most successful job-search initiatives that we know (Van Hoye, van Hooft, & Lievens, 2009).

Human capital—costs, future investments, and performance. A prime component of most employability models is some form of human capital: properties of a person that can be acquired through training and experience, and that can be assessed, documented, and sometimes even formally credited (Fugate et al., 2004). Age itself is often included in this category, though as a risk rather than a resource factor (Fugate et al., 2004; see also Latack et al., 1995). Other components include education, job performance, organization tenure, work experience, training, and knowledge, skills, and abilities (Fugate et al., 2004) with a particular focus on occupational expertise (Defillippi & Arthur, 1994; van der Heijde & van der Heijden, 2006). Especially relevant in this regard are "portable skills," that is, knowledge, skills, and abilities that are transferable to other contexts.

Older workers may lack—or at least be thought to lack—some major aspects of human capital, for instance by lacking an in-depth education of their profession's latest conceptualizations, methods, and practices (Patrickson & Ranzijn, 2003). On the other hand, older employees often have accumulated a higher tenure at the employing organization, and their loyalty and accumulated job- and organization-specific human capital justifies a certain status, security, and income (Becker, 1962; Munnell, Sass, Soto, & Zhivan, 2006; Valletta, 1999).

A downside of this status, however, is that older employees often enjoy considerably higher salaries and benefits than younger workers (e.g., Hirsch, Macpherson, & Hardy, 2000; Minda, 1997) and are thus more costly to an organization. Following cost-saving arguments, replacing older employees with younger ones is sometimes seen as a measure to reduce costs by decreasing wages and circumventing pension payouts. Since most people aim at earnings comparable to their last job when searching for reemployment, higher incomes in their last jobs might set this reservation wage of older workers at a higher level than that of younger workers (de Coen, Forrier, & Sels, 2015; Harackiewicz, Barron, & Elliot, 1998), thus enhancing their difficulties of finding adequate reemployment. Vansteenkiste, Deschacht, and Sels (2015) found a difference of 8 percent in the reemployment rate of younger (18- to 49-year-old) and older (50+-year-old) workers explained by the higher reservation wages of the latter.

On a related note, older employees are usually expected to have only a *limited time remaining* in the organization before retirement. Therefore, while organizational decision-makers may value older employees' tenure and long-term efforts in the organization, they may also argue that older employees have too little worktime left in the organization to warrant their inclusion in investments into the future (Hedge, Borman, & Lammlein, 2006; Roscigno, Mong, Byron, & Tester, 2007). While the validity of this assumption is debatable

in the face of higher voluntary turnover among younger employees (e.g., Adler & Hilber, 2009; Ng & Feldman, 2009), it may partly explain why older employees reportedly receive less investment (e.g., less training) in their human capital than younger employees (e.g., van Veldhoven & Dorenbosch, 2008), and employers often offer to their older employees only employability-enhancing practices that are either inexpensive or stipulated by state or collective agreements (Fleischmann, Koster, & Schippers, 2015). Moving beyond organizational factors, also some trends in the global economy endanger older workers' possibilities for human capital development. More often than their younger counterparts, older workers have tenures in "declining industries" and "shrinking occupations," that is, industries and occupations where work is becoming simpler due to offshoring, outsourcing, and technological advancement (Bosch & ter Weel, 2013). In such contexts, building up or even maintaining human capital is difficult.

Finally, many decision makers in organizations are concerned that *productivity declines with age* (Conen, Henkens, & Schippers, 2011; Greller & Simpson, 1999; Hedge et al., 2006; van Dalen, Henkens, & Schippers, 2010). While empirical data generally contradict this notion (Ng & Feldman, 2008), this stereotype is a relatively persistent component of the concerns brought forward against older workers (Posthuma & Campion, 2009; van Dalen et al., 2010). This stereotype may enhance the likelihood of older workers losing their employment and decreasing their likelihood of finding reemployment elsewhere.

Personal adaptability—learning and flexibility. Related to the notion of human capital is often the component of personal adaptability: the willingness and ability to change personal factors (e.g., knowledge, skills, abilities, dispositions, behavior) to meet the demands of the situation (Fugate et al., 2004, p. 21), either by proactive anticipation or by reactive flexibility (van der Heijde & van der Heijden, 2006).

The notion that "you can't teach an old dog new tricks" summarizes the stereotypes held against older workers in this regard. First, older workers are often seen as *less willing to learn* new skills (Maurer, Weiss, & Barbeite, 2003; Posthuma & Campion, 2009; Simpson, Greller, & Stroh, 2002; Wrenn & Maurer, 2004). While the accuracy of this stereotype is at least debatable (e.g., Fenwick, 2012; Greller, 2006), it can be explained, at least in part, by outdated career-stage conceptions assuming a reduced need for learning in the later stages of one's working life (Hall, 1996; Lippmann, 2008; Rubin & Brody, 2005) or that older workers are about to approach retirement anyway (Martin, Dymock, Billett, & Johnson, 2013).

Second, older workers have been found to be *less able to learn* (Kanfer & Ackerman, 2004; Maurer, Barbeite, Weiss, & Lippstreu, 2008) with results indicating a particular vulnerability under conditions of stereotype threat (Horton, Baker, Pearce, & Deakin, 2008). Even older workers themselves can be pessimistic about the benefits that work-based learning and training investments can have for their employability. In a study by van der Heijden, Gorgievski, and De Lange (2016), both the learning-conducive nature of work and the practical applicability of recently acquired training did not influence self-rated employability of older workers as much as it did that of younger workers. In any case, assumed lack of trainability further reduces the likelihood of organizations investing in the human capital development of older employees (Maurer & Rafuse, 2001; Ng & Feldman, 2008).

Such lack of training and new skill acquisition are particularly troublesome for older employees because the pattern of organization-specific, and thus nonportable, human capital that older employees often accumulate over a long tenure in their organization can become obsolete as soon as the organization undergoes major changes or as soon as these employees find themselves in the labor market (Becker, 1962; Lazear, 2003; Wrenn & Maurer, 2004).

A third concern is that older employees are too set in their ways and are *less willing to adapt* to changing work environments (Isaksson & Johansson, 2000; Posthuma & Campion, 2009). While some results suggest this stereotype itself to be misguided (Kunze, Boehm, & Bruch, 2013; Ng & Law, 2014), others have indeed found older workers less likely to portray certain activities that can help them deal with employment risks of the new economy, such as learning about and exploring their career opportunities (Elman & O'Rand, 2002). Also, they are less likely to adopt attitudes and behaviors that will help them survive in the flexible labor market (Lippmann, 2008). For example, older workers are less likely to change occupations as compared to younger workers, probably because of their job-specific human capital (Baumol, Blinder, & Wolff, 2003; Bosch & ter Weel, 2013). Applying this observation to the context of career transitions imposed by possible job-loss and a search for reemployment, older workers seem to have less ability to change in

order to fit into new career-related circumstances (Koen, Klehe, & van Vianen, 2013). This so-called career adaptability is an essential component of workers' employability and asset in today's changing society (also see Savickas 2002, 2005).

Identity. Finally, models of employability usually include a notion of identity, whether it is more self-centered career identity (Fugate et al., 2004) or identification with one's organization (Ashforth, Harrison, & Corley, 2008; van der Heijde & van der Heijden, 2006). Identity is often understood as narratives defining "who I am or want to be," and these self-narratives integrate people's past, present, and future and provide them with personal goals and aspirations (Fugate et al., 2004; Ibarra & Barbulescu, 2010). In the current context, identity will play a particular role as older workers usually strongly identify with their lifetime profession (Berger, 2006) and are more likely than younger workers to show extra role behaviors (Ng & Feldman, 2008) associated with identification with their organization (van der Heijde & van der Heijden, 2006). For older workers, letting go of their professional identity by changing jobs or organizations may thus be a particular challenge (Gray, Gabriel, & Goregaokar, 2015; Kira & Klehe, 2016; Lassus, Lopez, & Roscigno, 2015; Ranzijn, Carson, Winefield, & Price, 2006). In a similar vein, a step into early retirement, while more acceptable for older than younger workers, is not always an easy decision to make (Hanisch 1999).

In sum, older workers' actual employability and associated age-related stereotypes suggest that, for older workers, the possibility of job loss and unemployment may pose serious threats. Consequently, it seems likely that older workers face particularly high perceived and also objective job insecurity, more negative consequences of job loss, and more difficult reemployment trajectories. The following sections will address the empirical findings regarding these effects.

Before Job Loss: Age and Job Insecurity

Preceding an actual job loss, many employees experience a period of job insecurity. Job insecurity has been defined in various ways (see also Probst, Jiang, & Benson, this volume), with the most prominent distinction made between perceived and objective job insecurity.

Perceived job insecurity. Perceived job insecurity describes the "perception of a potential threat to continuity in [the] current job" (Heaney, Israel, & House, 1994, p. 1431) and a "powerlessness to maintain desired continuity in a threatened job situation" (Greenhalgh & Rosenblatt, 1984, p. 438). Relevant here is the subjective anticipation of an involuntary and stressful event (Greenhalgh & Rosenblatt, 1984). Quite recently, about a quarter of 50+-year-old European workers estimated their job security as poor, with great variations between countries, and about every second one of the 50+ workers in an economically struggling Greece worrying about the security of their current position (Hank & Erlinghagen, 2011). Also in the United States, the Great Recession has considerably decreased older workers' sense of financial security, both while working and in prospective retirement (Rix, 2011).

While perceived job insecurity is likely to be especially prevalent in the context of organizational change and downsizing (Gowing, Kraft, & Campbell Quick, 1998; Heaney et al., 1994; Parker, Chmiel, & Wall, 1997; Probst, 2003), it can also emerge in seemingly unthreatened job situations (Rosenblatt & Ruvio, 1996) and may differ between individuals even if they are exposed to the same objective situation. Consequently, perceived job insecurity might vary greatly depending on societal changes and public debates (e.g., Sersic & Trkulja, 2009) and individual differences (e.g., Kinnunen, Feldt, & Mauno, 2003). Furthermore, perceived job insecurity may be influenced by the comparison standard that workers employ. The result may be quite different, depending on whether older workers compare their objective job security to the objective job security of their younger colleagues; to the objective job security of their older colleagues, that is, the now-retired generation before them (e.g., Valletta, 1999), or to the objective job security that these workers might have expected when building their career in this organization (e.g., Lippmann, 2008).

Perceived job insecurity drives employees' perceptions, wellbeing, and reactions in a potentially threatening situation and leads to numerous negative consequences for both individuals and employing organizations. Among the immediate individual reactions are exhaustion (de Cuyper, Mäkikangas, Kinnunen, Mauno, & de Witte, 2012), psychological complaints (Griep et al., 2015), major or minor depressions (Burgard, Kalousova, & Seefeldt, 2012), a reduced sense of personal control (Glavin, 2013) and of experienced personal employability (de Cuyper et al., 2012), a decreased satisfaction with and involvement in the current job, and a decreased trust in and commitment to

the organization (Bal, Lange, Zacher, & van der Heijden, 2013). Long-term consequences include an overall decrease in performance, an overall increase in turnover intentions, and an impairment of mental as well as physical health (Glavin, 2015; Sverke, Hellgren, & Näswall, 2002).

The relationship between age and perceived job insecurity has evoked some speculation (e.g., De Witte, 1999; Sverke, Hellgren, & Näswall, 2006), but no findings that would point in either one or the other direction. Thus, age does not appear to predict perceived job insecurity. Yet, age does moderate the impact of perceived job insecurity on a number of adverse consequences. Compared to their younger colleagues, older employees usually suffer severely from the psychological and physiological health-related consequences of job insecurity, irrespective of whether this insecurity threatens the existence of the whole job (Glavin, 2015; Mandal, Ayyagari, & Gallo, 2011; Mauno, Ruokolainen, & Kinnunen, 2013) or of particular working conditions or resources that one values in one's job (Stynen, Forrier, Sels, & de Witte, 2015). At the same time, though, older employees are less likely to leave the organization when experiencing high perceived insecurity (Cheng & Chan, 2008). A likely reason for this mismatch between suffering and separation from the organization lies in older workers' increased dependency on their current employment (Greenhalgh & Rosenblatt, 1984). Older workers find themselves often in a vulnerable position with high "sunk costs," as they cannot easily leave the relationship due to factors such as familial and community ties, employment and pension benefits linked to seniority, and high job- and organization-specific human capital that appears to be "nonportable" to other potential employers (Becker, 1962; Minda, 1997). Combined with stereotypes against older workers (Posthuma & Campion, 2009), this situation may turn perceived job insecurity into a particularly threatening experience for older employees.

Objective job insecurity. While perceived job insecurity may give employees sleepless nights, it is employees' objective job insecurity that actually predicts the likelihood of job loss. Mohr (2000, p. 339) differentiates between four stages of objective job insecurity. The first stage is a state of public awareness that jobs in general might be insecure, for instance due to national debates about recession and unemployment. The second stage refers to objective job insecurity at the organizational level, which is reached when an organization's unstable situation is acknowledged. The third stage is "acute" objective job-insecurity at an individual level, when a real threat is perceived and when downsizing is obvious. Finally, the fourth stage of objective job-insecurity reflects anticipated job loss, when dismissals are already arranged.

Yet, any of these situations may not affect all workers equally. Although official unemployment rates (stage 1) are usually lower or comparable for older than for younger workers (e.g., Sincavage, 2004; Tatsiramos, 2009), the question remains—given the same organizational setting (stage 2)—whether older workers are at a lower, a comparable, or a higher risk of losing their jobs (stage 3). There are some indications that European employers, when having a higher percentage of older workers, apply employee development measures and also, in some cases, measures to accommodate workplaces to the older workers. However, employers' preferences seems to be exit measures toward retirement with their aging employees (van Dalen, Henkens, & Wang, 2015). Many countries forbid discrimination based on age during layoffs and issue regulations aimed at preventing such discrimination. While this should make age discrimination less likely to show, at least during mass layoffs, public (e.g., Wall Street Journal, March 11, 2009) and scientific (e.g., Henry & Jennings, 2004; Neumark, 2009; Neumark & Button, 2014; Roscigno et al., 2007) debates continue about the degree to which older employees are at a higher objective risk than younger colleagues to lose their employment.

In line with these assertions, some statistics (e.g., Tatsiramos, 2009) and a good number of successful legal cases indicate that age indeed may be a direct—and usually unlawful—predictor of layoffs (e.g., Henry & Jennings, 2004; Roscigno et al., 2007). Overall, however, the empirical data available draw a somewhat more refined picture. Combining the responses of more than 50,000 representative U.S. respondents collected in ten waves of Displaced Workers Surveys (DWSs) between 1984 and 2004, Munnell et al. (2006) found that the probability of being displaced declines with age. A closer analysis, however, revealed that it was not age, but organizational tenure, which protected employees (see also Johnson & Mommaerts, 2010; Munnell, Sass, & Zhivan, 2009). As soon as the authors controlled for tenure, age indeed showed a weak positive relationship with the likelihood of losing one's job. Similar protective effects of tenure have been reported by Valletta (1999), who found that tenure with the organization generally served as a good antidote against job loss. For the average participant of this sample, five additional years of tenure reduced the dismissal probability by nearly half. Yet, this protective effect of tenure significantly diminished with the year of data collection, suggesting that more tenured, thus often older, employees enjoy far less security today than long-tenured employees used to enjoy one or two decades earlier. The volatility of the global economy and, especially, the Great Recession in the first decade of the current century further decreased both workers' perceived (Rix, 2011) and objective security (Neumark & Button, 2014). Additionally worrisome is that older employees work more often than their younger colleagues in "shrinking occupations" (see Bosch & ter Weel, 2013). In summary, age can at points become a predictor of dismissal; yet overall, older—and particularly long-tenured—workers still enjoy more objective job-security than their younger colleagues, even though the protection by tenure seems to be decreasing. While this might change in the future when career mobility may become more of a norm among older workers, changing jobs late in one's career currently still increases the risk of displacement, given that mobile workers lose the protective shield of a long tenure with their organization.

Actual Job Loss: Age and the Job-Loss Experience

In their seminal model of coping with job loss, Latack et al. (1995) argued that people's primary appraisal of a job-loss situation as a loss or threat is largely a function of the discrepancy created between the goal or standard that people have come to expect and their actual situation. When people lose their jobs, they lose many of the benefits that work provides and that contribute to psychological and physical wellbeing (Jahoda, 1982; Warr, 1987; see also Paul, Hassel, & Moser, this volume). Among these losses are *manifest economic losses* in the form of a loss of income; pension benefits; health and further financial benefits (depending on the country one is working in); and *latent psychological losses* such as meaningful activities, a sense of purpose, social contacts, personal status, identity, and time structure (Creed & Machin, 2002; Creed & Reynolds, 2001; Creed & Watson, 2003; Paul & Batinic, 2010). Due to these manifest economic and latent psychological losses, job loss causes distress and can impair people's mental health (McKee-Ryan, Song, Wanberg, & Kinicki, 2005;

Murphy & Athanasou, 1999; Paul & Moser, 2009; Worach-Kardas & Kostrzewski, 2014). Job loss reduces workers' life, marital, and family satisfaction (Strom, 2003), and can eventually also impact workers' physical health (McKee-Ryan et al., 2005; Noelke & Beckfield, 2014).

The following section will address some of these experiences particularly in regard to older workers. When describing each of these losses, it is important to consider these losses not only on their own terms but also as a potentially threatening discrepancy between the standard that an employee has become used to during his or her working life and the feedback that is provided in the new situation (see Latack et al., 1995). In terms of the classical stress literature, this discrepancy reflects the primary appraisal of the situation ("how bad is it?"; Lazarus & Folkman, 1984). Adjusting control theory to the case of unemployment, Latack et al. (1995) argued that it will be this type of discrepancy appraisal that later motivates people to engage in a specific coping response.

Manifest functions—financial strain. "Money hadn't been an object with me through all my working life and now to be on the dole is devastating. I mean, I'm drawing on reserve now, all the time, I've gone into my shell, I don't go out, nothing. You don't want to afford it, can't afford it . . .. I found that when a lettuce was $1.95 I had to cut it out of my salad and just have a tomato, cucumber and onion and forget about the lettuce" (participants from Ranzijn et al., 2006, p. 474).

Money has been labeled "the most general means of controlling one's everyday life" (Frese, 1987, p. 213). Money not only allows one to buy the necessities of livelihood but is also needed for many more latent functions of our lives. For the unemployed, a lack of money often curbs engagement in meaningful activities (e.g., by being unable to pay for educational material, membership in a sports club, or admission to cultural events), social contacts (e.g., by being unable to go out, buy presents, or entertain friends), and social status (Frese, 1987; Willott & Griffin, 2004). Thus, one of the most imminent and frequently discussed issues of unemployment in general and among older workers in particular is the financial strain incurred by job loss. For older workers, this strain is usually a function of losses in (a) income, (b) pension buildup, (c) health benefits, and (d) savings.

Often, older workers have spent considerable time with their last employer, accumulating both seniority and organization-specific human capital

that justifies higher salaries (Becker, 1962). A loss of this income can therefore be particularly steep for older workers. Additionally, older workers face severe threats to their pension benefits. For one, a pension with a particular organization usually stops accumulating after displacement; and for the other, many organizational pension plans model the relationship between time worked and retirement pensions to be nonlinear, with pension wealth accruing most rapidly during the last years of employment. While the original idea of such plans may have been to increase the incentives for long-tenured employees with high organization-specific human capital to remain with their current organization, a job loss toward the end of this employment also implies that employees forgo those years with the highest pension accumulation (Haider & Stephens, 2001). In the end, their retirement funds may thus be considerably smaller than originally expected. The Great Recession in the first decade of this century made the situation even worse, at least for older workers in the United States. Munnell and Rutledge (2013, p. 139) describe how the financial outlook for older American workers deteriorated from two sides: "[T]he nature of today's retirement system left them exposed to declines in the value of equities and real estate. The asset market collapse led many workers to plan for a later retirement, only to find that the labor market did not accommodate these plans. Many more late-career workers experienced job loss than in previous downturns, and those jobless spells lasted longer than ever before."

Finally, in some countries, employers are also the prime purchaser of employee health insurance, and negotiate considerably cheaper deals than employees could negotiate on their own. Once laid-off workers' access to health insurance runs out, these people—despite their reduced income—face considerably higher costs for the same insurance benefits. As a consequence, job loss and unemployment may seriously affect older workers' savings (Chan & Stevens, 1999), sometimes even up to a degree that laid-off workers may be forced to sell their homes and spend their savings on bare survival (Ranzijn et al., 2006).

Social status. Besides providing us with financial income, work is a major source of latent psychological functions, such as social status and identity (e.g., Thiel, 2007), that is, "a person's location relative to others in the situation, the community, or the society as a whole" (Hewitt, 2000, p. 126). Status and identity are dynamic processes that change over time through negotiated interactions between the person and society (Goffman, 1959). In the context of older unemployed people, social identity may be particularly vulnerable to stigmata, deeply discrediting attributes that result in discriminatory attitudes and behaviors toward the stigmatized individual (Bos, Pryor, Reeder, & Stutterheim, 2013). Interview studies with aging workers (e.g., Berger, 2006; Lassus et al., 2015; Riach & Loretto, 2009) show that older job-seekers can become acutely aware of the barriers posed by age in finding adequate reemployment and that they start to feel treated as "old." Treated as "old," the informants felt devalued, cast aside, and degraded by potential employers (to cite one participant who said, "castaway, like an old shoe that is of no use anymore" Berger, 2006, p. 309). This experience can be particularly hurtful for older workers, given that laid-off older workers continue to identify with work and the work ethic to the same degree as when they had been employed, even after long periods of unemployment (Berger, 2006; Fraher & Gabriel, 2014; Rife & First, 1989).

Labeled as "old," with the associated stereotypes attached, older job-seekers easily experience "stereotype threat." Berger (2006) found that workers started to feel old and to question the value that they could add to a potential employer, thus contributing to a self-fulfilling prophecy (Buyens, Van Dijk, Dewilde, & De Vos, 2009; Horton et al., 2008; Kang & Chasteen, 2009). This way, job loss can pose a serious threat to the self (e.g., Garrett-Peters, 2009; Kasl & Cobb, 1971; Paul & Batinic, 2010), to a person's wellbeing (Creed & Macintyre, 2001), and to his or her performance during a possible application process for reemployment. Even when workers do not define themselves as old but believe their supervisors or colleagues have negative age-related stereotypes, intentions to retire become stronger (Bal et al., 2015). Simply believing that working life harbors negative stereotypes of age reduces older workers' motivation to work.

Collective purpose. In general, people strive to make a contribution and feel that they are useful and needed by other people (Deci & Ryan, 2000; Jahoda, 1982). What is more, several traditional career-stage models assume that making a contribution beyond one's own career interests, for instance mentoring and helping the next generation, are integral parts of the later stage of employees' organizational careers (e.g., Hall & Nougaim, 1968; Kanfer & Ackerman, 2004). Unemployment seriously hampers people's opportunity to do so and can thus make them feel obsolete (Parris & Vickers, 2010; Paul & Batinic, 2010), further impairing

their wellbeing (Creed & Bartrum, 2008; Creed & Macintyre, 2001). Often, older workers suffer deeply from the discovery that "a lifetime of learning and 'on the job' is wasted and useless" during unemployment and that "I cannot seem to find an outlet in these skills . . . I feel the need to be a part of a community, not just a job seeker" (Ranzijn et al., 2006, p. 473).

Social contacts. Another major drawback of unemployment is a decrement in social networks, the "regularly shared experiences and contacts with people outside the nuclear family" (Jahoda, 1982, p. 188) that "provide more information, more opportunity for judgment and rational appraisal of other human beings with their various foibles, opinions, and ways of life" (p. 26). Partially accounted for by poorer finances that allow for fewer social activities, several studies have shown that unemployed people lower their social activity and experience social isolation (e.g., Paul & Batinic, 2010; Underlid, 1996; Willott & Griffin, 2004).

Older unemployed in particular seem to entertain fewer social contacts (Creed & Macintyre, 2001; Paul & Batinic, 2010). Ranzijn and colleagues (2006) argued that the socially isolating effect of unemployment may be particularly harsh among older employees, because people tend to develop more friendships earlier in their lives; and later they deepen these friendships, expecting them to last (Carstensen, 1995). As one of their participants says, "[Y]ou don't have any office interaction, you don't have the after office interaction, you don't have anywhere else to go. If someone says to me, 'Hey you want to go down and buy dinner . . . ?' I want to say, 'Yeah, cool, great idea.' But then I think, 'Hang on, it's probably going to cost us $60,' and so I say, 'Ah no, got something else on, I've got to do this or do that, can't make it tonight.' So you become increasingly isolated" (p. 471).

Activity. Unemployment can also seriously affect people's general activity level. According to Jahoda (1982), being active—even being active due to external forces such as the need to earn a living— is better for a person's psychological wellbeing than being passive. However, the types of activities that people undertake during unemployment greatly influence their wellbeing during that time. Competence-serving activities, socializing, and active leisure activities in particular lead to better wellbeing than idling and passive leisure activities (e.g., Haworth & Ducker, 1991; Matz-Costa, Besen, Boone James, & Pitt-Catsouphes, 2014). Another benefit of these activities, particularly for unemployed people, is that they may foster the enjoyment of latent functions otherwise achieved by work, such as providing social contact, time structure, or collective purpose (e.g., Evans & Haworth, 1991). In sum, however, unemployed people are usually less active than employed people, and older people are usually less active than younger people (Paul & Batinic, 2010; Underlid, 1996). Taken together, being active might pose a severe challenge for older job-losers.

Time structure. Jahoda (1982) argued that a major latent function of work is that it shapes our experience of time, filling our days with planned activities. Without work, "days stretch long when there is nothing that has to be done; boredom and waste of time become the rule" (Jahoda, 1982, p. 22). In line with this argument, several studies showed that unemployed people reported lower levels of time structure than employed people (e.g., Berger, 2006; Paul & Batinic, 2010; Sousa-Ribeiro, Sverke, & Coimbra, 2014; Wanberg, Griffiths, & Gavin, 1997). As soon as people found work again (Wanberg, Griffiths, & Gavin, 1997) or engaged in training (Sousa-Ribeiro et al., 2014), their time structure significantly improved. At the same time, several studies showed that low levels of structured and purposeful time impaired people's mental health (e.g., Creed & Bartrum, 2008; Creed & Macintyre, 2001; Hepworth, 1980; Wanberg et al., 1997). Whether this effect is stronger or weaker among older than younger job-losers has not been examined yet. However, older unemployed workers in a qualitative study by Ranzijn et al. (2006) did not identify time structure as a major issue. This might be due to a declining time structure among older people in general (e.g., Paul & Batinic, 2010), possibly in connection with unemployed older workers being more likely to move toward early retirement.

Future outlook. Instead of the latent factors previously discussed, Fryer's agency restriction model assumes that unemployed people's reduced wellbeing is primarily a function of the financial hardship encountered and the fact that unemployment "cuts the unemployed person off from any future, making looking forward and planning very difficult" (Fryer, 1995, p. 270). While the older unemployed may engage different—more or less effective—narrative-coping strategies to deal with their job loss (Gabriel, Gray, & Goregaokar, 2010), what the unemployed might be missing is "the construction of prospective self-representations in terms of hopes and fears . . . a basis for anticipating future events, setting goals, planning, exploring options, making commitments, and subsequently guiding a developmental course" (Creed & Klisch, 2004, p. 252).

In fact, the future outlook that older job-losers have might be rather negative, as finding reemployment becomes increasingly difficult for older workers (e.g., Chan & Stevens, 2001); and even when they manage to do this, they usually face steep decreases in their future job security (A. H. Stevens, 1997) and in their wages (Couch, 1998; Couch, Jolly, & Placzek, 2009; Ruhm, 1991). Older unemployed workers are not immune to these dire outlooks (Berger, 2006). Ranzijn and colleagues (2006) outlined this aspect of unemployment in more detail, showing how older unemployed workers suffer from both a narrowed horizon and concerns about the future. Instead of building toward a comfortable retirement, many of these people suddenly and unexpectedly find themselves scraping by without a prospect of improvement and with less time and fewer opportunities to bring their financial retirement planning back into balance.

Wellbeing. Given the loss of manifest and latent benefits of work, it does not surprise that job loss and unemployment cause distress and impair people's mental health (Hyde, Hanson, Chungkham, Leineweber, & Westerlund, 2015; McKee-Ryan et al., 2005; Murphy & Athanasou, 1999; Riumallo-Herl, Basu, Stuckler, Courtin, & Avendano, 2014), irrespective of whether mental health is measured in terms of positive indicators such as subjective wellbeing or self-esteem, or negative indicators such as depression or anxiety (Paul & Moser, 2009). Moreover, the subjective meaning of involuntary job loss has a crucial role in job-loss-related wellbeing consequences, as job loss that people can attribute to external reasons, such as an economic downturn, are less harmful to wellbeing (Brand, 2015; Cohen & Janicki-Deverts, 2012; Mandal et al., 2011).

Facing the steep losses in finances, status, and identity; social contacts; and the ability to make a contribution, one might even assume that older workers will suffer more from unemployment than younger workers. On the other hand, older workers might feel less handicapped by the loss of activity and time structure, or might reframe the unemployment experience as a shift toward early retirement. The latter perspective would suggest that older people might actually suffer less.

Most early work on the relationship between age and wellbeing during unemployment assumed a U-shaped effect. That is, the middle-aged unemployed were usually assumed to suffer most from unemployment, while younger and older persons were thought to be less severely affected (e.g., Broomhall & Winefield, 1990; Hepworth, 1980). The tenacity of this assumption is largely based on a study by Warr and Jackson (1984), who found such an association among a sample of British blue-collar unemployed men. Warr and Jackson explained their finding with a combination of different reasons, including financial strains, family obligations, and early retirement.

Empirical findings regarding the relationship between age and mental health among unemployed workers are far less conclusive and include curvilinear, nonsignificant, positive, and also negative relationships (Paul & Moser, 2009). When meta-analytically examining the link between age and wellbeing among the unemployed, McKee-Ryan et al. (2005) found no significant linear relationship between age and either subjective physical wellbeing or psychological wellbeing in the form of mental health or life satisfaction. A further meta-analysis with a considerably larger collection of studies (Paul & Moser, 2009) replicated this finding and also found no indication of the proposed U-shaped effect of age on the unemployed person's wellbeing. If anything, results suggested the opposite, with particularly younger and older workers suffering more, even though results proved largely unstable. In sum, the mixed findings imply that in terms of well-eing, older workers suffer no less from job loss and unemployment than do younger workers (see also Brand, Levy, & Gallo, 2008; Falba, Sindelar, & Gallo, 2009; Gallo, Bradley, Siegel, & Kasl, 2000; Gallo, Bradley, Teng, & Kasl, 2006).

Physical health. Given the increased stress (Eliason & Storrie, 2009a) and a higher rate of self-destructive coping strategies (e.g., Ahs & Westerling, 2006), it does not surprise that unemployment also hampers people's physical health. Although the effect is weaker than that for psychological wellbeing, especially long-term unemployment fosters subjective complaints (Griep et al., 2015), psychosomatic symptoms (Paul & Moser, 2009), self-reported medical conditions (McKee-Ryan et al., 2005), the use of medical services and pension disability (Vahtera et al., 2005; Westin, Schlesselman, & Korper, 1989), and mortality (e.g., Lundin, Lundberg, Hallsten, Ottosson, & Hemmingsson, 2010; Noelke & Beckfield, 2014).

The role of age as a possible moderator in this relationship has not yet been sufficiently addressed.

Yet, there is good reason to believe that older workers will be at least as physically affected by unemployment as younger workers, if not more so. Older workers not only face the loss of financial benefits, longstanding social networks, and a lower likelihood of finding comparable reemployment elsewhere (as will be discussed more fully later in this chapter), but also these stress factors are matched by an escalating risk of chronic disease in general. In some countries, job loss may also restrict care access, making it harder for job-loss victims to get necessary medical treatment (Noelke & Beckfield, 2014), while ill individuals may especially be selected for displacement (Schmitz, 2011), further increasing the connection between job loss and physical health problems.

Individual studies showed that the negative impact of unemployment on physical health is a serious concern among older workers (e.g., Warr & Jackson, 1984). Drawing repeatedly on data from the U.S. Health and Retirement Survey, Gallo and colleagues (2000) found that involuntary job-loss was associated with numerous negative physical outcomes among workers aged 50 and older. Job loss during a two-year period predicted poorer subsequent self-reported performance on daily activities (e.g., walking different distances; climbing stairs; and lifting, pulling or pushing things), even after controlling for a host of other significant predictors two years earlier, such as baseline physical functioning, the prevalence of different medical conditions (hypertension, heart disease, cancer), smoking, obesity, age, gender, marital status, and education (Gallo et al., 2000). Involuntary job-loss was also associated with physical disability among older workers, even though effects were somewhat more consistent for women than for men (Gallo, Brand, Teng, Leo-Summers, & Byers, 2009).

Finally, long-term data collected from the same sample over six- and ten-year periods showed that job loss more than doubled older workers' risk of strokes (Gallo et al., 2004; Gallo et al., 2006) and heart attacks (Gallo et al., 2006), again after controlling for numerous potentially confounding variables.

In sum, the costs of job loss and unemployment among older workers are not merely a matter of finances or of a drop in wellbeing. Job loss and unemployment also bear substantial consequences on the unemployed person's physical health. Reemployment, in turn, significantly increased both physical and mental functioning (Gallo et al.,

2000), further supporting the notion of a causal relationship between unemployment and health.

After Job Loss: Coping and Unemployment

Given the results discussed in the preceding section, it is safe to say that the loss of manifest and latent psychological functions associated with job loss and subsequent unemployment can pose both a great loss to older workers and a serious threat regarding their future (see Latack et al., 1995). In other words, workers' primary appraisal of this situation can be rather negative. Latack and colleagues (1995, p. 323) employed a control theory framework to explain how people cope with job loss and unemployment and argued that the primary appraisal of a discrepancy between a desired and an actual state would motivate people to cope. *Coping* is defined as constantly changing cognitive and behavioral efforts to manage the internal and external demands of transactions that tax or exceed a person's resources (Latack et al., 1995, p. 313). Thus, people define certain *coping goals*, that is, desired end results that they seek to accomplish in response to the perceived loss or threat (Latack et al., 1995, p. 323). These coping goals in turn activate certain *coping strategies*, that is, cognitive and behavioral activities to accomplish these goals and to reduce the discrepancy experienced (see Figure 24.1).

Research often distinguishes between different types of coping strategies, such as cognitive versus behavioral coping strategies, control versus escape coping (Latack, 1986; Latack et al., 1995), problem-focused versus emotion-focused coping, or problem-focused versus symptom-focused coping strategies (Leana, Feldman, & Tan, 1998). Problem-focused coping strategies attempt to control the source of stress by defying the problem or generating alternative solutions and—in the context of unemployment—include activities aimed at finding new work. These coping strategies include, for example, job search, retraining, and relocating (Leana et al., 1998).

Symptom-focused coping strategies, in contrast, are aimed at lessening the emotional distress caused by the problem. In the context of unemployment, symptom-focused coping behaviors include steps such as seeking financial assistance to address the loss of income, or engaging in community activity in order to experience a common purpose (Leana et al., 1998). Symptom-focused coping could also imply adjusting one's personal standard, for example, when older workers who formerly strongly identified with their work decide to readjust their identities toward retirement (Berger, 2006; Kira & Klehe, 2016). Another common coping reaction is seeking social support in order to reestablish one's sense of social connectedness and status. Indeed, in satisfying humans' basic need for belonging (Baumeister & Leary, 1995), social support is a major resource in coping with stress in general and with unemployment in particular; it also helps older unemployed workers to prevail in their problem-focused coping response of searching for reemployment elsewhere (Rife & Belcher, 1993).

The last finding also highlights how problem- and symptom-focused coping strategies are not mutually exclusive (Leana et al., 1998). Rather, they are complementary, with high co-occurrences, and one coping strategy frequently serves multiple purposes and has multiple effects. A primarily problem-focused coping strategy, such as following a reemployment course aimed at older job-seekers, for example, can also alleviate some of the latent psychological losses of unemployment by providing participants with social support, a sense of daily purpose and a time structure, and improvement of their future outlook (Berger, 2006; Blustein, Kozan, & Connors-Kellgren, 2013; Garrett-Peters, 2009; Parris & Vickers, 2010; Riach & Loretto, 2009; see also Caplan, Vinokur, Price, & Vanryn, 1989). On the other hand, primarily symptom-focused coping strategies, such as voluntary work, may also serve problem-related objectives by increasing one's chances on the job market (Ranzijn et al., 2006).

In the following, we will first discuss a number of symptom-related coping strategies, moving from more proximal, and often less functional, stress-related coping strategies to strategies that the unemployed can undertake during their unemployment in order to reestablish the latent functions that might formerly have been associated with their work. None of these behaviors necessarily solves the unemployed's problem at hand, however, and older unemployed workers in particular confront decisions as to whether they want to seek reemployment, opt for self-employment, or retire (Kira & Klehe, 2016). We will therefore also discuss the considerations preceding this decision.

Stress-related coping reactions. Research has repeatedly pointed to the negative consequences of unemployment not only for unemployed people's psychological wellbeing but also for their physical health. These effects exceed those accounted for by stress alone. A portion of the decreased health and increased mortality of unemployed people has been attributed to increases in destructive coping behaviors (Henkel, 2011), such as smoking (Arcaya, Glymour, Christakis, Kawachi, & Subramanian, 2014), alcohol consumption (e.g., Catalano, Dooley, Wilson, & Hough, 1993), and suicidal behavior (e.g., Fanous, Prescott, & Kendler, 2004). While destructive in the longer term, many of these behaviors appear to offer some relief from the imminent stress associated with unemployment. Past research has repeatedly found age to moderate the effects of unemployment on the use of such strategies.

For example, an archival study based on Swedish registry data, combining nationwide accounts on plant closures, labor markets, and hospital admissions, found that displaced workers were significantly more likely than nondisplaced workers to face hospitalization due to alcohol abuse or, particularly among men, injuries from traffic accidents and self-harm (Eliason & Storrie, 2009b). Subgroup analyses, however, suggest that most of these effects are accounted for by younger workers, with results for workers of 50 years of age or older showing no significant difference between displaced and working people.

Another longitudinal study by Gallo, Bradley, Siegel, and Kasl (2001), with a focus on workers of more than 50 years of age, failed to find support for the general assumption of increased alcohol consumption among the older unemployed. Gallo et al. found no evidence that, among older respondents already drinking at least some alcohol, involuntary job-loss influenced the number of drinks consumed per day. Among previously abstinent participants, job loss was associated with a minor increase in drinking behavior. Yet for the vast majority of these former nondrinkers, consumption was light (less than one drink per day) and actually in a range usually considered healthy for older people (Scherr et al., 1992). Thus, older workers appear to be less susceptible to some dysfunctional coping reactions to job loss.

The same appears to be true for the most drastic response to unemployment, namely suicide. Overall, there appears to be a relatively stable link between unemployment and suicide in diverse countries (e.g., Collings & Blakely, 2001; Eliason & Storrie, 2009a; Kposowa, 2001; Kreitman & Platt, 1984; Laanani, Ghosn, Jougla, & Rey, 2015; Martikainen, Maki, & Jantti, 2007; Milner, Page, & LaMontagne, 2014; Morrell, Taylor, Quine, & Kerr, 1993; Preti & Miotto, 1999; Taylor, 2003; Voss, Nylen, Floderus, Diderichsen, & Terry, 2004; Yamasaki, Araki, Sakai, & Voorhees, 2009). Yet, these results appear to be particularly strong among young workers, with most effects diminishing with age. For example, Taylor (2003) compared the relationship between rates of unemployment and labor force participation and suicide rates among men of different ages in 20 countries across 20 years. In most of the developed economies studied, general suicide rates tended to be higher among older than among younger men, yet suicide rates also appeared to be less susceptible to labor market conditions among older men. While unemployment rates correlated positively with male youth suicide rates, the relationship was usually much weaker among older men. At the same time, results differed by country, and notable exceptions (depending to some extent on how the unemployment-suicide relationship had been calculated) to the general trend included the United States and Japan, where the unemployment-suicide relationship also held among older men.

An exception to the trend of less dysfunctional coping among the older unemployed is smoking (Arcaya et al., 2014), whether it is due to psychological stress associated with job loss, loss of balance between working life and leisure, or simple elimination of work-related smoking bans. Again, based on the Health and Retirement Survey sample already employed in earlier studies, Falba, Teng, Sindelar, and Gallo (2005) found that, among older workers, involuntary job-loss more than doubled the likelihood of relapse among former smokers. Among current smokers, job loss with continued unemployment after two years was associated with an average increase of five cigarettes smoked a day, also after controlling for other significant predictors such as prior smoking quantity, alcohol consumption, gender, and race. Given both the reduced finances available to unemployed workers and the often more severe consequences of smoking, particularly among older people, Falba et al. (2005, p. 1337) considered their findings to highlight "a potentially disastrous consequence of job loss."

Unemployment often accompanies a loss of physical activity when there are no more daily trips to work or physical movement relating to the execution of work tasks and moving about the workplace. Also, these trivial forms of daily activity play a role in fostering mental and physical health. Coping strategies focusing on increasing activity can, however, counteract the losses. An intervention study among older long-term unemployed in Germany, providing knowledge on healthy living and combined endurance and strength fitness training, had a long-term positive influence on both mental and physical health of the study participants (Kreuzfeld, Preuss, Weippert, & Stoll, 2013).

Symptom-focused coping—social participation.

Besides directly reacting to their level of stress, unemployed workers can also undertake several symptom-focused strategies that might help them obtain at least some of the psychological functions usually obtained from work. Research on different leisure activities (while people are still working) has found that volunteer work, for example, can provide people with mastery and community experiences (e.g., Mojza, Lorenz, Sonnentag, & Binnewies, 2010). Possibly because volunteering also increases social, physical, and cognitive activities, which are conductive to improved functioning among older workers (Anderson et al., 2014), positive affect and life satisfaction are higher (Pavlova & Silbereisen, 2012), and depression is less prevalent, among older workers engaging in formal volunteering or informal helping (Choi, Stewart, & Dewey, 2013). This idea has also been incorporated in prominent models of coping with unemployment, which assume that activity in community programs helps the unemployed and might thus be a viable approach to symptom-based coping (e.g., Leana & Feldman, 1990, 1992; Leana et al., 1998). In particular, volunteer work appears to be a valuable outlet for older workers, given earlier findings that older people in general (Frisch & Gerrard, 1981; Omoto, Snyder, & Martino, 2000), and the older unemployed in particular (Pavlova & Silbereisen, 2012; Riach & Loretto, 2009), turn to volunteer work out of altruistic service-related and community concerns.

Yet, empirical data show that unemployed people do not engage in social participation and volunteer work as much as can be expected in light of the preceding discussion. In general, declining economic prosperity and thus higher unemployment rates show a negative, rather than a positive, link to social participation (e.g., Lim & Sander, 2013; Meier & Stutzer, 2008; Putnam, 2000), that is, participation in leisure, religious, charity, community, civic, or professional groups or organizations. However, using panel data of more than 4,000 participants of the Wisconsin Longitudinal Study (WLS), Brand and Burgard (2008) found that such a decrement in social participation was particularly true for midcareer employees who lost jobs in their late thirties to early fifties. Employees losing jobs in their fifties or early sixties showed no decrement in

regular, extra-work social involvement compared to continuously employed workers. Their social participation in the form of social or leisure activities or religious, community, civic, or professional groups was comparable to that of continuously employed people.

Regarding volunteer work in particular, Brand and Burgard (2008) again found low activity among unemployed midcareer workers. For older workers, however, results were more promising. Among older men, the engagement in charitable work remained comparable to that of workers who had not lost their employment. Older women who lost their jobs engaged in more charitable work than their employed counterparts, suggesting that volunteering might contribute at least some latent functions that usually are associated with work.

It seems that, especially for the older unemployed, social participation and volunteering are effective coping responses that they also rely on rather actively. However, results by Ranzijn et al. (2006, p. 473) call for caution in making this assumption. Their older unemployed participants, while frequently engaging in volunteer work, perceived such work primarily "as a way of increasing their job chances or . . . a way to do something useful until a 'real job' came along." Since most participants' sense of identity was derived from paid work, volunteering did not appear as a truly viable way of contributing but rather was a means to enhance their chances of reemployment.

Retirement. While coping reactions possibly help unemployed workers handle the symptoms of unemployment, they do not necessarily answer the fundamental question of how these workers will spend their future. A coping strategy open particularly to older workers is early retirement. Retirement in general does not come voluntarily to many workers (Steiber & Kohli, 2015). Early retirement in particular is not an easy decision to make (Hanisch 1999), particularly if people feel like they are being forced into a decision rather than making it on their own terms and in their own time (Hershey & Henkens, 2014; Warr, Butcher, Robertson, & Callinan, 2004; see also Falba et al., 2009). Still, early retirement may be a viable—and at points institutionally supported—alternative to seeking reemployment in the face of steep reemployment barriers (e.g., Chan & Stevens, 2001; Hutchens, 1988).

Dynamic models of retirement decisions assume that people decide at any point in time whether to continue working or to retire (e.g., Stock & Wise,

1990). Based upon economical reasoning, the like-lihood of withdrawal from the labor market is often linked to the financial resources one has in order to bridge the gap between job loss and retirement (Tatsiramos, 2010). In other words, when older workers lose their jobs—affecting their current and future earnings such as retirement benefits—they tend to reevaluate their retirement decisions (Chan & Stevens, 1999). This decision is influenced by the expected payoff of retiring versus continuing work with a new employer, likely for lower wages and reduced employer attachment (Kyyrä & Ollikainen, 2008).

Overall, the direction of this decision is not nec-essarily clear. On the one hand, the great financial costs associated with unemployment may force workers to work longer in order to restore their re-tirement wealth (Chan & Stevens, 1999, 2001). On the other hand, reemployment chances for older workers are usually considerably lower than for younger workers (Chan & Stevens, 1999, 2001), and early retirement may pose a more agreeable and less stigmatized alternative (Berger, 2006; Hetschko, Knabe, & Schöb, 2013).

Empirically, studies covering data from several decades and countries have documented a positive link between unemployment, particularly long-term unemployment, and early retirement among older workers. While Lee (1998) showed such a re-lationship already to be true more than a hundred years ago, more recent data by Chan and Stevens (2004) based on the U.S. Health and Retirement Survey demonstrate that displacement among older workers nearly doubles the probability of retirement within the following year. Kyyrä and Ollikainen (2008) pointed out that when given a viable choice, roughly half of the older unemployed rather wait for early retirement than try to find an alternative job.

Some of this pattern may be attributed to the steep reemployment barriers that older unemployed workers face (e.g., Chan & Stevens, 2001; Hutchens, 1988). Other parts may be attributed to social se-curity systems that for a long time supported early retirement with financial incentives. In these sys-tems, disability and unemployment insurance funds are often utilized as alternative pathways to early retirement, with eligibility criteria being loosened and coverage increased so as to accommodate older workers with limited prospects of reemployment (Taylor, 2003). Consequently, in countries with more generous unemployment insurance provisions for the older unemployed, these workers show par-ticularly high retirement rates (Hairault, Sopraseuth,

& Langot, 2010; Tatsiramos, 2009; see also Kyyrä & Ollikainen, 2008; Kyyrä & Wilke, 2007). What is more, organizations in such systems often actively take advantage of existing social security programs by shedding older, thus more expensive, employees through encouraging them to "take" early retire-ment, sometimes made acceptable by additional compensation. While maintaining an appearance of social responsibility, these types of workforce reductions have made unemployment insurance the most widely used route to early retirement in some countries (Cremer Lozachmeur, & Pestieau, 2009; Hutchens, 1999). What is more, such policies stand at odds with current international movements to raise not only the general retirement age but also the age of early retirement. Research in Austria and the Netherlands showed that raising the early retirement age does indeed increase the employ-ment rate among the affected age group—but also increases their unemployment rate (Staubli & Zweimüller, 2013) and their outflow to sickness/disability insurance schemes (Lammers, Bloemen, & Hochguertel, 2013).

Further, financial incentives for retirement alone cannot completely explain the higher retirement rate among the unemployed compared to employed older workers. A closer analysis of U.S. Health and Retirement Survey data showed that the increased retirement rate among the unemployed was largely independent from the financial utility of the retire-ment decision, and that forgone future earnings and pension gains upon possible reemployment hardly diminished the found effects (Chan & Stevens, 2004). Chan and Stevens (2004) concluded that frequent retirement decisions must be due to other, unmeasured, predictors.

Some of these predictors may be related to threats to unemployed people's status and identity. After all, older workers often continue to identify with their work and the work ethic after long periods of unemployment (Berger, 2006; Rife & First, 1989). Yet, the unemployed can develop different possible identities (McVittie, McKinlay, & Widdicombe, 2008), and older unemployed workers may eventu-ally decide to define themselves as retired or semi-retired in order to avoid the stigma associated with being unemployed (Berger, 2006; Frese, 1987). Such psychological withdrawal from the labor market and identity change toward retirement are viable options, particularly among workers without heavy financial commitments. Defining themselves as retired allowed these people a renewed sense of control over their lives (Jackson & Taylor, 1994) and even improved the mental health of unemployed older workers (Hetschko et al. 2013; Mandal & Roe, 2008).

In a similar line, but more closely related to Fryer's (1995) notion of having a future outlook, Frese and Mohr (1987) found both retired and reemployed older workers to report fewer financial problems, more hope for control, and subsequently less depression than continuously or repeatedly unemployed workers. Decreasing financial problems and increasing hope for control accounted for the difference in depression between the groups. Here, the notion of control warrants particular attention, given that retirees who consider retirement a viable option, rather than feeling forced to retire, experience more happiness and joy and are less likely to be lonely, depressed, or sad than retirees who feel that they have been forced into retirement (Calvo, Haverstick, & Sass, 2009; Dingemans & Henkens, 2014, 2015; Warr et al., 2004).

Self-employment. Zikic and Richardson (2007) concluded from a qualitative study that job loss is not necessarily always a negative phenomenon for older workers. On the contrary, some older unemployed participants spoke of their job loss as a "blessing in disguise." Zikic and Richardson pointed out that unemployment at an older age gave older workers an opportunity to reflect upon their careers and engage in activities such as career exploration, which in turn opened the avenue to alternative career paths such as self-employment, whether undertaken for its own sake or as an intermediate step before eventual retirement. Self-employment in the form of consultancy work, freelancing, or other types of outsourced jobs has been lauded for its numerous possible benefits, some of which may be particularly attractive to older workers. Among these benefits are manifest financial considerations (Platman, 2003) as well as latent functions concerning time-structure in the form of possibly working part-time, enjoying flexible hours, and accommodating working time to one's own schedule (e.g., Fuchs, 1982; Platman, 2003). Self-employment may also serve status and identity purposes by shielding older workers from some of the discrimination experienced by regular job-seekers of the same age (Platman, 2003). In addition, self-employment provides older workers with an opportunity to derive self-esteem and satisfaction from work that allows them to use their skills and experiences and to remain connected, challenged, and sought after (Platman, 2003), thus satisfying the latent work functions of maintaining social status and contacts while making a valuable

contribution. Finally, self-employment allows workers to pursue meaningful work opportunities that might have eluded them earlier in their careers (e.g., Garrett-Peters, 2009; Lassus et al., 2015; Zikic & Richardson, 2007).

At the same time, the idea of self-employment does not always match the reality of the situation, and self-employment itself can be a risky undertaking. Often, self-employed workers are rather unprotected in the labor market (Platman, 2003) and are vulnerable to rapid and unforeseen changes in commissions. Given that self-employed workers often are required to deliver their work on demand, whatever their own circumstances or needs, if they want to remain viable partners, control over their own time presented as one of the advantages of self-employment often proves to be more of an ideal than a reality (Platman, 2003). Also, self-employment often requires a fair amount of financial capital in order to set up and to keep one's skill-set updated (Platman, 2003). As a consequence, start-up companies of the formerly unemployed have on average fewer employees than other start-ups, are often single-person enterprises, and operate in less-capital-intensive sectors (Quentier, 2014). Self-employment therefore takes in the formerly unemployed, often in volatile and vulnerable low-entry- and low-exit-barriers sectors while also failing to generate employment to others.

Representative U.S. data from different decades showed that older workers are more likely to be self-employed than younger workers (Fuchs, 1982; Zissimopoulos & Karoly, 2009). However, late-career self-employment is particularly common among those older workers in general, and older unemployed workers in particular, who have been self-employed before (Fuchs, 1982; Zissimopoulos & Karoly, 2009) and who are relatively wealthy or have received a mentionable lump sum of money (e.g., through inheritances or pension cash-outs). In addition, unemployed workers were more likely to choose self-employment if they were older, married, held a bachelor's degree (rather than no degree or a master's degree), and enjoyed government health insurance (Zissimopoulos & Karoly, 2009). Also macro-level economic fluctuations and gender influence willingness of the older unemployed to engage in self-employment (Biehl, Gurley-Calvez, & Hill, 2014). While the attractiveness of waged and salaried jobs persisted during the relatively short-lived 2001 dot-com recession, older unemployed men assessed that the Great Recession rendered such jobs scarcer and riskier. Consequently, they became more likely to engage in self-employment. The unemployed women, in their turn, became less likely to engage in self-employment after the Great Recession. Like men, they recognized the precariousness of waged and salaried jobs, but still preferred not to become self-employed during difficult financial times.

Searching for reemployment. Finally, searching for reemployment, or job search (Manroop & Richardson, 2015), is likely the most obvious and usually the most promising reaction to unemployment (see also Song, Sun, & Li, this volume). Kanfer, Wanberg, and Kantrowitz (2001) defined job-search behavior as the outcome of a dynamic self-regulated process in which individuals undertake a variety of activities and use a variety of personal resources to obtain employment. In other words, job search is a goal-directed behavior, influenced by numerous factors such as personality, motives, social context, and biographical variables. When discussing this goal-directed behavior, it will be helpful to distinguish between the *intensity* with which people search for reemployment, and the development of this intensity over time (i.e., their persistence), and the *strategies* by which they do so (Kanfer et al., 2001; see also van Hoye, this volume). The latter is particularly relevant given that older job-seekers are often considered to be inexperienced in how to perform a successful job-search (Rogers & O'Rourke, 2004). Often having worked in one occupation and organization for a long time, the concern is that these people may have lost track of the current labor market and lack necessary job-search skills (Hooyman & Kiyak, 2005).

Job-search intensity. The vast majority of the job-search literature has focused on the intensity with which unemployed people seek reemployment, for example, by measuring how often job seekers undertake activities such as "prepare a resume," "read the classified advertisements," "send out an application," or simply asking people how much time they invest per day in their job-search.

In a meta-analytic investigation of the predictors of job-search intensity, Kanfer et al. (2001) found a weak negative relationship between age and both the intensity with which people searched for jobs and employment outcomes (e.g., status, number of job offers, search duration). In this analysis, they distinguished biographical antecedents of job search, such as age, from more psychological antecedents such as self-evaluations (e.g., self-efficacy), personality, and the social context in which the job-search occurs (e.g., job seekers' networks).

They argued that biographical antecedents, while distinct from the motivational processes underlying job-search behavior, may bring about differences in the other antecedents, such as employment commitment and financial need influencing job-search motivation. For example, older job-seekers may lose their self-efficacy to find reemployment in the face of age discrimination, yet might also experience a lower need for direct financial earnings. Reemployment self-efficacy, in turn, stimulates intensive job search also among the older unemployed (de Coen, Forrier, de Cuyper, & Sels, 2015).

There also are compensatory resources that can foster job-search intensity among the older unemployed. For example, having a proactive personality moderates the connection between age and job-search intensity, such that "relatively older job seekers with a more proactive personality engaged to the same extent in job search behaviours as relatively younger older job seekers" (Zacher 2013, p. 1156). Moreover, among mature-aged job seekers, a proactive personality also fosters job-search self-efficacy, which promotes resilience in an intensive job search (Zacher & Bock, 2014). In sum, age has a very small impact on job-search intensity, which can hardly explain the well-reported difficulties older workers have with finding reemployment.

Job-search strategies. Besides considering the intensity with which people search for reemployment, one also needs to consider the qualitative nature of this search, even though the research on different job-search strategies is currently far less advanced than the research on job-search intensity (e.g., Crossley & Highhouse, 2005; van Hooft, Wanberg, & van Hoye, 2013). The behaviors usually addressed in measures of job-search intensity include relatively formal preparatory and actual job-search behaviors, such as updating and sending out one's resume. Qualitatively different approaches to a job search include: (a) using a focused, exploratory, or haphazard job-search strategy (Crossley & Highhouse, 2005); (b) employing the Internet during the search (e.g., Fountain, 2005); and (c) relying on social networks during the search (e.g., Wanberg, Kanfer, & Banas, 2000).

Based on earlier research on information seeking during a job search (C. K. Stevens & Turban, 2001), Crossley and Highhouse (2005) proposed a differentiation of three job-search strategies. A *focused search strategy* involves concentrating search efforts on a small number of carefully screened potential employers. People using this approach often identify top choices early in their search and only apply for jobs that fit their needs, qualifications, and interests. An *exploratory search strategy* involves examining several potential employment options and actively gathering job-related information from sources that may be available. Inherent in the use of an exploratory strategy is the openness to opportunities that arise. Job seekers using an exploratory strategy are dedicated to their search and are motivated to fully explore their options. Finally, a *haphazard job-search strategy* involves passively gathering information both inside and outside of one's area of expertise and employing a trial and error approach, often switching tactics without any clear rationale. Crossley and Highhouse argued that job seekers using this strategy often have low and unclear employment standards and tend to settle for the first acceptable job that comes along. Regarding the relationship of age with the use of these different strategies, research suggests that older unemployed workers do not differ from younger unemployed workers in regard to the use of the more promising focused and exploratory strategies that have been linked to a higher number of job offers (Crossley & Highhouse, 2005; Koen, Klehe, van Vianen, Zikic, & Nauta, 2010). At the same time, research has found older workers to be less likely to use a haphazard job-search strategy, which is usually associated with a lower quality of the reemployment found (Crossley & Highhouse, 2005; Koen et al., 2010). In sum, these results do not support the concern that older unemployed workers would employ less optimal search strategies than younger job-seekers.

The same has been found for the use of online resources during the job search. In contrast to the time when many older workers searched for their first job, the Internet has become a major source of information for job seekers regarding not only open positions but also current norms and expectations toward applicants during the application process. The Internet has also grown into a medium by which to announce one's own experience and availability on the labor market and to send out one's own application. Consequently, searching for a job without using the Internet is almost unthinkable these days, and using the Internet in a job search has also been connected to a higher likelihood for finding reemployment and a shorter duration of unemployment (Suvankulov, Lau, & Chau, 2012). Searching for a job online can also serve as a way to find out whether the applicant is able to use the Internet and has desirable skills associated with modern technology (Fountain, 2005). As

online job-searches have become the rule rather than the exception, with an accompanying stereotype that older job-seekers may be less up-to-date regarding current technology, one can imagine that older job-seekers are at a disadvantage compared to younger ones. Findings on the use of the Internet in job searches by older job-seekers are contradictory. While Fountain (2005) found no significant relationship between age and online job-searches there are, however, also indications on older job-seekers using the Internet far less in their job searches when compared to young job-seekers (Green, Li, Owen, & Hoyos, 2012). Used to in-person job interviews, older job-seekers may experience online job applications as impersonal, findindg it hard to convey their uniqueness and make sure they stand out among the applicants (Lassus et al., 2015).

A final type of job-search behavior to be examined is networking, that is, using private and professional networks as a source of finding and pursuing job leads (see also Forret, this handbook). Several studies have shown the usefulness of networking behaviors, not only over the course of a regular career (e.g., Forret & Dougherty, 2004; Kuijpers, Schyns, & Scheerens, 2006; Wolff & Moser, 2009) but also during job searches. It has even been suggested that 60% to 90% of job seekers find their job through a personal network (Logue, 1993). Several studies have shown that networks are a good resource, and networking is a very effective strategy in finding reemployment (Giles, Park, & Cai, 2006; Lambert, Eby, & Reeves, 2006; Lindsay, Greig, & McQuaid, 2005; Petrucci, Blau, & McClendon, 2015; Wanberg et al., 2000; Zikic & Klehe, 2006). The advantage of a social or professional network in searching for a job lies in its exclusiveness. Different from jobs announced via job advertisements, jobs distributed via networks are not available to everyone. Because friends and former business acquaintances know something about the skills, qualifications, and employment history of the person searching for a job, they are more likely to share jobs that fit the job seeker's abilities and aspirations (Fountain, 2005). Nevertheless, some research suggests that even though networking intensity in a job search results in job offers, the jobs actually received through social networks and informal contacts may be lower in status and in perceived fit with the job and the organization (van Hoye et al., 2009).

People typically have developed a professional network around the age of 40 (Greenhaus, Callanan, & Godshalk, 2000), implying that older workers can benefit more from a professional network compared to younger workers. However, several studies (Dex, Willis, Paterson, & Sheppard, 2000; Greenhaus et al., 2000; Zikic & Klehe, 2006) showed that networking activities often decrease with age. Yet, other studies did not find a significant relationship between age and the intensity of networking job-searches (e.g., Lambert et al., 2006; Van Hoye et al., 2009; Wanberg et al., 2000). It seems reasonable to assume the relevant difference may lie in the quality of the networks employed.

Network quality describes the diversity and information value of a job seeker's network. Although Lambert and colleagues (2006) found no age differences in network intensity, they did find a curvilinear effect for age and network diversity: middle-aged workers reported greater diversity among their network contacts than did younger or older workers. Similar results were reported by Van Hoye et al. (2009), who found that older job-seekers enjoyed a smaller network size with weaker ties and particularly ties to lower-status individuals (i.e., people of lower educational, occupational, and general status) than younger job-seekers. They further found that a large network size was associated with a greater likelihood of finding reemployment and a higher quality of reemployment. Networking activity per se was only helpful when the unemployed relied on a network of weak ties and when their network consisted of high-status individuals. In other words, spending much time on finding reemployment through networking does not necessarily mean that the networking is done effectively. For example, one might use a few high-quality connections within a network that lead to reemployment, or alternately use numerous low-quality connections that do not lead anywhere.

Taken together, these results imply that older job-seekers use their networks as often as younger job-seekers when searching for reemployment, although the quality of their networks might be poorer. This finding might explain some of the difficulties of older job-seekers with finding reemployment.

Gaining Reemployment

Job searching is usually seen as the best coping strategy available for finding reemployment. However, studies have shown that job searches may not be equally effective for older workers, and that older job-seekers face greater obstacles in their search for reemployment than younger job-seekers, particularly if they are striving toward high-quality employment (Conen et al., 2011; Heywood & Jirjahn,

2015; Maestas & Li, 2006; Oesch & Baumann, 2015; Wagenaar, Kompier, Houtman, van den Bossche, & Taris, 2015; Wanberg, Watt, & Rumsey, 1996). The following sections will first address the likelihood and speed of reemployment, followed by a discussion of the quality of reemployment.

Reemployment likelihood and speed. In comparison to younger workers, older unemployed workers are less likely to find reemployment within a given period of time (Kanfer et al., 2001; Vansteenkiste et al., 2015). They take longer to find reemployment (Chan & Stevens, 2001; Wanberg, Kanfer, Hamann, & Zhang, 2015); and they are more likely to exhaust their unemployment benefits (e.g., U.S. Department of Labor Statistics 2006) and to become long-term unemployed (Botric, 2009; Heidenreich, 2015). Using three waves of U.S. Health and Retirement Survey data, Chan and Stevens (2001) found that among 55-year-old workers who had been working at the first time of assessment, only 50% of the men and 46% of the women who lost their jobs were working again a year later; the percentage rose to 61% and 55% in the following year and then remained stable for about four years. While we are not aware of comparable data among younger workers, return rates for workers losing their jobs in their sixties were even lower. Given that the employment rate among workers in their fifties who had not lost their jobs slowly decreased from 100% to about 80% during the same period, the employment rate of workers losing their jobs in their fifties remained 20% below the employment rate of similar nondisplaced workers for at least four years following job loss.

One might argue that this employment gap could in part be due to older workers showing a slightly lower job-search intensity than younger workers (Kanfer et al., 2001; Wanberg et al., 2015) or to older employees understanding unemployment as a step toward early retirement. However, results (e.g., Heyma, van der Werff, Nauta, & van Sloten, 2014; Maestas & Li, 2006; Wanberg et al., 1996) suggest that these factors alone cannot explain the reemployment gap between older job-seekers. In one study, only one-third of the difference in reemployment rates of younger job-seekers (ages 18 to 49) and older job-seekers (ages 50-plus) was explained by such observable factors as job-search behavior, wage-setting behavior, attitudinal variables, and personal variables (Vansteenkiste et al., 2015). Again relying on U.S. Health and Retirement Survey data, Maestas and Li showed that when controlling for job-search intensity, the success rate among older job-seekers was lower than the success rate among younger job-seekers. Similarly, Wanberg et al. (1996) found a significant interaction between job-search intensity and age. Given the same job-search intensity, older job-seekers had considerably lower chances of finding reemployment. Of note is that job seekers who were intensely looking for a job experienced a success rate far below the one achieved by younger job-seekers. While Munnell et al. (2006) found that this trend has declined in recent decades, at least for employees who had not yet reached their sixties at the time of data collection, the existence of this gap is still relatively persistent—and becomes more worrisome when one also considers the role of tenure in this equation. While older workers are generally less likely to turn over than younger workers (Ng & Feldman, 2009), and while a high tenure is a relatively good protector against losing one's job in the first place (Munnell et al., 2006; Valletta, 1999), a high tenure at the last job decreases the likelihood that an unemployed individual will find a new job (Munnell et al., 2006). A possible reason may be that the same organization-specific human capital that helped employees to build a successful career and that increased their tenure with their last employer (Becker, 1962) may appear inadequate for alternative employers. Combined with stereotypes about older workers' willingness and ability to learn and to adapt to changing working conditions (Isaksson & Johansson, 2000; Maurer et al., 2003; Maurer et al., 2008; Posthuma & Campion, 2009; Simpson et al., 2002; Wrenn & Maurer, 2004), this makes it particularly difficult for long-tenured unemployed older workers to find comparable reemployment. Another finding regarding tenure that seems troubling is that formerly displaced workers often face substantial employment instability in their subsequent jobs (Stevens, 1997). Lacking the protective shield of tenure, these workers can experience repeated job losses over the next several years and may thus find themselves working under constant job insecurity.

Reemployment quality. Older workers are not only less likely than younger workers to find reemployment but also less likely to find high-quality jobs when they do become reemployed (Koeber & Wright, 2001; Lippmann, 2008; see also Virick & McKee-Ryan, this volume). Even though older job-changers have been documented as finding jobs with less strain, less physical effort, and more time flexibility than in their previous jobs (Johnson & Kawachi, 2007), finding jobs that match their

old jobs in terms of education level (Sum, Trubskyy, Khatiwada, McLaughlin, & Palma, 2011), earnings, and benefits is more unlikely. Results consistently showed significant earnings reductions for older job-seekers upon reemployment (e.g., Johnson & Mommaerts, 2010; Koeber & Wright, 2001; Ruhm, 1991; Schirle, 2012; A. H. Stevens, 1997; Zwick, 2012). Again relying on data from the 1992 U.S. Health and Retirement Survey, Couch (1998) found that the average displaced worker in his or her fifties experienced a loss in earnings of nearly 40%. Little of these lost earnings were replaced through pension income, and the rate of health insurance coverage was 16% lower for displaced workers compared to nondisplaced workers. Chan and Stevens (2001) also used waves of the early U.S. Health and Retirement Survey (1992, 1994, and 1996) and found that among reemployed, displaced older workers, the initial earning losses of 32% still ranged from 23% to 29% six or more years after displacement. In a later study, Chan and Stevens (2004) showed that men aged 50 to 75 years who experienced displacement and were reemployed faced average wage losses of 50% in the year after job loss. The estimated earnings reductions were still 40% four years after job displacement.

Extending these findings by including further years of the Health and Retirement Survey, Haider and Stephens (2001) showed that reemployment is not only unable to make up for the loss in earnings, but that the loss in fringe benefits is as large as the loss in direct earnings. They also found that when differences in earning losses disappear, it is not because of displaced individuals returning to their predisplacement earnings, but because nondisplaced workers begin to retire.

In addition, related to the notion of organization-specific expertise being rewarded in the former organization but not in the new organization upon reemployment, Munnell et al. found that each year of job tenure in the old job was associated with additional reemployment wage loss of 1–2%. Likely due to similar expertise-related reasons, both Ruhm (1991) and Couch et al. (2009) found that earnings reductions among older workers were particularly large when workers gained reemployment outside of their career jobs or industry.

Explaining the Employment Gap: Discrimination

Summing up, discussion in this article likely draws a somewhat bleak picture of the situation of older workers who experience job insecurity, job loss, and attempt to regain regular and acceptable reemployment. Latack et al (1995) argued that people's resources—or lack thereof—influence all of these areas, including the primary appraisal of the situation as one of loss or threat (in our model "discrepancies"), the coping goals that people set themselves (e.g., whether people even strive toward reemployment or rather opt for retirement instead), and finally the strategies that they choose in order to obtain these goals (in our model, the "coping reactions"). In this context, age is usually seen as a lacking resource (Latack et al., 1995) or a "risk factor," exposing job-seeking workers to the accompanying stereotypes and discrimination (Posthuma & Campion, 2009).

About 60% of older American workers indicate age discrimination to be real (AARP 2002, 2007), with higher discrimination perceived by workers who are currently unemployed and looking for a job. Similar findings have been reported in other countries (e.g., Duncan & Loretto, 2004) as well as in audit and correspondence studies, a more controlled method of testing for the effect of age discrimination. In these studies, pairs of applicants apply for the same job or send out résumés. These applicants are matched on all characteristics except for age (as far as that is possible, of course, given that age usually correlates with tenure and experience). Measures of outcomes include the likelihood of being invited for an interview or other expressions of interest in hiring. Via this method, several authors (e.g., Ahmed, Andersson, & Hammarstedt, 2012; Bentinck, Brown, & Wall, 1999; Bendick, Jackson, & Romero, 1996; Lahey, 2008a; Riach, 2015) found consistent evidence of age discrimination against older workers for various white-collar, entry-level management, sales, and service positions. Finally, analyses of the distribution of young versus older hires across industries and occupations (Hutchens, 1988) suggest that hiring opportunities decline with age. An analysis of U.S. legal cases on age discrimination suggests that the employment chances of workers above the age of 50 are often prone to discriminatory practices (Roscigno et al., 2007).

Age discrimination is obviously also addressed legally in many countries, but given that, at least in the United States, more people are going to sue their employer for discrimination at layoff rather than at hiring, Lahey (2008b) argued that antidiscrimination laws may actually make organizations hire *fewer* older workers, since they don't want to be sued for releasing these people later on. Some of the reasons for such discrimination are again to be seen in the stereotypes held against older workers. Moreover, discriminatory attitudes toward older employees can be implicit, placing them beyond the awareness and control of employers harboring them. A study by Malinen and Johnston (2013) shows that precisely such implicit age biases can be both negative and resistant to interventions.

Regarding the costs argument brought forward against hiring older job seekers, past research has found that the likelihood of finding reemployment for older workers and the income that they can expect from reemployment are not independent. For one, while it is true that older workers often have to accept considerably lower salaries at a new job than at the jobs they held before the job loss (Johnson & Mommaerts, 2010), older workers are still relatively expensive to hire. In a study combining different representative U.S. data-sources (e.g., from quarterly workforce indicators) for the year 2005, Adler and Hilber (2009) found that while new hires aged 55 to 64 earned 30% less than the average nondisplaced worker aged 55 to 64, they still earned 27% more than new hires of all ages—with relevant consequences to their chances for reemployment. The less a certain industry and labor market paid for older new hires compared to existing workers of the same age group, the more likely were older job-seekers being hired. At the same time, the more the older new hires were paid relative to younger new hires, the fewer older job-seekers were being hired in the respective industry and labor market. On a related note, Adler and Hilber found significant industry differences, with hiring rates for older job-seekers being particularly low in well-earning industries such as utilities, information, and management. In a similar line, Hirsch et al. (2000) found that occupations with steep wage profiles related to age were less likely to have a high proportion of older workers and were even less likely to hire new older workers, with somewhat similar findings emerging for the provision of pension coverage. Scott, Berger, and Garen (1995) found that the probability of new hires at ages 55–64 was significantly lower in firms with healthcare plans than in those without, and it was also significantly lower in firms with relatively costly plans than in those with less costly plans (see also Mendenhall, Kalil, Spindel, & Hart, 2008).

In short, particularly where older workers would fare relatively well, yet consequently also become relatively expensive, organizations hesitate to hire older workers because of cost-saving concerns. The same is true for jobs with high physical demands and jobs with up-to-date skill-sets and high training requirements. Probably because of the belief that people over the age of 50 lack the ability to learn and develop new skills, and that skills become obsolete over time (Wrenn & Maurer, 2004), employers are not likely to hire older workers for jobs that require training in order for employees to learn new skills (Hirsch et al., 2000). Hirsch et al. (2000) also found that older workers were less likely to work in and to be hired for occupations requiring computer use, and that older men in particular were less likely to be hired for occupations requiring a high numerical aptitude. In sum, cost considerations and age stereotypes may prevent organizations from hiring older workers. Drawing policy implications from such observations is not, however, straightforward. Heywood, Jirjahn, and Tsertsvadze (2011) found that several factors (e.g., use of deferred compensation) that reduced the likelihood of employers employing older workers on a full-time basis advanced the possibilities of employing older workers for part-time jobs.

Conclusions and Recommendations

Whereas the growing employment flexibility of our current society can signify opportunity for some, it can mean increased instability, uncertainty, midlife career changes, and long spells of unemployment for others. In the face of longer working lives, faster changes in employment and employment conditions, and stigmatizing stereotypes about age, older workers face a difficult situation when it comes to job loss and searching for reemployment (Koeber, 2002; Lippmann, 2008; Wagenaar et al., 2015; Wanberg et al., 2015). These differences hardly emerge while older workers are still employed, particularly for those older workers with a long tenure in their organization who enjoy appreciation, high financial benefits for their investment in the organization, and high organization-specific human capital. Given enough tenure, older workers usually face a lower probability of being displaced than younger workers. Yet, as soon as older workers do lose their jobs, difficulties are likely to arise (e.g., Conen et al., 2011).

The most straightforward advice given to unemployed workers is to seek reemployment. Yet in the case of older workers, even very intensive job-search efforts are less likely to pay dividends. Older workers face a considerably harder situation on the regular labor market, because the organization-specific human capital that made them valuable employees at their old job might not be equally valued by potential new employers. More often than young workers, older workers are employed in professions and industries declining under pressures from globalization and deregulation, thus making it more difficult for them to find satisfactory reemployment in their field of work. Even when older job-seekers do find reemployment, it is usually in exchange for a steep decline in earnings and benefits.

Early research (Warr & Jackson, 1984) assumed that older workers would suffer less from job loss than their younger colleagues, but results show that this assumption is not tenable. Rather, older workers seem to face a somewhat different array of threats and opportunities than those experienced by younger workers. On the one hand, given sufficient financial resources and opportunities, older workers may move into early retirement or self-employment. On the other hand, however, there are employer-side barriers at individual, organizational, industry, and societal levels both leading to and prolonging unemployment among older workers (Lassus, 2015). Signals from all these levels can make older job-seekers acutely aware of the stigma of being "old" that they now have to face. After a career with a high identification with their work and decades of experience, these workers may now feel obsolete and unwanted. Moreover, the valuable professional contribution that they are used to making and are still eager to make is about to go to waste, while the future holds little promise about any improvements in this situation. Despite the facts that, firstly, many of the employment barriers originate from the older workers' environments (Lassus, 2015) and that, secondly, in the maintenance of employability both contextual (Zacher, 2015) and individual proactive career behaviors (Kooij, 2015) play important roles, it is relevant to ask: What can older workers themselves do to secure their potential to remain in paid employment?

The basic answer, we believe, is for workers, employed or displaced, to face the situation of possible unemployment at an older working age, to adjust their expectations to the reality of a less stable career, and to prepare accordingly (e.g., Fournier, Zimmermann, & Gauthier, 2011; Hall & Mirvis, 1995; Lippmann, 2008). Given the relevance of employability in today's changing labor market in order to both remain employed and, if that fails, to enjoy better chances when searching for reemployment, we believe that workers in general, and older workers in particular, need to actively and continuously invest in their employability (Lo Presti & Pluviano, 2015).

Employees' employability in the form of human and social capital, work-related identity, and adaptability (e.g., Fugate et al., 2004) likely plays a major role at several stages along the process outlined in Figure 24.1. A high internal employability at the employing organization makes people less likely to lose their job in the first place. Once unemployed, however, a high employability may also affect how people cope with the situation and how effective such coping turns out to be in order to find reemployment elsewhere, to make up for lost work functions, or to adjust one's own personal standard. For example, job seekers with widely sought-after human capital will be more likely to engage in a job search and may also be more likely to find a job. People with strong social capital in the form of a large network filled with many high-status connections may find networking during a job search a particularly easy approach, and they may furthermore turn out to be particularly adept at it (Van Hoye et al., 2009). And finally, given that job searching, particularly among older job-seekers, is a process troubled with setbacks and disappointments, job seekers with a strong sense of career-related identity will be more likely to persist. Additionally, they may be more likely to continue to represent the image of a desirable employee to potential employers, thus leading to more success during the job search as well. Finally, a high adaptability will likely help workers to explore and envision alternative career options, thus possibly turning this difficult experience into an opportunity for unforeseen personal success (Gabriel et al., 2010; Zikic & Klehe, 2006; Zikic & Richardson, 2007).

Yet, one might also believe that a high employability does not necessarily lead people to more successfully search for reemployment elsewhere. The same could be argued, for example, for the decision to become self-employed, with high human capital enhancing the chances that one has something valuable to offer to the market, good social networks enhancing knowledge regarding whom to best offer it to, and high adaptability and identity helping the newly self-employed worker to successfully manage and persist in the face of emerging difficulties. While such relationships have not been sufficiently tested yet, we would also assume that a high adaptability may, for example, help unemployed workers to redefine themselves and their role in society, thus facilitating, for example, a move into early retirement or finding avenues other than work to make

up for the now-missing work functions. One might also assume that people with high social capital will enjoy more social connections that allow them to remain active, receive some form of social status, and make a meaningful contribution in other spheres than paid work, whether it be in professional associations or nonprofessional community organizations. A high human capital in the respective domains may further enhance their attractiveness to these communities.

In contrast to this perspective stand stereotypes about older people, which represent them as costly to employ, poor performers, unwilling and unable to learn, resistant to change, and not likely to last for long (Posthuma & Campion, 2009). These stereotypes may contribute to the likelihood of job loss and to the likelihood of finding reemployment. Yet, stereotypes and discrimination likely also impact the perceived loss of work functions, for instance by making older job-seekers acutely aware of the stigmata associated with age (Berger, 2006; Riach & Loretto, 2009) and discouraging a search for reemployment elsewhere or suggesting early retirement. The best that workers can do about these stereotypes, we would argue, is to prove them to be blatantly wrong and to actively work on their own employability. While this might not solve the problem of stereotypes per se, it might give the job seeker in question an opportunity to be understood as the exception, rather than the norm. The options available to workers, however, will likely differ greatly, depending on whether they are still employed or already face a dire unemployment situation.

Employed workers. Employed workers, including older workers, are in an easier situation in so far as regular employment often offers multiple avenues for actively tending to and increasing one's employability. Many of these avenues might not sound revolutionary per se, but in fact propose that older workers continue doing the same or at least similar things that we usually expect younger workers to do when they are trying to establish themselves in an organization or profession.

Possibilities include: (a) receive training on transferable skills, (b) find challenging and visible assignments, (c) network, and (d) expect to be flexible. Continuous learning through challenging assignments and successful participation in professional training allow for human capital development, counteracting the stereotype that older workers would be less motivated and able to learn. In many organizations, older employees may actually need to show *more* motivation to learn and claim equal rights to training and developmental opportunities. Stereotypes and resulting age discrimination may otherwise prevent them from enjoying the training opportunities reserved for younger employers (Maurer & Rafuse, 2001). Yet, training opportunities do not always need to be initiated by the organization alone. Additional training besides the job (or possibly in exchange for a reduced number of work hours) can both help to keep workers' skill-sets up to date and signal to potential future employers that the current job-seeker is willing and able to learn.

Beside official trainings, one can and should also strive to engage in continuous learning on the job (e.g., Hall & Mirvis, 1995), which has the advantage of usually being faster, less costly, directly job-related, and usually more under the workers' own control. One such approach would be to accumulate different types of experiences by actively seeking out challenging and particularly visible assignments. Such assignments help the person to both grow and develop their skill-set (De Rue & Wellman, 2009; Dragoni, Tesluk, Russell, & Oh, 2009) and at the same time can serve as signals to both present and possible future employers that this person is willing to challenge him- or herself, to learn and grow (De Pater, Van Vianen, Bechtoldt, & Klehe, 2009), and that he or she is apparently also able to handle different types of tasks, employing different types of skill-sets. A study by Picchio and van Ours (2013) confirms that on-the-job training is, indeed, related to employment among older workers.

Finally, older workers tend to underuse their social networks. The extension and maintenance of social networks, particularly professional networks, is often a valuable investment. Relevant in this regard are not only network connections to people within one's own organization, and thus people who may also not be faring well and might face the same threatening situations, but also connections to people outside of the organization, whether it be through professional associations or contacts to business partners, customers, or even competitors.

Unemployed workers. Once the ax has fallen and workers already find themselves unemployed, the further development of employability often becomes more difficult. Unemployment is often associated with a decrease in employability in the form of dwindling job-specific skills, fewer trainings and updates, deteriorating networks, and a reduced career identity in the form of a growing perception by oneself and others that the connection to the former job, profession, and employment overall. Yet again, workers are not fully defenseless. They may have to decide whether to search for regular reemployment, start self-employment, retire, or find a combination of these options. In any case, particularly when searching for reemployment or considering self-employment, older workers will quickly learn that new employers are often relatively unwilling to pay salaries comparable to the ones that workers enjoyed before the job loss. High-reservation wages, that is, wages below which workers are willing to accept a job, have been suggested as one factor contributing to the low success rate of older job-searchers (e.g., de Coen, Forrier, & Sels, 2010; Maestas & Li, 2006; Vansteenkiste et al., 2015).

At the same time, unemployed people can try to visibly enhance their human and social capital in the form of formal trainings or professional networking (Blustein et al., 2013; Garrett-Peters, 2009; Lassus et al., 2015; Riach & Loretto, 2009). A major aspect in this regard is the emphasis on "visible," as such visibility will be needed in order to defeat the stereotypes that older job-seekers will encounter during their job search. Given that older job-seekers are often acutely aware of the handicapping factor of "age" as they conduct their job search, they sometimes also try to downplay or hide this factor or even distort information in order to at least be invited for an interview (Berger, 2009; Gabriel et al., 2010; Parris & Vickers, 2010).

Overall, however, the situation for most older job-seekers is relatively bleak in that they have greater difficulty finding employment (Koeber & Wright, 2001; Lassus, 2015). The rapid changes and rise of the service economy have undoubtedly affected all workers. Much of what determines the reemployment success of older workers is the degree to which they are able and prepared to cope with career-related changes (Lippmann, 2008). The ability to remain an attractive employee on the labor market, that is, employability, and as a subcomponent thereof, to cope and adjust to these changes, appears to be the crux of reemployment success for older workers (Lippmann, 2008).

The difficulties older workers experience in finding reemployment may become less so when they can better respond and adapt to the changes of modern technology and the ever-changing labor market. Some will continue to find it difficult to find reemployment, but with increased employability and an adaptable mindset, job loss, job search, and subsequent reemployment may become easier over time.

Acknowlegments

This work has been financed by a grant from the German Research Foundation (KL 2366/2-1). Parts of this work are based on an earlier chapter published in the *Oxford Handbook of Work and Aging*.

References

AARP. (2002). *Staying ahead of the curve: The AARP work- and career study*. Washington, DC: AARP.

AARP. (2007). *Staying ahead of the curve: The AARP work- and career study*. Washington, DC: AARP.

Adler, G., & Hilber, D. (2009). Industry hiring patterns of older workers. *Research on Aging, 31*, 69–88.

Ahmed, A. M., Andersson, L., & Hammarstedt, M. (2012). Does age matter for employability?: A field experiment on ageism in the Swedish labour market. *Applied Economics Letters, 19*, 403–406.

Ahs, A. M. H., & Westerling, R. (2006). Mortality in relation to employment status during different levels of unemployment. *Scandinavian Journal of Public Health, 34*, 159–167.

Anderson, N. D., Damianakis, T., Kröger, E., Wagner, L. M., Dawson, D. R., Binns, M. A., . . . Cook, S. L. (2014). The benefits associated with volunteering among seniors: A critical review and recommendations for future research. *Psychological Bulletin, 140*, 1505–1533.

Arcaya, M., Glymour, M. M., Christakis, N. A., Kawachi, I., & Subramanian, S. V. (2014). Individual and spousal unemployment as predictors of smoking and drinking behavior. *Social Science & Medicine (1982), 110*, 89–95.

Ashforth, B. E., Harrison, S. H., & Corley, K. G. (2008). Identification in organizations: An examination of four fundamental questions. *Journal of Management, 34*, 325–374.

Bal, P. M., Lange, A. H. de, van der Heijden, B. I. J. M., Zacher, H., Oderkerk, F. A., & Otten, S. (2015). Young at heart, old at work?: Relations between age, (meta-)stereotypes, self-categorization, and retirement attitudes. *Journal of Vocational Behavior, 91*, 35–45.

Bal, P. M., Lange, A. H. de, Zacher, H., & van der Heijden, B. I. J. M. (2013). A lifespan perspective on psychological contracts and their relations with organizational commitment. *European Journal of Work and Organizational Psychology, 22*, 279–292.

Baumeister, R. F., & Leary, M. R. (1995). The need to belong: Desire for interpersonal attachments as a fundamental human motivation. *Psychological Bulletin, 117*, 497–529.

Baumol, W. J., Blinder, A. S., & Wolff, E. N. (2003). *Downsizing in America: Reality, causes, and consequences*. New York: Russell Sage Foundation Publications.

Becker, G. S. (1962). Investment in human capital: A theoretical analysis. *Journal of Political Economy, 70*, 9–49.

Bendick, M., Brown, L. E., & Wall, K. (1999). No foot in the door: An experimental study of employment discrimination against older workers. *Journal of Aging and Social Policy, 10*, 5–23.

Bendick, M., Jackson, C. W., & Romero, J. H. (1996). Employment discrimination against older workers: An experimental study of hiring practices. *Journal of Aging and Social Policy, 8*, 25–46.

Berger, E. D. (2006). "Aging" identities: Degradation and negotiation in the search for employment. *Journal of Aging Studies, 20*, 303–316.

Berger, E. D. (2009). Managing age discrimination: An examination of the techniques used when seeking employment. *Gerontologist, 49*, 317–332.

Biehl, A. M., Gurley-Calvez, T., & Hill, B. (2014). Self-employment of older Americans: Do recessions matter? *Small Business Economics, 42*, 297–309.

Blustein, D. L., Kozan, S., & Connors-Kellgren, A. (2013). Unemployment and underemployment: A narrative analysis about loss. *Journal of Vocational Behavior, 82*, 256–265.

Bos, A. E. R., Pryor, J. B., Reeder, G. D., & Stutterheim, S. E. (2013). Stigma: Advances in theory and research. *Basic and Applied Social Psychology, 35*, 1–9.

Bosch, N., & ter Weel, B. (2013). Labour-market outcomes of older workers in the Netherlands: Measuring job prospects using the occupational age structure. *De Economist, 161*, 199–218.

Botric, V. (2009). Unemployed and long-term unemployed in Croatia: Evidence from Labour Force Survey. *Revija Za Socijalnu Politiku, 16*, 25–44.

Brand, J. E. (2015). The far-reaching impact of job loss and unemployment. *Annual Review of Sociology, 41*, 359–375.

Brand, J. E., & Burgard, S. A. (2008). Job displacement and social participation over the lifecourse: Findings for a cohort of joiners. *Social Forces, 87*, 211–242.

Brand, J. E., Levy, B. R., & Gallo, W. T. (2008). Effects of layoffs and plant closings on subsequent depression among older workers. *Research on Aging, 30*, 701–721.

Broomhall, H. S., & Winefield, A. H. (1990). A comparison of the affective well-being of young and middle-aged unemployed men matched for length of unemployment. *British Journal of Medical Psychology, 63*, 43–52.

Burgard, S. A., Kalousova, L., & Seefeldt, K. S. (2012). Perceived job insecurity and health: the Michigan Recession and Recovery Study. *Journal of Occupational and Environmental Medicine/American College of Occupational and Environmental Medicine, 54*, 1101–1106.

Buyens, D., Van Dijk, H., Dewilde, T., & De Vos, A. (2009). The aging workforce: perceptions of career ending. *Journal of Managerial Psychology, 24*, 102–117.

Calvo, E., Haverstick, K., & Sass, S. A. (2009). Gradual retirement, sense of control, and retirees' happiness. *Research on Aging, 31*, 112–135.

Cameron, K., Freeman, S., & Mishra, A. (1991). Best practices in white-collar downsizing: Managing contradictions. *Academy of Management Executive, 5*, 57–73.

Caplan, R. D., Vinokur, A. D., Price, R. H., & Vanryn, M. (1989). Job seeking, reemployment, and mental-health—a randomized field experiment in coping with job loss. *Journal of Applied Psychology, 74*, 759–769.

Carstensen, L. L. (1995). Evidence for a life-span theory of socioemotional selectivity. *Current Directions in Psychological Science, 4*, 151–156.

Catalano, R., Dooley, D., Wilson, G., & Hough, R. (1993). Job loss and alcohol-abuse—a test using data from the Epidemiologic Catchment-Area Project. *Journal of Health and Social Behavior, 34*, 215–225.

Chan, S. W., & Stevens, A. H. (1999). Employment and retirement following a late-career job loss. *American Economic Review, 89*, 211–216.

Chan, S. W., & Stevens, A. H. (2001). Job loss and employment patterns of older workers. *Journal of Labor Economics, 19*, 484–521.

Chan, S. W., & Stevens, A. H. (2004). How does job loss affect the timing of retirement? *Contributions to Economic*

Analysis & Policy, 3, Article 5. Downloaded at: https://www.degruyter.com/downloadpdf/j/bejeap.2003.3.issue-1/bejeap.2004.3.1.1187/bejeap.2004.3.1.1187.pdf

Cheng, G. H. L., & Chan, D. K. S. (2008). Who suffers more from job insecurity? A meta-analytic review. *Applied Psychology—an International Review—Psychologie Appliquee—Revue Internationale, 57*, 272–303.

Choi, K.-S., Stewart, R., & Dewey, M. (2013). Participation in productive activities and depression among older Europeans: Survey of Health, Ageing and Retirement in Europe (SHARE). *International Journal of geriatric psychiatry, 28*, 1157–1165.

Cohen, S., & Janicki-Deverts, D. (2012). Who's stressed?: Distributions of psychological stress in the United States in probability samples from 1983, 2006, and 20091. *Journal of Applied Social Psychology, 42*, 1320–1334.

Conen, W. S., Henkens, K., & Schippers, J. J. (2011). Are employers changing their behavior toward older workers? An analysis of employers' surveys 2000–2009. *Journal of Aging & Social Policy, 23*, 141–158.

Collings, S., & Blakely, T. A. (2001). Unemployment and suicide among 25–64 year olds: Some results from the New Zealand Census Mortality Study. *Australian and New Zealand Journal of Psychiatry, 35*, A4–A5.

Couch, K. A. (1998). Late life job displacement. *Gerontologist, 38*, 7–17.

Couch, K. A., Jolly, N. A., & Placzek, D. W. (2009). Earnings losses of older displaced workers: A detailed analysis with administrative data. *Research on Aging, 31*, 17–40.

Creed, P. A., & Bartrum, D. A. (2008). Personal control as a mediator and moderator between life strains and psychological well-being in the unemployed. *Journal of Applied Social Psychology, 38*, 460–481.

Creed, P. A., & Klisch, J. (2004). Future outlook and financial strain: Testing the personal agency and latent deprivation models of unemployment and well-being. *International Journal of Psychology, 39*, 382–383.

Creed, P. A., & Machin, M. A. (2002). Access to the latent benefits of employment for unemployed and underemployed individuals. *Psychological Reports, 90*, 1208–1210.

Creed, P. A., & Macintyre, S. R. (2001). The relative effects of deprivation of the latent and manifest benefits of employment on the wellbeing of unemployed people. *Australian Journal of Psychology, 53*, 75–75.

Creed, P. A., & Reynolds, J. (2001). Economic deprivation, experiential deprivation and social loneliness in unemployed and employed youth. *Journal of Community & Applied Social Psychology, 11*, 167–178.

Creed, P. A., & Watson, T. (2003). Age, gender, psychological wellbeing and the impact of losing the latent and manifest benefits of employment in unemployed people. *Australian Journal of Psychology, 55*, 95–103.

Cremer, H., Lozachmeur, J. M., & Pestieau, P. (2009). Use and misuse of unemployment benefits for early retirement. *European Journal of Political Economy, 25*, 174–185.

Crossley, C. D., & Highhouse, S. (2005). Relation of job search and choice process with subsequent satisfaction. *Journal of Economic Psychology, 26*, 255–268.

de Coen, A. N., Forrier, A., de Cuyper, N., & Sels, L. (2015). Job seekers' search intensity and wage flexibility: Does age matter? *Ageing and Society, 35*, 346–366.

de Coen, A. N., Forrier, A., & Sels, L. (2010). The Impact of Age on the Reservation Wage: The Role of Employability. *SSRN Electronic Journal.*

de Coen, A. N., Forrier, A., & Sels, L. (2015). The impact of age on the reservation wage: the role of employment efficacy and work intention: a study in the Belgian context. *Journal of Applied Gerontology: The Official Journal of the Southern Gerontological Society, 34*, NP83–112.

de Cuyper, N., Mäkikangas, A., Kinnunen, U., Mauno, S., & de Witte, H. (2012). Cross-lagged associations between perceived external employability, job insecurity, and exhaustion: Testing gain and loss spirals according to the Conservation of Resources Theory. *Journal of Organizational Behavior, 33*, 770–788

De Pater, I. E., Van Vianen, A. E. M., Bechtoldt, M. N., & Klehe, U.-C. (2009). Employees' challenging job experiences and supervisors' evaluations of promotability. *Personnel Psychology, 62*, 297–325.

De Rue, D. S., & Wellman, N. (2009). Developing leaders via experience: The role of developmental challenge, learning orientation, and feedback availability. *Journal of Applied Psychology, 94*, 859–875.

De Witte, H. (1999). Job insecurity and psychological well-being: Review of the literature and exploration of some unresolved issues. *European Journal of Work and Organizational Psychology, 8*, 155–177.

Deci, E. L., & Ryan, R. M. (2000). The "What" and "Why" of Goal Pursuits: Human Needs and the Self-Determination of Behavior. *Psychological Inquiry, 11*, 227–268.

Defillippi, R. J., & Arthur, M. B. (1994). The boundaryless career—a competence-based perspective. *Journal of Organizational Behavior, 15*, 307–324.

Dex, S., Willis, J., Paterson, R., & Sheppard, E. (2000). Freelance workers and contract uncertainty: The effects of contractual changes in the television industry. *Work Employment and Society, 14*, 283–305.

Dingemans, E., & Henkens, K. (2014). Involuntary retirement, bridge employment, and satisfaction with life: A longitudinal investigation. *Journal of Organizational Behavior, 35*, 575–591.

Dingemans, E., & Henkens, K. (2015). How do retirement dynamics influence mental well-being in later life? A 10-year panel study. *Scandinavian Journal of Work, Environment & Health, 41*, 16–23.

Donkin, R. (2010). *The Future of Work.* New York, NY: Palgrave Macmillan.

Dragoni, L., Tesluk, P. E., Russell, J. E. A., & Oh, I. S. (2009). Understanding managerial development: Integrating developmental assignments, learning orientation, and access to developmental opportunities in predicting managerial competencies. *Academy of Management Journal, 52*, 731–743.

Duncan, C., & Loretto, W. (2004). Never the right age? Gender and age-based discrimination in employment. *Gender Work and Organization, 11*, 95–115.

Eliason, M., & Storrie, D. (2009a). Does job loss shorten life? *Journal of Human Resources, 44*, 277–302.

Eliason, M., & Storrie, D. (2009b). Job loss is bad for your health—Swedish evidence on cause-specific hospitalization following involuntary job loss. *Social Science & Medicine, 68*, 1396–1406.

Elman, C., & O'Rand, A. M. (2002). Perceived job insecurity and entry into work-related education and training among adult workers. *Social Science Research, 31*, 49–76.

Evans, S. T., & Haworth, J. T. (1991). Variations in personal activity, access to categories of experience and psychological well-being in unemployed youn adults. *Leisure Studies, 10*, 249–264.

Falba, T. A., Sindelar, J. L., & Gallo, W. T. (2009). Work expectations, realizations, and depression in older workers. *Journal of Mental Health Policy and Economics, 12*, 175–186.

Falba, T. A., Teng, H. M., Sindelar, J. L., & Gallo, W. T. (2005). The effect of involuntary job loss on smoking intensity and relapse. *Addiction, 100*, 1330–1339.

Fanous, A. H., Prescott, C. A., & Kendler, K. S. (2004). The prediction of thoughts of death or self-harm in a population-based sample of female twins. *Psychological Medicine, 34*, 301–312.

Fenwick, T. (2012). Older professional workers and continuous learning in new capitalism. *Human Relations, 65*, 1001–1020.

Fleischmann, M., Koster, F., & Schippers, J. (2015). Nothing ventured, nothing gained!: How and under which conditions employers provide employability-enhancing practices to their older workers. *International Journal of Human Resource Management, 26*, 2908–2925.

Forret, M. L., & Dougherty, T. W. (2004). Networking behaviors and career outcomes: Differences for men and women? *Journal of Organizational Behavior, 25*, 419–437.

Fountain, C. (2005). Finding a job in the Internet Age. *Social Forces, 83*, 1235–1262.

Fournier, G., Zimmermann, H., & Gauthier, C. (2011). Instable career paths among workers 45 and over: Insight gained from long-term career trajectories. *Journal of Aging Studies, 25*, 316–327.

Fraher, A. L., & Gabriel, Y. (2014). Dreaming of Flying When Grounded: Occupational Identity and Occupational Fantasies of Furloughed Airline Pilots. *Journal of Management Studies, 51*, 926–951.

Frese, M. (1987). Alleviating depression in the unemployed—adequate financial support, hope and early retirement. *Social Science & Medicine, 25*, 213–215.

Frese, M., & Mohr, G. (1987). Prolonged unemployment and depression in older workers—a longitudinal study of intervening variables. *Social Science & Medicine, 25*, 173–178.

Frisch, M. B., & Gerrard, M. (1981). Natural helping systems—a survey of Red Cross volunteers. *American Journal of Community Psychology, 9*, 567–579.

Fryer, D. (1995). Labor-market disadvantage, deprivation and mental-health. *Psychologist, 8*, 265–272.

Fuchs, V. R. (1982). Self-employment and labor-force participation of older males. *Journal of Human Resources, 17*, 339–357.

Fugate, M., Kinicki, A. J., & Ashforth, B. E. (2004). Employability: A psycho-social construct, its dimensions, and applications. *Journal of Vocational Behavior, 65*, 14–38.

Gabriel, Y., Gray, D. E., & Goregaokar, H. (2010). Temporary Derailment or the End of the Line?: Managers Coping with Unemployment at 50. *Organization Studies, 31*, 1687–1712.

Gallo, W. T., Bradley, E. H., Falba, T. A., Dubin, J. A., Cramer, L. D., Bogardus, S. T., & Kasl, S. V. (2004). Involuntary job loss as a risk factor for subsequent myocardial infarction and stroke: Findings from the Health and Retirement Survey. *American Journal of Industrial Medicine, 45*, 408–416.

Gallo, W. T., Bradley, E. H., Siegel, M., & Kasl, S. V. (2000). Health effects of involuntary job loss among older workers: Findings from the health and retirement survey. *Journals of Gerontology Series B—Psychological Sciences and Social Sciences, 55*, S131–S140.

Gallo, W. T., Bradley, E. H., Siegel, M., & Kasl, S. V. (2001). The impact of involuntary job loss on subsequent alcohol consumption by older workers: Findings from the health and retirement survey. *Journals of Gerontology Series B—Psychological Sciences and Social Sciences, 56*, S3–S9.

Gallo, W. T., Bradley, E. H., Teng, H. M., & Kasl, S. V. (2006). The effect of recurrent involuntary job loss on the depressive symptoms of older US workers. *International Archives of Occupational and Environmental Health, 80*, 109–116.

Gallo, W. T., Brand, J. E., Teng, H. M., Leo-Summers, L., & Byers, A. L. (2009). Differential impact of involuntary job loss on physical disability among older workers—does predisposition matter? *Research on Aging, 31*, 345–360.

Gallo, W. T., Teng, H. M., Falba, T. A., Kasl, S. V., Krumholz, H. M., & Bradley, E. H. (2006). The impact of late career job loss on myocardial infarction and stroke: A 10 year follow up using the Health and Retirement Survey. *Occupational and Environmental Medicine, 63*, 683–687.

Garrett-Peters, R. (2009). "If I don't have to work anymore, who am I?": Job loss and collaborative self-concept repair. *Journal of Contemporary Ethnography, 38*, 547–583.

Giles, J., Park, A., & Cai, F. (2006). Reemployment of dislocated workers in urban China: The roles of information and incentives. *Journal of Comparative Economics, 34*, 582–607.

Glavin, P. (2013). The Impact of Job Insecurity and Job Degradation on the Sense of Personal Control. *Work and Occupations, 40*, 115–142.

Glavin, P. (2015). Perceived Job Insecurity and Health: Do Duration and Timing Matter? *Sociological Quarterly, 56*, 300–328.

Goffman, E. (1959). *The presentation of self in everyday life.* New York: Doubleday.

Gowing, M. K., Kraft, J. D., & Campbell Quick, J. (Eds.). (1998). *The new organizational reality: Downsizing, restructuring, and revitalization.* Washington, DC: American Psychological Association.

Gray, D. E., Gabriel, Y., & Goregaokar, H. (2015). Coaching unemployed managers and professionals through the trauma of unemployment: Derailed or undaunted? *Management Learning, 46*, 299–316.

Green, A. E., Li, Y., Owen, D., & Hoyos, M. de. (2012). Inequalities in use of the Internet for job search: Similarities and contrasts by economic status in Great Britain. *Environment and Planning A, 44*, 2344–2358.

Greenhalgh, L., & Rosenblatt, Z. (1984). Job insecurity: Toward conceptual clarity. *Academy of Management Review, 3*, 438–448.

Greenhaus, J. H., Callanan, G. A., & Godshalk, V. M. (2000). *Career management* (3rd ed.). Fort Worth, TX: Dryden.

Greller, M. M. (2006). Hours invested in professional development during late career as a function of career motivation and satisfaction. *Career Development International, 11*, 544–559.

Greller, M. M., & Simpson, P. (1999). In search of late career: A review of contemporary social science research applicable to the understanding of late career. *Human Resource Management Review, 9*, 309–348.

Griep, Y., Kinnunen, U., Nätti, J., de Cuyper, N., Mauno, S., Mäkikangas, A., & de Witte, H. (2015). The effects of unemployment and perceived job insecurity: a comparison of their association with psychological and somatic complaints, self-rated health and life satisfaction. *International Archives of Occupational and Environmental Health*, *89*(1), 147–162.

Haider, S. J., & Stephens, M. J. (2001). The impact of displacement on older workers (DRU-2631-NIA—Labor and population program working paper series 01–13—prepared for the National Institute on Aging). Santa Monica, CA: RAND.

Hairault, J.-O., Sopraseuth, T., & Langot, F. (2010). Distance to retirement and older workers' employment: The case for delaying the retirement age. *Journal of the European Economic Association*, *8*, 1034–1076.

Hall, D. T. (1996). *The career is dead—long live the career*. San Francisco, CA: Jossey-Bass.

Hall, D. T., & Mirvis, P. H. (1995). The new career contract: Developing the whole person at midlife and beyond. *Journal of Vocational Behavior*, *47*, 269–289.

Hall, D. T., & Nougaim, K. (1968). An examination of Maslow's need hierarchy in an organizational setting. *Organizational Behavior and Human Performance*, *3*, 12–35.

Hanisch, K. A. (1999). Job loss and unemployment research from 1994 to 1998: A review and recommendations for research and interventions. *Journal of Vocational Behavior*, *55*, 188–220.

Hank, K., & Erlinghagen, M. (2011). Perceptions of job security in Europe's ageing workforce. *Social Indicators Research*, *103*, 427–442.

Harackiewicz, J. M., Barron, K. E., & Elliot, A. J. (1998). Rethinking achievement goals: When are they adaptive for college students and why? *Educational Psychologist*, *33*, 1–21.

Haworth, J. T., & Ducker, J. (1991). Psychological well-being and access to categories of experience in unemployed young adults. *Leisure Studies*, *10*, 265–274.

Heaney, C. A., Israel, B. A., & House, J. S. (1994). Chronic job insecurity among automobile workers—Effects on job-satisfaction and health. *Social Science & Medicine*, *38*, 1431–1437.

Hedge, J. W., Borman, W. C., & Lammlein, S. E. (2006). *The aging workforce: Realities, myths, and implications for organizations*. Washington, DC: American Psychological Association.

Heidenreich, M. (2015). The end of the honeymoon: The increasing differentiation of (long-term) unemployment risks in Europe. *Journal of European Social Policy*, *25*, 393–413.

Henkel, D. (2011). Unemployment and substance use: A review of the literature (1990–2010). *Current Drug Abuse Reviews*, *4*, 4–27.

Henry, E. G., & Jennings, J. P. (2004). Age discrimination in layoffs: Factors of injustice. *Journal of Business Ethics*, *54*, 217–224.

Hepworth, S. J. (1980). Moderating factors of the psychological impact of unemployment. *Journal of Occupational Psychology*, *53*, 139–146.

Hershey, D. A., & Henkens, K. (2014). Impact of different types of retirement transitions on perceived satisfaction with life. *The Gerontologist*, *54*, 232–244.

Hetschko, C., Knabe, A., & Schöb, R. (2013). Changing identity: Retiring from unemployment. *The Economic Journal*, *124*, 149–166.

Hewitt, J. P. (2000). *Self and society: A symbolic interactionist social psychology* (8th ed.). Boston: Allyn & Bacon.

Heyma, A., van der Werff, S., Nauta, A., & van Sloten, G. (2014). What makes older job-seekers attractive to employers? *De Economist*, *162*, 397–414.

Heywood, J. S., & Jirjahn, U. (2015). The German labor market for older workers in comparative perspective. Research Papers in Economics, Universität Trier, No. 2/15.

Heywood, J. S., Jirjahn, U., & Tsertsvadze, G. (2011). Part-time work and the hiring of older workers. *Applied Economics*, *43*, 4239–4255.

Hirsch, B. T., Macpherson, D. A., & Hardy, M. A. (2000). Occupational age structure and access for older workers. *Industrial & Labor Relations Review*, *53*, 401–418.

Hooyman, N. R., & Kiyak, A. H. (2005). *Social gerontology: A multidisciplinary perspective* (7th ed.). Boston: Allyn & Bacon.

Horton, S., Baker, J., Pearce, G. W., & Deakin, J. M. (2008). On the malleability of performance—Implications for seniors. *Journal of Applied Gerontology*, *27*, 446–465.

Hutchens, R. M. (1988). Do job opportunities decline with age. *Industrial & Labor Relations Review*, *42*, 89–99.

Hutchens, R. M. (1999). Social security benefits and employer behavior: evaluating social security early retirement benefits as a form of unemployment insurance. *International Economic Review*, *40*, 659–678.

Hyde, M., Hanson, L. M., Chungkham, H. S., Leineweber, C., & Westerlund, H. (2015). The impact of involuntary exit from employment in later life on the risk of major depression and being prescribed anti-depressant medication. *Aging & Mental Health*, *19*, 381–389.

Ibarra, H., & Barbulescu, R. (2010). Identity as narrative: Prevalence, effectiveness, and consequences of narrative identity work in macro work role transitions. *Academy of Management Review*, *35*, 135–154.

Isaksson, K., & Johansson, G. (2000). Adaptation to continued work and early retirement following downsizing: Long-term effects and gender differences. *Journal of Occupational & Organizational Psychology*, *73*, 241–256.

Jackson, P. R., & Taylor, P. E. (1994). Factors Associated with Employment Status in Later Working Life. *Work, Employment & Society*, *8*, 553–567. doi:10.1177/095001709484004

Jahoda, M. (1982). *Employment and unemployment: A social psychological analysis*. New York: Cambridge University Press.

Johnson, R. W., & Kawachi, J. (2007). Job Changes at Older Ages: Effects on Wages, Benefits, and Other Job Attributes. *SSRN Electronic Journal*. doi:10.2139/ssrn.1299189

Johnson, R. W., & Mommaerts, C. (2010). Age differences in job displacement, job search, and reemployment. *SSRN Electronic Journal*.

Kanfer, R., & Ackerman, P. L. (2004). Aging, adult development, and work motivation. *Academy of Management Review*, *29*, 440–458.

Kanfer, R., Wanberg, C. R., & Kantrowitz, T. M. (2001). Job search and employment: A personality-motivational analysis and meta-analytic review. *Journal of Applied Psychology*, *86*, 837–855.

Kang, S. K., & Chasteen, A. L. (2009). The moderating role of age-group identification and perceived threat on stereotype threat among older adults. *International Journal of Aging & Human Development*, *69*, 201–220.

Kasl, S. V., & Cobb, S. (1971). Some physical and mental health effects of job loss: A preliminary report. *Pakistan Medical Forum*, *6*, 95–106.

Kinnunen, U., Feldt, T., & Mauno, S. (2003). Job insecurity and self-esteem: Evidence from cross-lagged relations in a 1-year longitudinal sample. *Personality and Individual Differences*, *35*, 617–632.

Kira, M., & Klehe, U.-C. (2016). Self-Definition Threats and Potential for Growth among Mature-Aged Job Loss Victims. *Human Resource Management Review, 26*, 242–259.

Koeber, C. (2002). Corporate restructuring, downsizing, and the middle class: The process and meaning of worker displacement in the "new" economy. *Qualitative Sociology, 25*, 217–246.

Koeber, C., & Wright, D. W. (2001). Wage bias in worker displacement: How industrial structure shapes the job loss and earnings decline of older American workers. *Journal of Socio-Economics, 30*, 343–352.

Koen, J., Klehe, U.-C., & van Vianen, A. E. M. (2013). Employability among the long-term unemployed: A futile quest or worth the effort? *Journal of Vocational Behavior, 82*, 37–48.

Koen, J., Klehe, U.-C., van Vianen, A. E. M., Zikic, J., & Nauta, A. (2010). Job-search strategies and reemployment quality: The impact of career adaptability. *Journal of Vocational Behavior, 77*, 126–139.

Kooij, D. T. A. M. (2015). Successful aging at work: The active role of employees. *Work, Aging and Retirement, 1*, 309–319.

Kposowa, A. J. (2001). Unemployment and suicide: A cohort analysis of social factors predicting suicide in the US National Longitudinal Mortality Study. *Psychological Medicine, 31*, 127–138.

Kreitman, N., & Platt, S. (1984). Suicide, unemployment, and domestic gas detoxification in Britain. *Journal of Epidemiology and Community Health, 38*, 1–6.

Kreuzfeld, S., Preuss, M., Weippert, M., & Stoll, R. (2013). Health effects and acceptance of a physical activity program for older long-term unemployed workers. *International Archives of Occupational and Environmental Health, 86*, 99–105.

Kuijpers, M. A. C. T., Schyns, B., & Scheerens, J. (2006). Career competencies for career success. *Career Development Quarterly, 55*, 168–178.

Kunze, F., Boehm, S., & Bruch, H. (2013). Age, resistance to change, and job performance. *Journal of Managerial Psychology, 28*, 741–760.

Kyyrä, T., & Ollikainen, V. (2008). To search or not to search? The effects of UI benefit extension for the older unemployed. *Journal of Public Economics, 92*, 2048–2070.

Kyyrä, T., & Wilke, R. A. (2007). Reduction in the long-term unemployment of the elderly: A success story from Finland. *Journal of the European Economic Association, 5*, 154–182.

Laanani, M., Ghosn, W., Jougla, E., & Rey, G. (2015). Impact of unemployment variations on suicide mortality in Western European countries (2000–2010). *Journal of Epidemiology and Community Health, 69*, 103–109.

Lahey, J. N. (2008a). Age, women, and hiring—An experimental study. *Journal of Human Resources, 43*, 30–56.

Lahey, J. N. (2008b). State age protection laws and the age discrimination in employment act. *Journal of Law & Economics, 51*, 433–460.

Lambert, T. A., Eby, L. T., & Reeves, M. P. (2006). Predictors of networking intensity and network quality among white-collar job seekers. *Journal of Career Development, 32*, 351–365.

Lammers, M., Bloemen, H., & Hochguertel, S. (2013). Job search requirements for older unemployed: Transitions to employment, early retirement and disability benefits. *European Economic Review, 58*, 31–57.

Lassus, L. A. P. (2015). Over the hill, under siege: Labor force graying, labor market pushes, and consequences for life chances. *Sociology Compass, 9*, 814–827.

Lassus, L. A. P., Lopez, S., & Roscigno, V. J. (2015). Aging workers and the experience of job loss. *Research in Social Stratification and Mobility, 41*, 81–91.

Latack, J. C. (1986). Coping with job stress—Measures and future-directions for scale development. *Journal of Applied Psychology, 71*, 377–385.

Latack, J. C., Kinicki, A. J., & Prussia, G. E. (1995). An integrative process model of coping with job loss. *Academy of Management Review, 20*, 311–342.

Lazarus, R. S., & Folkman, S. (1984). *Stress, appraisal, and coping*. New York: Springer.

Lazear, E. (2003). *Firm-Specific Human Capital: A Skill-Weights Approach*. Cambridge, MA: National Bureau of Economic Research.

Leana, C. R., & Feldman, D. C. (1990). Individual responses to job loss—Empirical-findings from 2 field studies. *Human Relations, 43*, 1155–1181.

Leana, C. R., & Feldman, D. C. (1992). *Coping with job loss: How individuals, organizations, and communities respond to layoffs*. New York: Macmillan/Lexington Books.

Leana, C. R., Feldman, D. C., & Tan, G. Y. (1998). Predictors of coping behavior after a layoff. *Journal of Organizational Behavior, 19*, 85–97.

Lee, C. H. (1998). Long-term unemployment and retirement in early-twentieth-century America. *Journal of Economic History, 58*, 844–856.

Lim, C., & Sander, T. (2013). Does misery love company? Civic engagement in economic hard times. *Social Science Research, 42*, 14–30.

Lindsay, C., Greig, M., & McQuaid, R. W. (2005). Alternative job search strategies in remote rural and peri-urban labour markets: The role of social networks. *Sociologia Ruralis, 45*, 53–70.

Lippmann, S. (2008). Rethinking risk in the new economy: Age and cohort effects on unemployment and re-employment. *Human Relations, 61*, 1259–1292.

Lo Presti, A., & Pluviano, S. (2015). Looking for a route in turbulent waters: Employability as a compass for career success. *Organizational Psychology Review*.

Logue, C. H. (1993). *Outplace yourself: Secrets of an executive outplacement counselor*. Holbrook, MA: Adams Publishing.

Lundin, A., Lundberg, I., Hallsten, L., Ottosson, J., & Hemmingsson, T. (2010). Unemployment and mortality—A longitudinal prospective study on selection and causation in 49321 Swedish middle-aged men. *Journal of Epidemiology and Community Health, 64*, 22–28.

Maestas, N., & Li, X. (2006). Discouraged workers? Job search outcomes of older workers (Working paper, Michigan Retirement Research Center Research, Paper No. WP 2006-133). RAND Corporation.

Malinen, S., & Johnston, L. (2013). Workplace ageism: Discovering hidden bias. *Experimental Aging Research, 39*, 445–465.

Mandal, B., Ayyagari, P., & Gallo, W. T. (2011). Job loss and depression: the role of subjective expectations. *Social science & Medicine (1982), 72*, 576–583.

Mandal, B., & Roe, B. (2008). Job loss, retirement and the mental health of older Americans. *Journal of Mental Health Policy and Economics, 11*, 167–176.

Manroop, L., & Richardson, J. (2015). Job search: A multidisciplinary review and research agenda. *International Journal of Management Reviews, 18*, 206–227.

Martikainen, P., Maki, N., & Jantti, M. (2007). The effects of unemployment on mortality following workplace downsizing and workplace closure: A register-based follow-up study of Finnish men and women during economic boom and recession. *American Journal of Epidemiology, 165,* 1070–1075.

Martin, G., Dymock, D., Billett, S., & Johnson, G. (2013). In the name of meritocracy: Managers' perceptions of policies and practices for training older workers. *Ageing and Society,* 1–27.

Matz-Costa, C., Besen, E., Boone James, J., & Pitt-Catsouphes, M. (2014). Differential impact of multiple levels of productive activity engagement on psychological well-being in middle and later life. *Gerontologist, 54,* 277–289.

Mauno, S., Ruokolainen, M., and Kinnunen, U. (2013). Does aging make employees more resilient to job stress? Age as a moderator in the job stressor-well-being relationship in three Finnish occupational samples. *Aging & Mental Health, 17,* 411–422.

Maurer, T. J., Barbeite, F. G., Weiss, E. M., & Lippstreu, M. (2008). New measures of stereotypical beliefs about older workers' ability and desire for development—Exploration among employees age 40 and over. *Journal of Managerial Psychology, 23,* 395–418.

Maurer, T. J., & Rafuse, N. E. (2001). Learning, not litigating: Managing employee development and avoiding claims of age discrimination. *Academy of Management Executive, 15,* 110–121.

Maurer, T. J., Weiss, E. M., & Barbeite, F. G. (2003). A model of involvement in work-related learning and development activity: The effects of individual, situational, motivational, and age variables. *Journal of Applied Psychology, 88,* 707–724.

McFadyen, R. G. (1995). Coping with threatened identities: Unemployed people's self-categorizations. *Current Psychology, 14,* 233–256.

McKee-Ryan, F. M., Song, Z. L., Wanberg, C. R., & Kinicki, A. (2005). Psychological and physical well-being during unemployment: A meta-analytic study. *Journal of Applied Psychology, 90,* 53–76.

McVittie, C., McKinlay, A., & Widdicombe, S. (2008). Passive and active non-employment: Age, employment and the identities of older non-working people. *Journal of Aging Studies, 22,* 248–255.

Meier, S., & Stutzer, A. (2008). Is volunteering rewarding in itself? *Economica, 75,* 39–59.

Mendenhall, R., Kalil, A., Spindel, L. J., & Hart, C. M. D. (2008). Job loss at mid-life: Managers and executives face the "New Risk Economy." *Social Forces, 87,* 185–209.

Milner, A., Page, A., & LaMontagne, A. D. (2014). Cause and effect in studies on unemployment, mental health and suicide: A meta-analytic and conceptual review. *Psychological Medicine, 44,* 909–917.

Minda, G. (1997). Opportunistic downsizing of aging workers: The 1990s version of age and pension discrimination in employment. *Hastings Law Journal, 48,* 511–576.

Mohr, G. B. (2000). The changing significance of different stressors after the announcement of bankruptcy: a longitudinal investigation with special emphasis on job insecurity. *Journal of Organizational Behavior, 21,* 337–359.

Mojza, E. J., Lorenz, C., Sonnentag, S., & Binnewies, C. (2010). Daily recovery experiences: The role of volunteer work during leisure time. *Journal of Occupational Health Psychology, 15,* 60–74.

Morrell, S., Taylor, R., Quine, S., & Kerr, C. (1993). Suicide and unemployment in Australia 1907–1990. *Social Science & Medicine, 36,* 749–756.

Munnell, A. H., & Rutledge, M. S. (2013). The effects of the Great Recession on the retirement security of older workers. *ANNALS of the American Academy of Political and Social Science, 650,* 124–142.

Munnell, A. H., Sass, S., Soto, M., & Zhivan, N. (2006). Has the displacement of older workers increased? 8th Annual Joint Conference of the Retirement Research Consortium "Pathways to a Secure Retirement." Washington, DC.

Munnell, A. H., Sass, S. S., & Zhivan, N. (2009). Why are older workers at greater risk of displacement? Center for Retirement Research at Boston College, Brief IB#9-10. Retrieved from http://crr.bc.edu/wp-content/uploads/2009/05/IB_9-10-508.pdf.

Murphy, G. C., & Athanasou, J. A. (1999). The effect of unemployment on mental health. *Journal of Occupational and Organizational Psychology, 72,* 83–99.

Neumark, D. (2009). The Age Discrimination in Employment Act and the challenge of population aging. *Research on Aging, 31,* 41–68.

Neumark, D., & Button, P. (2014). Did age discrimination protections help older workers weather the Great Recession? *Journal of Policy Analysis and Management, 33,* 566–601.

Ng, T. W. H., & Feldman, D. C. (2008). The relationship of age to ten dimensions of job performance. *Journal of Applied Psychology, 93,* 392–423.

Ng, T. W. H., & Feldman, D. C. (2009). Re-examining the relationship between age and voluntary turnover. *Journal of Vocational Behavior, 74,* 283–294.

Ng, E. S. W., & Law, A. (2014). Keeping up! Older workers' adaptation in the workplace after age 55. *Canadian Journal on Aging = La revue canadienne du vieillissement, 33,* 1–14.

Noelke, C., & Beckfield, J. (2014). Recessions, job loss, and mortality among older US adults. *American Journal of Public Health, 104,* e126–e134.

Oesch, D., & Baumann, I. (2015). Smooth transition or permanent exit?: Evidence on job prospects of displaced industrial workers. *Socio-Economic Review, 13,* 101–123.

Omoto, A. M., Snyder, M., & Martino, S. C. (2000). Volunteerism and the life course: Investigating age-related agendas for action. *Basic and Applied Social Psychology, 22,* 181–197.

Parker, S. K., Chmiel, N., & Wall, T. D. (1997). Work characteristics and employee well-being within a context of strategic downsizing. *Journal of Occupational Health Psychology, 4,* 289–303.

Parris, M. A., & Vickers, M. H. (2010). "Look at Him . . . He's Failing": Male executives' experiences of redundancy. *Employee Responsibilities and Rights Journal, 22,* 345–357.

Patrickson, M., & Ranzijn, R. (2003). Employability of older workers. *Equal Opportunities International, 22,* 50–63.

Paul, K. I., & Batinic, B. (2010). The need for work: Jahoda's latent functions of employment in a representative sample of the German population. *Journal of Organizational Behavior, 31,* 45–64.

Paul, K. I., & Moser, K. (2009). Unemployment impairs mental health: Meta-analyses. *Journal of Vocational Behavior, 74,* 264–282.

Pavlova, M. K., & Silbereisen, R. K. (2012). Participation in voluntary organizations and volunteer work as a compensation for the absence of work or partnership? Evidence from two German samples of younger and older adults. *Journals of Gerontology. Series B, Psychological Sciences and Social Sciences, 67,* 514–524.

Petrucci, T., Blau, G., & McClendon, J. (2015). Effect of age, length of unemployment, and problem-focused coping on positive reemployment expectations. *Journal of Employment Counseling, 52*, 171–177.

Picchio, M., & van Ours, J. C. (2013). Retaining through training even for older workers. *Economics of Education Review, 32*, 29–48. doi:10.1016/j.econedurev.2012.08.004

Platman, K. (2003). The self-designed career in later life: A study of older portfolio workers in the United Kingdom. *Ageing and Society, 23*, 281–302.

Posthuma, R. A., & Campion, M. A. (2009). Age stereotypes in the workplace: Common stereotypes, moderators, and future research directions. *Journal of Management, 35*, 158–188.

Preti, A., & Miotto, P. (1999). Suicide and unemployment in Italy, 1982–1994. *Journal of Epidemiology and Community Health, 53*, 694–701.

Probst, T. M. (2003). Exploring employee outcomes of organizational restructuring—A solomon four-group study. *Group and Organization Management, 28*, 416–439.

Probst, T. M. (2005). Countering the negative effects of job insecurity through participative decision making: Lessons from the demand-control model. *Journal of Occupational Health Psychology, 10*, 320–329.

Putnam, R. (2000). *Bowling alone: The collapse and revival of American community*: Simon & Schuster.

Quentier, J. M. (2014). Self-employment start-ups and value creation: An empirical analysis of German micro data. *Journal of Competitiveness Studies*, 37–57.

Ranzijn, R., Carson, E., Winefield, A. H., & Price, D. (2006). On the scrap-heap at 45: The human impact of mature-aged unemployment. *Journal of Occupational and Organizational Psychology, 79*, 467–479.

Riach, P. A. (2015). A field experiment investigating age discrimination in four European labour markets. *International Review of Applied Economics, 29*, 608–619.

Riach, K., & Loretto, W. (2009). Identity work and the "unemployed" worker: Age, disability and the lived experience of the older unemployed. *Work, Employment & Society, 23*, 102–119.

Rife, J. C., & Belcher, J. R. (1993). Social support and job search intensity among older unemployed workers: Implications for employment counselors. *Journal of Employment Counseling, 30*, 98–107.

Rife, J. C., & First, R. J. (1989). Discouraged older workers—An exploratory study. *International Journal of Aging & Human Development, 29*, 195–203.

Riumallo-Herl, C., Basu, S., Stuckler, D., Courtin, E., & Avendano, M. (2014). Job loss, wealth and depression during the Great Recession in the USA and Europe. *International Journal of Epidemiology, 43*, 1508–1517.

Rix, S. E. (2011). *Recovering from the Great Recession: Long struggle ahead for older Americans. Insight on the Issue. 50, May, 2011.* Washington.

Rogers, M. E., & O'Rourke, N. (2004). Health, job loss, and programs for older workers in Canada. *Canadian Journal of Career Development, 3*, 35–42.

Roscigno, V. J., Mong, S., Byron, R., & Tester, G. (2007). Age discrimination, social closure and employment. *Social Forces, 86*, 313–334.

Rosenblatt, Z., & Ruvio, A. (1996). A test of a multidimensional model of job insecurity: The case of Israeli teachers. *Journal of Organizational Behavior, 17*, 587–605.

Rubin, B. A., & Brody, C. J. (2005). Contradictions of commitment in the new economy: Insecurity, time, and technology. *Social Science Research, 34*, 843–861.

Ruhm, C. (1991). Are workers permanently scarred by job displacements? *American Economic Review, 81*, 319–324.

Savickas, M. L. (2002). Career construction: A developmental theory of vocational behavior. In D. Brown & associates (Eds.), *Career choice and development* (pp. 149–205). San Francisco, CA: John Wiley & Sons.

Savickas, M. L. (2005). The theory and practice of career construction. In S. D. Brown & R. W. Lent (Eds.), *Career development and counseling: Putting theory and research to work* (pp. 42–70). Hoboken, NJ: John Wiley & Sons.

Scherr, P. A., Lacroix, A. Z., Wallace, R. B., Berkman, L., Curb, J. D., Cornoni-Huntley, J., . . . Hennekens, C. H. (1992). Light to moderate alcohol-consumption and mortality in the elderly. *Journal of the American Geriatrics Society, 40*, 651–657.

Schirle, T. (2012). Wage losses of displaced older men: Does selective retirement bias results? *Canadian Public Policy, 38*, 1–13.

Schmitz, H. (2011). Why are the unemployed in worse health?: The causal effect of unemployment on health. *Labour Economics, 18*, 71–78.

Scott, F. A., Berger, M. C., & Garen, J. E. (1995). Do health-insurance and pension costs reduce the job opportunities of older workers. *Industrial & Labor Relations Review, 48*, 775–791.

Sersic, D. M., & Trkulja, J. (2009). Job insecurity as a research subject in psychology: Theories, definitions, findings. *Drustvena Istrazivanja, 18*, 523–545.

Simpson, P. A., Greller, M. M., & Stroh, L. K. (2002). Variations in human capital investment activity by age. *Journal of Vocational Behavior, 61*, 109–138.

Sincavage, J. R. (2004). The labor force and unemployment: Three generations of change. *Monthly Labor Review, 127*, 34–41.

Sousa-Ribeiro, M., Sverke, M., & Coimbra, J. L. (2014). Perceived quality of the psychosocial environment and well-being in employed and unemployed older adults: The importance of latent benefits and environmental vitamins. *Economic and Industrial Democracy, 35*, 629–652.

Sparrow, P. R. (2000). The new employment contract: Psychological implications of future work. In R. J. Burke and C. L. Cooper (Eds.), *The organization in crisis: downsizing, restructuring, and privatization,* 165–187. Oxford, UK: Blackwell.

Staubli, S., & Zweimüller, J. (2013). Does raising the early retirement age increase employment of older workers? *Journal of Public Economics, 108*, 17–32.

Steiber, N., & Kohli, M. (2015). You can't always get what you want: Actual and preferred ages of retirement in Europe. *Ageing and Society*, 1–34.

Stevens, A. H. (1997). Persistent effects of job displacement: The importance of multiple job losses. *Journal of Labor Economics, 15*, 165–188.

Stevens, C. K., & Turban, D. B. (2001). Impact of job seekers' search strategies and tactics on search success. Paper presented at the 16th annual conference of the Society for Industrial and Organizational Psychology, San Diego, CA, April.

Stock, J. H., & Wise, D. A. (1990). Pensions, the option value of work, and retirement. *Econometrica, 58*, 1151–1180.

Strom, S. (2003). Unemployment and families: A review of research. *Social Service Review, 77*, 399–430.

Stynen, D., Forrier, A., Sels, L., & de Witte, H. (2015). The relationship between qualitative job insecurity and OCB: Differences across age groups. *Economic and Industrial Democracy, 36*, 383–405.

Sum, A., Trubskyy, M., Khatiwada, I., McLaughlin, J., & Palma, S. (2011). The job dislocation and re-employment experiences of America's older workers during the great recessionary period of 2007–2009: The economic consequences for the dislocated and the rest of U.S. Society. Retrieved from ERPN Resources, Center for Labor Market Studies, Northeastern University. http://50.87.169.168/OJS/ojs-2.4.4-1/index.php/EPRN/article/view/1989.

Suvankulov, F., Lau, M. C. K., & Chau, F. H. C. (2012). Job search on the Internet and its outcome. *Internet Research, 22*, 298–317.

Sverke, M., Hellgren, J., & Näswall, K. (2002). No security: A meta-analysis and review of job insecurity and its consequences. *Journal of Occupational Health Psychology, 7*, 242–264.

Sverke, M., Hellgren, J., & Näswall, K. (2006). *Job insecurity: A literature review* (1:2006). Stockholm, Sweden: National Institute for Working Life.

Tatsiramos, K. (2009). Unemployment insurance in Europe: Unemployment duration and subsequent employment stability. *Journal of the European Economic Association, 7*, 1225–1260.

Tatsiramos, K. (2010). Job displacement and the transitions to re-employment and early retirement for non-employed older workers. *European Economic Review, 54*, 517–535.

Taylor, P. (2003). Age, labour market conditions and male suicide rates in selected countries. *Ageing and Society, 23*, 25–40.

Tetrick, L. E., & Barling, J. (Eds.). (1995). *Changing employment relations: Behavioral and social perspectives*. Washington, DC: American Psychological Association.

Thiel, D. (2007). Class in construction: London building workers, dirty work and physical cultures. *British Journal of Sociology, 58*, 227–251.

Underlid, K. (1996). Activity during unemployment and mental health. *Scandinavian Journal of Psychology, 37*, 269–281.

U.S. Department of Labor Statistics. (2006). *Extended mass layoffs in 2005* (Report 997. http://www.bls.gov/mls/mlsreport997.pdf.

Vahtera, J., Kivimaki, M., Forma, P., Wikstrom, J., Halmeenmaki, T., Linna, A., & Pentti, J. (2005). Organisational downsizing as a predictor of disability pension: The 10-town prospective cohort study. *Journal of Epidemiology and Community Health, 59*, 238–242.

Valletta, R. G. (1999). Declining job security. *Journal of Labor Economics, 17*, S170–S197.

van Dalen, H. P., Henkens, K., & Schippers, J. (2010). Productivity of older workers: Perceptions of employers and employees. *Population and Development Review, 36*, 309–330.

van Dalen, H. P., Henkens, K., & Wang, M. (2015). Recharging or retiring older workers? Uncovering the age-based strategies of European employers. *The Gerontologist, 55*, 814–824.

van der Heijden, B. I. J. M., Gorgievski, M. J., & De Lange, A. H. (2016). Learning at the workplace and sustainable employability: a multi-source model moderated by age. *European Journal of Work and Organizational Psychology, 25*, 13–30. http://dx.doi.org/10.1080/1359432X.2015.100713

van der Heijde, C. M., & van der Heijden, B. I. J. M. (2006). A competence-based and multidimensional operationalization and measurement of employability. *Human Resource Management, 45*, 449–476.

van Hooft, E. A. J., Wanberg, C. R., & van Hoye, G. (2013). Moving beyond job search quantity: Towards a conceptualization and self-regulatory framework of job search quality. *Organizational Psychology Review, 3*, 3–40.

Van Hoye, G., van Hooft, E. A. J., & Lievens, F. (2009). Networking as a job search behaviour: A social network perspective. *Journal of Occupational and Organizational Psychology, 82*, 661–682.

van Veldhoven, M., & Dorenbosch, L. (2008). Age, proactivity and career development. *Career Development International, 13*, 112–131.

Vansteenkiste, S., Deschacht, N., & Sels, L. (2015). Why are unemployed aged fifty and over less likely to find a job?: A decomposition analysis. *Journal of Vocational Behavior, 90*, 55–65.

Voss, M., Nylen, L., Floderus, B., Diderichsen, F., & Terry, P. D. (2004). Unemployment and early cause-specific mortality: A study based on the Swedish twin registry. *American Journal of Public Health, 94*, 2155–2161.

Wagenaar, A. F., Kompier, M. A. J., Houtman, I. L. D., van den Bossche, S. N. J., & Taris, T. W. (2015). Who gets fired, who gets re-hired: The role of workers' contract, age, health, work ability, performance, work satisfaction and employee investments. *International Archives of Occupational and Environmental Health, 88*, 321–334.

Wanberg, C. R., Griffiths, R. F., & Gavin, M. B. (1997). Time structure and unemployment: A longitudinal investigation. *Journal of Occupational and Organizational Psychology, 70*, 75–95.

Wanberg, C. R., Kanfer, R., & Banas, J. T. (2000). Predictors and outcomes of networking intensity among unemployed job seekers. *Journal of Applied Psychology, 85*, 491–503.

Wanberg, C. R., Kanfer, R., Hamann, D. J., & Zhang, Z. (2015). Age and reemployment success after job loss: An integrative model and meta-analysis. *Psychological Bulletin*.

Wanberg, C. R., Watt, J. D., & Rumsey, D. J. (1996). Individuals without jobs: An empirical study of job-seeking behavior and reemployment. *Journal of Applied Psychology, 81*, 76–87.

Warr, P. B. (1987). *Work, unemployment and mental health*. Oxford, UK: Oxford University Press.

Warr, P. B., Butcher, V., Robertson, I., & Callinan, M. (2004). Older people's well-being as a function of employment, retirement, environmental characteristics and role preference. *British Journal of Psychology, 95*, 297–324.

Warr, P. B., & Jackson, P. (1984). Men without jobs—Some correlates of age and length of unemployment. *Journal of Occupational Psychology, 57*, 77–85.

Westin, S., Schlesselman, J. J., & Korper, M. (1989). Long-term effects of a factory closure—unemployment and disability during 10 years follow-up. *Journal of Clinical Epidemiology, 42*, 435–441.

Willott, S., & Griffin, C. (2004). Redundant men: Constraints on identity change. *Journal of Community & Applied Social Psychology, 14*, 53–69.

Wolff, H. G., & Moser, K. (2009). Effects of networking on career success: A longitudinal study. *Journal of Applied Psychology, 94*, 196–206.

Worach-Kardas, H., & Kostrzewski, S. (2014). Quality of life and health state of long-term unemployed in older production age. *Applied Research in Quality of Life, 9,* 335–353.

Wrenn, K. A., & Maurer, T. J. (2004). Beliefs about older workers' learning and development behavior in relation to beliefs about malleability of skills, age-related decline, and control. *Journal of Applied Social Psychology, 34,* 223–242.

Yamasaki, A., Araki, S., Sakai, R., & Voorhees, A. S. (2009). Suicide mortality of young, middle-aged and elderly males and females in Japan for the years 1953–96: Time series analysis for the effects of unemployment, female labour force, young and aged population, primary industry and population density. *Industrial Health, 47,* 343–344.

Zacher, H. (2013). Older job seekers' job search intensity: The interplay of proactive personality, age and occupational future time perspective. *Ageing and Society, 33,* 1139–1166.

Zacher, H. (2015). The importance of a precise definition, comprehensive model, and critical discussion of successful aging at work. *Work, Aging and Retirement, 1,* 320–333.

Zacher, H., & Bock, A. (2014). Mature age job seekers: The role of proactivity. *Journal of Managerial Psychology, 29,* 1082–1097.

Zwick, T. (2012). Earnings losses after non-employment increase with age. *Schmalenbach Business Review, 64,* 2–19.

Zikic, J., & Klehe, U.-C. (2006). Job loss as a blessing in disguise: The role of career exploration and career planning in predicting reemployment quality. *Journal of Vocational Behavior, 69,* 391–409.

Zikic, J., & Richardson, J. (2007). Unlocking the careers of business professionals following job loss: Sensemaking and career exploration of older workers. *Canadian Journal of Administrative Sciences—Revue Canadienne Des Sciences De L Administration, 24,* 58–73.

Zissimopoulos, J. M., & Karoly, L. A. (2009). Labor-force dynamics at older ages—Movements into self-employment for workers and nonworkers. *Research on Aging, 31,* 89–111.

Nontraditional Employment: The Careers of Temporary Workers

Nele De Cuyper, Rita Fontinha, *and* Hans De Witte

Abstract

This chapter focuses upon the careers of temporary workers. Temporary employment for many workers presents a route to permanent employment. Other workers, however, get trapped into temporary employment or cycle between unstable jobs and spells of unemployment. Predictors of such transitions are multiple. We selected two broad categories, namely perceived employability from the area of career research and health and well-being from the area of occupational health and well-being research. The overall conclusion is that the association between temporary employment and both perceived employability and health and well-being is inconclusive. This suggests that there are boundary conditions that may make some temporary workers successful and others not. Risk factors include dynamics related to the dual labor market, including lower job quality, lower investments on the part of employers, and negative stereotyping of temporary workers as second-class citizens. On the positive side, many temporary workers have learned to manage their careers in the sense that they invest in training and in continuous job search.

Key Words: careers, employability, health and well-being, human capital, temporary employment, training

Introduction

Labor market experts, academics and practitioners alike, have observed a growth in different forms of nontraditional employment. This growth is not matched with a similar growth in more traditional forms of employment (Kalleberg, 2009). While the trend away from traditional employment is generally acknowledged, some see this trend as "gradual but continuing" (Gallagher & Sverke, 2005), and others as "extraordinary" (Marler, Barringer, & Milkovich, 2002). One reason for these varying reports relates to fairly large international differences—for example, in the incidence of nontraditional employment. By way of illustration, the incidence of temporary employment in Europe varies from around 4% in Luxembourg up to 25% in Spain, the average being about 14% (De Cuyper et al., 2008). A further reason for the different views on the growth in nontraditional employment should be sought in the diversification

of the nontraditional workforce (Kalleberg, 2009). This has led to a blurring of boundaries between traditional and nontraditional employment and, with blurring boundaries, to different definitions about nontraditional employment.

In the broadest sense, *non-traditional employment* refers to all forms of dependent (i.e., waged work)[1] employment that deviate in one or multiple ways from the standard form of employment. The standard form of employment includes permanent full-time employment with one employer during regular working hours (De Cuyper et al., 2008). Non-traditional employment presents a way to achieve flexibility in organizations in two ways (Reilly, 1998; Sels & Van Hootegem, 2001): Temporal flexibility and contractual flexibility. Temporal flexibility concerns the hours people work, be it the number of hours or time schedules. Examples are part-time work, overtime work, and shift work (e.g., day shifts, night shifts, weekend work). Contractual flexibility concerns the intake and exit of employees. Perhaps the most widespread form of contractual flexibility is the use of temporary employment (versus permanent employment). This chapter focuses on forms of contractual flexibility, temporary employment in particular. Temporary employment has particular resonance in the context of the theme of this book— job loss and job search. Temporary workers know for sure that they will have to engage in job search in the near future when their contract expires.

Temporary employment has been a topic of considerable debate. In the pessimistic view, temporary employment is seen as entirely driven by employers' demand for flexibility (Burgess & Connell, 2006; Kalleberg, Reynolds, & Marsden, 2003), with few if any benefits for the workers. Temporary employment would land workers in "precarious" jobs in terms of pay, job security, and job quality, for example. This has led to concerns about health and well-being among temporary workers (see e.g., Bardasi & Francesconi, 2004; Saloniemi, Virtanen, & Vahtera, 2004). In a next step, this may result in a series of "dead-end" jobs, so that temporary workers cycle between spells of unemployment and short periods of precarious work (see also Probst, Jiang, & Benson as well as Virick & McKee-Ryan, this volume). In the more optimistic view, temporary employment is seen as the exemplification of a change in patterns of individual careers (De Cuyper & De Witte, 2008a), much along new career paradigms such as the "boundaryless career" and the free-agent perspective (Forrier & Sels, 2003; Forrier, Sels, & Stynen, 2009; see also van Vianen & Klehe, this volume). The idea is that temporary employment, desired by workers or not, brings along opportunities for skill development and exploration for many workers (Kalleberg, 2000). This, in turn, may present a steppingstone for future career development.

We believe that both views have their merits and can be integrated to good effect. Accordingly, the key question in this chapter is as follows: Understanding the risks associated with temporary employment, what are the boundary conditions that would make temporary employment more harmful, less harmful, or even beneficial for future career development? The structure of this chapter is as follows: We set off with an overview of definitions regarding temporary employment. We continue with an overview of possible career paths of temporary workers, namely transitions to permanent employment, temporary employment, or unemployment. In

a next step, we highlight two main routes to successful transitions that have particular relevance for temporary workers: Perceived employability and health and well-being. Finally, we inspect a set of boundary conditions that may strengthen or instead weaken the association between temporary employment and perceived employability and health and well-being. These conditions come in five strands related to the individual, the heterogeneity of the temporary workforce, job resources, organizational investments, and labor market dynamics.

Temporary Employment: Definition, Facts, and Figures

One problem in temporary work research, as with research about non-traditional employment in general, relates to differences in vocabulary and the types of employment that fall under the heading of temporary employment across studies (De Cuyper et al., 2008).

Regarding vocabulary, differences are mostly tied to countries and continents: The dominant term in the United States and Canada is *contingent employment; temporary, fixed-term or non-permanent employment* in Europe; and *casual employment* in Australia and New Zealand[2] (De Cuyper et al., 2008). For the sake of consistency, we use the term *temporary employment* throughout this chapter.

Regarding types of temporary employment, a critical difference tied to objective characteristics of the contract[3] concerns direct-hire versus market-mediated temporary employment (Cranford, Vosko, & Zukewich, 2003; Feldman, 2005; Kalleberg, 2000; see Figure 25.1). Direct-hire temporary workers are hired by the organization at which they perform work. Direct-hire temporary employment comes in different grades of stability (OECD, 2002): Daily or on-call contracts are at the lower end and training and probationary contracts at the higher end. Fixed-term contracts and replacement contracts are situated in between (Aronsson, Gustafsson, & Dallner, 2002). Note that some of the less stable temporary contracts are chosen by workers who engage in temporary jobs aside another main activity (e.g., students), whereas other workers, particularly the less skilled, are forced into unstable temporary contracts (see, e.g., Silla, Gracia, & Peiró, 2005).

Market-mediated temporary employment involves a tripartite employment relationship: The workers are hired by a third party to perform work at the user or client organization (Barling & Gallagher, 1996; Connelly & Gallagher, 2004;

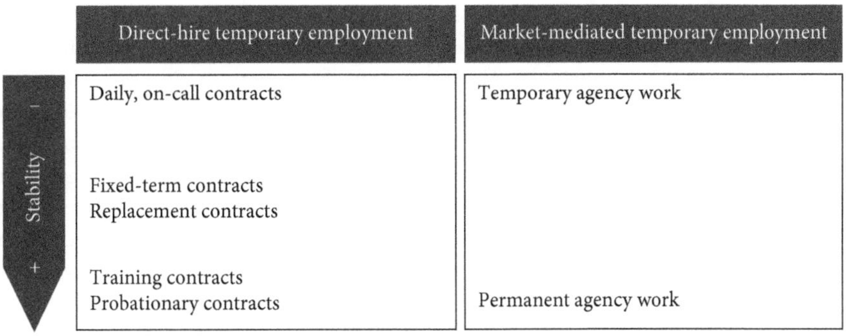

Direct-hire temporary employment	Market-mediated temporary employment
Daily, on-call contracts	Temporary agency work
Fixed-term contracts Replacement contracts	
Training contracts Probationary contracts	Permanent agency work

Stability − → +

Figure 25.1 Types of temporary employment.

Gallagher & McLean Parks, 2001; Kalleberg, 2000). The most prototypical example is agency work: Agency workers are hired by the agency on a temporary or permanent basis, depending on national legislation. For example, agency workers are always temporarily employed in Belgium, whereas most agency workers have a permanent contract in Sweden (De Cuyper, De Witte, & Isaksson, 2005). This has implications at the level of risk distribution and stability of contract. Permanent agency workers are paid, though somewhat less, also in between assignments: The financial risk is shared between agency and agency worker. Temporary agency workers get paid for the work they do: The financial risk lies with the worker. Some compensatory mechanisms may exist: For example, temporary agency workers may seek (financial) stability by working for multiple agencies. Because of their specific tripartite employment relationship, we treat temporary agency workers as a special case of temporary workers.

What binds the different vocabulary and the different types of temporary employment is the lack of ongoing employment. The OECD (2002, p. 170) provides the following definition: Temporary employment refers to "dependent employment of limited duration." Limited duration may take different forms: The contract may expire when a specific condition is met, as when a permanent worker returns to work in the case of replacement contracts. Otherwise, the ending date is set well in advance, as in the case of fixed-term contract workers (De Cuyper, et al., 2005). In contrast, permanent or open-ended employment contracts are valid until further notice. The idea of ongoing employment has implications at the level of statutory benefits and entitlements such as minimum wage, unemployment insurance, protection against unfair dismissal and paid leave; benefits and entitlements that

are more common and extensive among permanent compared with temporary workers (OECD, 2002). This is perhaps most explicit in the case of casual workers in Australia: Casual workers are not entitled to paid holiday or sick leave, public holidays, notice of dismissal, or redundancy payment (Kryger, 2004; Murtough & Waite, 2000).

Data collected by the OECD suggest that the percentage of temporary workers relative to dependent employment is substantial (see www.oecd.org), particularly in Europe (14%) and Canada (13%) but perhaps less so in the United States (8%). Recent figures for Australia are lacking, but OECD figures from 2005 suggest a relatively low incidence of temporary employment (5%). Note, however, that figures should be interpreted with considerable caution. First, figures for temporary employment are probably different when one is using national statistics based on country-specific interpretations. Second, all figures may mask substantial regional an international differences or differences according to the profiles of workers. Consider, for example, the differences between European countries: The United Kingdom (6%), Luxembourg (7%), and Belgium (8%) score well below the European average; Finland (15%) and Germany (15%) come close to the average; and Portugal (22%) and particularly Spain (25%) score above the average. The most obvious example in the area of workers' profiles concerns age: Temporary employment is much more common among the youngest age group (e.g., 40% in Europe), but the incidence of temporary employment drops in later career stages (e.g., 10% in the age group between 25 and 54).

The Special Case of Temporary Agency Workers

The number of agency workers almost doubled from 1999 to 2009, from 5 to 9 million (CIETT,

2011), and this evolution is expected to continue given the obvious benefits of agency work for employers (Kalleberg, 2000). Although the rise in agency work is substantial, its share relative to the total working population is modest, also in comparison to other forms of temporary employment (CIETT, 2011): 2% in Europe and 1% in North America. These averages mask substantial variation across countries. For example, Greece, Slovenia, and Poland are below the European average, with less than 0.5% temporary agency workers in the total working population. Germany, Belgium, and France have average rates, and The Netherlands (3%) and particularly the United Kingdom (4%) are clearly above the average.

The Careers of Temporary Workers: Transitions from Temporary Employment

An evaluation of whether temporary employment is a threat or instead an incentive for the careers of workers basically concerns possible transitions out of temporary employment. These transitions can be positive—for example, transitions to permanent or otherwise desired employment; or they may be negative—for example, transitions to unemployment or cycling between unstable jobs and spells of unemployment. Here we address the question as to whether temporary employment is a steppingstone to more stable employment or instead a dead end for future career success.

Transitions to permanent employment are an important indicator of career success for temporary workers: Indeed, many temporary workers see temporary employment as a route to permanent employment (De Cuyper & De Witte, 2008b; De Cuyper, Notelaers, & De Witte, 2009a). Taking the perspective of employers, temporary employment is sometimes seen as a Human Resource instrument for selection. It is used to "screen" temporary workers, who are hired on a permanent basis upon satisfactory performance and upon a demonstrated person-organization fit (Gagliarducci, 2005; Korpi & Levin, 2001; Tunny & Mangan, 2004). Accordingly, a substantial share of the temporary workforce moves into permanent employment within a reasonable time (OECD, 2002): Percentages range from 21% in France to 56% in Austria (1996–1997). More recent figures that are comparable across countries are hard to find and subject to bias—for example owing to differences in definitions of temporary

employment, the use of different data sources and methods across studies, and differences in legislation. However, studies providing anecdotal evidence arrive at similar conclusions. For example, Dekker (2001) concludes that temporary employment often presents an entry into permanent employment in Germany, The Netherlands, and to a lesser extent also in the United Kingdom. Chalmers and Kalb (2000), in a similar vein, establish that casual employment facilitates access to regular employment, particularly in comparison with unemployment. Booth, Francesconi, and Frank (2000) add to these findings by highlighting that the steppingstone function is common among fixed-term contract workers but less so for seasonal and on-call workers. That is to say, temporary employment may land some temporary workers into permanent jobs, but not workers in the most precarious forms of temporary employment in terms of contract stability and duration.

Relative to the share of temporary workers who find permanent employment, the share of those moving into unemployment in a time span of 1 to 2 years is fairly small, ranging from about 7% in Portugal to about 25% in Germany and France (OECD, 2002). Retrospective data aggregated over the OECD countries tie in with these findings: About two in three temporary workers were also employed a year previously. Among those not working, a considerable percentage were pursuing full-time studies (OECD, 2002). This clearly attests to the fairly high level of continuity in the work experiences of temporary workers. Hence the problem may not be that temporary employment increases the chance of ending up unemployed; what could be a problem instead is that some temporary workers get trapped in temporary jobs (see, e.g., Aronsson & Göransson, 1999): Between 25% and 50% of the temporary workforce were still employed on temporary contracts 2 years later.

In all, although we definitely acknowledge that some temporary workers may cycle between unemployment and temporary employment, this should not be presented as a general conclusion. To the contrary, most temporary workers seem to be able to keep a foot in employment, but sometimes only in the form of a chain of temporary contracts. An important factor here seems to be stability of contract (cf. Booth et al., 2000). Given the considerable variation across countries (cf. OECD, 2002), other factors may relate to the general state and structure of the labor market and country-specific legislation.

The Special Case of Temporary Agency Workers

While transitions from temporary agency work (versus from regular temporary work) to permanent employment are fewer (Amuedo-Dorantes, Malo, & Muñoz-Bullón, 2008), the steppingstone function of temporary agency work is generally acknowledged (CIETT, 2011): Temporary agency work may first present a steppingstone from unemployment to employment and then to permanent employment. The picture advanced by Storrie (2002) aligns with this view: Close to 20% of a large sample of agency workers from Germany, France, The Netherlands, Spain, and the United Kingdom are subsequently hired by the client organization, the majority on a permanent contract. Somewhat less than 20% found a permanent job with another employer, so that, in total, temporary agency work led to permanent employment for a considerable share of the temporary agency workers. Accordingly, temporary agency work for many workers is a lever for subsequent and in many cases more stable employment.

Predictors of Successful Transitions: Perceived Employability and Health and Well-Being

The key question to be addressed in the next sections concerns predictors of transitions. In this respect, we advance two main routes, successful transitions being conditional upon perceived employability and health and well-being. We selected these routes for two reasons. First, they come from two clearly distinct streams of literature: Career research and occupational health research. Second, both employability and health and well-being have been central concerns in the area of temporary work research (De Cuyper et al., 2008).

Route 1: Perceived Employability

Perceived employability is advanced as an upcoming critical resource for workers (Silla, De Cuyper, Gracia, Peiró, & De Witte, 2008; see also Klehe, de Pater, Koen & Kira, this volume). This is because changes in the labor market along with changes in the employee-employer relationship and the patterns of individual careers have induced a sense of insecurity among the workers, particularly temporary workers (Kalleberg, 2009). Unlike permanent workers, temporary workers cannot rely on security provided by the employer (De Cuyper & De Witte, 2006, 2007, 2008a; De Cuyper, Notelaers, & De Witte, 2009b).

Perceived employability may well provide a response. Perceived employability concerns the workers' perceptions of available job opportunities, either with the current employer (i.e., on the internal labor market; internal perceived employability) or with another employer (i.e., on the external labor market; external perceived employability; Berntson, Sverke, & Marklund, 2006; De Cuyper & De Witte, 2010; Rothwell & Arnold, 2007). The assumption is that perceived employability provides the workers with an alternative form of security, namely employment security rather than job security (Forrier & Sels, 2003). Perceived employability is built on a proactive attitude vis-à-vis the internal and the external labor market (Wittekind, Raeder, & Grote, 2010), so that employable workers are more likely to see, seek, and pursue career opportunities in defense of potential job loss. A plausible assumption therefore is that perceived employability may help temporary workers to achieve career success. Temporary employment implies both opportunities and threats to employability.

The positive view sees perceived employability as the result of employee investments. Temporary workers know for sure that they will have to leave their employers when their contracts expire. This induces the need to explore alternatives (De Cuyper et al., 2009b; Forrier & Sels, 2003). In other words, job loss is common among the temporary workforce, so temporary workers have learned to cope with job loss by investing in their marketability and by continuously inspecting the pool of potential job alternatives. The result is that they also see more job opportunities. In this perspective, temporary employment presents an exemplary case of career entrepreneurship, even though some temporary workers may have been forced to accept career self-management as a way to survive the labor market rather than as a free choice.

The negative view that temporary workers are likely to be less employable is built on dual labor market dynamics (Doeringer & Piore, 1971), both internal and external to the current organization (see e.g., Berntson et al., 2006). Regarding the internal labor market, the idea is that the core workforce of permanent workers gets access to privileges that are not available for peripheral workers, including temporary workers. One of these privileges relates to internal career ladders. That is to say, career opportunities are reserved for the permanent workers. To the extent that temporary workers are aware of such policies, this affects their perceptions of internal employability negatively. Regarding the external labor market, temporary workers start from a notoriously weaker negotiation position: Other employers may see temporary status as a negative signal, and they may be inclined to select core workers with shown records in other organizations first (Korpi & Levin, 2001). That is to say, when temporary workers have to compete for jobs with permanent workers, they are likely to lose. To the extent that temporary workers know, sometimes through experience, or think that they are less likely to be hired by employers, this affects their perceptions of external employability negatively. This is particularly so when the pool of potential rivals is large, as is the case in times of high unemployment or labor market recession.

Few studies to date have addressed the relationship between temporary employment and perceived employability. Most studies to date did not establish a significant relationship between temporary versus permanent employment and perceived employability (Berntson et al., 2006; De Cuyper et al., 2009b; De Cuyper, Mauno, Kinnunen, & Mäkikangas, 2011; De Cuyper, De Witte, Krausz, Mohr, & Rigotti, 2010). One exception is the study by De Cuyper and De Witte (2010): Temporary workers perceived themselves to be more employable, both on the internal and the external labor market.

Route 2: Health and Well-Being

Occupational health researchers have expressed concerns about temporary workers' health and well-being: The idea is that temporary employment associates with poorer working conditions (e.g., limited access to statutory benefits and entitlements) and with poorer job quality (e.g., fewer resources). This ultimately leads to poorer health and well-being among temporary versus permanent workers. Poorer health and well-being, in turn, may induce selection mechanisms on the part of employers who are inclined to select "the healthiest worker" from the pool of available workers, based on the "healthy worker—productive worker" (Taris & Schreurs, 2009; Zelenski, Murphy, & Jenkins, 2008) association. That is to say, to the extent that temporary employment relates to poorer health, this affects their career opportunities negatively.

Evidence on the relationship between temporary employment and psychological well-being and general health is mixed. For example, temporary workers compared with permanent workers report better (Liukkonen, Virtanen, Kivimäki, Pentii, & Vahtera, 2004) or poorer (Virtanen, Kivimäki, Elovainio, Vahtera, & Cooper, 2001; Virtanen, Vahtera, Kivimäki, Pentii, & Ferrie, 2002) psychological well-being. The meta-analysis by Virtanen et al. (2005) suggests that the relationship between temporary employment and psychological well-being is negative, though it is weak to moderate depending on the specific type of contract and the well-being indicator. However, the pattern of results reported in a large European project— PSYCONES (Guest, Isaksson, & De Witte, 2010)—does not support this picture. Rather to the contrary: Psychological well-being among temporary workers is as good in terms of life satisfaction and better in that they report lower irritation, depression, and anxiety and higher job satisfaction compared with permanent workers. In a similar vein, temporary workers report better (Liukkonen et al., 2004; Martens, Nijhuis, van Boxtel, & Knottnerus, 1999) or comparable general health (Artazcoz, Benach, Borrell, & Cortèz, 2005; Bardasi & Francesconi, 2004; Bernhard-Oettel, Sverke, & De Witte, 2005; De Cuyper & De Witte, 2006, 2007; Virtanen, Liukkonen, Vahtera, Kivimäki, & Koskenvuo, 2003). In the meta-analyses by Virtanen and colleagues (2005), no significant relationship between temporary employment and general health was established.

Conclusion

In sum, we established that temporary employment carries both threats and opportunities in terms of perceived employability, which aligns with the observation that most studies to date did not establish significant differences. In a similar vein, we tend to conclude that although selection mechanisms involving poor health may exist to some extent (Virtanen et al., 2002), they may be fairly weak and not a threat for the careers of temporary workers. Also, the evidence is mixed, with many studies reporting nonsignificant differences.

The Special Case of Agency Workers

Similar to regular temporary work research, the general assumption is that temporary agency work brings along specific stressors which then negatively affect temporary workers' health and well-being (Gimeno, Benavides, Amick, Benach, & Martinez, 2004), as is demonstrated in some studies (Rogers, 1995; Rogers & Henson, 1997; Yeh, Ko, Chang, & Chen, 2007). However, there is also evidence to the contrary, with temporary agency workers reporting fewer health problems and less sickness absence compared to permanent workers (Virtanen et al.,

2001). As with regular temporary workers, results for health and well-being are mixed.

Boundary Conditions

The mixed results on the relationship between temporary (versus permanent) employment and both perceived employability and health and well-being suggests some moderating factors. These factors may be bound to the individual's career investments, the heterogeneity of the temporary workforce, job resources, the organization, or the labor market, examples of which are provided below. Note that we do not aim at providing an exhaustive overview. Instead, our aim is to highlight some key issues that have been noted in the realm of temporary work research.

The Individual's Career Investments

Investments in the career made by the individual present a critical condition for both perceived employability and health and well-being, and, in a next step, also for career success. A case in point is training. Training boosts perceptions of employability (Forrier et al., 2009; Guest, 2000; Van Dam, 2004) and gives the worker a sense of competence and mastery, both critical to health and well-being. The implication is that perceived employability and health and well-being are conditional upon the individual's willingness to invest in training.

In this respect, Campbell (2001) and Forrier and Sels (2003) observe that temporary workers are, more than permanent workers, inclined to pay for training themselves. Moreover, the training objectives pursued by temporary workers emphasize opportunities for career development, whereas permanent workers' training objectives are related to personal development. That is to say, many temporary workers have embraced training as a form of investment in their careers. To the extent that they do, training is definitely a factor strengthening perceptions of employability and possibly also health and well-being and future career success among temporary workers.

Heterogeneity of Contracts

Much of the debate in the area of temporary employment has concerned the large heterogeneity of the temporary workforce in relation to workers' health and well-being. This heterogeneity is reflected in a number of objective contract characteristics related to stability (Virtanen et al., 2005). The general observation is that workers on stable contracts—for example, contracts of longer duration—fare better. For example, Guest and Clinton (2005) conclude that fixed-term workers report equal or higher levels of job satisfaction as compared with permanent workers, while seasonal, casual, and temporary agency workers are least satisfied. Similarly, Virtanen et al. (2003) do not find differences between fixed-term contracts and permanent contracts in self-reported health, while seasonal workers report more health problems.

Heterogeneity may also concern subjective aspects, most notably volition. The hypothesis is that temporary workers who voluntarily accept a temporary assignment report better health than those who are forced into temporary employment (De Cuyper & De Witte, 2008b; Krausz, 2000; Tan & Tan, 2002). This is based on the general idea of agency; that is, some workers are temporarily employed because they want to experience a sense of control, which then lead to increased health and well-being. This idea has found some support (Krausz, 2000), even though relationships are weak to moderate.

De Cuyper and De Witte (2008b) argue that a more complete account of volition would also embrace the specific motives for accepting temporary employment. Such motives concern voluntary reasons (e.g., accepting temporary employment because the worker does not want a long-term commitment), involuntary reasons (e.g., accepting temporary employment because no permanent jobs are available), reasons related to exploration of skills (e.g., accepting temporary employment because the worker aims to gain experience in different jobs and organizations), and steppingstone motives (e.g., accepting temporary employment because it may lead to permanent employment). They establish that many temporary workers see temporary employment as a steppingstone to desired employment, mostly in the form of a permanent contract. This was more important than any other motive. This aligns with the study by De Clerck, De Cuyper and De Witte (2006), who observed that about 80% of workers agree with steppingstone motives. De Jong and colleagues (De Jong, De Cuyper, De Witte, Silla, & Bernhard-Oettel, 2009) have demonstrated that more than one temporary worker in five highlighted *only* steppingstone motives as a reason for accepting a temporary contract.

Steppingstone motives may be seen in the context of job search strategies: Temporary workers who value these motives may be highly motivated to increase their chances on a permanent contract by showing their intentions to become good organizational citizens—for example, by expressing commitment to the organization, excelling in performance or engaging in extra-role behavior. Employers may interpret such behaviors as a positive signal, and they may be likely to hire these workers on a more permanent basis. On a related note, De Cuyper and De Witte (2010) have demonstrated that temporary workers were more likely to use various forms of impression management (i.e., behavior by the individual attempting to control or manipulate others' impressions)—for example, exemplification, self-promotion, and flattering from the category of self-focused, job-focused, and supervisor-focused impression management. They may do so to further promote the image of an excellent worker—an image that may lead to the permanent position to which they aspire.

In all, the relationship between temporary employment and health and well-being is strengthened for workers on stable contracts and a preference for temporary employment. Furthermore, transition chances into permanent employment may increase among workers who value steppingstone motives in accepting a temporary assignment, probably because they are highly motivated.

Job Resources

Employability and health and well-being may be conditional upon resources provided in the current job. First, resourceful jobs may provide the workers with opportunities to learn and to develop, whereas lack of resources may thwart all development or, worse, may lead to a reduction of available resources. The latter reflects the idea advanced by Hobfoll (1989, 2001) in his conservation of resources theory: Available resources attract new resources, so that ultimately caravans of resources are formed. Conversely, loss of resources may trigger a process that ultimately leads to a loss spiral. Second, resources have been related to workers' health and well-being—for example, in the many studies inspired by the job demand resources model (Bakker & Demerouti, 2007).

The dominant discourse is that temporary employment provides the workers with relatively few resources (Beard & Edwards, 1995; Sverke, Gallagher & Hellgren, 2000). This idea is grounded in the flexible firm model (Atkinson, 1984)—namely the view that the organization is built in layers, with permanent workers at the core and temporary workers at the periphery. Permanent workers are employed in jobs with many resources as a way to bind them to the organization so as to secure continuity in the organization. Research has generally supported the hypothesis of fewer resources, felt job security (Beard & Edwards, 1995; Bernhard-Oettel et al., 2005; De Cuyper & De Witte, 2006, 2007; De Cuyper et al., 2010; De Witte & Näswall, 2003; Mauno & Kinnunen, 2002; Parker, Griffin, Sprigg, & Wall, 2002), autonomy (Benach, Gimeno, & Benavides, 2002; De Cuyper et al., 2010; Goudswaard & Andries, 2002), and aspects of control over the working situation (Aronsson et al., 2002; Parker et al., 2002), in particular among temporary workers.

Those temporary workers who are employed in high-quality jobs may have more opportunities for career progression, although the general picture is that lack of resources presents a threat to employability and health and well-being among temporary workers.

The Organization

The workers' perceived employability may also be stimulated by factors at the level of the organization, for example human resource (HR) practices. In this respect, access to training has particular resonance as a way to boost the workers' employability. The general idea, based on insights from human capital theory (Becker, 1993), is that employers invest less in training for temporary compared with permanent workers. Employers invest with a view on a return on these investments, which is less likely among temporary workers (Aronsson et al., 2002; Forrier & Sels, 2003).

Research generally supports the idea of lower participation in training funded by the employer among temporary compared with permanent workers (Aronsson et al., 2002; Arulampalam & Booth, 1998; Campbell, 2001; Connell & Burgess, 2001; De Feyter, Smulders, & de Vroome, 2001; Delsen, 1998; Forrier & Sels, 2003; OECD, 2002), particularly where general rather than job-specific training is concerned (Rix, Davies, Gaunt, Hare, & Cobbolds, 1999). Aronsson et al. (2002) have established one exception on the general norm of lower training participation among temporary workers, namely among workers on probationary contracts (i.e., workers who transition to permanent employment upon successful performance).

The Labor Market

The profiles of temporary workers are, in general, not in demand on the labor market, particularly not in the contemporary knowledge-based economy that highly values experience and specialist knowledge. Temporary workers are, on average, younger, with little work experience, and they are somewhat less educated (OECD, 2002). This problem is exacerbated by the tendency of stigmatization of temporary workers as peripheral or second-class workers (Boyce, Ryan, Imus, & Morgeson, 2007). These factors may increase the risk of becoming unemployed.

Conclusion

There are many factors that may strengthen or weaken the relationship between temporary employment on the one hand and perceived employability, health and well-being, and future career success on the other. On the positive side, temporary workers who acknowledge the importance of training, as many do, and who accept their assignment with the idea that this may land them in a permanent job, fare better. On the negative side, many temporary workers are employed in jobs with few resources, they often have limited access to high commitment HR practices, and their profiles are often not in demand in the labor market. These factors present a threat for employability, health and well-being, and future career success.

The Special Case of Agency Workers

Many of the factors discussed above are also relevant in the specific case of agency workers. Perhaps investments on the part organizations require some further comment in the sense that the tripartite employment relationship that is characteristic for temporary agency workers presents a further risk (Eurofond, 2007): Client organizations generally see few gains in providing training to agency workers because a return on investments is highly unlikely. A further risk is that training responsibility is scattered across the client organization and the agency, with no party taking up full responsibility.

These risks should be balanced against factors that lead agencies to invest in training, mostly factors related to business strategy: Well-trained agency workers can be placed on better-paying jobs and are likely to increase client satisfaction, which then binds the client to the agency (Fontinha, Chambel, & De Cuyper, 2013). Agency workers themselves are well aware of the importance of training, even to the extent that access to training is one of the main reasons why employees in Brazil and the United States choose agency work (CIETT, 2011).

At a more general level, and leaving training investments on the part of the agency aside, temporary agency workers are clearly also at risk where the relationship with the client is concerned: Client organizations see their relationship with temporary agency workers as transactional and restricted to minimum terms and conditions as stipulated in the formal employment contract. The result is that temporary agency workers, even more than directly hired workers, are marginalized (Burgess & Connell, 2006), which shows in terms of compensation, both wages and fringe benefits (Nollen, 1996).

Conclusions

The central question in this chapter concerns the situation of temporary workers in terms of future career transitions, predictors of such transitions, and the boundary conditions that may further the careers of temporary workers. Our aim now is to bring the evidence together in a model that may inspire future research (Figure 25.2).

In terms of future career transitions, a major concern is that temporary employment is a dead-end route that often results in unemployment or, at the very least, the trapping of workers in temporary jobs. In the more optimistic view, however, temporary employment is portrayed as an entry to the primary labor market, with quick upward mobility in the first few career stages and stabilization in the next (Scherer, 2004). Figures from the OECD show that a considerable share of the temporary workforce makes "negative" transitions, but "positive" transitions into permanent employment in a relatively short time are more common. Nevertheless, some caution is warranted in interpreting these figures, as little is known about temporary workers who feel trapped into temporary employment: They have a foothold in employment but perhaps not in the most stable jobs. We also believe that employment, be it temporary or otherwise, may lead to the accumulation of human capital, particularly in comparison to unemployment; this argument is often neglected in research on temporary work (see also Lindsay, this volume, for a similar debate in reference to unemployment interventions). Indeed, most temporary workers are compared with permanent workers, whereas another and critical reference group may also be the unemployed. In all, our conclusion is that temporary employment for many workers presents a steppingstone to permanent or otherwise desired employment. A minority of the workers, however, get stuck in temporary employment or end up unemployed.

In terms of predictors of future career success, we focused upon perceived employability and health and well-being so as to capture a career and

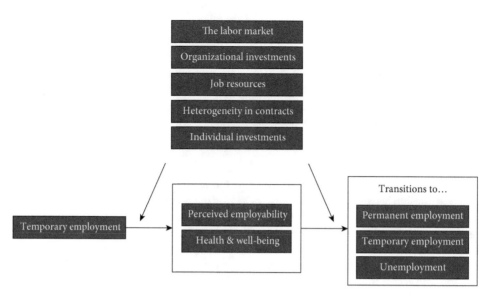

Figure 25.2 The careers of temporary workers.

occupational health perspective, respectively; We see both as critical conditions for achieving career success. The literature shows that the relationships between temporary employment and both perceived employability and health and well-being are inconclusive. This may suggest that temporary employment is beneficial for some workers and a risk for others. An important question, then, concerns boundary conditions.

In terms of such boundary conditions, we distinguished both opportunities and risk factors, and at different levels: Training investments on the part of the individual, volition and motives as indicators of the heterogeneity of the temporary workforce, job resources, training investments on the part of the organization, and the larger context.

On the positive side, temporary workers are, to a certain extent, entrepreneurs of their own careers. For example, they take responsibility for job-related training and skill development more than permanent workers do. Also, many temporary workers may pursue their ambition to transition to the core segment of the labor market; indeed, many temporary workers are motivated to gain a permanent contract, and they may do so by showing attitudes and behavior that are sought also in future permanent workers. This may, in some cases, take the form of intentional behavior directed toward creating a favorable impression. In this sense, temporary workers demonstrate proactivity and self-management, and they may have embraced a continuous job search as a way of building a career. These are critical career

competencies in the current era of change and flexibility; these factors may strengthen the relationship between temporary employment and both perceived employability and health and well-being (see also van Vianen & Klehe, this volume).

On the negative side, we established that employers tend to invest substantially less in temporary compared with permanent workers. For example, access to and participation in employer-funded training and job resources signaled labor market segmentation. To the extent that workers receive fewer employer entitlements and are employed in jobs of poorer quality, they may feel less employable and they may report poorer health and well-being. A further risk factor is that the profiles of temporary workers are not in demand in the labor market; temporary workers are, on average, somewhat less skilled, with little experience. This problem is exacerbated by negative stereotyping about "the" temporary worker. Indeed, some employers may see temporary work status as a negative signal, which places temporary workers in a weaker position both on the internal and the external labor market.

In all, our conclusion is that some factors hamper career success whereas others enhance it. Negative aspects include dynamics related to the dual labor market, including the lower level of investment on the part of employers—for example, in terms of training and job/organization resources and stereotyping. Positive aspects are built on the observation that temporary workers have to comply with job changes and have learned to be proactive—for example, by investing in training and career competencies. Possibly the negative and positive views address different contingents of temporary workers: The negative view may be dominant among temporary workers on the most unstable contracts or with the weakest occupational profiles, and vice versa for the positive view. In this respect, Silla et al. (2005) demonstrated that heterogeneity is a critical issue in temporary work research—a hypothesis that has received some attention in relation to employees' health and well-being but not yet where the careers of temporary workers are concerned.

The Special Case of Temporary Agency Workers

In many aspects, the situation of temporary agency workers mirrors the situation of other temporary workers. On the negative side, investments in temporary agency workers, too, are relatively few, particularly on the part of the client organization. The relationship between client organization and agency worker in many cases is transactional and limited to what is required from a legal point of view. The result could be that temporary agency workers are less committed and less willing to go beyond the minimum performance. On the positive side, like other temporary workers, agency workers are motivated by the prospect of transitioning to permanent employment. They may want to increase such transition chances by displaying excellent attitudes and behaviours in an attempt to influence hiring decisions. In this respect, successful transitions from temporary agency work to permanent employment with the client organization or another organization are relatively common. A further positive feature of temporary agency work, unlike regular temporary work, is that agency workers can rely on the agency for whom they are the single most critical asset for competitive advantage: The agency may invest in temporary agency workers, for example in the form of training or other HR practices that promote excellent performance so as to provide better service to client organizations *and* to bind the workers to the agency.

Future Directions

Perhaps the most general direction for future research could be to probe different aspects related to the careers of temporary workers in more detail. While the careers of temporary workers have received some attention, the efforts are overall scattered with little theoretical input (for an overview, see De Cuyper et al., 2008). In response, we advanced a model (Figure 25.2) that may inspire future research. We realize, however, that our model is not exhaustive and should be probed in much more detail. We provide some examples below.

First, we highlighted some aspects that we considered as inputs for perceived employability, health and well-being, and ultimately also labor market transitions—namely investment in training by the worker, steppingstone motives, investments on the part of the organization, and labor market dynamics. However, other factors may be equally important though perhaps less prominent in temporary work research. Examples are career competencies (see, e.g., Van der Heijde & Van der Heijden, 2006), employability dispositions (see, e.g., Fugate & Kinicki, 2008; Fugate, Kinicki, & Ashforth, 2004), or social capital (see, e.g., Adler & Kwon, 2002).

Second, we advanced "positive"—from temporary to permanent—and "negative"—from temporary to unemployment—labor market transitions as outcomes in our model. This presents a fairly quantitative approach vis-à-vis career outcomes. Future research may want to include more qualitative indicators of labor market transitions and career success, for example indicators that probe employment quality or subjective career success.

Finally, and perhaps most critically, not included in the model but critical in career research are more structural variables, for example the general economic situation (see, e.g., Forrier et al., 2009) or country-specific rules and legislation in particular. When demand for labor is slowing down, as in times of economic recession, temporary workers may find themselves in a notoriously weaker position than when the labor market is picking up: Organizations may be less inclined to hire temporary workers on a more stable basis, thus limiting the chances for upward transition; they may thus further reduce other investments in the temporary workforce. In a similar vein, country-specific laws and practices vis-à-vis temporary employment may affect the careers of temporary workers. Consider the example of the Dutch Flexibility and Security Act (Flexicurity, 01/1999), which includes the obligation to hire temporary workers on a permanent basis after three consecutive temporary contracts (De Jong & Schalk, 2005). Such a policy provides more protection compared with more liberal labor markets, with the United Kingdom as an example (Guest & Clinton, 2005). That is to say, variables at the macro level may be critical in understanding the careers of temporary workers. This obviously calls for contextualization both in time and in place.

Practical Implications

Given our general conclusion about boundary conditions that provide both opportunities and risks for future career development among temporary workers, an obvious advice for temporary workers and career counselors is to exploit the opportunities and to reduce the risks associated with temporary employment. For employers, we believe it is important to treat temporary workers with respect. A summary of hands-on practical implications is shown in Table 25.1.

The Workers

In terms of exploiting the opportunities, workers may want to make the most of the steppingstone function of temporary employment, which we think is triple. First, temporary employment may present an escape route out of unemployment. It is a way to keep foot in the labor market. Second, for many workers, temporary employment ultimately leads to permanent employment. Third, temporary employment leads to human capital accumulation, knowledge of the labor market and the development of career competencies that is without parallels among the unemployed. Accordingly, our advice is to set stereotypes vis-à-vis temporary employment ("just a temp") or too high ambitions ("my first job should be my ideal job") aside and instead see it as a way to enter and also actively explore the labor market with likely quick upward mobility. This may require a fairly proactive attitude and learning orientation—for example, by asking questions of colleagues so as to increase knowledge or by investing in training, preferably training of general skills that are transferable from one job to the next. Successful temping may also be conditional upon flexibility—for example, in the sense of accepting a diverse set of jobs in different types of organizations so as to increase one's options. It may also require an investment in training on the part of the worker, preferably training in general skills that are transferable from one job to the next.

In terms of reducing risks associated with temporary employment, workers should regularly check how much their current jobs and organizations contribute to their development, with development being interpreted in the broadest sense—namely, in terms of general and job-specific knowledge, skills, and attitudes but also in terms of social capital, for example. When this evaluation is negative in all areas, they should avoid falling in the dead-end trap—staying in temporary jobs with no career and development prospects.

Counselors

The main tasks for counselors is to coach temporary workers to exploit all opportunities associated

Table 25.1. Practical Implications for Workers, Counselors, and Employers

Some Tips and Tricks for . . .		
Workers	Counselors	Employers

1. Set stereotypes and too high ambitions aside: they will not land you in a job.	1. Nurture "knowing how" competencies.
	  a. Map all job and career opportunities.
	  b. Map training opportunities.
	  c. Share labor market knowledge.
	  d. . . .
		1. Treat temporary workers with respect so that you will be treated with respect., and not as "just the temp."
		  a. Invite them for company events.
		  b. Introduce them to the work floor.
		  c. Provide them with feedback.
		  d. . . .

2. See temporary employment as a stepping stone that drives your motivation.		

3. Be proactive: ask questions, follow training.	2. Nurture "knowing why" competencies.
	  a. Map weaknesses and strengths.
	  b. . . .
		2. See the potential of temporary workers.
		  a. Temporary workers are clients.
		  b. Temporary workers may be potential permanent workers.
		  c. Solicit feedback: temporary workers may have worked for your competitor.
		  d. Be open for new ideas temporary workers bring in.

4. Be flexible: accept different jobs in different organizations, even if they do not match your ideal.		

5. Avoid the "dead-end job" trap: leave an assignment before you feel locked in.	3. Nurture "knowing whom" competencies.
	  a. Share contacts.
	  b. Show/teach workers how to mingle.
	  c. Demonstrate the potential of new social media.	

with temporary employment—for example, in terms of knowing how (i.e., increasing one's human capital), knowing why (i.e., increasing one's self-awareness in terms of possible jobs and career paths), and knowing-whom (i.e., increasing one's social capital) (for a discussion of these competencies, see DeFillippi & Arthur, 1994).

Knowing-how competencies can be stimulated in many ways: Counselors may advise workers to accept jobs in different domains or sectors to broaden their scope, they may help workers to find their way in the complex landscape of training, they may share their often inside knowledge of the labor market, and so on. Knowing-why competencies relate to the question "Who am I and who do I want to be?" Counselors may help workers to identify their strengths and weaknesses and to find out what drives satisfactory employment in their specific case. This likely strengthens motivation, and with motivation and the resulting positive attitudes, also chances to transition to more stable employment. Finally, with respect to knowing-whom competencies, counselors in many cases have a fairly broad network of former clients and organizations with which they collaborate. Therefore they are in a unique position to share their contacts with their clients. They may also teach workers how to expand their networks—for example, by showing them the latest evolutions in social media and how these are used in job applications.

The Employer

The main advice to employers is to treat temporary workers fairly and with respect, which may show in fairly small things—for example, inviting them along with their permanent coworkers on company events; introducing them to the work floor; appointing someone they may turn to with questions, both work-related and administrative; providing them with feedback so that they can learn; soliciting their feedback; and so on. This may bring along some benefits. First, many employers have used temporary employment, deliberately or not, as a screening tool for permanent employment: If the temporary worker had a bad experience, he or she may not be interested, which then implies a new recruitment process. Second, temporary workers may also be (future) customers and are therefore critical for the company's image. Finally, but perhaps most important, temporary workers who are treated with respect are much more likely to reciprocate with hard work than those who have the sense of being "just a temp"

in the organization. Workers who are treated well and with respect may also be more likely to bring in and share knowledge from earlier jobs and organizations.

The Special Case of Agency Workers

The agency is yet another party to the employment relationship in the specific case of temporary agency work. Our advice for agencies is not to see temporary agency workers as expendable but instead as critical human capital that should be nurtured. This may require considerable investments in training, but this training may lead to multiple gains: It may bind workers *and* client organizations to the agency, and it is clearly a strength in the face of increasing competition among different agencies to attract both workers and client organizations.

Notes

1. The definition of nontraditional employment as a form of dependent employment or waged work excludes forms of self-employment and volunteer work. The reason for excluding these forms from this definition and from this chapter is that they are built on entirely different laws and regulations and on different research traditions.
2. Note that casual employment is the best available equivalent to temporary employment, even though it is distinct in important respects. For more information, we refer the reader to De Cuyper et al., 2008.
3. We realize that other factors may also be important in distinguishing types of temporary employment—for example, issues related to volition. We discuss these factors in more detail in later parts of this chapter.

References

Adler, P. S., & Kwon, S. (2002). Social capital: Prospects for a new concept. *Academy of Management Review, 27*, 17–40.

Amuedo-Dorantes, C., Malo, M. A., & Muñoz-Bullón, F. (2008). The role of temporary help agency employment on temp-to-perm transitions. *Journal of Labor Research, 29*, 138–161.

Aronsson, G., & Göransson, S. (1999). Permanent employment but not in a preferred occupation: Psychological and medical aspects, research implications. *Journal of Occupational Health Psychology, 4*, 152–163.

Aronsson, G., Gustafsson, K., & Dallner, M. (2002). Work environment and health in different types of temporary jobs. *European Journal of Work and Organizational Psychology, 11*, 151–175.

Artazcoz, L., Benach, J., Borrell, C., & Cortèz, I. (2005). Social inequalities in the impact of flexible employment on different domains of psychosocial health. *Journal of Epidemiological Community Health, 59*, 761–767.

Arulampalam, W., & Booth, A. L. (2002). Training and labour market flexibility: Is there a trade-off? *British Journal of Industrial Relations, 36*, 521–536.

Atkinson, J. (1984). Manpower strategies for flexible organizations. *Personnel Management, August*, 28–31.

Bakker, A. B., & Demerouti, E. (2007). The job demands-resources model: State of the art. *Journal of Managerial Psychology, 22*, 209–328.

Bardasi, E., & Francesconi, M. (2004). The impact of atypical employment on individual well-being: Evidence from a panel of British workers. *Social Science and Medicine, 58*, 1671–1688.

Barling, J., & Gallagher, D. G. (1996). Part-time employment. *International Review of Industrial and Organizational Psychology, 11*, 241–77.

Beard, K. M., & Edwards, J. R. (1995). Employees at risk: Contingent work and the psychological experience of contingent workers. In Cooper, C. I. and Rousseau, D. M. (Eds.), *Trends in Organizational Behavior*, Vol. 2 (pp. 1–126). Chichester, UK: Wiley.

Becker, G. (1993). *Human Capital: A theoretical and empirical analysis with special reference to education* (3rd Ed). Chicago: University of Chicago Press.

Benach, J., Gimeno, D., & Benavides, F. G. (2002). *Types of employment and health in the European Union*. European Foundation for the Improvement of Living and Working Conditions. Office for Official Publications in the European Community. Luxembourg.

Bernhard-Oettel, C., Sverke, M., & De Witte, H. (2005). Comparing three alternative types of employment with permanent full-time work: How do employment contract and perceived job conditions relate to health complaints? *Work and Stress, 19*, 301–318.

Berntson, E., Sverke, M., & Marklund, S. (2006). Predicting perceived employability: Human capital or labour market opportunities? *Economic and Industrial Democracy, 27*, 223–244.

Booth, A., Francesconi, M., & Frank, J. (2000). Temporary workers: New evidence on their pay, conditions and prospects. *Future of Work Bulletin, 1*, 2–4.

Boyce, S., Ryan, M., Imus, L., & Morgeson, F. P. (2007). "Temporary worker, permanent loser?" A model of the stigmatization of temporary workers. *Journal of Management, 33*, 5–29.

Burgess, J., & Connell, J. (2006). Temporary work and human resources management: Issues, challenges and responses. *Personnel Review, 35*, 129–140.

Campbell, I. (2001). Casual employees and the training deficit: Exploring employer calculations and choices. *International Journal of Employment Studies, 9*, 61–101.

Chalmers, J., & Kalb, G. (2000). *The transition from unemployment to work. Are casual jobs a shortcut to permanent employment?* Social Policy Research Center, Discussion Paper No. 109, October.

CIETT (2011). *The agency work industry around the world: Economic report*. International Confederation of Private Employment Agencies. Brussels, Belgium.

Connell, J., & Burgess, J. (2001). Skill, training and workforce restructuring in Australia: An overview. *International Journal of Employment Studies, 9*, 1–24.

Connelly, C. E., & Gallagher, D. G. (2004). Managing contingent workers: Adapting to new realities In R. J. Burke & C. L. Cooper (Eds.), *Leading in turbulent times* (pp. 143–164). Malden, MA: Blackwell.

Cranford, C. J., Vosko, L. F., & Zukewich, N. (2003). The gender of precarious employment in Canada. *Industrial Relations, 58*, 454–482.

De Clerck, V., De Cuyper, N., & De Witte, H. (2006). Motieven voor tijdelijk werk en uitzendarbeid. Waarom accepteren tijdelijke werknemers en uitzendkrachten een "flexible" contract? (Motives for accepting temporary employment and temporary agency work). *Over. Werk, 1–2*, 147–151.

De Cuyper, N., de Jong, J., De Witte, H., Isaksson, K., Rigotti, T., & Schalk, R. (2008). Literature review of theory and research on the psychological impact of temporary employment: Towards a conceptual model. *International Journal of Management Reviews, 10*, 25–51.

De Cuyper, N., & De Witte, H. (2006). The impact of job insecurity and contract type on attitudes, well-being and behavioural reports: a psychological contract perspective. *Journal of Occupational and Organizational Psychology, 79*, 395–409.

De Cuyper, N., & De Witte, H. (2007). Job insecurity among temporary versus permanent workers: Effects on job satisfaction, organizational commitment, life satisfaction and self-rated performance. *Work and Stress, 21*, 65–84.

De Cuyper, N., & De Witte, H. (2008a). Job insecurity and employability among temporary workers: A theoretical approach based on the psychological contract, in K. Näswall, J. Hellgren, & M. Sverke (Eds.), *The individual in the changing working life* (pp. 88–107). Cambridge, UK: Cambridge University Press.

De Cuyper, N., & De Witte, H. (2008b). Volition and reasons for accepting temporary employment: Associations with attitudes, well-being and behavioural intentions. *European Journal of Work & Organizational Psychology, 17*, 363–387.

De Cuyper, N., & De Witte, H. (2010). Impress to become employable. The case of temporary workers. *Journal of Career Development, 37*, 635–652.

De Cuyper, N., De Witte, H., & Isaksson, K. (2005). Employment contracts: How to deal with diversity?, in N. De Cuyper, K. Isaksson, & H. De Witte (Eds.), *Employment contracts and Well-being among European Workers* (pp. 15–34). Hampshire, UK: Ashgate Publishing.

De Cuyper, N., De Witte, H., Krausz, M., Mohr, G., & Rigotti, T. (2010). Individual and organizational outcomes of employment contracts, in D. Guest, K. Isaksson, & H. De Witte (Eds.), *Employment contracts, psychological contracts and worker well-being: An international study*. Oxford, UK: Oxford University Press.

De Cuyper, N., Mauno, S., Kinnunen, U., & Mäkikangas, A. (2011). The role of job resources in the relation between perceived employability and turnover intention: A prospective two-sample study. *Journal of Vocational Behavior, 78*, 253–263.

De Cuyper, N., Notelaers, G., & De Witte, H. (2009a). Transitioning between temporary and permanent employment: A two-wave study on the entrapment, the stepping stone and the selection hypothesis. *Journal of Occupational and Organizational Psychology, 82*, 67–88.

De Cuyper, N., Notelaers, G., & De Witte, H. (2009b). Job insecurity and employability among fixed term contract workers, temporary agency workers and permanent workers: Associations with employees' attitudes. *Journal of Occupational Health Psychology, 14*, 193–205.

De Feyter, M., Smulders, P., & de Vroome, E. (2001). De inzetbaarheid van mannelijke en vrouwelijke werknemers. Kenmerken van invloed (The employability of male and female employees. Characteristics of influence). *Tijdschrift voor Arbeidsvraagstukken 17*, 47–59.

DeFillippi, R., & Arthur, M. (1994). The boundaryless career: A competency-based perspective. *Journal of Organizational Behavior, 15*, 307–324.

De Jong, J., De Cuyper, N., De Witte, H., Silla, I., & Bernhard-Oettel, C. (2009). Motives for accepting temporary employment: A typology. *International Journal of Manpower, 30*, 237–252.

De Jong, J., & Schalk, R. (2005). Temporary employment in The Netherlands: Between flexibility and Security, in De Cuyper, N., Isaksson, K. and De Witte, H. (Eds.), *Employment contracts and well-being among European workers* (pp. 119–152). Aldershot, UK: Ashgate.

Dekker, R. (2001). *A phase they are going through: Transitions from non-regular to regular jobs in Germany, the Netherlands and Great Britain.* Tilburg, The Netherlands: Tilburg University.

Delsen, L. (1998). Zijn externe flexibiliteit en employability strijdig? (Are external flexibility and employability incompatible?). *Tijdschrift voor HRM, 2*, 27–46.

De Witte, H., & Näswall, K. (2003). "Objective" vs "subjective" job insecurity: Consequences of temporary work for job satisfaction and organizational commitment in four European countries. *Economic and Industrial Democracy, 24*, 149–188.

Doeringer, P. B., & Piore, M. J. (1971). *Internal labour markets and manpower analysis.* Lexington, MA: Heath Lexington Books.

Eurofound. (2007). *Impact of training on people's employability.* European Foundation for the Improvement of Living and Working Conditions. Available at: www.eurofound.europa.eu

Feldman, D. C. (2005). Toward a new taxonomy for understanding the nature and consequences of contingent employment. *Career Development International, 11*, 28–47.

Fontinha, R., Chambel, M. J., & De Cuyper, N. (2013). Training and the commitment of outsourced IT workers: Psychological contract fulfillment as a mediator. *Journal of Career Development*, online publication.

Forrier, A., & Sels, L. (2003). Temporary employment and employability: Training opportunities and efforts of temporary and permanent employees in Belgium. *Work, Employment and Society, 17*, 641–666.

Forrier, A., Sels, L., & Stynen, D. (2009). Career mobility at the intersection between agent and structure: A conceptual model. *Journal of Occupational and Organizational Psychology, 82*, 739–759.

Fugate, M., & Kinicki, A. J. (2008). A dispositional approach to employability. Development of a measure and test of implications for employee reactions to organizational change. *Journal of Occupational and Organizational Psychology, 81*, 503–527.

Fugate, M., Kinicki, A. J., & Ashforth, B. E. (2004). Employability: A psycho-social construct, its dimensions, and applications. *Journal of Vocational Behavior, 65*, 14–38.

Gagliarducci, S. (2005). The dynamics of repeated temporary jobs. *Labour Economics, 12*, 429–448.

Gallagher, D. G., & McLean Parks, J. (2001). I pledge thee my troth . . . contingently: Commitment and the contingent work relationship. *Human Resource Management Review, 11*, 181–208.

Gallagher, D. G., & Sverke, M. (2005). Contingent employment contracts: Are existing employment theories still relevant? *Economic and Industrial Democracy, 26*, 181–203.

Gimeno, D., Benavides, F. G., Amick, B. C., Benach, J., & Martinez, J. M. (2004). Psychological factors and work related sickness absence among permanent and non-permanent employees. *Journal of Epidemiology and Community Health, 58*, 870–876.

Goudswaard, A., & Andries, F. (2002). *Employment status and working conditions.* Luxembourg: European Foundation for the Improvement of Working and Living Conditions, Office for Official Publications of the European Community.

Guest, D. (2000). Management and the insecure workforce: The search for a new psychological contract, In E. Heery & J. Salmon (Eds.), *The insecure workforce* (pp. 140–154). London: Routledge.

Guest, D., & Clinton, M. (2005). Contracting in the UK: Current research evidence on the impact of flexible employment and the nature of psychological contracts, In De Cuyper, N., Isaksson, K. and De Witte, H. (Eds.), *Employment contracts and well-being among European workers* (pp. 201–224). Aldershot, UK: Ashgate.

Guest, D., Isaksson, K., & De Witte, H. (2010). *Employment contracts, psychological contracts, and employee well-being. An international study.* Oxford, UK: Oxford University Press.

Hobfoll, S. E. (1989). Conservation of resources: A new attempt at conceptualizing stress. *American Psychologist, 44*, 513–524.

Hobfoll, S. E. (2001). The influence of culture, community, and the nested-self in the stress process: Advancing conservation of resources theory. *Applied Psychology: An International Review, 50*, 337–421.

Kalleberg, A. L. (2000). Nonstandard employment relations: Part-time, temporary and contract work. *Annual Review of Sociology, 26*, 341–365.

Kalleberg A. L (2009). Precarious work, insecure workers: Employment relations in transition. *American Sociological Review, 74*, 1–22.

Kalleberg, A. L., Reynolds, J., & Marsden, P. V. (2003). Externalizing employment: Flexible staffing arrangements in US organizations. *Social Science Research, 32*, 525–552.

Korpi, T., & Levin, H. (2001). Precarious footing: Temporary employment as a stepping stone out of unemployment in Sweden. *Work, Employment & Society, 15*, 127–148.

Krausz, M. (2000). Effects of short- and long-term preference for temporary work upon psychological outcomes. *International Journal of Manpower, 21*, 635–647.

Kryger, T. (2004). *Casual employment: Trends and characteristics.* Research Note No. 53. Department of Parliamentary Services, Canberra, ACT.

Liukkonen, V., Virtanen, P., Kivimäki, M., Pentii, J., & Vahtera, J. (2004). Social capital in working life and the health of employees. *Social Science and Medicine, 59*, 2447–2458.

Marler, J. H., Barringer, M. W., & Milkovich, G. T. (2002). Boundaryless and traditional contingent employees: Worlds apart. *Journal of Organizational Behavior, 23*, 425–453.

Martens, M. F. J., Nijhuis, F. J. N., van Boxtel, M. P. J., & Knottnerus, J. A. (1999). Flexible work schedules and mental and physical health. A study of a working population with non-traditional working hours. *Journal of Organizational Behavior, 20*, 35–46.

Mauno, S., & Kinnunen, U. (2002). Perceived job insecurity among dual earner couples: Do its antecedents vary according to gender, economic sector and the measure used. *Journal of Occupational and Organizational Psychology, 75*, 295–314.

Murtough, G., & Waite, M. (2000). *The diversity of casual contract employment.* The Productivity Commission, Canberra, ACT.

Nollen, S. D. (1996). Negative aspects of temporary employment. *Journal of Labor Research, 27*, 567–582.

OECD. (2002). Employment Outlook. Paris: Organization for Economic Co-operation and Development.

Parker, S. K., Griffin, M. A., Sprigg, C. A., & Wall, T. A. (2002). Effect of temporary contracts on perceived work characteristics and job strain: A longitudinal study. *Personnel Psychology*, *55*, 689–717.

Reilly, P. A. (1998). Balancing flexibility—Meeting the interests of employer and employee. *European Journal of Work and Organizational Psychology*, *7*, 7–22.

Rix, A., Davies, K., Gaunt, R., Hare, A., & Cobbolds, S. (1999). *The training and development of flexible workers* (p. 118). London: Department for Education and Employment Research.

Rogers, J. K. (1995). Just a temp: Experience and structure of alienation in temporary clerical employment. *Work and Occupations*, *22*, 137–166.

Rogers, J. K., & Henson, K. D. (1997). "Hey, why don't you wear a shorter skirt?" Structural vulnerability and the organization of sexual harassment in temporary clerical employment. *Gender & Society*, *1*, 215–237.

Rothwell, A., & Arnold, J. (2007). Self-perceived employability: Development and validation of a scale. *Personnel Review*, *36*, 23–41.

Saloniemi, A., Virtanen, P., & Vahtera, J. (2004). The work environment in fixed-term jobs: Are poor psychosocial conditions inevitable? *Work, Employment and Society*, *18*, 193–208.

Scherer, S. (2004). Stepping stones or traps? The consequences of labour market entry positions on future careers in West Germany, Great Britain and Italy. *Work, Employment and Society*, *18*, 369–394.

Sels, S., & Van Hootegem, G. (2001). Seeking the balance between flexibility and security. A rising issue in the low countries. *Work, Employment and Society*, *15*, 327–352.

Silla, I., De Cuyper, N., Gracia, F., Peiró, J. M., & De Witte, H. (2008). Job insecurity and well-being: Moderation by employability. *Journal of Happiness Studies*, *10*, 739–751.

Silla, I., Gracia, F., & Peiró, J. M. (2005). Job insecurity and health-related outcomes among different types of temporary workers. *Economic and Industrial Democracy*, *26*, 89–117.

Storrie, D. (2002). *Temporary agency work in the European Union*. Luxembourg: Office for Official Publications of the European Communities.

Sverke, M., Gallagher, D. G., & Hellgren, J. (2000). Alternative work arrangements: Job stress, well-being, and work attitudes among employees with different employment contracts, In K. Isaksson, L. Hogsted, C. Eriksson, and T. Theorell (Eds.), *Health effects of the new labour market*. New York: Plenum.

Tan, H., & Tan, C. (2002). Temporary employees in Singapore: What drives them? *The Journal of Psychology*, *136*, 83–102.

Taris, T., & Schreurs, P. (2009). Well-being and organizational performance: An organizational-level test of the happy-productive worker hypothesis. *Work & Stress*, *23*, 120–136.

Tunny, G., & Mangan, J. (2004). Stepping stones to permanent employment in the public service. *Labour*, *18*, 591–614.

Van Dam, K. (2004). Antecedents and consequences of employability orientation. *European Journal of Work and Organisational Psychology*, *13*, 29–51.

Van der Heijde, C. M., & Van der Heijden, B. I. J. M. (2006). A competence-based and multidimensional operationalization and measurement of employability. *Human Resource Management*, *45*, 449–476.

Virtanen, M., Kivimäki, M., Elovainio, M., Vahtera, J., & Cooper, C. L. (2001). Contingent employment, health and sickness absence. *Scandinavian Journal of Work Environment and Health, 2001, 27*, 365–72.

Virtanen, M., Kivimäki, M., Joensuu, M., Virtanen, P., Elovainio, M., & Vahtera, J. (2005). Temporary employment and health: A review. *International Journal of Epidemiology*, *34*, 610–622.

Virtanen, P., Liukkonen, V., Vahtera, J., Kivimäki, M., & Koskenvuo, M. (2003). Health inequalities in the workforce: The labour market core–periphery structure. *International Journal of Epidemiology*, *32*, 1015–1021.

Virtanen, P., Vahtera, J., Kivimäki, M., Pentii, J., & Ferrie, J. (2002). Employment security and health. *Journal of Epidemiology and Community Health*, *56*, 569–574.

Wittekind, A., Raeder, S., & Grote, G. (2010). A longitudinal study of determinants of perceived employability. *Journal of Organizational Behavior*, *31*, 566–586.

Yeh, Y.-J. Y., Ko, J.-J. R., Chang, Y.-S., & Chen, C.-H. V. (2007). Job stress and work attitudes between temporary and permanently employed nurses. *Stress and Health*, *23*, 111–120.

Zelenski, J. M., Murphy, S. A., & Jenkins, D. A. (2008). The happy-productive worker thesis revisited. *Journal of Happiness Studies*, *9*, 521–537.

International Job Search

Jelena Zikic, Derin Kent, *and* Julia Richardson

Abstract

As globalization and integration of national economies continues unabated, an increasing number of people are looking for work outside oftheir home countries. Moreover, rather than waiting to be sent overseas by an employer, as might be the case for corporate expatriate assignees, a growing number of people are independently engaging in international job search. In this chapter, we review the literature on these international job seekers, focusing specifically on immigrants and self-initiated expatriates. First, we consider the diverse motives and contextual factors that drive this international job search; second, we look at the personal and cultural factors serving as antecedents for specific job-search behaviors. We then consider how job-search behaviors—in combination with personal factors and host country contexts—influence international job-search outcomes. Throughout this discussion we identify similarities and differences between immigrants and self-initiated expatriates while acknowledging that the boundaries between different groups of international job seekers are blurred. We conclude the chapter with a discussion of areas for future research.

Key Words: international job search, job seekers, expatriates, job-search behaviors, immigrants

International job seekers (IJSs) offer a wealth of knowledge and experience and can have a significant impact on local labor markets and economies, not only in countries such as Canada and Australia, with traditionally high numbers of immigrants, but also in many other countries experiencing an influx of foreign labor (Kogan, 2006; The Economist, 2011). Yet just as IJSs impact on local economies, relocating to another country to find work also has a major impact on their own personal and professional lives (Carr, Inkson, & Thorn, 2005). Indeed, looking for and then accepting a job outside of one's home country constitutes a major career and life transition.

The challenges of managing and integrating immigrants and other international job seekers into local economies is an increasingly important area of concern for management scholars, practitioners, and government policymakers in particular (Alboim & McIssac, 2007; Chiswick,

Lee, & Miller 2005; Kogan, 2006). Yet where job search is concerned, much of the existing literature has focused on domestic/local job seekers—that is, individuals searching for work in their home country. Addressing this gap is crucial, given current labor shortages in advanced as well as developing economies and the forces of globalization calling for more internationally mobile and experienced professionals (The Economist, 2011). As organizations and national economies strive to become more globally connected, understanding how IJSs search for work and how they integrate and leverage their international expertise, language skills, and networks is paramount.

Who Are International Job Seekers?

Surprisingly little is known about career progression and the obstacles that IJSs face as they attempt to pursue careers outside oftheir home country (Bhagat & London, 1999; Salaff, Greve,

& Ping, 2002; Turchick-Hakak, Holzinger, & Zikic, 2010). Therefore, seeking to address this gap, this chapter will focus on two specific groups of IJSs: immigrants and self-initiated expatriates (SIEs).

For the purposes of this chapter, IJS are defined as individuals who are seeking *permanent* employment outside of their home country. SIEs, on the other hand, are people who, independent of an employer, are also seeking employment outside of their home country albeit on a *temporary* basis (Doherty, Richardson, and Thorn, 2013). These definitions notwithstanding, we acknowledge that the boundaries between SIEs and immigrants are blurred. For example, SIEs may at some point decide to stay on permanently in a particular host country and consequently become immigrants, whereas immigrants may remain in their host country only for a short period of time, which would mean that they might be better considered as SIEs. Other characteristics often cited as distinguishing these two groups are country of origin (i.e., migrants typically moving from developing countries to developed ones or places clear labor shortages are identified) (The Economist, 2011), reason for the move (i.e., immigrants being pushed out of necessity versus personal choice for SIEs); and what might be referred to as "social" distinctions (e.g., the term *immigrant* is more likely to have a negative connotation than the term *self-initiated expatriate*) (Al Ariss, 2010). In addition, three other distinguishing factors should be noted: (1) depending on their official status (immigrant or temporary worker), these two groups may face potentially different structural barriers and/or facilitating factors in the new labor market; (2) immigrants are more likely to move to another country with their families and after a long period of planning. By comparison, SIEs may encounter opportunities to expatriate somewhat serendipitously, and their decision to move may be made relatively quickly (Richardson, 2008; Richardson & Mallon, 2005). Similarly, as noted above, SIEs generally see their respective moves as being relatively brief, perhaps for a few months or a few years, after which they will either return to their home country and/or move on elsewhere (Doherty et al., 2013). A further distinguishing feature between immigrants and SIEs relates to their official status. SIEs are unlikely to become citizens of a host country and are more likely to have temporary work visas. Immigration, however, usually requires citizenship or—at least in countries such as Canada, Australia, and New Zealand—permanent residency.

The blurred boundaries between immigrants and SIEs notwithstanding, for the purposes of this chapter they are considered IJSs because they both engage in *international* job-search activities. For example, both groups engage in an independent search for employment beyond the boundaries of their home country. They both provide examples of international mobility and self-initiated international careers (Tams & Arthur, 2007). As a further note of clarification, however, the review does not attend to corporate expatriates, or individuals sent by their employer outside of their home country for a temporary work assignment (Yan, Zhu, & Hall, 2002). While the members of this group also work internationally, they do not conduct an international job search per se because their relocation is managed by their employer and/ or after collaboration with a manager or other organizational agents (Cappellen & Janssens, 2008; Doherty, Dickmann, & Mills, 2011).

The existing literature often deals more broadly with motivational, structural or career-related issues facing international job seekers. Very few articles focus more narrowly on the intricacies of the international job-search process itself. Therefore this review is organized as shown in the Model presented in Figure 26.1.

As shown in the Model, we examine preentry factors, comprising an exploration of the contextual circumstances/influences impacting on IJSs experiences of job search, such as host country immigration policies, and the concomitant job-search outcomes, such as whether or not such an individual is able to find employment commensurate with his or her experience/qualifications. We then examine the diverse range of motives impacting on IJSs decision to seek a job outside of their home country. This section addresses a fairly wide range of potential motives but also acknowledges the connectivity of motives and how they may change over time and according to individual life circumstances. Next we look at antecedents and moderators of the international job search. In doing so we consider factors that are part of the job seeker's social milieu as antecedents and moderators of job search. We also consider moderators between job search and outcomes as those factors inherent in the context or environment in which the job seeker is immersed. As we argue, these moderating factors may change depending on the location and resources available to the respective job seeker. We then examine the different job-search strategies of SIEs and immigrants, followed by a discussion of the potential outcomes of international job search. This latter discussion

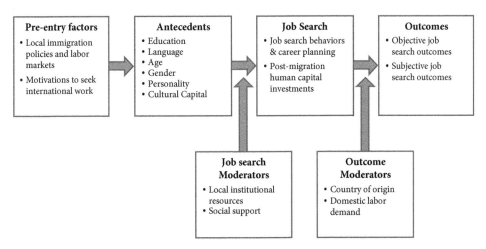

Figure 26.1 Process model of international job search.

addresses both objective and subjective outcomes such as earnings, career development, and job satisfaction. The chapter concludes with a general discussion of the findings and a separate section indicating specific areas for future research.

Preentry factors Facing International Job Seekers
Local Immigration Policies and the Labor Market

In examining the experiences of IJSs, several contextual and motivational variables must be considered. Their entry to a particular country, and hence their ability to search for work and engage in their new host country's labor market, is dependent on local immigration policies and employment requirements. These requirements will vary by host country, and their implications will be different depending on the IJS's country or region of origin. For example, Canada's policy on attracting skilled migrants is informed by human capital theory, favoring individuals who have general skills and experience (i.e., a certain level of education/ credentials) as opposed to those with specific skills in market demand (Hawthorne, 2008). Conversely, Australia has abandoned the human capital model and moved to a more pragmatic and national interest–based approach. Accordingly, its immigration policy favors strong vocational-level English, education, and experience that is valued by local employers (e.g., local or internationally recognized schooling), and qualifications that are currently in demand in the respective job market. In Australia, then, the focus is on screening for specific employment attributes (Hawthorne, 2008).

The Canadian and Australian examples show how countries may vary in regard to the demands and requirements for immigration (Lawrence, 2004), from very specific and constrained immigration policies to more liberal ones. In either case, we observe how contextual factors affect both the type of individual to whom the respective authorities will grant entry and whom they will allow to search for work and in which employment contexts. Clearly, prior to the start of the job-search process, migrants and SIEs must meet the demands of rigorous bureaucratic systems that will decide whether they will be allowed to enter and search for work in the respective host country's labor market.

It is also worth noting that there are substantial differences within local labor markets and their related institutions (e.g., industrial relations, earnings dispersions, gender inequalities, career structures, and unemployment rates) (Reitz, 2002). Labor markets are also closely connected to other societal institutions, such as legal, political, educational, and welfare systems. Therefore, even prior to the start of the job-search process, IJSs must navigate the influences of the respective systems. For example, they must have a clear understanding of whether or not their educational qualifications will be "recognized" and whether they will be able to compete with locally qualified job seekers. They must also be aware of the impact of political trends on the host country's labor market, such as what might happen if a host country government changed or if new labor laws were introduced.

Another disadvantage that IJSs may encounter in competing with local job seekers is the "liability-of-foreignness" effect (Harvey, Novicevic, Buckley,

& Fung, 2005), a topic that Derous and Ryan address in more detail in this volume. The liability-of-foreignness hypothesis might equally apply to immigrants and SIEs, because both groups must manage the liability of being foreign in pursuing job opportunities in a country that is not their home country. Indeed, IJSs may lack legitimacy and therefore face more challenges in finding a job than their local counterparts, who are locally qualified and experienced and thus more familiar with the local labor market (Brekke & Mastekaasa, 2008; Constant, Kahanec, & Zimmermann, 2009; Millar & Choi, 2008).

Motivations to Engage in International Job Search

Any discussion of the motivation to seek employment outside of one's home country would not be complete without some acknowledgement of the neoclassical economic "push-pull" theory of migration (King, 2012), which is based on the idea of utility maximization. That is to say, it rests on an underlying assumption that IJSs will seek out employment in another country according to perceived "push" factors in their home country, such as lack of employment opportunities, societal and/or civil unrest, and so on, and "pull" factors in the prospective host country, such as increased employment opportunities, financial reward, and/or better overall living standards. In the case of immigrants, then, immigration would occur when individual actors "rationally" weigh up the pros and cons of either staying in their home country or looking for a job in another country. Criticisms of this theory notwithstanding (see, for example, King, 2012), it has had a significant impact on the thinking of scholars and practitioners. For example, Cerdin and Abdeljalil (2007) have proposed a typology of motivations to find a job outside of one's home country using the push/pull model, based on Lewin's field theory (1951). According to their study of immigrants' decisions to migrate to and work in France, immigrants experienced "contradictory forces" (e.g., Baruch, 1995; Baruch et al., 2007), given the push factors such as the political and economic situation in their home country (i.e., "desperate migration") and the challenges and opportunities of travel and cultural immersion in France (i.e., "dream migration").

Migrants are typically seen as relocating outside their home country for economic reasons (Chiswick, 2000), which distinguishes them from refugees or/and those who move because of the immigration

decisions of others, such as family members ("tied movers"). In addition to economic factors, however, both SIEs and immigrants are invariably motivated toward international job search by a broad range of factors (Peltokorpi & Froese, 2009; Richardson & Mallon, 2005; Richardson, McBey, & McKenna, 2009; Thorn, 2009; Zikic, Bonache, & Cerdin, 2010). For example, in a study of New Zealanders living abroad, Jackson, et al. (2005) identified 25 factors influencing subjects' decisions to look for a job overseas. The authors then carried out a principal-components analysis identifying five key motivations: economic, career, family, lifestyle, and culture. Yet these themes did not account for all of the reported motivations, suggesting that other factors may also come into play. Therefore the authors explored other influences and subsequently identified a further 31 possible motivations, or "submotives" (Thorn, 2009). Thorn (2009) subsequently identified 56 submotives for engaging in international job search among a group of SIEs, of which the first six were travel, partner from the host country, better remuneration, adventure, further professional development, and improved overall economic situation. In the same study, Thorn (2009) also reported that women rated cultural and travel opportunities and relationship issues as more important to them, whereas men were more concerned with career and economic issues. Similarly, those who went to Asia were motivated by economic reasons, while those who moved to Oceania, North America, and Africa were motivated primarily by opportunities for career development. Cultural and travel experiences were most salient for those who went to Europe. Studies of SIE academics (see, for example, Doherty, 2010; Richardson et al., 2009; Richardson & Mallon, 2005; Selmer & Lauring, 2010) and SIE voluntary overseas development workers (Hudson & Inkson, 2006) also found diverse motivations to look for a job outside of their home country, ranging from "a search for adventure," providing children with different cultural experiences, career advancement, and "escape" from a difficult work situation, among others.

Taken together the findings of the studies cited above indicate a broad range of potential motivating factors impacting on IJSs' decisions to seek employment outside of their home country. Adding further to the complexity, motivations may also change over time, with some having more or less influence than others, depending on life stage. Therefore whereas the "push-pull" theory of motivations has come under some criticism (King, 2012), it is clear that further theoretical development is required to explain the connections between the different motivations and their evolution according to individual life circumstances.

Antecedents of International Job Search
Gender

Drawing on Hawthorne's (2008) Canada-Australia comparative study introduced above, female migrants have been found to have significantly worse employment outcomes than male migrants and Canadian-born migrants of either gender. These findings may reflect constraints of gender roles, where females may be less commonly viewed as "principal" applicants in immigrating families and their careers more likely to be viewed as of secondary importance. Moreover, given the lack of extended family and social support in the host country, it may be that females are more likely to take the role of homemaker. Suto (2008), for example, has described such career choices as giving rise to *compromised careers* and suggests that immigrant women's downward career mobility can be partly attributed to lack of social support.

Turning to the experiences of SIEs and the theme of gender, Tharenou (2010) has reported that many women engage in SIE precisely in order to *avoid* discrimination or limited professional opportunities in their home countries. Indeed, moving overseas (albeit for a temporary period) was viewed by many women in Tharenou's study as a way to enhance both their earning capacity and overall career opportunities. On a similar note, Bozionelos (2009) found that female SIE nurses in Saudi Arabia reported greater career satisfaction (a subjective marker of career success) and earning capacity than they expected they would have had they remained in their home country. Richardson (2009) has also reported that female SIE academics in universities in the United Arab Emirates believed that they had greater earning capacity and professional opportunities there than in their home country, Britain. Compared with immigrant women, then, this suggests that female SIEs may be motivated to undertake an international job search in order to enhance their professional development and earning capacity.

Age

Research on immigrants suggests that where age is concerned, career outcomes often depend on the level of demand in the particular field. In general, graduate male migrants age 25 to 44 did best

in Canada and Australia. Moreover, they did much better than young graduates aged 15 to 24, who did especially poorly if they were from non-English-speaking countries. Where SIEs are concerned, there is unfortunately very little evidence about the impact of age on SIE job-search outcomes. Yet in a study of older female SIEs, Myers (2011) found that age does appear to limit opportunities to engage in SIE. In fact, she suggested that age may be an impetus for self-initiated expatriation, where some people may want to experience something new or different as they grow older. On a similar note, in their study of a group of SIEs working for Voluntary Service Overseas, Hudson and Inkson (2006) found that age was not seen as a limitation to SIE. Indeed, the participants in their study ranged from 29 to 67 years of age.

Personality

While both nonimmigrants and immigrants are generally motivated by life and career opportunities, immigrants, according to Chiswick (2000), tend to be more ambitious and assertive, with a stronger inclination toward entrepreneurial activities than those who remain in their home country. In addition, some research suggests that immigrants' job searches may be highly dependent on their personality characteristics (e.g., Boneva & Frieze, 2001). The same might also be said of SIEs who tend to be highly qualified professionals with at least a bachelor's degree (Doherty, 2010; Richardson, 2008; Selmer & Lauring, 2010). For example, some studies suggest that immigrants may differ from nonmigrants, proposing what the authors suggest is an "migrant personality" (Boneva & Frieze, 2001), which comprises specific personality factors such as a greater need for power and work achievement, which together amplify the individuals' desire to migrate to what they perceive to be more advantageous socioeconomic contexts. This research complements work on local job seekers, who are thought to engage in varying amounts of job-seeking behaviors based on the "Big Five" personality characteristics, especially conscientiousness and extraversion (Kanfer et al., 2001).

Focusing on SIEs, Hudson and Inkson (2006) found that voluntary overseas development workers had "higher levels of the Big Five personality characteristic 'openness' than the normative general population" (p. 310). They also reported higher levels of "agreeableness." However, IJSs are embedded within a general transition phase, as they are coping simultaneously with settlement and work-related stressors in the new country, both of which demand a high degree of self-reliance and proactivity (Bhagat & London, 1999; Hudson & Inkson, 2006; Richardson, 2009; Richardson & Zikic, 2007). Having a proactive personality may, therefore, be an important antecedent of workplace adjustment and career success for local and international job seekers alike (Brown et al., 2006; Siebert, Kraimer, & Linden, 2001), because proactive individuals are relatively unconstrained by situational forces and are able to change and influence the environment (Bandura, 1986, 2001; Bateman & Crant, 1993).

In the case of IJSs, then, their ability to navigate and adapt to the new labor market is very much based on whether they are able to be active career agents and to intentionally exert influence over the new environment. For example, proactive immigrants are likely to manage various structural environmental barriers, such as lack of recognition for foreign education, more effectively. Empirical investigations have demonstrated not only that proactive individuals in general are more successful in their careers (Siebert et al., 2001) but also that they are able to adapt more easily to their respective environments.

Education

In a job-search meta-analysis by Kanfer et al. (2001), higher levels of education were positively related to increased job-search activity. The review also reported a small but significant positive relationship with employment outcomes, those with more education being both more likely to find employment and having a shorter duration of unemployment. While education is typically seen as an important predictor of job-search success and higher-quality reemployment for local job seekers (Wanberg, Hough, & Song, 2002), in the case of IJSs their foreign human capital and foreign labor market experience may have the opposite effect. For instance, several studies show that in the Canadian labor market, human capital acquired abroad is often discounted or at least accorded less value than it might have been in the IJS's home country (Boyd & Thomas, 2001; Kustec et al., 2007; Reitz, 2001a, 2005; Richardson, 2009; Richardson et al., 2009; Richardson & Zikic, 2007). Research also suggests that immigrants experience longer periods of unemployment and often poorer reemployment outcomes compared with local job seekers (Weiner, 2008). This is often described as a "transition penalty"—a

longer period of adjustment as they establish themselves in a new country (Lochhead, 2003).

Focusing specifically on immigrants, existing foreign human capital may also limit their ability to find work in their respective occupation (e.g., Chiswick & Miller, 2009b). Indeed, some researchers have reported that preimmigration labor market experience *diminishes* the likelihood of an immigrant finding a job that is commensurate with her or his skills and qualifications. This may also create a situation where immigrants are likely to have more years of schooling than native-born workers employed in the same occupation precisely because of the limited transferability of their overseas experience. As a result, they are also more likely to work in lower-paying occupations than locals (Chiswick & Miller, 2009a). Labor economists in particular suspect that this is because local employers may be unsure of how to value foreign work experience (Chiswick & Miller, 2009a). The emerging literature on the experiences of SIEs suggests a similar theme, although it is notable that studies addressing the experiences of SIEs from this perspective comprised only those who had secured employment *before* arrival in the host country (see for example, Richardson, 2009; Richardson et al., 2009; Richardson & Zikic, 2007). A key finding in these studies was that SIEs believed that their experience and credentials had been sufficient to get them their jobs but were being undervalued for the purposes of promotion after arrival and thus impacted negatively on their future career prospects.

Language Proficiency

Another important antecedent of international job-search and reemployment outcomes is proficiency in the local language and understanding of local communication and interpersonal skills, particularly those specific to the workplace (e.g., occupational jargon and business etiquette) (Chiswick & Miller, 2009b; Cohen-Goldner & Eckstein, 2008; Thompson, 2000). Proficiency in English was cited as a key factor in determining access to high-paying occupations among immigrants to the United States and to better individual-job matches (Chiswick & Miller, 2009b). Several studies have also confirmed that knowledge of the local language led to higher earnings in both white- and blue-collar occupations and to increased chances of attaining high-skill employment (Cohen-Goldner & Eckstein, 2008; Thompson, 2000). Finally, when asked about barriers for hiring immigrant professionals, employers cited poor language skills as the number one barrier (Weiner, 2008).

Continuing with the theme of language proficiency, in some countries knowledge of the local language has become one of the most highly valued criteria impacting on employers' willingness to recruit immigrants. In Australia, for example, a new immigration policy is weighted toward applicants having vocational-level English, which is awarded significantly more points than conversational-level English (Hawthorne, 2008). Similarly, for SIEs looking for opportunities in non-English-speaking countries, knowledge of English (often their mother tongue) is essential for their job-search success. A study of western English-speaking SIEs in Taiwan (Tzeng, 2010), for example, found that many were hired without adequate skills or experience because local employers believed that it would be easier to teach an English-speaking westerner technology skills than teaching English and western cultural skills to local employees. The study also reported that English-speaking western employees were given positions where they would be required to interact with foreign clients, and that they often saw themselves as a "bridge" between the local employer and the clients. Some firms also deployed western employees as "figureheads" to create a "brand image" of being "western." Moreover, reflecting the same experiences as immigrant professionals discussed earlier, some researchers have noted the impact of SIEs' linguistic ability on cross-cultural adjustment, particularly on opportunities for promotion and/or job security. For example, even while their English language skills had not prevented them from getting their positions, a study of international faculty in Canada (Richardson et al., 2009) found that faculty for whom English was a second language reported more difficulty in meeting requirements for tenure and promotion than those of their counterparts who had English as their first language.

Research on immigrants to English-speaking countries has consistently identified inferior objective labor market outcomes for immigrant professionals from non-English-speaking countries (Hawthorne, 2008). They have also reported that increased competency in English leads to increased job "matching," understood as closer match between the immigrants' professional qualifications and experience and their employment in the host country (Chiswick & Miller, 2009a). Yet in studies of SIE academics who have moved from English-speaking to non-English-speaking countries, competency in the host language was *not* a prerequisite

for professional development. In one study, for example, SIE British academics in Turkey and the United Arab Emirates indicated that whereas competency in Turkish or Arabic was helpful for interactions outside of work, it was not a requirement for their jobs because English was the medium of instruction in all of the institutions in which the participants worked (Richardson, 2008). By comparison, the preliminary but unreported findings of a study of internationally mobile SIE mining engineers conducted by the third author of this chapter indicates that opportunities to engage in self-initiated expatriation are directly impacted by the engineers' competency in the potential host country's language. The rationale for this is that their work involves working directly with the host country's nationals. Whereas the same might be said of the SIE British academics in Richardson's (2008) study, the important difference is that in the professional context—that is, universities—the language used is English.

Cultural Capital

Another antecedent of successful international job search is job seekers' cultural capital, namely their ability to acculturate or integrate and adapt to aspects of the host society's culture. Thus, in addition to language proficiency, IJSs' success in the local labor market will depend on their accumulated knowledge of socially valued norms, beliefs, and behaviors (Bourdieu, 1986; Garnett, Guppy, & Veenstra, 2008). Someone who is more acculturated into the local culture is also likely to build rapport with locals, generating perceptions of social similarities and trustworthiness (Garnett et al., 2008; Tzeng, 2010). Therefore, as they become more acculturated, IJSs' ability to search for job opportunities in the new labor market will increase (Ackers & Gill, 2008; Bhagat & London, 1999; Bozionelos, 2009; Forstenlechner, 2010; Forstenlechner & Al-Waqfi, 2010; Inkson & Myers, 2003; Richardson, 2009; Richardson & Mallon, 2005).

Moderators
Social Support

Like local job search, international job search and job-search outcomes are embedded in and shaped by relational influences. In particular, in the course of a career transition such as a period of unemployment, social support has a positive impact on job-search behaviors and employment outcomes (Gowan, Riordan, & Gatewood, 1999;

Zikic & Klehe, 2006). As a result, IJSs who are able to draw on various sources of social support are likely to engage in more job-search behaviors and obtain better career outcomes than their more socially isolated counterparts (Peltokorpi & Froese, 2009; Richardson, 2009; Richardson & McKenna, 2006). For example, in a comparative study of SIEs and organizational expatriates (i.e., those sent overseas by an employer) working in the corporate sector in Japan, Peltokorpi and Froese (2009) pointed to the value of preexisting social networks for facilitating adjustment. Social support, then, aids IJSs in searching for new career options and adjusting to the host country by providing them with feelings of security, understanding, and help needed during times of transition and crisis (Peltokorpi & Froese, 2009; Schweizer, Schnegg, & Berzborn, 1999; Walker, Wasserman, & Wellman, 1994). This is an especially pressing concern for immigrants and SIEs who face heightened family and career demands and responsibilities during their transition (Richardson, 2006, 2009; Richardson & McKenna, 2006; Suto, 2008). Lack of social support in the new country also significantly affects immigrant professionals' and SIEs' ability to adapt and may lead to poorer work adjustment and downward career mobility (Peltokorpi & Froese, 2009; Suto, 2008; Wang & Sangaland, 2005). For a more detailed exploration of the impact of networks on job-search experiences and outcomes, see Forret (this volume).

Local Institutional Resources

Local institutional and governmental resources and services are important moderators for international job-search and integration outcomes. For example, studies of SIEs in the United Arab Emirates and Austria (Forstenlechner, 2010; Forstenlechner & Al-Waqfi, 2010) have identified the impact of perceptions of systemic injustice toward foreigners in local labor markets on SIEs' willingness to remain. Taking Canada as another example, government departments are often required to coordinate between each other and provide information and support for immigrants (it is notable, however, that no such service is available for SIEs). Several such partnerships have recently been established to bring together diverse groups of stakeholders to address relatively high levels of underemployment among immigrant professionals. Many of these local institutions are seeking to alleviate the barriers to labor market entry by educating potential migrants about local labor

market conditions prior to their arrival (Weiner, 2008). Such initiatives may also help to shape more realistic expectations and encourage immigrants to undertake more effective job-search strategies. For example, the Canadian government currently provides immigrants with online tools where they can input their credentials and be given realistic information about integration into the Canadian labor force. In this way, prospective immigrants can start the credentialing process before they move to Canada, thus speeding up the transition process and allowing for more effective job-search outcomes.

The Canadian government is also promoting general language training, although it does not provide training for workplace-specific language skills and broader communication skills. Some universities in Canada, however, have started to address this gap; for example, Ryerson University in Toronto has established a program geared toward Intercultural Communication in the Canadian workplace, and York University, also in Toronto, has created an Internationally Educated Professionals or "Bridging" Program. These programs also provide students with career management skills, again free of charge, and offer them opportunities for internships in local business organizations. Training programs such as these—especially those that include some form of mentoring, bridging, apprenticeship, or internship—are having a positive impact on individuals' career transition and enabling immigrants to be job-ready so that they can be more effective in their job-search activities. Many of these programs are also seeking to increase participants' local social capital, which further supports more effective job search. In this respect, many of these programs echo Reitz's (2001b) contention that institutional change is an essential element in the assignment of value to foreign human capital and the economic role of immigrants.

Finally, in addition to government and educational institutions, local unions are also seeking to support immigrants' entry to local labor markets. Harcourt, Lam, Harcourt, and Flynn (2008) described unions as primarily inclusive in their treatment of immigrant and ethnic minorities. The authors concluded that unions do have a positive effect on adoption of Equal Employment Opportunities practices (such as seeking information for compliance purposes) yet do not seem to have a significant effect on reducing some of the problems in IJS's access to jobs.

Job-Search Strategies
Job-Search Behaviors and Career Planning

As mentioned earlier, the majority of studies in the job-search literature focus on contextual issues facing IJSs, whereas comparatively few address their job-search *behaviors*. Those who do, however, have traditionally compared three different behaviors: (1) use of social networks (i.e., family or friends), (2) use of recruitment agencies, and (3) use of newspaper ads and the Internet (e.g., Fang et al., 2010; Frijters, Shields, & Wheatley Price, 2005; Greve, Salaff, & Chan, 2008).

In the case of immigrants, these studies confirm the *liability of foreignness* hypothesis, whereby lean media job-search methods such as mailed/emailed responses to newspaper ads and online postings provide better employment outcomes for immigrants than rich media methods such as visiting recruitment agencies in person (Fang et al., 2010; Greve, et al., 2008). This research suggests that immigrants' liability of foreignness stems primarily from their lack of familiarity with the local environment and lack of local contacts to facilitate entry into the local labor market. Therefore lean methods enable them to conceal their foreignness—that is, the traits that might be viewed negatively by employers (Greve et al., 2008). In addition, while an Internet job search may require some computer literacy, it is usually fairly easy to do and allows for multiple job applications to be sent, often free of charge, while also avoiding negative labeling, as employers may be more focused on objective data (e.g., skills and experience listed in the résumé). The use of recruitment agencies also has a negative impact on employment outcomes (lower wage satisfaction). Fang et al. (2010) has suggested that agencies may see immigrants as unfit for the best jobs and offer lower-skill, often temporary employment.

Turning to SIE's, there is a paucity of empirical evidence about their experiences of job search. However, of the studies that have addressed this theme, albeit in a tangential rather than a direct manner, Richardson and Mallon (2006) point to the impact of social networking on SIEs' ability to secure overseas positions. For example, they report how SIE British academics had drawn on contacts they had made at academic conferences or people they already knew in the host country as a means of finding their respective positions. Indeed, several of the academics in their study indicated that they would not have considered seeking out a position in their host country had they not had an existing social contact there. It is notable that none of the participants in their study had used job-search agencies. Moreover, in a study of Italian faculty seeking to return to Italy after spending a number of years in the United Kingdom, Gill (2005) reported widespread agreement that social connections in the respective institutions were essential for securing a position. This finding suggests that social networks have an important influence on IJSs who are seeking to *return* to their home country from overseas as well as those who are seeking a position outside of their home country.

Whereas some of the SIEs in the studies noted above had existing contacts in the host country, immigrants often arrive in their host country without an established network of contacts (Carr et al., 2005; Turchik-Hakak, Holzinger, & Zikic, 2010; Zikic et al., 2010). As Forret shows in this volume, professional networks take time to establish, which gives domestic job seekers—particularly more mature job seekers with more work experience—an advantage over IJSs (Turchik-Hakak et al., 2010). However, unlike the experience of some local job seekers (e.g., Wanberg, 2002), social networking and the use of agents is often less effective for IJSs. That is, while immigrants may be more likely to use social networks, their contacts are often within the same ethnic group and/or with other immigrants. While these networks act as a source of support and trust, especially in the settlement phase (Boyd, 1989; Hagan, 1998) they often lead to temporary, ethnic-enclave labor, or clerical work, or what have recently been called "survival" jobs (Greve et al., 2008). Pang (1999), for example, found that enclave social networks had a negative impact on job satisfaction among young Chinese adults participating in the British labor market. In spite of their strong professional qualifications and training, most of the young Chinese adults in that study were engaged in low-quality employment in the Chinese catering industry. Similarly, Bauder (2006) found that many South Asian immigrants in Vancouver, Canada, obtained work as taxi drivers using their ethnic network referrals. Yet the advantage of using these ethnic social networks is that it allows the respective job seeker to bypass the recruitment and selection process in nonethnic organizations, which most commonly require a demonstration of language proficiency, such as writing a résumé, communicating by email, and being interviewed.

In a study of highly qualified Latin American immigrant professionals in Canada who had obtained local MBA degrees, Turchik-Hakak et al. (2010) reported that networks with other Latin Americans facilitated success in the job market and were instrumental in helping them to find their first jobs in their field. While these homophilious networks (i.e., networks composed of people similar to themselves, usually a minority) (Ibarra, 1993) may be highly beneficial in the early phase of a transition, they may be of limited value when it comes to further professional development and advancement in larger organizational hierarchies owing to the very small number of minorities in high-ranking organizational positions. Therefore, whereas the role of personal contacts for job search and future career development seems pivotal for SIEs—at least for Richardson and Mallon's (2006) group of SIE British academics—they appear to be less effective where immigrants are concerned. Moreover, while intraethnic ties between professionals, as was the case with the Latin American sample in Turchick-Hakak et al.'s, (2010) study, provided job-relevant information and were of benefit for some job seekers, when it came to upward mobility, strong ties within one's ethnic group may not be enough (Drever & Hoffmesister, 2008).

Given the discussion thus far, it seems that some immigrants may view intra-ethnic and professional ties as a secure gateway into certain occupations and particularly for jobs dominated by their respective ethnic group. However, in the case of immigrant professionals and depending on the labor market, economy and geographic region of origin, these occupations may not furnish opportunities that are commensurate with the individual's level of education and experience. Indeed, Drever and Hoffmeister (2008) have reported that less assimilated immigrants in Germany tended to rely more heavily on their intraethnic networks to find employment. Consequently these researchers advise creating new ties with host country nationals in order to better integrate into the economy; they also suggest perhaps even cutting or limiting homophilious networks. Similarly, other researchers have reported the positive effects of bridging social ties (ties with host contacts) on immigrants' employment experiences and prospects (Kanas, van Tubergen, & van der Lippe, 2011). Kanas et al. (2011) suggest that social contacts with locals provide crucial resources to immigrants, such as information and influence, that further facilitate their employment chances. Focusing specifically on SIEs, Richardson and McKenna (2006) have also reported the importance of strong relationships with host country

nationals as a means of facilitating adjustment and a greater sense of "rootedness." By comparison, they also found that those SIEs who had a strong relationship with their home country (in this case Britain) were less likely to report a sense of belonging in the host country and expected to return to Britain much sooner. As noted above, Gill (2005) also noted the importance of social connections for *returning* SIEs.

Based on the above findings, it seems that some IJSs, such as immigrants, may draw initially on familiar social contacts because they do not have the resources or the familiarity with the local labor market to search as broadly as domestic job seekers (Frijters et al., 2005). Some IJSs may also need time to "learn" local job-search techniques, given their lack of familiarity with local networking and/or Internet job-search strategies. While social contacts in general are often cited as the primary method for obtaining jobs among domestic job seekers (Franzen & Hangartner, 2006; Granovetter, 1995; van Hoye, van Hooft, & Lievens, 2009) and were essential for the SIE academics in the reported studies, this method, while still useful, has a different and more complex meaning among immigrants.

Postmigration Investment in Human Capital

In addition to establishing destination-relevant social networks in their job search, IJSs must find ways to signal familiarity with their new labor market by obtaining *local* human capital. It is during this process that host country education can play a decisive role. By obtaining local educational credentials, IJSs are signaling to the labor market that they are informed about and committed to adopting local business practices and local occupational norms (Banerjee & Verma, 2009; Greve et al., 2008; Kanas et al., 2011). For many IJSs then, obtaining local human capital is an integral part of the job-search process. Indeed, it at the heart of initiatives such as the bridging programs, introduced above, that seek to provide immigrant professionals with a "local" educational qualification.

Numerous studies (see, for example, Chiswick & Miller, 2009; Cohen-Goldner & Eckstein, 2008; Kanas et al., 2011) link postimmigration credentials and experience to increased employment opportunities for both male and female immigrants. Cohen-Goldner and Eckstein (2008), for example, found that participation in white-collar job training in the host country (in this case among male immigrants to Israel from the Soviet

Union) was positively related to higher wages and, more importantly, to an increased probability of securing a higher occupation-relevant job offer. They further suggest that because this kind of postmigration investment seems to have long-term benefits, it makes economic sense for immigrants to undertake training in the host country as soon as possible after arrival. The authors also note that many immigrants are drawn in by the initial high returns from non–occupation-specific work in the host country, but that they must find opportunities for either gaining experience in specific occupations or undertake white-collar training opportunities for longer-term optimal returns. In examining propensities to seek postmigration education, Banerjee and Verma (2009) found that immigrants were more likely to seek postimmigration education (any form of professional formal instruction) if they were younger rather than older, had higher levels of education prior to their immigration (up to undergraduate), their foreign work experience had been unrecognized by Canadian employers or professional groups, and they had proficiency in English or French.

Turning to SIEs, while comparatively little is known about their job-search strategies, the existing literature suggests a number of important themes relating to their investment in expanding their human capital after expatriation. First, in some studies, when asked about the primary motives for self-initiated expatriation, career development was mentioned by only a minority (Hudson & Inkson, 2006; Richardson & Mallon, 2005). For example, for voluntary overseas development workers, a "search for adventure" and/or challenge was a primary driver alongside other motivators, such as a desire for personal change, a "search for meaning," or a general feeling that "the time was right." While some of the SIEs in Richardson and Mallon's (2006) study indicated that theu had considered the potential impact of the move on their career trajectory, it was rarely considered a significant issue. Rather, the most common reason was a "search for adventure," where many interviewees had made the decision to expatriate relatively quickly without specific concern about how such a move would impact on their career development. Yet when asked to evaluate the impact of SIE on their careers, the majority felt that it had had a positive impact—particularly in terms of acquiring "international experience" and a better understanding of different approaches to pedagogy, expanded research opportunities, and collegial networks. Thus these SIEs had gained what

they felt was significant human capital, but more as a result of being in the host country.

Another study of SIEs (Jokinen, Suutari, & Brewster, 2008) working in the corporate sector rather than the academic sector also reported perceptions of having gained increased "career capital" as a result of their international experience. Furthermore, in a study of American expatriates in East Asia, Vance (2005) presented a longer-range model reporting how exposure to and immersion in foreign cultures during earlier career stages had a positive impact on long-term career outcomes.

While the findings reported above might suggest some element of strategic career planning, Richardson and Mallon's (2005) study of SIEs reported the impact of serendipity on SIEs' decisions to move and their subsequent job-search and career experiences. Several SIE academics indicated that they had not particularly been looking for an overseas position but had accepted an offer that had "turned up out of the blue," perhaps through a chance meeting at an academic conference or when they had been "browsing" a website or professional maagazine. A later study of SIE academics in Canada suggested a similar finding; few of the participants in Richardson, McBey, and McKenna's (2009) study reported specific "career planning" activities and instead spoke of the impact of "serendipity" on their decision to look for a job overseas. To be sure, it may be that the paucity of career planning may be a feature of SIE academic careers rather than SIE careers more generally. Yet Inkson et al. (1997) and Inkson and Myers (2005) also reported widespread evidence of the role of serendipity and lack of career planning among young New Zealanders during their first postuniversity overseas work experiences (i.e., their "Big Overseas Experience").

International Job-Search Outcomes

Given the structural barriers encountered in destination labor markets, research on immigrants has adopted a broad conception of job-search success. Below we first consider objective job-search outcomes and then subjective ones.

Objective Job-Search Outcomes

What constitutes "success" in a domestic job search may not necessarily apply or translate to international job search. In addition to typical job-search outcomes such as reemployment speed, job-search offers, and interviews (Saks, 2005), indicators of international job-search success must be seen in close relation to the specific structural barriers encountered by IJSs in the local labor market. Outcomes of international job search are dependent on the specific geographic location, type of occupation (e.g., regulated versus unregulated), previous foreign work experience, and existing local social network, to name but a few; each outcome must be viewed in the context of these. In particular, we must acknowledge that much of the existing research in the area has been conducted in countries that have traditionally welcomed large numbers of immigrants, such as Canada, Australia, and the United States (e.g., Hawthorne, 2008; Reitz, 2001a); therefore the majority of empirical research leading to the outcomes reviewed below is based on data from those geographical regions.

Finding a Job in One's Field of Study and Career Development/Promotion

Finding a job in one's professional field may be a particularly important marker of objective job-search success for the IJS since, compared with local job seekers, immigrants are more likely to end up working outside of their field of study or experience (often taking jobs that are below their level of competency), both of which may lead to long-term downward career mobility (see, for example, Chiswick, Lee, & Miller, 2005; Reitz, 2001a). Furthermore, as noted earlier, empirical research has suggested that having higher levels of preimmigration labor market experience may actually diminish immigrants' chances of finding work that is commensurate with their educational qualifications and professional competencies (Chiswick & Miller, 2009a). Yet in the case of SIEs, research suggests a fairly widespread perception that "foreign" or "international" experience will support rather than detract from career advancement. Indeed, according to several studies (Jokinen, Suutaari, & Brewster, 2008; Richardson et al., 2009; Richardson, & Mallon, 2006; Selmer & Lauring, 2010; Thorn, 2009), SIEs believed that acquiring such experience would be an asset in the contemporary job market. It may be, therefore, that certain kinds of international experience—such as experience gained in specific regions—may be more valuable or more "recognized" than others.

Returning to the problem of when international experience is unrecognized or devalued, how can IJSs obtain job-search success if their human capital is judged to be incompatible with the local labor market? Sometimes this incompatibility is also due to technological change and general lack of transferability of knowledge and experience between national contexts (Chiswick & Miller, 2009b;

Friedberg, 2000; Richardson, 2009). For example, experience of working with a particular culture or ethnic group may have little value if that group does not exist or is a minority in the new "home" country. Similarly, despite the current rhetoric about the globalization of certain HRM practices, the extent to which they are indeed transferable across national boundaries may be limited (McKenna, Richardson, Singh, & Xu, 2010).

It may also be that the respective foreign human capital may be of lower quality, as might be the case in comparing some graduate degrees from different countries/institutions. However, such differences are often difficult to judge owing to the potential lack of knowledge or familiarity with the respective country's/institution's educational and professional institutions (Freidberg, 2000; Reitz, 2001). There is research showing that there may in fact be some discrimination involved in how foreign human capital is evaluated (Banerjee & Verma, 2009). For example, some researchers have argued that some Canadian employers' demands for job applicants to have "Canadian experience" (Bauder, 2003; Nwosu, 2006; Ralston, 1998) and preferences for some accents over others (Creese & Kambere, 2003; Purkiss et al., 2006; Scassa, 1994) are manifestations of discrimination. To be sure, there are certain jobs where lack of local experience and knowledge of local cultures and customs can be a legitimate reason not to hire a foreign candidate. Yet we must also acknowledge the possibility of prejudice (Essess et al., 2006) and concomitant discrimination. Similarly, while having a local accent may be advantageous in certain professions, in most occupations accents have little impact on performance (Scassa, 1994). In particular, job interviews have been identified as occasions when accents may cause candidates to be undervalued regardless of the content of the interview (Purkiss et al., 2006; Scassa, 1994).

Our review of the SIE and immigrant literatures suggests that some IJSs may be more "objectively successful" than others in the sense that they have obtained a job in their field of study that is commensurate with their experience and qualifications (e.g., Chiswick & Miller, 2009a,b; Cohen-Goldner & Eckstein, 2008; Doherty, 2010; Forstenlechner & Al-Waqfi, 2010; Friedberg, 2000; Richardson, 2009; Selmer & Lauring, 2010). Indeed, as noted above, with the exception of young New Zealanders going overseas for their postuniversity overseas work experience, much of the literature on SIEs focuses on those who secured a job before they arrived in the host country rather than after they arrived, as is the case for many (if not all) immigrants. Generally, among SIEs and immigrants, more objective success in the destination labor market was obtained by those individuals who had studied in western and internationally recognized schools and had gained their experience in western countries (Freidberg, 2000; Hawthorne, 2008; Reitz, 2001a; Thompson, 2000). Moreover, those who studied more "technical" or "scientific" topics (which are believed to transfer across contexts more easily—see Hawthorne, 2008; Leong & Leung, 2004; Reitz, 2001) and those with higher levels of education were more likely to have experienced this form of objective success in finding a position (Chiswick & Miller, 2009b; Hawthorne, 2008, Thompson 2000). Some studies also indicate that, depending on the immigrants' country of origin and especially for highly regulated professions such as medicine, little or no previous work experience may be an advantage rather than a disadvantage (Zikic & Richardson, 2011). One rationale for this is that local labor market "gatekeepers" may believe that it would be easier to "mold" and educate less experienced IJSs according to local occupational and business standards than would be the case with their more experienced counterparts. It may also be that these typically younger newcomers with limited work experience arrive without families and thus have more time and energy to invest in obtaining local human capital.

Earnings

Like experience-relevant work, earnings are often seen as a primary measure of IJSs' objective success in the local labor market. Focusing specifically on newer cohorts of immigrants to Canada, research has suggested that despite increased levels of education, their labor force participation rates and earnings relative to individuals born in Canada are declining (Reitz, 2001). Indeed, Frenette and Morissette (2005) have found that the earnings gap is especially wide between male immigrants and Canadian-born workers; the relative earnings gap between these two groups doubled between 1980 and 2000. After a period of 15 years, the earnings of earlier cohorts of immigrants had nearly converged with the earnings of those born in Canada. While more recent immigrant cohorts are increasing their earnings at a faster rate than previous cohorts, the relative speed of the increase does not compensate for the initial loss. Moreover, as Frenette and Morissette (2005) point out, more recent arrivals are significantly more educated than earlier cohorts. These researchers also found that new entrants to

the Canadian labor market are worse off and had relatively reduced earnings growth compared with experienced workers regardless of their local or foreign origin. Thus these issues may be related to broader systemic issues that are not unique to international job search, such as employers offering lower-paid entry-level jobs.

Reitz (2001b) also discusses the reasons for the reported decline in immigrants' earnings, emphasizing the role of increasing levels of education among the Canadian-born workforce and employers making "sharper distinctions" between foreign-born and locally born groups' skills. This, Reitz (2001b) suggests, further decreases the perceived value accorded to foreign education and work experience. It may also be that despite the putative transferability of knowledge across national boundaries, the current "knowledge economy" requires more specific forms of knowledge and experience derived from local rather than international work experiences.

Recent empirical work comparing the experiences of immigrants in Canada and Australia suggests that immigrant economic integration is not completely at the mercy of global shifts in labor market structures and may be influenced to a significant degree by national policy. Hawthorne (2008), for example, found that compared with the stagnating and even declining labor market outcomes of immigrants to Canada, immigrants to Australia experienced gains in employment, earnings, and use of credentials and skills. Moreover, this trend was particularly visible among the traditionally disadvantaged non−west European immigrants, older individuals, and females. This finding may be due to the recent change in Australian immigration policy strongly favoring experience that is locally valued by employers (e.g. local or internationally recognized schooling), qualifications currently in market demand, and strong English language skills. The same study also found that graduate migrants as well as graduate degree holders were more likely to secure professional employment than their diploma-holding counterparts.

In interpreting earnings outcomes for various groups of migrants, we must also acknowledge the potential differences between regulated and nonregulated professions. Individuals working in regulated professions require credentialing—certification that they have passed all the professional requirements to work in a particular field (Weiner, 2008). By comparison, individuals working in nonregulated professions may voluntarily undergo a more general assessment of their knowledge and qualifications to earn the requisite recognition from employers and clients (Reitz, 2005). The effect of regulation on an international job seeker's prospects in the host country can vary according to two factors: the ease of credential recognition and assessment in his or her respective field and the extent to which that recognition is communicated to potential employers and accepted by them. More often than not, IJSs from regulated professions encounter more difficulty in having their qualifications recognized in host countries and hence are more likely to encounter problems finding work that is commensurate with their professional status prior to immigration (Hall & Sadouzai, 2010). The difficulties in obtaining certification for a regulated profession have been described in a number of studies and reports, suggesting a lack of clear information about the credentialing process and requirements, exorbitant licensing fees and examinations, subjective evaluations of foreign qualifications, requirements for local work experience or for training and upgrading, and a lack of opportunities and financial support for such upgrading (Alboim & McIsaac, 2007; Galarneau & Morissette, 2008; Weiner, 2008). Additionally, regulation of professions may be undertaken by state regulators, state-licensed professional regulators, professional representative bodies, or some combination thereof, making it especially frustrating for internationally trained professionals who must navigate the often ad hoc and uncoordinated demands of these institutions (Weiner, 2008).

Subjective International Job-Search Outcomes

Thus far we have focused on objective job-search outcomes such as earnings and career advancement. While much of the literature on the job-search success of IJSs focuses on objective outcomes, it is also important to consider subjective job-search outcomes, such as career satisfaction, professional fulfillment, and so on. For instance, Greve et al. (2008) suggest that a primary need for successful IJSs is the "reconstruct[ion] of their biographies." Thus, IJSs must understand what kinds of signals are recognized by local employers. In each labor market, local institutions and employers have certain sets of expectations regarding what a "proper" candidate would look like, which means that both SIEs and immigrants may have to learn to first transform their human capital into what is acceptable and expected in the local labor market. Depending on a number of factors, such as family situation or personality, IJSs may experience a lack of subjective success; their responses to such feeling may range from those reflecting high levels of proactivity, an "adaptable" attitude, or an extremely unhappy and frustrated one (Zikic et al., 2010). However, it is clear that for some immigrants, it often takes a long time to achieve subjective job-search success.

In terms of causes for these negative subjective job-search outcomes, some authors go as far as to claim that employers and regulatory groups purposefully devalue immigrant labor and exclude them from high-status occupations to reproduce social privileges (Bauder, 2003). This deskilling and nonrecognition of foreign qualifications and requirements is said to be a labor market barrier that shackles immigrants to survival jobs, thus further detracting from their sense of fulfillment and overall job/professional satisfaction. Given the potential negative impact on individual identity and long-term career mobility, survival jobs are not a desirable outcome of a job-search endeavor. Often the type of job experience gained during a survival job contributes little if anything to the individual's qualifications, level of experience, or financial aspirations. In this regard, it may well be that such activities detract from the individual's overall job-search competencies and sense of fulfillment precisely because of the concomitant demands in terms of time and energy. In the Canadian context, requirement for local labor market experience (i.e., Canadian experience) for almost any type of job allows employers to differentiate between domestic job seekers (i.e., Canadian-born) and immigrants. Accordingly, some IJSs—particularly immigrants— have access only to low-skilled or voluntary work at the start of their postmigration careers, thus limiting their chances of subjective success (Bauder, 2003).

Moderators of Job-Search Outcome
Time in Host Country and Job-Search Outcomes

In general it seems that long-established (resident for 10 or more years) graduate immigrants experience similar unemployment rates as those born in the host country. This finding seems to suggest that there is indeed a "transition penalty" (Leon, 2003), but that migrants are able to catch up with locals as time passes. Where SIEs are concerned, our review has not come up with any specific findings regarding the impact of time spent in the host country on earning capacity or professional development.

Country of Origin and Job-Search Outcomes

Empirical data suggest that immigrants from western countries benefit most from immigration and Asians/Africans least. Schooling obtained abroad also provides more returns to those from western countries, while Asians and Africans experience the lowest returns (Friedberg, 2000). Experience earned abroad is also linked to negative earnings for eastern Europeans and confers zero value to migrant westerners, individuals from the former Soviet Union, Asians, and Africans. Local experience confers higher earnings premiums to westerners and Soviets, with other immigrant groups benefiting substantially less. In general, male non-European immigrants earn between 15% and 25% less than most European immigrants. As well, some Europeans earn less than others (Reitz, 2001). The extent to which inequities are due to racial discrimination versus the actual devaluation of foreign human capital because of limitations in transferability remains a question for further exploration. Research on SIEs has, to date, not yet explored differentials in earning capacity relating to country of origin, although our review suggests that it is a theme that merits attention.

Occupation-Specific Market Demand and Job-Search Outcomes

It is notable that job-search outcomes for migrants vary by occupation-specific market demand (Wanberg et al., 2002). For example, recent decades have seen an increased demand for migrants in technical occupations, so it is perhaps not surprising that they achieve somewhat better professional and economic outcomes than individuals in fields experiencing less demand (Banerjee & Verma, 2009). Indeed, this argument has been supported by the new policies of Australian immigration authorities mentioned in Hawthorne's report (2008). Studies of SIE academics (Richardson, 2008; Richardson et al., 2009) have also connected labor market demand with the ability of SIEs to obtain jobs outside their home countries. In a study of SIE academics in Canadian uuniversities (Richardson et al., 2009), interviewees reported that the shortage of academics in Canada was an important incentive for them to apply for their current positions. Many academics in the study also predicted that this shortage would continue to impact recruitment trends for faculty from outside Canada. Similarly the expansion of higher education in some parts of the world, such as the Middle and Far East, has also been cited as expanding opportunities for SIEs in academia more generally (Richardson, 2009).

Conclusion

While acknowledging that international job seekers comprise a highly diverse group, for the purposes of this review we have focused on two specific groups of international job seekers: immigrants (typically white-collar workers) and self-initiated expatriates. Other groups of IJSs—such as migrant seasonal workers (e.g., fruit pickers) or temporary migrant (project-based) workers (e.g., construction workers)—may have presented other themes for discussion. Yet focusing on these two groups allows an in-depth comparison of the job-search process, outcomes, and associated variables. That said, we also acknowledge that the boundaries between different groups of international job seekers are blurred. This clearly draws our attention to the "problem of definition" as a broader concept and one that has been debated at length in the literature on global mobility more generally (see for example, Doherty, et al., 2013, for a discussion of the problem of defining and distinguishing SIEs from other groups of mobile professionals). Acknowledging the blurred boundaries between different groupings of IJSs where immigrants and SIEs are concerned, we have shown some of the differences in the job-search experiences of the two groups. For example, we have shown how SIEs seem to report more objective and subjective job-search outcomes than their immigrant counterparts. Yet one of the factors clearly distinguishing the two groups and perhaps explaining some of the above findings may be different motivations for leaving their home country, challenges experienced in the host country labor market, and overall expectations of potential outcomes. For example, as Al-Ariss (2010) has suggested, immigration may be seen more as an escape from difficult circumstances in the respective home country and/or an opportunity to enhance one's economic status. By comparison, self-initiated expatriation may be viewed more as an opportunity for adventure or a search for a different cultural experience rather than as an opportunity for increased earnings and/or professional advancement. Interestingly, however, while SIEs seem to do less explicit planning for their move, the majority still appear to secure jobs before leaving. In their case then, their job search takes place in their home country rather than in the host country, which means that they are explicitly conducting their search "at a distance" rather than in the local labor market, which is the case for immigrants.

Future Directions

Although the findings and themes reported in this chapter provide some understanding of the existing literature on these two groups of international job seekers, our overall conclusion is that international job search remains a relatively underresearched theme overall. For example, the SIE literature has focused either on specific occupational groups such as academics or does not distinguish sufficiently between occupational groups (i.e., speaking of "managerial" or "corporate" SIEs). The need for a more nuanced body of research on corporate/managerial SIEs seems to be especially important given the potential differences between different employment sectors. For example, it might be that there are differences in SIE job-search experiences between those looking for work in different industries or fields. As for research on the job-search experiences of immigrants, there is a growing body of research on labor market barriers and challenges encountered by immigrants in the host country and much less focus on their specific job-search behaviors and success factors. Similarly, much focus is given to immigrant professionals as opposed to the job-search experiences of other types of immigrants (e.g., blue collar immigrant and those seeking temporary work, etc.).

Indeed, future work might explore the differences and similarities between a broader range of IJSs both with regard to their job-search experiences and outcomes. It might also be fruitful to develop an understanding of the extent to which individuals move from one type of job-search activity/grouping to another. Moreover, whereas our study has considered some of the influences on the outcomes of international job search—such as gender, age, and language proficiency—future research might explore the different ways in which governments could support IJSs through government and public policy initiatives. In particular, a broader comparison of initiatives might be helpful in providing a more nuanced understanding of the impact of support systems. For example, whereas we have made comparisons between western countries such as Canada and Australia, further comparisons might be made focusing on initiatives in nonwestern countries, such as Singapore (Tan, 2012). Taken as a whole then,

it is clear that within the field of international job search more generally, there are a number of avenues requiring further exploration.

Practical Implications Checklist

- Research and exploration of career options and job-search process can start in the home country and while preparing for this major career transition.
- Strategic planning and starting job-search process before reaching the host country will help in creating realistic expectations of the local labor market.
- IJSs should rely on the web and various social networking tools and web job-search tools while in the host country and trying to prepare for local job search.
- Obtaining additional local human capital will increase chances of job-search success in the host country.
- Engaging in mentoring and other ways of increasing local social capital will increase job-search success for IJSs.
- Local career counselors must understand specific job-search barriers faced by IJs and focus on coaching them in terms of local employer needs and specific local business culture requirements.
- Local career counselors must especially be prepared to understand and coach by focusing on cultural differences and communication styles.
- Cultural intelligence training will benefit job seekers, employers, and counselors as well as anyone involved in the IJS's job-seeking process.
- Local organizations can tap into the IJS talent pool by using local agencies serving immigrants and foreign workers as well as local bridging programs (e.g., marketing your job openings through organizations that work directly with skilled immigrants) (e.g., hireimmigrants.com).
- In order to better source foreign talent, local employers can broaden their recruitment strategy by participating in specific networking and coaching events as well as participating in mentoring programs (e.g., hireimmigrants.com).
- Local employers can benefit from hiring IJSs in terms of reducing a shortage of talent and skills, increasing innovation and problem

solving, and helping them connect to global markets and diverse local customer groups.

- Successful integration of IJSs into local workplace can be achieved by providing cultural sensitivity training to both local employees as well newcomers; by offering language training and communication/presentation skills training as part of the training and development for new hires with international backgrounds, and by encouraging local employees to mentor international hires for their mutual benefit and learning (e.g., Maytree foundation: hireimmigrants.com).

References

Ackers, H. K., & Gill, B. (2008). *Moving people and knowledge: Scientific mobility in an enlarging European Union.* Northampton, MA: Edward Elgar.

Al Ariss, A. (2010). Modes of engagement: Migration, self-initiated expatriation, and career development. *Career Development International, 15*, 338–368.

Alboim, N., & McIsaac, E. (2007). Making the connections: Ottawa's role in immigrant employment. *IRPP Choices, 13*, 1–24.

Bandura, A. (1986). Social foundations of thought and action: A social cognitive theory. Englewood Cliffs, NJ: Prentice- Hall.

Bandura, A. (2001). Social cognitive theory: An agentic perspective. *Annual Review of Psychology, 52*, 1–26.

Banerjee, R., & Verma, A. (2009). "Determinants and effects of post-migration education among new immigrants in Canada." CLSRN Working Papers.

Baruch, Y. (1995). Business globalization—The human resource management aspect. *Human Systems Management, 14*, 313–326.

Baruch, Y., Budhwar, P., & Khatri, N. (2007). Brain drain: Inclination to stay abroad after studies. *Journal of World Business, 42*, 99–112.

Bateman, T. S., & Crant, M. J. (2006) The proactive component of organizational behaviour: A measure and correlates. *Journal of Organizational Behavior, 14*, 103–118.

Bauder, H. (2003). "Brain abuse," or the devaluation of immigrant labour in Canada. *Antipode, 35*, 699–717.

Bauder, H. (2006). Origin, employment status and attitudes towards work: Immigrants in Vancouver, Canada. *Work, Employment and Society, 20*, 709–729.

Bhagat, R. S., & London, M. (1999). Getting started and getting ahead: Career dynamics of immigrants. *Human Resource Management Review, 9*, 349–365.

Boneva, B. S., & Frieze, I. H. (2001). Toward a concept of a migrant personality. *Journal of Social Issues, 57*, 477–491.

Bourdieu, P. (1986) "The forms of capital." In J. Richardson (Ed.), *Handbook of theory and research for the sociology of education* (pp. 241–258). New York: Greenwood.

Boyd, M. (1989). Family and personal networks in international migration: Recent developments and new agendas. *International Migration Review*, 638–670.

Boyd, M., & Thomas, D. (2001). Match or mismatch? The labour market performances of foreign-born engineers. *Population Research and Policy Review, 20*, 107–133.

Bozionelos, N. (2009). Expatriation outside the boundaries of the multinational corporation: Expatriate nurses in Saudi Arabia. *Human Resource Management, 48*, 111–134.

Brekke, I., & Mastekaasa, A. (2008). Highly educated immigrants in the Norweigan labour market: Permanent disadvantage? *Work, Employment and Society, 22*, 507–526.

Brown, D. J., Cober, R. T., Kane, K., Levy, P. E., & Shalhoop, J. (2006). Proactive personality and the successful job search: A field investigation with college graduates. *Journal of Applied Psychology, 91*, 717–726.

Cappellen, T., & Janssens, M. (2008). Global managers' career competencies. *Career Development International, 13*, 514–537.

Carr, S. C., Inkson, K., & Thorn, K. (2005). From global careers to talent flow: Reinterpreting "brain drain." *Journal of World Business, 40*, 386–398.

Cerdin, J.-L., & Abdeljalil, M. (2007). "The success of highly qualified foreigners in France." Paper presented at the Annual Meeting of the Academy of Management. Philadelphia.

Chiswick, B. R. (2000). "Are immigrants favorably self-selected?" IZA Discussion Paper Series. Bonn.

Chiswick, B. R., Lee, Y. L., & Miller, P. W. (2005). A longitudinal analysis of immigrant occupational mobility: A test of the immigrant assimilation hypothesis. *International Migration Review, 39*, 332–350.

Chiswick, B. R., & Miller, P. W. (2009a). Earnings and occupational attainment among immigrants. *Industrial Relations, 48*, 454–465.

Chiswick, B. R., & Miller, P. W. (2009b). The international transferability of immigrants' human capital skills. *Economics of Education Review, 28*, 162–169.

Cohen-Goldner, S., & Eckstein, Z. (2008). Labor mobility of immigrants: Training, experience, language, and opportunities. *International Economic Review, 49*, 837–872.

Constant, A., Kahanec, M., & Zimmermann K. (2009). Attitudes towards immigrants, other integration barriers, and their veracity. *International Journal of Manpower, 30*, 5–19.

Creese, G., & Kambere, E. N. (2003). What colour is your English? *Canadian Review of Sociology and Anthropology, 40*, 565–573.

Doherty, N. (2010). "Self-initiated expatriates—Mavericks of the global milieu?" Paper presented at the Annual Meeting of the Academy of Management. Montreal.

Doherty, N., Dickmann, M., & Mills, T. (2011). Exploring the motives of company-backed and self-initiated expatriates. *International Journal of Human Resource Management, 22*(3), 595–611.

Doherty, N., Richardson, J., & Thorn, K. (2013). Self-initiated expatriation and self-initiated expatriates: clarification of the research stream. *Career Development International, 18*(1), 97–112

Drever, A. I., & Hoffmeister, O. (2008). Immigrants and social networks in a job-scarce environment: The case of Germany. *International Migration Review, 42*, 425–448.

Essess, V. M., Dietz, J., & Bhardwaj, A. (2006). The role of prejudice in the discounting of immigrant skills. In R. Mahalingam (Ed.), *Cultural psychology of immigrants* (pp. 113–130). Mahwah, NJ: Erlbaum.

Fang, T., Samnani, A.-K., Novicevic, M. M., & Bing, M. A. (2010). "Liability-of-foreignness effects on job success of immigrant job seekers." 15th International Metropolis Conference. The Hague.

Forstenlechner, I. (2010). Exploring expatriates' behavioural reaction to institutional injustice on host country level. *Personnel Review, 39*, 178–194.

Forstenlechner, I., & Al-Waqfi, M. A. (2010). A job interview for Mo, but none for Mohammed. *Personnel Review, 39*, 767–784.

Franzen, A., & Hangartner, D. (2006) Social networks and labour market outcomes: The non-monetary benefits of social capital. *European Sociological Review, 22*, 353–368.

Frenette, M., & Morissette, R. (2005). Will they ever converge? Earnings of immigrant and Canadian-born workers over the last two decades. *International Migration Review, 39*, 228–257.

Friedberg, R. M. (2000). You can't take it with you? Immigration assimilation and the portability of human capital. *Journal of Labour Economics, 18*, 221–251.

Frijters, P., Shields, M. A., & Wheatley Price, S. (2005). Job search methods and their success: A comparison of immigrants and natives in the UK. *The Economic Journal, 115*, F359–F376.

Galarneau, D., & Morissette, R. (December 2005). Immigrants' education and required job skills. *Perspectives on Labour and Income*, 5–18.

Garnett, B., Guppy, N., & Veenstra, G. (2008). Careers open to talent: Educational credentials, cultural talent, and skilled employment. *Sociological Forum, 23*, 144–164.

Gill, B. (2005). Homeward bound? The experience of return mobility for Italian scientists. *Innovation, 18*, 319–341.

Gowan, M. A., Riordan, C. M., & Gatewood, R. D. (1999). Test of a model of coping with involuntary job loss following a company closing. *Journal of Applied Psychology, 84*, 75–86.

Granovetter, M. S. (1995). *Getting a job: A study of contacts and careers.* Chicago: University of Chicago Press.

Greve, A., Salaff, J. W. & Chan, E. (2008). "Immigrants and job search: An institutional perspective." Proceedings of the 13th International ITA Workshop (pp. 88–108), Krakow, Poland.

Hagan, J. M. (1998). Social networks, gender, and immigrant incorporation: Resources and constraints. *American Sociological Review, 63*, 55–67.

Hall, P. V., & Sadouzai, T. (2010). The value of "experience" and the labour market entry of new immigrants to Canada. *Canadian Public Policy, 36*, 181–198.

Harcourt, M., Lam, H., Harcourt, S., & Flynn, M. (2008). Discrimination in hiring against immigrants and ethnic minorities: The effect of unionization. *The International Journal of Human Resource Management, 19*, 98–115.

Harvey, M., Novicevic, M., Buckley, M., & Fung, H. (2005). Reducing inpatriate liability of foreignness by addressing stigmatization and stereotype threats. *Journal of World Business, 40*, 267–280.

Hawthorne, L. (2008). The impact of economic selection policy on labour market outcomes for degree-qualified migrants in Canada and Australia. *IRPP Choices, 14*, 1–50.

Hudson, S., & Inkson, K. (2006). Volunteer overseas development workers: The hero's adventure and personal transformation. *Career Development International, 11*, 304–320.

Ibarra, H. (1993). Personal networks of women and minorities in management: A conceptual framework. *Academy of Management Review, 18*, 56–88.

Inkson, K., Arthur, M. B., Pringle, J., & Barry, S. (1997). Expatriate assignment versus overseas experience: International human resource development. *Journal of World Business, 32*(4), 351–368.

Inkson, K., & Myers, B. (2003). The big OE: Self directed travel and career development. *Career Development International, 8*, 170–181.

Jackson, D.J.R., Carr, S. C., Edwards, M., Thorn, K., Allfree, N., Hooks, J. & Inkson, K. (2005). Exploring the dynamics of New Zealand's talent flow. *New Zealand Journal of Psychology, 34*, 110–116

Jokinen, T., Brewster, C., & Suutari, V. (2008). Career capital during international work experiences: Contrasting self-initiated expatriate experiences and assignees expatriation. *The International Journal of Human Resource Management, 19*(6), 979–998.

Kanas, A., van Tubergen, F., & van der Lippe, T. (2011). The role of social contacts in the employment status of immigrants: A panel study of immigrants in Germany. *International Sociology, 26*, 95–122.

Kanfer, R., Wanberg, C. R., & Kantrowitz. T. M. (2001). Job search and employment: A personality-motivational analysis and meta-analytic review. *Journal of Applied Psychology, 86*, 837–855.

King, R. (2012). "Theories and typologies of migration: An overview and primer." Willy Brandt Series of Working Papers in International Migration and Ethnic Relations, 3/12. Available at: http://www.mah.se/upload/Forskningscentrum/MIM/WB/WB%203.12.pdf

Kogan, I. (2006). Labor markets and economic incorporation among recent immigrants in Europe. *Social Forces, 85*, 697–721.

Kustec, S., Thompson, E., & Xue, L. (2007). Foreign credentials: The tools for research. *Canadian Issues, 26*, 26–30.

Lawrence, M. K. (2004). Immigration, skills and the labor market: International evidence. *Journal of Population Economics, 7*, 501–534.

Leong, F.T.L., & Leung, K. (2004). Academic careers in Asia: A cross-cultural analysis. *Journal of Vocational Behavior, 64*, 346–357.

Lewin, K. (1951). *Field theory in social science: Selected theoretical papers.* D. Cartwright. New York: Harper & Row.

Lochhead, C. (2003). "The transition penalty: Unemployment among recent immigrants to Canada." CLBC Commentary.

Maytree Foundation. (August 8, 2012). "Deloitte's three ideas to boost immigrant success." Available at: http://www.hireimmigrants.ca/success-stories/cultural-training-deloitte/

McKenna, S., Richardson, J., Singh, P., & Xu, J. J. (2010). Negotiating and resisting HRM: A Chinese case study. *International Journal of Human Resources Management, 21*, 851–872.

Millar, C.C.J.M., & Choi, C. J. (2008). Worker identity, the liability of foreignness, the exclusion of local managers and unionism: A conceptual analysis. *Journal of Organizational Change Management, 21*, 460–470.

Myers, B. (2011). "Older women: Travelling and working at the edge." Paper presented at the Equality, Diversity and Inclusion Conference, Auckland University, 7–8 February, 2011.

Nwosu, L. N. (2006). The experience of domestic violence among Nigerian-Canadian women in Toronto. *Canadian Woman Studies, 25*, 99–106.

Pang, M. (1999). The employment situation of young Chinese adults in the British labour market. *Personnel Review, 28*, 41–55.

Peltokorpi, V., & Froese, F. J. (2009). Organizational expatriates and self-initiated expatriates: Who adjusts better to work and life in Japan? *International Journal of Human Resource Management, 20*, 1096–1112.

Purkiss, S.L.S., Perrewé, P. L., Gillespie, T. L., Mayes, B. T., & Ferris, G. R. (2006). Implicit sources of bias in employment interview judgments and decisions. *Organizational Behavior and Human Decision Processes, 101*, 152–167.

Ralston, H. (1998). Race, class, gender and multiculturalism in Canada and Australia. *Race, Gender and Class, 5*, 14–29.

Reitz, J. G. (2001a). Immigrant skill utilization in the Canadian labour market: Implications of human capital research. *Journal of International Migration and Integration, 2*, 347–378.

Reitz, J. G. (2001b). Immigrant success in the knowledge economy: Institutional change and the immigrant experience in Canada, 1970–1995. *Journal of International Migration and Integration, 2*, 347–378.

Reitz, J. G. (2002). Host societies and the reception of immigrants: Research themes, emerging theories and methodological issues. *The International Migration Review, 36*, 1005–1019.

Reitz, J. G. (2005). Tapping Immigrants' skills: New directions for Canadian immigration policy in the knowledge economy. *Law and Business Review of the Americas, 11*, 409–432.

Richardson, J. (2006). International mobility: Family matters. *Personnel Review, 35*, 469–486.

Richardson, J. (2008). *The independent expatriate: Academics abroad*, VDM Publishers.

Richardson, J. (2009). Geographical flexibility—A cautionary note. *British Journal of Management, 20*, 160–170.

Richardson, J., & Mallon M. (2005). Self-directed expatriation: Career interrupted? *Journal of World Business, 40*, 409–420.

Richardson, J. McBey, K., & McKenna, S. (2009). "Internationalizing Canadian universities: Where do international faculty fit in?" In R. Trilokekar, G. A. Jones & A. Shubert (Eds.), *Canada's universities go global* (pp. 277–296). Lorimer.

Richardson, J., & Zikic, J. (2007). The darker side of an international academic career. *Career Development International, 12*, 163–186.

Salaff, J., Greve, A., & Ping, L.X.L. (2002). Paths into the economy: Structural barriers and the job hunt for skilled PRC migrants in Canada. *The International Journal of Human Resource Management, 13*, 450–464.

Saks, A. M., (2005). "Job search success: A review and integration of the predictors, behaviours, and outcomes." In S. Brown and R. Lent (Eds.), *Career development and counseling: Putting theory and research to work* (pp. 155–179). Hoboken, NJ: Wiley.

Scassa, T. Language standards, ethnicity and discrimination. (1994). *Canadian Ethnic Studies, 26*, 105–121.

Schweizer, T., Schnegg, M., & Berzborn, S. (1998). Personal networks and social support in a multiethnic community of southern California. *Social Networks 20*, 1–21.

Selmer, J., & Lauring, J. (2010). Self-initiated academic expatriates: Inherent demographics and reasons to expatriate. *European Management Review, 7*, 169–179.

Siebert, S. E., Kraimer, M. L., & Liden, R. C. (2001). A social capital theory of career success. *Academy of Management Journal, 44*, 219–238.

Suto, M. (2008). Compromised careers: The occupational transition of immigration and resettlement. *Work, 32*, 417–429.

Tams, S., & Arthur, M. B. (2007). Studying careers across cultures: Distinguishing international, cross-cultural and globalization perspectives. *Career Development International, 12*, 86–98.

Tan, M. (2012). Foreign talent policy had an impact on impact gap. *The Straits Times*. Available at: http://www.spp.nus.edu.sg/ips/docs/media/yr2012/p2012/ST_Foreign%20talent%20policy%20had%20effect%20on%20income%20gap_170112.pdf

Tharenou, P. (2010) Women's self-initiated expatriation as a career option and its ethical issues. *Journal of Business Ethics, 95*, 73–88.

The Economist. (2011). Migration after the crash: Moving out, on and back. August 27.

Thompson, E. N. (2000). "Immigrant occupational skill outcomes and the role of region-of-origin-specific human capital." Applied Research Branch Research Paper W-00-8E. Ottawa: Human Resources Development Canada.

Thorn, K. (2009). The relative importance of motives for international self-initiated mobility. *Career Development International, 14*, 441–464.

Turchick-Hakak, L., Holzinger, I., & Zikic, J. (2010). Barriers and paths to success: Latin American MBAs' views of employment in Canada. *Journal of Managerial Psychology, 25*, 159–176.

Tzeng, R. (2010). Cultural capital and cross-border career ladders: Western professional migrants in Taiwan. *International Sociology, 25*, 123–143.

Van Hoye, G., van Hooft, E.A.J., & Lievens, F. (2009). Networking as a job search behaviour: A social network perspective. *Journal of Occupational and Organizational Psychology, 82*, 661–682.

Vance, C. M. (2005). The personal quest for building global competence: A taxonomy of self-initiating career path strategies for gaining business experience abroad. *Journal of World Business, 40*, 374–385.

Walker, J., Wasserman, S., & Wellman, B. (1994). Statistical models for social support networks. In S. Wasserman and J. Galaskiewicz (Eds.), *Advances in social network analysis* (pp. 53–78). Thousand Oaks, CA: Sage.

Wanberg, C. R., Hough, L. A., & Song, Z. (2002). Predictive validity of a multidisciplinary model of reemployment success. *Journal of Applied Psychology, 87*, 1100–1120.

Wang, X., & Sangaland, P. J. (2005). Work adjustment and job satisfaction of Filipino immigrant employees in Canada. *Canadian Journal of Administrative Sciences, 22*, 243–254.

Weiner, N. (2008). Breaking down barriers to labour market integration of newcomers to Toronto. *IRPP Choices, 14*,.

Yan, A., Zhu, G. & Hall, D. (2002). International assignments for career building: A model of agency relationships and psychological contracts, *Academy of Management Review, 27*, 373–391.

Zikic, J., Bonache, J., & Cerdin, J.-L. (2010). Crossing national boundaries: A typology of qualified immigrants' career orientations. *Journal of Organizational Behaviour, 31*, 667–686.

Zikic, J., & Klehe, U.-C. (2006). Job loss as a blessing in disguise: The role of career exploration and career planning in predicting reemployment quality. *Journal of Vocational Behavior, 69*, 391–409.

Zikic, J. & Richardson, J. (2011). "No country for 'old' men? Exploring the careers of international medical graduates in Canada." Paper presented at the Annual Meeting of the Academy of Management, San Antonio.

By Any Other Name: Discrimination in Resume Screening

Eva Derous *and* Ann Marie Ryan

Abstract

This chapter discusses perspectives and empirical findings on ethnic discrimination during the resume screening phase. First, the labor market position of ethnic minorities is discussed and two prominent hypotheses on the disadvantaged labor market position of ethnic minorities are presented, namely the human capital versus hiring discrimination hypothesis. Second, several theoretical perspectives are discussed that illustrate why resume screening might be vulnerable to biased decision making. Third, we turn our attention to influences on hiring discrimination that reside in the applicant, the job/organization, and recruiter. Finally, this chapter ends with a critical reflection on some practical recommendations (such as anonymous resume screening) and future research directions on hiring discrimination during resume screening, including new technologies such as video resumes.

Key Words: hiring discrimination, ethnic minorities, anonymous resume-screening

Introduction

Juliet:
"What's in a name? that which we call a rose
By any other name would smell as sweet;
So Romeo would, were he not Romeo call'd,
Retain that dear perfection which he owes
Without that title. Romeo, doff thy name,
And for that name which is no part of thee
Take all myself." *(Shakespeare, 1600)*

Imagine Anna and Aisha, who apply for a job as management assistant. Anna and Aisha's resumes show that they are about the same age and that they have about the same educational background and work experience. Aisha's name, however, betrays that she is of Arabic descent, whereas Anna's name sounds very Caucasian. Would Anna and Aisha have the same chance to be invited for a job interview when employers screen their resumes? Repeatedly, hiring discrimination based on ethnic-sounding names is reported in both the United States (Bertrand & Mullainathan, 2004) and western Europe

(Zegers De Beijl, 2000). As a result, organizations as well as political parties across the world (e.g., the Netherlands, Belgium, France, Sweden) argue about ways to avert hiring discrimination, such as anonymous resume-screening.

Typically, within the personnel selection domain, a fair amount of attention goes to adverse impact and test bias (Outtz, 2009). While the adverse impact[1] of selection tools is well investigated, researchers have paid less attention to the adverse impact of the resume screening phase (Derous & Ryan, 2012) despite the fact that concerns have been voiced about judgmental biases toward ethnic out-groups during this phase (Derous, Nguyen, & Ryan, 2009). This is a remarkable observation, since resume screening involves one of the first selection hurdles applicants undergo, thereby determining both the quality and quantity of the applicant pool as well as individual applicants' job search success.

In the present chapter we discuss current psychological perspectives and empirical findings on ethnic discrimination *during the resume screening phase*. We start with highlighting some recent and consistent findings on the labor market position of ethnic minorities across the world. Next, we present two prominent hypotheses on the disadvantaged labor market position of ethnic minorities, namely the human capital versus hiring discrimination hypothesis. Subsequently, several theoretical perspectives illustrate *why* resume screening might be particularly vulnerable to biased decision making. Specifically, we discuss predictions from the realistic group theory, social categorization/identity, impression formation, stereotype-threat, and ego-depletion theories. We then turn our attention to determinants of hiring discrimination in resume screening that have been researched recently and discuss the unique and interactive effects of applicant, job, and recruiter characteristics. Throughout this chapter, theoretical perspectives and hypotheses are illustrated with available research evidence. Finally, we conclude with practical implications and further research opportunities.

Labor Market Position of Ethnic Minorities

A literature review by Sidanius and Pratto (1999) estimated that—worldwide—ethnic majority applicants are 24% more likely to be hired than ethnic minority applicants. Recent labor market statistics of the Organization for Economic Co-Operation and Development (OECD) also show that ethnic minorities[2] have a much weaker labor market position than the host population (OECD, 2011, 2012). Whereas in most OECD countries unemployment rates increased in 2009 for both foreign- and native-born persons, ethnic minorities were much more affected by unemployment than their native counterparts. In several countries the unemployment rate among ethnic minorities appeared close or even more than 15% (e.g., Belgium, Sweden, and France) and the unemployment rate was more than twice the level observed for the native-born population (e.g., Belgium, the Netherlands, Sweden, Switzerland, and Finland). Remarkably, unemployment seems less determined by birth status in the United States and other settlement countries (e.g., Australia, Canada) than in nonsettlement countries (e.g., Belgium, the Netherlands, and France). However, despite these statistics, several studies in settlement countries like the United States also showed significantly lower labor market outcomes for ethnic minorities compared with ethnic majorities (Bertrand & Mullainathan, 2004).

Differences in labor market position also depend on the particular ethnic minority group and dominant culture under consideration. For instance, in several western European countries, the level of unemployment is highest among individuals of North-African descent (like Moroccans) compared with other ethnic minority groups with the same level of education, whereas other ethnic minorities (like Mexicans) are most disadvantaged in other countries (such as the United States) (Alba, 2005; Meurs, Pailhé, & Simon, 2008). For instance, recent OECD estimates show that the country of origin explains about 23% of the variance in African minorities' unemployment rates, whereas an additional 40% could be explained by the country of residence. Although considerable, this still leaves about 36.5% of the variance to be explained by other factors.

Educational attainment seems to further complicate this picture. In all OECD countries, native-born persons with high educational qualifications have higher employment rates compared with foreign-born persons with the same qualifications, which seems to point to employment discrimination. For instance, in the Netherlands, unemployment rates are still higher for all ethnic minority groups regardless of their educational level (CBS, 2012; Jungbluth, 2007). Yet among the highly qualified nonwestern minorities, the unemployment level is *more than five times* higher than that of Dutch natives with comparable educational levels (Forum, 2012). A more diverse pattern emerges for the less educated ethnic minorities. According to recent OECD statistics (OECD, 2011), ethnic minority migrants with low educational qualifications might have much lower employment rates than their native-born counterparts in many OECD countries (such as the Netherlands, the United Kingdom, and Denmark), whereas the reverse appears in countries that have a high demand for low-skilled jobs that are not taken up by native workers (such as the United States, southern Europe, and South-Africa).

Further, it takes on average longer for ethnic minorities to get a job, and they often have to accept lower-level positions compared with equally qualified ethnic majorities. Statistics signal overqualification and large differentials in earnings with respect to comparable ethnic minorities. This is currently pronounced in southern Europe (Italy, Greece, and Spain) and in some northern European countries (Denmark and Sweden).

Human Capital Versus Hiring Discrimination

Two prominent hypotheses are set forward that may explain differential labor market outcomes of ethnic minorities compared with majorities—that is, the human capital hypothesis and the hiring discrimination hypothesis. Basic support for the likelihood of human capital deficits vis-à-vis hiring discrimination against ethnic minority applicants is provided in the literature.

Human Capital

The *human capital hypothesis* explains lower labor market outcomes of ethnic minorities compared with ethnic majorities by means of ethnic minorities' poorer levels of job competencies (KSAOs) and work-related attitudes versus those of ethnic majorities (e.g., te Nijenhuis, De Jong, Evers, & Van der Flier, 2004). Despite slight intergenerational improvements, the educational level and language proficiencies of many ethnic minorities are generally substantially lower than those of ethnic majorities (te Nijenhuis & van der Flier, 2003). De Meijer, Born, Terlouw, and Van der Molen (2006) showed that ethnic majority-minority score differences on several personnel selection devices at the Dutch police (i.e., cognitive ability tests, personality questionnaires, assessment center, job interviews) depended on minorities' lower language proficiency. If personnel selection tests include a substantial verbal component, they may measure language proficiency instead of the psychological construct of interest, which may lead to an underestimation of the ability of nonnative speakers vis-à-vis native speakers (te Nijenhuis & van der Flier, 2003). Yet poor human capital in terms of oral and writing skills may hinder test performance as well as the applicants' general job-search process and outcomes (van Hooft, Born, Taris, & Van der Flier, 2004). During the early screening phase, applicants typically need to present themselves to future employers via resumes; these depend heavily on written language capabilities and interviews, which rely on oral expression.

To further investigate the human capital hypothesis in the resume screening context, Hiemstra, Derous, Serlie, and Born (2012a) compared actual resumes of better-educated ethnic minority and majority entrants on several resume characteristics (i.e., academic performance, work experience, extracurricular activities, and resume presentation) through a blind review process among real recruiters. As expected, professional recruiters rated ethnic minorities' resumes significantly lower on several items (like having held supervisory positions, or organizational internships), which supports the idea that differential job access of nonwestern ethnic job entrants could be party explained by less human capital compared with their Dutch native counterparts. However, because socioeconomic status was controlled for (in the sense that applicants were all highly educated), differences could also be explained by the way in which ethnic minority job entrants *presented* themselves in their resume. That is, ethnic minorities might also differ from ethnic majorities in *reported* human capital (i.e., what they chose to indicate) rather than in what capital they actually possessed. However, the Hiemstra et al. resume screening study, cannot fully exclude hiring discrimination as an alternative explanation for minority-majority evaluation differences. Specifically, any mediocre quality of minorities' resumes (e.g., less interesting organizational internships) could also reflect previously discriminatory acts against that minority applicant (e.g., fewer chances to get interesting organizational internships).

The human capital hypothesis would further postulate that, when the human capital of ethnic minorities becomes more similar to that of ethnic majorities, subgroup differences would diminish. Yet research consistently shows that even well-educated ethnic minorities on average remain unemployed *much longer* (Vandevenne & Lenaers, 2007), receive significantly *lower job suitability* scores during recruitment and selection (de Meijer et al., 2006; Hiemstra et al., 2012a), and occupy *lower-level jobs* once they are accepted for a job (Junghbluth, 2007) as compared with equally qualified majorities. In sum, human capital factors (like educational level, level of language proficiency, work-related attitudes, competencies, and job-search strategies) may explain some but not all of the observed differences in ethnic minorities and majorities' labor market outcomes. Hiring discrimination has been suggested as an alternative to the human capital hypothesis in explaining the generally lower labor market position of ethnic minorities (Jungbluth, 2007; Nievers, Andriessen, Faulk, & Dagevos, 2010; Zegers De Beijl, 2000).

Hiring Discrimination

The *hiring discrimination hypothesis* explains lower labor market outcomes of ethnic minorities compared with equally qualified ethnic majorities by means of ethnic majority raters' prejudiced attitudes and reactions toward ethnic majorities (Derous, Ryan, & Nguyen, 2012a; Hiemstra et al., 2012a). Specifically, the hiring discrimination hypothesis would posit lower job suitability and person ratings of minority applicants when minority and majority applicants are equally qualified for the same job position.

"Unique people, equal opportunities" is the adage of the Equal Treatment Commission in the Netherlands, which pertains to the fairness of employment decisions. Despite the omnipresent and long-standing antidiscrimination regulations and guidelines, both in the United States (e.g., Principles, 2003; Standards, 1999; Uniform Guidelines, 1978) and in western Europe (e.g., the ILO International Labor Standards; the Netherlands' General Act of Equal Treatment, 1994), minority applicants are still denied labor market access to a larger extent than their majority counterparts. A series of audit tests conducted by the International Labor Organization (ILO) in four European countries (Belgium, Germany, the Netherlands, and Spain) showed a net discrimination of 30%, meaning that in 1 out of 3 applications, ethnic minority applicants did not pass the first hurdle of the selection procedure. That is, selection rates of ethnic minorities were disproportionally lower than those of equally qualified majorities (Zegers de Beijl, 2000). The number of employment discrimination complaints also increased after 9/11, both in the United States and the rest of the western world. For instance, from 2004 until 2008, Dutch antidiscrimination offices received about 405 complaints per year from nonwestern migrants about ethnic/religious employment discrimination. Most of these complaints were lodged by people of Arabic (Moroccan) origin. In support of this, several studies also showed that majority members think of ethnic minority people in a stereotypical way as less tolerant, more inferior, lazier, less educated, more dishonest, and less trustworthy than other ethnic minorities (IPSOS/CEOOR, 2009).

FORMS OF DISCRIMINATION

Discrimination comes in many forms. Following legal definitions of discrimination (e.g., ILO Convention, 1958), hiring discrimination can be described as any distinction, exclusion, or preference made on the basis of job-irrelevant characteristics (including ethnicity, sex, color, religion, and so on) that relate to access to employment, which has the effect of nullifying or impairing equality of opportunity or treatment. Both case law and social

science definitions of racial/ethnic discrimination (e.g., National Research Council, 2004) additionally differentiate between *direct forms* of discrimination (i.e., differential treatment on the basis of race/ethnicity that disadvantages members of this racial/ethnic group) and more *indirect forms* of discrimination (i.e., treatment on the basis of inadequately justified factors other than race/ethnicity that disadvantages members of a particular racial/ethnic group). Direct forms of hiring discrimination are highly susceptible to legal sanctions and can occur when an applicant is not hired for a job because of his or her ethnic background. More subtle, indirect forms of hiring discrimination occur when a recruitment or selection practice involves factors that co-vary with ethnicity, as hiring practices that use certain recruiting sources where minorities have less access to or selection tools that screen out more minorities because of unrelated factors (like computer skills on a job that does not require computer skills).

A further distinction is made between *formal discrimination* and *interpersonal discrimination*, which is somewhat similar to Dovidio and Gaertner's (2000) distinction between overt and subtle discrimination (Hebl, Foster, Mannix, & Dovidio, 2002). Formal discrimination is marked by explicit negative behaviors toward equally qualified members of a stigmatized group as compared with members of a nonstigmatized group, like outright refusal to employ stigmatized individuals. Interpersonal discrimination, on the other hand, is the more subtle expression of exclusion through interpersonal nonverbal/verbal behaviors (like less smiling, avoiding contact, terminating interpersonal interactions sooner, showing negativity and less interest). Contrary to formal discrimination that is clearly prohibited, there are no explicit laws against interpersonal discrimination.

ACTUAL VERSUS PERCEIVED DISCRIMINATION

So far, we have considered actual hiring discrimination, which may be different from applicants' perceived hiring discrimination. *Actual* hiring discrimination typically involves differential hiring outcomes (e.g., test scores, selection rates) between the majority group and identified minority groups (Derous & Ryan, 2012), whereas *perceived* hiring discrimination involves applicants' ("perceptions of substantive and statistically demonstrable differences in treatment that results in an unfavorable selection evaluation or decision, based upon protected minority group membership"

(Anderson, 2011, p. 230)). Imagine a hiring practice that differentially affects the withdrawal rate of ethnic minorities and majorities from a selection procedure. Arvey, Gordon, Massengrill, and Mussio (1975), for instance, registered a significantly higher dropout rate for ethnic minorities as compared with ethnic majorities in a civil service position selection procedure. Specifically, the time lag between an application and invitation for the selection interview differentially affected the dropout rates of ethnic minorities and majorities in such a way that long delays even halved the number of minority applicants. In line with predictions from signaling theory, applicants try to mind-read organizations (Bangerter, Roulin, & König, 2012) and try to detect the selection criteria when they complete tests (Kleinmann, Ingold, Lievens, Jansen, Melchers, & König, 2011). One possible explanation for the Arvey findings would be that African Americans might have misinterpreted long delays as an organizational sign of their not being competent enough for the job and/or organization. Some applicants might interpret long delays as discriminatory (e.g., "It takes long before they inform me about the testing outcome probably because I am an African American"). Because withdrawal is more under the individual control than under the organization's control, it is not considered as a form of actual discrimination. Withdrawal, however, might be a manifestation of applicants' perceived job discrimination regardless of the level of actual discrimination.

This example shows that actual and perceived hiring discrimination can be unrelated: An applicant may perceive being discriminated against when in fact no actual discrimination against that person took place. Perceived hiring discrimination, however, may be important as it might affect applicants' complaints and case initiation as well as job-search behavior regardless of the level of actual discrimination. Applicants usually complain less about the discriminatory nature of resume screening than about that of other selection devices like ability testing, assessment centers, and the job interview. The applicant perceptions' literature shows that resumes are generally perceived as one of the least invasive selection devices (Stone-Romero, Stone, & Hyatt, 2003): Applicants are usually quite favorably disposed toward resume screening because of its perceived job relevance (Hausknecht, Day, & Thomas, 2004). Also, any violation of distributive and procedural justice rules might be more apparent in later phases of the selection procedure and also

seen as more egregious, as applicants have already passed several selection hurdles and put more time and effort in their application. On the other hand, any biased decision making in resume screening often remains invisible to the applicant. Thus actual discrimination during the resume screening phase may be reported less readily, partly because it remains undisclosed to applicants and more difficult to prove on an individual basis.

As a final point regarding the human capital and hiring discrimination hypotheses is the importance of acknowledging that hiring discrimination explanations of ethnic minority-majority score differences during resume screening might go hand in hand with human capital explanations. Both can operate in a given context, as when an ethnic minority candidate is rated lower than other applicants because of a lack of human capital but also lower than similarly less qualified majority applicants because of discrimination. Further, human capital and discriminatory practices can interact. A study of Watkins and Johnston (2000), for instance, showed that unfair hiring outcomes during resume screening depended on both applicants' physical attractiveness (manipulated with a head-and-shoulder photograph attached to the resume) and applicants' resume quality (with either mediocre or good job qualifications). Applicants' attractiveness had a positive impact on hiring intentions, but only when the quality of the application was mediocre and not so anymore when the resume quality was high. Dovidio and Gaertner (2000) also showed that hiring discrimination is much stronger in ambiguous situations (i.e., when the quality of job applicants' profiles is moderate). Much as in resume screening, stereotype-based biases and general information-processing errors also have more influence in low-structured, more ambiguous interview settings compared with high-structured, less ambiguous ones (e.g., Avery, Richeson, Hebl, & Ambady, 2009; Moscoso, 2000). Indeed, meta-analytic findings (Huffcutt, Conway, Roth, & Stone, 2001; Huffcutt & Roth, 1998) showed that the adverse impact of unstructured job interviews is generally higher than that of structured interviews. This is not to say that structured interviews are completely free from bias. The type of questions/constructs measured (e.g., intellectual abilities versus personality constructs), the use of a structured scoring system, and individual differences in recruiters' information processing and attitudes might also affect the adverse impact of assessment tools. Notwithstanding these findings, ambiguous selection settings might overall be more prone to biases than less ambiguous, more structured ones. Like the interview, resume screening can vary in the level of structure brought to the evaluation task.

Hiring Discrimination During Resume screening

The creation of a resume is one of the first steps applicants take in their job-search process. Resumes are a specific type of biographical data that represents a culmination of applicants' life and work experiences that are considered applicable for a work context. Generally resumes show the connection between a targeted job and one's work/life experiences and prior work roles. They identify and quantify applicants' previous accomplishments and work performances (Cole, Field, & Stafford, 2005; Greenhaus & Callanan, 2006). The format of resumes can vary from a written resume (e.g., a paper resume including text and eventually pictures) to a multimedia resume that additionally includes videotaped messages and even animations. Hence the information provided in resumes can be static as in paper resumes or more dynamic, including both visual and vocal information, as in video resumes.

It is commonly accepted that resumes are one of the most important sources of information that personnel decision makers consider when they initially screen applicants for jobs (Piotrowski & Armstrong, 2006). We turn our attention to several social-psychological theories that explain why resume screening may be particularly vulnerable to biased decision making, taking into consideration individuals' cognitive-affective reactions toward ethnic out-group members.

Social-Psychological Perspectives

Many studies have shown that biased decision making and prejudiced reactions result from (1) conflicts between groups because of a competition over valued and limited resources (*realistic group conflict and competition theories*), (2) people's tendency to classify others into simple categories and to more strongly identify with those who are perceived as similar to themselves, like in-group members (*social categorization/identification theories*), (3) the way in which people form their impressions about others (*impression formation theories*), and (4) the degree to which stigma evokes attention deficits such as ego depletion in perceivers/decision makers. Few studies, however, have applied each of these perspectives to the act of resume screening; that is considered here.

REALISTIC GROUP CONFLICT AND COMPETITION THEORIES

The *realistic group conflict theory* (Sherif, Harvey, White, Hood, & Sherif, 1961) and *group competition theory* (Blalock, 1982) are among the oldest and most straightforward social-psychological theories explaining intergroup prejudice and discrimination. These theories assume that social groups exist; have a shared, common history; that these groups are in a zero-sum competition over valued resources (either material or symbolic); and that a group's perceived threats from loss of such resources may result in negative intergroup reactions and out-group derogation. Several studies have shown support for these theories. In times of economic recession, for example, job shortages do foster ethnic discrimination in the labor market. Hence hiring discrimination against minorities would be more prevalent in a sluggish economy than a buoyant economy. However, even when the economy goes well, employment rates of ethnic minorities appear significantly lower than those of ethnic majorities (e.g., Andriessen Dagevos, Nievers, & Boog, 2007), which would run counter to predictions from the realistic conflict theory. It has been suggested that symbolic threats to the self or ingroup may even be more powerful than economic threats. For instance, social/political events (like the 9/11 attack) may also increase any negative reactions toward minorities (Oswald, 2005) and explain lower job suitability scores for individuals belonging to an ethnic minority. Indeed, using the minimal group paradigm, Tajfel, Billig, Bundy, and Flament (1971) contested the necessity for a zero-sum competition and the actual existence of real groups with a shared history for discrimination. When people are placed in a minimal group condition (i.e., when in-groups and out-groups are formed in an arbitrary and temporary way) and when they are allowed to allocate restricted resources to any member except for themselves (i.e., not in a zero-sum way), they still show ethnocentric and discriminatory reactions toward outgroup members.

SOCIAL CATEGORIZATION AND SOCIAL IDENTITY THEORY

Building further on these experimental findings, the *social categorization and social identity theory* (Tajfel & Turner, 1986) suggest that people's need for a positive identity (self/group) and their tendency to protect a positive social identity may instigate in-group favoritism to the detriment of out-group members. Hence, to preserve a positive self/group identity, majority members may employ discriminatory practices against out-group members to compensate for the felt "symbolic" threats (Crocker, Major, & Steele, 1998). Thus, according to these theories, any combination of perceived actual/symbolic threats and social group identity may even be more impactful than realistic conflicts of interests like job shortages. The social identity theory further posits that strongly identified out-group members may be more subject to out-group derogation and hiring discrimination: Ethnic minorities who strongly identify with their own groups may strive for their group interests and be perceived by majority members as an attack to the legitimacy of the status quo. For instance, in a resume screening study, Derous et al. (2009) showed that resumes of highly ethnic-identified applicants (with both ethnic names and affiliations) were rated lower on job suitability than their less ethnically identified counterparts, thus supporting this assumption.

IMPRESSION FORMATION THEORIES

In addition, *impression formation theories* like the continuum model (Fiske, Lin, & Neuberg, 1999) and the dual process model (Brewer & Harasty Feinstein, 1999) are worth considering, as they may explain why resume screening is particularly vulnerable to biased decision making. Both impression formation theories propose a dual-process model of category-based, schematic reactions versus more specific, individuating reactions to others, but the suggested mechanisms along which this happens differ somewhat. According to the Brewer's branching model of dual processing (Brewer & Harasty Feinstein, 1999), a perceiver will engage either in category-based processing when the target individual is of little interest to that person, or will engage in individuating processing if the perceiver is interested in attending to the target individual. The continuum model (Fiske et al., 1999), on the other hand, suggests one dimension of impression formation, representing a continuum with at one side category-based processing and at the other side attribute-oriented processing. Category-based processing of information about a target individual implies that impressions are formed almost entirely on the basis of stereotypes and category-based information that is readily available about the category that person seems to belongs to. The other side of the continuum reflects individuation, meaning that impression formation is based on specific, attribute-based information about the target person. According to Fiske and colleagues, people

tend to believe the first things that come to their minds. A person will first try to categorize, and only when that fails (i.e., a target person does not seem to fit well into the ready-made category) will he or she engage in more individuating processing. According to Fiske et al., movement along this continuum (from category-based to individualized, attribute-based evaluations) is not completely beyond the perceiver's control but might also depend on the perceiver's motivation and attention. For instance, social norms and feelings of pressure (like time constraints) might affect people's motivation to individuate and respond without prejudice (e.g., Brief, Dietz, Cohen, Pugh, & Vaslow, 2000; Derous et al., 2012a). The moderating role of situational moderators (in job/organization/culture) and rater characteristics are discussed briefly further on in this chapter.

Despite dictated motivational control over the impression-formation processes, Brewer's and Fiske et al.'s impression formation models first and foremost suggest that any tendency to categorize another person as a member of an out-group rather than an individual appears rather automatically and might be much stronger when relatively limited information about that individual is available, which may lead to a less personalized perception of out-group members. In the case of resume screening, job applicants are typically judged on a limited amount of information, usually only a one- or two-page resume. In line with predictions from impression formation theories, when a limited amount of information is available about a job candidate, recruiters might more easily rely on heuristic cues (i.e., first impressions, physical attractiveness) in making their judgments, which may result in biased decision making about the applicant. On the other hand, when more personalized information about a candidate becomes available and such information is not consistent with inferences drawn from the ready-made category, a more fully informed decision about the applicant could result, which might counter any stereotypical information processing.

Upcoming multimedia applications, like the use of video resumes and social network media (e.g., Facebook, LinkedIn) provide an interesting dilemma regarding the early screening of out-group applicants. Following the dual processing theories, one would expect more individuating information to become available during the initial screening phase, which should lead to *less categorization effects* and stigmatization of out-group members (i.e., the individuating hypothesis), particularly if this information seems somewhat inconsistent with inferences drawn from the ready-made category the person was placed into. However, more job-irrelevant, stigmatizing information about the applicant might become available through video resumes and related recruitment media (like skin color, ethnic-sounding speech, or any other ethnic marker), so that one could expect *greater categorization* effects instead of individualization (i.e., the categorization hypothesis). These seemingly contradictory predictions stemming from impression formation theories have been specified as the "video resume dilemma" (Derous, Taveirne, & Hiemstra, 2012). Empirical studies on the potentially discriminatory effects of video resumes provide support for both the individuating hypothesis (i.e., regarding ethnic minorities in a Dutch sample) (Hiemstra, Derous, Serlie, & Born, 2012b) and the categorization hypothesis (i.e., regarding physically unattractive applicants in a Belgian sample) (Derous et al., 2012), thus fueling the video resume dilemma. These findings further suggest that discriminatory effects of recruitment media might depend also on type of stigma and potentially other context characteristics. Clearly technological changes and innovative screening methods pose new challenges in the area of applicant screening that require further research (Lievens & Harris, 2003).

SELF-REGULATION AND ATTENTION
DEFICIT THEORIES

During the last decades, cognitive psychologists have tried to further unravel the underlying mechanisms that might explain the effect of social stigma on perceivers' biased decision making.

Stigmas (like ethnic cues) may trigger negative stereotypes, which may be difficult to suppress and in turn may lead to negative evaluations of stigmatized persons. Ego-depletion has been put forward in the literature to explain these effects (Baumeister, Bratslavsky, Muraven, & Tice, 1998). Baumeister and colleagues (1998), suggested that ego depletion makes people more vulnerable to prejudiced reactions, because the suppression of stereotypic thoughts requires self-regulation. Ego depletion builds upon the idea that self-regulation draws on some limited mental resources that subsequently may affect one's behavior.

When applied to the act of resume screening, one can consider that recruiters first have to screen several resumes and have to attend to multiple cues while engaging in self-control (like suppressing stigma-related information and focusing on job-related competencies), which subsequently may hinder recruiters' rating and ranking of applicants. In terms of attention deficit models, attention to the stigmatized applicant (e.g., as revealing from resume information) may interfere with recruiters' working memory processes by dividing the recruiter's attention between the stigma and job-relevant information (e.g., Muraven & Baumeister, 2000; Shomstein & Yantis, 2004), thereby *impairing* recruiters' executive cognitive attention. This interference may prevent recruiters from focusing on job-relevant information when making decisions and may even lead them to remember more job-irrelevant, stigma-related information. However, because it is socially unacceptable to focus on stigmatizing marks and recruiters are trained to focus on job-relevant information, they may also choose to avert their attention from the stigma, hence suppressing stereotypes. Nonetheless, trying to be "objective" or to "suppress stereotypes" may ironically result in impaired memory for job-relevant individuating information and might instigate a higher recall for the job-irrelevant, stigma-related information regarding the applicant (also known as the "white bear" or "rebound effect") (Wegner, 1994, 2003), which again could explain biased decision making during the resume screening phase (e.g., Macrae, Bodenhausen, Milne, & Jetten, 1994).

The limited resource model on self-control and ego depletion (Muraven & Baumeister, 2007) has recently been challenged by Inzlicht and Schmeichel (2012), who propose a process model that posits that ego-depletion might further be driven by subjective perceptions: perceivers' beliefs, moods, and motivations might mitigate depletion of cognitive resources. Specifically, according to Inzlicht and Schmeichel, exerting self-control in one task might initiate shifts in subjective perceptions (like motivation and attention) that reduce self-control in a subsequent task. Govorun and Payne (2006) showed that ego-depleting effects might particularly pertain to people who have strong stereotypes against stigmatized individuals. Also, in a series of four experiments, Gailliot, Plant, Butz, and Baumeister (2007) showed that stereotype suppression resulted in poorer subsequent self-control, but particularly so among people whose motivation to suppress stereotypes I was low. The good news is that self-control exercises (which are unrelated to the type of stereotypes/prejudice measured) can counter such ego-depleting effects (Gaillot et al., 2007). We can learn from these findings that individual differences in recruiters' prejudiced beliefs, attitudes, and motivations are equally important to consider, as these might considerably affect attentional biases and discriminatory reactions toward stigmatized candidates above and beyond depletion of cognitive resources. The effect of recruiter characteristics such as one's motivation to respond without prejudice on hiring decisions is further discussed below.

Now that we have looked more closely at several social-cognitive mechanisms that may underlie discriminatory hiring decisions during the resume screening phase, it is time to turn our attention to specific sources of information that might affect biased decision making during resume screening.

Determinants of Hiring Discrimination During Resume Screening

Research has shown that factors that trigger biased resume screening and hiring discrimination may reside in the applicant (e.g., ethnicity, gender, socioeconomic status), the job/organization (e.g., job client contact, diversity climate), and the recruiter (e.g., information processing, prejudiced attitudes). However, hiring discrimination might also depend on much broader factors, like the dominant cultural paradigm in the "host" country that refers to the type of acculturation that is expected by host nationals from ethnic minorities (e.g., representing society as a "cultural melting" pot versus a "salad bowl"), the status of the immigrant group in the host country, and the cultural values and the economic and political situation in the host country. Whereas many more factors might be at play than factors in the applicant, the job/organization, and the recruiter, we limit our discussion here to these three sources.

APPLICANT CHARACTERISTICS

Ethnicity appears to be one of the most investigated applicant characteristics in the literature on hiring discrimination. According to the *ethnic prominence hypothesis* (EP), ethnicity is the most influential factor in discrimination because of the greater salience and threat associated with ethnicity as compared with other stigmatizing characteristics (Levin, Sinclair, Veniegas, & Taylor, 2002). Bertrand and Mullainathan (2004), for instance, conducted a correspondence audit test in the United States, showing that resumes with African American–sounding names received 50% fewer callbacks for follow-up interviews than those with typically White-sounding names (Bertrand & Mullainathan, 2004). The correspondence audit technique (i.e., a kind of employment audit using

application letters or resumes) allows researchers to compare labor market outcomes of applicants who are equally qualified for a job (i.e., identical in all productive characteristics) but different in demographic variables (e.g., ethnicity and gender). By sending out matched applications to the same job opening and counting the callbacks (i.e., rejections or invitations), one may investigate whether recruiters' differential treatment of subgroups of applicants is attributable to hiring discrimination. Recently conducted correspondence audit tests in Europe (e.g., Belgium: Segers, Decoster, & Derous, 2012; Sweden: Carlsson & Rooth, 2008; Germany: Kaas & Manger, 2011; United Kingdom: Wood, Hales, Purdon, Sejersen, & Hayllar, 2009) also show the prominence of ethnic markers on resumes. For instance, correspondence audit tests in the Netherlands (Derous et al., 2012) have shown that the odds for rejection were significantly higher for applicants with ethnic-sounding names as compared with those with a Dutch-sounding name. Carlsson and Rooth (2008) showed that Swedish-named applicants were more often invited for an application interview than those with Middle Eastern–sounding names. Correspondence audit tests on ethnic labor market discrimination typically consider an ethnic-sounding name as an ethnic marker.

Resumes, however, might contain more ethnic markers than ethnic-sounding names. Applicants' affiliations with sociocultural groups are less well investigated but also appear to be strong predictors that may operate in more subtle ways than ethnic-sounding names (Cole, Rubin, Feild, & Giles, 2007; Derous et al., 2009; Dovidio & Gaertner, 2000). Cole and colleagues (2007) showed that if asked directly, recruiters considered extracurricular affiliations as the least important resume characteristic in judging applicants' employability. Actual employability ratings, however, showed exactly the opposite picture. Affiliations seem to affect recruiters' information processing and ethnic affiliations may even lower minorities' job suitability ratings (Dovidio & Gaertner, 2000), but this may also depend on the particular cultural setting. Derous et al. (2009) found stronger discriminatory effects of Arab affiliations on resumes in an American sample compared with a Dutch sample, which they explained by different patterns in acculturation and immigration across the Netherlands and the United States (Derous et al., 2009). Specifically, the long-standing immigration history in the United States may have socialized Americans to associate ethnic affiliations with minorities' ethnic identity more strongly than ethnic names when these pieces of proxy information for group identity coexist. However, ethnic-sounding names alone may be enough to conjure the association of ethnic identity in nonsettlement countries that lack such a deeply rooted immigration tradition as in the United States (Derous et al., 2009). Given the globalization and increased international recruitment (see Zikic, Kent, & Richardson, this volume), an interesting pathway for further research would therefore consider cultural differences in the effect of ethnic markers on discriminatory hiring decisions.

Generally, studies consider the effects of only one ethnic identifier at a time, such as one's ethnic-sounding name or ethnic affiliations. However, resumes commonly reflect multiple ethnic identifiers simultaneously, like one's name and affiliations. Combined effects of multiple ethnic identifiers should be considered as majorities' discriminatory reactions towards ethnic minorities might depend on perceived strength of ethnic minorities' identification with their ethnic in-group, as reflected by the number of ethnic identifiers on applicants' resumes. Specifically, one could expect strong ethnic identification of minority members leading to stronger discriminatory effects from majority members (Kaiser & Pratt-Hyatt, 2009). The *ethnic identification (EI) hypothesis* stresses the importance of considering such within-category effects. This hypothesis specifically considers the strength of identification with an ethnic group as an influential factor in judging people. Applied to the act of resume screening we expect ethnic majority recruiters to reject ethnic minority applicants in proportion to their ties with an out-group. In support of this hypothesis, research has shown that recruiters report most negative attitudes toward highly identified ethnic minority applicants compared with their less ethnically identified counterparts. For instance, a lab experiment (Derous et al., 2009) and a correspondence audit test (Derous & Ryan, 2012), both conducted in the Netherlands, showed most negative hiring outcomes for ethnic minority applicants with an ethnic-sounding minority name and non-Dutch minority affiliations. The lab study (Derous et al., 2009) employed a scenario test in which participants were asked to evaluate fictitious job applicants' job suitability ratings on the basis of a resume screening activity. As hypothesized, significant two-way interactions between name and affiliation were found such that job suitability ratings were the lowest for highly identified Arabic

profiles (i.e., applicants having both an Arabic-sounding name and Arabic affiliations) compared with the other three applicant profiles (with either an Arabic-sounding name or Arabic affiliations or both a native Dutch-sounding name and Dutch affiliations). The correspondence audit test (Derous & Ryan, 2012) supported these lab findings in an actual field setting. This audit consisted of a 2 (name: Arab-sounding versus Dutch-sounding) by 2 (affiliation: Arab versus Dutch) by 2 (gender: male vs. female) mixed-factor design. Name and affiliation were measures within subjects whereas gender was the between-subjects factor in the design. In line with lab findings, the odds for rejection were significantly (i.e., four to six times) higher for resumes with ethnic minority identifiers (i.e., Arabic names and affiliations) as compared with ethnic majority identifiers (i.e., Dutch names and affiliations). As discussed further on, applicant gender moderated these findings.

Other types of ethnic identifiers that have been investigated in application settings other than resume screening, such as the job interview, include skin color (e.g., Wade, Judkins-Romano, & Blue, 2004), ethnic/religious attire (e.g., King & Ahmad, 2010), and ethnic speech (e.g., Purkiss, Perrewe, Gillespie, Mayers, & Ferris, 2006). The study findings of Wade and colleagues revealed that fair-skinned applicants received better hiring outcomes than their dark-skinned counterparts (Wade et al., 2004). The study by Purkiss and colleagues, however, showed that ethnic speech interacted with ethnic-sounding names, such that the applicant with the ethnic-sounding name (i.e., Hispanic), speaking with an ethnic accent (i.e., Hispanic) was viewed less positively by interviewers than the ethnic-named applicant speaking without an accent and the Anglo-named applicant (with or without an Hispanic accent). Whereas Wade et al. and Purkiss et al. showed evidence for formal discrimination (with lower interview ratings and less job offers), King and Ahmad did not: Religious clothing did not affect the number of interview offers. However, the investigators showed negative effects of religious attire on interpersonal discrimination such that confederate applicants and observers rated interactions between applicants and potential employers/recruiters more negatively when applicants wore Muslim attire (i.e., a hijab and abaya) than when their clothing did not convey a particular religion. Given the increased use of dynamic resume displays in social media (such as video resumes), some of these ethnic markers (like skin color, ethnic attire, and ethnic accents) may become as prominent as one's ethnic-sounding name and affiliations. Therefore, a study of the combined effects of visual and auditory identifiers like skin color and ethnic speech will be an interesting avenue for further research.

Ethnic minorities may also hold other stigmatized identities than ethnicity (Derous & Ryan, 2012), and theoretical predictions differ on how multiple minority, characteristics affect categorization and hiring decisions. Three competing hypotheses that have been tested within the context of resume screening are set forward on categorization effects (Derous et al., 2012): the ethnic prominence/identification hypothesis, the multiple minority hypothesis, and the subordinate male target hypothesis. As mentioned, the *ethnic prominence/identification hypothesis* states that ethnicity is a more influential factor in decision making than other social category information (ethnic prominence) and that a stronger ethnic identification may lead to more out-group derogation (ethnic identification). By considering ethnicity as the most prominent factor in decision making, this hypothesis offers an interesting but possibly incomplete picture of social categorization. Opponents to the ethnic prominence/identification hypothesis stress that applicants belong to multiple social groups and that those with multiple stigmatized identities (such as being female[3] and an ethnic minority member) may experience greater discrimination than those with just one (such as being female). Theories on multiple categorization usually consider the intersectional effects of two or more social categories to which one may belong.

The *multiple minority status hypothesis* (MMS, also referred to as the double- or multiple-jeopardy hypothesis) would suggest that other stigmatizing characteristics may have additive or moderating effects on ethnic discrimination. Double jeopardy is most often discussed in terms of the status of minority women and would suggest that resumes of minority women would be rated lower than those of minority men. Bendick, Jackson, and Reinoso (1994), for instance, reported that African American women were more likely to encounter discrimination than African American men and White individuals. However, this finding is not consistently reported. Hosoda et al. (2003) found the opposite with female African American applicants being preferred to their male and White counterparts when they applied for high-status jobs. Furthermore and with few exceptions, the intersectional effects of

other minority characteristics—such as applicants' socioeconomic status, sexual orientation, or physical disability—are less well investigated and also in need of further research. For instance, in one of our audit studies (Derous et al., 2012), we manipulated job applicants' socioeconomic status on applicant resumes by varying the applicants' addresses and schools (i.e., in upscale neighborhoods versus lower-class neighborhoods). However, no moderating effects were found for socioeconomic status on hiring outcomes, which is in line with earlier findings of Bertrand and Mullainathan (2004) but inconsistent with those from other studies (e.g., Jussim, Coleman, & Lerch, 1987). The category salience of applicants' socioeconomic status may have depended on our manipulation of socioeconomic status as well as on the nature of the screening phase. Maybe socioeconomic markers may become more prominent during the interview phase when recruiters meet the applicant in person than upon initial resume screening (preinterview phase), when recruiters have to infer applicants' socioeconomic status from paper resumes. Also, type of school and place of living may not be as strong markers for social class as one's physical appearance (like the type of clothing one wears) and one's accent (e.g., whether one speaks standard English or nongrammatical English) (see Jussim et al., 1987). Clearly more research is needed to investigate discriminatory effects of the multiple minority status of applicants (e.g., crossing ethnicity with gender or socioeconomic status) in the preinterview phase.

Finally, the *subordinate male target (SMT) hypothesis* also focuses on the intersection of ethnicity and gender but suggests that ethnic minority men suffer the most discrimination because threat and conflict are primarily related to intergroup competition among men in society (Sidanius & Pratto, 1999). In their meta-analysis, Sidanius and Pratto showed that the level of employment discrimination against minority males was substantially greater than the employment discrimination against minority females. For instance, in many western European countries, among which the Netherlands, stereotypes of Arab men are more negative than those of Arab females, which would be in support of the SMT rather than the MMS. These findings suggest that the viability of the MMS or SMT might also depend on the particular ethnic minority group that is studied (e.g., Arabs, Asians, etc.) and that one should take this into consideration. Indeed, research on differential effects of applicant characteristics has shown some inconsistent results. For instance, in one correspondence audit test (Derous & Ryan, 2012), we found that the two-way interaction between ethnic identifiers (i.e., name and affiliation) on resumes was qualified by the three-way interaction of ethnic name and affiliation with applicants' gender. Closer inspection of the data showed that male applicants with an Arab-sounding name and Dutch affiliations were rejected more often than female applicants with an Arab-sounding name and Dutch affiliations, supporting the subordinate male target hypothesis. Prejudice might be more directed toward minority men than women because of the status differences in gender in Dutch society. Particularly, female Arabs are generally perceived as less threatening than male Arabs. However, some studies have suggested that the viability of the EP/EI, MMT or SMT hypotheses might also depend on other factors than applicant characteristics, such as job/organization characteristics. This is considered next.

JOB/ORGANIZATION CHARACTERISTICS

Kulik, Roberson, and Perry's (2007) called for more research on the relative role of multiple categories in hiring decisions considering contextual cues, such as job and organizational characteristics that might affect those roles (e.g., job status, client contact, and diversity climate). For instance, employment discrimination against minorities might be most intensively manifested in situations where majority group members are directly or symbolically threatened by the advancement of minority members, such as in high-status, high-demand jobs. That is, ethnic minorities are typically expected to apply for low-status/low-demand jobs instead of high-status/high-demand jobs. When ethnic majorities do not do so, they might violate expectations about the social/ethnic group that perceivers initially categorized them into. As a result, highly educated ethnic minorities may be perceived as more threatening to (highly educated) ethnic majorities than their lower educated counterparts because of the competition of jobs and the larger attack to the legitimacy of the status quo. Hence, one would expect more discrimination against minority applicants who apply for high status/high-demand jobs than against those who apply for lower status jobs. However, studies have also shown the opposite. In a resume screening study, Hosoda et al. (2003) showed that White applicants were more likely to be selected for high status/high demand jobs than equally qualified African American applicants. However, applicant gender moderated findings,

showing a clear advantage for African American women over African American men, White men, and White women. The difficulties overcome to get in such a position (i.e., applying for a high-status/high-demand job) might have been perceived as much higher for ethnic minority females compared with their White and male counterparts.

Client contact may complicate findings to a further extent. In an employment audit study on obesity and hiring discrimination, Rooth (2009) and Ägerström and Rooth (2011) found that an obese job applicant (manipulated with pictures attached to paper resumes) was called less often to be interviewed in occupations that included personal contacts with customers, such as sales and restaurant jobs. Similarly, in June 2011, a Belgian court convicted a temporary work agency for keeping records of commissioning clients who refused hiring ethnic minority applicants (i.e., the so-called BBB files[4]). These files also listed extra information such as "often works with the police," "no scum," or "BBB or other nationality but no Arabs." Notably, among these clients were dozens of national and international companies who either blamed their individual workers (who had already left the company by then) or their external clients for any discriminatory action.

An employment audit study that investigated ethnic discrimination in the Swedish labor market (Carlsson & Rooth, 2008) demonstrated the lowest callback ratios for ethnic minorities with a Middle Eastern–sounding name who applied for occupations with frequent customer contacts (e.g., restaurant workers and shop sales assistants). These findings support anecdotal information on hiring discrimination being justified by client demands. Specifically, by not hiring minority staff, employers might safeguard their organizations against any negative reactions of majority clients. However, mixed results on the effect of client contact on hiring outcomes of ethnic minorities have also been reported. For instance, less discriminatory effects were found for front-office jobs like business sales assistants, leaving us with some puzzling findings. Similar findings have been reported in an Australian audit study conducted by Booth, Leigh, and Varganova (2012) with few differences in callback rate across jobs with and without customer contact. In support of this, we did not find client contact to trigger ethnic discrimination either, and this was observed in both field and lab studies (Derous et al., 2012). The two field studies consisted of two correspondence audit studies that were conducted in a large Dutch city. In one study we used a 2 (applicant ethnicity: Dutch majority versus Arab minority) by 2 (applicant gender: male versus female) by 2 (job client contact: high versus low external client contact) mixed factorial design, with applicant ethnicity and gender as the within-subjects factors and job client contact as the between-subjects factor. We selected a pool of job advertisements in the service sector covering jobs at a semiskilled level (i.e., low-demand/low-status). Correspondence audit study 2 was similar to the first study but varied socioeconomic status, ethnicity, and client contact (gender was kept constant as male). Evidence was found for the ethnic prominence hypothesis, as no moderating effect was found for applicants' gender (correspondence audit study 1) or socioeconomic status (correspondence audit study 2). Interestingly, the amount of external client contact played no mitigating role. Employers seemed particularly reluctant to invite ethnic minority (i.e., Arab) applicants further in the selection process regardless of the amount of external client contact.

Correspondence audit tests are unobtrusive measures that offer a great amount of control because applicants' interpersonal style, appearance, and behavior are controlled for. However, correspondence tests are also limited in that they only register callbacks; they do not allow researchers to examine unobserved factors such as raters' characteristics (e.g., prejudice) Therefore, in a follow-up study in the lab, we investigated the combined effects of job client contact with applicant ethnicity and rater prejudice (i.e., modern racism). Modern racism is a form of subtle prejudice introduced by the political psychologist John McConahay (1983), who built on the idea that old-fashioned and blatant forms of racial/ethnic discrimination have been replaced by more subtle forms owing to the changing norms in society about expressing prejudice against others. Modern racism suggests that individuals will discriminate only when they can point to an alternative justification for their action. It is expected that people who score high on modern racism will be more attuned to normative standards about expression of traditional racist views; therefore they will be more likely *not* to display their prejudice when it can be easily detected (i.e., appears blatant) and to display any prejudice where it cannot be easily detected, as when there is a business justification for their discriminatory behavior. As in the correspondence audit studies, we investigated hiring discrimination in the context of a low-demand job.

Results of this lab study showed a main effect for ethnicity. However, ethnicity did not interact with amount of external client contact (high versus low) and the three-way interaction between ethnicity, raters' modern racism against Arabs, and amount of client contact was not significant. It was therefore concluded that client contact did not serve as a business justification for prejudiced recruiters to display hiring discrimination. One explanation for these null findings may be in the changing demographic makeup of the organization's clients, with a more diverse clientele that organizations need to reach and to serve compared with two decennia ago. Hiring discrimination may further be contingent upon the complex and simultaneous interplay of several other context characteristics. To complicate this picture, studies also showed broader organizational characteristics (such as organizational structure, culture, climate, leadership, human resources practices) to affect minority-majority differences in hiring outcomes. As mentioned by Cox (1994) almost two decades ago, the organization's culture may either hinder or promote tolerance for diversity. When an organization's culture tolerates business justifications of discriminatory behavior, highly prejudiced individuals may feel safe in expressing their attitudes. This was demonstrated by Brief et al. (2000). In their seminal paper, Brief and colleagues reported two lab experiments, each of which showed that obedience to authority moderated majorities' expression of modern racism on discriminatory hiring intentions. Participants were assigned randomly to either a no-justification condition or a business-justification condition. As expected, participants in the business-justification condition selected fewer African American applicants, but particularly so when participants scored high on modern racism. No prejudice effects were found for illegitimate authority figures and in the no-justification condition, which implies that modern racism might be held in check in the absence of any business justification for discrimination. Clearly, the organization's characteristics (e.g., organizational culture, organizational norms, and diversity policies) may impact individual-level discriminatory decision making. However, as shown, this trigger most likely also interacts with recruiters' prejudiced attitudes and propensity to discriminate against minority applicants.

RECRUITER CHARACTERISTICS

The sociopsychological literature has identified prejudice and stereotypical beliefs as the main determinants of any discriminatory practices. Related factors also mentioned are anxiety of the unknown, dissimilarities in beliefs, self and group preservation (e.g., need to uphold individual or group status, dominance, or power), and personality characteristics (e.g., ethnocentrism, authoritarianism) (Derous & Ryan, 2006). As illustrated above, latest research on ego-depletion also suggests that detrimental effects of stereotype suppression depends on individual differences in attitudes, beliefs, and motivations to avoid prejudice (e.g., Inzlicht & Schmeichel, 2012). Contrary to the large amount of studies on prejudiced decision making in the sociopsychological and organizational literature, research on hiring discrimination has often failed to consider individual differences in recruiters' tendency to discriminate. Investigating individual's propensity to discriminate is important, however, as it may provide some practical guidance on the selection, appraisal, and training of recruiters.

Building further on social categorization/identity theories and following Byrne's well-known similarity-attraction paradigm (Byrne, 1997), many studies have investigated the effects of actual and perceived demographic similarity among employees on several work-related outcomes (e.g., Chattopadhyay, Tluchowska, & George, 2004). Demographic characteristics—such as employees' ethnicity or race—are very salient and may, in turn, activate one's own racial/ethnic identity. Studies that have investigated recruiters' perceived similarity with the applicant, however, mainly considered the job interview (e.g., Graves & Powell, 1996; Howard & Ferris, 1996; McFarland, Ryan, Sacco, & Kriska, 2004; Sacco, Scheu, Ryan, & Schmitt, 2003). Despite similarity-attraction effects in many social and work-related settings (e.g., Riordan, Schaffer, & Stewart, 2005), evidence for demographic similarity effects in hiring settings is rather mixed. For instance, Sacco et al. (2003) could not find any effect of demographic (racial) similarity on interview scores when they used a sophisticated multi-level analysis technique. However, McFarland et al. (2004) did find racial similarity effects: African American interviewers rated African American applicants more favorably, but only when the interview panel was predominantly Black (McFarland et al., 2004). Devendorf and Highhouse (2008) further showed that applicants' perceived similarity as well as prototype similarity to prospective coworkers both enhanced applicants' attraction to the potential employer. In a different though somewhat related vein, Garcia, Posthuma, and Colella (2008)

further demonstrated that interviewers are not biased in favor of applicants whom they liked the most and that actual demographic similarity did not impact their hiring judgments. Instead, interviewers' perceived person–organization fit assessments had larger effects on their hiring recommendations. A recent study of McCarthy, Van Iddekinge, and Campion (2010) might explain previously mixed findings. McCarthy et al. investigated whether three widely used structured interviews (i.e., experienced-based interviewing, situational interviewing, and past-behavioral interviewing) were resistant to demographic similarity effects on hiring outcomes. These authors proposed that demographic similarity effects might depend on the structure of the employment interview, with only trivial effects if interviews are highly structured. This hypothesis was derived from impression formation theories (Fiske et al., 1999), discussed earlier in this chapter, suggesting that "highly structured interviews facilitate the acquisition and use of individuating information, which, in turn, overrides initial perceptions and provides resistance against demographic similarity effects" (McCarthy et al., 2010, p. 336).

Effects of similarity on attraction have been well established in the broad domain of interpersonal interactions and have been much investigated in the context of job interviews (e.g., Devendorf & Highhouse, 2008; McCarthy et al., 2010; McCarthy & Cheng, 2013, this volume). Possibly because of any lack of systematic effects in the interview literature and/or the lack of face-to-face interactions in traditional resume screening settings, studies have not considered actual and perceived similarity-attraction effects among (majority) recruiters and (minority) applicants during the early resume screening phase. Instead, some researchers have turned their attention towards recruiters' prejudiced attitudes against minority applicants, such as modern racism beliefs (McConahay, 1983; McConahay, Hardee, & Batts, 1981). On the one hand, modern racists do not endorse discrimination as a practice, but, on the other hand, they do believe that ethnic minorities are making too many demands that challenge the status quo. However and again, mixed results have been reported on the effects of self-reported modern racism and discriminatory behavior during resume screening, with some studies showing direct negative effects on discriminatory behavior against ethnic minority applicants (Blommaert, van Tubergen, & Coenders, 2011; Derous, Ryan, & Serlie, 2014), while others not (Brief et al., 2000; Derous et al., 2009; Son Hing,

Chung-Yan, Hamilton, & Zanna, 2008; Ziegert & Hanges, 2005).

We posit at least four reasons that may explain mixed findings regarding the effects of recruiters' prejudiced attitudes. First and as recently suggested by Talaska, Fiske, and Chaiken (2008), despite the fact that emotions and cognitions are strongly interrelated, it is posited that *emotions* (e.g., toward out-groups) might be better predictors of direct, immediate forms of discrimination that approximate face-to-face interactions (directed toward an actual person), whereas *cognitions* (like stereotypes) might be better predictors of hypothetical, more abstract forms of discrimination (directed toward a fictional person or out-group in general). Because the early screening phase for the most part considers the screening of "paper people," [5] one could expect cognitive prejudices to be somewhat stronger determinants of hiring discrimination than emotions in this phase. Thus the effect of prejudice on hiring discrimination could be contingent upon the prejudice measure (capturing more emotional than cognitive aspects) and the level of abstraction of the target/type of discrimination (direct/concrete versus abstract/hypothetical discrimination). This—to the best of our knowledge—has not been considered as yet and is an interesting avenue for further research.

The relation of modern racism with discriminatory hiring decisions may further depend on the *degree of contextual ambiguity* recruiters have to deal with. The attributional-ambiguity effect suggests that recruiters would not be discriminating in unambiguous situations where bias would be obviously and directly attributable to the recruiter (i.e., because of their desire not to appear prejudiced). However, in more ambiguous situations when one's behavior could be justified by external factors, one might more readily engage in any discriminatory behavior. As mentioned, one such excuse for discriminatory evaluations of ethnic minorities may involve applicants' moderate job qualifications. For instance, modern racism may negatively affect ethnic minorities' job suitability ratings when job applicants' qualifications are moderately relevant for the job (creating ambiguity in the applicants' profile) whereas no effects are expected if applicants' qualifications are highly relevant for the job position.

Third, socially desirable responding may affect the predictive strength of explicit prejudice measures like modern racism. The broad normative climate in western society has turned against explicit expressions of racial/ethnic prejudice (e.g., Dovidio

& Gaertner, 2000; Hodson, Dovidio, & Gaertner, 2002). Individual difference variables (like modern racism) reflect group and social norms that gradually become internalized by the individual. As such, they are not entirely the product of individual preferences acquired over time (Crandall, Eshleman, & O'Brien, 2002). Conversely, social norms may affect whether individuals show their true faces. For instance, people may feel the desire to respond without prejudice because of concerns of how others would evaluate them if they were to respond with prejudice (Plant & Devine, 1998). In a simulated lab study, we showed that recruiters' motivation not to be perceived as prejudiced moderated the effect of ethnicity on job suitability ratings. Job suitability ratings of applicants with Arabic-sounding names were significantly higher for those who were externally motivated to respond without prejudice.

Finally, because explicit expressions of prejudice (like modern racism and motivation to respond without prejudice) are susceptible to socially desirable responding, researchers have directed their attention toward more implicit ways of measuring prejudice, such as the Implicit Association Test (IAT) (Greenwald, McGhee, & Schwartz, 1998). This test is an association-based implicit measure that assumes that more closely related concepts and attributes of the self are more quickly processed than less related concepts and attributes. There is a great deal of evidence for the construct and criterion-related validity of IATs, both theoretically as well as empirically (e.g., Rudman, 2008; Uhlmann, Leavitt, Menges, Koopman, Howe, & Johnson, 2012). However, the use and value of the IAT has also been criticized—for instance, for being related only to micro-level behavior (like spatial distance, eye contact, smiling) instead of macro-level behavior (like work-related evaluations) (Landy, 2008). Lately, however, some studies have demonstrated that recruiting behavior may be affected to a larger extent by implicit prejudice than had previously been thought. Both scenario-based studies (e.g., Rudman & Glick, 2001; Yogeeswaran & Dasgupta, 2010; Ziegert & Hanges, 2005) as well as correspondence audits (e.g., Rooth, 2009; 2010) show empirical evidence that the IAT does predict discriminatory behavior at a macro-level (like hiring rates and job suitability ratings), even outside the psychological lab, and at the micro-level (like eye contact and smiling). It is further suggested that automatically activated prejudice (e.g., as captured by the IAT) would particularly affect hiring outcomes when recruiters have to work under time pressure, experience ambiguity, or are inattentive to their task (Bertrand, Chugh, & Mullainathan, 2005), which is another interesting avenue for further research. Clearly, given the sensitive nature of prejudice, we suggest that further research should pay more attention to unobtrusive research methods.

In Conclusion

Back into the nineties, shifting demographics and a tightening labor market were predicted to bring about a "war for talent," which would automatically lead into an increased recruitment of minorities (Rynes & Barber, 1990). As expected, organizations' war for talented workers is one of today's most urgent business challenges, yet some talent pools remain underexplored. Specifically, labor market integration of ethnic minorities appears challenging and both human capital and hiring discrimination have been put forward as potential explanations for the lower labor market position of individuals belonging to an ethnic minority group. The main goal of this chapter is to contrast theoretical perspectives with empirical findings on ethnic discrimination during early recruitment and more specifically regarding the resume-screening phase. Resume screening is one of the most frequently used screening tools in personnel assessment. But apparently the adverse impact of resume screening has been considered to a considerable lesser extent than to that of other assessment tools. This chapter aimed to address this literature gap. To achieve this goal, we have compared theoretical predictions with currently available research evidence, with a particular highlighting of our own research on ethnic discrimination.

We started with an excerpt from Shakespeare's *Romeo and Juliet*. Romeo and Juliet's story ends tragically, leading to a considerable loss for both the Montague and Capulet families. Obviously, companies too might lose considerable human capital during the prehire phase, when screeners may be blinded by job-irrelevant characteristics such as applicants' ethnic-sounding names. What should matter is what something is, not what it is being called. However, a rose—or, in this case, a resume—by any other (ethnic) name does not smell as sweet as Shakespeare's Juliet suggested. Applicants' ethnic identifiers do matter, and discriminatory effects can be large. Yet we have illustrated that resume screening is very complex and that hiring discrimination may depend on many more factors than names, including the ways in which we can (or cannot) measure biased decision making.

Future Research Directions

Future research, therefore, should consider the complexity of resume screening and biased decision-making in particular by documenting and investigating intersectional effects of applicant, rater, job, organizational, and cultural characteristics on hiring decisions. Several directions for further research have already been mentioned. On top of these suggestions, the following research questions present some additional and fruitful avenues for further research:

1. **Are hiring outcomes of minorities affected by the specific sociocultural context in which resume screening takes place?** A first question relates to the effect of broader societal factors on resume screening practices, such as the type of acculturation that is expected, the cultural values of a particular society, and status of the immigrant group in the society. For instance, members of the same ethnic minority group might not be regarded equally across cultures. Ethnic discrimination may depend on ethnic minorities' perceived acculturation patterns. In a related vein, the economic and legal setting in which recruitment takes place may affect whether discriminatory effects show-up. Investigating sociocultural effects is important, for example, for international recruitment practices.

2. **Will members of the same (ethnic) minority group always be treated in the same way?** Traditional lines of research typically focus on one minority characteristic (e.g., ethnicity only), thereby considering minority groups as monolithic categories. Hiring decisions, however, might depend on diversity *across* and *within* minority categories. For instance, one may consider both multiple categorization effects of different minority characteristics (such as intersection of ethnicity with gender) as well as within categorization effects of ethnic markers (such as the intersection of ethnic-sounding names with affiliations) on hiring outcomes. Empirical studies have just started to explore these theoretical assumptions and empirical outcomes of both types of categorization effects.

3. **How will discrimination be affected by emerging and future resume forms and resume uses?** A third question relates to the future of resume screening. Many companies still request traditional resumes as part of their application package. Others rely on social networks and online applications for gauging job applicants' job suitability. It seems rather unlikely that paper resumes would disappear; however, they might come in another way, such as through blogs, videos, and portfolios as posted on

personal websites. Technological advances impact assessment practices in organizations with video resumes being one of the latest trends in HR. Video resumes (sometimes also called video interviews) are short videotaped messages in which applicants present themselves to potential employers. While they may offer an alternative or supplement to traditional paper resumes, concerns have been voiced about their validity, the equivalence with paper resumes, the potential for biased decision making, and unlawful discrimination (Derous et al., 2012b). For instance, some groups might be advantaged while others might be disadvantaged by the use of video resumes. Empirical research is lagging behind the rate at which video resumes are being adopted and is much needed.

4. What methods to avert hiring discrimination during resume screening are most promising? A final question relates to ways to stop hiring discrimination. Anonymous resume-screening (blotting names; hiding one's ethnic background) may be one way to overcome hiring discrimination during the resume screening phase. However, this practice is much debated and highly contested, particularly by ethnic minority members. Applying is not going on a blind date: sooner or later, employers meet the applicant, as during the job interview. In many western countries, employers are not allowed to register the applicants' ethnicity for privacy-related issues. While, at first sight this might protect the ethnic minority applicant against biased decision making in the earliest phase, it could—paradoxically—also lead to *more* instead of less hiring discrimination. Specifically, there might be many more "hidden" cues of one's ethnicity (or any other minority characteristic) on resumes beyond obvious signals (such as ethnic-sounding names, birthplaces, or one's mastery of languages) that can prompt discrimination. Less visible ethnic markers on resumes like one's affiliations to sociocultural groups as well as applicants' strength of ethnic out-group identification seem equally important to consider. Further research on these subtle markers is needed.

However, another important factor to consider is the recruiter. Recruiters' ethnic attitudes clearly matter. Therefore, more research is needed on methods to screen recruiters on their propensity to discriminate as well as to investigate whether recruiters can be trained to avert biased decision making (Derous et al., 2012a). Maybe, some implicit measures could be used too, to alert recruiters on their hidden attitudes. Further research, therefore, can consider the context of resume screening.

Practical recommendations

What recommendations can practitioners take away from the psychological research on bias in resume screening? Our overall recommendation for practice is that both job seekers and career counselors and recruiters/organizations might benefit if they were more aware of all blatant and subtle factors that might instigate biased decision making in resume screening:

1. As demonstrated by many studies, applicant names are clear markers of ethnicity. Ethnic names might interact with other ethnic identifiers on resumes (like affiliations) as well as with other applicant characteristics that co-vary with applicants' ethnicity (like applicants' gender) and even with applicants' attire and ethnic accent (e.g., when video resumes are used). Organizations should attempt to educate those involved in any type of applicant screening as to potential biases that may enter in where ethnicity is conveyed indirectly. In general, training those who screen resumes should be undertaken.

2. Career counselors might make ethnic minorities more aware of these indirect indicators and might guide ethnic minority job seekers in how to best present their competencies, such as by providing training on how to write a resume or to make videotaped resumes.

3. From the recruiters' point of view, anonymous resume screening has often been suggested to avoid bias. However, considering the effect of subtle markers, blotting candidate names may be only a partially effective intervention. One way to deal with this is through the use of structured checklists. Recruiters might use a structured sifting process with competency and experience checklists or testimonials. This approach resembles in a way the blind auditions musicians do when they apply for jobs (e.g., in orchestras like the YouTube Symphony orchestra [http://www.youtube.com/user/symphony]). Similarly, automated screening processes that are part of applicant tracking systems have value in terms of efficiently processing large numbers of applications, but may also have value in reducing attention to ethnic identifiers.

4. As illustrated, recruiters' prejudice, attitudes and motivations might also affect their decision making. Considering this, a recommendation is to screen recruiters on their propensity to discriminate. However, this may be difficult to enact, as those who screen resumes may be in

that role because of technical job expertise or hiring authority. Identifying prejudiced attitudes, however, can be important in increasing awareness of recruiters.

5. Organizations often enact policies to promote a diverse workforce. In terms of resume screening, holding recruiters accountable for their decisions is important. At the start of this chapter we noted that human capital differences provide one explanation for differences in hiring rates; thus, recruiters may hire lower proportions of individuals from an ethnic minority group because of differences in human capital. Still, organizations should develop policies and procedures to detect any discriminatory screening practices. Coupled with efforts at increasing recruiter awareness and training, holding resume screeners accountable for their actions can make a difference in reducing bias in resume screening.

Notes

1. The term *adverse impact* is often used generally to refer to the possibility of unfairness in employment-related decision making against any subgroup (like ethnic minorities). In its original sense, *adverse impact* is a legal term that refers to a substantially different selection rate for one group relative to another group (like ethnic minorities vs. ethnic majorities) (e.g., Tippins, 2010).

2. It is a complex and difficult endeavor to come to a clear and straightforward definition of *ethnic minority*. Often, the notion "ethnic minority" is used interchangeably with the terms *foreign-born, migrant, national minority,* and even *non-White* (with a different racial background) or *nonwestern* workers. It is also frequently used in a restricted sense referring to those who were born in, or are citizens of, another country. For instance, in the Netherlands population statistics use the term *western migrants* (i.e., *westerse allochtonen*) versus *nonwestern migrants* (i.e., *niet-westerse allochtonen*) instead of *ethnic minority. Ethnic minority* seems more a sociological/psychological notion/categorization than a legal one. For instance, international law does not provide a single legal definition of *ethnic minority.* However, Recommendation 1201 (1993) of the Parliamentary Assembly of the Council of Europe as well as the European Charter for Regional or Minority Languages has defined national minorities "a group of people within a given national state, (a) that is numerically smaller than the rest of the population of that state or any part of that state, (b) that is not in a dominant position in that state, (c) that has a culture, language, religion, race and so on that is distinct from that of the majority of the population, (d) whose members want to preserve their specificity or cultural heritance, (e) whose members are citizens of the state they have the status of a minority in, and (f) whose members have a long-term presence in the state/part of the state they are a minority in." According to the United Nations, ethnic minority status should be based on both objective criteria (like nondominance in terms of numbers and/or political power and possession of distinct ethnic characteristics) and subjective criteria of self-definition (like one's will to preserve distinct characteristics). The same definition as proposed by the United Nations and European Commission is used throughout this chapter. Specifically, we refer to ethnic minorities as "a social group of people that have a common cultural/ethnic inheritance other than that of the dominant host majority, that want to preserve this inheritance, who are settled in a certain geographic area they are a minority in, and who are in a disadvantaged labor market position compared with the dominant/majority population and therefore form the object for government policy regarding labor market integration and employability."

3. Generally, females have lower labor market outcomes than males (e.g., lower wages, less promotions, and so on). Even without being a numerical minority, females are still considered as a less dominant group in society as compared with males.

4. The BBB-files were named after a pure breed of Belgian cows, named *Blanc Bleu Belge*. Similarly, the code BBR (i.e., *Bleu Blanc Rouge*) was used in France by the same temporary agency for indicating clients who did not want ethnic minorities to work for them.

5. The notion of "paper people" includes both static resume information (like paper resumes and biographic data) as well as more dynamic resume information (like video resumes and social media).

References

Ägerström, J., & Rooth, D.-O. (2011). The role of automatic obesity stereotypes in real hiring discrimination. *Journal of Applied Psychology, 96,* 790–805. doi: 10.1037/a0021594

Alba, R. (2005). Bright vs. blurred boundaries: Second-generation assimilation and exclusion in France, Germany, and the United States. *Ethnic and Racial Studies, 1,* 20–49. doi:10.1080/0141987042000280003

Anderson, N. (2011). Perceived job discrimination: Toward a model of applicant propensity to case initiation in selection. *International Journal of Selection and Assessment, 19,* 229–244. http://dx.doi.org/10.1111/j.1468-2389.2011.00551.x

Andriessen, I., Dagevos, J., Nievers, E., & Boog, I. (2007). *Discriminatiemonitor niet-Westerse allochtonen op de arbeidsmarkt 2007* [Discrimination of non-western migrants on the labor market 2007]. The Hague: Sociaal en Cultureel Planbureau/Art.1.

American Educational Research Association, American Psychological Association & National Council on Measurement in Education, (1999). *Standards for educational and psychological testing* (2nd ed.). Washington, DC: American Educational Research Association.

Arvey, R. D., Gordon, M. E., Massengrill, D. P., & Mussio, S. J. (1975). Differential dropout rates of minority and majority job candidates due to "time lags" between selection procedures. *Personnel Psychology, 28,* 175–180.

Avery, D. R., Hernandez, M., & Hebl, M. R. (2004). Who's watching the race? Racial salience in recruitment advertising. *Journal of Applied Social Psychology, 34,* 146–161. doi: 10.1111/j.1559-1816.2004.tb02541.x

Avery, D. R., Richeson, J. A., Hebl, M. R., & Ambady, N. (2009). It does not have to be uncomfortable: The role of behavioral scripts in Black–White interracial interactions. *Journal of Applied Psychology, 94,* 1382–1393. doi: 10.1037/a0016208

Bangerter, A, Roulin, N., & König,C. J. (2012). Personnel selection as a signaling game. *Journal of Applied Psychology, 97*, 719–738. doi: 10.1037/a0026078

Baumeister, R. F., Bratslavsky, E., Muraven, M., & Tice, D. M. (1998). Ego depletion: Is the active self a limited resource? *Journal of Personality and Social Psychology, 74*, 1252–1265. doi:10.1037/0022-3514.74.5.1252

Bendick, M. Jr., Jackson, C., & Reinoso, V. (1994). Measuring employment discrimination through controlled experiments. *Review of Black Political Economy, 23*, 25–48. doi: 10.1007/BF02895739

Bertrand, M., Chugh, D., & Mullainathan, S. (2005). New approaches to discrimination: Implicit discrimination. *American Economic Review, 95*, 94–98.

Bertrand, M., & Mullainathan, S. (2004). Are Emily and Greg more employable than Lakeisha and Jamal? A field experiment on labor market discrimination. *The American Economic Review, 94*, 991–1031. doi: 10.1257/0002828042002561

Blalock, H. M. (1982). *Race and ethnic relations*. Englewood Cliffs, NJ: Prentice Hall.

Blommaert, L., van Tubergen, F., & Coenders, M. (2012). Implicit and explicit interethnic attitudes and ethnic discrimination in hiring. *Social Science Research, 41*, 61–73. doi:10.1016/j.ssresearch.2011.09.007

Booth, A., L., Leigh, A., & Varganova, E. (2012). Does ethnic discrimination vary across minority groups? Evidence from a field experiment. *Oxford Bulletin of Economics and Statistics, 74*, 547–573. doi: 10.1111/j.1468-0084.2011.00664.x.

Brewer, M. B., & Harasty Feinstein, A. S. (1999). Dual processes in the cognitive representation of persons and social categories. In S. Chaiken, & Y. Trope (Eds.), *Dual process theories in social psychology* (pp. 255–270). New York: Guilford Press.

Brief, A. P., Dietz, J., Cohen, R. R., Pugh, S. D., & Vaslow, J. B. (2000). Just doing business: Modern racism and obedience to authority as explanations for employment discrimination. *Organizational Behavior and Human Decision Processes, 81*, 72–97. doi:10.1006/obhd.1999.2867

Byrne, D. (1997). An overview (and underview) of research and theory within the attraction paradigm. *Journal of Social and Personal Relationships, 14*, 417–431. doi: 10.1177/0265407597143008

Carlsson, M., & Rooth, D.-O. (2008). Is it your foreign name or foreign qualifications? An experimental study of ethnic discrimination in hiring. (IZA Discussion Paper No. 3810). Available at: http://www.iza.org/en/webcontent/webcontent/links/whoiswho/wiwDetail?key=911

CBS Statline. (2012). Centraal Bureau voor de Statistiek. Retrieved January 12, 2012. Available at: http://Statline.cbs.nl

Chattopadhyay, P., Tluchowska, M., & George, E. (2004). Identifying the ingroup: A closer look at the influence of demographic dissimilarity on employee social identity. *Academy of Management Review, 29*, 180–202. Available at: http://www.jstor.org/stable/20159028

Cole, M. S., Feild, H. S., & Stafford, J. O. (2005). Validity of resume reviewers' inferences concerning applicant personality based on resume evaluation. *International Journal of Selection and Assessment, 13*, 321–324. doi: 10.1111/j.1468-2389.2005.00329.x

Cole, M. S., Rubin, R. S., Feild, H. S., & Giles, W. F. (2007). Recruiters' perceptions and use of applicant resume information: Screening the recent graduate. *Applied Psychology—An International Review, 56*, 319–343. doi:10.1111/j.1464-0597.2007.00288.x

Cox, T. (1994). *Cultural diversity in organizations: Theory, research, and practice*. San Francisco: Berrett-Koehler.

Crandall, C. S., Eshleman, A., & O'Brien, L. (2002). Social norms and the expression and suppression of prejudice: The struggle for internalization. *Journal of Personality and Social Psychology, 82*, 359–378. doi: 10.1037/0022-3514.82.3.359

De Meijer, L. A. L., Born, M. Ph., Terlouw, G., & Van der Molen, H. T. (2006). Applicant and method factors related to ethnic score differences in personnel selection: A study among the Dutch police. *Human Performance, 19*, 219–251.

Derous, E., & Nguyen, H.-H. D., & Ryan, A. M. (2009). Hiring discrimination against Arab minorities: Interactions between prejudice and job characteristics. *Human Performance, 22*, 297–320. doi: 10.1080/08959280903120261

Derous, E., & Ryan, A. M. (2006). Religious discrimination. In J. H. Greenhaus and G. A. Callanan (Eds.), *Encyclopedia of career development* (pp. 686–690). Thousand Oaks, CA: Sage.

Derous, E., & Ryan, A. M. (2012). Documenting the adverse impact of resume screening: Degree of ethnic identification matters. *International Journal of Selection and Assessment, 20*, 464–474. doi: 10.1111/ijsa.12009

Derous, E., Ryan, A. M., & Nguyen, H.-H. D. (2012a). Multiple categorization in resume screening: Examining effects on hiring against Arab applicants in field and lab settings. *Journal of Organizational Behavior, 33*, 544–570. doi 10.1002/job.769

Derous, E., Ryan, A. M & Serlie, A. W. (2014). Double Jeopardy upon Resume-screening: When Achmed is less Employable than Aïsha. *Personnel Psychology.* Advance online publication. doi: 10.1111/peps.12078

Derous, E., Taveirne, A, & Hiemstra, A. M. F. (2012, April). Differential effects of video versus paper resumes on personality ratings. In E, Derous & A. Buijsrogge (Chairs), Assessing video resumes: Valuable and/or vulnerable to biased decision-making? Symposium conducted at the 27th Annual Conference of the Society for Industrial and Organizational Psychology, San Diego, CA.

Devendorf, S. A., & Highhouse, S. (2008). Applicant-employee similarity and attraction to an employer. *Journal of Occupational and Organizational Psychology, 81*, 607–617. doi: 10.1348/096317907X248842

Dovidio, J. F., & Gaertner, S. L. (2000). Aversive racism and selection decisions: 1989 and 1999. *Psychological Science, 11*, 315–319. doi: 10.1111/1467–9280.00262

Equal Employment Opportunity Commission (EEOC), Civil Service Commission, Department of Labor & Department of Justice. (1987). Uniform guidelines on employee selection procedures. Federal Register, *43*, 38290–39315.

Fiske, S. T., Lin, M., & Neuberg, S. L. (1999). The continuum model, ten years later. In S. Chaiken, & Y. Trope (Eds.), *Dual process theories in social psychology* (pp. 231–254). New York: Guilford Press.

Gailliot, M. T., Plant, E. A., Butz, D. A., & Baumeister, R. F. (2007). Increasing self-regulatory strength can reduce the depleting effect of suppressing stereotypes. *Personality and Social Psychology Bulletin, 33*, 281–294. doi: 10.1177/0146167206296101

Garcia, M. F., Posthuma, R. A., & Colella, A. (2008). Fit perceptions in the employment interview: The role of similarity, liking, and expectations. *Journal of Occupational* and *Organizational Psychology*, *81*, 173–189. doi: 10.1348/096317907X238708

Govorun, O., & Payne, B. K. (2006). Ego–depletion and prejudice: Separating automatic and controlled components. *Social Cognition*, *24*, 111–136.

Graves, L. M. & Powell, G. N. (1996). Sex similarity, quality of the employment interview and recruiters' evaluation of actual applicants. *Journal of Occupational and Organizational Psychology*, *69*, 243–261. doi: 10.1111/j.2044–8325.1996.tb00613.x

Greenhaus, J., & Callanan, G. A. (Eds.) (2006). *Encyclopedia of career development* (pp. 686–690). Thousand Oaks, CA: Sage.

Greenwald, A., McGhee, D. E., Schwartz, J. L. K., (1998). Measuring individual differences in implicit cognition: the Implicit Association Test. *Journal of Personality and Social Psychology*, *74*, 1464–1480. doi: 10.1037/0022-3514.74.6.1464

Hausknecht, J. P., Day, D. V., & Thomas, S. C. (2004). Applicant reactions to selection procedures: An updated model and meta-analysis. *Personnel Psychology*, *57*, 639–683. doi: 10.1111/j.1744-6570.2004.00003.x

Hebl, M. R., Foster, J. M., Mannix, L. M., & Dovidio, J. F. (2002). Formal and interpersonal discrimination: A field study examination of applicant bias. *Personality and Social Psychological Bulletin*, *28*, 815–825. doi: 10.1177/0146167202289010

Hiemstra, A. M. F., Derous, E., Serlie, A. W., & Born, M. Ph. (2012a). Ethnicity effects in graduates' resume content. *Applied Psychology: An International Review*, *62*, 427–453. Doi: 10.1111/j.1464-0597.2012.00487.x

Hiemstra, A. M. F., Derous, E., Serlie, M. Ph., & Born, M. Ph. (2012b). Perceived and actual discriminatory effects in video resume screening. In E. Derous and A. Buijsrogge (Chairs). *Assessing video resumes: Valuable and/or vulnerable to biased decision-making?* Symposium conducted at the 27th Annual Conference of the Society for Industrial and Organizational Psychology, San Diego, CA.

Hodson, G., Dovidio, J. F., & Gaertner, S. L. (2002). Processes in racial discrimination: Differential weighting of conflicting information. *Personality and Social Psychology Bulletin*, *28*, 460–471. doi: 10.1177/0146167202287004

Hosoda, M., Stone, D. L., & Stone-Romero, E. F. (2003). The interactive effects of race, gender, and job type job suitability ratings and selection decisions. *Journal of Applied Social Psychology*, *33*, 145–178. doi: 10.1111/j.1559-1816.2003.tb02077.x

Howard, J. L., & Ferris, G. R. (1996). The employment interview context: Social and situational influences on interviewer decisions. *Journal of Applied Social Psychology 26*, 112–136. doi: 10.1111/j.1559-1816.1996.tb01841.x

Huffcutt, A. I., & Roth, P. L. (1998). Racial group differences in employment interview evaluations. *Journal of Applied Psychology*, *83*, 179–189. doi: 10.1037/0021-9010.83.2.179

Huffcutt, A. I., Conway, J. M., Roth, P. L., & Stone, N. J. (2001). Identification and meta-analytic assessment of psychological constructs measured in employment interviews. *Journal of Applied Psychology*, *86*, 897–913. doi: 10.1037/0021-9010.86.5.897

Inzlicht, M., & Schmeichel, B. J. (2012). What is ego depletion? Toward a mechanistic revision of the resource model of self-control. *Perspectives on Psychological Science*, *7*, 450–463. doi: 10.1177/1745691612454134.

IPSOS/CEOOR. (2009). *Tolerance barometer: How tolerant are Belgians towards ethnic minorities?* Brussels: IPSOS/Centre for Equal Opportunities and Opposition to Racism. Available at: http://www.diversiteit.be

Jungbluth, P. (2007). Onverzilverde talent. *Hoogopgeleide allochtonen op zoek naar werk* [Higher-educated migrants looking for a job]. Nijmegen: FORUM Instituut voor Multiculturele Ontwikkeling.

Jussim, L. J., Coleman, L. M., & Lerch, L. (1987). The nature of stereotypes: A comparison and integration of three theories. *Journal of Personality and Social Psychology*, *52*, 536–546. Retrieved from http://www.apa.org/pubs/journals/psp/index.aspx

Kaas, L., & Manger, C. (2011). Ethnic discrimination in Germany's labour market: A field experiment. *German Economic Review*, *13*, 1–20. DOI: 10.1111/j.1468-0475.2011.00538.x

Kaiser, C. R., & Pratt-Hyatt, J. S. (2009). Distributing prejudice unequally: Do Whites direct their prejudice toward strongly identified minorities? *Journal of Personality and Social Psychology*, *96*, 432–445. doi: 10.1037/a0012877

King, E. B., & Ahmad, A. S. (2010). An experimental field study of interpersonal discrimination toward Muslim job applicants. *Personnel Psychology*, *63*, 881–906. doi: 10.1111/j.1744-6570.2010.01199.x

King, E. B., Madera, J. M., Hebl, M. R., Knight, J. L. & Mendoza, S. A. (2007). What's in a name? A multiracial investigation of the role of occupational stereotypes in selection decisions. *Journal of Applied Social Psychology*, *36*, 1145–1159. doi:10.1111/j.0021-9029.2006.00035.x

Kleinmann, M., Ingold, P. V., Lievens, F., Jansen, A., Melchers, K. G., & König, C. J. (2011). A different look at why selection procedures work: The role of candidates' ability to identify criteria. *Organizational Psychology Review*, *1*, 128–146. doi: 10.1177/2041386610387000

Kulik, C. T., Roberson, L., & Perry, E. L. (2007). The multiple-category problem: Category activation and inhibition in the hiring process. *Academy of Management Review*, *32*, 529–548. Available at: http://www.aom.pace.edu/amr/

Landy, F. J. (2008). Stereotypes, bias, and personnel decisions: Strange and stranger. *Industrial and Organizational Psychology: Perspectives on Science and Practice*, *1*, 379–392. doi:10.1111/j.1754-9434.2008.00071.x

Levin, S., Sinclair, S., Veniegas, R. C., & Taylor, P. L. (2002). Perceived discrimination in the context of multiple group memberships. *Psychological Science*, *13*, 557–560. doi: 10.1111/1467–9280.00498

Lievens, F., & Harris, M. M. (2003). Research on internet recruiting and testing: Current status and future directions. In C. L. Cooper & I. T. Robertson (Eds.), *International review of industrial and organizational psychology* (Vol. *18*, pp. 131–165). Chichester, UK: Wiley.

Macrae, C. N., Bodenhausen, G. V., Milne, A. B., & Jetten, J. (1994). Out of mind but back in sight: Stereotypes on the rebound. *Journal of Personality and Social Psychology*, *67*, 808–817. doi: 10.1037/0022-3514.67.5.808

Macrae, C. N., Bodenhausen, G. V., Milne, A. B., & Wheeler, V. (1996). On resisting the temptation for simplification: Counterintentional consequences of stereotype suppression on social memory. *Social Cognition*, *14*, 1–20. doi: 10.1521/soco.1996.14.1.1

McCarthy, J. M., Van Iddekinge, C. H., & Campion, M. A. (2010). Are highly structured job interviews resistant to demographic similarity effects? *Personnel Psychology, 63*, 325–359. doi: 10.1111/j.1744-6570.2010.01172.x

McConahay, J. B. (1983). Modern racism and modern discrimination: The effects of race, racial attitudes, and context on simulated hiring decisions. *Personality and Social Psychology Bulletin, 9*, 551–558. doi: 10.1177/0146167283094004

McConahay, J. B., Hardee, B. B., & Batts, V. (1981). Has racism declined in America? It depends on who is asking and what is asked. *Journal of Conflict Resolution, 25*, 563–579. doi: 10.1177/002200278102500401

McFarland, L. A., Ryan, A. M., Sacco, J. M, & Kriska, S. D. (2004). Examination of structured interview ratings across time: The effects of applicant race, rater race, and panel composition. *Journal of Management, 30*, 435–452. doi: 10.1016/j.jm.2003.09.004

Meurs, D., Pailhé, A., & Simon P. (2008), Discrimination despite integration: Immigrants and the second generation in education and the labour market in France. In C. Bonifazi, M Okólski, J. Schoorl and P. Simon (Eds.), *International migration in Europe: New trends and new methods of analysis* (pp. 247–272). Amsterdam: Amsterdam University Press.

Moscoso, S. (2000). Selection interview: A review of validity evidence, adverse impact and applicant reactions. *International Journal of Selection and Assessment, 8*, 237–247. doi: 10.1111/1468–2389.00153

Muraven, M., & Baumeister, R. F. (2007). Self-regulation and depletion of limited resources. Does self-control resemble a muscle? *Psychological Bulletin, 126*, 247–259. doi: 10.1037/0033-2909.126.2.247

National Research Council. (2004). *Measuring racial discrimination*. Washington, DC: National Academies Press.

Nievers, E., Andriessen, I., Faulk, L., & Dagevos, J. (2010). *Discriminatiemonitor niet-westerse immigranten op de arbeidsmarkt 2010* [Discrimination of non-western migrants on the labor market 2007]. The Hague: Sociaal en Cultureel Planbureau.

OECD. (2011). *International migration outlook 2011*, Paris: OECD Publications. doi: 10.1787/migr_outlook-2011-en

OECD. (2012). *OECD factbook 2011–2012: Economic, environmental and social statistics*. Paris: OECD Publications. doi: 10.1787/factbook-2011-en

Oswald, D. L. (2005). Understanding anti-Arab reactions post-9/11: The role of threats, social categories and personal ideologies. *Journal of Applied Social Psychology, 35*, 1775–1799. doi: 10.1111/j.1559–1816.2005.tb02195.x

Outtz, J. L. (2009). *Adverse impact: Implications for organizational staffing and high stakes selection*. New York: Taylor & Francis.

Piotrowski, C., & Armstrong, T. (2006). Current recruitment and selection practices: A national survey of Fortune 1000 firms. *North American Journal of Psychology, 8*, 489–496.

Plant, E. A., & Devine, P. G. (1998). Internal and external motivation to respond without prejudice. *Journal of Personality and Social Psychology, 75*, 811–832. doi: 10.1037/0022-3514.75.3.811

Purkiss, S. L. S., Perrewe, P. L., Gillespie, T. L., Mayes, B. T., & Ferris, G. R. (2006). Implicit sources of bias in employment interview judgments and decisions. *Organizational Behavior and Human Decision Processes, 101*, 152–167. doi:10.1016/j.obhdp.2006.06.005

Riordan, C. M., Schaffer, B. S., & Stewart, M. M. (2005). Relational demography within groups: Through the lens of discrimination. In R. L. Dipboye & A. Colella (Eds.), *Discrimination at work: The psychological and organizational bases* (pp. 11–35) (SIOP Frontiers Series). Mahwah, NJ: Erlbaum.

Rooth, D. O. (2009). Obesity, attractiveness, and differential treatment in hiring. A field experiment. *Journal of Human Resources, 44*, 710–735.

Rooth, D. O. (2010). Automatic associations and discrimination in hiring: Real-world evidence. *Labour Economics 17*, 523–534. doi:10.1016/j.labeco.2009.04.005

Rudman, L. A. (2008). The validity of the implicit association test is a scientific certainty. *Industrial and Organizational Psychology: Perspectives on Science and Practice, 1*, 426–429. doi: 10.1111/j.1754-9434.2008.00081.x

Rudman, L. A., & Glick, P. (2001). Prescriptive gender stereotypes and backlash toward agentic women. *Journal of Social Issues, 57*, 743–762. doi: 10.1111/0022-4537.00239

Rynes, S. L., & Barber, A. E. (1990). Applicant attraction strategies: An organizational perspective. *Academy of Management Review, 15*, 286–310.

Sacco, J. M., Scheu, C. R., Ryan, A. M., & Schmitt, N. (2003). An investigation of race and sex similarity effects in interviews: A multilevel approach to relational demography. *Journal of Applied Psychology, 88*, 852–865. doi: 10.1037/0021-9010.88.5.852

Segers, S., Decoster, J., & Derous, E. (2012, June). Selecting-out minority applicants: Findings from a Belgian audit study. In R. H. Searle (Chair). *Unseen and unexpected: New insights into discrimination from a European Context*. Symposium conducted at the IWP 2012 International Conference, Sheffield, UK.

Sherif, M., Harvey, O. J., White, B. J., Hood, W. R. & Sherif, C. (1961). *Intergroup conflict and cooperation: The robbers' cave experiment*. Norman: Institute of Group Relations, University of Oklahoma.

Shomstein, S., & Yantis, S. (2004). Control of attention shifts between vision and audition in human cortex. *Journal of Neuroscience, 24*, 10702–10706. doi: 10.1523/JNEUROSCI.2939-04.2004

Sidanius, J., & Pratto, F. (1999). *Social dominance: An intergroup theory of social hierarchy and oppression*. New York: Cambridge University Press.

Society for Industrial and Organizational Psychology (SIOP). (2003). *Principles for the validation and use of personnel selection procedures* (4th ed.). Bowling Green, OH: Author.

Son Hing, L., Chung-Yan, G. A., Hamilton, L. K., & Zanna, M. P. (2008). A two-dimensional model that employs explicit and implicit attitudes to characterize prejudice. *Journal of Personality and Social Psychology 94*, 971–987. doi: 10.1037/0022-3514.94.6.971

Stone-Romero, E. F., Stone, D. L., & Hyatt, D. (2003). Personnel selection procedures and invasion of privacy. *Journal of Social Issues, 59*, 343–368. doi: 10.1111/1540–4560.00068

Tajfel, H., Billig, M. G., & Bundy, R. P., & Flament, C. (1971). Social categorization and intergroup behavior. *European Journal of Social Psychology, 1*, 149–178. doi: 10.1002/ejsp.2420010202

Tajfel, H., & Turner, J. C. (1986). The social identity theory of intergroup behavior. In S. Worchel & W. G. Austin (Eds.), *Psychology of intergroup relations* (pp. 7–24). Chicago: Nelson-Hall.

Talaska, C. A., Fiske, S. T., & Chaiken, S. (2008). Legitimating racial discrimination: A meta-analysis of the racial attitude–behavior literature shows that emotions, not beliefs, best predict discrimination. *Social Justice Research: Social Power in Action 21*, 263–296. doi: 10.1007/s11211-008-0071-2

Te Nijenhuis, J., De Jong, M.-J., Evers, A., & van der Flier, H. (2004). Are cognitive differences between immigrant and majority groups diminishing? *European Journal of Personality, 18*, 405–434. doi: 10.1002/per.511

Te Nijenhuis, J., & van der Flier, H. (2003). Immigrant–majority group differences in cognitive performance: Jensen effects, cultural effects, or both? *Intelligence, 31*, 443–459. Available at: http://dx.doi.org/10.1016/S0160-2896

Tippins, N. T. (2010). Adverse impact in employee selection procedures from the perspective of an organizational consultant. In J. L. Outtz (Ed.), *Adverse impact: Implications for organizational staffing and high stakes selection* (pp. 201–225). New York: Routledge.

Uhlmann, E. L., Leavitt, K., Menges, J. I., Koopman, J., Howe, M., & Johnson, R. E. (2012). Getting explicit about the implicit: A taxonomy of implicit measures and guide for their use in organizational research. *Organizational Research Methods, 15*, 553–601. doi: 10.1177/1094428112442750

Vandevenne, G., & Lenaers, S. (2007) (Ed.). *Allochtoon talent aan het werk. Kansen van hooggeschoolde allochtonen bij arbeidsmarktintrede* [Labour market opportunities for high-educated ethnic minorities upon organizational entry]. Diepenbeek, Belgium: Expertisecentrum Gelijke Onderwijskansen.

Van Hooft, E. A. J., Born, M. Ph., Taris, T. W., & van der Flier, H. (2004). Job search behavior and the theory of planned behavior: Minority—majority group differences in The Netherlands. *Journal of Vocational Behavior, 65*, 366–390. doi:10.1016/j.jvb.2003.09.001

Wade, T. J., Judkins–Romano, M., & Blue, L. (2004). The effect of African American skin color on hiring preferences. *Journal of Applied Social Psychology, 34*, 2550–2558. doi: 10.1111/j.1559-1816.2004.tb01991.x

Watkins, L. M., & Johnston, L. (2000). Screening job applicants: The impact of physical attractiveness and application quality. *International Journal of Selection and Assessment, 8*, 76–84. doi: 10.1111/1468-2389.00135

Wegner, D. M. (1994). Ironic processes of thought control. *Psychological Review, 101*, 34–52.

Wegner, D. M., & Schneider, D. J. (2003). "The White Bear Story." *Psychological Inquiry, 14*, 326–329. doi: 10.1080/1047840X.2003.9682900

Wood, M., Hales, J., Purdon, S., Sejersen, T., & Hayllar, O. (2009). A test for racial discrimination in recruitment practice in British cities. (Research Report No 607). Retrieved from the National Centre for Social Research website. Available at: http://www.natcen.ac.uk/media/664762/a%20test%20of%20racial%20discrumination%20in%20recruitment%20practice%20research%20report.pdf

Yogeeswaran, K., & Dasgupta, N. (2010). Will the "real" American please stand up? The effect of implicit national prototypes on discriminatory behavior and judgments. *Personality and Social Psychology Bulletin, 36*, 1332–1345. doi: 10.1177/0146167210380928

Zegers De Beijl, R. Z. (2000). *Documenting discrimination against migrant workers in the labor market: A comparative study of four European countries.* Geneva: International Labor Organization.

Ziegert, J. C., & Hanges, P. J. (2005). Employment discrimination: The role of implicit attitudes, motivation and a climate for racial bias. *Journal of Applied Psychology, 90*, 553–562. doi: 10.1037/0021-9010.90.3.553

Programs to Support Job-Search and End Spells of Unemployment

The Evaluation of Reemployment Programs: Between Impact Assessment and Theory-Based Approaches

Arie Glebbeek *and* Els Sol

Abstract

In spite of a much improved labor market, the outcome of a leading evaluation report on reemployment programs in the Netherlands turned out negative. This result might be due to limitations of the evaluation method used by the researchers, who had to content themselves with a nonexperimental approach. Currently, for many evaluation researchers, the experimental method stands out as the superior design, especially when combined with a meta-analysis over several trials. We show, however, that experimental evaluations do not solve the uncertainties in this field. Meta-analyses of evaluation studies in Europe and the United States produced strikingly mixed results. Efforts to trace their diversity to variations in reemployment programs have not been very successful. This is mainly because of the "black box character" of many experimental evaluations, which offer little information about the content of the programs. Following "realistic evaluation," we argue for a focus on the theories behind these programs in evaluation research. To this end, reemployment services are depicted in twelve core (mediating) mechanisms.

Key Words: reemployment services, realistic evaluation, experimental versus nonexperimental designs, meta-analysis, intervention strategies, mediating mechanisms, active labor market policy

In previous chapters we have seen how psychological insights have been brought to bear on the design of reemployment services. Especially the JOBS program, described by Price and Vinokur (this volume), can be regarded as an exercise in applied psychology. These and other rigorously tested interventions have repeatedly shown encouraging results. But do these interventions also work on a larger scale and systematically? And how can we establish that? This chapter deals with the issue of evaluation. It is written from a socioeconomic perspective, since the large majority of the evaluations in this field are conducted by economists and econometricians. Yet this approach is not principally different from the testing strategies we encounter in the psychological literature. You will therefore find the present chapter clearly in line with the other

parts of this handbook, many of its methodological topics being familiar to psychologists. This holds especially for the application of experimental designs, the use of meta-analysis, and the recognition of explanatory mechanisms. We illustrate our discussion with the evaluation of reemployment services in the Netherlands, where for 10 years an extensive practice of these services has arisen.

Nice Success or Manifest Failure? The Ambiguities of the Dutch Reemployment Experience

In 2008, the Dutch government sent the *Reemployment Policy Review* to parliament. The debate that followed can be called memorable for several reasons. First, it is highly unlikely for a government to be heavily criticized in spite of the favorable overall outcome of a policy. Second, the debate paved the way for a very substantial reduction of reemployment efforts. Third, it demonstrated the power of scientific evaluation research.

A Brief History

From the crisis of the 1980s, the Netherlands had to deal with relatively high unemployment and disability rates and a correspondingly large share of social security expenditures in the national income. Because of this, the country was even called the "sick man of Europe." Since then successive governments have strongly promoted a "work work work" strategy, with an increasing focus on reemploying the unemployed, the sick, and the disabled. Around the turn of the century, a quasimarket for commercially operating reemployment companies was created to this end. Ten years on, the Netherlands is the country with the lowest unemployment rate and an above average labor force participation within the European Union.

This turnaround is described in the *Policy Review*. The number of unemployment and social assistance benefits sharply decreased after the 2001–2004 recession. The number of disability benefits fell slightly. The share of the long-term unemployed in total unemployment has fallen below the European average. Especially the decrease in the number of welfare recipients to the lowest level in decades is considered a "historical landmark." The Dutch government writes that "these positive developments cannot be automatically attributed to the re-employment policy. However, it is likely that the re-employment policy has also contributed to this" (Ministry of Social Affairs and Employment, 2008, p. 40). The *Policy Review* then presents a table showing that the results of reemployment courses have increased over the years.[1] Of those who started a reemployment course in 2002, some 26% had found a job 2 years later. Of those who started a course in 2004, the corresponding figure was 41%. "Therefore, the results have increased by more than half. This means that we are on course towards achieving the objective" (p. 40). To give a glimpse of what is to follow: These figures represent what researchers call the *gross effectiveness* of a policy.

So Secretary Piet Hein Donner and Assistant Secretary Ahmed Aboutaleb came home with some good macro figures. You would expect that they would look forward to the debate with confidence and that approval would be given to the policy conducted. However, nothing was further from the truth. Members of the "Second Chamber"

(i.e., the parliament) clashed vehemently with the government about the disappointing results of the reemployment policy. "Billions are disappearing into thin air, I do not understand that you accept this without any questions asked," said a spokesman for the leftist opposition. And the spokesman of the ruling party (the secretary's party) said: "These figures are shocking. Tax money is being wasted. The government is far too optimistic." Newspaper headlines expressed this mood with equal emphasis: "Reemployment rarely results in a job" and "Helping one unemployed individual find a job costs EUR 537,000."[2] The subsequent (right-wing) cabinet lead by Mr. Rutte was therefore of the opinion (2010) that a large part of the reemployment budget could be cut without any noticeable damage.

At some point in the *Policy Review*, the members of government were forced to consider the *net effectiveness* of the programs. The idea is that some of the unemployed would have found a job anyway, without reemployment aid, which means that it comes down to estimating the added value of the reemployment services. What would have happened without them? It was mainly economists who, in recent years, emphasized net effectiveness as the only correct measure of effectiveness (e.g., De Koning, 2003; Koning & Heyma, 2009); these voices were especially influential in a departmental report by the Committee on the Future of Labour Market Policy (2001). The fact that the secretaries of state could not get around this in their review shows that economists enjoy the "power to define." This in itself is worth noting. Evaluation research has been described, in the words of Wildavsky (1979) as "speaking truth to power." The turn in the *Policy Review* apparently shows that it is possible for an evaluation science to acquire so much authority that even a government has to listen.

Regarding net effectiveness, the message was clearly less positive. The *Policy Review* pointed to the results of econometric research which allegedly proved that the added value of reemployment courses, on average, was only a few percentage points. It was these results that the newspapers and the political debate focused on. Therefore there is every reason to look more closely at these results and, as a corollary, to discuss the ways in which reemployment programs can be evaluated in greater depth.

We do this by first presenting the three main approaches to impact evaluation in the next section. One of the three, the nonexperimental approach, will subsequently be illustrated by the Dutch case.

The difficulties involved in this case and similar cases drive many evaluation researchers toward the experimental approach. However, an international tour, discussed further on, shows that this often merely shifts the problem and leaves many questions unanswered. Whether the third approach—the "realistic evaluation"—provides a solution remains to be seen. At this time, this approach has few exemplary instances to show. Nevertheless we present, as a first in this field, questions that a realistic reemployment evaluation should answer. Our conclusion is that this would bring a welcome reorientation to evaluation research.

Impact Evaluation: Three Principal Approaches

In the field of impact evaluation, the dominant question is: To what extent can a measured effect be attributed to the intervention with certainty? This is the *internal validity* of the evaluation design. In addition, there is the *external validity* that concerns generalization: To what extent will the effect also occur at other times, in other places, and in other groups? There is tension between the attention given to internal and external validity, as will become clear.

The design of an evaluation is crucial to be able to determine these impacts. Three approaches can be differentiated:

1. The experimental design. In the dominant view, this is the ideal design, or the "gold standard" of policy evaluation.

2. The nonexperimental design. Within this design, often an attempt is made to approach the certainty of the experimental design as much as possible with the aid of statistical methods. In a majority of opinions, this counts as the second-best alternative.

3. Theory-based ("realistic") evaluation. This, too, could be regarded as a second-best alternative to experimental design, but according to some major proponents (Pawson & Tilley, 1997), it is an even better alternative. Authors who are more inclined to compromise view this approach as a corollary of 1 and 2 and argue that it supplements them (e.g., Van der Knaap, Leeuw, Bogaerts, & Nijssen, 2008).

Apart from these, a macroeconomic perspective can be discerned. In this perspective one tries to answer the question of how effects of specific measures add up to the aggregate level. The two polar cases are displacement (i.e., other persons lose their jobs or opportunities) and positive spillovers (i.e., other persons benefit as well). According to this macro framework, the results of a specific program will be overestimated when displacement occurs and underestimated when third parties benefit from the program. Things get even more complicated when one assumes an impact on wages, which affects the overall level of employment. Some economists therefore theorize that micro-level evaluations like experiments can be dead wrong if such equilibrium effects are neglected (cf. Cahuc & Le Barbanchon, 2010). Reemployment policy evaluations only rarely reach this level (but see Blundelll, Costa Dias, Meghir, & Van Reenen, 2004; De Koning, 2001); therefore we refrain from it in this review. This perspective makes it understandable, however, why experimental evaluations are less common in macro-oriented fields like economics and sociology than in clinical fields like medicine and psychology. As most readers will acknowledge, the experimental design very much belongs to the core business of psychologists.

Finally, it is important to note that *systematic reviews* or *metaevaluations* are becoming increasingly important in the field of policy evaluation. The abundance of studies has created a need for policymakers (and scientists) to make up the balance of all these studies from time to time. In the past, this took place especially in a *narrative* sense: A researcher would write a literature overview in which he mainly made his own choices and determined the emphasis himself. Objections arose against the subjectivity of this approach, as a result of which systematic reviews must now comply with strict rules regarding the search strategy (databases, search terms), selection of studies, and the weighting of the results. If, in addition, an attempt is made to calculate an average effect across all the selected studies, a *meta-analysis* is performed. The advance of the meta-analyses has further strengthened the dominance of the experimental design. Meta-analysts need a selection criterion for the studies they wish to include in their synthesis. The studies with the "strongest designs" are preferred in this regard. Thus, a *hierarchy of evidence* has been created, where experimental designs are at the top of the list and many "weaker" designs are not even addressed. These other types of studies are therefore not accepted as evidence and, in scientific terms, remain invisible.

1. *Experimental research.* The key point of this design is the wish to ensure internal validity by

excluding any systematic influence caused by any factor other than the policy. This is done by randomly allocating those who will participate in a program and those who will form the control group of nonparticipants. The standard abbreviation for this approach has therefore become RCT: *randomized controlled trial*. Designing, implementing, and preserving the trial usually takes considerable effort, but it has proved to be a feasible approach for large social programs as well (Hollister, 2008; Oakley et al., 2003). According to the proponents, a big advantage is that the design can be easily explained to politicians and other outsiders and that the results are more easily accepted than those of other tests (Burtless, 1995). This is particularly important for social programs, because they always take place in a political arena where there are usually parties that have a vested or ideological interest in disputing the results of evaluations. This is undeniably the case in the field of reemployment services. For leftwing critics, this is a surrogate policy that discharges the government from the duty to create real jobs, whereas for conservatives it is an excess of the welfare state that undermines the unemployed person's own responsibility. Only unequivocal and "incontrovertible" results of experiments would be able to break through political bias and deadlocks.

A full RCT even makes demands with regard to the awareness of the participants. To counteract motivation effects, it is preferred that the participants not know which group they belong to ("double blind"). In medical science, where this design is widely used, it is customary to give the control group a placebo. However, so far nobody has managed to figure out how to get people to participate in a pseudo–reemployment program (a program without content) (unless you, as some Dutch critics would suggest in view of the results mentioned above, feel that all reemployment programs are actually pseudo).

2. *Nonexperimental research*. Usually, in this approach, too, the impact of the policy is measured by the difference in comparison to a control group which, for the sake of clarity, is better called the "comparison group" here. The intention is to make the comparison group as similar as possible to the intervention group and, where this is not possible, to correct the differences by statistical means.[3] The preequating of the groups is the *matching* method. For each participant in a reemployment program a nonparticipant is sought that is as

similar as possible (in terms of age, gender, ethnicity, education, work experience, duration of unemployment, etc.). The seemingly endless list of variables that can be devised here makes matching a task that is almost impossible from the outset, which is why the method has fallen into disuse over the years. More recently, however, it has made a comeback in the form of *propensity score matching*, whereby the long series of measured variables is first reduced to a distance measure, after which members of both groups are matched based on this distance measure. This distance is usually calculated in relation to the chances to participate in the program. Thus, the likelihood of being included in a reemployment program is a weighted combination of age, sex, education, etc., with the likelihood of some combinations being much greater than that of others. These differences in likelihood probably say much about the underlying differences in labor market opportunities. Through this convenient procedure, the groups have been made comparable on the basis of the most relevant measured characteristics.

However, conducting statistical corrections afterward is the most common nonexperimental method. Suppose that participants of reemployment programs differ from nonparticipants in terms of the duration of their unemployment. By including unemployment duration as a control variable in the impact estimation (usually a regression equation), its influence is neutralized and the "net effect" (added value) of participation remains in the coefficient of the participation variable. All this is of course provided that these effects can be estimated using the linear model of regression analysis, but terms for nonlinear relationships and interaction effects can also be included. The regression models can become highly complex and sophisticated, but the approach is essentially not different from the standard practice of social scientists to correct for all kinds of "confounding variables" in explanatory statistical analysis.

A major complication occurs because in reemployment programs events are spread over time. The duration of a reemployment program can be different for each person and the inflow occurs at different times. The same applies to the result of getting a job. In impact evaluations, several outcomes can be used as a success criterion: the finding of a job, the quality of that job, the amount of time it took to find the job, and the income earned through the job. All those criteria need to be observed in some real-time interval. When the observation period is over (i.e., the survey is closed), some participants are employed and others are not. Some of the latter will soon find a job and some never will. However, we do not know this: the data are *censored*. Grouping all non–job finders together is a rough procedure and would result in incorrect estimates of the predictors (the independent variables). Therefore it is better to include the differing time periods more directly in the impact estimates. To this end, the observed time period is subdivided into many small time boxes and the conditional probability that a person finds a job is estimated for each of those boxes ("conditional" means: given the person's characteristics and whether or not he is participating in a reemployment program). This way, more consideration is given to the influence of time, whereby the time dependency can be modelled in several ways (linear, curvilinear, indefinite, etc.). Accordingly, the distorting effect of the observations all ending at one single point in time is reduced. Furthermore, cofactors that change over time (such as the economy) can be connected to the time periods as covariates. It is also possible to make time periods infinitely small (this is called a *continuous time* model as opposed to *discrete time* periods). Econometricians who conduct these time-sensitive analyses call them econometric duration models and usually present them together with an impressive series of formulas. But, also in other scientific disciplines (biology, sociology, demography, medicine) similar models are applied, often under different names (survival analysis, event-history analysis). By comparison, the duration models that econometricians apply in reemployment studies are mostly a simple variety.

Using the statistical tools of the social sciences, the *measured differences* between the treatment group and the comparison group can thus be tackled effectively. However, the *unmeasured differences* are the big issue. Participants of reemployment programs vary in motivation, presentation, language skills, physical and psychological health, social skills, self-control and a whole series of other characteristics. They probably also differ from nonparticipants in these respects. Participation in a reemployment program is *selective* and *endogenous* if there is no random assignment. It results from self-selection or selection by bureaucrats, who want to deliver "tailor-made work" and do not want to include candidates who in their view are certain to fail or can easily find reemployment without help. The "soft" personal characteristics that are linked to this selection are undeniably highly important for the success of

reemployment programs. However, they are usually not recorded anywhere, certainly not in administrative files, and are therefore usually not visible for evaluation researchers. In evaluation jargon, this is called the *unobserved heterogeneity*. This is the Achilles' heel of the nonexperimental approach.

However, to the tools and tricks of non-experimentalists belongs the surprising claim of mainly econometricians, that statistical corrections can be used for unmeasured characteristics as well. This is where many researchers give up, but the claim is serious. Usually a so-called *instrumental variable* is sought, which is connected to participation in a program but not to its outcome, and to which the unmeasured differences "stick," as it were. A more sophisticated version of this, which can be explained convincingly, is Heckman's two-step correction. In the first step, participation in a reemployment program is estimated through a regression model. It can be reasonably assumed that the unmeasured differences between the unemployed are reflected in the unexplained variance or error term of this selection equation. If the individual error terms (i.e. the residuals or a derivative thereof) can now be included in the substantial equation in which the outcome of the program is estimated, unmeasured differences are still represented (Heckman, 1979) (see, for well-considered discussions, Bushway, Johnson, & Slocum, 2007; Winship & Mare, 1992). This approach is based on a series of assumptions and is often not practicable. Moreover, the results of these corrections appear to be sensitive to the model specification. Nonexperimental results also often differ substantially from the estimates obtained from an experimental design (Glazerman, Levy, & Myers, 2003; Pirog, Buffardi, Chrisinger, Singh, & Briney, 2009). Nevertheless, proponents believe these statistical corrections constitute a powerful weapon. And in the absence of an RCT there is always the ultimate argument of "We have to do something."

3. *Theory-based ("realistic") evaluation.* Through the years, supporters of this approach have argued that the one-sided focus on impact assessment leaves too many questions unanswered. Why did the effect occur (or not)? Does this apply in general, or were there special circumstances? And what does this say about the underlying theory of the intervention? Advocates of theory-based evaluation keep pointing out that policies are always based on underlying theoretical ideas. Therefore an evaluation is only instructive if those theoretical ideas or—a somewhat stricter

term—the *policy theories* themselves can be assessed. Being able to *explain* the obtained results is for this a necessary condition (Chen, 1990; Weiss, 1997). In the chapter by Price and Vinokur, this volume, concerning the JOBS program, we learn about the usefulness of this approach. However, within the "black box" mode of impact evaluation, such an explanation is often impossible to give (cf. Mosley & Sol, 2001). Thus in the evaluation of the Dutch reemployment policy, essential explanatory questions have remained unanswered. Does the alleged ineffectiveness of reemployment programs apply in general or only to a specific approach? Are the underlying assumptions and ideas incorrect or were they just poorly implemented? Does the problem mainly lie with the reemployment companies or were the clients not up to the task? Was the creation of a "market" for reemployment services a good idea after all? And, last but not least, does little added value ("net effectiveness") mean that reemployment services are *unnecessary* or *ineffective*?

British sociologists Pawson and Tilley (1997) gave these criticisms a powerful boost with their book *Realistic Evaluation*, which can already be characterized as a "modern classic." They argue that, in spite of its high standing, the results of an RCT are often anticlimactic. All the efforts made to establish and maintain this demanding research design result in little more than a simple difference score. For Pawson and Tilley, evaluating means *understanding what has happened*, and without an answer to "why" questions this understanding cannot occur. They add, importantly, that usually the confusion only increases if multiple RCTs are performed. Sometimes an experiment shows a positive result, the next time this is curiously lacking. "*Most things have been found sometimes to work*" (Pawson & Tilley, p. 10). This is because in social policy, whether a measure can be successful or not depends decisively on the conditions. In experimental designs, it is those very conditions that are regarded as disturbing factors that should be neutralised as much as possible. "The explanatory capacity of experimental evaluation rests on an irresolvable paradox. . . . The method . . . seeks to discount in design and evidence precisely that which needs to be addressed in explanation" (Pawson & Tilley, p. 31).

This becomes very clear in the role of facilitating conditions. Pawson and Tilley argue that no policy measure can do without the help of favorable circumstances. In reemployment research, the role of motivation is a striking example of this. Most reemployment professionals will endorse the view that motivation of the client is an indispensable condition for a reemployment program to succeed. However, for conventional evaluation researchers such motivation is a variable that should be controlled for. In a plea for more RCTs in labor market policy, Dutch economist De Beer (2001) exemplified his objection to nonrandom assignment as follows: "If participants are generally more motivated than non-participants, the effect of the instrument is *overstated*" (p. 74). Pawson and Tilley would find this an absurd position and, in their book, it seems that they already anticipated De Beer's elucidation:

> Quasi-experimentation's method of random allocation, or efforts to mimic it as closely as possible, represents an endeavour to cancel out differences, to find out whether a program will work without the added advantage of special conditions liable to enable it to do so. This is absurd. It is an effort to write out what is essential to a program—social conditions favourable to its success. *(Pawson & Tilley, 1997, p. 52)*

A "realistic" evaluation should a priori assume that policy measures can only be successful under certain conditions. We may call this the principle of *conditional effectiveness*. This seems particularly relevant to the field of reemployment programs, because the results here obviously depend on the cooperation of clients and other stakeholders (notably employers and benefits officers). Social policy always involves a change in behavior. Behavioral change results from changes in the resources and reasoning of all concerned. What we need, according to Pawson and Tilley, is a methodology that seeks to understand what a program actually offers to incite a change in behavior of the actors, and why not every situation is suitable to effect that change. Their proposed method of realistic evaluation is centred on so-called CMO chains: configurations of *contexts, mechanisms, and outcomes*.

The mechanisms are the ways in which a behavioral change can be brought about. In a paper of a later date, Pawson (2003) suggested that these can essentially be divided in material, cognitive, social, and emotional mechanisms (p. 472). Exactly how these mechanisms work is often not visible but is a matter of theoretical assumptions. The policy theories of reemployment are, in other words, arguments about the initiation and development of mechanisms. If the policy theories are complete, they also identify the main conditions under which these mechanisms may or may not occur. This way, the context and the mechanism together ensure that a particular outcome is achieved: *context + mechanism = outcome*. In analytical terms, the context is therefore to be understood as the moderator of the relationship between a program and the outcome.

The main question of evaluation can now be easily summarized in the motto "*What works for whom under what circumstances?*" Below (as in the chapter by Price & Vinokur, this volume), we will see that this key question is not fundamentally incompatible with the RCT approach; in practice, however, this will not be easy. Pawson and Tilley (1997) are even more skeptical about compatibility. They stress that the methodology of internal validity, net effectiveness and randomization distracts from the key question in stead of bringing us closer to it. By demanding absolute certainty that the measured effect can be attributed to the program and nothing but the program, the supporting conditions that should enable the effect go out of sight. In this sense, a tension exists between the pursuit of internal and external validity. Whoever tries to maximize the former will lose in regard to the latter.

The Evaluation of Dutch Reemployment Policy

How has Dutch reemployment policy been evaluated? In the Netherlands, for many years scholars have complained about the reluctance of politicians to establish or promote experimental evaluations in the field of social security. At last the government agreed to an experiment that has started in 2012. The evaluation of the reemployment programs in the *Policy Review* is therefore not based on an experimental design.

The unfavorable judgment of the added value of reemployment programs is mainly based on nonexperimental impact evaluations carried out by econometricians. This discipline has clearly captured the authoritative evaluations in this field in the Netherlands. The primary study on which the *Policy Review* is based was conducted by the Foundation for Economic Research (SEO) commissioned by the Council for Work and Income (Groot et al., 2008). A few other studies on which the picture was based are mentioned as well, but it is reasonable and clarifying to zoom in on this dominant study. The report is illustrative of the problems nonexperimental evaluations run into.

The study is based on administrative data. Combining various benefits registrations has created an impressive database. It includes everyone who received a social benefit in the period from 1999 till 2006. Information is added about the use of reemployment services and (if applicable) the reason for no longer receiving the benefit. The longitudinal nature of the data made it possible to use an econometric duration model (see above) as a basis for the estimates of the impact of the reemployment services.

No matter how impressive and large the records and no matter how sophisticated the statistical analysis, it is not experimental data. The main problem for the researchers is that a true control group of unemployed people who do not participate in a reemployment program is lacking. This is further complicated by the fact that, over time, most of the unemployed persons are eligible for some form of reemployment counselling and, as a result, comparison to non-participants often boils down to a comparison with later participants. The researchers are compelled to resort to this and their analysis therefore essentially relies on the fact that some of the unemployed joined a reemployment course earlier than others (Groot et al., 2008, appendix). Since exact dates are available, technically a model can still be estimated of the use made of reemployment services (at some point in time) in relation to the duration of the benefit. However, the researchers themselves perfectly know that the time of entrance into a reemployment course is *selective* (Groot et al., p. 4).

We would like to highlight this point, because the implication for policy evaluation is fundamental. Evaluation researchers generally assume that selectivity can work both ways: overestimating or underestimating the results. In regard to the former, program officers may indeed prefer to select the most promising individuals in order to make their program a success. In that case the results seem better than they would have been in a larger group. The second possibility, however, is also realistic and puts evaluation research in a somewhat paradoxical situation. Program officers are generally motivated and encouraged to deliver "customized solutions." They are considered to use their tools where and when they are needed most. Thus, officers do not offer reemployment programs if they feel the unemployed person has a good chance of finding a job him/herself. Suppose that officers can deliver a perfectly customized solution and use tools in such a way that the differences in opportunities between the unemployed are canceled out. The result can only be that the bivariate relationship between the tools and the outcome disappears (cf. Wotschack, Glebbeek, & Wittek, 2013). We do not intend to suggest that this tailor-made work is always provided in actual practice or that it always must have this result, but the degree to which such selectivity plays a role is usually not known. Moreover, we dare to say that equalizing opportunities is the ideal or guideline of policy implementation in very many cases. Therefore the irony is that the better the officers do their job, the harder it is for researchers to prove an impact. We can identify this as *the ideal of zero correlation: If the use of a policy instrument neutralizes starting conditions perfectly, the correlation between intervention and outcome will tend to be zero.*

This places the low impact estimates of the reemployment evaluation in a different light. Obviously selectivity can be partly eliminated from the data by controlling statistically for characteristics and prospects of the unemployed. And, of course, this is what happened in the studies we are discussing here. "By taking into account the selective use of reemployment instruments in the model, a pure effect can still be calculated," the report said (Groot et al., 2008, p. 101). And: the selectivity "is at least in part corrected . . . by relating the probability of the resumption of work to the probability of the use of reemployment tools" (p. 102). The latter clearly refers to an application of the Heckman correction that we mentioned above. This passage in the methodological annex, however, was probably copied from another report, because the main text states that this did not occur (p. 4). Corrections were made for a whole series of measured characteristics of the unemployed, like age, sex, education, region, ethnic group, benefit duration and "distance to the labor market" (an administrative category). All practitioners, however, will point to the importance of the unmeasured characteristics: motivation, presentation, self-confidence and health. What's more, these "soft characteristics" are also emphasised in a literature review enclosed with the evaluation (Gelderblom & De Koning, 2007). In short, despite all statistical efforts, the uneasy feeling remains that selectivity in policy implementation has affected the impact estimates in unknown ways. This selectivity is therefore a severe bias for researchers indeed—but, as we argued, for policy practitioners it is the very core of their business and professionalism. The sobering point we want to make is that evaluation research generally works against the grain, because time and again

researchers need to seek corrections for what policy practice pursues as ideal.

All this is not intended as criticism of the researchers—they "had to do something"—but it does indicate that the seemingly destructive image that has been created around reemployment services is not based on strong empirical grounds. This has also been emphasized by fellow researchers in the discussion following the *Policy Review*. For instance, Dutch labor economist Borghans (2008) writes in a response: "Econometricians have put a great deal of effort into developing techniques for comparing people in cases where no randomisation had taken place. These methods often use unintentional coincidences that occur in reemployment practice. Because these coincidences are often very minor, the power of these methods is not very great" (p. 8).

This conclusion leads Borghans to make a direct plea for RCTs. Only if participants and nonparticipants are truly comparable by randomization, solid conclusions can be drawn. This completes the circle: Nonexperimental methods were developed to overcome the practical difficulties of RCTs, but their deficiencies push researchers back to experimental design. To this conclusion Borghans adds a firm rebuke to policy makers: "Therefore, the unwillingness to let participation in reemployment programs be partly determined by chance means for benefit recipients that the whims of the politicians decide whether they can/should participate in a program nobody knows the effectiveness of" (Borghans, 2008, p. 9).

We could agree with this conclusion were it not that another problem immediately arises. Borghans's formulation suggests that we will know once and for all after an RCT has been conducted. Let us organise a trial and determine indisputably whether reemployment services work or not. We believe this is an illusion. Besides the internal validity, one also has to account for the external validity of evaluation research. And in this regard, we cannot but conclude that there is a great deal of variation among seemingly similar policies. Reemployment services do not constitute a homogeneous intervention but in practice represent a wide variety of approaches and instruments (e.g. Groothoff et al., 2008; Sol et al., 2011). In addition to these varying approaches, the groups of participants and—highly essential to this policy—labor market conditions vary. Therefore new RCTs will constantly be needed to determine the efficacy of specific approaches for specific target groups under specific circumstances. Without the guidance of more substantive ideas or theories, we would get lost in this forest of RCTs as well. Let us examine this by looking across the Dutch border and considering the results of studies that are indeed based on the experimental method.

Evaluation of Reemployment Programs: A Global View

The story so far could create the impression that experiments are rare and that scholars everywhere insist on them in vain. However, this is not true if we look at other countries. Especially in America, experimental evaluations have often been conducted, also in the field of social policy and labor market policy. This is partly due to a greater skepticism about government interference in the United States, which makes politicians more often insist that it is unequivocally demonstrated that new programs "actually work." Accordingly large-scale experiments have been conducted with training programs (Friedlander, Greenberg, & Robins, 1997), job search assistance and reemployment bonuses (Meyer, 1995) and welfare-to-work programs. The latter are more comparable to the Dutch reemployment services than the traditional training programs, since they also tend to focus on the shortest route to a job and include many similar elements (orientation, activation, help with finding jobs, and enhancing job readiness).

In a series of meta-analyses, the balance of these welfare-to-work experiments was made up (Ashworth, Cebulla, Greenberg, & Walker, 2004; Greenberg & Cebulla, 2008; Greenberg, Deitch, & Hamilton, 2010). For instance, Greenberg and Cebulla (2008) used 27 evaluation studies from a total of 71 mandatory programs conducted between 1982 and 1996 in the United States as a basis, whereas Greenberg et al. (2010) zoom in on 28 of these programs that were evaluated by one single institution (MDRC) with an identical approach. These 28 programs ran in eleven states and two Canadian provinces and included over 100,000 participants. "All the studies used random assignment research designs, resulting in probably the most extensive and most reliable database of findings about welfare-to-work programs ever assembled" (Greenberg et al., p. 2). The individual studies were carried forward to the stage of cost-benefit analysis—a stage that is rarely reached in this field (cf. Card, Kluve, & Weber, 2010, p. 476)—making them exemplary from an evaluation point of view. The authors consider these costs and benefits from three different viewpoints: the participants, the government budget, and society at large.[4] In this

regard they establish that just examining whether the unemployed have found jobs or have improved their income, whilst ignoring the administrative costs of the policy ("which is often the case"), easily leads to erroneous conclusions about the return for government and society (Greenberg & Cebulla, p. 136).

With this warning in mind, it should come as no surprise that the general conclusion on the cost-effectiveness of the programs is not one to arouse jubilation. "The net benefits from a typical welfare-to-work intervention, accumulated over several years, are fairly modest for the program group, even smaller from the perspectives of society as a whole" (Greenberg & Cebulla, 2008, p. 122). This corresponds with the familiar picture from the earlier evaluations that positive effects of such programs on earnings and welfare dependency range from minimal to modest (e.g. Friedlander et al., 1997). The authors state, however, that all this pertains to an *average* program. "Many welfare-to-work programs *are* cost-beneficial, some highly so" (Greenberg & Cebulla, p. 139).

In reading these meta-analyses, Pawson and Tilley's (1997) characterization inevitably comes to mind: *Most things have been found sometimes to work.* Some programs had positive results, some negative, and others insignificant, and all of this seen from each of the different viewpoints. Greenberg et al. (2010) divided their twenty-eight programs into six types, and within each of them they made up the cost-benefit ratio from the perspectives of participants, government, and society. In thirteen of the eighteen cells, both programs with a positive and a negative result occur (Greenberg et al., Table 4). A similar variation in outcomes is observed if we do not use the cost-benefit ratio but the direct effects for the participants as a basis (income improvement, getting off welfare). Here, too, the results of the experiments appear to be "widely dispersed" (Ashworth et al., 2004, pp. 202–204). Greenberg and Cebulla (2008) report that, from a societal point of view, 58% of the programs had a positive and 42% a negative result. Their conclusion is, therefore, that "the variation in findings across the 50 cost-benefit analyses in our sample is *enormous*" (Greenberg & Cebulla, p. 122, our emphasis)—therewith crushing the hope of Borghans and many others that RCTs would determine the effectiveness of reemployment programs once and for all.

Obviously one can try to figure out if this variation can be attributed to certain features of the programs or their environment, and that is what is done in these meta-analyses. The welfare-to-work experiments have a reputation for providing clear indications in this regard and are therefore considered by some to be the "best experiences" of the use of RCTs in social policy (Hollister, 2008). This is largely due to their contrasting of "work first" (cf. Lindsay, this volume) with "human capital" elements (e.g. schooling, training), "showing that the work-first approach was more effective" (Hollister, p. 406). This is also the conclusion of Ashworth et al. (2004) in their meta-analysis— "the relative success of the "tough love" approach" (p. 209)—but they immediately add a whole series of qualifications to this result. Greenberg et al. (2010) go a step further in weakening the argument by pointing out that work-first programs are generally beneficial to the government but often do not really increase the incomes of the participants. Mixed programs, which include training, perform a little better in their analysis (pp. 14–15, 21). Our reading of the meta-analyses is that they have not uncovered many consistent patterns in the studies. In general, they offer few concrete reference points for the selection or improvement of reemployment programs; the findings have a high degree of "it could be that." Obviously this has everything to do with the large variation in outcomes but also with the fact that the programs are divided only into broad categories and that the active mechanisms are not tested or assessed. After fifteen years of experimenting, Ashworth et al. therefore admit: "To conclude, the search for a best-practice model of welfare-to-work has only just begun" (p. 211).

Although welfare-to-work programs in the United States are still widespread, the enthusiasm to evaluate these using RCTs has decreased (Greenberg & Cebulla, 2008, p. 116). This is perhaps significant, but we do not wish to speculate about it here. In recent years the use of experiments has found acceptance in Europe, albeit on a lesser scale than in the United States. Therefore when we shift our view to European reemployment programs, we will examine experimental and nonexperimental evaluations jointly.

Kluve (2010) offers the most comprehensive overview of evaluation research of European "active labor market programs." Note that this policy is broader than the welfare-to-work programs discussed above—they also include training and subsidized employment—but reemployment courses are reasonably well distinguished. For his meta-analysis, Kluve used 137 evaluations from nineteen European countries. The outcome measures of the studies are not cost-benefit ratios but individual job opportunities, which Kluve simply classifies as "positive," "negative," and "insignificant" owing to a lack of comparable effect sizes. His study provides the familiar picture of mixed results again. Of the evaluations, 55% estimated a positive impact, 21% a negative effect, and 24% an insignificant effect (p. 907). This is true, even if we have a look at the category of "Services and sanctions" (see below), which is closest to what happens in reemployment courses. Here, positive and insignificant results alternate, although it seems at first sight that the positive results are predominant (p. 908) (Table 29.2). The studies on which the Dutch reemployment *Policy Review* was based (see above) are not included in the database.

The purpose of Kluve's meta-analysis is now to trace the variation found in outcomes back to (1) the program type, (2) the evaluation design, (3) institutional features of labor markets, and (4) the economic situation in the country at the time of the study. His findings are more pronounced than those of the American meta-evaluations, which may be caused by the greater dispersion of policies in relation to the welfare-to-work programs.

The program type stands out as an explanatory factor. Kluve distinguishes four types: (1) services and sanctions, (2) training, (3) private sector incentives, and (4) public sector employment. Of these, the subsidized jobs in the public sector score worst, followed by traditional training programs. The results of incentives for the private sector (i.e., wage costs subsidies and grants to start one's own business) are significantly better. The same holds for the "services and sanctions" category, which comprises all measures aimed at enhancing job-search efficiency. These include job-search courses, job clubs, vocational guidance, counseling and monitoring, and sanctions in the case of non-compliance with job-search requirements. Work-first programs (see Lindsay, this volume) are not mentioned explicitly by Kluve but undoubtedly belong to the same category. It is important to note that the effects of these program types are assessed by a much narrower measure (i.e., individual employment probabilities) than the cost-benefit ratios for the various stakeholders in the American studies. However, this limitation does not prevent Kluve from drawing a powerful conclusion: "This implies that modern private sector incentive schemes are the ones that work, and that modern types of 'Services and Sanctions' are particularly effective.

This is certainly good news for the public employment services" (Kluve, 2010, p. 916). It would also have been news for the Dutch politicians referred to at the beginning of this chapter.

Finally, Card, Kluve, and Weber (2010) merged European and American studies in a meta-analysis. They compiled a database of ninety-seven evaluations from twenty-six countries, the vast majority of which were of recent date (the year 2000 or later). Because different types of programs and groups of participants can be distinguished within the studies, the researchers were eventually able to use 199 different impact estimates as their basis. Apart from that, the approach is the same as that of Kluve (2010) and the results are broadly the same. The effects of the active labor market programs vary widely, but within them, subsidized jobs seem to do worse and approaches focused on direct reemployment (job-search assistance and sanctions) seem to do better.

A puzzling result is the finding that the outcome measure matters. These measures vary among the studies in the database, ranging from unemployment duration to employment chances and average quarterly earnings. "Evaluations . . . that measure outcomes based on time in registered unemployment appear to show more positive short-term results than evaluations based on employment and earnings" (Card et al., 2010, p. F475). The authors suggest in a footnote (p. F467) that assignment to a program may induce people to leave the benefit system without moving to a job. This reminds us of a much-cited article by Black, Smith, Burger, and Noel (2003), who found that reemployment programs also may have a deterrent effect, a result that was later repeated by Graversen and Van Ours (2008).

However, an important addition to the previous meta-analyses is that, in a subset of studies, the researchers could also examine the effects in the medium and long term. This results in a significant shift of the estimated outcomes in a positive direction. "Indeed, it appears that many programs with insignificant or even negative impacts after only a year have significantly positive impact estimates after 2 or 3 years. Classroom and on-the-job training programs appear to be particularly likely to yield more favourable medium-term than short-term impact estimates" (Card et al., 2010, p. F475). Therefore some interventions seem to need time to reach their potential. This observation corresponds with a recent evaluation of welfare-to-work programs by Dyke, Heinrich, Mueser, Troske, and Jeon (2006), who monitored more than 130,000 welfare mothers in two American states for a period of 4 years on the basis of administrative data. It also corresponds with the evaluation of the long-term effects of the famous California's Greater Avenues to Independence (GAIN) program (Hotz, Imbens, & Klerman, 2006). Both studies found that more intensive training programs in the long term yield greater and more lasting results than short-term work-first approaches. "These results suggest that the current emphasis on work-first activities is misplaced and argue for a greater emphasis on training activities designed to enhance participants' human capital" (Dyke et al., p. 569). This is in clear contrast with the conclusion of Kluve and the message of the old welfare-to-work studies. What is the cause of this difference? Is it indeed the longer observation period? Can it lie in the quality and implementation of specific programs? Does the fact that the criterion is not job opportunity, but earned income, play a role? Or are the results of Dyke et al. still the effect of a selectivity bias in the data, which in this case could only be combated with a nonexperimental estimation method? No answers can be given. Therefore we can a least say that after all these impact evaluations, much uncertainty about key questions of labor market policy remains.

In view of the above, what is the balance? Here we feel a certain reluctance, because a critical assessment should not be interpreted as a negative judgment of the work conducted by researchers. On the contrary, the methodological quality of many studies is undeniably high. Impact evaluations and the meta-analyses based on them rely increasingly on an impressive amount of data and are commendable for the quality and accuracy of the analysis. Still, we think it is fair to say that the result of all these efforts is disappointing. The outcomes of evaluations vary widely and only few of them have been successfully related to the design of the programs. This is no wonder, since these programs have been described too superficially to achieve this end. Besides, quality differences in the performance are ignored and it remains particularly unclear which mechanisms can and cannot be activated by the programs. In the impact evaluations we examined, the lack of explanations for the results is striking. In cases where effects are established, their causes remain unclear. The average impact evaluation really does not provide any indication as to how the outcomes should be interpreted in terms of the intervention that took place. The usual composition of the studies is a detailed description of the data, the evaluation design and the details of the statistical analysis, followed by a relatively brief account of the results and a minimal interpretation. It is therefore not unreasonable to say that the cost-benefit ratio of this evaluation method is unsatisfactory.

Toward More Realistic Evaluations?

We are not the first to plead for a more substantive focus in the research into the effectiveness of reemployment programs. Also traditional evaluation researchers recognize the importance of more focus on the content of the programs (e.g. Friedlander et al., 1997). Ashworth et al. (2004) even believe that this stage has arrived with the advance of meta-analyses, because "meta-analysis changes the form of the evaluation question from the narrow "Does it work?" to the more useful: "What works best, when and where, and for whom?"" (p. 211). We will not take a position on whether this optimism is justified, but we welcome the formulation. Incidentally, we have noticed that the realistic evaluation question of "What works for whom under what circumstances" is now widely accepted among reemployment researchers as the relevant question to ask (Koning & Heyma, 2009; Koning, 2012).

Let us return to the Dutch example of reemployment policy. As we saw, this policy has been condemned as ineffective on the basis of econometric impact evaluations. Even if we, with all the methodological reservations we have, accept the results of these evaluations, important questions remain unanswered. Where did the reemployment strategy fail? Was it not possible to provide the unemployed with the required skills? Or did this succeed, but have they been unwilling to act on these skills? Or—another possibility—did the social and personal circumstances of the unemployed form a barrier to finding work? These are just some of the problems that can play a role on the supply side. Obviously there are also factors on the demand side. Are employers reluctant to hire long-term unemployed in spite of their improved skills? Or do they want to, but are there simply too many competitors for the positions (and therefore, by implication, not enough jobs)? Or is the basic problem, classically, the inability to match supply and demand in the labor market?

We believe that without including explanatory questions of this type in the evaluations, reemployment research will not improve. Whether this "opening of the black box" can take place in combination with experimental methods (as advocated by Ashworth et al.) or whether these

approaches are incompatible (as argued by Pawson and Tilley) is not our primary concern. It is important to move toward the explanatory mechanisms and demonstrate that this will result in feasible and informative evaluations. Psychologists have shown that it is entirely possible to combine the experimental design with a test of the mediating psychological and behavioral mechanisms like increased self-efficacy and intensified job search (e.g., Eden & Aviram, 1993; Van Hooft & Noordzij, 2009; Van Ryn & Vinokur, 1992; see also Latham, Mawritz, & Locke, this volume; Price & Vinokur, this volume). Whether such a combination is also feasible for social and economic mechanisms and for the role of "contextual" factors remains to be seen. For even though traditional evaluation research has come under heavy criticism, the "realistic" alternative has yet to prove itself.[5]

In this chapter we can only outline a framework for such a realistic evaluation of reemployment policy. To this end, it is particularly the substantive ideas and/or mechanisms (underlying reemployment policy) we want to put forward. Expectations are that empirical research conducted on the basis of this framework will be completed in 2014 (cf. Sol et al., 2011).

Based on the principles of realistic evaluation, we have started a research project in collaboration with four reemployment companies in the Netherlands with the aim of further opening the black box. These four are all commercial (for profit) companies that need to win contracts from local authorities or social security offices with the purpose of making unemployed people find jobs. The policy theory behind this "market" for reemployment services is that companies that are fully ("no cure no pay") or partly ("no cure less pay") paid by result will make the unemployed try harder (and the employers less reluctant), and will develop more effective and innovative methods to achieve this (Struyven & Steurs, 2005). Three of the four companies are leading companies in this reemployment market; the fourth is a small niche player known for its innovative approach.

We have mapped the reemployment counseling strategies used by these companies thoroughly on the basis of documents, interviews, and observations. In particular, the "field visit days" of the researchers appeared to be an important way to truly get in touch with the subject. We subsequently ordered our findings based on the method, recommended by Pawson and Tilley (1997), of the teacher-learner cycle (cf. also Nanninga & Glebbeek, 2011). We have consistently fed reconstructions back to the companies, asking whether we accurately described their approach and their concerns. Is this how you think it works? Are these the thoughts behind your routines? Do these convey the main reemployment mechanisms?

The research has resulted in a conceptual framework for opening the reemployment services black box, consisting of *38 key problems, 34 basic tools, 9 intermediate goals, and 12 core mechanisms* (see Tables 28.1 and 28.2). This framework essentially describes reemployment service and its conceptual basis. We then started an empirical study of the four companies, in which over 1,000 clients in their reemployment courses are carefully monitored for two years. Consultants of the companies record on a weekly basis what has happened with their clients and how they assess their progress—or lack thereof—on a range of important issues (e.g., skills, presentation, motivation, health, and behavior). The conceptual framework was converted into a web-based research tool in which these data are recorded in a standardised way. The starting condition (at intake) and the end result of the courses are accurately recorded as well. It has already become clear that there is a wide variation in the progress and outcomes of the reemployment courses. This variation is especially useful for the researchers to be able to assess the underlying ideas of reemployment services in regard to their validity and scope. After all, there is no "control group" in this research. Realistic evaluation exploits the *within-program variation* in its results to detect the determinants of success and failure, and to test the underlying theories represented by the mechanisms and the ensuing CMO configurations (Pawson & Tilley, 1997, pp. 43, 113).

The *twelve core mechanisms* constitute the essence of the reemployment policy theories. Each of these mechanisms is linked to an *intervention claim*, which succinctly expresses why it is thought that participation in a reemployment course can be beneficial for an unemployed person. The mechanisms are all focused on solving a problem that prevents the unemployed from finding work—or at least on making this problem manageable. This is not always a *sufficient condition* for returning to a job, but it is often a *necessary condition*. In other words, the mechanisms are often directly focused on achieving an *intermediate goal*. Table 28.2 provides an overview of the identified mechanisms and their respective intervention claims.

To arrive at these twelve mechanisms, we combined the inductively gathered materials from the reemployment companies (Table 28.1) with the conceptual framework suggested by Pawson (2003). In his view, policy instruments can be classified according to the level at which they seek to elicit and maintain behavioral change: material, cognitive, social, or emotional. We elaborated on Pawson's suggestion in that we propose a trade-off between feasibility and durability of the intervention. That is, it can be fairly easy to change a person's behavior by offering a material incentive, but his behavior may fall back as soon as the incentive disappears. This is less likely when the intervention has changed the cognitive patterns of this person and even still less likely when his social network or personal identity has changed. In these last instances we can have more confidence in the durability of the intervention, although clearly this level is more difficult to attain. Table 28.3 depicts this trade-off and arranges the interventions by their appropriate level. Using this conceptual tool, it became apparent how the reemployment instruments could be reduced to a more basic set of core mechanisms.

At the material level, finding practical solutions to a host of practical problems stands out as a major activity reemployment staff conducts on behalf of their unemployed clients. Such facilitation can be offered to employers as well, for instance when they are relieved from formal procedures and paperwork. Clearly financial incentives for employers are an important instrument at this level. (Financial compensation can be offered to the unemployed as well, but in the Netherlands this is uncommon.) The threat with sanctions is another (though mostly implicit) option in this range. Information about vacancies and workers should also be placed in this sphere. Although information affects knowing, this is not what psychologists understand by cognitive processes. Providing labor market information is more like a material incentive—it reduces search costs and reveals the gains that can be had by entering into a contract.

Cognition refers to the mental processes involved in perceiving, attending to, remembering, thinking about and making sense of oneself and others (Moskowitz, 2005). A great many reemployment activities are directed at this level. At the surface this means trying to foster new habits (and shaking off old ones) by engaging the unemployed in all kinds of activities, work and nonwork alike. Such activation is meant to improve the physical and mental condition and to make the unemployed accustomed to daily routines and a rhythm of work again. One step deeper the course may

Table 28.1. Key Issues, Intermediate Goals, and Basic Tools of Reemployment Services

Focus	Problem Type	Key Problems	Intermediate Goals	Basic Tools
Supply-side (employees)	A. Personal characteristics unfavorable to the labour market	1. Age (usually too old) 2. Gender (usually female) 3. Ethnicity (nonwestern, non-Dutch background) 4. Occupational disability 5. Past detention 6. Welfare dependency		
	B. Personal and social barriers	7. Unstable housing situation 8. Disrupted family 9. Financial debts 10. Addiction problems 11. Child-care needs 12. Poor integration 13. Poor mental state 14. Sickness (nonoccupational disability)	Eliminating practical barriers	1. Practical support 2. Debt settlement 3. Help with housing 4. Arranging child care 5. Help with transport
			Health promotion	6. Specialist help 7. Help with personal care 8. Fitness
	C. Poor personal fitness	15. Behavioral problems 16. Self-confidence 17. Self-esteem 18. Self-efficacy 19. Motivation (unwillingness) 20. Self-care/hygiene 21. Physical condition	Increasing motivation	9. Financial sanctions 10. Financial incentives 11. Self-esteem/self-confidence 12. Social approval 13. Sense of purpose
			Reorientation	14. Career orientation 15. Career test 16. Competence profile
	D. Lack of labor (market) skills	22. Work experience 23. Employee skills 24. Rhythm of work 25. Language deficiency 26. Application skills 27. Education 28. Social skills 29. Presentation 30. Small network 31. Insufficient insight into talents, skills, desires	Improving job search	17. Search training 18. Application training 19. Presentation training 20. Network training
			Enhancing employee skills	21. "Work First" 22. Traineeship 23. Work placement
			Improving knowledge	24. Schooling/Training 25. Language course 26. Work training program
Demand-side (employers)	E. Negative image of the unemployed	32. Statistical discrimination by employers 33. Prejudices against people on welfare	Compensation	27. Subsidies
	F. Lack of adaptability	34. Insufficient capacity to adjust the work organisation 35. Insufficient knowledge or skills to deal with people with disabilities and/or abnormal behavior	Adaptation	28. Workplace adjustment 29. Adjustment of work processes 30. Job coaching

Table 28.1. Continued

Focus	Problem Type	Key Problems	Intermediate Goals	Basic Tools
Matching supply and demand	G Information problems	36. Employers and unemployed cannot find each other	Finding job openings	31. Networking by staff 32. Job hunting by staff
		37. Employers have no insight into the skills, knowledge, and talents of the unemployed	Matching/ counseling	33. Matching tools 34. (Intensive) counseling
		38. The unemployed lack understanding of the fit between their own wishes/skills and the needs of the employer		

Source: Sol et al., 2011.

try to change the ways of thinking and customary interpretations of the unemployed persons. This holds the promise that their job search will become more self-directed and resistant against the inevitable setbacks of economic life. The self-efficacy principle (see Kanfer & Bufton, this volume; Latham et al., this volume; Price & Vinokur, this volume) stands out as a prime example of such a cognitive mechanism that will mediate (and moderate) the major outcomes of reemployment counseling. The claim that such counseling must seek to change these cognitive processes is at the heart of the psychological interference with this policy domain.[6]

Sociologists point at the social rewards reemployment courses should try to offer to their clients. Obtaining social approval can be regarded as a fundamental human desire, on equal footing with achieving economic goals (Brennan & Pettit, 2004; Lindenberg, 2001). Changing the sources and content of social approval can therefore be seen as a powerful but challenging course of action. To be sure, many reemployment courses make use of their social context and try to create an atmosphere in which participants support and stimulate each other and get motivated by social rewards. It is far more difficult, however, to maintain this influence outside the course, as participants fall back on their existing social networks. A more enduring effect would be realized if these existing networks could be permanently affected too, but this is only seldom within the reach of reemployment services. (Possibly, the effort of coaching on the job qualifies for such an influence.)

The most durable effect is obtained when the emotional level is reached, that is when the desired behavior is firmly rooted in a person's identity or personality. Usually this can be secured only by socialization processes, such as those that take place in childhood or when entering an occupation. It may be too ambitious for reemployment counseling to aim for this level, and we might leave this cell empty accordingly. Reading the chapter by Price and Vinokur (this volume), we nevertheless presume that self-efficacy training may qualify as a candidate. Thus in Table 28.3 we provided for its cautious inclusion within brackets.

It is unnecessary to discuss all these mechanisms here at length. Three illustrations will suffice to point out that it will be instructive to put these mechanisms at the heart of evaluation efforts. Only through considering the workings of these kinds of mechanisms will we be able to understand the limits and possibilities of reemployment policies.

Take the *facilitation mechanism*. Unemployed persons who are at a great distance from the labor market are often confronted with multiple problems, such as a combination of addiction, debts, and a chaotic domestic life. These can have an obstructing effect on finding a job. The barriers are reinforced by the fact that the infrastructure that provides services in these areas is fragmented, confusing, and inaccessible to the unemployed. Many reemployment professionals work from the assumption that these barriers should be removed before entry into a job can be an option. Thus we find these professionals busy arranging all sorts of practical matters for their clients. An interesting question for evaluation poses itself almost immediately: Can professionals really succeed in removing these barriers? And if so, does this indeed improve the job chances of the unemployed?

Table 28.2. Twelve Core Mechanisms in Reemployment with Their Corresponding Intervention Claims

Reference Point	Mechanism	Intervention Claim
Supply side	Facilitation mechanism	"Frontline staff are often able to provide solutions for practical problems that obstruct the reemployment of an unemployed person."
	Sanctioning mechanism ("stick")	"Reemployment programmes are essential to track and control the unemployed who are unwilling to work, so that their cost-benefit balance tips to the side of accepting work."
	Information mechanism	"Obtaining vacancies and revealing individual skills are necessary, because long-term unemployed and their suitable employers are often unable to find each other."
	Job-search skills mechanism	"Many unemployed are unfamiliar with the job search process and have to learn how to look for jobs, how to apply for them, and how to present themselves acceptably to an employer."
	Activation mechanism	"Practical activities not directly focused on a job are an effective and often necessary intermediate step to help the unemployed regain the daily rhythm and energy level required for paid work."
	Goal-orientation mechanism	"It is possible to change the negative or unreal expectations and convictions of the unemployed concerning their chances to find a job, and redirect them towards the necessary steps for obtaining reemployment."
	Coaching mechanism	"By assisting the unemployed person (and his employer and colleagues) in the workplace, adaptation and habituation can occur, making it possible to bridge a gap that cannot be bridged in one step."
	Social approval mechanism	"Since unemployed persons who participate in a re-employment course receive positive feedback from colleagues and supervisors for the first time in years, they (re)discover that going to work is an indispensable way to fulfil their social needs."
	Self-efficacy mechanism	"It is possible to break the negative self-image and low self-esteem of the unemployed person, and foster a sense of competence that guards against setbacks and helps to persist in the job search process."
Demand side	Compensation mechanism ("carrot")	"The long-term unemployed are hampered by a lack of productivity that can be compensated by providing a financial subsidy to the employer."
	Trust mechanism	"Reemployment consultants know how to build a good relationship with employers by providing them with expert and honest advice, making them receptive to their advocacy for the unemployed."
Focused on matching supply and demand	Matching mechanism	"Establishing direct links between employers and the unemployed is an effective way to adjust their preferences and to remove their mutual ignorance and fear."

Source: Sol et al., 2011

Second, the *job-search-skills mechanism*. Although reemployment programs are not training programs,[7] almost all of them try to offer learning experiences to the participants. This is because the programs seek to effect a change in behavior. Their aim is to teach the unemployed certain behaviors and to make them refrain from others. This change in behavior has a cognitive component (self-awareness, reorientation, new knowledge and skills) and a routine component (breaking off habits and habituation). Many reemployment companies believe that group training programs provide an appropriate

Table 28.3 Focus and Level of Intervention of the Twelve Core Mechanisms for Reemployment

Level of intervention	Supply-side	Demand-side
Material	• Compensation • Facilitation • Information • Matching • Sanctioning	• Compensation • Facilitation • Information • Matching
Cognitive	• Job search skills • Activation • Goal orientation • Self efficacy • Coaching	• Trust • Coaching
Social	• Social approval • [Coaching]	
Emotional	• [Self efficacy]	

Durability

context for this. By working in groups the unemployed learn (again) how to keep appointments and cooperate with others. Getting and giving feedback is also an important component of the learning mechanism. Until now, evaluations have given us little insight in whether such learning really takes place in reemployment courses. This is all the more important as learning goals should be distinguished from performance goals (cf. Latham et al., this volume; Van Hooft, this volume). Van Hooft and Noordzij (2009) claim that in the standard practice of reemployment counselling, performance goals and results-oriented guiding techniques come to override learning goals (p. 1588). If this claim is correct, it may offer an interesting explanation for the alleged lack of success of Dutch reemployment courses.

As is shown by the tables, the majority of mechanisms concern the supply side of the labor market. That is because most reemployment activities try to enhance the employability of the unemployed. However, reemployment activities can be directed toward the demand side as well. The *trust mechanism* is an instance of this. Employers have difficulties in judging the individual qualities of unemployed persons and they will therefore resort to prejudices or statistical discrimination. This is not surprising, since they do not like taking risks with their personnel and want to feel comfortable about whom they take in. The long-term unemployed are

often unable to get rid of their stigma on their own. They need someone to mediate and/or put in a good word for them. When reemployment professionals gain the confidence of the employers, they may be able to perform this classic intermediary role.

Taken together, the twelve mechanisms of Table 28.2 constitute the claim of reemployment policy. By making them explicit, we have opened up the black box of these policies to a considerable degree. The mechanisms may provide a checklist to practitioners, like the management and staff of reemployment companies, for evaluating their own practices and identifying the strong and weak points in their courses (see also Box 1). To scientific evaluators they convey the message that we would like to know if and when these mechanisms occur in order to be able to explain the successes and failures of reemployment programs.

The fact that most mechanisms focus on *intermediate* goals has important implications for the evaluation of their effectiveness. For example, a client can be made employable (intermediate goal) but not be able to find employment (ultimate goal) simply because there are no vacancies. Then, despite the disappointing outcome, a number of mechanisms still appear to have worked in accordance with the theory. Thus "no result" does not mean that the policy theory should be automatically rejected but rather that one or more critical conditions for achieving the ultimate goal were lacking

(Glebbeek, 2005; Pawson & Tilley, 1997). Both the relationships between intervention and intermediate goals, and those between intermediate and ultimate goals, are in other words context-dependent. Thus to find the appropriate *CMO configurations* that specify and improve the policy theory, intermediate goals should be taken into account. Impact evaluations that look only at the ultimate goal and ignore the intermediate process teach us little about whether or not mechanisms work and do not further our knowledge of reemployment policies. It is our claim and expectation that an evaluation of the mechanisms identified above will provide us with the necessary progress.

In the end, not only the workings of the mechanisms but also their necessary and supportive conditions should be part of the intervention theory. Thus the "C" for "context" in realistic evaluation is identical to what psychologists call moderators. Latham, Mawritz, and Locke (this volume) identified five moderators for the goal-orientation mechanism: ability, commitment, feedback, complexity, and situational variables (among which the condition of the economy). Accordingly all twelve core mechanisms will have their specific moderators—that is, conditions that can only be discovered when evaluation research is directed to their functioning.

One condition stands out, however: *There must be jobs around to fill.* We have already noticed that reemployment services are mainly oriented toward the supply side of the labor market. This is in accordance with the dominant policy orientation since the 1980s, which entailed a shift from macroeconomic demand-management to the behavior and institutions of the supply side. For critics of this policy, this shift marks the transition from "full employment" to "full employability" (Mitchell & Muysken, 2008). The latter is described as a digression "forcing unemployed individuals into a relentless succession of training programs designed to address deficiencies in skills and character" (p. 4). To these critics the denounced failure of the Dutch reemployment policy will therefore come as no surprise. "Most welfare-to-work schemes are little more than a cruel joke, precisely because there is no job for most welfare leavers" (Mitchell & Muysken, p. 20).[8]

Conclusion

Reemployment counseling has definitively become a field of applied psychology. Many courses offered to the unemployed make use of insights from cognitive psychology and social learning theory,

with varying degrees of professionalism. This certainly holds true for the Netherlands (cf. Groothoff et al., 2008), where, since the 1990s, an extensive practice of reemployment services has developed.

Dutch reemployment policy has been judged to be ineffective on the basis of evaluation studies. The added value ("net effectiveness") was alleged to be small. This national experience is not only interesting in itself but also shows that scientific evaluations matter. Based on the negative verdict, funding for reemployment services in the Netherlands has been reduced.

These evaluations had therefore better be right. In this chapter, we have discussed the main evaluation study in more detail and we can say that technically speaking it was conducted in a state-of-the-art fashion. The econometric arsenal of nonexperimental research was widely and judiciously placed in position. Nevertheless, uncertainties are associated with this study and similar ones. To find a comparison group, coincidences in the data must be used, and the correction for selectivity requires disputable assumptions. The prevailing opinion in the field is that nonexperimental estimates can sometimes be way off the mark. As a consequence, we never know whether or not we are dealing with such a case. Moreover, the irony of the situation remains: The Dutch labor market and benefit dependency developed favorably in the period involved. As a colleague of ours once put it: "So, we must have done *something* right!?"

This chapter has provided a picture of the three main approaches to impact evaluation. We think the reader now will have a good idea of what these approaches are about. When it comes to solely determining added value in an undisputed manner, the experimental approach has the best credentials. No one disputes that a randomized controlled trial is superior in terms of internal validity. But this chapter has sought to make clear that this in itself is not sufficient. We cannot be satisfied with the results of experimental evaluations. The meta-analyses show that the experiments have only shifted the problem: the uncertainty is now at the level of conflicting studies. Moreover, they teach us little about the content and quality of reemployment programs, and as a result provide few suggestions for improvement. We believe that continuing along this path will not take us much further.

In the spirit of realistic evaluation, we have emphasized that it is vital to include the guiding ideas behind reemployment services in the evaluations. We certainly do not rule out that this can be combined

Box 1. Advice for Reemployment Practitioners

The Dutch experience has shown that reemployment services are vulnerable to external evaluations. Many practitioners were confident about the successes of their approach. But when the econometricians came around, they had no convincing evidence to show. It is important, therefore, that reemployment practitioners build their own evaluation culture and provide themselves with facts and figures that lend support to their claims.

In the evidence-based policy framework, four levels of recognition for interventions are often distinguished: (1) theoretically sound, (2) probable effectiveness, (3) established effectiveness, and (4) established cost-effectiveness. The case for the first two levels can be made by reemployment practitioners themselves provided that their approach has been accurately described and documented. Establishing credibility is important not only to politicians and evaluation researchers but also the clients and commissioners of reemployment services.

In brief, we offer the following suggestions:
- Try to be a learning organization. Invest in your own proof of effectiveness. Do not depend only on external evaluations.
- Be explicit about the theory behind your approach. Try to formulate this theory as a set of principal mechanisms and main supportive conditions.
- Consider each case as a test of your theory. After each course, make sure to document why it was a success or why it has failed. At regular intervals, evaluate what these successes and failures imply for your theory.
- Don't be reluctant to put your approach to the test in a randomized controlled trial. Make sure, however, that the trial provides for the measurement of mediating (explanatory) mechanisms and the fulfilment of theoretically required, necessary conditions. In short, the trial should be a fair application of your intervention theory.

---

with an experimental approach—with sufficient time, resources and inspiration, a "best of both worlds" can probably be achieved (cf. Van der Knaap et al., 2008). However, the priority is an approach that enables an *explanation* of the findings. Because if we—for the sake of argument—accept the Dutch evaluation and conclude that reemployment policy has led to nothing, we need to know where in the chain it went wrong. Did reemployment programs fail because of a difficult labor market or is it an illusion to think that you can change people's behaviour effectively through a course? Have we been unable to gain the trust of employers or are the motivation and discipline of the unemployed demonstrably inadequate? And which barriers are most likely to occur under what labor market conditions?

In short, what is needed is to test the underlying ideas (mechanisms) of a policy. This way, evaluation will become more like explanatory research that is concerned with scientific theories (Vaessen & Leeuw, 2010). In the last section we have shown what kind of ideas are at stake in this field, and we have proposed a set of mechanisms by which reemployment can be characterized. We realize that this makes our contribution highly programmatic in nature. Time and experience will tell whether

"breaking open the black box" of reemployment services leads to valuable insights.

Notes

1. In the Netherlands reemployment programs generally take the form of 'trajectories' or "courses" consisting of several phases: intake, diagnosis, orientation, preparation of a personal action plan, teaching employability skills, job-search assistance, and interview training and, when successful, placement and job coaching.
2. Quotations are from *De Volkskrant*, January 30, April 3, and November 20, 2008.
3. This is sometimes called the *quasiexperimental design*, but because of the need to somehow correct for nonrandomization, it definitively belongs to the nonexperimental category.
4. Note that this last viewpoint accounts for the macro-level effects we recognized in the second section of this chapter.
5. See Pawson and Manzano-Santaella (2012) for a critical appraisal of allegedly "realistic" evaluations. For theory-based evaluations in general, a preliminary balance was drawn by Weiss (1997) and more recently by Coryn, Noakes, Westine, and Schröter (2011).
6. This claim was made very explicit by Eden and Aviram (1993): "There is much that applied psychologists can do for the unemployed. . . . Helping people to regain their GSE [= general self-efficacy] is help of the noblest kind and is ultimately the most effective, because it truly helps people to help themselves" (p. 359).
7. Following established practice, we distinguish labor market schooling and training from reemployment services.

However, they are part of the wider category of active labor market programs (cf. Kluve, 2010).

8. The negative evaluation of reemployment policy has not changed the overall commitment of the Dutch government to supply-side measures. In the proposed reform on dismissal law (2013), a large role is again reserved for reemployment services.

References

Ashworth, K., Cebulla, A., Greenberg, D., & Walker, R. (2004). Meta-evaluation: Discovering what works best in welfare provision. *Evaluation, 10*(2), 193–216.

Black, D. A., Smith, J. A., Berger, M. C., & Noel, B. J. (2003). Is the threat of reemployment services more effective than the services themselves? Evidence from random assignment in the UI system. *American Economic Review, 93*(4), 1313–1327.

Blundell, R., Costa Dias, M., Meghir, C., & Van Reenen, J. (2004). Evaluating the employment impact of a mandatory job search program. *Journal of the European Economic Association, 2*(4), 569–606.

Borghans, L. (2008). Tijd voor maatwerk in arbeidsmarktbeleid [It's time for customisation in labour market policy]. *Economisch Statistische Berichten, 93*(4533S), 4–9.

Brennan, G., & Pettit, P. (2004). *The economy of esteem. An essay on civil and political society.* Oxford, UK: Oxford University Press.

Burtless, G. (1995). The case for randomized field trials in economic and policy research, *Journal of Economic Perspectives, 9*(2), 63–84.

Bushway, S., Johnson, B. D., & Slocum, L. A. (2007). Is the magic still there? The use of the Heckman two-step correction for selection bias in criminology. *Journal of Quantitative Criminology, 23*(2), 151–178.

Cahuc, P., & Le Barbanchon, T. (2010). Labor market policy evaluation in equilibrium: Some lessons of the job search and matching model. *Labour Economics, 17*(1), 196–205.

Card, D., Kluve, J., & Weber, A. (2010). Active labour market policy evaluations: A meta-analysis. *The Economic Journal, 120*(548), F452–F477.

Chen, H. T. (1990). *Theory-driven evaluations.* Newbury Park, CA: Sage.

Committee on the Future of Labour Market Policy (2001). *Aan de slag. Eindrapport van de werkgroep Toekomst van het arbeidsmarktbeleid* [Final report of the committee on the future of labour market policy]. The Hague, The Netherlands: Ministry of Social Affairs and Employment (SZW).

Coryn, C. L. S., Noakes, L. A., Westine, C. D., & Schröter, D. C. (2011). A systematic review of theory-driven evaluation practice from 1990 to 2009. *American Journal of Evaluation, 32*(2), 199–226.

De Beer, P. T. (2001). Beoordeling van evaluatie-onderzoeken [An assessment of evaluation studies]. Appendix 4. In *Committee on the future of labour market policy.* The Hague, The Netherlands: Ministry of Social Affairs and Employment (SZW).

De Koning, J. (2001). Aggregate impact analysis of active labour market policy. A literature review. *International Journal of Manpower, 22*(8), 707–735.

De Koning, J. (2003). Wat niet weet, wat niet deert: over de decentralisatie en uitbesteding van het arbeidsmarktbeleid [If you don't know, it does not hurt: about the decentralization and outsourcing of labour market policy]. Inaugural lecture, Erasmus University. Rotterdam: SEOR.

Dyke, A., Heinrich, C. J., Mueser, P. R., Troske, K. R., & Jeon, K. S. (2006). The effects of welfare-to-work program activities on labor market outcomes. *Journal of Labor Economics, 24*(3), 567–607.

Eden, D., & Aviram, A. (1993). Self-efficacy training to speed reemployment: Helping people to help themselves. *Journal of Applied Psychology, 78*(3), 352–360.

Friedlander, D., Greenberg, D. H., & Robins, P. K. (1997). Evaluating government training programs for the economically disadvantaged. *Journal of Economic Literature, 35*(4), 1809–1855.

Gelderblom, A., & De Koning, J. (2007). *Effecten van "zachte" kenmerken op de reïntegratie van de WWB, WW en AO populatie: een literatuurstudie* [Effects of "soft" characteristics on the re-employment chances of persons on unemployment, welfare and disability benefits: A literature review]. Rotterdam: SEOR.

Glazerman, S., Levy, D. M., & Myers, D. (2003). Nonexperimental versus experimental estimates of earnings impacts. *Annals of the American Academy of Political and Social Science, 589,* 63–93.

Glebbeek, A. C. (2005). De onrealistische evaluatie van arbeidsmarktbeleid [The unrealistic evaluation of labour market policy]. *Tijdschrift voor Arbeidsvraagstukken, 21*(1), 38–48.

Graversen, B. K., & Van Ours, J. C. (2008). How to help unemployed find jobs quickly: Experimental evidence from a mandatory activation program. *Journal of Public Economics, 92*(10–11), 2020–2035.

Greenberg, D., & Cebulla, A. (2008). The cost-effectiveness of welfare-to-work programs: A meta-analysis. *Public Budgeting & Finance, 28*(2), 112–145.

Greenberg, D., Deitch, V., & Hamilton, G. (2010). A synthesis of random assignment benefit-cost studies of welfare-to-work programs. *Journal of Benefit-Cost Analysis, 1*(1), 1–28.

Groot, I., De Graaf-Zijl, M., Hop, P., Kok, L., Fermin, B., Ooms, D., & Zwinkels, W. (2008). *De lange weg naar werk. Beleid voor langdurig uitkeringsgerechtigden in de WW en de WWB* [It's a long road to a job. Dutch policies for long-term unemployment and welfare beneficiaries]. The Hague: The Council for Work and Income (RWI).

Groothoff, J. W., Brouwer, S., Bakker, R. H., Overweg, K., Schellekens, J., Abma, F., . . . Pierik, B. (2008). *BIMRA: Beoordelen van interventies en meetinstrumenten bij reïntegratie naar arbeid, eindrapportage* [BIMRA: Assessment of interventions and measuring instruments for re-employment counselling]. Groningen: University of Groningen/UMCG.

Heckman, J. J. (1979). Sample selection bias as a specification error. *Econometrica, 47*(1): 153–161.

Hollister, R. G. (2008). The role of random assignment in social policy research. *Journal of Policy Analysis and Management, 27*(2), 402–409.

Hotz, V. J., Imbens, G. W., & Klerman, J. A. (2006). Evaluating the differential effects of alternative welfare-to-work training components: A reanalysis of the California GAIN program. *Journal of Labor Economics, 24*(3), 521–566.

Kluve, J. (2010). The effectiveness of European active labor market programs. *Labour Economics, 17*(6), 904–918.

Koning, P. (2012). Leren re-integreren [Learning how to re-employ]. *TPEdigitaal, 6*(2), 28–43.

Koning, P., & Heyma, A. (2009). Aansturing van klantmanagers voor een effectief re-integratiebeleid [Caseworkers and the effectiveness of active labour market policies]. *Tijdschrift voor Arbeidsvraagstukken, 25*(4), 440–455.

Lindenberg, S. M. (2001). Intrinsic motivation in a new light. *Kyklos, 54*(2–3), 317–342.

Meyer, B. D. (1995). Lessons from the U.S. unemployment insurance experiments. *Journal of Economic Literature, 33*(1), 91–131.

Ministry of Social Affairs and Employment (2008). *Beleidsdoorlichting re-integratie* [Re-employment policy review]. The Hague: Ministry of Social Affairs and Employment (SZW).

Mitchell, W., & Muysken, J. (2008). *Full employment abandoned. Shifting sands and policy failures.* Cheltenham, UK: Edward Elgar.

Moskowitz, G. B. (2005). *Social cognition. Understanding self and others.* New York: Guilford Press.

Mosley, H., & Sol, E. (2001). Evaluation of active labour market policies and trends in implementation regimes. In J. de Koning & H. Mosley (Eds.), *Active labour market policy and unemployment* (pp. 163–178). Cheltenham, UK: Edward Elgar.

Nanninga, M., & Glebbeek, A. C. (2011). Employing the teacher-learner cycle in realistic evaluation: A case study of the social benefits of young people's playing fields. *Evaluation, 17*(1), 73–87.

Oakley, A., Strange, V., Toroyan, T., Wiggins, M., Roberts, I., & Stephenson, J. (2003). Using random allocation to evaluate social interventions: Three recent U.K. examples. *Annals of the American Academy of Political and Social Science, 589,* 170–189.

Pawson, R. (2003). Nothing as practical as a good theory. *Evaluation, 9*(4), 471–490.

Pawson, R., & Manzano-Santaella, A. (2012). A realist diagnostic workshop. *Evaluation, 18*(2), 176–191.

Pawson, R., & Tilley, N. (1997). *Realistic evaluation.* London, UK: Sage.

Pirog, M. A., Buffardi, A. L., Chrisinger, C. K., Singh, P., & Briney, J. (2009). Are the alternatives to randomized assignment nearly as good? Statistical corrections to nonrandomized evaluations. *Journal of Policy Analysis and Management, 28*(1), 169–172.

Sol, C. C. A. M., Glebbeek, A. C., Edzes, A. J. E., Busschers, I., De Bok, H. I., Engelsman, J. S., & Nysten, C. E. R. (2011). *"Fit or unfit." Naar expliciete re-integratietheorieën* ["Fit or unfit." Towards explicit re-employment theories]. RVO-5. Amsterdam: University of Amsterdam.

Struyven, L., & Steurs, G. (2005). Design and redesign of a quasi-market for the reintegration of jobseekers: Empirical evidence from Australia and the Netherlands. *Journal of European Social Policy, 15*(3), 211–229.

Vaessen, J., & Leeuw, F. L. (Eds.). (2010). *Mind the gap. Perspectives on policy evaluation and the social sciences.* New Brunswick, NJ: Transaction.

Van der Knaap, L. M., Leeuw, F. L., Bogaerts, S., & Nijssen, L. T. J. (2008). Combining Campbell standards and the realist evaluation approach: The best of two worlds? *American Journal of Evaluation, 29*(1), 48–57.

Van Hooft, E. A. J., & Noordzij, G. (2009). The effects of goal orientation on job search and reemployment: A field experiment among unemployed job seekers. *Journal of Applied Psychology, 94*(6), 1581–1590.

Van Ryn, M., & Vinokur, A. M. (1992). How did it work? An examination of the mechanisms through which an intervention for the unemployed promoted job-search behavior. *American Journal of Community Psychology, 20*(5), 577–597.

Weiss, C. H. (1997). How can theory-based evaluation make greater headway? *Evaluation Review, 21*(4), 501–524.

Wildavsky, A. B. (1979). *Speaking truth to power: The art and craft of policy analysis.* Boston: Little, Brown.

Winship, C., & Mare, R. D. (1992). Models for sample selection bias. *Annual Review of Sociology, 18,* 327–350.

Wotschack, P., Glebbeek, A. C., & Wittek, R. P. M. (2013). Strong boundary control, weak boundary control, and tailor made solutions. The role of household governance structures in work-family time allocation and mismatch. Manuscript under review. Berlin: Social Science Research Center (WZB).

Job Loss: Outplacement Programs

William A. Borgen *and* Lee D. Butterfield

Abstract

Outplacement counseling (OPC) is a form of career counseling that organizations offer to displaced workers to help them deal with job loss, develop job search skills, and successfully transition back into employment. Despite the fact this is a multimillion-dollar business, little is known about its effectiveness, whose best interests are being served (the organization's or the individual recipient's), and the measures of success being used. This chapter reviews the history of outplacement; typical services offered by OPC firms; measures of success; individual characteristics that increase participation in and success with OPC; what helps, hinders, or would have helped individual recipients; challenges related to OPC; directions for future outplacement counseling research; where OPC stands today; and what is needed for OPC to help the vulnerable population it is intended to serve.

Key Words: outplacement counseling, career counseling, counseling displaced workers, history of outplacement counseling, outplacement counseling research

The History of Outplacement Counseling

Outplacement counseling (OPC) is a specialized form of career counseling offered to employees when an employer has decided to terminate an employee for cause or poor fit or due to a downsizing, merger, closure, or restructuring. It is "a process of helping employees who have been terminated or whose jobs have been eliminated, to face their job loss with renewed self-confidence, to learn effective job search strategies and techniques, and to conduct a successful job search campaign" (Pickman, 1994, p. 1). It is an interesting area because it spans the worlds and academic disciplines of both business and counseling psychology. From the organization's perspective, the decision to offer OPC to terminated employees is a business one intended to help management "deal with the sensitive and often traumatic problem of the employee who must be released or the staff that must be reduced" (Mirabile, 1985, p. 40). It also has the potential to result in considerable cost savings for the organization (Challenger, 2005). From the individual

OPC recipient's perspective, it is a service that is expected to offer psychological support, targeted skills training, and help in finding a new job (Butterfield & Borgen, 2005; Spears, Buhrfeind, & Pennebaker, 1994).

OPC began in the 1960s, although who should be credited with its origins is unclear (Pickman, 1994). What is clear is that it was initially offered only to executives and high-level professionals as a way of minimizing wrongful dismissal lawsuits. Organizations feared that the longer an executive was out of work, the greater the likelihood of a lawsuit (Burdett, 1988). More recently OPC has been provided in order to minimize costly disruptions within an organization by facilitating a smooth transition process, reducing lawsuits and grievances, increasing the morale of the remaining employees, and maintaining the organization's public image as a caring, ethical, and socially responsible employer (Aquilanti & Leroux, 1999; Burdett, 1988; Mirabile, 1985; Wooten, 1996). A 2009 survey by the British Columbia Human Resources Management

Association (HRMA) found that employers are using OPC services to assist/support management, mitigate the possibility of legal action, minimize the negative effect on remaining staff, demonstrate corporate responsibility, and assist the terminated employee (HRMA, 2009). Beugre (1998) suggests that, when workers are displaced because of a major workplace change or business reengineering initiative, the provision of OPC services is a distributive justice issue. He cautions that it is not simply a matter of providing OPC services to terminated employees but also of ensuring that the process and procedures leading to the decision and resulting action of dismissal are seen as fair by employees and those who leave the organization.

The growth of OPC was slow until the 1970s, when OPC services were first offered to middle management, technical professionals, and eventually clerical and blue-collar workers (Neinas, 1987; Pickman, 1994). Outplacement services then exploded in the 1980s and 1990s with the advent of massive corporate downsizings, mergers, acquisitions, globalization, increased competition, and falling stock prices as well as changes in legislation, the employment environment, social conditions, the economy, and corporate social responsibility. Pickman also reported that the OPC industry had grown into a $750 million (US) industry by the early 1990s. Yet as Wooten (1996) has pointed out, relatively little is known about it.

The 2009 HRMA survey of 211 organizations in western Canada found that 41% of organizations planned reductions in staff because of decreases in the volume of business or in order to decrease overall operating costs. Respondents reported that they planned to offer OPC services to all levels of staff, although it continues to remain more common at the executive and management levels. Nearly a quarter of respondents (24%) stated they planned to offer OPC services to more levels of staff in the future. These data and the ongoing pressure that organizations are experiencing to remain competitive, reduce costs, and maximize shareholder returns make it likely that OPC services will continue to be needed now and in the future. Strewler (1997) echoes this sentiment in her review of the evolution of outplacement support centers in the United States; these range from corporate-specific career centers to more centralized multicorporate career centers that are better able to address a greater spectrum of needs across the employment-unemployment-employment transition.

There is evidence that OPC services are useful. Tzafrir and colleagues (2006) conducted a study with workers who were being downsized in a large metalwork factory in Israel. Management, with the cooperation of unions and government, offered an extensive job counseling and retraining program. The purpose of the study was to assess how the implementation of the program would affect the responses of employees who were being laid off and those who remained. The dependent variable in the study was termed *effective response*, which included measures of anxiety and present feelings. Intervening variables were labeled as *individual's cost* and included economic cost, cost of a new job, and quality-of-life cost. Independent variables included a range of factors that together were described as *worker employability*. The study found that the job counseling and training programs lowered dismissed workers' level of anxiety irrespective of age, education, preparation, and work orientation.

Services Offered by a Typical OPC Firm

The components provided by OPC programs have been outlined by many authors over several years. Some have provided general descriptions of the components of OPC programs. Pickman (1994) suggests that a comprehensive OPC program begins by counseling the person who has been terminated on how to deal with the emotional impact of job loss. Later, OPC provides career assessment and helps the client develop his or her job-search materials (such as a resumé, cover letter, etc.). Then interview skills training is offered, along with help in developing marketing strategies and instructing clients about the effectiveness of job-search techniques (e.g., networking, responding to newspaper ads, etc.). Pickman also mentions that coaching is offered related to the use of executive search or job placement agencies; often office space, secretarial services, and library resources are made available to the client. Throughout the process the OPC consultant offers support and encouragement. Not mentioned by Pickman is help with salary negotiations at the point when a position is offered to the client. Aquilanti and Leroux (1999) indicate that services "vary from firm to firm depending on the programs that are purchased by the employer. Some programs offer in-depth one-on-one counseling with psychological assessment, while others offer rudimentary counseling with a concentration on job search techniques" (p. 179). These authors reviewed four OPC-related models and their elements. The models discussed were (1) Latack and Dozier's

(1996) Career Growth Model, (2) Mirabile's (1985) Stages of Transition Counseling Model, (3) Kirk's (1994) Holistic Outplacement Model, and (4) the Aquilanti Integrated Model (AIM) (1999).

The Career Growth Model (Latack & Dozier, 1996) is described as consisting of three components, including the individual's characteristics, the individual's environment, and the individual's transition process. Individual factors that are seen to reduce stress and sustain motivation include level of job satisfaction, being in midcareer, and staying active. The two most important environmental factors are financial issues and level of support from colleagues, friends, and family. Transition issues viewed as being salient are the length of time of unemployment and the person's success in being able to move beyond initial grief and loss reactions. In this model, counselors help clients manage their stress, with the aim of keeping it at a moderate level.

The Stages of Transition Counseling Model (Mirabile, 1985) involves five stages: (1) comfort, (2) reflection, (3) clarification, (4) direction, and (5) perspective shift. Counselors provide support, encouragement, and assistance as participants progress through the stages of the model, but as Aquilanti and Leroux (1999) point out, few specifics are provided regarding the strategies or tools that would be effective for the counselor to use. The Holistic Outplacement Model (Kirk, 1994) involves three elements: (1) regaining equilibrium, (2) career development, and (3) job hunting. The counselor's role in this model is described as being the "empathetic listener" (p. 180) and as helping clients to regain their equilibrium. As the clients progress through the model, the counselors assist them by using a number of interventions—such as small group discussions, role plays, and stress-reducing exercises—with the aim of keeping stress at more acceptable levels, managing financial concerns, and building self-esteem. As with the other two models, the specifics regarding how the counselor assists clients in moving from reacting to job loss to effectively engaging in job search are not provided.

Based on what they viewed as theoretical or practical gaps in previously developed models, Aquilanti and Leroux (1999) also introduced the Aquilanti Integrated Model of Outplacement (AIM). This model utilizes Super's Life Span Theory, Kübler-Ross's Grief Theory, and Parker and Lewis's Transition Cycle Model. The Aquilanti Integrated Model consists of four phases: (1) loss, grieving, and transition; (2) personal development; (3) job search; and (4) ongoing counseling and support.

Counselors start their work with clients by creating a trusting, empathic, and safe relationship with them. This is considered a key element in helping clients to be successful in their outplacement process and to reach a level of engagement that will enable them to make further progress toward reemployment. A major role of the counselors is to determine the client's readiness to move forward in the process. After the first phase, the counselors guide clients through a personal development process that consists of assessment, addressing personal stress, and organizing financial planning. Next, a job-search phase is implemented, which consists of the following key elements: (1) informational interviews, (2) resumé preparation, (3) networking, and (4) practicing interview skills. Last, clients are provided with ongoing counseling and support throughout their transition into their new career/ life situation. This is considered to be a critical part of the model, and no specific length of time is designated for this final phase.

Other authors, including Bowers (1997), have outlined a similar range of services in their reviews of OPC. Feldman and Leana (2000) found that most programs included psychologist-assisted counseling, the services of placement consultants, word-processing support (e.g., administrative support to type resumés, application letters, etc.), office support (e.g., office space for the client to use, including a computer, telephone, etc.), and access to computer databases. Gowan and Nassar-McMillan (2001), in focusing on group outplacement services, found that these programs centered around three components: self-awareness activities (individual career assessments, group career assessment feedback sessions, and one-on-one counseling), action-oriented activities (job search workshops and resumé writing workshops), and training activities (enrolling in a job training program).

Kieselbach and colleagues (2009) describe the results of an investigation regarding OPC in Belgium, Italy, Germany, The Netherlands, and Spain. Although there were many results in common across these countries, there were also differences based on the level of understanding and acceptance of outplacement services and the extent to which unemployment was seen as an individual or collective responsibility. The authors found that common elements in outplacement programs included initial sessions to introduce the counselors and the program, group counseling to facilitate the exchange of information regarding effective ways to apply for work, the development of improved resumés, the exchange of information regarding labor market possibilities, individual counseling to establish a framework for understanding each individual along with their strengths and challenges, and practical training related to enhancing job interviewing skills.

Kieselbach and associates (2009) also provide a list of best practices across Belgium, Italy, Germany, The Netherlands, and Spain. First, they suggest that counseling should be initiated early in the process, starting prior to dismissal of employees if possible. In the case of companywide restructuring and downsizing it is particularly important for professionally trained counselors to be involved in the initial communication process with employees regarding what will happen in the company. This can be effective in reducing fear and animosity among employees, reducing the number of rumors that are spread, and providing a foundation for subsequent OPC activities.

Second, Kieselbach and coworkers (2009) suggest that it is important for the OPC service to provide a detailed analysis of the employees' employment-related needs and requirements. This will help to ensure that the service is tailored as much as possible to the needs of each individual. Third, as is suggested in several studies related to unemployment, it is important to offer services to lay the foundation for a systematic approach to job search. This provides employees with a greater sense of control regarding the job search and is a needed component in helping the employee to connect with ongoing reemployment.

Fourth, since most employees in a company that is facing restructuring may want to avoid dismissal and may improve their productivity as a way of warding off job loss, psychological support is vital in facing the prospect of dismissal, coping with it more effectively, and managing the changes that accompany the transition to unemployment.

Fifth, it is important that employees participate in OPC services voluntarily if they are to more fully commit to engage in the process. Kieselbach and colleagues (2009) found this to vary across the five countries they studied. It seemed to work most effectively in settings where the service was viewed as a form of compensation to the employees. They suggest that these services should be a part of a company's corporate social responsibility. Sixth, OPC service providers need to help employees to be active in their job search. This is essential in setting the trajectory for employees engaging in more independent job-search activity after the outplacement service activities have ended.

Seventh, as appropriate, it is helpful for OPC service providers to facilitate experience for employees in temporary positions and/or in seeking further training (Kieselbach et al., 2009).

Eighth, once the layoff takes place, it is important to utilize a variety of strategies to support employees who have lost their jobs. This often requires a level of psychological assistance that goes beyond training in assisting individuals in adjusting to their transition from employment to unemployment.

Ninth, in terms of connecting with reemployment, the authors suggest that it may be important to develop more creative networks of communication to connect employment offers with those who are seeking reemployment. It is also important to assist individuals with their occupational transition once reemployment has occurred.

Finally, Kieselbach and coworkers note that best practice may be compromised for financial reasons. For example, in terms of the type of service provided, often individual counseling is provided only to managers and collective counseling to employees, with mixed results.

Measures of Success for OPC Services

According to a recent review of selected OPC firms' websites and the scholarly literature, there appear to be four primary criteria used to evaluate the success of OPC services: (1) the length of time it takes the displaced worker to find new employment, (2) the percentage of terminated workers who find new employment within a designated period of time; (3) measures of success for OPC consultants; and (4) client satisfaction with the OPC services offered (Davenport, 1984; Feldman & Leana, 2000; Foxman & Polsky, 1990; Luciano, 1996; Wooten, 1996). These criteria strike us as being insufficient for several reasons. First, there is an inherent conflict of interest between the goals of the organization that hired the OPC firm and the needs of the individual receiving the OPC services (Burdett, 1988), which is discussed in more detail further on in this chapter. Fast reemployment of the terminated worker serves the interests of the organization that hires the OPC firm, since it reduces the fees owing to the OPC firm as well as the likelihood of a lawsuit. However, the clients receiving OPC services are often best served by taking time to contemplate future goals, both personal and professional, assessing the need for retraining, and/or positioning themselves for the *right* new job that meets those goals, not just *any* job (see also Virick & McKee-Ryan, this volume). Second, the OPC firm actually has two clients: the hiring organization and the displaced worker. The definitions of success appear to deal only with the measures benefiting the organization, but they do not address the criteria for evaluating success as it pertains to the individual recipient. Third, the literature has not established a relationship between the speed of acquiring a new job and individual client satisfaction with the OPC services received. Indeed, Davenport (1984) states:

> Time pressures dictate that outplacement services produce results, that is, new employment, quickly. This attitude, coupled with the terminee's wish to put the termination in the past, encourages abbreviated attention to grief issues, exploration, and preventive behavioral changes and focuses instead on task-oriented matters—resumé writing, interviewing skills, contacts with employers, and so forth. (p. 189)

Finally, these measures do not address the satisfaction of the displaced worker in the new job, long-range performance in that job, or worker adjustment (Davenport, 1984). These measures of success and the challenges associated with them are discussed in more detail next.

Other measures of success include individual OPC clients' satisfaction with the services provided by the OPC firm. Feldman and Leana (2000) studied individual OPC clients' satisfaction with the services provided using both quantitative and open-ended questions to gather data about their experiences from a purposive sample, finding that 75% of the 517 senior managers who participated were either satisfied or very satisfied with the services they received. However, the investigators also reported that 36% of participants reported accepting new jobs at a lower hierarchical level than the one they held at the time they were terminated; 44% of participants reported receiving less pay in their new jobs; 87% reported skill underutilization in their new jobs; and 56% reported being underemployed. The authors discussed the six job outcomes commonly related to underemployment: (1) job satisfaction, (2) organizational commitment, (3) fulfillment of psychological contracts, (4) organizational trust, (5) careerist attitudes towards work ("the belief that one does not get ahead mainly on the basis of merit" [p. 68]), and (6) continued job-hunting behavior. The researchers found that participants reported decreased job satisfaction and organizational commitment in their new positions compared with their previous positions; lower trust, less commitment to their careers, and increased cynicism towards employers due to breaches of the psychological employment contracts; and increased job-hunting activities resulting in voluntarily leaving their new jobs. As Feldman and Leana point out, this activity is often motivated both by a desire for more rewarding work and fear that problems arising in the early months of a new job may not be resolved.

A trend appears to be emerging with respect to employment following participation in OPC services. As already indicated, Feldman and Leana (2000) reported that the majority of individuals who participated in an OPC process were satisfied. They also suggested, however, that the participants may have become reemployed in positions with lower salaries—that is, positions where they were underemployed. Other studies, such as that of Gowan and Nassar-McMillan (2001), found no difference in employment rates among participants who had engaged or had not engaged in specific activities in an OPC service. More recently, Kieselbach and associates (2009) found that people who had participated in OPC services tended to take longer to find employment. This was further elucidated by Westaby (2004), who found that "displaced managers and executives participating in programs that demonstrated higher levels of outplacement support took more time to find reemployment, had greater likelihood of reemployment, and had higher salaries in new jobs than individuals participating in programs with lower levels of outplacement support" (p. 19). Taken together, these studies suggest that time to reemployment may not be a simple variable to measure. Older studies of programs where the focus may have been on quick rather than sustainable reemployment, may have used a different yardstick to consider the success of OPC programs.

Luciano's (1996) study used as the measure of success how valuable the participants found each of 11 OPC services offered. The results were in the form of participant rankings of the OPC services, from most valuable to least valuable, as follows: meeting with a consultant, word processing support, support or focus groups, research books and materials, computerized databases, job posting, job lead bank/databases, personal computers, office equipment (e.g., fax, copier), job search manual, and career center.

Wooten's (1996) study picked up on questions raised by Pickman (1994) and explored the relationship between service components of OPC and client satisfaction. He defined the client in his study as "an employee whose job was terminated and who was looking for a job" (p. 108). The service components he examined in an 11-item pencil-and-paper inventory included consultant relationship, clarity of expectations, job-search training, job-search preparation, positive focus, offices, library materials, office equipment, computer software, administrative support, and client satisfaction. The sample of 68 clients was 91% male and 9% female, all of them executives, receiving services from the same national OPC firm in 23 cities in the United States. The results indicated that outplacement content components (job search training, preparation) and process components (consultant relationship, clarity of expectation, assistance in maintaining focus) were better predictors of client satisfaction as compared with contextual components (library, software, administrative support).

Wooten's (1996) and Luciano's (1997) studies both rated clients' satisfaction based on the OPC services provided. Butterfield and Borgen's (2005) study suggests that these measures of success may also be insufficient. Using the Critical Incident Technique (CIT) (Butterfield, Borgen, Amundson & Maglio, 2005; Flanagan, 1954; Woolsey, 1986), these authors asked individual recipients of OPC services what services helped them, what services were not helpful, and whether there were services that would have helped had they been available (the "wish list"). The six wish list categories that emerged are discussed further on. Participants reported receiving structured, task-focused programs that did not meet their emotional needs, a finding that is consistent with Feldman and Leana (2000), who found that meeting with psychologists was the least utilized but most highly valued OPC service in their sample and meeting with placement consultants was the most utilized but least valued service. In this study, psychologists provided counseling support to individual clients who were feeling helpless, depressed, and unmotivated. Placement consultants in this study assisted OPC clients in organizing their job search.

Foxman and Polsky (1990) suggest that the definition of success for any career consultant is "seeing a client move through an effective job search, find the job or opportunity he or she wants and take the skills learned in the job search process to the new job to better manage his or her career" (p. 30). Since OPC consultants are in fact career consultants, it is interesting that little was found in the literature that reflects these values as important measures of success for effective OPC services.

Combined, these studies suggest that the four most prevalent measures of success (percentage of terminated workers obtaining new employment within a specified time, speed of obtaining new employment, definition of success for OPC consultants and client satisfaction with the OPC services offered) are insufficient to ensure the needs of the displaced workers receiving OPC services are being met. Given that OPC services are being offered to individuals at a time of high vulnerability and emotional shock, these results suggest that measures of success should be expanded to include what is needed by the individual recipients, not just what is being offered by the OPC firms or what is viewed to be best for the organization retaining the OPC firm.

Individual Characteristics That Increase Participation and Success with OPC

In considering individual attributes with respect to the effectiveness of program offerings, Martin and Lekan (2008) found that individual OPC client characteristics were important determining factors in the perception of outplacement effectiveness both during and after the employment transition. The study found that agreeableness, conscientiousness, and openness to experience were particularly important. The authors suggest that these three variables could signal the client's readiness to engage in the outplacement services and indicate an ability on the part of the client to put the job transition into a broader life perspective. Kieselbach and associates (2009) suggested that workers who have come to the realization that their dismissal is unavoidable may be more likely to participate and benefit from OPC programs. They stated that workers who were unable to avoid dismissal and saw that the whole process was fair valued the offer of outplacement services. This practice is already in place in the Netherlands, where affected workers are offered transition counseling early in the course of business changes; the researchers found that these workers felt more confident from the beginning of the process, which reduced their stress and anxiety and positively influenced their decision to participate and succeed in OPC (p. 75).

Gowan and Nassar-McMillan (2001) studied individual differences in outplacement-related activities, exploring sex, age, and race. Their results suggest that women are more likely to engage in outplacement services to relieve their stress and anxiety by using symptom-focused coping strategies, such as social support, and men are more likely to participate in outplacement services to use problem-solving strategies, such as job-searching activities (p. 187). Gowan and Nassar-McMillan also found that there may be some differences due to race. They reported African Americans are more likely to participate in OPC activities for the more formal sources of job search, such as employment agencies, media announcements, and job-search workshops. The literature indicates that Caucasians who have longer tenure are more likely to use more informal sources to find employment, such as employee referrals (Caldwell & Spivey, 1983; as cited in Gowan & Nassar-McMillan, 2001, p. 188). Gowan and Nassar-McMillan (2001) also found age differences with respect to the use of OPC services. They reported that older individuals have more difficulty finding reemployment and were more likely to participate in outplacement services.

Parris and Vickers (2007) and Gribble and Miller (2009) also underscore the importance of taking into account the experience of the individual employee. These studies found conflicting experiences on the part of employees who participated in OPC services. Although the employees appreciated the use of office services and the receipt of proactive support, the absence of effective and tailored counseling skills on the part of service providers and the lack of more personal treatment through the job-loss process were found to be not helpful. This suggests that individual differences need to be taken into account in designing OPC programs for particular individuals.

Kieselbach and associates (2006), in their studies in Europe, found that the most vulnerable groups of employees and thus most likely to have problems finding reemployment were people 40 years of age and older with low qualification and education levels who had specific job skills and long employment with a single employer. The researchers reported that many in this group were not able to find new work and that they were mainly women, suggesting that there is a considerable gender issue that needs to be addressed by OPC firms in serving these individuals so as to maximize the success of their programs.

Kanfer and Hulin (1985) studied a group of 35 employees laid off due to organizational budget issues, some of whom attended in-house OPC meetings and some of whom did not. Regardless of attendance at OPC sessions, the researchers' findings suggested that people with low self-confidence were less likely to find employment after job loss, possibly because they engaged in fewer job-search activities. Wooten (1996) suggests that individuals with clearer expectations of the OPC program were more satisfied with the program; he offers this as a possible explanation for the findings of his study: "Perhaps the greater the clarity, the more the involvement and the subsequent satisfaction" (p. 113).

What Helps Individual Recipients of OPC Services?

Aquilanti and Leroux (1999) suggest that counselors can help unemployed individuals deal with their grief and anger through empathy and active listening (p. 180). They also state that gainful employment can be achieved by learning job-search skills and that the rapport between clients and counselors is key to the clients' outplacement success (p. 186).

Feldman and Leana (2000) found that 52% of participants benefited from counseling from a psychologist; 69% benefited from word processing support; 69% benefited from the use of office equipment; 79% benefited from a group support/strategy session; 85% benefited from the use of a resource/library/computer database; 86% benefited from career development materials; and 98% benefited from meetings with consultants.

Butterfield and Borgen (2005) reported on helpful categories in their Critical Incident Technique (CIT) study. The helpful categories were: (1) OPC representative's activities/actions; (2) job-search skills training; (3) OPC program elements and design; (4) assessments; (5) reference materials; (6) OPC representative's traits/characteristics; (7) access to offices, supplies, equipment; (8) secretarial/administrative services; (9) relationship with OPC representative; and (10) OPC office environment and location. It is important to note, however, that often what was helpful for some participants was not helpful for others. An example of this is "Access to offices, supplies, equipment," where 47% of participants thought this was helpful while 53% did not. This tension was observed in many of the categories, which, as noted earlier, suggests having a "one size fits all" program may not meet every individual client's needs.

Kieselbach and colleagues (2009) found that affected workers who are offered transition counseling early in the course of business changes feel more confident from the beginning of the process, which reduced their stress and anxiety and positively influenced their decision to participate and succeed in outplacement services (p. 75).

Saam and Wodtke (1995) examined a specific strategy for enhancing the outcome of OPC programs. They studied the "effectiveness of a structured cognitive stress reduction program for unemployed managers involved in an outplacement program" (p. 1). The study compared a control group of managers who received unstructured advice about stress management to a group of managers who received structured weekly counseling using a cognitively based stress reduction program. These researchers found that the managers who received the structured stress management counseling obtained reemployment significantly faster and showed a reduction in levels of stress, anxiety, and anger as compared with the control group.

Last, Spera and coworkers (1994) explored the impact of writing about the experience of unemployment on subsequent reemployment activity among 63 recently unemployed professionals who were receiving OPC services. They found that the people who were assigned to write about their feelings and thoughts related to their job loss were reemployed more quickly than those who wrote about nontraumatic issues or who did not write at all. They highlighted the importance of people working through the psychological issues related to job loss before engaging in job search activities in order to increase the likelihood of subsequent reemployment. Their findings support Feldman and Leana's (2000) and Butterfield and Borgen's (2005) results related to the underutilized helpfulness of psychological counseling.

What Is Not Helpful for OPC Recipients?

What is not considered helpful by recipients of OPC services can be categorized in two ways: individual characteristics and contextual factors influencing the recipients and the nature of the service itself. In terms of individual characteristics, the psychological trauma associated with job loss can influence readiness to participate in OPC services (Amundson & Borgen, 1987; Borgen & Amundson, 1987). As individuals make the transition from employment to unemployment, a range of grieving and job search–related burnout responses can greatly impact participants' readiness to engage in OPC activities. Regarding environmental or contextual influences, financial pressures and lack of social support have been documented to increase the stress of the transition to and the experience of unemployment (Amundson & Borgen, 1987; Borgen & Amundson, 1987; Borgen, 1997; Latack & Dozier, 1986). Like the individual variables, these outside factors can impact participants' readiness and ability to effectively engage in services offered to them.

Regarding the nature of the OPC service, Feldman and Leana (2000) found that many participants expected that the placement consultants would find a job for them rather than help them to develop and organize their own job-search activities. Another area of service that participants thought was less helpful was the computer services. Feldman and Leana (2000) suggested that participants from top-level management positions were not impressed with the computer services that were available to them. Consistent with Butterfield and Borgen's (2005) results, these services were seen as being inadequate and outdated, given the advent of home offices and computers. Similarly, high-level executive participants found the generic networking support services offered to be of little use. These services were seen as perhaps being more helpful to employees in less specialized positions.

The largest hindering category reported by Butterfield and Borgen (2005) was that of OPC program elements and design, with 80% of participants citing hindering incidents in that category. Hindering categories constituted related incidents and services that participants stated were not useful or helpful during the OPC experience. Examples of incidents that were not useful or helpful included the menu of services (e.g., services focused only on hard job search skills that did not include support for the emotional side of job loss, or they were of only limited variety); lack of flexibility (e.g., start-to-finish progression through a "canned" program, with everybody getting the same formula); and specific components that did not work for individuals (e.g., the entrepreneurial option, training in resumé writing, long-distance telephone conversations with the OPC representative that consisted mostly of progress reports on the workbook material).

The second largest hindering category comprised the OPC representative's activities/actions, cited by 73% of participants (Butterfield & Borgen, 2005). Examples of incidents from this category included ineffective services (e.g., help picking out a new career when the client had already decided on a career direction); the OPC representative acting unilaterally (e.g., setting up a whole schedule of meetings without consulting the client); inappropriate comments (e.g., dropping the names of important clients the OPC firm or representative was serving); and one-on-ones (e.g., OPC representative's questions lacked depth and did not go beneath the surface, showing disregard for the client's emotional state). The third largest hindering category was reference materials, with 67% of participants stating they did not find them helpful. Participants reported feeling overwhelmed by the sheer volume of the reference materials they were given. That translated into either not reading the material or not engaging in the exercises. Participants stated that the OPC firm expected too much too soon from them, and they felt unimportant because no attempt was made to customize the material to meet their specific needs.

Taken together, it would seem that in order to be more effective for the displaced workers, OPC services need to tailor their activities more to the individual needs of participants and to provide the counseling support that individuals need to help them cope with their psychological reactions to their situations more effectively.

What Individual OPC Recipients Would Like to Receive in the Way of Services

Little was found in the literature regarding what individual OPC clients would like to receive in the way of services, as most studies have focused on the extent to which these individuals were satisfied with the services that were actually rendered. Only the study by Butterfield and Borgen (2005) asked participants whether there were OPC services they would like to have received but were not offered in their program. Participants cited a total of 194 "wish list" items that were grouped into six new categories (there were no helping or hindering items in these categories): (1) tailored/flexible services, (2) structured/hands-on services, (3) counseling skills/services, (4) group work, (5) closure/follow-up at the end of their OPC program, and (6) technical skills assessment and upgrading. Participants in this study stressed the need to have OPC services tailored to meet their specific needs (e.g., a person who wants to open his or her own business needs entrepreneurial support and services, not necessarily skill training in writing résumés or job interviews). In addition, technical skills assessment and upgrading was important to those clients who needed to improve their skills or to develop new skills in order to be competitive in the job market, which they believed would be more useful to them than the "one size fits all" program offered by the OPC firm. Participants also commented on the value of connection and support through the availability of group work in their OPC program and through the need for follow-up by their OPC representative once they finished the program. Having lost their work team

and work-related connections owing to job loss, it was difficult for the participants not to have some closure and a check-in by the OPC representative sometime after the services ended. Finally, these participants stressed the need for the OPC representative to have counseling skills and for counseling services to be offered as part of the program. Before moving on to job skills training or skills assessment and upgrading, participants needed help in dealing with the anger, shock, grief, and loss associated with their job loss. Although all of these components of OPC are written about in the literature in terms of best practices (e.g., Davenport, 1984; Pickman, 1994), it appears many OPC firms do not routinely offer them to individual clients.

Challenges Related to OPC

There are several challenges inherent in offering OPC services. A major issue relates to the context in which the service is offered. OPC services are offered by employers who are releasing employees from their place of work. A historic motivation for employers to offer these services has been to reduce legal and other costs related to a reduction in their workforce. A good outcome for employers, then, is often measured by a smooth transition to a reduced number of employees and former employees being reemployed by other employers.

From an employee's perspective, they are placed in a difficult psychological and financial career-related transition. They are then invited to participate in a program offered by the employer who is terminating them. A second issue that appears to be an ongoing challenge is the tension between offering more extended counseling-related support to terminated employees over the time needed to regain comparable sustained employment compared with the pressure to offer a service in a more time-limited and less costly fashion. This tension between offering "cookie cutter" generic programs and more extended tailored programs has yet to be resolved.

Another challenge is that workers are often unaware of OPC services prior to being offered them at the point when their employment is terminated (Butterfield & Borgen, 2005). They do not know what to expect, and often they have expectations that the OPC services are not able to meet. Participants reported feeling confused and worried about the proposed program and were unsure about what the program may have to offer them that would suit their individual needs. They also may not see themselves in a position to make negative comments about the services they are offered, given that they will likely need a letter of reference from the employer who is funding the services.

As stated earlier, there also appears to be a challenge related to the evaluation of OPC services. Most often, evaluations are conducted by the employers who pay for the services rather than by the employees who receive them. Given the difference in perception of successful outcomes by employers and employees already discussed, this can be problematic.

Much of the recent literature related to OPC programs centers on the need for counseling-related support. One ongoing challenge arising from the OPC literature is that some OPC consultants may not have the educational background or experience to offer the counseling services that recipients of OPC services say are needed. Pickman (1994) stressed the need for OPC consultants to possess specific personality attributes or attitudes in order to be most effective. These include genuine respect for other people, curiosity, excellent communication skills, professionalism, and knowledge about job search, business, and counseling. The studies surveyed highlight the importance of OPC consultants possessing counseling skills or referring individual clients to counseling services elsewhere to help the clients with all aspects of their transition from employment to unemployment and back into employment. Often it seems that organizations make arrangements for their terminated employees to receive counseling services from the organization's Employee Assistance Program (EAP) provider. However, terminated employees are often uncomfortable with the idea of seeking EAP services (for many of the same reasons they are uncomfortable receiving OPC services). Often OPC firms offer the services of a registered psychologist, but this is generally to conduct assessments rather than to provide counseling/psychological support during the transition.

There is also the issue of who is the client. In fact, both the corporation that hires the OPC firm and the individual who has been terminated are clients. This raises the potential for conflict and for conflict-of-interest issues to arise (Burdett, 1988). As Burdett points out, it is in the best interests of the corporation for the terminated employee to find employment quickly. On the other hand, it may be in the individual client's best interests to take a long-term perspective and find the job that is right rather than one that is expedient. There can also be misunderstanding on the part of the individual OPC client about what information is released back to the former employer by the OPC firm, which can inhibit the individual's willingness to participate in OPC services and discuss sensitive issues (Burdett, 1988; Butterfield & Borgen, 2005).

Directions for Further Research

OPC services are being offered within the context of rapidly evolving and ongoing changes to labor markets around the world. At their heart, OPC services raise the question regarding the employer's responsibility in assisting employees to find sustainable employment following layoffs that have occurred as a result of organizational restructuring and downsizing. Within an environment of ongoing organizational change, it is expected that the need for the services will grow. Therefore research regarding the attitudes of employers toward continuing to offer or perhaps expand the scope of these services is important.

Much of the literature over the past decade has suggested directions for future research centered on the refinement and tailoring of programs to more specific groups of employees. Gowan and Nassar-McMillan (2001) suggested more investigation was needed into the relationship between reemployment and the use of various types of outplacement-related activities, given their finding that men and women and different age groups had different needs and expectations. As stated earlier, these authors also found no difference in employment rates among participants who had engaged or had not engaged in specific activities in an OPC service. Other literature, such as the writings of Kieselbach and coworkers (2009), found that people who had participated in OPC services tended to take longer to find employment but that the employment they found was more sustainable, suggesting that the complexities related to reemployment require further study. Finally, Martin and Lekan (2008) suggested that further research needs to be conducted regarding what types of transition counseling work best with different personality types to positively affect participant outcomes.

Much has been written in the earlier OPC literature about future research needed to develop a more complete understanding of the effectiveness of OPC, its impact on those individual clients who would best benefit from receiving OPC, and what services are most useful to individuals. A summary of these calls for further research is offered here as it appears from our review of the existing literature that little research has been conducted to address these areas. Pickman (1994, pp. 132–133) stated the need for studies that look at the long-term effect of receiving outplacement, if indeed there are any. He also suggested quality outcome studies are needed regarding the effectiveness of using outplacement, as well as the need for studies related to counseling issues as they relate to the delivery of OPC services. He asks about the relation (if any) between "successful counseling outcomes and counselor gender, age, sex, educational background . . . [and] what methods or approaches work best for which type of client" (p. 132). He cites the need to research many organizational questions related to downsizing and OPC that remain unanswered, such as what the long-term effect is of downsizing on a company's morale and productivity, what factors help an organization implement a successful downsizing, what leadership is needed during downsizing, as well as optimal processes involved in downsizing and how people within the organization are apt to react to the downsizing. Finally, Pickman suggests the field of OPC has an opportunity to contribute to the creation of career development theories for adults at all stages in their careers as an adjunct to most theories currently in use that were focused on young adults.

A number of researchers have suggested there is a need to better understand the individual characteristics of recently terminated employees that define their likelihood of participating in and benefiting from OPC programs. Wooten (1996) found that OPC program content and processes were more important predictors of client satisfaction than context. He speculates that individual client self-efficacy and personality variables need to be understood in order to determine their role in mediating or accounting for these relationships. Latack and Dozier's (1986) results that suggested an individual's "previous job satisfaction, being in the mid-career stage, and maintaining high activity levels" (as cited in Aquilanti & Leroux, 1999, p. 179) might influence the extent to which people benefit from OPC. The extent to which race affects the OPC experience is not known, although Gowan and Nassar-McMillan (2001) suggested it may impact success rates of OPC service. Luciano (1997) suggests that additional person and situational variables need to be studied, possibly including all of the "Big Five" personality traits (openness, conscientiousness, extraversion, agreeableness, and neuroticism) as well as potential interactions.

Other researchers have suggested there is a need to understand the role of "counseling" in OPC programs (Butterfield & Borgen, 2005). Borgen and Amundson (1984) suggest that the psychological transition to uemployment, including grieving reactions, may start while people are still employed. They may begin to withdraw from coworkers as part of a more general process of detachment from the workplace that they will be leaving. Davenport (1984) writes of the need for research "to determine whether present programs meet the needs of outplaced workers" (p. 189).

Butterfield and Borgen (2005) suggest two areas for further research. First, they found that participants' experiences with OPC services, both positive and negative, seemed to be associated with the individual OPC representatives with whom the clients worked rather than with the OPC firm or the program components offered. Further research would be helpful around the possible relationship between the individual clients' perceived positive or negative experiences with OPC and their interpersonal relationship with their OPC consultants. Second, these researchers found that participants expressed high levels of emotion as they talked about aspects of the OPC services they received that were not helpful to them, particularly with respect to their relationship with their OPC representative and that person's behaviors and characteristics. Additional information in this area would assist corporate clients to decide which services they want to provide for their departing employees and guide OPC firms in deciding on the mix of services for individual clients.

Feldman and Leana (2000) suggest we need to know more about the expectations downsized managers bring to the OPC experience. They point out that many managers come to OPC programs with the expectation that the purpose is to find them a job rather than to help them develop and implement a job search strategy. The relationship between individual client expectations and satisfaction with OPC services is important to address. They also suggest that it is important for OPC programs to be tailored to the need of the individual and the individual's level in the work hierarchy at the time of termination. An example they cite is that generic networking skills training is useful for lower-level employees but may not be useful to upper-level managers. Knowing what services are needed and tailoring them accordingly is a theme that was also found in the Butterfield and Borgen (2005) study.

Last, it struck us as we reviewed the literature that most of the studies focused on the OPC experiences of executives and senior managers. Given the trend toward offering OPC services to people at all levels within the organization, research that includes workers other than senior managers is needed to ensure the needs of all individual recipients are being met.

Where Does OPC Stand Today and What Is Needed?

After reviewing the scholarly literature currently available related to OPC, several things stand out for us. First, OPC cannot be separated from the experience of unemployment. Aquilanti and Leroux (1999) and others acknowledge the shock, grief, anger, and despair that often accompany loss of one's job. The need for psychological or counseling services is often great, given the emotional reactions experienced by the person who has lost his or her job (Amundson & Borgen, 1988; Butterfield & Borgen, 2005; Pickman, 1994). Second, it is also clear that individual recipients of OPC services would like to receive services not always offered by OPC firms, who tend to sell a "package" of services to the employer or organization that is paying for their services (Butterfield & Borgen, 2005). Third, there is support for the importance of conducting individual needs assessments as part of the OPC process that is also echoed in the career counseling literature (e.g., Borgen, 1999; Kieselbach et al., 2009). What appears to be lacking is an OPC model that incorporates these important elements in addition to the components traditionally offered by OPC firms. The Aquilanti Integrated Model (AIM) of outplacement (Aquilanti & Leroux, 1999) strikes us as a particularly useful model on which to build to add these additional elements.

As previously mentioned, Aquilanti and Leroux's (1999) first phase deals with loss, grieving, and transition. They highlight the need to know when a candidate requires a referral for counseling services and offer some markers suggesting when such a referral is warranted. Given the criticality of helping individual OPC recipients deal with the emotional rollercoaster related to job loss (Amundson & Borgen, 1988), we believe that as a minimum all OPC counselors need to have excellent communication and active listening skills that include empathy. By hearing the individual client's needs and understanding their requirements and readiness, the OPC counselor is better able to determine the client's needs and tailor the services accordingly.

Acquilanti and Leroux's second phase focuses on personal development. This includes assessments of the individual's values as well as interests, personality, and other inventories. To this we would suggest adding a needs analysis as part of determining the candidate's readiness for growth, as suggested by Borgen (1999) and Kieselbach and colleagues (2009). This would be helpful in addressing the wish list items identified by the participants in Butterfield and Borgen's (2005) study, particularly their stated desire for tailored services that meet their specific needs. This addition would also serve the findings reported by Parris and Vickers (2007), Gribble and Miller (2009), and Gowan and Nassar-McMillan (2001) regarding the different needs of OPC recipients related to race and gender and individual experience. As part of this expanded assessment component, technical skills assessment and technical upgrading could be included for those who need it (Butterfield & Borgen, 2005).

Phase three of Aquilanti and Leroux's AIM (1999) is the job search. Here they mention the importance of informational interviews, resumé preparation, networking, and interview skills. To this we would propose adding the elements mentioned by Pickman (1994), as well as salary negotiations.

Finally, phase four of the AIM (Aquilanti & Leroux, 1999) is ongoing counseling and support. We believe that this would also incorporate the coaching advocated by Pickman (1994). As written, it appears that this is intended to be ongoing counseling and support during the job-search phase and includes reflection on the part of the candidate after each job interview as well as encouragement by the OPC representative. We would add to this stage the inclusion of closure and follow-up at the point where OPC services are being concluded. The participants in the study conducted by Butterfield and Borgen (2005) mentioned how lost they felt when their OPC services ended, either because they found a job or because their OPC service time or funds had been exhausted and there was no further contact with the OPC representative. Having lost their employment relationships, losing their connection with their OPC counselors represented a double blow. This could be incorporated during the final phase of the AIM model by incorporating an action planning component (Borgen & Maglio, 2007). This is also good practice from a counseling psychology/counseling process perspective in the final stage of individual counseling. Hackney and Cormier (2009) and Borgen (1999) stress the ethical and professional reasons to discuss and make arrangements for professional contact once the formal work has been concluded. If these elements were added to the AIM of outplacement and utilized by OPC firms in providing services, we believe that the needs of the individual OPC clients would be better served.

Conclusion

In summary, it can be seen that OPC services have evolved greatly since their inception, both in terms of the range of employees served and the scope of services offered. There remains an ongoing tension involving the relative importance of serving the needs of employers or employees in offering OPC. In terms of the sustainability of the service, it will likely be of increased importance to work toward viewing OPC as being effective when it sets out to serve the needs of both groups. That will facilitate the original purpose of protecting the reputation of employers and helping to maximize the effective use of employees' skills and abilities.

The questions that remain outstanding are many. Given that OPC is a multimillion-dollar industry and is serving a vulnerable population (unexpectedly unemployed individuals), we believe that it is important to focus more research on the effectiveness of OPC services. The research that does exist suggests that individual OPC clients' needs for counseling-related services are probably not being met effectively, individual OPC clients perceive a conflict of interest regarding the role of the terminating employer and whose interests the OPC firm is serving, and the existing measures of success appear to focus more on the needs of the employers needs than those of the individual recipients. In addition, little is known about the credentials of OPC consultants and how they facilitate services across the two disciplines of business and counseling psychology—including career planning and skills development—and how well they are able to meet the needs of individual OPC recipients. As researchers and career counseling professionals, we need more information about these services and the people who provide them. We have an ethical obligation to ensure that no harm is being done, either to the firms hiring OPC consultants or, most important, to the individual recipients of these services.

References

Amundson, N. E., & Borgen, W. A. (1987). Coping with unemployment: What helps and hinders. *Journal of Employment Counseling, 24,* 97–106.

Amundson, N. E., & Borgen, W. A. (1988). Factors that help and hinder in group employment counseling. *Journal of Employment Counseling, 25,* 104–114.

Aquilanti, T. M., & Leroux, J. (1999). An integrated model of outplacement counseling. *Journal of Employment Counseling, 36*(4), 177–192.

Beugre, C.D. (1998). Implementing business process reengineering: The role of organizational justice. *The Journal of Applied Behavioral Science, 34*(3), 347–360.

Borgen, W.A. (1997). People caught in changing career opportunities: A counseling process. *Journal of Employment Counseling, 34,* 133–143.

Borgen, W. A. (1999). Implementing 'Starting Points': A follow-up study. *Journal of Employment Counseling, 36,* 98–114.

Borgen, W. A., & Amundson, N. E. (1984). *The experience of unemployment.* Toronto, ON: Nelson Canada.

Borgen, W. A., & Amundson, N. E. (1987). The dynamics of unemployment. *Journal for Counseling and Development, 66,* 180–184.

Borgen, W. A., & Maglio, A. T. (2007). Putting action back into action planning: Experiences of career clients. *Journal of Employment Counseling, 44,* 173–184.

Bowers, S. (1997). Identity formation in outplacement and career management counsellors. In A. J. Pickman (Ed.) Special Challenges in Career Management. Mahwah, New Jersey: Lawrence Erlbaum Associates.

Burdett, J. O. (1988). Easing the way out: Consultants and counselors help terminated executives strategically and psychologically. *Personnel Administrator, 33,* 157–166.

Butterfield, L. D., & Borgen, W. A. (2005). Outplacement counseling from the client's perspective. *The Career Development Quarterly, 53*(4), 306–316.

Butterfield, L. D., Borgen, W. A., Amundson, N. E., & Maglio, A. T. (2005). Fifty years of the Critical Incident Technique: 1954–2004 and beyond. *Qualitative Research, 5*(4), 475–497.

Challenger, J. A. (2005). Return on investment of high quality outplacement programs. *Economic Perspectives,* 2Q, Federal Reserve Bank of Chicago.

Davenport, D. W. (1984). Outplacement counseling: Whither the counselor? *The Vocational Guidance Quarterly, 32,* 185–190.

Feldman, D. C., & Leana, C. R. (2000). Whatever happened to laid-off executives? A study of reemployment challenges after downsizing. *Organizational Dynamics, 29*(1), 64–75.

Flanagan, J. (1954). The critical incident technique. *Psychological Bulletin, 51,* 327–358.

Foxman, L. D., & Polsky, W. L. (1990). Outplacement results in success. *Personnel Journal, 69,* 30–37.

Gowan, M. A., & Nassar-McMillan, S. C. (2001). Examination of individual differences in participation in outplacement program. *Journal of Employment Counseling, 38,* 185–196.

Gribble, L. C., Miller, P. (2009). Employees in outplacement services, do they really get the help they need? *Australian Journal of Career Development, 18,* 18–28.

Hackney, H. L., & Cormier, S. (2009). *The professional counselor: A process guide to helping.* Upper Saddle River, NJ: Pearson Education.

Human Resources Management Association (2009). *Outplacement practices in B.C. 2009: Survey report.* Available at: http://www.bchrma.org/pdf.outplacement.pdf (Retrieved December 29, 2010.)

Kanfer, R., & Hulin, C. L. (1985). Individual differences in successful job searches following lay-off. *Personnel Psychology, 38*(4), 835–847.

Kieselbach, T., Bagnara, S., Birk, R., De Witte, H., Jeurissen, R., . . . Schaufeli, W. (2006). *Social Convoy and Sustainable*

Employability: Innovative Strategies for Outplacement/ Replacement Counselling—Final Report. EU research project (2000–2004) supported by the European Commission (DG Research). ISBN 3-88722-677-1.

Kieselbach, T., Bagnara, S., De Witte, H., Lemkow, L., & Schaufeli, W. (Eds.) (2009). *Coping with occupational transitions: An empirical study with employees facing job loss in five European countries.* Wiesbaden, Germany: Springer Science + Business Media.

Kirk, J. J. (1994). Putting outplacement in its place. *Journal of Employment Counseling, 31,* 10–18.

Latack, J. C., & Dozier, J. B. (1986). After the ax falls: Job loss as a career transition. *Academy of Management Review, 11,* 375–392.

Luciano, J. M. (1997). Involuntary job loss: An examination of the factors that predict reemployment and satisfaction with outplacement services. *Dissertation Abstracts International, 58*(05), 1811A. (University Microfilms No. 9733825).

Martin, H. J., & Lekan, D. F. (2008). Individual differences in outplacement success. *Career Development International, 13,* 425–439.

Mirabile (1985). Outplacement as transition counseling. *Journal of Employment Counseling, 22* (1), 39–45.

Neinas, C. C. (1987). Outplacement services for the blue-collar worker. *Journal of Career Development, 14,* 80–89.

Parris, M. A., & Vickers, M. H. (Eds.) (2007). Stories of ambivalence: Australian executives' experiences of outplacement services. In M. A. Parris & M. H. Vickers (Eds.), *Proceedings of the 15th International Conference 2007* (pp. 108–113). Fort Lauderdale, FL: Association on Employment Practices and Principles.

Pickman, A. J. (1994). *The complete guide to outplacement counseling.* Hillsdale, NJ: Lawrence Erlbaum.

Saam, R. H., & Wodtke, K. H. (1995). A cognitive stress reduction program for recently unemployed managers. *The Career Development Quarterly, 44,* 43–45.

Spera, S. P., Buhrfeind, E. D., & Pennebaker, J. W. (1994). Expressive writing and coping with job loss. *Academy of Management Journal, 37*(3), 722–733.

Strewler, J. (1997). New models for career centers. In A. J. Pickman (Ed.) *Special Challenges in Career Management.* Mahwah, NJ: Lawrence Erlbaum Associates.

Tzafrir, S. S., Mano-Negrin, R., Harel, G. H., & Rom-Nagy, D. (2006). Downsizing and the impact of job counseling and retraining on effective employee responses. *Career Development International, 11,* 125–144.

Westaby, J. D. (2004). The impact of outplacement programs on reemployment criteria: A longitudinal study of displaced managers and executives. *Journal of Employment Counseling, 41,* 19–28.

Woolsey, L. (1986). The critical incident technique: An innovative method of research. *Canadian Journal of Counselling, 20,* 242–254.

Wooten, K. C. (1996). Predictors of client satisfaction in executive outplacement: Implications for service delivery. *Journal of Employment Counseling, 33,* 106–116.

Work First Versus Human Capital Development in Employability Programs

Colin Lindsay

Abstract

Policymakers across advanced welfare states have prioritized programs to enhance the employability of unemployed people and help them to find and sustain work. In this regard, analysts have drawn attention to the difference between Work First and Human Capital Development (HCD) models. The former seek to direct people to any available job as quickly as possible; the latter seek to improve long-term employability through investments in human capital (typically via education and training). This chapter deploys a framework for comparing Work First– and HCD-oriented approaches to employability, identifying differences in rationales, content, and outcomes. A key conclusion is that policymakers (and indeed researchers) need to adopt a broader, more holistic view of the factors affecting the unemployed. A better understanding can inform the development of programs that combine Work First and HCD elements and address the problems that explain why some people face prolonged periods excluded from the workplace.

Key Words: work first, human capital, employability, activation, active labor market policies, welfare reform

Introduction

Policymakers have adopted a range of strategies to promote unemployed job seekers' employability and help them to find and sustain work. But there are considerable differences in how the "employability gap" encountered by people experiencing unemployment is understood and characterized (McQuaid & Lindsay, 2005), and this has informed fundamentally different active labor market policies and employability programs. In assessing the content and outcomes of different programs, analysts have suggested that a distinction can be drawn between approaches broadly focused on Work First and Human Capital Development (HCD). The former programs work on the assumption that "any job is better than no job" (Layard, 2003, p. 5), so that services are designed to place people into any available job opportunity as quickly as possible; the latter seek to improve the long-term employability of the unemployed through human capital

investment (for example, through training and personal development).

These distinctions matter because, as shown below, Work First– and HCD-type programs tend to produce different outcomes in the immediate and longer terms, contingent on the existing employability of participants, demand in local and national labor markets, and employer needs. There is also considerable debate about whether Work First or HCD programs (and their immediate impacts) are more effective at promoting long-term labor market participation and socioeconomic inclusion (Daguerre & Etherington, 2009).

Following this introduction, this chapter provides a definition and discussion of Work First and HCD approaches to employability, drawing on US, UK, and other literature, and clearly distinguishing the key features of each model. Drawing on Lindsay et al.'s (2007) framework, the discussion below specifically addresses the key features and differences of Work First and HCD approaches in terms of: their rationale, targets, and priorities; the "intervention model" or content of programs; and how they negotiate relationships with individuals and the labor market. The chapter then provides a brief discussion of "what works" in employability strategies—especially the impact of Work First and HCD models—drawing on evaluation evidence from the United Kingdom, United States, and other countries. The chapter concludes by noting the increasing dominance of Work First in many developed economies/member states of the Organization for Economic Co-operation and Development (OECD) and considers whether these approaches are fit for purpose in an era of high unemployment. The chapter then goes on to identify future directions for research.

Defining Work First and HCD Approaches to Employability

Many authors have sought to differentiate between Work First and HCD approaches to promoting the employability of those excluded from the labor market (Bruttel & Sol, 2006; Lindsay et al., 2007; Peck & Theodore, 2000, 2001; Sol & Hoogtanders, 2005; Tang & Cheung, 2007). Lindsay et al. (2007), drawing on previous work by Peck and Theodore (2000) and others, provide a model comparing Work First and HCD that makes distinctions across five dimensions: the rationale for employability programs, their targets (what the policy or program is seeking to achieve for the individual), the intervention model deployed (the content and structure of services to improve

employability), how they mediate the relationship between individuals and the labor market, and how employability programs themselves engage with individuals. Table 30.1 presents an adapted version of Lindsay et al.'s (2007) framework and provides the basis for the following discussion.

Rationale and "Program Targets" of Work First and HCD

First, in terms of the rationale and sought outcomes (or program targets) associated with the two models, there are clear differences. By definition, the prioritization of an immediate return to work is fundamental to the Work First approach. In terms of targets, Work First programs place "an emphasis on job seekers, wherever possible, moving quickly towards any kind of work" (Lindsay, 2010, p. 126). The stated aims of such programs often explicitly focus on "immediate labor market entry" (Mitchell et al., 2007, p. 294), prioritizing "labor market attachment on the premise that any job is better than none" (Mead, 2003, p. 442) and emphasizing the negative consequences of individuals experiencing prolonged periods without work.

The rationale for Work First is therefore closely related to "hysteresis" theories in labor economics. These theories posit that "duration dependency" (the increased likelihood of continued exclusion among the long-term unemployed due to the deterioration of skills and work habits) is important in explaining high levels of structural unemployment (see, for example, Layard, 2000). The logical conclusion of such a position is that employability programs should seek to move people into the regular labor market

Table 30.1. Features of Work First and Human Capital Development (HCD) programs

	Work First Approaches	HCD Approaches
Rationale	Facilitating quick return to labor market by job search and work-focused training	Improving long-term employability through improved education, skills, health, and personal development
Program targets	Immediate emphasis on job entry; focus on getting people into work quickly	Sustainable transitions to work at range of skill levels with progression routes once in work
Intervention model	Job search central and constant; short-term training; focus on immediate activity	Long-term training; integrated with social care, education, and health Personal adviser support
Relationship to labor market	Demand-responsive; seeks to insert job seekers into available opportunities	Up-skills job seeker to expand range of opportunities; supports progression in workplace
Relationship with individuals	Use of benefit restrictions, sanctions, and/or financial top-ups to encourage job entry; emphasis on compulsion	Encourages voluntary participation by demonstrating benefits of high-quality HCD opportunities; emphasis on trust

as quickly as possible in order to limit unemployment duration. As Lindsay (2010, p. 124) notes, such thinking has informed a number of supply-side employability policies, "from keeping benefit replacement rates relatively low to increasing compulsion upon the unemployed to re-engage in the labor market, for example through Work First activation." Accordingly, an important challenge to the rationale for Work First models is that there seems to be evidence that labor demand fluctuations are more powerful in explaining long-term unemployment rises than is duration dependency and hysteresis. Webster (2005) has shown that changes in long-term unemployment in the United Kingdom largely mirror trends in general rates of worklessness (once time lags are accounted for), suggesting that high long-term unemployment is more a function of labor market weaknesses than the declining skills and aspirations of the unemployed.

Among some US social theorists in particular, an alternative theoretical foundation to justify Work First programs is found in the "dependency culture" or "underclass" thesis, whereby a demoralized and demotivated workless class is seen as making conscious choices to avoid job opportunities (Mead, 2003). Evidence for these claims has proved elusive, as people excluded from the labor market consistently report similar attitudes and aspirations to those in work (Beatty et al., 2010; Fletcher, 2007). This would explain why, in times of economic recovery, many alleged underclass members make their way back into work, having been given the opportunity to do so by expanding labor market demand (Freeman, 2000). Nor has the underclass thesis been able to explain why regions and localities that have hemorrhaged jobs during periods of industrial restructuring continue to report high levels of worklessness when compared with more economically resilient neighboring labor markets. For Ritchie et al. (2005, p. 43) "these understandings of an underclass caused by individual and behavioral problems fail to take into account the structural causes of worklessness"; but it is clear that accounts of unemployment focusing on the individual continue to inform Work First responses that seek to press job seekers into employment through a mix of "carrots and sticks" (Castonguay, 2009).

The rationale and targets for HCD-oriented approaches tend to be quite different. Of course, there remains a focus on getting unemployed people back to work, but HCD models arguably deemphasize immediate labor market integration, instead prioritizing the development of skills that will enable people to find *suitable* employment (Hagelund & Kavli, 2009). Accordingly, "HCD approaches are distinguished by the rationale that job seekers will often require substantial support (potentially over a prolonged period) in order to improve their long-term employability (with the implication that this will require substantial investments in the education, skills and health of individuals)" (Lindsay et al., 2007, p. 541). Program targets are less concerned with the immediate placement of clients into any job and more focused on sustainable transitions and progression through education as well as pre-work and in-work training. Central to the HCD model is the idea that substantial gains in employability and skills, placed alongside support for the establishment of continuing development and progression routes at work, can solve the problem of "revolving door" participation in employability programs, whereby lower-skilled people tend to cycle between periods of unemployment, Work First programs, and temporary, low-quality jobs (Peck & Theodore, 2000).

"Intervention Models"

Work First and HCD approaches also differ significantly in their content or intervention models. It has been noted that job-search assistance/job matching is central to the content of Work First (Ochel, 2005) and in some cases is the only provision offered under these programs (Bruttel & Sol, 2006). Under Work First, the prioritization of job matching is key to facilitating the immediate returns to work that define the program targets for such initiatives (see above). Policymakers opting for Work First may also be hoping to tap a potential "deterrence effect," whereby the threat of immediate, extensive, compulsory job-search activity is meant to discourage unemployed people from claiming benefits in the first place (Daguerre & Etherington, 2009). Some Work First providers would argue that their programs might also include training, but in most cases these activities tend to be short-term, with a focus on improving the individual's motivation and generic skills (Daguerre, 2007). In summary, Sol and Hoogtanders (2005, p. 147) have provided what is often cited as a standard definition of Work First:

> Work First programs seek to move people out of welfare and into unsubsidized jobs as quickly as possible, and job search itself is a central activity in these programs. . . . For those who fail to get a job straight away, Work First provides additional

activities directed at addressing those factors impeding employment. These activities might include education, training and work experience. In the context of Work First, they generally are short-term, closely monitored and either combined with or immediately followed by additional job search. . . . In addition, Work First uses sanctions as a main component in its approach, rather than trust.

Some analysts have consistently suggested that a feature of Work First programs is the manner in which they restrict access to human capital development for participants (Deprez & Butler, 2007). As Goldrick-Rab and Shaw (2005, p. 293) note with reference to US welfare reforms: "Work First emphasizes rapid job placement as the strategy of choice in achieving stable employment and moving out of poverty. As such, it cements a gradual movement away from the human capital philosophy that . . . emphasizes skills and education as the most effective long-term path to economic self-sufficiency." Ridzi (2009, p. 10) agrees that the US model of Work First activation "de-emphasizes education, training and even career advancement under the pretext that motivating people to take any job they can will jumpstart the long and arduous process of climbing the career ladder from the very bottom up."

An archetypal skills-based, HCD-oriented approach suggests a different intervention model. Here, the aim is to facilitate the development of skills and attributes that will equip people to find and retain suitable jobs and advance through in-work progression routes (Peck & Theodore, 2001). Its intervention model therefore requires strong links to well-funded skills-focused employability services (including, if necessary, long-term education and training). Skills development opportunities may be linked to extensive accreditation (Hagelund & Kavli, 2009). Lindsay et al. (2007) suggest that HCD approaches also tend to better integrate employability and training provision with a range of other holistic services addressing the full range of barriers to work faced by job seekers (for example, health problems, substance dependency, or complex caring responsibilities). The HCD intervention model requires the use of professionals—such as "personal advisers" (PAs) or case managers—capable of working with clients in a holistic way to improve their employability and empowered to direct them to appropriate learning and development opportunities (Lødemel & Trickey, 2001). It is again important to note that PA services are also

a key element of Work First interventions; but, as Mazzeo et al. (2003) argue with reference to US welfare reform measures, even when intensive adviser assistance is offered under such programs, there remains a strong emphasis on immediate, compulsory, work-based activity as the outcome being sought for the unemployed.

Relationship to the Labor Market

Another distinctive feature of the Work First model is that it seeks to respond to, rather than adapt, existing labor market opportunities. The assumption is that employability programs should be demand-responsive, placing job seekers into opportunities that already exist in the "regular" labor market. As shown below, this means that Work First approaches tend to run into trouble in labor markets where demand is weak and perform more poorly during eras of economic crisis. Work First therefore assumes that the sole role of the employer is to provide a job opportunity; it is the responsibility of the individual (perhaps assisted by an employability program) to offer the skills required by the employer (Ray et al., 2009). Another consistent theme in how Work First programs connect with the labor market relates to the downplaying of concerns with the quality and sustainability of job outcomes. There tends to be a focus on "quick re-entry in the labor market regardless of the quality of employment" (Daguerre & Etherington, 2009, p. 11). As Handler (2006, p. 119) notes, referring to the US context: "A Work First strategy . . . encourages recipients to take any job, even a low-wage entry-level job."

Conversely, HCD approaches focus on achieving high-quality, sustainable outcomes, prioritizing measures to promote continuous skills development and in-work progression (Lindsay et al., 2007). HCD models might therefore involve the establishment of "intermediate labor markets"– that is, a subsidized and/or supported employment environment where more disadvantaged program participants can make gradual progress in developing skills and integrating into a workplace environment, equipping them to make the transition to work in the "real" economy (Gregg, 2009). HCD approaches might also involve partnership between employability program providers and employers to ensure that participants entering work are given the support needed to sustain transitions and to identify opportunities for progression and in-work training (Ray et al., 2009). It is notable that national activation regimes where social partnership structures inform the development of employability programs (for example, through advisory councils bringing together employers, trade unions, and policymakers in countries like Denmark) appear more often to report HCD-oriented interventions characterized by substantial investment in vocational training and in-work support (Serrano Pascual & Magnusson, 2007). At a most basic level, HCD-oriented employability programs are more likely to seek to match participants to workplaces and job roles to which they are suited and where there is some opportunity for personal development and advancement, disputing the Work First assumption that "the aim is not to establish a long-term career goal but to reinforce the belief that any job is a first career step, no matter how precarious this employment might be" (Sol & Hoogtanders, 2005, p. 147).

Relationship with Individuals

A final defining feature of Work First approaches to employability relates to their far more *dirigiste* relationship with individual program participants. Work First is informed by an understanding of labor market exclusion that sees behavioral and attitudinal failings as key, so that behavior-shaping incentives and punitive measures are required. Accordingly, compulsory work-related activity is enforced by the threat of sanctions that can be applied to welfare benefits. For Daguerre (2007, p. 5), under Work First, "welfare claimants are faced with sanctions if they do not comply with work requirements and do not develop the 'right' attitude to employment." At one extreme, Work First can be equated with workfare (as practiced in the United States and some other countries)—programs that mandate unpaid work activities in return for benefits or other forms of financial support (Crisp & Fletcher, 2008). Under many other compulsory Work First models, "non-compliance with work requirements can lead to substantial benefit sanctions, if not blanket denial of benefit entitlement" (Daguerre & Etherington, 2009, p. 11). Work First approaches therefore tend to be accompanied by generally greater conditionality and less generosity in the welfare benefits system (i.e., benefits are set at a low level and are more difficult to access) (Daguerre, 2008); but they also place a strong emphasis on in-work incentives, such as tax credits that top up low wages for former program participants (Lindsay, 2010).

Sol and Hoogtanders (2005) suggest that similar levels of compulsion and conditionality are less common in HCD-oriented models, where providers hope that an emphasis on choice and quality in

services will negate the need for punitive measures. There are examples of HCD-oriented programs that have retained strong elements of compulsion (Hagelund & Kavli, 2009); but for Dean (2003, p. 442), the human capital approach "is characteristically (but not necessarily) predicated on voluntary participation." Trust, rather than coercion, is the basis of relationships that employability program providers seek to build with participants (Lødemel & Trickey, 2001). The assumption is that job seekers will respond positively to the opportunity to choose an appropriate skills development or work experience intervention, so that in many cases financial threats or incentives will be unnecessary. Finally, the greater emphasis on choice and voluntarism that generally defines HCD-oriented approaches means that they may be better placed to help job seekers to cope with non–work-related issues while participating in employability programs. As noted above, Work First is generally more associated with imposing activity on program participants—as Carpenter et al. (2007, p. 164) note, "people's life goals may at times conflict with a Work First strategy"—whereas there may be more scope to cope with (for example) caring roles or health problems under voluntary HCD-oriented programs.

It is of course important to reiterate that the Work First and HCD-oriented approaches discussed above are ideal types and that most actual employability programs will exhibit elements of both models. As Dean (2009, p. 110) notes in his comparison of Work First and HCD concepts, "welfare-to-work regimes are invariably hybrid in nature, reflecting contested discourses of responsibility and the inherent instability of the ethical foundations of welfare." Dean (2009, p. 110) notes that the US welfare reform agenda "is generally held to exemplify the Work First approach, [but] initiatives taken in certain states under the Workforce Investment Act of 1998 provide isolated examples of a human capital approach." Similarly, Lindsay et al. (2007) see the United Kingdom's recent welfare-to-work programs as a hybrid, with some HCD elements surviving within an increasingly Work First–dominated agenda. Riach & Loretto (2009, p. 104) share this analysis of UK policy as "characterized by a Work First tactic," but with something of "an HCD orientation [that theoretically] will benefit people with multiple disadvantages."

While most employability interventions will fall into a hybrid category, there is a general consensus that liberal welfare states (such as the United Kingdom and United States) tend to offer the most Work First–oriented programs, while some social democratic welfare states (such as Sweden) are perhaps at the opposite end of the spectrum, emphasizing training and HCD (Daguerre, 2008; Dean, 2009). However, since the 1990s, there has arguably been a shift towards more Work First–oriented approaches in many developed nations, irrespective of welfare regime traditions. Across many states belonging to the Organisation for Economic Co-operation and Development (OECD), "the Work First attitude has penetrated public institutions, with the public employment service often quickly matching clients to available jobs, as opposed to helping them invest in their human resources and skills and move towards more sustainable long-term careers" (Froy & Giguere, 2010, p. 27).

Given this context, and the evidence that these two models are a useful starting point for discussing the rationale and content of employability programs, an obvious next issue is to discuss the evidence on what types of intervention work best under what circumstances and the appropriateness of Work First and HCD strategies in responding to the post-2008 crisis and accompanying high levels of worklessness.

What Works? Work First Versus HCD

In terms of achieving immediate (if sometimes temporary) reductions in welfare rolls, Work First strategies have been seen as more effective than HCD-oriented models. Layard (2004, p. 5) argues that the evidence supports "Work First over training first" as a means of promoting immediate transitions off welfare benefits. Advocates of Work First point to the reduced welfare rolls that often follow a tightening of welfare eligibility requirements and increased compulsion and conditionality. Evidence reviews of the impact of active labor market policies (ALMPs) have produced mixed results but tend to be more positive toward Work First interventions. De Koning (2007) provides a descriptive report of the results of 130 evaluation studies, concluding that there is strong evidence of positive effects from a combination of sanctions and financial incentives, while training programs have a more mixed record. Kluwe (2006), using probit modeling to provide a meta-analysis of 137 "observations" (i.e., quantifiable evaluation outcomes) from 95 different studies of employability programs, concludes that the impact of training programs was positive but modest, whereas "services and sanctions" showed significantly better performance. Accordingly, both studies argue that while there are positive employment effects associated with some HCD-oriented

programs, the classic measures associated with Work First—sanctions and intensified job search—are most effective in quickly reducing welfare rolls. Given that such Work First measures are also inevitably cheap to implement, they may also be considered more cost-effective in the short term (Daguerre & Etherington, 2009). Indeed, as noted above, there is evidence of deterrence effects associated with increased compulsion and conditionality, so that welfare rolls decline even before the implementation of policy changes (Kvist & Pedersen, 2007).

Ochel (2005, p. 87) conducted a structured evidence review summarizing 18 evaluation studies of employability programs across five countries, suggesting that those mixing Work First and HCD elements were the best performers but generally confirming "the superiority of Work First programs over human capital investment" in achieving both exits from welfare and job entries. Martin's (2000, p. 93) review of evidence on training initiatives in Canada, Sweden, and the United States focused mainly on the findings of eight large-scale evaluations and found that some programs "have yielded low or even negative rates of return for participants when the estimated program effects on earnings or employment are compared with the cost of achieving those effects." Furthermore, HCD models have been criticized as encouraging "lock-in" effects, where unemployed people concentrating on participating in training may pass up opportunities to move into employment. However, Meadows (2006) notes that supposed lock-in effects associated with training in fact often represent the reality that job seekers wish to concentrate on, so that they complete (hopefully) useful training prior to moving toward work. Furthermore, doubts have been cast on claims that Work First approaches are a panacea for the problems of worklessness. First, while we might expect that rule changes limiting access to benefits and increasing compulsion will result in fewer claimants, it is not clear that such measures improve employability or chances of exiting benefits *to employment* (see, for example, Manning, 2009). And when Work First participants do enter employment, many evaluations have concluded that the same people would have found work anyway. Evaluations of ALMPs targeting a range of workless claimants in the United Kingdom—from young people to those with health problems—have identified significant "deadweight" effects (where the same person, or another member of the targeted group, would have found a job even in the absence of ALMP), indicating that the *additional* job impacts of such programs were limited (Blundell et al., 2003; National Audit Office, 2010; Van Reenen, 2004).

It also appears that time frame matters in evaluating the benefits of Work First– and HCD-oriented approaches. Gaps in longitudinal data represent a major problem in assessing the extent to which Work First and HCD offer long-term benefits, so that former participants are able to retain employment and progress in the workplace. However, there is some evidence that HCD initiatives continue to amortize (or provide a return on) human capital investments in the long run (Green & Hasluck, 2009). For example, Meager (2009) points to evidence from the small number of evaluations in Sweden, the United Kingdom, the United States, and elsewhere that have sought to follow training participants for more than a year after the completion of programs; he argues that there appears to be a "slow burn" impact of some investments in human capital that may continue to add to participants' employability over a prolonged period. Indeed, some studies of HCD programs have found little by way of job impact in the short term but significant positive effects in the long term. Positive long-term impacts of training-focused employability programs were reported in the 1990s in both the United Kingdom (Payne et al., 1996) and the United States (Hotz et al., 2006). Card et al.'s (2010) meta-analysis of more than 90 evaluations across 26 countries found that HCD program impacts were more powerful after two to three years than in the immediate-term with regard to positive employment effects and progression in the labor market reported by completers. Meadows's (2006) review of ALMPs similarly concludes that Work First services have a larger impact for less cost in the short term, while (well-resourced) HCD programs may have better long-term impacts on sustainability and progression:

> Over longer periods of time, and particularly over a period of five years or more, the effect of training increases and continues to grow. Moreover, those who have entered employment after a period of training seem to have better rates of job retention than those who have entered from Work First provision, probably because they are better able to match the skill requirements of the jobs they are doing. *(Meadows, 2006, p. 25)*

The corollary of the failure of some Work First programs to deliver long-term, sustainable outcomes is that participants may find themselves "cycling" between activation programs, short-term jobs, and periods of unemployment (Daguerre & Etherington, 2009). Lindsay (2010, p. 129), reviewing evidence from the United Kingdom's New Deal ALMPs during the 2000s, notes: "While initial job entry figures were encouraging, the New Deal programs soon faced an increasing problem of 'revolving door' participation, with clients moving from activation into short-term employment, and then back into unemployment, eventually repeating their participation in activation." These are potentially serious failings of Work First models (or indeed any other intervention that does not result in participants making sustainable progress in the labor market). It is difficult to square the positive evaluations of Work First programs as being effective at helping people into work with the reality that many "successful completers" will be back on benefits (and possibly again the target for Work First programs) within a year (Finn, 2011). There is also a risk that such employability programs will fail to offer routes out of poverty and into decent work. There remains a concern that "Work First programs are pitched in such a way that . . . interventions are far too brief and modest in scope to allow participants an opportunity to move into stable, high-quality jobs" (Peck & Theodore 2000, p. 132). As Ridzi (2009, p. 10) notes in examining US Work First programs, there is evidence that the lack of training provided can leave "successful" participants "permanently stranded in the low wage labor market."

There are also some concerns that a decisive shift toward Work First approaches to employability may result in *deskilling*, or at least reinforce processes of polarization in access to skills development that appear to increasingly define labor markets in the United States, United Kingdom, and beyond (Autor, 2010; Goos et al., 2009). In the United States, some evaluations have pointed to the deskilling effects of Work First programs, which can direct people with potentially valuable and transferable skills toward short-term, basic activation programs of little relevance to their needs. Participants have reported a "degradation of their intellect and technical abilities" as a result of mandatory participation in such programs (Gingrich, 2008, p. 388). Clearly there is a danger of a much more serious "lock-in" effect here, whereby participants in employability program are forced to undertake compulsory work of limited value rather than refreshing and applying existing skill sets. Certainly, large groups of low-wage employees in welfare states such as the United Kingdom report that they are unable to utilize their existing skills at work (Wright & Sissons, 2012), suggesting that Work First may be feeding the unemployed into unproductive positions characterized by underemployment and few opportunities for progression. This is an inefficient use of both human capital and public money. Furthermore, given the evidence that underemployment can produce negative socioeconomic and psychological outcomes for those at the bottom end of the labor market (see Virick & McKee-Ryan, this volume) there is a risk that, for some among the unemployed, Work First will do more harm than good.

Finally, both Work First and HCD models to employability assume a "supply side" approach—they seek to improve employment outcomes by intervening at the individual level, so that job seekers are adapted to better match the demands of employers and the labor market. Where labor demand is weak, such supply-side models will run into trouble. As Macnicol (2008, p. 592) notes, "improving employability does not by itself create jobs." This is particularly problematic for Work First programs, which are based on the assumption that there are accessible entry-level jobs into which the unemployed can be quickly placed. Yet there is substantial evidence to suggest that the impact of Work First programs is shaped by local labor market demand. For example, McVicar and Podivinsky (2009) and others have shown that the impact of New Deal employability programs has varied significantly across regions of the United Kingdom. In areas where mass job losses followed from the decline of traditional industries in the 1980s and 1990s and where economic regeneration remains incomplete, the performance of such programs has been least effective (Lindsay, 2010). North et al. (2009, p. 1038) criticize the "long-term neglect of demand-side issues" within the employability policy agenda in the United Kingdom (and some other OECD states), which largely fails to address issues around the amount and quality of work available; in particular, "Work First approaches remain constrained by the fact that, for many disadvantaged in the labor market and living in areas of concentrated worklessness, the low-paid entry-level jobs on offer provide few prospects for developing skills and moving out of poverty" (North et al., 2009, p. 1037).

It has proved difficult for Work First advocates to engage with these criticisms, because demand-side barriers to employment do not square with assumptions behind the Work First model: content (with its strong focus on job search), understanding of the labor market (which sees employers as the end recipients of employable candidates rather than proactive partners in providing appropriate opportunities), or approach to dealing with individuals (which relies on behavioral incentives and sanctions to "encourage" people into work). In an attempt to "individualize a collective problem" (Lindsay, 2007), it assumes that the problem of unemployment is a problem of the unemployed. Yet as Peck (1999) notes, it seems fanciful to argue that, for example, unemployment is five times higher in some of the United Kingdom's postindustrial areas than in wealthy suburbs, where opportunities are plentiful, because of a shared "local deficiency in the work ethic" in the former communities: "It is a straightforward reflection of job availability. In depressed areas, even the most active of active welfare-to-work policies will struggle to achieve results in the face of a shortage of jobs" (Peck, 1999, p. 357).

As noted above, to some extent the same critique can be directed at HCD-oriented employability programs, which similarly focus their resources on the individual, sometimes with little sense of connection to the level or characteristics of job demand in local labor markets. However, advocates of HCD can at least point to a rationale and intervention model that emphasize *long-term* employability benefits and transferable skills. Accordingly, even if HCD programs fail to help unemployed people move into work in the immediate term because of weak labor markets, they might be more likely to deliver skills that are applicable within future workplace contexts. In comparison, Work First programs often have little by way of skills content; in the context of the 2008–2009 recession and continuing economic crisis, they are likely to try to force some job seekers into opportunities that simply do not exist. The result may be that vulnerable workless people are forced off benefits as a result of a tightening of eligibility and conditionality while not being offered sustainable progression routes from welfare to work. A strengthening of Work First during the ongoing economic crisis may mean fewer people in the welfare benefits system, but "they may not be in employment either" (Lindsay & Houston, 2011, p. 714). Given the fragility of many local, regional, and national labor markets in an era of prolonged economic crisis, the rationale and added value of Work First programs (which are based on an assumption of healthy labor demand) is questionable. Even the OECD—previously a strong advocate of Work First—argues that "it is advisable to shift from a 'Work First' approach to active labor market policy to a 'Train First' approach for those at high risk of long-term unemployment in the context of the downturn" (Froy & Giguere, 2010, p. 13).

The discussion above highlights how the evaluation of Work First– and HCD-oriented approaches to employability remains contested territory. A number of reviews of evaluation evidence have pointed to the apparent superiority in immediate outcomes delivered by Work First employability programs while criticizing potential lock-in effects associated with HCD-oriented training (i.e., in line with their core objectives, Work First programs get people into paid employment more quickly). However, the research question informing such studies appears somewhat "loaded"; by definition, programs aiming to facilitate immediate job entry at all costs are more likely to report these outcomes than initiatives seeking to enhance human capital and provide more gradual (but perhaps also more sustainable) transitions to work. There is evidence that deterrence effects and compulsory job-search activities mean that Work First programs can push people off benefits and into work more quickly than would otherwise have happened. But for Work First to work, such programs need the right kind of participants (ideally those relatively close to the labor market and with fewer disadvantages) and the right kind of economic conditions (where there are ample entry-level job opportunities). We have also seen above that HCD-oriented training interventions may offer important routes into work for hard-to-reach groups as well as longer-term benefits for participants who can develop transferable skills that can lead to higher-quality employment.

Conclusions

Policymakers across the OECD and beyond are concerned to develop interventions that enhance the employability of unemployed and inactive groups and provide routes into work. Comparing Work First and HCD models of employability allows us to consider how the different rationales and content of ALMPs can shape how they connect with individuals and the labor market and the outcomes achieved for participants. As noted above, most ALMP regimes will be something of a hybrid combining elements of Work First and HCD (Castonguay, 2009). However, this chapter has noted that distinctive aims and approaches associated with

specific employability programs can be identified as being more Work First– or HCD-oriented. This matters, because of the different outcomes (contingent on individual characteristics and labor market conditions) that tend to be reported by these different kinds of programs and because the balance between Work First and HCD within employability programs continues to shift. Indeed, there is some evidence to suggest that the Work First model has enjoyed a position of increasing dominance in the United States, United Kingdom, and many other OECD countries (Froy & Giguere, 2010). Even those employability-focused programs that target hard-to-reach groups some distance from the labor market tend to be judged against job-entry targets (Castonguay, 2009). Policymakers faced with spiraling unemployment and shrinking budgets for public services may be increasingly tempted to pursue the cheaper option of Work First–oriented employability programs (Driver, 2009).

The evidence suggests that if the best results are to be achieved, a degree of balance will be required between Work First and HCD within employability programs. In the short term, Work First measures can help direct those unemployed people who are close to being job ready toward opportunities in buoyant labor markets (Daguerre & Etherington, 2009). On the other hand, where Work First is applied to job seekers facing multiple and complex barriers to employment, the evidence suggests that it is unlikely to produce sustainable positive outcomes and at best will result in driving people off welfare without work or into patterns of cycling between low-quality jobs and unemployment. In short, "Work First activation, which focuses on increasing motivation, generic skills and job-search effort, is not equal to the task of addressing the range of barriers faced by the most disadvantaged" (Lindsay, 2010, p. 139). Indeed, none of the narrowly focused policy evaluations discussed above deal with the potential broader social costs of Work First programs that seek to push people off benefits and into low-paid jobs. For those denied access to benefits (for example, as a result of falling foul of Work First sanctions) and indeed those trying to cope with the transition to entry-level, low-wage work, there may be increased risks of poverty. The social cost of poverty and inequality is a matter of considerable debate and beyond the scope of this chapter, but there is evidence to suggest that experiences of poverty feed into pressures on health, social work, and criminal justice budgets (Wilkinson & Pickett, 2009). At the very least, Work First approaches must be complemented by more HCD-oriented training and personal development for those who need more intensive support if they are to be assisted toward sustained, good-quality job outcomes. Yet for some analysts, Work First is synonymous with, indeed facilitates, polarized labor markets that offer few routes out of poverty for those at the bottom (Peck & Theodore, 2000).

More generally, both Work First and HCD elements of employability programs will work better if they are integrated with policies to promote more and better jobs in depressed labor markets and strategies to encourage employers to provide sustainable progression routes and training in the workplace. The latter workplace strategies are important if job seekers are to avoid the "revolving door" of participation in employability programs followed by temporary jobs without prospects, followed by unemployment, and then repeated participation in employability programs. The former policies to stimulate job growth are even more essential, because in an era of economic crisis, supply-side employability programs will inevitably run up against the problem of limited labor demand. There must be a coherent attempt to link the demand and supply sides of the employability equation so that we no longer "individualize the collective problem" of unemployment (McQuaid & Lindsay, 2005). Only by taking meaningful action to stimulate job growth—especially in those regions and localities hit hardest by recession and economic crisis—will policymakers ensure that those targeted by Work First programs will be able to move into the promised "unsubsidized jobs as quickly as possible" (Sol & Hoogtanders, 2005, p. 14), or that those benefiting from human capital development initiatives will be able to deploy their new skills within decent jobs, with opportunities for progression.

Our collective complicity in "individualizing" the problem of unemployment has legitimated a policy agenda that seeks to shift responsibility from the state to the individual victim of job loss. Yet we know from previous economic crises that "unemployment has to be examined as a characteristic of the society in which we live, not just of those members of it who happen to be out of work at any one time" (Sinfield, 1981, p. 122). There is a fundamental need to reconnect with the idea of collective solutions to unemployment that identify active roles for employers and policymakers in providing opportunity as well as the responsibilities of the individual to take up opportunities to work and/or train (Lindsay, 2010).

Future Directions

A number of research questions remain open. There is broad agreement on the need for a combination of Work First– and HCD-oriented approaches to employability, depending on individuals' barriers to employment and the labor market context (Castonguay, 2009; Daguerre & Etherington, 2009). However, as noted above, there remains considerable debate on what combination of policies works best in which circumstances. There is a need for further comparative and (crucially) longitudinal research to measure the impacts of different combinations of policies over time, across different labor markets, and on specific client groups. As noted above, the small number of studies that have sought to capture the long-term progression of participants after ALMP participation have challenged the assumed superiority of Work First interventions, identifying "slow burn" benefits from HCD. There is a need for much more longitudinal research on these issues. Much of the research agenda on employability programs also starts from the assumption that initiatives will either succeed or fail in delivering predicted positive outcomes; yet we have seen above that there may be *negative* consequences associated with different models of employability provision (ranging from lock-in effects associated with some training interventions to an increased risk of poverty and exclusion from the application of sanctions or as a result of forcing individuals to accept low-paid work). There is a need to broaden the research agenda to assess *all* the costs and benefits associated with Work First and HCD approaches to promoting employability, especially from the perspective of program participants.

At the level of the individual, there is a need to deploy multidimensional models for understanding and assessing employability (see McQuaid & Lindsay, 2005, for discussion) that capture a range of personal characteristics and barriers, so that we can match unemployed people to programs more effectively. Such models and assessment tools must engage with the full range of individual barriers, personal circumstances and external (including labor market) factors that shape employability trajectories. There may also be benefits in capturing psychological data (such as measures of individual coping strategies) in order to gain a better understanding of which interventions might work best for ALMP participants. Andersen's (2011) research with Danish ALMP completers has identified potential relationships between individuals' different coping strategies and the effects of employability interventions, concluding that such psychological measures should be used by PAs to ensure that the unemployed are directed toward appropriate programs. There is scope for further research on how coping strategies and other individual traits shape the outcomes achieved by ALMP participants in order to inform the personalization of services to the needs and characteristics of unemployed people.

Finally, as emphasized throughout this chapter, debates on employability policy remain too narrowly focused on the supply side of the labor market. The outcomes achieved by participants in both Work First– and HCD-oriented employability programs are contingent on a number of broader factors, including the extent and nature of local labor demand, the sustainability and quality of job opportunities, and the support provided by employers. If policy researchers are to inform this debate, they must adopt a broad-based and holistic approach to the study of employability—one that helps policymakers to grapple with the combination of individual, social, workplace, and labor market problems that are at the heart of the ongoing unemployment crisis in many communities. And if policymakers are to achieve their aim of helping unemployed people move from welfare to work, there must be a renewed commitment to addressing the full range of barriers that leave some people excluded from the world of work for prolonged periods. There must also be a thorough, critical assessment of the long-term benefits of both Work First and HCD interventions for individuals and economies. For example, future evaluations need to tackle directly the critique of Peck (1999) and others that Work First ALMPs do little more than facilitate (if necessary by compulsion) the churning of the low-skilled between low-wage jobs at the bottom of the labor market, with few participants permanently escaping the risk of recurring unemployment or poverty.

Key Points

• Both Work First and HCD programs play an important role in ALMPs designed to improve the employability of unemployed people. But in many OECD states, Work First programs have come to be seen as more cost-effective and play an increasingly prominent role.

• A number of evaluations have pointed to the cost-effectiveness of Work First programs in producing quicker job entries. While there is

mixed evidence as to the effectiveness of HCD, concerns have been raised that long-term human capital–oriented programs can produce "lock-in" effects, thus discouraging job seekers from taking up employment opportunities.

• However, this chapter has pointed to the need for more extensive research and evaluation before selecting Work First– and/or HCD-oriented employability programs. There is a need to consider the potential negative impacts of programs (for example, the socioeconomic and psychological effects on Work First participants who may find themselves churning between repeated periods of unemployment, ALMP participation, and insecure low-paid work). There is also a need to consider the long-term benefits of all programs, and especially HCD-oriented interventions, that may amortize investments in individuals' skills and employability over a longer time period.

• In order to evaluate effectively both Work First and HCD approaches, policymakers need to adopt a broad-based understanding of employability, which reflects how individual (including psychological) characteristics, personal circumstances, and external factors—such as the quality and quantity of jobs available—shape people's trajectories in the labor market.

References

Andersen, S. H. (2011). Exiting unemployment: How do program effects depend on individual coping strategies? *Journal of Economic Psychology, 32*(2), 248–258.

Autor, D. (2010). *The polarization of job opportunities in the US job market.* Washington DC: Center for American Progress.

Beatty, C., Fothergill, S., Houston, D., Powell, R., & Sissons, P. (2010). Bringing incapacity benefit numbers down: To what extent do women need a different approach? *Policy Studies, 31*(2), 143–162.

Blundell, R., Reed, H., Van Reenen, J., & Shephard, A. (2003). The impact of the New Deal for Young People on the labour market: A four year assessment. In R. Dickens, P. Gregg, & J. Wadsworth (Eds.), *The labour market under New Labour: The state of working Britain* (pp. 17–31). Basingstoke: Palgrave.

Bruttel, O., & Sol, E. (2006). Work First as a European model? Evidence from Germany and the Netherlands. *Policy and Politics, 34*(1), 69–89.

Card, D., Kluwe, J., & Weber, A. (2010). Active labour market policy evaluations: A meta-analysis. *Economic Journal, 120,* F452–F477.

Carpenter, M., Freda, B., & Speeden, S. (2007). *Beyond the workfare state: Labour markets, equalities and human rights.* Bristol, UK: Policy Press.

Castonguay, J. (2009). *Benchmarking carrots and sticks: Developing a model for the evaluation of work-based employment programs.* Amsterdam: University of Amsterdam.

Crisp, R., & Fletcher, D. (2008). *A comparative review of work-fare programs in the United States, Canada and Australia*. London: Department for Work and Pensions.

Daguerre, A. (2007). *Active labour market policies and welfare reform*. Basingstoke, UK: Palgrave.

Daguerre, A. (2008). The second phase of US welfare reform, 2000–2006: Blaming the poor again? *Social Policy and Administration, 42*(4), 362–378.

Daguerre, A., & Etherington, D. (2009). *Active labour market policies in international context: What works best? Lessons for the UK*. Norwich, UK: Stationery Office.

De Koning, J. (2007). *The evaluation of active labour market policies: Measures, public-private partnership and benchmarking*. Aldershot, UK: Edward Elgar.

Dean, H. (2003). Re-conceptualising welfare-to-work for people with multiple problems and needs. *Journal of Social Policy, 32*(4), 441–459

Dean, H. (2009). The ethics of welfare-to-work. In K. Schneider & H. Otto (Eds.), *From employability towards capability* (pp. 97–116). Luxembourg: Inter-Actions.

Deprez, L., & Butler, S. (2007). The capability approach and women's economic security: Access to higher education under welfare reform. In M. Walker & E. Unterhalter (Eds.), *Amartya Sen's capability approach and social justice in education*. New York: Palgrave.

Driver, S. (2009). Work to be done? Welfare reform from Blair to Brown. *Policy Studies, 30*(1), 69–84.

Finn, D. (2011). Welfare to work after the recession: from the New Deals to the Work Programme. In C. Holden, M. Kilkey, & G. Ramia (Eds.), *Social Policy Review 23* (pp. 127–145). Bristol, UK: Policy Press.

Fletcher, D. R. (2007). A culture of worklessness? Historical insights from the Manor and Park area of Sheffield. *Policy and Politics, 35*(1), 65–85.

Freeman, R. (2000). The US underclass in a booming economy. *World Economics, 1*(2), 89–100.

Froy, F., & Giguere, S. (2010). *Putting in place jobs that last*. Paris: OECD.

Gingrich, L. G. (2008). Social exclusion and double jeopardy: The management of lone mothers in the market-state social field. *Social Policy and Administration, 42*(4), 379–395.

Goldrick-Rab, S., & Shaw, K. (2005). Racial and ethnic differences in the impact of Work-First reforms on access to postsecondary education. *Educational Evaluation and Policy Analysis, 27*(4), 291–307.

Goos, M., Manning, A., & Salomons, A. (2009). Job polarisation in Europe. *American Economic Review Papers and Proceedings, 99*(2), 58–63.

Green A. E., & Hasluck, C. (2009). Action to reduce worklessness: What works? *Local Economy, 24*(1), 73–82.

Gregg, P. (2009). Job guarantees: Easing the pain of long-term unemployment. *Public Policy Research, 16*(3), 174–179.

Hagelund, A., & Kavli, H. (2009). In work is out of sight: Activation and citizenship for new refugees. *Journal of European Social Policy, 19*(3), 259–270.

Handler, J. (2006). Ending welfare as we know it: Welfare reform in the US. In P. Henman & M. Fenger (Eds.), *Administering welfare reform: International transformations in welfare governance* (pp. 117–136). Bristol, UK: Policy Press.

Hotz, J., Imbens, G., & Klerman, J. (2006). Evaluating the differential effects of alternative welfare-to-work training components: A re-analysis of the California GAIN program. *Journal of Labor Economics, 24*(3), 521–566.

Kluwe, J. (2006). *The effectiveness of European active labor market policy*. Bonn: Institute for the Study of Labor.

Kvist, J., & Pedersen, L. (2007). Danish activation policies. *National Institute Economic Review, 202,* 99–112.

Layard, R. (2000). Welfare-to-work and the New Deal. *World Economics, 1*(2), 29–39.

Layard, R. (2003). *Happiness: Has social science a clue?* Lionel Robbins Memorial Lecture 3. London: Centre for Economic Performance.

Layard, R. (2004). *Good jobs and bad jobs*. London: Centre for Economic Performance.

Lindsay, C. (2007). The United Kingdom's "Work First" welfare state and activation regimes in Europe. In A. Serrano Pascual & L. Magnusson (Eds.), *Reshaping welfare states and activation regimes in Europe* (pp. 35–70). Brussels: Peter Lang.

Lindsay, C. (2010). Re-connecting with "what unemployment means": Employability, the experience of unemployment and priorities for policy in an era of crisis. In I. Greener, C. Holden, & M. Kilkey (Eds.), *Social Policy Review 22* (pp. 121–147). Bristol, UK: Policy Press.

Lindsay, C., & Houston, D. (2011). Fit for purpose? Welfare reform and challenges for health and labour market policy in the UK. *Environment and Planning A, 43*(3), 703–721.

Lindsay, C., McQuaid, R. W., & Dutton, M. (2007). New approaches to employability in the UK: combining "Human Capital Development" and "Work First" strategies? *Journal of Social Policy, 36*(4), 539–560.

Lødemel, I., & Trickey, H. (2001). *An offer you can't refuse: Workfare in international perspective*. Bristol, UK: Policy Press.

Macnicol, J. (2008). Older men and work in the 21st century: What can the history of retirement tell us? *Journal of Social Policy, 37*(4), 579–595.

Manning, A. (2009). You can't always get what you want: The impact of the UK jobseekers' allowance. *Labour Economics, 16*(3), 230–250.

Martin, J. P. (2000). What works among active labour market policies: Evidence from OECD countries' experiences. *OECD Proceedings: Policies Towards Full Employment*, 191–219.

Mazzeo, C., Rab, S., & Eachus, S. (2003). Work-first or work-only: Welfare reform, state policy, and access to postsecondary education. *Annals of the American Academy of Political and Social Science, 586,* 144–171.

McQuaid, R. W., & Lindsay, C. (2005). The concept of employability. *Urban Studies, 42*(2), 197–219.

McVicar, D., & Podivinsky, J. M. (2009). How well has the New Deal for Young People worked in the UK regions? *Scottish Journal of Political Economy, 56*(2), 167–195.

Mead, L. M. (2003). Welfare caseload change: An alternative approach. *Policy Studies Journal, 3,* 163–185.

Meadows, P. (2006). *What works with tackling worklessness?* London: London Development Agency.

Meager, N. (2009). The role of training and skills development in active labour market policies. *International Journal of Training and Development, 13*(1), 1–18.

Mitchell, A., Lightman, E., & Herd, D. (2007). Work-first and immigrants in Toronto. *Social Policy and Society, 6*(3), 293–307.

National Audit Office (2010). *Support to incapacity benefit claimants through Pathways to Work*. London: National Audit Office.

North, D., Syrett, S., & Etherington, D. (2009). Tackling concentrated worklessness: Integrating governance and policy across and within spatial scales. *Environment and Planning C: Government and Policy, 27*(6), 1022–1039.

Ochel, W. (2005). Welfare-to-work experiences with specific work-first programmes in 23 selected countries. *International Social Security Review, 58*(4), 67–93.

Payne, J., Casey, B., Payne, C., & Connolly, S. (1996). *Long-term unemployment individual risk factors and outcomes*. London: Policy Studies Institute.

Peck, J. (1999). New labourers? Making a New Deal for the workless class. *Environment and Planning C: Government and Policy, 17*(3), 345–372.

Peck, J., & Theodore, N. (2000). Beyond employability. *Cambridge Journal of Economics, 24* (6), 729–749.

Peck, J., & Theodore, N. (2001). Exporting workfare/importing welfare-to-work: Exploring the politics of third way policy transfer. *Political Geography, 20*(4), 427–460.

Ray, K., Hoggart, L., Taylor, R., Vegeris, S., & Campbell-Barr, V. (2009). Rewarding responsibility? Long-term unemployed men and the welfare-to-work agenda. *Environment and Planning C: Government and Policy, 27*(6), 975–990.

Riach, K., & Loretto, W. (2009). Identity work and the "unemployed" worker: Age, disability and the lived experience of the older unemployed. *Work Employment and Society, 23*(1), 102–119.

Ridzi, F. (2009). *Selling welfare reform: Work-First and the new common sense of employment*. New York: New York University Press.

Ritchie, H., Casebourne, J., & Rick, J. (2005). *Understanding workless people and communities, DWP Research Report 255*. Leeds, UK: Corporate Document Services.

Serrano Pascual, A., & Magnusson, L. (2007). *Reshaping welfare states and activation regimes in Europe*. Brussels: Peter Lang.

Sinfield, A. (1981). Unemployment in an unequal society. In B. Showler & A. Sinfield (Eds.), *The workless state* (pp. 122–166). Oxford, UK: Martin Robertson.

Sol, E., & Hoogtanders, Y. (2005). Steering by contract in the Netherlands: New approaches to labour market integration. In E. Sol & M. Westerveld (Eds.), *Contractualism in employment services* (pp. 139–166). The Hague: Kluwer.

Tang, K. L., & Cheung, C. (2007). Programme effectiveness in activating welfare recipients to work: The case of Hong Kong. *Social Policy and Administration, 41*(7), 747–767.

Van Reenen, J. (2004). Active labour market policies and the British New Deal for the young unemployed in context. In R. Blundell, D. Card, & R. Freeman (Eds.), *Seeking a premier economy* (pp. 461–496). Chicago: University of Chicago Press.

Webster, D. (2005). Long-term unemployment, the invention of hysteresis and the misdiagnosis of structural unemployment in the UK. *Cambridge Journal of Economics, 29*(6), 975–995.

Wilkinson, R., & Pickett, K. (2009). *The spirit level: why more equal societies almost always do better*. London: Allen Lane.

Wright, J., & Sissons, P. (2012). *The skills dilemma: skills under-utilisation and low-wage work*. London: Work Foundation.

The JOBS Program: Impact on Job Seeker Motivation, Reemployment, and Mental Health

Richard H. Price *and* Amiram D. Vinokur

Abstract

JOBS is a research-based program delivered in a group format and designed to aid unemployed job seekers in their search for employment. The program has demonstrated positive impacts on job-search skills, motivation, reemployment rates, and mental health. The JOBS program was designed and tested in large-scale randomized trials at the Institute for Social Research at the University of Michigan. The positive effect of JOBS has been replicated in a number of national and international settings. Research, theory, and principles for best practice in the implementation of JOBS are discussed, as well as future directions for research and new applications.

Key Words: coping with unemployment, reemployment, job search, intervention, mental health, cost benefit

We are living in an era of global change comparable to earlier major social transitions marked by world wars and the Great Depression. These eras of transition have major impacts on individuals and on family life (Elder, 1995; Price, 1992). Dramatic economic, technological, and political changes are producing a wide range of transitions in working life, including involuntary job loss, forced retirement, and dramatically changed economic circumstances (Price, 2006; Price & Burgard, 2006, 2008). Job loss has well-documented multiple impacts on individuals, including depression, increases in family conflict and violence, alcohol and drug abuse, and family turmoil (Barling, 1990; Vinokur, 1997; see also in this volume Bambra & Eikemo, McKee-Ryan & Maitoza, Paul, Hassel, & Moser, and Sinfield).

In attempting to make the transition back to paid employment, job losers are faced with a set of critical challenges. They may have had no previous experience in job-search and may be unfamiliar with the critical skills required for success. Many may not have the capacity to identify their own marketable skills or to locate where these skills are sought in the marketplace. As commonplace as it may seem today, they may not have a ready ability to use their personal social networks effectively to identify job leads or mobilize support from others. Job losers may not have had experience making a convincing presentation of their credentials or know what might especially interest a prospective employer. None of these skills are taught in any standard school curriculum or in the workplace.

Some of these skills can be found in a handbook aimed at helping job seekers find new employment (Bolles, 2011). But even some familiarity with the needed skills will not be adequate unless the job seeker also has the knowledge and confidence to enact them and can rebound from the inevitable rejections and failures encountered during the job-search process.

These substantial job-search challenges are further compounded by the fact that many people experiencing job loss have had their confidence shaken or may even be mildly depressed. In addition they are often dealing with stresses and strains in family life that comes with job loss, including economic strain and disruption of familiar family roles and routines (Jahoda, 1982). Searching for a job inevitably involves many rejections and refusals before any glimpse of possible success can be seen. Therefore any effective program designed to aid unemployed people in the challenging and multifaceted task of job-search must not only focus on what job-search skills are needed but also offer them a safe and supportive learning environment where confidence as well as skills can be built. Since job-search is an interpersonal and social process requiring the acquisition of unfamiliar new behaviors, there must also be opportunities for social modeling and active learning designed to fit the unique circumstances of the individual.

In this chapter we present the conceptual model and delivery protocol of the JOBS program, which is designed to help unemployed individuals gain paid employment. We also describe research on the JOBS program demonstrating its effectiveness and identify a number of factors that make it effective. We also report our experience in disseminating JOBS both in the United States and a number of international settings. Finally, we discuss future directions for research on JOBS, considering both applications to new populations and research aimed at identifying underlying social psychological principles that make programs like JOBS effective.

The JOBS Model

Transitions, including the experience of job loss, are almost always times of elevated risk (Elder and O' Rand, 1995). They are also natural opportunities for prevention programs that support people experiencing a risky transition. Our program of research on job loss was motivated by our sense that helping people navigate these transitions could contribute in useful ways to their lives and well-being. The program grew out of programs of research on stress and unemployment supported by grants from the National Institute of Mental Health and conducted at the Institute for Social Research at the University of Michigan in the late 1960s by Cobb, Kasl, and French (Cobb, & Kasl, 1977). In the early 1980s this research continued, largely focusing on the mental health consequences of unemployment as assessed in a large community study (Kessler, House, & Turner, 1987) and also in another large community study of Vietnam Veterans (Vinokur, Caplan, & Williams, 1987). As this

research went forward, we turned our attention to the development of an intervention program to help unemployed workers seek a way back to the marketplace and at the same time protect their mental health. We therefore designed the JOBS intervention program for anyone seeking a job, with a focus on those currently unemployed.

Furthermore, the JOBS program was designed to be delivered to groups of job seekers with eight to twenty participants using a workshop format that allows for extensive interaction between the participants and two group facilitators. We implemented the program in various settings including community centers, social service agencies, union halls, churches, and community colleges.

It was clear that in a successful intervention the emotional and psychological needs of the job seekers must be addressed along with the need to learn job seeking skills, since most job seekers have recently endured the stressful, sometimes traumatic, experience of job loss. Thus the intervention protocol includes heavy reliance on (1) self-esteem and confidence boosting techniques and (2) the participants' own record of strengths by giving them visible opportunities to realize, show, and build on their personal resources. The attention to the emotional needs of the job seekers and the reliance on their strengths emphasized in the JOBS program sets it apart from past efforts to accelerate the return of the unemployed to the job market in the Job Club program (Azrin, & Beasalel, 1982).

This emphasis on designing the JOBS programming in ways that address the emotional needs of the participants has the dual goal of making the participants' job-search more persistent and effective and at the same time preventing the deterioration in mental health often observed among the unemployed. Our research and that of others has already shown that job loss and unemployment places the person at risk for having a high level of depressive symptoms or developing a major depression. It has also been shown that reemployment brings with it a restoration to the normal level of mental health that existed prior to the unemployment. In designing the JOBS program with the dual goal of creating effective job-search and addressing the emotional needs of unemployed job seekers, we intended it to be a preventive intervention for those especially at risk for depression as a result of job loss.

Most generally, the design the JOBS program was based on a combination of social psychological evidence-based principles for successful behavioral change (Caplan, Vinokur, & Price, 1997). The most general principle that applied to the design of the JOBS intervention was that successful behavioral outcomes are achieved through the combination of techniques that build up relevant skills and the motivation to use them. We then designed principles and techniques to maximize the acquisition of skills involved in job-search as well as those to enhance and maintain the motivation of the job seekers. For building skills, we applied the principles of active learning through modeling and the use of role-playing exercises. For enhancing motivation, we applied techniques that build job-search self-efficacy. To safeguard motivation and self-efficacy, we applied principles of inoculation against setbacks. Finally to ensure effective delivery, we taught trainers to provide unconditional positive regard, supportive positive feedback, and moderate self-disclosure as well as to model skillful behaviors before having participants engage in role-play exercises.

Of major importance in the implementation of the JOBS program is the appropriate selection and training of facilitators. The group facilitators must be experienced in the use of active teaching processes involving group problem solving and modeling appropriate behaviors. Facilitators are not simple conveyors of information but experts in navigating the group processes according to the JOBS protocol, with the ability to connect emotionally with the participants. They provide appropriate social support and guidance as well as promoting rewarding interactions among the participants. To select potentially successful trainers we looked for persons who are empathic and socially skilled as well as able to adapt and facilitate social interactions in a group setting. We have often resorted to auditions where we asked candidates to enact various training episodes or sections from our intervention protocol while our staff played the role of unemployed workshop participants. Overall, our trainers came from diverse backgrounds with these skills as the major criterion for selection. Finally, we paired female and male facilitators in delivering the program together to each group of unemployed persons because this would provide additional role model similarity for participants.

Figure 31.1 shows the conceptual framework underlying the JOBS program that guides both delivery and research. The framework describes the (1) intervention itself, (2) mediating processes produced by the program and reemployment, and (3) the economic and mental health outcomes for the individual job seeker.

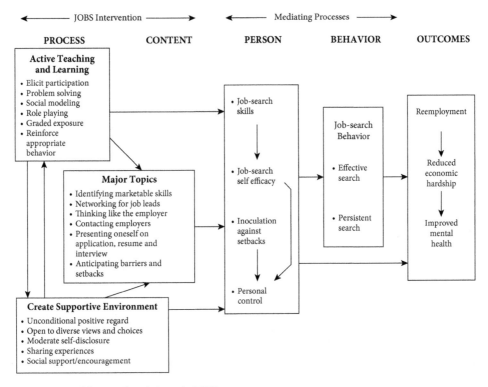

Figure 31.1 A conceptual framework underlying the JOBS program.

The intervention itself is described in Figure 31.1 combines two types of processes designed to maximize the acquisition of required skills. One process is that of active teaching and learning that involves eliciting job-search information from the participants themselves thus relying on their resources and strengths. In this process the trainers engage the participants in problem solving discussions followed by modeling various job-search behaviors, and role playing practice. The facilitators provide a variety of opportunities for social modeling, role playing in pairs and in groups, graded exposure to new tasks to promote mastery and positive reinforcement of appropriate behaviors, always avoiding critical or negative feedback. The program is designed to create a social environment where the participant feels positive regard rather than being judged by others, where a variety of views and choices are considered appropriate, where there is a positive norm for sharing experiences with one another and mutual support and encouragement.

The content of the intervention includes participants identifying their own marketable skills, networking for job leads, self presentation to prospective employers, and anticipating the setbacks and barriers that they will inevitably encounter.

Our conceptual framework indicates two mediating processes need to be completed to result in successful outcomes. One process involves the job seeker as a person who acquires the job-search skills thereby also developing job-search self-efficacy. The other process involves the effectiveness and persistence of the job-search behavior itself. Job-search behavior that is effective and persistent leads to reemployment, the reduction of economic hardship, and improvement mental health.

The overall result is that the JOBS program is carefully designed to increase participant's sense of job-search self-efficacy and their ability to cope with the setbacks encountered in the job-search process. Both of the research program we turn to next and the actual design and implementation of the program we describe later are guided by the model in Figure 31.1.

The JOBS Research Program

Our program of research has followed the prevention research cycle (Price, Friedland, Choi, & Caplan, 1998) moving from (1) risk-factor research with vulnerable populations to identify modifiable risk factors, to (2) randomized preventive efficacy trials to test the impact of interventions aimed at reducing potentially modifiable risk factors. The goal of the prevention research cycle is to combine the tools of epidemiology to identify populations at risk with the power of randomized trials to evaluate efficacy of prevention efforts aimed at reducing adverse health and mental health outcomes and finally to conduct services research to guide effective program implementation and dissemination. For successful efficacy trials, research moves to (3) effectiveness trials to test the impact of interventions with various vulnerable populations in actual service settings and varied national and cultural contexts. In both efficacy and effectiveness trials additional research is undertaken to identify the mechanisms by which interventions have their effects. When positive effectiveness trials are obtained, (4) dissemination strategies for successful programs are undertaken.

Risk-Factor Research: Unemployment Risks to Individuals and Families

Results from a community epidemiology survey in a sample of high unemployment census tracts in southeastern Michigan established that job losers showed significant elevations of depression, anxiety, and self-reported physical illness (Kessler, House, & Turner, 1987). In addition, social support of spouses reduced the psychosocial impact and social isolation associated with job loss among the unemployed (Kessler, Turner, & House, 1988). In a set of analyses designed to identify key processes that intervene in the relationship between unemployment and poor mental health, Kessler, Turner, and House (1987) identified financial strain as a critical mediating factor. Price, van Ryn, and Vinokur (1992), Vinokur, Price, and Schul (1995), and Vinokur and Schul (1997) corroborated these epidemiological findings and also identified other modifiable vulnerability factors, including elevated depressive symptoms, and low sense of mastery.

Taken together, these findings were critical in the design of the Michigan Prevention Research Center (MPRC) preventive trials. A later study of 756 persons experiencing job loss over a period of 2 years by Price, Choi, and Vinokur (2002) clarified still further links in the chain of adversity between job loss and poor health. Their study shows that depression is an immediate response to job loss, but that loss of personal control and increases in financial hardship both play a critical role in subsequent reports of poor health and declines in social and emotional functioning. Together these studies show how the interplay of adverse life events such as job loss trigger depression, economic hardship, and the erosion of personal control, leading to deteriorating social and emotional functioning and poor health (see also, in this volume, both Bambra & Eikemo and Paul et al.)

The negative effects of job loss radiate well beyond the unemployed individual. The stressful circumstances of job loss and economic strain powerfully influence intimate relationships in the family (see also McKee-Ryan & Maitoza, this volume). Vinokur, Price, and Caplan (1996) studied the impact of financial strain on couples in terms of changes in providing social support, such as help, advice and understanding, and engaging in social undermining behavior, such as criticism and insults. A unique feature of their studies has been measurement of support and undermining both provided and received by each partner, allowing more reliable combined estimates of support and undermining processes in the relationship. Their results demonstrated that financial strain results in a decrease in social support and an increase in social undermining in couples, which, in turn, increases both depressive symptoms and marital dissatisfaction. It should be noted that the decrease in marital satisfaction may account for a documented increase in marital separation and divorce (Stack, 1981). The effects of social undermining in these analyses were significantly stronger than those of social support, particularly with respect to symptoms of depression. These findings are consistent with Vinokur and van Ryn (1993). The effects of unemployment on family process suggest that reemployment can have equally important positive effects on the well-being of family members.

Randomized Trials: Tests of JOBS Efficacy

Our approach to test the efficacy of the JOBS program has striven to design sequential trials in which each new trial capitalizes on knowledge derived from the last (Caplan, Vinokur, & Price, 1997; Price, Friedland, & Vinokur, 1998). Designed using behavioral science principles to enhance skill, motivation, and a sense of self-efficacy in job-search, the JOBS program was delivered by trained facilitators in a group format to unemployed workers. The efficacy of the program was tested in large-scale randomized trials with a 2-year follow-up and measurement of economic status, mental health, and family relationship outcomes. JOBS also served as a laboratory to study human coping with adversity— that is, the study of cognitive, emotional, and behavioral adjustment that takes place following a stressful event (Hobfoll, 1989). Unlike most other evaluations of social program innovations, JOBS

was designed not only to measure impact but also to measure the underlying psychosocial processes by which the program had its effects, both in providing knowledge to improve the program and also in testing hypotheses concerning the role of support, skill, self-efficacy, and inoculation against setbacks in coping with adversity.

Results of the first JOBS randomized trial (Caplan, Vinokur, Price, & van Ryn, 1989) indicated that, compared with control group participants, the program produced higher motivation to persist in job-search efforts, more rapid and higher rates reemployment, and reduction in mental health problems. Furthermore, a benefit cost analysis (Vinokur, van Ryn, Gramlich, & Price, 1991) demonstrated that the JOBS program provided economic benefits to recipients and increases in government revenues (taxes paid on income that followed reemployment) that far exceeded the cost of delivery. This benefit-cost study has clear policy implications for the economic benefits of science based job-search programs if implemented with high quality and fidelity to their original design.

After demonstrating beneficial effects of the first JOBS efficacy trial, we then conducted additional risk-factor analyses of these preventive efficacy trial data and were able to demonstrate that the beneficial mental health effects of the JOBS intervention were primarily experienced by an identifiable subgroup of individuals who were at highest risk for later episodes of depression unless they received the JOBS intervention (Price, van Ryn, & Vinokur, 1992). These individuals were characterized by elevated levels of depressive symptoms, high levels of financial strain, and low levels of social assertiveness. These findings led to critical design changes in our preventive intervention to prospectively test the hypothesis that it is these individuals, who are not only at higher risk for significant deterioration in mental health but are also most likely to benefit from the JOBS preventive intervention.

The second JOBS efficacy trial study provided a replication of the results of the first JOBS experiment with several enhancements and new extensions. In particular, the delivery procedures that involve active teaching and learning and inoculation against setbacks were emphasized and expanded. The results of the second efficacy trial (Vinokur, Price, & Schul, 1995) demonstrated that the JOBS intervention significantly decreased depression, improved role and emotional functioning, and also increased rates and quality of reemployment, which, in turn, had a major impact on decreasing financial strain. The preventive impact of the second enhanced JOBS intervention on depression was also demonstrated, using measures obtained from spouses and other significant others who reported on the job seeker's mental health and role and emotional functioning. In addition, the second efficacy trial of JOBS significantly increased the sense of mastery among the participants, and this increase in mastery had a preventive impact on depression symptoms. Finally, the extended JOBS II field experiment demonstrated that the intervention primarily improved the mental health and the reemployment outcomes of the high-risk respondents. A 2-year follow-up of the JOBS II randomized trial (Vinokur, Schul, Vuori, & Price, 2000) demonstrated that the program had an impact on a wide range of psychosocial outcomes including motivation, mental health, and physical health; it also provided economic benefits through higher-paying and higher-quality jobs.

Individual Mechanisms Underlying JOBS Effectiveness

One of the distinctive features of our research program has been the development of measurement and analysis techniques that allow the identification of those factors most important in producing positive outcomes in preventive trials. For example, early in our program of research on the effects of the JOBS program, van Ryn and Vinokur (1992) identified increases in the sense of job search self-efficacy as a critical mediator produced by the JOBS intervention that increased job-search motivation, reemployment, and positive mental health outcomes.

As our program of research has continued, additional individual psychosocial processes have been uncovered that account for the effectiveness of the JOBS program. Vuori and Vinokur (2005) identified job-search preparedness, the combination of job-search self-efficacy and inoculation against setbacks, as a key factor in unemployed populations in Finland who benefited from the jobs intervention. Price, Vinokur and Friedland (2002) identified the role of job seeker as a resource in undertaking the complex social task of successful job search. That is, teaching unemployed persons that the task of job search is greatly enhanced when the individual recognizes that job search is a "job in itself" and that the role of job seeker is one that can be understood and played skillfully to increase the chances of finding a good job. Job search is often stressful and filled with failures and setbacks. Vinokur and Schul (1997) reported that JOBS increased resilience and

inoculation against setbacks protecting job seekers from distress and depression not only in their current job search but subsequently in the event of a second job loss. Finally, Choi, Price and Vinokur (2003) showed that group processes that enhance self efficacy were key ingredients in group-based aspects of the JOBS intervention.

Group Influences on Job-Search Self-Efficacy, Motivation, Reemployment, and Mental Health

Some of the positive effects of the JOBS program are due to individual psychological changes, but some are due to the way group processes that are designed into the delivery of the JOBS program. Choi, Price, and Vinokur (2003) focused on identifying JOBS program group influences on job-search self-efficacy, since there is a large literature on social learning theory suggesting that efficacy processes are important in meeting challenging tasks (Bandura, 1977; Gist & Mitchell, 1992). Earlier MPRC research by Vinokur and Schul (2002) had shown that individual job-search self-efficacy was a key mediator linking job seekers experience in the program to reemployment and improved mental health outcomes. Thus it was crucial to see which elements of the group process in the JOBS program actually influenced this key change in participant motivation. Interestingly, some influences on job-search self-efficacy came from both individual-level experiences and from the group itself. Seeing participation in the group as a positive experience and the leadership of the group as supportive was influential at the individual level, while the open climate of the group itself and both gender and educational diversity were positive influences on people's job-search self-efficacy at the group level. It is often assumed that groups need to be specialized by educational level or gender to be effective. Our results suggest the opposite. Perhaps a wider variety of educational backgrounds and having both men and women in the group provides a useful range of role models for participants.

A second important question is how do group perceptions of key features of the JOBS program influence later distress, depression, and reemployment? The JOBS program was designed to address five major psychosocial issues every time the intervention was delivered by (1) employing active learning methods, (2) ensuring skilled trainer delivery, (3) preparing participants for setbacks, (4) providing a supportive learning environment, and finally (5) providing explicit instruction in job-search skills. Vuori, Price, Mutanen, and Malmberg-Heimonen (2005) examined the degree to which each of these aspects of the JOBS group process influenced both reemployment and mental health. Not all features of the group process were equally influential. Indeed, trainer skills were particularly important in reducing depressive symptoms and in producing higher levels of reemployment. Of particular importance was the finding that group emphasis on preparation for setbacks had a much more substantial impact on the reduction of distress and depression and was especially powerful in helping those at highest risk for depression. Earlier studies at the individual level of analysis also showed that those with elevated depressive symptoms benefitted from JOBS with better protected mental health outcomes than their control-group counterparts (Vinokur, Price, & Schul, 1995).

Demonstrations of Effectiveness in Service Settings

Our research program follows the public health distinction between preliminary efficacy trials aimed at demonstrating impact under more controlled, experimentally ideal conditions and later effectiveness trials aimed at demonstrating wider impact over time with different populations; it was implemented under a range of actual organizational and service delivery conditions. Effectiveness trials are an essential test of the robustness of the program and the range of populations for which it is appropriate. The findings reported below demonstrate that the JOBS intervention has demonstrated broad effectiveness with a variety of outcomes, populations, and modes of service delivery.

LARGE-SCALE IMPLEMENTATION

In an early effectiveness trial, Price, Friedland, Choi and Caplan (1998) reported a large-scale demonstration conducted in three cities in California and serving over 6,500 unemployed persons. The demonstration showed that the JOBS program could be implemented on a large scale, training human service workers in three demographically diverse communities, and could be implemented with high quality. A subsequent cross-level study (Choi, Price, & Vinokur, 2003) of the supportive and skill-building group process in the Winning New Jobs (WNJ) program, the implementation program of JOBS in California, demonstrated that the carefully designed group learning environment engendered by the program produced increases in self-efficacy in participants that was critical for subsequent successful job search.

WELFARE-TO-WORK CLIENTS

Effectiveness trials have also been conducted with welfare clients as part of government welfare-to-work initiatives. From 2000 to 2002 workshops were implemented and evaluated within the "From the Ground Up" program of the Department of Social Services of Baltimore County, Maryland. At present, the program is still ongoing in its original format. The workshops provided job-search skills to the welfare-to-work clients and were evaluated on the mental health and employment outcomes of participating clients. The evaluation included baseline data collected from 1,756 program applicants of whom 1,543 entered and participated in the program and 213 applicants who did not participate. The workshop produced positive impacts on participants increasing their motivation and readiness to engage in job-search. Workshops also improved mental health, reduced depressive symptoms, and increased participant sense of personal control. Follow-up assessments after clients' participation in the comprehensive "From the Ground Up" program, which included the JOBS workshop, demonstrated that participation improved the mental health and well-being of the participating clients and also facilitated their entry into the workforce.

International Dissemination of JOBS: Finland, China, and Ireland

As the scientific evidence began to accumulate on the effectiveness of the JOBS program, we began to receive the inquiries from a variety of countries interested in the implementation of the program (Price, 2006). In some cases, these inquiries led to long-term scientific collaborations and to program and policy impacts in the collaborating nations. In other cases, JOBS contributions primarily involved the dissemination of behavioral science knowledge and the training of service providers in other countries. In all cases we worked intensively with our partners in training the people who delivered the program. Cultural adaptations consisted largely of translation of the training manual into the native language of facilitators and participants and adapting examples in the manual and program so that they were appropriate to the cultural setting. However, we found that the group-based process for active learning, the overall program structure, and the ordering of topics in the JOBS program were well accepted in all the international settings in which the program was implemented. Below we briefly describe three major scientific collaborations in Finland, the People's Republic of China, and Ireland. In addition to the dissemination projects described below, JOBS has been disseminated by collaborators in the Netherlands, Sweden, and South Korea.

FINLAND

Collaboration in Finland began with preliminary discussions and scientific exchanges with Jukka Vuori, of the Finnish Institute of Occupational Health. It and the Ministry of Labor in Finland later supported an initial randomized trial in Turku and a large-scale nationwide dissemination of the JOBS program called "Työhön." Analysis of the randomized trial in Turku showed that the program replicated the effects obtained in the United States and, in addition, was effective with individuals experiencing chronic long-term unemployment (Vuori, Silvonen, Vinokur, & Price, 2002). Further analyses on mediating mechanisms responsible for program's effectiveness showed that it had its effects through increased job seeker motivation and job-search preparation (Vuori & Vinokur, 2005). The program was then disseminated on a national scale. A cross-level analysis of the national program identified critical group-level processes in the intervention that influenced job-search motivation and mental health (Vuori, et al, 2005). A description of the cultural adaptation of the program and its implementation is available as well (Vuori & Price, 2006). Vuori and his colleagues at the Finnish Institute of Occupational Health have extended this program of research by adopting the JOBS model and creating new programs across the life course, including adolescents making the transition to work and persons approaching retirement.

PEOPLE'S REPUBLIC OF CHINA

In the last two decades, the transformation of the Chinese economy from state socialism to a market economy has brought significant benefits and dramatic economic growth but also significant strains and dislocations that have had substantial impact on Chinese workers. Employees in State Owned Enterprises are being laid off in large numbers and are feeling the impact of increasing job insecurity, job loss and distress. The impact of this economic transformation in Chinese society has been documented in a survey of workers in seven Chinese cities (Price & Fang, 2002) and found to vary from generation to generation. While the younger generation of workers searching for jobs is intensely worried about their future and show high levels of distress, middle-aged workers who survived the Cultural Revolution feel relatively secure, while the elderly are deeply discouraged by their prospects for the future. In collaboration with the National Academy of Sciences of the People's Republic of China, implementation of the JOBS program in China was undertaken in seven cities and data were collected not only from unemployed job seekers who participated in the program but also from their spouses or significant others. Data on the family dynamics of unemployed Chinese workers and their spouses have yielded interesting cross-cultural comparisons between US and Chinese couples (Price, Choi, & Lim, 2006).

IRELAND

While economic growth and prosperity has been the rule among urban areas in much of Ireland, rural Ireland and particularly Northern Ireland continue to experience chronic unemployment and worker discouragement, with related health, mental health, and alcohol problems. We have undertaken a partnership with Professor Margaret Barry and her colleagues at the National University of Ireland and Anne Sheridan in the Irish Health Service to implement the JOBS program with experimental trials both in Northern Ireland and in the Republic of Ireland. The research results indicate that the JOBS program is effective not only with chronically unemployed Irish workers but also with service recipients in the mental health system (Barry, 2005). Encouraged by these results, the Irish government is planning to expand JOBS services.

JOBS in Practice: Protocol for Training and Delivery

Below we briefly describe the protocol for training group facilitators and delivery of JOBS. It is important to note at the outset that this description or even access to the materials described here do not constitute an adequate basis for successful delivery of the JOBS program. Intensive training of group facilitators and follow-up training and monitoring for quality delivery of JOBS is essential.

OVERVIEW

The JOBS Program is a group-based psychological educational intervention that has the dual goals of promoting reemployment and enhancing the coping capacities of unemployed workers and their families. At the core of the program design are three broad theoretical principles that involve the acquisition of job-search self-efficacy (Bandura, 1997) and inoculation against setbacks (Meichenbaum, 1985) using active learning processes (Zimmerman, 2001). A more detailed description is provided in Price and Vinokur (1995). The intervention offers a system for delivery and evaluation of a job-search skill enhancement workshop for unemployed job seekers 17 to 65 years of age. Through a series of interactive sessions the JOBS Program helps participants identify effective job-search strategies, improve job-search skills, learn how to overcome setbacks in the job-search process, increase confidence to implement one's job-search skills, and remain motivated to engage and persist in job-search activities until they become reemployed.

PROGRAM DESIGN

The actual design of the JOBS program involved a group learning situation with twelve to twenty participants per group occurring in five 4-hour sessions during a 1-week period (see manual by Curran, Wishart, & Gingrich, 1999). Participants were recruited in unemployment offices and learning groups were facilitated by male-female trainer pairs that had been carefully trained to deliver a standardized group protocol. Unlike other job-search programs, the focus was on the group participants rather than the trainer, participant-to-participant interactions were emphasized, effective behavior was reinforced and criticism eliminated; furthermore, participants were supported rather than challenged, being taught the idea that "believing you can do it"; that is, engagement in a successful job-search was emphasized. Throughout the program participants went through a series of active learning cycles beginning with trainers presenting a topic such as finding job leads, then role modeling effective job-search tactics, followed by participants practicing their new skills within the group, all of which this was followed by debriefing and group discussion of the newly learned skills (Curran et al,, 1999). A schematic presentation of the cycles is displayed in Figure 31.2.

How It Works

The JOBS program is delivered during five half-day sessions in employment offices, social service settings, community settings, and outplacement programs. Because social support is crucial to participants' ability to learn new skills and face job-market challenges, the program is delivered to groups of twelve to twenty job seekers. JOBS workshop leaders use active learning methods to engage participants rather than didactic teaching techniques. Workshop leaders model by example

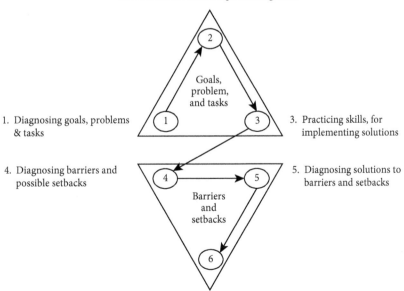

Cycles of the Active Teaching and Learning Intervention Process

2. Diagnosing solutions for problems and needed activities and skills for implementing them

Goals, problem, and tasks

1. Diagnosing goals, problems & tasks

3. Practicing skills, for implementing solutions

4. Diagnosing barriers and possible setbacks

5. Diagnosing solutions to barriers and setbacks

Barriers and setbacks

6. Practicing skills to overcome barriers and setbacks

Figure 31.2 Cycles of the active teaching and learning process in JOBS.

and reinforce supportive behavior and effective job-search activities and skills and work to create a supportive learning environment through exercises that provide opportunities for participants to learn from and support each other.

Workshop leaders help participants discover principles of successful and unsuccessful job-search strategies, model and role-play effective job-search activities and techniques, such as job interview, and encourage active participation. Program participants are engaged in problem-solving processes to help them cope with unemployment-related stress, the job-search process, and the inevitable setbacks they will encounter. Because the program is designed with a heavy reliance on group discussions and interactions among the participants involving social support, members are encouraged to raise their individual concerns and receive support and advice from both the workshop leaders and other group members. Thus, the program accommodates the individual needs of the participants. Recruitment begins in central organizational settings such as state employment offices, various social service organizations, or outplacement programs in human resources departments.

TRAINING WORKSHOP FACILITATORS

JOBS program workshop facilitators must be trained by master trainers from the Michigan Prevention Research Center. Workshop leaders should be carefully chosen by the master trainer or agency personnel to have demonstrated skills or experience in group facilitation and collaboration. They should be rigorously trained to be able to co-train together and to build trust among program participants. Training teams should consist of pairs of co-trainers. In some contexts male/female co-trainers may be preferred. The training is provided in a 2-week course followed by another week of later feedback from a master trainer observing actual delivery of the program. A program manual, *JOBS: A Manual for Teaching People Successful Job-Search Strategies*, outlines techniques for selecting and hiring workshop leaders; it describes the training, design, and delivery of the Mock Job-Search Seminar and Trainer's Forum. One program manual is required for each workshop leader as it also includes implementation and evaluation materials for the five-session job-search intervention.

WHAT PARTICIPANTS GAIN

Figure 31.3 provides a portrait of what participants gain by attending the JOBS workshop and a more detailed rationale for the way the JOBS program

has been designed (also see Price & Vinokur, 1995). JOBS is designed to produce improved job-search skills, increased confidence, increased awareness of appropriate strategies for coping with stress and setbacks, and increased motivation for job-search. First and foremost, it is essential to have especially skilled trainers who can generate trust, are perceived as credible, and can generate participation while also increasing participants' motivation and confidence in their own abilities. High levels of active participation stand in contrast to more didactic and passive approaches to teaching job-search skills. Increased participation not only increases engagement but also improves opportunities for skill acquisition, opens people up to a range of possible strategies, and increases confidence. The program provides a safe and supportive learning environment where trainers encourage and support participants and encourage participants to support each other. Group exercises are done in a supportive atmosphere that not only enhances learning and minimizes dropouts but also enhances an approach where participants are more likely to risk trying out new ideas. Problem-solving strategies help participants to be ready when setbacks occur by learning how to reframe their experience and devise ways to identify and overcome barriers. Knowing how to successfully deal with problems that confront one in the job-search process is a key coping strategy for dealing with stressful encounters.

Support Materials

The JOBS manual for training and delivery can be found at: http://www.isr.umich.edu/src/seh/mprc/PDFs/Jobs%20Manual.pdf

It consists of five chapters and is accompanied by two videotapes. The five chapters of the manual and the videotapes are described below.

The JOBS implementation manual is Chapter 1 (110 single-spaced pages), which provides a thorough description of how trainers should be trained for high-quality delivery of the JOBS program. The jobs implementation manual covers topics such as selecting and hiring trainers, the orientation and description of the training process, the description of intervention seminar training, the trainers forum for follow-up training of trainers to fine-tuned trainer skills, and logistical material on locating and working with sites as well as a bibliography.

The JOBS workshop protocol is Chapter 2 (78 pages) with detailed script to guide trainers during initial training and throughout the delivery process. It describes in detail how each day of the training program is laid out, how sessions work, and covers

JOB SEARCH SKILLS	INCREASED CONFIDENCE	INCREASED AWARENESS	INCREASED MOTIVATION
An improved set of specific job search skills and an expanded range of job search ideas.	in their ability to use those job search skills and motivation to put the skills/ideas into action.	of strategies for managing the stress and setbacks that are inherent in a job search.	to use those strategies when faced with stress or setbacks.

Strategies Used to Accomplish the Workshop's Goals

PARTICIPATION	SAFE & SUPPORTIVE ENVIRONMENT	PROBLEM SOLVING STRATEGIES	SKILLED TRAINERS
• Allows for a maximum level of interaction among participants • Fun, highly interactive format • Participants rehearse new skills	• Trainers encourage supportive behavior among the participants • Group exercises provide opportunities for participants to demonstrate supportive behavior	• Group problem-solving process • Participant anticipates barriers to job search challenges and prepares solutions	• Trainers guide and encourage • Engage participants in the workshop • Encourage participants to try out new behaviors • Expert at helping participants feel comfortable interacting with each other
Why?	*Why?*	*Why?*	*Why?*
• Improves skill acquisition • Expands range of strategies • Increases confidence • Increases likelihood of using skills	• Engages participants in workshop • Increases likelihood that participants remain in the workshop • Increases likelihood participants will try out new ideas	• Participants are prepared more rapidly when setbacks occur • Helps participants cope with stress • Increases likelihood participant will persevere in job search	• Increases likelihood participants will listen to trainer feedback • Increases participants confidence in abilities • Increases motivation

Figure 31.3 What participants gain by attending the JOBS workshop.

the following: Session 1—teaching of participants to discover his or her job skills; Session 2—dealing with obstacles to employment; Session 3—finding job openings; Session 4—designing resumes, creating contacts, and interviewing; and Session 5—a review of the complete job interview and planning for setbacks in the job-search process

HANDOUTS FOR PARTICIPANTS

Chapter 3 of the manual consists of approximately forty detailed handouts for the participants to accompany each of the detailed session descriptions and behavioral scripts for each of the five training sessions in the jobs program.

QUALITY ASSESSMENT AND MONITORING INSTRUMENT

Chapter 4 provides pre- and posttest rating scales for participants that provide opportunities to check for improved quality of delivery from administration to administration of the JOBS program.

PROTOCOLS AND CHECKLISTS FOR OBSERVERS TO MONITOR QUALITY IN THE DELIVERY OF THE JOBS PROGRAM

These assessments in Chapter 5 specify trainer tasks, detailed trainer activities, and expected group

behavior for every training session for participants of the JOBS intervention. This is followed by a set a rating scales allowing observers to assess additional characteristics of the quality of training on multiple dimensions. The behavioral checklist, pre- and posttest assessment, and observer rating scales allow systematic data-based feedback to trainers to maintain and improve quality from delivery to delivery of the JOBS program.

Videotapes

In addition to the five chapters in the overall JOBS manual, two training videotapes are available. They were produced during the Wining New Jobs (WNJ) implementation project in California. The first, titled "From Within Themselves," is designed give trainers a general orientation to delivering the JOBS program through observation and to provide an opportunity for discussion in training sessions. A second videotape, titled "Path to the Future," is designed to give administrators in agencies delivering the JOBS program clear idea of the role of administrators in supporting the JOBS program. Both training videos involve interviews with actual participants to provide a highly credible set of supportive materials for implementing the JOBS program.

Future Directions for Research and Practice with the JOBS Program

A Need to Investigate the Effects of Additional Mechanisms and Mediators

While the research to date focused on and demonstrated the effects of two key mediators, job-search efficacy and inoculation against setbacks, there are other potential mechanisms that may be identified in the intervention process and need to be tested in future research. Most of these mechanisms are briefly reviewed here. One such mechanism is *Implementation Intentions*. In several sections of the intervention, participants were encouraged to develop concrete plans of action to which they commit themselves, such as developing job leads and arranging for job interviews. These preparations amount to the development of implementation intentions, which, has been shown by Gollwitzer (1996) to increase the likelihood that an intended action would actually be performed. Participants were also asked to announce their plans to the group. Such *public commitment* has been suggested in the literature to enhance the adherence to the commitment to act (Pelz, 1958). In addition various procedures were introduced to enhance *identification with the trainers* as stronger identification is shown to produce greater acceptance of communication from the source—that is, the workshop leaders (Kelman, 1958). Thus the protocol includes statements by the workshop leaders that made them more likable using moderate self-disclosure (Derlaga, Harris, & Chaikin, 1973) and enhancing their referent and expert power (French & Raven, 1968). For example, when the workshop leaders introduced themselves to the participants they told them of their own background and experiences with job loss and unemployment (enhancing referent power). They also made the participants know of the extensive training they received in preparation for delivering the workshop and the long training experience they have with the JOBS workshops (enhancing expert power).

Studies show that when individuals' *self-esteem is enhanced,* their defensiveness is reduced, and they become more open and receptive to new information and ideas (Sherman & Cohen, 2002). We therefore embedded in the JOBS protocol various procedures to enhance the participants' self-esteem. For example, various activities and exercises were designed to have the participants experience success, followed by workshop leaders providing *specific and individual positive feedback* with praising or appreciative comments on the behavior and performance of the workshop members.

Another mechanism that appears in the literature to facilitate receptivity to new ideas and attitude change is the *repetition of arguments* that support the information provided during group discussion (Brauer, Judd, & Gliner, 1995). Workshop leaders were trained to encourage the group members to elaborate on information and ideas raised in the group, which resulted in argument repetition.

Recent studies have demonstrated the importance of *reciprocal social support*. The positive effects of social support are more pronounced when the support is being reciprocated, that is, when the receiver has the opportunity to also provide support to the giver (Nahum-Shani, Bamberger, & Bacharach, in press; Nadler, 1998). The JOBS workshop participants not only encouraged socially supportive interactions among themselves but the various small group role playing exercises included procedures for everyone to provide supportive comments to the others.

Last but not least, a rich literature documents the impressive effects of *self-fulfilling prophecies* on motivation and performance (also referred to as the Pygmalion effect; Eden, 1990). Here we view prophesies as *expectations of success*. The JOBS program included steps to increase the self fulfilling prophesies of both the workshop leaders and the participants. The training of the leaders included communication of information on past successes of the program in various settings and how able and talented are most job seekers who participate in the workshop to make the most of it. Similar information about expected success was also communicated to the participants. All of these communications had the goal of creating expectations of success that will generate the self fulfilling prophecies of successful coping. It is for future research to determine which and how much each of these mechanisms built into the delivery protocol of JOBS plays a role in achieved level of final outcomes.

A Need for Cross-Level Analyses and Adaptive Treatments in Intervention Research

What have we learned about the active ingredients of the JOBS program that makes it work? Both our studies of the way JOBS program influences individual psychological mediators (Vinokur & Schul, 1997, 2002) and group mediated processes (Choi, Price, & Vinokur, 2003; Vuori, et al., 2005) show that *job-search self efficacy*, and *inoculation against setbacks* are clearly important intermediate outcomes leading to effective job search and reemployment. However a number of *enabling conditions* in the JOBS program are crucial for learning these skills. These enabling conditions include an atmosphere of trust, an open group climate for sharing ideas, encouragement and modeling new and more effective behaviors, an emphasis on support and absence of criticism are all critical enabling conditions for effective program delivery.

Disentangling which of these are individual meditational processes versus group mediated effects will be a continuing and challenging research agenda. *Cross-level studies* need to be conducted to understand what aspect of interventions like JOBS are due to contextual variables and what aspects are due to individual change. Identifying the individual and the group level effects is essential for future designs that may include adaptive interventions and to other designs that will be delivered as internet web based interventions. The methodologies are now widely available to accomplish this (Bryk & Raudenbush, 1992). Price (2003) has argued that intervention research should take advantage of this cross-level research approach in future work.

Our results also make it clear that some unemployed participants in JOBS are particularly vulnerable to depression (Price, van Ryn, & Vinokur, 1992; Vinokur, Price, & Schul, 1995), and results reported by Vuori and his colleagues (Vuori et al., 2005) also make it very clear that some elements of the JOBS group experience will be particularly helpful to subpopulations at risk for depression. Inoculation against setbacks was a particularly important element of the group process for people at high risk for depression. These results suggests the possibility that researchers should consider designs in which *adaptive treatments* (Cronbach & Snow, 1977) are available providing greater emphasis on one group technique or practice for particular vulnerable subgroups, tailoring the intervention for maximal impact.

New Populations That Could Benefit from JOBS Core Ingredients

Thus far the majority of our research and intervention work has focused on job losers seeking to obtain new employment. However we believe that the basic JOBS model can be provided to a wide range of populations attempting to make the transition to gainful employment. First there are a number of employment transitions throughout the life cycle in addition to assisting unemployed

workers that could be addressed. For example, unemployed youth attempting to enter the workforce for the first time are in need of support in making the transition (O'Higgins, 2001). At the other end of the life cycle, working life is being transformed in ways that suggest that the elderly may continue to seek paid employment for considerably longer than has traditionally been the case (Kite & Johnson, 1988). At the same time, the labor market for full-time paid employment is dramatically changing and nonstandard jobs and part-time employment are much more prevalent in the workforce (Friedland & Price, 2003; Price & Burgard, 2008). These jobs often lack benefits or a regular schedule, and millions of workers are part of a new nonstandard job market, where transitions in and out of jobs will need to be skillfully navigated A variety of special populations not currently employed could also be beneficiaries of the JOBS program and benefit from paid employment either on a part-time or full-time basis in ways that can be crucial for rehabilitation and well-being. For example, disabled persons reentering the workforce after illness or injury (DePoy & Gilson, 2004) face special challenges in obtaining employment and could in many instances greatly benefit. Indeed, we already have evidence that the JOBS program can be effective with persons in the welfare-to-work population. In addition, employment is critical in the rehabilitation of incarcerated individuals returning to the community who also face special challenges in obtaining jobs and without employment are at higher risk of recidivism (Maruna, 2001). In a similar vein, employment is critical for returning soldiers who seek reintegration into civilian life after completing their military service.

Transferring What We Have Learned to Help Navigate Other Risky Transitions in the Life Course

The transition from unemployment back to the workforce is just one of a number of risky life transitions in the life course where interventions with some of the same core ingredients as JOBS could be beneficial. Our research suggests that at least five intervention ingredients may be important in helping a wide variety of populations confronting a risky life transition. Interventions would clearly require (1) *specific normative knowledge and skills* that address the particular transition the person is experiencing. In the case of job search, specific knowledge about self-presentation to prospective employers and how to identify job leads are examples. At least as important as substantive information in such groups is the skill with which the groups are conducted. In addition, (2) *Skilled and well-trained group leaders* are essential to the effectiveness of such groups. Programs of this sort are not impromptu affairs and group leader training and skill is essential. (3) An *active learning and teaching style* including role playing, modeling, peer- to peer- discussion, and positive feedback is critical so that participants can practice the requisite skills, to see a variety of interaction styles and solutions modeled for the same problems, and gain confidence in their own approaches. In addition, (4) a *positive reinforcing style of teaching* is essential. The detailed knowledge being offered in the group has to be provided in ways that are both encouraging and nonthreatening to people who are usually feeling vulnerable in their life circumstances. Purely didactic approaches or implicit blaming are likely to be ineffective and even destructive. Finally, most life transitions and their aftermath contain many setbacks and failed attempts that must be overcome. It is reasonable to hypothesize that (5) *teaching people to plan to cope with anticipated setbacks during the transition* is a critical ingredient in the success of both the JOBS program and in other similar programs involving charting a new direction in the life course.

A Delicate Balance

Practitioners often feel that they face a delicate balance in maintaining fidelity to evidence-based practices or engaging in creative adaptation to local circumstances or particular populations in delivering the JOBS program (Price et al., 1998). On the one hand, practitioners attempting to use evidence-based practices will quite appropriately be urged to maintain fidelity to the core features of a practice that has previously been validated by rigorous research. On the other hand, practitioners know that they must also adapt their practices to the particular characteristics of populations they serve and cope with the challenging practical circumstances of limited funds and staff available to deliver programs. Finding ways of managing the fidelity-adaptation dilemma in the case of JOBS will continue to be a challenge for practitioners attempting to implement programs aimed at behavior change (Mayer & Davidson, 2000).

At the same time, the creativity and innovativeness of practitioners in the field is often not well appreciated. As end users of research based innovations such as JOBS, practitioners can be creative and resourceful innovators who develop variations on the basic intervention model that opens the way for new applications with different populations. In fact, von Hippel (1988, 2005) shows that the vast majority of innovations are created not by inventors, but by end-users of a new social technology or invention who find creative new uses and adaptations.

There seems no simple solution to the fidelity–adaptation dilemma (Blakeley et al., 1987). On the one hand, researchers will quite appropriately expect practitioners to maintain fidelity to carefully designed research-based protocols with demonstrated research effectiveness. Practitioners, on the other hand, spurred by creativity and the necessity of constrained resources, will borrow, adapt, and reinvent proven programs such as JOBS to fit constrained local circumstances or different cultural expectations. Perhaps the most appropriate strategy is to create communities of practice where there are opportunities for practitioners and researchers to join forces in a partnership to study innovative applications of programs like JOBS and thus to learn from each other more about how and for whom a particular helping program works best.

References

Azrin, N. H., & Beasalel, V. B. (1982). *Finding a job*. Berkeley, CA: Ten Speed Press.

Bandura, A. (1977). Self-efficacy: Toward a unifying theory of behavioral change. *Psychological Review*, 84, 91–215.

Bandura, A. (1997). *Self-efficacy. The exercise of control*. New York: Freeman.

Barling, J. (1990). *Employment, stress and family functioning*. West Sussex, UK: Wiley.

Barry, M. (2005). *Preliminary findings for the "Winning New Jobs" programme in Ireland*. Galway: Centre for Health Promotion Studies, National University of Ireland.

Brauer, M., Judd, C. M., & Gliner, M. D. (1995). The effects of repeated attitude expressions on attitude polarization during group discussions. *Journal of Personality and Social Psychology*, 68, 1014–1029.

Blakely, C. H., Mayer, J. P., Gottschalk, R. G., Schmitt, N., Davidson, W. S., Roitman, D. B., & Emshoff, J. G. (1987). The fidelity-adaptation debate: Implications for the implementation of public sector social programs. *American Journal of Community Psychology*, 15, 253–268.

Bolles, R. N. (2011) *What color is your parachute? A practical guide for job-hunters and career changers*. Berkeley, CA: Ten Speed Press.

Bryk, A. S. & Raudenbush, S. W. (1992). *Hierarchical linear models: Applications and data analysis methods*. Newbury Park, CA: Sage.

Caplan, R. D., Vinokur, A. D., & Price, R. H. (1997). From job loss to reemployment: Field experiments in prevention-focused coping. In G. W. Albee & T. P. Gullotta (Eds.), *Primary prevention works* (vol. 16, pp. 341–379). Thousand Oaks, CA: Sage.

Caplan, R. D., Vinokur, A. D., Price, R. H., & van Ryn, M. (1989). Job seeking, reemployment, and mental health: A randomized field experiment in coping with job loss. *Journal of Applied Psychology*, 74(5), 759–769.

Choi, J., Price, R. H., & Vinokur, A. D. (2003). Self-efficacy changes in groups: Effects of diversity, leadership, and group climate. *Journal of Organizational Behavior*, 24(4), 357–372.

Cobb, S., & Kasl, S. V. (1977). *Termination: The consequences of job loss.* (DHEW NIOSH Publication No. 77-224P. Cincinnati, OH: NIOSH.

Cronbach, L. J. & Snow, R. E. (1977). *Aptitudes and instructional methods: A handbook for research on interactions.* New York: Irvington.

Curran, J., Wishart, P. & Gingrich, J. (1999). *JOBS: A manual for teaching people successful job-search strategies.* Michigan Prevention Research Center, Institute for Social Research, University of Michigan, Ann Arbor, MI. (Replaces JOBS manual by J. Curran, 1992).

DePoy, E., & Gilson, S. F. (2004). *Rethinking disability: Principles for professional and social change.* Pacific Grove, CA: Wadsworth.

Derlaga, V. J., Harris, M. S., & Chaikin, A. L. (1973). Self-disclosure, reciprocity, liking and deviant. *Journal of Experimental Social Psychology*, 9, 277–284.

Eden, D. (1990) *Pygmalion in management: Productivity as a self-fulfilling prophecy.* Lexington MA: Lexington Books.

Elder, G. H. Jr. (1995). The life course paradigm: Social change and individual development. In P. Moen, P., G. H. Elder Jr., & K. Luscher (Eds.), *Examining lives in context* (pp. 101–139). Washington, DC: American Psychological Association.

Elder, Glen H. Jr., & O'Rand, Angela M. (1995) Adult lives in a changing society. In K. S. Cook, G. A. Fine, & J. S. House (Eds.), *Sociological perspectives on social psychology.* Needham Heights, MA: Allyn and Bacon.

French, J. R. P. Jr., & Raven, B. (1968). The bases of social power. In D. Cartwright & A. Zander (Eds.), *Group dynamics* (3rd ed., pp. 259–269). New York: Harper & Row.

Friedland, D. S., & Price, R. H. (2003). Underemployment: Consequences for the health and well-being of workers. *American Journal of Community Psychology*, 32 (1/2), 33–45.

Gist, M. E., & Mitchell, T. M. (1992). Self-efficacy: A theoretical analysis of its determinants and malleability. *The Academy of Management Review*, 17, 183–211.

Gollwitzer, P. M. (1996). The volitional benefits of planning. In P. M. Gollwitzer & J. A. Bargh (Eds.), *The psychology of action: Linking cognition and motivation to behavior* (pp. 287–312). New York: Guilford.

Hobfoll, S. E. (1989). Conservation of resources: A new attempt at conceptualizing stress. *American Psychologist*, 44, 513–524.

Jahoda, M. (1982). *Employment and unemployment.* Cambridge, UK: Cambridge University Press.

JOBS II. (1995). *Manual for questionnaire measures: JOBS II project preventive intervention for the unemployed.* Ann Arbor, MI: Michigan Prevention Research Center, Institute for Social Research, University of Michigan.

JOBS Video Tape 1. (2000). *Winning new jobs: Path to the future.* Ann Arbor, MI: University of Michigan Institute for Social Research, Michigan Prevention Research Center. (Information video for service providers/organizational audiences.)

JOBS Video Tape 2. (2001). *From within themselves: Training for the winning new jobs program.* Ann Arbor, MI: University of Michigan Institute for Social Research, Michigan Prevention Research Center. (Training video for "training the trainer" for the WNJ program.)

Kelman, H. C. (1958). Compliance, identification, and internalization: three processes of attitude change. *Journal of Conflict Resolution.* 2, 51–60.

Kessler, R. C., House, J. S., & Turner, J. B. (1987). Unemployment and health in a community sample. *Journal of Health and Social Behavior*, 28, 51–59.

Kessler, R. C., Turner, B., & House, J. S. (1988). Effects of unemployment on health in a community survey: Main, modifying, and mediating effects. *Journal of Social Issues*, 44(4), 69–86.

Kessler, R., Turner, J., & House, J. (1987). Intervening processes in the relationship between unemployment and health. *Psychological Medicine*, 17(4), 949–961.

Kite, M. E., & Johnson, B. T. (1988). Attitudes towards older and younger adults: A meta-analysis. *Psychology and Aging*, 3(3), 232–244.

Maruna, S. (2001). *Making good: How ex-convicts reform and rebuild their lives.* Washington, DC: American Psychological Association.

Meichenbaum, D. (1985). *Stress inoculation training.* New York: Pergamon.

Mayer, J. P., & Davidson, W. S. II. (2000). Dissemination of innovation as social change. In J. Rappaport & E. Seidman (Eds.), *Handbook of community psychology* (pp. 421–438). New York: Kluwer Academic/Plenum.

Nadler, A., (1998) Relationship, esteem and achievement perspectives on autonomous and dependent help seeking. In S. A. Karabenick (Ed.), *Strategic help seeking: Implications for learning and teaching* (pp. 61–95). Mahwah, NJ: Erlbaum.

Nahum-Shani, I., Bamberger, P., & Bacharach, S. B. (in press). Social support and well-being among blue collar workers: The conditioning effects of perceived patterns of supportive exchange. *Journal of Health and Social Behavior.*

O'Higgins, N. (2001). *Youth unemployment and employment policy: A global perspective.* Geneva: International Labor Organization.

Pelz, E. B. (1958). Some factors in group decision. In. E. F. Maccoby, T. M. Newcomb, & E. L. Hartley (Eds.), *Reading in social psychology* (3d ed., pp. 212–219). New York: Holt, Rinehart and Winston.

Price, R. H. (1992). Psychosocial impact of job loss on individuals and families. *Current Directions in Psychological Science*, 1(1), 9–11.

Price, R. H. (October 2003). Systems within systems: Putting program implementation in organizational context. *Prevention and Treatment.* Available at: http://journals.apa.org/prevention/volume6/toc-oct-03.html

Price, R. H. (2006). The transformation of work in America: New health vulnerabilities for American workers. In E. Lawler & J. O' Toole, (Eds.), *The new American workplace.* Alexandria VA: Society for Human Resource Management Press.

Price, R. H. (2006). Cultural collaboration: Implementing the JOBS program in China, California, and Finland. In C. M. Hosman (Ed.), *Proceedings of the London Second World Conference on the Promotion of Mental Health and Prevention of Mental and Behavioural Disorders.* London: World Federation for Mental Health.

Price, R. H., & Burgard, S. (2006). The new employment contract and worker health in the United States. Paper presented at the Health Effects of a Nonhealth Policy conference, Bethesda, MD.

Price, R. H., & Burgard, S. A. (2006). Nonstandard work and health: Who is at risk and who benefits? Paper presented at the Health Effects of a Nonhealth policy conference, Ann Arbor, MI.

Price, R. H., & Burgard, S. A. (2008). The new employment contract and worker health in the United States. In *Making Americans healthier: Social and economic policy as health policy* (pp. 201–208). New York: Russell Sage Foundation.

Price, R. H., Choi, J., & Vinokur, A. D. (2002). Links in the chain of adversity following job loss: How financial strain and loss of personal control lead to depression, impaired functioning, and poor health. *Journal of Occupational Health Psychology*, 7(4), 302–312.

Price, R. H., Choi, J. N., & Lim, S. (2006). Beyond the iron rice bowl: Life stage and family dynamics in unemployed Chinese workers. In Malcolm Warner & Grace Lee (Eds.), *Unemployment in China*. New York: Routledge Curzon.

Price, R. H. & Fang, Liluo. (2002). Unemployed Chinese workers: The survivors, the worried young and the discouraged old. *International Journal of Human Resource Management*, 13(3), 416–430.

Price, R. H., Friedland, D. S., Choi, J., & Caplan, R. D. (1998). Job loss and work transitions in a time of global economic change. In X. Arriaga & S. Oskamp (Eds.), *Addressing community problems* (pp. 195–222). Thousand Oaks, CA: Sage.

Price, R. H., Friedland, D. S., & Vinokur, A. D. (1998). Job loss: Hard times and eroded identity. In J. Harvey (Ed.), *Perspectives on loss: A source book* (pp. 303–316). Philadelphia: Taylor & Francis.

Price, R. H., van Ryn, M., & Vinokur, A. D. (1992). Impact of preventive job-search intervention on the likelihood of depression among the unemployed. *Journal of Health and Social Behavior*, 33(2), 158–167.

Price, R. H., & Vinokur, A. D. (1995). Supporting career transitions in time of organizational downsizing: The Michigan JOBS program. In M. London (Ed.), *Employees, careers, and job creation: Developing growth-oriented human resource strategies and programs* (pp. 191–209). San Francisco: Jossey-Bass.

Price, R. H., Vinokur, A. D., & Friedland, D. S. (2002). The job seeker role as resource in achieving reemployment and enhancing mental health new directions. In A. Maney & J. Ramos (Eds.), *Socioeconomic conditions, stress and mental health disorders: Toward a new synthesis of research and public policy*. Washington, DC: National Institute of Mental Health. Available at: http://www.mhsip.org/nimhdoc/socioeconmh_home.htm

Sherman, D. K., & Cohen, G. L. (2002). Accepting threatening information: Self-affirmation and the reduction of defensive biases. *Current Directions in Psychological Science*, 11, 119–123.

Stack, S. (1981). Divorce and suicide: A time series analysis. 1933–1970. *Journal of Family Issues*. 2, 77–90.

van Ryn, M., & Vinokur, A. D. (1992). How did it work? An examination of the mechanism through which a community intervention influenced job-search behavior among an unemployed sample. *American Journal of Community Psychology*, 20(5), 577–599.

Vinokur, A. D. (1997). Job security: Unemployment. In J. M. Stellman (Ed.), *Encyclopedia of occupational health and safety* (4th ed., pp. 34.31–34.32). Geneva: International Labor Office.

Vinokur, A., Caplan, R. D., & Williams, C. C. (1987). Effects of recent and past stresses on mental health: Coping with unemployment among Vietnam veterans and non-veterans. *Journal of Applied Social Psychology*, 17(8), 710–730.

Vinokur, A. D., Price, R. H., & Caplan, R. D. (1996). Hard times and hurtful partners: How financial strain affects depression and relationship satisfaction of unemployed persons and their spouses. *Journal of Personality and Social Psychology*, 71(1), 166–179.

Vinokur, A. D., Price, R. H., & Schul, Y. (1995). Impact of the JOBS intervention on unemployed workers varying in risk for depression. *American Journal of Community Psychology*, 23(1), 39–74.

Vinokur, A. D., & Schul, Y. (1997). Mastery and inoculation against setbacks as active ingredients in the JOBS intervention for the unemployed. *Journal of Consulting and Clinical Psychology*, 65(5), 867–877.

Vinokur, A. D., & Schul, Y. (2002). The web of coping resources and pathways to reemployment following a job loss. *Journal of Occupational Health Psychology*, 7(1), 68–83.

Vinokur, A. D., Schul, Y., Vuori, J., & Price, R. H. (2000). Two years after a job loss: Long term impact of the JOBS program on reemployment and mental health. *Journal of Occupational Health Psychology*, 5(1), 32–47.

Vinokur, A. D., van Ryn, M., Gramlich, E. M., & Price, R. H. (1991). Long-term follow-up and benefit-cost analysis of the jobs program: A preventive intervention for the unemployed. *Journal of Applied Psychology*, 76(2), 213–219.

Vinokur, A. D., & van Ryn, M. (1993). Social support and undermining in close relationships: Their independent effects on the mental health of unemployed persons. *Journal of Personality and Social Psychology*, 65(2), 350–359.

von Hippel, E. von. (1988). *The sources of innovation*. New York: Oxford University Press.

von Hippel, E. von. (2005). *Democratizing innovation*. Cambridge, MA: MIT Press.

Vuori, J., & Price, R. H. (2006). Promoting re-employment and mental health: A cross-cultural case study. In M. Barry & R. Jenkins, (Eds.) *Implementing mental health promotion*. Edinburgh: Elsevier.

Vuori, J., Silvonen, J., Vinokur, A. D., & Price, R. H. (2002). The Työhön job-search program in Finland: Benefits for the unemployed with risk of depression or discouragement. *Journal of Occupational Health Psychology*, 7(1), 5–19.

Vuori, J., Price, R. H., Mutanen, P., & Malmberg-Heimonen, I. (2005). Effective group training techniques in job-search training. *Journal of Occupational Health Psychology*, 10, 261–275.

Vuori, J. & Vinokur A. D. (2005) Job-search preparedness as a mediator of the effects of the Työhön Job-search Intervention on re-employment and mental health. *Journal of Organizational Behavior*, 26, 275–291.

Zimmerman, J. (2001). Theories of self-regulated learning and academic achievement: An overview and analysis. In B. J. Zimmerman & D. Schunk (Eds.), *Self-regulated learning and academic achievement* (pp. 1–39). Mahwah, NJ Erlbaum.

INDEX

A

ABCX model, of stressors in
    unemployment, 90–91
Abdeljalil, M., 484
Abele, A. E., 231, 232
ability, as moderator of goal setting, 131
Abrahamsen, B., 368
absenteeism, and job insecurity, 39, 113
academic performance, and success of
    school-to-work transition, 395–396
accents, and outcomes of international
    job search, 492
Accountancy Magazine, 299
Ackerman, P. L., 148
activation, of unemployed individuals,
    159–160, 168
active *vs.* preparatory job-search
    behaviors, 263–264, 317, 389, 418
activity level, and job loss among older
    workers, 440–441, 444–445
Adams, C. E., 216–217
adaptability
    and career transitions, 224
    and older job seekers, 435–436
Addison, J. T., 46
Adler, G., 452
adverse impact, definition of, 518*n*1
affective attitudes, and job search, 191, 315,
    342–343
affective events theory, 145, 146
affective reactions
    to job insecurity, 39
    to job search, 132
age
    age discrimination, 451–453
    and career-growth goals, 366
    and coping with career
        interruptions, 233
    and coping with identity threat, 228
    and desire for reemployment, 150
    diversity of in labor market, 144
    and effects of job loss on mental
        health, 62–64
    and experience of job loss, 438–443
    and experience of repeated
        unemployment, 100
    and generational impact of
        unemployment, 102–104
    as human capital, 434–435
    and international job search, 485
    and job interview process, 331–332

and job search, 5
and job-search strategies, 152
and perceived job insecurity, 37, 48*n*2
research agenda for age-related
    differences, 155
and underemployment, 361
variations in job search, 143
see also older job seekers
agency-restriction model, 71, 72, 76, 88
agency theory, and research on
    unemployment, 18–19
agency workers, and temporary
    employment, 467–468, 469, 470–
    471, 473, 475, 477
Ägerström, J., 512
aggression, and unemployment, 74
Agrawal, A., 287
Ahmad, A. S., 510
Ajzen, I., 22
    broader context of job search, 198
    measures of intention and behavior, 191
    social-cognitive perspective on job loss
        and job search, 145
    social pressure to search for
        employment, 186
    theory of planned behavior, 182, 321
    theory of reasoned action, 146–147
alcohol consumption, and
    unemployment, 73, 92–93, 116, 444
Aldag, R. J., 260
Aletraris, L., 42
Allen, R. E., 382
    job information sources, 389
alternative activities, and motivation
    theory, 169–170
amotivation, 164
Amundson, N. E., 557
analysis and methodology, post-World
    War II improvements in, 14
Anand, N., 284
Andersen, R., 362–363
Andersen, S. H., 570–571
Anderson, C. A., 38
Anderson, N., 341
anger, as reaction to job interviews, 342
Anong, S. T., 89
anticipated job loss
    comprehensive model of, 35*f*
    difficulties in researching, 79*n*6
    effects on health and well-being, 103
    prevalence of, 31–32

vs. job insecurity, 48*n*1
see also job loss
anxiety, and job interviews, 340–341,
    344–345, 346*t*
apathy, among the unemployed, 11
applicant attraction, predictors of,
    312–314, 317
applicant characteristics, and hiring
    discrimination, 509–512
appraisals, primary and secondary of
    events, 146, 150
Aquilanti, T. M., 548, 549, 553, 558
Aquilanti Integrated Model of
    outplacement services, 549, 558
Archer, J., 150
Armitage, C. J., 186, 191
Aronsson, G., 472
Artazcoz, L., 93
Arthur, M. B., 277
Arvey, R. D., 505
Ashforth, B. E., 131, 264
    career planning, 384
    career planning and development, 386
    employment-fit perceptions, 392
    job information sources, 389
    job satisfaction, 391
    job-search dynamics, 268
    job-search intensity, 389
    job-search outcomes, 390
    personality traits and school-to-work
        transition, 395
    person-job fit, 364, 411
    school-to-work transition and success
        spiral, 393
    sequential model of job search
        behavior, 421
Ashworth, K., 534, 536
Assertive Job-Hunting Survey, 263
assertive job-search behaviors, 263–264
attention deficit theory, and biased
    decision making, 508–509
attitudinal reactions
    to job insecurity, 39
    to job loss, 74–75
    to underemployment, 367–368
attractiveness
    and job interview process, 332
    and type of employment, 334
attributional retraining, 345
attribution theory, and
    underemployment, 369

Austin, E. J., 383–384
Austin, J. T., 423
Austria
    Marienthal study, origins of, 10
    Marienthal study, summary of, 11
autonomous motivation, 164–165, 166
    quality of motivation, 170–171
    and refusal to job search, 169–170
    and self-regulation, 211
autonomous regulation, 164
autonomy, psychological need for,
    160–162
Autor, David H., 293
Avey, J. B., 407
Axtell, C. M., 41
Aycan, Z., 134–135

B
Baker, Wayne, 276
Bakke, E. W.
    research on unemployment and
        families, 87
    studies in Greenwich, 11–12
    study in New Haven, Connecticut, 12
Bakker, A. B., 208–209
Bambra, Clare, 3
    "Insecurity, Unemployment, and
        Health: A Social Epidemiological
        Perspective," 111–125
    Work, Worklessness, and the Political
        Economy of Health, 123n1
Banai, M., 34
    job insecurity and job-search
        behaviors, 41
Banas, J. T.
    job-search intensity and job
        satisfaction, 391
Bandura, A.
    goal setting theory, 133
    self-efficacy, 23, 423
    social-cognitive perspective on job loss
        and job search, 145
    theories of self-efficacy, 147, 148
Banks, M. H.
    expectancy-value theory, 22
    unemployment and mental health, 19
Barber, A. E., 260
    job-search dynamics, 268
    recruitment process, 312
    sequential model of change, 322
    theoretical models of job-search
        behavior, 420
Barling, J., 45
Baron, J. N., 278
Barrick, M. R., 332, 335, 336, 337, 344
Barros, E., 425
Barry, Margaret, 582
Bartum, D., 16
Bartunek, J. M., 285
Baruch, Y., 277
Basbug, G., 283
    job-search behavior and
        underemployment, 363

job-to-job search outcomes, 409
    self-regulatory model of job-search
        behavior, 423
Batenburg, R., 362
Batinic, B., 72
Bauder, H., 489
Bauer, T. N., 339
    justice in job interviews, 342, 345
    underemployment and turnover
        behavior, 368
Baumeister, Roy F., 215
    ego depletion and prejudiced
        reactions, 508
    self-presentation, 303
Bayer, U., 151
Beach, L. R., 262
Beal, D. J., 425
Beaverstock, Jonathan V., 304
behavior
    actions taken, 171–173
    intention-behavior gap, 206–208, 208t
    and intrinsic and extrinsic work goals,
        172–173
behavior, motivations for, 162–171, 163f
    controlled regulation, 163–164
    internalization, 163
    intrinsic motivation, 162
    motivation and job-search intensity,
        164–167
    and notion of "self," 167–169
    quality of motivation as moderating
        factor, 170–171, 211
    refusal to job search, 169–170
behavioral consequences, of job
    insecurity, 40–41
behavioral coping theory, 194
behavioral intentions vs. behavioral goals,
    146–147
belief in a just world (BJW), and response
    to job loss, 23–24
Benach, J., 93
Bendick, M., Jr., 511
benefits system, stabilizing quality of, 105
Benson, Wendi, 2
    "Job Insecurity and Anticipated Job
        Loss: A Primer and Exploration of
        Possible Interventions," 31–53
Berg, J. M., 227
Berger, M. C., 452
    evaluating reemployment programs, 535
Bertrand, M., 509, 511
Beugre, C. D., 548
Beveridge, William, 99
Bibliography of Unemployment and the
    Unemployed (1909), 10
Billig, M. G., 506
Black, D. A., 535
Black, M. D., 216
Blackburn, M., 46
Blakely, T., 115
Blau, G., 33–34
    grieving job loss, 150
    job-search intensity, 389

preparatory vs. active job-search
    behaviors, 153, 263, 281
Blonk, R. W. B., 192
    dissatisfaction as motivator in job
        search, 196
    multiwave longitudinal study of job-
        search dynamics, 424
Blustein, D. L., 394, 396
Bohnert, D., 287
Bolino, M. C.
    underemployment and job
        performance, 368
Booth, A., 468
Bordia, P., 45
Borgatti, S. P., 276
Borgen, William A., 6
    "Job Loss: Outplacement Programs,"
        547–560
    outplacement programs, 552
Borghans, L., 532
Born, M. P., 191, 192
    dissatisfaction as motivator in job
        search, 196
    employment position and job
        search, 200
    multiwave longitudinal study of job-
        search dynamics, 424
    psychological distress after job loss, 362
    resume screening, discrimination
        in, 503
Borrell, C., 93
Boswell, Wendy R., 4–5
    "Employed Job Seekers and Job-to-Job
        Search," 401–416
    job search and networking goals, 277
    job-to-job search outcomes, 408
    leverage-seeking job searches,
        409–410, 411
    self-efficacy and job-search, 390
Boudreau, J. W., 406, 407, 409
Bourbonnais, C., 37
Bowers, S., 549
Boyar, S. L., 425
Bozionellos, N., 281, 282, 285, 485
Bradley, E. H., 444
Brady, D., 106
Brand, J. E., 40, 445
Brasher, E. E., 153–154, 284
Brass, D. J., 278
Breaugh, J. A., 312
Brenner, M. H., 14
Brett, J. M., 280
Bretz, R. D., 406, 408
Brewer, M. B., 507
Brewington, J., 46
Brief, A. P., 513
Brokenshire, R., 197
Brooks, N. G., 228
Brown, D. W., 278, 283
Brown, S., 151
Brown, S. D., 147
Brown, T. C., 133
Brunswick, E., 336

Buch, K., 149
Büchel, F., 365, 425
Budworth, M. H., 134
Bufton, Gina M., 3
"Job Loss and Job Search: A Social-
Cognitive and Self-Regulation
Perspective," 143–158
Bundy, R. P., 506
Burchell, B., 16
Burdett, J. O., 556
Burgard, S. A., 40, 445
Burger, J. M., 344
Burke, R. J., 367
Burnett, J. R., 337
Burt, R., 279
Burt, Ronald S., 300
Butterfield, Lee D., 6
"Job Loss: Outplacement Programs,"
547–560
outplacement programs, 552
Butts, M., 281
Butz, D. A., 508
Byrne, D., 514

C

Cable, D. M., 266
Caldwell, D. F., 344
calling, identity and a sense of, 225,
226, 227
Campbell, I., 471
Campion, J. E., 346
Campion, M. A., 335, 339
candidate reactions to job
interviews, 343
improving interview skills, 346
structured interviews and
discrimination, 514
Cantillon, Bea, 106
Caplan, R. D., 22
job loss in marriages, 89–90
large-scale implementation of JOBS
Program, 581
reemployment interventions, 150
unemployment and marital strain, 579
Cappelli, Peter, 307n3
Caranikas-Walker, F., 196
Card, D., 535, 567
Cardador, M. T., 227
career, definition of, 223
career adaptability, 234–236, 237–239
career aspirations, impact of
unemployment on, 102–103
career development
and outcomes of international job
search, 492–493
social-cognitive career theory, 147
Career Development Quarterly, 381
career exploration, and school-to-work
transition, 383–384
Career Growth Model of outplacement
services, 549
career history, and perceived job
insecurity, 39

career identity, 277
career interruptions, 232–234
career issues, and underemployment,
369–370
career mobility, theory of, 365
career planning and development
and international job search, 489–490
and school-to-work transition, 383–387
careers
individual career investments and
temporary employment, 471
mental models of, 230–234
of temporary workers, 468–469, 474f
career success, mental models of, 230–234
career trajectories
and economic and labor market
circumstances, 223–224
career transitions, 4–5
and adaptability, 224
identity and coping during,
228–230, 234f
Carlier, O., 231
Carlsson, M., 509
Carnegie Trust, research on unemployed
youth, 13
Carpenter, M., 565
Carroll, G. R., 283
Cartledge, N., 137
Carver, C. S., 135, 137, 148
Caska, B. A., 196
Catalano, R. A., 15
causal attributions, and response to job
loss, 22–23
Cebulla, A., 533
Cerdin, J.-L., 484
certification, and international job search,
493–494
Chaiken, S., 515
challenge-hindrance theory, 196
Chalmers, J., 468
Chan, D. K.-S., 40, 41, 48n2
Chan, S. W., 446
older job seekers and reemployment,
450, 451
Chapman, D. S., 312, 313, 314, 341
Chapple, K., 279
Chatzisarantis, N. L. D., 217
chemistry, interpersonal, 301–302
Chen, C., 338
Chen, P. Y., 153–154, 284
Cheng, Bonnie Hayden, 4
"Through the Looking Glass:
Employment Interviews from the
Lens of Job Candidates," 329–357
Cheng, G. H.-L., 40, 41, 48n2
Chia, S. L., 42
Chicoine, E., 168
child abuse or neglect, and
unemployment, 74
child development, effects of family job
loss on, 94
children, effects of unemployment
on, 93–94

China, JOBS Program in, 582
Chiswick, B. R., 485
Chiu, S., 338
Choi, J., 578, 580, 581
Cianci, A. M., 131–132
Clark, A., 37
Clerkin, Thomas A., 306
client companies
and the use of headhunters, 304–305
see also headhunters
Clinton, M., 471
clothing and style of dress, and interview
process, 333, 348
Cobb, S., 21, 576
cognition, and discrimination, 515
cognitive interference theories, and job
interview anxiety, 340–341
cognitive processes, and reemployment
program activities, 537, 539
cognitive reactions
to job insecurity, 39
to job search, 196
cognitive-transactional model of stress, 34
Cohen-Goldner, S., 490
coherence, sense of in unemployment, 75
Cole, M. S., 509
Colella, A., 514
collective purpose, and job loss among
older workers, 440
collectivism
as contextual factor in job search, 200
and individual consequences of job
loss, 66–67
Collison, J., 46
commitment, as moderator of goal
setting, 131
communication
alleviating effects of job insecurity via
enhanced, 46–47
importance of in outplacement
programs, 558
verbal and nonverbal in interviews,
336–337
competence
knowing-how competencies, 477
networking and maintaining, 277
psychological need for, 160–162,
186–187
complexity, as moderator of goal
setting, 131
components and phases of job search, 4
confidence, and career adaptability, 234,
235, 236
Conger, J. A., 284
Connelly, B. L., 319
Conner, M., 186, 191
conscientiousness, and job search, 315, 395
conservation of resources theory, 366, 369
and comprehensive model of job
insecurity, 35
and on-the-job resources, 472
contextual ambiguity, and
discrimination, 515

contextual-level motivating factors in job
    search, 192–193, 193–197, 198–201
contingency headhunters
    see headhunters
contingency workers, and
    underemployment, 362
contract employment
    effects on families, 89
    heterogeneity of contracts, 471–472
    and perceived job insecurity, 38
contractual flexibility, 465–466
control, and career adaptability, 234, 236
controlled motivation, 164–165, 166
    quality of motivation, 170–171
    and refusal to job search, 169–170
    and self regulation, 211
controlled regulation, 163–164
control theory
    empirical research on, 137
    future research, 139–140
    implications for job search, 135–139
    negative feedback loop, 135–136, 136f,
        137–138, 138
    and theories of motivation, 129
    vs. goal setting, 138–139
Converse, P. D., 215
Conway, N., 281
coping with job loss
    gender differences in, 362
    mediating and modifying
        variables of, 15
    older workers and, 443–450
    and phase model of
        self-categorization, 422
    protective resources for, 91–92
    strategies for, 67–68
    transactional model of stress and
        coping, 146
Cormier, S., 558
Cortes, I., 93
cost-effectiveness of reemployment
    programs, evaluating, 533
Côté, S., 132, 151, 387, 390, 395
Couch, K. A., 451
counseling services, as part of
    outplacement programs, 550, 555, 556
country of origin, and international job
    search outcome, 495
Coverdill, James E., 4
    "Contingency Headhunters: What
        They Do–and What Their Activities
        Tell Us About Jobs, Careers, and the
        Labor Market," 293–310
    job turnover process, 405
Cox, T., 513
Cox, T. H., Jr., 280
credential inflation, 362
Creed, P. A., 16
    job search among high school
        students, 192
    learning goal orientation, 316
    outcomes of job-search behavior, 394
    self-regulation in job search, 315

crime and unemployment, 106
criteria, headhunting and ability to
    identify, 305–306
Cropanzano, R.
    affective events theory, 146
    social-cognitive perspective on job loss
        and job search, 145
Crosby, F., 364
Cross, R., 276
Crossley, C. D., 166
    affective attitudes, 315
    economic rational choice theory,
        194–195
    job-search intensity, 390, 408
    job-search strategies, 448
Crown, W. H., 361
cultural capital, and international job
    search, 487
culture, as contextual factor in job search,
    200–201
curiosity
    and career adaptability, 234, 236
    and intrinsic motivation, 162
cybernetic control theory, 148, 209

D

Daguerre, A., 565
daily routine, coping with change in,
    149, 162
Dalbert, C., 23
Daly, C. L., 260
Darity, W., Jr., 366
Darnold, T. C., 335
Davenport, P. R.
    expectancy theory, 320
    expectancy-value theory, 22
    outplacement programs, 551, 557
Davey, K. M., 281
Davis, J. H., 47
Davy, J. A., 41
Dawson, S., 23
day-reconstruction method, and studying
    job search, 426
Deacon, Alan, 101
Dean, H., 565
De Beer, P. T., 530
De Boer, B. J., 208–209
Debrun, X., 104
Debus, M. E.
    job insecurity and social safety
        net, 44–45
    organizational performance and
        perceived job insecurity, 36
Deci, E. L., 148
    autonomous *vs.* controlled choices, 211
    self-determination theory, 160, 168
    self-regulation/job-search
        questionnaire, 164
decision-making, and career adaptability,
    234–235, 236
decision-making theory, and job-search
    strategies, 262
De Clerck, V., 471

De Cuyper, Nele, 5, 38
    "Nontraditional Employment: The
        Careers of Temporary Workers,"
        465–480
    reasons for accepting temporary
        employment, 471
    temporary workers and impression
        management, 472
DeGroot, T., 337
Deitch, C., 361
De Janasz, S., 288
De Jong, G. F., 362
De Jong, M., 200
de Jonge, J., 20
Dekker, R., 468
De Koning, J., 566
De Lange, A. H., 436
Delery, John E., 302
demands-abilities job fit, 364–365
demographics
    demographic characteristics and job
        interviews, 331–332
    further research on moderating effects
        of, 76–77
    and job-to-job search, 407
    moderator effects and interventions, 76
    and perceived job insecurity, 37, 48n2
DeNisi, A. S., 46
De Pater, Irene E., 5
    "Too Old to Tango? Job Loss and
        Job Search among Older Workers,
        433–464
depression
    and JOBS Program model, 576
    and JOBS Program research, 578
    unemployment as risk factor for
        suicide, 79n7
deprivation theory, and research on
    unemployment, 17–18
Derous, Eva, 5
    "By Any Other Name: Discrimination
        in Resume Screening," 501–522
    impression management behaviors, 336
    resume screening, discrimination
        in, 503
Deschacht, N., 435
deservingness, and response to job
    loss, 23–24
DeShon, R. P., 215
despair, among the unemployed, 11
Deutsch, R., 208
DeVaney, S. A., 89
Devendorf, S. A., 514
DeVinney, L. C., 363
De Witte, Hans, 5
    autonomous *vs.* controlled
        motivation, 166
    credential inflation, 362
    impression management behaviors, 336
    motivation for job search, 164
    "Nontraditional Employment: The
        Careers of Temporary Workers,"
        465–480

reasons for accepting temporary
employment, 471
subjective job insecurity, 33
temporary employees and job
insecurity, 38
temporary workers and impression
management, 472
De Witte, S., 164
Diamond, Peter, 253*n1*
diary study
of job-search dynamics, 424
of job-search efforts, 170
dimensions of job-search behavior, 260
Dineen, B. R., 313
Dipboye, R. L., 322
interview formats, 341
physical attractiveness in job
candidates, 332
direct-hire temporary workers, 466
disabilities
impact of unemployment on workers
with, 102, 103
and underemployment, 362
discrimination
actual *vs.* perceived, 504–506
discriminatory questions in job
interviews, 341
forms of, 504
hiring discrimination, 503–506
and international job search, 492
in job layoffs, 438
and job search among older workers,
451–453
modern manifestations of, 513, 514–515
discrimination, in resume screening,
501–502, 506, 516, 518*n*5
and applicant characteristics, 509–512
determinants of, 509
future research directions, 516–517
human capital hypothesis *vs.* hiring
discrimination hypothesis, 503–506
job and organizational characteristics,
512–513
labor market position of ethnic
minorities, 502
methods to avert, 517
practical recommendations for
avoiding, 517–518
recruiter characteristics, 513–516,
517–518, 518*n*4
social-psychological perspectives,
506–509
dissatisfaction, as motivating factor in job
search, 196–197
distal *vs.* proximal goals, 130–131
distancing strategies, 149
Doherty, F., 192, 394
Dolton, P., 365
domestic violence, and unemployment,
74, 92–93
Donnelly, D. P., 404
Dooley, C. D., 15
Dorr, S., 366

Dossett, D. L., 132
Dougherty, T. W., 281
antecedents of networking behavior,
282–283
outcomes of networking behavior, 285
preinterview impressions, 322
Dovidio, J. F., 504
Dozier, J. B.
Career Growth Model of outplacement
services, 549
outplacement programs, 557
positive effects of job loss, 149, 150
Dreher, G. F., 280
Dreher, George F., 306
Drever, A. I., 490
Dries, N., 231
drug use, and unemployment, 92–93
Dunford, B. B., 409
Dustin, S. L., 335
Dutton, J. E., 285
Dweck, C. S., 215
Dyke, A., 535
dynamics of job-search process, 268–269

E
Eales, M. J., 115
earning potential, effect of
underemployment on, 367
Eby, L. T., 149
career competencies, 281
models of career success, 231
outcomes of networking behavior, 285
Eckstein, Z., 244, 490
economic costs of high
unemployment, 99–100
economic development, and individual
consequences of job loss, 65
economic downturns, increased mental
illness during, 14–15
economic hardship
in context of job search, 195
effects on families, 88–89
economic job-search theory, 243–244, 253
basic model with stationarity
assumption, 244–246
endogenous job-search effort, 249
job search while employed, 248–249
and labor market policy, 250–251
nonstationarity with anticipation,
247–248
nonstationarity without
anticipation, 246
and personality, 251–253
search frictions, 243, 253*n1*
social networks and informal search
channels, 249–250
economic markets
and career adaptability, 230, 234–236
effect on career trajectories, 223–224
economic rational choice theory,
194–195
economic stabilizers of unemployment,
104–105

education
and career planning and development,
384–385
educational attainment and family
unemployment, 94
and effects of job loss on mental
health, 61
and international job search, 486
and labor market position of ethnic
minorities, 502
and underemployment, 362–363
effort
and dimensions of job search, 260–262
and goal setting theory, 132
ego depletion, and prejudiced
reactions, 508
Eikemo, Terje A., 3
"Insecurity, Unemployment, and
Health: A Social Epidemiological
Perspective," 111–125
Eisenberg, P., 13
duration of unemployment, 62
theoretical approaches to studying
unemployment, 16, 17
Ellis, R. A., 264
emergency funds, availability to
families, 88–89
emotion
and discrimination, 515
suppression of in interviews, 342–343
emotional contagion theory, 323
emotional model of job search behavior,
421–422
emotion-focused coping, 20
employability
defining approaches to, 562–566, 562*t*
efficacy of approaches, 566–569
enhancing, 43–44
full employment *vs.* full
employability, 542
maintaining, 277
maintaining among employed workers,
454–455
maintaining among older workers, 454
maintaining among unemployed
workers, 455
of older job seekers, 434–436
and temporary employment
transitions, 469–471
employability programs, work first
vs. human capital development
approaches, 561–562
employed job seekers, 401, 403
antecedents of job search, 406–408,
410–411
directions for future research, 410–413
implications for employers, 413–414
methodology and analysis of research
on, 412–413
operationalizing search, 403
outcomes, 411–412
outcomes of search, 408–410
overview of process used, 402*f*

employed job seekers (*cont.*)
 push-and-pull factors influencing, 406
 researching dynamic process of, 412
 search and turnover process models,
  403–406
 vs. job turnover, 405–406
employees, impediments to
  satisfaction, 300
employers, and treatment of temporary
  employees, 477
employment
 and environmental factors in
  well-being, 19–20
 full employment *vs.* full
  employability, 542
 lifetime employability, concept of, 43
 manifest and latent functions of, 18
 orientations toward, 224
 setting employment goals, 182, 184
 skill utilization and quality of, 72
 social pressure to search for, 186,
  191, 192
 standard *vs.* nontraditional form
  of, 465
employment, temporary, 465–466,
  473–475
 agency workers, 467–468
 careers of temporary workers, 474f
 definition and statistics, 466–467,
  477n1, 477n2, 477n3
 future directions for research, 475–476
 moderating factors, 471–473
 practical implications regarding,
  476–477, 476t
 reasons for accepting, 471, 476
 transitions and careers, 468–469
 transitions and perceived employability,
  469–471
 types of, 467f
employment agencies, *vs.* headhunting
  firms, 295, 297
employment commitment, 194
employment contract, and perceived job
  insecurity, 38
employment position, in context of job
  search, 199–200
employment security *vs.* job security, 469
endogenous job-search effort, 249
Ensel, W. M., 279
entitlement, and response to job
  loss, 23–24
environmental factors, in mental
  health, 19–20
equilibrium theory of coping, and
  underemployment, 365–366
Erdogan, B., 368, 370
Erlinghagen, M., 39
ethnic-enclave labor, 489
ethnic identification hypothesis, and
  discrimination, 510, 511
ethnicity
 as contextual factor in job search,
  200–201

as determinant of hiring
  discrimination, 509
 diversity of in labor market, 144
 and job interview process, 331–332
 and underemployment, 362
 see also ethnic minorities
ethnic minorities
 definition of, 518n2
 and job search, 5
 labor market position of, 502
ethnic prominence hypothesis, and
  discrimination, 509, 511
evaluation design, principal
  approaches, 527
events, primary and secondary appraisals
  of, 146, 150
expectancy theory, 320–321
expectancy-value theory, and research on
  unemployment, 21–22, 193–194
Expectations and Actions
  (Feather), 22
experience sampling method
 and study of job-search dynamics,
  424–425
 using in future research, 78
experimental research, and impact
  evaluation, 527–528, 532
exploration, and career adaptability,
  234–235
exploratory job-search strategy, 262,
  418, 449
external regulation, 163
extraversion, and job search, 315, 395
extrinsic motivation, 171
 and self-regulation, 211
eye contact, maintaining in interviews,
  348–349

F

facilitators and trainers, in JOBS
  Program, 577, 578, 582–585
fairness, and job interviews, 341–342
Falba, T. A., 444
Falbe, C. M., 338
families
 adaptation to stress, 90–91
 family formation, and
  unemployment, 73–74
 family resilience and coping with job
  loss, 91
 further research on effects of job
  loss on, 77
 health consequences of
  unemployment, 114
 implications of job insecurity for, 40
 neglect and abuse, and
  unemployment, 74
 risks of unemployment to, 578–579
 as support systems, 44
families, and unemployment
 cascade of stressors, 90–91
 directions for future research, 94–95
 effects of Great Recession, 87

effects of reduced household income,
  88–89, 95
 family outcomes, 93–94
 family resilience and coping with job
  loss, 91
 identities and family roles, 92–93
 male *vs.* female unemployment, 93
 pathways of affect, 88f
 protective resources for coping with job
  loss, 91–92
 research perspectives on, 87–88
 stress and mental health effects, 89–90
family situation, as contextual factor in
  job search, 200
Fang, T., 489
Farley, J. A., 264
Faulconbridge, James R., 304
Feather, Norman, 2
 autonomous *vs.* controlled
  motivation, 166
 expectancy theory, 320, 321
 grounding research in theory, 160
 "Historical Background to Research on
  Job Loss, Unemployment, and Job
  Search," 9–29
 quality of employment, 72
feedback
 control theory and negative feedback
  loop, 135–136, 136f, 137–138, 138
 as moderator of goal setting, 131–132
Feij, J. A., 381, 392
Feldman, D. C., 39
 career issues and
  underemployment, 370
 cognitive appraisals of job loss, 196
 concept of underemployment, 359
 coping with job loss, 149
 education and work experience, 384
 models of career success, 231
 outplacement services, 549, 551, 552,
  553–554, 557
 psychological distress after job loss, 362
 relative deprivation theory and
  underemployment, 364
 school-to-work transition, 380, 381
 theoretical approaches to effects of
  underemployment, 369
 underemployment, 366
 underemployment and job
  performance, 368
Feldt, T., 90
Felps, W., 407
Fernandez, R. M., 284
Ferrera, M., 117
Ferrie, J., 113
Ferris, Gerald R., 281
 impression management, 302
 political skill inventory, 283
financial insecurity, in context of job
  search, 195
financial strain, for older workers in job
  loss, 439
Fineman, S., 17, 21

Fink, S. L., 17
Finland, JOBS Program in, 582
Finlay, William, 4
  "Contingency Headhunters: What
    They Do--and What Their Activities
    Tell Us About Jobs, Careers, and the
    Labor Market," 293–310
  job turnover process, 405
Fireman, S., 404
first impressions, in job interviews, 335
Fishbein, J., 22
  broader context of job search, 198
  determinants of behavior, 193
  social-cognitive perspective on job loss
    and job search, 145
  theory of reasoned action, 146–147
Fisher, Dan, 297
Fiske, S. T., 507, 515
Flament, C., 506
flexibility
  and older job seekers, 435–436
  and temporary employment, 465–466
Flinders program of research, 15, 22
Flynn, M., 488
focal phenomena, and selecting research
  designs, 424–425
focused job-search strategy, 262, 418,
  448–449
Folkman, S., 20
  primary and secondary appraisals of
    job loss, 150
  social-cognitive perspective on job loss
    and job search, 145
  transactional model of stress and
    coping, 146
Fontinha, Rita, 5
  "Nontraditional Employment: The
    Careers of Temporary Workers,"
    465–480
Foo, M.-D.
  unemployment and marriages, 90
Fordyce Letter, The, 295, 297, 307n4
Forret, Monica, 4
  "Networking as a Job- Search Behavior
    and Career Management Strategy,"
    275–292
  establishing professional networks, 489
  gender roles and unemployment, 233
Forrier, A., 471
Forsythe, S. M., 333
Fort, I., 151
Fountain, C., 449
Fox, S., 339
Foxman, L. D., 552
Francesconi, M., 468
Frank, J., 468
Franke, M., 344
Franzen, A., 275
Frayne, C. A., 133
Frenette, M., 493
Frese, M., 67, 68, 132, 447
Friedland, D. S., 580, 581
Froese, F. J., 488

Fryer, D. M., 10, 11
  agency-restriction model, 71, 72, 76,
    88, 162, 441
  agency theory, 18–19
  future orientation and coping with job
    loss, 447
  research on positive effects of job
    loss, 77–78
  unemployment and health, 114
Fugate, M., 131
  goal setting theory, 132
  job-search goals, 387
Full Employment in a Free Society
  (Beveridge), 99
Fullerton, A. S., 37
Furda, J., 45
future orientation
  in context of job search, 200–201
  and job loss among older workers, 441

G

Gaertner, S. L., 504
Gailliot, M. T., 508
Galesic, M., 424, 425
Galic, Z.
  analytic strategies, 425
  multiwave longitudinal study of job-
    search dynamics, 424, 425
Gallo, W. T., 444
Galor, O., 365
Galunic, C., 279
Garcia, M. F., 514
Gardner, Richard G., 4–5
  "Employed Job Seekers and Job-to-Job
    Search," 401–416
Gardner, Timothy M., 307n5
Garen, J. E., 452
Gatewood, R. D.
  coping with job loss, 149
  engagement in non-work activities, 210
Gault, J., 386
Gebel, M., 232
Geisinger, K. F., 264
gender
  and effects of job loss on mental health,
    60–61, 76, 233
  and international job search, 485
  and interventions for consequences of
    job loss, 75–76
  and job interview process, 331–332
  job loss and masculine identity, 92–93
  and labor market outcomes, 518n3
  male *vs.* female unemployment, 93
  and type of employment, 334
  and underemployment, 361–362
  and unemployment rates, 79n2
  and use of outplacement services, 552–553
  and verbal self-guidance in job search,
    134–135
generational impact of unemployment,
  102–104
Gerhart, B., 332
Gersick, C. J., 285

Giannnantonio, C. M., 260
Gill, B., 489, 490
Gilliland, S. W., 342, 345
Gini score of income distribution, 79n4
Glebbeck, Arie, 5–6
  "The Evaluation of Reemployment
    Programs: Between Impact
    Assessment and Theory-Based
    Approaches," 525–545
globalization, and hiring
  discrimination, 510
global job markets, and recent economic
  downturns, 360
global-level motivating factors in job
  search, 192–193, 197–198
goal-establishment system, in self-
  regulation, 209–211
goal maintenance strategies, 214
goals
  goal conflicts, 210–211
  goal-establishment phase of job search,
    182, 184
  goal proximity, 210
  goal specificity, 209–210
  and intrinsic and extrinsic work goals,
    172–173
  learning goal orientation, 213
  multiple goals, 211
  performance goal orientation,
    212–213, 213f
  subconscious goal primes, 217
goal setting
  and career planning and
    development, 387
  checklist for job seekers, 139
  generating reemployment intentions
    and goals, 146–147
  proximal *vs.* distal goals, 130–131
  SMART goals, 139
goal setting theory, 130–135, 130f
  functional *vs.* dysfunctional self-talk,
    133–135
  future research, 139–140
  and generating reemployment goals, 147
  goal setting research, 132–135
  and job interviews, 342
  moderator variables, 131–132
  and motivation for job search, 196
  and theories of motivation, 129
  vs. control theory, 138–139
goal-shielding implementation intentions,
  214, 217
goal specificity, in goal setting theory, 132
goal-striving phase, of job-search process,
  184, 185, 209, 212–215
goal theory, and control theory, 135–137
Goffin, R., 340
Goldney, R. D., 18
Goldrick-Rab, S., 564
Goldsmith, A. H., 366
Gollwitzer, P. M., 151, 423, 586
Gordon, J. R., 228
Gordon, M. E., 505

Gorgievski, M. J., 436
Gould, S., 281, 384, 386
Govorun, O., 508
Gowan, M. A.
  coping with job loss, 149
  engagement in non-work activities, 210
  outplacement services, 549, 551,
    552–553, 556, 557, 558
grade-point-average, and success of
  school-to-work transition, 395–396
Granovetter, M. S., 265, 278
Grau, A., 287
Graversen, B. K., 535
Gray, M., 95
Great Depression, studies on job loss and
  job search, 9–13
Greater Avenues to Independence
  program, 535
Great Recession
  and financial outlook for older
    workers, 439
  and job availability in economic
    recovery, 568
  longstanding unemployment from, 87
  mass layoff events during, 35–36
  and objective job security, 438
  and perceived job insecurity, 437
  and recent history of job loss and job
    search, 1
  recovery of global job markets from, 360
  and self-employment for older workers,
    447–448
Greenberg, D., 533
Greenhalgh, L., 33
  job insecurity, 44
  organizational norms of fairness, 47
  organizational performance and
    perceived job insecurity, 36
Greve, A., 494
Grey, A., 37
Gribble, L. C., 553, 558
grievances, and perceived job
  insecurity, 39
Griffeth, R. W., 196
group competition theory, and
  discrimination, 506
Guest, D., 281, 471
Gutek, B. A., 92

H
Hackett, G., 147
Hackney, H. L., 558
Hagger, M. S., 217
Haider, S. J., 451
Hall, Sarah J. E., 304
Halvari, H., 169
Hamann, D. J., 154
Hambrick, D. C., 129–130
Hamilton, J. E., 94
Hamori, Monika, 298
  results of headhunting, 306
  work and practices of
    headhunters, 307n3

Handler, J., 564
handshake, in job interview, 319, 335,
  336–337
Hangartner, D., 275
haphazard job-search strategy, 262,
  418, 449
Harcourt, M., and S. Harcourt, 488
Harriman, D., 130
Harrison, R., 16–17
Hart, David, 307n5
Hartley, J., 15, 21
Hartman, K., 383–384, 385
Harvey, J., 361
  job attitudes and
    underemployment, 368
  measurement issues and research on
    underemployment, 370
  relative deprivation theory and
    underemployment, 364
Hassel, Alice, 2–3
  "Individual Consequences of Job Loss
    and Unemployment," 57–85
Hausknecht, J. P., 339, 345
Hawkinson, Paul, 307n4
Hawthorne, L., 485, 493
headhunters
  business relationships with client
    companies, 296–297, 304–305
  evaluating prospective candidates,
    301–302
  financial footing of industry, 295–296
  identifying job candidates, 297–299,
    300–301
  impression management, 299–300,
    302–304
  insights provided by, 300–304
  and job turnover process, 405
  matching clients and candidates,
    299–300, 308n12
  methods of building clientele, 296–297
  in other countries, 299, 304, 305
  practical advice on, 306–307
  source companies, 307n8, 308n9
  structural holes and headhunting
    practices, 300
  work and practices of, 293–295, 307n3
headhunters, directions for future
  research, 304–307
  candidates and source companies, 305
  client companies, 304–305
  headhunting firms, 304
  impression management, 305–306
  producing candidates, 306
health
  international variation in job security
    and, 122
  and job insecurity, 111–114
  perceived status as motivator in job
    search, 197
  self-reported health and health
    behaviors, 116
  self-reported health and
    unemployment, 118, 121t, 122

  and temporary employment
    transitions, 470
  unemployment and health, 114–116
  welfare-state regimes and, 116–118
health care benefits, and hiring of older
  workers, 452
health care utilization, and job
  insecurity, 113
Hebl, M. R., 333
Heinrich, C. J., 535
Heinrichs, N., 366
Hellgren, J., 33
Hennessey, H. W., 280–281
Heywood, J. S., 453
Hiemstra, A. M. F., 503
Highhouse, S., 166
  job-search strategies, 448
  recruiter characteristics and
    discrimination, 514
high school graduates, school-to-work
  transition, 394
Hilber, G., 452
Hill, J. M. M., 16–17
hiring discrimination, 503–506, 509–516
hiring expectations, 314, 320
Hirsch, B. T., 452
historical background, of research on job
  loss and job search
  agency theory, 18–19
  deprivation theory, 17–18
  early twentieth-century concerns, 10
  expectancy-value theory, 21–22
  fourteenth-century attitudes, 9–10
  implications of research, 25
  improvements in methodology and
    analysis, 14
  in post-World War II era to
    1990s, 14–16
  significance of research, 24–25
  stage theories, 16–17
  stress and coping models, 20–21
  studies from Great Depression, 9–13
  theoretical approaches, 16–24
  vitamin model, 19–20
Hobfoll, S. E., 35
  conservation of resources theory, 472
  theoretical approaches to effects of
    underemployment, 369
Hoffmeister, O., 490
Holistic Outplacement Model, 549
Hollenbeck, J. R., 137
Holtom, Brooks C., 294, 368
Hom, P. W., 196, 404
Hoogtanders, Y., 563–564, 565
Hosoda, M., 511, 512
hostility, and unemployment, 74
Hough, L., 132, 363
House, J. S., 15
  job insecurity and worker health, 40
  unemployment and mental health, 578
household size, as contextual factor in job
  search, 200
Howard, A., 21

Howe, G. W., 89–90
Hua, S. S., 132
Huang, T., 336
Hudson, S., 485
Huffcutt, A. I., 331, 336, 339
Huffman, M. L., 279–280, 389
Hughes, L. W., 407
Hulin, C. L., 38, 553
human capital
    competitive advantage of, 301
    and international job seekers, 486,
        490–491
    measures to enhance, 455
    and older job seekers, 434–435, 454
human capital attainment
    and career competencies, 277
    and family unemployment, 94
human capital development, vs. work first
        approach to employability, 561–562,
        569–570, 571
    defining approaches, 562–566, 562t
    future directions for research, 570–571
    intervention models, 563–564
    program efficacy, 566–569
    rationale and targets of approaches,
        562–563
    relationship to individual participants,
        565–566
    relationship to labor market, 564–565
human capital theory, and
        underemployment, 365
Human Development Index (HDI), 79n3
hypoegoic self-regulation, 216–217
hysteresis, theory of, 366, 562

I
Ibrahim, S., 40
identified regulation, 164
identity
    coping with identity threat, 228–230
    and early retirement, 446–447
    and job loss among older workers,
        439–440
    and phase model of
        self-categorization, 422
    work-related identity threats,
        225–228
identity, vocational, 165, 224–230
identity and coping during career
        transitions model (ICCT), 230
identity change, and school-to-work
        transition, 380
identity theory, and effects of job
        loss, 92–93
Ilgen, D. R., 148
immigrants
    and local institutional resources,
        488, 490
    and underemployment, 362
    see also international job seekers;
        international job search
immigration policies, and international
        job search, 483–484

immigration status, and perceived job
        insecurity, 37
impact evaluation, of reemployment
        programs, 527–531
implementation intentions, 214, 217
Implicit Association Test, 515–516
implicit personality theory, 332
impression formation theories, and
        discrimination, 507–508
impression management
    future research, 305–306
    and headhunters, 299–300, 302–304
    and job interview behavior, 334–336
    and preparing for interviews, 348–349
income distribution
    Gini score to measure, 79n4
    and impact of unemployment, 106
income inequality, and individual
        consequences of job loss, 65
incongruence model, 76
individual antecedents, of perceived job
        insecurity, 37–39
individualism
    and consequences of job loss, 66–67
    as contextual factor in job search, 200
inductive theory building, 129–130
Industrial Age, and concept of
        unemployment, 58
industry sector, and perceived job
        insecurity, 37
informal search channels, and economic
        job-search theory, 249–250
Inkson, K., 277, 485, 491
insecure employment
    see job insecurity
insecurity, sources of feeling, 12
instrumental attitudes, and job search, 191
integrated regulation, 164
intensity, and dimensions of job search,
        260–262
intention-behavior gap, 206–208, 208t
intention-behavior moderators
    and goal establishment, 209–211
    and goal striving, 212–215
intentions, implementation intentions,
        214, 217
interdependence theory, and job
        interviews, 335
internalization, and autonomous job
        search, 163
international job search, 495–496
    antecedents of, 485–487
    career development and promotion,
        492–493
    future directions for research, 496
    immigration policies and labor market,
        483–484
    moderators of, 487–488
    moderators of outcome, 494–495
    motivations to engage in, 484–485
    objective outcomes, 491–492
    postmigration investment in human
        capital, 490–491

practical implications checklist,
        496–497
    process of, 483f
    search strategies, 489–490
    subjective outcomes, 494
international job seekers, 481, 495–496
    backgrounds of, 481–483
    challenges to, 5
    earnings of, 493–494
    future directions for research, 496
    practical implications checklist,
        496–497
Internet
    and job search among older
        workers, 449
    and job-to-job search, 412
internships, and school-to-work
        transition, 384–385
interval job-search strategy, 419
interventions
    and approaches to employability, 563–
        564, 565–566
    for consequences of job loss, 75–76
    and job-search behaviors and
        success, 419
    JOBS Program content, 578
    JOBS Program protocols, 576
    reemployment interventions, 236
    verbal self-guidance in job search,
        133–135
interviews
    candidate checklist for practice,
        347–349
    candidate preferences, 339–340
    candidate responses, 340–342
    comprehensive model of
        performance, 331
    discriminatory questions in, 341
    hiring discrimination and structure
        of, 505
    improving interview skills, 344
    interview anxiety, 340–341,
        344–345, 346t
    interview structure, significance of,
        333–334, 338
    and preinterview impressions, 322–323
    reciprocal processes in, 323–324
    and studying episodes of job
        search, 426
    type of job, significance of, 334
    verbal and nonverbal communication
        in, 336–337
interviews, from the candidate
        perspective, 329–331, 346–347
    candidate behaviors, 334–339
    candidate characteristics, 331–334
    candidate reactions, 339–343
    candidate recommendations,
        343–346, 347t
    checklist for practice, 347–349
    conceptual framework, 330f
intrinsic motivation, 162, 171, 211
introjected regulation, 163–164

intuition, and decision-making, 235
Inzlicht, M., 508
Ireland, JOBS Program in, 582
Isaksson, K., 33

J

Jackson, C., 511
Jackson, D. J. R., 484
Jackson, P. R.
  age and effects of job loss, 442
  duration of unemployment, 62
  unemployment and mental health, 19
Jackson, S. E., 345
Jacquet, F., 151
Jahoda, Marie
  activity level, importance of, 440
  and agency theory, 18–19
  attitude toward employment, 72
  defining unemployment, 59
  and deprivation theory, 17–18
  effects of long-term unemployment, 14
  job-search motives, 160
  latent-deprivation model, 70, 71
  latent functions of employment, 114
  Marienthal and other studies by, 11, 57
  mediating processes, 76
  origins of Marienthal study, 10
  research on unemployment and
    families, 87
  theoretical approaches to studying
    unemployment, 16, 17
  time structure and work, 441
  underemployment, 366
Jaidi, Y., 318, 321
Jarrett, J. E., 10
Jenn, Nancy Garrison, 307n6
Jensen, L., 361
Jeon, K. S., 535
Jeurissen, T., 20
Jiang, Lixin, 2
  "Job Insecurity and Anticipated Job
    Loss: A Primer and Exploration of
    Possible Interventions," 31–53
Jirjahn, U., 453
Job, V., 215
job agencies, employee-client
    relationships, 78
job assessment, and preparing for
    interviews, 348
job attendance, self-management of, 133
job attitudes
  and job-to-job search, 412
  and underemployment, 367–368
job availability, and employability
    programs, 568
job candidate behaviors, and interview
    process, 334–339, 337
  candidate sincerity, 338
  directions for future research, 338–339
  first impressions, 335
  general impressions, 335–336
  identifying and practicing
    behaviors, 349

impression management behaviors,
    334–336
  moderating factors, 337–338
  nonverbal and verbal communication,
    336–337
job candidate characteristics, and
    interview process, 331–334
  demographic characteristics, 331–332
  directions for future research, 334
  interview structure, significance of,
    333–334
  physical appearance, 332–333
  style of dress, 333, 348
  type of job, significance of, 334
  weight, 332–333
job candidate reactions, and interview
    process, 339–343
  directions for future research, 342–343
  interview anxiety, 340–341,
    344–345, 346t
  justice in job interviews, 341–342
  preference for types of interviews,
    339–340
  responses to interviews, 340–342
job candidate recommendations, and
    interview process, 343–346
  improving interview skills, 344
  increasing perceptions of justice,
    345–346
  reducing anxiety, 344–345, 346t
job characteristics
  and applicant attraction, 313
  and discrimination in resume
    screening, 512–513
job choice, predictors of, 312–314, 317
job creation, governmental, 160
job information sources, 388–389
job insecurity
  affective vs. cognitive, 34
  alleviating effects via enhanced
    communication, 46–47
  alleviating effects via enhanced
    control, 45–46
  alleviating effects via enhanced
    employability, 43–44
  alleviating effects via enhanced support
    systems, 44–45
  alleviating effects via organizational
    justice and trust, 47
  alleviating negative effects of, 43t
  attenuating adverse safety
    outcomes, 47–48
  behavioral consequences of, 40–41
  and career trajectories, 224
  cognitive, attitudinal, and affective
    reactions to, 39
  comprehensive model of, 34–35, 35f
  consequences of, 39–42
  defining, 111–112
  dimensionality of, 2, 33
  evidence for positive outcomes, 42
  and health, 111–114
  implications for well-being, 40

individual antecedents, 37–39
  and industry sector, 37
  measures of, 33–34
  mental and physical reactions to, 437
  moderating effects of perceived, 42–48
  nature of, 32–34
  objective insecurity, 437–438
  and older workers, 436–438
  organizational antecedents, 36–37
  organizational consequences, 42
  perceived insecurity, 436–437
  prevalence of, 31–32
  proximity to organizational core, 38
  psychological effects of, 15–16
  qualitative vs. quantitative, 33–34
  socioeconomic antecedents, 35–36
  sources of feeling, 12
  stages of, 33
  subjective vs.objective insecurity, 32–33
  vs. anticipated job loss, 48m
  and work-related identity threats,
    225–228
job insecurity, a social epidemiological
    perspective on
  explaining job insecurity and
    health, 114
  international variation in job insecurity
    and health, 122
  job insecurity and health, 111–114
  social protections in welfare-state
    regimes, 117–118, 118f
  unemployment and health, 114–116
  welfare state regimes and health,
    116–118
job interviews, and multidimensionality
    of job search, 266–267
job interviews, from the candidate
    perspective, 329–331, 346–347
  candidate behaviors, 334–339
  candidate characteristics, 331–334
  candidate reactions, 339–343
  candidate recommendations,
    343–346, 347t
  checklist for practice, 347–349
  conceptual framework, 330f
job loss
  benefits of writing about, 554
  and career trajectories, 224
  causal attributions and response
    to, 22–23
  consequences of, 2–3
  effects on child development, 94
  effects on work identity and well-being,
    226, 228
  financial and psychological impacts of,
    438–439
  frequency of, 143–144
  future research on positive effects
    of, 77–78
  grieving process and, 150
  and identity theory, 92–93
  increased recognition of context, 144
  personal and societal costs of, 15

positive effects of, 77–78, 149–150
potential benefits for older
  workers, 447
reactions to, 149, 575–576
research agenda, 154–155
self-efficacy and response to, 23
self-regulation perspective on, 148–150
social-cognitive perspective on, 148–150
social-cognitive process model of, 145f
and social-cognitive theory, 146
and stages of grief, 417–418
theoretical perspectives on, 3–4
and underemployment, 360
and work-related identity threats,
  225–228
see also anticipated job loss;
  unemployment
job loss, among older workers, 433–434,
  453–455
advantages and challenges of, 453
aftereffects of, 438–443
and age discrimination, 451–453
coping with job loss, 443–450
employability and associated
  stereotypes, 434–436
and maintaining employability, 454
perceived *vs.* objective job insecurity,
  436–438
process model, 434f
job loss, and families
cascade of stressors, 90–91
directions for future research, 94–95
effects of Great Recession, 87
effects of reduced household income,
  88–89, 95
family outcomes, 93–94
family resilience and coping, 91
identities and family roles, 92–93
male *vs.* female unemployment, 93
pathways of affect, 88f
protective resources for coping with job
  loss, 91–92
research perspectives on, 87–88
stress and mental health effects, 89–90
job loss, historical background of
  research, 9–29
agency theory, 18–19
deprivation theory, 17–18
early twentieth-century concerns, 10
expectancy-value theory, 21–22
fourteenth-century attitudes, 9–10
implications of research, 25
improvements in methodology and
  analysis, 14
in post-World War II era to
  1990s, 14–16
significance of research, 24–25
stage theories, 16–17
stress and coping models, 20–21
studies from the Great
  Depression, 9–13
theoretical approaches, 16–24
vitamin model, 19–20

job loss, individual consequences of
and age, 62–64
attitudes, 74–75
causal effects on mental health, studies
  of, 68–70
coping strategies, 67–68
differences across national
  borders, 65–67
differences among countries, 65–67
duration of unemployment, 62, 63f
explaining negative mental health
  effects, 70–72
gaps in research, 76–79
and gender, 60–61
hostility and aggression, 74
on mental health, 59–60
moderators of effects on mental
  health, 60–64
physical health and health
  behavior, 72–73
practical conclusions of research, 75–76
sexual behavior and family
  formation, 73–74
and socioeconomic status, 61–62
job loss and underemployment
prevalence of, 360
research perspectives on, 363–366
job performance, and
  underemployment, 368
job-person fit, and applicant
  attraction, 314
job previews, 305–306, 314
*JOBS: A Manual for Teaching People
  Successful Job-Search Strategies,*
  584–585
job satisfaction
after job-to-job search, 409
impediments to, 300
sources of feeling, 12
and temporary employment, 471
job search
affective *vs.* instrumental attitudes, 191
among temporary workers, 469
basic model with stationarity
  assumption, 244–246
characteristics of, 181–182
checklist for, 139
clarity and intensity of, 132,
  164–167, 185
components and phases of, 4
control theory and, 135–139
definition of, 181, 422
demands of, 575–576
duration of, 143–144
effect of economic hardship on, 89
effort and intensity, defining, 403
facilitating or impending factors, 193
financial and other costs of, 305
generating reemployment intentions
  and goals, 146–147
goal setting theory, 130–135
goal setting *vs.* control theory, 138–139
habits and routines, significance of, 217

increased recognition of context, 144
individual salient beliefs motivating,
  192–193
integrating with recruitment, 316–318
intensity and effort, among older job
  seekers, 448
intensity and effort, defining, 403
international job search strategies,
  489–490
interventions and outcomes, 150–152
measurement issues and research on,
  153–154
and mindfulness training, 217
and mindset of unlimited
  willpower, 215
and modern self-regulation models,
  167–169
motivational and self-regulatory
  perspectives on, 183f
multiple job options, 211
outcomes of networking for, 284–285
perceived behavioral control over,
  186–187, 192
personal attitude toward, 186
potential for lowered mental health, 67
predictors of behaviors and outcomes,
  315–316
process of, 182–184
procrastination and, 235–236
refusal to search, 169–170
research agenda, 154–155
search clarity, 151
and self-efficacy, 133–135, 390
self-regulated job search, 147–148, 206
significance of motivation in, 164–167
significance of quality in, 185
social-cognitive process model of, 145f
and social influences, 152–153
studying episodes of behavior, 425–426
temporal considerations in, 152
theoretical approaches to, 318–322
theoretical perspectives on, 3–4
theories of motivation, 129–130
and verbal self-guidance, 133–135
vs. recruitment, 316t
see also job-to-job search
job search, among older workers, 433–
  434, 453–455
advantages and challenges of, 453
and age discrimination, 451–453
employability and associated
  stereotypes, 434–436
and maintaining employability, 454
process model, 434f
job search, and school-to-work transition,
  379–381, 394–396, 398
career planning and development,
  383–387
defining success of, 381
education and work experience,
  384–385
implications for research and practice,
  396–398

job search, and school-to-work transition (*cont.*)
  integrative model of, 382, 383*f*
  interrelatedness of stages, 394, 396
  intervention framework, 397*t*
  job information sources, 388–389
  job-search intensity, 389–390
  job-search stage, 387–392
  key challenges, 382
  stakeholders in success of, 396
  work adjustment, 392–396
job search, historical background of research, 9–29
  agency theory, 18–19
  deprivation theory, 17–18
  early twentieth-century concerns, 10
  expectancy-value theory, 21–22
  fourteenth-century attitudes, 9–10
  implications of research, 25
  improvements in methodology and analysis, 14
  in post-World War II era to 1990s, 14–16
  significance of research, 24–25
  stage theories, 16–17
  stress and coping models, 20–21
  studies from the Great Depression, 9–13
  theoretical approaches, 16–24
  vitamin model, 19–20
job-search behavior
  predictors of, 315–316
  and underemployment, 363
job-search behavior, a theory of planned, 183*f*, 184–187, 191–201
  characteristics of, 205–206
  conceptualizing self-regulation in, 209–216
  contextual and global-level motivating factors, 192–201
  empirical support for core relationships, 187, 188*t*–190*t*, 191–192
  intention-behavior gap, 206–208
  intention-behavior moderators, and goal establishment, 209–211
  intention-behavior moderators, and goal striving, 212–215
  job attainment, 187
  job-search intention, 185–187, 187, 191
  motivational and self-regulatory perspectives on, 207*t*
  nonconscious self-regulation, 216–217
  practical suggestions regarding, 201, 218
  predictors of job-search intention, 191–192
  self-regulation, functioning of, 208–209
  theoretical underpinnings, 185–187
job-search behavior,
  multidimensionality of
  behaviors and sources, 261*t*
  content and direction of behavior, 262–268

definition and dimensions, 260
dynamics and persistence, 268–269
effort and intensity, 260–262
future research directions, 271–273
implications for employment counselors, 270–271
implications for job seekers, 270
informal and formal sources of information, 264–265, 418
job interviews, 266–267
job-search strategies, 262–263
networking, 265
preparatory and active behaviors, 263–264
quality of job-search behaviors, 267–268
relationships within and between dimensions, 269–270
specific behaviors and sources, 265–267
vs. unidimensionality, 259–260, 273
job-search behavior, of the unemployed
  analytic strategies for studying, 425
  antecedents and outcomes of, 419–420
  categorizing behavior, 418–419
  dynamic nature of, 420
  methodologies of research into search dynamics, 424–425
  studying episodes of behavior, 425–426
  theoretical models of dynamics in, 420–423
  unique aspects, 417–418
job-search research
  future directions of, 322–324
  integrating with recruitment research, 311–312, 316–318, 317–318, 324, 325
  literature overview, 314–315
  practical implications of, 324–325
  recommendations for individuals and organizations, 325
  signaling theory, 318–320
job search strategies, among older workers, 448–450
job-search theory, and underemployment, 366
job security
  and organizational tenure, 438
  vs. employment security, 469
job-seeking behavior
  and expectancy-value theory, 21–22
JOBS Program, 6
  adaptation of, 588
  benefits to participants, 584, 585*f*
  conceptual framework of, 577*f*
  cycles of active teaching and learning, 583*f*
  delivery of, 583–584
  and demands of job search, 575–576
  design of, 583
  effectiveness in service settings, 581
  future directions for research and practice, 586–588
  group influences of, 580–581, 587
  international dissemination of, 581–582

mechanisms underlying effectiveness of, 580
model of, 576–578
protocol for training and delivery, 582–585
research program, 578–582
and risks of unemployment, 578–579
support materials, 584–585
tests of efficacy, 579–580
job tenure, and perceived job insecurity, 37–38
job-to-job search, 401, 403
  antecedents of, 406–408, 410–411
  directions for future research, 410–413
  implications for employers, 413–414
  methodology and analysis of research on, 412–413
  operationalizing search, 403
  outcomes, 408–410, 411–412
  overview of process, 402*f*
  researching dynamic process of, 412
  search and turnover process models, 403–406
  vs. job turnover, 405–406
Johnston, L., 452, 505
Jones, L. P., 78
Jordan, Michael, 131
Judge, T. A., 406
justice, in job interviews, 341–342, 345–346
justice, organizational, 47

K

Kacmar, K. Michelle, 302
Kalb, G., 468
Kalil, A., 94
Kammeyer-Mueller, J. D., 395
Kanfer, F.
  social-cognitive perspective on job loss and job search, 145
  theories of self-regulation, 147
Kanfer, Ruth, 3
  defining job search, 138, 260, 388, 448
  education and job search, 486
  effect of economic hardship on job search, 89
  employment position and job search, 199
  evaluating reemployment, 154
  goal setting theory, 139, 140
  intensity of job search, 185
  "Job Loss and Job Search: A Social-Cognitive and Self-Regulation Perspective," 143–158
  job-search dynamics, 269–270
  job-search effort and intensity, 261
  job-search intensity, 389
  job-search intensity and job satisfaction, 391
  measuring job-search intensity, 153
  outplacement programs, 553
  perceived financial need, 195
  personality traits and job search, 146

personality traits and school-to-work transition, 395
preparatory and active job search behaviors, 263
resource allocation model, 148
self-regulation model, introduction of, 420
underemployment, 363
volitional job seeking, 168
Kantrowitz, T. M.
  defining job search, 138, 448
  effect of economic hardship on job search, 89
Kapoor, R., 104
Karasek, R. A., 16
Karl, K., 287
Kasl, S., 21
Kasl, S. V., 444, 576
Keaveny, T. J., 382, 389
Kelloway, E. K., 45
Kelvin, P., 9–10
Kent, Derin, 5
  "International Job Search," 481–499
Kernan, M. C., 137
Kerr, C., 101
Kessler, R. C., 15
  stress and coping models, 21
  unemployment and mental health, 578
Khapova, S. N., 227
Khatiwada, I., 361, 362
Kieselbach, T., 549–550, 551, 552, 553, 556, 558
King, E. B., 510
Kinicki, A. J., 41
  coping with job loss, 149, 365
  goal setting theory, 131, 132
  job-search goals, 387
  well-being during unemployment, 58
Kinnunen, U., 44, 90
Kira, Mari, 5
  "Too Old to Tango? Job Loss and Job Search among Older Workers," 433–464
Kirk, J. J., 549
Kirnan, J. P., 264
Kitanaka, Anna, 307n7
Klehe, Ute-Christine
  advance notice of redundancy, 46
  career planning and development, 385, 386
  focused job search strategy, 151
  goal setting theory, 132
  job insecurity and job search behaviors, 41
  "New Economy Careers Demand Adaptive Mental Models and Resources," 223–241
  reemployment quality, 363, 391
  research on positive effects of job loss, 78
  results of mandatory reemployment course, 165

"Too Old to Tango? Job Loss and Job Search among Older Workers," 433–464
"What to Expect: The Oxford Handbook of Job Loss and Job Search," 1–6
Klein, H. J., 131–132
Kleinmann, M.
  job insecurity and social safety net, 44–45
  organizational performance and perceived job insecurity, 36
Kluve, J., 534, 535
Kluwe, J., 566
Knerr, C. S., 137
knowing-how competencies, 477
Koen, Jesse, 5
  career adaptability, 234
  focused job search strategy, 151
  goal setting theory, 132
  mandatory skill training, 236
  reemployment quality, 363
  research on positive effects of job loss, 78
  results of mandatory reemployment course, 165
  "Too Old to Tango? Job Loss and Job Search among Older Workers," 433–464
  use of job search strategies, 262
Koestner, R., 168
König, C.
  job insecurity and social safety net, 44–45
  organizational performance and perceived job insecurity, 36
König, C. J., 42
Konrad, A. M., 278, 283
Krieshok, T. S., 216
Kriska, S. D., 336
Kristof-Brown, A., 344
Kubler-Ross, E., 150
Kulik, C. T., 512
Kyyrä, T., 446

L

labor market
  active labor market policies, and employability, 566–567, 569
  and approaches to employability, 564–565
  balance of power in, 100
  and career adaptability, 234–236
  demand as contextual factor in job search, 199
  and economic job search theory, 243–244
  effect on career trajectories, 223–224
  ethnic-enclave labor, 489
  and individual consequences of job loss, 66
  international deregulation of, 112
  and international job search, 483–484

and job-to-job search, 407–408
occupation-specific demand and international job search, 495
position of ethnic minorities in and psychological impacts of job insecurity and loss, 16
and reemployment programs, 543n7
and temporary workers, 472–473
and work first approach to employability, 562–563
labor market policy, and job search behavior, 250–251
labor unions, and international job seekers, 488
LaFrance, M., 341
Lahey, J. N., 452
Lam, H., 488
Lambert, T. A., 450
Lancaster, 244
language proficiency, and international job search, 486–487
Lasker, B., 11
László, K. D., 114
Latack, J. C., 149
  Career Growth Model of outplacement services, 549
  coping with job loss, 438, 439, 443
  outplacement programs, 557
  positive effects of job loss, 149
  reactions to job loss, 452
latent deprivation theory, 70, 71, 114
Latham, Gary P., 3
  expectancy theory, 320
  goal primes, 217
  "Goal Setting and Control Theory: Implications for Job Search," 129–141
  goal setting research, 132, 133
  social-cognitive perspective on job loss and job search, 145
  verbal self-guidance, 134
Lay, C. H., 197
Layard, R., 566
layoffs, and workload of remaining employees, 100
Lazarsfeld, Paul
  duration of unemployment, 62
  Marienthal study, 57
  origins of Marienthal study, 10
  stages of unemployment effects, 13
  theoretical approaches to studying unemployment, 16, 17
Lazarus, R. S., 20
  primary and secondary appraisals of job loss, 150
  social-cognitive perspective on job loss and job search, 145
  stress and coping models, 21
  transactional model of stress and coping, 146
leader-member exchange theory, 44
Leana, C. R.
  cognitive appraisals of job loss, 196

Leana, C. R. (*cont.*)
  coping with job loss, 149
  outplacement services, 549, 551, 552, 553–554, 557
  psychological distress after job loss, 362
  relative deprivation theory and underemployment, 364
learning, and older job seekers, 435–436
learning goal orientation, 213
learning goals, and goal setting theory, 131
learning model of job search behavior, 421
Leary, M. R., 216–217
Leavitt, T. D., 361
Lee, C. H., 446
Lee, F. K., 187
Lee, Jeong-Yeon, 306
Lee, T. H., 410
Lee, T. W.
  job attitudes and underemployment, 368
  turnover process, 404, 408, 410
Lee, Tae Heon, 294
Lee, Thomas W., 294, 307n1
leisure activities, and fulfilling a sense of calling, 227
Lekan, D. F., 552, 556
Lekes, N., 168
Lens, W., 164, 166
Lent, R. W., 147
LePine, M. A., 390
Leroux, J., 548, 549, 553, 558
Leroy, N., 151
Levashina, J., 335, 339
leverage-seeking job searches, 409–410
Levy, M. L., 89–90
Lewin, K.
  field theory, 484
  theoretical approaches to studying unemployment, 16
Li, Xian, 5
  "Job-Search Behavior of the Unemployed: A Dynamic Perspective," 417–429
  older job seekers and reemployment, 450–451
liability of foreignness effect, 483–484, 489
Lievens, F., 337, 338
"life design" career approach, 224
lifetime employability, concept of, 43
Lilly, R. S., 369
limited resource model, and biased decision making, 508
limiting long-term illness, and unemployment, 116
Lin, N., 279
Lindsay, Colin, 6
  "Work First *versus* Human Capital Development in Employability Programs," 561–574
LMSI, and access to income-earning activities, 79n5
Lo, I., 336

local institutional resources, and international job seekers, 488
Locke, Edwin A., 3
  control theory and job search, 135, 137
  "Goal Setting and Control Theory: Implications for Job Search," 129–141
  goal setting theory, 147
  social-cognitive perspective on job loss and job search, 145
Lockwood, A., 281
long-term illness, and unemployment, 116
Lord, R. G., 137
Loretto, W., 565
Louis-Guerin, C., 40
Lubbers, R., 395
Luciano, J. M., 551, 552, 557
Luksyte, A., 365, 369–370
Luthans, F., 280–281, 284

M

Macan, T., 341, 343
MacDermid, S. M., 425
Macnicol, J., 568
Madamba, A. B., 362
Maertz, C. P., 425
Maestas, N., 450
Mainiero, L. A., 233
Maitoza, Robyn, 3
  "Job Loss, Unemployment, and Families," 87–98
Malinen, S., 452
Mallinckrodt, B., 367
Mallon, M., 489, 490, 491
Malmberg-Heimonen, I., 581
Maloles, C. M., 42
Mannix, L. M., 333
Marcia, J. E., 165
Marienthal study
  effects of unemployment, 57
  origins of, 10
  significance of economic development, 65
  summary and historical background of, 11
market-mediated temporary employment, 466–467
marriages
  effect of economic hardship on, 89–90
  job loss and loss of identity, 92–93
  "rigid" *vs.* "flexible" roles in, 92
  social support in coping with job loss, 91
  stress and mental health effects of unemployment, 89–90
Martin, H. J., 552, 556
Martinez, Tomás, 297
Massengrill, D. P., 505
Mauno, S., 38
Maurer, T. J., 344
Mawritz, Mary B., 3
  "Goal Setting and Control Theory: Implications for Job Search," 129–141

maximizing job search strategy, 262–263
Mayer, R. C., 47
Maynard, D. C., 364, 365
  job attitudes and underemployment, 368
  underemployment and turnover behavior, 368
Mazzeo, C., 564
McBey, K., 491
McCallum, S., 285
McCarthy, Julie M., 4
  discriminatory questions in job interviews, 341–342
  job interview anxiety, 340
  structured interviews and discrimination, 514
  "Through the Looking Glass: Employment Interviews from the Lens of Job Candidates," 329–357
McConahay, John, 513
McConnell, A. R., 229
McCool, Joseph Daniel, 307n3
McCoy, L., 33–34
McCubbin, H. I., 90
McDonnell, Anthony, 301
McFadyen, R. G., 420
McFarland, L. A., 336, 514
McKay, R. A., 216
McKee-Ryan, Frances M., 3, 4
  age and effects of job loss, 442
  age and individual consequences of job loss, 63
  causal effects of job loss on mental health, 69
  coping with job loss, 67
  duration of unemployment, 62
  equilibrium theory of coping, 365
  job attitudes and underemployment, 367, 368
  "Job Loss, Unemployment, and Families," 87–98
  job loss and gender, 61
  measurement issues and research on underemployment, 370
  "Reemployment Quality, Underemployment, and Career Outcomes," 359–375
  relative deprivation theory and underemployment, 364
  significance of unemployment protection, 65–66
  theoretical approaches to effects of underemployment, 369
  well-being during unemployment, 58
  work-role centrality, 227
McKenna, S., 490, 491
McVicar, D., 568
Meadows, P., 566, 567
Meager, N., 567
means-testing, and social protections for the unemployed, 117–118
measurement issues
  in evaluating reemployment programs, 535

and research on reemployment, 153–154
and research on underemployment, 370
mechanisms of change
  in JOBS Program, 580, 586
  and reemployment programs, 537, 539, 540t, 541–542, 541t
  and theory-based research, 530
Meichenbaum, D., 133
Meijman, T., 45
mental health
  of children in unemployed households, 93–94
  and duration of unemployment, 62, 63f
  effects of job loss on, 438–439
  effects of unemployment on, 57–58
  environmental factors in, 19
  explaining negative effects of job loss, 70–72
  and individual consequences of job loss, 59–60
  influence of JOBS Program, 580–581
  and JOBS Program model, 576
  and JOBS Program research, 578
  moderators of effects of job loss on, 60–64
  and perceived job insecurity, 437
  and stress in families, 89–90
  unemployment as risk factor for suicide, 79n7, 115
  vs. physical health in coping with job loss, 69–70
mental illness
  impact of unemployment on workers with, 102, 103
  increases during economic downturns, 14–15
Mertens, A., 365
Merton, R., 364
metaevaluations, and impact evaluation, 527
Metcalfe, J., 208, 214
methodology and analysis
  of job-to-job search, 412–413
  post-World War II improvements in, 14
Michael, J., 281
  dependency and management, 283
  outcomes of networking behavior, 285
"migrant personality," and international job seekers, 485
Mikkelsen, A., 45
Miller, P., 553, 558
Millman, Z., 134
mindfulness, and self-regulation, 217
minimum income for healthy living, concept of, 123
minority groups and job search, 5
  barriers to building and utilizing social networks, 279–280
  and practices of headhunting firms, 297–298
  use of informal job information sources, 264–265
Mischel, W., 208, 214

Mitchell, Terence R., 132
  turnover process, 404
  voluntary employee turnover, 294, 307n1
Mobley, W. H., 403
Mohr, G. B., 33
  coping with job loss, 67
  job loss among older workers, 447
  stages of objective job insecurity, 437–438
Moller, A. C., 211
money, impact on everyday life, 439
monitoring function, of self-regulation, 209, 212–213
Monmouthshire study, 11
moral norms, and social pressure to search for employment, 186, 192
Morgeson, F. P., 343
Morisette, R., 493
Morris, J. N., 123
Morrison, E. W., 278, 381, 382
  career planning and development, 383
  education and work experience, 384
  personality traits and school-to-work transition, 395
  work adjustment for new graduates, 392
mortality
  and job insecurity, 113
  and unemployment, 115–116
Mortensen, Dale T., 244, 253n1
Moser, Klaus, 2–3
  "dark side" of networking, 287
  "Individual Consequences of Job Loss and Unemployment," 57–85
  measurement of networking behavior, 281
  outcomes of networking behavior, 284, 285
motivation
  autonomous regulation, 164
  and candidate reactions to interviews, 342
  contextual and global-level factors, 192–201
  controlled regulation, 163–164
  and controlled regulation, 163–164
  and duration of unemployment, 167
  energetic basis of, 160–162
  to engage in international job search, 484–485
  extrinsic motivation, 171
  importance to job search, 182
  influence of JOBS Program, 580–581
  internalization, 163, 164
  intrinsic motivation, 162, 171
  and job search outcomes, 152
  of job seekers in JOBS Program, 577
  motivational perspectives on job search, 183f, 184, 207t
  as predictor in job search, 315–316
  quality of as moderating factor, 170–171, 211

and self-determination theory, 163f
  significance in job search, 164–167
  sources of, 138
  target and alternative activities, 169–170
  see also autonomous motivation; controlled motivation
motivation, theories of
  goal setting theory, 130–135, 130f, 138–139
  goal setting theory and control theory, 129, 138–139
  inductive theory building, 129–130
motivational profiles, 170–171
Motowidlo, S. J., 337
Motta Veiga, Serge P. da, 4
  "Who is Searching for Whom? Integrating Recruitment and Job Search Research," 311–328
Mowday, R. T., 404
Moynihan, L. M., 390
Mueser, P. R., 535
Mullainathan, S., 509, 511
multidimensionality, of job search behavior
  behaviors and sources, 261t
  content and direction of behavior, 262–268
  definition and dimensions, 260
  dynamics and persistence, 268–269
  effort and intensity, 260–262
  future research directions, 271–273
  implications for employment counselors, 270–271
  implications for job seekers, 270
  informal and formal sources of information, 264–265, 418
  job interviews, 266–267
  networking, 265
  preparatory and active behaviors, 263–264
  quality of job-search behaviors, 267–268
  relationships within and between dimensions, 269–270
  specific behaviors and sources, 265–267
  vs. unidimensionality, 259–260, 273
multiple minority status hypothesis, and discrimination, 511
multiple self-aspect framework, 229
multiwave longitudinal study, of job-search dynamics, 424
Munnell, A. H., 438
  financial outlook for older workers, 439
  older job seekers and job search intensity, 451
  older job seekers and reemployment quality, 451
Muntaner, C., 40
Muraven, M., 211
Mussio, S. J., 505
Mutanen, P., 581
Myers, B., 485

Nakamura, Alice O., 293
names, and ethnicity in hiring discrimination, 509–510, 517
Nassar-McMillan, S. C., 549, 551, 552–553, 556, 557, 558
Näswell, K., 33
Natti, J., 44
Nauta, A.
    focused job search strategy, 151
    goal setting theory, 132
    reemployment quality, 363
    research on positive effects of job loss, 78
Naylor, J. C., 148
needs-supplies job fit, 364–365
nepotism, and "dark side" of networking, 287–288
networking, 275–276, 288
    agenda for future research, 286–288
    antecedents of networking behavior, 282–284
    barriers faced by women and minority groups, 279–280
    and building contacts, 278–279
    components of networking behavior, 276–277
    "dark side" of, 287–288
    and developing career competencies, 277–278
    implications of research for counselors, 286
    implications of research for individuals, 285–286
    implications of research for organizations, 286
    intraethnic networks, 490
    measurement of networking behavior, 280–282
    and multidimensionality of job search, 265
    and older job seekers, 449–450, 454
    outcomes for job search, 284–285
    training and coaching for, 288
    types of networking behavior, 281
Networking for People Who Hate Networking (Zack), 275
neuroticism, and job search, 315, 395
Newton, P., 381
Ng, T. W. H., 231
    education and work experience, 384
    school-to-work transition, 380, 381
Niessen, C., 366
Nixon, D. R., 407
Noe, R. A., 313
Noel, B. J., 535
nonconscious self-regulation, 216–217
nonexperimental research, and impact evaluation, 527, 528–529, 532
nontraditional employment, temporary workers, 465–468, 473–475
    agency workers, 467–468
    careers of, 468–469
    careers of temporary workers, 474f
    definition and statistics, 466–467, 477n1, 477n2, 477n3
    future directions for research, 475–476
    moderating factors, 471–473
    practical implications regarding, 476–477, 476t
    reasons for accepting temporary work, 471, 476
    transitions and perceived employability, 469–471
    types of, 467f
nonwestern countries, further research on effects of job loss in, 77
Noordzij, G., 131
    goals of reemployment programs, 541
    learning goal orientation, 213
    performance goal orientation, 212–213
Norman, P., 211
Nyklicek, I., 20

obesity, stigma of, 332–333
O'Brien, G. E., 12, 15
    effects of employment, 18
    expectancy-value theory, 22, 320, 321
    quality of employment, 72
O'Callaghan, F., 192, 394
occupational status, and underemployment, 362–363
occupation and social status, 114–115
    effects on health, 112
    and job loss among older workers, 439–440
occupation-specific market demand, and international job search, 495
Ochel, W., 566
older job seekers, 433–434, 453–455
    advantages and challenges of, 453
    and age discrimination, 451–453
    challenges to, 5
    effect of stereotypes on, 440
    employability and associated stereotypes, 434–436
    maintaining employability, 454
    process model, 434f
    see also age
older workers
    and aftereffects of job loss, 438–443
    coping with job loss, 443–450
    and job insecurity, 436–438
Ollikainen, V., 446
operating function, of self-regulation, 209, 213–215
oppositional defiance, and refusal to job search, 169–170
optimism, and coping with job loss, 67–68
Orbell, S., 211
organizational antecedents, of perceived job insecurity, 36–37
organizational characteristics
    and applicant attraction, 313
    and discrimination in resume screening, 512–513, 518
organizational consequences, of job insecurity, 42
organizational identity, 225–226, 227, 228–230
organizational justice and trust, and effects of job insecurity, 47
organizational participation, and effects of job insecurity, 45
organizational performance, and perceived job insecurity, 36
organizational resources, and temporary workers, 472
organizational safety climate, 47–48
organizational tenure, and job security, 438
Ouellette, J. A., 216
outcome expectancy, 194
outplacement programs, 559
    benefits to individuals, 553–554
    directions for future research, 556–558
    history of, 547–548
    individual participation and success with, 552–553
    measuring success of, 550–552
    models of, 549
    participant wishes for, 555
    present status and needs of, 558–559
    related challenges, 555–556
    services typically offered, 548–550
    unhelpful characteristics and factors, 554–555
Oxford Handbook of Job Loss and Job Search, The
    career transitions, 4–5
    components and phases of job search, 4
    consequences of job loss and unemployment, 2–3
    historical perspective, 2
    job insecurity, 2
    programs supporting job search, 5–6
    rationale behind, 1–2
    scope and structure of, 2–6
    special populations, 5
    theoretical perspectives, 3–4

Pang, M., 489
parents
    further research on effects of job loss on, 77
    and mental health of children in unemployed households, 93–94
Parker, A., 276
Parker, S. K., 41, 47
Paronto, M. E., 339
Parris, M. A., 553, 558
part-time employment, motivation for, 165
Patterson, J. M., 90
Paul, Karsten I., 2–3

"Individual Consequences of Job Loss and Unemployment," 57–85
Pawson, R., 530, 531, 533, 536
Payne, B. K., 508
Payne, R. L., 10
  agency-restriction model, 162
  research on positive effects of job loss, 77–78
  stress and coping models, 21
Peck, J., 568, 571
Peeters, H., 337, 338
Peiró, J. M., 368, 381
Peltokorpi, V., 488
Peluchette, J., 287
Penley, L. E., 281
pension benefits, and hiring of older workers, 452
Pepermans, R., 231
perceived alternatives, and applicant attraction, 314
performance goal orientation, 212–213, 213f
performance-related variables, and perceived job insecurity, 39
Perry, E. L., 512
persistence
  and goal setting theory, 132
  and job search process, 184, 268–269
personal-agency theory, and research on unemployment, 18–19
personality
  and employed job seekers, 406, 407
  implicit personality theory, 332
  and international job search, 485–486
  and job search behavior, 251–253, 315
  and networking behavior, 283
  and older job seekers, 448
  and perceived job insecurity, 37
personality theory, and underemployment, 369
person-job fit
  and applicant attraction, 314
  and underemployment, 364–365
pessimism, and coping with job loss, 67–68
Petriglieri, J. L., 228
Pfeffer, J., 280
phase model of self-categorization and coping, 422
Phillips, J., 260
physical appearance, and job interview process, 332–333
physical health
  and consequences of job loss, 72–73
  effects of job loss on, 438–439
  and job insecurity, 40
  and job loss among older workers, 442–443
  and perceived job insecurity, 437
Picchio, M., 455
Pickman, A. J., 548, 556–557
Pilgrim Trust, research on unemployment, 13
Pinder, C. C., 320

Pissarides, 244
Pissarides, Christopher A., 253n1
planned behavior, theory of
  characteristics of, 205–206
  conceptualizing self-regulation in, 209–216
  contextual and global-level motivating factors, 192–201
  empirical support for core relationships, 187, 188t–190t, 191–192
  and employed job seekers, 407
  intention-behavior gap, 206–208
  intention-behavior moderators, and goal establishment, 209–211
  intention-behavior moderators, and goal striving, 212–215
  motivation and self-regulation in job search, 182, 183f
  nonconscious self-regulation, 216–217
  planned job search behavior, 184–187, 191–201
  practical suggestions regarding, 201, 218
  recruitment and job search, 321–322
  self-regulation, functioning of, 208–209
  significance of intention, 185–187
  theoretical underpinnings, 185–187
  and turnover process, 405
planning
  and career adaptability, 234–235, 236
  and goal setting theory, 132
Plant, E. A., 508
Ployhart, R. E., 343
Podgursky, M., 46
Podivinsky, J. M., 568
Podolny, J. M., 278, 279
point job search strategy, 419
political attitudes, changes with unemployment, 74
political construction of unemployment, 105–106
Pollmann-Schult, M., 425
Polsky, W. L., 552
Pontusson, J., 38
Posthuma, R. A., 514
posttraumatic growth, further research on, 77
poverty
  and efficacy of employability programs, 569, 571
  and wider impacts of unemployment, 106
Poverty in the United Kingdom: A Survey of Household Resources and Standards of Living. (Townsend), 100
Power Networking (Fisher & Vilas), 275
Powers, T. A., 168
Powers, W., 135, 138
Pratto, F., 502, 511
pregnancy, and job interview process, 333
prejudice, modern manifestations of, 513, 514–515
preparatory *vs.* active job search behaviors, 263–264, 317, 389, 418

prevocational programs, and school-to-work transition, 386
Price, Richard H., 6
  reemployment interventions, 150
  stress and coping models, 21
  "The JOBS Program: Impact on Job Seeker Motivation, Reemployment, and Mental Health," 575–590
Pritchard, R. D., 148
problem-focused coping strategies, 443
problem-solving coping, 20
Probst, Tahira M., 2
  "Job Insecurity and Anticipated Job Loss: A Primer and Exploration of Possible Interventions," 31–53
procrastination, and job search, 235–236
professional identity, 225, 226, 227
  coping with threat to, 228–230
  and early retirement, 446–447
  and older workers, 436, 454
programs supporting job search, 5–6
promotion potential
  and outcomes of international job search, 492–493
  and underemployment, 365
Proost, K., 336, 342
protean career theory, 224, 277
proximal *vs.* distal goals, 130–131
Prus, Robert C., 300
Prusak, L., 276
Prussia, G. E., 132
  coping with job loss, 149
  dissatisfaction as motivator in job search, 196
  job-search goals, 387
Psychological Impact of Unemployment, The (Feather), 9, 20
psychological impacts
  of job insecurity, 15–16
  of unemployment, 15
psychological need satisfaction, 160–162
psychological stress, and coping models, 20–21
psychological vulnerabilities, awakening of, 161
public services, impact of unemployment on, 102
Purkiss, S. L. S., 510

Q

quality of job-search behaviors, 267–268
Quirin, J. J., 404

R

race
  and job interview process, 331–332
  and perceived job insecurity, 37
  and underemployment, 362
  and use of outplacement services, 552–553
racism, modern manifestations of, 513, 514–515

randomized controlled trials, and impact evaluation, 528, 532

Rantakeisu, U., 115

Ranzijn, R., 440, 441, 445

Rasmussen, K. G., 337

Realistic Evaluation (Pawson & Tilley), 530

realistic group conflict theory, and discrimination, 506

reasoned action, theory of, 146–147

recruiter behavior, and applicant attraction, 314

recruiter characteristics, and discrimination, 513–516, 517–518, 518n4

recruitment
and applicant attraction, 313–314
externalization of, 296
integrating with job search, 316–318
theoretical approaches to, 318–322
three phases of, 312
vs. job search, 316t
see also headhunters

recruitment research
future directions of, 322–324
integrating with job search research, 311–312, 317–318, 324, 325
overview of literature, 312–313
practical implications of, 324–325
recommendations for individuals and organizations, 325
signaling theory, 318–320

Redington, J., 386

reemployment
age and desire for, 150
effect of economic hardship on job search, 89
generating intentions and goals, 146–147
and improved functioning, 442–443
influence of JOBS Program, 580–581
interventions and outcomes, 150–152
of long-term unemployed, 236
measurement issues and research on, 153–154
older workers and quality of, 451
older workers gaining, 450–451
research agenda, 154–155
search for among older workers, 448
speed of, 166–167
and writing about previous job loss, 554

Reemployment Policy Review, the Netherlands, 525–527, 542–543, 543n1, 544n8

reemployment programs
issues, goals, and tools of, 538t–539t
and labor market, 543n7
social support and, 539

reemployment programs, evaluation of, 525, 542–543
distinguishing types of programs, 534
evaluation of Dutch reemployment policy, 531–533

a global view, 533–536
impact evaluation, 527–531, 543n3
Reemployment Policy Review, the Netherlands, 525–527, 542–543, 543n1, 544n8
transition to more realistic evaluations, 536–537, 539–542, 540t, 541t

reemployment quality
and career outcomes, 359–360, 371
multidimensional construct of, 420

Rees, A., 418

regulation
autonomous regulation, 164
external regulation, 163
introjected regulation, 163–164
regulated professions and international job search, 493–494
and self-determination theory, 163f

Reinoso, V., 511

Reisel, W. D., 34
job insecurity and job search behaviors, 41
organizational consequences of job insecurity, 42
perceptions of job insecurity, 45

Reitman, F., 367

Reitz, J. G., 488, 493

relatedness, psychological need for, 160–162

relative deprivation theory, and underemployment, 363–364

research
on anticipated job loss, 79n6
focal phenomena and selecting study designs, 424–425
gaps in, 76–79
using new methods in, 78–79

reservation wages, 151, 455
and economic job search theory, 243–244
and older job seekers, 435

resignation, among the unemployed, 11

resilience, of family in coping with job loss, 91

responsibility, unemployed individuals taking, 168–169

resume screening, discrimination in, 501–502, 506, 516, 518n5
and applicant characteristics, 509–512
determinants of, 509
future research directions, 516–517
human capital hypothesis *vs.* hiring discrimination hypothesis, 503–506
job and organizational characteristics, 512–513
labor market position of ethnic minorities, 502
methods to avert, 517
practical recommendations for avoiding, 517–518
recruiter characteristics, 513–516, 517–518, 518n4

social-psychological perspectives, 506–509

retirement and retired individuals
impact of unemployment on, 103–104
job loss and early retirement, 445–447

Reubens, Beatrice, 101

revenue, government
impact of high unemployment rates on, 102

Reynolds, Smooch S., 307n3

Rhodes, V., 150

Riach, K., 565

Richards, E. W., 379
internships, 385
prevocational programs, 386

Richardson, Julia, 5
benefits of job loss to older workers, 447
"International Job Search," 481–499
language proficiency and international job search, 487
self-initiated expatriate job search, 489, 490, 491

Ridzi, F., 564, 567

Riordan, C. M., 149, 210

Ritchie, H., 563

Roberson, L., 512

Rodan, S., 279

Rodriquez, D., 361

Roehling, M. V., 390

Rogerson, 244

role reframing, and sense of calling, 227

roles, loss of in family life and work, 92–93

Rooth, D. -O., 509, 512

Rosen, S., 365

Rosenbaum, J. E., 379–380

Rosenblatt, Z., 33
job insecurity, 44
organizational norms of fairness, 47
organizational performance and perceived job insecurity, 36

Rosenfeld, Paul, 302

Rosenkrantz, S. A., 280–281

Roskies, E., 40

Ross, W. H., 287

Rossi, A., 364

Roth, P. L., 331

Rotundo, M., 363

routine, coping with change in, 149, 162

Rowntree, B. S., 11

Roznowski, M., 38

Ruhm, C., 451

rural environments, effects of job loss in, 77

Rutledge, M. S., 439

Ryan, Ann Marie, 5
"By Any Other Name: Discrimination in Resume Screening," 501–522
candidate reactions to job interviews, 343
impression management behaviors, 336

Ryan, R. M., 148, 211

Ryan, Richard
  self-determination theory, 160, 168
Rynes, S. L., 260
  expectancy theory, 320
  physical attractiveness in job
    candidates, 332

S

Saam, R. H., 553–554
Sacco, J. M., 514
safety outcomes, and organizational safety
  climate, 47–48
Saks, Alan M., 4
  career exploration and planning, 384
  career planning and development, 386
  discriminatory questions in job
    interviews, 341–342
  employment-fit perceptions, 392
  goal setting theory, 132, 138
  job information sources, 388–389
  job satisfaction, 391
  "Job Search and the School-to-Work
    Transition," 379–400
  job search clarity, 151
  job search dynamics, 268
  job search goals and behaviors, 316
  job-search intensity, 389–390
  job-search intervention framework, 397
  job-search objectives, 403
  job-search outcomes, 388, 390
  measurement of networking
    behavior, 282
  multidimensionality of job search
    behavior, 272
  outcomes of networking behavior, 284
  personality traits and school-to-work
    transition, 395
  person-job fit, 364, 411
  sequential model of job search
    behavior, 421
  specific job-search behaviors, 266
  successful school-to-work
    transition, 393
  use of informal job sources, 264
Saksvik, P. O., 45
salient beliefs about job search, 192–193
Samtani, A., 282
  antecedents of networking
    behavior, 283
  job search behavior and
    underemployment, 363
  job-to-job search outcomes, 409
  self-regulatory model of job
    search-behavior, 423
Sanchez, R. J., 342
satisfaction
  feelings of job satisfaction, 12
  psychological need satisfaction,
    160–162
satisficing job search strategy, 262–263
Savickas, M. L., 383
Schaller, J., 94
Schaufeli, W. B., 20

Scheck, C. L., 41
Scheier, M. F., 135, 137, 148
Schlaegel, C., 287
Schlager, T., 386
Schleicher, D. J., 343
Schlenker, J. A., 92
Schmeichel, B. J., 215, 508
Schneer, J. A., 367
school-to-work transition, 379–381,
  394–396, 398
  career planning and development,
    383–387
  defining success of, 381
  education and work experience,
    384–385
  implications for research and practice,
    396–398
  integrative model of, 382, 383f
  interrelatedness of stages, 394, 396
  intervention framework, 397t
  job information sources, 388–389
  job-search intensity, 389–390
  job-search stage, 387–392
  key challenges of, 382
  stakeholders in success of, 396
  work adjustment, 392–396
Schoorman, F. D., 47
Schreurs, B., 321, 336
Schul, Y.
  perceived health status as motivator in
    job search, 197
  unemployment and mental health,
    578, 580
Schwab, D. P., 260, 391
Schweiger, D. M., 46
Scott, F. A., 452
Scott, R. A., 21
search frictions, 253$n1$
Secrets of Savvy Networking, The
  (RoAne), 275
Segers-Noij, M., 342
Seijts, G., 131–132
self, notion of in modern self-regulation
  models, 167–169
self-aspects, accessing multiple, 229, 239$n1$
self-assessment, and job interviews,
  347–348
self-categorization, 422
self-determination theory, 148
  and autonomous regulation, 164
  and behavior, 171–173
  and controlled regulation, 163–164
  grounding unemployment research
    in, 160
  intrinsic and extrinsic work goals,
    172–173
  and job search intention, 191
  motivation and job search intensity,
    164–167
  and motivation behind behavior,
    162–171
  notion of "self" in modern self-
    regulation models, 167–169

  and predictors of job search intention,
    185–187
  and psychological need satisfaction,
    160–162
  and quality of motivation, 170–171
  and refusal to job search, 169–170
  types of motivation and regulation, 163f
self-efficacy
  influence of JOBS Program, 580–581
  and job search, 315, 387, 390
  and pursuit of goals, 132, 133–135
  and reducing anxiety in interviews, 344
  and reemployment programs,
    539, 557$n6$
  and response to job loss, 23
  and self-regulatory model of job search
    behavior, 422–423
self-employment
  and job loss among older workers,
    447–448, 454
  vs. reemployment, 150
self-endorsed choices, and refusal to job
  search, 169–170
self-esteem
  enhancement of in JOBS Program, 586
  and networking behavior, 283
  and self-regulatory model of job search
    behavior, 422–423
self-initiated expatriates, 495–496
  antecedents of international job search,
    485–487
  backgrounds of, 482
  career development and promotion,
    492–493
  earnings, 493–494
  future directions for research, 496
  immigration policies and labor market,
    483–484
  international job search strategies,
    489–490
  moderators of international job search,
    487–488
  moderators of job search outcome,
    494–495
  motivations to engage in international
    job search, 484–485
  objective job-search outcomes, 491–492
  postmigration investment in human
    capital, 491
  practical implications checklist,
    496–497
  subjective outcomes of job search, 494
self-regulation
  conceptualizing in planned job search
    behavior, 209–216
  and dynamics of job search, 269
  functioning of, 208–209
  goal conflicts, 210–211
  and goal maintenance, 214
  and goal proximity, 210
  and goal specificity, 209–210
  hypoegoic self-regulation, 216–217
  intention-behavior gap, 206–208, 208t

self-regulation (*cont.*)
    intention-behavior moderators, and
        goal establishment, 209–211
    intention-behavior moderators, and
        goal striving, 212–215
    in job search, 315–316
    and mindfulness, 217
    monitoring function, 209, 212–213
    and multiple goals, 211
    nonconscious self-regulation, 216–217
    operating function, 213–215
    perspectives on job search, 207*f*
    self-regulatory model of job search
        behavior, 422–423
    significance of in job search, 206
    strength model of, 215
    and willpower, 215
self-regulation theory
    and biased decision making, 508–509
    defined, 145
    and job loss and job search, 154–155, 182
    notion of "self" in modern, 167–169
    perspective on job loss and job search,
        145–148
    perspectives on job search, 183*f*
    and reactions to job loss, 146
    and reemployment outcomes, 150–152
    self-regulated job search, 147–148
    and social influences in job search,
        152–153
    and temporal considerations in job
        search, 152
self-talk, functional *vs.* dysfunctional,
    133–135
Sels, L.
    individual career investments, 471
    older job seekers and higher reservation
        wages, 435
sequential model of job search behavior,
    420–421
Serlie, A. W., 503
Sersic, D. M., 424, 425
services, impact of unemploymen on, 102
sexual behavior, and
    unemployment, 73–74
Shahani-Denning, C., 341
Shamir, B., 76
Shantz, A., 217
Shaw, S., 564
Sheeran, P., 206, 211
Sheffield program of research, 15, 19, 20
Sheridan, Anne, 582
Sherman, J., 92
Sicherman, N., 365
Sidanius, J., 502, 511
Siegel, M., 444
Sieverding, M., 341
signaling theory, 318–320
Silla, I., 475
similarity-attraction paradigm, 279
Simmons, H. S., 282
Sinclair, R. R., 36
Sindelar, J. L., 444

Sinfield, Adrian, 3
    "Unemployment and Its Wider
        Impact," 99–109
situational variables
    and goal setting theory, 132
    and job-to-job search, 407
skill training
    and career adaptability, 236, 435–436
    and outplacement programs, 555
    potential deskilling effects of, 567–568
skill utilization, and quality of
    employment, 72
Slack, T., 361
Slocum, J. W., 42
Smith, J. A., 535
Smith, P., 40
smoking, and unemployment, 444
social capital
    and career competencies, 277
    competitive advantage of, 301
    measures to enhance, 455
    and older job seekers, 434
social categorization and social identity
    theory, 506–507
social-cognitive career theory, 209,
    223–224
    defined, 147
    and reemployment outcomes, 151
social cognitive theory
    defined, 145
    and goal setting theory, 133
    and job loss and job search, 154–155
    perspective on job loss and job search,
        145–148, 145*f*
    and reactions to job loss, 146
    and reemployment outcomes, 150–152
    and social influences in job search,
        152–153
    and temporal considerations in job
        search, 152
social cohesion, and individual
    consequences of job loss, 65
social construction of unemployment,
    105–106
social contacts, and job loss among older
    workers, 440
social costs of high
    unemployment, 99–100
social epidemiology, defined, 111
social epidemiology, perspective on
    unemployment
    explaining job insecurity and
        health, 114
    international variation in job insecurity
        and health, 122
    job insecurity and health, 111–114
    self-reported health and health
        behaviors, 116
    self-reported health and
        unemployment, 118, 121*t*, 122
    social protections in welfare-state
        regimes, 117–118, 118*f*
    unemployment and health, 114–116

unemployment and mortality, 115–116
    unemployment and suicide, 115
    welfare state regimes and health,
        116–118
    welfare state regimes and social
        protections, 119–120*t*
social identity theory, 227
social influences, and job search, 152–153
social influence theory, and job
    interviews, 335, 336
social insurance, and social protections
    for the unemployed, 117–118
socialization, and work adjustment for
    new graduates, 392–393, 393–394
social media
    and future research on networking, 287
    potentially discriminatory effects of,
        507–508
    and signaling theory, 320
social networks
    barriers faced by women and minority
        groups, 279–280
    characteristics of, 278–279
    and economic job search theory,
        249–250
    and older workers, 455
social participation, and coping with job
    loss, 445
social pressure, to search for employment,
    186, 191, 192
social protections in welfare-state regimes,
    117–118, 118*f*, 119–120*t*
social-psychological perspectives, on
    discrimination, 506–509
social safety net
    and perceived job insecurity, 44–45
social stabilizers of unemployment,
    104–105
social status and occupation, 114–115
    effects on health, 112
    and job loss among older workers,
        439–440
social support
    and coping with job loss, 91, 195–196
    and international job search, 487–488
    in JOBS Program, 586
    and reemployment programs, 539
social undermining
    and coping with job loss, 91
socioeconomic antecedents, of perceived
    job insecurity, 35–36
socioeconomic contexts, of job-search
    interventions, 419–420
socioeconomic status, and effects of job
    loss, 61–62
Soelberg, P. O., 260
Sol, Els, 5–6
    defining work first approaches, 563–564
    employability programs, 565
    "The Evaluation of Reemployment
        Programs: Between Impact
        Assessment and Theory-Based
        Approaches," 525–545

Song, Zhaoli, 5
  analytic strategies, 425
  distress and job search efforts, 318
  gender, and family distress in job
      loss, 93
  goal setting theory, 132
  intention-behavior consistency, 214
  job search and distress, 422
  job search behavior and
      underemployment, 363
  "Job-Search Behavior of the
      Unemployed: A Dynamic
      Perspective," 417–429
  unemployment and marriages, 90
  well-being during unemployment, 58
Sora, B., 47
Sorensen, K. L., 231
sources of job information, formal and
      informal, 264–265, 418
Soylu, A., 37
Spalter-Roth, R., 361
special populations, in job loss and job
      search, 5
Spector, P. E., 339
Spence, M., 319
Spencer, D. G., 404
Spera, S. P., 554
Spitzmuller, C., 365, 369–370
Spurk, D., 231, 232
stabilizers, social and economic, 104–105
Stages of Transition Counseling
      Model, 549
stage theories, and research on
      unemployment, 16–17
Stansbury, Jason, 307n5
Stanton, J. M., 315, 390
Star, S. A., 363
start-control, self-regulation, 209
Staufenbiel, T., 42
Steel, R. P., 137–138
Steers, R. M., 404
Steffy, B. D., 385
  job-search intensity and job
      satisfaction, 391
  personality traits and school-to-work
      transition, 395
Stephens, M. J., 451
stereotypes
  effect on older job seekers, 440
  mitigating use of, 155
  of older workers, 434–436, 454
Stevens, A. H., 94
  job loss and early retirement, 446
  older job seekers and reemployment,
      450, 451
Stevens, C. K.
  job search behavior and job
      attainment, 187
  job search strategies, 262
Stevens, N. D., 382, 387
Stewart, G. L., 335
stop-control, self-regulation, 208, 209
Storrie, D., 469

Stouffer, S. A., 363
Strack, F., 208
Straits, B. C., 279–280
strategies
  coping with job loss, 443
  job search, 262–263
  and job search among older workers,
      448–450
strength model, of self-regulation, 215
stress
  adaptation to by families, 90–91
  and comprehensive model of job
      insecurity, 34
  and mental health in families, 89–90
  protective resources for coping
      with, 91–92
stress and coping models, and research on
      unemployment, 20–21
stressors, cascade of in
      unemployment, 90–91
stress-related coping reactions, 443–445
Strewler, J., 548
Stroh, L. K., 280
Ström, S., 93–94
structural holes, and headhunting
      practices, 300
students and job search
  dynamics and persistence, 268–269
  high school students, 192
  resources available, 388
  use of informal job information
      sources, 264–265
Stumpf, S. A., 383–384, 385
Sturges, J., 281
subconscious goal primes, 217
subordinate male target hypothesis, and
      discrimination, 511
success, mental models of, 230–234, 586
Suchman, E. A., 363
suicide, and unemployment as risk factor
      for, 79n7, 115, 444
Sullivan, Sherry, 277
  developing diverse social networks, 282
  social media and networking, 287
Sulliven, S. E., 233
Sum, A., 361, 362
Sun, S., 90
Sun, Shu Hua, 5
  "Job-Search Behavior of the
      Unemployed: A Dynamic
      Perspective," 417–429
Super, D. E., 223
support systems, and alleviating effects of
      job insecurity, 44–45
Sussman, S., 94
Suto, M., 485
Sverke, M., 33
Sverko, B.
  analytic strategies, 425
  multiwave longitudinal study of job-
      search dynamics, 424
Swaim, P., 46
Swami, V., 333

Swider, B. W., 335
  job search and networking goals, 277
  job-to-job search and withdrawal
      behavior, 410
  job-to-job search outcomes, 408
  symptom-focused coping strategies, 443,
      445–450

T
Tajfel, H., 506
Talaska, C. A., 515
talent, headhunter search for, 300–301
Tam, H., 361
Tan, G. Y., 196
Tan, H. H., 323
target activities, and motivation theory,
      169–170
Taris, T. W., 191, 192
  dissatisfaction as motivator in job
      search, 196
  employment position and job
      search, 200
  multiwave longitudinal study of job-
      search dynamics, 424
  perceived health status as motivator in
      job search, 197
  psychological distress after job loss, 362
  school-to-work transition, 381
Tate, F. B., 216–217
Tatum, G. S., 33–34
taxes, and high unemployment rates, 102
Taylor, K., 151
Taylor, M. S., 264
  career exploration, 384
  career planning
      internships, 385, 386
  school-to-work transition, 381
Taylor, P., 444
Taylor, S. E., 21
technology changes, and perceived job
      insecurity, 36
temporal considerations, in job search,
      152, 465–466
temporary employment, 465–466,
      473–475
  agency workers, 467–468
  careers of temporary workers, 474f
  definition and statistics, 466–467,
      477n1, 477n2, 477n3
  future directions for research, 475–476
  moderating factors, 471–473
  practical implications regarding,
      476–477, 476t
  reasons for accepting, 471, 476
  transitions and careers, 468–469
  transitions and perceived employability,
      469–471
  types of, 467f
temporary workers
  career interruptions and, 232
  challenges to, 5
  and job insecurity, 112
  and perceived job insecurity, 38

Teng, H. M., 444
Teo, A. C., 283
Terpstra, David E., 293, 305
Tews, M. J., 334
Tharenou, P., 485
Thatcher, Margaret, 101
theoretical approaches to effects of
    underemployment, 369
theoretical approaches to effects of
    unemployment, 16–24
  cautions when applying, 23
  deprivation theory, 17–18
  stage theories, 16–17
theoretical perspectives on job loss and
    job search, 3–4
theories of motivation
  goal setting theory, 130–135, 130f
  goal setting theory and control
    theory, 129
  inductive theory building, 129–130
theory-based research, and impact
    evaluation, 529–531
theory building, inductive, 129–130
Therborn, Goran, 100
Thompson, J. A., 283
Thorn, K., 484
Tichy, N. M., 279
Tidd, S. T., 368
Tiggemann, M., 18
Tilley, N., 530, 531, 533, 536
time in host country, and international
    job search outcome, 494
time structure
  and job loss among older workers, 441
  research on importance in daily
    life, 18
Tivendell, J., 37
tokenism theory, 280
Torres, L., 279–280, 389
Tosti-Kharas, J., 226
Townsend, P., 100
trainers and facilitators, in JOBS
    Program, 577, 578, 582–585
training, employability and investments
    in, 471
transactional model of stress and
    coping, 146
"transitional penalty," and international
    job search, 486
Troske, K. R., 535
trust, organizational, 47
Truxillo, D. M., 339
  expectations in job interviews, 342
  underemployment and job
    performance, 368
Tsai, W., 336, 338
Tsertsvadze, G., 453
Turban, Daniel B., 4
  job search behavior and job
    attainment, 187
  multidimensionality of job search, 266
  reciprocal processes in interviews, 323
  self-regulation in job search, 315

"Who is Searching for Whom?
    Integrating Recruitment and Job
    Search Research," 311–328
Turchik-Hakak, L., 490
Turner, J. B., 15, 578
Turner, N., 41
Turner, R. G., 361
Turnley, W. H., 364, 366, 370
turnover behaviors, and
    underemployment, 368
turnover process, models of, 403–406
Tzafrir, S. S., 548

U
Uhlendorff, Arne, 3–4
  "Economic Job Search and Decision-
    making Models," 243–255
Ullah, P., 22, 195
underemployment
  among high-risk groups, 360–362
  and career outcomes, 359–360, 371
  education and occupational status,
    362–363
  and equilibrium theory of coping,
    365–366
  future research directions, 369–370
  and human capital theory, 365
  and job performance, 368
  and job search behavior, 363
  and job search theory, 366
  outcomes of, 366–368
  and perceived job insecurity, 36, 89
  person-job fit, 364–365
  and relative deprivation theory,
    363–364
  and theory of career mobility, 365
  theory of hysteresis, 366
  withdrawal and turnover behaviors, 368
underemployment and job loss, research
    perspectives on, 363–366
Unemployed Man, The (Bakke), 11–12
unemployed persons
  "activation" of, 159–160, 168
  future research with, 78–79
  identity changes among long-term, 230
  maintaining employability among, 455
  and notion of taking responsibility,
    168–169
  psychological need frustration among,
    161–162
  relationships with job agency
    personnel, 78
  social protections in welfare-state
    regimes, 117–118, 118f
unemployed persons, job-search
    behavior of
  analytic strategies for studying, 425
  antecedents and outcomes, 419–420
  categorizing behavior, 418–419
  dynamic nature of, 420
  methodologies of research into search
    dynamics, 424–425
  studying episodes of behavior, 425–426

theoretical models of dynamics in,
    420–423
  unique aspects, 417–418
unemployment
  adaptability during long-term, 235–236
  attitudes among the unemployed, 11
  cascade of stressors in, 90–91
  causal attributions and response
    to, 22–23
  chronic nature of in society, 57, 59
  consequences of, 2–3
  defining, 59
  and disruption of daily routine,
    149, 162
  duration and motivational
    regulation, 167
  effects of long-term, 13, 14, 15
  effects on children, 93–94
  effects on work identity and well-being,
    226, 228
  future research on positive effects
    of, 77–78
  gender and rates of, 79n2
  history of, 58–59
  identity changes in long-term, 230
  individualizing collective problem of,
    568, 570
  magnitude of effects of, 12–13
  meta-analyses examining, 57–58
  negative effects on well-being, 19
  normalization of, 64
  prior unemployment and perceived job
    insecurity, 39
  and psychological need frustration,
    161–162
  risks to individuals and families, 578–579
  societal differences in preventing and
    containing, 100–101
  and suicide, 115
  theoretical approaches to, 16
  vs. nonparticipation in labor force, 246
  worldwide increase in, 143
  see also anticipated job loss; job loss
unemployment, and families
  cascade of stressors, 90–91
  directions for future research, 94–95
  effects of Great Recession, 87
  effects of reduced household income,
    88–89, 95
  family outcomes, 93–94
  family resilience and coping with job
    loss, 91
  identities and family roles, 92–93
  male *vs.* female unemployment, 93
  pathways of affect, 88f
  protective resources for coping with job
    loss, 91–92
  research perspectives on, 87–88
  stress and mental health effects, 89–90
unemployment, a social epidemiological
    perspective on
  explaining job insecurity and
    health, 114

international variation in job insecurity and health, 122
job insecurity and health, 111–114
self-reported health and health behaviors, 116
self-reported health and unemployment, 118, 121t, 122
social protections in welfare-state regimes, 117–118, 118f
unemployment and health, 114–116
unemployment and mortality, 115–116
unemployment and suicide, 115
welfare state regimes and health, 116–118
welfare state regimes and social protections, 119–120t
unemployment, historical background of research, 9–29
agency theory, 18–19
deprivation theory, 17–18
early twentieth-century concerns, 10
expectancy-value theory, 21–22
fourteenth-century attitudes, 9–10
implications of research, 25
improvements in methodology and analysis, 14
in post-World War II era to 1990s, 14–16
significance of research, 24–25
stage theories, 16–17
stress and coping models, 20–21
studies from the Great Depression, 9–13
theoretical approaches, 16–24
vitamin model, 19–20
unemployment, individual consequences of
and age, 62–64
attitudes, 74–75
causal effects on mental health, studies of, 68–70
coping strategies, 67–68
differences across national borders, 65–67
differences among countries, 65–67
duration of unemployment, 62, 63f
explaining negative mental health effects, 70–72
gaps in research, 76–79
and gender, 60–61
hostility and aggression, 74
on mental health, 59–60
moderators of effects on mental health, 60–64
physical health and health behavior, 72–73
practical conclusions of research, 75–76
sexual behavior and family formation, 73–74
and socioeconomic status, 61–62
unemployment, wider impacts of
across generations, 102–104
crime and unemployment, 106

differences across societies and over time, 100–101
impact on public and other services, 102
labor market, balance of power in, 100
modifying, 104–106
political and social construct of unemployment, 105–106
poverty and unemployment, 106
research questions, 107
social and economic costs, 99–100, 106–107
social and economic stabilizers, 104–105, 106–107
unemployment benefits
conditional distribution of, 159–160
and individual consequences of job loss, 65
and job-search behavior, 418, 419
as route to early retirement, 446
unemployment research, 160
Unger, J. B., 94
union membership, and perceived job insecurity, 38
universalism, and social protections for the unemployed, 117–118
Uy, M. A., 90

V

Vallerand, R. J.
hierarchical model of motivation, 185, 193, 198
Valletta, R. G., 438
Vance, C. M., 491
Vancouver, J. B., 423
Van den Berg, Gerard J., 3–4
"Economic Job Search and Decision-making Models," 243–255
Van den Broeck, Anja, 3
"Understanding the Motivational Dynamics Among Unemployed Individuals: Refreshing Insights from the Self-Determination Theory Perspective," 159–179
Van der Flier, H., 191, 192
dissatisfaction as motivator in job search, 196
employment position and job search, 200
multiwave longitudinal study of job-search dynamics, 424
psychological distress after job loss, 362
Van der Heijden, B. I. J. M, 436
Van Der Werfhorst, H. G., 362–363
Van Dijke, M. H., 342
Van Hooft, Edwin A. J., 3
antecedents of networking behavior, 283
control theory and job search, 138
demographics and job-to-job search, 407
goal setting theory, 131
goals of reemployment programs, 541
goal specificity, 210

interpersonal factors in job-search, 152–153
job-search behavior and underemployment, 363
job-search dynamics and persistence, 269
job-search intensity, 408
job-search theory and underemployment, 366
job-to-job search and job satisfaction, 409
job-to-job search outcomes, 409
"Motivation and Self-Regulation in Job Search: A Theory of Planned Job Search Behavior," 181–204
multiwave longitudinal study of job-search dynamics, 424
psychological distress after job loss, 362
quality of job-search behaviors, 267
self-regulatory model of job-search behavior, 423
"Self-Regulatory Perspectives in the Theory of Planned Job Search Behavior: Deliberate and Automatic Self-Regulation Strategies to Facilitate Job Seeking," 205–221
stop- control and start-control self-regulation, 208–209
theory of planned behavior, 321
theory of planned behavior and job turnover process, 405
underemployment, 360
"What to Expect: The Oxford Handbook of Job Loss and Job Search," 1–6
Van Hoye, Greet, 4
antecedents of networking behavior, 282
"Job-Search Behavior as a Multidimensional Construct: A Review of Different Job-Search Behaviors and Sources," 259–274
job-search goals and behaviors, 316
job-search objectives, 403
measurement of networking behavior, 282
networking and older job seekers, 450
networking and social networks, 278, 279
outcomes of networking behavior, 284
types of job-search goals, 138
underemployment, 360
Van Iddekinge, C. H., 331
candidate reactions to job interviews, 343
structured interviews and discrimination, 514
Van Ours, J. C., 455, 535
Van Ryn, M., 133
mechanisms in JOBS Program, 580
reemployment interventions, 150
unemployment and mental health, 578, 579

Vansteenkiste, Maarten, 3
  autonomous *vs.* controlled
    motivation, 166
  older job seekers and higher reservation
    wages, 435
  refusal to job search, 169
Van Vianen, Annelies E. M., 3
  focused job-search strategy, 151
  goal setting theory, 132
  "New Economy Careers Demand
    Adaptive Mental Models and
    Resources," 223–241
  reemployment quality, 363
  research on positive effects of job
    loss, 78
  results of mandatory reemployment
    course, 165
Vansteenkiste , Maarten
  "Understanding the Motivational
    Dynamics Among Unemployed
    Individuals: Refreshing Insights
    from the Self-Determination Theory
    Perspective," 159–179
Vaughan, J. C., 279
verbal and nonverbal communication, in
    interviews, 336–337
verbal self-guidance, 133–135, 140, 344–345
Vickers, M. H., 553, 558
video resumes, potentially discriminatory
    effects of, 507–508, 510–511, 517
Vignoles, A., 365
Vinokur, Amiram D., 6
  expectancy-value theory, 22
  job-search self-efficacy, 133
  perceived health status as motivator in
    job search, 197
  reemployment interventions, 150
  "The JOBS Program: Impact on Job
    Seeker Motivation, Reemployment,
    and Mental Health," 575–590
Virick, Meghna, 4
  "Reemployment Quality,
    Underemployment, and Career
    Outcomes," 359–375
Virtanen, M., 470
Virtanen, P., 471
vitamin model, and research on
    unemployment, 19–20
vocational identity
  and early retirement, 446–447
  formation of, 165, 396
  and older workers, 436
Vohs, K. D., 215
volunteer work, and coping with job
    loss, 445
Von Grumbko, J., 342
Von Hippel, E., 588
Vroom, V. H., 320
Vuori, J., 580, 581, 582, 587

W
Wade, T. J., 510
wages, reservation, 151, 455

Wallace, M., 37
Walsh, F., 91
Walsh, K., 228
Walton, G. M., 215
Wanberg, C. R.
  analytic strategies, 425
  antecedents of networking behavior,
    282, 283
  broader context of job search, 199, 200
  career exploration, 384
  cognitive appraisals of job loss, 196
  control theory and job search, 138
  defining job search, 448
  diary study of job-search efforts,
    170, 210
  effect of economic hardship on job
    search, 89
  evaluating reemployment, 154
  goal setting theory, 132
  job attitudes and
    underemployment, 367
  job-search behavior and
    underemployment, 363
  job-search clarity, 387
  job-search dynamics and
    persistence, 269
  job-search intensity, 422
  job-search intensity and job
    satisfaction, 391
  job-to-job search outcomes, 409
  measurement of networking behavior,
    281–282
  motivations and intensity in job search,
    152, 197
  multiwave longitudinal and diary
    studies of job-search dynamics, 424
  older job seekers and job search
    intensity, 451
  outcomes of networking behavior, 284
  personality traits and school-to-work
    transition, 395
  recruiters and job seekers, 318
  self-regulation model, introduction
    of, 420
  self-regulatory model of job search
    behavior, 423
  underemployment, 360, 363
  well-being during unemployment, 58
Wanous, J. P., 266
Ward-Cook, K., 33–34
Warr, P. B., 15
  age and effects of job loss, 442
  duration of unemployment, 62
  effects of employment, 18
  psychological need frustration, 161–162
  requirements for psychological
    health, 45
  vitamin model, 19–20, 70–71, 72
Waters, L. E., 41
Watkins, L. M., 505
Weber, A., 535
websites, and applicant attraction, 313
Webster, D., 563

Weekley, J. A., 339
weight, and job interview process, 332–333
Weinberg, N., 284
Weiss, H. M.
  affective events theory, 146
  social-cognitive perspective on job loss
    and job search, 145
  studying episodes of job-search
    behavior, 425
welfare-state regimes
  and health, 116–118
  social protection for unemployed, 117–
    118, 119–120t
  typologies of, 117, 118f
welfare-to-work programs, evaluations of,
    534, 535, 581
well-being
  career interruptions and, 232–234
  consequences of job insecurity for, 40
  environmental factors in, 19–20
  and job loss among older workers,
    441–442
  and on-the-job resources, 472
  and psychological need satisfaction,
    161–162
  and quality of motivation, 170–171
  and temporary employment, 466
  and temporary employment
    transitions, 470
Werbel, J. D., 384
  career planning and development, 385
  job-search intensity, 389
  job-search intensity and job
    satisfaction, 391
West, M., 381
Westaby, J. D., 551
Westman, M., 90, 93
Westphal, James D., 305
Whelan, C. T., 15
Whitaker, W. M., 361
Whitehall II study, 113
Whitely, W. T., 381
Wightman, P., 94
Williams, R. M., 363
willpower, and self-regulation, 215
Winefield, A. H., 14
  effects of employment, 18
  effects of underemployment, 366–367
  theoretical approaches to studying
    unemployment, 16
Wise, L., 404
withdrawal behavior, and
    underemployment, 368
Wodtke, K. H., 553–554
Wolff, H. G., 281
  "dark side" of networking, 287
  outcomes of networking behavior,
    284, 285
women and job search
  barriers to building and utilizing social
    networks, 279–280
  clothing style in job interviews, 333
  practices of headhunting firms, 297–298